D0142669

# Calculus Volume 2

SENIOR CONTRIBUTING AUTHORS

**EDWIN "JED" HERMAN, UNIVERSITY OF WISCONSIN-STEVENS POINT**

**GILBERT STRANG, MASSACHUSETTS INSTITUTE OF TECHNOLOGY**

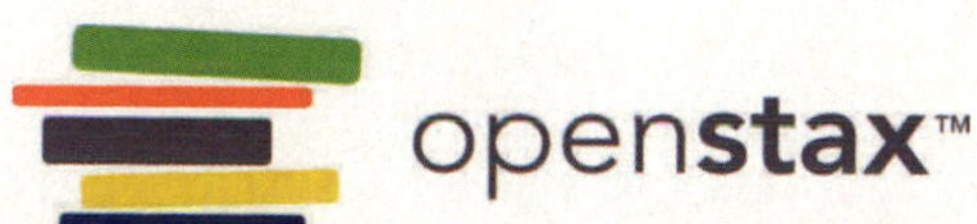


ISBN: 978-1-938168-06-2

**OpenStax**
Rice University
6100 Main Street MS-375
Houston, Texas 77005

To learn more about OpenStax, visit https://openstax.org.
Individual print copies and bulk orders can be purchased through our website.



| | |
|---|---|
| **HARDCOVER BOOK ISBN-13** | **978-1-938168-06-2** |
| **PAPERBACK BOOK ISBN-13** | **978-1-947172-82-1** |
| **B&W PAPERBACK BOOK ISBN-13** | **978-1-50669-807-6** |
| **DIGITAL VERSION ISBN-13** | **978-1-947172-14-2** |
| **Revision Number** | **C2-2016-002(03/17)-LC** |
| **Original Publication Year** | **2016** |

Printed by
XanEdu
4750 Venture Drive, Suite 400
Ann Arbor, MI 48108
800-562-2147
www.xanedu.com

## OpenStax

OpenStax provides free, peer-reviewed, openly licensed textbooks for introductory college and Advanced Placement® courses and low-cost, personalized courseware that helps students learn. A nonprofit ed tech initiative based at Rice University, we're committed to helping students access the tools they need to complete their courses and meet their educational goals.

## Rice University

OpenStax, OpenStax CNX, and OpenStax Tutor are initiatives of Rice University. As a leading research university with a distinctive commitment to undergraduate education, Rice University aspires to path-breaking research, unsurpassed teaching, and contributions to the betterment of our world. It seeks to fulfill this mission by cultivating a diverse community of learning and discovery that produces leaders across the spectrum of human endeavor.

## Foundation Support

OpenStax is grateful for the tremendous support of our sponsors. Without their strong engagement, the goal of free access to high-quality textbooks would remain just a dream.

Laura and John Arnold Foundation (LJAF) actively seeks opportunities to invest in organizations and thought leaders that have a sincere interest in implementing fundamental changes that not only yield immediate gains, but also repair broken systems for future generations. LJAF currently focuses its strategic investments on education, criminal justice, research integrity, and public accountability.

The William and Flora Hewlett Foundation has been making grants since 1967 to help solve social and environmental problems at home and around the world. The Foundation concentrates its resources on activities in education, the environment, global development and population, performing arts, and philanthropy, and makes grants to support disadvantaged communities in the San Francisco Bay Area.

Calvin K. Kazanjian was the founder and president of Peter Paul (Almond Joy), Inc. He firmly believed that the more people understood about basic economics the happier and more prosperous they would be. Accordingly, he established the Calvin K. Kazanjian Economics Foundation Inc, in 1949 as a philanthropic, nonpolitical educational organization to support efforts that enhanced economic understanding.

Guided by the belief that every life has equal value, the Bill & Melinda Gates Foundation works to help all people lead healthy, productive lives. In developing countries, it focuses on improving people's health with vaccines and other life-saving tools and giving them the chance to lift themselves out of hunger and extreme poverty. In the United States, it seeks to significantly improve education so that all young people have the opportunity to reach their full potential. Based in Seattle, Washington, the foundation is led by CEO Jeff Raikes and Co-chair William H. Gates Sr., under the direction of Bill and Melinda Gates and Warren Buffett.

The Maxfield Foundation supports projects with potential for high impact in science, education, sustainability, and other areas of social importance.

Our mission at The Michelson 20MM Foundation is to grow access and success by eliminating unnecessary hurdles to affordability. We support the creation, sharing, and proliferation of more effective, more affordable educational content by leveraging disruptive technologies, open educational resources, and new models for collaboration between for-profit, nonprofit, and public entities.

The Bill and Stephanie Sick Fund supports innovative projects in the areas of Education, Art, Science and Engineering.

# Table of Contents

# PREFACE

Welcome to *Calculus Volume 2*, an OpenStax resource. This textbook was written to increase student access to high-quality learning materials, maintaining highest standards of academic rigor at little to no cost.

## About OpenStax

OpenStax is a nonprofit based at Rice University, and it's our mission to improve student access to education. Our first openly licensed college textbook was published in 2012, and our library has since scaled to over 20 books for college and AP courses used by hundreds of thousands of students. Our adaptive learning technology, designed to improve learning outcomes through personalized educational paths, is being piloted in college courses throughout the country. Through our partnerships with philanthropic foundations and our alliance with other educational resource organizations, OpenStax is breaking down the most common barriers to learning and empowering students and instructors to succeed.

## About OpenStax's Resources

### Customization

*Calculus Volume 2* is licensed under a Creative Commons Attribution Non-Commercial ShareAlike (CC BY-NC-SA) license, which means that you can distribute, remix, and build upon the content, as long as you provide attribution to OpenStax and its content contributors.

Because our books are openly licensed, you are free to use the entire book or pick and choose the sections that are most relevant to the needs of your course. Feel free to remix the content by assigning your students certain chapters and sections in your syllabus, in the order that you prefer. You can even provide a direct link in your syllabus to the sections in the web view of your book.

Faculty also have the option of creating a customized version of their OpenStax book through the aerSelect platform. The custom version can be made available to students in low-cost print or digital form through their campus bookstore. Visit your book page on openstax.org for a link to your book on aerSelect.

### Errata

All OpenStax textbooks undergo a rigorous review process. However, like any professional-grade textbook, errors sometimes occur. Since our books are web based, we can make updates periodically when deemed pedagogically necessary. If you have a correction to suggest, submit it through the link on your book page on openstax.org. Subject matter experts review all errata suggestions. OpenStax is committed to remaining transparent about all updates, so you will also find a list of past errata changes on your book page on openstax.org.

### Format

You can access this textbook for free in web view or PDF through openstax.org, and for a low cost in print.

## About *Calculus Volume 2*

*Calculus* is designed for the typical two- or three-semester general calculus course, incorporating innovative features to enhance student learning. The book guides students through the core concepts of calculus and helps them understand how those concepts apply to their lives and the world around them. Due to the comprehensive nature of the material, we are offering the book in three volumes for flexibility and efficiency. Volume 2 covers integration, differential equations, sequences and series, and parametric equations and polar coordinates.

### Coverage and Scope

Our *Calculus Volume 2* textbook adheres to the scope and sequence of most general calculus courses nationwide. We have worked to make calculus interesting and accessible to students while maintaining the mathematical rigor inherent in the subject. With this objective in mind, the content of the three volumes of *Calculus* have been developed and arranged to provide a logical progression from fundamental to more advanced concepts, building upon what students have already learned and emphasizing connections between topics and between theory and applications. The goal of each section is to enable students not just to recognize concepts, but work with them in ways that will be useful in later courses and future careers. The organization and pedagogical features were developed and vetted with feedback from mathematics educators dedicated to the project.

#### Volume 1

Chapter 1: Functions and Graphs

Chapter 2: Limits

Chapter 3: Derivatives

Chapter 4: Applications of Derivatives

Chapter 5: Integration

Chapter 6: Applications of Integration

**Volume 2**

Chapter 1: Integration

Chapter 2: Applications of Integration

Chapter 3: Techniques of Integration

Chapter 4: Introduction to Differential Equations

Chapter 5: Sequences and Series

Chapter 6: Power Series

Chapter 7: Parametric Equations and Polar Coordinates

**Volume 3**

Chapter 1: Parametric Equations and Polar Coordinates

Chapter 2: Vectors in Space

Chapter 3: Vector-Valued Functions

Chapter 4: Differentiation of Functions of Several Variables

Chapter 5: Multiple Integration

Chapter 6: Vector Calculus

Chapter 7: Second-Order Differential Equations

## Pedagogical Foundation

Throughout *Calculus Volume 2* you will find examples and exercises that present classical ideas and techniques as well as modern applications and methods. Derivations and explanations are based on years of classroom experience on the part of long-time calculus professors, striving for a balance of clarity and rigor that has proven successful with their students. Motivational applications cover important topics in probability, biology, ecology, business, and economics, as well as areas of physics, chemistry, engineering, and computer science. **Student Projects** in each chapter give students opportunities to explore interesting sidelights in pure and applied mathematics, from showing that the number e is irrational, to calculating the center of mass of the Grand Canyon Skywalk or the terminal speed of a skydiver. **Chapter Opening Applications** pose problems that are solved later in the chapter, using the ideas covered in that chapter. Problems include the hydraulic force against the Hoover Dam, and the comparison of the relative intensity of two earthquakes. **Definitions, Rules,** and **Theorems** are highlighted throughout the text, including over 60 **Proofs** of theorems.

## Assessments That Reinforce Key Concepts

In-chapter **Examples** walk students through problems by posing a question, stepping out a solution, and then asking students to practice the skill with a "Check Your Learning" component. The book also includes assessments at the end of each chapter so students can apply what they've learned through practice problems. Many exercises are marked with a **[T]** to indicate they are suitable for solution by technology, including calculators or Computer Algebra Systems (CAS). Answers for selected exercises are available in the **Answer Key** at the back of the book. The book also includes assessments at the end of each chapter so students can apply what they've learned through practice problems.

## Early or Late Transcendentals

*Calculus Volume 2* is designed to accommodate both Early and Late Transcendental approaches to calculus. Exponential and logarithmic functions are presented in Chapter 2. Integration of these functions is covered in Chapters 1 for instructors who want to include them with other types of functions. These discussions, however, are in separate sections that can be skipped for instructors who prefer to wait until the integral definitions are given before teaching the calculus derivations of exponentials and logarithms.

## Comprehensive Art Program

Our art program is designed to enhance students' understanding of concepts through clear and effective illustrations, diagrams, and photographs.

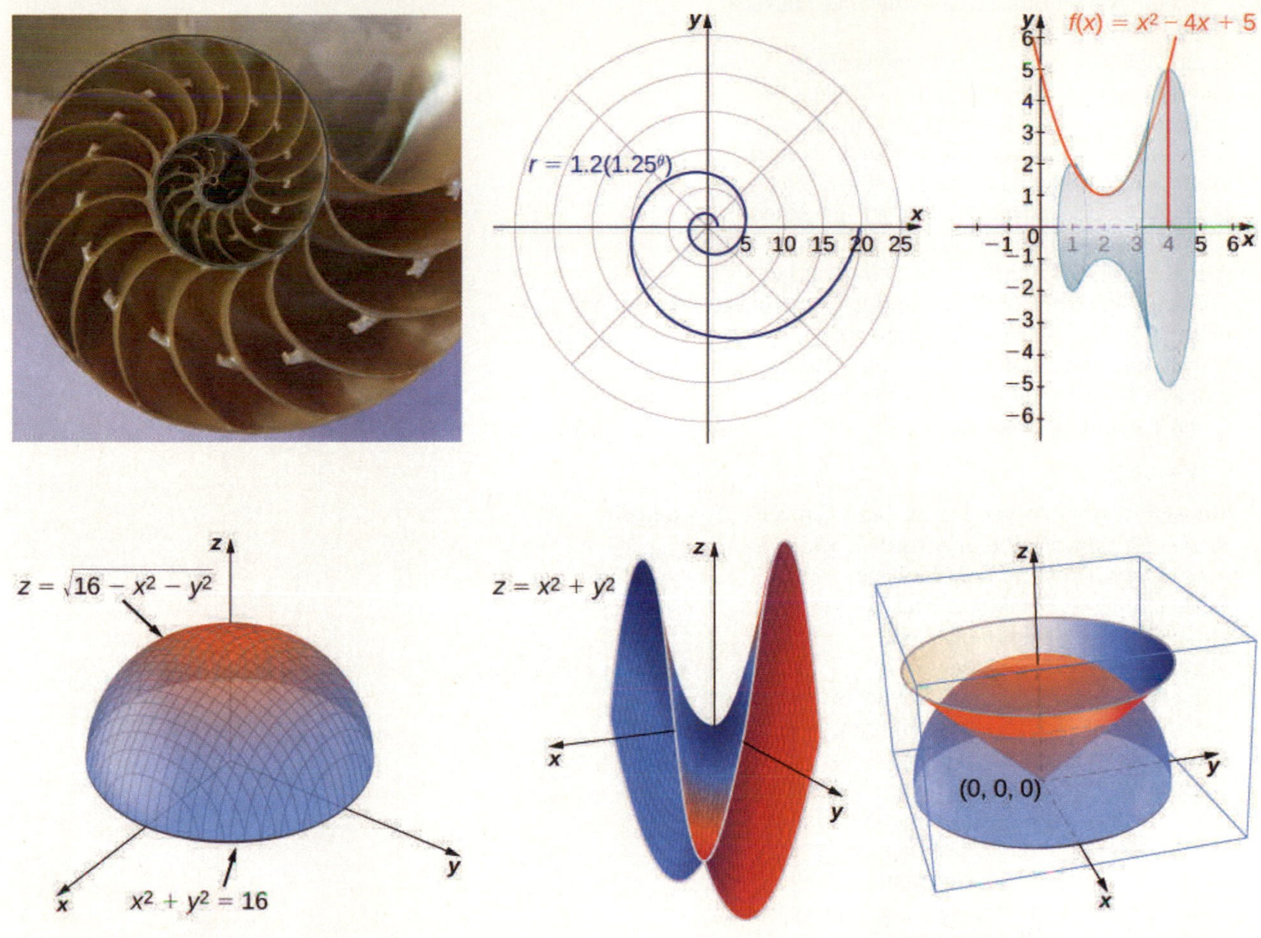


# Additional Resources

## Student and Instructor Resources

We've compiled additional resources for both students and instructors, including Getting Started Guides, an instructor solution manual, and PowerPoint slides. Instructor resources require a verified instructor account, which can be requested on your openstax.org log-in. Take advantage of these resources to supplement your OpenStax book.

## Partner Resources

OpenStax Partners are our allies in the mission to make high-quality learning materials affordable and accessible to students and instructors everywhere. Their tools integrate seamlessly with our OpenStax titles at a low cost. To access the partner resources for your text, visit your book page on openstax.org.

# About The Authors

## Senior Contributing Authors

**Gilbert Strang, Massachusetts Institute of Technology**
Dr. Strang received his PhD from UCLA in 1959 and has been teaching mathematics at MIT ever since. His Calculus online textbook is one of eleven that he has published and is the basis from which our final product has been derived and updated for today's student. Strang is a decorated mathematician and past Rhodes Scholar at Oxford University.

**Edwin "Jed" Herman, University of Wisconsin-Stevens Point**
Dr. Herman earned a BS in Mathematics from Harvey Mudd College in 1985, an MA in Mathematics from UCLA in 1987, and a PhD in Mathematics from the University of Oregon in 1997. He is currently a Professor at the University of Wisconsin-Stevens Point. He has more than 20 years of experience teaching college mathematics, is a student research mentor, is experienced in course development/design, and is also an avid board game designer and player.

## Contributing Authors

Catherine Abbott, Keuka College
Nicoleta Virginia Bila, Fayetteville State University
Sheri J. Boyd, Rollins College
Joyati Debnath, Winona State University
Valeree Falduto, Palm Beach State College
Joseph Lakey, New Mexico State University
Julie Levandosky, Framingham State University
David McCune, William Jewell College
Michelle Merriweather, Bronxville High School
Kirsten R. Messer, Colorado State University - Pueblo
Alfred K. Mulzet, Florida State College at Jacksonville
William Radulovich (retired), Florida State College at Jacksonville
Erica M. Rutter, Arizona State University
David Smith, University of the Virgin Islands
Elaine A. Terry, Saint Joseph's University
David Torain, Hampton University

## Reviewers

Marwan A. Abu-Sawwa, Florida State College at Jacksonville
Kenneth J. Bernard, Virginia State University
John Beyers, University of Maryland
Charles Buehrle, Franklin & Marshall College
Matthew Cathey, Wofford College
Michael Cohen, Hofstra University
William DeSalazar, Broward County School System
Murray Eisenberg, University of Massachusetts Amherst
Kristyanna Erickson, Cecil College
Tiernan Fogarty, Oregon Institute of Technology
David French, Tidewater Community College
Marilyn Gloyer, Virginia Commonwealth University
Shawna Haider, Salt Lake Community College
Lance Hemlow, Raritan Valley Community College
Jerry Jared, The Blue Ridge School
Peter Jipsen, Chapman University
David Johnson, Lehigh University
M.R. Khadivi, Jackson State University
Robert J. Krueger, Concordia University
Tor A. Kwembe, Jackson State University
Jean-Marie Magnier, Springfield Technical Community College
Cheryl Chute Miller, SUNY Potsdam
Bagisa Mukherjee, Penn State University, Worthington Scranton Campus
Kasso Okoudjou, University of Maryland College Park
Peter Olszewski, Penn State Erie, The Behrend College
Steven Purtee, Valencia College
Alice Ramos, Bethel College
Doug Shaw, University of Northern Iowa
Hussain Elalaoui-Talibi, Tuskegee University
Jeffrey Taub, Maine Maritime Academy
William Thistleton, SUNY Polytechnic Institute
A. David Trubatch, Montclair State University
Carmen Wright, Jackson State University
Zhenbu Zhang, Jackson State University

# 1 | INTEGRATION

**Figure 1.1** Iceboating is a popular winter sport in parts of the northern United States and Europe. (credit: modification of work by Carter Brown, Flickr)

## Chapter Outline



## Introduction

Iceboats are a common sight on the lakes of Wisconsin and Minnesota on winter weekends. Iceboats are similar to sailboats, but they are fitted with runners, or "skates," and are designed to run over the ice, rather than on water. Iceboats can move very quickly, and many ice boating enthusiasts are drawn to the sport because of the speed. Top iceboat racers can attain speeds up to five times the wind speed. If we know how fast an iceboat is moving, we can use integration to determine how far it travels. We revisit this question later in the chapter (see **Example 1.27**).

Determining distance from velocity is just one of many applications of integration. In fact, integrals are used in a wide variety of mechanical and physical applications. In this chapter, we first introduce the theory behind integration and use integrals to calculate areas. From there, we develop the Fundamental Theorem of Calculus, which relates differentiation and integration. We then study some basic integration techniques and briefly examine some applications.

# 1.1 | Approximating Areas

## Learning Objectives

**1.1.1** Use sigma (summation) notation to calculate sums and powers of integers.
**1.1.2** Use the sum of rectangular areas to approximate the area under a curve.
**1.1.3** Use Riemann sums to approximate area.

Archimedes was fascinated with calculating the areas of various shapes—in other words, the amount of space enclosed by the shape. He used a process that has come to be known as the *method of exhaustion*, which used smaller and smaller shapes, the areas of which could be calculated exactly, to fill an irregular region and thereby obtain closer and closer approximations to the total area. In this process, an area bounded by curves is filled with rectangles, triangles, and shapes with exact area formulas. These areas are then summed to approximate the area of the curved region.

In this section, we develop techniques to approximate the area between a curve, defined by a function $f(x)$, and the *x*-axis on a closed interval $[a, b]$. Like Archimedes, we first approximate the area under the curve using shapes of known area (namely, rectangles). By using smaller and smaller rectangles, we get closer and closer approximations to the area. Taking a limit allows us to calculate the exact area under the curve.

Let's start by introducing some notation to make the calculations easier. We then consider the case when $f(x)$ is continuous and nonnegative. Later in the chapter, we relax some of these restrictions and develop techniques that apply in more general cases.

## Sigma (Summation) Notation

As mentioned, we will use shapes of known area to approximate the area of an irregular region bounded by curves. This process often requires adding up long strings of numbers. To make it easier to write down these lengthy sums, we look at some new notation here, called **sigma notation** (also known as **summation notation**). The Greek capital letter $\Sigma$, sigma, is used to express long sums of values in a compact form. For example, if we want to add all the integers from 1 to 20 without sigma notation, we have to write

$$1 + 2 + 3 + 4 + 5 + 6 + 7 + 8 + 9 + 10 + 11 + 12 + 13 + 14 + 15 + 16 + 17 + 18 + 19 + 20.$$

We could probably skip writing a couple of terms and write

$$1 + 2 + 3 + 4 + \cdots + 19 + 20,$$

which is better, but still cumbersome. With sigma notation, we write this sum as

$$\sum_{i=1}^{20} i,$$

which is much more compact.

Typically, sigma notation is presented in the form

$$\sum_{i=1}^{n} a_i$$

where $a_i$ describes the terms to be added, and the *i* is called the *index*. Each term is evaluated, then we sum all the values, beginning with the value when $i = 1$ and ending with the value when $i = n$. For example, an expression like $\sum_{i=2}^{7} s_i$ is interpreted as $s_2 + s_3 + s_4 + s_5 + s_6 + s_7$. Note that the index is used only to keep track of the terms to be added; it does not factor into the calculation of the sum itself. The index is therefore called a *dummy variable*. We can use any letter we like for the index. Typically, mathematicians use *i, j, k, m,* and *n* for indices.

Let's try a couple of examples of using sigma notation.

## Example 1.1

### Using Sigma Notation

a. Write in sigma notation and evaluate the sum of terms $3^i$ for $i = 1, 2, 3, 4, 5.$

b. Write the sum in sigma notation:

$$1 + \frac{1}{4} + \frac{1}{9} + \frac{1}{16} + \frac{1}{25}.$$

### Solution

a. Write

$$\begin{aligned}\sum_{i=1}^{5} 3^i &= 3 + 3^2 + 3^3 + 3^4 + 3^5 \\ &= 363.\end{aligned}$$

b. The denominator of each term is a perfect square. Using sigma notation, this sum can be written as $\sum_{i=1}^{5} \frac{1}{i^2}.$

**1.1** Write in sigma notation and evaluate the sum of terms $2^i$ for $i = 3, 4, 5, 6.$

The properties associated with the summation process are given in the following rule.

### Rule: Properties of Sigma Notation

Let $a_1, a_2, \ldots, a_n$ and $b_1, b_2, \ldots, b_n$ represent two sequences of terms and let $c$ be a constant. The following properties hold for all positive integers $n$ and for integers $m$, with $1 \le m \le n.$

1.

$$\sum_{i=1}^{n} c = nc \quad (1.1)$$

2.

$$\sum_{i=1}^{n} ca_i = c\sum_{i=1}^{n} a_i \quad (1.2)$$

3.

$$\sum_{i=1}^{n} (a_i + b_i) = \sum_{i=1}^{n} a_i + \sum_{i=1}^{n} b_i \quad (1.3)$$

4.

$$\sum_{i=1}^{n} (a_i - b_i) = \sum_{i=1}^{n} a_i - \sum_{i=1}^{n} b_i \quad (1.4)$$

5.

$$\sum_{i=1}^{n} a_i = \sum_{i=1}^{m} a_i + \sum_{i=m+1}^{n} a_i \tag{1.5}$$

### Proof

We prove properties 2. and 3. here, and leave proof of the other properties to the Exercises.

2. We have

$$\begin{aligned}\sum_{i=1}^{n} ca_i &= ca_1 + ca_2 + ca_3 + \cdots + ca_n \\ &= c(a_1 + a_2 + a_3 + \cdots + a_n) \\ &= c\sum_{i=1}^{n} a_i.\end{aligned}$$

3. We have

$$\begin{aligned}\sum_{i=1}^{n} (a_i + b_i) &= (a_1 + b_1) + (a_2 + b_2) + (a_3 + b_3) + \cdots + (a_n + b_n) \\ &= (a_1 + a_2 + a_3 + \cdots + a_n) + (b_1 + b_2 + b_3 + \cdots + b_n) \\ &= \sum_{i=1}^{n} a_i + \sum_{i=1}^{n} b_i.\end{aligned}$$

□

A few more formulas for frequently found functions simplify the summation process further. These are shown in the next rule, for **sums and powers of integers**, and we use them in the next set of examples.

### Rule: Sums and Powers of Integers

1. The sum of $n$ integers is given by

$$\sum_{i=1}^{n} i = 1 + 2 + \cdots + n = \frac{n(n+1)}{2}.$$

2. The sum of consecutive integers squared is given by

$$\sum_{i=1}^{n} i^2 = 1^2 + 2^2 + \cdots + n^2 = \frac{n(n+1)(2n+1)}{6}.$$

3. The sum of consecutive integers cubed is given by

$$\sum_{i=1}^{n} i^3 = 1^3 + 2^3 + \cdots + n^3 = \frac{n^2(n+1)^2}{4}.$$

## Example 1.2

### Evaluation Using Sigma Notation

Write using sigma notation and evaluate:

a. The sum of the terms $(i-3)^2$ for $i = 1, 2, \ldots, 200$.

b. The sum of the terms $\left(i^3 - i^2\right)$ for $i = 1, 2, 3, 4, 5, 6.$

### Solution

a. Multiplying out $(i - 3)^2,$ we can break the expression into three terms.

$$\begin{aligned}\sum_{i=1}^{200} (i-3)^2 &= \sum_{i=1}^{200} \left(i^2 - 6i + 9\right) \\ &= \sum_{i=1}^{200} i^2 - \sum_{i=1}^{200} 6i + \sum_{i=1}^{200} 9 \\ &= \sum_{i=1}^{200} i^2 - 6\sum_{i=1}^{200} i + \sum_{i=1}^{200} 9 \\ &= \frac{200(200+1)(400+1)}{6} - 6\left[\frac{200(200+1)}{2}\right] + 9(200) \\ &= 2{,}686{,}700 - 120{,}600 + 1800 \\ &= 2{,}567{,}900\end{aligned}$$

b. Use sigma notation property iv. and the rules for the sum of squared terms and the sum of cubed terms.

$$\begin{aligned}\sum_{i=1}^{6} \left(i^3 - i^2\right) &= \sum_{i=1}^{6} i^3 - \sum_{i=1}^{6} i^2 \\ &= \frac{6^2(6+1)^2}{4} - \frac{6(6+1)(2(6)+1)}{6} \\ &= \frac{1764}{4} - \frac{546}{6} \\ &= 350\end{aligned}$$

**1.2** Find the sum of the values of $4 + 3i$ for $i = 1, 2, \ldots, 100.$

## Example 1.3

### Finding the Sum of the Function Values

Find the sum of the values of $f(x) = x^3$ over the integers $1, 2, 3, \ldots, 10.$

### Solution

Using the formula, we have

$$\begin{aligned}\sum_{i=0}^{10} i^3 &= \frac{(10)^2(10+1)^2}{4} \\ &= \frac{100(121)}{4} \\ &= 3025.\end{aligned}$$

**1.3** Evaluate the sum indicated by the notation $\sum_{k=1}^{20} (2k + 1)$.

## Approximating Area

Now that we have the necessary notation, we return to the problem at hand: approximating the area under a curve. Let $f(x)$ be a continuous, nonnegative function defined on the closed interval $[a, b]$. We want to approximate the area $A$ bounded by $f(x)$ above, the $x$-axis below, the line $x = a$ on the left, and the line $x = b$ on the right (**Figure 1.2**).

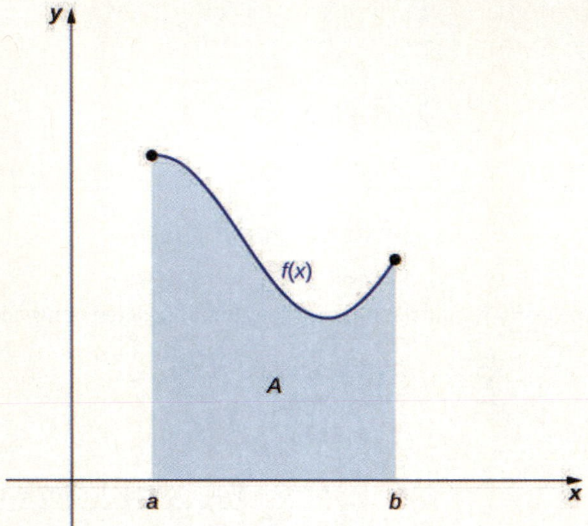


**Figure 1.2** An area (shaded region) bounded by the curve $f(x)$ at top, the $x$-axis at bottom, the line $x = a$ to the left, and the line $x = b$ at right.

How do we approximate the area under this curve? The approach is a geometric one. By dividing a region into many small shapes that have known area formulas, we can sum these areas and obtain a reasonable estimate of the true area. We begin by dividing the interval $[a, b]$ into $n$ subintervals of equal width, $\frac{b-a}{n}$. We do this by selecting equally spaced points $x_0, x_1, x_2, \ldots, x_n$ with $x_0 = a$, $x_n = b$, and

$$x_i - x_{i-1} = \frac{b-a}{n}$$

for $i = 1, 2, 3, \ldots, n$.

We denote the width of each subinterval with the notation $\Delta x$, so $\Delta x = \frac{b-a}{n}$ and

$$x_i = x_0 + i\Delta x$$

for $i = 1, 2, 3, \ldots, n$. This notion of dividing an interval $[a, b]$ into subintervals by selecting points from within the interval is used quite often in approximating the area under a curve, so let's define some relevant terminology.

### Definition

A set of points $P = \{x_i\}$ for $i = 0, 1, 2, \ldots, n$ with $a = x_0 < x_1 < x_2 < \cdots < x_n = b$, which divides the interval $[a, b]$ into subintervals of the form $[x_0, x_1], [x_1, x_2], \ldots, [x_{n-1}, x_n]$ is called a **partition** of $[a, b]$. If the subintervals all have the same width, the set of points forms a **regular partition** of the interval $[a, b]$.

We can use this regular partition as the basis of a method for estimating the area under the curve. We next examine two methods: the left-endpoint approximation and the right-endpoint approximation.

### Rule: Left-Endpoint Approximation

On each subinterval $[x_{i-1}, x_i]$ (for $i = 1, 2, 3, \ldots, n$), construct a rectangle with width $\Delta x$ and height equal to $f(x_{i-1})$, which is the function value at the left endpoint of the subinterval. Then the area of this rectangle is $f(x_{i-1})\Delta x$. Adding the areas of all these rectangles, we get an approximate value for $A$ (**Figure 1.3**). We use the notation $L_n$ to denote that this is a **left-endpoint approximation** of $A$ using $n$ subintervals.

$$A \approx L_n = f(x_0)\Delta x + f(x_1)\Delta x + \cdots + f(x_{n-1})\Delta x \tag{1.6}$$

$$= \sum_{i=1}^{n} f(x_{i-1})\Delta x$$

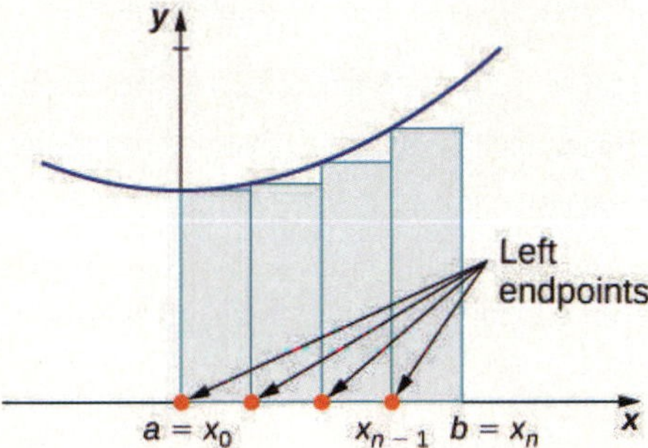


**Figure 1.3** In the left-endpoint approximation of area under a curve, the height of each rectangle is determined by the function value at the left of each subinterval.

The second method for approximating area under a curve is the right-endpoint approximation. It is almost the same as the left-endpoint approximation, but now the heights of the rectangles are determined by the function values at the right of each subinterval.

### Rule: Right-Endpoint Approximation

Construct a rectangle on each subinterval $[x_{i-1}, x_i]$, only this time the height of the rectangle is determined by the function value $f(x_i)$ at the right endpoint of the subinterval. Then, the area of each rectangle is $f(x_i)\Delta x$ and the approximation for $A$ is given by

$$A \approx R_n = f(x_1)\Delta x + f(x_2)\Delta x + \cdots + f(x_n)\Delta x \tag{1.7}$$

$$= \sum_{i=1}^{n} f(x_i)\Delta x.$$

The notation $R_n$ indicates this is a **right-endpoint approximation** for $A$ (**Figure 1.4**).

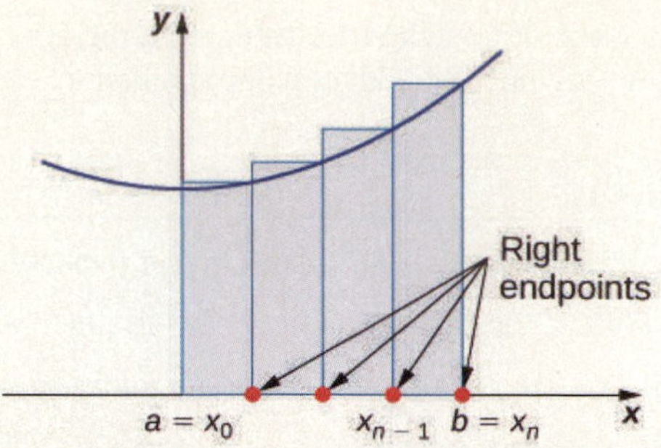


**Figure 1.4** In the right-endpoint approximation of area under a curve, the height of each rectangle is determined by the function value at the right of each subinterval. Note that the right-endpoint approximation differs from the left-endpoint approximation in **Figure 1.3**.

The graphs in **Figure 1.5** represent the curve $f(x) = \frac{x^2}{2}$. In graph (a) we divide the region represented by the interval $[0, 3]$ into six subintervals, each of width 0.5. Thus, $\Delta x = 0.5$. We then form six rectangles by drawing vertical lines perpendicular to $x_{i-1}$, the left endpoint of each subinterval. We determine the height of each rectangle by calculating $f(x_{i-1})$ for $i = 1, 2, 3, 4, 5, 6$. The intervals are $[0, 0.5], [0.5, 1], [1, 1.5], [1.5, 2], [2, 2.5], [2.5, 3]$. We find the area of each rectangle by multiplying the height by the width. Then, the sum of the rectangular areas approximates the area between $f(x)$ and the $x$-axis. When the left endpoints are used to calculate height, we have a left-endpoint approximation. Thus,

$$\begin{aligned}
A \approx L_6 &= \sum_{i=1}^{6} f(x_{i-1})\Delta x = f(x_0)\Delta x + f(x_1)\Delta x + f(x_2)\Delta x + f(x_3)\Delta x + f(x_4)\Delta x + f(x_5)\Delta x \\
&= f(0)0.5 + f(0.5)0.5 + f(1)0.5 + f(1.5)0.5 + f(2)0.5 + f(2.5)0.5 \\
&= (0)0.5 + (0.125)0.5 + (0.5)0.5 + (1.125)0.5 + (2)0.5 + (3.125)0.5 \\
&= 0 + 0.0625 + 0.25 + 0.5625 + 1 + 1.5625 \\
&= 3.4375.
\end{aligned}$$

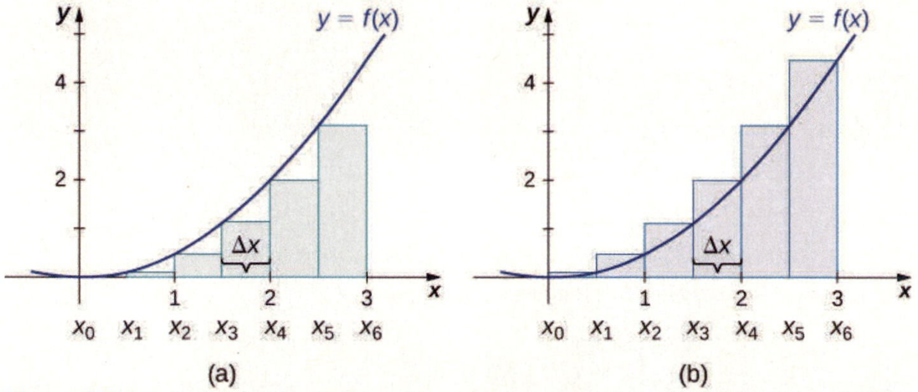

**Figure 1.5** Methods of approximating the area under a curve by using (a) the left endpoints and (b) the right endpoints.

In **Figure 1.5**(b), we draw vertical lines perpendicular to $x_i$ such that $x_i$ is the right endpoint of each subinterval, and calculate $f(x_i)$ for $i = 1, 2, 3, 4, 5, 6$. We multiply each $f(x_i)$ by $\Delta x$ to find the rectangular areas, and then add them. This is a right-endpoint approximation of the area under $f(x)$. Thus,

$$\begin{aligned}
A \approx R_6 &= \sum_{i=1}^{6} f(x_i)\Delta x = f(x_1)\Delta x + f(x_2)\Delta x + f(x_3)\Delta x + f(x_4)\Delta x + f(x_5)\Delta x + f(x_6)\Delta x \\
&= f(0.5)0.5 + f(1)0.5 + f(1.5)0.5 + f(2)0.5 + f(2.5)0.5 + f(3)0.5 \\
&= (0.125)0.5 + (0.5)0.5 + (1.125)0.5 + (2)0.5 + (3.125)0.5 + (4.5)0.5 \\
&= 0.0625 + 0.25 + 0.5625 + 1 + 1.5625 + 2.25 \\
&= 5.6875.
\end{aligned}$$

## Example 1.4

### Approximating the Area Under a Curve

Use both left-endpoint and right-endpoint approximations to approximate the area under the curve of $f(x) = x^2$ on the interval $[0, 2]$; use $n = 4$.

### Solution

First, divide the interval $[0, 2]$ into $n$ equal subintervals. Using $n = 4$, $\Delta x = \frac{(2-0)}{4} = 0.5$. This is the width of each rectangle. The intervals $[0, 0.5], [0.5, 1], [1, 1.5], [1.5, 2]$ are shown in **Figure 1.6**. Using a left-endpoint approximation, the heights are $f(0) = 0,\ f(0.5) = 0.25,\ f(1) = 1,\ f(1.5) = 2.25$. Then,

$$\begin{aligned}
L_4 &= f(x_0)\Delta x + f(x_1)\Delta x + f(x_2)\Delta x + f(x_3)\Delta x \\
&= 0(0.5) + 0.25(0.5) + 1(0.5) + 2.25(0.5) \\
&= 1.75.
\end{aligned}$$

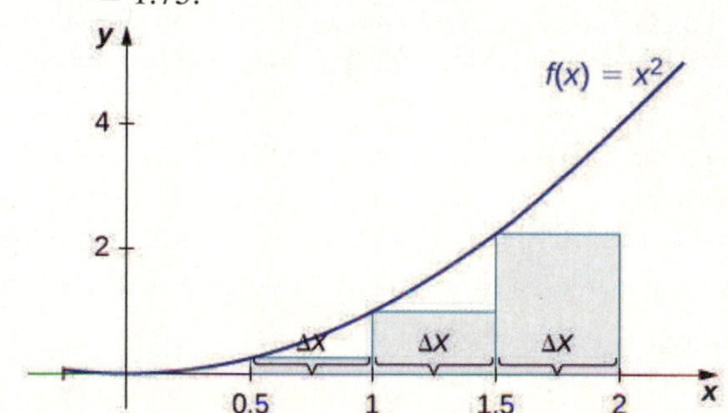


**Figure 1.6** The graph shows the left-endpoint approximation of the area under $f(x) = x^2$ from 0 to 2.

The right-endpoint approximation is shown in **Figure 1.7**. The intervals are the same, $\Delta x = 0.5$, but now use the right endpoint to calculate the height of the rectangles. We have

$$\begin{aligned}
R_4 &= f(x_1)\Delta x + f(x_2)\Delta x + f(x_3)\Delta x + f(x_4)\Delta x \\
&= 0.25(0.5) + 1(0.5) + 2.25(0.5) + 4(0.5) \\
&= 3.75.
\end{aligned}$$

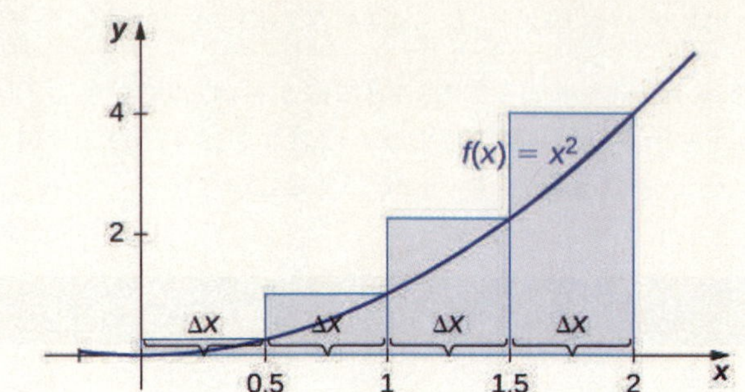


**Figure 1.7** The graph shows the right-endpoint approximation of the area under $f(x) = x^2$ from 0 to 2.

The left-endpoint approximation is 1.75; the right-endpoint approximation is 3.75.

**1.4** Sketch left-endpoint and right-endpoint approximations for $f(x) = \frac{1}{x}$ on $[1, 2]$; use $n = 4$. Approximate the area using both methods.

Looking at **Figure 1.5** and the graphs in **Example 1.4**, we can see that when we use a small number of intervals, neither the left-endpoint approximation nor the right-endpoint approximation is a particularly accurate estimate of the area under the curve. However, it seems logical that if we increase the number of points in our partition, our estimate of $A$ will improve. We will have more rectangles, but each rectangle will be thinner, so we will be able to fit the rectangles to the curve more precisely.

We can demonstrate the improved approximation obtained through smaller intervals with an example. Let's explore the idea of increasing $n$, first in a left-endpoint approximation with four rectangles, then eight rectangles, and finally 32 rectangles. Then, let's do the same thing in a right-endpoint approximation, using the same sets of intervals, of the same curved region. **Figure 1.8** shows the area of the region under the curve $f(x) = (x-1)^3 + 4$ on the interval $[0, 2]$ using a left-endpoint approximation where $n = 4$. The width of each rectangle is

$$\Delta x = \frac{2-0}{4} = \frac{1}{2}.$$

The area is approximated by the summed areas of the rectangles, or

$$\begin{aligned} L_4 &= f(0)(0.5) + f(0.5)(0.5) + f(1)(0.5) + f(1.5)0.5 \\ &= 7.5. \end{aligned}$$

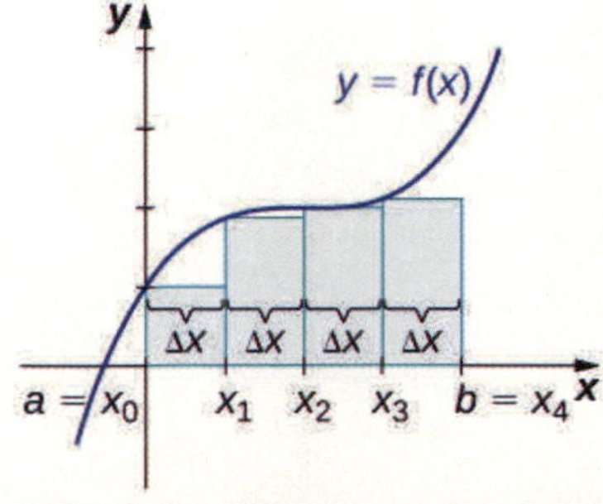


**Figure 1.8** With a left-endpoint approximation and dividing the region from $a$ to $b$ into four equal intervals, the area under the curve is approximately equal to the sum of the areas of the rectangles.

**Figure 1.9** shows the same curve divided into eight subintervals. Comparing the graph with four rectangles in **Figure 1.8** with this graph with eight rectangles, we can see there appears to be less white space under the curve when $n = 8$. This white space is area under the curve we are unable to include using our approximation. The area of the rectangles is

$$\begin{aligned} L_8 &= f(0)(0.25) + f(0.25)(0.25) + f(0.5)(0.25) + f(0.75)(0.25) \\ &\quad + f(1)(0.25) + f(1.25)(0.25) + f(1.5)(0.25) + f(1.75)(0.25) \\ &= 7.75. \end{aligned}$$

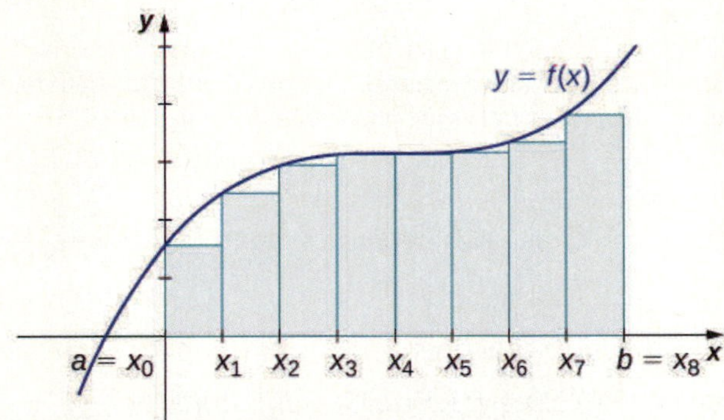


**Figure 1.9** The region under the curve is divided into $n = 8$ rectangular areas of equal width for a left-endpoint approximation.

The graph in **Figure 1.10** shows the same function with 32 rectangles inscribed under the curve. There appears to be little white space left. The area occupied by the rectangles is

$$\begin{aligned} L_{32} &= f(0)(0.0625) + f(0.0625)(0.0625) + f(0.125)(0.0625) + \cdots + f(1.9375)(0.0625) \\ &= 7.9375. \end{aligned}$$

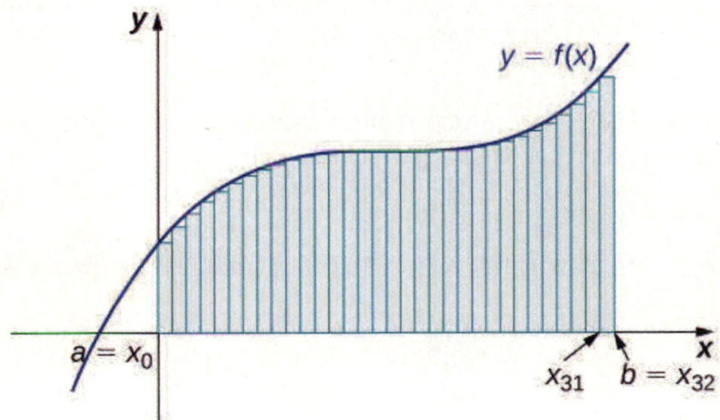


**Figure 1.10** Here, 32 rectangles are inscribed under the curve for a left-endpoint approximation.

We can carry out a similar process for the right-endpoint approximation method. A right-endpoint approximation of the same curve, using four rectangles (**Figure 1.11**), yields an area

$$\begin{aligned} R_4 &= f(0.5)(0.5) + f(1)(0.5) + f(1.5)(0.5) + f(2)(0.5) \\ &= 8.5. \end{aligned}$$

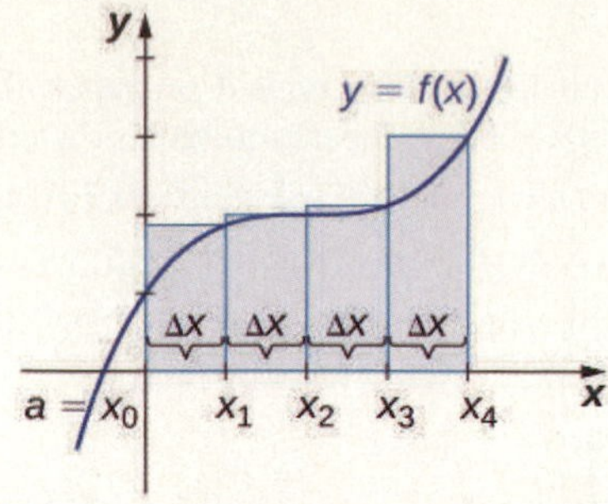


**Figure 1.11** Now we divide the area under the curve into four equal subintervals for a right-endpoint approximation.

Dividing the region over the interval $[0, 2]$ into eight rectangles results in $\Delta x = \frac{2-0}{8} = 0.25$. The graph is shown in **Figure 1.12**. The area is

$$\begin{aligned} R_8 &= f(0.25)(0.25) + f(0.5)(0.25) + f(0.75)(0.25) + f(1)(0.25) \\ &+ f(1.25)(0.25) + f(1.5)(0.25) + f(1.75)(0.25) + f(2)(0.25) \\ &= 8.25. \end{aligned}$$

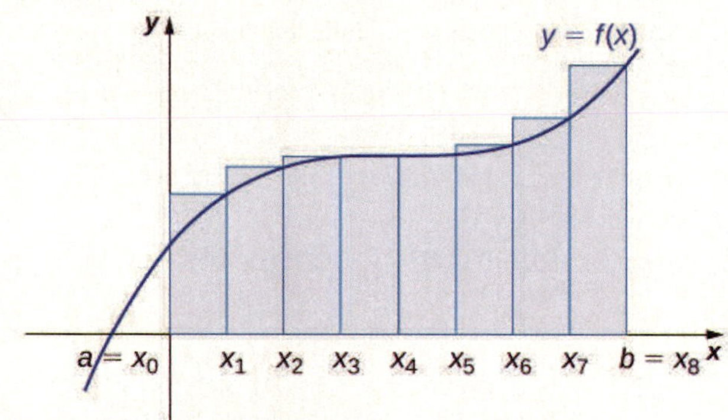


**Figure 1.12** Here we use right-endpoint approximation for a region divided into eight equal subintervals.

Last, the right-endpoint approximation with $n = 32$ is close to the actual area (**Figure 1.13**). The area is approximately

$$\begin{aligned} R_{32} &= f(0.0625)(0.0625) + f(0.125)(0.0625) + f(0.1875)(0.0625) + \cdots + f(2)(0.0625) \\ &= 8.0625. \end{aligned}$$

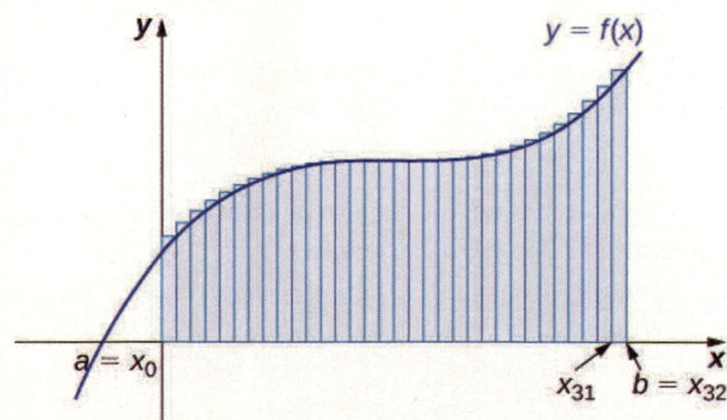


**Figure 1.13** The region is divided into 32 equal subintervals for a right-endpoint approximation.

Based on these figures and calculations, it appears we are on the right track; the rectangles appear to approximate the area under the curve better as $n$ gets larger. Furthermore, as $n$ increases, both the left-endpoint and right-endpoint approximations appear to approach an area of 8 square units. **Table 1.1** shows a numerical comparison of the left- and right-endpoint methods. The idea that the approximations of the area under the curve get better and better as $n$ gets larger and larger is very important, and we now explore this idea in more detail.

| Values of $n$ | Approximate Area $L_n$ | Approximate Area $R_n$ |
|---|---|---|
| $n = 4$ | 7.5 | 8.5 |
| $n = 8$ | 7.75 | 8.25 |
| $n = 32$ | 7.94 | 8.06 |

**Table 1.1** Converging Values of Left- and Right-Endpoint Approximations as $n$ Increases

## Forming Riemann Sums

So far we have been using rectangles to approximate the area under a curve. The heights of these rectangles have been determined by evaluating the function at either the right or left endpoints of the subinterval $[x_{i-1}, x_i]$. In reality, there is no reason to restrict evaluation of the function to one of these two points only. We could evaluate the function at any point $c_i$ in the subinterval $[x_{i-1}, x_i]$, and use $f(x_i^*)$ as the height of our rectangle. This gives us an estimate for the area of the form

$$A \approx \sum_{i=1}^{n} f(x_i^*)\Delta x.$$

A sum of this form is called a Riemann sum, named for the 19th-century mathematician Bernhard Riemann, who developed the idea.

### Definition

Let $f(x)$ be defined on a closed interval $[a, b]$ and let $P$ be a regular partition of $[a, b]$. Let $\Delta x$ be the width of each subinterval $[x_{i-1}, x_i]$ and for each $i$, let $x_i^*$ be any point in $[x_{i-1}, x_i]$. A **Riemann sum** is defined for $f(x)$ as

$$\sum_{i=1}^{n} f(x_i^*)\Delta x.$$

Recall that with the left- and right-endpoint approximations, the estimates seem to get better and better as $n$ get larger and larger. The same thing happens with Riemann sums. Riemann sums give better approximations for larger values of $n$. We are now ready to define the area under a curve in terms of Riemann sums.

### Definition

Let $f(x)$ be a continuous, nonnegative function on an interval $[a, b]$, and let $\sum_{i=1}^{n} f(x_i^*)\Delta x$ be a Riemann sum for $f(x)$. Then, the **area under the curve** $y = f(x)$ on $[a, b]$ is given by

$$A = \lim_{n \to \infty} \sum_{i=1}^{n} f(x_i^*)\Delta x.$$

 See a **graphical demonstration (http://www.openstaxcollege.org/l/20_riemannsums)** of the construction of a Riemann sum.

Some subtleties here are worth discussing. First, note that taking the limit of a sum is a little different from taking the limit of a function $f(x)$ as $x$ goes to infinity. Limits of sums are discussed in detail in the chapter on **Sequences and Series**; however, for now we can assume that the computational techniques we used to compute limits of functions can also be used to calculate limits of sums.

Second, we must consider what to do if the expression converges to different limits for different choices of $\{x_i^*\}$. Fortunately, this does not happen. Although the proof is beyond the scope of this text, it can be shown that if $f(x)$ is continuous on the closed interval $[a, b]$, then $\lim_{n \to \infty} \sum_{i=1}^{n} f(x_i^*)\Delta x$ exists and is unique (in other words, it does not depend on the choice of $\{x_i^*\}$).

We look at some examples shortly. But, before we do, let's take a moment and talk about some specific choices for $\{x_i^*\}$. Although any choice for $\{x_i^*\}$ gives us an estimate of the area under the curve, we don't necessarily know whether that estimate is too high (overestimate) or too low (underestimate). If it is important to know whether our estimate is high or low, we can select our value for $\{x_i^*\}$ to guarantee one result or the other.

If we want an overestimate, for example, we can choose $\{x_i^*\}$ such that for $i = 1, 2, 3,\ldots, n,$ $f(x_i^*) \geq f(x)$ for all $x \in [x_{i-1}, x_i]$. In other words, we choose $\{x_i^*\}$ so that for $i = 1, 2, 3,\ldots, n,$ $f(x_i^*)$ is the maximum function value on the interval $[x_{i-1}, x_i]$. If we select $\{x_i^*\}$ in this way, then the Riemann sum $\sum_{i=1}^{n} f(x_i^*)\Delta x$ is called an **upper sum**. Similarly, if we want an underestimate, we can choose $\{x_i^*\}$ so that for $i = 1, 2, 3,\ldots, n,$ $f(x_i^*)$ is the minimum function value on the interval $[x_{i-1}, x_i]$. In this case, the associated Riemann sum is called a **lower sum**. Note that if $f(x)$ is either increasing or decreasing throughout the interval $[a, b]$, then the maximum and minimum values of the function occur at the endpoints of the subintervals, so the upper and lower sums are just the same as the left- and right-endpoint approximations.

## Example 1.5

### Finding Lower and Upper Sums

Find a lower sum for $f(x) = 10 - x^2$ on $[1, 2]$; let $n = 4$ subintervals.

#### Solution

With $n = 4$ over the interval $[1, 2], \Delta x = \frac{1}{4}$. We can list the intervals as $[1, 1.25], [1.25, 1.5], [1.5, 1.75], [1.75, 2]$. Because the function is decreasing over the interval $[1, 2]$, **Figure 1.14** shows that a lower sum is obtained by using the right endpoints.

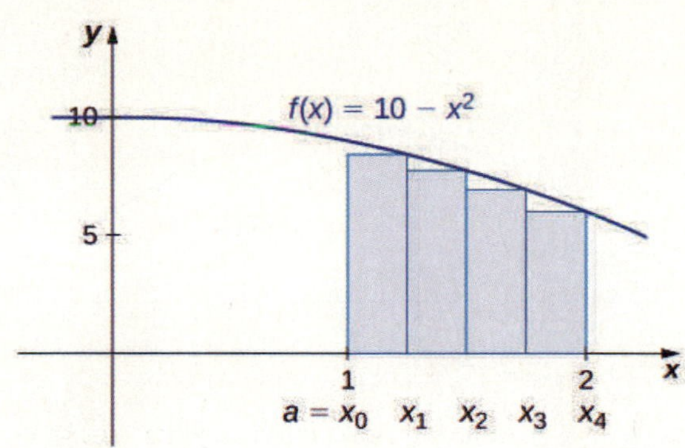


**Figure 1.14** The graph of $f(x) = 10 - x^2$ is set up for a right-endpoint approximation of the area bounded by the curve and the $x$-axis on $[1, 2]$, and it shows a lower sum.

The Riemann sum is

$$\begin{aligned}\sum_{k=1}^{4}\left(10 - x^2\right)(0.25) &= 0.25\left[10 - (1.25)^2 + 10 - (1.5)^2 + 10 - (1.75)^2 + 10 - (2)^2\right] \\ &= 0.25[8.4375 + 7.75 + 6.9375 + 6] \\ &= 7.28.\end{aligned}$$

The area of 7.28 is a lower sum and an underestimate.

**1.5**

a. Find an upper sum for $f(x) = 10 - x^2$ on $[1, 2]$; let $n = 4$.

b. Sketch the approximation.

## Example 1.6

### Finding Lower and Upper Sums for $f(x) = \sin x$

Find a lower sum for $f(x) = \sin x$ over the interval $[a, b] = \left[0, \frac{\pi}{2}\right]$; let $n = 6$.

#### Solution

Let's first look at the graph in **Figure 1.15** to get a better idea of the area of interest.

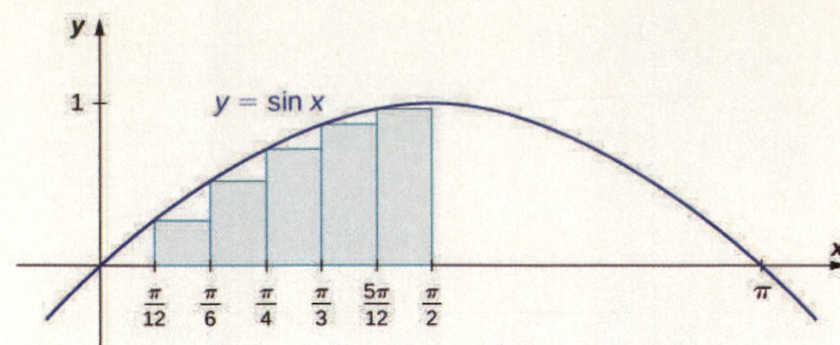


**Figure 1.15** The graph of $y = \sin x$ is divided into six regions: $\Delta x = \frac{\pi/2}{6} = \frac{\pi}{12}$.

The intervals are $\left[0, \frac{\pi}{12}\right], \left[\frac{\pi}{12}, \frac{\pi}{6}\right], \left[\frac{\pi}{6}, \frac{\pi}{4}\right], \left[\frac{\pi}{4}, \frac{\pi}{3}\right], \left[\frac{\pi}{3}, \frac{5\pi}{12}\right]$, and $\left[\frac{5\pi}{12}, \frac{\pi}{2}\right]$. Note that $f(x) = \sin x$ is increasing on the interval $\left[0, \frac{\pi}{2}\right]$, so a left-endpoint approximation gives us the lower sum. A left-endpoint approximation is the Riemann sum $\sum_{i=0}^{5} \sin x_i \left(\frac{\pi}{12}\right)$. We have

$$\begin{aligned} A &\approx \sin(0)\left(\frac{\pi}{12}\right) + \sin\left(\frac{\pi}{12}\right)\left(\frac{\pi}{12}\right) + \sin\left(\frac{\pi}{6}\right)\left(\frac{\pi}{12}\right) + \sin\left(\frac{\pi}{4}\right)\left(\frac{\pi}{12}\right) + \sin\left(\frac{\pi}{3}\right)\left(\frac{\pi}{12}\right) + \sin\left(\frac{5\pi}{12}\right)\left(\frac{\pi}{12}\right) \\ &= 0.863. \end{aligned}$$

**1.6** Using the function $f(x) = \sin x$ over the interval $\left[0, \frac{\pi}{2}\right]$, find an upper sum; let $n = 6$.

# 1.1 EXERCISES

1. State whether the given sums are equal or unequal.

   a. $\sum_{i=1}^{10} i$ and $\sum_{k=1}^{10} k$

   b. $\sum_{i=1}^{10} i$ and $\sum_{i=6}^{15} (i-5)$

   c. $\sum_{i=1}^{10} i(i-1)$ and $\sum_{j=0}^{9} (j+1)j$

   d. $\sum_{i=1}^{10} i(i-1)$ and $\sum_{k=1}^{10} \left(k^2-k\right)$

In the following exercises, use the rules for sums of powers of integers to compute the sums.

2. $\sum_{i=5}^{10} i$

3. $\sum_{i=5}^{10} i^2$

Suppose that $\sum_{i=1}^{100} a_i = 15$ and $\sum_{i=1}^{100} b_i = -12$. In the following exercises, compute the sums.

4. $\sum_{i=1}^{100} (a_i + b_i)$

5. $\sum_{i=1}^{100} (a_i - b_i)$

6. $\sum_{i=1}^{100} (3a_i - 4b_i)$

7. $\sum_{i=1}^{100} (5a_i + 4b_i)$

In the following exercises, use summation properties and formulas to rewrite and evaluate the sums.

8. $\sum_{k=1}^{20} 100\left(k^2 - 5k + 1\right)$

9. $\sum_{j=1}^{50} \left(j^2 - 2j\right)$

10. $\sum_{j=11}^{20} \left(j^2 - 10j\right)$

11. $\sum_{k=1}^{25} \left[(2k)^2 - 100k\right]$

Let $L_n$ denote the left-endpoint sum using $n$ subintervals and let $R_n$ denote the corresponding right-endpoint sum. In the following exercises, compute the indicated left and right sums for the given functions on the indicated interval.

12. $L_4$ for $f(x) = \frac{1}{x-1}$ on $[2, 3]$

13. $R_4$ for $g(x) = \cos(\pi x)$ on $[0, 1]$

14. $L_6$ for $f(x) = \frac{1}{x(x-1)}$ on $[2, 5]$

15. $R_6$ for $f(x) = \frac{1}{x(x-1)}$ on $[2, 5]$

16. $R_4$ for $\frac{1}{x^2+1}$ on $[-2, 2]$

17. $L_4$ for $\frac{1}{x^2+1}$ on $[-2, 2]$

18. $R_4$ for $x^2 - 2x + 1$ on $[0, 2]$

19. $L_8$ for $x^2 - 2x + 1$ on $[0, 2]$

20. Compute the left and right Riemann sums—$L_4$ and $R_4$, respectively—for $f(x) = (2 - |x|)$ on $[-2, 2]$. Compute their average value and compare it with the area under the graph of $f$.

21. Compute the left and right Riemann sums—$L_6$ and $R_6$, respectively—for $f(x) = (3 - |3 - x|)$ on $[0, 6]$. Compute their average value and compare it with the area under the graph of $f$.

22. Compute the left and right Riemann sums—$L_4$ and $R_4$, respectively—for $f(x) = \sqrt{4 - x^2}$ on $[-2, 2]$ and compare their values.

23. Compute the left and right Riemann sums—$L_6$ and $R_6$, respectively—for $f(x) = \sqrt{9 - (x-3)^2}$ on $[0, 6]$ and compare their values.

Express the following endpoint sums in sigma notation but do not evaluate them.

24. $L_{30}$ for $f(x) = x^2$ on $[1, 2]$

25. $L_{10}$ for $f(x) = \sqrt{4 - x^2}$ on $[-2, 2]$

26. $R_{20}$ for $f(x) = \sin x$ on $[0, \pi]$

27. $R_{100}$ for $\ln x$ on $[1, e]$

In the following exercises, graph the function then use a calculator or a computer program to evaluate the following left and right endpoint sums. Is the area under the curve between the left and right endpoint sums?

28. **[T]** $L_{100}$ and $R_{100}$ for $y = x^2 - 3x + 1$ on the interval $[-1, 1]$

29. **[T]** $L_{100}$ and $R_{100}$ for $y = x^2$ on the interval $[0, 1]$

30. **[T]** $L_{50}$ and $R_{50}$ for $y = \frac{x+1}{x^2 - 1}$ on the interval $[2, 4]$

31. **[T]** $L_{100}$ and $R_{100}$ for $y = x^3$ on the interval $[-1, 1]$

32. **[T]** $L_{50}$ and $R_{50}$ for $y = \tan(x)$ on the interval $\left[0, \frac{\pi}{4}\right]$

33. **[T]** $L_{100}$ and $R_{100}$ for $y = e^{2x}$ on the interval $[-1, 1]$

34. Let $t_j$ denote the time that it took Tejay van Garteren to ride the $j$th stage of the Tour de France in 2014. If there were a total of 21 stages, interpret $\sum_{j=1}^{21} t_j$.

35. Let $r_j$ denote the total rainfall in Portland on the $j$th day of the year in 2009. Interpret $\sum_{j=1}^{31} r_j$.

36. Let $d_j$ denote the hours of daylight and $\delta_j$ denote the increase in the hours of daylight from day $j - 1$ to day $j$ in Fargo, North Dakota, on the $j$th day of the year. Interpret $d_1 + \sum_{j=2}^{365} \delta_j$.

37. To help get in shape, Joe gets a new pair of running shoes. If Joe runs 1 mi each day in week 1 and adds $\frac{1}{10}$ mi to his daily routine each week, what is the total mileage on Joe's shoes after 25 weeks?

38. The following table gives approximate values of the average annual atmospheric rate of increase in carbon dioxide ($CO_2$) each decade since 1960, in parts per million (ppm). Estimate the total increase in atmospheric $CO_2$ between 1964 and 2013.

| Decade | Ppm/y |
|---|---|
| 1964–1973 | 1.07 |
| 1974–1983 | 1.34 |
| 1984–1993 | 1.40 |
| 1994–2003 | 1.87 |
| 2004–2013 | 2.07 |

**Table 1.2** Average Annual Atmospheric $CO_2$ Increase, 1964–2013 ***Source***: **http://www.esrl.noaa.gov/gmd/ccgg/trends/.**

39. The following table gives the approximate increase in sea level in inches over 20 years starting in the given year. Estimate the net change in mean sea level from 1870 to 2010.

| Starting Year | 20-Year Change |
|---|---|
| 1870 | 0.3 |
| 1890 | 1.5 |
| 1910 | 0.2 |
| 1930 | 2.8 |
| 1950 | 0.7 |
| 1970 | 1.1 |
| 1990 | 1.5 |

**Table 1.3** Approximate 20-Year Sea Level Increases, 1870–1990 ***Source*: http://link.springer.com/article/10.1007%2Fs10712-011-9119-1**

40. The following table gives the approximate increase in dollars in the average price of a gallon of gas per decade since 1950. If the average price of a gallon of gas in 2010 was $2.60, what was the average price of a gallon of gas in 1950?

| Starting Year | 10-Year Change |
|---|---|
| 1950 | 0.03 |
| 1960 | 0.05 |
| 1970 | 0.86 |
| 1980 | −0.03 |
| 1990 | 0.29 |
| 2000 | 1.12 |

**Table 1.4** Approximate 10-Year Gas Price Increases, 1950–2000 ***Source*: http://epb.lbl.gov/homepages/Rick_Diamond/docs/lbnl55011-trends.pdf.**

41. The following table gives the percent growth of the U.S. population beginning in July of the year indicated. If the U.S. population was 281,421,906 in July 2000, estimate the U.S. population in July 2010.

| Year | % Change/Year |
|---|---|
| 2000 | 1.12 |
| 2001 | 0.99 |
| 2002 | 0.93 |
| 2003 | 0.86 |
| 2004 | 0.93 |
| 2005 | 0.93 |
| 2006 | 0.97 |
| 2007 | 0.96 |
| 2008 | 0.95 |
| 2009 | 0.88 |

**Table 1.5** Annual Percentage Growth of U.S. Population, 2000–2009 ***Source*:** **http://www.census.gov/popest/data.**

(*Hint:* To obtain the population in July 2001, multiply the population in July 2000 by 1.0112 to get 284,573,831.)

In the following exercises, estimate the areas under the curves by computing the left Riemann sums, $L_8$.

42.

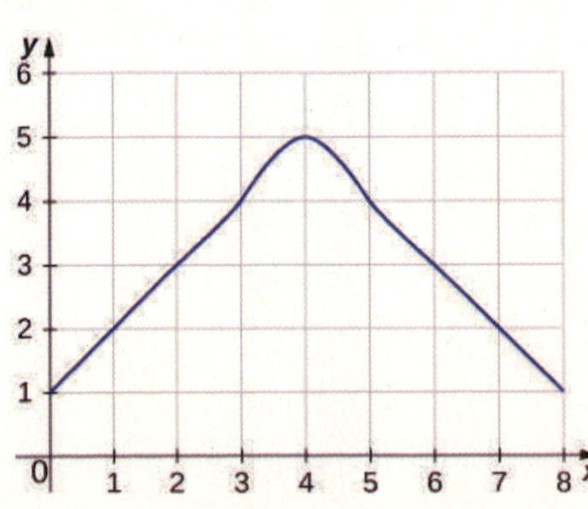


43.

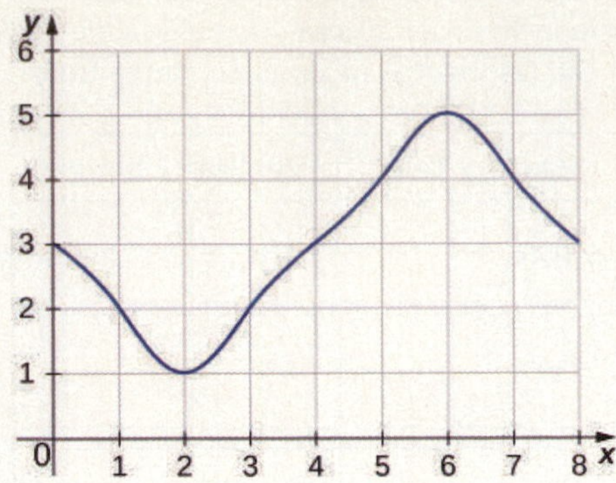


44.

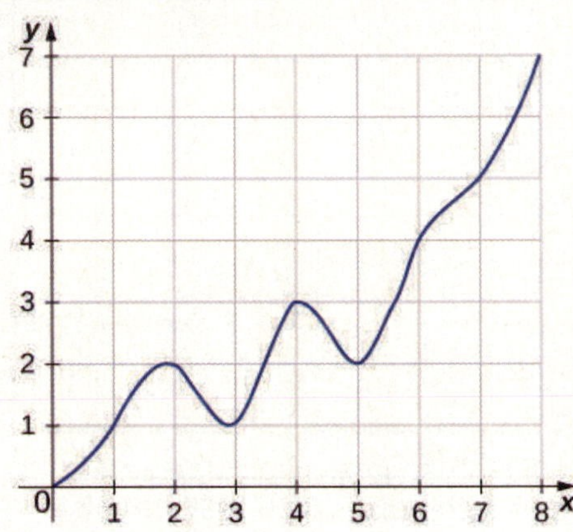


45.

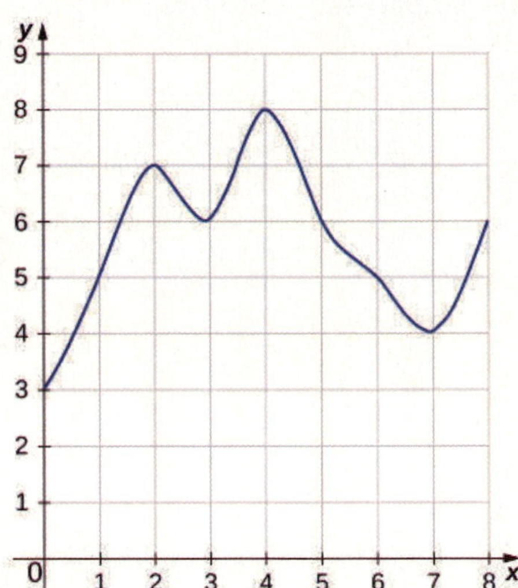


46. **[T]** Use a computer algebra system to compute the Riemann sum, $L_N$, for $N = 10, 30, 50$ for $f(x) = \sqrt{1 - x^2}$ on $[-1, 1]$.

47. **[T]** Use a computer algebra system to compute the Riemann sum, $L_N$, for $N = 10, 30, 50$ for $f(x) = \frac{1}{\sqrt{1 + x^2}}$ on $[-1, 1]$.

48. **[T]** Use a computer algebra system to compute the Riemann sum, $L_N$, for $N = 10, 30, 50$ for $f(x) = \sin^2 x$ on $[0, 2\pi]$. Compare these estimates with $\pi$.

In the following exercises, use a calculator or a computer program to evaluate the endpoint sums $R_N$ and $L_N$ for $N = 1,10,100$. How do these estimates compare with the exact answers, which you can find via geometry?

49. **[T]** $y = \cos(\pi x)$ on the interval $[0, 1]$

50. **[T]** $y = 3x + 2$ on the interval $[3, 5]$

In the following exercises, use a calculator or a computer program to evaluate the endpoint sums $R_N$ and $L_N$ for $N = 1,10,100$.

51. **[T]** $y = x^4 - 5x^2 + 4$ on the interval $[-2, 2]$, which has an exact area of $\frac{32}{15}$

52. **[T]** $y = \ln x$ on the interval $[1, 2]$, which has an exact area of $2\ln(2) - 1$

53. Explain why, if $f(a) \geq 0$ and $f$ is increasing on $[a, b]$, that the left endpoint estimate is a lower bound for the area below the graph of $f$ on $[a, b]$.

54. Explain why, if $f(b) \geq 0$ and $f$ is decreasing on $[a, b]$, that the left endpoint estimate is an upper bound for the area below the graph of $f$ on $[a, b]$.

55. Show that, in general, $R_N - L_N = (b - a) \times \frac{f(b) - f(a)}{N}$.

56. Explain why, if $f$ is increasing on $[a, b]$, the error between either $L_N$ or $R_N$ and the area $A$ below the graph of $f$ is at most $(b - a)\frac{f(b) - f(a)}{N}$.

57. For each of the three graphs:

a. Obtain a lower bound $L(A)$ for the area enclosed by the curve by adding the areas of the squares *enclosed completely* by the curve.

b. Obtain an upper bound $U(A)$ for the area by adding to $L(A)$ the areas $B(A)$ of the squares *enclosed partially* by the curve.

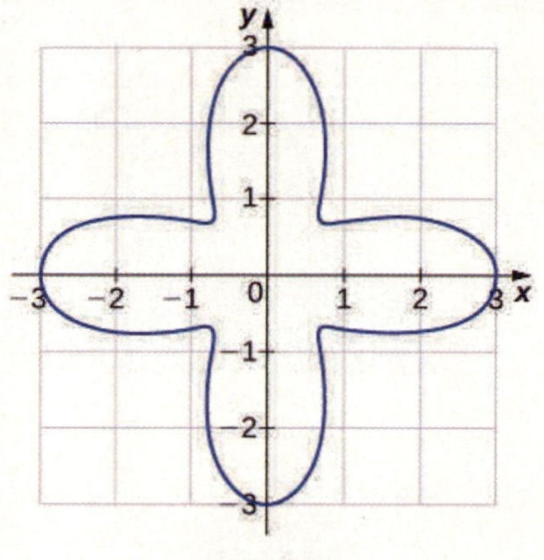


Graph 1

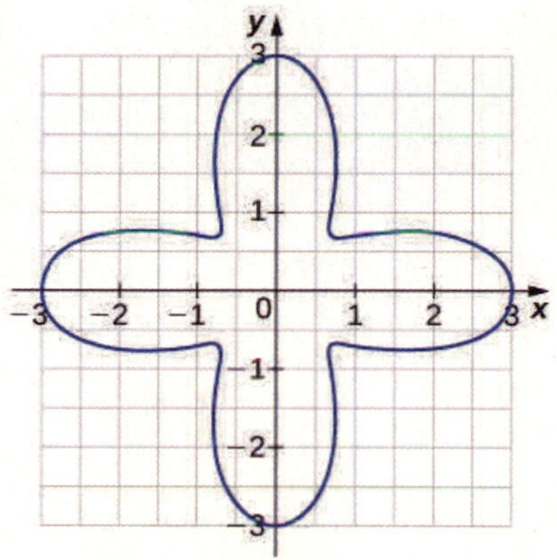


Graph 2

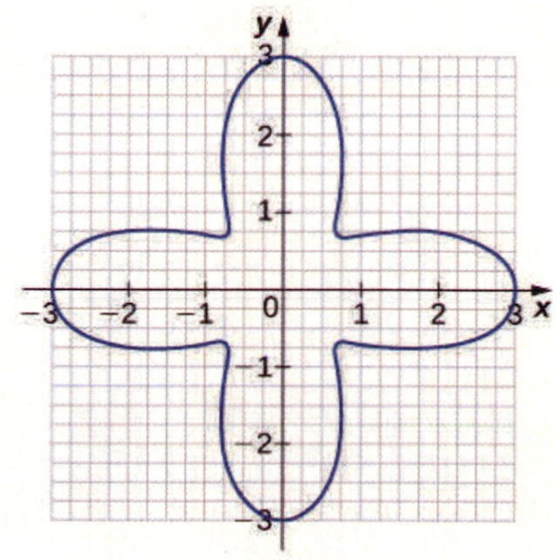


Graph 3

58. In the previous exercise, explain why $L(A)$ gets no smaller while $U(A)$ gets no larger as the squares are subdivided into four boxes of equal area.

59. A unit circle is made up of $n$ wedges equivalent to the inner wedge in the figure. The base of the inner triangle is 1 unit and its height is $\sin\left(\frac{\pi}{n}\right)$. The base of the outer triangle is $B = \cos\left(\frac{\pi}{n}\right) + \sin\left(\frac{\pi}{n}\right)\tan\left(\frac{\pi}{n}\right)$ and the height is $H = B\sin\left(\frac{2\pi}{n}\right)$. Use this information to argue that the area of a unit circle is equal to $\pi$.

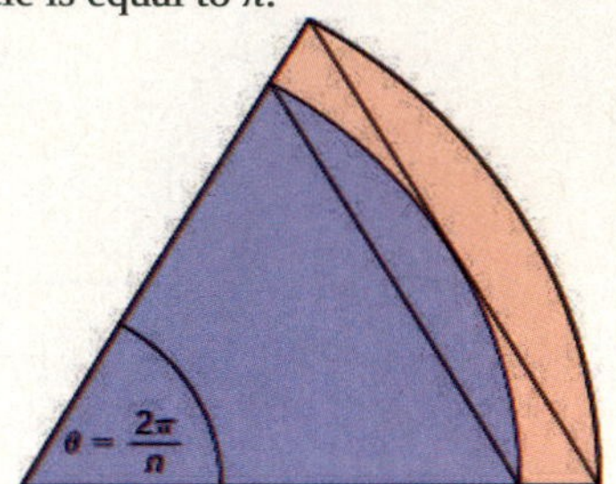

# 1.2 | The Definite Integral

## Learning Objectives

**1.2.1** State the definition of the definite integral.
**1.2.2** Explain the terms integrand, limits of integration, and variable of integration.
**1.2.3** Explain when a function is integrable.
**1.2.4** Describe the relationship between the definite integral and net area.
**1.2.5** Use geometry and the properties of definite integrals to evaluate them.
**1.2.6** Calculate the average value of a function.

In the preceding section we defined the area under a curve in terms of Riemann sums:

$$A = \lim_{n \to \infty} \sum_{i=1}^{n} f(x_i^*)\Delta x.$$

However, this definition came with restrictions. We required $f(x)$ to be continuous and nonnegative. Unfortunately, real-world problems don't always meet these restrictions. In this section, we look at how to apply the concept of the area under the curve to a broader set of functions through the use of the definite integral.

## Definition and Notation

The definite integral generalizes the concept of the area under a curve. We lift the requirements that $f(x)$ be continuous and nonnegative, and define the definite integral as follows.

### Definition

If $f(x)$ is a function defined on an interval $[a, b],$ the **definite integral** of *f* from *a* to *b* is given by

$$\int_a^b f(x)dx = \lim_{n \to \infty} \sum_{i=1}^{n} f(x_i^*)\Delta x, \quad (1.8)$$

provided the limit exists. If this limit exists, the function $f(x)$ is said to be integrable on $[a, b],$ or is an **integrable function**.

The integral symbol in the previous definition should look familiar. We have seen similar notation in the chapter on **Applications of Derivatives (http://cnx.org/content/m53602/latest/)** , where we used the indefinite integral symbol (without the *a* and *b* above and below) to represent an antiderivative. Although the notation for indefinite integrals may look similar to the notation for a definite integral, they are not the same. A definite integral is a number. An indefinite integral is a family of functions. Later in this chapter we examine how these concepts are related. However, close attention should always be paid to notation so we know whether we're working with a definite integral or an indefinite integral.

Integral notation goes back to the late seventeenth century and is one of the contributions of Gottfried Wilhelm Leibniz, who is often considered to be the codiscoverer of calculus, along with Isaac Newton. The integration symbol ∫ is an elongated S, suggesting sigma or summation. On a definite integral, above and below the summation symbol are the boundaries of the interval, $[a, b].$ The numbers *a* and *b* are *x*-values and are called the **limits of integration**; specifically, *a* is the lower limit and *b* is the upper limit. To clarify, we are using the word *limit* in two different ways in the context of the definite integral. First, we talk about the limit of a sum as $n \to \infty.$ Second, the boundaries of the region are called the *limits of integration*.

We call the function $f(x)$ the **integrand**, and the *dx* indicates that $f(x)$ is a function with respect to *x*, called the **variable of integration**. Note that, like the index in a sum, the variable of integration is a dummy variable, and has no impact on the computation of the integral. We could use any variable we like as the variable of integration:

$$\int_a^b f(x)dx = \int_a^b f(t)dt = \int_a^b f(u)du$$

Previously, we discussed the fact that if $f(x)$ is continuous on $[a, b]$, then the limit $\lim_{n \to \infty} \sum_{i=1}^{n} f(x_i^*)\Delta x$ exists and is unique. This leads to the following theorem, which we state without proof.

### Theorem 1.1: Continuous Functions Are Integrable

If $f(x)$ is continuous on $[a, b]$, then $f$ is integrable on $[a, b]$.

Functions that are not continuous on $[a, b]$ may still be integrable, depending on the nature of the discontinuities. For example, functions with a finite number of jump discontinuities on a closed interval are integrable.

It is also worth noting here that we have retained the use of a regular partition in the Riemann sums. This restriction is not strictly necessary. Any partition can be used to form a Riemann sum. However, if a nonregular partition is used to define the definite integral, it is not sufficient to take the limit as the number of subintervals goes to infinity. Instead, we must take the limit as the width of the largest subinterval goes to zero. This introduces a little more complex notation in our limits and makes the calculations more difficult without really gaining much additional insight, so we stick with regular partitions for the Riemann sums.

## Example 1.7

### Evaluating an Integral Using the Definition

Use the definition of the definite integral to evaluate $\int_0^2 x^2\, dx.$ Use a right-endpoint approximation to generate the Riemann sum.

#### Solution

We first want to set up a Riemann sum. Based on the limits of integration, we have $a = 0$ and $b = 2$. For $i = 0, 1, 2, \ldots, n,$ let $P = \{x_i\}$ be a regular partition of $[0, 2]$. Then

$$\Delta x = \frac{b-a}{n} = \frac{2}{n}.$$

Since we are using a right-endpoint approximation to generate Riemann sums, for each $i$, we need to calculate the function value at the right endpoint of the interval $[x_{i-1}, x_i]$. The right endpoint of the interval is $x_i$, and since $P$ is a regular partition,

$$x_i = x_0 + i\Delta x = 0 + i\left[\frac{2}{n}\right] = \frac{2i}{n}.$$

Thus, the function value at the right endpoint of the interval is

$$f(x_i) = x_i^2 = \left(\frac{2i}{n}\right)^2 = \frac{4i^2}{n^2}.$$

Then the Riemann sum takes the form

$$\sum_{i=1}^{n} f(x_i)\Delta x = \sum_{i=1}^{n} \left(\frac{4i^2}{n^2}\right)\frac{2}{n} = \sum_{i=1}^{n} \frac{8i^2}{n^3} = \frac{8}{n^3}\sum_{i=1}^{n} i^2.$$

Using the summation formula for $\sum_{i=1}^{n} i^2,$ we have

$$\begin{aligned}\sum_{i=1}^{n} f(x_i)\Delta x &= \frac{8}{n^3}\sum_{i=1}^{n} i^2 \\ &= \frac{8}{n^3}\left[\frac{n(n+1)(2n+1)}{6}\right] \\ &= \frac{8}{n^3}\left[\frac{2n^3+3n^2+n}{6}\right] \\ &= \frac{16n^3+24n^2+n}{6n^3} \\ &= \frac{8}{3}+\frac{4}{n}+\frac{1}{6n^2}.\end{aligned}$$

Now, to calculate the definite integral, we need to take the limit as $n \to \infty$. We get

$$\begin{aligned}\int_0^2 x^2\,dx &= \lim_{n\to\infty}\sum_{i=1}^{n} f(x_i)\Delta x \\ &= \lim_{n\to\infty}\left(\frac{8}{3}+\frac{4}{n}+\frac{1}{6n^2}\right) \\ &= \lim_{n\to\infty}\left(\frac{8}{3}\right)+\lim_{n\to\infty}\left(\frac{4}{n}\right)+\lim_{n\to\infty}\left(\frac{1}{6n^2}\right) \\ &= \frac{8}{3}+0+0=\frac{8}{3}.\end{aligned}$$

**1.7** Use the definition of the definite integral to evaluate $\int_0^3 (2x-1)dx.$ Use a right-endpoint approximation to generate the Riemann sum.

## Evaluating Definite Integrals

Evaluating definite integrals this way can be quite tedious because of the complexity of the calculations. Later in this chapter we develop techniques for evaluating definite integrals *without* taking limits of Riemann sums. However, for now, we can rely on the fact that definite integrals represent the area under the curve, and we can evaluate definite integrals by using geometric formulas to calculate that area. We do this to confirm that definite integrals do, indeed, represent areas, so we can then discuss what to do in the case of a curve of a function dropping below the $x$-axis.

### Example 1.8

#### Using Geometric Formulas to Calculate Definite Integrals

Use the formula for the area of a circle to evaluate $\int_3^6 \sqrt{9-(x-3)^2}\,dx.$

#### Solution

The function describes a semicircle with radius 3. To find

$$\int_3^6 \sqrt{9 - (x - 3)^2}dx,$$

we want to find the area under the curve over the interval $[3, 6]$. The formula for the area of a circle is $A = \pi r^2$. The area of a semicircle is just one-half the area of a circle, or $A = \left(\frac{1}{2}\right)\pi r^2$. The shaded area in **Figure 1.16** covers one-half of the semicircle, or $A = \left(\frac{1}{4}\right)\pi r^2$. Thus,

$$\begin{aligned}\int_3^6 \sqrt{9 - (x - 3)^2} &= \frac{1}{4}\pi(3)^2 \\ &= \frac{9}{4}\pi \\ &\approx 7.069.\end{aligned}$$

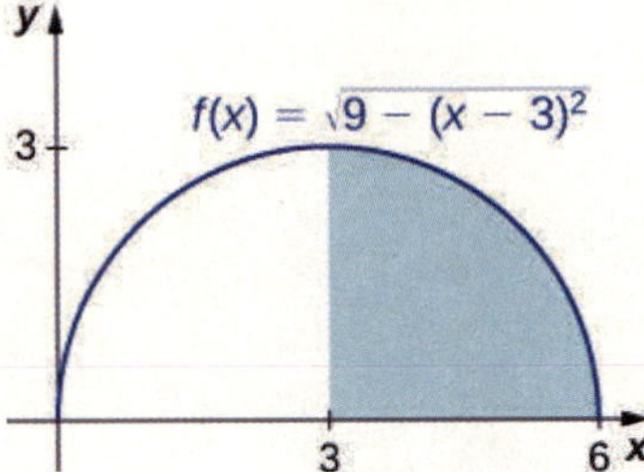


**Figure 1.16** The value of the integral of the function $f(x)$ over the interval $[3, 6]$ is the area of the shaded region.

**1.8** Use the formula for the area of a trapezoid to evaluate $\int_2^4 (2x + 3)dx.$

## Area and the Definite Integral

When we defined the definite integral, we lifted the requirement that $f(x)$ be nonnegative. But how do we interpret "the area under the curve" when $f(x)$ is negative?

### Net Signed Area

Let us return to the Riemann sum. Consider, for example, the function $f(x) = 2 - 2x^2$ (shown in **Figure 1.17**) on the interval $[0, 2]$. Use $n = 8$ and choose $\{x_i^*\}$ as the left endpoint of each interval. Construct a rectangle on each subinterval of height $f(x_i^*)$ and width $\Delta x$. When $f(x_i^*)$ is positive, the product $f(x_i^*)\Delta x$ represents the area of the rectangle, as before. When $f(x_i^*)$ is negative, however, the product $f(x_i^*)\Delta x$ represents the *negative* of the area of the rectangle. The Riemann sum then becomes

$$\sum_{i=1}^{8} f(x_i^*)\Delta x = (\text{Area of rectangles above the } x\text{-axis}) - (\text{Area of rectangles below the } x\text{-axis})$$

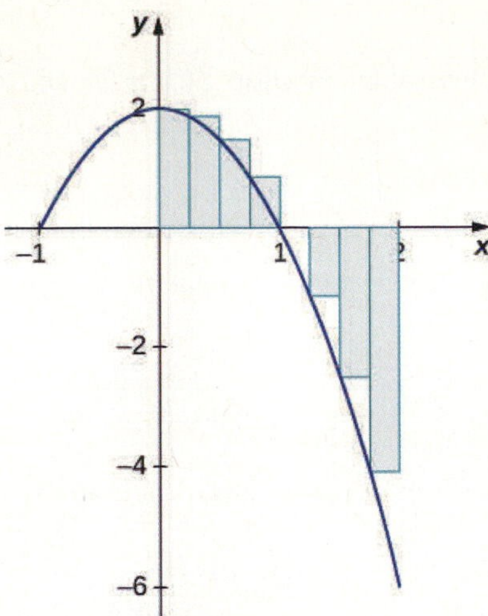


**Figure 1.17** For a function that is partly negative, the Riemann sum is the area of the rectangles above the *x*-axis less the area of the rectangles below the *x*-axis.

Taking the limit as $n \to \infty$, the Riemann sum approaches the area between the curve above the *x*-axis and the *x*-axis, less the area between the curve below the *x*-axis and the *x*-axis, as shown in **Figure 1.18**. Then,

$$\begin{aligned}\int_0^2 f(x)dx &= \lim_{n \to \infty} \sum_{i=1}^{n} f(c_i)\Delta x \\ &= A_1 - A_2.\end{aligned}$$

The quantity $A_1 - A_2$ is called the **net signed area**.

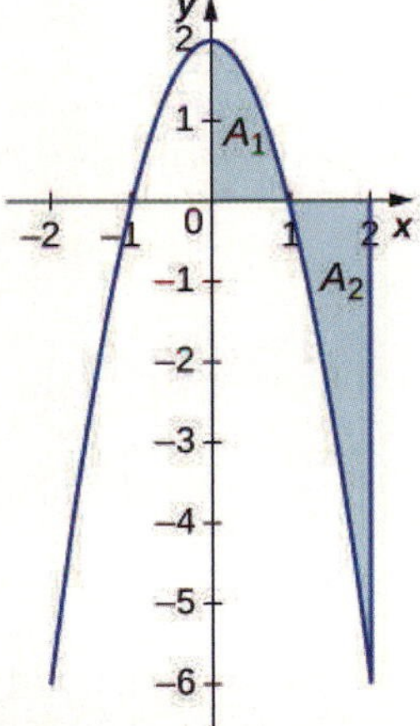


**Figure 1.18** In the limit, the definite integral equals area $A_1$ less area $A_2$, or the net signed area.

Notice that net signed area can be positive, negative, or zero. If the area above the *x*-axis is larger, the net signed area is positive. If the area below the *x*-axis is larger, the net signed area is negative. If the areas above and below the *x*-axis are equal, the net signed area is zero.

## Example 1.9

### Finding the Net Signed Area

Find the net signed area between the curve of the function $f(x) = 2x$ and the x-axis over the interval $[-3, 3]$.

### Solution

The function produces a straight line that forms two triangles: one from $x = -3$ to $x = 0$ and the other from $x = 0$ to $x = 3$ (**Figure 1.19**). Using the geometric formula for the area of a triangle, $A = \frac{1}{2}bh,$ the area of triangle $A_1$, above the axis, is

$$A_1 = \frac{1}{2}3(6) = 9,$$

where 3 is the base and $2(3) = 6$ is the height. The area of triangle $A_2$, below the axis, is

$$A_2 = \frac{1}{2}(3)(6) = 9,$$

where 3 is the base and 6 is the height. Thus, the net area is

$$\int_{-3}^{3} 2xdx = A_1 - A_2 = 9 - 9 = 0.$$

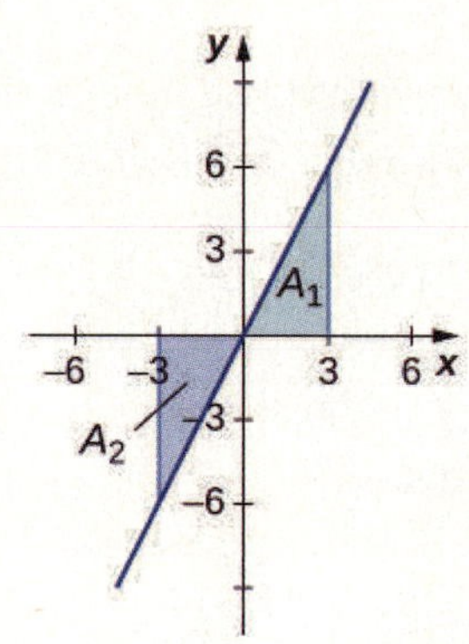


**Figure 1.19** The area above the curve and below the x-axis equals the area below the curve and above the x-axis.

**Analysis**

If $A_1$ is the area above the x-axis and $A_2$ is the area below the x-axis, then the net area is $A_1 - A_2$. Since the areas of the two triangles are equal, the net area is zero.

**1.9** Find the net signed area of $f(x) = x - 2$ over the interval $[0, 6]$, illustrated in the following image.

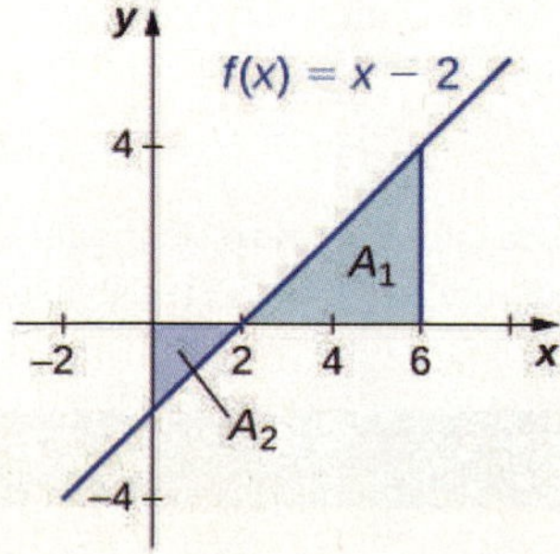


## Total Area

One application of the definite integral is finding displacement when given a velocity function. If $v(t)$ represents the velocity of an object as a function of time, then the area under the curve tells us how far the object is from its original position. This is a very important application of the definite integral, and we examine it in more detail later in the chapter. For now, we're just going to look at some basics to get a feel for how this works by studying constant velocities.

When velocity is a constant, the area under the curve is just velocity times time. This idea is already very familiar. If a car travels away from its starting position in a straight line at a speed of 75 mph for 2 hours, then it is 150 mi away from its original position (**Figure 1.20**). Using integral notation, we have

$$\int_0^2 75dt = 150.$$

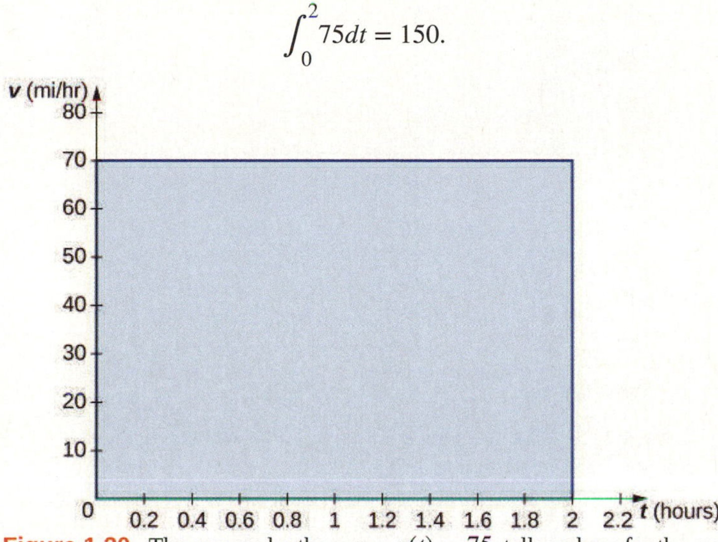


**Figure 1.20** The area under the curve $v(t) = 75$ tells us how far the car is from its starting point at a given time.

In the context of displacement, net signed area allows us to take direction into account. If a car travels straight north at a speed of 60 mph for 2 hours, it is 120 mi north of its starting position. If the car then turns around and travels south at a speed of 40 mph for 3 hours, it will be back at it starting position (**Figure 1.21**). Again, using integral notation, we have

$$\begin{aligned} \int_0^2 60dt + \int_2^5 -40dt &= 120 - 120 \\ &= 0. \end{aligned}$$

In this case the displacement is zero.

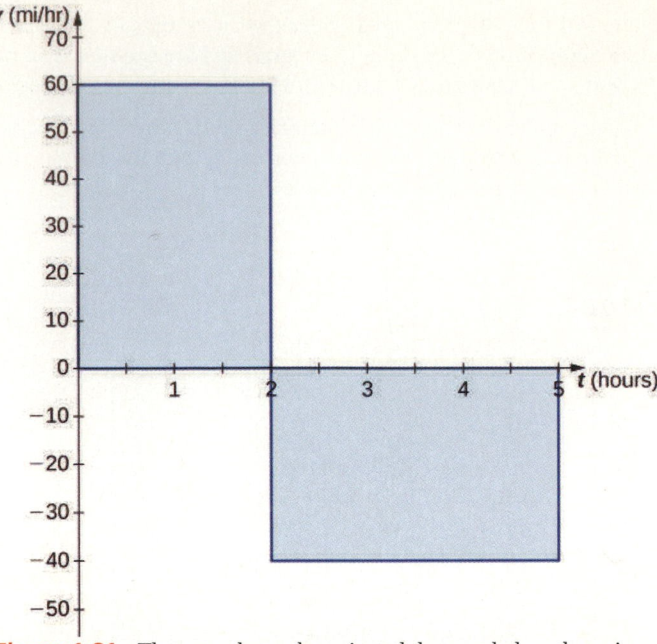


**Figure 1.21** The area above the axis and the area below the axis are equal, so the net signed area is zero.

Suppose we want to know how far the car travels overall, regardless of direction. In this case, we want to know the area between the curve and the *x*-axis, regardless of whether that area is above or below the axis. This is called the **total area**.

Graphically, it is easiest to think of calculating total area by adding the areas above the axis and the areas below the axis (rather than subtracting the areas below the axis, as we did with net signed area). To accomplish this mathematically, we use the absolute value function. Thus, the total distance traveled by the car is

$$\begin{aligned}\int_0^2 |60|dt + \int_2^5 |-40|dt &= \int_0^2 60dt + \int_2^5 40dt \\ &= 120 + 120 \\ &= 240.\end{aligned}$$

Bringing these ideas together formally, we state the following definitions.

## Definition

Let $f(x)$ be an integrable function defined on an interval $[a, b]$. Let $A_1$ represent the area between $f(x)$ and the *x*-axis that lies *above* the axis and let $A_2$ represent the area between $f(x)$ and the *x*-axis that lies *below* the axis. Then, the **net signed area** between $f(x)$ and the *x*-axis is given by

$$\int_a^b f(x)dx = A_1 - A_2.$$

The **total area** between $f(x)$ and the *x*-axis is given by

$$\int_a^b |f(x)|dx = A_1 + A_2.$$

## Example 1.10

### Finding the Total Area

Find the total area between $f(x) = x - 2$ and the $x$-axis over the interval $[0, 6]$.

#### Solution

Calculate the $x$-intercept as $(2, 0)$ (set $y = 0,$ solve for $x$). To find the total area, take the area below the $x$-axis over the subinterval $[0, 2]$ and add it to the area above the $x$-axis on the subinterval $[2, 6]$ (**Figure 1.22**).

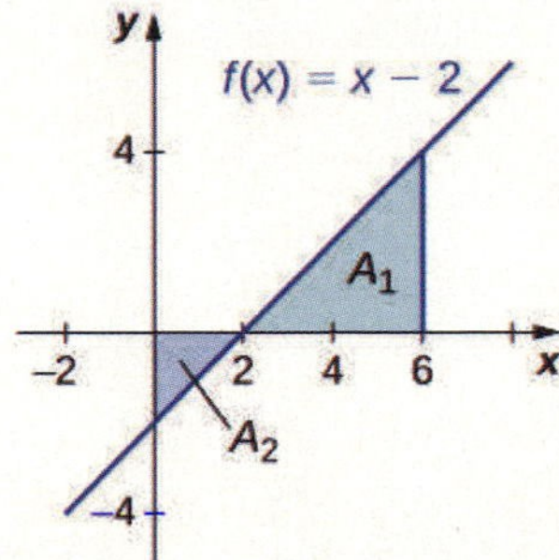


**Figure 1.22** The total area between the line and the x-axis over $[0, 6]$ is $A_2$ plus $A_1$.

We have

$$\int_0^6 |(x-2)|dx = A_2 + A_1.$$

Then, using the formula for the area of a triangle, we obtain

$$A_2 = \frac{1}{2}bh = \frac{1}{2} \cdot 2 \cdot 2 = 2$$
$$A_1 = \frac{1}{2}bh = \frac{1}{2} \cdot 4 \cdot 4 = 8.$$

The total area, then, is

$$A_1 + A_2 = 8 + 2 = 10.$$

**1.10** Find the total area between the function $f(x) = 2x$ and the $x$-axis over the interval $[-3, 3]$.

## Properties of the Definite Integral

The properties of indefinite integrals apply to definite integrals as well. Definite integrals also have properties that relate to the limits of integration. These properties, along with the rules of integration that we examine later in this chapter, help us manipulate expressions to evaluate definite integrals.

### Rule: Properties of the Definite Integral

1.

$$\int_a^a f(x)dx = 0 \tag{1.9}$$

If the limits of integration are the same, the integral is just a line and contains no area.

2.

$$\int_b^a f(x)dx = -\int_a^b f(x)dx \quad (1.10)$$

If the limits are reversed, then place a negative sign in front of the integral.

3.

$$\int_a^b [f(x) + g(x)]dx = \int_a^b f(x)dx + \int_a^b g(x)dx \quad (1.11)$$

The integral of a sum is the sum of the integrals.

4.

$$\int_a^b [f(x) - g(x)]dx = \int_a^b f(x)dx - \int_a^b g(x)dx \quad (1.12)$$

The integral of a difference is the difference of the integrals.

5.

$$\int_a^b cf(x)dx = c\int_a^b f(x) \quad (1.13)$$

for constant $c$. The integral of the product of a constant and a function is equal to the constant multiplied by the integral of the function.

6.

$$\int_a^b f(x)dx = \int_a^c f(x)dx + \int_c^b f(x)dx \quad (1.14)$$

Although this formula normally applies when $c$ is between $a$ and $b$, the formula holds for all values of $a$, $b$, and $c$, provided $f(x)$ is integrable on the largest interval.

## Example 1.11

### Using the Properties of the Definite Integral

Use the properties of the definite integral to express the definite integral of $f(x) = -3x^3 + 2x + 2$ over the interval $[-2, 1]$ as the sum of three definite integrals.

#### Solution

Using integral notation, we have $\int_{-2}^{1}\left(-3x^3 + 2x + 2\right)dx$. We apply properties 3. and 5. to get

$$\begin{aligned}\int_{-2}^{1}\left(-3x^3+2x+2\right)dx &= \int_{-2}^{1}-3x^3\,dx+\int_{-2}^{1}2x\,dx+\int_{-2}^{1}2\,dx\\ &= -3\int_{-2}^{1}x^3\,dx+2\int_{-2}^{1}x\,dx+\int_{-2}^{1}2\,dx.\end{aligned}$$

**1.11** Use the properties of the definite integral to express the definite integral of $f(x)=6x^3-4x^2+2x-3$ over the interval $[1, 3]$ as the sum of four definite integrals.

## Example 1.12

### Using the Properties of the Definite Integral

If it is known that $\int_0^8 f(x)dx = 10$ and $\int_0^5 f(x)dx = 5,$ find the value of $\int_5^8 f(x)dx.$

#### Solution

By property 6.,

$$\int_a^b f(x)dx = \int_a^c f(x)dx + \int_c^b f(x)dx.$$

Thus,

$$\begin{aligned}\int_0^8 f(x)dx &= \int_0^5 f(x)dx + \int_5^8 f(x)dx\\ 10 &= 5+\int_5^8 f(x)dx\\ 5 &= \int_5^8 f(x)dx.\end{aligned}$$

**1.12** If it is known that $\int_1^5 f(x)dx = -3$ and $\int_2^5 f(x)dx = 4,$ find the value of $\int_1^2 f(x)dx.$

### Comparison Properties of Integrals

A picture can sometimes tell us more about a function than the results of computations. Comparing functions by their graphs as well as by their algebraic expressions can often give new insight into the process of integration. Intuitively, we might say that if a function $f(x)$ is above another function $g(x),$ then the area between $f(x)$ and the $x$-axis is greater than the area between $g(x)$ and the $x$-axis. This is true depending on the interval over which the comparison is made. The properties of definite integrals are valid whether $a < b, a = b,$ or $a > b.$ The following properties, however, concern only the case $a \le b,$ and are used when we want to compare the sizes of integrals.

### eorem 1.2: Comparison Theorem

i. If $f(x) \geq 0$ for $a \leq x \leq b$, then

$$\int_a^b f(x)dx \geq 0.$$

ii. If $f(x) \geq g(x)$ for $a \leq x \leq b$, then

$$\int_a^b f(x)dx \geq \int_a^b g(x)dx.$$

iii. If *m* and *M* are constants such that $m \leq f(x) \leq M$ for $a \leq x \leq b$, then

$$m(b - a) \leq \int_a^b f(x)dx \leq M(b - a).$$

## Example 1.13

### Comparing Two Functions over a Given Interval

Compare $f(x) = \sqrt{1 + x^2}$ and $g(x) = \sqrt{1 + x}$ over the interval $[0, 1]$.

#### Solution

Graphing these functions is necessary to understand how they compare over the interval $[0, 1]$. Initially, when graphed on a graphing calculator, $f(x)$ appears to be above $g(x)$ everywhere. However, on the interval $[0, 1]$, the graphs appear to be on top of each other. We need to zoom in to see that, on the interval $[0, 1]$, $g(x)$ is above $f(x)$. The two functions intersect at $x = 0$ and $x = 1$ (**Figure 1.23**).

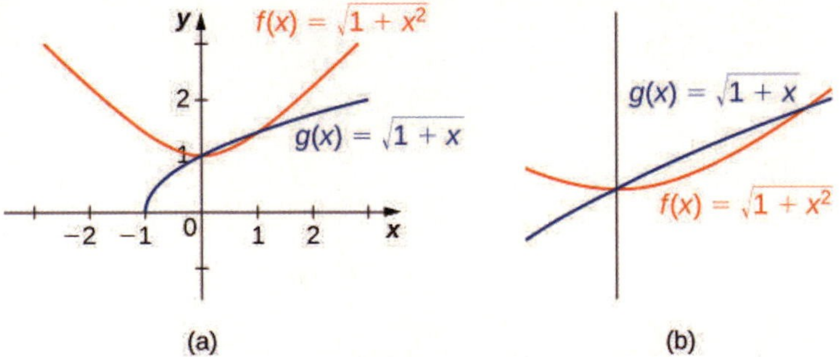


**Figure 1.23** (a) The function $f(x)$ appears above the function $g(x)$ except over the interval $[0, 1]$ (b) Viewing the same graph with a greater zoom shows this more clearly.

We can see from the graph that over the interval $[0, 1]$, $g(x) \geq f(x)$. Comparing the integrals over the specified interval $[0, 1]$, we also see that $\int_0^1 g(x)dx \geq \int_0^1 f(x)dx$ (**Figure 1.24**). The thin, red-shaded area shows just how much difference there is between these two integrals over the interval $[0, 1]$.

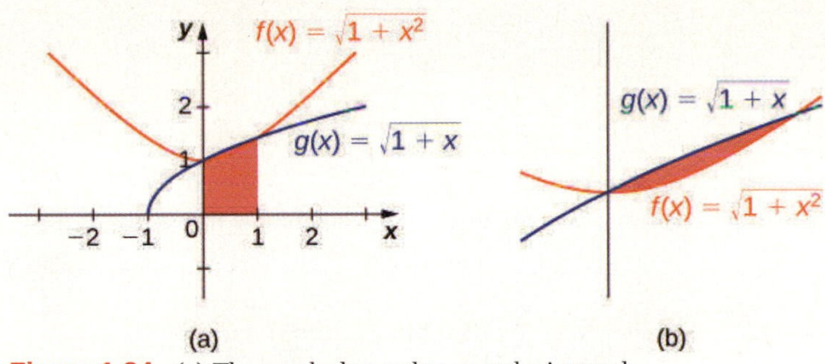


**Figure 1.24** (a) The graph shows that over the interval $[0, 1]$, $g(x) \geq f(x)$, where equality holds only at the endpoints of the interval. (b) Viewing the same graph with a greater zoom shows this more clearly.

## Average Value of a Function

We often need to find the average of a set of numbers, such as an average test grade. Suppose you received the following test scores in your algebra class: 89, 90, 56, 78, 100, and 69. Your semester grade is your average of test scores and you want to know what grade to expect. We can find the average by adding all the scores and dividing by the number of scores. In this case, there are six test scores. Thus,

$$\frac{89 + 90 + 56 + 78 + 100 + 69}{6} = \frac{482}{6} \approx 80.33.$$

Therefore, your average test grade is approximately 80.33, which translates to a B− at most schools.

Suppose, however, that we have a function $v(t)$ that gives us the speed of an object at any time $t$, and we want to find the object's average speed. The function $v(t)$ takes on an infinite number of values, so we can't use the process just described. Fortunately, we can use a definite integral to find the average value of a function such as this.

Let $f(x)$ be continuous over the interval $[a, b]$ and let $[a, b]$ be divided into $n$ subintervals of width $\Delta x = (b - a)/n$. Choose a representative $x_i^*$ in each subinterval and calculate $f(x_i^*)$ for $i = 1, 2, \ldots, n$. In other words, consider each $f(x_i^*)$ as a sampling of the function over each subinterval. The average value of the function may then be approximated as

$$\frac{f(x_1^*) + f(x_2^*) + \cdots + f(x_n^*)}{n},$$

which is basically the same expression used to calculate the average of discrete values.

But we know $\Delta x = \frac{b - a}{n}$, so $n = \frac{b - a}{\Delta x}$, and we get

$$\frac{f(x_1^*) + f(x_2^*) + \cdots + f(x_n^*)}{n} = \frac{f(x_1^*) + f(x_2^*) + \cdots + f(x_n^*)}{\frac{(b - a)}{\Delta x}}.$$

Following through with the algebra, the numerator is a sum that is represented as $\sum_{i=1}^{n} f(x_i^*)$, and we are dividing by a fraction. To divide by a fraction, invert the denominator and multiply. Thus, an approximate value for the average value of the function is given by

$$\frac{\sum_{i=1}^{n} f(x_i^*)}{\frac{(b-a)}{\Delta x}} = \left(\frac{\Delta x}{b-a}\right) \sum_{i=1}^{n} f(x_i^*)$$
$$= \left(\frac{1}{b-a}\right) \sum_{i=1}^{n} f(x_i^*) \Delta x.$$

This is a Riemann sum. Then, to get the *exact* average value, take the limit as $n$ goes to infinity. Thus, the average value of a function is given by

$$\frac{1}{b-a} \lim_{n \to \infty} \sum_{i=1}^{n} f(x_i) \Delta x = \frac{1}{b-a} \int_a^b f(x) dx.$$

## Definition

Let $f(x)$ be continuous over the interval $[a, b]$. Then, the **average value of the function** $f(x)$ (or $\mathbf{f_{ave}}$) on $[a, b]$ is given by

$$f_{\text{ave}} = \frac{1}{b-a} \int_a^b f(x) dx.$$

## Example 1.14

### Finding the Average Value of a Linear Function

Find the average value of $f(x) = x + 1$ over the interval $[0, 5]$.

#### Solution

First, graph the function on the stated interval, as shown in **Figure 1.25**.

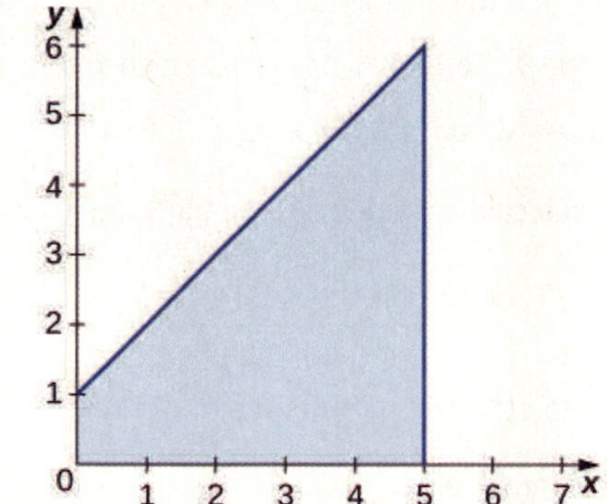


**Figure 1.25** The graph shows the area under the function $f(x) = x + 1$ over $[0, 5]$.

The region is a trapezoid lying on its side, so we can use the area formula for a trapezoid $A = \frac{1}{2}h(a + b)$, where $h$ represents height, and $a$ and $b$ represent the two parallel sides. Then,

$$\begin{aligned}\int_0^5 x + 1dx &= \frac{1}{2}h(a+b) \\ &= \frac{1}{2}\cdot 5\cdot (1+6) \\ &= \frac{35}{2}.\end{aligned}$$

Thus the average value of the function is

$$\frac{1}{5-0}\int_0^5 x + 1dx = \frac{1}{5}\cdot\frac{35}{2} = \frac{7}{2}.$$

**1.13** Find the average value of $f(x) = 6 - 2x$ over the interval $[0, 3]$.

# 1.2 EXERCISES

In the following exercises, express the limits as integrals.

60. $\lim_{n \to \infty} \sum_{i=1}^{n} (x_i^*)\Delta x$ over $[1, 3]$

61. $\lim_{n \to \infty} \sum_{i=1}^{n} \left(5(x_i^*)^2 - 3(x_i^*)^3\right)\Delta x$ over $[0, 2]$

62. $\lim_{n \to \infty} \sum_{i=1}^{n} \sin^2(2\pi x_i^*)\Delta x$ over $[0, 1]$

63. $\lim_{n \to \infty} \sum_{i=1}^{n} \cos^2(2\pi x_i^*)\Delta x$ over $[0, 1]$

In the following exercises, given $L_n$ or $R_n$ as indicated, express their limits as $n \to \infty$ as definite integrals, identifying the correct intervals.

64. $L_n = \frac{1}{n}\sum_{i=1}^{n} \frac{i-1}{n}$

65. $R_n = \frac{1}{n}\sum_{i=1}^{n} \frac{i}{n}$

66. $L_n = \frac{2}{n}\sum_{i=1}^{n} \left(1 + 2\frac{i-1}{n}\right)$

67. $R_n = \frac{3}{n}\sum_{i=1}^{n} \left(3 + 3\frac{i}{n}\right)$

68. $L_n = \frac{2\pi}{n}\sum_{i=1}^{n} 2\pi\frac{i-1}{n}\cos\left(2\pi\frac{i-1}{n}\right)$

69. $R_n = \frac{1}{n}\sum_{i=1}^{n} \left(1 + \frac{i}{n}\right)\log\left(\left(1 + \frac{i}{n}\right)^2\right)$

In the following exercises, evaluate the integrals of the functions graphed using the formulas for areas of triangles and circles, and subtracting the areas below the *x*-axis.

70.

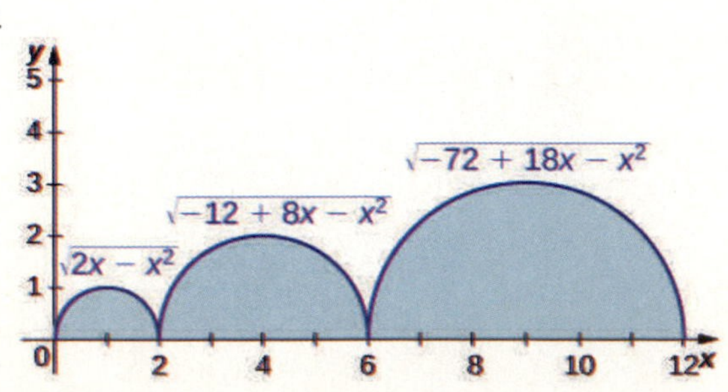


71.

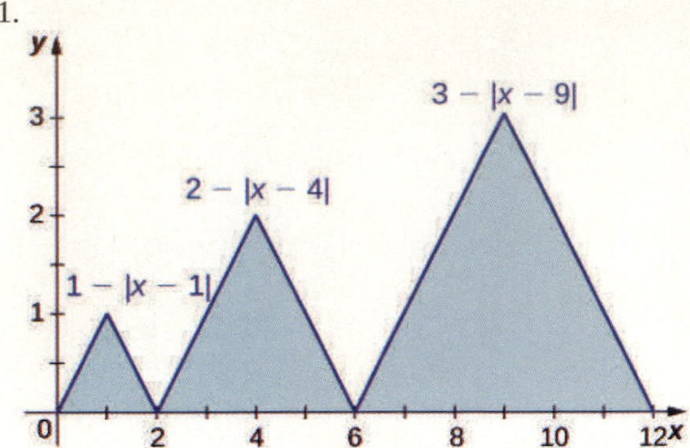


72.

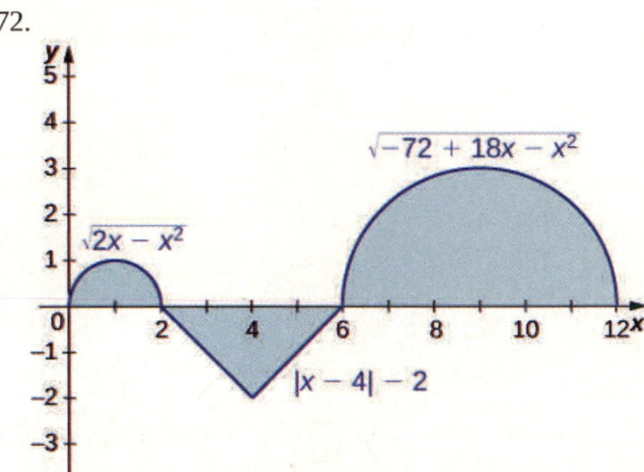


73.

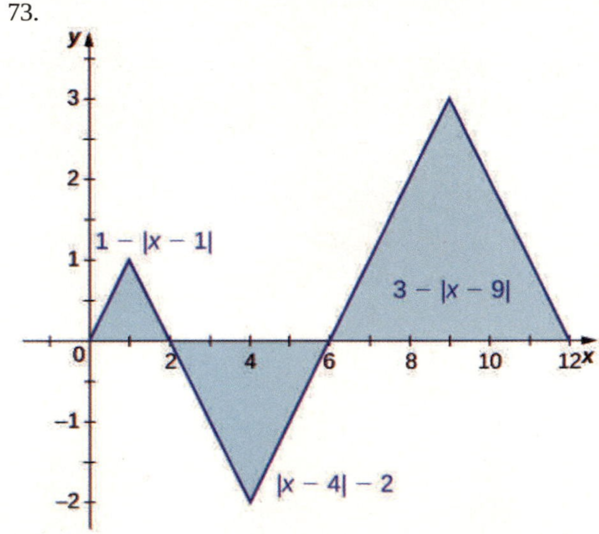

74.

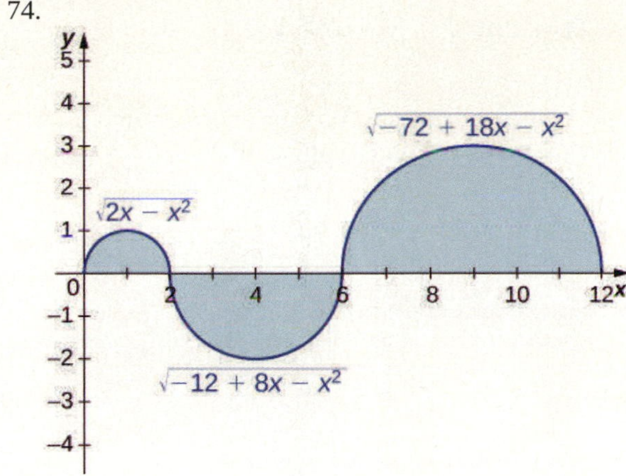


75.

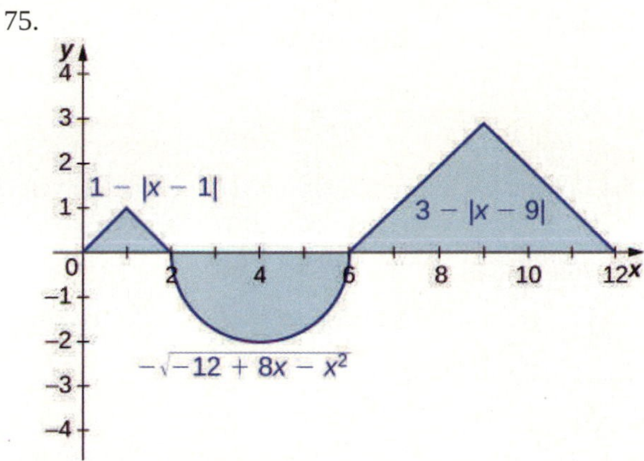


In the following exercises, evaluate the integral using area formulas.

76. $\int_0^3 (3-x)dx$

77. $\int_2^3 (3-x)dx$

78. $\int_{-3}^3 (3-|x|)dx$

79. $\int_0^6 (3-|x-3|)dx$

80. $\int_{-2}^2 \sqrt{4-x^2}dx$

81. $\int_1^5 \sqrt{4-(x-3)^2}dx$

82. $\int_0^{12} \sqrt{36-(x-6)^2}dx$

83. $\int_{-2}^3 (3-|x|)dx$

In the following exercises, use averages of values at the left ($L$) and right ($R$) endpoints to compute the integrals of the piecewise linear functions with graphs that pass through the given list of points over the indicated intervals.

84. $\{(0,0),(2,1),(4,3),(5,0),(6,0),(8,3)\}$ over $[0,8]$

85. $\{(0,2),(1,0),(3,5),(5,5),(6,2),(8,0)\}$ over $[0,8]$

86. $\{(-4,-4),(-2,0),(0,-2),(3,3),(4,3)\}$ over $[-4,4]$

87. $\{(-4,0),(-2,2),(0,0),(1,2),(3,2),(4,0)\}$ over $[-4,4]$

Suppose that $\int_0^4 f(x)dx = 5$ and $\int_0^2 f(x)dx = -3$, and $\int_0^4 g(x)dx = -1$ and $\int_0^2 g(x)dx = 2$. In the following exercises, compute the integrals.

88. $\int_0^4 (f(x)+g(x))dx$

89. $\int_2^4 (f(x)+g(x))dx$

90. $\int_0^2 (f(x)-g(x))dx$

91. $\int_2^4 (f(x)-g(x))dx$

92. $\int_0^2 (3f(x)-4g(x))dx$

93. $\int_2^4 (4f(x)-3g(x))dx$

In the following exercises, use the identity $\int_{-A}^A f(x)dx = \int_{-A}^0 f(x)dx + \int_0^A f(x)dx$ to compute the integrals.

94. $\int_{-\pi}^{\pi} \frac{\sin t}{1+t^2}dt$ (*Hint*: $\sin(-t) = -\sin(t)$)

95. $\int_{-\sqrt{\pi}}^{\sqrt{\pi}} \frac{t}{1+\cos t} dt$

96. $\int_1^3 (2-x)dx$ (*Hint:* Look at the graph of *f*.)

97. $\int_2^4 (x-3)^3 dx$ (*Hint:* Look at the graph of *f*.)

In the following exercises, given that $\int_0^1 x dx = \frac{1}{2}$, $\int_0^1 x^2 dx = \frac{1}{3}$, and $\int_0^1 x^3 dx = \frac{1}{4}$, compute the integrals.

98. $\int_0^1 \left(1 + x + x^2 + x^3\right) dx$

99. $\int_0^1 \left(1 - x + x^2 - x^3\right) dx$

100. $\int_0^1 (1-x)^2 dx$

101. $\int_0^1 (1-2x)^3 dx$

102. $\int_0^1 \left(6x - \frac{4}{3}x^2\right) dx$

103. $\int_0^1 \left(7 - 5x^3\right) dx$

In the following exercises, use the **comparison theorem**.

104. Show that $\int_0^3 \left(x^2 - 6x + 9\right) dx \geq 0$.

105. Show that $\int_{-2}^3 (x-3)(x+2) dx \leq 0$.

106. Show that $\int_0^1 \sqrt{1+x^3} dx \leq \int_0^1 \sqrt{1+x^2} dx$.

107. Show that $\int_1^2 \sqrt{1+x} dx \leq \int_1^2 \sqrt{1+x^2} dx$.

108. Show that $\int_0^{\pi/2} \sin t dt \geq \frac{\pi}{4}$. (*Hint*: $\sin t \geq \frac{2t}{\pi}$ over $\left[0, \frac{\pi}{2}\right]$)

109. Show that $\int_{-\pi/4}^{\pi/4} \cos t dt \geq \pi\sqrt{2}/4$.

In the following exercises, find the average value $f_{\text{ave}}$ of $f$ between $a$ and $b$, and find a point $c$, where $f(c) = f_{\text{ave}}$.

110. $f(x) = x^2$, $a = -1$, $b = 1$

111. $f(x) = x^5$, $a = -1$, $b = 1$

112. $f(x) = \sqrt{4 - x^2}$, $a = 0$, $b = 2$

113. $f(x) = (3 - |x|)$, $a = -3$, $b = 3$

114. $f(x) = \sin x$, $a = 0$, $b = 2\pi$

115. $f(x) = \cos x$, $a = 0$, $b = 2\pi$

In the following exercises, approximate the average value using Riemann sums $L_{100}$ and $R_{100}$. How does your answer compare with the exact given answer?

116. **[T]** $y = \ln(x)$ over the interval $[1, 4]$; the exact solution is $\frac{\ln(256)}{3} - 1$.

117. **[T]** $y = e^{x/2}$ over the interval $[0, 1]$; the exact solution is $2(\sqrt{e} - 1)$.

118. **[T]** $y = \tan x$ over the interval $\left[0, \frac{\pi}{4}\right]$; the exact solution is $\frac{2\ln(2)}{\pi}$.

119. **[T]** $y = \frac{x+1}{\sqrt{4-x^2}}$ over the interval $[-1, 1]$; the exact solution is $\frac{\pi}{6}$.

In the following exercises, compute the average value using the left Riemann sums $L_N$ for $N = 1, 10, 100$. How does the accuracy compare with the given exact value?

120. **[T]** $y = x^2 - 4$ over the interval $[0, 2]$; the exact solution is $-\frac{8}{3}$.

121. **[T]** $y = xe^{x^2}$ over the interval $[0, 2]$; the exact solution is $\frac{1}{4}\left(e^4 - 1\right)$.

122. **[T]** $y = \left(\frac{1}{2}\right)^x$ over the interval $[0, 4]$; the exact solution is $\frac{15}{64\ln(2)}$.

123. **[T]** $y = x\sin(x^2)$ over the interval $[-\pi, 0]$; the exact solution is $\frac{\cos(\pi^2) - 1}{2\pi}$.

124. Suppose that $A = \int_0^{2\pi} \sin^2 t dt$ and $B = \int_0^{2\pi} \cos^2 t dt$. Show that $A + B = 2\pi$ and $A = B$.

125. Suppose that $A = \int_{-\pi/4}^{\pi/4} \sec^2 t dt = \pi$ and $B = \int_{-\pi/4}^{\pi/4} \tan^2 t dt$. Show that $A - B = \frac{\pi}{2}$.

126. Show that the average value of $\sin^2 t$ over $[0, 2\pi]$ is equal to 1/2 Without further calculation, determine whether the average value of $\sin^2 t$ over $[0, \pi]$ is also equal to 1/2.

127. Show that the average value of $\cos^2 t$ over $[0, 2\pi]$ is equal to 1/2. Without further calculation, determine whether the average value of $\cos^2(t)$ over $[0, \pi]$ is also equal to 1/2.

128. Explain why the graphs of a quadratic function (parabola) $p(x)$ and a linear function $\ell(x)$ can intersect in at most two points. Suppose that $p(a) = \ell(a)$ and $p(b) = \ell(b)$, and that $\int_a^b p(t)dt > \int_a^b \ell(t)dt$. Explain why $\int_c^d p(t) > \int_c^d \ell(t)dt$ whenever $a \le c < d \le b$.

129. Suppose that parabola $p(x) = ax^2 + bx + c$ opens downward $(a < 0)$ and has a vertex of $y = \frac{-b}{2a} > 0$. For which interval $[A, B]$ is $\int_A^B \left(ax^2 + bx + c\right)dx$ as large as possible?

130. Suppose $[a, b]$ can be subdivided into subintervals $a = a_0 < a_1 < a_2 < \cdots < a_N = b$ such that either $f \ge 0$ over $[a_{i-1}, a_i]$ or $f \le 0$ over $[a_{i-1}, a_i]$. Set $A_i = \int_{a_{i-1}}^{a_i} f(t)dt$.

a. Explain why $\int_a^b f(t)dt = A_1 + A_2 + \cdots + A_N$.

b. Then, explain why $\left|\int_a^b f(t)dt\right| \le \int_a^b |f(t)|dt$.

131. Suppose $f$ and $g$ are continuous functions such that $\int_c^d f(t)dt \le \int_c^d g(t)dt$ for every subinterval $[c, d]$ of $[a, b]$. Explain why $f(x) \le g(x)$ for all values of $x$.

132. Suppose the average value of $f$ over $[a, b]$ is 1 and the average value of $f$ over $[b, c]$ is 1 where $a < c < b$. Show that the average value of $f$ over $[a, c]$ is also 1.

133. Suppose that $[a, b]$ can be partitioned. taking $a = a_0 < a_1 < \cdots < a_N = b$ such that the average value of $f$ over each subinterval $[a_{i-1}, a_i] = 1$ is equal to 1 for each $i = 1, \ldots, N$. Explain why the average value of $f$ over $[a, b]$ is also equal to 1.

134. Suppose that for each $i$ such that $1 \le i \le N$ one has $\int_{i-1}^{i} f(t)dt = i$. Show that $\int_0^N f(t)dt = \frac{N(N+1)}{2}$.

135. Suppose that for each $i$ such that $1 \le i \le N$ one has $\int_{i-1}^{i} f(t)dt = i^2$. Show that $\int_0^N f(t)dt = \frac{N(N+1)(2N+1)}{6}$.

136. **[T]** Compute the left and right Riemann sums $L_{10}$ and $R_{10}$ and their average $\frac{L_{10} + R_{10}}{2}$ for $f(t) = t^2$ over $[0, 1]$. Given that $\int_0^1 t^2 dt = 0.\overline{33}$, to how many decimal places is $\frac{L_{10} + R_{10}}{2}$ accurate?

137. **[T]** Compute the left and right Riemann sums, $L_{10}$ and $R_{10}$, and their average $\frac{L_{10}+R_{10}}{2}$ for $f(t)=\left(4-t^2\right)$ over $[1, 2]$. Given that $\int_1^2 \left(4-t^2\right)dt = 1.\overline{66}$, to how many decimal places is $\frac{L_{10}+R_{10}}{2}$ accurate?

138. If $\int_1^5 \sqrt{1+t^4}\,dt = 41.7133...$, what is $\int_1^5 \sqrt{1+u^4}\,du$?

139. Estimate $\int_0^1 t\,dt$ using the left and right endpoint sums, each with a single rectangle. How does the average of these left and right endpoint sums compare with the actual value $\int_0^1 t\,dt$?

140. Estimate $\int_0^1 t\,dt$ by comparison with the area of a single rectangle with height equal to the value of $t$ at the midpoint $t=\frac{1}{2}$. How does this midpoint estimate compare with the actual value $\int_0^1 t\,dt$?

141. From the graph of $\sin(2\pi x)$ shown:

a. Explain why $\int_0^1 \sin(2\pi t)dt = 0$.

b. Explain why, in general, $\int_a^{a+1} \sin(2\pi t)dt = 0$ for any value of $a$.

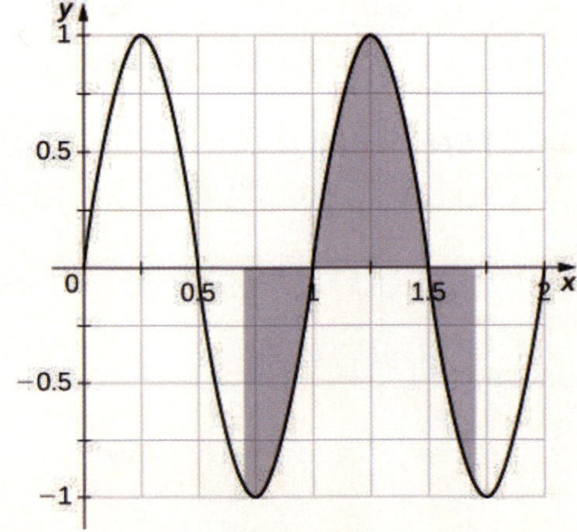


142. If $f$ is 1-periodic $(f(t+1)=f(t))$, odd, and integrable over $[0, 1]$, is it always true that $\int_0^1 f(t)dt = 0$?

143. If $f$ is 1-periodic and $\int_0^1 f(t)dt = A$, is it necessarily true that $\int_a^{1+a} f(t)dt = A$ for all $A$?

# 1.3 | The Fundamental Theorem of Calculus

## Learning Objectives

1.3.1 Describe the meaning of the Mean Value Theorem for Integrals.
1.3.2 State the meaning of the Fundamental Theorem of Calculus, Part 1.
1.3.3 Use the Fundamental Theorem of Calculus, Part 1, to evaluate derivatives of integrals.
1.3.4 State the meaning of the Fundamental Theorem of Calculus, Part 2.
1.3.5 Use the Fundamental Theorem of Calculus, Part 2, to evaluate definite integrals.
1.3.6 Explain the relationship between differentiation and integration.

In the previous two sections, we looked at the definite integral and its relationship to the area under the curve of a function. Unfortunately, so far, the only tools we have available to calculate the value of a definite integral are geometric area formulas and limits of Riemann sums, and both approaches are extremely cumbersome. In this section we look at some more powerful and useful techniques for evaluating definite integrals.

These new techniques rely on the relationship between differentiation and integration. This relationship was discovered and explored by both Sir Isaac Newton and Gottfried Wilhelm Leibniz (among others) during the late 1600s and early 1700s, and it is codified in what we now call the **Fundamental Theorem of Calculus**, which has two parts that we examine in this section. Its very name indicates how central this theorem is to the entire development of calculus.

Isaac Newton's contributions to mathematics and physics changed the way we look at the world. The relationships he discovered, codified as Newton's laws and the law of universal gravitation, are still taught as foundational material in physics today, and his calculus has spawned entire fields of mathematics. To learn more, read a **brief biography (http://www.openstaxcollege.org/l/20_newtonbio)** of Newton with multimedia clips.

Before we get to this crucial theorem, however, let's examine another important theorem, the Mean Value Theorem for Integrals, which is needed to prove the Fundamental Theorem of Calculus.

## The Mean Value Theorem for Integrals

The **Mean Value Theorem for Integrals** states that a continuous function on a closed interval takes on its average value at the same point in that interval. The theorem guarantees that if $f(x)$ is continuous, a point $c$ exists in an interval $[a, b]$ such that the value of the function at $c$ is equal to the average value of $f(x)$ over $[a, b]$. We state this theorem mathematically with the help of the formula for the average value of a function that we presented at the end of the preceding section.

### Theorem 1.3: The Mean Value Theorem for Integrals

If $f(x)$ is continuous over an interval $[a, b]$, then there is at least one point $c \in [a, b]$ such that

$$f(c) = \frac{1}{b-a}\int_a^b f(x)dx. \tag{1.15}$$

This formula can also be stated as

$$\int_a^b f(x)dx = f(c)(b-a).$$

### Proof

Since $f(x)$ is continuous on $[a, b]$, by the extreme value theorem (see **Maxima and Minima (http://cnx.org/content/m53611/latest/)** ), it assumes minimum and maximum values—$m$ and $M$, respectively—on $[a, b]$. Then, for all $x$ in $[a, b]$, we have $m \le f(x) \le M$. Therefore, by the comparison theorem (see **The Definite Integral**), we have

$$m(b-a) \le \int_a^b f(x)dx \le M(b-a).$$

Dividing by $b-a$ gives us

$$m \le \frac{1}{b-a}\int_a^b f(x)dx \le M.$$

Since $\frac{1}{b-a}\int_a^b f(x)dx$ is a number between $m$ and $M$, and since $f(x)$ is continuous and assumes the values $m$ and $M$ over $[a, b]$, by the Intermediate Value Theorem (see **Continuity (http://cnx.org/content/m53489/latest/)** ), there is a number $c$ over $[a, b]$ such that

$$f(c) = \frac{1}{b-a}\int_a^b f(x)dx,$$

and the proof is complete.

□

## Example 1.15

### Finding the Average Value of a Function

Find the average value of the function $f(x) = 8 - 2x$ over the interval $[0, 4]$ and find $c$ such that $f(c)$ equals the average value of the function over $[0, 4]$.

#### Solution

The formula states the mean value of $f(x)$ is given by

$$\frac{1}{4-0}\int_0^4 (8-2x)dx.$$

We can see in **Figure 1.26** that the function represents a straight line and forms a right triangle bounded by the $x$- and $y$-axes. The area of the triangle is $A = \frac{1}{2}(\text{base})(\text{height})$. We have

$$A = \frac{1}{2}(4)(8) = 16.$$

The average value is found by multiplying the area by $1/(4-0)$. Thus, the average value of the function is

$$\frac{1}{4}(16) = 4.$$

Set the average value equal to $f(c)$ and solve for $c$.

$$\begin{aligned} 8 - 2c &= 4 \\ c &= 2 \end{aligned}$$

At $c = 2, f(2) = 4$.

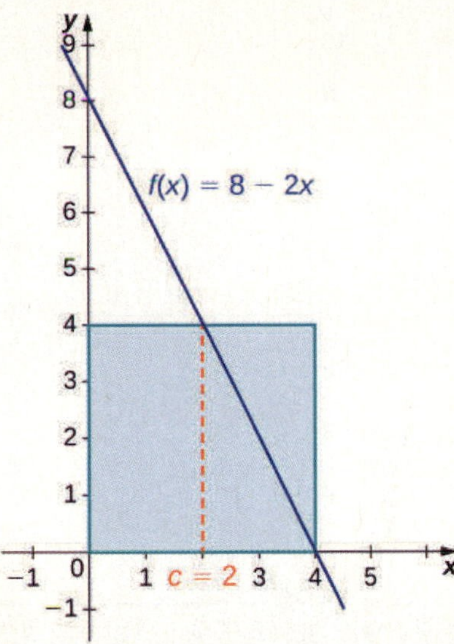


**Figure 1.26** By the Mean Value Theorem, the continuous function $f(x)$ takes on its average value at $c$ at least once over a closed interval.

**1.14** Find the average value of the function $f(x) = \frac{x}{2}$ over the interval $[0, 6]$ and find $c$ such that $f(c)$ equals the average value of the function over $[0, 6]$.

## Example 1.16

### Finding the Point Where a Function Takes on Its Average Value

Given $\int_0^3 x^2\,dx = 9,$ find $c$ such that $f(c)$ equals the average value of $f(x) = x^2$ over $[0, 3]$.

#### Solution

We are looking for the value of $c$ such that

$$f(c) = \frac{1}{3-0}\int_0^3 x^2\,dx = \frac{1}{3}(9) = 3.$$

Replacing $f(c)$ with $c^2$, we have

$$\begin{aligned} c^2 &= 3 \\ c &= \pm\sqrt{3}. \end{aligned}$$

Since $-\sqrt{3}$ is outside the interval, take only the positive value. Thus, $c = \sqrt{3}$ (**Figure 1.27**).

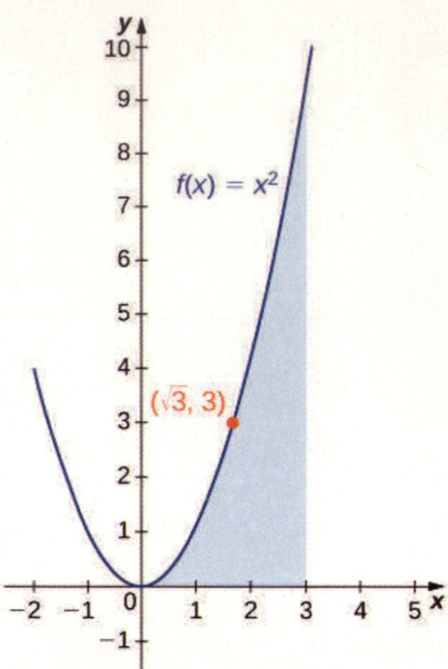


**Figure 1.27** Over the interval $[0, 3]$, the function $f(x) = x^2$ takes on its average value at $c = \sqrt{3}$.

**1.15** Given $\int_0^3 (2x^2 - 1)dx = 15$, find $c$ such that $f(c)$ equals the average value of $f(x) = 2x^2 - 1$ over $[0, 3]$.

## Fundamental Theorem of Calculus Part 1: Integrals and Antiderivatives

As mentioned earlier, the Fundamental Theorem of Calculus is an extremely powerful theorem that establishes the relationship between differentiation and integration, and gives us a way to evaluate definite integrals without using Riemann sums or calculating areas. The theorem is comprised of two parts, the first of which, the **Fundamental Theorem of Calculus, Part 1**, is stated here. Part 1 establishes the relationship between differentiation and integration.

### Theorem 1.4: Fundamental Theorem of Calculus, Part 1

If $f(x)$ is continuous over an interval $[a, b]$, and the function $F(x)$ is defined by

$$F(x) = \int_a^x f(t)dt, \tag{1.16}$$

then $F'(x) = f(x)$ over $[a, b]$.

Before we delve into the proof, a couple of subtleties are worth mentioning here. First, a comment on the notation. Note that we have defined a function, $F(x)$, as the definite integral of another function, $f(t)$, from the point $a$ to the point $x$. At first glance, this is confusing, because we have said several times that a definite integral is a number, and here it looks like it's a function. The key here is to notice that for any particular value of $x$, the definite integral is a number. So the function $F(x)$ returns a number (the value of the definite integral) for each value of $x$.

Second, it is worth commenting on some of the key implications of this theorem. There is a reason it is called the *Fundamental* Theorem of Calculus. Not only does it establish a relationship between integration and differentiation, but also it guarantees that any integrable function has an antiderivative. Specifically, it guarantees that any continuous function has an antiderivative.

### Proof

Applying the definition of the derivative, we have

$$\begin{aligned} F'(x) &= \lim_{h \to 0} \frac{F(x+h) - F(x)}{h} \\ &= \lim_{h \to 0} \frac{1}{h}\left[\int_a^{x+h} f(t)dt - \int_a^x f(t)dt\right] \\ &= \lim_{h \to 0} \frac{1}{h}\left[\int_a^{x+h} f(t)dt + \int_x^a f(t)dt\right] \\ &= \lim_{h \to 0} \frac{1}{h}\int_x^{x+h} f(t)dt. \end{aligned}$$

Looking carefully at this last expression, we see $\frac{1}{h}\int_x^{x+h} f(t)dt$ is just the average value of the function $f(x)$ over the interval $[x, x+h]$. Therefore, by **The Mean Value Theorem for Integrals**, there is some number $c$ in $[x, x+h]$ such that

$$\frac{1}{h}\int_x^{x+h} f(x)dx = f(c).$$

In addition, since $c$ is between $x$ and $h$, $c$ approaches $x$ as $h$ approaches zero. Also, since $f(x)$ is continuous, we have $\lim_{h \to 0} f(c) = \lim_{c \to x} f(c) = f(x)$. Putting all these pieces together, we have

$$\begin{aligned} F'(x) &= \lim_{h \to 0} \frac{1}{h}\int_x^{x+h} f(x)dx \\ &= \lim_{h \to 0} f(c) \\ &= f(x), \end{aligned}$$

and the proof is complete.

□

## Example 1.17

### Finding a Derivative with the Fundamental Theorem of Calculus

Use the **Fundamental Theorem of Calculus, Part 1** to find the derivative of

$$g(x) = \int_1^x \frac{1}{t^3 + 1}dt.$$

#### Solution

According to the Fundamental Theorem of Calculus, the derivative is given by

$$g'(x) = \frac{1}{x^3 + 1}.$$

**1.16** Use the Fundamental Theorem of Calculus, Part 1 to find the derivative of $g(r) = \int_0^r \sqrt{x^2 + 4}dx.$

## Example 1.18

### Using the Fundamental Theorem and the Chain Rule to Calculate Derivatives

Let $F(x) = \int_1^{\sqrt{x}} \sin t dt.$ Find $F'(x).$

#### Solution

Letting $u(x) = \sqrt{x},$ we have $F(x) = \int_1^{u(x)} \sin t dt.$ Thus, by the Fundamental Theorem of Calculus and the chain rule,

$$\begin{aligned} F'(x) &= \sin(u(x))\frac{du}{dx} \\ &= \sin(u(x)) \cdot \left(\frac{1}{2}x^{-1/2}\right) \\ &= \frac{\sin\sqrt{x}}{2\sqrt{x}}. \end{aligned}$$

**1.17** Let $F(x) = \int_1^{x^3} \cos t dt.$ Find $F'(x).$

## Example 1.19

### Using the Fundamental Theorem of Calculus with Two Variable Limits of Integration

Let $F(x) = \int_x^{2x} t^3 dt.$ Find $F'(x).$

#### Solution

We have $F(x) = \int_x^{2x} t^3 dt.$ Both limits of integration are variable, so we need to split this into two integrals. We get

$$\begin{aligned} F(x) &= \int_x^{2x} t^3 dt \\ &= \int_x^0 t^3 dt + \int_0^{2x} t^3 dt \\ &= -\int_0^x t^3 dt + \int_0^{2x} t^3 dt. \end{aligned}$$

Differentiating the first term, we obtain

$$\frac{d}{dx}\left[-\int_0^x t^3\,dt\right] = -x^3.$$

Differentiating the second term, we first let $u(x) = 2x$. Then,

$$\begin{aligned}\frac{d}{dx}\left[\int_0^{2x} t^3\,dt\right] &= \frac{d}{dx}\left[\int_0^{u(x)} t^3\,dt\right] \\ &= (u(x))^3\frac{du}{dx} \\ &= (2x)^3 \cdot 2 \\ &= 16x^3.\end{aligned}$$

Thus,

$$\begin{aligned}F'(x) &= \frac{d}{dx}\left[-\int_0^x t^3\,dt\right] + \frac{d}{dx}\left[\int_0^{2x} t^3\,dt\right] \\ &= -x^3 + 16x^3 \\ &= 15x^3.\end{aligned}$$

**1.18** Let $F(x) = \int_x^{x^2} \cos t\,dt$. Find $F'(x)$.

## Fundamental Theorem of Calculus, Part 2: The Evaluation Theorem

The Fundamental Theorem of Calculus, Part 2, is perhaps the most important theorem in calculus. After tireless efforts by mathematicians for approximately 500 years, new techniques emerged that provided scientists with the necessary tools to explain many phenomena. Using calculus, astronomers could finally determine distances in space and map planetary orbits. Everyday financial problems such as calculating marginal costs or predicting total profit could now be handled with simplicity and accuracy. Engineers could calculate the bending strength of materials or the three-dimensional motion of objects. Our view of the world was forever changed with calculus.

After finding approximate areas by adding the areas of $n$ rectangles, the application of this theorem is straightforward by comparison. It almost seems too simple that the area of an entire curved region can be calculated by just evaluating an antiderivative at the first and last endpoints of an interval.

### Theorem 1.5: The Fundamental Theorem of Calculus, Part 2

If $f$ is continuous over the interval $[a, b]$ and $F(x)$ is any antiderivative of $f(x)$, then

$$\int_a^b f(x)dx = F(b) - F(a). \tag{1.17}$$

We often see the notation $F(x)|_a^b$ to denote the expression $F(b) - F(a)$. We use this vertical bar and associated limits $a$ and $b$ to indicate that we should evaluate the function $F(x)$ at the upper limit (in this case, $b$), and subtract the value of the function $F(x)$ evaluated at the lower limit (in this case, $a$).

The **Fundamental Theorem of Calculus, Part 2** (also known as the **evaluation theorem**) states that if we can find an antiderivative for the integrand, then we can evaluate the definite integral by evaluating the antiderivative at the endpoints of the interval and subtracting.

### Proof

Let $P = \{x_i\},\ i = 0, 1,\ldots, n$ be a regular partition of $[a, b]$. Then, we can write

$$\begin{aligned} F(b) - F(a) &= F(x_n) - F(x_0) \\ &= [F(x_n) - F(x_{n-1})] + [F(x_{n-1}) - F(x_{n-2})] + \ldots + [F(x_1) - F(x_0)] \\ &= \sum_{i=1}^{n} [F(x_i) - F(x_{i-1})]. \end{aligned}$$

Now, we know $F$ is an antiderivative of $f$ over $[a, b]$, so by the Mean Value Theorem (see **The Mean Value Theorem (http://cnx.org/content/m53612/latest/)** ) for $i = 0, 1,\ldots, n$ we can find $c_i$ in $[x_{i-1}, x_i]$ such that

$$F(x_i) - F(x_{i-1}) = F'(c_i)(x_i - x_{i-1}) = f(c_i)\Delta x.$$

Then, substituting into the previous equation, we have

$$F(b) - F(a) = \sum_{i=1}^{n} f(c_i)\Delta x.$$

Taking the limit of both sides as $n \to \infty$, we obtain

$$\begin{aligned} F(b) - F(a) &= \lim_{n \to \infty} \sum_{i=1}^{n} f(c_i)\Delta x \\ &= \int_a^b f(x)dx. \end{aligned}$$

□

## Example 1.20

### Evaluating an Integral with the Fundamental Theorem of Calculus

Use **The Fundamental Theorem of Calculus, Part 2** to evaluate

$$\int_{-2}^{2} (t^2 - 4)dt.$$

### Solution

Recall the power rule for **Antiderivatives (http://cnx.org/content/m53621/latest/)** :

$$\text{If } y = x^n, \int x^n\,dx = \frac{x^{n+1}}{n+1} + C.$$

Use this rule to find the antiderivative of the function and then apply the theorem. We have

$$\begin{aligned}\int_{-2}^{2}(t^2-4)dt &= \frac{t^3}{3}-4t\Big|_{-2}^{2} \\ &= \left[\frac{(2)^3}{3}-4(2)\right]-\left[\frac{(-2)^3}{3}-4(-2)\right] \\ &= \left(\frac{8}{3}-8\right)-\left(-\frac{8}{3}+8\right) \\ &= \frac{8}{3}-8+\frac{8}{3}-8 \\ &= \frac{16}{3}-16 \\ &= -\frac{32}{3}.\end{aligned}$$

**Analysis**

Notice that we did not include the "+ $C$" term when we wrote the antiderivative. The reason is that, according to the Fundamental Theorem of Calculus, Part 2, *any* antiderivative works. So, for convenience, we chose the antiderivative with $C = 0.$ If we had chosen another antiderivative, the constant term would have canceled out. This always happens when evaluating a definite integral.

The region of the area we just calculated is depicted in **Figure 1.28**. Note that the region between the curve and the *x*-axis is all below the *x*-axis. Area is always positive, but a definite integral can still produce a negative number (a net signed area). For example, if this were a profit function, a negative number indicates the company is operating at a loss over the given interval.

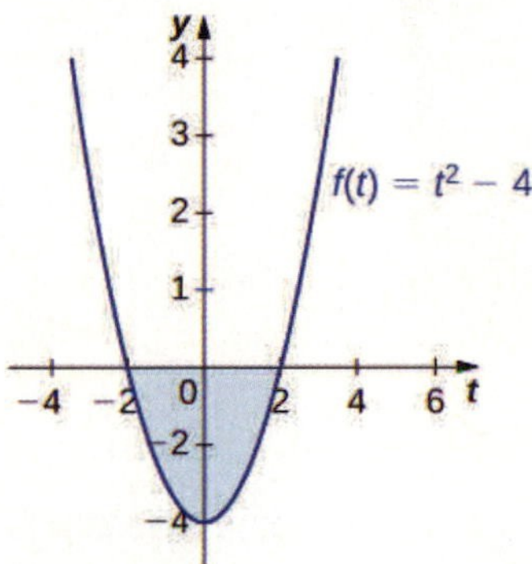


**Figure 1.28** The evaluation of a definite integral can produce a negative value, even though area is always positive.

## Example 1.21

### Evaluating a Definite Integral Using the Fundamental Theorem of Calculus, Part 2

Evaluate the following integral using the Fundamental Theorem of Calculus, Part 2:

$$\int_{1}^{9}\frac{x-1}{\sqrt{x}}dx.$$

**Solution**

First, eliminate the radical by rewriting the integral using rational exponents. Then, separate the numerator terms by writing each one over the denominator:

$$\int_1^9 \frac{x-1}{x^{1/2}}dx = \int_1^9 \left(\frac{x}{x^{1/2}} - \frac{1}{x^{1/2}}\right)dx.$$

Use the properties of exponents to simplify:

$$\int_1^9 \left(\frac{x}{x^{1/2}} - \frac{1}{x^{1/2}}\right)dx = \int_1^9 \left(x^{1/2} - x^{-1/2}\right)dx.$$

Now, integrate using the power rule:

$$\begin{aligned}\int_1^9 \left(x^{1/2} - x^{-1/2}\right)dx &= \left(\frac{x^{3/2}}{\frac{3}{2}} - \frac{x^{1/2}}{\frac{1}{2}}\right)\Bigg|_1^9 \\ &= \left[\frac{(9)^{3/2}}{\frac{3}{2}} - \frac{(9)^{1/2}}{\frac{1}{2}}\right] - \left[\frac{(1)^{3/2}}{\frac{3}{2}} - \frac{(1)^{1/2}}{\frac{1}{2}}\right] \\ &= \left[\frac{2}{3}(27) - 2(3)\right] - \left[\frac{2}{3}(1) - 2(1)\right] \\ &= 18 - 6 - \frac{2}{3} + 2 \\ &= \frac{40}{3}.\end{aligned}$$

See **Figure 1.29**.

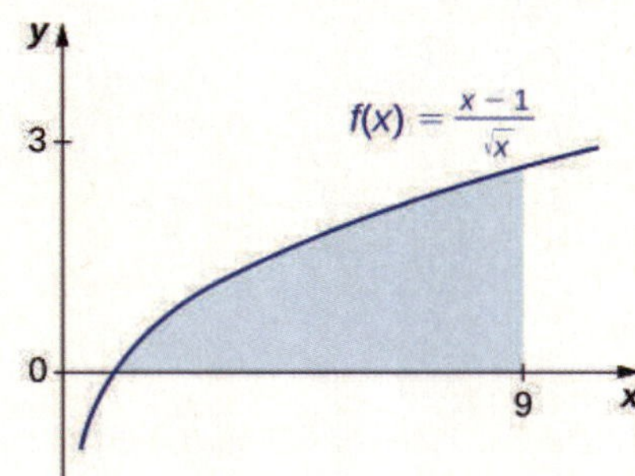


**Figure 1.29** The area under the curve from $x = 1$ to $x = 9$ can be calculated by evaluating a definite integral.

**1.19** Use **The Fundamental Theorem of Calculus, Part 2** to evaluate $\int_1^2 x^{-4}\,dx.$

## Example 1.22

### A Roller-Skating Race

James and Kathy are racing on roller skates. They race along a long, straight track, and whoever has gone the farthest after 5 sec wins a prize. If James can skate at a velocity of $f(t) = 5 + 2t$ ft/sec and Kathy can skate at a velocity of $g(t) = 10 + \cos\left(\frac{\pi}{2}t\right)$ ft/sec, who is going to win the race?

### Solution

We need to integrate both functions over the interval $[0, 5]$ and see which value is bigger. For James, we want to calculate

$$\int_0^5 (5 + 2t)dt.$$

Using the power rule, we have

$$\begin{aligned}\int_0^5 (5 + 2t)dt &= \left(5t + t^2\right)\Big|_0^5 \\ &= (25 + 25) = 50.\end{aligned}$$

Thus, James has skated 50 ft after 5 sec. Turning now to Kathy, we want to calculate

$$\int_0^5 10 + \cos\left(\frac{\pi}{2}t\right)dt.$$

We know $\sin t$ is an antiderivative of $\cos t$, so it is reasonable to expect that an antiderivative of $\cos\left(\frac{\pi}{2}t\right)$ would involve $\sin\left(\frac{\pi}{2}t\right)$. However, when we differentiate $\sin\left(\frac{\pi}{2}t\right)$, we get $\frac{\pi}{2}\cos\left(\frac{\pi}{2}t\right)$ as a result of the chain rule, so we have to account for this additional coefficient when we integrate. We obtain

$$\begin{aligned}\int_0^5 10 + \cos\left(\frac{\pi}{2}t\right)dt &= \left(10t + \frac{2}{\pi}\sin\left(\frac{\pi}{2}t\right)\right)\Big|_0^5 \\ &= \left(50 + \frac{2}{\pi}\right) - \left(0 - \frac{2}{\pi}\sin 0\right) \\ &\approx 50.6.\end{aligned}$$

Kathy has skated approximately 50.6 ft after 5 sec. Kathy wins, but not by much!

**1.20** Suppose James and Kathy have a rematch, but this time the official stops the contest after only 3 sec. Does this change the outcome?

# Student PROJECT

## A Parachutist in Free Fall

**Figure 1.30** Skydivers can adjust the velocity of their dive by changing the position of their body during the free fall. (credit: Jeremy T. Lock)

Julie is an avid skydiver. She has more than 300 jumps under her belt and has mastered the art of making adjustments to her body position in the air to control how fast she falls. If she arches her back and points her belly toward the ground, she reaches a terminal velocity of approximately 120 mph (176 ft/sec). If, instead, she orients her body with her head straight down, she falls faster, reaching a terminal velocity of 150 mph (220 ft/sec).

Since Julie will be moving (falling) in a downward direction, we assume the downward direction is positive to simplify our calculations. Julie executes her jumps from an altitude of 12,500 ft. After she exits the aircraft, she immediately starts falling at a velocity given by $v(t) = 32t$. She continues to accelerate according to this velocity function until she reaches terminal velocity. After she reaches terminal velocity, her speed remains constant until she pulls her ripcord and slows down to land.

On her first jump of the day, Julie orients herself in the slower "belly down" position (terminal velocity is 176 ft/sec). Using this information, answer the following questions.

1. How long after she exits the aircraft does Julie reach terminal velocity?
2. Based on your answer to question 1, set up an expression involving one or more integrals that represents the distance Julie falls after 30 sec.
3. If Julie pulls her ripcord at an altitude of 3000 ft, how long does she spend in a free fall?
4. Julie pulls her ripcord at 3000 ft. It takes 5 sec for her parachute to open completely and for her to slow down, during which time she falls another 400 ft. After her canopy is fully open, her speed is reduced to 16 ft/sec. Find the total time Julie spends in the air, from the time she leaves the airplane until the time her feet touch the ground.

On Julie's second jump of the day, she decides she wants to fall a little faster and orients herself in the "head down" position. Her terminal velocity in this position is 220 ft/sec. Answer these questions based on this velocity:

5. How long does it take Julie to reach terminal velocity in this case?
6. Before pulling her ripcord, Julie reorients her body in the "belly down" position so she is not moving quite as fast when her parachute opens. If she begins this maneuver at an altitude of 4000 ft, how long does she spend in a free fall before beginning the reorientation?

Some jumpers wear " wingsuits" (see **Figure 1.31**). These suits have fabric panels between the arms and legs and allow the wearer to glide around in a free fall, much like a flying squirrel. (Indeed, the suits are sometimes called "flying squirrel suits.") When wearing these suits, terminal velocity can be reduced to about 30 mph (44 ft/sec), allowing the wearers a much longer time in the air. Wingsuit flyers still use parachutes to land; although the vertical velocities are within the margin of safety, horizontal velocities can exceed 70 mph, much too fast to land safely.

**Figure 1.31** The fabric panels on the arms and legs of a wingsuit work to reduce the vertical velocity of a skydiver's fall. (credit: Richard Schneider)

Answer the following question based on the velocity in a wingsuit.

7. If Julie dons a wingsuit before her third jump of the day, and she pulls her ripcord at an altitude of 3000 ft, how long does she get to spend gliding around in the air?

# 1.3 EXERCISES

144. Consider two athletes running at variable speeds $v_1(t)$ and $v_2(t)$. The runners start and finish a race at exactly the same time. Explain why the two runners must be going the same speed at some point.

145. Two mountain climbers start their climb at base camp, taking two different routes, one steeper than the other, and arrive at the peak at exactly the same time. Is it necessarily true that, at some point, both climbers increased in altitude at the same rate?

146. To get on a certain toll road a driver has to take a card that lists the mile entrance point. The card also has a timestamp. When going to pay the toll at the exit, the driver is surprised to receive a speeding ticket along with the toll. Explain how this can happen.

147. Set $F(x) = \int_1^x (1 - t)dt$. Find $F'(2)$ and the average value of $F'$ over $[1, 2]$.

In the following exercises, use the Fundamental Theorem of Calculus, Part 1, to find each derivative.

148. $\frac{d}{dx}\int_1^x e^{-t^2}\,dt$

149. $\frac{d}{dx}\int_1^x e^{\cos t}\,dt$

150. $\frac{d}{dx}\int_3^x \sqrt{9 - y^2}dy$

151. $\frac{d}{dx}\int_4^x \frac{ds}{\sqrt{16 - s^2}}$

152. $\frac{d}{dx}\int_x^{2x} tdt$

153. $\frac{d}{dx}\int_0^{\sqrt{x}} tdt$

154. $\frac{d}{dx}\int_0^{\sin x} \sqrt{1 - t^2}dt$

155. $\frac{d}{dx}\int_{\cos x}^1 \sqrt{1 - t^2}dt$

156. $\frac{d}{dx}\int_1^{\sqrt{x}} \frac{t^2}{1 + t^4}dt$

157. $\frac{d}{dx}\int_1^{x^2} \frac{\sqrt{t}}{1 + t}dt$

158. $\frac{d}{dx}\int_0^{\ln x} e^t\,dt$

159. $\frac{d}{dx}\int_1^{e^2} \ln u^2\,du$

160. The graph of $y = \int_0^x f(t)dt$, where $f$ is a piecewise constant function, is shown here.

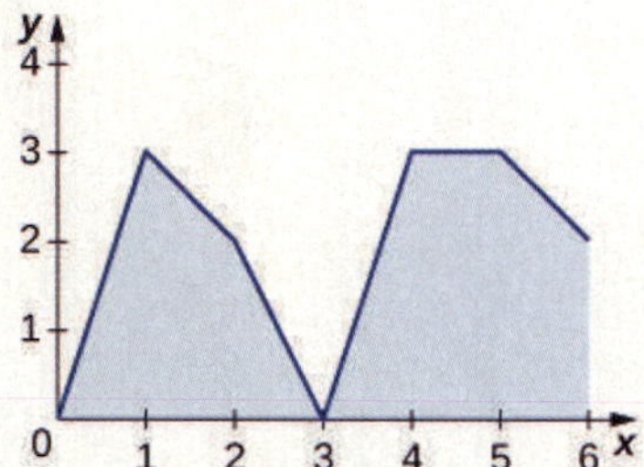


a. Over which intervals is $f$ positive? Over which intervals is it negative? Over which intervals, if any, is it equal to zero?
b. What are the maximum and minimum values of $f$?
c. What is the average value of $f$?

161. The graph of $y = \int_0^x f(t)dt$, where $f$ is a piecewise constant function, is shown here.

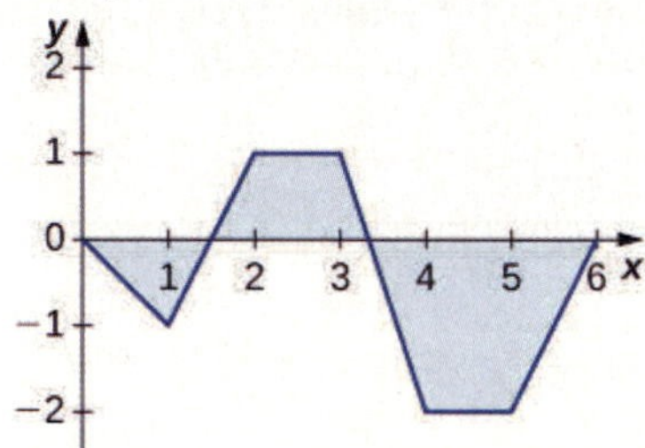


a. Over which intervals is $f$ positive? Over which intervals is it negative? Over which intervals, if any, is it equal to zero?
b. What are the maximum and minimum values of $f$?
c. What is the average value of $f$?

162. The graph of $y = \int_0^x \ell(t)dt$, where $\ell$ is a piecewise linear function, is shown here.

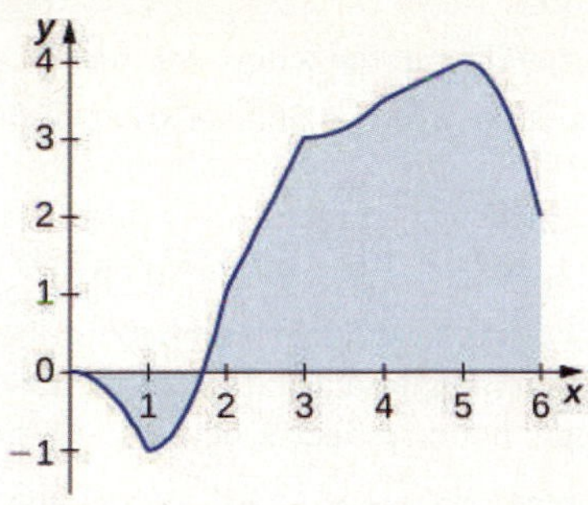

a. Over which intervals is $\ell$ positive? Over which intervals is it negative? Over which, if any, is it zero?
b. Over which intervals is $\ell$ increasing? Over which is it decreasing? Over which, if any, is it constant?
c. What is the average value of $\ell$?

163. The graph of $y = \int_0^x \ell(t)dt$, where $\ell$ is a piecewise linear function, is shown here.

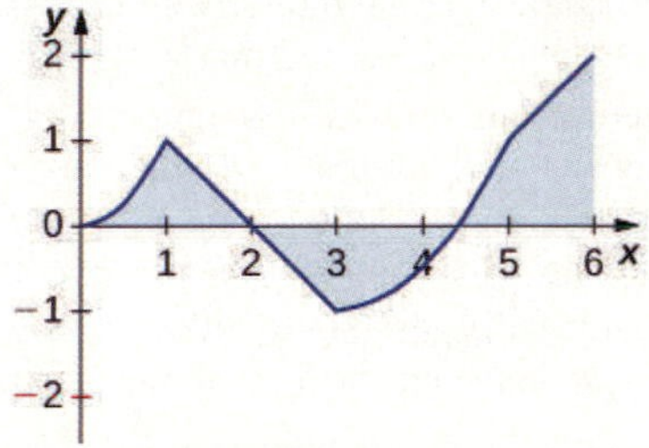

a. Over which intervals is $\ell$ positive? Over which intervals is it negative? Over which, if any, is it zero?
b. Over which intervals is $\ell$ increasing? Over which is it decreasing? Over which intervals, if any, is it constant?
c. What is the average value of $\ell$?

In the following exercises, use a calculator to estimate the area under the curve by computing $T_{10}$, the average of the left- and right-endpoint Riemann sums using $N = 10$ rectangles. Then, using the Fundamental Theorem of Calculus, Part 2, determine the exact area.

164. **[T]** $y = x^2$ over $[0, 4]$

165. **[T]** $y = x^3 + 6x^2 + x - 5$ over $[-4, 2]$

166. **[T]** $y = \sqrt{x^3}$ over $[0, 6]$

167. **[T]** $y = \sqrt{x} + x^2$ over $[1, 9]$

168. **[T]** $\int (\cos x - \sin x)dx$ over $[0, \pi]$

169. **[T]** $\int \frac{4}{x^2}dx$ over $[1, 4]$

In the following exercises, evaluate each definite integral using the Fundamental Theorem of Calculus, Part 2.

170. $\int_{-1}^{2} \left(x^2 - 3x\right)dx$

171. $\int_{-2}^{3} \left(x^2 + 3x - 5\right)dx$

172. $\int_{-2}^{3} (t + 2)(t - 3)dt$

173. $\int_{2}^{3} \left(t^2 - 9\right)\left(4 - t^2\right)dt$

174. $\int_{1}^{2} x^9\, dx$

175. $\int_{0}^{1} x^{99}\, dx$

176. $\int_{4}^{8} \left(4t^{5/2} - 3t^{3/2}\right)dt$

177. $\int_{1/4}^{4} \left(x^2 - \frac{1}{x^2}\right)dx$

178. $\int_{1}^{2} \frac{2}{x^3}dx$

179. $\int_{1}^{4} \frac{1}{2\sqrt{x}}dx$

180. $\int_{1}^{4} \frac{2 - \sqrt{t}}{t^2}dt$

181. $\int_{1}^{16} \frac{dt}{t^{1/4}}$

182. $\int_{0}^{2\pi} \cos\theta d\theta$

183. $\int_{0}^{\pi/2} \sin\theta d\theta$

184. $\int_0^{\pi/4} \sec^2 \theta d\theta$

185. $\int_0^{\pi/4} \sec\theta \tan\theta$

186. $\int_{\pi/3}^{\pi/4} \csc\theta \cot\theta d\theta$

187. $\int_{\pi/4}^{\pi/2} \csc^2 \theta d\theta$

188. $\int_1^2 \left(\frac{1}{t^2} - \frac{1}{t^3}\right) dt$

189. $\int_{-2}^{-1} \left(\frac{1}{t^2} - \frac{1}{t^3}\right) dt$

In the following exercises, use the evaluation theorem to express the integral as a function $F(x)$.

190. $\int_a^x t^2 \, dt$

191. $\int_1^x e^t \, dt$

192. $\int_0^x \cos t dt$

193. $\int_{-x}^x \sin t dt$

In the following exercises, identify the roots of the integrand to remove absolute values, then evaluate using the Fundamental Theorem of Calculus, Part 2.

194. $\int_{-2}^3 |x| dx$

195. $\int_{-2}^4 \left|t^2 - 2t - 3\right| dt$

196. $\int_0^\pi |\cos t| dt$

197. $\int_{-\pi/2}^{\pi/2} |\sin t| dt$

198. Suppose that the number of hours of daylight on a given day in Seattle is modeled by the function $-3.75\cos\left(\frac{\pi t}{6}\right) + 12.25,$ with $t$ given in months and $t = 0$ corresponding to the winter solstice.

a. What is the average number of daylight hours in a year?

b. At which times $t_1$ and $t_2,$ where $0 \le t_1 < t_2 < 12,$ do the number of daylight hours equal the average number?

c. Write an integral that expresses the total number of daylight hours in Seattle between $t_1$ and $t_2$.

d. Compute the mean hours of daylight in Seattle between $t_1$ and $t_2,$ where $0 \le t_1 < t_2 < 12,$ and then between $t_2$ and $t_1,$ and show that the average of the two is equal to the average day length.

199. Suppose the rate of gasoline consumption in the United States can be modeled by a sinusoidal function of the form $\left(11.21 - \cos\left(\frac{\pi t}{6}\right)\right) \times 10^9$ gal/mo.

a. What is the average monthly consumption, and for which values of $t$ is the rate at time $t$ equal to the average rate?

b. What is the number of gallons of gasoline consumed in the United States in a year?

c. Write an integral that expresses the average monthly U.S. gas consumption during the part of the year between the beginning of April $(t = 3)$ and the end of September $(t = 9)$.

200. Explain why, if $f$ is continuous over $[a, b],$ there is at least one point $c \in [a, b]$ such that $f(c) = \frac{1}{b-a}\int_a^b f(t) dt.$

201. Explain why, if $f$ is continuous over $[a, b]$ and is not equal to a constant, there is at least one point $M \in [a, b]$ such that $f(M) = \frac{1}{b-a}\int_a^b f(t) dt$ and at least one point $m \in [a, b]$ such that $f(m) < \frac{1}{b-a}\int_a^b f(t) dt.$

202. Kepler's first law states that the planets move in elliptical orbits with the Sun at one focus. The closest point of a planetary orbit to the Sun is called the *perihelion* (for Earth, it currently occurs around January 3) and the farthest point is called the *aphelion* (for Earth, it currently occurs around July 4). Kepler's second law states that planets sweep out equal areas of their elliptical orbits in equal times. Thus, the two arcs indicated in the following figure are swept out in equal times. At what time of year is Earth moving fastest in its orbit? When is it moving slowest?

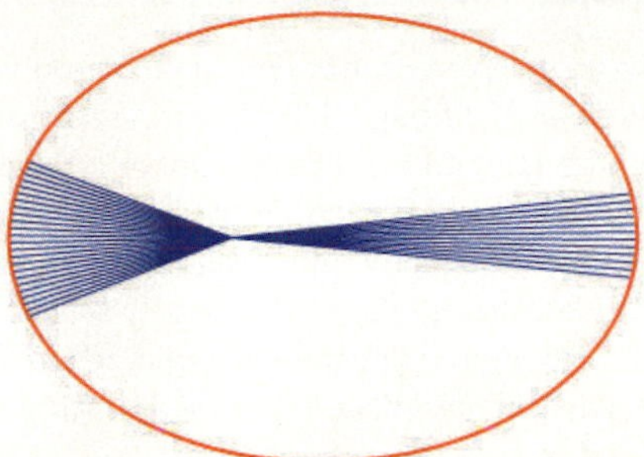

203. A point on an ellipse with major axis length $2a$ and minor axis length $2b$ has the coordinates $(a\cos\theta,\ b\sin\theta),\ 0 \le \theta \le 2\pi$.

a. Show that the distance from this point to the focus at $(-c,\ 0)$ is $d(\theta) = a + c\cos\theta,$ where $c = \sqrt{a^2 - b^2}$.
b. Use these coordinates to show that the average distance $\bar{d}$ from a point on the ellipse to the focus at $(-c,\ 0),$ with respect to angle $\theta$, is $a$.

204. As implied earlier, according to Kepler's laws, Earth's orbit is an ellipse with the Sun at one focus. The perihelion for Earth's orbit around the Sun is 147,098,290 km and the aphelion is 152,098,232 km.

a. By placing the major axis along the $x$-axis, find the average distance from Earth to the Sun.
b. The classic definition of an astronomical unit (AU) is the distance from Earth to the Sun, and its value was computed as the average of the perihelion and aphelion distances. Is this definition justified?

205. The force of gravitational attraction between the Sun and a planet is $F(\theta) = \dfrac{GmM}{r^2(\theta)},$ where $m$ is the mass of the planet, $M$ is the mass of the Sun, $G$ is a universal constant, and $r(\theta)$ is the distance between the Sun and the planet when the planet is at an angle $\theta$ with the major axis of its orbit. Assuming that $M$, $m$, and the ellipse parameters $a$ and $b$ (half-lengths of the major and minor axes) are given, set up—but do not evaluate—an integral that expresses in terms of $G, m, M, a, b$ the average gravitational force between the Sun and the planet.

206. The displacement from rest of a mass attached to a spring satisfies the simple harmonic motion equation $x(t) = A\cos(\omega t - \phi),$ where $\phi$ is a phase constant, $\omega$ is the angular frequency, and $A$ is the amplitude. Find the average velocity, the average speed (magnitude of velocity), the average displacement, and the average distance from rest (magnitude of displacement) of the mass.

# 1.4 | Integration Formulas and the Net Change Theorem

## Learning Objectives

**1.4.1** Apply the basic integration formulas.
**1.4.2** Explain the significance of the net change theorem.
**1.4.3** Use the net change theorem to solve applied problems.
**1.4.4** Apply the integrals of odd and even functions.

In this section, we use some basic integration formulas studied previously to solve some key applied problems. It is important to note that these formulas are presented in terms of *indefinite* integrals. Although definite and indefinite integrals are closely related, there are some key differences to keep in mind. A definite integral is either a number (when the limits of integration are constants) or a single function (when one or both of the limits of integration are variables). An indefinite integral represents a family of functions, all of which differ by a constant. As you become more familiar with integration, you will get a feel for when to use definite integrals and when to use indefinite integrals. You will naturally select the correct approach for a given problem without thinking too much about it. However, until these concepts are cemented in your mind, think carefully about whether you need a definite integral or an indefinite integral and make sure you are using the proper notation based on your choice.

## Basic Integration Formulas

Recall the integration formulas given in the **table in Antiderivatives (http://cnx.org/content/m53621/latest/#fs-id1165043092431)** and the rule on properties of definite integrals. Let's look at a few examples of how to apply these rules.

### Example 1.23

#### Integrating a Function Using the Power Rule

Use the power rule to integrate the function $\int_1^4 \sqrt{t}(1+t)dt$.

#### Solution

The first step is to rewrite the function and simplify it so we can apply the power rule:

$$\begin{aligned}\int_1^4 \sqrt{t}(1+t)dt &= \int_1^4 t^{1/2}(1+t)dt \\ &= \int_1^4 \left(t^{1/2}+t^{3/2}\right)dt.\end{aligned}$$

Now apply the power rule:

$$\begin{aligned}\int_1^4 \left(t^{1/2}+t^{3/2}\right)dt &= \left(\frac{2}{3}t^{3/2}+\frac{2}{5}t^{5/2}\right)\Big|_1^4 \\ &= \left[\frac{2}{3}(4)^{3/2}+\frac{2}{5}(4)^{5/2}\right]-\left[\frac{2}{3}(1)^{3/2}+\frac{2}{5}(1)^{5/2}\right] \\ &= \frac{256}{15}.\end{aligned}$$

**1.21** Find the definite integral of $f(x) = x^2 - 3x$ over the interval $[1, 3]$.

## The Net Change Theorem

The **net change theorem** considers the integral of a *rate of change*. It says that when a quantity changes, the new value equals the initial value plus the integral of the rate of change of that quantity. The formula can be expressed in two ways. The second is more familiar; it is simply the definite integral.

### Theorem 1.6: Net Change Theorem

The new value of a changing quantity equals the initial value plus the integral of the rate of change:

$$F(b) = F(a) + \int_a^b F'(x)dx \tag{1.18}$$

or

$$\int_a^b F'(x)dx = F(b) - F(a).$$

Subtracting $F(a)$ from both sides of the first equation yields the second equation. Since they are equivalent formulas, which one we use depends on the application.

The significance of the net change theorem lies in the results. Net change can be applied to area, distance, and volume, to name only a few applications. Net change accounts for negative quantities automatically without having to write more than one integral. To illustrate, let's apply the net change theorem to a velocity function in which the result is displacement.

We looked at a simple example of this in **The Definite Integral**. Suppose a car is moving due north (the positive direction) at 40 mph between 2 p.m. and 4 p.m., then the car moves south at 30 mph between 4 p.m. and 5 p.m. We can graph this motion as shown in **Figure 1.32**.

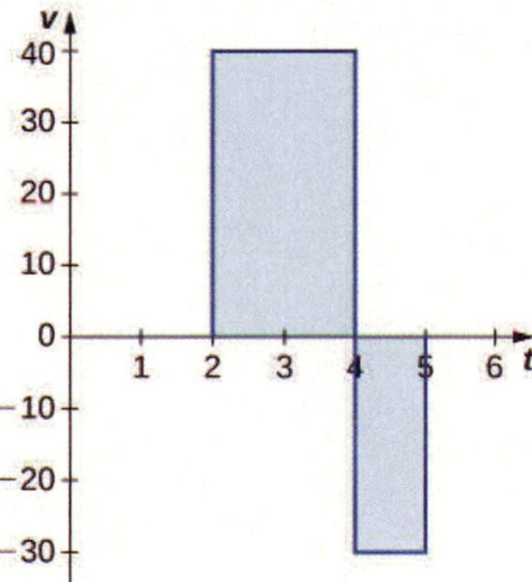


**Figure 1.32** The graph shows speed versus time for the given motion of a car.

Just as we did before, we can use definite integrals to calculate the net displacement as well as the total distance traveled. The net displacement is given by

$$\begin{aligned}\int_2^5 v(t)dt &= \int_2^4 40dt + \int_4^5 -30dt \\ &= 80 - 30 \\ &= 50.\end{aligned}$$

Thus, at 5 p.m. the car is 50 mi north of its starting position. The total distance traveled is given by

$$\begin{aligned}\int_2^5 |v(t)|dt &= \int_2^4 40dt + \int_4^5 30dt \\ &= 80 + 30 \\ &= 110.\end{aligned}$$

Therefore, between 2 p.m. and 5 p.m., the car traveled a total of 110 mi.

To summarize, net displacement may include both positive and negative values. In other words, the velocity function accounts for both forward distance and backward distance. To find net displacement, integrate the velocity function over the interval. Total distance traveled, on the other hand, is always positive. To find the total distance traveled by an object, regardless of direction, we need to integrate the absolute value of the velocity function.

## Example 1.24

### Finding Net Displacement

Given a velocity function $v(t) = 3t - 5$ (in meters per second) for a particle in motion from time $t = 0$ to time $t = 3,$ find the net displacement of the particle.

### Solution

Applying the net change theorem, we have

$$\begin{aligned}\int_0^3 (3t - 5)dt &= \frac{3t^2}{2} - 5t\Big|_0^3 \\ &= \left[\frac{3(3)^2}{2} - 5(3)\right] - 0 \\ &= \frac{27}{2} - 15 \\ &= \frac{27}{2} - \frac{30}{2} \\ &= -\frac{3}{2}.\end{aligned}$$

The net displacement is $-\frac{3}{2}$ m (**Figure 1.33**).

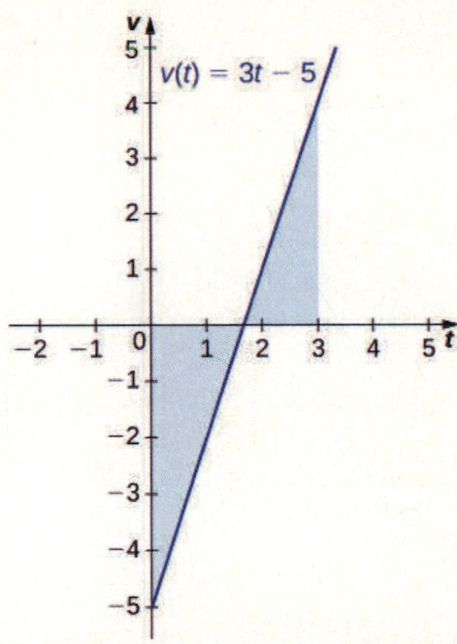


**Figure 1.33** The graph shows velocity versus time for a particle moving with a linear velocity function.

## Example 1.25

### Finding the Total Distance Traveled

Use **Example 1.24** to find the total distance traveled by a particle according to the velocity function $v(t) = 3t - 5$ m/sec over a time interval $[0, 3]$.

### Solution

The total distance traveled includes both the positive and the negative values. Therefore, we must integrate the absolute value of the velocity function to find the total distance traveled.

To continue with the example, use two integrals to find the total distance. First, find the $t$-intercept of the function, since that is where the division of the interval occurs. Set the equation equal to zero and solve for $t$. Thus,

$$\begin{aligned} 3t - 5 &= 0 \\ 3t &= 5 \\ t &= \frac{5}{3}. \end{aligned}$$

The two subintervals are $\left[0, \frac{5}{3}\right]$ and $\left[\frac{5}{3}, 3\right]$. To find the total distance traveled, integrate the absolute value of the function. Since the function is negative over the interval $\left[0, \frac{5}{3}\right]$, we have $|v(t)| = -v(t)$ over that interval. Over $\left[\frac{5}{3}, 3\right]$, the function is positive, so $|v(t)| = v(t)$. Thus, we have

$$\begin{aligned}\int_0^3 |v(t)|dt &= \int_0^{5/3} -v(t)dt + \int_{5/3}^3 v(t)dt \\ &= \int_0^{5/3} 5 - 3tdt + \int_{5/3}^3 3t - 5dt \\ &= \left(5t - \frac{3t^2}{2}\right)\Big|_0^{5/3} + \left(\frac{3t^2}{2} - 5t\right)\Big|_{5/3}^3 \\ &= \left[5\left(\frac{5}{3}\right) - \frac{3(5/3)^2}{2}\right] - 0 + \left[\frac{27}{2} - 15\right] - \left[\frac{3(5/3)^2}{2} - \frac{25}{3}\right] \\ &= \frac{25}{3} - \frac{25}{6} + \frac{27}{2} - 15 - \frac{25}{6} + \frac{25}{3} \\ &= \frac{41}{6}.\end{aligned}$$

So, the total distance traveled is $\frac{14}{6}$ m.

**1.22** Find the net displacement and total distance traveled in meters given the velocity function $f(t) = \frac{1}{2}e^t - 2$ over the interval $[0, 2]$.

## Applying the Net Change Theorem

The net change theorem can be applied to the flow and consumption of fluids, as shown in **Example 1.26**.

## Example 1.26

### How Many Gallons of Gasoline Are Consumed?

If the motor on a motorboat is started at $t = 0$ and the boat consumes gasoline at the rate of $5 - t^3$ gal/hr, how much gasoline is used in the first 2 hours?

### Solution

Express the problem as a definite integral, integrate, and evaluate using the Fundamental Theorem of Calculus. The limits of integration are the endpoints of the interval $[0, 2]$. We have

$$\begin{aligned}\int_0^2 (5 - t^3)dt &= \left(5t - \frac{t^4}{4}\right)\Big|_0^2 \\ &= \left[5(2) - \frac{(2)^4}{4}\right] - 0 \\ &= 10 - \frac{16}{4} \\ &= 6.\end{aligned}$$

Thus, the motorboat uses 6 gal of gas in 2 hours.

## Example 1.27

### Chapter Opener: Iceboats

**Figure 1.34** (credit: modification of work by Carter Brown, Flickr)

As we saw at the beginning of the chapter, top iceboat racers (**Figure 1.1**) can attain speeds of up to five times the wind speed. Andrew is an intermediate iceboater, though, so he attains speeds equal to only twice the wind speed. Suppose Andrew takes his iceboat out one morning when a light 5-mph breeze has been blowing all morning. As Andrew gets his iceboat set up, though, the wind begins to pick up. During his first half hour of iceboating, the wind speed increases according to the function $v(t) = 20t + 5.$ For the second half hour of Andrew's outing, the wind remains steady at 15 mph. In other words, the wind speed is given by

$$v(t) = \begin{cases} 20t + 5 & \text{for } 0 \le t \le \frac{1}{2} \\ 15 & \text{for } \frac{1}{2} \le t \le 1. \end{cases}$$

Recalling that Andrew's iceboat travels at twice the wind speed, and assuming he moves in a straight line away from his starting point, how far is Andrew from his starting point after 1 hour?

### Solution

To figure out how far Andrew has traveled, we need to integrate his velocity, which is twice the wind speed. Then

$$\text{Distance } = \int_0^1 2v(t)dt.$$

Substituting the expressions we were given for $v(t),$ we get

$$\begin{aligned}
\int_0^1 2v(t)dt &= \int_0^{1/2} 2v(t)dt + \int_{1/2}^1 2v(t)dt \\
&= \int_0^{1/2} 2(20t+5)dt + \int_{1/3}^1 2(15)dt \\
&= \int_0^{1/2} (40t+10)dt + \int_{1/2}^1 30dt \\
&= \left[20t^2+10t\right]\Big|_0^{1/2} + [30t]\Big|_{1/2}^1 \\
&= \left(\frac{20}{4}+5\right) - 0 + (30-15) \\
&= 25.
\end{aligned}$$

Andrew is 25 mi from his starting point after 1 hour.

**1.23** Suppose that, instead of remaining steady during the second half hour of Andrew's outing, the wind starts to die down according to the function $v(t) = -10t + 15$. In other words, the wind speed is given by

$$v(t) = \begin{cases} 20t+5 & \text{for } 0 \le t \le \frac{1}{2} \\ -10t+15 & \text{for } \frac{1}{2} \le t \le 1. \end{cases}$$

Under these conditions, how far from his starting point is Andrew after 1 hour?

## Integrating Even and Odd Functions

We saw in **Functions and Graphs (http://cnx.org/content/m53472/latest/)** that an even function is a function in which $f(-x) = f(x)$ for all $x$ in the domain—that is, the graph of the curve is unchanged when $x$ is replaced with $-x$. The graphs of even functions are symmetric about the $y$-axis. An odd function is one in which $f(-x) = -f(x)$ for all $x$ in the domain, and the graph of the function is symmetric about the origin.

Integrals of even functions, when the limits of integration are from $-a$ to $a$, involve two equal areas, because they are symmetric about the $y$-axis. Integrals of odd functions, when the limits of integration are similarly $[-a, a]$, evaluate to zero because the areas above and below the $x$-axis are equal.

### Rule: Integrals of Even and Odd Functions

For continuous even functions such that $f(-x) = f(x)$,

$$\int_{-a}^{a} f(x)dx = 2\int_0^a f(x)dx.$$

For continuous odd functions such that $f(-x) = -f(x)$,

$$\int_{-a}^{a} f(x)dx = 0.$$

## Example 1.28

### Integrating an Even Function

Integrate the even function $\int_{-2}^{2}(3x^8 - 2)dx$ and verify that the integration formula for even functions holds.

#### Solution

The symmetry appears in the graphs in **Figure 1.35**. Graph (a) shows the region below the curve and above the $x$-axis. We have to zoom in to this graph by a huge amount to see the region. Graph (b) shows the region above the curve and below the $x$-axis. The signed area of this region is negative. Both views illustrate the symmetry about the $y$-axis of an even function. We have

$$\begin{aligned}\int_{-2}^{2}(3x^8 - 2)dx &= \left(\frac{x^9}{3} - 2x\right)\Big|_{-2}^{2} \\ &= \left[\frac{(2)^9}{3} - 2(2)\right] - \left[\frac{(-2)^9}{3} - 2(-2)\right] \\ &= \left(\frac{512}{3} - 4\right) - \left(-\frac{512}{3} + 4\right) \\ &= \frac{1000}{3}.\end{aligned}$$

To verify the integration formula for even functions, we can calculate the integral from 0 to 2 and double it, then check to make sure we get the same answer.

$$\begin{aligned}\int_{0}^{2}(3x^8 - 2)dx &= \left(\frac{x^9}{3} - 2x\right)\Big|_{0}^{2} \\ &= \frac{512}{3} - 4 \\ &= \frac{500}{3}\end{aligned}$$

Since $2 \cdot \frac{500}{3} = \frac{1000}{3}$, we have verified the formula for even functions in this particular example.

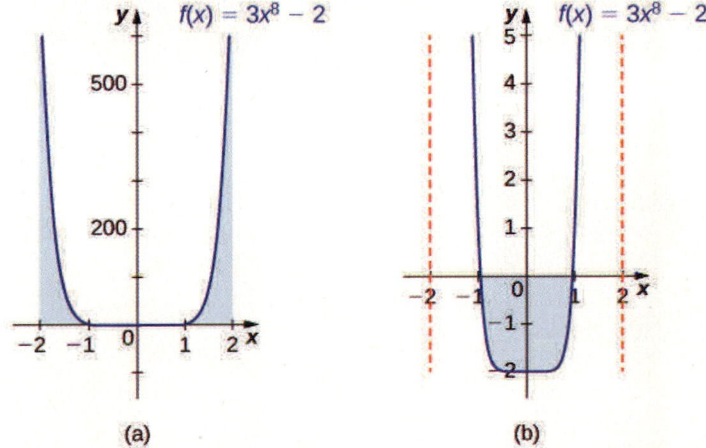


**Figure 1.35** Graph (a) shows the positive area between the curve and the $x$-axis, whereas graph (b) shows the negative area between the curve and the $x$-axis. Both views show the symmetry about the $y$-axis.

## Example 1.29

### Integrating an Odd Function

Evaluate the definite integral of the odd function $-5\sin x$ over the interval $[-\pi, \pi]$.

### Solution

The graph is shown in **Figure 1.36**. We can see the symmetry about the origin by the positive area above the $x$-axis over $[-\pi, 0]$, and the negative area below the $x$-axis over $[0, \pi]$. We have

$$\begin{aligned}\int_{-\pi}^{\pi} -5\sin x\,dx &= -5(-\cos x)\big|_{-\pi}^{\pi} \\ &= 5\cos x\big|_{-\pi}^{\pi} \\ &= [5\cos\pi] - [5\cos(-\pi)] \\ &= -5 - (-5) \\ &= 0.\end{aligned}$$

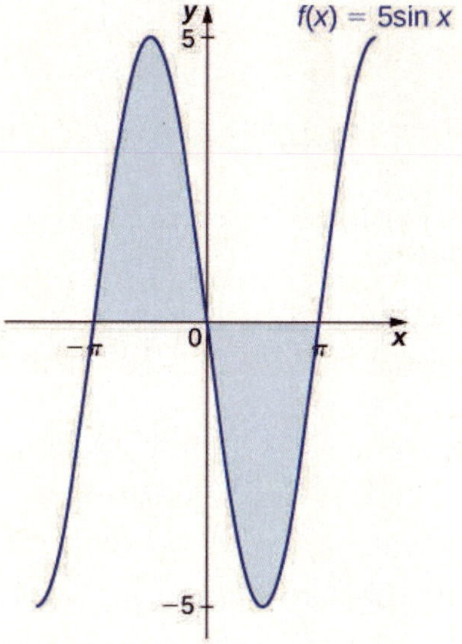

**Figure 1.36** The graph shows areas between a curve and the $x$-axis for an odd function.

**1.24** Integrate the function $\int_{-2}^{2} x^4\,dx.$

# 1.4 EXERCISES

Use basic integration formulas to compute the following antiderivatives.

207. $\int\left(\sqrt{x} - \frac{1}{\sqrt{x}}\right)dx$

208. $\int\left(e^{2x} - \frac{1}{2}e^{x/2}\right)dx$

209. $\int\frac{dx}{2x}$

210. $\int\frac{x-1}{x^2}dx$

211. $\int_0^{\pi}(\sin x - \cos x)dx$

212. $\int_0^{\pi/2}(x - \sin x)dx$

213. Write an integral that expresses the increase in the perimeter $P(s)$ of a square when its side length $s$ increases from 2 units to 4 units and evaluate the integral.

214. Write an integral that quantifies the change in the area $A(s) = s^2$ of a square when the side length doubles from $S$ units to $2S$ units and evaluate the integral.

215. A regular $N$-gon (an $N$-sided polygon with sides that have equal length $s$, such as a pentagon or hexagon) has perimeter $Ns$. Write an integral that expresses the increase in perimeter of a regular $N$-gon when the length of each side increases from 1 unit to 2 units and evaluate the integral.

216. The area of a regular pentagon with side length $a > 0$ is $pa^2$ with $p = \frac{1}{4}\sqrt{5 + \sqrt{5 + 2\sqrt{5}}}$. The Pentagon in Washington, DC, has inner sides of length 360 ft and outer sides of length 920 ft. Write an integral to express the area of the roof of the Pentagon according to these dimensions and evaluate this area.

217. A dodecahedron is a Platonic solid with a surface that consists of 12 pentagons, each of equal area. By how much does the surface area of a dodecahedron increase as the side length of each pentagon doubles from 1 unit to 2 units?

218. An icosahedron is a Platonic solid with a surface that consists of 20 equilateral triangles. By how much does the surface area of an icosahedron increase as the side length of each triangle doubles from $a$ unit to $2a$ units?

219. Write an integral that quantifies the change in the area of the surface of a cube when its side length doubles from $s$ unit to $2s$ units and evaluate the integral.

220. Write an integral that quantifies the increase in the volume of a cube when the side length doubles from $s$ unit to $2s$ units and evaluate the integral.

221. Write an integral that quantifies the increase in the surface area of a sphere as its radius doubles from $R$ unit to $2R$ units and evaluate the integral.

222. Write an integral that quantifies the increase in the volume of a sphere as its radius doubles from $R$ unit to $2R$ units and evaluate the integral.

223. Suppose that a particle moves along a straight line with velocity $v(t) = 4 - 2t$, where $0 \le t \le 2$ (in meters per second). Find the displacement at time $t$ and the total distance traveled up to $t = 2$.

224. Suppose that a particle moves along a straight line with velocity defined by $v(t) = t^2 - 3t - 18$, where $0 \le t \le 6$ (in meters per second). Find the displacement at time $t$ and the total distance traveled up to $t = 6$.

225. Suppose that a particle moves along a straight line with velocity defined by $v(t) = |2t - 6|$, where $0 \le t \le 6$ (in meters per second). Find the displacement at time $t$ and the total distance traveled up to $t = 6$.

226. Suppose that a particle moves along a straight line with acceleration defined by $a(t) = t - 3$, where $0 \le t \le 6$ (in meters per second). Find the velocity and displacement at time $t$ and the total distance traveled up to $t = 6$ if $v(0) = 3$ and $d(0) = 0$.

227. A ball is thrown upward from a height of 1.5 m at an initial speed of 40 m/sec. Acceleration resulting from gravity is $-9.8$ m/sec$^2$. Neglecting air resistance, solve for the velocity $v(t)$ and the height $h(t)$ of the ball $t$ seconds after it is thrown and before it returns to the ground.

228. A ball is thrown upward from a height of 3 m at an initial speed of 60 m/sec. Acceleration resulting from gravity is $-9.8$ m/sec$^2$. Neglecting air resistance, solve for the velocity $v(t)$ and the height $h(t)$ of the ball $t$ seconds after it is thrown and before it returns to the ground.

229. The area $A(t)$ of a circular shape is growing at a constant rate. If the area increases from $4\pi$ units to $9\pi$ units between times $t = 2$ and $t = 3$, find the net change in the radius during that time.

230. A spherical balloon is being inflated at a constant rate. If the volume of the balloon changes from $36\pi$ in.$^3$ to $288\pi$ in.$^3$ between time $t = 30$ and $t = 60$ seconds, find the net change in the radius of the balloon during that time.

231. Water flows into a conical tank with cross-sectional area $\pi x^2$ at height $x$ and volume $\frac{\pi x^3}{3}$ up to height $x$. If water flows into the tank at a rate of 1 m$^3$/min, find the height of water in the tank after 5 min. Find the change in height between 5 min and 10 min.

232. A horizontal cylindrical tank has cross-sectional area $A(x) = 4\left(6x - x^2\right)m^2$ at height $x$ meters above the bottom when $x \le 3$.

a. The volume $V$ between heights $a$ and $b$ is $\int_a^b A(x)dx$. Find the volume at heights between 2 m and 3 m.
b. Suppose that oil is being pumped into the tank at a rate of 50 L/min. Using the chain rule, $\frac{dx}{dt} = \frac{dx}{dV}\frac{dV}{dt}$, at how many meters per minute is the height of oil in the tank changing, expressed in terms of $x$, when the height is at $x$ meters?
c. How long does it take to fill the tank to 3 m starting from a fill level of 2 m?

233. The following table lists the electrical power in gigawatts—the rate at which energy is consumed—used in a certain city for different hours of the day, in a typical 24-hour period, with hour 1 corresponding to midnight to 1 a.m.

| Hour | Power | Hour | Power |
|---|---|---|---|
| 1 | 28 | 13 | 48 |
| 2 | 25 | 14 | 49 |
| 3 | 24 | 15 | 49 |
| 4 | 23 | 16 | 50 |
| 5 | 24 | 17 | 50 |
| 6 | 27 | 18 | 50 |
| 7 | 29 | 19 | 46 |
| 8 | 32 | 20 | 43 |
| 9 | 34 | 21 | 42 |
| 10 | 39 | 22 | 40 |
| 11 | 42 | 23 | 37 |
| 12 | 46 | 24 | 34 |

Find the total amount of power in gigawatt-hours (gW-h) consumed by the city in a typical 24-hour period.

234. The average residential electrical power use (in hundreds of watts) per hour is given in the following table.

| Hour | Power | Hour | Power |
|---|---|---|---|
| 1 | 8 | 13 | 12 |
| 2 | 6 | 14 | 13 |
| 3 | 5 | 15 | 14 |
| 4 | 4 | 16 | 15 |
| 5 | 5 | 17 | 17 |
| 6 | 6 | 18 | 19 |
| 7 | 7 | 19 | 18 |
| 8 | 8 | 20 | 17 |
| 9 | 9 | 21 | 16 |
| 10 | 10 | 22 | 16 |
| 11 | 10 | 23 | 13 |
| 12 | 11 | 24 | 11 |

a. Compute the average total energy used in a day in kilowatt-hours (kWh).
b. If a ton of coal generates 1842 kWh, how long does it take for an average residence to burn a ton of coal?
c. Explain why the data might fit a plot of the form $p(t) = 11.5 - 7.5\sin\left(\frac{\pi t}{12}\right)$.

235. The data in the following table are used to estimate the average power output produced by Peter Sagan for each of the last 18 sec of Stage 1 of the 2012 Tour de France.

| Second | Watts | Second | Watts |
|---|---|---|---|
| 1 | 600 | 10 | 1200 |
| 2 | 500 | 11 | 1170 |
| 3 | 575 | 12 | 1125 |
| 4 | 1050 | 13 | 1100 |
| 5 | 925 | 14 | 1075 |
| 6 | 950 | 15 | 1000 |
| 7 | 1050 | 16 | 950 |
| 8 | 950 | 17 | 900 |
| 9 | 1100 | 18 | 780 |

**Table 1.6** Average Power Output ***Source*:** **sportsexercisengineering.com**

Estimate the net energy used in kilojoules (kJ), noting that 1W = 1 J/s, and the average power output by Sagan during this time interval.

236. The data in the following table are used to estimate the average power output produced by Peter Sagan for each 15-min interval of Stage 1 of the 2012 Tour de France.

| Minutes | Watts | Minutes | Watts |
|---|---|---|---|
| 15 | 200 | 165 | 170 |
| 30 | 180 | 180 | 220 |
| 45 | 190 | 195 | 140 |
| 60 | 230 | 210 | 225 |
| 75 | 240 | 225 | 170 |
| 90 | 210 | 240 | 210 |
| 105 | 210 | 255 | 200 |
| 120 | 220 | 270 | 220 |
| 135 | 210 | 285 | 250 |
| 150 | 150 | 300 | 400 |

**Table 1.7** Average Power Output ***Source*****: sportsexercisengineering.com**

Estimate the net energy used in kilojoules, noting that 1W = 1 J/s.

237. The distribution of incomes as of 2012 in the United States in $5000 increments is given in the following table. The $k$th row denotes the percentage of households with incomes between $\$5000xk$ and $5000xk + 4999$. The row $k = 40$ contains all households with income between $200,000 and $250,000 and $k = 41$ accounts for all households with income exceeding $250,000.

| | | | |
|---|---|---|---|
| 0 | 3.5 | 21 | 1.5 |
| 1 | 4.1 | 22 | 1.4 |
| 2 | 5.9 | 23 | 1.3 |
| 3 | 5.7 | 24 | 1.3 |
| 4 | 5.9 | 25 | 1.1 |
| 5 | 5.4 | 26 | 1.0 |
| 6 | 5.5 | 27 | 0.75 |
| 7 | 5.1 | 28 | 0.8 |
| 8 | 4.8 | 29 | 1.0 |
| 9 | 4.1 | 30 | 0.6 |
| 10 | 4.3 | 31 | 0.6 |
| 11 | 3.5 | 32 | 0.5 |
| 12 | 3.7 | 33 | 0.5 |
| 13 | 3.2 | 34 | 0.4 |
| 14 | 3.0 | 35 | 0.3 |
| 15 | 2.8 | 36 | 0.3 |
| 16 | 2.5 | 37 | 0.3 |
| 17 | 2.2 | 38 | 0.2 |
| 18 | 2.2 | 39 | 1.8 |
| 19 | 1.8 | 40 | 2.3 |
| 20 | 2.1 | 41 | |

**Table 1.8** Income Distributions ***Source*: http://www.census.gov/prod/2013pubs/p60-245.pdf**

**Table 1.8** Income Distributions ***Source*: http://www.census.gov/prod/2013pubs/p60-245.pdf**

a. Estimate the percentage of U.S. households in 2012 with incomes less than $55,000.
b. What percentage of households had incomes exceeding $85,000?
c. Plot the data and try to fit its shape to that of a graph of the form $a(x+c)e^{-b(x+e)}$ for suitable $a, b, c$.

238. Newton's law of gravity states that the gravitational force exerted by an object of mass $M$ and one of mass $m$ with centers that are separated by a distance $r$ is $F = G\frac{mM}{r^2}$, with $G$ an empirical constant $G = 6.67x10^{-11}\,m^3/(kg \cdot s^2)$. The work done by a variable force over an interval $[a, b]$ is defined as $W = \int_a^b F(x)dx$. If Earth has mass $5.97219 \times 10^{24}$ and radius 6371 km, compute the amount of work to elevate a polar weather satellite of mass 1400 kg to its orbiting altitude of 850 km above Earth.

239. For a given motor vehicle, the maximum achievable deceleration from braking is approximately 7 m/sec$^2$ on dry concrete. On wet asphalt, it is approximately 2.5 m/sec$^2$. Given that 1 mph corresponds to 0.447 m/sec, find the total distance that a car travels in meters on dry concrete after the brakes are applied until it comes to a complete stop if the initial velocity is 67 mph (30 m/sec) or if the initial braking velocity is 56 mph (25 m/sec). Find the corresponding distances if the surface is slippery wet asphalt.

240. John is a 25-year old man who weighs 160 lb. He burns $500 - 50t$ calories/hr while riding his bike for $t$ hours. If an oatmeal cookie has 55 cal and John eats $4t$ cookies during the $t$th hour, how many net calories has he lost after 3 hours riding his bike?

241. Sandra is a 25-year old woman who weighs 120 lb. She burns $300 - 50t$ cal/hr while walking on her treadmill. Her caloric intake from drinking Gatorade is $100t$ calories during the $t$th hour. What is her net decrease in calories after walking for 3 hours?

242. A motor vehicle has a maximum efficiency of 33 mpg at a cruising speed of 40 mph. The efficiency drops at a rate of 0.1 mpg/mph between 40 mph and 50 mph, and at a rate of 0.4 mpg/mph between 50 mph and 80 mph. What is the efficiency in miles per gallon if the car is cruising at 50 mph? What is the efficiency in miles per gallon if the car is cruising at 80 mph? If gasoline costs $3.50/gal, what is the cost of fuel to drive 50 mi at 40 mph, at 50 mph, and at 80 mph?

243. Although some engines are more efficient at given a horsepower than others, on average, fuel efficiency decreases with horsepower at a rate of $1/25$ mpg/horsepower. If a typical 50-horsepower engine has an average fuel efficiency of 32 mpg, what is the average fuel efficiency of an engine with the following horsepower: 150, 300, 450?

244. **[T]** The following table lists the 2013 schedule of federal income tax versus taxable income.

| Taxable Income Range | The Tax Is … | … Of the Amount Over |
|---|---|---|
| $0–$8925 | 10% | $0 |
| $8925–$36,250 | $892.50 + 15% | $8925 |
| $36,250–$87,850 | $4,991.25 + 25% | $36,250 |
| $87,850–$183,250 | $17,891.25 + 28% | $87,850 |
| $183,250–$398,350 | $44,603.25 + 33% | $183,250 |
| $398,350–$400,000 | $115,586.25 + 35% | $398,350 |
| > $400,000 | $116,163.75 + 39.6% | $400,000 |

**Table 1.9** Federal Income Tax Versus Taxable Income ***Source*: http://www.irs.gov/pub/irs-prior/i1040tt--2013.pdf.**

Suppose that Steve just received a $10,000 raise. How much of this raise is left after federal taxes if Steve's salary before receiving the raise was $40,000? If it was $90,000? If it was $385,000?

245. **[T]** The following table provides hypothetical data regarding the level of service for a certain highway.

| Highway Speed Range (mph) | Vehicles per Hour per Lane | Density Range (vehicles/mi) |
|---|---|---|
| > 60 | < 600 | < 10 |
| 60–57 | 600–1000 | 10–20 |
| 57–54 | 1000–1500 | 20–30 |
| 54–46 | 1500–1900 | 30–45 |
| 46–30 | 1900–2100 | 45–70 |
| <30 | Unstable | 70–200 |

**Table 1.10**

a. Plot vehicles per hour per lane on the $x$-axis and highway speed on the $y$-axis.
b. Compute the average decrease in speed (in miles per hour) per unit increase in congestion (vehicles per hour per lane) as the latter increases from 600 to 1000, from 1000 to 1500, and from 1500 to 2100. Does the decrease in miles per hour depend linearly on the increase in vehicles per hour per lane?
c. Plot minutes per mile (60 times the reciprocal of miles per hour) as a function of vehicles per hour per lane. Is this function linear?

For the next two exercises use the data in the following table, which displays bald eagle populations from 1963 to 2000 in the continental United States.

| Year | Population of Breeding Pairs of Bald Eagles |
|---|---|
| 1963 | 487 |
| 1974 | 791 |
| 1981 | 1188 |
| 1986 | 1875 |
| 1992 | 3749 |
| 1996 | 5094 |
| 2000 | 6471 |

**Table 1.11** Population of Breeding Bald Eagle Pairs ***Source*: http://www.fws.gov/Midwest/eagle/population/chtofprs.html.**

246. **[T]** The graph below plots the quadratic $p(t) = 6.48t^2 - 80.3\,1t + 585.69$ against the data in preceding table, normalized so that $t = 0$ corresponds to 1963. Estimate the average number of bald eagles per year present for the 37 years by computing the average value of $p$ over $[0, 37]$.

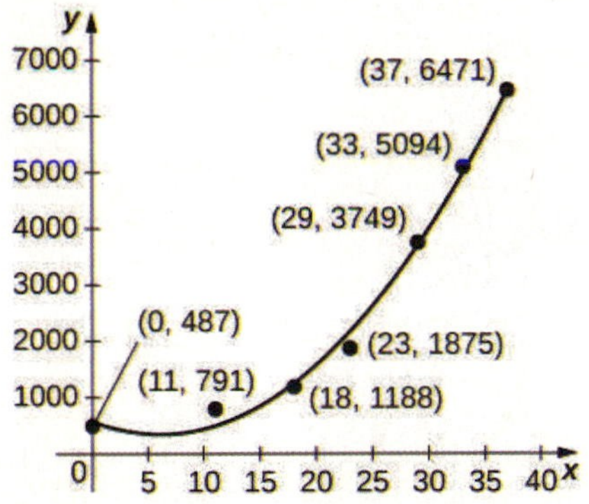


247. **[T]** The graph below plots the cubic $p(t) = 0.07t^3 + 2.42t^2 - 25.63t + 521.23$ against the data in the preceding table, normalized so that $t = 0$ corresponds to 1963. Estimate the average number of bald eagles per year present for the 37 years by computing the average value of $p$ over $[0, 37]$.

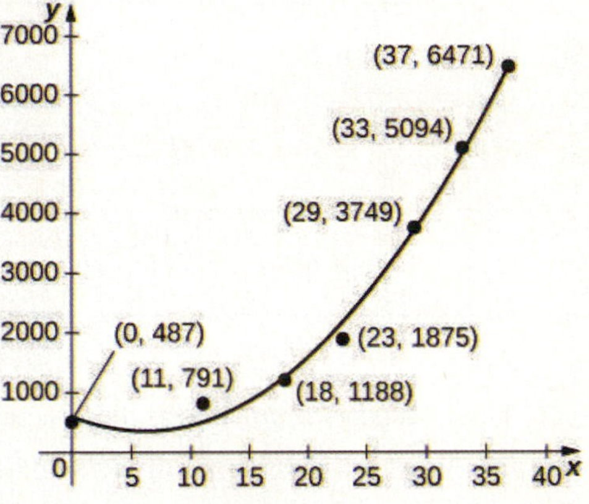


248. **[T]** Suppose you go on a road trip and record your speed at every half hour, as compiled in the following table. The best quadratic fit to the data is $q(t) = 5x^2 - 11x + 49$, shown in the accompanying graph. Integrate $q$ to estimate the total distance driven over the 3 hours.

| Time (hr) | Speed (mph) |
|---|---|
| 0 (start) | 50 |
| 1 | 40 |
| 2 | 50 |
| 3 | 60 |

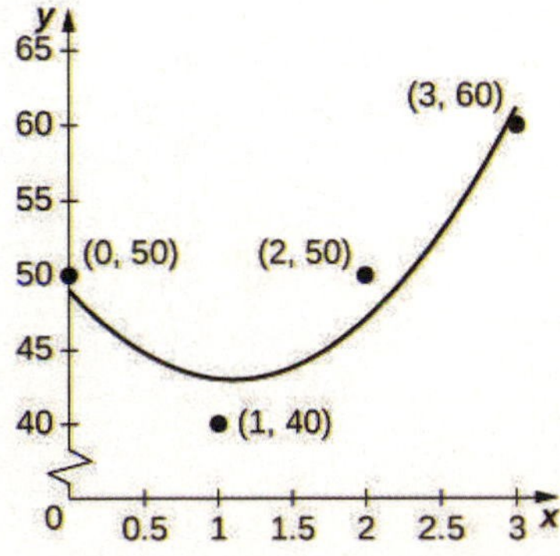


As a car accelerates, it does not accelerate at a constant rate; rather, the acceleration is variable. For the following exercises, use the following table, which contains the acceleration measured at every second as a driver merges onto a freeway.

| Time (sec) | Acceleration (mph/sec) |
|---|---|
| 1 | 11.2 |
| 2 | 10.6 |
| 3 | 8.1 |
| 4 | 5.4 |
| 5 | 0 |

249. **[T]** The accompanying graph plots the best quadratic fit, $a(t) = -0.70t^2 + 1.44t + 10.44$, to the data from the preceding table. Compute the average value of $a(t)$ to estimate the average acceleration between $t = 0$ and $t = 5$.

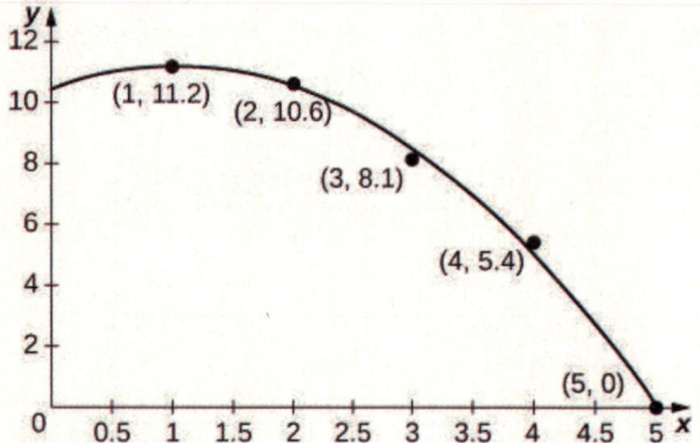


250. **[T]** Using your acceleration equation from the previous exercise, find the corresponding velocity equation. Assuming the final velocity is 0 mph, find the velocity at time $t = 0$.

251. **[T]** Using your velocity equation from the previous exercise, find the corresponding distance equation, assuming your initial distance is 0 mi. How far did you travel while you accelerated your car? (*Hint:* You will need to convert time units.)

252. **[T]** The number of hamburgers sold at a restaurant throughout the day is given in the following table, with the accompanying graph plotting the best cubic fit to the data, $b(t) = 0.12t^3 - 2.13t^3 + 12.13t + 3.91$, with $t = 0$ corresponding to 9 a.m. and $t = 12$ corresponding to 9 p.m. Compute the average value of $b(t)$ to estimate the average number of hamburgers sold per hour.

| Hours Past Midnight | No. of Burgers Sold |
|---|---|
| 9 | 3 |
| 12 | 28 |
| 15 | 20 |
| 18 | 30 |
| 21 | 45 |

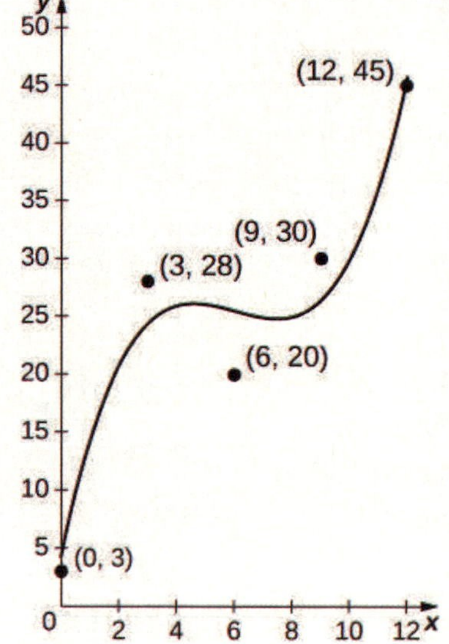

253. **[T]** An athlete runs by a motion detector, which records her speed, as displayed in the following table. The best linear fit to this data, $\ell(t) = -0.068t + 5.14,$ is shown in the accompanying graph. Use the average value of $\ell(t)$ between $t = 0$ and $t = 40$ to estimate the runner's average speed.

| Minutes | Speed (m/sec) |
|---|---|
| 0 | 5 |
| 10 | 4.8 |
| 20 | 3.6 |
| 30 | 3.0 |
| 40 | 2.5 |

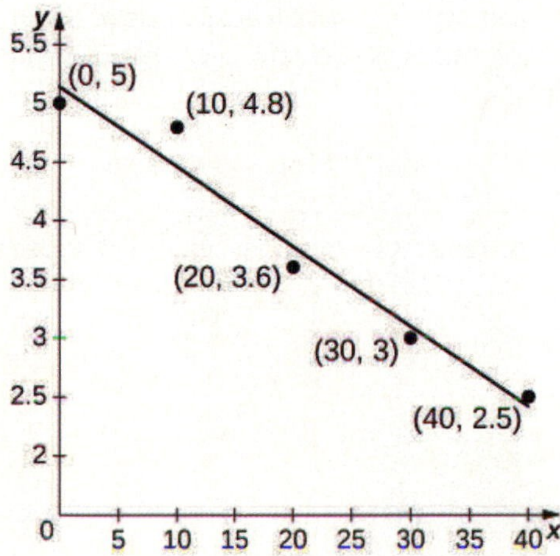

# 1.5 | Substitution

## Learning Objectives

1.5.1 Use substitution to evaluate indefinite integrals.
1.5.2 Use substitution to evaluate definite integrals.

The Fundamental Theorem of Calculus gave us a method to evaluate integrals without using Riemann sums. The drawback of this method, though, is that we must be able to find an antiderivative, and this is not always easy. In this section we examine a technique, called **integration by substitution**, to help us find antiderivatives. Specifically, this method helps us find antiderivatives when the integrand is the result of a chain-rule derivative.

At first, the approach to the substitution procedure may not appear very obvious. However, it is primarily a visual task—that is, the integrand shows you what to do; it is a matter of recognizing the form of the function. So, what are we supposed to see? We are looking for an integrand of the form $f[g(x)]g'(x)dx$. For example, in the integral $\int (x^2 - 3)^3 2x dx$, we have $f(x) = x^3$, $g(x) = x^2 - 3$, and $g'(x) = 2x$. Then,

$$f[g(x)]g'(x) = (x^2 - 3)^3 (2x),$$

and we see that our integrand is in the correct form.

The method is called *substitution* because we substitute part of the integrand with the variable *u* and part of the integrand with *du*. It is also referred to as **change of variables** because we are changing variables to obtain an expression that is easier to work with for applying the integration rules.

### Theorem 1.7: Substitution with Indefinite Integrals

Let $u = g(x)$, , where $g'(x)$ is continuous over an interval, let $f(x)$ be continuous over the corresponding range of *g*, and let $F(x)$ be an antiderivative of $f(x)$. Then,

$$\begin{aligned} \int f[g(x)]g'(x)dx &= \int f(u)du \\ &= F(u) + C \\ &= F(g(x)) + C. \end{aligned} \tag{1.19}$$

## Proof

Let *f*, *g*, *u*, and *F* be as specified in the theorem. Then

$$\begin{aligned} \frac{d}{dx}F(g(x)) &= F'(g(x))g'(x) \\ &= f[g(x)]g'(x). \end{aligned}$$

Integrating both sides with respect to *x*, we see that

$$\int f[g(x)]g'(x)dx = F(g(x)) + C.$$

If we now substitute $u = g(x)$, and $du = g'(x)dx$, we get

$$\begin{aligned} \int f[g(x)]g'(x)dx &= \int f(u)du \\ &= F(u) + C \\ &= F(g(x)) + C. \end{aligned}$$

□

Returning to the problem we looked at originally, we let $u = x^2 - 3$ and then $du = 2xdx$. Rewrite the integral in terms of $u$:

$$\int \underbrace{\left(x^2 - 3\right)}_{u}^{3} (2\underbrace{xdx}_{du}) = \int u^3 du.$$

Using the power rule for integrals, we have

$$\int u^3 du = \frac{u^4}{4} + C.$$

Substitute the original expression for $x$ back into the solution:

$$\frac{u^4}{4} + C = \frac{\left(x^2 - 3\right)^4}{4} + C.$$

We can generalize the procedure in the following Problem-Solving Strategy.

### Problem-Solving Strategy: Integration by Substitution

1. Look carefully at the integrand and select an expression $g(x)$ within the integrand to set equal to $u$. Let's select $g(x)$. such that $g'(x)$ is also part of the integrand.
2. Substitute $u = g(x)$ and $du = g'(x)dx$. into the integral.
3. We should now be able to evaluate the integral with respect to $u$. If the integral can't be evaluated we need to go back and select a different expression to use as $u$.
4. Evaluate the integral in terms of $u$.
5. Write the result in terms of $x$ and the expression $g(x)$.

## Example 1.30

### Using Substitution to Find an Antiderivative

Use substitution to find the antiderivative of $\int 6x\left(3x^2 + 4\right)^4 dx$.

#### Solution

The first step is to choose an expression for $u$. We choose $u = 3x^2 + 4$. because then $du = 6xdx$., and we already have $du$ in the integrand. Write the integral in terms of $u$:

$$\int 6x\left(3x^2 + 4\right)^4 dx = \int u^4 du.$$

Remember that $du$ is the derivative of the expression chosen for $u$, regardless of what is inside the integrand. Now we can evaluate the integral with respect to $u$:

$$\begin{aligned}\int u^4\,du &= \frac{u^5}{5}+C\\ &= \frac{\left(3x^2+4\right)^5}{5}+C.\end{aligned}$$

**Analysis**

We can check our answer by taking the derivative of the result of integration. We should obtain the integrand. Picking a value for $C$ of 1, we let $y = \frac{1}{5}\left(3x^2+4\right)^5 + 1$. We have

$$y = \frac{1}{5}\left(3x^2+4\right)^5 + 1,$$

so

$$\begin{aligned}y' &= \left(\frac{1}{5}\right)5\left(3x^2+4\right)^4 6x\\ &= 6x\left(3x^2+4\right)^4.\end{aligned}$$

This is exactly the expression we started with inside the integrand.

**1.25** Use substitution to find the antiderivative of $\int 3x^2\left(x^3-3\right)^2 dx.$

Sometimes we need to adjust the constants in our integral if they don't match up exactly with the expressions we are substituting.

## Example 1.31

### Using Substitution with Alteration

Use substitution to find the antiderivative of $\int z\sqrt{z^2-5}\,dz.$

#### Solution

Rewrite the integral as $\int z\left(z^2-5\right)^{1/2} dz.$ Let $u = z^2-5$ and $du = 2z\,dz.$ Now we have a problem because $du = 2z\,dz$ and the original expression has only $z\,dz.$ We have to alter our expression for $du$ or the integral in $u$ will be twice as large as it should be. If we multiply both sides of the $du$ equation by $\frac{1}{2}$. we can solve this problem. Thus,

$$\begin{aligned}u &= z^2-5\\ du &= 2z\,dz\\ \frac{1}{2}du &= \frac{1}{2}(2z)dz = z\,dz.\end{aligned}$$

Write the integral in terms of $u$, but pull the $\frac{1}{2}$ outside the integration symbol:

$$\int z\left(z^2-5\right)^{1/2} dz = \frac{1}{2}\int u^{1/2}\,du.$$

Integrate the expression in $u$:

$$\begin{aligned}\frac{1}{2}\int u^{1/2}\,du &= \left(\frac{1}{2}\right)\frac{u^{3/2}}{\frac{3}{2}} + C \\ &= \left(\frac{1}{2}\right)\left(\frac{2}{3}\right)u^{3/2} + C \\ &= \frac{1}{3}u^{3/2} + C \\ &= \frac{1}{3}\left(z^2-5\right)^{3/2} + C.\end{aligned}$$

**1.26** Use substitution to find the antiderivative of $\int x^2\left(x^3+5\right)^9 dx.$

## Example 1.32

### Using Substitution with Integrals of Trigonometric Functions

Use substitution to evaluate the integral $\int \frac{\sin t}{\cos^3 t}\,dt.$

### Solution

We know the derivative of $\cos t$ is $-\sin t,$ so we set $u = \cos t.$ Then $du = -\sin t\,dt.$ Substituting into the integral, we have

$$\int \frac{\sin t}{\cos^3 t}\,dt = -\int \frac{du}{u^3}.$$

Evaluating the integral, we get

$$\begin{aligned}-\int \frac{du}{u^3} &= -\int u^{-3}\,du \\ &= -\left(-\frac{1}{2}\right)u^{-2} + C.\end{aligned}$$

Putting the answer back in terms of $t$, we get

$$\begin{aligned}\int \frac{\sin t}{\cos^3 t}\,dt &= \frac{1}{2u^2} + C \\ &= \frac{1}{2\cos^2 t} + C.\end{aligned}$$

**1.27** Use substitution to evaluate the integral $\int \frac{\cos t}{\sin^2 t} dt.$

Sometimes we need to manipulate an integral in ways that are more complicated than just multiplying or dividing by a constant. We need to eliminate all the expressions within the integrand that are in terms of the original variable. When we are done, $u$ should be the only variable in the integrand. In some cases, this means solving for the original variable in terms of $u$. This technique should become clear in the next example.

## Example 1.33

### Finding an Antiderivative Using *u*-Substitution

Use substitution to find the antiderivative of $\int \frac{x}{\sqrt{x-1}} dx.$

**Solution**

If we let $u = x - 1,$ then $du = dx.$ But this does not account for the $x$ in the numerator of the integrand. We need to express $x$ in terms of $u$. If $u = x - 1,$ then $x = u + 1.$ Now we can rewrite the integral in terms of $u$:

$$\begin{aligned}\int \frac{x}{\sqrt{x-1}} dx &= \int \frac{u+1}{\sqrt{u}} du \\ &= \int \sqrt{u} + \frac{1}{\sqrt{u}} du \\ &= \int \left(u^{1/2} + u^{-1/2}\right) du.\end{aligned}$$

Then we integrate in the usual way, replace $u$ with the original expression, and factor and simplify the result. Thus,

$$\begin{aligned}\int \left(u^{1/2} + u^{-1/2}\right) du &= \frac{2}{3}u^{3/2} + 2u^{1/2} + C \\ &= \frac{2}{3}(x-1)^{3/2} + 2(x-1)^{1/2} + C \\ &= (x-1)^{1/2}\left[\frac{2}{3}(x-1) + 2\right] + C \\ &= (x-1)^{1/2}\left(\frac{2}{3}x - \frac{2}{3} + \frac{6}{3}\right) \\ &= (x-1)^{1/2}\left(\frac{2}{3}x + \frac{4}{3}\right) \\ &= \frac{2}{3}(x-1)^{1/2}(x+2) + C.\end{aligned}$$

**1.28** Use substitution to evaluate the indefinite integral $\int \cos^3 t \sin t \, dt.$

## Substitution for Definite Integrals

Substitution can be used with definite integrals, too. However, using substitution to evaluate a definite integral requires a change to the limits of integration. If we change variables in the integrand, the limits of integration change as well.

### Theorem 1.8: Substitution with Definite Integrals

Let $u = g(x)$ and let $g'$ be continuous over an interval $[a, b]$, and let $f$ be continuous over the range of $u = g(x)$. Then,

$$\int_a^b f(g(x))g'(x)dx = \int_{g(a)}^{g(b)} f(u)du.$$

Although we will not formally prove this theorem, we justify it with some calculations here. From the substitution rule for indefinite integrals, if $F(x)$ is an antiderivative of $f(x)$, we have

$$\int f(g(x))g'(x)dx = F(g(x)) + C.$$

Then

$$\begin{aligned} \int_a^b f[g(x)]g'(x)dx &= F(g(x))\Big|_{x=a}^{x=b} \\ &= F(g(b)) - F(g(a)) \\ &= F(u)\Big|_{u=g(a)}^{u=g(b)} \\ &= \int_{g(a)}^{g(b)} f(u)du, \end{aligned} \tag{1.20}$$

and we have the desired result.

## Example 1.34

### Using Substitution to Evaluate a Definite Integral

Use substitution to evaluate $\int_0^1 x^2\left(1 + 2x^3\right)^5 dx.$

#### Solution

Let $u = 1 + 2x^3$, so $du = 6x^2 dx$. Since the original function includes one factor of $x^2$ and $du = 6x^2 dx$, multiply both sides of the $du$ equation by $1/6$. Then,

$$\begin{aligned} du &= 6x^2 dx \\ \frac{1}{6}du &= x^2 dx. \end{aligned}$$

To adjust the limits of integration, note that when $x = 0,\ u = 1 + 2(0) = 1,$ and when $x = 1,\ u = 1 + 2(1) = 3.$ Then

$$\int_0^1 x^2\left(1 + 2x^3\right)^5 dx = \frac{1}{6}\int_1^3 u^5 du.$$

Evaluating this expression, we get

$$\begin{aligned}\frac{1}{6}\int_1^3 u^5\,du &= \left(\frac{1}{6}\right)\left(\frac{u^6}{6}\right)\Big|_1^3 \\ &= \frac{1}{36}\left[(3)^6 - (1)^6\right] \\ &= \frac{182}{9}.\end{aligned}$$

**1.29** Use substitution to evaluate the definite integral $\int_{-1}^{0} y(2y^2 - 3)^5\,dy.$

## Example 1.35

### Using Substitution with an Exponential Function

Use substitution to evaluate $\int_0^1 xe^{4x^2 + 3}\,dx.$

#### Solution

Let $u = 4x^3 + 3.$ Then, $du = 8xdx.$ To adjust the limits of integration, we note that when $x = 0,\ u = 3,$ and when $x = 1,\ u = 7.$ So our substitution gives

$$\begin{aligned}\int_0^1 xe^{4x^2+3}\,dx &= \frac{1}{8}\int_3^7 e^u\,du \\ &= \frac{1}{8}e^u\Big|_3^7 \\ &= \frac{e^7 - e^3}{8} \\ &\approx 134.568.\end{aligned}$$

**1.30** Use substitution to evaluate $\int_0^1 x^2 \cos\left(\frac{\pi}{2}x^3\right)dx.$

Substitution may be only one of the techniques needed to evaluate a definite integral. All of the properties and rules of integration apply independently, and trigonometric functions may need to be rewritten using a trigonometric identity before we can apply substitution. Also, we have the option of replacing the original expression for $u$ after we find the antiderivative, which means that we do not have to change the limits of integration. These two approaches are shown in **Example 1.36**.

## Example 1.36

### Using Substitution to Evaluate a Trigonometric Integral

Use substitution to evaluate $\int_0^{\pi/2} \cos^2 \theta \, d\theta.$

#### Solution

Let us first use a trigonometric identity to rewrite the integral. The trig identity $\cos^2 \theta = \frac{1 + \cos 2\theta}{2}$ allows us to rewrite the integral as

$$\int_0^{\pi/2} \cos^2 \theta d\theta = \int_0^{\pi/2} \frac{1 + \cos 2\theta}{2} d\theta.$$

Then,

$$\begin{aligned} \int_0^{\pi/2} \left(\frac{1 + \cos 2\theta}{2}\right) d\theta &= \int_0^{\pi/2} \left(\frac{1}{2} + \frac{1}{2}\cos 2\theta\right) d\theta \\ &= \frac{1}{2}\int_0^{\pi/2} d\theta + \int_0^{\pi/2} \cos 2\theta d\theta. \end{aligned}$$

We can evaluate the first integral as it is, but we need to make a substitution to evaluate the second integral. Let $u = 2\theta.$ Then, $du = 2d\theta,$ or $\frac{1}{2}du = d\theta.$ Also, when $\theta = 0,$ $u = 0,$ and when $\theta = \pi/2,$ $u = \pi.$ Expressing the second integral in terms of $u$, we have

$$\begin{aligned} \frac{1}{2}\int_0^{\pi/2} d\theta + \frac{1}{2}\int_0^{\pi/2} \cos 2\theta d\theta &= \frac{1}{2}\int_0^{\pi/2} d\theta + \frac{1}{2}\left(\frac{1}{2}\right)\int_0^{\pi} \cos u du \\ &= \frac{\theta}{2}\bigg|_{\theta = 0}^{\theta = \pi/2} + \frac{1}{4}\sin u\bigg|_{u = 0}^{u = \theta} \\ &= \left(\frac{\pi}{4} - 0\right) + (0 - 0) = \frac{\pi}{4}. \end{aligned}$$

# 1.5 EXERCISES

254. Why is $u$-substitution referred to as *change of variable*?

255. 2. If $f = g \circ h$, when reversing the chain rule, $\frac{d}{dx}(g \circ h)(x) = g'(h(x))h'(x)$, should you take $u = g(x)$ or $u = h(x)$?

In the following exercises, verify each identity using differentiation. Then, using the indicated $u$-substitution, identify $f$ such that the integral takes the form $\int f(u)du$.

256. $\int x\sqrt{x+1}dx = \frac{2}{15}(x+1)^{3/2}(3x-2) + C;\ u = x+1$

257. $\int \frac{x^2}{\sqrt{x-1}}dx(x > 1) = \frac{2}{15}\sqrt{x-1}\left(3x^2 + 4x + 8\right) + C;\ u = x-1$

258. $\int x\sqrt{4x^2+9}dx = \frac{1}{12}\left(4x^2+9\right)^{3/2} + C;\ u = 4x^2+9$

259. $\int \frac{x}{\sqrt{4x^2+9}}dx = \frac{1}{4}\sqrt{4x^2+9} + C;\ u = 4x^2+9$

260. $\int \frac{x}{(4x^2+9)^2}dx = -\frac{1}{8(4x^2+9)};\ u = 4x^2+9$

In the following exercises, find the antiderivative using the indicated substitution.

261. $\int (x+1)^4 dx;\ u = x+1$

262. $\int (x-1)^5 dx;\ u = x-1$

263. $\int (2x-3)^{-7} dx;\ u = 2x-3$

264. $\int (3x-2)^{-11} dx;\ u = 3x-2$

265. $\int \frac{x}{\sqrt{x^2+1}}dx;\ u = x^2+1$

266. $\int \frac{x}{\sqrt{1-x^2}}dx;\ u = 1-x^2$

267. $\int (x-1)\left(x^2-2x\right)^3 dx;\ u = x^2-2x$

268. $\int \left(x^2-2x\right)\left(x^3-3x^2\right)^2 dx;\ u = x^3 = 3x^2$

269. $\int \cos^3 \theta d\theta;\ u = \sin\theta$ $\left(Hint\text{: } \cos^2\theta = 1 - \sin^2\theta\right)$

270. $\int \sin^3 \theta d\theta;\ u = \cos\theta$ $\left(Hint\text{: } \sin^2\theta = 1 - \cos^2\theta\right)$

In the following exercises, use a suitable change of variables to determine the indefinite integral.

271. $\int x(1-x)^{99} dx$

272. $\int t\left(1-t^2\right)^{10} dt$

273. $\int (11x-7)^{-3} dx$

274. $\int (7x-11)^4 dx$

275. $\int \cos^3\theta \sin\theta d\theta$

276. $\int \sin^7\theta \cos\theta d\theta$

277. $\int \cos^2(\pi t)\sin(\pi t)dt$

278. $\int \sin^2 x \cos^3 x dx$ $\left(Hint\text{: } \sin^2 x + \cos^2 x = 1\right)$

279. $\int t\sin\left(t^2\right)\cos\left(t^2\right)dt$

280. $\int t^2\cos^2\left(t^3\right)\sin\left(t^3\right)dt$

281. $\int \frac{x^2}{\left(x^3-3\right)^2}dx$

282. $\int \frac{x^3}{\sqrt{1-x^2}}dx$

283. $\displaystyle\int \frac{y^5}{\left(1-y^3\right)^{3/2}}dy$

284. $\displaystyle\int \cos\theta(1-\cos\theta)^{99}\sin\theta d\theta$

285. $\displaystyle\int \left(1-\cos^3\theta\right)^{10}\cos^2\theta\sin\theta d\theta$

286. $\displaystyle\int (\cos\theta-1)\left(\cos^2\theta-2\cos\theta\right)^3\sin\theta d\theta$

287. $\displaystyle\int \left(\sin^2\theta-2\sin\theta\right)\left(\sin^3\theta-3\sin^2\theta\right)^3\cos\theta d\theta$

In the following exercises, use a calculator to estimate the area under the curve using left Riemann sums with 50 terms, then use substitution to solve for the exact answer.

288. **[T]** $y=3(1-x)^2$ over $[0, 2]$

289. **[T]** $y=x\left(1-x^2\right)^3$ over $[-1, 2]$

290. **[T]** $y=\sin x(1-\cos x)^2$ over $[0, \pi]$

291. **[T]** $y=\dfrac{x}{\left(x^2+1\right)^2}$ over $[-1, 1]$

In the following exercises, use a change of variables to evaluate the definite integral.

292. $\displaystyle\int_0^1 x\sqrt{1-x^2}dx$

293. $\displaystyle\int_0^1 \frac{x}{\sqrt{1+x^2}}dx$

294. $\displaystyle\int_0^2 \frac{t}{\sqrt{5+t^2}}dt$

295. $\displaystyle\int_0^1 \frac{t}{\sqrt{1+t^3}}dt$

296. $\displaystyle\int_0^{\pi/4} \sec^2\theta\tan\theta d\theta$

297. $\displaystyle\int_0^{\pi/4} \frac{\sin\theta}{\cos^4\theta}d\theta$

In the following exercises, evaluate the indefinite integral $\int f(x)dx$ with constant $C=0$ using $u$-substitution. Then, graph the function and the antiderivative over the indicated interval. If possible, estimate a value of $C$ that would need to be added to the antiderivative to make it equal to the definite integral $F(x)=\int_a^x f(t)dt,$ with $a$ the left endpoint of the given interval.

298. **[T]** $\displaystyle\int (2x+1)e^{x^2+x-6}dx$ over $[-3, 2]$

299. **[T]** $\displaystyle\int \frac{\cos(\ln(2x))}{x}dx$ on $[0, 2]$

300. **[T]** $\displaystyle\int \frac{3x^2+2x+1}{\sqrt{x^3+x^2+x+4}}dx$ over $[-1, 2]$

301. **[T]** $\displaystyle\int \frac{\sin x}{\cos^3 x}dx$ over $\left[-\frac{\pi}{3}, \frac{\pi}{3}\right]$

302. **[T]** $\displaystyle\int (x+2)e^{-x^2-4x+3}dx$ over $[-5, 1]$

303. **[T]** $\displaystyle\int 3x^2\sqrt{2x^3+1}dx$ over $[0, 1]$

304. If $h(a)=h(b)$ in $\int_a^b g'(h(x))h(x)dx,$ what can you say about the value of the integral?

305. Is the substitution $u=1-x^2$ in the definite integral $\displaystyle\int_0^2 \frac{x}{1-x^2}dx$ okay? If not, why not?

In the following exercises, use a change of variables to show that each definite integral is equal to zero.

306. $\displaystyle\int_0^{\pi} \cos^2(2\theta)\sin(2\theta)d\theta$

307. $\displaystyle\int_0^{\sqrt{\pi}} t\cos\left(t^2\right)\sin\left(t^2\right)dt$

308. $\displaystyle\int_0^1 (1-2t)dt$

309. $\displaystyle\int_0^1 \frac{1-2t}{\left(1+\left(t-\frac{1}{2}\right)^2\right)} dt$

310. $\displaystyle\int_0^{\pi} \sin\left(\left(t-\frac{\pi}{2}\right)^3\right)\cos\left(t-\frac{\pi}{2}\right)dt$

311. $\displaystyle\int_0^2 (1-t)\cos(\pi t)dt$

312. $\displaystyle\int_{\pi/4}^{3\pi/4} \sin^2 t \cos t dt$

313. Show that the average value of $f(x)$ over an interval $[a, b]$ is the same as the average value of $f(cx)$ over the interval $\left[\frac{a}{c}, \frac{b}{c}\right]$ for $c > 0$.

314. Find the area under the graph of $f(t) = \frac{t}{\left(1+t^2\right)^a}$ between $t = 0$ and $t = x$ where $a > 0$ and $a \neq 1$ is fixed, and evaluate the limit as $x \to \infty$.

315. Find the area under the graph of $g(t) = \frac{t}{\left(1-t^2\right)^a}$ between $t = 0$ and $t = x,$ where $0 < x < 1$ and $a > 0$ is fixed. Evaluate the limit as $x \to 1$.

316. The area of a semicircle of radius 1 can be expressed as $\int_{-1}^{1} \sqrt{1-x^2}dx$. Use the substitution $x = \cos t$ to express the area of a semicircle as the integral of a trigonometric function. You do not need to compute the integral.

317. The area of the top half of an ellipse with a major axis that is the $x$-axis from $x = -1$ to $a$ and with a minor axis that is the $y$-axis from $y = -b$ to $b$ can be written as $\int_{-a}^{a} b\sqrt{1-\frac{x^2}{a^2}}dx$. Use the substitution $x = a\cos t$ to express this area in terms of an integral of a trigonometric function. You do not need to compute the integral.

318. **[T]** The following graph is of a function of the form $f(t) = a\sin(nt) + b\sin(mt)$. Estimate the coefficients $a$ and $b$, and the frequency parameters $n$ and $m$. Use these estimates to approximate $\int_0^{\pi} f(t)dt$.

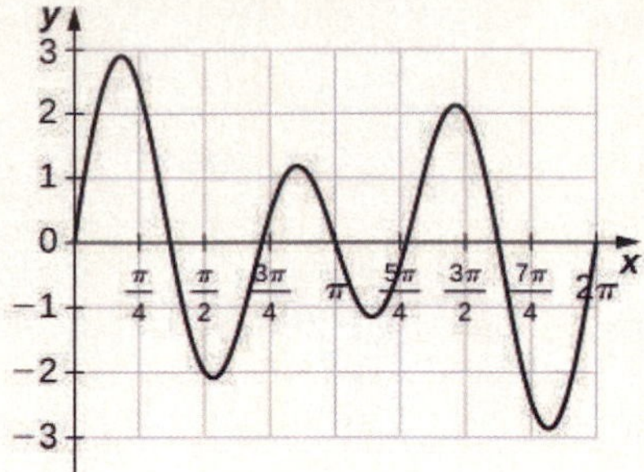


319. **[T]** The following graph is of a function of the form $f(x) = a\cos(nt) + b\cos(mt)$. Estimate the coefficients $a$ and $b$ and the frequency parameters $n$ and $m$. Use these estimates to approximate $\int_0^{\pi} f(t)dt$.

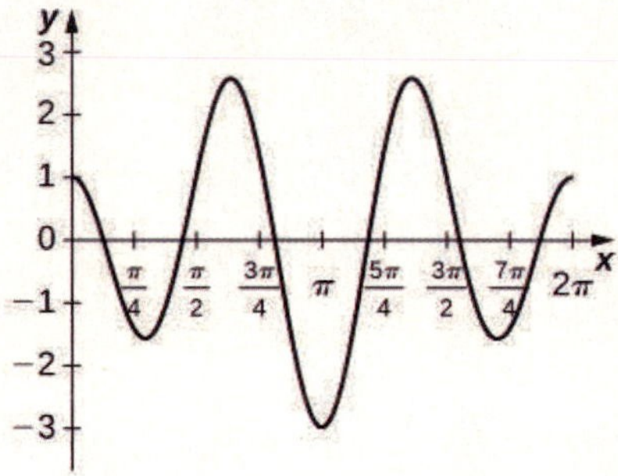

# 1.6 | Integrals Involving Exponential and Logarithmic Functions

## Learning Objectives

**1.6.1** Integrate functions involving exponential functions.

**1.6.2** Integrate functions involving logarithmic functions.

Exponential and logarithmic functions are used to model population growth, cell growth, and financial growth, as well as depreciation, radioactive decay, and resource consumption, to name only a few applications. In this section, we explore integration involving exponential and logarithmic functions.

## Integrals of Exponential Functions

The exponential function is perhaps the most efficient function in terms of the operations of calculus. The exponential function, $y = e^x$, is its own derivative and its own integral.

### Rule: Integrals of Exponential Functions

Exponential functions can be integrated using the following formulas.

$$\begin{aligned} \int e^x\,dx &= e^x + C \\ \int a^x\,dx &= \frac{a^x}{\ln a} + C \end{aligned} \tag{1.21}$$

### Example 1.37

#### Finding an Antiderivative of an Exponential Function

Find the antiderivative of the exponential function $e^{-x}$.

#### Solution

Use substitution, setting $u = -x$, and then $du = -1dx$. Multiply the $du$ equation by $-1$, so you now have $-du = dx$. Then,

$$\begin{aligned} \int e^{-x}dx &= -\int e^u\,du \\ &= -e^u + C \\ &= -e^{-x} + C. \end{aligned}$$

**1.31** Find the antiderivative of the function using substitution: $x^2 e^{-2x^3}$.

A common mistake when dealing with exponential expressions is treating the exponent on $e$ the same way we treat exponents in polynomial expressions. We cannot use the power rule for the exponent on $e$. This can be especially confusing when we have both exponentials and polynomials in the same expression, as in the previous checkpoint. In these cases, we should always double-check to make sure we're using the right rules for the functions we're integrating.

## Example 1.38

### Square Root of an Exponential Function

Find the antiderivative of the exponential function $e^x\sqrt{1+e^x}$.

**Solution**

First rewrite the problem using a rational exponent:

$$\int e^x\sqrt{1+e^x}dx = \int e^x(1+e^x)^{1/2}dx.$$

Using substitution, choose $u = 1 + e^x.u = 1 + e^x$. Then, $du = e^x dx$. We have (**Figure 1.37**)

$$\int e^x(1+e^x)^{1/2}dx = \int u^{1/2}du.$$

Then

$$\int u^{1/2}du = \frac{u^{3/2}}{3/2} + C = \frac{2}{3}u^{3/2} + C = \frac{2}{3}(1+e^x)^{3/2} + C.$$

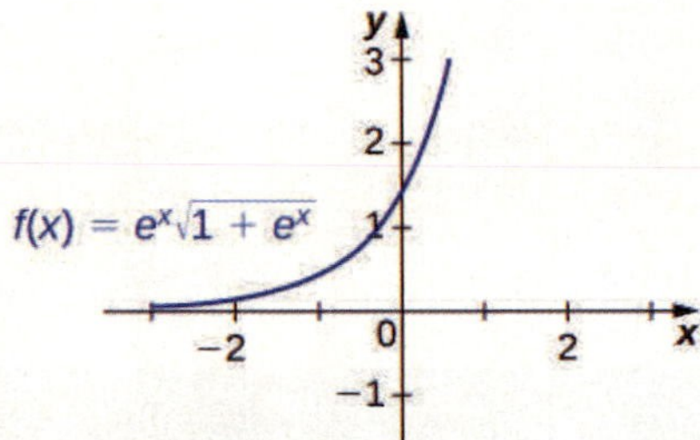


**Figure 1.37** The graph shows an exponential function times the square root of an exponential function.

**1.32** Find the antiderivative of $e^x(3e^x - 2)^2$.

## Example 1.39

### Using Substitution with an Exponential Function

Use substitution to evaluate the indefinite integral $\int 3x^2 e^{2x^3}dx$.

**Solution**

Here we choose to let *u* equal the expression in the exponent on *e*. Let $u = 2x^3$ and $du = 6x^2 dx$.. Again, *du* is off by a constant multiplier; the original function contains a factor of $3x^2$, not $6x^2$. Multiply both sides of the equation by $\frac{1}{2}$ so that the integrand in *u* equals the integrand in *x*. Thus,

$$\int 3x^2 e^{2x^3}dx = \frac{1}{2}\int e^u du.$$

Integrate the expression in $u$ and then substitute the original expression in $x$ back into the $u$ integral:

$$\frac{1}{2}\int e^u du = \frac{1}{2}e^u + C = \frac{1}{2}e^{2x^3} + C.$$

**1.33** Evaluate the indefinite integral $\int 2x^3 e^{x^4} dx$.

As mentioned at the beginning of this section, exponential functions are used in many real-life applications. The number $e$ is often associated with compounded or accelerating growth, as we have seen in earlier sections about the derivative. Although the derivative represents a rate of change or a growth rate, the integral represents the total change or the total growth. Let's look at an example in which integration of an exponential function solves a common business application.

A price–demand function tells us the relationship between the quantity of a product demanded and the price of the product. In general, price decreases as quantity demanded increases. The marginal price–demand function is the derivative of the price–demand function and it tells us how fast the price changes at a given level of production. These functions are used in business to determine the price–elasticity of demand, and to help companies determine whether changing production levels would be profitable.

## Example 1.40

### Finding a Price–Demand Equation

Find the price–demand equation for a particular brand of toothpaste at a supermarket chain when the demand is 50 tubes per week at $2.35 per tube, given that the marginal price—demand function, $p'(x)$, for $x$ number of tubes per week, is given as

$$p'(x) = -0.015e^{-0.01x}.$$

If the supermarket chain sells 100 tubes per week, what price should it set?

#### Solution

To find the price–demand equation, integrate the marginal price–demand function. First find the antiderivative, then look at the particulars. Thus,

$$\begin{aligned} p(x) &= \int -0.015e^{-0.01x} dx \\ &= -0.015\int e^{-0.01x} dx. \end{aligned}$$

Using substitution, let $u = -0.01x$ and $du = -0.01dx$. Then, divide both sides of the $du$ equation by $-0.01$. This gives

$$\begin{aligned} \frac{-0.015}{-0.01}\int e^u du &= 1.5\int e^u du \\ &= 1.5e^u + C \\ &= 1.5e^{-0.01x} + C. \end{aligned}$$

The next step is to solve for $C$. We know that when the price is $2.35 per tube, the demand is 50 tubes per week. This means

$$\begin{aligned} p(50) &= 1.5e^{-0.01(50)} + C \\ &= 2.35. \end{aligned}$$

Now, just solve for $C$:

$$\begin{aligned} C &= 2.35 - 1.5e^{-0.5} \\ &= 2.35 - 0.91 \\ &= 1.44. \end{aligned}$$

Thus,

$$p(x) = 1.5e^{-0.01x} + 1.44.$$

If the supermarket sells 100 tubes of toothpaste per week, the price would be

$$p(100) = 1.5e^{-0.01(100)} + 1.44 = 1.5e^{-1} + 1.44 \approx 1.99.$$

The supermarket should charge $1.99 per tube if it is selling 100 tubes per week.

## Example 1.41

### Evaluating a Definite Integral Involving an Exponential Function

Evaluate the definite integral $\int_1^2 e^{1-x}\,dx.$

#### Solution

Again, substitution is the method to use. Let $u = 1 - x,$ so $du = -1dx$ or $-du = dx.$ Then $\int e^{1-x}dx = -\int e^u du.$ Next, change the limits of integration. Using the equation $u = 1 - x,$ we have

$$\begin{aligned} u &= 1 - (1) = 0 \\ u &= 1 - (2) = -1. \end{aligned}$$

The integral then becomes

$$\begin{aligned} \int_1^2 e^{1-x}dx &= -\int_0^{-1} e^u du \\ &= \int_{-1}^0 e^u du \\ &= e^u|_{-1}^0 \\ &= e^0 - \left(e^{-1}\right) \\ &= -e^{-1} + 1. \end{aligned}$$

See **Figure 1.38**.

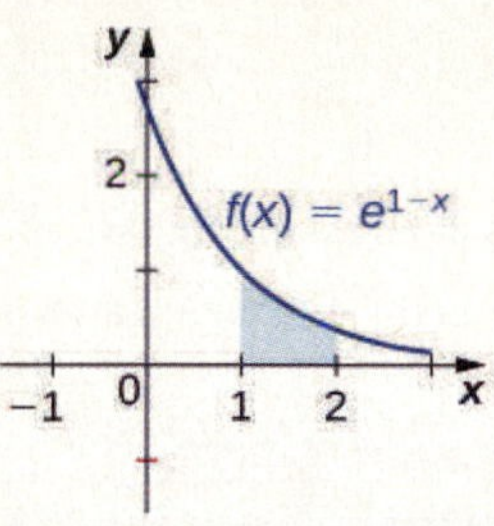


**Figure 1.38** The indicated area can be calculated by evaluating a definite integral using substitution.

**1.34** Evaluate $\int_0^2 e^{2x}\,dx.$

## Example 1.42

### Growth of Bacteria in a Culture

Suppose the rate of growth of bacteria in a Petri dish is given by $q(t) = 3^t,$ where $t$ is given in hours and $q(t)$ is given in thousands of bacteria per hour. If a culture starts with 10,000 bacteria, find a function $Q(t)$ that gives the number of bacteria in the Petri dish at any time $t$. How many bacteria are in the dish after 2 hours?

### Solution

We have

$$Q(t) = \int 3^t\,dt = \frac{3^t}{\ln 3} + C.$$

Then, at $t = 0$ we have $Q(0) = 10 = \frac{1}{\ln 3} + C,$ so $C \approx 9.090$ and we get

$$Q(t) = \frac{3^t}{\ln 3} + 9.090.$$

At time $t = 2,$ we have

$$\begin{aligned} Q(2) &= \frac{3^2}{\ln 3} + 9.090 \\ &= 17.282. \end{aligned}$$

After 2 hours, there are 17,282 bacteria in the dish.

**1.35** From **Example 1.42**, suppose the bacteria grow at a rate of $q(t) = 2^t.$ Assume the culture still starts with 10,000 bacteria. Find $Q(t).$ How many bacteria are in the dish after 3 hours?

## Example 1.43

### Fruit Fly Population Growth

Suppose a population of fruit flies increases at a rate of $g(t) = 2e^{0.02t}$, in flies per day. If the initial population of fruit flies is 100 flies, how many flies are in the population after 10 days?

### Solution

Let $G(t)$ represent the number of flies in the population at time $t$. Applying the net change theorem, we have

$$\begin{aligned} G(10) &= G(0) + \int_0^{10} 2e^{0.02t}\,dt \\ &= 100 + \left[\frac{2}{0.02}e^{0.02t}\right]\Bigg|_0^{10} \\ &= 100 + \left[100e^{0.02t}\right]\Big|_0^{10} \\ &= 100 + 100e^{0.2} - 100 \\ &\approx 122. \end{aligned}$$

There are 122 flies in the population after 10 days.

**1.36** Suppose the rate of growth of the fly population is given by $g(t) = e^{0.01t}$, and the initial fly population is 100 flies. How many flies are in the population after 15 days?

## Example 1.44

### Evaluating a Definite Integral Using Substitution

Evaluate the definite integral using substitution: $\int_1^2 \frac{e^{1/x}}{x^2}dx$.

### Solution

This problem requires some rewriting to simplify applying the properties. First, rewrite the exponent on $e$ as a power of $x$, then bring the $x^2$ in the denominator up to the numerator using a negative exponent. We have

$$\int_1^2 \frac{e^{1/x}}{x^2}dx = \int_1^2 e^{x^{-1}} x^{-2}\,dx.$$

Let $u = x^{-1}$, the exponent on $e$. Then

$$\begin{aligned} du &= -x^{-2}\,dx \\ -du &= x^{-2}\,dx. \end{aligned}$$

Bringing the negative sign outside the integral sign, the problem now reads

$$-\int e^u\, du.$$

Next, change the limits of integration:

$$u = (1)^{-1} = 1$$
$$u = (2)^{-1} = \frac{1}{2}.$$

Notice that now the limits begin with the larger number, meaning we must multiply by −1 and interchange the limits. Thus,

$$\begin{aligned} -\int_1^{1/2} e^u\, du &= \int_{1/2}^{1} e^u\, du \\ &= e^u \Big|_{1/2}^{1} \\ &= e - e^{1/2} \\ &= e - \sqrt{e}. \end{aligned}$$

**1.37** Evaluate the definite integral using substitution: $\int_1^2 \frac{1}{x^3} e^{4x^{-2}} dx.$

## Integrals Involving Logarithmic Functions

Integrating functions of the form $f(x) = x^{-1}$ result in the absolute value of the natural log function, as shown in the following rule. Integral formulas for other logarithmic functions, such as $f(x) = \ln x$ and $f(x) = \log_a x,$ are also included in the rule.

### Rule: Integration Formulas Involving Logarithmic Functions

The following formulas can be used to evaluate integrals involving logarithmic functions.

$$\begin{aligned} \int x^{-1} dx &= \ln|x| + C \\ \int \ln x\, dx &= x\ln x - x + C = x(\ln x - 1) + C \\ \int \log_a x\, dx &= \frac{x}{\ln a}(\ln x - 1) + C \end{aligned} \qquad \textbf{(1.22)}$$

## Example 1.45

### Finding an Antiderivative Involving $\ln x$

Find the antiderivative of the function $\frac{3}{x - 10}.$

### Solution

First factor the 3 outside the integral symbol. Then use the $u^{-1}$ rule. Thus,

$$\begin{aligned}\int \frac{3}{x-10}dx &= 3\int \frac{1}{x-10}dx \\ &= 3\int \frac{du}{u} \\ &= 3\ln|u| + C \\ &= 3\ln|x-10| + C,\ x \neq 10.\end{aligned}$$

See **Figure 1.39**.

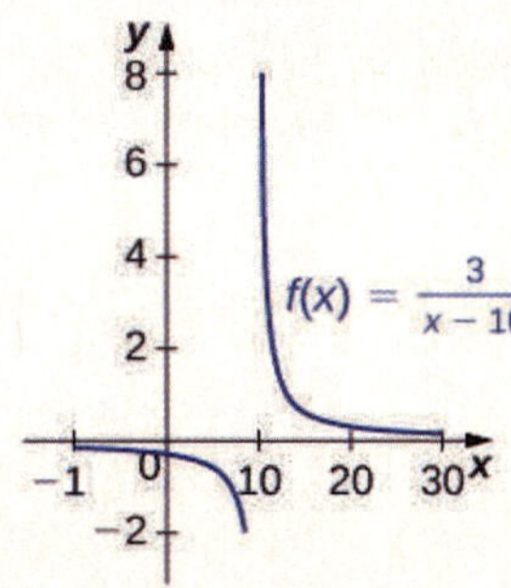


**Figure 1.39** The domain of this function is $x \neq 10$.

**1.38** Find the antiderivative of $\frac{1}{x+2}$.

## Example 1.46

### Finding an Antiderivative of a Rational Function

Find the antiderivative of $\frac{2x^3+3x}{x^4+3x^2}$.

### Solution

This can be rewritten as $\int (2x^3+3x)(x^4+3x^2)^{-1}dx$. Use substitution. Let $u = x^4+3x^2$, then $du = 4x^3+6x$. Alter $du$ by factoring out the 2. Thus,

$$\begin{aligned} du &= (4x^3+6x)dx \\ &= 2(2x^3+3x)dx \\ \frac{1}{2}du &= (2x^3+3x)dx. \end{aligned}$$

Rewrite the integrand in $u$:

$$\int (2x^3 + 3x)(x^4 + 3x^2)^{-1} dx = \frac{1}{2} \int u^{-1} du.$$

Then we have

$$\begin{aligned} \frac{1}{2} \int u^{-1} du &= \frac{1}{2} \ln|u| + C \\ &= \frac{1}{2} \ln\left|x^4 + 3x^2\right| + C. \end{aligned}$$

## Example 1.47

### Finding an Antiderivative of a Logarithmic Function

Find the antiderivative of the log function $\log_2 x$.

#### Solution

Follow the format in the formula listed in the rule on integration formulas involving logarithmic functions. Based on this format, we have

$$\int \log_2 x dx = \frac{x}{\ln 2}(\ln x - 1) + C.$$

**1.39** Find the antiderivative of $\log_3 x$.

**Example 1.48** is a definite integral of a trigonometric function. With trigonometric functions, we often have to apply a trigonometric property or an identity before we can move forward. Finding the right form of the integrand is usually the key to a smooth integration.

## Example 1.48

### Evaluating a Definite Integral

Find the definite integral of $\int_0^{\pi/2} \frac{\sin x}{1 + \cos x} dx$.

#### Solution

We need substitution to evaluate this problem. Let $u = 1 + \cos x$, , so $du = -\sin x\, dx$. Rewrite the integral in terms of $u$, changing the limits of integration as well. Thus,

$$u = 1 + \cos(0) = 2$$
$$u = 1 + \cos\left(\frac{\pi}{2}\right) = 1.$$

Then

$$\begin{aligned}\int_0^{\pi/2} \frac{\sin x}{1+\cos x} &= -\int_2^1 u^{-1}\,du \\ &= \int_1^2 u^{-1}\,du \\ &= \ln|u||_1^2 \\ &= [\ln 2 - \ln 1] \\ &= \ln 2.\end{aligned}$$

# 1.6 EXERCISES

In the following exercises, compute each indefinite integral.

320. $\int e^{2x}dx$

321. $\int e^{-3x}dx$

322. $\int 2^x dx$

323. $\int 3^{-x}dx$

324. $\int \frac{1}{2x}dx$

325. $\int \frac{2}{x}dx$

326. $\int \frac{1}{x^2}dx$

327. $\int \frac{1}{\sqrt{x}}dx$

In the following exercises, find each indefinite integral by using appropriate substitutions.

328. $\int \frac{\ln x}{x}dx$

329. $\int \frac{dx}{x(\ln x)^2}$

330. $\int \frac{dx}{x\ln x}\ (x > 1)$

331. $\int \frac{dx}{x\ln x\ln(\ln x)}$

332. $\int \tan\theta\, d\theta$

333. $\int \frac{\cos x - x\sin x}{x\cos x}dx$

334. $\int \frac{\ln(\sin x)}{\tan x}dx$

335. $\int \ln(\cos x)\tan x dx$

336. $\int xe^{-x^2}dx$

337. $\int x^2 e^{-x^3}dx$

338. $\int e^{\sin x}\cos x dx$

339. $\int e^{\tan x}\sec^2 x dx$

340. $\int e^{\ln x}\frac{dx}{x}$

341. $\int \frac{e^{\ln(1-t)}}{1-t}dt$

In the following exercises, verify by differentiation that $\int \ln x\, dx = x(\ln x - 1) + C,$ then use appropriate changes of variables to compute the integral.

342. $\int \ln x dx$ (*Hint*: $\int \ln x dx = \frac{1}{2}\int x\ln\left(x^2\right)dx$)

343. $\int x^2 \ln^2 x\, dx$

344. $\int \frac{\ln x}{x^2}dx$ (*Hint*: Set $u = \frac{1}{x}$.)

345. $\int \frac{\ln x}{\sqrt{x}}dx$ (*Hint*: Set $u = \sqrt{x}$.)

346. Write an integral to express the area under the graph of $y = \frac{1}{t}$ from $t = 1$ to $e^x$ and evaluate the integral.

347. Write an integral to express the area under the graph of $y = e^t$ between $t = 0$ and $t = \ln x,$ and evaluate the integral.

In the following exercises, use appropriate substitutions to express the trigonometric integrals in terms of compositions with logarithms.

348. $\int \tan(2x)dx$

349. $\int \frac{\sin(3x) - \cos(3x)}{\sin(3x) + \cos(3x)}dx$

350. $\int \frac{x\sin\left(x^2\right)}{\cos\left(x^2\right)}dx$

351. $\int x\csc\left(x^2\right)dx$

352. $\int \ln(\cos x)\tan x\, dx$

353. $\int \ln(\csc x)\cot x dx$

354. $\int \frac{e^x - e^{-x}}{e^x + e^{-x}} dx$

In the following exercises, evaluate the definite integral.

355. $\int_1^2 \frac{1 + 2x + x^2}{3x + 3x^2 + x^3} dx$

356. $\int_0^{\pi/4} \tan x\, dx$

357. $\int_0^{\pi/3} \frac{\sin x - \cos x}{\sin x + \cos x} dx$

358. $\int_{\pi/6}^{\pi/2} \csc x dx$

359. $\int_{\pi/4}^{\pi/3} \cot x dx$

In the following exercises, integrate using the indicated substitution.

360. $\int \frac{x}{x - 100} dx;\ u = x - 100$

361. $\int \frac{y - 1}{y + 1} dy;\ u = y + 1$

362. $\int \frac{1 - x^2}{3x - x^3} dx;\ u = 3x - x^3$

363. $\int \frac{\sin x + \cos x}{\sin x - \cos x} dx;\ u = \sin x - \cos x$

364. $\int e^{2x}\sqrt{1 - e^{2x}} dx;\ u = e^{2x}$

365. $\int \ln(x)\frac{\sqrt{1 - (\ln x)^2}}{x} dx;\ u = \ln x$

In the following exercises, does the right-endpoint approximation overestimate or underestimate the exact area? Calculate the right endpoint estimate $R_{50}$ and solve for the exact area.

366. **[T]** $y = e^x$ over $[0, 1]$

367. **[T]** $y = e^{-x}$ over $[0, 1]$

368. **[T]** $y = \ln(x)$ over $[1, 2]$

369. **[T]** $y = \frac{x + 1}{x^2 + 2x + 6}$ over $[0, 1]$

370. **[T]** $y = 2^x$ over $[-1, 0]$

371. **[T]** $y = -2^{-x}$ over $[0, 1]$

In the following exercises, $f(x) \geq 0$ for $a \leq x \leq b$. Find the area under the graph of $f(x)$ between the given values $a$ and $b$ by integrating.

372. $f(x) = \frac{\log_{10}(x)}{x};\ a = 10,\ b = 100$

373. $f(x) = \frac{\log_2(x)}{x};\ a = 32,\ b = 64$

374. $f(x) = 2^{-x};\ a = 1,\ b = 2$

375. $f(x) = 2^{-x};\ a = 3,\ b = 4$

376. Find the area under the graph of the function $f(x) = xe^{-x^2}$ between $x = 0$ and $x = 5$.

377. Compute the integral of $f(x) = xe^{-x^2}$ and find the smallest value of $N$ such that the area under the graph $f(x) = xe^{-x^2}$ between $x = N$ and $x = N + 10$ is, at most, 0.01.

378. Find the limit, as $N$ tends to infinity, of the area under the graph of $f(x) = xe^{-x^2}$ between $x = 0$ and $x = 5$.

379. Show that $\int_a^b \frac{dt}{t} = \int_{1/b}^{1/a} \frac{dt}{t}$ when $0 < a \leq b$.

380. Suppose that $f(x) > 0$ for all $x$ and that $f$ and $g$ are differentiable. Use the identity $f^g = e^{g \ln f}$ and the chain rule to find the derivative of $f^g$.

381. Use the previous exercise to find the antiderivative of $h(x) = x^x(1 + \ln x)$ and evaluate $\int_2^3 x^x(1 + \ln x)dx$.

382. Show that if $c > 0$, then the integral of $1/x$ from $ac$ to $bc$ $(0 < a < b)$ is the same as the integral of $1/x$ from $a$ to $b$.

The following exercises are intended to derive the fundamental properties of the natural log starting from the *definition* $\ln(x) = \int_1^x \frac{dt}{t}$, using properties of the definite integral and making no further assumptions.

383. Use the identity $\ln(x) = \int_1^x \frac{dt}{t}$ to derive the identity $\ln\left(\frac{1}{x}\right) = -\ln x$.

384. Use a change of variable in the integral $\int_1^{xy} \frac{1}{t}dt$ to show that $\ln xy = \ln x + \ln y$ for $x,\ y > 0$.

385. Use the identity $\ln x = \int_1^x \frac{dt}{x}$ to show that $\ln(x)$ is an increasing function of $x$ on $[0,\ \infty)$, and use the previous exercises to show that the range of $\ln(x)$ is $(-\infty,\ \infty)$. Without any further assumptions, conclude that $\ln(x)$ has an inverse function defined on $(-\infty,\ \infty)$.

386. Pretend, for the moment, that we do not know that $e^x$ is the inverse function of $\ln(x)$, but keep in mind that $\ln(x)$ has an inverse function defined on $(-\infty,\ \infty)$. Call it $E$. Use the identity $\ln xy = \ln x + \ln y$ to deduce that $E(a + b) = E(a)E(b)$ for any real numbers $a$, $b$.

387. Pretend, for the moment, that we do not know that $e^x$ is the inverse function of $\ln x$, but keep in mind that $\ln x$ has an inverse function defined on $(-\infty,\ \infty)$. Call it $E$. Show that $E'(t) = E(t)$.

388. The sine integral, defined as $S(x) = \int_0^x \frac{\sin t}{t}dt$ is an important quantity in engineering. Although it does not have a simple closed formula, it is possible to estimate its behavior for large $x$. Show that for $k \geq 1,\ |S(2\pi k) - S(2\pi(k + 1))| \leq \frac{1}{k(2k + 1)\pi}$.

(*Hint*: $\sin(t + \pi) = -\sin t$)

389. **[T]** The normal distribution in probability is given by $p(x) = \frac{1}{\sigma\sqrt{2\pi}}e^{-(x - \mu)^2/2\sigma^2}$, where $\sigma$ is the standard deviation and $\mu$ is the average. The *standard normal distribution* in probability, $p_s$, corresponds to $\mu = 0$ and $\sigma = 1$. Compute the left endpoint estimates $R_{10}$ and $R_{100}$ of $\int_{-1}^{1} \frac{1}{\sqrt{2\pi}}e^{-x^{2/2}}dx.$

390. **[T]** Compute the right endpoint estimates $R_{50}$ and $R_{100}$ of $\int_{-3}^{5} \frac{1}{2\sqrt{2\pi}}e^{-(x - 1)^2/8}$.

# 1.7 | Integrals Resulting in Inverse Trigonometric Functions

**Learning Objectives**

1.7.1 Integrate functions resulting in inverse trigonometric functions

In this section we focus on integrals that result in inverse trigonometric functions. We have worked with these functions before. Recall from **Functions and Graphs (http://cnx.org/content/m53472/latest/)** that trigonometric functions are not one-to-one unless the domains are restricted. When working with inverses of trigonometric functions, we always need to be careful to take these restrictions into account. Also in **Derivatives (http://cnx.org/content/m53494/latest/)** , we developed formulas for derivatives of inverse trigonometric functions. The formulas developed there give rise directly to integration formulas involving inverse trigonometric functions.

## Integrals that Result in Inverse Sine Functions

Let us begin this last section of the chapter with the three formulas. Along with these formulas, we use substitution to evaluate the integrals. We prove the formula for the inverse sine integral.

### Rule: Integration Formulas Resulting in Inverse Trigonometric Functions

The following integration formulas yield inverse trigonometric functions:

1.

$$\int \frac{du}{\sqrt{a^2 - u^2}} = \sin^{-1}\frac{u}{a} + C \quad (1.23)$$

2.

$$\int \frac{du}{a^2 + u^2} = \frac{1}{a}\tan^{-1}\frac{u}{a} + C \quad (1.24)$$

3.

$$\int \frac{du}{u\sqrt{u^2 - a^2}} = \frac{1}{a}\sec^{-1}\frac{u}{a} + C \quad (1.25)$$

### Proof

Let $y = \sin^{-1}\frac{x}{a}$. Then $a\sin y = x$. Now let's use implicit differentiation. We obtain

$$\begin{aligned} \frac{d}{dx}(a\sin y) &= \frac{d}{dx}(x) \\ a\cos y\frac{dy}{dx} &= 1 \\ \frac{dy}{dx} &= \frac{1}{a\cos y}. \end{aligned}$$

For $-\frac{\pi}{2} \le y \le \frac{\pi}{2}$, $\cos y \ge 0$. Thus, applying the Pythagorean identity $\sin^2 y + \cos^2 y = 1$, we have $\cos y = \sqrt{1 = \sin^2 y}$. This gives

$$\begin{aligned}\frac{1}{a\cos y} &= \frac{1}{a\sqrt{1-\sin^2 y}}\\ &= \frac{1}{\sqrt{a^2-a^2\sin^2 y}}\\ &= \frac{1}{\sqrt{a^2-x^2}}.\end{aligned}$$

Then for $-a \le x \le a,$ we have

$$\int \frac{1}{\sqrt{a^2-u^2}}du = \sin^{-1}\left(\frac{u}{a}\right) + C.$$

□

## Example 1.49

### Evaluating a Definite Integral Using Inverse Trigonometric Functions

Evaluate the definite integral $\displaystyle\int_0^1 \frac{dx}{\sqrt{1-x^2}}.$

### Solution

We can go directly to the formula for the antiderivative in the rule on integration formulas resulting in inverse trigonometric functions, and then evaluate the definite integral. We have

$$\begin{aligned}\int_0^1 \frac{dx}{\sqrt{1-x^2}} &= \sin^{-1} x\Big|_0^1\\ &= \sin^{-1} 1 - \sin^{-1} 0\\ &= \frac{\pi}{2} - 0\\ &= \frac{\pi}{2}.\end{aligned}$$

**1.40** Find the antiderivative of $\displaystyle\int \frac{dx}{\sqrt{1-16x^2}}.$

## Example 1.50

### Finding an Antiderivative Involving an Inverse Trigonometric Function

Evaluate the integral $\displaystyle\int \frac{dx}{\sqrt{4-9x^2}}.$

### Solution

Substitute $u = 3x$. Then $du = 3dx$ and we have

$$\int \frac{dx}{\sqrt{4 - 9x^2}} = \frac{1}{3} \int \frac{du}{\sqrt{4 - u^2}}.$$

Applying the formula with $a = 2$, we obtain

$$\begin{aligned} \int \frac{dx}{\sqrt{4 - 9x^2}} &= \frac{1}{3} \int \frac{du}{\sqrt{4 - u^2}} \\ &= \frac{1}{3} \sin^{-1}\left(\frac{u}{2}\right) + C \\ &= \frac{1}{3} \sin^{-1}\left(\frac{3x}{2}\right) + C. \end{aligned}$$

**1.41** Find the indefinite integral using an inverse trigonometric function and substitution for $\int \frac{dx}{\sqrt{9 - x^2}}$.

## Example 1.51

### Evaluating a Definite Integral

Evaluate the definite integral $\int_0^{\sqrt{3}/2} \frac{du}{\sqrt{1 - u^2}}$.

#### Solution

The format of the problem matches the inverse sine formula. Thus,

$$\begin{aligned} \int_0^{\sqrt{3}/2} \frac{du}{\sqrt{1 - u^2}} &= \sin^{-1} u \Big|_0^{\sqrt{3}/2} \\ &= \left[\sin^{-1}\left(\frac{\sqrt{3}}{2}\right)\right] - \left[\sin^{-1}(0)\right] \\ &= \frac{\pi}{3}. \end{aligned}$$

## Integrals Resulting in Other Inverse Trigonometric Functions

There are six inverse trigonometric functions. However, only three integration formulas are noted in the rule on integration formulas resulting in inverse trigonometric functions because the remaining three are negative versions of the ones we use. The only difference is whether the integrand is positive or negative. Rather than memorizing three more formulas, if the integrand is negative, simply factor out $-1$ and evaluate the integral using one of the formulas already provided. To close this section, we examine one more formula: the integral resulting in the inverse tangent function.

## Example 1.52

### Finding an Antiderivative Involving the Inverse Tangent Function

Find an antiderivative of $\int \frac{1}{1+4x^2}dx.$

#### Solution

Comparing this problem with the formulas stated in the rule on integration formulas resulting in inverse trigonometric functions, the integrand looks similar to the formula for $\tan^{-1}u + C$. So we use substitution, letting $u = 2x$, then $du = 2dx$ and $1/2du = dx$. Then, we have

$$\frac{1}{2}\int \frac{1}{1+u^2}du = \frac{1}{2}\tan^{-1}u + C = \frac{1}{2}\tan^{-1}(2x) + C.$$

**1.42** Use substitution to find the antiderivative of $\int \frac{dx}{25+4x^2}.$

## Example 1.53

### Applying the Integration Formulas

Find the antiderivative of $\int \frac{1}{9+x^2}dx.$

#### Solution

Apply the formula with $a = 3$. Then,

$$\int \frac{dx}{9+x^2} = \frac{1}{3}\tan^{-1}\left(\frac{x}{3}\right) + C.$$

**1.43** Find the antiderivative of $\int \frac{dx}{16+x^2}.$

## Example 1.54

### Evaluating a Definite Integral

Evaluate the definite integral $\int_{\sqrt{3}/3}^{\sqrt{3}} \frac{dx}{1+x^2}.$

**Solution**

Use the formula for the inverse tangent. We have

$$\begin{aligned}\int_{\sqrt{3}/3}^{\sqrt{3}} \frac{dx}{1+x^2} &= \tan^{-1} x \Big|_{\sqrt{3}/3}^{\sqrt{3}} \\ &= \left[\tan^{-1}(\sqrt{3})\right] - \left[\tan^{-1}\left(\frac{\sqrt{3}}{3}\right)\right] \\ &= \frac{\pi}{6}.\end{aligned}$$

**1.44** Evaluate the definite integral $\int_0^2 \frac{dx}{4+x^2}$.

# 1.7 EXERCISES

In the following exercises, evaluate each integral in terms of an inverse trigonometric function.

391. $\int_0^{\sqrt{3}/2} \frac{dx}{\sqrt{1-x^2}}$

392. $\int_{-1/2}^{1/2} \frac{dx}{\sqrt{1-x^2}}$

393. $\int_{\sqrt{3}}^{1} \frac{dx}{\sqrt{1+x^2}}$

394. $\int_{1/\sqrt{3}}^{\sqrt{3}} \frac{dx}{1+x^2}$

395. $\int_1^{\sqrt{2}} \frac{dx}{|x|\sqrt{x^2-1}}$

396. $\int_1^{2/\sqrt{3}} \frac{dx}{|x|\sqrt{x^2-1}}$

In the following exercises, find each indefinite integral, using appropriate substitutions.

397. $\int \frac{dx}{\sqrt{9-x^2}}$

398. $\int \frac{dx}{\sqrt{1-16x^2}}$

399. $\int \frac{dx}{9+x^2}$

400. $\int \frac{dx}{25+16x^2}$

401. $\int \frac{dx}{|x|\sqrt{x^2-9}}$

402. $\int \frac{dx}{|x|\sqrt{4x^2-16}}$

403. Explain the relationship $-\cos^{-1}t + C = \int \frac{dt}{\sqrt{1-t^2}} = \sin^{-1}t + C.$ Is it true, in general, that $\cos^{-1}t = -\sin^{-1}t$?

404. Explain the relationship $\sec^{-1}t + C = \int \frac{dt}{|t|\sqrt{t^2-1}} = -\csc^{-1}t + C.$ Is it true, in general, that $\sec^{-1}t = -\csc^{-1}t$?

405. Explain what is wrong with the following integral: $\int_1^2 \frac{dt}{\sqrt{1-t^2}}.$

406. Explain what is wrong with the following integral: $\int_{-1}^{1} \frac{dt}{|t|\sqrt{t^2-1}}.$

In the following exercises, solve for the antiderivative $\int f$ of $f$ with $C = 0,$ then use a calculator to graph $f$ and the antiderivative over the given interval $[a, b]$. Identify a value of $C$ such that adding $C$ to the antiderivative recovers the definite integral $F(x) = \int_a^x f(t)dt.$

407. **[T]** $\int \frac{1}{\sqrt{9-x^2}}dx$ over $[-3, 3]$

408. **[T]** $\int \frac{9}{9+x^2}dx$ over $[-6, 6]$

409. **[T]** $\int \frac{\cos x}{4+\sin^2 x}dx$ over $[-6, 6]$

410. **[T]** $\int \frac{e^x}{1+e^{2x}}dx$ over $[-6, 6]$

In the following exercises, compute the antiderivative using appropriate substitutions.

411. $\int \frac{\sin^{-1} t dt}{\sqrt{1-t^2}}$

412. $\int \frac{dt}{\sin^{-1} t\sqrt{1-t^2}}$

413. $\int \frac{\tan^{-1}(2t)}{1+4t^2}dt$

414. $\int \frac{t\tan^{-1}\left(t^2\right)}{1+t^4}dt$

415. $\int \frac{\sec^{-1}\left(\frac{t}{2}\right)}{|t|\sqrt{t^2-4}}dt$

416. $\int \frac{t\sec^{-1}\left(t^2\right)}{t^2\sqrt{t^4-1}}dt$

In the following exercises, use a calculator to graph the antiderivative $\int f$ with $C=0$ over the given interval $[a, b]$. Approximate a value of $C$, if possible, such that adding $C$ to the antiderivative gives the same value as the definite integral $F(x)=\int_a^x f(t)dt$.

417. **[T]** $\int \frac{1}{x\sqrt{x^2-4}}dx$ over $[2, 6]$

418. **[T]** $\int \frac{1}{(2x+2)\sqrt{x}}dx$ over $[0, 6]$

419. **[T]** $\int \frac{(\sin x + x\cos x)}{1+x^2\sin^2 x}dx$ over $[-6, 6]$

420. **[T]** $\int \frac{2e^{-2x}}{\sqrt{1-e^{-4x}}}dx$ over $[0, 2]$

421. **[T]** $\int \frac{1}{x+x\ln^2 x}$ over $[0, 2]$

422. **[T]** $\int \frac{\sin^{-1}x}{\sqrt{1-x^2}}$ over $[-1, 1]$

In the following exercises, compute each integral using appropriate substitutions.

423. $\int \frac{e^x}{\sqrt{1-e^{2t}}}dt$

424. $\int \frac{e^t}{1+e^{2t}}dt$

425. $\int \frac{dt}{t\sqrt{1-\ln^2 t}}$

426. $\int \frac{dt}{t\left(1+\ln^2 t\right)}$

427. $\int \frac{\cos^{-1}(2t)}{\sqrt{1-4t^2}}dt$

428. $\int \frac{e^t\cos^{-1}\left(e^t\right)}{\sqrt{1-e^{2t}}}dt$

In the following exercises, compute each definite integral.

429. $\int_0^{1/2} \frac{\tan\left(\sin^{-1}t\right)}{\sqrt{1-t^2}}dt$

430. $\int_{1/4}^{1/2} \frac{\tan\left(\cos^{-1}t\right)}{\sqrt{1-t^2}}dt$

431. $\int_0^{1/2} \frac{\sin\left(\tan^{-1}t\right)}{1+t^2}dt$

432. $\int_0^{1/2} \frac{\cos\left(\tan^{-1}t\right)}{1+t^2}dt$

433. For $A>0$, compute $I(A)=\int_{-A}^{A} \frac{dt}{1+t^2}$ and evaluate $\lim_{a\to\infty} I(A)$, the area under the graph of $\frac{1}{1+t^2}$ on $[-\infty, \infty]$.

434. For $1<B<\infty$, compute $I(B)=\int_1^B \frac{dt}{t\sqrt{t^2-1}}$ and evaluate $\lim_{B\to\infty} I(B)$, the area under the graph of $\frac{1}{t\sqrt{t^2-1}}$ over $[1, \infty)$.

435. Use the substitution $u=\sqrt{2}\cot x$ and the identity $1+\cot^2 x=\csc^2 x$ to evaluate $\int \frac{dx}{1+\cos^2 x}$. (*Hint:* Multiply the top and bottom of the integrand by $\csc^2 x$.)

436. **[T]** Approximate the points at which the graphs of $f(x) = 2x^2 - 1$ and $g(x) = \left(1 + 4x^2\right)^{-3/2}$ intersect, and approximate the area between their graphs accurate to three decimal places.

437. 47. **[T]** Approximate the points at which the graphs of $f(x) = x^2 - 1$ and $f(x) = x^2 - 1$ intersect, and approximate the area between their graphs accurate to three decimal places.

438. Use the following graph to prove that $\int_0^x \sqrt{1 - t^2}dt = \frac{1}{2}x\sqrt{1 - x^2} + \frac{1}{2}\sin^{-1} x.$

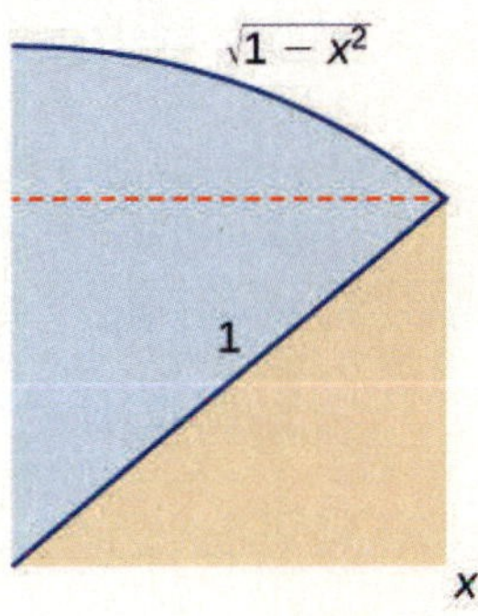

# CHAPTER 1 REVIEW

## KEY TERMS

**average value of a function** (or $f_{\text{ave}}$) the average value of a function on an interval can be found by calculating the definite integral of the function and dividing that value by the length of the interval

**change of variables** the substitution of a variable, such as *u*, for an expression in the integrand

**definite integral** a primary operation of calculus; the area between the curve and the *x*-axis over a given interval is a definite integral

**fundamental theorem of calculus** the theorem, central to the entire development of calculus, that establishes the relationship between differentiation and integration

**fundamental theorem of calculus, part 1** uses a definite integral to define an antiderivative of a function

**fundamental theorem of calculus, part 2** (also, **evaluation theorem**) we can evaluate a definite integral by evaluating the antiderivative of the integrand at the endpoints of the interval and subtracting

**integrable function** a function is integrable if the limit defining the integral exists; in other words, if the limit of the Riemann sums as *n* goes to infinity exists

**integrand** the function to the right of the integration symbol; the integrand includes the function being integrated

**integration by substitution** a technique for integration that allows integration of functions that are the result of a chain-rule derivative

**left-endpoint approximation** an approximation of the area under a curve computed by using the left endpoint of each subinterval to calculate the height of the vertical sides of each rectangle

**limits of integration** these values appear near the top and bottom of the integral sign and define the interval over which the function should be integrated

**lower sum** a sum obtained by using the minimum value of $f(x)$ on each subinterval

**mean value theorem for integrals** guarantees that a point *c* exists such that $f(c)$ is equal to the average value of the function

**net change theorem** if we know the rate of change of a quantity, the net change theorem says the future quantity is equal to the initial quantity plus the integral of the rate of change of the quantity

**net signed area** the area between a function and the *x*-axis such that the area below the *x*-axis is subtracted from the area above the *x*-axis; the result is the same as the definite integral of the function

**partition** a set of points that divides an interval into subintervals

**regular partition** a partition in which the subintervals all have the same width

**riemann sum** an estimate of the area under the curve of the form $A \approx \sum_{i=1}^{n} f(x_i^*)\Delta x$

**right-endpoint approximation** the right-endpoint approximation is an approximation of the area of the rectangles under a curve using the right endpoint of each subinterval to construct the vertical sides of each rectangle

**sigma notation** (also, **summation notation**) the Greek letter sigma ($\Sigma$) indicates addition of the values; the values of the index above and below the sigma indicate where to begin the summation and where to end it

**total area** total area between a function and the *x*-axis is calculated by adding the area above the *x*-axis and the area below the *x*-axis; the result is the same as the definite integral of the absolute value of the function

**upper sum** a sum obtained by using the maximum value of $f(x)$ on each subinterval

**variable of integration** indicates which variable you are integrating with respect to; if it is *x*, then the function in the integrand is followed by *dx*

# KEY EQUATIONS

- **Properties of Sigma Notation**

$$\sum_{i=1}^{n} c = nc$$

$$\sum_{i=1}^{n} ca_i = c\sum_{i=1}^{n} a_i$$

$$\sum_{i=1}^{n} (a_i + b_i) = \sum_{i=1}^{n} a_i + \sum_{i=1}^{n} b_i$$

$$\sum_{i=1}^{n} (a_i - b_i) = \sum_{i=1}^{n} a_i - \sum_{i=1}^{n} b_i$$

$$\sum_{i=1}^{n} a_i = \sum_{i=1}^{m} a_i + \sum_{i=m+1}^{n} a_i$$

- **Sums and Powers of Integers**

$$\sum_{i=1}^{n} i = 1 + 2 + \cdots + n = \frac{n(n+1)}{2}$$

$$\sum_{i=1}^{n} i^2 = 1^2 + 2^2 + \cdots + n^2 = \frac{n(n+1)(2n+1)}{6}$$

$$\sum_{i=0}^{n} i^3 = 1^3 + 2^3 + \cdots + n^3 = \frac{n^2(n+1)^2}{4}$$

- **Left-Endpoint Approximation**

$$A \approx L_n = f(x_0)\Delta x + f(x_1)\Delta x + \cdots + f(x_{n-1})\Delta x = \sum_{i=1}^{n} f(x_{i-1})\Delta x$$

- **Right-Endpoint Approximation**

$$A \approx R_n = f(x_1)\Delta x + f(x_2)\Delta x + \cdots + f(x_n)\Delta x = \sum_{i=1}^{n} f(x_i)\Delta x$$

- **Definite Integral**

$$\int_a^b f(x)dx = \lim_{n \to \infty} \sum_{i=1}^{n} f(x_i^*)\Delta x$$

- **Properties of the Definite Integral**

$$\int_a^a f(x)dx = 0$$

$$\int_b^a f(x)dx = -\int_a^b f(x)dx$$

$$\int_a^b [f(x) + g(x)]dx = \int_a^b f(x)dx + \int_a^b g(x)dx$$

$$\int_a^b [f(x) - g(x)]dx = \int_a^b f(x)dx - \int_a^b g(x)dx$$

$$\int_a^b cf(x)dx = c\int_a^b f(x) \text{ for constant } c$$

$$\int_a^b f(x)dx = \int_a^c f(x)dx + \int_c^b f(x)dx$$

- **Mean Value Theorem for Integrals**

If $f(x)$ is continuous over an interval $[a, b]$, then there is at least one point $c \in [a, b]$ such that $f(c) = \frac{1}{b-a}\int_a^b f(x)dx.$

- **Fundamental Theorem of Calculus Part 1**

  If $f(x)$ is continuous over an interval $[a, b]$, and the function $F(x)$ is defined by $F(x) = \int_a^x f(t)dt$, then $F'(x) = f(x).$

- **Fundamental Theorem of Calculus Part 2**

  If $f$ is continuous over the interval $[a, b]$ and $F(x)$ is any antiderivative of $f(x)$, then $\int_a^b f(x)dx = F(b) - F(a).$

- **Net Change Theorem**

  $F(b) = F(a) + \int_a^b F'(x)dx$ or $\int_a^b F'(x)dx = F(b) - F(a)$

- **Substitution with Indefinite Integrals**

  $\int f[g(x)]g'(x)dx = \int f(u)du = F(u) + C = F(g(x)) + C$

- **Substitution with Definite Integrals**

  $\int_a^b f(g(x))g'(x)dx = \int_{g(a)}^{g(b)} f(u)du$

- **Integrals of Exponential Functions**

  $\int e^x dx = e^x + C$

  $\int a^x dx = \frac{a^x}{\ln a} + C$

- **Integration Formulas Involving Logarithmic Functions**

  $\int x^{-1} dx = \ln|x| + C$

  $\int \ln x\, dx = x\ln x - x + C = x(\ln x - 1) + C$

  $\int \log_a x\, dx = \frac{x}{\ln a}(\ln x - 1) + C$

- **Integrals That Produce Inverse Trigonometric Functions**

  $\int \frac{du}{\sqrt{a^2 - u^2}} = \sin^{-1}\left(\frac{u}{a}\right) + C$

  $\int \frac{du}{a^2 + u^2} = \frac{1}{a}\tan^{-1}\left(\frac{u}{a}\right) + C$

  $\int \frac{du}{u\sqrt{u^2 - a^2}} = \frac{1}{a}\sec^{-1}\left(\frac{u}{a}\right) + C$

# KEY CONCEPTS

## 1.1 Approximating Areas

- The use of sigma (summation) notation of the form $\sum_{i=1}^{n} a_i$ is useful for expressing long sums of values in compact form.

- For a continuous function defined over an interval $[a, b]$, the process of dividing the interval into $n$ equal parts, extending a rectangle to the graph of the function, calculating the areas of the series of rectangles, and then summing the areas yields an approximation of the area of that region.
- The width of each rectangle is $\Delta x = \frac{b-a}{n}$.
- Riemann sums are expressions of the form $\sum_{i=1}^{n} f(x_i^*)\Delta x$, and can be used to estimate the area under the curve $y = f(x)$. Left- and right-endpoint approximations are special kinds of Riemann sums where the values of $\{x_i^*\}$ are chosen to be the left or right endpoints of the subintervals, respectively.
- Riemann sums allow for much flexibility in choosing the set of points $\{x_i^*\}$ at which the function is evaluated, often with an eye to obtaining a lower sum or an upper sum.

## 1.2 The Definite Integral

- The definite integral can be used to calculate net signed area, which is the area above the *x*-axis less the area below the *x*-axis. Net signed area can be positive, negative, or zero.
- The component parts of the definite integral are the integrand, the variable of integration, and the limits of integration.
- Continuous functions on a closed interval are integrable. Functions that are not continuous may still be integrable, depending on the nature of the discontinuities.
- The properties of definite integrals can be used to evaluate integrals.
- The area under the curve of many functions can be calculated using geometric formulas.
- The average value of a function can be calculated using definite integrals.

## 1.3 The Fundamental Theorem of Calculus

- The Mean Value Theorem for Integrals states that for a continuous function over a closed interval, there is a value $c$ such that $f(c)$ equals the average value of the function. See **The Mean Value Theorem for Integrals**.
- The Fundamental Theorem of Calculus, Part 1 shows the relationship between the derivative and the integral. See **Fundamental Theorem of Calculus, Part 1**.
- The Fundamental Theorem of Calculus, Part 2 is a formula for evaluating a definite integral in terms of an antiderivative of its integrand. The total area under a curve can be found using this formula. See **The Fundamental Theorem of Calculus, Part 2**.

## 1.4 Integration Formulas and the Net Change Theorem

- The net change theorem states that when a quantity changes, the final value equals the initial value plus the integral of the rate of change. Net change can be a positive number, a negative number, or zero.
- The area under an even function over a symmetric interval can be calculated by doubling the area over the positive *x*-axis. For an odd function, the integral over a symmetric interval equals zero, because half the area is negative.

## 1.5 Substitution

- Substitution is a technique that simplifies the integration of functions that are the result of a chain-rule derivative. The term ‘substitution’ refers to changing variables or substituting the variable *u* and *du* for appropriate expressions in the integrand.
- When using substitution for a definite integral, we also have to change the limits of integration.

### 1.6 Integrals Involving Exponential and Logarithmic Functions

- Exponential and logarithmic functions arise in many real-world applications, especially those involving growth and decay.
- Substitution is often used to evaluate integrals involving exponential functions or logarithms.

### 1.7 Integrals Resulting in Inverse Trigonometric Functions

- Formulas for derivatives of inverse trigonometric functions developed in **Derivatives of Exponential and Logarithmic Functions (http://cnx.org/content/m53584/latest/)** lead directly to integration formulas involving inverse trigonometric functions.
- Use the formulas listed in the rule on integration formulas resulting in inverse trigonometric functions to match up the correct format and make alterations as necessary to solve the problem.
- Substitution is often required to put the integrand in the correct form.

## CHAPTER 1 REVIEW EXERCISES

*True or False.* Justify your answer with a proof or a counterexample. Assume all functions $f$ and $g$ are continuous over their domains.

**439.** If $f(x) > 0,\ f'(x) > 0$ for all $x$, then the right-hand rule underestimates the integral $\int_a^b f(x)$. Use a graph to justify your answer.

**440.** $\int_a^b f(x)^2 dx = \int_a^b f(x)dx \int_a^b f(x)dx$

**441.** If $f(x) \le g(x)$ for all $x \in [a, b]$, then $\int_a^b f(x) \le \int_a^b g(x)$.

**442.** All continuous functions have an antiderivative.

Evaluate the Riemann sums $L_4$ and $R_4$ for the following functions over the specified interval. Compare your answer with the exact answer, when possible, or use a calculator to determine the answer.

**443.** $y = 3x^2 - 2x + 1$ over $[-1, 1]$

**444.** $y = \ln\left(x^2 + 1\right)$ over $[0, e]$

**445.** $y = x^2 \sin x$ over $[0, \pi]$

**446.** $y = \sqrt{x} + \frac{1}{x}$ over $[1, 4]$

Evaluate the following integrals.

**447.** $\int_{-1}^{1}\left(x^3 - 2x^2 + 4x\right)dx$

**448.** $\int_0^4 \frac{3t}{\sqrt{1 + 6t^2}}dt$

**449.** $\int_{\pi/3}^{\pi/2} 2\sec(2\theta)\tan(2\theta)d\theta$

**450.** $\int_0^{\pi/4} e^{\cos^2 x}\sin x \cos x\, dx$

Find the antiderivative.

**451.** $\int \frac{dx}{(x + 4)^3}$

**452.** $\int x\ln\left(x^2\right)dx$

**453.** $\int \frac{4x^2}{\sqrt{1 - x^6}}dx$

**454.** $\int \frac{e^{2x}}{1 + e^{4x}}dx$

Find the derivative.

**455.** $\frac{d}{dt}\int_0^t \frac{\sin x}{\sqrt{1 + x^2}}dx$

**456.** $\frac{d}{dx}\int_{1}^{x^3} \sqrt{4 - t^2}dt$

**457.** $\frac{d}{dx}\int_{1}^{\ln(x)} (4t + e^t)dt$

**458.** $\frac{d}{dx}\int_{0}^{\cos x} e^{t^2} dt$

The following problems consider the historic average cost per gigabyte of RAM on a computer.

| Year | 5-Year Change ($) |
|---|---|
| 1980 | 0 |
| 1985 | −5,468,750 |
| 1990 | −755,495 |
| 1995 | −73,005 |
| 2000 | −29,768 |
| 2005 | −918 |
| 2010 | −177 |

**459.** If the average cost per gigabyte of RAM in 2010 is $12, find the average cost per gigabyte of RAM in 1980.

**460.** The average cost per gigabyte of RAM can be approximated by the function $C(t) = 8,500,000(0.65)^t$, where $t$ is measured in years since 1980, and $C$ is cost in US$. Find the average cost per gigabyte of RAM for 1980 to 2010.

**461.** Find the average cost of 1GB RAM for 2005 to 2010.

**462.** The velocity of a bullet from a rifle can be approximated by $v(t) = 6400t^2 - 6505t + 2686,$ where $t$ is seconds after the shot and $v$ is the velocity measured in feet per second. This equation only models the velocity for the first half-second after the shot: $0 \le t \le 0.5$. What is the total distance the bullet travels in 0.5 sec?

**463.** What is the average velocity of the bullet for the first half-second?

# 2 | APPLICATIONS OF INTEGRATION

**Figure 2.1** Hoover Dam is one of the United States' iconic landmarks, and provides irrigation and hydroelectric power for millions of people in the southwest United States. (credit: modification of work by Lynn Betts, Wikimedia)

## Chapter Outline

# Introduction

The Hoover Dam is an engineering marvel. When Lake Mead, the reservoir behind the dam, is full, the dam withstands a great deal of force. However, water levels in the lake vary considerably as a result of droughts and varying water demands. Later in this chapter, we use definite integrals to calculate the force exerted on the dam when the reservoir is full and we examine how changing water levels affect that force (see **Example 2.28**).

Hydrostatic force is only one of the many applications of definite integrals we explore in this chapter. From geometric applications such as surface area and volume, to physical applications such as mass and work, to growth and decay models, definite integrals are a powerful tool to help us understand and model the world around us.

# 2.1 | Areas between Curves

## Learning Objectives

**2.1.1** Determine the area of a region between two curves by integrating with respect to the independent variable.

**2.1.2** Find the area of a compound region.

**2.1.3** Determine the area of a region between two curves by integrating with respect to the dependent variable.

In **Introduction to Integration**, we developed the concept of the definite integral to calculate the area below a curve on a given interval. In this section, we expand that idea to calculate the area of more complex regions. We start by finding the area between two curves that are functions of $x$, beginning with the simple case in which one function value is always greater than the other. We then look at cases when the graphs of the functions cross. Last, we consider how to calculate the area between two curves that are functions of $y$.

## Area of a Region between Two Curves

Let $f(x)$ and $g(x)$ be continuous functions over an interval $[a, b]$ such that $f(x) \geq g(x)$ on $[a, b]$. We want to find the area between the graphs of the functions, as shown in the following figure.

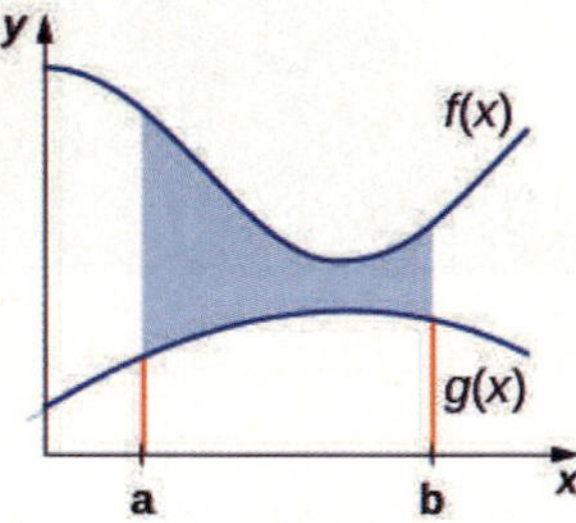


**Figure 2.2** The area between the graphs of two functions, $f(x)$ and $g(x)$, on the interval $[a, b]$.

As we did before, we are going to partition the interval on the $x$-axis and approximate the area between the graphs of the functions with rectangles. So, for $i = 0, 1, 2, \ldots, n$, let $P = \{x_i\}$ be a regular partition of $[a, b]$. Then, for $i = 1, 2, \ldots, n$, choose a point $x_i^* \in [x_{i-1}, x_i]$, and on each interval $[x_{i-1}, x_i]$ construct a rectangle that extends vertically from $g(x_i^*)$ to $f(x_i^*)$. **Figure 2.3**(a) shows the rectangles when $x_i^*$ is selected to be the left endpoint of the interval and $n = 10$. **Figure 2.3**(b) shows a representative rectangle in detail.

Use this **calculator (http://www.openstaxcollege.org/l/20_CurveCalc)** to learn more about the areas between two curves.

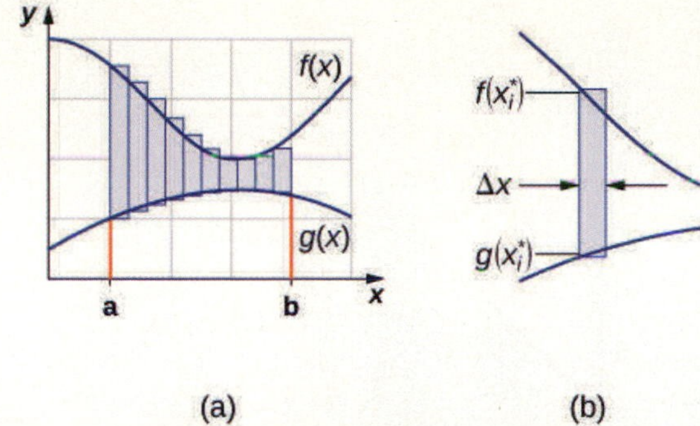


**Figure 2.3** (a)We can approximate the area between the graphs of two functions, $f(x)$ and $g(x)$, with rectangles. (b) The area of a typical rectangle goes from one curve to the other.

The height of each individual rectangle is $f(x_i^*) - g(x_i^*)$ and the width of each rectangle is $\Delta x$. Adding the areas of all the rectangles, we see that the area between the curves is approximated by

$$A \approx \sum_{i=1}^{n} \left[f(x_i^*) - g(x_i^*)\right]\Delta x.$$

This is a Riemann sum, so we take the limit as $n \to \infty$ and we get

$$A = \lim_{n \to \infty} \sum_{i=1}^{n} \left[f(x_i^*) - g(x_i^*)\right]\Delta x = \int_a^b \left[f(x) - g(x)\right]dx.$$

These findings are summarized in the following theorem.

### Theorem 2.1: Finding the Area between Two Curves

Let $f(x)$ and $g(x)$ be continuous functions such that $f(x) \geq g(x)$ over an interval $[a, b]$. Let $R$ denote the region bounded above by the graph of $f(x)$, below by the graph of $g(x)$, and on the left and right by the lines $x = a$ and $x = b$, respectively. Then, the area of $R$ is given by

$$A = \int_a^b \left[f(x) - g(x)\right]dx. \tag{2.1}$$

We apply this theorem in the following example.

## Example 2.1

### Finding the Area of a Region between Two Curves 1

If $R$ is the region bounded above by the graph of the function $f(x) = x + 4$ and below by the graph of the function $g(x) = 3 - \frac{x}{2}$ over the interval $[1, 4]$, find the area of region $R$.

#### Solution

The region is depicted in the following figure.

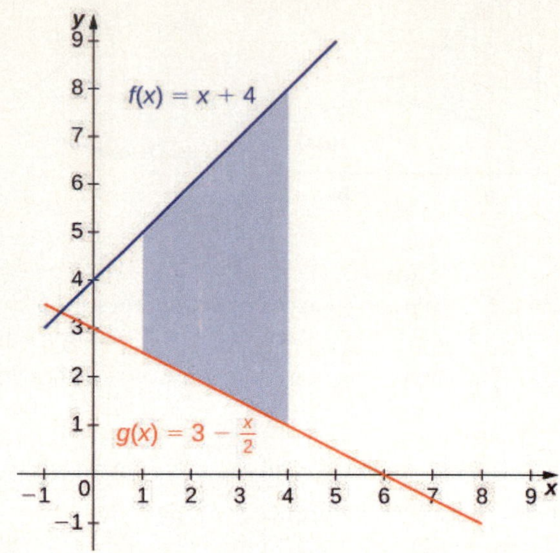


**Figure 2.4** A region between two curves is shown where one curve is always greater than the other.

We have

$$\begin{aligned} A &= \int_a^b [f(x) - g(x)]dx \\ &= \int_1^4 \left[(x+4) - \left(3 - \frac{x}{2}\right)\right]dx = \int_1^4 \left[\frac{3x}{2} + 1\right]dx \\ &= \left[\frac{3x^2}{4} + x\right]\Bigg|_1^4 = \left(16 - \frac{7}{4}\right) = \frac{57}{4}. \end{aligned}$$

The area of the region is $\frac{57}{4}$ units$^2$.

**2.1** If $R$ is the region bounded by the graphs of the functions $f(x) = \frac{x}{2} + 5$ and $g(x) = x + \frac{1}{2}$ over the interval $[1, 5]$, find the area of region $R$.

In **Example 2.1**, we defined the interval of interest as part of the problem statement. Quite often, though, we want to define our interval of interest based on where the graphs of the two functions intersect. This is illustrated in the following example.

## Example 2.2

### Finding the Area of a Region between Two Curves 2

If $R$ is the region bounded above by the graph of the function $f(x) = 9 - (x/2)^2$ and below by the graph of the function $g(x) = 6 - x$, find the area of region $R$.

### Solution

The region is depicted in the following figure.

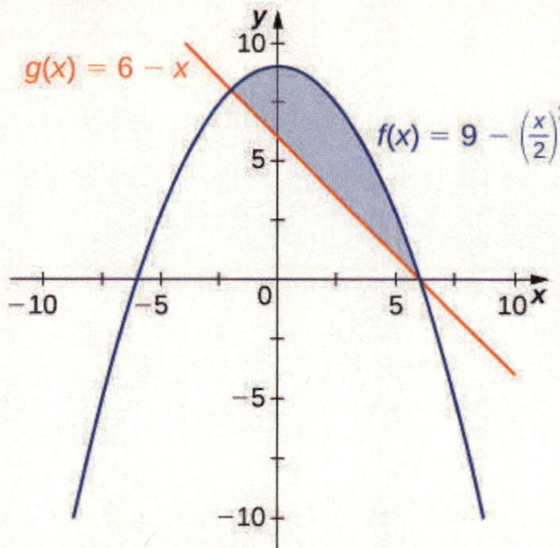


**Figure 2.5** This graph shows the region below the graph of $f(x)$ and above the graph of $g(x)$.

We first need to compute where the graphs of the functions intersect. Setting $f(x) = g(x),$ we get

$$\begin{aligned} f(x) &= g(x) \\ 9 - \left(\frac{x}{2}\right)^2 &= 6 - x \\ 9 - \frac{x^2}{4} &= 6 - x \\ 36 - x^2 &= 24 - 4x \\ x^2 - 4x - 12 &= 0 \\ (x - 6)(x + 2) &= 0. \end{aligned}$$

The graphs of the functions intersect when $x = 6$ or $x = -2,$ so we want to integrate from $-2$ to $6.$ Since $f(x) \geq g(x)$ for $-2 \leq x \leq 6,$ we obtain

$$\begin{aligned} A &= \int_a^b [f(x) - g(x)]dx \\ &= \int_{-2}^{6} \left[9 - \left(\frac{x}{2}\right)^2 - (6 - x)\right]dx = \int_{-2}^{6} \left[3 - \frac{x^2}{4} + x\right]dx \\ &= \left[3x - \frac{x^3}{12} + \frac{x^2}{2}\right]\Bigg|_{-2}^{6} = \frac{64}{3}. \end{aligned}$$

The area of the region is $64/3$ units$^2$.

**2.2** If $R$ is the region bounded above by the graph of the function $f(x) = x$ and below by the graph of the function $g(x) = x^4,$ find the area of region $R.$

## Areas of Compound Regions

So far, we have required $f(x) \geq g(x)$ over the entire interval of interest, but what if we want to look at regions bounded by the graphs of functions that cross one another? In that case, we modify the process we just developed by using the absolute value function.

### Theorem 2.2: Finding the Area of a Region between Curves That Cross

Let $f(x)$ and $g(x)$ be continuous functions over an interval $[a, b]$. Let $R$ denote the region between the graphs of $f(x)$ and $g(x)$, and be bounded on the left and right by the lines $x = a$ and $x = b$, respectively. Then, the area of $R$ is given by

$$A = \int_a^b |f(x) - g(x)|dx.$$

In practice, applying this theorem requires us to break up the interval $[a, b]$ and evaluate several integrals, depending on which of the function values is greater over a given part of the interval. We study this process in the following example.

### Example 2.3

#### Finding the Area of a Region Bounded by Functions That Cross

If $R$ is the region between the graphs of the functions $f(x) = \sin x$ and $g(x) = \cos x$ over the interval $[0, \pi]$, find the area of region $R$.

#### Solution

The region is depicted in the following figure.

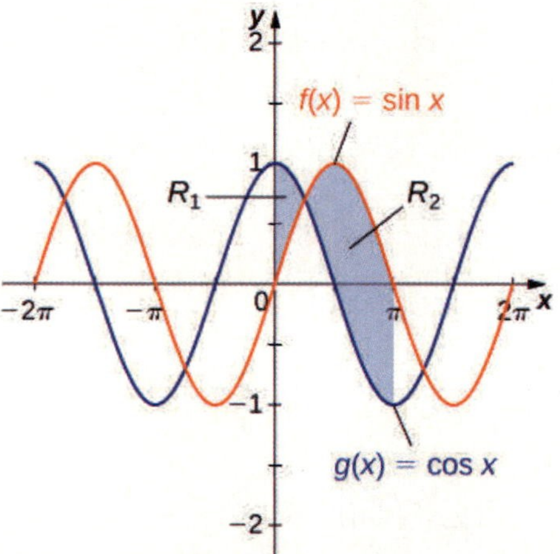


Figure 2.6 The region between two curves can be broken into two sub-regions.

The graphs of the functions intersect at $x = \pi/4$. For $x \in [0, \pi/4]$, $\cos x \geq \sin x$, so

$$|f(x) - g(x)| = |\sin x - \cos x| = \cos x - \sin x.$$

On the other hand, for $x \in [\pi/4, \pi]$, $\sin x \geq \cos x$, so

$$|f(x) - g(x)| = |\sin x - \cos x| = \sin x - \cos x.$$

Then

$$\begin{aligned} A &= \int_a^b |f(x) - g(x)|dx \\ &= \int_0^{\pi} |\sin x - \cos x|dx = \int_0^{\pi/4} (\cos x - \sin x)dx + \int_{\pi/4}^{\pi} (\sin x - \cos x)dx \\ &= [\sin x + \cos x]\Big|_0^{\pi/4} + [-\cos x - \sin x]\Big|_{\pi/4}^{\pi} \\ &= (\sqrt{2} - 1) + \left(1 + \sqrt{2}\right) = 2\sqrt{2}. \end{aligned}$$

The area of the region is $2\sqrt{2}$ units$^2$.

**2.3** If $R$ is the region between the graphs of the functions $f(x) = \sin x$ and $g(x) = \cos x$ over the interval $[\pi/2, 2\pi]$, find the area of region $R$.

## Example 2.4

### Finding the Area of a Complex Region

Consider the region depicted in **Figure 2.7**. Find the area of $R$.

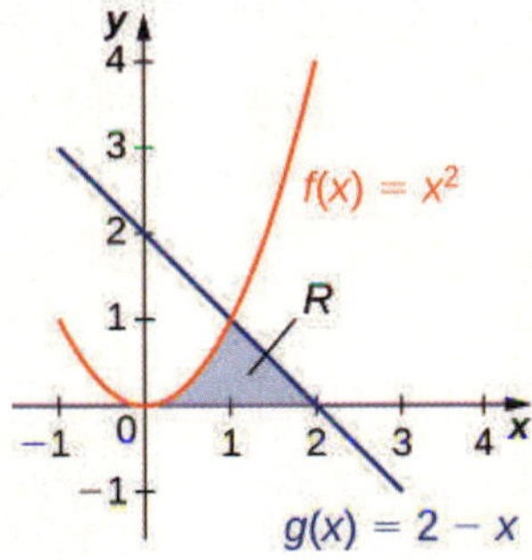


**Figure 2.7** Two integrals are required to calculate the area of this region.

### Solution

As with **Example 2.3**, we need to divide the interval into two pieces. The graphs of the functions intersect at $x = 1$ (set $f(x) = g(x)$ and solve for x), so we evaluate two separate integrals: one over the interval $[0, 1]$ and one over the interval $[1, 2]$.

Over the interval $[0, 1]$, the region is bounded above by $f(x) = x^2$ and below by the x-axis, so we have

$$A_1 = \int_0^1 x^2 dx = \frac{x^3}{3}\Big|_0^1 = \frac{1}{3}.$$

Over the interval $[1, 2]$, the region is bounded above by $g(x) = 2 - x$ and below by the $x$-axis, so we have

$$A_2 = \int_1^2 (2 - x)dx = \left[2x - \frac{x^2}{2}\right]\Big|_1^2 = \frac{1}{2}.$$

Adding these areas together, we obtain

$$A = A_1 + A_2 = \frac{1}{3} + \frac{1}{2} = \frac{5}{6}.$$

The area of the region is $5/6$ units$^2$.

**2.4** Consider the region depicted in the following figure. Find the area of $R$.

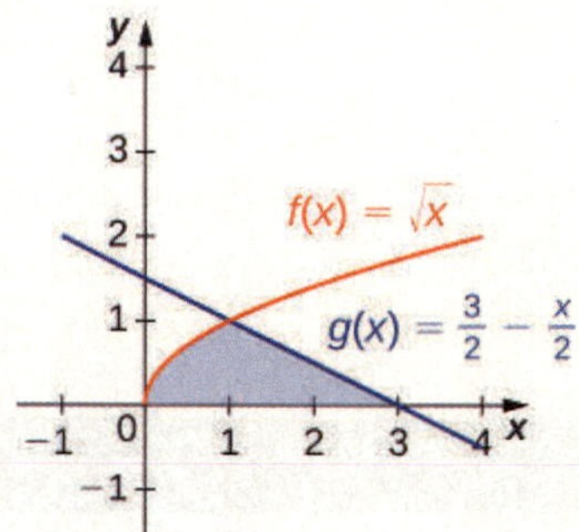


## Regions Defined with Respect to *y*

In **Example 2.4**, we had to evaluate two separate integrals to calculate the area of the region. However, there is another approach that requires only one integral. What if we treat the curves as functions of $y$, instead of as functions of $x$? Review **Figure 2.7**. Note that the left graph, shown in red, is represented by the function $y = f(x) = x^2$. We could just as easily solve this for $x$ and represent the curve by the function $x = v(y) = \sqrt{y}$. (Note that $x = -\sqrt{y}$ is also a valid representation of the function $y = f(x) = x^2$ as a function of $y$. However, based on the graph, it is clear we are interested in the positive square root.) Similarly, the right graph is represented by the function $y = g(x) = 2 - x$, but could just as easily be represented by the function $x = u(y) = 2 - y$. When the graphs are represented as functions of $y$, we see the region is bounded on the left by the graph of one function and on the right by the graph of the other function. Therefore, if we integrate with respect to $y$, we need to evaluate one integral only. Let's develop a formula for this type of integration.

Let $u(y)$ and $v(y)$ be continuous functions over an interval $[c, d]$ such that $u(y) \geq v(y)$ for all $y \in [c, d]$. We want to find the area between the graphs of the functions, as shown in the following figure.

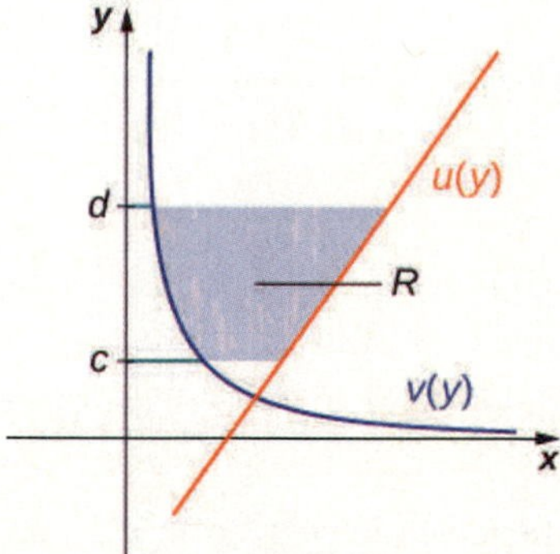


**Figure 2.8** We can find the area between the graphs of two functions, $u(y)$ and $v(y)$.

This time, we are going to partition the interval on the $y$-axis and use horizontal rectangles to approximate the area between the functions. So, for $i = 0, 1, 2,\ldots, n,$ let $Q = \{y_i\}$ be a regular partition of $[c, d]$. Then, for $i = 1, 2,\ldots, n,$ choose a point $y_i^* \in [y_{i-1}, y_i],$ then over each interval $[y_{i-1}, y_i]$ construct a rectangle that extends horizontally from $v(y_i^*)$ to $u(y_i^*)$. **Figure 2.9**(a) shows the rectangles when $y_i^*$ is selected to be the lower endpoint of the interval and $n = 10$. **Figure 2.9**(b) shows a representative rectangle in detail.

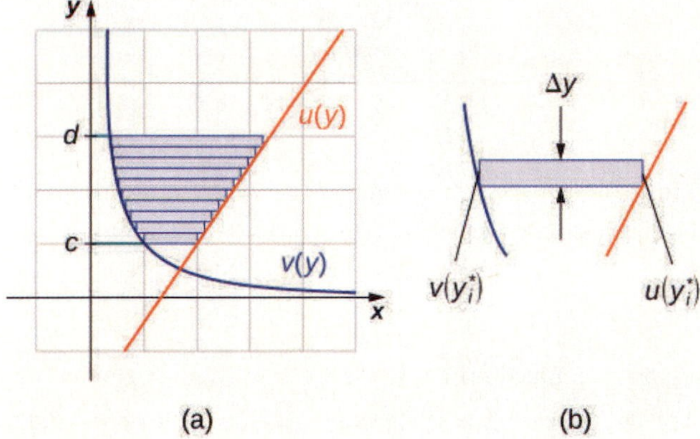


**Figure 2.9** (a) Approximating the area between the graphs of two functions, $u(y)$ and $v(y)$, with rectangles. (b) The area of a typical rectangle.

The height of each individual rectangle is $\Delta y$ and the width of each rectangle is $u(y_i^*) - v(y_i^*)$. Therefore, the area between the curves is approximately

$$A \approx \sum_{i=1}^{n} [u(y_i^*) - v(y_i^*)]\Delta y.$$

This is a Riemann sum, so we take the limit as $n \to \infty,$ obtaining

$$A = \lim_{n \to \infty} \sum_{i=1}^{n} [u(y_i^*) - v(y_i^*)]\Delta y = \int_c^d [u(y) - v(y)]dy.$$

These findings are summarized in the following theorem.

### Theorem 2.3: Finding the Area between Two Curves, Integrating along the *y*-axis

Let $u(y)$ and $v(y)$ be continuous functions such that $u(y) \ge v(y)$ for all $y \in [c, d]$. Let $R$ denote the region bounded on the right by the graph of $u(y),$ on the left by the graph of $v(y),$ and above and below by the lines $y = d$ and $y = c,$ respectively. Then, the area of $R$ is given by

$$A = \int_c^d [u(y) - v(y)]dy. \tag{2.2}$$

## Example 2.5

### Integrating with Respect to *y*

Let's revisit **Example 2.4**, only this time let's integrate with respect to $y$. Let $R$ be the region depicted in **Figure 2.10**. Find the area of $R$ by integrating with respect to $y$.

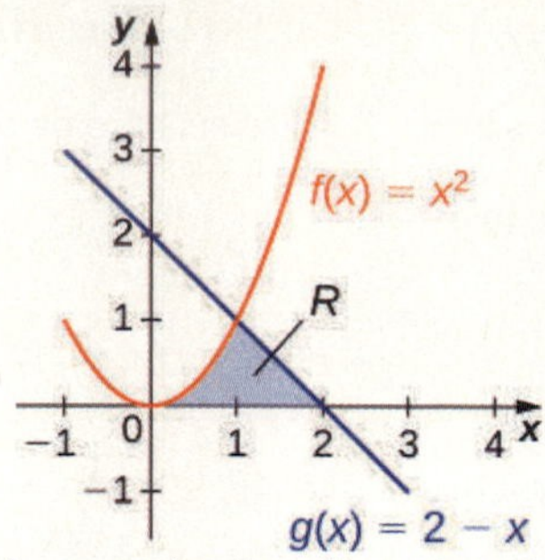


**Figure 2.10** The area of region $R$ can be calculated using one integral only when the curves are treated as functions of $y$.

### Solution

We must first express the graphs as functions of $y$. As we saw at the beginning of this section, the curve on the left can be represented by the function $x = v(y) = \sqrt{y}$, and the curve on the right can be represented by the function $x = u(y) = 2 - y$.

Now we have to determine the limits of integration. The region is bounded below by the $x$-axis, so the lower limit of integration is $y = 0$. The upper limit of integration is determined by the point where the two graphs intersect, which is the point $(1, 1)$, so the upper limit of integration is $y = 1$. Thus, we have $[c, d] = [0, 1]$.

Calculating the area of the region, we get

$$\begin{aligned} A &= \int_c^d [u(y) - v(y)]dy \\ &= \int_0^1 [(2 - y) - \sqrt{y}]dy = \left[2y - \frac{y^2}{2} - \frac{2}{3}y^{3/2}\right]\Big|_0^1 \\ &= \frac{5}{6}. \end{aligned}$$

The area of the region is $5/6$ units$^2$.

**2.5** Let's revisit the checkpoint associated with **Example 2.4**, only this time, let's integrate with respect to $y$. Let be the region depicted in the following figure. Find the area of $R$ by integrating with respect to $y$.

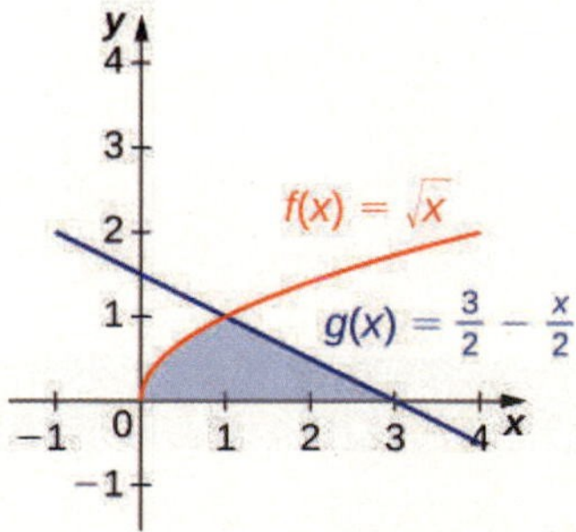

# 2.1 EXERCISES

For the following exercises, determine the area of the region between the two curves in the given figure by integrating over the $x$-axis.

1. $y = x^2 - 3$ and $y = 1$

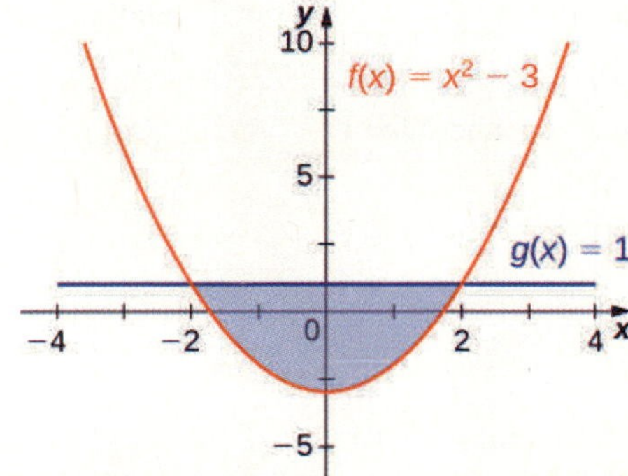


2. $y = x^2$ and $y = 3x + 4$

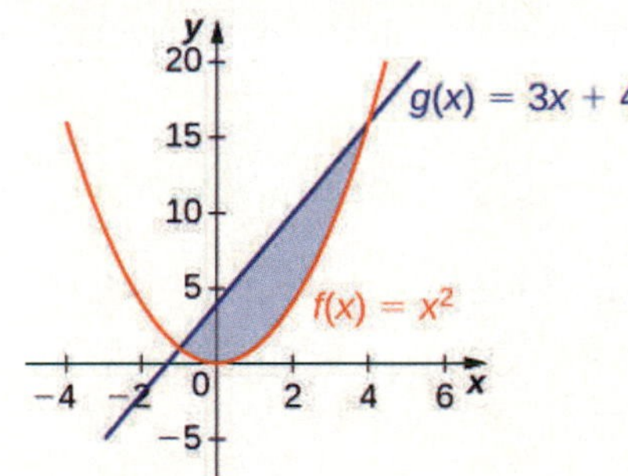


For the following exercises, split the region between the two curves into two smaller regions, then determine the area by integrating over the $x$-axis. Note that you will have two integrals to solve.

3. $y = x^3$ and $y = x^2 + x$

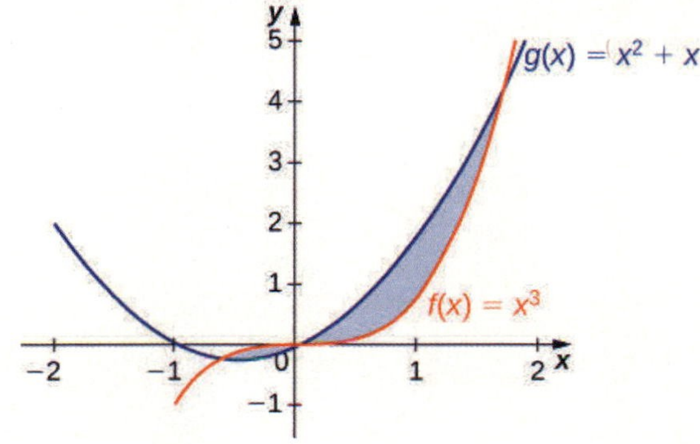


4. $y = \cos\theta$ and $y = 0.5$, for $0 \le \theta \le \pi$

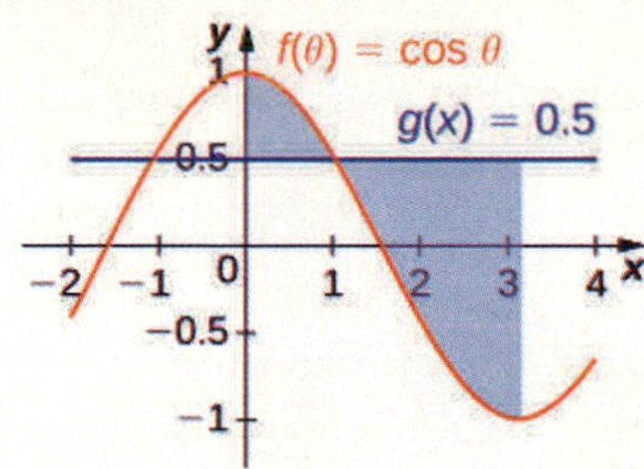


For the following exercises, determine the area of the region between the two curves by integrating over the $y$-axis.

5. $x = y^2$ and $x = 9$

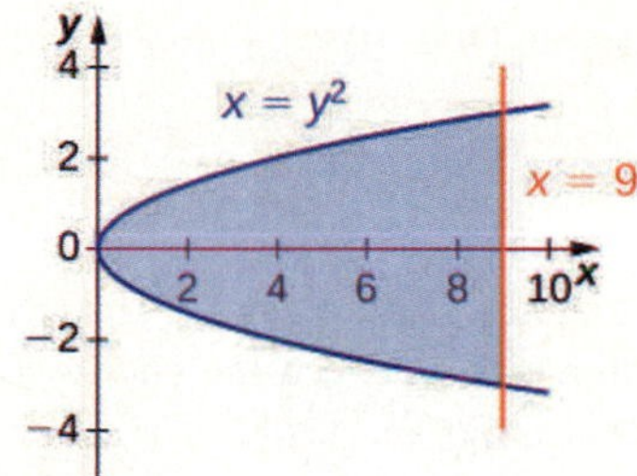


6. $y = x$ and $x = y^2$

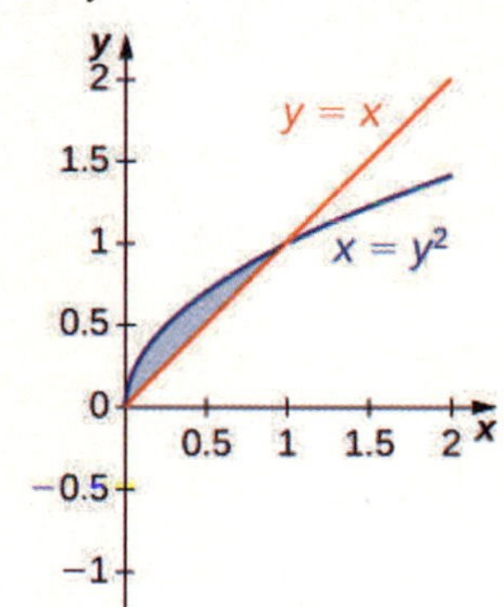


For the following exercises, graph the equations and shade the area of the region between the curves. Determine its area by integrating over the $x$-axis.

7. $y = x^2$ and $y = -x^2 + 18x$

8. $y = \frac{1}{x}$, $y = \frac{1}{x^2}$, and $x = 3$

9. $y = \cos x$ and $y = \cos^2 x$ on $x = [-\pi, \pi]$

10. $y = e^x$, $y = e^{2x-1}$, and $x = 0$

11. $y = e^x$, $y = e^{-x}$, $x = -1$ and $x = 1$

12. $y = e$, $y = e^x$, and $y = e^{-x}$

13. $y = |x|$ and $y = x^2$

For the following exercises, graph the equations and shade the area of the region between the curves. If necessary, break the region into sub-regions to determine its entire area.

14. $y = \sin(\pi x)$, $y = 2x$, and $x > 0$

15. $y = 12 - x$, $y = \sqrt{x}$, and $y = 1$

16. $y = \sin x$ and $y = \cos x$ over $x = [-\pi, \pi]$

17. $y = x^3$ and $y = x^2 - 2x$ over $x = [-1, 1]$

18. $y = x^2 + 9$ and $y = 10 + 2x$ over $x = [-1, 3]$

19. $y = x^3 + 3x$ and $y = 4x$

For the following exercises, graph the equations and shade the area of the region between the curves. Determine its area by integrating over the $y$-axis.

20. $x = y^3$ and $x = 3y - 2$

21. $x = 2y$ and $x = y^3 - y$

22. $x = -3 + y^2$ and $x = y - y^2$

23. $y^2 = x$ and $x = y + 2$

24. $x = |y|$ and $2x = -y^2 + 2$

25. $x = \sin y$, $x = \cos(2y)$, $y = \pi/2$, and $y = -\pi/2$

For the following exercises, graph the equations and shade the area of the region between the curves. Determine its area by integrating over the $x$-axis or $y$-axis, whichever seems more convenient.

26. $x = y^4$ and $x = y^5$

27. $y = xe^x$, $y = e^x$, $x = 0$, and $x = 1$

28. $y = x^6$ and $y = x^4$

29. $x = y^3 + 2y^2 + 1$ and $x = -y^2 + 1$

30. $y = |x|$ and $y = x^2 - 1$

31. $y = 4 - 3x$ and $y = \frac{1}{x}$

32. $y = \sin x$, $x = -\pi/6$, $x = \pi/6$, and $y = \cos^3 x$

33. $y = x^2 - 3x + 2$ and $y = x^3 - 2x^2 - x + 2$

34. $y = 2\cos^3(3x)$, $y = -1$, $x = \frac{\pi}{4}$, and $x = -\frac{\pi}{4}$

35. $y + y^3 = x$ and $2y = x$

36. $y = \sqrt{1 - x^2}$ and $y = x^2 - 1$

37. $y = \cos^{-1} x$, $y = \sin^{-1} x$, $x = -1$, and $x = 1$

For the following exercises, find the exact area of the region bounded by the given equations if possible. If you are unable to determine the intersection points analytically, use a calculator to approximate the intersection points with three decimal places and determine the approximate area of the region.

38. **[T]** $x = e^y$ and $y = x - 2$

39. **[T]** $y = x^2$ and $y = \sqrt{1 - x^2}$

40. **[T]** $y = 3x^2 + 8x + 9$ and $3y = x + 24$

41. **[T]** $x = \sqrt{4 - y^2}$ and $y^2 = 1 + x^2$

42. **[T]** $x^2 = y^3$ and $x = 3y$

43. **[T]** $y = \sin^3 x + 2$, $y = \tan x$, $x = -1.5$, and $x = 1.5$

44. **[T]** $y = \sqrt{1 - x^2}$ and $y^2 = x^2$

45. **[T]** $y = \sqrt{1 - x^2}$ and $y = x^2 + 2x + 1$

46. **[T]** $x = 4 - y^2$ and $x = 1 + 3y + y^2$

47. **[T]** $y = \cos x$, $y = e^x$, $x = -\pi$, and $x = 0$

48. The largest triangle with a base on the $x$-axis that fits inside the upper half of the unit circle $y^2 + x^2 = 1$ is given by $y = 1 + x$ and $y = 1 - x$. See the following figure. What is the area inside the semicircle but outside the triangle?

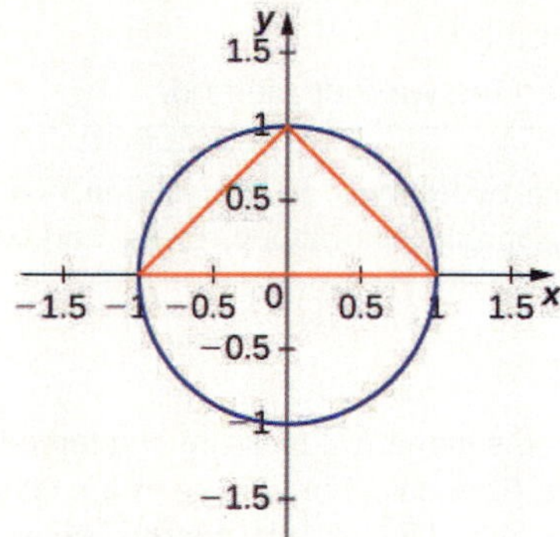

49. A factory selling cell phones has a marginal cost function $C(x) = 0.01x^2 - 3x + 229$, where $x$ represents the number of cell phones, and a marginal revenue function given by $R(x) = 429 - 2x$. Find the area between the graphs of these curves and $x = 0$. What does this area represent?

50. An amusement park has a marginal cost function $C(x) = 1000e^{-x} + 5$, where $x$ represents the number of tickets sold, and a marginal revenue function given by $R(x) = 60 - 0.1x$. Find the total profit generated when selling 550 tickets. Use a calculator to determine intersection points, if necessary, to two decimal places.

51. The tortoise versus the hare: The speed of the hare is given by the sinusoidal function $H(t) = 1 - \cos((\pi t)/2)$ whereas the speed of the tortoise is $T(t) = (1/2)\tan^{-1}(t/4)$, where $t$ is time measured in hours and the speed is measured in miles per hour. Find the area between the curves from time $t = 0$ to the first time after one hour when the tortoise and hare are traveling at the same speed. What does it represent? Use a calculator to determine the intersection points, if necessary, accurate to three decimal places.

52. The tortoise versus the hare: The speed of the hare is given by the sinusoidal function $H(t) = (1/2) - (1/2)\cos(2\pi t)$ whereas the speed of the tortoise is $T(t) = \sqrt{t}$, where $t$ is time measured in hours and speed is measured in kilometers per hour. If the race is over in 1 hour, who won the race and by how much? Use a calculator to determine the intersection points, if necessary, accurate to three decimal places.

For the following exercises, find the area between the curves by integrating with respect to $x$ and then with respect to $y$. Is one method easier than the other? Do you obtain the same answer?

53. $y = x^2 + 2x + 1$ and $y = -x^2 - 3x + 4$

54. $y = x^4$ and $x = y^5$

55. $x = y^2 - 2$ and $x = 2y$

For the following exercises, solve using calculus, then check your answer with geometry.

56. Determine the equations for the sides of the square that touches the unit circle on all four sides, as seen in the following figure. Find the area between the perimeter of this square and the unit circle. Is there another way to solve this without using calculus?

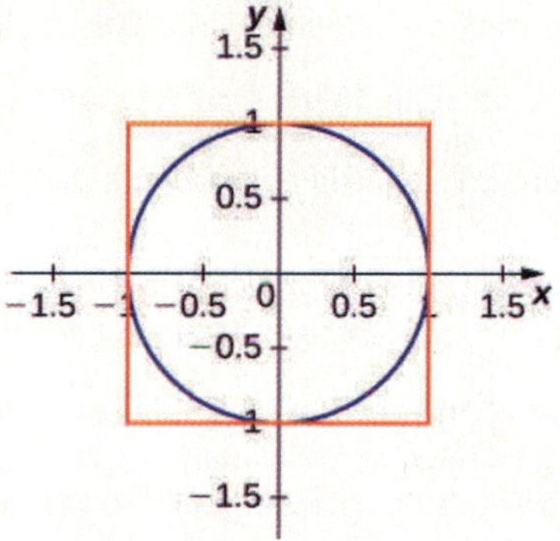

57. Find the area between the perimeter of the unit circle and the triangle created from $y = 2x + 1$, $y = 1 - 2x$ and $y = -\frac{3}{5}$, as seen in the following figure. Is there a way to solve this without using calculus?

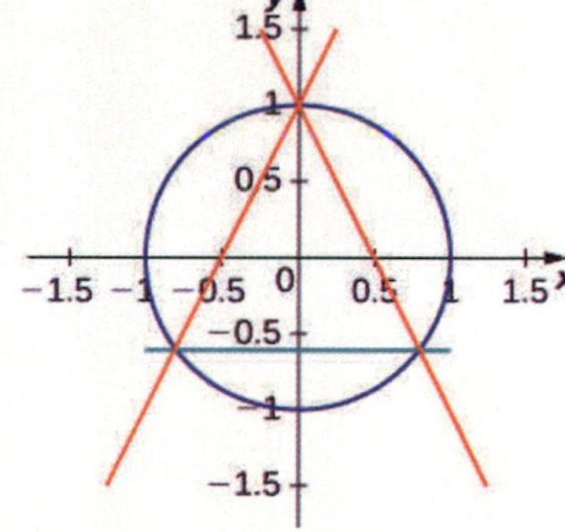

# 2.2 | Determining Volumes by Slicing

**Learning Objectives**

**2.2.1** Determine the volume of a solid by integrating a cross-section (the slicing method).
**2.2.2** Find the volume of a solid of revolution using the disk method.
**2.2.3** Find the volume of a solid of revolution with a cavity using the washer method.

In the preceding section, we used definite integrals to find the area between two curves. In this section, we use definite integrals to find volumes of three-dimensional solids. We consider three approaches—slicing, disks, and washers—for finding these volumes, depending on the characteristics of the solid.

## Volume and the Slicing Method

Just as area is the numerical measure of a two-dimensional region, volume is the numerical measure of a three-dimensional solid. Most of us have computed volumes of solids by using basic geometric formulas. The volume of a rectangular solid, for example, can be computed by multiplying length, width, and height: $V = lwh.$ The formulas for the volume of a sphere $\left(V = \frac{4}{3}\pi r^3\right),$ a cone $\left(V = \frac{1}{3}\pi r^2 h\right),$ and a pyramid $\left(V = \frac{1}{3}Ah\right)$ have also been introduced. Although some of these formulas were derived using geometry alone, all these formulas can be obtained by using integration.

We can also calculate the volume of a cylinder. Although most of us think of a cylinder as having a circular base, such as a soup can or a metal rod, in mathematics the word *cylinder* has a more general meaning. To discuss cylinders in this more general context, we first need to define some vocabulary.

We define the **cross-section** of a solid to be the intersection of a plane with the solid. A *cylinder* is defined as any solid that can be generated by translating a plane region along a line perpendicular to the region, called the *axis* of the cylinder. Thus, all cross-sections perpendicular to the axis of a cylinder are identical. The solid shown in **Figure 2.11** is an example of a cylinder with a noncircular base. To calculate the volume of a cylinder, then, we simply multiply the area of the cross-section by the height of the cylinder: $V = A \cdot h.$ In the case of a right circular cylinder (soup can), this becomes $V = \pi r^2 h.$

**Figure 2.11** Each cross-section of a particular cylinder is identical to the others.

If a solid does not have a constant cross-section (and it is not one of the other basic solids), we may not have a formula for its volume. In this case, we can use a definite integral to calculate the volume of the solid. We do this by slicing the solid into pieces, estimating the volume of each slice, and then adding those estimated volumes together. The slices should all be parallel to one another, and when we put all the slices together, we should get the whole solid. Consider, for example, the solid *S* shown in **Figure 2.12**, extending along the $x$-axis.

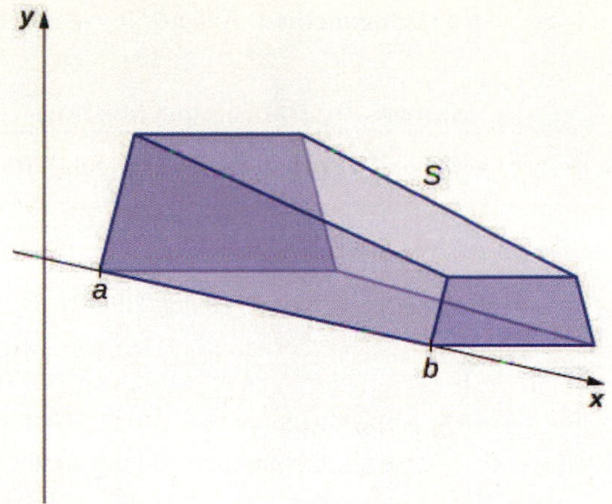


Figure 2.12 A solid with a varying cross-section.

We want to divide $S$ into slices perpendicular to the $x$-axis. As we see later in the chapter, there may be times when we want to slice the solid in some other direction—say, with slices perpendicular to the $y$-axis. The decision of which way to slice the solid is very important. If we make the wrong choice, the computations can get quite messy. Later in the chapter, we examine some of these situations in detail and look at how to decide which way to slice the solid. For the purposes of this section, however, we use slices perpendicular to the $x$-axis.

Because the cross-sectional area is not constant, we let $A(x)$ represent the area of the cross-section at point $x$. Now let $P = \{x_0, x_1 \ldots, X_n\}$ be a regular partition of $[a, b]$, and for $i = 1, 2,\ldots n,$ let $S_i$ represent the slice of $S$ stretching from $x_{i-1}$ to $x_i$. The following figure shows the sliced solid with $n = 3$.

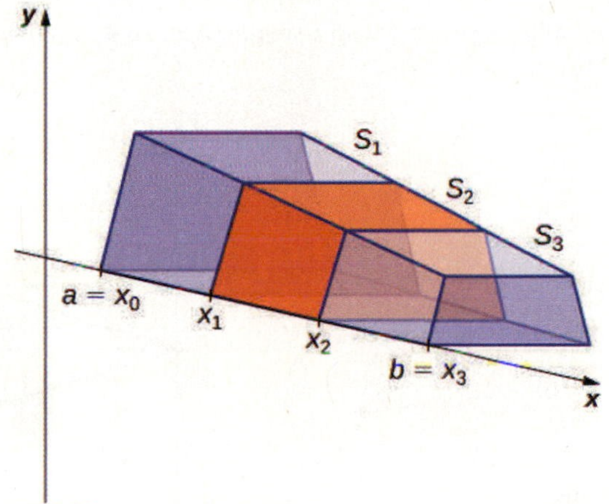


Figure 2.13 The solid $S$ has been divided into three slices perpendicular to the $x$-axis.

Finally, for $i = 1, 2,\ldots n,$ let $x_i^*$ be an arbitrary point in $[x_{i-1}, x_i]$. Then the volume of slice $S_i$ can be estimated by $V(S_i) \approx A(x_i^*)\Delta x$. Adding these approximations together, we see the volume of the entire solid $S$ can be approximated by

$$V(S) \approx \sum_{i=1}^{n} A(x_i^*)\Delta x.$$

By now, we can recognize this as a Riemann sum, and our next step is to take the limit as $n \to \infty$. Then we have

$$V(S) = \lim_{n \to \infty} \sum_{i=1}^{n} A(x_i^*)\Delta x = \int_a^b A(x)dx.$$

The technique we have just described is called the **slicing method**. To apply it, we use the following strategy.

## Problem-Solving Strategy: Finding Volumes by the Slicing Method

1. Examine the solid and determine the shape of a cross-section of the solid. It is often helpful to draw a picture if one is not provided.
2. Determine a formula for the area of the cross-section.
3. Integrate the area formula over the appropriate interval to get the volume.

Recall that in this section, we assume the slices are perpendicular to the $x$-axis. Therefore, the area formula is in terms of $x$ and the limits of integration lie on the $x$-axis. However, the problem-solving strategy shown here is valid regardless of how we choose to slice the solid.

## Example 2.6

### Deriving the Formula for the Volume of a Pyramid

We know from geometry that the formula for the volume of a pyramid is $V = \frac{1}{3}Ah$. If the pyramid has a square base, this becomes $V = \frac{1}{3}a^2 h,$ where $a$ denotes the length of one side of the base. We are going to use the slicing method to derive this formula.

#### Solution

We want to apply the slicing method to a pyramid with a square base. To set up the integral, consider the pyramid shown in **Figure 2.14**, oriented along the $x$-axis.

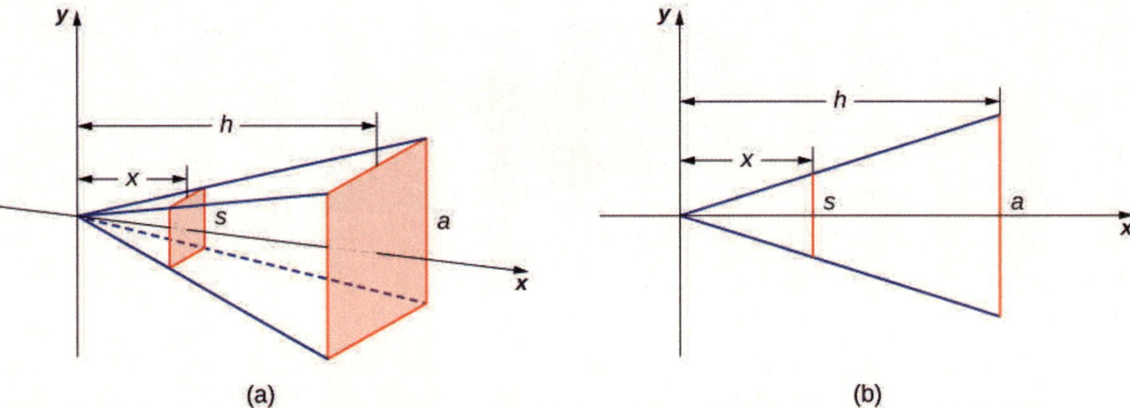


**Figure 2.14** (a) A pyramid with a square base is oriented along the $x$-axis. (b) A two-dimensional view of the pyramid is seen from the side.

We first want to determine the shape of a cross-section of the pyramid. We are know the base is a square, so the cross-sections are squares as well (step 1). Now we want to determine a formula for the area of one of these cross-sectional squares. Looking at **Figure 2.14**(b), and using a proportion, since these are similar triangles, we have

$$\frac{s}{a} = \frac{x}{h} \text{ or } s = \frac{ax}{h}.$$

Therefore, the area of one of the cross-sectional squares is

$$A(x) = s^2 = \left(\frac{ax}{h}\right)^2 \text{ (step 2).}$$

Then we find the volume of the pyramid by integrating from $0$ to $h$ (step 3):

$$\begin{aligned} V &= \int_0^h A(x)dx \\ &= \int_0^h \left(\frac{ax}{h}\right)^2 dx = \frac{a^2}{h^2}\int_0^h x^2 dx \\ &= \left[\frac{a^2}{h^2}\left(\frac{1}{3}x^3\right)\right]\Bigg|_0^h = \frac{1}{3}a^2 h. \end{aligned}$$

This is the formula we were looking for.

**2.6** Use the slicing method to derive the formula $V = \frac{1}{3}\pi r^2 h$ for the volume of a circular cone.

## Solids of Revolution

If a region in a plane is revolved around a line in that plane, the resulting solid is called a **solid of revolution**, as shown in the following figure.

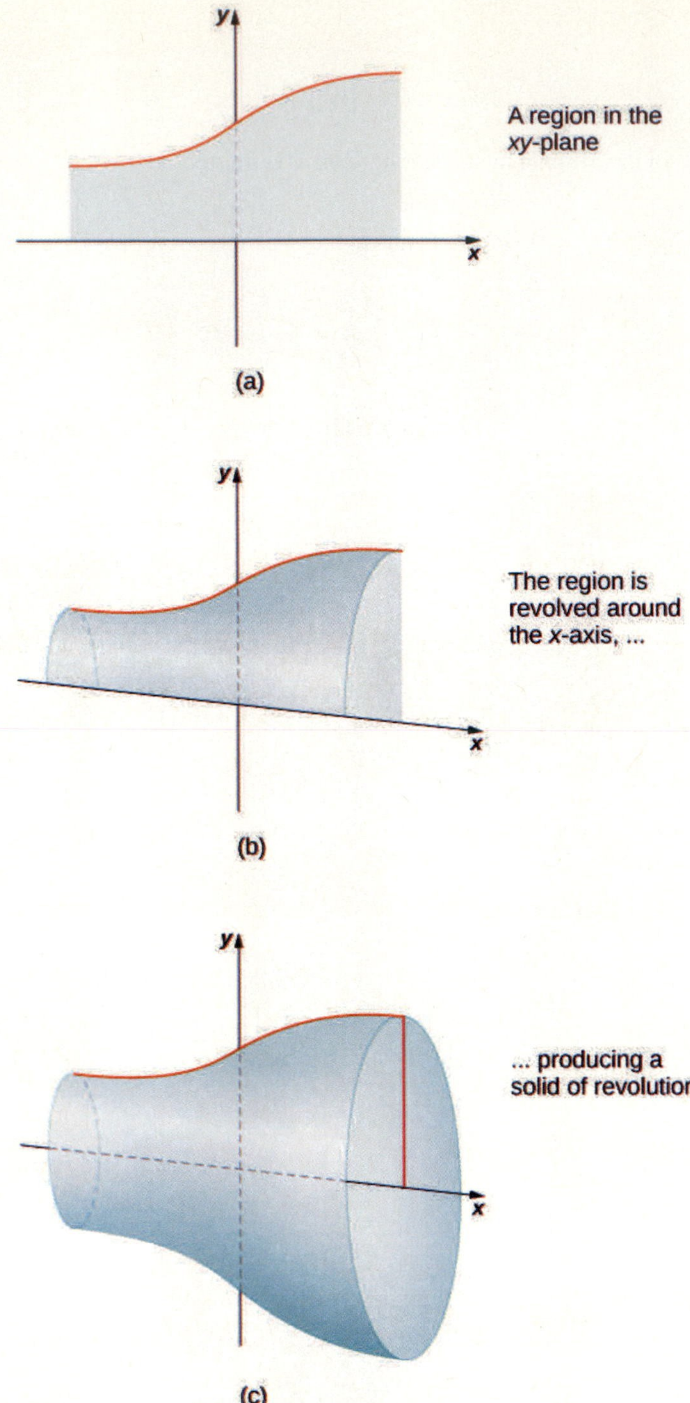


**Figure 2.15** (a) This is the region that is revolved around the $x$-axis. (b) As the region begins to revolve around the axis, it sweeps out a solid of revolution. (c) This is the solid that results when the revolution is complete.

Solids of revolution are common in mechanical applications, such as machine parts produced by a lathe. We spend the rest of this section looking at solids of this type. The next example uses the slicing method to calculate the volume of a solid of revolution.

Use an online **integral calculator (http://www.openstaxcollege.org/l/20_IntCalc2)** to learn more.

## Example 2.7

### Using the Slicing Method to find the Volume of a Solid of Revolution

Use the slicing method to find the volume of the solid of revolution bounded by the graphs of $f(x) = x^2 - 4x + 5,\ x = 1,$ and $x = 4,$ and rotated about the $x$-axis.

#### Solution

Using the problem-solving strategy, we first sketch the graph of the quadratic function over the interval $[1, 4]$ as shown in the following figure.

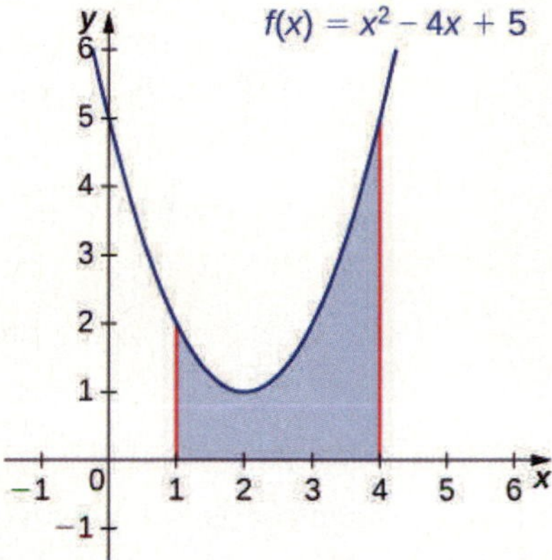


**Figure 2.16** A region used to produce a solid of revolution.

Next, revolve the region around the $x$-axis, as shown in the following figure.

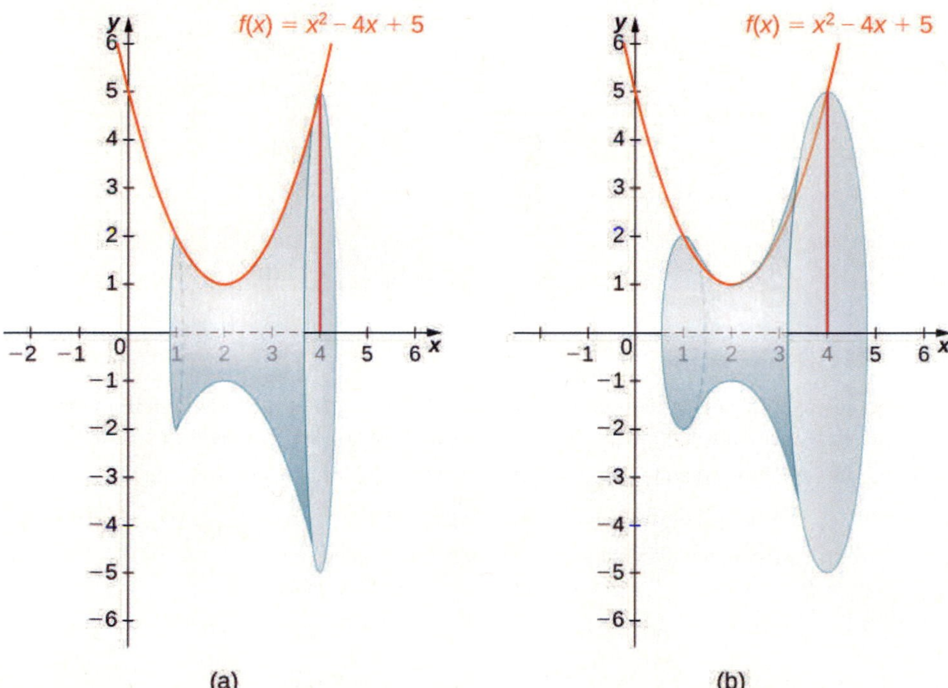


**Figure 2.17** Two views, (a) and (b), of the solid of revolution produced by revolving the region in **Figure 2.16** about the $x$-axis.

Since the solid was formed by revolving the region around the $x$-axis, the cross-sections are circles (step 1). The area of the cross-section, then, is the area of a circle, and the radius of the circle is given by $f(x)$. Use the formula for the area of the circle:

$$A(x) = \pi r^2 = \pi[f(x)]^2 = \pi\left(x^2 - 4x + 5\right)^2 \text{ (step 2).}$$

The volume, then, is (step 3)

$$\begin{aligned} V &= \int_a^h A(x)dx \\ &= \int_1^4 \pi\left(x^2 - 4x + 5\right)^2 dx = \pi \int_1^4 \left(x^4 - 8x^3 + 26x^2 - 40x + 25\right)dx \\ &= \pi\left(\frac{x^5}{5} - 2x^4 + \frac{26x^3}{3} - 20x^2 + 25x\right)\Bigg|_1^4 = \frac{78}{5}\pi. \end{aligned}$$

The volume is $78\pi/5$.

**2.7** Use the method of slicing to find the volume of the solid of revolution formed by revolving the region between the graph of the function $f(x) = 1/x$ and the $x$-axis over the interval $[1, 2]$ around the $x$-axis. See the following figure.

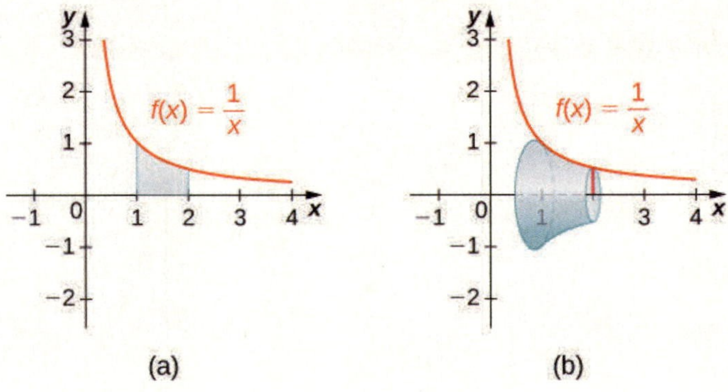


## The Disk Method

When we use the slicing method with solids of revolution, it is often called the **disk method** because, for solids of revolution, the slices used to over approximate the volume of the solid are disks. To see this, consider the solid of revolution generated by revolving the region between the graph of the function $f(x) = (x - 1)^2 + 1$ and the $x$-axis over the interval $[-1, 3]$ around the $x$-axis. The graph of the function and a representative disk are shown in **Figure 2.18**(a) and (b). The region of revolution and the resulting solid are shown in **Figure 2.18**(c) and (d).

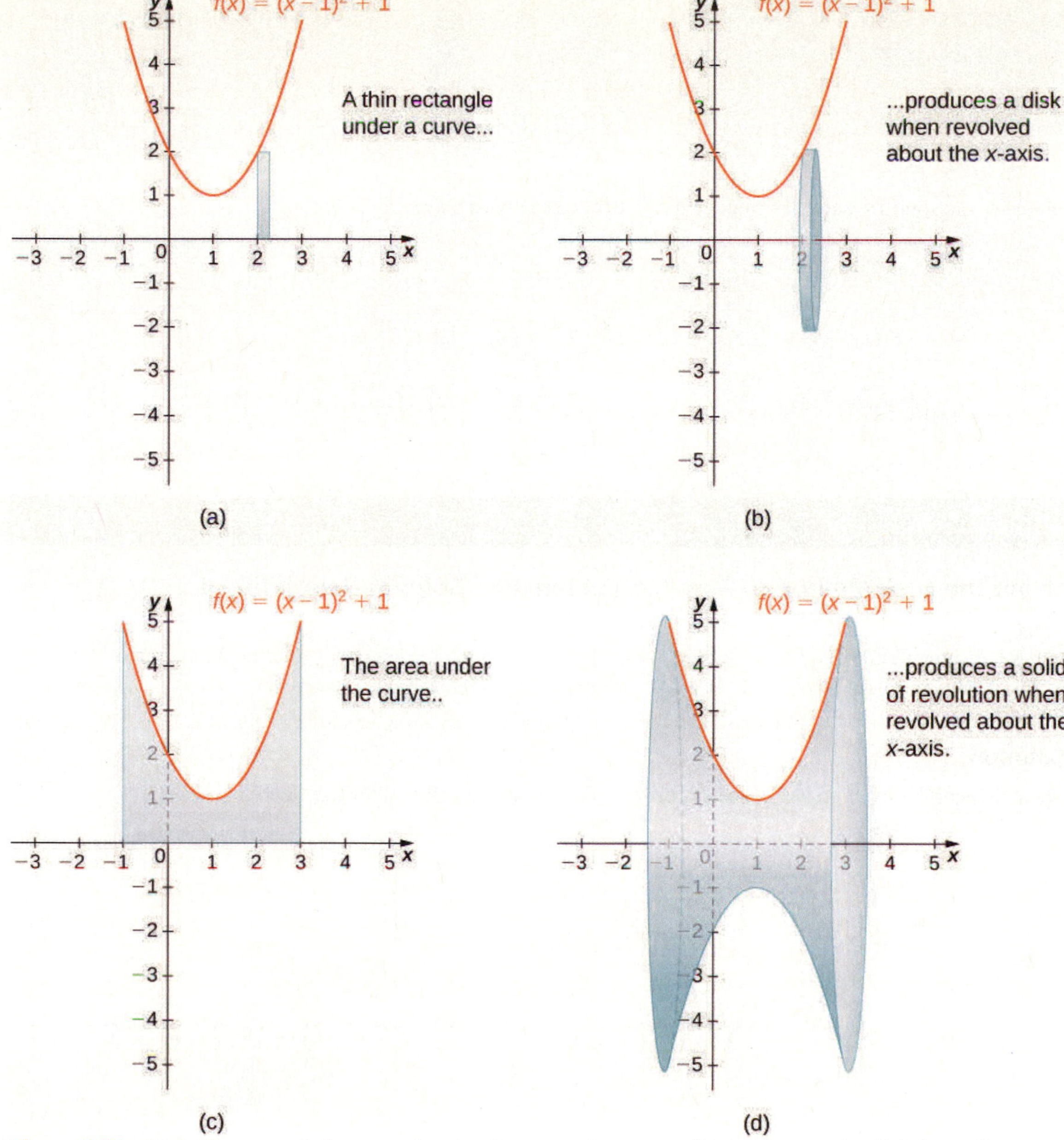


**Figure 2.18** (a) A thin rectangle for approximating the area under a curve. (b) A representative disk formed by revolving the rectangle about the $x$-axis. (c) The region under the curve is revolved about the $x$-axis, resulting in (d) the solid of revolution.

We already used the formal Riemann sum development of the volume formula when we developed the slicing method. We know that

$$V = \int_a^b A(x)dx.$$

The only difference with the disk method is that we know the formula for the cross-sectional area ahead of time; it is the area of a circle. This gives the following rule.

### Rule: The Disk Method

Let $f(x)$ be continuous and nonnegative. Define $R$ as the region bounded above by the graph of $f(x)$, below by the

$x$-axis, on the left by the line $x = a$, and on the right by the line $x = b$. Then, the volume of the solid of revolution formed by revolving $R$ around the $x$-axis is given by

$$V = \int_a^b \pi[f(x)]^2\, dx. \tag{2.3}$$

The volume of the solid we have been studying (Figure 2.18) is given by

$$\begin{aligned} V &= \int_a^b \pi[f(x)]^2\, dx \\ &= \int_{-1}^{3} \pi\left[(x-1)^2+1\right]^2 dx = \pi\int_{-1}^{3}\left[(x-1)^4+2(x-1)^2+1\right]^2 dx \\ &= \pi\left[\frac{1}{5}(x-1)^5+\frac{2}{3}(x-1)^3+x\right]\Bigg|_{-1}^{3} = \pi\left[\left(\frac{32}{5}+\frac{16}{3}+3\right)-\left(-\frac{32}{5}-\frac{16}{3}-1\right)\right] = \frac{412\pi}{15}\text{ units}^3. \end{aligned}$$

Let's look at some examples.

## Example 2.8

### Using the Disk Method to Find the Volume of a Solid of Revolution 1

Use the disk method to find the volume of the solid of revolution generated by rotating the region between the graph of $f(x) = \sqrt{x}$ and the $x$-axis over the interval $[1, 4]$ around the $x$-axis.

#### Solution

The graphs of the function and the solid of revolution are shown in the following figure.

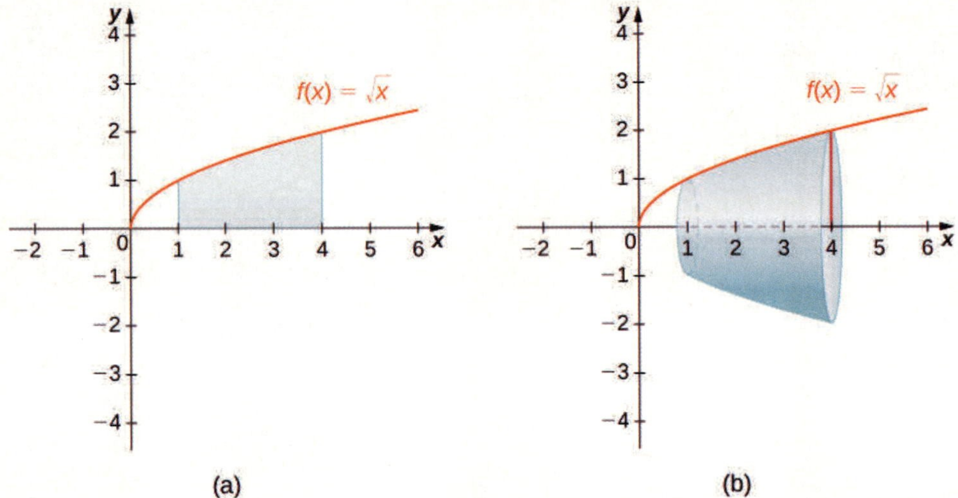


Figure 2.19 (a) The function $f(x) = \sqrt{x}$ over the interval $[1, 4]$. (b) The solid of revolution obtained by revolving the region under the graph of $f(x)$ about the $x$-axis.

We have

$$\begin{aligned} V &= \int_a^b \pi[f(x)]^2\, dx \\ &= \int_1^4 \pi[\sqrt{x}]^2 dx = \pi \int_1^4 x\, dx \\ &= \frac{\pi}{2}x^2\Big|_1^4 = \frac{15\pi}{2}. \end{aligned}$$

The volume is $(15\pi)/2$ units$^3$.

**2.8** Use the disk method to find the volume of the solid of revolution generated by rotating the region between the graph of $f(x) = \sqrt{4 - x}$ and the $x$-axis over the interval $[0, 4]$ around the $x$-axis.

So far, our examples have all concerned regions revolved around the $x$-axis, but we can generate a solid of revolution by revolving a plane region around any horizontal or vertical line. In the next example, we look at a solid of revolution that has been generated by revolving a region around the $y$-axis. The mechanics of the disk method are nearly the same as when the $x$-axis is the axis of revolution, but we express the function in terms of $y$ and we integrate with respect to $y$ as well. This is summarized in the following rule.

### Rule: The Disk Method for Solids of Revolution around the *y*-axis

Let $g(y)$ be continuous and nonnegative. Define $Q$ as the region bounded on the right by the graph of $g(y)$, on the left by the $y$-axis, below by the line $y = c$, and above by the line $y = d$. Then, the volume of the solid of revolution formed by revolving $Q$ around the $y$-axis is given by

$$V = \int_c^d \pi[g(y)]^2\, dy. \tag{2.4}$$

The next example shows how this rule works in practice.

## Example 2.9

### Using the Disk Method to Find the Volume of a Solid of Revolution 2

Let $R$ be the region bounded by the graph of $g(y) = \sqrt{4 - y}$ and the $y$-axis over the $y$-axis interval $[0, 4]$. Use the disk method to find the volume of the solid of revolution generated by rotating $R$ around the $y$-axis.

#### Solution

Figure 2.20 shows the function and a representative disk that can be used to estimate the volume. Notice that since we are revolving the function around the $y$-axis, the disks are horizontal, rather than vertical.

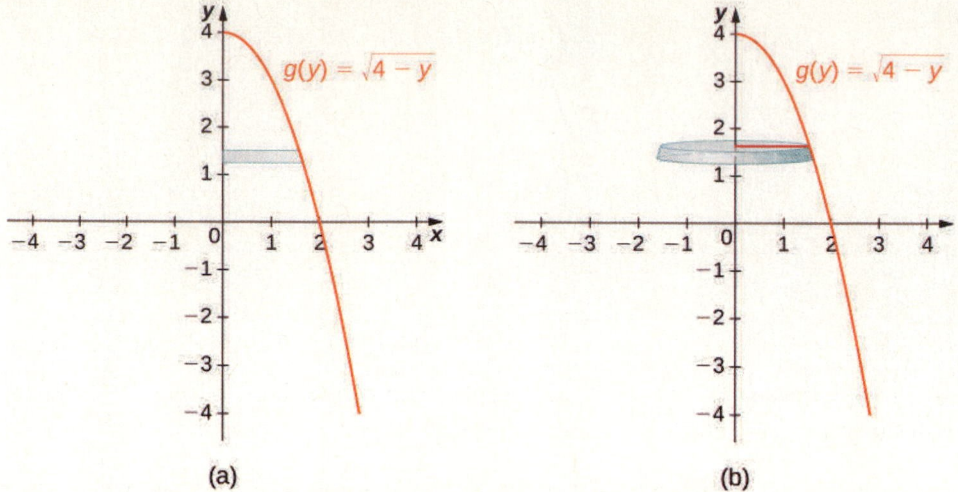


**Figure 2.20** (a) Shown is a thin rectangle between the curve of the function $g(y) = \sqrt{4 - y}$ and the $y$-axis. (b) The rectangle forms a representative disk after revolution around the $y$-axis.

The region to be revolved and the full solid of revolution are depicted in the following figure.

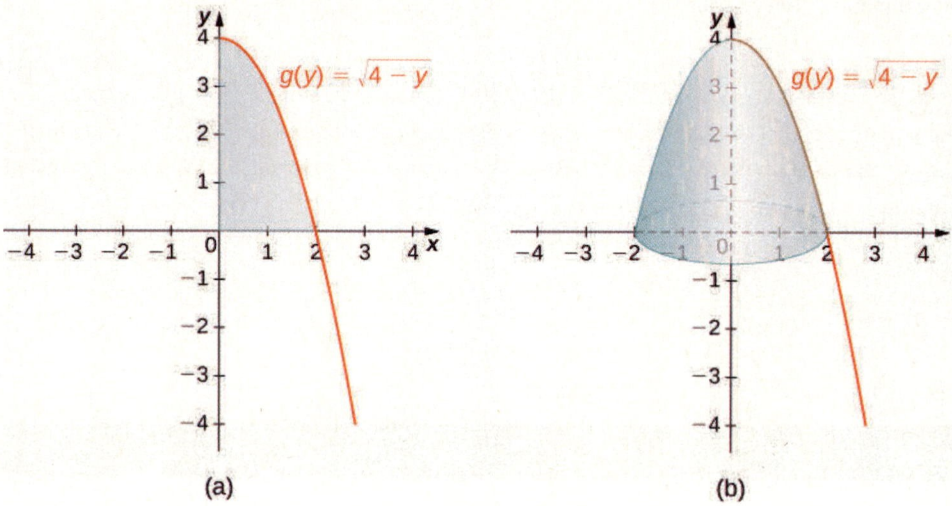


**Figure 2.21** (a) The region to the left of the function $g(y) = \sqrt{4 - y}$ over the $y$-axis interval $[0, 4]$. (b) The solid of revolution formed by revolving the region about the $y$-axis.

To find the volume, we integrate with respect to $y$. We obtain

$$\begin{aligned} V &= \int_c^d \pi[g(y)]^2 \, dy \\ &= \int_0^4 \pi\left[\sqrt{4 - y}\right]^2 dy = \pi \int_0^4 (4 - y)dy \\ &= \pi\left[4y - \frac{y^2}{2}\right]\Bigg|_0^4 = 8\pi. \end{aligned}$$

The volume is $8\pi$ units$^3$.

**2.9** Use the disk method to find the volume of the solid of revolution generated by rotating the region between the graph of $g(y) = y$ and the $y$-axis over the interval $[1, 4]$ around the $y$-axis.

## The Washer Method

Some solids of revolution have cavities in the middle; they are not solid all the way to the axis of revolution. Sometimes, this is just a result of the way the region of revolution is shaped with respect to the axis of revolution. In other cases, cavities arise when the region of revolution is defined as the region between the graphs of two functions. A third way this can happen is when an axis of revolution other than the $x$-axis or $y$-axis is selected.

When the solid of revolution has a cavity in the middle, the slices used to approximate the volume are not disks, but washers (disks with holes in the center). For example, consider the region bounded above by the graph of the function $f(x) = \sqrt{x}$ and below by the graph of the function $g(x) = 1$ over the interval $[1, 4]$. When this region is revolved around the $x$-axis, the result is a solid with a cavity in the middle, and the slices are washers. The graph of the function and a representative washer are shown in Figure 2.22(a) and (b). The region of revolution and the resulting solid are shown in Figure 2.22(c) and (d).

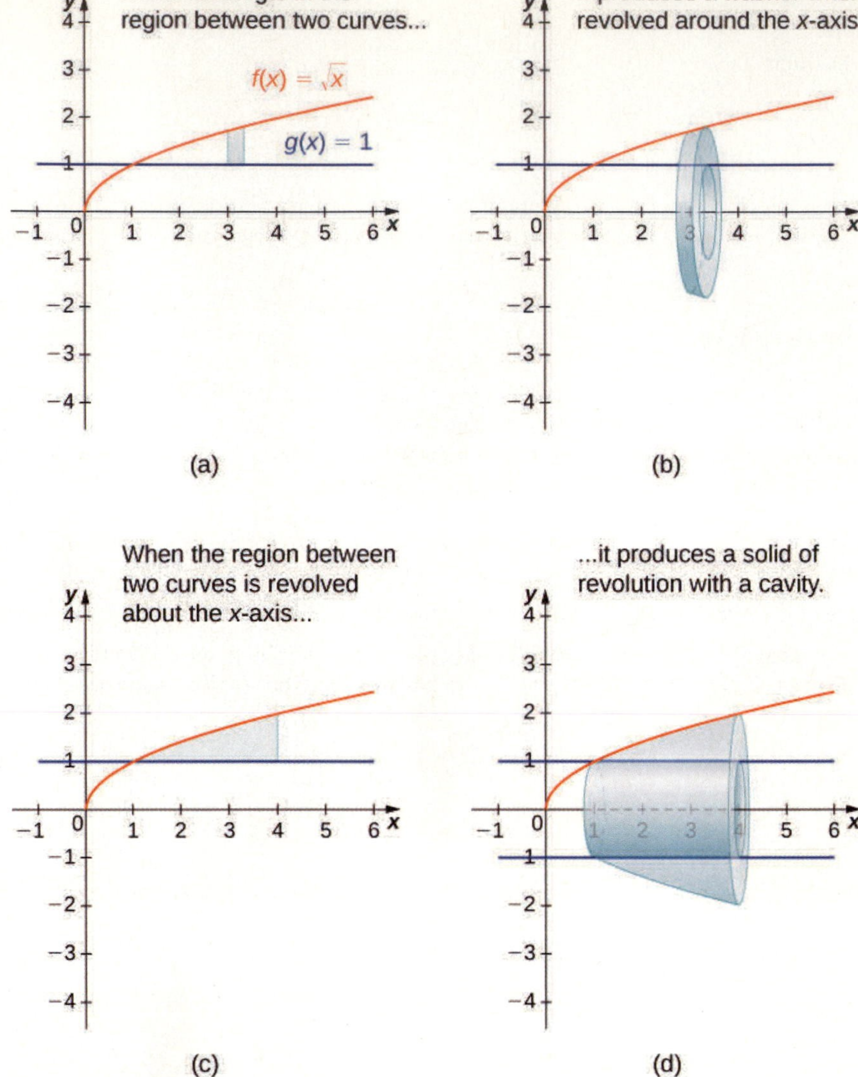


**Figure 2.22** (a) A thin rectangle in the region between two curves. (b) A representative disk formed by revolving the rectangle about the $x$-axis. (c) The region between the curves over the given interval. (d) The resulting solid of revolution.

The cross-sectional area, then, is the area of the outer circle less the area of the inner circle. In this case,

$$A(x) = \pi(\sqrt{x})^2 - \pi(1)^2 = \pi(x - 1).$$

Then the volume of the solid is

$$\begin{aligned} V &= \int_a^b A(x)dx \\ &= \int_1^4 \pi(x - 1)dx = \pi\left[\frac{x^2}{2} - x\right]\Big|_1^4 = \frac{9}{2}\pi \text{ units}^3. \end{aligned}$$

Generalizing this process gives the **washer method**.

### Rule: The Washer Method

Suppose $f(x)$ and $g(x)$ are continuous, nonnegative functions such that $f(x) \geq g(x)$ over $[a, b]$. Let $R$ denote the region bounded above by the graph of $f(x)$, below by the graph of $g(x)$, on the left by the line $x = a$, and on the right by the line $x = b$. Then, the volume of the solid of revolution formed by revolving $R$ around the $x$-axis is given by

$$V = \int_a^b \pi\left[(f(x))^2 - (g(x))^2\right]dx. \tag{2.5}$$

## Example 2.10

### Using the Washer Method

Find the volume of a solid of revolution formed by revolving the region bounded above by the graph of $f(x) = x$ and below by the graph of $g(x) = 1/x$ over the interval $[1, 4]$ around the $x$-axis.

### Solution

The graphs of the functions and the solid of revolution are shown in the following figure.

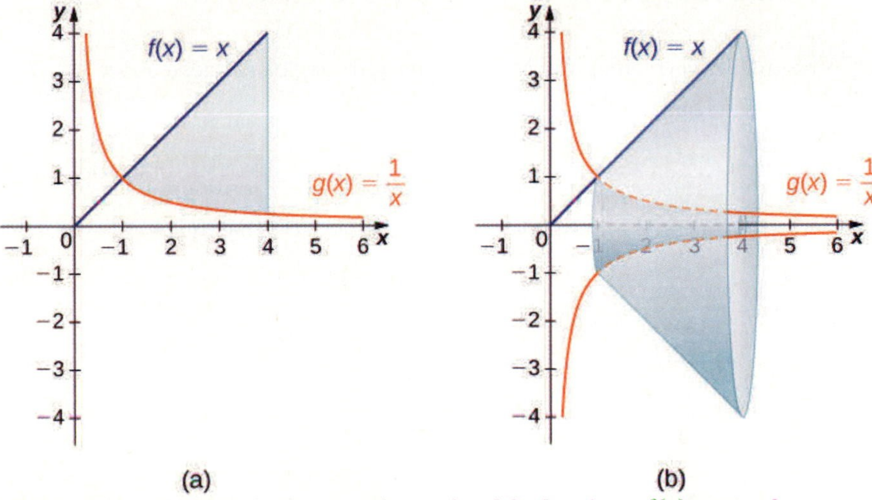


**Figure 2.23** (a) The region between the graphs of the functions $f(x) = x$ and $g(x) = 1/x$ over the interval $[1, 4]$. (b) Revolving the region about the $x$-axis generates a solid of revolution with a cavity in the middle.

We have

$$\begin{aligned} V &= \int_a^b \pi\left[(f(x))^2 - (g(x))^2\right]dx \\ &= \pi\int_1^4 \left[x^2 - \left(\frac{1}{x}\right)^2\right]dx = \pi\left[\frac{x^3}{3} + \frac{1}{x}\right]\Bigg|_1^4 = \frac{81\pi}{4}\text{ units}^3. \end{aligned}$$

**2.10** Find the volume of a solid of revolution formed by revolving the region bounded by the graphs of $f(x) = \sqrt{x}$ and $g(x) = 1/x$ over the interval $[1, 3]$ around the $x$-axis.

As with the disk method, we can also apply the washer method to solids of revolution that result from revolving a region around the $y$-axis. In this case, the following rule applies.

**Rule: The Washer Method for Solids of Revolution around the $y$-axis**

Suppose $u(y)$ and $v(y)$ are continuous, nonnegative functions such that $v(y) \leq u(y)$ for $y \in [c, d]$. Let $Q$ denote the region bounded on the right by the graph of $u(y)$, on the left by the graph of $v(y)$, below by the line $y = c$, and above by the line $y = d$. Then, the volume of the solid of revolution formed by revolving $Q$ around the $y$-axis is given by

$$V = \int_c^d \pi\left[(u(y))^2 - (v(y))^2\right]dy.$$

Rather than looking at an example of the washer method with the $y$-axis as the axis of revolution, we now consider an example in which the axis of revolution is a line other than one of the two coordinate axes. The same general method applies, but you may have to visualize just how to describe the cross-sectional area of the volume.

## Example 2.11

### The Washer Method with a Different Axis of Revolution

Find the volume of a solid of revolution formed by revolving the region bounded above by $f(x) = 4 - x$ and below by the $x$-axis over the interval $[0, 4]$ around the line $y = -2$.

#### Solution

The graph of the region and the solid of revolution are shown in the following figure.

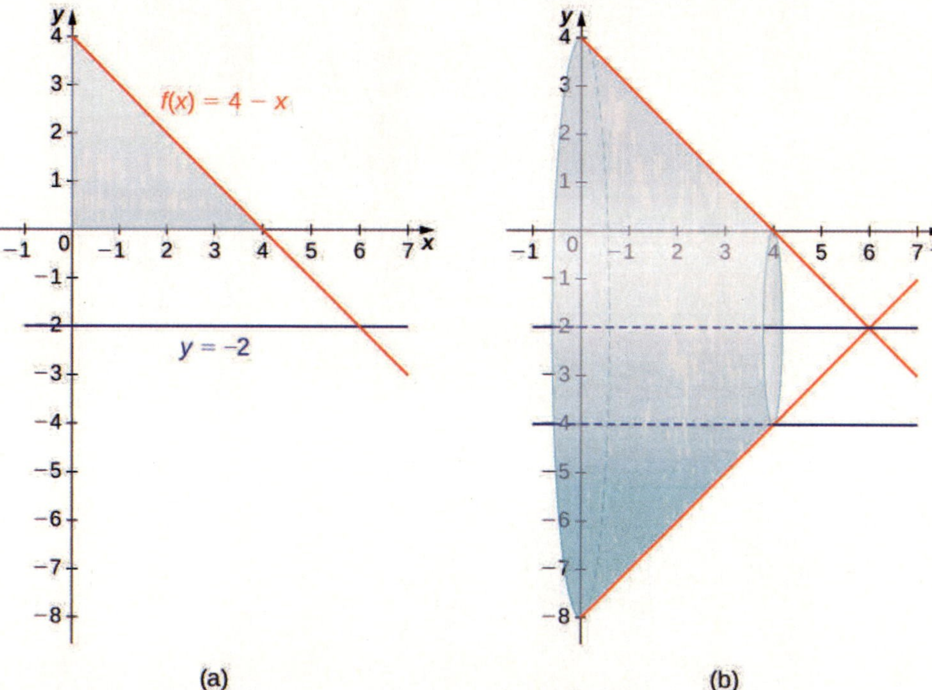


**Figure 2.24** (a) The region between the graph of the function $f(x) = 4 - x$ and the $x$-axis over the interval $[0, 4]$. (b) Revolving the region about the line $y = -2$ generates a solid of revolution with a cylindrical hole through its middle.

We can't apply the volume formula to this problem directly because the axis of revolution is not one of the coordinate axes. However, we still know that the area of the cross-section is the area of the outer circle less the area of the inner circle. Looking at the graph of the function, we see the radius of the outer circle is given by $f(x)+2,$ which simplifies to

$$f(x)+2=(4-x)+2=6-x.$$

The radius of the inner circle is $g(x)=2.$ Therefore, we have

$$\begin{aligned} V &= \int_0^4 \pi\left[(6-x)^2-(2)^2\right]dx \\ &= \pi\int_0^4 \left(x^2-12x+32\right)dx = \pi\left[\frac{x^3}{3}-6x^2+32x\right]\Bigg|_0^4 = \frac{160\pi}{3}\text{ units}^3. \end{aligned}$$

**2.11** Find the volume of a solid of revolution formed by revolving the region bounded above by the graph of $f(x)=x+2$ and below by the $x$-axis over the interval $[0,3]$ around the line $y=-1.$

# 2.2 EXERCISES

58. Derive the formula for the volume of a sphere using the slicing method.

59. Use the slicing method to derive the formula for the volume of a cone.

60. Use the slicing method to derive the formula for the volume of a tetrahedron with side length $a$.

61. Use the disk method to derive the formula for the volume of a trapezoidal cylinder.

62. Explain when you would use the disk method versus the washer method. When are they interchangeable?

For the following exercises, draw a typical slice and find the volume using the slicing method for the given volume.

63. A pyramid with height 6 units and square base of side 2 units, as pictured here.

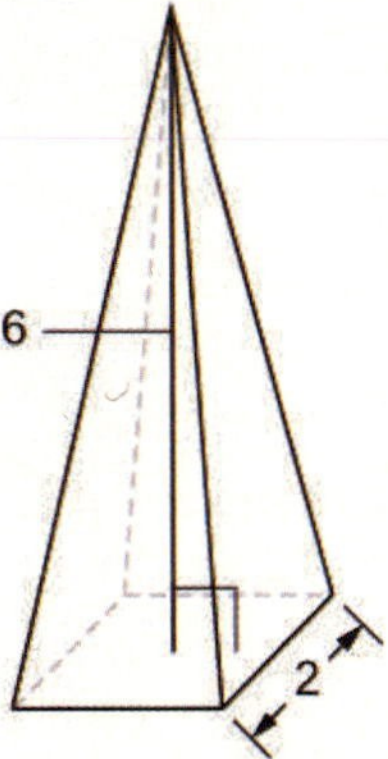


64. A pyramid with height 4 units and a rectangular base with length 2 units and width 3 units, as pictured here.

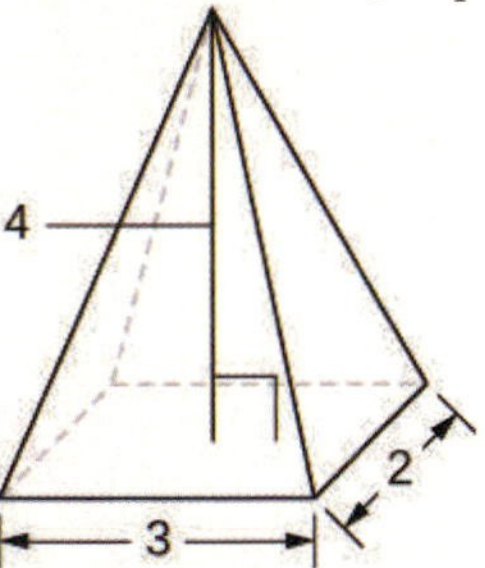


65. A tetrahedron with a base side of 4 units, as seen here.

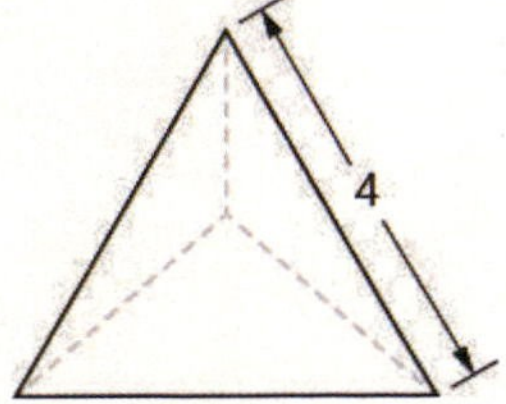


66. A pyramid with height 5 units, and an isosceles triangular base with lengths of 6 units and 8 units, as seen here.

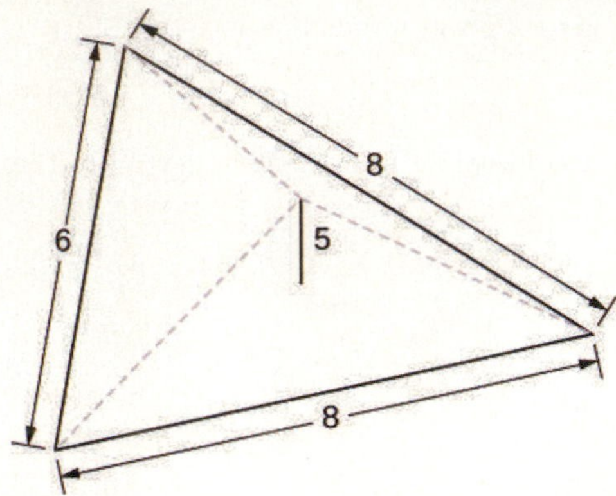


67. A cone of radius $r$ and height $h$ has a smaller cone of radius $r/2$ and height $h/2$ removed from the top, as seen here. The resulting solid is called a *frustum*.

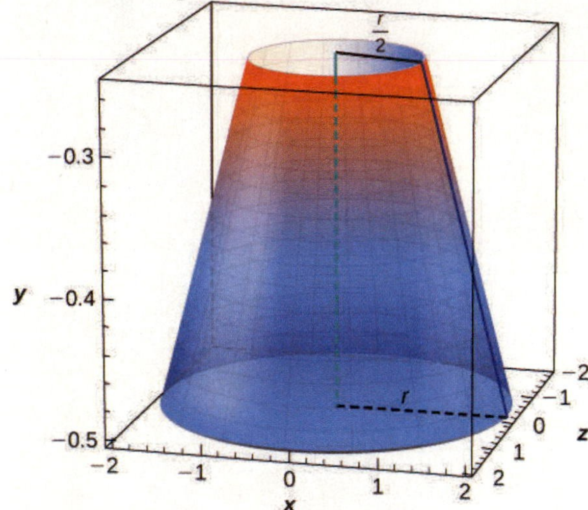


For the following exercises, draw an outline of the solid and find the volume using the slicing method.

68. The base is a circle of radius $a$. The slices perpendicular to the base are squares.

69. The base is a triangle with vertices $(0, 0)$, $(1, 0)$, and $(0, 1)$. Slices perpendicular to the $xy$-plane are semicircles.

70. The base is the region under the parabola $y = 1 - x^2$ in the first quadrant. Slices perpendicular to the $xy$-plane are squares.

71. The base is the region under the parabola $y = 1 - x^2$ and above the $x$-axis. Slices perpendicular to the $y$-axis are squares.

72. The base is the region enclosed by $y = x^2$ and $y = 9$. Slices perpendicular to the $x$-axis are right isosceles triangles.

73. The base is the area between $y = x$ and $y = x^2$. Slices perpendicular to the $x$-axis are semicircles.

For the following exercises, draw the region bounded by the curves. Then, use the disk method to find the volume when the region is rotated around the $x$-axis.

74. $x + y = 8,\ x = 0,$ and $y = 0$

75. $y = 2x^2,\ x = 0,\ x = 4,$ and $y = 0$

76. $y = e^x + 1,\ x = 0,\ x = 1,$ and $y = 0$

77. $y = x^4,\ x = 0,$ and $y = 1$

78. $y = \sqrt{x},\ x = 0,\ x = 4,$ and $y = 0$

79. $y = \sin x,\ y = \cos x,$ and $x = 0$

80. $y = \frac{1}{x},\ x = 2,$ and $y = 3$

81. $x^2 - y^2 = 9$ and $x + y = 9,\ y = 0$ and $x = 0$

For the following exercises, draw the region bounded by the curves. Then, find the volume when the region is rotated around the $y$-axis.

82. $y = 4 - \frac{1}{2}x,\ x = 0,$ and $y = 0$

83. $y = 2x^3,\ x = 0,\ x = 1,$ and $y = 0$

84. $y = 3x^2,\ x = 0,$ and $y = 3$

85. $y = \sqrt{4 - x^2},\ y = 0,$ and $x = 0$

86. $y = \frac{1}{\sqrt{x + 1}},\ x = 0,$ and $x = 3$

87. $x = \sec(y)$ and $y = \frac{\pi}{4},\ y = 0$ and $x = 0$

88. $y = \frac{1}{x + 1},\ x = 0,$ and $x = 2$

89. $y = 4 - x,\ y = x,$ and $x = 0$

For the following exercises, draw the region bounded by the curves. Then, find the volume when the region is rotated around the $x$-axis.

90. $y = x + 2,\ y = x + 6,\ x = 0,$ and $x = 5$

91. $y = x^2$ and $y = x + 2$

92. $x^2 = y^3$ and $x^3 = y^2$

93. $y = 4 - x^2$ and $y = 2 - x$

94. **[T]** $y = \cos x,\ y = e^{-x},\ x = 0,$ and $x = 1.2927$

95. $y = \sqrt{x}$ and $y = x^2$

96. $y = \sin x,\ y = 5 \sin x,\ x = 0$ and $x = \pi$

97. $y = \sqrt{1 + x^2}$ and $y = \sqrt{4 - x^2}$

For the following exercises, draw the region bounded by the curves. Then, use the washer method to find the volume when the region is revolved around the $y$-axis.

98. $y = \sqrt{x},\ x = 4,$ and $y = 0$

99. $y = x + 2,\ y = 2x - 1,$ and $x = 0$

100. $y = \sqrt[3]{x}$ and $y = x^3$

101. $x = e^{2y},\ x = y^2,\ y = 0,$ and $y = \ln(2)$

102. $x = \sqrt{9 - y^2},\ x = e^{-y},\ y = 0,$ and $y = 3$

103. Yogurt containers can be shaped like frustums. Rotate the line $y = \frac{1}{m}x$ around the $y$-axis to find the volume between $y = a$ and $y = b$.

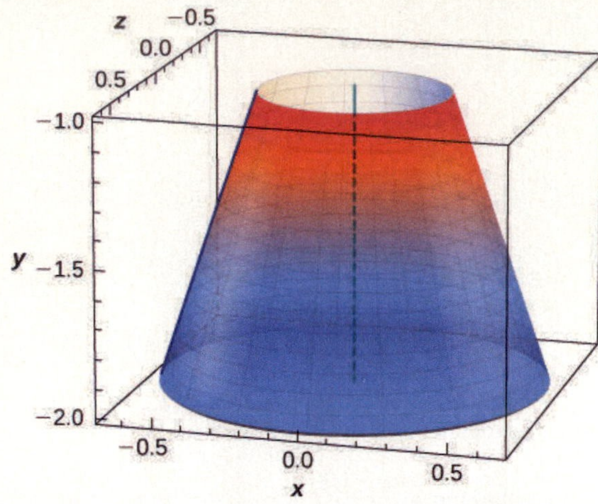

104. Rotate the ellipse $\left(x^2/a^2\right) + \left(y^2/b^2\right) = 1$ around the $x$-axis to approximate the volume of a football, as seen here.

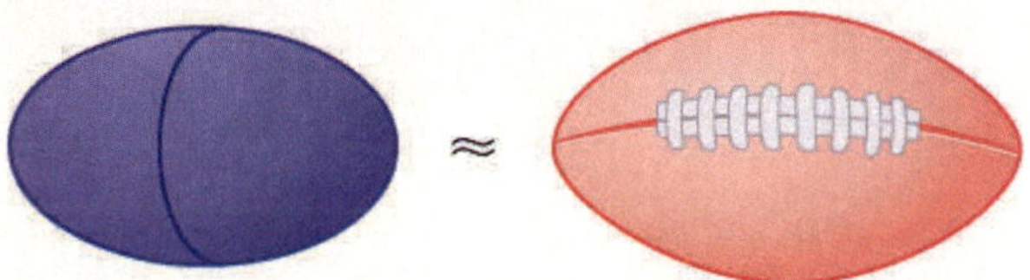

105. Rotate the ellipse $\left(x^2/a^2\right) + \left(y^2/b^2\right) = 1$ around the $y$-axis to approximate the volume of a football.

106. A better approximation of the volume of a football is given by the solid that comes from rotating $y = \sin x$ around the $x$-axis from $x = 0$ to $x = \pi$. What is the volume of this football approximation, as seen here?

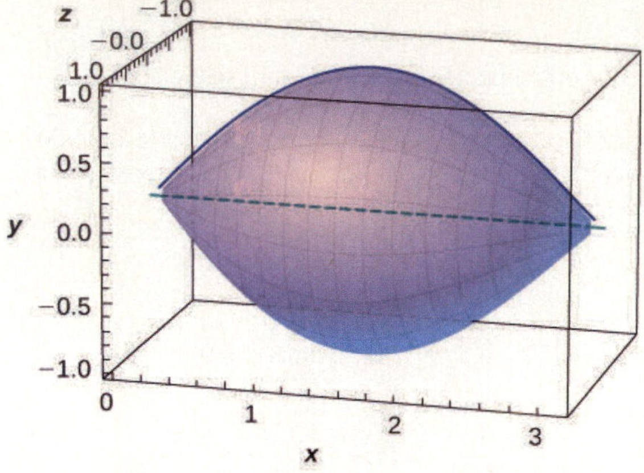


107. What is the volume of the Bundt cake that comes from rotating $y = \sin x$ around the $y$-axis from $x = 0$ to $x = \pi$?

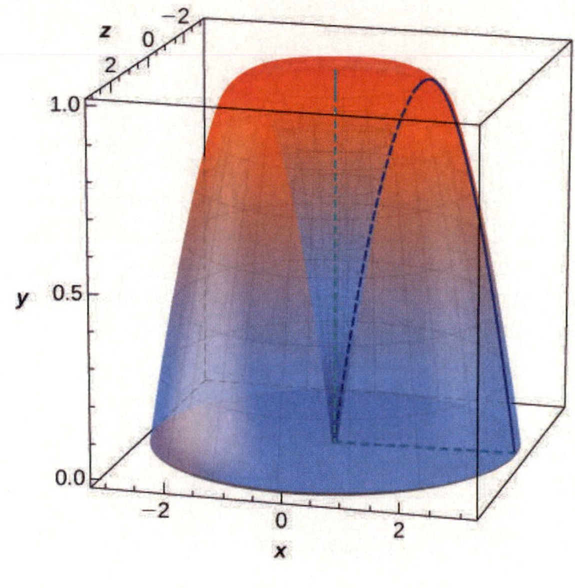

For the following exercises, find the volume of the solid described.

108. The base is the region between $y = x$ and $y = x^2$. Slices perpendicular to the $x$-axis are semicircles.

109. The base is the region enclosed by the generic ellipse $\left(x^2/a^2\right) + \left(y^2/b^2\right) = 1$. Slices perpendicular to the $x$-axis are semicircles.

110. Bore a hole of radius $a$ down the axis of a right cone and through the base of radius $b$, as seen here.

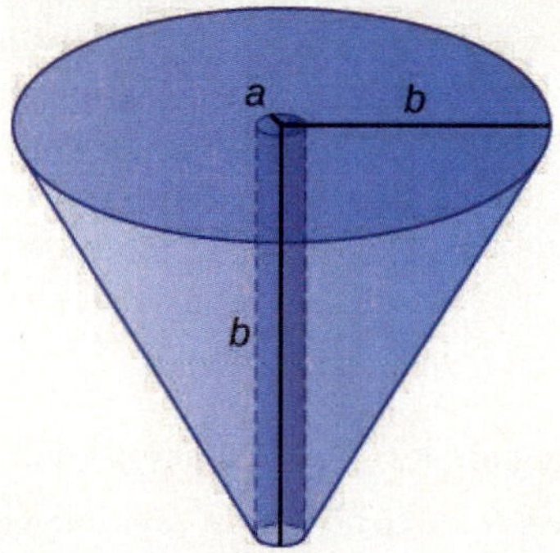


111. Find the volume common to two spheres of radius $r$ with centers that are $2h$ apart, as shown here.

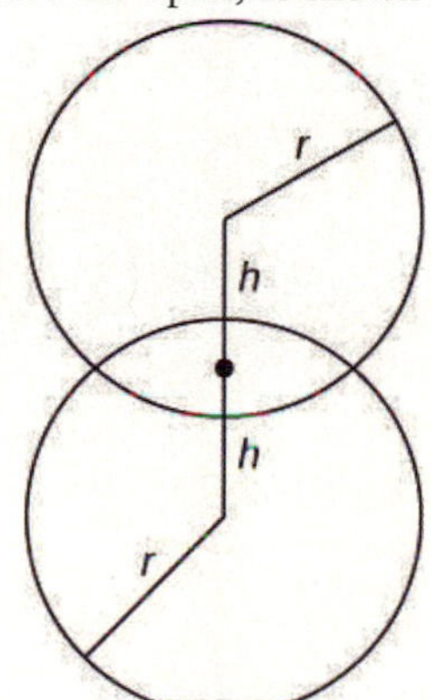


112. Find the volume of a spherical cap of height $h$ and radius $r$ where $h < r$, as seen here.

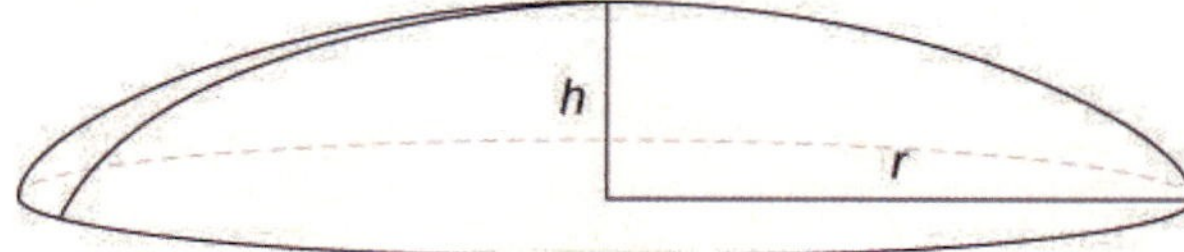


113. Find the volume of a sphere of radius $R$ with a cap of height $h$ removed from the top, as seen here.

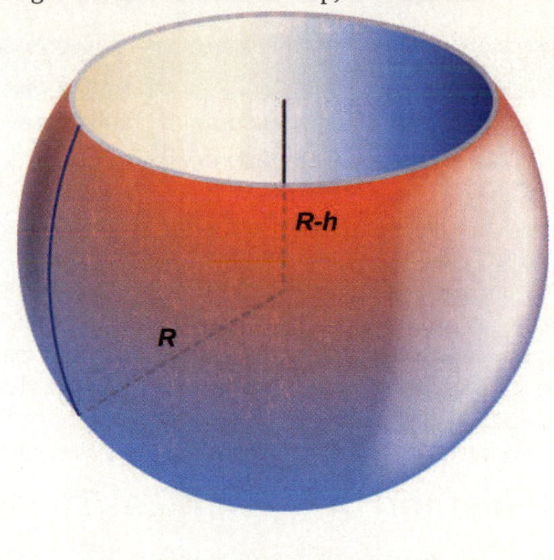

# 2.3 | Volumes of Revolution: Cylindrical Shells

## Learning Objectives

**2.3.1** Calculate the volume of a solid of revolution by using the method of cylindrical shells.
**2.3.2** Compare the different methods for calculating a volume of revolution.

In this section, we examine the method of cylindrical shells, the final method for finding the volume of a solid of revolution. We can use this method on the same kinds of solids as the disk method or the washer method; however, with the disk and washer methods, we integrate along the coordinate axis parallel to the axis of revolution. With the method of cylindrical shells, we integrate along the coordinate axis *perpendicular* to the axis of revolution. The ability to choose which variable of integration we want to use can be a significant advantage with more complicated functions. Also, the specific geometry of the solid sometimes makes the method of using cylindrical shells more appealing than using the washer method. In the last part of this section, we review all the methods for finding volume that we have studied and lay out some guidelines to help you determine which method to use in a given situation.

## The Method of Cylindrical Shells

Again, we are working with a solid of revolution. As before, we define a region $R$, bounded above by the graph of a function $y = f(x)$, below by the $x$-axis, and on the left and right by the lines $x = a$ and $x = b$, respectively, as shown in Figure 2.25(a). We then revolve this region around the $y$-axis, as shown in Figure 2.25(b). Note that this is different from what we have done before. Previously, regions defined in terms of functions of $x$ were revolved around the $x$-axis or a line parallel to it.

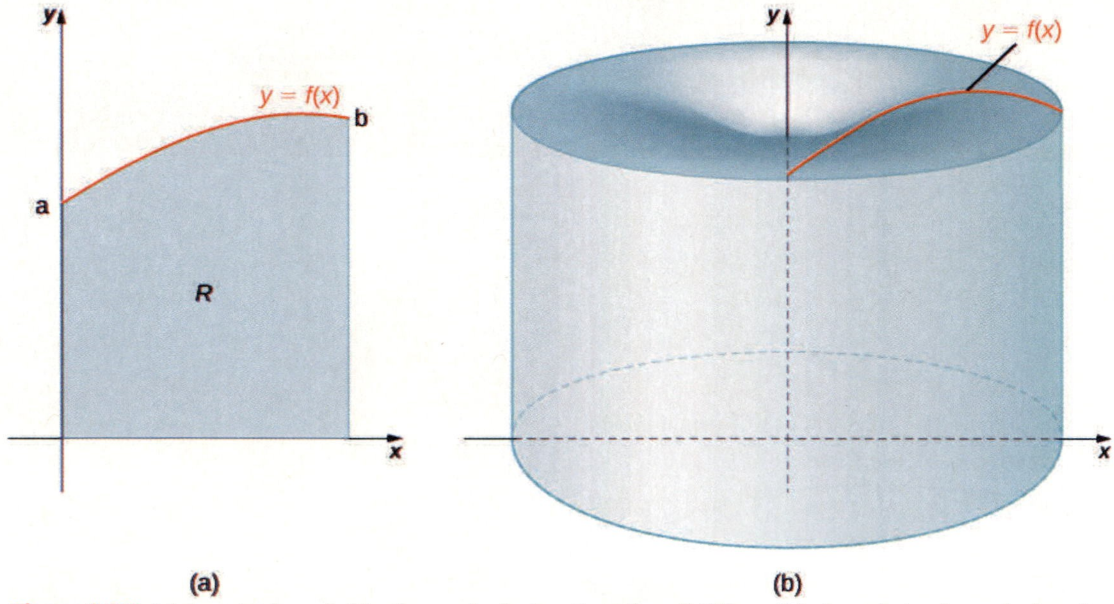


**Figure 2.25** (a) A region bounded by the graph of a function of $x$. (b) The solid of revolution formed when the region is revolved around the $y$-axis.

As we have done many times before, partition the interval $[a, b]$ using a regular partition, $P = \{x_0, x_1, \ldots, x_n\}$ and, for $i = 1, 2, \ldots, n$, choose a point $x_i^* \in [x_{i-1}, x_i]$. Then, construct a rectangle over the interval $[x_{i-1}, x_i]$ of height $f(x_i^*)$ and width $\Delta x$. A representative rectangle is shown in Figure 2.26(a). When that rectangle is revolved around the $y$-axis, instead of a disk or a washer, we get a cylindrical shell, as shown in the following figure.

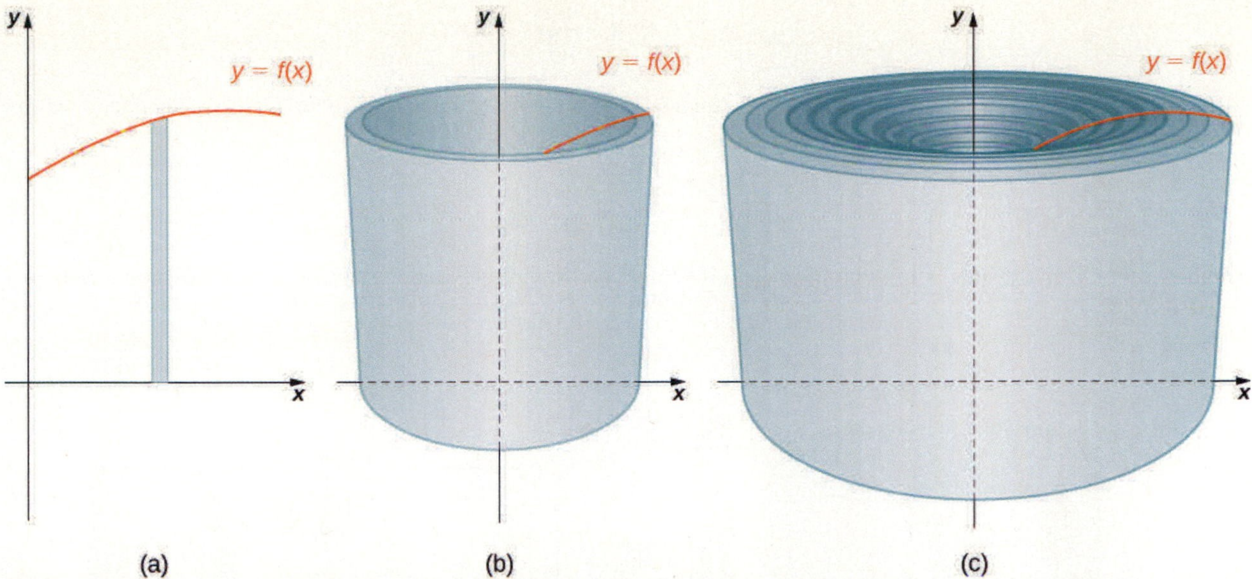


**Figure 2.26** (a) A representative rectangle. (b) When this rectangle is revolved around the $y$-axis, the result is a cylindrical shell. (c) When we put all the shells together, we get an approximation of the original solid.

To calculate the volume of this shell, consider **Figure 2.27**.

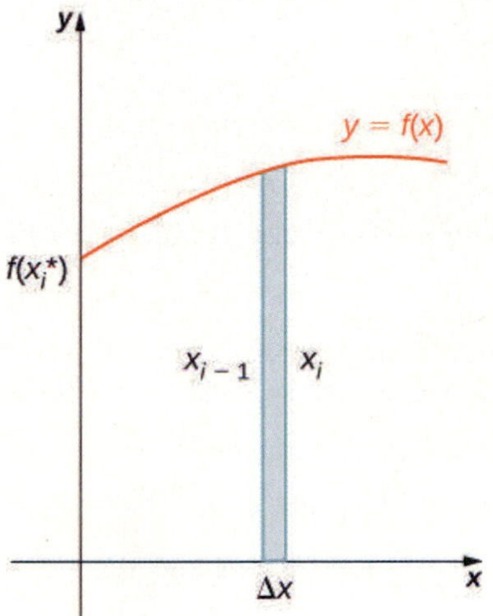


**Figure 2.27** Calculating the volume of the shell.

The shell is a cylinder, so its volume is the cross-sectional area multiplied by the height of the cylinder. The cross-sections are annuli (ring-shaped regions—essentially, circles with a hole in the center), with outer radius $x_i$ and inner radius $x_{i-1}$. Thus, the cross-sectional area is $\pi x_i^2 - \pi x_{i-1}^2$. The height of the cylinder is $f(x_i^*)$. Then the volume of the shell is

$$\begin{aligned} V_{\text{shell}} &= f(x_i^*)(\pi x_i^2 - \pi x_{i-1}^2) \\ &= \pi f(x_i^*)\left(x_i^2 - x_{i-1}^2\right) \\ &= \pi f(x_i^*)(x_i + x_{i-1})(x_i - x_{i-1}) \\ &= 2\pi f(x_i^*)\left(\frac{x_i + x_{i-1}}{2}\right)(x_i - x_{i-1}). \end{aligned}$$

Note that $x_i - x_{i-1} = \Delta x,$ so we have

$$V_{\text{shell}} = 2\pi f(x_i^*)\left(\frac{x_i + x_{i-1}}{2}\right)\Delta x.$$

Furthermore, $\frac{x_i + x_{i-1}}{2}$ is both the midpoint of the interval $[x_{i-1}, x_i]$ and the average radius of the shell, and we can approximate this by $x_i^*$. We then have

$$V_{\text{shell}} \approx 2\pi f(x_i^*)x_i^*\ \Delta x.$$

Another way to think of this is to think of making a vertical cut in the shell and then opening it up to form a flat plate (**Figure 2.28**).

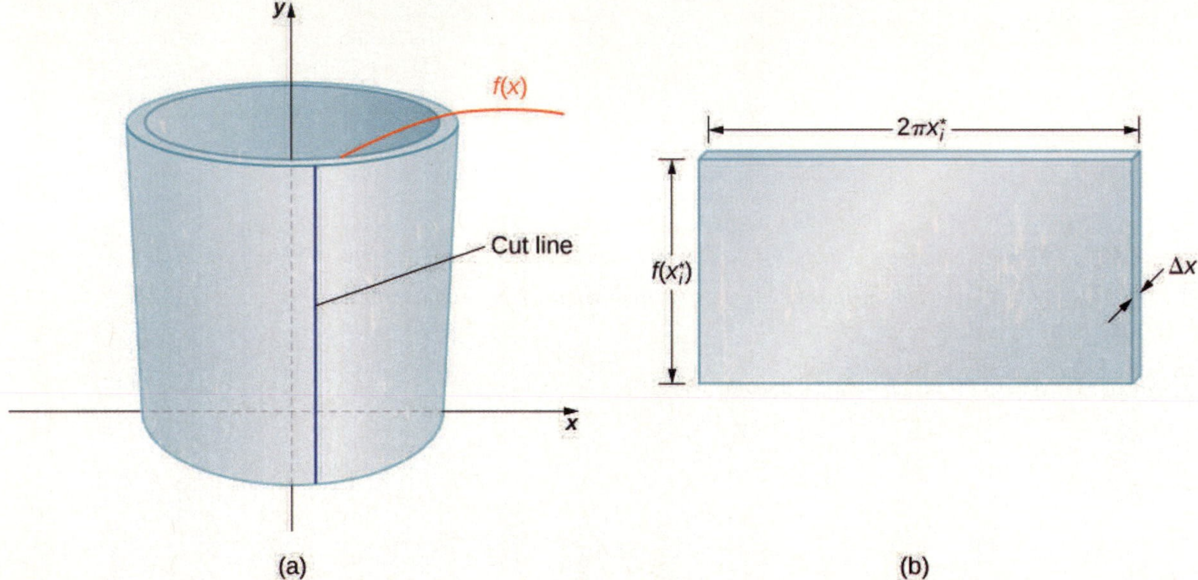


**Figure 2.28** (a) Make a vertical cut in a representative shell. (b) Open the shell up to form a flat plate.

In reality, the outer radius of the shell is greater than the inner radius, and hence the back edge of the plate would be slightly longer than the front edge of the plate. However, we can approximate the flattened shell by a flat plate of height $f(x_i^*)$, width $2\pi x_i^*$, and thickness $\Delta x$ (**Figure 2.28**). The volume of the shell, then, is approximately the volume of the flat plate. Multiplying the height, width, and depth of the plate, we get

$$V_{\text{shell}} \approx f(x_i^*)(2\pi x_i^*)\Delta x,$$

which is the same formula we had before.

To calculate the volume of the entire solid, we then add the volumes of all the shells and obtain

$$V \approx \sum_{i=1}^{n}\left(2\pi x_i^*\ f(x_i^*)\Delta x\right).$$

Here we have another Riemann sum, this time for the function $2\pi x f(x)$. Taking the limit as $n \to \infty$ gives us

$$V = \lim_{n \to \infty}\sum_{i=1}^{n}\left(2\pi x_i^*\ f(x_i^*)\Delta x\right) = \int_a^b \left(2\pi x f(x)\right)dx.$$

This leads to the following rule for the **method of cylindrical shells.**

### Rule: The Method of Cylindrical Shells

Let $f(x)$ be continuous and nonnegative. Define $R$ as the region bounded above by the graph of $f(x)$, below by the $x$-axis, on the left by the line $x = a$, and on the right by the line $x = b$. Then the volume of the solid of revolution formed by revolving $R$ around the $y$-axis is given by

$$V = \int_a^b (2\pi x f(x))dx. \tag{2.6}$$

Now let's consider an example.

## Example 2.12

### The Method of Cylindrical Shells 1

Define $R$ as the region bounded above by the graph of $f(x) = 1/x$ and below by the $x$-axis over the interval $[1, 3]$. Find the volume of the solid of revolution formed by revolving $R$ around the $y$-axis.

#### Solution

First we must graph the region $R$ and the associated solid of revolution, as shown in the following figure.

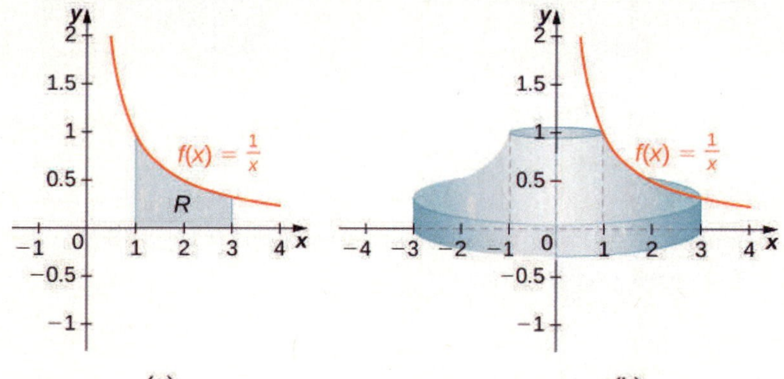


**Figure 2.29** (a) The region $R$ under the graph of $f(x) = 1/x$ over the interval $[1, 3]$. (b) The solid of revolution generated by revolving $R$ about the $y$-axis.

Then the volume of the solid is given by

$$\begin{aligned} V &= \int_a^b (2\pi x f(x))dx \\ &= \int_1^3 \left(2\pi x\left(\frac{1}{x}\right)\right)dx \\ &= \int_1^3 2\pi\, dx = 2\pi x\Big|_1^3 = 4\pi \text{ units}^3. \end{aligned}$$

**2.12** Define $R$ as the region bounded above by the graph of $f(x) = x^2$ and below by the $x$-axis over the interval $[1, 2]$. Find the volume of the solid of revolution formed by revolving $R$ around the $y$-axis.

## Example 2.13

### The Method of Cylindrical Shells 2

Define $R$ as the region bounded above by the graph of $f(x) = 2x - x^2$ and below by the $x$-axis over the interval $[0, 2]$. Find the volume of the solid of revolution formed by revolving $R$ around the $y$-axis.

#### Solution

First graph the region $R$ and the associated solid of revolution, as shown in the following figure.

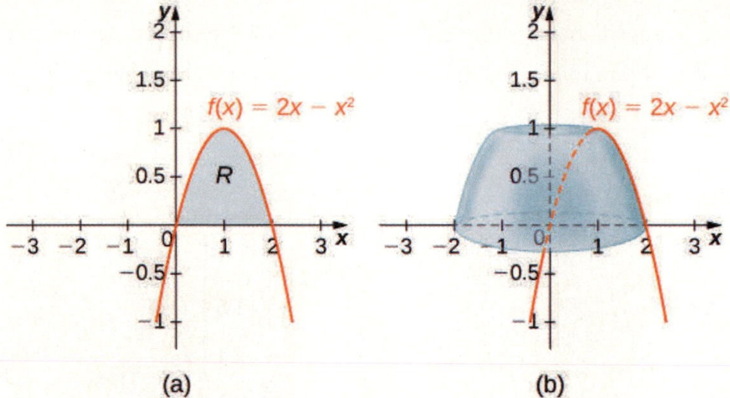


**Figure 2.30** (a) The region $R$ under the graph of $f(x) = 2x - x^2$ over the interval $[0, 2]$. (b) The volume of revolution obtained by revolving $R$ about the $y$-axis.

Then the volume of the solid is given by

$$\begin{aligned} V &= \int_a^b (2\pi x f(x))dx \\ &= \int_0^2 \left(2\pi x\left(2x - x^2\right)\right)dx = 2\pi\int_0^2 \left(2x^2 - x^3\right)dx \\ &= 2\pi\left[\frac{2x^3}{3} - \frac{x^4}{4}\right]\Big|_0^2 = \frac{8\pi}{3}\text{ units}^3. \end{aligned}$$

**2.13** Define $R$ as the region bounded above by the graph of $f(x) = 3x - x^2$ and below by the $x$-axis over the interval $[0, 2]$. Find the volume of the solid of revolution formed by revolving $R$ around the $y$-axis.

As with the disk method and the washer method, we can use the method of cylindrical shells with solids of revolution, revolved around the $x$-axis, when we want to integrate with respect to $y$. The analogous rule for this type of solid is given here.

**Rule: The Method of Cylindrical Shells for Solids of Revolution around the $x$-axis**

Let $g(y)$ be continuous and nonnegative. Define $Q$ as the region bounded on the right by the graph of $g(y)$, on the left by the $y$-axis, below by the line $y = c$, and above by the line $y = d$. Then, the volume of the solid of revolution formed by revolving $Q$ around the $x$-axis is given by

$$V = \int_c^d (2\pi y g(y))dy.$$

## Example 2.14

### The Method of Cylindrical Shells for a Solid Revolved around the x-axis

Define $Q$ as the region bounded on the right by the graph of $g(y) = 2\sqrt{y}$ and on the left by the $y$-axis for $y \in [0, 4]$. Find the volume of the solid of revolution formed by revolving $Q$ around the $x$-axis.

#### Solution

First, we need to graph the region $Q$ and the associated solid of revolution, as shown in the following figure.

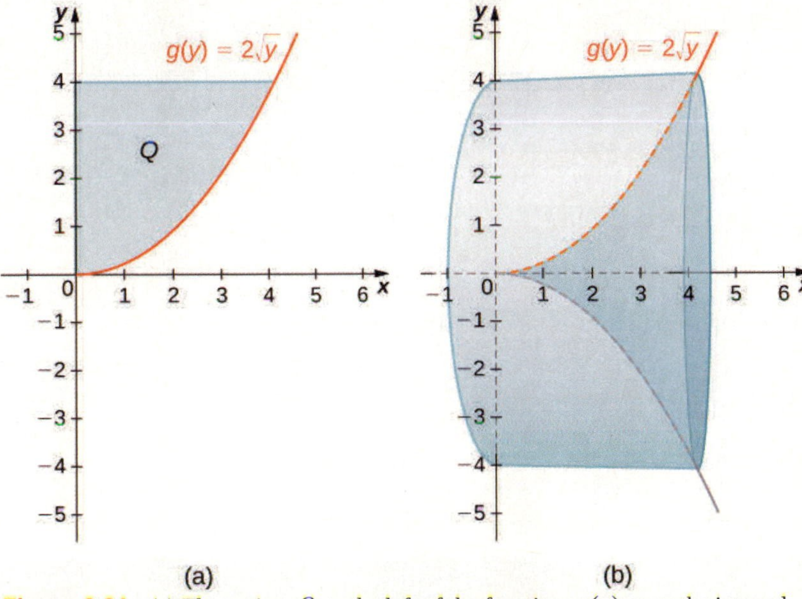


**Figure 2.31** (a) The region $Q$ to the left of the function $g(y)$ over the interval $[0, 4]$. (b) The solid of revolution generated by revolving $Q$ around the $x$-axis.

Label the shaded region $Q$. Then the volume of the solid is given by

$$\begin{aligned} V &= \int_c^d (2\pi y g(y))dy \\ &= \int_0^4 (2\pi y(2\sqrt{y}))dy = 4\pi \int_0^4 y^{3/2} dy \\ &= 4\pi \left[\frac{2y^{5/2}}{5}\right]\Bigg|_0^4 = \frac{256\pi}{5} \text{ units}^3. \end{aligned}$$

**2.14** Define $Q$ as the region bounded on the right by the graph of $g(y) = 3/y$ and on the left by the $y$-axis for $y \in [1, 3]$. Find the volume of the solid of revolution formed by revolving $Q$ around the $x$-axis.

For the next example, we look at a solid of revolution for which the graph of a function is revolved around a line other than one of the two coordinate axes. To set this up, we need to revisit the development of the method of cylindrical shells. Recall that we found the volume of one of the shells to be given by

$$\begin{aligned} V_{\text{shell}} &= f(x_i^*)(\pi x_i^2 - \pi x_{i-1}^2) \\ &= \pi f(x_i^*)\left(x_i^2 - x_{i-1}^2\right) \\ &= \pi f(x_i^*)(x_i + x_{i-1})(x_i - x_{i-1}) \\ &= 2\pi f(x_i^*)\left(\frac{x_i + x_{i-1}}{2}\right)(x_i - x_{i-1}). \end{aligned}$$

This was based on a shell with an outer radius of $x_i$ and an inner radius of $x_{i-1}$. If, however, we rotate the region around a line other than the $y$-axis, we have a different outer and inner radius. Suppose, for example, that we rotate the region around the line $x = -k$, where $k$ is some positive constant. Then, the outer radius of the shell is $x_i + k$ and the inner radius of the shell is $x_{i-1} + k$. Substituting these terms into the expression for volume, we see that when a plane region is rotated around the line $x = -k$, the volume of a shell is given by

$$\begin{aligned} V_{\text{shell}} &= 2\pi f(x_i^*)\left(\frac{(x_i + k) + (x_{i-1} + k)}{2}\right)\left((x_i + k) - (x_{i-1} + k)\right) \\ &= 2\pi f(x_i^*)\left(\left(\frac{x_i + x_{i-2}}{2}\right) + k\right)\Delta x. \end{aligned}$$

As before, we notice that $\frac{x_i + x_{i-1}}{2}$ is the midpoint of the interval $[x_{i-1}, x_i]$ and can be approximated by $x_i^*$. Then, the approximate volume of the shell is

$$V_{\text{shell}} \approx 2\pi\left(x_i^* + k\right)f(x_i^*)\Delta x.$$

The remainder of the development proceeds as before, and we see that

$$V = \int_a^b \left(2\pi(x + k)f(x)\right)dx.$$

We could also rotate the region around other horizontal or vertical lines, such as a vertical line in the right half plane. In each case, the volume formula must be adjusted accordingly. Specifically, the $x$-term in the integral must be replaced with an expression representing the radius of a shell. To see how this works, consider the following example.

## Example 2.15

### A Region of Revolution Revolved around a Line

Define $R$ as the region bounded above by the graph of $f(x) = x$ and below by the $x$-axis over the interval $[1, 2]$. Find the volume of the solid of revolution formed by revolving $R$ around the line $x = -1$.

#### Solution

First, graph the region $R$ and the associated solid of revolution, as shown in the following figure.

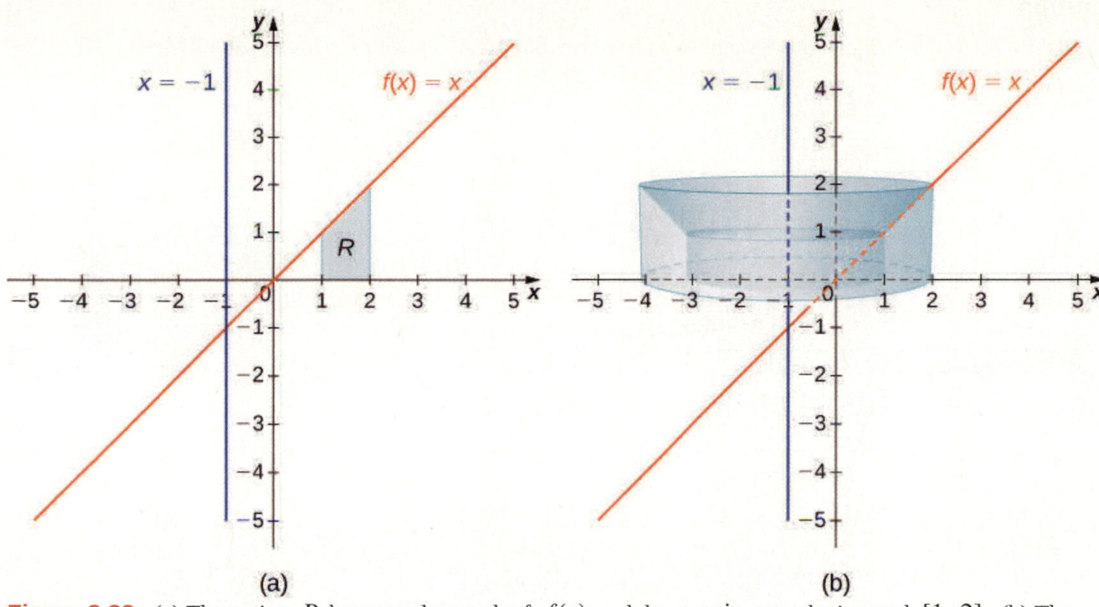


**Figure 2.32** (a) The region $R$ between the graph of $f(x)$ and the $x$-axis over the interval $[1, 2]$. (b) The solid of revolution generated by revolving $R$ around the line $x = -1$.

Note that the radius of a shell is given by $x + 1$. Then the volume of the solid is given by

$$\begin{aligned} V &= \int_1^2 (2\pi(x+1)f(x))dx \\ &= \int_1^2 (2\pi(x+1)x)dx = 2\pi\int_1^2 \left(x^2 + x\right)dx \\ &= 2\pi\left[\frac{x^3}{3} + \frac{x^2}{2}\right]\Bigg|_1^2 = \frac{23\pi}{3}\text{ units}^3. \end{aligned}$$

**2.15** Define $R$ as the region bounded above by the graph of $f(x) = x^2$ and below by the $x$-axis over the interval $[0, 1]$. Find the volume of the solid of revolution formed by revolving $R$ around the line $x = -2$.

For our final example in this section, let's look at the volume of a solid of revolution for which the region of revolution is bounded by the graphs of two functions.

## Example 2.16

### A Region of Revolution Bounded by the Graphs of Two Functions

Define $R$ as the region bounded above by the graph of the function $f(x) = \sqrt{x}$ and below by the graph of the function $g(x) = 1/x$ over the interval $[1, 4]$. Find the volume of the solid of revolution generated by revolving $R$ around the $y$-axis.

### Solution

First, graph the region $R$ and the associated solid of revolution, as shown in the following figure.

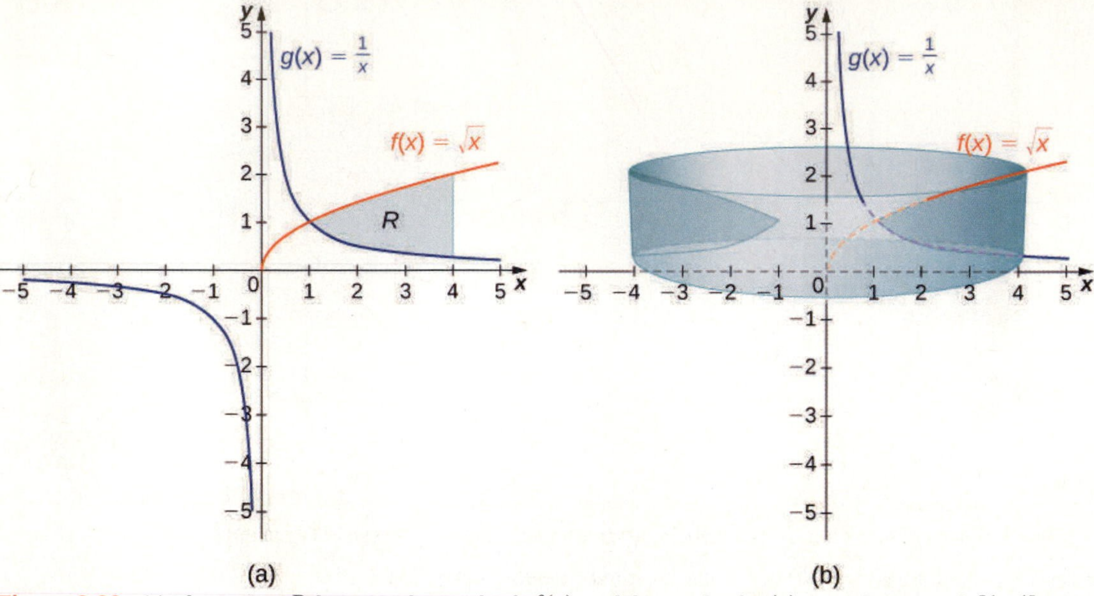


**Figure 2.33** (a) The region $R$ between the graph of $f(x)$ and the graph of $g(x)$ over the interval $[1, 4]$. (b) The solid of revolution generated by revolving $R$ around the $y$-axis.

Note that the axis of revolution is the $y$-axis, so the radius of a shell is given simply by $x$. We don't need to make any adjustments to the $x$-term of our integrand. The height of a shell, though, is given by $f(x) - g(x)$, so in this case we need to adjust the $f(x)$ term of the integrand. Then the volume of the solid is given by

$$\begin{aligned} V &= \int_1^4 (2\pi x(f(x) - g(x)))dx \\ &= \int_1^4 \left(2\pi x\left(\sqrt{x} - \frac{1}{x}\right)\right)dx = 2\pi \int_1^4 \left(x^{3/2} - 1\right)dx \\ &= 2\pi\left[\frac{2x^{5/2}}{5} - x\right]\Bigg|_1^4 = \frac{94\pi}{5} \text{ units}^3. \end{aligned}$$

**2.16** Define $R$ as the region bounded above by the graph of $f(x) = x$ and below by the graph of $g(x) = x^2$ over the interval $[0, 1]$. Find the volume of the solid of revolution formed by revolving $R$ around the $y$-axis.

## Which Method Should We Use?

We have studied several methods for finding the volume of a solid of revolution, but how do we know which method to use? It often comes down to a choice of which integral is easiest to evaluate. **Figure 2.34** describes the different approaches for solids of revolution around the $x$-axis. It's up to you to develop the analogous table for solids of revolution around the $y$-axis.

Comparing the Methods for Finding the Volume of a Solid Revolution around the *x*-axis

| Compare | Disk Method | Washer Method | Shell Method |
|---|---|---|---|
| Volume formula | $V = \int_a^b \pi[f(x)]^2\,dx$ | $V = \int_a^b \pi[(f(x))^2 - (g(x))^2]\,dx$ | $V = \int_c^d 2\pi y\, g(y)\,dy$ |
| Solid | No cavity in the center | Cavity in the center | With or without a cavity in the center |
| Interval to partition | $[a, b]$ on $x$-axis | $[a, b]$ on $x$-axis | $[c, d]$ on $y$-axis |
| Rectangle | Vertical | Vertical | Horizontal |
| Typical region | 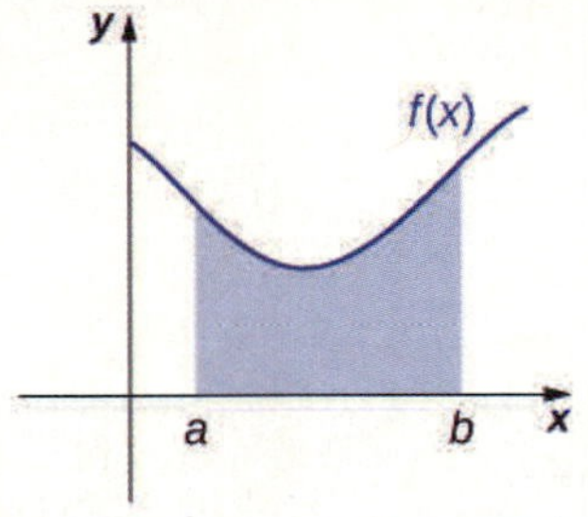 y f(x) a b x | 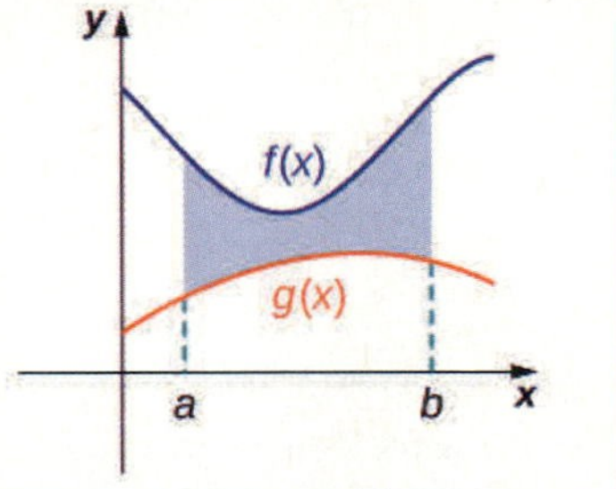 y f(x) g(x) a b x | 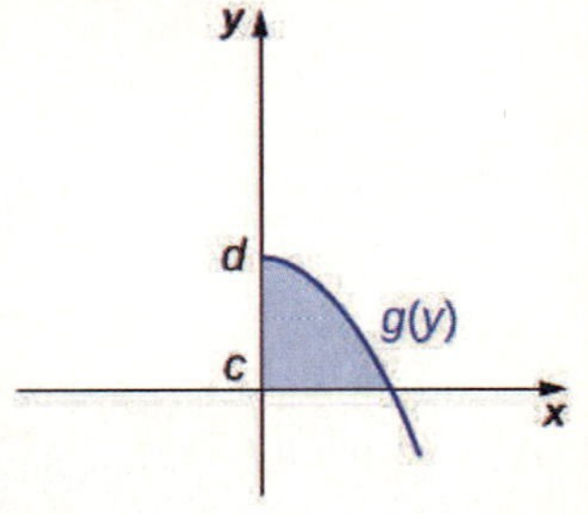 y d c g(y) x |
| Typical element | 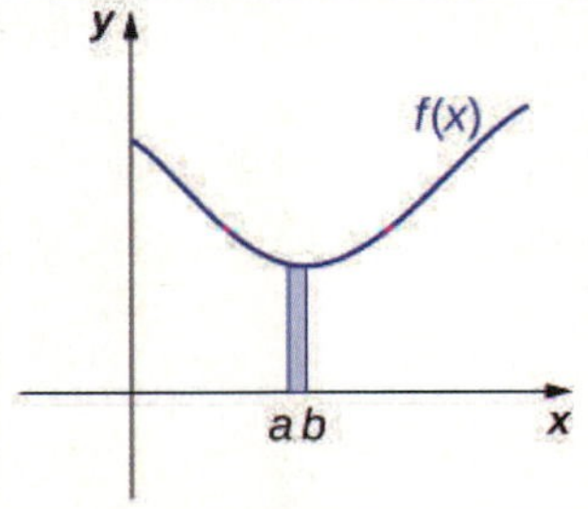 y f(x) a b x | 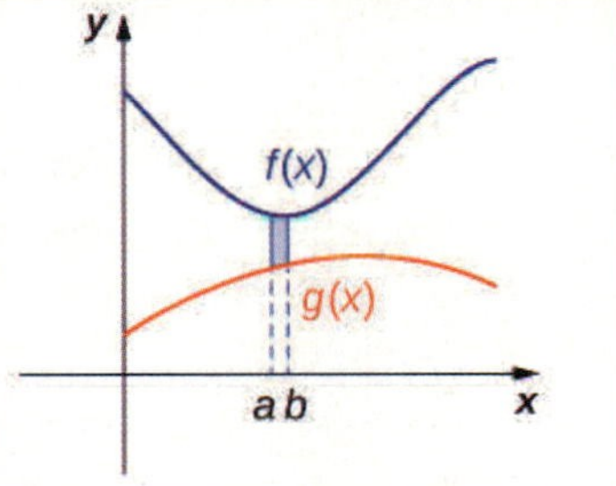 y f(x) g(x) a b x | 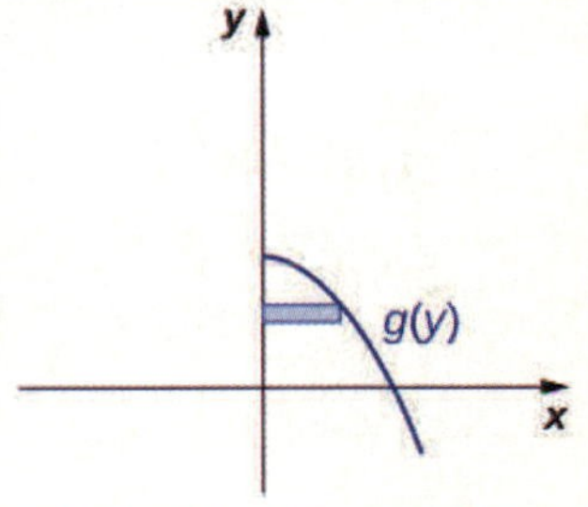 y g(y) x |

Figure 2.34

Let's take a look at a couple of additional problems and decide on the best approach to take for solving them.

## Example 2.17

### Selecting the Best Method

For each of the following problems, select the best method to find the volume of a solid of revolution generated by revolving the given region around the $x$-axis, and set up the integral to find the volume (do not evaluate the integral).

a. The region bounded by the graphs of $y = x$, $y = 2 - x$, and the $x$-axis.

b. The region bounded by the graphs of $y = 4x - x^2$ and the $x$-axis.

### Solution

a. First, sketch the region and the solid of revolution as shown.

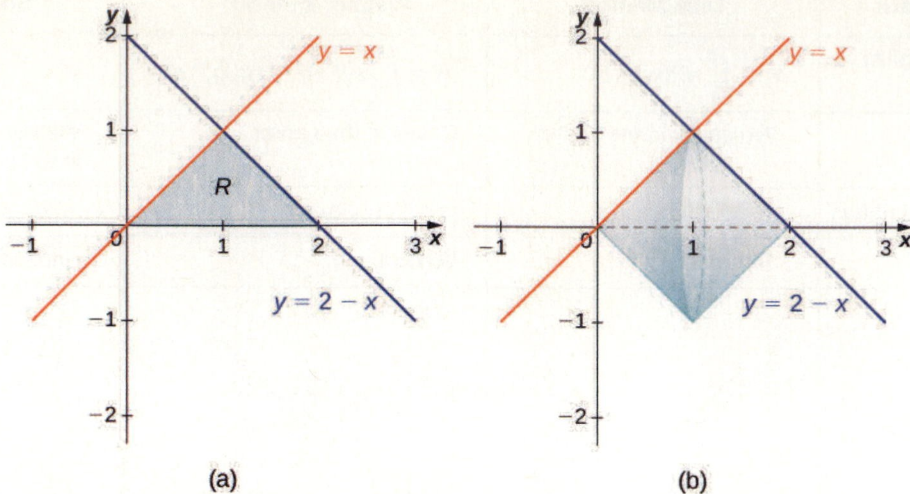


**Figure 2.35** (a) The region $R$ bounded by two lines and the $x$-axis. (b) The solid of revolution generated by revolving $R$ about the $x$-axis.

Looking at the region, if we want to integrate with respect to $x$, we would have to break the integral into two pieces, because we have different functions bounding the region over $[0, 1]$ and $[1, 2]$. In this case, using the disk method, we would have

$$V = \int_0^1 \left(\pi x^2\right)dx + \int_1^2 \left(\pi(2 - x)^2\right)dx.$$

If we used the shell method instead, we would use functions of $y$ to represent the curves, producing

$$\begin{aligned} V &= \int_0^1 (2\pi y[(2 - y) - y])dy \\ &= \int_0^1 (2\pi y[2 - 2y])dy. \end{aligned}$$

Neither of these integrals is particularly onerous, but since the shell method requires only one integral, and the integrand requires less simplification, we should probably go with the shell method in this case.

b. First, sketch the region and the solid of revolution as shown.

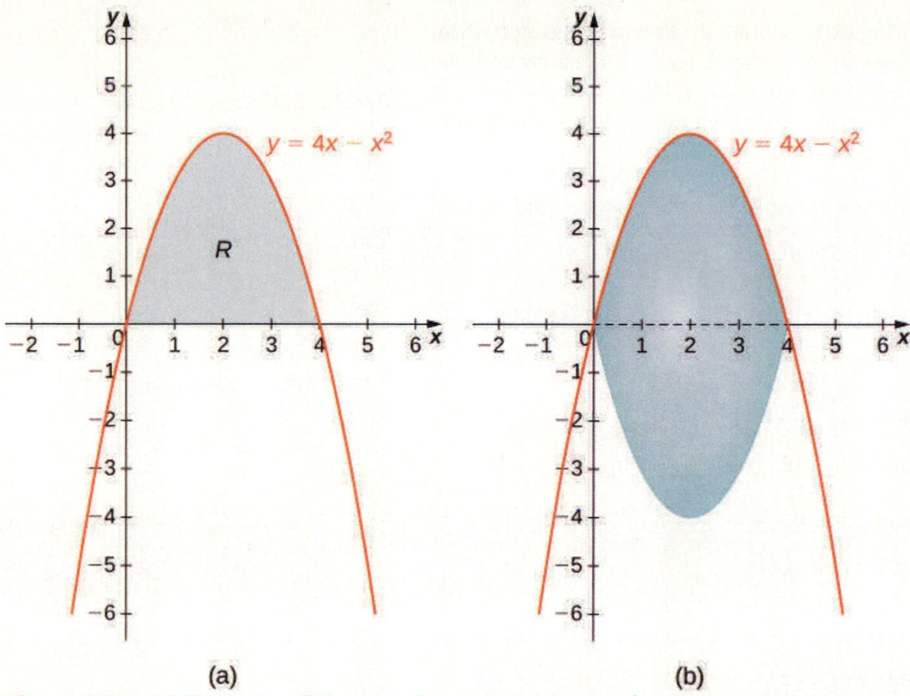


**Figure 2.36** (a) The region $R$ between the curve and the $x$-axis. (b) The solid of revolution generated by revolving $R$ about the $x$-axis.

Looking at the region, it would be problematic to define a horizontal rectangle; the region is bounded on the left and right by the same function. Therefore, we can dismiss the method of shells. The solid has no cavity in the middle, so we can use the method of disks. Then

$$V = \int_0^4 \pi\left(4x - x^2\right)^2 dx.$$

**2.17** Select the best method to find the volume of a solid of revolution generated by revolving the given region around the $x$-axis, and set up the integral to find the volume (do not evaluate the integral): the region bounded by the graphs of $y = 2 - x^2$ and $y = x^2$.

## 2.3 EXERCISES

For the following exercise, find the volume generated when the region between the two curves is rotated around the given axis. Use both the shell method and the washer method. Use technology to graph the functions and draw a typical slice by hand.

114. **[T]** Over the curve of $y = 3x$, $x = 0$, and $y = 3$ rotated around the $y$-axis.

115. **[T]** Under the curve of $y = 3x$, $x = 0$, and $x = 3$ rotated around the $y$-axis.

116. **[T]** Over the curve of $y = 3x$, $x = 0$, and $y = 3$ rotated around the $x$-axis.

117. **[T]** Under the curve of $y = 3x$, $x = 0$, and $x = 3$ rotated around the $x$-axis.

118. **[T]** Under the curve of $y = 2x^3$, $x = 0$, and $x = 2$ rotated around the $y$-axis.

119. **[T]** Under the curve of $y = 2x^3$, $x = 0$, and $x = 2$ rotated around the $x$-axis.

For the following exercises, use shells to find the volumes of the given solids. Note that the rotated regions lie between the curve and the $x$-axis and are rotated around the $y$-axis.

120. $y = 1 - x^2$, $x = 0$, and $x = 1$

121. $y = 5x^3$, $x = 0$, and $x = 1$

122. $y = \frac{1}{x}$, $x = 1$, and $x = 100$

123. $y = \sqrt{1 - x^2}$, $x = 0$, and $x = 1$

124. $y = \dfrac{1}{1 + x^2}$, $x = 0$, and $x = 3$

125. $y = \sin x^2$, $x = 0$, and $x = \sqrt{\pi}$

126. $y = \dfrac{1}{\sqrt{1 - x^2}}$, $x = 0$, and $x = \dfrac{1}{2}$

127. $y = \sqrt{x}$, $x = 0$, and $x = 1$

128. $y = \left(1 + x^2\right)^3$, $x = 0$, and $x = 1$

129. $y = 5x^3 - 2x^4$, $x = 0$, and $x = 2$

For the following exercises, use shells to find the volume generated by rotating the regions between the given curve and $y = 0$ around the $x$-axis.

130. $y = \sqrt{1 - x^2}$, $x = 0$, and $x = 1$

131. $y = x^2$, $x = 0$, and $x = 2$

132. $y = e^x$, $x = 0$, and $x = 1$

133. $y = \ln(x)$, $x = 1$, and $x = e$

134. $x = \dfrac{1}{1 + y^2}$, $y = 1$, and $y = 4$

135. $x = \dfrac{1 + y^2}{y}$, $y = 0$, and $y = 2$

136. $x = \cos y$, $y = 0$, and $y = \pi$

137. $x = y^3 - 4y^2$, $x = -1$, and $x = 2$

138. $x = ye^y$, $x = -1$, and $x = 2$

139. $x = \cos ye^y$, $x = 0$, and $x = \pi$

For the following exercises, find the volume generated when the region between the curves is rotated around the given axis.

140. $y = 3 - x$, $y = 0$, $x = 0$, and $x = 2$ rotated around the $y$-axis.

141. $y = x^3$, $y = 0$, and $y = 8$ rotated around the $y$-axis.

142. $y = x^2$, $y = x$, rotated around the $y$-axis.

143. $y = \sqrt{x}$, $x = 0$, and $x = 1$ rotated around the line $x = 2$.

144. $y = \dfrac{1}{4 - x}$, $x = 1$, and $x = 2$ rotated around the line $x = 4$.

145. $y = \sqrt{x}$ and $y = x^2$ rotated around the $y$-axis.

146. $y = \sqrt{x}$ and $y = x^2$ rotated around the line $x = 2$.

147. $x = y^3$, $y = \frac{1}{x}$, $x = 1$, and $y = 2$ rotated around the $x$-axis.

148. $x = y^2$ and $y = x$ rotated around the line $y = 2$.

149. **[T]** Left of $x = \sin(\pi y)$, right of $y = x$, around the $y$-axis.

For the following exercises, use technology to graph the region. Determine which method you think would be easiest to use to calculate the volume generated when the function is rotated around the specified axis. Then, use your chosen method to find the volume.

150. **[T]** $y = x^2$ and $y = 4x$ rotated around the $y$-axis.

151. **[T]** $y = \cos(\pi x)$, $y = \sin(\pi x)$, $x = \frac{1}{4}$, and $x = \frac{5}{4}$ rotated around the $y$-axis.

152. **[T]** $y = x^2 - 2x$, $x = 2$, and $x = 4$ rotated around the $y$-axis.

153. **[T]** $y = x^2 - 2x$, $x = 2$, and $x = 4$ rotated around the $x$-axis.

154. **[T]** $y = 3x^3 - 2$, $y = x$, and $x = 2$ rotated around the $x$-axis.

155. **[T]** $y = 3x^3 - 2$, $y = x$, and $x = 2$ rotated around the $y$-axis.

156. **[T]** $x = \sin\left(\pi y^2\right)$ and $x = \sqrt{2}y$ rotated around the $x$-axis.

157. **[T]** $x = y^2$, $x = y^2 - 2y + 1$, and $x = 2$ rotated around the $y$-axis.

For the following exercises, use the method of shells to approximate the volumes of some common objects, which are pictured in accompanying figures.

158. Use the method of shells to find the volume of a sphere of radius $r$.

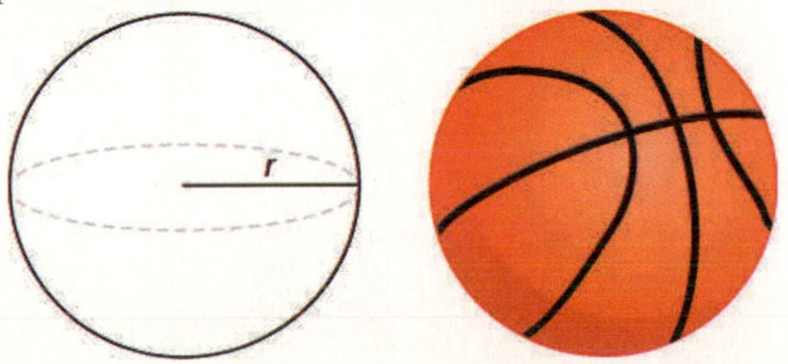


159. Use the method of shells to find the volume of a cone with radius $r$ and height $h$.

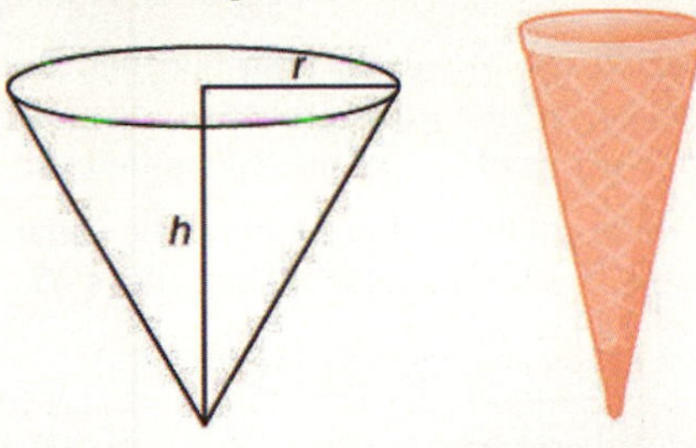


160. Use the method of shells to find the volume of an ellipse $\left(x^2/a^2\right) + \left(y^2/b^2\right) = 1$ rotated around the $x$-axis.

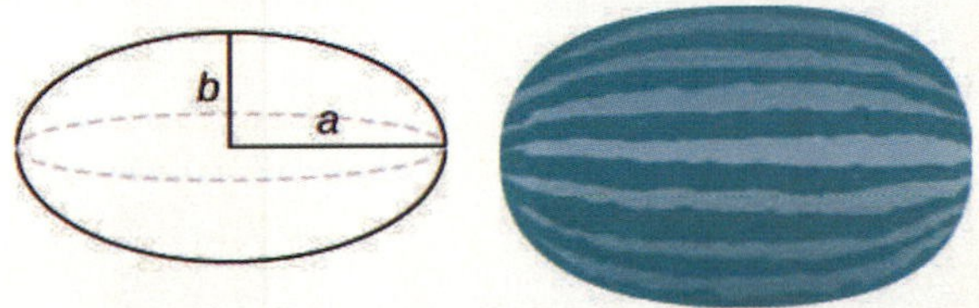


161. Use the method of shells to find the volume of a cylinder with radius $r$ and height $h$.

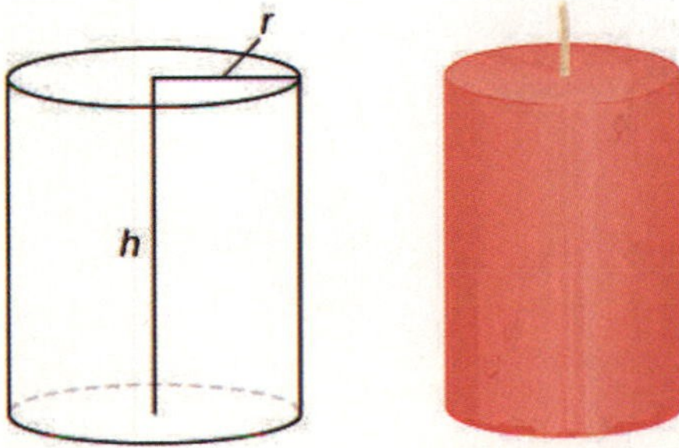


162. Use the method of shells to find the volume of the donut created when the circle $x^2 + y^2 = 4$ is rotated around the line $x = 4$.

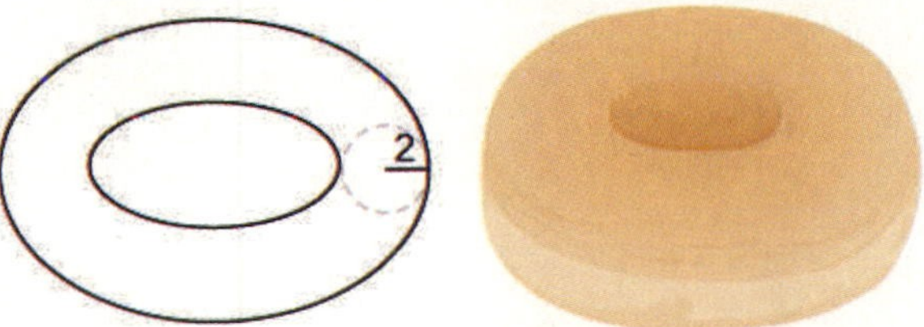


163. Consider the region enclosed by the graphs of $y = f(x)$, $y = 1 + f(x)$, $x = 0$, $y = 0$, and $x = a > 0$. What is the volume of the solid generated when this region is rotated around the $y$-axis? Assume that the function is defined over the interval $[0, a]$.

164. Consider the function $y = f(x)$, which decreases from $f(0) = b$ to $f(1) = 0$. Set up the integrals for determining the volume, using both the shell method and the disk method, of the solid generated when this region, with $x = 0$ and $y = 0$, is rotated around the $y$-axis. Prove that both methods approximate the same volume. Which method is easier to apply? (*Hint:* Since $f(x)$ is one-to-one, there exists an inverse $f^{-1}(y)$.)

# 2.4 | Arc Length of a Curve and Surface Area

## Learning Objectives

**2.4.1** Determine the length of a curve, $y = f(x)$, between two points.

**2.4.2** Determine the length of a curve, $x = g(y)$, between two points.

**2.4.3** Find the surface area of a solid of revolution.

In this section, we use definite integrals to find the arc length of a curve. We can think of **arc length** as the distance you would travel if you were walking along the path of the curve. Many real-world applications involve arc length. If a rocket is launched along a parabolic path, we might want to know how far the rocket travels. Or, if a curve on a map represents a road, we might want to know how far we have to drive to reach our destination.

We begin by calculating the arc length of curves defined as functions of $x$, then we examine the same process for curves defined as functions of $y$. (The process is identical, with the roles of $x$ and $y$ reversed.) The techniques we use to find arc length can be extended to find the surface area of a surface of revolution, and we close the section with an examination of this concept.

## Arc Length of the Curve y = f(x)

In previous applications of integration, we required the function $f(x)$ to be integrable, or at most continuous. However, for calculating arc length we have a more stringent requirement for $f(x)$. Here, we require $f(x)$ to be differentiable, and furthermore we require its derivative, $f'(x)$, to be continuous. Functions like this, which have continuous derivatives, are called *smooth*. (This property comes up again in later chapters.)

Let $f(x)$ be a smooth function defined over $[a, b]$. We want to calculate the length of the curve from the point $(a, f(a))$ to the point $(b, f(b))$. We start by using line segments to approximate the length of the curve. For $i = 0, 1, 2,\ldots, n$, let $P = \{x_i\}$ be a regular partition of $[a, b]$. Then, for $i = 1, 2,\ldots, n$, construct a line segment from the point $(x_{i-1}, f(x_{i-1}))$ to the point $(x_i, f(x_i))$. Although it might seem logical to use either horizontal or vertical line segments, we want our line segments to approximate the curve as closely as possible. Figure 2.37 depicts this construct for $n = 5$.

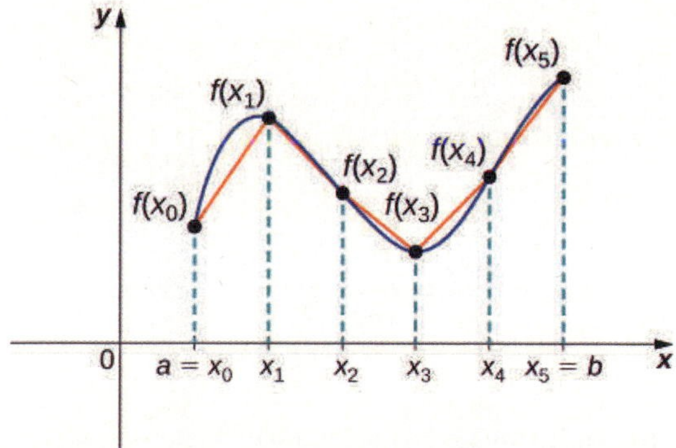


**Figure 2.37** We can approximate the length of a curve by adding line segments.

To help us find the length of each line segment, we look at the change in vertical distance as well as the change in horizontal distance over each interval. Because we have used a regular partition, the change in horizontal distance over each interval is given by $\Delta x$. The change in vertical distance varies from interval to interval, though, so we use $\Delta y_i = f(x_i) - f(x_{i-1})$ to represent the change in vertical distance over the interval $[x_{i-1}, x_i]$, as shown in Figure 2.38. Note that some (or all) $\Delta y_i$ may be negative.

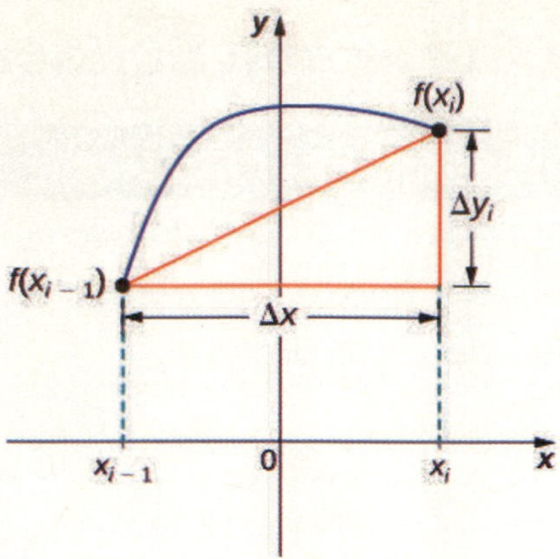


**Figure 2.38** A representative line segment approximates the curve over the interval $[x_{i-1}, x_i]$.

By the Pythagorean theorem, the length of the line segment is $\sqrt{(\Delta x)^2 + (\Delta y_i)^2}$. We can also write this as $\Delta x\sqrt{1 + ((\Delta y_i)/(\Delta x))^2}$. Now, by the Mean Value Theorem, there is a point $x_i^* \in [x_{i-1}, x_i]$ such that $f'(x_i^*) = (\Delta y_i)/(\Delta x)$. Then the length of the line segment is given by $\Delta x\sqrt{1 + [f'(x_i^*)]^2}$. Adding up the lengths of all the line segments, we get

$$\text{Arc Length} \approx \sum_{i=1}^{n} \sqrt{1 + [f'(x_i^*)]^2}\,\Delta x.$$

This is a Riemann sum. Taking the limit as $n \to \infty$, we have

$$\text{Arc Length} = \lim_{n \to \infty} \sum_{i=1}^{n} \sqrt{1 + [f'(x_i^*)]^2}\,\Delta x = \int_a^b \sqrt{1 + [f'(x)]^2}\,dx.$$

We summarize these findings in the following theorem.

### Theorem 2.4: Arc Length for $y = f(x)$

Let $f(x)$ be a smooth function over the interval $[a, b]$. Then the arc length of the portion of the graph of $f(x)$ from the point $(a, f(a))$ to the point $(b, f(b))$ is given by

$$\text{Arc Length} = \int_a^b \sqrt{1 + [f'(x)]^2}\,dx. \tag{2.7}$$

Note that we are integrating an expression involving $f'(x)$, so we need to be sure $f'(x)$ is integrable. This is why we require $f(x)$ to be smooth. The following example shows how to apply the theorem.

## Example 2.18

### Calculating the Arc Length of a Function of $x$

Let $f(x) = 2x^{3/2}$. Calculate the arc length of the graph of $f(x)$ over the interval $[0, 1]$. Round the answer to three decimal places.

### Solution

We have $f'(x) = 3x^{1/2}$, so $[f'(x)]^2 = 9x$. Then, the arc length is

$$\begin{aligned}\text{Arc Length} &= \int_a^b \sqrt{1 + [f'(x)]^2}\, dx \\ &= \int_0^1 \sqrt{1 + 9x}\, dx.\end{aligned}$$

Substitute $u = 1 + 9x$. Then, $du = 9\, dx$. When $x = 0$, then $u = 1$, and when $x = 1$, then $u = 10$. Thus,

$$\begin{aligned}\text{Arc Length} &= \int_0^1 \sqrt{1 + 9x}\, dx \\ &= \frac{1}{9}\int_0^1 \sqrt{1 + 9x} 9dx = \frac{1}{9}\int_1^{10} \sqrt{u}\, du \\ &= \frac{1}{9} \cdot \frac{2}{3} u^{3/2}\Big|_1^{10} = \frac{2}{27}\left[10\sqrt{10} - 1\right] \approx 2.268 \text{ units.}\end{aligned}$$

**2.18** Let $f(x) = (4/3)x^{3/2}$. Calculate the arc length of the graph of $f(x)$ over the interval $[0, 1]$. Round the answer to three decimal places.

Although it is nice to have a formula for calculating arc length, this particular theorem can generate expressions that are difficult to integrate. We study some techniques for integration in **Introduction to Techniques of Integration**. In some cases, we may have to use a computer or calculator to approximate the value of the integral.

## Example 2.19

### Using a Computer or Calculator to Determine the Arc Length of a Function of *x*

Let $f(x) = x^2$. Calculate the arc length of the graph of $f(x)$ over the interval $[1, 3]$.

### Solution

We have $f'(x) = 2x$, so $[f'(x)]^2 = 4x^2$. Then the arc length is given by

$$\text{Arc Length} = \int_a^b \sqrt{1 + [f'(x)]^2}\, dx = \int_1^3 \sqrt{1 + 4x^2}\, dx.$$

Using a computer to approximate the value of this integral, we get

$$\int_1^3 \sqrt{1 + 4x^2}\, dx \approx 8.26815.$$

**2.19** Let $f(x) = \sin x$. Calculate the arc length of the graph of $f(x)$ over the interval $[0, \pi]$. Use a computer or calculator to approximate the value of the integral.

## Arc Length of the Curve $x = g(y)$

We have just seen how to approximate the length of a curve with line segments. If we want to find the arc length of the graph of a function of $y,$ we can repeat the same process, except we partition the $y$-axis instead of the $x$-axis. **Figure 2.39** shows a representative line segment.

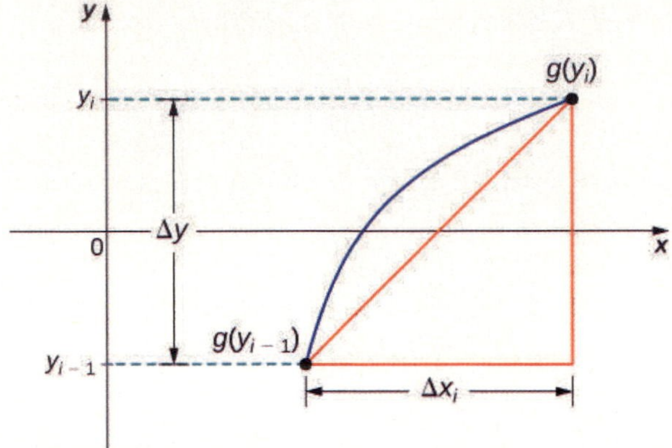


**Figure 2.39** A representative line segment over the interval $[y_{i-1}, y_i]$.

Then the length of the line segment is $\sqrt{(\Delta y)^2 + (\Delta x_i)^2},$ which can also be written as $\Delta y\sqrt{1 + ((\Delta x_i)/(\Delta y))^2}$. If we now follow the same development we did earlier, we get a formula for arc length of a function $x = g(y)$.

### Theorem 2.5: Arc Length for $x = g(y)$

Let $g(y)$ be a smooth function over an interval $[c, d]$. Then, the arc length of the graph of $g(y)$ from the point $(c, g(c))$ to the point $(d, g(d))$ is given by

$$\text{Arc Length} = \int_c^d \sqrt{1 + [g'(y)]^2}\, dy. \tag{2.8}$$

## Example 2.20

### Calculating the Arc Length of a Function of $y$

Let $g(y) = 3y^3$. Calculate the arc length of the graph of $g(y)$ over the interval $[1, 2]$.

#### Solution

We have $g'(y) = 9y^2,$ so $[g'(y)]^2 = 81y^4$. Then the arc length is

$$\text{Arc Length} = \int_c^d \sqrt{1 + [g'(y)]^2}\, dy = \int_1^2 \sqrt{1 + 81y^4}\, dy.$$

Using a computer to approximate the value of this integral, we obtain

$$\int_1^2 \sqrt{1 + 81y^4}\, dy \approx 21.0277.$$

**2.20** Let $g(y) = 1/y$. Calculate the arc length of the graph of $g(y)$ over the interval $[1, 4]$. Use a computer or calculator to approximate the value of the integral.

## Area of a Surface of Revolution

The concepts we used to find the arc length of a curve can be extended to find the surface area of a surface of revolution. **Surface area** is the total area of the outer layer of an object. For objects such as cubes or bricks, the surface area of the object is the sum of the areas of all of its faces. For curved surfaces, the situation is a little more complex. Let $f(x)$ be a nonnegative smooth function over the interval $[a, b]$. We wish to find the surface area of the surface of revolution created by revolving the graph of $y = f(x)$ around the $x$-axis as shown in the following figure.

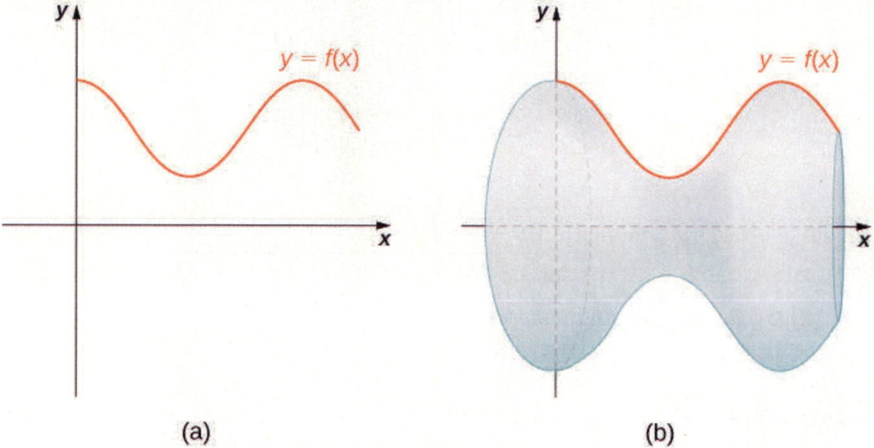


Figure 2.40 (a) A curve representing the function $f(x)$. (b) The surface of revolution formed by revolving the graph of $f(x)$ around the $x$-axis.

As we have done many times before, we are going to partition the interval $[a, b]$ and approximate the surface area by calculating the surface area of simpler shapes. We start by using line segments to approximate the curve, as we did earlier in this section. For $i = 0, 1, 2,\ldots, n$, let $P = \{x_i\}$ be a regular partition of $[a, b]$. Then, for $i = 1, 2,\ldots, n$, construct a line segment from the point $(x_{i-1}, f(x_{i-1}))$ to the point $(x_i, f(x_i))$. Now, revolve these line segments around the $x$-axis to generate an approximation of the surface of revolution as shown in the following figure.

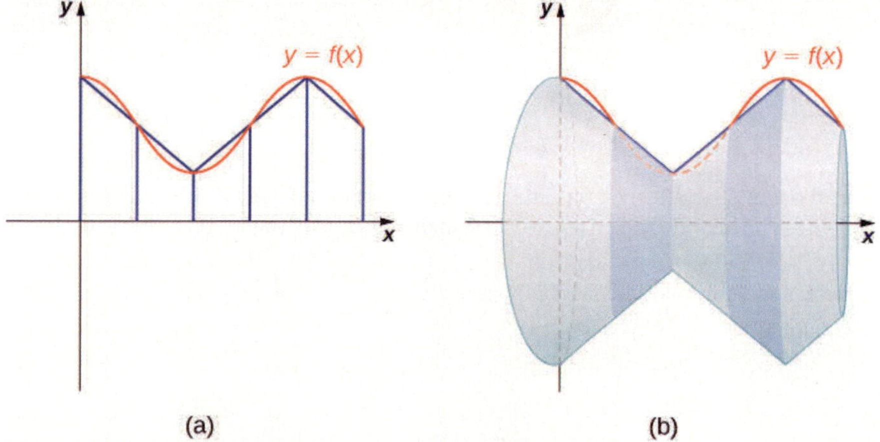


Figure 2.41 (a) Approximating $f(x)$ with line segments. (b) The surface of revolution formed by revolving the line segments around the $x$-axis.

Notice that when each line segment is revolved around the axis, it produces a band. These bands are actually pieces of cones (think of an ice cream cone with the pointy end cut off). A piece of a cone like this is called a **frustum** of a cone.

To find the surface area of the band, we need to find the lateral surface area, $S,$ of the frustum (the area of just the slanted outside surface of the frustum, not including the areas of the top or bottom faces). Let $r_1$ and $r_2$ be the radii of the wide end and the narrow end of the frustum, respectively, and let $l$ be the slant height of the frustum as shown in the following figure.

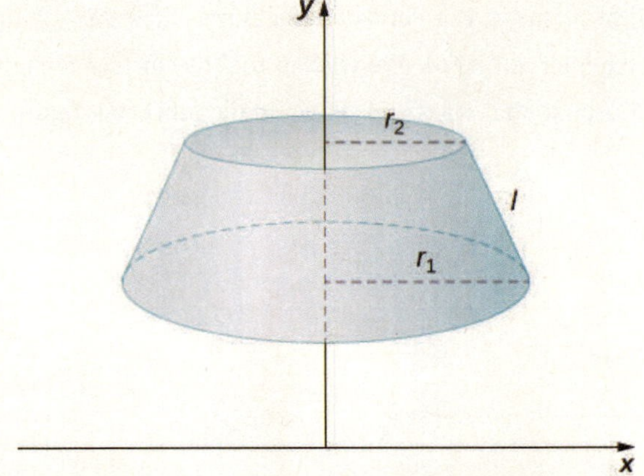


**Figure 2.42** A frustum of a cone can approximate a small part of surface area.

We know the lateral surface area of a cone is given by

$$\text{Lateral Surface Area} = \pi rs,$$

where $r$ is the radius of the base of the cone and $s$ is the slant height (see the following figure).

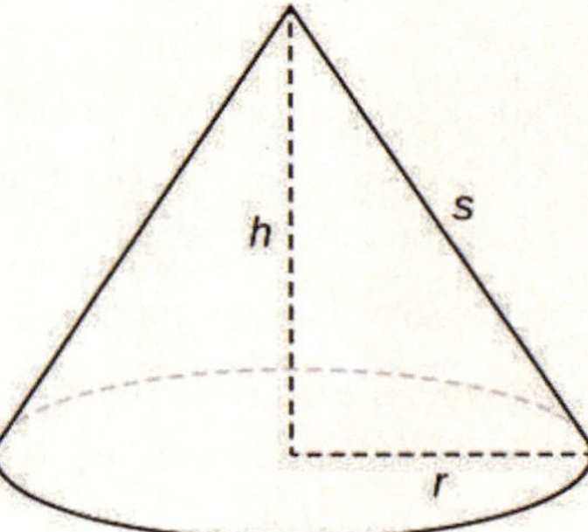


**Figure 2.43** The lateral surface area of the cone is given by $\pi rs.$

Since a frustum can be thought of as a piece of a cone, the lateral surface area of the frustum is given by the lateral surface area of the whole cone less the lateral surface area of the smaller cone (the pointy tip) that was cut off (see the following figure).

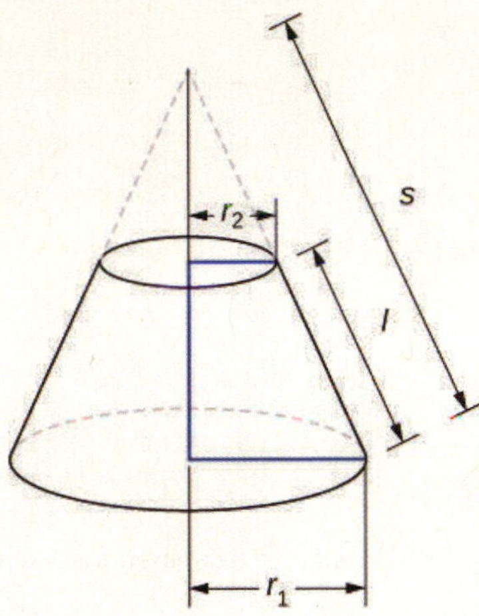


**Figure 2.44** Calculating the lateral surface area of a frustum of a cone.

The cross-sections of the small cone and the large cone are similar triangles, so we see that

$$\frac{r_2}{r_1} = \frac{s - l}{s}.$$

Solving for $s$, we get

$$\begin{aligned}
\frac{r_2}{r_1} &= \frac{s-l}{s} \\
r_2 s &= r_1(s - l) \\
r_2 s &= r_1 s - r_1 l \\
r_1 l &= r_1 s - r_2 s \\
r_1 l &= (r_1 - r_2)s \\
\frac{r_1 l}{r_1 - r_2} &= s.
\end{aligned}$$

Then the lateral surface area (SA) of the frustum is

$$\begin{aligned}
S &= \text{(Lateral SA of large cone)} - \text{(Lateral SA of small cone)} \\
&= \pi r_1 s - \pi r_2 (s - l) \\
&= \pi r_1 \left(\frac{r_1 l}{r_1 - r_2}\right) - \pi r_2 \left(\frac{r_1 l}{r_1 - r_2} - l\right) \\
&= \frac{\pi r_1^2 l}{r_1 - r_2} - \frac{\pi r_1 r_2 l}{r_1 - r_2} + \pi r_2 l \\
&= \frac{\pi r_1^2 l}{r_1 - r_2} - \frac{\pi r_1 r_2 l}{r_1 - r_2} + \frac{\pi r_2 l(r_1 - r_2)}{r_1 - r_2} \\
&= \frac{\pi r_1^2 l}{r_1 - r_2} - \frac{\pi r_1 r_2 l}{r_1 - r_2} + \frac{\pi r_1 r_2 l}{r_1 - r_2} - \frac{\pi r_2{}^2 l}{r_1 - r_2} \\
&= \frac{\pi\left(r_1^2 - r_2^2\right)l}{r_1 - r_2} = \frac{\pi(r_1 - r_2)(r_1 + r_2)l}{r_1 - r_2} = \pi(r_1 + r_2)l.
\end{aligned}$$

Let's now use this formula to calculate the surface area of each of the bands formed by revolving the line segments around the $x$-axis. A representative band is shown in the following figure.

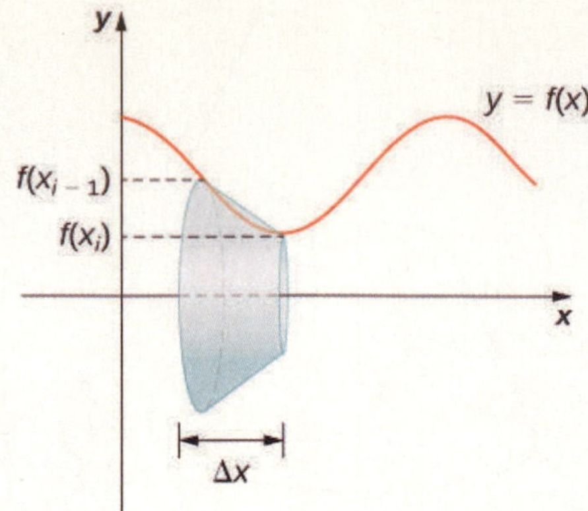


**Figure 2.45** A representative band used for determining surface area.

Note that the slant height of this frustum is just the length of the line segment used to generate it. So, applying the surface area formula, we have

$$\begin{aligned} S &= \pi(r_1 + r_2)l \\ &= \pi\big(f(x_{i-1}) + f(x_i)\big)\sqrt{\Delta x^2 + (\Delta y_i)^2} \\ &= \pi\big(f(x_{i-1}) + f(x_i)\big)\Delta x\sqrt{1 + \left(\frac{\Delta y_i}{\Delta x}\right)^2}. \end{aligned}$$

Now, as we did in the development of the arc length formula, we apply the Mean Value Theorem to select $x_i^* \in [x_{i-1}, x_i]$ such that $f'(x_i^*) = (\Delta y_i)/\Delta x$. This gives us

$$S = \pi\big(f(x_{i-1}) + f(x_i)\big)\Delta x\sqrt{1 + \big(f'(x_i^*)\big)^2}.$$

Furthermore, since $f(x)$ is continuous, by the Intermediate Value Theorem, there is a point $x_i^{**} \in [x_{i-1}, x_i]$ such that $f(x_i^{**}) = (1/2)\big[f(x_{i-1}) + f(x_i)\big],$ so we get

$$S = 2\pi f(x_i^{**})\Delta x\sqrt{1 + \big(f'(x_i^*)\big)^2}.$$

Then the approximate surface area of the whole surface of revolution is given by

$$\text{Surface Area} \approx \sum_{i=1}^{n} 2\pi f(x_i^{**})\Delta x\sqrt{1 + \big(f'(x_i^*)\big)^2}.$$

This *almost* looks like a Riemann sum, except we have functions evaluated at two different points, $x_i^*$ and $x_i^{**}$, over the interval $[x_{i-1}, x_i]$. Although we do not examine the details here, it turns out that because $f(x)$ is smooth, if we let $n \to \infty,$ the limit works the same as a Riemann sum even with the two different evaluation points. This makes sense intuitively. Both $x_i^*$ and $x_i^{**}$ are in the interval $[x_{i-1}, x_i],$ so it makes sense that as $n \to \infty,$ both $x_i^*$ and $x_i^{**}$ approach $x.$ Those of you who are interested in the details should consult an advanced calculus text.

Taking the limit as $n \to \infty,$ we get

$$\text{Surface Area} = \lim_{n \to \infty} \sum_{i=1}^{n} 2\pi f(x_i^{**})\Delta x\sqrt{1 + \big(f'(x_i^*)\big)^2} = \int_a^b \left(2\pi f(x)\sqrt{1 + \big(f'(x)\big)^2}\right)dx.$$

As with arc length, we can conduct a similar development for functions of $y$ to get a formula for the surface area of surfaces of revolution about the $y$-axis. These findings are summarized in the following theorem.

### Theorem 2.6: Surface Area of a Surface of Revolution

Let $f(x)$ be a nonnegative smooth function over the interval $[a, b]$. Then, the surface area of the surface of revolution formed by revolving the graph of $f(x)$ around the $x$-axis is given by

$$\text{Surface Area} = \int_a^b \left(2\pi f(x)\sqrt{1 + (f'(x))^2}\right)dx. \quad (2.9)$$

Similarly, let $g(y)$ be a nonnegative smooth function over the interval $[c, d]$. Then, the surface area of the surface of revolution formed by revolving the graph of $g(y)$ around the $y$-axis is given by

$$\text{Surface Area} = \int_c^d \left(2\pi g(y)\sqrt{1 + (g'(y))^2}\right)dy.$$

## Example 2.21

### Calculating the Surface Area of a Surface of Revolution 1

Let $f(x) = \sqrt{x}$ over the interval $[1, 4]$. Find the surface area of the surface generated by revolving the graph of $f(x)$ around the $x$-axis. Round the answer to three decimal places.

#### Solution

The graph of $f(x)$ and the surface of rotation are shown in the following figure.

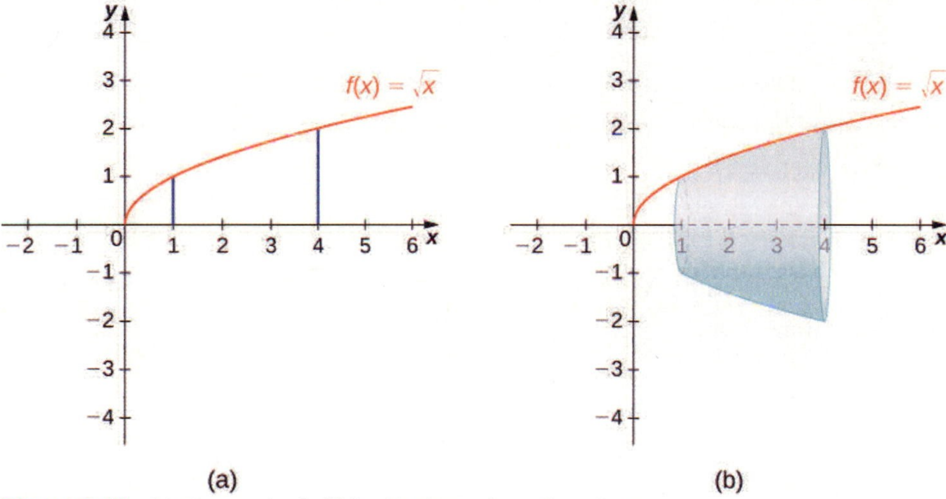


**Figure 2.46** (a) The graph of $f(x)$. (b) The surface of revolution.

We have $f(x) = \sqrt{x}$. Then, $f'(x) = 1/(2\sqrt{x})$ and $(f'(x))^2 = 1/(4x)$. Then,

$$\begin{aligned}\text{Surface Area} &= \int_a^b \left(2\pi f(x)\sqrt{1+(f'(x))^2}\right)dx \\ &= \int_1^4 \left(2\pi\sqrt{x}\sqrt{1+\frac{1}{4x}}\right)dx \\ &= \int_1^4 \left(2\pi\sqrt{x+\frac{1}{4}}\right)dx.\end{aligned}$$

Let $u = x + 1/4.$ Then, $du = dx.$ When $x = 1,$ $u = 5/4,$ and when $x = 4,$ $u = 17/4.$ This gives us

$$\begin{aligned}\int_0^1 \left(2\pi\sqrt{x+\frac{1}{4}}\right)dx &= \int_{5/4}^{17/4} 2\pi\sqrt{u}\,du \\ &= 2\pi\left[\frac{2}{3}u^{3/2}\right]\Big|_{5/4}^{17/4} = \frac{\pi}{6}\left[17\sqrt{17} - 5\sqrt{5}\right] \approx 30.846.\end{aligned}$$

**2.21** Let $f(x) = \sqrt{1 - x}$ over the interval $[0, 1/2].$ Find the surface area of the surface generated by revolving the graph of $f(x)$ around the $x$-axis. Round the answer to three decimal places.

## Example 2.22

### Calculating the Surface Area of a Surface of Revolution 2

Let $f(x) = y = \sqrt[3]{3x}.$ Consider the portion of the curve where $0 \le y \le 2.$ Find the surface area of the surface generated by revolving the graph of $f(x)$ around the $y$-axis.

#### Solution

Notice that we are revolving the curve around the $y$-axis, and the interval is in terms of $y,$ so we want to rewrite the function as a function of $y$. We get $x = g(y) = (1/3)y^3.$ The graph of $g(y)$ and the surface of rotation are shown in the following figure.

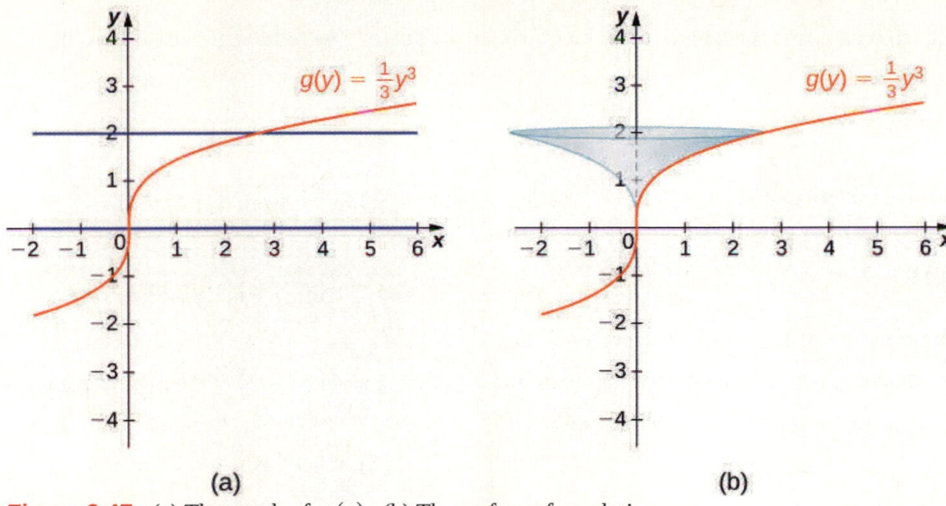


**Figure 2.47** (a) The graph of $g(y)$. (b) The surface of revolution.

We have $g(y) = (1/3)y^3$, so $g'(y) = y^2$ and $(g'(y))^2 = y^4$. Then

$$\begin{aligned} \text{Surface Area} &= \int_c^d \left(2\pi g(y)\sqrt{1 + (g'(y))^2}\right)dy \\ &= \int_0^2 \left(2\pi\left(\frac{1}{3}y^3\right)\sqrt{1 + y^4}\right)dy \\ &= \frac{2\pi}{3}\int_0^2 \left(y^3\sqrt{1 + y^4}\right)dy. \end{aligned}$$

Let $u = y^4 + 1$. Then $du = 4y^3\,dy$. When $y = 0$, $u = 1$, and when $y = 2$, $u = 17$. Then

$$\begin{aligned} \frac{2\pi}{3}\int_0^2 \left(y^3\sqrt{1 + y^4}\right)dy &= \frac{2\pi}{3}\int_1^{17} \frac{1}{4}\sqrt{u}\,du \\ &= \frac{\pi}{6}\left[\frac{2}{3}u^{3/2}\right]\Bigg|_1^{17} = \frac{\pi}{9}\left[(17)^{3/2} - 1\right] \approx 24.118. \end{aligned}$$

**2.22** Let $g(y) = \sqrt{9 - y^2}$ over the interval $y \in [0, 2]$. Find the surface area of the surface generated by revolving the graph of $g(y)$ around the $y$-axis.

# 2.4 EXERCISES

For the following exercises, find the length of the functions over the given interval.

165. $y = 5x$ from $x = 0$ to $x = 2$

166. $y = -\frac{1}{2}x + 25$ from $x = 1$ to $x = 4$

167. $x = 4y$ from $y = -1$ to $y = 1$

168. Pick an arbitrary linear function $x = g(y)$ over any interval of your choice $(y_1, y_2)$. Determine the length of the function and then prove the length is correct by using geometry.

169. Find the surface area of the volume generated when the curve $y = \sqrt{x}$ revolves around the $x$-axis from $(1, 1)$ to $(4, 2)$, as seen here.

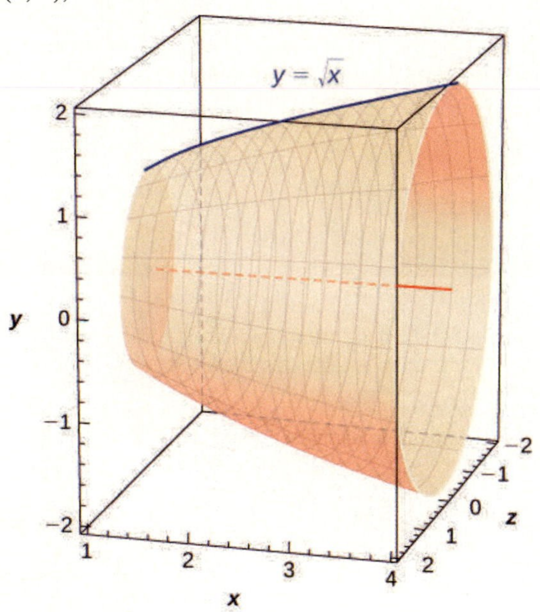


170. Find the surface area of the volume generated when the curve $y = x^2$ revolves around the $y$-axis from $(1, 1)$ to $(3, 9)$.

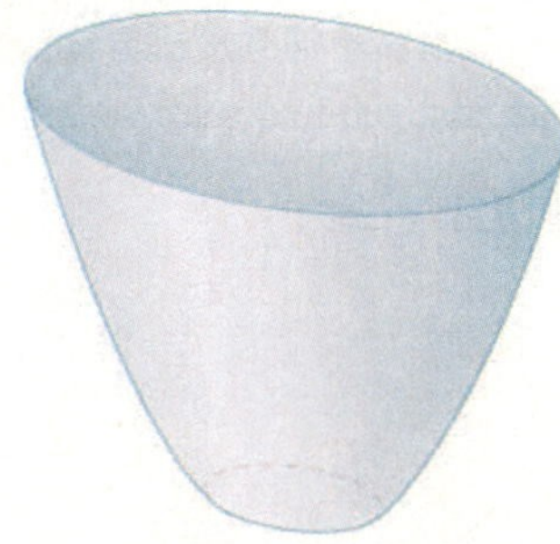

For the following exercises, find the lengths of the functions of $x$ over the given interval. If you cannot evaluate the integral exactly, use technology to approximate it.

171. $y = x^{3/2}$ from $(0, 0)$ to $(1, 1)$

172. $y = x^{2/3}$ from $(1, 1)$ to $(8, 4)$

173. $y = \frac{1}{3}(x^2 + 2)^{3/2}$ from $x = 0$ to $x = 1$

174. $y = \frac{1}{3}(x^2 - 2)^{3/2}$ from $x = 2$ to $x = 4$

175. **[T]** $y = e^x$ on $x = 0$ to $x = 1$

176. $y = \frac{x^3}{3} + \frac{1}{4x}$ from $x = 1$ to $x = 3$

177. $y = \frac{x^4}{4} + \frac{1}{8x^2}$ from $x = 1$ to $x = 2$

178. $y = \frac{2x^{3/2}}{3} - \frac{x^{1/2}}{2}$ from $x = 1$ to $x = 4$

179. $y = \frac{1}{27}(9x^2 + 6)^{3/2}$ from $x = 0$ to $x = 2$

180. **[T]** $y = \sin x$ on $x = 0$ to $x = \pi$

For the following exercises, find the lengths of the functions of $y$ over the given interval. If you cannot evaluate the integral exactly, use technology to approximate it.

181. $y = \frac{5 - 3x}{4}$ from $y = 0$ to $y = 4$

182. $x = \frac{1}{2}(e^y + e^{-y})$ from $y = -1$ to $y = 1$

183. $x = 5y^{3/2}$ from $y = 0$ to $y = 1$

184. **[T]** $x = y^2$ from $y = 0$ to $y = 1$

185. $x = \sqrt{y}$ from $y = 0$ to $y = 1$

186. $x = \frac{2}{3}(y^2 + 1)^{3/2}$ from $y = 1$ to $y = 3$

187. **[T]** $x = \tan y$ from $y = 0$ to $y = \frac{3}{4}$

188. **[T]** $x = \cos^2 y$ from $y = -\frac{\pi}{2}$ to $y = \frac{\pi}{2}$

189. **[T]** $x = 4^y$ from $y = 0$ to $y = 2$

190. **[T]** $x = \ln(y)$ on $y = \frac{1}{e}$ to $y = e$

For the following exercises, find the surface area of the volume generated when the following curves revolve around the $x$-axis. If you cannot evaluate the integral exactly, use your calculator to approximate it.

191. $y = \sqrt{x}$ from $x = 2$ to $x = 6$

192. $y = x^3$ from $x = 0$ to $x = 1$

193. $y = 7x$ from $x = -1$ to $x = 1$

194. **[T]** $y = \frac{1}{x^2}$ from $x = 1$ to $x = 3$

195. $y = \sqrt{4 - x^2}$ from $x = 0$ to $x = 2$

196. $y = \sqrt{4 - x^2}$ from $x = -1$ to $x = 1$

197. $y = 5x$ from $x = 1$ to $x = 5$

198. **[T]** $y = \tan x$ from $x = -\frac{\pi}{4}$ to $x = \frac{\pi}{4}$

For the following exercises, find the surface area of the volume generated when the following curves revolve around the $y$-axis. If you cannot evaluate the integral exactly, use your calculator to approximate it.

199. $y = x^2$ from $x = 0$ to $x = 2$

200. $y = \frac{1}{2}x^2 + \frac{1}{2}$ from $x = 0$ to $x = 1$

201. $y = x + 1$ from $x = 0$ to $x = 3$

202. **[T]** $y = \frac{1}{x}$ from $x = \frac{1}{2}$ to $x = 1$

203. $y = \sqrt[3]{x}$ from $x = 1$ to $x = 27$

204. **[T]** $y = 3x^4$ from $x = 0$ to $x = 1$

205. **[T]** $y = \frac{1}{\sqrt{x}}$ from $x = 1$ to $x = 3$

206. **[T]** $y = \cos x$ from $x = 0$ to $x = \frac{\pi}{2}$

207. The base of a lamp is constructed by revolving a quarter circle $y = \sqrt{2x - x^2}$ around the $y$-axis from $x = 1$ to $x = 2$, as seen here. Create an integral for the surface area of this curve and compute it.

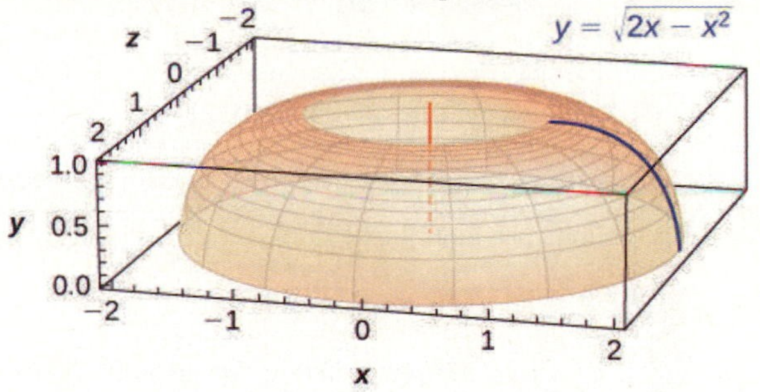


208. A light bulb is a sphere with radius $1/2$ in. with the bottom sliced off to fit exactly onto a cylinder of radius $1/4$ in. and length $1/3$ in., as seen here. The sphere is cut off at the bottom to fit exactly onto the cylinder, so the radius of the cut is $1/4$ in. Find the surface area (not including the top or bottom of the cylinder).

209. **[T]** A lampshade is constructed by rotating $y = 1/x$ around the $x$-axis from $y = 1$ to $y = 2$, as seen here. Determine how much material you would need to construct this lampshade—that is, the surface area—accurate to four decimal places.

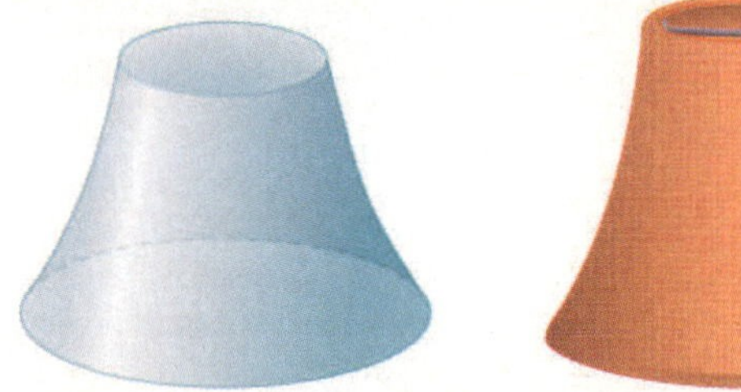

210. **[T]** An anchor drags behind a boat according to the function $y = 24e^{-x/2} - 24$, where $y$ represents the depth beneath the boat and $x$ is the horizontal distance of the anchor from the back of the boat. If the anchor is 23 ft below the boat, how much rope do you have to pull to reach the anchor? Round your answer to three decimal places.

211. **[T]** You are building a bridge that will span 10 ft. You intend to add decorative rope in the shape of $y = 5|\sin((x\pi)/5)|$, where $x$ is the distance in feet from one end of the bridge. Find out how much rope you need to buy, rounded to the nearest foot.

For the following exercises, find the exact arc length for the following problems over the given interval.

212. $y = \ln(\sin x)$ from $x = \pi/4$ to $x = (3\pi)/4$. (*Hint:* Recall trigonometric identities.)

213. Draw graphs of $y = x^2$, $y = x^6$, and $y = x^{10}$. For $y = x^n$, as $n$ increases, formulate a prediction on the arc length from $(0, 0)$ to $(1, 1)$. Now, compute the lengths of these three functions and determine whether your prediction is correct.

214. Compare the lengths of the parabola $x = y^2$ and the line $x = by$ from $(0, 0)$ to $\left(b^2, b\right)$ as $b$ increases. What do you notice?

215. Solve for the length of $x = y^2$ from $(0, 0)$ to $(1, 1)$. Show that $x = (1/2)y^2$ from $(0, 0)$ to $(2, 2)$ is twice as long. Graph both functions and explain why this is so.

216. **[T]** Which is longer between $(1, 1)$ and $(2, 1/2)$: the hyperbola $y = 1/x$ or the graph of $x + 2y = 3$?

217. Explain why the surface area is infinite when $y = 1/x$ is rotated around the $x$-axis for $1 \le x < \infty$, but the volume is finite.

# 2.5 | Physical Applications

## Learning Objectives

**2.5.1** Determine the mass of a one-dimensional object from its linear density function.
**2.5.2** Determine the mass of a two-dimensional circular object from its radial density function.
**2.5.3** Calculate the work done by a variable force acting along a line.
**2.5.4** Calculate the work done in pumping a liquid from one height to another.
**2.5.5** Find the hydrostatic force against a submerged vertical plate.

In this section, we examine some physical applications of integration. Let's begin with a look at calculating mass from a density function. We then turn our attention to work, and close the section with a study of hydrostatic force.

## Mass and Density

We can use integration to develop a formula for calculating mass based on a density function. First we consider a thin rod or wire. Orient the rod so it aligns with the $x$-axis, with the left end of the rod at $x = a$ and the right end of the rod at $x = b$ (**Figure 2.48**). Note that although we depict the rod with some thickness in the figures, for mathematical purposes we assume the rod is thin enough to be treated as a one-dimensional object.

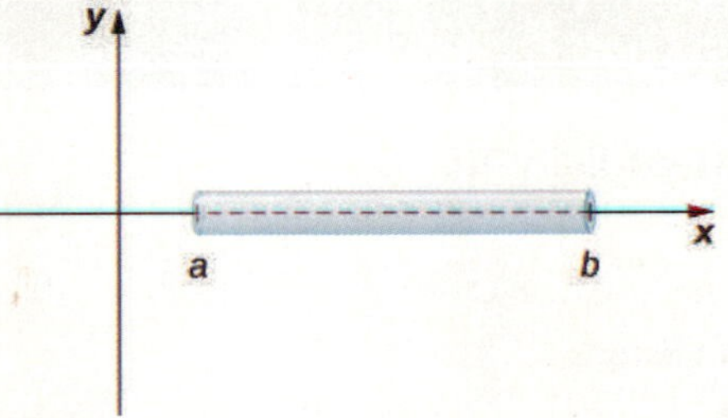


**Figure 2.48** We can calculate the mass of a thin rod oriented along the $x$-axis by integrating its density function.

If the rod has constant density $\rho,$ given in terms of mass per unit length, then the mass of the rod is just the product of the density and the length of the rod: $(b - a)\rho.$ If the density of the rod is not constant, however, the problem becomes a little more challenging. When the density of the rod varies from point to point, we use a linear **density function**, $\rho(x),$ to denote the density of the rod at any point, $x.$ Let $\rho(x)$ be an integrable linear density function. Now, for $i = 0, 1, 2,\ldots, n$ let $P = \{x_i\}$ be a regular partition of the interval $[a, b],$ and for $i = 1, 2,\ldots, n$ choose an arbitrary point $x_i^* \in [x_{i-1}, x_i].$ **Figure 2.49** shows a representative segment of the rod.

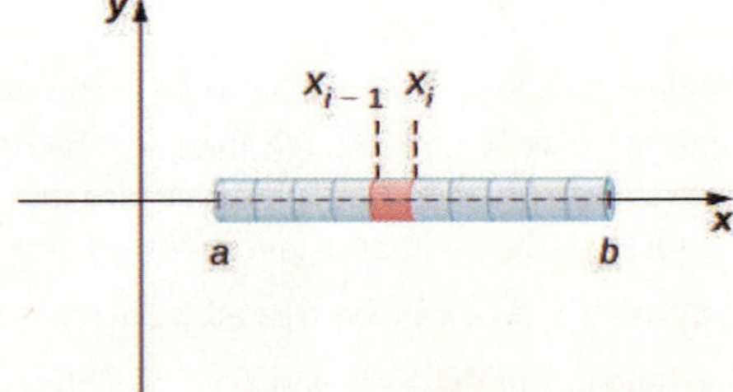


**Figure 2.49** A representative segment of the rod.

The mass $m_i$ of the segment of the rod from $x_{i-1}$ to $x_i$ is approximated by

$$m_i \approx \rho(x_i^*)(x_i - x_{i-1}) = \rho(x_i^*)\Delta x.$$

Adding the masses of all the segments gives us an approximation for the mass of the entire rod:

$$m = \sum_{i=1}^{n} m_i \approx \sum_{i=1}^{n} \rho(x_i^*)\Delta x.$$

This is a Riemann sum. Taking the limit as $n \to \infty$, we get an expression for the exact mass of the rod:

$$m = \lim_{n \to \infty} \sum_{i=1}^{n} \rho(x_i^*)\Delta x = \int_a^b \rho(x)dx.$$

We state this result in the following theorem.

### Theorem 2.7: Mass–Density Formula of a One-Dimensional Object

Given a thin rod oriented along the $x$-axis over the interval $[a, b]$, let $\rho(x)$ denote a linear density function giving the density of the rod at a point $x$ in the interval. Then the mass of the rod is given by

$$m = \int_a^b \rho(x)dx. \tag{2.10}$$

We apply this theorem in the next example.

## Example 2.23

### Calculating Mass from Linear Density

Consider a thin rod oriented on the $x$-axis over the interval $[\pi/2, \pi]$. If the density of the rod is given by $\rho(x) = \sin x$, what is the mass of the rod?

#### Solution

Applying **Equation 2.10** directly, we have

$$m = \int_a^b \rho(x)dx = \int_{\pi/2}^{\pi} \sin x\, dx = -\cos x|_{\pi/2}^{\pi} = 1.$$

**2.23** Consider a thin rod oriented on the $x$-axis over the interval $[1, 3]$. If the density of the rod is given by $\rho(x) = 2x^2 + 3$, what is the mass of the rod?

We now extend this concept to find the mass of a two-dimensional disk of radius $r$. As with the rod we looked at in the one-dimensional case, here we assume the disk is thin enough that, for mathematical purposes, we can treat it as a two-dimensional object. We assume the density is given in terms of mass per unit area (called *area density*), and further assume the density varies only along the disk's radius (called *radial density*). We orient the disk in the $xy$-plane, with the center at the origin. Then, the density of the disk can be treated as a function of $x$, denoted $\rho(x)$. We assume $\rho(x)$ is integrable. Because density is a function of $x$, we partition the interval from $[0, r]$ along the $x$-axis. For $i = 0, 1, 2,\ldots, n$, let $P = \{x_i\}$ be a regular partition of the interval $[0, r]$, and for $i = 1, 2,\ldots, n$, choose an arbitrary point $x_i^* \in [x_{i-1}, x_i]$. Now, use the partition to break up the disk into thin (two-dimensional) washers. A disk and a representative washer are depicted in the following figure.

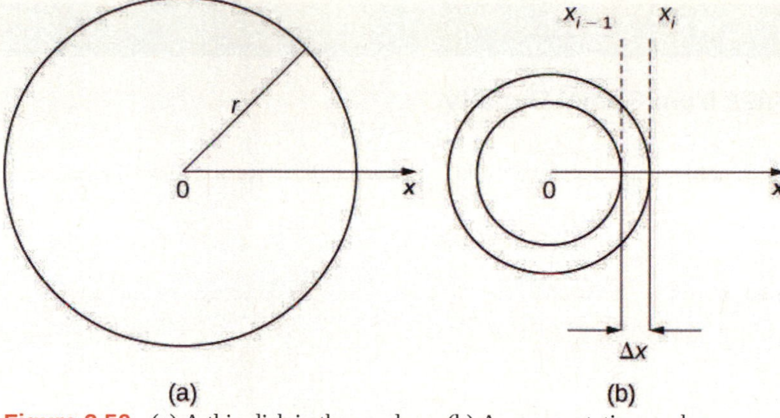


**Figure 2.50** (a) A thin disk in the *xy*-plane. (b) A representative washer.

We now approximate the density and area of the washer to calculate an approximate mass, $m_i$. Note that the area of the washer is given by

$$\begin{aligned} A_i &= \pi(x_i)^2 - \pi(x_{i-1})^2 \\ &= \pi\left[x_i^2 - x_{i-1}^2\right] \\ &= \pi(x_i + x_{i-1})(x_i - x_{i-1}) \\ &= \pi(x_i + x_{i-1})\Delta x. \end{aligned}$$

You may recall that we had an expression similar to this when we were computing volumes by shells. As we did there, we use $x_i^* \approx (x_i + x_{i-1})/2$ to approximate the average radius of the washer. We obtain

$$A_i = \pi(x_i + x_{i-1})\Delta x \approx 2\pi x_i^* \Delta x.$$

Using $\rho(x_i^*)$ to approximate the density of the washer, we approximate the mass of the washer by

$$m_i \approx 2\pi x_i^* \rho(x_i^*)\Delta x.$$

Adding up the masses of the washers, we see the mass $m$ of the entire disk is approximated by

$$m = \sum_{i=1}^{n} m_i \approx \sum_{i=1}^{n} 2\pi x_i^* \rho(x_i^*)\Delta x.$$

We again recognize this as a Riemann sum, and take the limit as $n \to \infty$. This gives us

$$m = \lim_{n \to \infty} \sum_{i=1}^{n} 2\pi x_i^* \rho(x_i^*)\Delta x = \int_0^r 2\pi x \rho(x) dx.$$

We summarize these findings in the following theorem.

### Theorem 2.8: Mass–Density Formula of a Circular Object

Let $\rho(x)$ be an integrable function representing the radial density of a disk of radius $r$. Then the mass of the disk is given by

$$m = \int_0^r 2\pi x \rho(x) dx. \tag{2.11}$$

## Example 2.24

### Calculating Mass from Radial Density

Let $\rho(x) = \sqrt{x}$ represent the radial density of a disk. Calculate the mass of a disk of radius 4.

#### Solution

Applying the formula, we find

$$\begin{aligned} m &= \int_0^r 2\pi x \rho(x) dx \\ &= \int_0^4 2\pi x \sqrt{x} dx = 2\pi \int_0^4 x^{3/2} dx \\ &= 2\pi \frac{2}{5} x^{5/2} \Big|_0^4 = \frac{4\pi}{5}[32] = \frac{128\pi}{5}. \end{aligned}$$

**2.24** Let $\rho(x) = 3x + 2$ represent the radial density of a disk. Calculate the mass of a disk of radius 2.

## Work Done by a Force

We now consider work. In physics, work is related to force, which is often intuitively defined as a push or pull on an object. When a force moves an object, we say the force does work on the object. In other words, work can be thought of as the amount of energy it takes to move an object. According to physics, when we have a constant force, work can be expressed as the product of force and distance.

In the English system, the unit of force is the pound and the unit of distance is the foot, so work is given in foot-pounds. In the metric system, kilograms and meters are used. One newton is the force needed to accelerate $1$ kilogram of mass at the rate of $1$ m/sec$^2$. Thus, the most common unit of work is the newton-meter. This same unit is also called the *joule*. Both are defined as kilograms times meters squared over seconds squared $\left(\text{kg} \cdot \text{m}^2/\text{s}^2\right)$.

When we have a constant force, things are pretty easy. It is rare, however, for a force to be constant. The work done to compress (or elongate) a spring, for example, varies depending on how far the spring has already been compressed (or stretched). We look at springs in more detail later in this section.

Suppose we have a variable force $F(x)$ that moves an object in a positive direction along the *x*-axis from point $a$ to point $b$. To calculate the work done, we partition the interval $[a, b]$ and estimate the work done over each subinterval. So, for $i = 0, 1, 2, \ldots, n,$ let $P = \{x_i\}$ be a regular partition of the interval $[a, b],$ and for $i = 1, 2, \ldots, n,$ choose an arbitrary point $x_i^* \in [x_{i-1}, x_i]$. To calculate the work done to move an object from point $x_{i-1}$ to point $x_i,$ we assume the force is roughly constant over the interval, and use $F(x_i^*)$ to approximate the force. The work done over the interval $[x_{i-1}, x_i],$ then, is given by

$$W_i \approx F(x_i^*)(x_i - x_{i-1}) = F(x_i^*)\Delta x.$$

Therefore, the work done over the interval $[a, b]$ is approximately

$$W = \sum_{i=1}^{n} W_i \approx \sum_{i=1}^{n} F(x_i^*)\Delta x.$$

Taking the limit of this expression as $n \to \infty$ gives us the exact value for work:

$$W = \lim_{n \to \infty} \sum_{i=1}^{n} F(x_i^*)\Delta x = \int_a^b F(x)dx.$$

Thus, we can define work as follows.

**Definition**

If a variable force $F(x)$ moves an object in a positive direction along the $x$-axis from point $a$ to point $b$, then the **work** done on the object is

$$W = \int_a^b F(x)dx. \quad (2.12)$$

Note that if $F$ is constant, the integral evaluates to $F \cdot (b - a) = F \cdot d$, which is the formula we stated at the beginning of this section.

Now let's look at the specific example of the work done to compress or elongate a spring. Consider a block attached to a horizontal spring. The block moves back and forth as the spring stretches and compresses. Although in the real world we would have to account for the force of friction between the block and the surface on which it is resting, we ignore friction here and assume the block is resting on a frictionless surface. When the spring is at its natural length (at rest), the system is said to be at equilibrium. In this state, the spring is neither elongated nor compressed, and in this equilibrium position the block does not move until some force is introduced. We orient the system such that $x = 0$ corresponds to the equilibrium position (see the following figure).

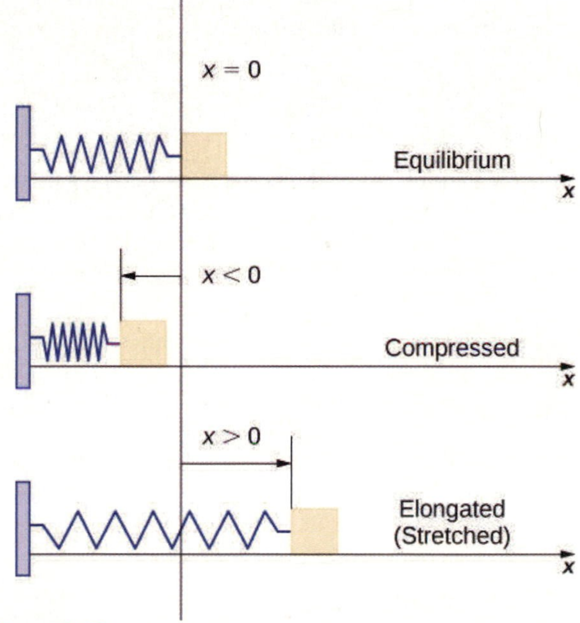


**Figure 2.51** A block attached to a horizontal spring at equilibrium, compressed, and elongated.

According to **Hooke's law**, the force required to compress or stretch a spring from an equilibrium position is given by $F(x) = kx$, for some constant $k$. The value of $k$ depends on the physical characteristics of the spring. The constant $k$ is called the *spring constant* and is always positive. We can use this information to calculate the work done to compress or elongate a spring, as shown in the following example.

## Example 2.25

### The Work Required to Stretch or Compress a Spring

Suppose it takes a force of $10$ N (in the negative direction) to compress a spring $0.2$ m from the equilibrium position. How much work is done to stretch the spring $0.5$ m from the equilibrium position?

#### Solution

First find the spring constant, $k$. When $x = -0.2,$ we know $F(x) = -10,$ so

$$\begin{aligned} F(x) &= kx \\ -10 &= k(-0.2) \\ k &= 50 \end{aligned}$$

and $F(x) = 50x$. Then, to calculate work, we integrate the force function, obtaining

$$W = \int_a^b F(x)dx = \int_0^{0.5} 50x\,dx = 25x^2\Big|_0^{0.5} = 6.25.$$

The work done to stretch the spring is $6.25$ J.

**2.25** Suppose it takes a force of $8$ lb to stretch a spring $6$ in. from the equilibrium position. How much work is done to stretch the spring $1$ ft from the equilibrium position?

## Work Done in Pumping

Consider the work done to pump water (or some other liquid) out of a tank. Pumping problems are a little more complicated than spring problems because many of the calculations depend on the shape and size of the tank. In addition, instead of being concerned about the work done to move a single mass, we are looking at the work done to move a volume of water, and it takes more work to move the water from the bottom of the tank than it does to move the water from the top of the tank.

We examine the process in the context of a cylindrical tank, then look at a couple of examples using tanks of different shapes. Assume a cylindrical tank of radius $4$ m and height $10$ m is filled to a depth of 8 m. How much work does it take to pump all the water over the top edge of the tank?

The first thing we need to do is define a frame of reference. We let $x$ represent the vertical distance below the top of the tank. That is, we orient the $x$-axis vertically, with the origin at the top of the tank and the downward direction being positive (see the following figure).

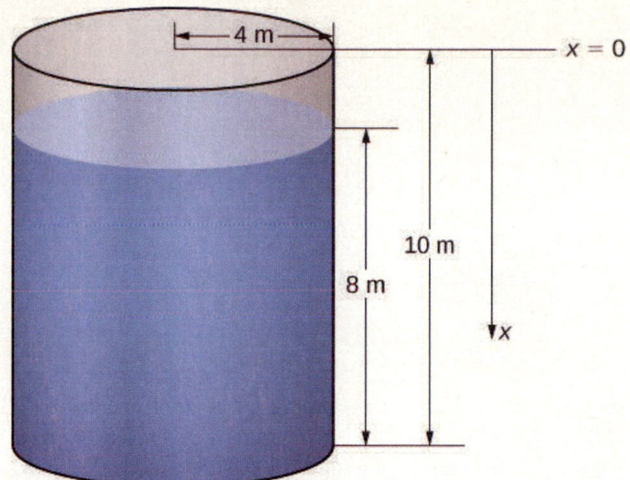


**Figure 2.52** How much work is needed to empty a tank partially filled with water?

Using this coordinate system, the water extends from $x = 2$ to $x = 10$. Therefore, we partition the interval $[2, 10]$ and look at the work required to lift each individual "layer" of water. So, for $i = 0, 1, 2,\ldots, n,$ let $P = \{x_i\}$ be a regular partition of the interval $[2, 10],$ and for $i = 1, 2,\ldots, n,$ choose an arbitrary point $x_i^* \in [x_{i-1}, x_i].$ **Figure 2.53** shows a representative layer.

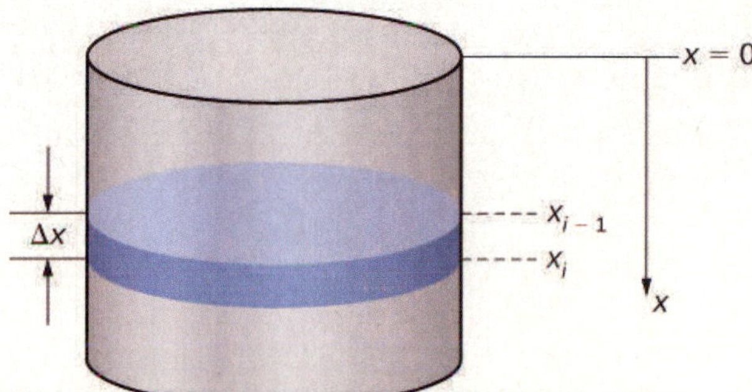


**Figure 2.53** A representative layer of water.

In pumping problems, the force required to lift the water to the top of the tank is the force required to overcome gravity, so it is equal to the weight of the water. Given that the weight-density of water is $9800 \text{ N/m}^3$, or $62.4 \text{ lb/ft}^3$, calculating the volume of each layer gives us the weight. In this case, we have

$$V = \pi(4)^2 \Delta x = 16\pi \Delta x.$$

Then, the force needed to lift each layer is

$$F = 9800 \cdot 16\pi \Delta x = 156{,}800\pi \Delta x.$$

Note that this step becomes a little more difficult if we have a noncylindrical tank. We look at a noncylindrical tank in the next example.

We also need to know the distance the water must be lifted. Based on our choice of coordinate systems, we can use $x_i^*$ as an approximation of the distance the layer must be lifted. Then the work to lift the $i$th layer of water $W_i$ is approximately

$$W_i \approx 156{,}800\pi x_i^* \Delta x.$$

Adding the work for each layer, we see the approximate work to empty the tank is given by

$$W = \sum_{i=1}^{n} W_i \approx \sum_{i=1}^{n} 156{,}800\pi x_i^* \ \Delta x.$$

This is a Riemann sum, so taking the limit as $n \to \infty$, we get

$$\begin{aligned} W &= \lim_{n \to \infty} \sum_{i=1}^{n} 156{,}800\pi x_i^* \ \Delta x \\ &= 156{,}800\pi \int_2^{10} x dx \\ &= 156{,}800\pi \left[\frac{x^2}{2}\right]\Bigg|_2^{10} = 7{,}526{,}400\pi \approx 23{,}644{,}883. \end{aligned}$$

The work required to empty the tank is approximately 23,650,000 J.

For pumping problems, the calculations vary depending on the shape of the tank or container. The following problem-solving strategy lays out a step-by-step process for solving pumping problems.

### Problem-Solving Strategy: Solving Pumping Problems

1. Sketch a picture of the tank and select an appropriate frame of reference.
2. Calculate the volume of a representative layer of water.
3. Multiply the volume by the weight-density of water to get the force.
4. Calculate the distance the layer of water must be lifted.
5. Multiply the force and distance to get an estimate of the work needed to lift the layer of water.
6. Sum the work required to lift all the layers. This expression is an estimate of the work required to pump out the desired amount of water, and it is in the form of a Riemann sum.
7. Take the limit as $n \to \infty$ and evaluate the resulting integral to get the exact work required to pump out the desired amount of water.

We now apply this problem-solving strategy in an example with a noncylindrical tank.

## Example 2.26

### A Pumping Problem with a Noncylindrical Tank

Assume a tank in the shape of an inverted cone, with height $12$ ft and base radius $4$ ft. The tank is full to start with, and water is pumped over the upper edge of the tank until the height of the water remaining in the tank is $4$ ft. How much work is required to pump out that amount of water?

#### Solution

The tank is depicted in **Figure 2.54**. As we did in the example with the cylindrical tank, we orient the $x$-axis vertically, with the origin at the top of the tank and the downward direction being positive (step 1).

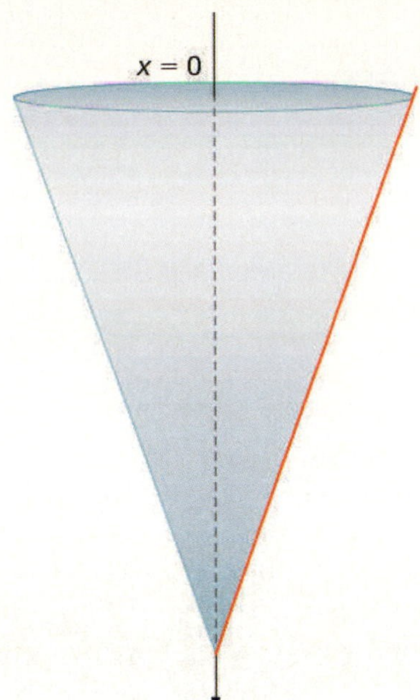


**Figure 2.54** A water tank in the shape of an inverted cone.

The tank starts out full and ends with 4 ft of water left, so, based on our chosen frame of reference, we need to partition the interval $[0, 8]$. Then, for $i = 0, 1, 2,\ldots, n,$ let $P = \{x_i\}$ be a regular partition of the interval $[0, 8],$ and for $i = 1, 2,\ldots, n,$ choose an arbitrary point $x_i^* \in [x_{i-1}, x_i]$. We can approximate the volume of a layer by using a disk, then use similar triangles to find the radius of the disk (see the following figure).

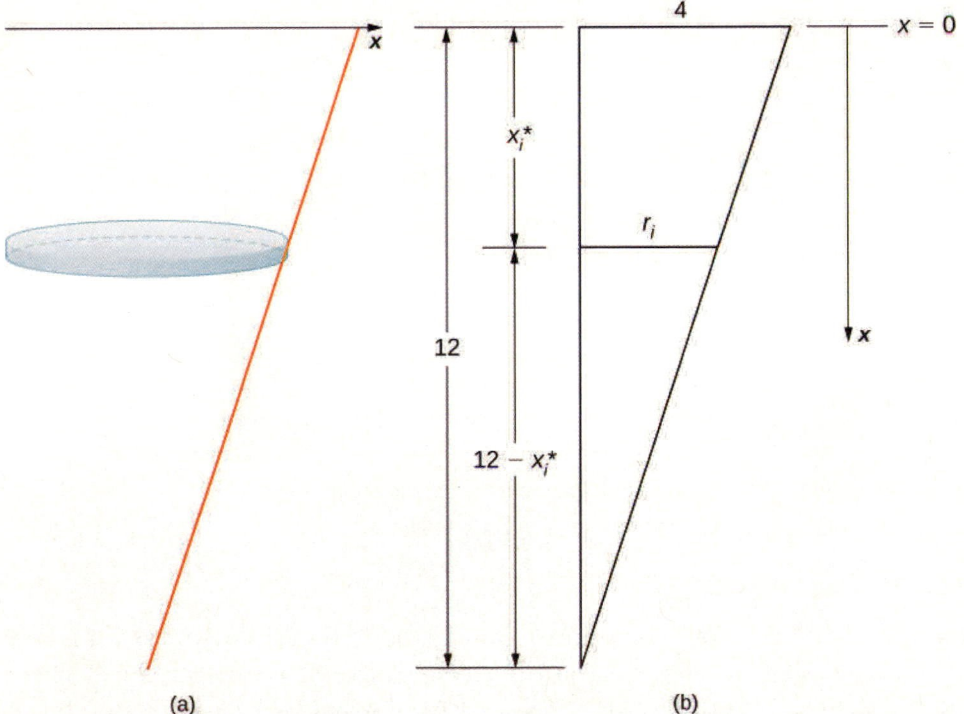


**Figure 2.55** Using similar triangles to express the radius of a disk of water.

From properties of similar triangles, we have

$$\begin{aligned} \frac{r_i}{12 - x_i^*} &= \frac{4}{12} = \frac{1}{3} \\ 3r_i &= 12 - x_i^* \\ r_i &= \frac{12 - x_i^*}{3} \\ &= 4 - \frac{x_i^*}{3}. \end{aligned}$$

Then the volume of the disk is

$$V_i = \pi\left(4 - \frac{x_i^*}{3}\right)^2 \Delta x \text{ (step 2).}$$

The weight-density of water is $62.4 \text{ lb/ft}^3$, so the force needed to lift each layer is approximately

$$F_i \approx 62.4\pi\left(4 - \frac{x_i^*}{3}\right)^2 \Delta x \text{ (step 3).}$$

Based on the diagram, the distance the water must be lifted is approximately $x_i^*$ feet (step 4), so the approximate work needed to lift the layer is

$$W_i \approx 62.4\pi x_i^* \left(4 - \frac{x_i^*}{3}\right)^2 \Delta x \text{ (step 5).}$$

Summing the work required to lift all the layers, we get an approximate value of the total work:

$$W = \sum_{i=1}^{n} W_i \approx \sum_{i=1}^{n} 62.4\pi x_i^* \left(4 - \frac{x_i^*}{3}\right)^2 \Delta x \text{ (step 6).}$$

Taking the limit as $n \to \infty$, we obtain

$$\begin{aligned} W &= \lim_{n \to \infty} \sum_{i=1}^{n} 62.4\pi x_i^* \left(4 - \frac{x_i^*}{3}\right)^2 \Delta x \\ &= \int_0^8 62.4\pi x\left(4 - \frac{x}{3}\right)^2 dx \\ &= 62.4\pi \int_0^8 x\left(16 - \frac{8x}{3} + \frac{x^2}{9}\right) dx = 62.4\pi \int_0^8 \left(16x - \frac{8x^2}{3} + \frac{x^3}{9}\right) dx \\ &= 62.4\pi\left[8x^2 - \frac{8x^3}{9} + \frac{x^4}{36}\right]\Bigg|_0^8 = 10{,}649.6\pi \approx 33{,}456.7. \end{aligned}$$

It takes approximately 33,450 ft-lb of work to empty the tank to the desired level.

**2.26** A tank is in the shape of an inverted cone, with height 10 ft and base radius 6 ft. The tank is filled to a depth of 8 ft to start with, and water is pumped over the upper edge of the tank until 3 ft of water remain in the tank. How much work is required to pump out that amount of water?

## Hydrostatic Force and Pressure

In this last section, we look at the force and pressure exerted on an object submerged in a liquid. In the English system, force is measured in pounds. In the metric system, it is measured in newtons. Pressure is force per unit area, so in the English system we have pounds per square foot (or, perhaps more commonly, pounds per square inch, denoted psi). In the metric system we have newtons per square meter, also called *pascals*.

Let's begin with the simple case of a plate of area $A$ submerged horizontally in water at a depth *s* (**Figure 2.56**). Then, the force exerted on the plate is simply the weight of the water above it, which is given by $F = \rho As,$ where $\rho$ is the weight density of water (weight per unit volume). To find the **hydrostatic pressure**—that is, the pressure exerted by water on a submerged object—we divide the force by the area. So the pressure is $p = F/A = \rho s.$

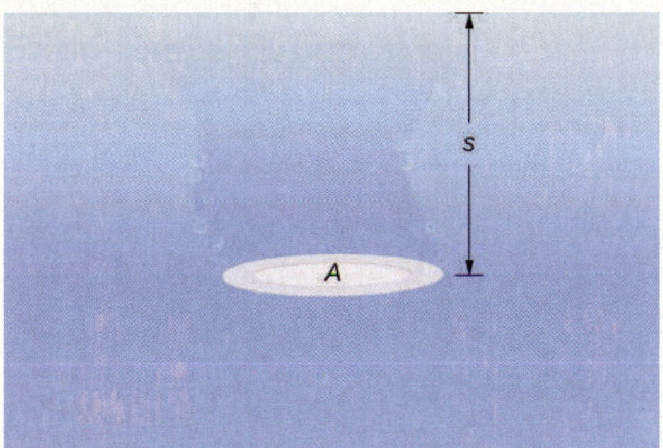


**Figure 2.56** A plate submerged horizontally in water.

By Pascal's principle, the pressure at a given depth is the same in all directions, so it does not matter if the plate is submerged horizontally or vertically. So, as long as we know the depth, we know the pressure. We can apply Pascal's principle to find the force exerted on surfaces, such as dams, that are oriented vertically. We cannot apply the formula $F = \rho As$ directly, because the depth varies from point to point on a vertically oriented surface. So, as we have done many times before, we form a partition, a Riemann sum, and, ultimately, a definite integral to calculate the force.

Suppose a thin plate is submerged in water. We choose our frame of reference such that the *x*-axis is oriented vertically, with the downward direction being positive, and point $x = 0$ corresponding to a logical reference point. Let $s(x)$ denote the depth at point *x*. Note we often let $x = 0$ correspond to the surface of the water. In this case, depth at any point is simply given by $s(x) = x.$ However, in some cases we may want to select a different reference point for $x = 0,$ so we proceed with the development in the more general case. Last, let $w(x)$ denote the width of the plate at the point $x.$

Assume the top edge of the plate is at point $x = a$ and the bottom edge of the plate is at point $x = b.$ Then, for $i = 0, 1, 2,\ldots, n,$ let $P = \{x_i\}$ be a regular partition of the interval $[a, b],$ and for $i = 1, 2,\ldots, n,$ choose an arbitrary point $x_i^* \in [x_{i-1}, x_i].$ The partition divides the plate into several thin, rectangular strips (see the following figure).

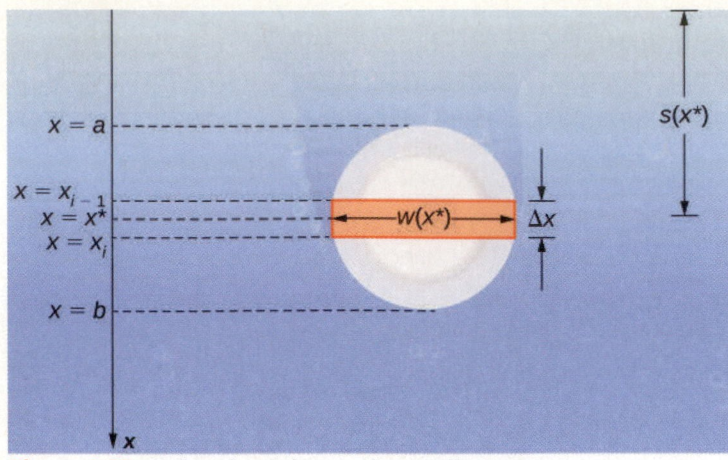


**Figure 2.57** A thin plate submerged vertically in water.

Let's now estimate the force on a representative strip. If the strip is thin enough, we can treat it as if it is at a constant depth, $s(x_i^*)$. We then have

$$F_i = \rho A s = \rho\left[w(x_i^*)\Delta x\right]s(x_i^*).$$

Adding the forces, we get an estimate for the force on the plate:

$$F \approx \sum_{i=1}^{n} F_i = \sum_{i=1}^{n} \rho\left[w(x_i^*)\Delta x\right]s(x_i^*).$$

This is a Riemann sum, so taking the limit gives us the exact force. We obtain

$$F = \lim_{n \to \infty} \sum_{i=1}^{n} \rho\left[w(x_i^*)\Delta x\right]s(x_i^*) = \int_a^b \rho w(x)s(x)dx. \quad (2.13)$$

Evaluating this integral gives us the force on the plate. We summarize this in the following problem-solving strategy.

### Problem-Solving Strategy: Finding Hydrostatic Force

1. Sketch a picture and select an appropriate frame of reference. (Note that if we select a frame of reference other than the one used earlier, we may have to adjust **Equation 2.13** accordingly.)
2. Determine the depth and width functions, $s(x)$ and $w(x)$.
3. Determine the weight-density of whatever liquid with which you are working. The weight-density of water is $62.4 \text{ lb/ft}^3$, or $9800 \text{ N/m}^3$.
4. Use the equation to calculate the total force.

## Example 2.27

### Finding Hydrostatic Force

A water trough 15 ft long has ends shaped like inverted isosceles triangles, with base 8 ft and height 3 ft. Find the force on one end of the trough if the trough is full of water.

#### Solution

Figure 2.58 shows the trough and a more detailed view of one end.

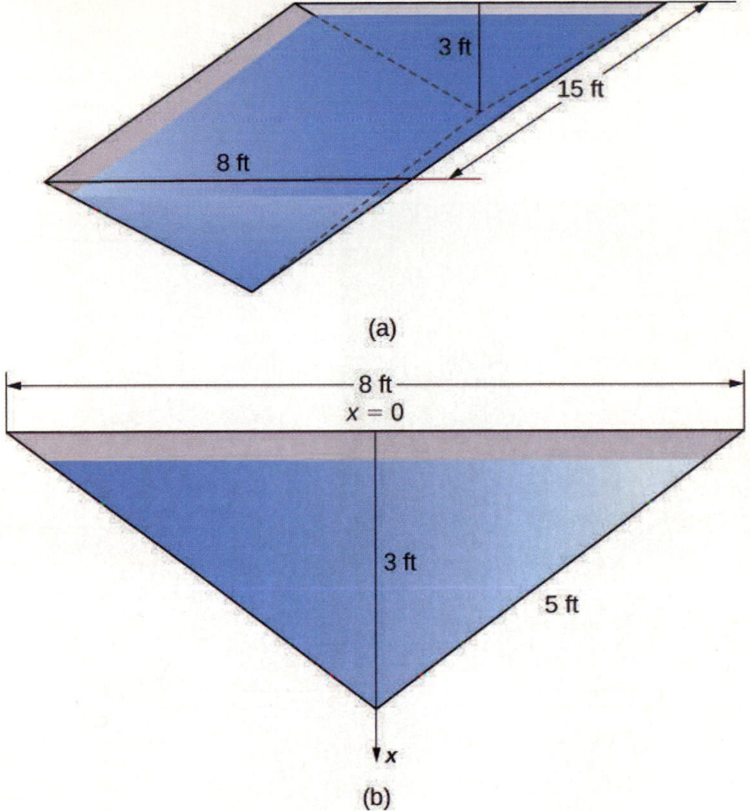


Figure 2.58 (a) A water trough with a triangular cross-section. (b) Dimensions of one end of the water trough.

Select a frame of reference with the $x$-axis oriented vertically and the downward direction being positive. Select the top of the trough as the point corresponding to $x = 0$ (step 1). The depth function, then, is $s(x) = x.$ Using similar triangles, we see that $w(x) = 8 - (8/3)x$ (step 2). Now, the weight density of water is $62.4$ lb/ft$^3$ (step 3), so applying Equation 2.13, we obtain

$$\begin{aligned} F &= \int_a^b \rho w(x)s(x)dx \\ &= \int_0^3 62.4\left(8 - \frac{8}{3}x\right)x\,dx = 62.4\int_0^3 \left(8x - \frac{8}{3}x^2\right)dx \\ &= 62.4\left[4x^2 - \frac{8}{9}x^3\right]\Big|_0^3 = 748.8. \end{aligned}$$

The water exerts a force of 748.8 lb on the end of the trough (step 4).

**2.27** A water trough 12 m long has ends shaped like inverted isosceles triangles, with base 6 m and height 4 m. Find the force on one end of the trough if the trough is full of water.

## Example 2.28

### Chapter Opener: Finding Hydrostatic Force

We now return our attention to the Hoover Dam, mentioned at the beginning of this chapter. The actual dam is arched, rather than flat, but we are going to make some simplifying assumptions to help us with the calculations. Assume the face of the Hoover Dam is shaped like an isosceles trapezoid with lower base $750$ ft, upper base $1250$ ft, and height $750$ ft (see the following figure).

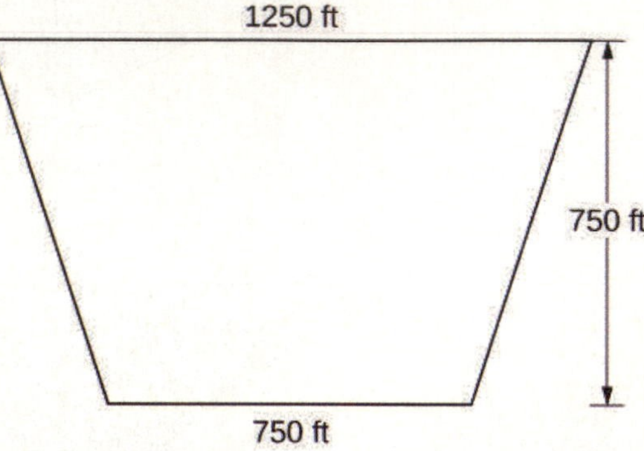


When the reservoir is full, Lake Mead's maximum depth is about 530 ft, and the surface of the lake is about 10 ft below the top of the dam (see the following figure).

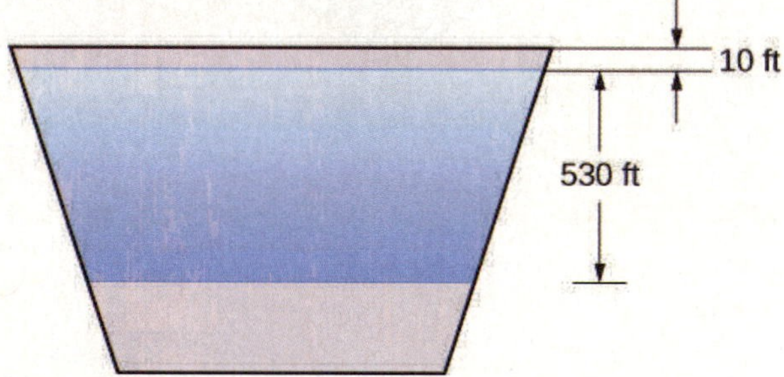


**Figure 2.59** A simplified model of the Hoover Dam with assumed dimensions.

a. Find the force on the face of the dam when the reservoir is full.
b. The southwest United States has been experiencing a drought, and the surface of Lake Mead is about 125 ft below where it would be if the reservoir were full. What is the force on the face of the dam under these circumstances?

### Solution

a. We begin by establishing a frame of reference. As usual, we choose to orient the $x$-axis vertically, with the downward direction being positive. This time, however, we are going to let $x = 0$ represent the top of the dam, rather than the surface of the water. When the reservoir is full, the surface of the water is $10$ ft below the top of the dam, so $s(x) = x - 10$ (see the following figure).

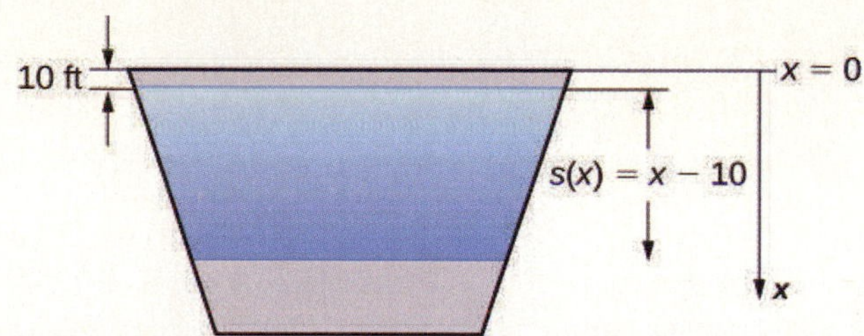


**Figure 2.60** We first choose a frame of reference.

To find the width function, we again turn to similar triangles as shown in the figure below.

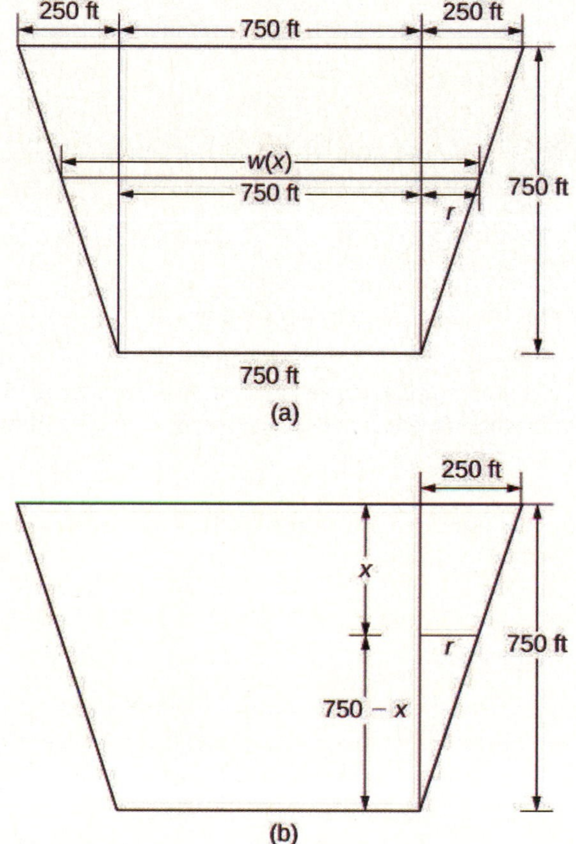


**Figure 2.61** We use similar triangles to determine a function for the width of the dam. (a) Assumed dimensions of the dam; (b) highlighting the similar triangles.

From the figure, we see that $w(x) = 750 + 2r$. Using properties of similar triangles, we get $r = 250 - (1/3)x$. Thus,

$$w(x) = 1250 - \frac{2}{3}x \text{ (step 2).}$$

Using a weight-density of $62.4 \text{ lb/ft}^3$ (step 3) and applying **Equation 2.13**, we get

$$\begin{aligned} F &= \int_a^b \rho w(x)s(x)dx \\ &= \int_{10}^{540} 62.4\left(1250 - \frac{2}{3}x\right)(x - 10)dx = 62.4\int_{10}^{540} -\frac{2}{3}\left[x^2 - 1885x + 18750\right]dx \\ &= -62.4\left(\frac{2}{3}\right)\left[\frac{x^3}{3} - \frac{1885x^2}{2} + 18750x\right]\Bigg|_{10}^{540} \approx 8{,}832{,}245{,}000 \text{ lb} = 4{,}416{,}122.5 \text{ t}. \end{aligned}$$

Note the change from pounds to tons $(2000 \text{ lb} = 1 \text{ ton})$ (step 4). This changes our depth function, $s(x)$, and our limits of integration. We have $s(x) = x - 135.$ The lower limit of integration is $135.$ The upper limit remains $540.$ Evaluating the integral, we get

$$\begin{aligned} F &= \int_a^b \rho w(x)s(x)dx \\ &= \int_{135}^{540} 62.4\left(1250 - \frac{2}{3}x\right)(x - 135)dx \\ &= -62.4\left(\frac{2}{3}\right)\int_{135}^{540} (x - 1875)(x - 135)dx = -62.4\left(\frac{2}{3}\right)\int_{135}^{540} \left(x^2 - 2010x + 253125\right)dx \\ &= -62.4\left(\frac{2}{3}\right)\left[\frac{x^3}{3} - 1005x^2 + 253125x\right]\Bigg|_{135}^{540} \approx 5{,}015{,}230{,}000 \text{ lb} = 2{,}507{,}615 \text{ t}. \end{aligned}$$

**2.28** When the reservoir is at its average level, the surface of the water is about 50 ft below where it would be if the reservoir were full. What is the force on the face of the dam under these circumstances?

To learn more about Hoover Dam, see this **article (http://www.openstaxcollege.org/l/20_HooverDam)** published by the History Channel.

# 2.5 EXERCISES

For the following exercises, find the work done.

218. Find the work done when a constant force $F = 12$ lb moves a chair from $x = 0.9$ to $x = 1.1$ ft.

219. How much work is done when a person lifts a 50 lb box of comics onto a truck that is 3 ft off the ground?

220. What is the work done lifting a 20 kg child from the floor to a height of 2 m? (Note that 1 kg equates to 9.8 N)

221. Find the work done when you push a box along the floor 2 m, when you apply a constant force of $F = 100\,\text{N}$.

222. Compute the work done for a force $F = 12/x^2$ N from $x = 1$ to $x = 2$ m.

223. What is the work done moving a particle from $x = 0$ to $x = 1$ m if the force acting on it is $F = 3x^2$ N?

For the following exercises, find the mass of the one-dimensional object.

224. A wire that is 2 ft long (starting at $x = 0$) and has a density function of $\rho(x) = x^2 + 2x$ lb/ft

225. A car antenna that is 3 ft long (starting at $x = 0$) and has a density function of $\rho(x) = 3x + 2$ lb/ft

226. A metal rod that is 8 in. long (starting at $x = 0$) and has a density function of $\rho(x) = e^{1/2x}$ lb/in.

227. A pencil that is 4 in. long (starting at $x = 2$) and has a density function of $\rho(x) = 5/x$ oz/in.

228. A ruler that is 12 in. long (starting at $x = 5$) and has a density function of $\rho(x) = \ln(x) + (1/2)x^2$ oz/in.

For the following exercises, find the mass of the two-dimensional object that is centered at the origin.

229. An oversized hockey puck of radius 2 in. with density function $\rho(x) = x^3 - 2x + 5$

230. A frisbee of radius 6 in. with density function $\rho(x) = e^{-x}$

231. A plate of radius 10 in. with density function $\rho(x) = 1 + \cos(\pi x)$

232. A jar lid of radius 3 in. with density function $\rho(x) = \ln(x + 1)$

233. A disk of radius 5 cm with density function $\rho(x) = \sqrt{3x}$

234. A 12 -in. spring is stretched to 15 in. by a force of 75 lb. What is the spring constant?

235. A spring has a natural length of 10 cm. It takes 2 J to stretch the spring to 15 cm. How much work would it take to stretch the spring from 15 cm to 20 cm?

236. A 1 -m spring requires 10 J to stretch the spring to 1.1 m. How much work would it take to stretch the spring from 1 m to 1.2 m?

237. A spring requires 5 J to stretch the spring from 8 cm to 12 cm, and an additional 4 J to stretch the spring from 12 cm to 14 cm. What is the natural length of the spring?

238. A shock absorber is compressed 1 in. by a weight of 1 t. What is the spring constant?

239. A force of $F = 20x - x^3$ N stretches a nonlinear spring by $x$ meters. What work is required to stretch the spring from $x = 0$ to $x = 2$ m?

240. Find the work done by winding up a hanging cable of length 100 ft and weight-density 5 lb/ft.

241. For the cable in the preceding exercise, how much work is done to lift the cable 50 ft?

242. For the cable in the preceding exercise, how much additional work is done by hanging a 200 lb weight at the end of the cable?

243. **[T]** A pyramid of height 500 ft has a square base 800 ft by 800 ft. Find the area $A$ at height $h$. If the rock used to build the pyramid weighs approximately $w = 100\,\text{lb/ft}^3$, how much work did it take to lift all the rock?

244. **[T]** For the pyramid in the preceding exercise, assume there were $1000$ workers each working $10$ hours a day, $5$ days a week, $50$ weeks a year. If the workers, on average, lifted 10 100 lb rocks $2$ ft/hr, how long did it take to build the pyramid?

245. **[T]** The force of gravity on a mass $m$ is $F = -\left((GMm)/x^2\right)$ newtons. For a rocket of mass $m = 1000\text{ kg},$ compute the work to lift the rocket from $x = 6400$ to $x = 6500$ km. (*Note*: $G = 6 \times 10^{-17}\text{ N m}^2/\text{kg}^2$ and $M = 6 \times 10^{24}$ kg.)

246. **[T]** For the rocket in the preceding exercise, find the work to lift the rocket from $x = 6400$ to $x = \infty$.

247. **[T]** A rectangular dam is $40$ ft high and $60$ ft wide. Compute the total force $F$ on the dam when

a. the surface of the water is at the top of the dam and
b. the surface of the water is halfway down the dam.

248. **[T]** Find the work required to pump all the water out of a cylinder that has a circular base of radius $5$ ft and height $200$ ft. Use the fact that the density of water is $62$ lb/ft$^3$.

249. **[T]** Find the work required to pump all the water out of the cylinder in the preceding exercise if the cylinder is only half full.

250. **[T]** How much work is required to pump out a swimming pool if the area of the base is $800$ ft$^2$, the water is $4$ ft deep, and the top is $1$ ft above the water level? Assume that the density of water is $62$ lb/ft$^3$.

251. A cylinder of depth $H$ and cross-sectional area $A$ stands full of water at density $\rho$. Compute the work to pump all the water to the top.

252. For the cylinder in the preceding exercise, compute the work to pump all the water to the top if the cylinder is only half full.

253. A cone-shaped tank has a cross-sectional area that increases with its depth: $A = \left(\pi r^2 h^2\right)/H^3$. Show that the work to empty it is half the work for a cylinder with the same height and base.

# 2.6 | Moments and Centers of Mass

## Learning Objectives

2.6.1 Find the center of mass of objects distributed along a line.
2.6.2 Locate the center of mass of a thin plate.
2.6.3 Use symmetry to help locate the centroid of a thin plate.
2.6.4 Apply the theorem of Pappus for volume.

In this section, we consider centers of mass (also called *centroids*, under certain conditions) and moments. The basic idea of the center of mass is the notion of a balancing point. Many of us have seen performers who spin plates on the ends of sticks. The performers try to keep several of them spinning without allowing any of them to drop. If we look at a single plate (without spinning it), there is a sweet spot on the plate where it balances perfectly on the stick. If we put the stick anywhere other than that sweet spot, the plate does not balance and it falls to the ground. (That is why performers spin the plates; the spin helps keep the plates from falling even if the stick is not exactly in the right place.) Mathematically, that sweet spot is called the *center of mass of the plate*.

In this section, we first examine these concepts in a one-dimensional context, then expand our development to consider centers of mass of two-dimensional regions and symmetry. Last, we use centroids to find the volume of certain solids by applying the theorem of Pappus.

## Center of Mass and Moments

Let's begin by looking at the center of mass in a one-dimensional context. Consider a long, thin wire or rod of negligible mass resting on a fulcrum, as shown in Figure 2.62(a). Now suppose we place objects having masses $m_1$ and $m_2$ at distances $d_1$ and $d_2$ from the fulcrum, respectively, as shown in Figure 2.62(b).

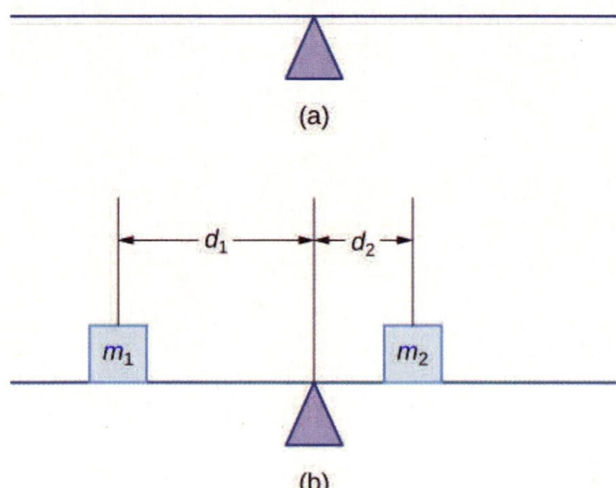


Figure 2.62 (a) A thin rod rests on a fulcrum. (b) Masses are placed on the rod.

The most common real-life example of a system like this is a playground seesaw, or teeter-totter, with children of different weights sitting at different distances from the center. On a seesaw, if one child sits at each end, the heavier child sinks down and the lighter child is lifted into the air. If the heavier child slides in toward the center, though, the seesaw balances. Applying this concept to the masses on the rod, we note that the masses balance each other if and only if $m_1 d_1 = m_2 d_2$.

In the seesaw example, we balanced the system by moving the masses (children) with respect to the fulcrum. However, we are really interested in systems in which the masses are not allowed to move, and instead we balance the system by moving the fulcrum. Suppose we have two point masses, $m_1$ and $m_2$, located on a number line at points $x_1$ and $x_2$, respectively (Figure 2.63). The center of mass, $\bar{x}$, is the point where the fulcrum should be placed to make the system balance.

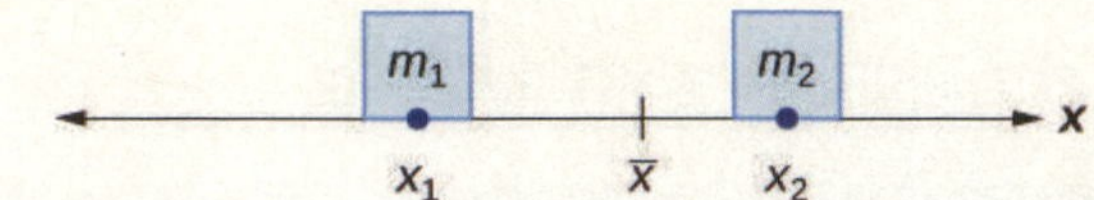


**Figure 2.63** The center of mass $\bar{x}$ is the balance point of the system.

Thus, we have

$$\begin{aligned} m_1|x_1 - \bar{x}| &= m_2|x_2 - \bar{x}| \\ m_1(\bar{x} - x_1) &= m_2(x_2 - \bar{x}) \\ m_1\bar{x} - m_1x_1 &= m_2x_2 - m_2\bar{x} \\ \bar{x}(m_1 + m_2) &= m_1x_1 + m_2x_2 \\ \bar{x} &= \frac{m_1x_1 + m_2x_2}{m_1 + m_2}. \end{aligned}$$

The expression in the numerator, $m_1x_1 + m_2x_2,$ is called the *first moment of the system with respect to the origin.* If the context is clear, we often drop the word *first* and just refer to this expression as the **moment** of the system. The expression in the denominator, $m_1 + m_2,$ is the total mass of the system. Thus, the **center of mass** of the system is the point at which the total mass of the system could be concentrated without changing the moment.

This idea is not limited just to two point masses. In general, if *n* masses, $m_1, m_2,\ldots, m_n,$ are placed on a number line at points $x_1, x_2,\ldots, x_n,$ respectively, then the center of mass of the system is given by

$$\bar{x} = \frac{\sum_{i=1}^{n} m_i x_i}{\sum_{i=1}^{n} m_i}.$$

### Theorem 2.9: Center of Mass of Objects on a Line

Let $m_1, m_2,\ldots, m_n$ be point masses placed on a number line at points $x_1, x_2,\ldots, x_n,$ respectively, and let $m = \sum_{i=1}^{n} m_i$ denote the total mass of the system. Then, the moment of the system with respect to the origin is given by

$$M = \sum_{i=1}^{n} m_i x_i \tag{2.14}$$

and the center of mass of the system is given by

$$\bar{x} = \frac{M}{m}. \tag{2.15}$$

We apply this theorem in the following example.

## Example 2.29

### Finding the Center of Mass of Objects along a Line

Suppose four point masses are placed on a number line as follows:

$m_1 = 30$ kg, placed at $x_1 = -2$ m $\quad m_2 = 5$ kg, placed at $x_2 = 3$ m

$m_3 = 10$ kg, placed at $x_3 = 6$ m $\quad m_4 = 15$ kg, placed at $x_4 = -3$ m.

Find the moment of the system with respect to the origin and find the center of mass of the system.

### Solution

First, we need to calculate the moment of the system:

$$\begin{aligned} M &= \sum_{i=1}^{4} m_i x_i \\ &= -60 + 15 + 60 - 45 = -30. \end{aligned}$$

Now, to find the center of mass, we need the total mass of the system:

$$\begin{aligned} m &= \sum_{i=1}^{4} m_i \\ &= 30 + 5 + 10 + 15 = 60 \text{ kg}. \end{aligned}$$

Then we have

$$\bar{x} = \frac{M}{m} = \frac{-30}{60} = -\frac{1}{2}.$$

The center of mass is located 1/2 m to the left of the origin.

**2.29** Suppose four point masses are placed on a number line as follows:

$m_1 = 12$ kg, placed at $x_1 = -4$ m $\quad m_2 = 12$ kg, placed at $x_2 = 4$ m

$m_3 = 30$ kg, placed at $x_3 = 2$ m $\quad m_4 = 6$ kg, placed at $x_4 = -6$ m.

Find the moment of the system with respect to the origin and find the center of mass of the system.

We can generalize this concept to find the center of mass of a system of point masses in a plane. Let $m_1$ be a point mass located at point $(x_1, y_1)$ in the plane. Then the moment $M_x$ of the mass with respect to the *x*-axis is given by $M_x = m_1 y_1$. Similarly, the moment $M_y$ with respect to the *y*-axis is given by $M_y = m_1 x_1$. Notice that the *x*-coordinate of the point is used to calculate the moment with respect to the *y*-axis, and vice versa. The reason is that the *x*-coordinate gives the distance from the point mass to the *y*-axis, and the *y*-coordinate gives the distance to the *x*-axis (see the following figure).

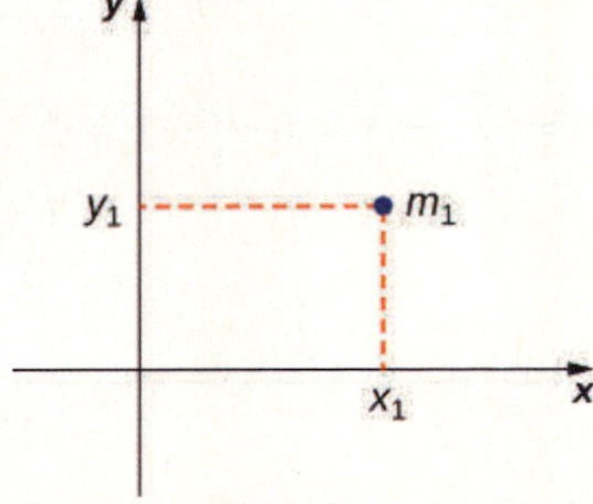


**Figure 2.64** Point mass $m_1$ is located at point $(x_1, y_1)$ in the plane.

If we have several point masses in the *xy*-plane, we can use the moments with respect to the *x*- and *y*-axes to calculate the

$x$- and $y$-coordinates of the center of mass of the system.

### Theorem 2.10: Center of Mass of Objects in a Plane

Let $m_1, m_2, \ldots, m_n$ be point masses located in the $xy$-plane at points $(x_1, y_1), (x_2, y_2), \ldots, (x_n, y_n)$, respectively, and let $m = \sum_{i=1}^{n} m_i$ denote the total mass of the system. Then the moments $M_x$ and $M_y$ of the system with respect to the $x$- and $y$-axes, respectively, are given by

$$M_x = \sum_{i=1}^{n} m_i y_i \quad \text{and} \quad M_y = \sum_{i=1}^{n} m_i x_i. \tag{2.16}$$

Also, the coordinates of the center of mass $(\bar{x}, \bar{y})$ of the system are

$$\bar{x} = \frac{M_y}{m} \quad \text{and} \quad \bar{y} = \frac{M_x}{m}. \tag{2.17}$$

The next example demonstrates how to apply this theorem.

## Example 2.30

### Finding the Center of Mass of Objects in a Plane

Suppose three point masses are placed in the $xy$-plane as follows (assume coordinates are given in meters):

$$\begin{aligned} m_1 &= 2\text{ kg, placed at } (-1, 3), \\ m_2 &= 6\text{ kg, placed at } (1, 1), \\ m_3 &= 4\text{ kg, placed at } (2, -2). \end{aligned}$$

Find the center of mass of the system.

### Solution

First we calculate the total mass of the system:

$$m = \sum_{i=1}^{3} m_i = 2 + 6 + 4 = 12\text{ kg}.$$

Next we find the moments with respect to the $x$- and $y$-axes:

$$\begin{aligned} M_y &= \sum_{i=1}^{3} m_i x_i = -2 + 6 + 8 = 12, \\ M_x &= \sum_{i=1}^{3} m_i y_i = 6 + 6 - 8 = 4. \end{aligned}$$

Then we have

$$\bar{x} = \frac{M_y}{m} = \frac{12}{12} = 1 \text{ and } \bar{y} = \frac{M_x}{m} = \frac{4}{12} = \frac{1}{3}.$$

The center of mass of the system is $(1, 1/3)$, in meters.

**2.30** Suppose three point masses are placed on a number line as follows (assume coordinates are given in meters):

$$\begin{aligned} m_1 &= 5 \text{ kg, placed at } (-2, -3), \\ m_2 &= 3 \text{ kg, placed at } (2, 3), \\ m_3 &= 2 \text{ kg, placed at } (-3, -2). \end{aligned}$$

Find the center of mass of the system.

## Center of Mass of Thin Plates

So far we have looked at systems of point masses on a line and in a plane. Now, instead of having the mass of a system concentrated at discrete points, we want to look at systems in which the mass of the system is distributed continuously across a thin sheet of material. For our purposes, we assume the sheet is thin enough that it can be treated as if it is two-dimensional. Such a sheet is called a **lamina**. Next we develop techniques to find the center of mass of a lamina. In this section, we also assume the density of the lamina is constant.

Laminas are often represented by a two-dimensional region in a plane. The geometric center of such a region is called its **centroid**. Since we have assumed the density of the lamina is constant, the center of mass of the lamina depends only on the shape of the corresponding region in the plane; it does not depend on the density. In this case, the center of mass of the lamina corresponds to the centroid of the delineated region in the plane. As with systems of point masses, we need to find the total mass of the lamina, as well as the moments of the lamina with respect to the *x*- and *y*-axes.

We first consider a lamina in the shape of a rectangle. Recall that the center of mass of a lamina is the point where the lamina balances. For a rectangle, that point is both the horizontal and vertical center of the rectangle. Based on this understanding, it is clear that the center of mass of a rectangular lamina is the point where the diagonals intersect, which is a result of the **symmetry principle**, and it is stated here without proof.

### Theorem 2.11: The Symmetry Principle

If a region $R$ is symmetric about a line $l$, then the centroid of $R$ lies on $l$.

Let's turn to more general laminas. Suppose we have a lamina bounded above by the graph of a continuous function $f(x)$, below by the $x$-axis, and on the left and right by the lines $x = a$ and $x = b$, respectively, as shown in the following figure.

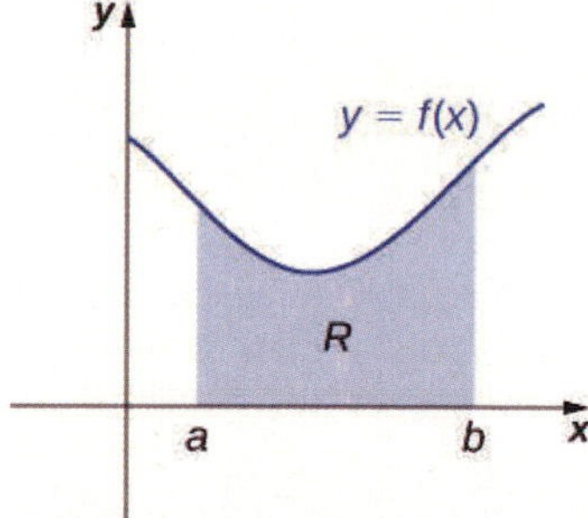


**Figure 2.65** A region in the plane representing a lamina.

As with systems of point masses, to find the center of mass of the lamina, we need to find the total mass of the lamina, as well as the moments of the lamina with respect to the *x*- and *y*-axes. As we have done many times before, we approximate these quantities by partitioning the interval $[a, b]$ and constructing rectangles.

For $i = 0, 1, 2,\ldots, n,$ let $P = \{x_i\}$ be a regular partition of $[a, b]$. Recall that we can choose any point within the interval $[x_{i-1}, x_i]$ as our $x_i^*$. In this case, we want $x_i^*$ to be the $x$-coordinate of the centroid of our rectangles. Thus, for $i = 1, 2,\ldots, n,$ we select $x_i^* \in [x_{i-1}, x_i]$ such that $x_i^*$ is the midpoint of the interval. That is, $x_i^* = (x_{i-1} + x_i)/2.$

Now, for $i = 1, 2,\ldots, n,$ construct a rectangle of height $f(x_i^*)$ on $[x_{i-1}, x_i]$. The center of mass of this rectangle is

$\left(x_i^*, \left(f(x_i^*)\right)/2\right)$, as shown in the following figure.

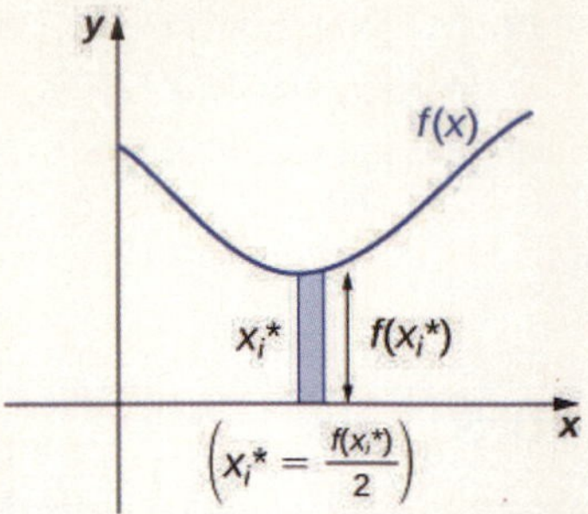


**Figure 2.66** A representative rectangle of the lamina.

Next, we need to find the total mass of the rectangle. Let $\rho$ represent the density of the lamina (note that $\rho$ is a constant). In this case, $\rho$ is expressed in terms of mass per unit area. Thus, to find the total mass of the rectangle, we multiply the area of the rectangle by $\rho$. Then, the mass of the rectangle is given by $\rho f(x_i^*)\Delta x$.

To get the approximate mass of the lamina, we add the masses of all the rectangles to get

$$m \approx \sum_{i=1}^{n} \rho f(x_i^*)\Delta x.$$

This is a Riemann sum. Taking the limit as $n \to \infty$ gives the exact mass of the lamina:

$$m = \lim_{n \to \infty} \sum_{i=1}^{n} \rho f(x_i^*)\Delta x = \rho \int_a^b f(x)dx.$$

Next, we calculate the moment of the lamina with respect to the *x*-axis. Returning to the representative rectangle, recall its center of mass is $\left(x_i^*, \left(f(x_i^*)\right)/2\right)$. Recall also that treating the rectangle as if it is a point mass located at the center of mass does not change the moment. Thus, the moment of the rectangle with respect to the *x*-axis is given by the mass of the rectangle, $\rho f(x_i^*)\Delta x$, multiplied by the distance from the center of mass to the *x*-axis: $\left(f(x_i^*)\right)/2$. Therefore, the moment with respect to the *x*-axis of the rectangle is $\rho\left(\left[f(x_i^*)\right]^2/2\right)\Delta x$. Adding the moments of the rectangles and taking the limit of the resulting Riemann sum, we see that the moment of the lamina with respect to the *x*-axis is

$$M_x = \lim_{n \to \infty} \sum_{i=1}^{n} \rho \frac{\left[f(x_i^*)\right]^2}{2}\Delta x = \rho \int_a^b \frac{\left[f(x)\right]^2}{2}dx.$$

We derive the moment with respect to the *y*-axis similarly, noting that the distance from the center of mass of the rectangle to the *y*-axis is $x_i^*$. Then the moment of the lamina with respect to the *y*-axis is given by

$$M_y = \lim_{n \to \infty} \sum_{i=1}^{n} \rho x_i^* f(x_i^*)\Delta x = \rho \int_a^b x f(x)dx.$$

We find the coordinates of the center of mass by dividing the moments by the total mass to give $\bar{x} = M_y/m$ and $\bar{y} = M_x/m$. If we look closely at the expressions for $M_x$, $M_y$, and $m$, we notice that the constant $\rho$ cancels out when $\bar{x}$ and $\bar{y}$ are calculated.

We summarize these findings in the following theorem.

### Theorem 2.12: Center of Mass of a Thin Plate in the *xy*-Plane

Let *R* denote a region bounded above by the graph of a continuous function $f(x)$, below by the *x*-axis, and on the left and right by the lines $x = a$ and $x = b$, respectively. Let $\rho$ denote the density of the associated lamina. Then we can make the following statements:

i. The mass of the lamina is

$$m = \rho \int_a^b f(x)dx. \tag{2.18}$$

ii. The moments $M_x$ and $M_y$ of the lamina with respect to the *x*- and *y*-axes, respectively, are

$$M_x = \rho \int_a^b \frac{[f(x)]^2}{2} dx \text{ and } M_y = \rho \int_a^b x f(x)dx. \tag{2.19}$$

iii. The coordinates of the center of mass $(\bar{x}, \bar{y})$ are

$$\bar{x} = \frac{M_y}{m} \text{ and } \bar{y} = \frac{M_x}{m}. \tag{2.20}$$

In the next example, we use this theorem to find the center of mass of a lamina.

## Example 2.31

### Finding the Center of Mass of a Lamina

Let $R$ be the region bounded above by the graph of the function $f(x) = \sqrt{x}$ and below by the *x*-axis over the interval $[0, 4]$. Find the centroid of the region.

### Solution

The region is depicted in the following figure.

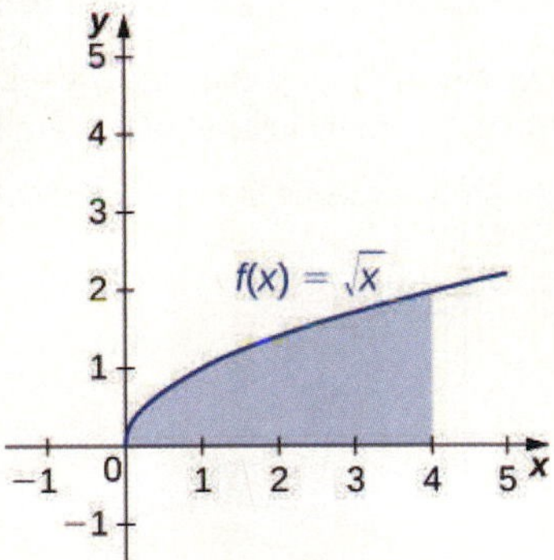


**Figure 2.67** Finding the center of mass of a lamina.

Since we are only asked for the centroid of the region, rather than the mass or moments of the associated lamina, we know the density constant $\rho$ cancels out of the calculations eventually. Therefore, for the sake of convenience, let's assume $\rho = 1$.

First, we need to calculate the total mass:

$$\begin{aligned} m &= \rho \int_a^b f(x)dx = \int_0^4 \sqrt{x}\, dx \\ &= \frac{2}{3}x^{3/2}\Big|_0^4 = \frac{2}{3}[8 - 0] = \frac{16}{3}. \end{aligned}$$

Next, we compute the moments:

$$\begin{aligned} M_x &= \rho \int_a^b \frac{[f(x)]^2}{2} dx \\ &= \int_0^4 \frac{x}{2} dx = \frac{1}{4} x^2 \Big|_0^4 = 4 \end{aligned}$$

and

$$\begin{aligned} M_y &= \rho \int_a^b x f(x) dx \\ &= \int_0^4 x\sqrt{x} dx = \int_0^4 x^{3/2} dx \\ &= \frac{2}{5} x^{5/2} \Big|_0^4 = \frac{2}{5}[32 - 0] = \frac{64}{5}. \end{aligned}$$

Thus, we have

$$\bar{x} = \frac{M_y}{m} = \frac{64/5}{16/3} = \frac{64}{5} \cdot \frac{3}{16} = \frac{12}{5} \text{ and } \bar{y} = \frac{M_x}{y} = \frac{4}{16/3} = 4 \cdot \frac{3}{16} = \frac{3}{4}.$$

The centroid of the region is $(12/5, 3/4)$.

**2.31** Let $R$ be the region bounded above by the graph of the function $f(x) = x^2$ and below by the $x$-axis over the interval $[0, 2]$. Find the centroid of the region.

We can adapt this approach to find centroids of more complex regions as well. Suppose our region is bounded above by the graph of a continuous function $f(x)$, as before, but now, instead of having the lower bound for the region be the $x$-axis, suppose the region is bounded below by the graph of a second continuous function, $g(x)$, as shown in the following figure.

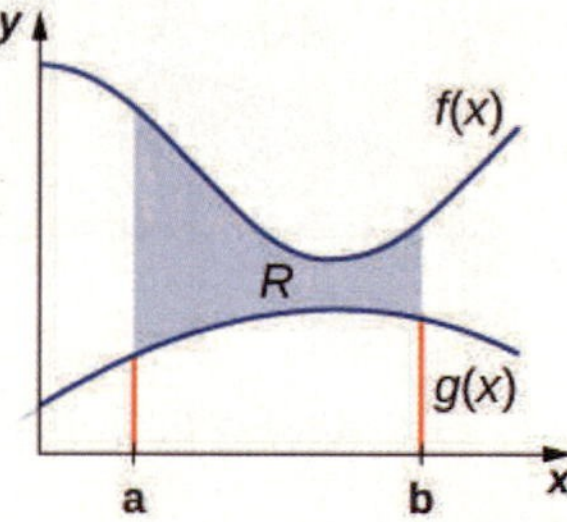


**Figure 2.68** A region between two functions.

Again, we partition the interval $[a, b]$ and construct rectangles. A representative rectangle is shown in the following figure.

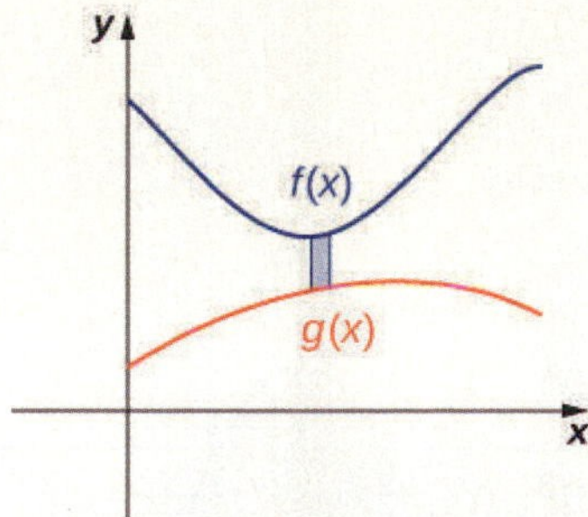


**Figure 2.69** A representative rectangle of the region between two functions.

Note that the centroid of this rectangle is $\left(x_i^*, \left(f(x_i^*) + g(x_i^*)\right)/2\right)$. We won't go through all the details of the Riemann sum development, but let's look at some of the key steps. In the development of the formulas for the mass of the lamina and the moment with respect to the *y*-axis, the height of each rectangle is given by $f(x_i^*) - g(x_i^*)$, which leads to the expression $f(x) - g(x)$ in the integrands.

In the development of the formula for the moment with respect to the *x*-axis, the moment of each rectangle is found by multiplying the area of the rectangle, $\rho\left[f(x_i^*) - g(x_i^*)\right]\Delta x$, by the distance of the centroid from the *x*-axis, $\left(f(x_i^*) + g(x_i^*)\right)/2$, which gives $\rho(1/2)\left\{\left[f(x_i^*)\right]^2 - \left[g(x_i^*)\right]^2\right\}\Delta x$. Summarizing these findings, we arrive at the following theorem.

### Theorem 2.13: Center of Mass of a Lamina Bounded by Two Functions

Let $R$ denote a region bounded above by the graph of a continuous function $f(x)$, below by the graph of the continuous function $g(x)$, and on the left and right by the lines $x = a$ and $x = b$, respectively. Let $\rho$ denote the density of the associated lamina. Then we can make the following statements:

i. The mass of the lamina is

$$m = \rho\int_a^b [f(x) - g(x)]dx. \tag{2.21}$$

ii. The moments $M_x$ and $M_y$ of the lamina with respect to the *x*- and *y*-axes, respectively, are

$$M_x = \rho\int_a^b \frac{1}{2}\left([f(x)]^2 - [g(x)]^2\right)dx \text{ and } M_y = \rho\int_a^b x[f(x) - g(x)]dx. \tag{2.22}$$

iii. The coordinates of the center of mass $(\bar{x}, \bar{y})$ are

$$\bar{x} = \frac{M_y}{m} \text{ and } \bar{y} = \frac{M_x}{m}. \tag{2.23}$$

We illustrate this theorem in the following example.

## Example 2.32

### Finding the Centroid of a Region Bounded by Two Functions

Let $R$ be the region bounded above by the graph of the function $f(x) = 1 - x^2$ and below by the graph of the function $g(x) = x - 1$. Find the centroid of the region.

### Solution

The region is depicted in the following figure.

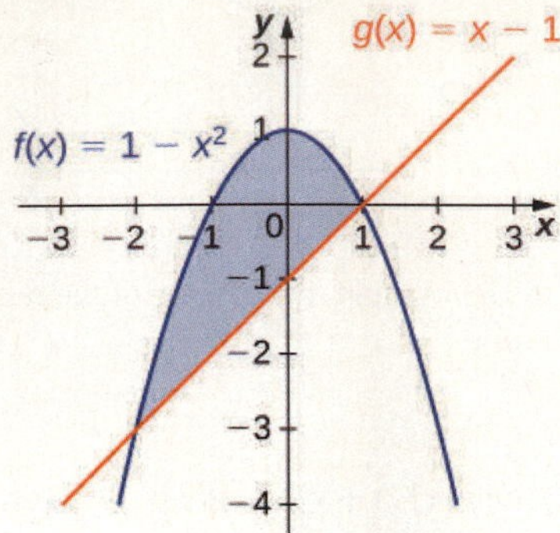


**Figure 2.70** Finding the centroid of a region between two curves.

The graphs of the functions intersect at $(-2, -3)$ and $(1, 0),$ so we integrate from −2 to 1. Once again, for the sake of convenience, assume $\rho = 1$.

First, we need to calculate the total mass:

$$\begin{aligned} m &= \rho\int_a^b [f(x) - g(x)]dx \\ &= \int_{-2}^{1} [1 - x^2 - (x - 1)]dx = \int_{-2}^{1} (2 - x^2 - x)dx \\ &= \left[2x - \frac{1}{3}x^3 - \frac{1}{2}x^2\right]\Big|_{-2}^{1} = \left[2 - \frac{1}{3} - \frac{1}{2}\right] - \left[-4 + \frac{8}{3} - 2\right] = \frac{9}{2}. \end{aligned}$$

Next, we compute the moments:

$$\begin{aligned} M_x &= \rho\int_a^b \frac{1}{2}\left([f(x)]^2 - [g(x)]^2\right)dx \\ &= \frac{1}{2}\int_{-2}^{1} \left(\left(1 - x^2\right)^2 - (x - 1)^2\right)dx = \frac{1}{2}\int_{-2}^{1} \left(x^4 - 3x^2 + 2x\right)dx \\ &= \frac{1}{2}\left[\frac{x^5}{5} - x^3 + x^2\right]\Big|_{-2}^{1} = -\frac{27}{10} \end{aligned}$$

and

$$\begin{aligned} M_y &= \rho\int_a^b x[f(x) - g(x)]dx \\ &= \int_{-2}^{1} x\left[(1 - x^2) - (x - 1)\right]dx = \int_{-2}^{1} x\left[2 - x^2 - x\right]dx = \int_{-2}^{1} \left(2x - x^4 - x^2\right)dx \\ &= \left[x^2 - \frac{x^5}{5} - \frac{x^3}{3}\right]\Big|_{-2}^{1} = -\frac{9}{4}. \end{aligned}$$

Therefore, we have

$$\bar{x} = \frac{M_y}{m} = -\frac{9}{4} \cdot \frac{2}{9} = -\frac{1}{2} \text{ and } \bar{y} = \frac{M_x}{y} = -\frac{27}{10} \cdot \frac{2}{9} = -\frac{3}{5}.$$

The centroid of the region is $(-(1/2), -(3/5))$.

**2.32** Let $R$ be the region bounded above by the graph of the function $f(x) = 6 - x^2$ and below by the graph of the function $g(x) = 3 - 2x$. Find the centroid of the region.

## The Symmetry Principle

We stated the symmetry principle earlier, when we were looking at the centroid of a rectangle. The symmetry principle can be a great help when finding centroids of regions that are symmetric. Consider the following example.

### Example 2.33

#### Finding the Centroid of a Symmetric Region

Let $R$ be the region bounded above by the graph of the function $f(x) = 4 - x^2$ and below by the $x$-axis. Find the centroid of the region.

#### Solution

The region is depicted in the following figure.

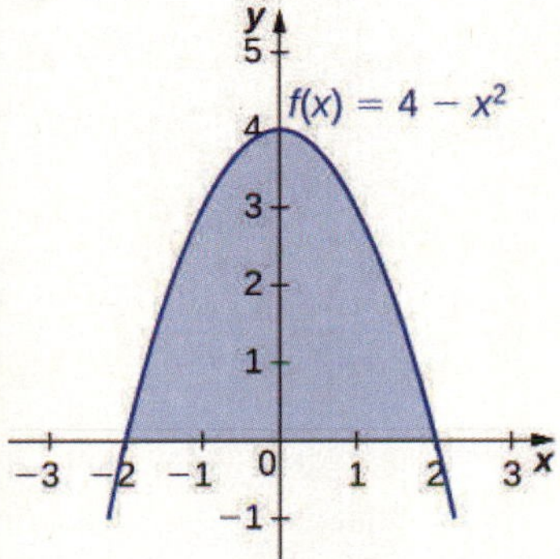


**Figure 2.71** We can use the symmetry principle to help find the centroid of a symmetric region.

The region is symmetric with respect to the $y$-axis. Therefore, the $x$-coordinate of the centroid is zero. We need only calculate $\bar{y}$. Once again, for the sake of convenience, assume $\rho = 1$.

First, we calculate the total mass:

$$\begin{aligned} m &= \rho \int_a^b f(x)dx \\ &= \int_{-2}^{2} \left(4 - x^2\right)dx \\ &= \left[4x - \frac{x^3}{3}\right]\Big|_{-2}^{2} = \frac{32}{3}. \end{aligned}$$

Next, we calculate the moments. We only need $M_x$:

$$\begin{aligned} M_x &= \rho\int_a^b \frac{[f(x)]^2}{2}dx \\ &= \frac{1}{2}\int_{-2}^{2}\left[4-x^2\right]^2 dx = \frac{1}{2}\int_{-2}^{2}\left(16-8x^2+x^4\right)dx \\ &= \frac{1}{2}\left[\frac{x^5}{5}-\frac{8x^3}{3}+16x\right]\Big|_{-2}^{2} = \frac{256}{15}. \end{aligned}$$

Then we have

$$\bar{y} = \frac{M_x}{y} = \frac{256}{15}\cdot\frac{3}{32} = \frac{8}{5}.$$

The centroid of the region is $(0, 8/5)$.

**2.33** Let $R$ be the region bounded above by the graph of the function $f(x) = 1 - x^2$ and below by $x$-axis. Find the centroid of the region.

# Student PROJECT

## The Grand Canyon Skywalk

The Grand Canyon Skywalk opened to the public on March 28, 2007. This engineering marvel is a horseshoe-shaped observation platform suspended 4000 ft above the Colorado River on the West Rim of the Grand Canyon. Its crystal-clear glass floor allows stunning views of the canyon below (see the following figure).

**Figure 2.72** The Grand Canyon Skywalk offers magnificent views of the canyon. (credit: 10da_ralta, Wikimedia Commons)

The Skywalk is a cantilever design, meaning that the observation platform extends over the rim of the canyon, with no visible means of support below it. Despite the lack of visible support posts or struts, cantilever structures are engineered to be very stable and the Skywalk is no exception. The observation platform is attached firmly to support posts that extend 46 ft down into bedrock. The structure was built to withstand 100-mph winds and an 8.0-magnitude earthquake within 50 mi, and is capable of supporting more than 70,000,000 lb.

One factor affecting the stability of the Skywalk is the center of gravity of the structure. We are going to calculate the center of gravity of the Skywalk, and examine how the center of gravity changes when tourists walk out onto the observation platform.

The observation platform is U-shaped. The legs of the U are 10 ft wide and begin on land, under the visitors' center, 48 ft from the edge of the canyon. The platform extends 70 ft over the edge of the canyon.

To calculate the center of mass of the structure, we treat it as a lamina and use a two-dimensional region in the *xy*-plane to represent the platform. We begin by dividing the region into three subregions so we can consider each subregion separately. The first region, denoted $R_1$, consists of the curved part of the U. We model $R_1$ as a semicircular annulus, with inner radius 25 ft and outer radius 35 ft, centered at the origin (see the following figure).

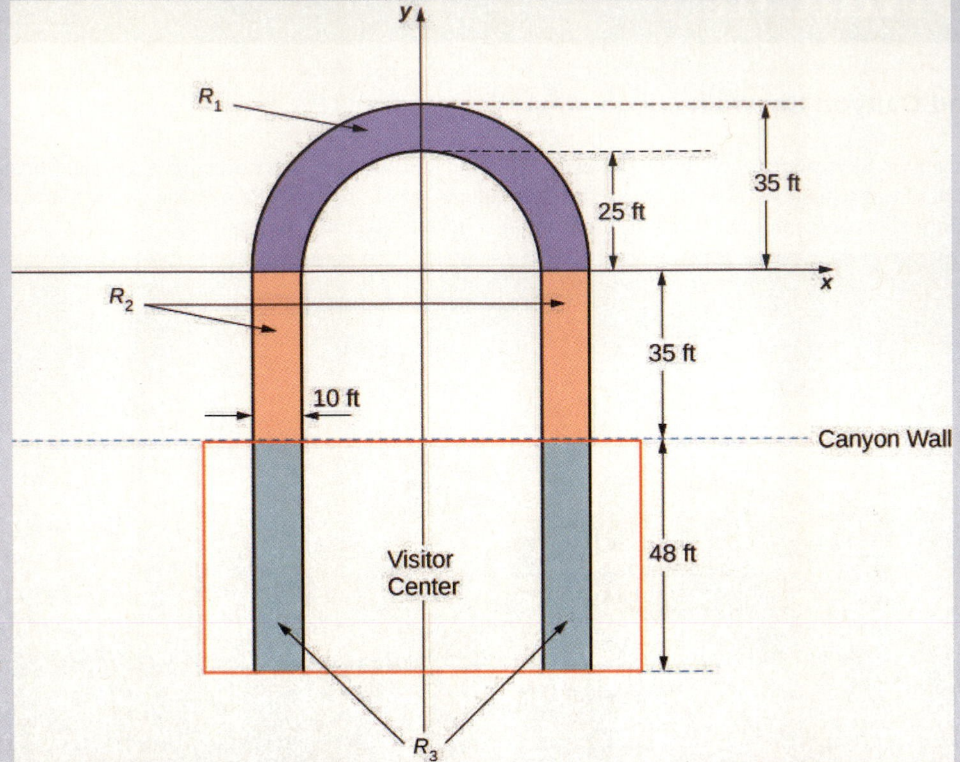


**Figure 2.73** We model the Skywalk with three sub-regions.

The legs of the platform, extending 35 ft between $R_1$ and the canyon wall, comprise the second sub-region, $R_2$. Last, the ends of the legs, which extend 48 ft under the visitor center, comprise the third sub-region, $R_3$. Assume the density of the lamina is constant and assume the total weight of the platform is 1,200,000 lb (not including the weight of the visitor center; we will consider that later). Use $g = 32 \text{ ft/sec}^2$.

1. Compute the area of each of the three sub-regions. Note that the areas of regions $R_2$ and $R_3$ should include the areas of the legs only, not the open space between them. Round answers to the nearest square foot.
2. Determine the mass associated with each of the three sub-regions.
3. Calculate the center of mass of each of the three sub-regions.
4. Now, treat each of the three sub-regions as a point mass located at the center of mass of the corresponding sub-region. Using this representation, calculate the center of mass of the entire platform.
5. Assume the visitor center weighs 2,200,000 lb, with a center of mass corresponding to the center of mass of $R_3$. Treating the visitor center as a point mass, recalculate the center of mass of the system. How does the center of mass change?
6. Although the Skywalk was built to limit the number of people on the observation platform to 120, the platform is capable of supporting up to 800 people weighing 200 lb each. If all 800 people were allowed on the platform, and all of them went to the farthest end of the platform, how would the center of gravity of the system be affected? (Include the visitor center in the calculations and represent the people by a point mass located at the farthest edge of the platform, 70 ft from the canyon wall.)

## Theorem of Pappus

This section ends with a discussion of the **theorem of Pappus for volume**, which allows us to find the volume of particular kinds of solids by using the centroid. (There is also a theorem of Pappus for surface area, but it is much less useful than the theorem for volume.)

### Theorem 2.14: Theorem of Pappus for Volume

Let $R$ be a region in the plane and let $l$ be a line in the plane that does not intersect $R$. Then the volume of the solid of revolution formed by revolving $R$ around $l$ is equal to the area of $R$ multiplied by the distance $d$ traveled by the centroid of $R$.

### Proof

We can prove the case when the region is bounded above by the graph of a function $f(x)$ and below by the graph of a function $g(x)$ over an interval $[a, b]$, and for which the axis of revolution is the $y$-axis. In this case, the area of the region is $A = \int_a^b [f(x) - g(x)]dx$. Since the axis of rotation is the $y$-axis, the distance traveled by the centroid of the region depends only on the $x$-coordinate of the centroid, $\bar{x}$, which is

$$\bar{x} = \frac{M_y}{m},$$

where

$$m = \rho \int_a^b [f(x) - g(x)]dx \text{ and } M_y = \rho \int_a^b x[f(x) - g(x)]dx.$$

Then,

$$d = 2\pi \frac{\rho \int_a^b x[f(x) - g(x)]dx}{\rho \int_a^b [f(x) - g(x)]dx}$$

and thus

$$d \cdot A = 2\pi \int_a^b x[f(x) - g(x)]dx.$$

However, using the method of cylindrical shells, we have

$$V = 2\pi \int_a^b x[f(x) - g(x)]dx.$$

So,

$$V = d \cdot A$$

and the proof is complete.

□

## Example 2.34

### Using the Theorem of Pappus for Volume

Let $R$ be a circle of radius 2 centered at $(4, 0)$. Use the theorem of Pappus for volume to find the volume of the torus generated by revolving $R$ around the $y$-axis.

### Solution

The region and torus are depicted in the following figure.

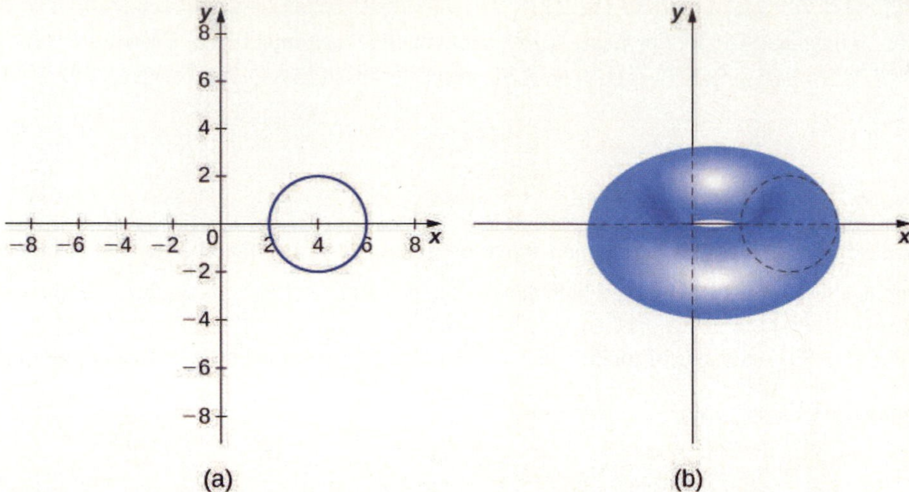


**Figure 2.74** Determining the volume of a torus by using the theorem of Pappus. (a) A circular region $R$ in the plane; (b) the torus generated by revolving $R$ about the $y$-axis.

The region $R$ is a circle of radius 2, so the area of $R$ is $A = 4\pi$ units$^2$. By the symmetry principle, the centroid of $R$ is the center of the circle. The centroid travels around the $y$-axis in a circular path of radius 4, so the centroid travels $d = 8\pi$ units. Then, the volume of the torus is $A \cdot d = 32\pi^2$ units$^3$.

**2.34** Let $R$ be a circle of radius 1 centered at $(3, 0)$. Use the theorem of Pappus for volume to find the volume of the torus generated by revolving $R$ around the $y$-axis.

# 2.6 EXERCISES

For the following exercises, calculate the center of mass for the collection of masses given.

254. $m_1 = 2$ at $x_1 = 1$ and $m_2 = 4$ at $x_2 = 2$

255. $m_1 = 1$ at $x_1 = -1$ and $m_2 = 3$ at $x_2 = 2$

256. $m = 3$ at $x = 0, 1, 2, 6$

257. Unit masses at $(x, y) = (1, 0), (0, 1), (1, 1)$

258. $m_1 = 1$ at $(1, 0)$ and $m_2 = 4$ at $(0, 1)$

259. $m_1 = 1$ at $(1, 0)$ and $m_2 = 3$ at $(2, 2)$

For the following exercises, compute the center of mass $\bar{x}$.

260. $\rho = 1$ for $x \in (-1, 3)$

261. $\rho = x^2$ for $x \in (0, L)$

262. $\rho = 1$ for $x \in (0, 1)$ and $\rho = 2$ for $x \in (1, 2)$

263. $\rho = \sin x$ for $x \in (0, \pi)$

264. $\rho = \cos x$ for $x \in \left(0, \frac{\pi}{2}\right)$

265. $\rho = e^x$ for $x \in (0, 2)$

266. $\rho = x^3 + xe^{-x}$ for $x \in (0, 1)$

267. $\rho = x \sin x$ for $x \in (0, \pi)$

268. $\rho = \sqrt{x}$ for $x \in (1, 4)$

269. $\rho = \ln x$ for $x \in (1, e)$

For the following exercises, compute the center of mass $(\bar{x}, \bar{y})$. Use symmetry to help locate the center of mass whenever possible.

270. $\rho = 7$ in the square $0 \le x \le 1, \quad 0 \le y \le 1$

271. $\rho = 3$ in the triangle with vertices $(0, 0)$, $(a, 0)$, and $(0, b)$

272. $\rho = 2$ for the region bounded by $y = \cos(x)$, $y = -\cos(x)$, $x = -\frac{\pi}{2}$, and $x = \frac{\pi}{2}$

For the following exercises, use a calculator to draw the region, then compute the center of mass $(\bar{x}, \bar{y})$. Use symmetry to help locate the center of mass whenever possible.

273. **[T]** The region bounded by $y = \cos(2x)$, $x = -\frac{\pi}{4}$, and $x = \frac{\pi}{4}$

274. **[T]** The region between $y = 2x^2$, $y = 0$, $x = 0$, and $x = 1$

275. **[T]** The region between $y = \frac{5}{4}x^2$ and $y = 5$

276. **[T]** Region between $y = \sqrt{x}$, $y = \ln(x)$, $x = 1$, and $x = 4$

277. **[T]** The region bounded by $y = 0$, $\frac{x^2}{4} + \frac{y^2}{9} = 1$

278. **[T]** The region bounded by $y = 0$, $x = 0$, and $\frac{x^2}{4} + \frac{y^2}{9} = 1$

279. **[T]** The region bounded by $y = x^2$ and $y = x^4$ in the first quadrant

For the following exercises, use the theorem of Pappus to determine the volume of the shape.

280. Rotating $y = mx$ around the $x$-axis between $x = 0$ and $x = 1$

281. Rotating $y = mx$ around the $y$-axis between $x = 0$ and $x = 1$

282. A general cone created by rotating a triangle with vertices $(0, 0)$, $(a, 0)$, and $(0, b)$ around the $y$-axis. Does your answer agree with the volume of a cone?

283. A general cylinder created by rotating a rectangle with vertices $(0, 0)$, $(a, 0)$, $(0, b)$, and $(a, b)$ around the $y$-axis. Does your answer agree with the volume of a cylinder?

284. A sphere created by rotating a semicircle with radius $a$ around the $y$-axis. Does your answer agree with the volume of a sphere?

For the following exercises, use a calculator to draw the region enclosed by the curve. Find the area $M$ and the centroid $(\overline{x}, \overline{y})$ for the given shapes. Use symmetry to help locate the center of mass whenever possible.

285. **[T]** Quarter-circle: $y = \sqrt{1 - x^2}$, $y = 0$, and $x = 0$

286. **[T]** Triangle: $y = x$, $y = 2 - x$, and $y = 0$

287. **[T]** Lens: $y = x^2$ and $y = x$

288. **[T]** Ring: $y^2 + x^2 = 1$ and $y^2 + x^2 = 4$

289. **[T]** Half-ring: $y^2 + x^2 = 1$, $y^2 + x^2 = 4$, and $y = 0$

290. Find the generalized center of mass in the sliver between $y = x^a$ and $y = x^b$ with $a > b$. Then, use the Pappus theorem to find the volume of the solid generated when revolving around the *y*-axis.

291. Find the generalized center of mass between $y = a^2 - x^2$, $x = 0$, and $y = 0$. Then, use the Pappus theorem to find the volume of the solid generated when revolving around the *y*-axis.

292. Find the generalized center of mass between $y = b\sin(ax)$, $x = 0$, and $x = \frac{\pi}{a}$. Then, use the Pappus theorem to find the volume of the solid generated when revolving around the *y*-axis.

293. Use the theorem of Pappus to find the volume of a torus (pictured here). Assume that a disk of radius $a$ is positioned with the left end of the circle at $x = b$, $b > 0$, and is rotated around the *y*-axis.

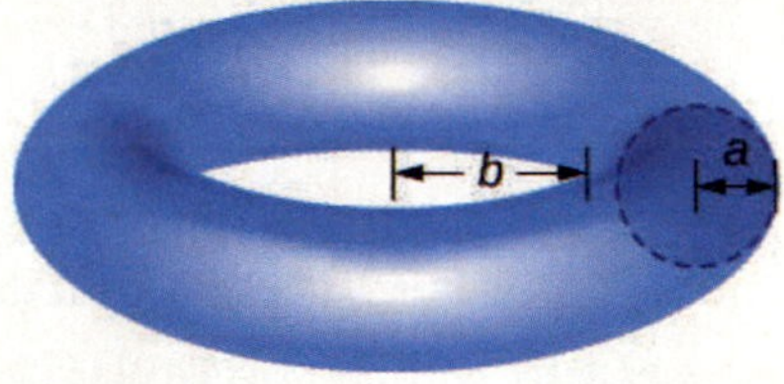


294. Find the center of mass $(\overline{x}, \overline{y})$ for a thin wire along the semicircle $y = \sqrt{1 - x^2}$ with unit mass. (*Hint:* Use the theorem of Pappus.)

# 2.7 | Integrals, Exponential Functions, and Logarithms

**Learning Objectives**

- **2.7.1** Write the definition of the natural logarithm as an integral.
- **2.7.2** Recognize the derivative of the natural logarithm.
- **2.7.3** Integrate functions involving the natural logarithmic function.
- **2.7.4** Define the number $e$ through an integral.
- **2.7.5** Recognize the derivative and integral of the exponential function.
- **2.7.6** Prove properties of logarithms and exponential functions using integrals.
- **2.7.7** Express general logarithmic and exponential functions in terms of natural logarithms and exponentials.

We already examined exponential functions and logarithms in earlier chapters. However, we glossed over some key details in the previous discussions. For example, we did not study how to treat exponential functions with exponents that are irrational. The definition of the number $e$ is another area where the previous development was somewhat incomplete. We now have the tools to deal with these concepts in a more mathematically rigorous way, and we do so in this section.

For purposes of this section, assume we have not yet defined the natural logarithm, the number $e$, or any of the integration and differentiation formulas associated with these functions. By the end of the section, we will have studied these concepts in a mathematically rigorous way (and we will see they are consistent with the concepts we learned earlier).

We begin the section by defining the natural logarithm in terms of an integral. This definition forms the foundation for the section. From this definition, we derive differentiation formulas, define the number $e$, and expand these concepts to logarithms and exponential functions of any base.

## The Natural Logarithm as an Integral

Recall the power rule for integrals:

$$\int x^n \, dx = \frac{x^{n+1}}{n+1} + C, \quad n \neq -1.$$

Clearly, this does not work when $n = -1$, as it would force us to divide by zero. So, what do we do with $\int \frac{1}{x} dx$? Recall from the Fundamental Theorem of Calculus that $\int_1^x \frac{1}{t} dt$ is an antiderivative of $1/x$. Therefore, we can make the following definition.

**Definition**

For $x > 0$, define the natural logarithm function by

$$\ln x = \int_1^x \frac{1}{t} dt. \tag{2.24}$$

For $x > 1$, this is just the area under the curve $y = 1/t$ from $1$ to $x$. For $x < 1$, we have $\int_1^x \frac{1}{t} dt = -\int_x^1 \frac{1}{t} dt$, so in this case it is the negative of the area under the curve from $x$ to $1$ (see the following figure).

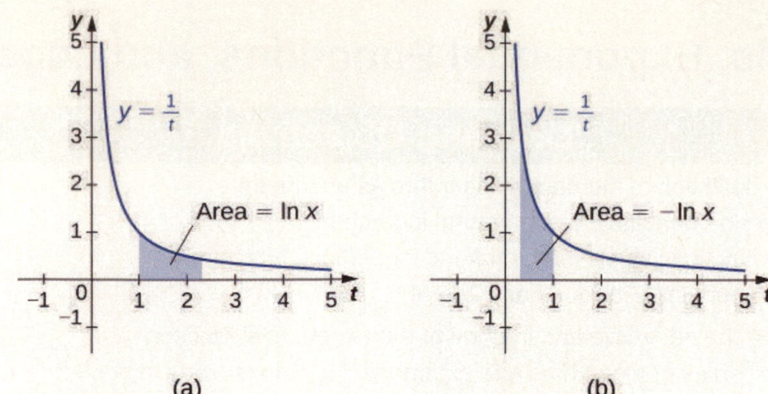


**Figure 2.75** (a) When $x > 1,$ the natural logarithm is the area under the curve $y = 1/t$ from $1$ to $x$. (b) When $x < 1,$ the natural logarithm is the negative of the area under the curve from $x$ to $1$.

Notice that $\ln 1 = 0$. Furthermore, the function $y = 1/t > 0$ for $x > 0$. Therefore, by the properties of integrals, it is clear that $\ln x$ is increasing for $x > 0$.

## Properties of the Natural Logarithm

Because of the way we defined the natural logarithm, the following differentiation formula falls out immediately as a result of to the Fundamental Theorem of Calculus.

### Theorem 2.15: Derivative of the Natural Logarithm

For $x > 0,$ the derivative of the natural logarithm is given by

$$\frac{d}{dx}\ln x = \frac{1}{x}.$$

### Theorem 2.16: Corollary to the Derivative of the Natural Logarithm

The function $\ln x$ is differentiable; therefore, it is continuous.

A graph of $\ln x$ is shown in **Figure 2.76**. Notice that it is continuous throughout its domain of $(0, \infty)$.

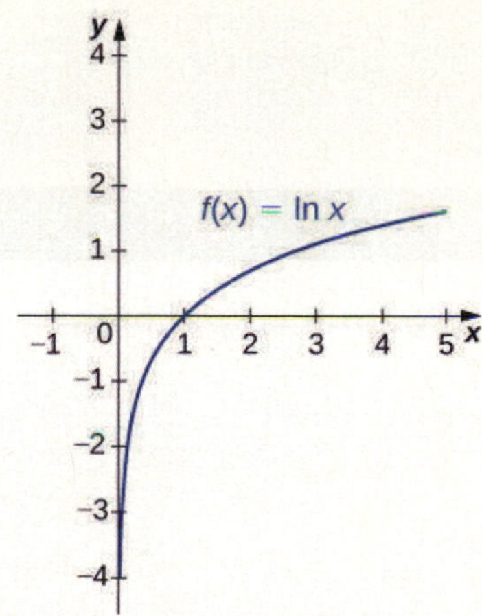


**Figure 2.76** The graph of $f(x) = \ln x$ shows that it is a continuous function.

## Example 2.35

### Calculating Derivatives of Natural Logarithms

Calculate the following derivatives:

a. $\frac{d}{dx}\ln\left(5x^3 - 2\right)$

b. $\frac{d}{dx}(\ln(3x))^2$

### Solution

We need to apply the chain rule in both cases.

a. $\frac{d}{dx}\ln\left(5x^3 - 2\right) = \frac{15x^2}{5x^3 - 2}$

b. $\frac{d}{dx}(\ln(3x))^2 = \frac{2(\ln(3x)) \cdot 3}{3x} = \frac{2(\ln(3x))}{x}$

**2.35** Calculate the following derivatives:

a. $\frac{d}{dx}\ln\left(2x^2 + x\right)$

b. $\frac{d}{dx}\left(\ln\left(x^3\right)\right)^2$

Note that if we use the absolute value function and create a new function $\ln|x|,$ we can extend the domain of the natural logarithm to include $x < 0.$ Then $(d/(dx))\ln|x| = 1/x.$ This gives rise to the familiar integration formula.

### Theorem 2.17: Integral of (1/*u*) *du*

The natural logarithm is the antiderivative of the function $f(u) = 1/u$:

$$\int \frac{1}{u}du = \ln|u| + C.$$

## Example 2.36

### Calculating Integrals Involving Natural Logarithms

Calculate the integral $\int \frac{x}{x^2+4}dx.$

### Solution

Using $u$ -substitution, let $u = x^2 + 4.$ Then $du = 2x\,dx$ and we have

$$\int \frac{x}{x^2+4}dx = \frac{1}{2}\int \frac{1}{u}du\frac{1}{2}\ln|u| + C = \frac{1}{2}\ln\left|x^2+4\right| + C = \frac{1}{2}\ln\left(x^2+4\right) + C.$$

**2.36** Calculate the integral $\int \frac{x^2}{x^3+6}dx.$

Although we have called our function a "logarithm," we have not actually proved that any of the properties of logarithms hold for this function. We do so here.

### Theorem 2.18: Properties of the Natural Logarithm

If $a, b > 0$ and $r$ is a rational number, then

i. $\ln 1 = 0$

ii. $\ln(ab) = \ln a + \ln b$

iii. $\ln\left(\frac{a}{b}\right) = \ln a - \ln b$

iv. $\ln(a^r) = r\ln a$

### Proof

i. By definition, $\ln 1 = \int_1^1 \frac{1}{t}dt = 0.$

ii. We have

$$\ln(ab) = \int_1^{ab} \frac{1}{t}dt = \int_1^a \frac{1}{t}dt + \int_a^{ab} \frac{1}{t}dt.$$

Use $u$-substitution on the last integral in this expression. Let $u = t/a.$ Then $du = (1/a)dt.$ Furthermore, when $t = a,\ u = 1,$ and when $t = ab,\ u = b.$ So we get

$$\ln(ab) = \int_1^a \frac{1}{t}dt + \int_a^{ab} \frac{1}{t}dt = \int_1^a \frac{1}{t}dt + \int_1^{ab} \frac{a}{t}\cdot\frac{1}{a}dt = \int_1^a \frac{1}{t}dt + \int_1^b \frac{1}{u}du = \ln a + \ln b.$$

iii. Note that

$$\frac{d}{dx}\ln(x^r) = \frac{rx^{r-1}}{x^r} = \frac{r}{x}.$$

Furthermore,

$$\frac{d}{dx}(r\ln x) = \frac{r}{x}.$$

Since the derivatives of these two functions are the same, by the Fundamental Theorem of Calculus, they must differ by a constant. So we have

$$\ln(x^r) = r\ln x + C$$

for some constant $C$. Taking $x = 1,$ we get

$$\begin{aligned} \ln(1^r) &= r\ln(1) + C \\ 0 &= r(0) + C \\ C &= 0. \end{aligned}$$

Thus $\ln(x^r) = r\ln x$ and the proof is complete. Note that we can extend this property to irrational values of $r$ later in this section.

Part iii. follows from parts ii. and iv. and the proof is left to you.

□

## Example 2.37

### Using Properties of Logarithms

Use properties of logarithms to simplify the following expression into a single logarithm:

$$\ln 9 - 2\ln 3 + \ln\left(\frac{1}{3}\right).$$

#### Solution

We have

$$\ln 9 - 2\ln 3 + \ln\left(\frac{1}{3}\right) = \ln\left(3^2\right) - 2\ln 3 + \ln\left(3^{-1}\right) = 2\ln 3 - 2\ln 3 - \ln 3 = -\ln 3.$$

**2.37** Use properties of logarithms to simplify the following expression into a single logarithm:

$$\ln 8 - \ln 2 - \ln\left(\frac{1}{4}\right).$$

## Defining the Number *e*

Now that we have the natural logarithm defined, we can use that function to define the number $e$.

**Definition**

The number $e$ is defined to be the real number such that

$$\ln e = 1.$$

To put it another way, the area under the curve $y = 1/t$ between $t = 1$ and $t = e$ is $1$ (**Figure 2.77**). The proof that such a number exists and is unique is left to you. (*Hint*: Use the Intermediate Value Theorem to prove existence and the fact that

$\ln x$ is increasing to prove uniqueness.)

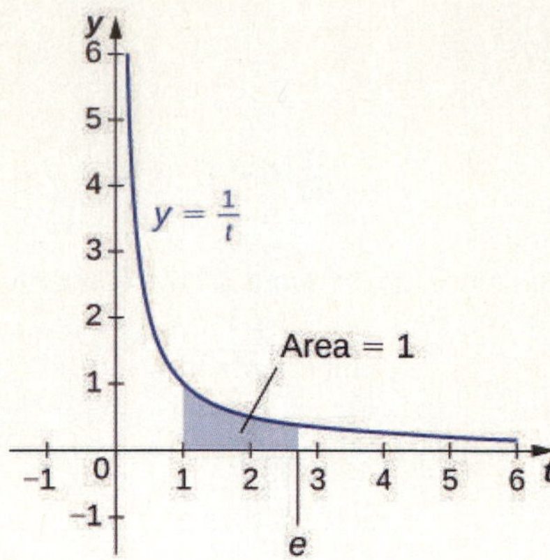


Figure 2.77 The area under the curve from $1$ to $e$ is equal to one.

The number $e$ can be shown to be irrational, although we won't do so here (see the Student Project in **Taylor and Maclaurin Series**). Its approximate value is given by

$$e \approx 2.71828182846.$$

## The Exponential Function

We now turn our attention to the function $e^x$. Note that the natural logarithm is one-to-one and therefore has an inverse function. For now, we denote this inverse function by $\exp x$. Then,

$$\exp(\ln x) = x \text{ for } x > 0 \text{ and } \ln(\exp x) = x \text{ for all } x.$$

The following figure shows the graphs of $\exp x$ and $\ln x$.

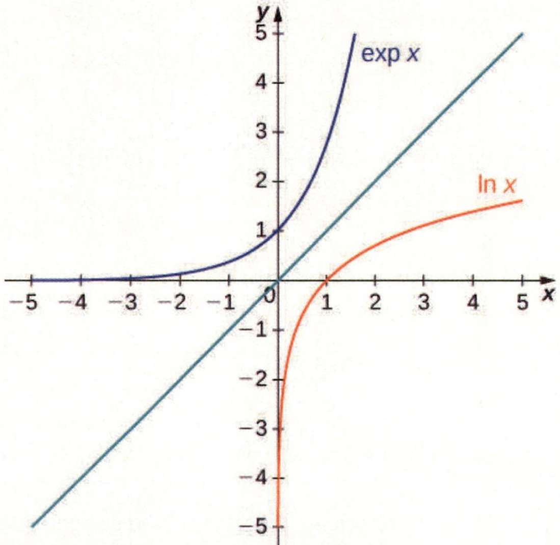


Figure 2.78 The graphs of $\ln x$ and $\exp x$.

We hypothesize that $\exp x = e^x$. For rational values of $x$, this is easy to show. If $x$ is rational, then we have $\ln(e^x) = x \ln e = x$. Thus, when $x$ is rational, $e^x = \exp x$. For irrational values of $x$, we simply define $e^x$ as the inverse function of $\ln x$.

### Definition

For any real number $x$, define $y = e^x$ to be the number for which

$$\ln y = \ln(e^x) = x. \tag{2.25}$$

Then we have $e^x = \exp(x)$ for all $x$, and thus

$$e^{\ln x} = x \text{ for } x > 0 \text{ and } \ln(e^x) = x \tag{2.26}$$

for all $x$.

## Properties of the Exponential Function

Since the exponential function was defined in terms of an inverse function, and not in terms of a power of $e$, we must verify that the usual laws of exponents hold for the function $e^x$.

### Theorem 2.19: Properties of the Exponential Function

If $p$ and $q$ are any real numbers and $r$ is a rational number, then

i. $e^p e^q = e^{p+q}$

ii. $\frac{e^p}{e^q} = e^{p-q}$

iii. $(e^p)^r = e^{pr}$

### Proof

Note that if $p$ and $q$ are rational, the properties hold. However, if $p$ or $q$ are irrational, we must apply the inverse function definition of $e^x$ and verify the properties. Only the first property is verified here; the other two are left to you. We have

$$\ln(e^p e^q) = \ln(e^p) + \ln(e^q) = p + q = \ln\left(e^{p+q}\right).$$

Since $\ln x$ is one-to-one, then

$$e^p e^q = e^{p+q}.$$

□

As with part iv. of the logarithm properties, we can extend property iii. to irrational values of $r$, and we do so by the end of the section.

We also want to verify the differentiation formula for the function $y = e^x$. To do this, we need to use implicit differentiation. Let $y = e^x$. Then

$$\begin{aligned} \ln y &= x \\ \frac{d}{dx}\ln y &= \frac{d}{dx}x \\ \frac{1}{y}\frac{dy}{dx} &= 1 \\ \frac{dy}{dx} &= y. \end{aligned}$$

Thus, we see

$$\frac{d}{dx}e^x = e^x$$

as desired, which leads immediately to the integration formula

$$\int e^x\,dx = e^x + C.$$

We apply these formulas in the following examples.

## Example 2.38

### Using Properties of Exponential Functions

Evaluate the following derivatives:

a. $\frac{d}{dt}e^{3t}e^{t^2}$

b. $\frac{d}{dx}e^{3x^2}$

### Solution

We apply the chain rule as necessary.

a. $\frac{d}{dt}e^{3t}e^{t^2} = \frac{d}{dt}e^{3t+t^2} = e^{3t+t^2}(3+2t)$

b. $\frac{d}{dx}e^{3x^2} = e^{3x^2}6x$

**2.38** Evaluate the following derivatives:

a. $\frac{d}{dx}\left(\frac{e^{x^2}}{e^{5x}}\right)$

b. $\frac{d}{dt}\left(e^{2t}\right)^3$

## Example 2.39

### Using Properties of Exponential Functions

Evaluate the following integral: $\int 2xe^{-x^2}\,dx.$

### Solution

Using $u$-substitution, let $u = -x^2$. Then $du = -2x\,dx,$ and we have

$$\int 2xe^{-x^2}\,dx = -\int e^u\,du = -e^u + C = -e^{-x^2} + C.$$

**2.39** Evaluate the following integral: $\int \frac{4}{e^{3x}} dx.$

## General Logarithmic and Exponential Functions

We close this section by looking at exponential functions and logarithms with bases other than $e$. Exponential functions are functions of the form $f(x) = a^x$. Note that unless $a = e$, we still do not have a mathematically rigorous definition of these functions for irrational exponents. Let's rectify that here by defining the function $f(x) = a^x$ in terms of the exponential function $e^x$. We then examine logarithms with bases other than $e$ as inverse functions of exponential functions.

### Definition

For any $a > 0$, and for any real number $x$, define $y = a^x$ as follows:

$$y = a^x = e^{x \ln a}.$$

Now $a^x$ is defined rigorously for all values of $x$. This definition also allows us to generalize property iv. of logarithms and property iii. of exponential functions to apply to both rational and irrational values of $r$. It is straightforward to show that properties of exponents hold for general exponential functions defined in this way.

Let's now apply this definition to calculate a differentiation formula for $a^x$. We have

$$\frac{d}{dx}a^x = \frac{d}{dx}e^{x \ln a} = e^{x \ln a} \ln a = a^x \ln a.$$

The corresponding integration formula follows immediately.

### Theorem 2.20: Derivatives and Integrals Involving General Exponential Functions

Let $a > 0$. Then,

$$\frac{d}{dx}a^x = a^x \ln a$$

and

$$\int a^x dx = \frac{1}{\ln a}a^x + C.$$

If $a \neq 1$, then the function $a^x$ is one-to-one and has a well-defined inverse. Its inverse is denoted by $\log_a x$. Then,

$$y = \log_a x \text{ if and only if } x = a^y.$$

Note that general logarithm functions can be written in terms of the natural logarithm. Let $y = \log_a x$. Then, $x = a^y$. Taking the natural logarithm of both sides of this second equation, we get

$$\begin{aligned} \ln x &= \ln(a^y) \\ \ln x &= y \ln a \\ y &= \frac{\ln x}{\ln a} \\ \log x &= \frac{\ln x}{\ln a}. \end{aligned}$$

Thus, we see that all logarithmic functions are constant multiples of one another. Next, we use this formula to find a differentiation formula for a logarithm with base $a$. Again, let $y = \log_a x$. Then,

$$\begin{aligned}\frac{dy}{dx} &= \frac{d}{dx}(\log_a x)\\ &= \frac{d}{dx}\left(\frac{\ln x}{\ln a}\right)\\ &= \left(\frac{1}{\ln a}\right)\frac{d}{dx}(\ln x)\\ &= \frac{1}{\ln a}\cdot\frac{1}{x}\\ &= \frac{1}{x\ln a}.\end{aligned}$$

### Theorem 2.21: Derivatives of General Logarithm Functions

Let $a > 0$. Then,

$$\frac{d}{dx}\log_a x = \frac{1}{x\ln a}.$$

## Example 2.40

### Calculating Derivatives of General Exponential and Logarithm Functions

Evaluate the following derivatives:

a. $\frac{d}{dt}\left(4^t\cdot 2^{t^2}\right)$

b. $\frac{d}{dx}\log_8\left(7x^2+4\right)$

#### Solution

We need to apply the chain rule as necessary.

a. $\frac{d}{dt}\left(4^t\cdot 2^{t^2}\right) = \frac{d}{dt}\left(2^{2t}\cdot 2^{t^2}\right) = \frac{d}{dt}\left(2^{2t+t^2}\right) = 2^{2t+t^2}\ln(2)(2+2t)$

b. $\frac{d}{dx}\log_8\left(7x^2+4\right) = \frac{1}{\left(7x^2+4\right)(\ln 8)}(14x)$

**2.40** Evaluate the following derivatives:

a. $\frac{d}{dt}4^{t^4}$

b. $\frac{d}{dx}\log_3\left(\sqrt{x^2+1}\right)$

## Example 2.41

### Integrating General Exponential Functions

Evaluate the following integral: $\int \frac{3}{2^{3x}} dx.$

### Solution

Use $u$-substitution and let $u = -3x$. Then $du = -3dx$ and we have

$$\int \frac{3}{2^{3x}} dx = \int 3 \cdot 2^{-3x} dx = -\int 2^u du = -\frac{1}{\ln 2} 2^u + C = -\frac{1}{\ln 2} 2^{-3x} + C.$$

**2.41** Evaluate the following integral: $\int x^2 2^{x^3} dx.$

# 2.7 EXERCISES

For the following exercises, find the derivative $\frac{dy}{dx}$.

295. $y = \ln(2x)$

296. $y = \ln(2x + 1)$

297. $y = \frac{1}{\ln x}$

For the following exercises, find the indefinite integral.

298. $\int \frac{dt}{3t}$

299. $\int \frac{dx}{1 + x}$

For the following exercises, find the derivative $dy/dx$. (You can use a calculator to plot the function and the derivative to confirm that it is correct.)

300. **[T]** $y = \frac{\ln(x)}{x}$

301. **[T]** $y = x\ln(x)$

302. **[T]** $y = \log_{10} x$

303. **[T]** $y = \ln(\sin x)$

304. **[T]** $y = \ln(\ln x)$

305. **[T]** $y = 7\ln(4x)$

306. **[T]** $y = \ln\left((4x)^7\right)$

307. **[T]** $y = \ln(\tan x)$

308. **[T]** $y = \ln(\tan(3x))$

309. **[T]** $y = \ln\left(\cos^2 x\right)$

For the following exercises, find the definite or indefinite integral.

310. $\int_0^1 \frac{dx}{3 + x}$

311. $\int_0^1 \frac{dt}{3 + 2t}$

312. $\int_0^2 \frac{x\,dx}{x^2 + 1}$

313. $\int_0^2 \frac{x^3\,dx}{x^2 + 1}$

314. $\int_2^e \frac{dx}{x\ln x}$

315. $\int_2^e \frac{dx}{(x\ln(x))^2}$

316. $\int \frac{\cos x\,dx}{\sin x}$

317. $\int_0^{\pi/4} \tan x\,dx$

318. $\int \cot(3x)dx$

319. $\int \frac{(\ln x)^2\,dx}{x}$

For the following exercises, compute $dy/dx$ by differentiating $\ln y$.

320. $y = \sqrt{x^2 + 1}$

321. $y = \sqrt{x^2 + 1}\sqrt{x^2 - 1}$

322. $y = e^{\sin x}$

323. $y = x^{-1/x}$

324. $y = e^{(ex)}$

325. $y = x^e$

326. $y = x^{(ex)}$

327. $y = \sqrt{x}\sqrt[3]{x}\sqrt[6]{x}$

328. $y = x^{-1/\ln x}$

329. $y = e^{-\ln x}$

For the following exercises, evaluate by any method.

330. $\int_5^{10} \frac{dt}{t} - \int_{5x}^{10x} \frac{dt}{t}$

331. $\int_1^{e^{\pi}} \frac{dx}{x} + \int_{-2}^{-1} \frac{dx}{x}$

332. $\frac{d}{dx}\int_x^1 \frac{dt}{t}$

333. $\frac{d}{dx}\int_x^{x^2} \frac{dt}{t}$

334. $\frac{d}{dx}\ln(\sec x + \tan x)$

For the following exercises, use the function $\ln x$. If you are unable to find intersection points analytically, use a calculator.

335. Find the area of the region enclosed by $x = 1$ and $y = 5$ above $y = \ln x$.

336. **[T]** Find the arc length of $\ln x$ from $x = 1$ to $x = 2$.

337. Find the area between $\ln x$ and the $x$-axis from $x = 1$ to $x = 2$.

338. Find the volume of the shape created when rotating this curve from $x = 1$ to $x = 2$ around the $x$-axis, as pictured here.

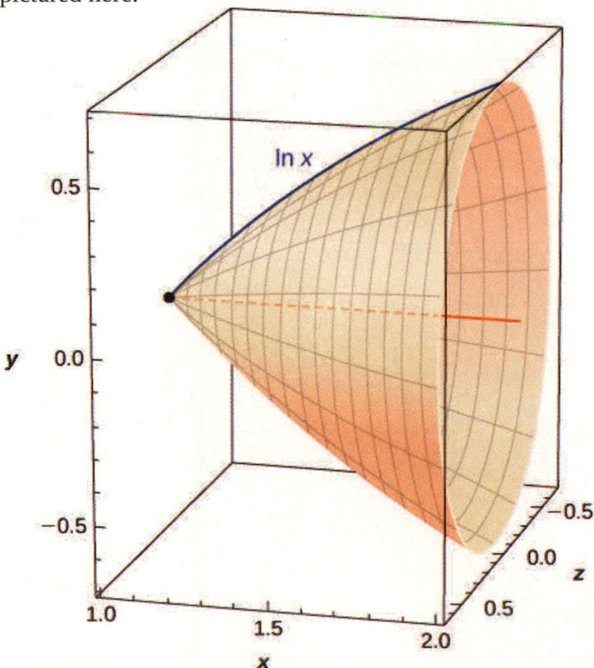


339. **[T]** Find the surface area of the shape created when rotating the curve in the previous exercise from $x = 1$ to $x = 2$ around the $x$-axis.

If you are unable to find intersection points analytically in the following exercises, use a calculator.

340. Find the area of the hyperbolic quarter-circle enclosed by $x = 2$ and $y = 2$ above $y = 1/x$.

341. **[T]** Find the arc length of $y = 1/x$ from $x = 1$ to $x = 4$.

342. Find the area under $y = 1/x$ and above the $x$-axis from $x = 1$ to $x = 4$.

For the following exercises, verify the derivatives and antiderivatives.

343. $\frac{d}{dx}\ln\left(x + \sqrt{x^2 + 1}\right) = \frac{1}{\sqrt{1 + x^2}}$

344. $\frac{d}{dx}\ln\left(\frac{x - a}{x + a}\right) = \frac{2a}{\left(x^2 - a^2\right)}$

345. $\frac{d}{dx}\ln\left(\frac{1 + \sqrt{1 - x^2}}{x}\right) = -\frac{1}{x\sqrt{1 - x^2}}$

346. $\frac{d}{dx}\ln\left(x + \sqrt{x^2 - a^2}\right) = \frac{1}{\sqrt{x^2 - a^2}}$

347. $\int \frac{dx}{x\ln(x)\ln(\ln x)} = \ln(\ln(\ln x)) + C$

# 2.8 | Exponential Growth and Decay

## Learning Objectives

2.8.1 Use the exponential growth model in applications, including population growth and compound interest.

2.8.2 Explain the concept of doubling time.

2.8.3 Use the exponential decay model in applications, including radioactive decay and Newton's law of cooling.

2.8.4 Explain the concept of half-life.

One of the most prevalent applications of exponential functions involves growth and decay models. Exponential growth and decay show up in a host of natural applications. From population growth and continuously compounded interest to radioactive decay and Newton's law of cooling, exponential functions are ubiquitous in nature. In this section, we examine exponential growth and decay in the context of some of these applications.

## Exponential Growth Model

Many systems exhibit exponential growth. These systems follow a model of the form $y = y_0 e^{kt}$, where $y_0$ represents the initial state of the system and $k$ is a positive constant, called the *growth constant*. Notice that in an exponential growth model, we have

$$y' = ky_0 e^{kt} = ky. \tag{2.27}$$

That is, the rate of growth is proportional to the current function value. This is a key feature of exponential growth. **Equation 2.27** involves derivatives and is called a *differential equation*. We learn more about differential equations in **Introduction to Differential Equations**.

### Rule: Exponential Growth Model

Systems that exhibit **exponential growth** increase according to the mathematical model

$$y = y_0 e^{kt},$$

where $y_0$ represents the initial state of the system and $k > 0$ is a constant, called the *growth constant*.

Population growth is a common example of exponential growth. Consider a population of bacteria, for instance. It seems plausible that the rate of population growth would be proportional to the size of the population. After all, the more bacteria there are to reproduce, the faster the population grows. **Figure 2.79** and **Table 2.1** represent the growth of a population of bacteria with an initial population of $200$ bacteria and a growth constant of $0.02.$ Notice that after only $2$ hours ($120$ minutes), the population is $10$ times its original size!

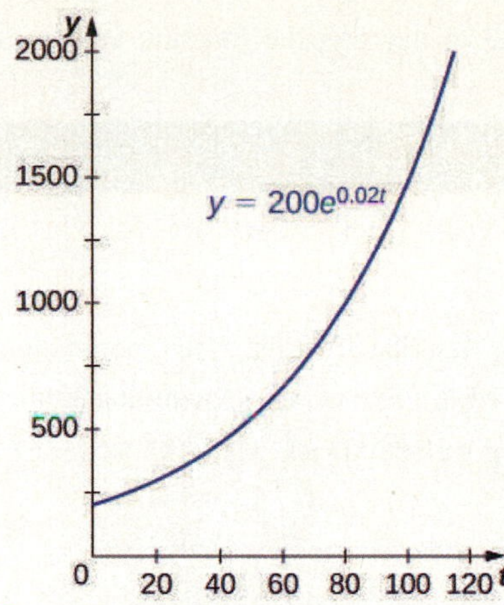


**Figure 2.79** An example of exponential growth for bacteria.

| Time (min) | Population Size (no. of bacteria) |
|---|---|
| 10 | 244 |
| 20 | 298 |
| 30 | 364 |
| 40 | 445 |
| 50 | 544 |
| 60 | 664 |
| 70 | 811 |
| 80 | 991 |
| 90 | 1210 |
| 100 | 1478 |
| 110 | 1805 |
| 120 | 2205 |

**Table 2.1** Exponential Growth of a Bacterial Population

Note that we are using a continuous function to model what is inherently discrete behavior. At any given time, the real-world population contains a whole number of bacteria, although the model takes on noninteger values. When using exponential growth models, we must always be careful to interpret the function values in the context of the phenomenon we are modeling.

## Example 2.42

### Population Growth

Consider the population of bacteria described earlier. This population grows according to the function $f(t) = 200e^{0.02t}$, where $t$ is measured in minutes. How many bacteria are present in the population after 5 hours (300 minutes)? When does the population reach 100,000 bacteria?

### Solution

We have $f(t) = 200e^{0.02t}$. Then

$$f(300) = 200e^{0.02(300)} \approx 80{,}686.$$

There are 80,686 bacteria in the population after 5 hours.

To find when the population reaches 100,000 bacteria, we solve the equation

$$\begin{aligned} 100{,}000 &= 200e^{0.02t} \\ 500 &= e^{0.02t} \\ \ln 500 &= 0.02t \\ t &= \frac{\ln 500}{0.02} \approx 310.73. \end{aligned}$$

The population reaches 100,000 bacteria after 310.73 minutes.

**2.42** Consider a population of bacteria that grows according to the function $f(t) = 500e^{0.05t}$, where $t$ is measured in minutes. How many bacteria are present in the population after 4 hours? When does the population reach 100 million bacteria?

Let's now turn our attention to a financial application: compound interest. Interest that is not compounded is called *simple interest*. Simple interest is paid once, at the end of the specified time period (usually 1 year). So, if we put \$1000 in a savings account earning 2% simple interest per year, then at the end of the year we have

$$1000(1 + 0.02) = \$1020.$$

Compound interest is paid multiple times per year, depending on the compounding period. Therefore, if the bank compounds the interest every 6 months, it credits half of the year's interest to the account after 6 months. During the second half of the year, the account earns interest not only on the initial \$1000, but also on the interest earned during the first half of the year. Mathematically speaking, at the end of the year, we have

$$1000\left(1 + \frac{0.02}{2}\right)^2 = \$1020.10.$$

Similarly, if the interest is compounded every 4 months, we have

$$1000\left(1 + \frac{0.02}{3}\right)^3 = \$1020.13,$$

and if the interest is compounded daily (365 times per year), we have \$1020.20. If we extend this concept, so that the interest is compounded continuously, after $t$ years we have

$$1000\lim_{n \to \infty}\left(1 + \frac{0.02}{n}\right)^{nt}.$$

Now let's manipulate this expression so that we have an exponential growth function. Recall that the number $e$ can be expressed as a limit:

$$e = \lim_{m \to \infty}\left(1 + \frac{1}{m}\right)^{m}.$$

Based on this, we want the expression inside the parentheses to have the form $(1 + 1/m)$. Let $n = 0.02m$. Note that as $n \to \infty$, $m \to \infty$ as well. Then we get

$$1000\lim_{n \to \infty}\left(1 + \frac{0.02}{n}\right)^{nt} = 1000\lim_{m \to \infty}\left(1 + \frac{0.02}{0.02m}\right)^{0.02mt} = 1000\left[\lim_{m \to \infty}\left(1 + \frac{1}{m}\right)^{m}\right]^{0.02t}.$$

We recognize the limit inside the brackets as the number $e$. So, the balance in our bank account after $t$ years is given by $1000e^{0.02t}$. Generalizing this concept, we see that if a bank account with an initial balance of $\$P$ earns interest at a rate of $r\%$, compounded continuously, then the balance of the account after $t$ years is

$$\text{Balance} = Pe^{rt}.$$

## Example 2.43

### Compound Interest

A 25-year-old student is offered an opportunity to invest some money in a retirement account that pays $5\%$ annual interest compounded continuously. How much does the student need to invest today to have $\$1$ million when she retires at age $65$? What if she could earn $6\%$ annual interest compounded continuously instead?

### Solution

We have

$$\begin{aligned} 1{,}000{,}000 &= Pe^{0.05(40)} \\ P &= 135{,}335.28. \end{aligned}$$

She must invest $\$135{,}335.28$ at $5\%$ interest.

If, instead, she is able to earn $6\%$, then the equation becomes

$$\begin{aligned} 1{,}000{,}000 &= Pe^{0.06(40)} \\ P &= 90{,}717.95. \end{aligned}$$

In this case, she needs to invest only $\$90{,}717.95$. This is roughly two-thirds the amount she needs to invest at $5\%$. The fact that the interest is compounded continuously greatly magnifies the effect of the $1\%$ increase in interest rate.

**2.43** Suppose instead of investing at age $25\sqrt{b^2 - 4ac}$, the student waits until age $35$. How much would she have to invest at $5\%$? At $6\%$?

If a quantity grows exponentially, the time it takes for the quantity to double remains constant. In other words, it takes the same amount of time for a population of bacteria to grow from $100$ to $200$ bacteria as it does to grow from $10{,}000$ to $20{,}000$ bacteria. This time is called the doubling time. To calculate the doubling time, we want to know when the quantity reaches twice its original size. So we have

$$\begin{aligned} 2y_0 &= y_0 e^{kt} \\ 2 &= e^{kt} \\ \ln 2 &= kt \\ t &= \frac{\ln 2}{k}. \end{aligned}$$

### Definition

If a quantity grows exponentially, the **doubling time** is the amount of time it takes the quantity to double. It is given by

$$\text{Doubling time} = \frac{\ln 2}{k}.$$

## Example 2.44

### Using the Doubling Time

Assume a population of fish grows exponentially. A pond is stocked initially with 500 fish. After 6 months, there are 1000 fish in the pond. The owner will allow his friends and neighbors to fish on his pond after the fish population reaches 10,000. When will the owner's friends be allowed to fish?

### Solution

We know it takes the population of fish 6 months to double in size. So, if $t$ represents time in months, by the doubling-time formula, we have $6 = (\ln 2)/k$. Then, $k = (\ln 2)/6$. Thus, the population is given by $y = 500e^{((\ln 2)/6)t}$. To figure out when the population reaches 10,000 fish, we must solve the following equation:

$$\begin{aligned} 10{,}000 &= 500e^{(\ln 2/6)t} \\ 20 &= e^{(\ln 2/6)t} \\ \ln 20 &= \left(\frac{\ln 2}{6}\right)t \\ t &= \frac{6(\ln 20)}{\ln 2} \approx 25.93. \end{aligned}$$

The owner's friends have to wait 25.93 months (a little more than 2 years) to fish in the pond.

**2.44** Suppose it takes 9 months for the fish population in **Example 2.44** to reach 1000 fish. Under these circumstances, how long do the owner's friends have to wait?

## Exponential Decay Model

Exponential functions can also be used to model populations that shrink (from disease, for example), or chemical compounds that break down over time. We say that such systems exhibit exponential decay, rather than exponential growth. The model is nearly the same, except there is a negative sign in the exponent. Thus, for some positive constant $k$, we have $y = y_0 e^{-kt}$.

As with exponential growth, there is a differential equation associated with exponential decay. We have

$$y' = -ky_0 e^{-kt} = -ky.$$

### Rule: Exponential Decay Model

Systems that exhibit **exponential decay** behave according to the model

$$y = y_0 e^{-kt},$$

where $y_0$ represents the initial state of the system and $k > 0$ is a constant, called the *decay constant*.

The following figure shows a graph of a representative exponential decay function.

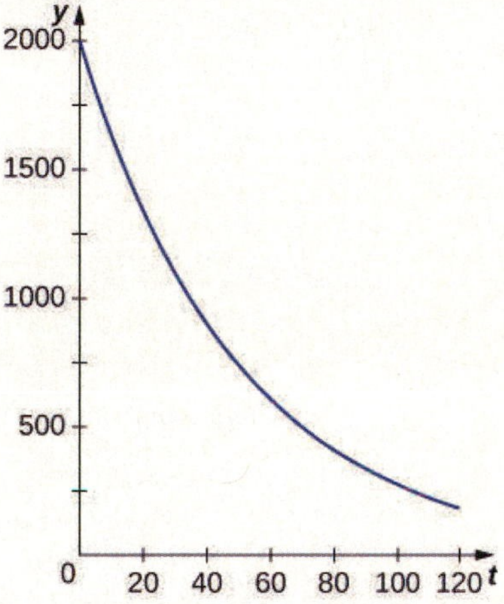


**Figure 2.80** An example of exponential decay.

Let's look at a physical application of exponential decay. Newton's law of cooling says that an object cools at a rate proportional to the difference between the temperature of the object and the temperature of the surroundings. In other words, if $T$ represents the temperature of the object and $T_a$ represents the ambient temperature in a room, then

$$T' = -k(T - T_a).$$

Note that this is not quite the right model for exponential decay. We want the derivative to be proportional to the function, and this expression has the additional $T_a$ term. Fortunately, we can make a change of variables that resolves this issue. Let $y(t) = T(t) - T_a$. Then $y'(t) = T'(t) - 0 = T'(t),$ and our equation becomes

$$y' = -ky.$$

From our previous work, we know this relationship between $y$ and its derivative leads to exponential decay. Thus,

$$y = y_0 e^{-kt},$$

and we see that

$$\begin{aligned} T - T_a &= (T_0 - T_a)e^{-kt} \\ T &= (T_0 - T_a)e^{-kt} + T_a \end{aligned}$$

where $T_0$ represents the initial temperature. Let's apply this formula in the following example.

## Example 2.45

### Newton's Law of Cooling

According to experienced baristas, the optimal temperature to serve coffee is between $155°F$ and $175°F$. Suppose coffee is poured at a temperature of $200°F$, and after $2$ minutes in a $70°F$ room it has cooled to $180°F$. When is the coffee first cool enough to serve? When is the coffee too cold to serve? Round answers to the nearest half minute.

### Solution

We have

$$\begin{aligned} T &= (T_0 - T_a)e^{-kt} + T_a \\ 180 &= (200 - 70)e^{-k(2)} + 70 \\ 110 &= 130e^{-2k} \\ \frac{11}{13} &= e^{-2k} \\ \ln \frac{11}{13} &= -2k \\ \ln 11 - \ln 13 &= -2k \\ k &= \frac{\ln 13 - \ln 11}{2}. \end{aligned}$$

Then, the model is

$$T = 130e^{(\ln 11 - \ln 13/2)t} + 70.$$

The coffee reaches $175°F$ when

$$\begin{aligned} 175 &= 130e^{(\ln 11 - \ln 13/2)t} + 70 \\ 105 &= 130e^{(\ln 11 - \ln 13/2)t} \\ \frac{21}{26} &= e^{(\ln 11 - \ln 13/2)t} \\ \ln \frac{21}{26} &= \frac{\ln 11 - \ln 13}{2}t \\ \ln 21 - \ln 26 &= \frac{\ln 11 - \ln 13}{2}t \\ t &= \frac{2(\ln 21 - \ln 26)}{\ln 11 - \ln 13} \approx 2.56. \end{aligned}$$

The coffee can be served about $2.5$ minutes after it is poured. The coffee reaches $155°F$ at

$$\begin{aligned} 155 &= 130e^{(\ln 11 - \ln 13/2)t} + 70 \\ 85 &= 130e^{(\ln 11 - \ln 13)t} \\ \frac{17}{26} &= e^{(\ln 11 - \ln 13)t} \\ \ln 17 - \ln 26 &= \left(\frac{\ln 11 - \ln 13}{2}\right)t \\ t &= \frac{2(\ln 17 - \ln 26)}{\ln 11 - \ln 13} \approx 5.09. \end{aligned}$$

The coffee is too cold to be served about $5$ minutes after it is poured.

**2.45** Suppose the room is warmer $(75°F)$ and, after $2$ minutes, the coffee has cooled only to $185°F$. When is the coffee first cool enough to serve? When is the coffee be too cold to serve? Round answers to the nearest half minute.

Just as systems exhibiting exponential growth have a constant doubling time, systems exhibiting exponential decay have a constant half-life. To calculate the half-life, we want to know when the quantity reaches half its original size. Therefore, we have

$$\begin{aligned} \frac{y_0}{2} &= y_0 e^{-kt} \\ \frac{1}{2} &= e^{-kt} \\ -\ln 2 &= -kt \\ t &= \frac{\ln 2}{k}. \end{aligned}$$

*Note*: This is the same expression we came up with for doubling time.

### Definition

If a quantity decays exponentially, the **half-life** is the amount of time it takes the quantity to be reduced by half. It is given by

$$\text{Half-life} = \frac{\ln 2}{k}.$$

## Example 2.46

### Radiocarbon Dating

One of the most common applications of an exponential decay model is carbon dating. Carbon-14 decays (emits a radioactive particle) at a regular and consistent exponential rate. Therefore, if we know how much carbon was originally present in an object and how much carbon remains, we can determine the age of the object. The half-life of carbon-14 is approximately 5730 years—meaning, after that many years, half the material has converted from the original carbon-14 to the new nonradioactive nitrogen-14. If we have 100 g carbon-14 today, how much is left in 50 years? If an artifact that originally contained 100 g of carbon now contains 10 g of carbon, how old is it? Round the answer to the nearest hundred years.

### Solution

We have

$$\begin{aligned} 5730 &= \frac{\ln 2}{k} \\ k &= \frac{\ln 2}{5730}. \end{aligned}$$

So, the model says

$$y = 100e^{-(\ln 2/5730)t}.$$

In 50 years, we have

$$\begin{aligned} y &= 100e^{-(\ln 2/5730)(50)} \\ &\approx 99.40. \end{aligned}$$

Therefore, in 50 years, 99.40 g of carbon-14 remains.

To determine the age of the artifact, we must solve

$$\begin{aligned} 10 &= 100e^{-(\ln 2/5730)t} \\ \frac{1}{10} &= e^{-(\ln 2/5730)t} \\ t &\approx 19035. \end{aligned}$$

The artifact is about $19,000$ years old.

**2.46** If we have $100$ g of $\text{carbon-14},$ how much is left after. years? If an artifact that originally contained $100$ g of carbon now contains $20g$ of carbon, how old is it? Round the answer to the nearest hundred years.

## 2.8 EXERCISES

*True or False*? If true, prove it. If false, find the true answer.

348. The doubling time for $y = e^{ct}$ is $(\ln(2))/(\ln(c))$.

349. If you invest $500, an annual rate of interest of 3% yields more money in the first year than a 2.5% continuous rate of interest.

350. If you leave a 100°C pot of tea at room temperature (25°C) and an identical pot in the refrigerator (5°C), with $k = 0.02$, the tea in the refrigerator reaches a drinkable temperature (70°C) more than 5 minutes before the tea at room temperature.

351. If given a half-life of $t$ years, the constant $k$ for $y = e^{kt}$ is calculated by $k = \ln(1/2)/t$.

For the following exercises, use $y = y_0 e^{kt}$.

352. If a culture of bacteria doubles in 3 hours, how many hours does it take to multiply by 10?

353. If bacteria increase by a factor of 10 in 10 hours, how many hours does it take to increase by 100?

354. How old is a skull that contains one-fifth as much radiocarbon as a modern skull? Note that the half-life of radiocarbon is 5730 years.

355. If a relic contains 90% as much radiocarbon as new material, can it have come from the time of Christ (approximately 2000 years ago)? Note that the half-life of radiocarbon is 5730 years.

356. The population of Cairo grew from 5 million to 10 million in 20 years. Use an exponential model to find when the population was 8 million.

357. The populations of New York and Los Angeles are growing at 1% and 1.4% a year, respectively. Starting from 8 million (New York) and 6 million (Los Angeles), when are the populations equal?

358. Suppose the value of $1 in Japanese yen decreases at 2% per year. Starting from $1 = ¥250, when will $1 = ¥1?

359. The effect of advertising decays exponentially. If 40% of the population remembers a new product after 3 days, how long will 20% remember it?

360. If $y = 1000$ at $t = 3$ and $y = 3000$ at $t = 4$, what was $y_0$ at $t = 0$?

361. If $y = 100$ at $t = 4$ and $y = 10$ at $t = 8$, when does $y = 1$?

362. If a bank offers annual interest of 7.5% or continuous interest of 7.25%, which has a better annual yield?

363. What continuous interest rate has the same yield as an annual rate of 9%?

364. If you deposit $5000 at 8% annual interest, how many years can you withdraw $500 (starting after the first year) without running out of money?

365. You are trying to save $50,000 in 20 years for college tuition for your child. If interest is a continuous 10%, how much do you need to invest initially?

366. You are cooling a turkey that was taken out of the oven with an internal temperature of 165°F. After 10 minutes of resting the turkey in a 70°F apartment, the temperature has reached 155°F. What is the temperature of the turkey 20 minutes after taking it out of the oven?

367. You are trying to thaw some vegetables that are at a temperature of 1°F. To thaw vegetables safely, you must put them in the refrigerator, which has an ambient temperature of 44°F. You check on your vegetables 2 hours after putting them in the refrigerator to find that they are now 12°F. Plot the resulting temperature curve and use it to determine when the vegetables reach 33°F.

368. You are an archaeologist and are given a bone that is claimed to be from a Tyrannosaurus Rex. You know these dinosaurs lived during the Cretaceous Era (146 million years to 65 million years ago), and you find by radiocarbon dating that there is 0.000001% the amount of radiocarbon. Is this bone from the Cretaceous?

369. The spent fuel of a nuclear reactor contains plutonium-239, which has a half-life of 24,000 years. If 1 barrel containing 10 kg of plutonium-239 is sealed, how many years must pass until only 10$g$ of plutonium-239 is left?

For the next set of exercises, use the following table, which features the world population by decade.

| Years since 1950 | Population (millions) |
|---|---|
| 0 | 2,556 |
| 10 | 3,039 |
| 20 | 3,706 |
| 30 | 4,453 |
| 40 | 5,279 |
| 50 | 6,083 |
| 60 | 6,849 |

*Source*: http://www.factmonster.com/ipka/A0762181.html.

370. **[T]** The best-fit exponential curve to the data of the form $P(t) = ae^{bt}$ is given by $P(t) = 2686e^{0.01604t}$. Use a graphing calculator to graph the data and the exponential curve together.

371. **[T]** Find and graph the derivative $y'$ of your equation. Where is it increasing and what is the meaning of this increase?

372. **[T]** Find and graph the second derivative of your equation. Where is it increasing and what is the meaning of this increase?

373. **[T]** Find the predicted date when the population reaches 10 billion. Using your previous answers about the first and second derivatives, explain why exponential growth is unsuccessful in predicting the future.

For the next set of exercises, use the following table, which shows the population of San Francisco during the 19th century.

| Years since 1850 | Population (thousands) |
|---|---|
| 0 | 21.00 |
| 10 | 56.80 |
| 20 | 149.5 |
| 30 | 234.0 |

*Source*: http://www.sfgenealogy.com/sf/history/hgpop.htm.

374. **[T]** The best-fit exponential curve to the data of the form $P(t) = ae^{bt}$ is given by $P(t) = 35.26e^{0.06407t}$. Use a graphing calculator to graph the data and the exponential curve together.

375. **[T]** Find and graph the derivative $y'$ of your equation. Where is it increasing? What is the meaning of this increase? Is there a value where the increase is maximal?

376. **[T]** Find and graph the second derivative of your equation. Where is it increasing? What is the meaning of this increase?

# 2.9 | Calculus of the Hyperbolic Functions

## Learning Objectives

**2.9.1** Apply the formulas for derivatives and integrals of the hyperbolic functions.

**2.9.2** Apply the formulas for the derivatives of the inverse hyperbolic functions and their associated integrals.

**2.9.3** Describe the common applied conditions of a catenary curve.

We were introduced to hyperbolic functions in **Introduction to Functions and Graphs (http://cnx.org/content/m53472/latest/)** , along with some of their basic properties. In this section, we look at differentiation and integration formulas for the hyperbolic functions and their inverses.

## Derivatives and Integrals of the Hyperbolic Functions

Recall that the hyperbolic sine and hyperbolic cosine are defined as

$$\sinh x = \frac{e^x - e^{-x}}{2} \text{ and } \cosh x = \frac{e^x + e^{-x}}{2}.$$

The other hyperbolic functions are then defined in terms of $\sinh x$ and $\cosh x$. The graphs of the hyperbolic functions are shown in the following figure.

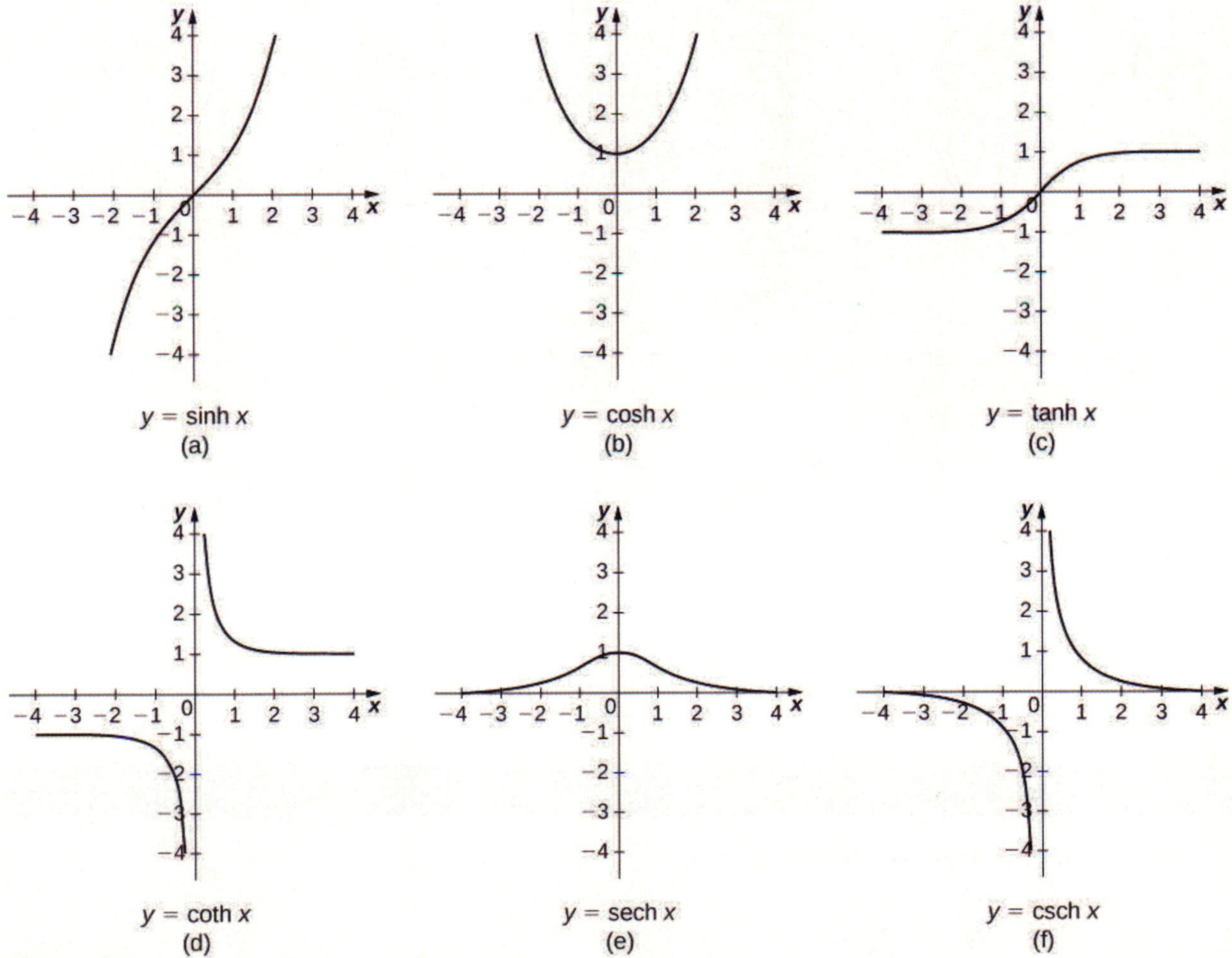


**Figure 2.81** Graphs of the hyperbolic functions.

It is easy to develop differentiation formulas for the hyperbolic functions. For example, looking at $\sinh x$ we have

$$\begin{aligned}\frac{d}{dx}(\sinh x) &= \frac{d}{dx}\left(\frac{e^x - e^{-x}}{2}\right) \\ &= \frac{1}{2}\left[\frac{d}{dx}(e^x) - \frac{d}{dx}(e^{-x})\right] \\ &= \frac{1}{2}[e^x + e^{-x}] = \cosh x.\end{aligned}$$

Similarly, $(d/dx)\cosh x = \sinh x$. We summarize the differentiation formulas for the hyperbolic functions in the following table.

| $f(x)$ | $\frac{d}{dx}f(x)$ |
|---|---|
| $\sinh x$ | $\cosh x$ |
| $\cosh x$ | $\sinh x$ |
| $\tanh x$ | $\text{sech}^2\, x$ |
| $\coth x$ | $-\text{csch}^2\, x$ |
| $\text{sech}\, x$ | $-\text{sech}\, x \tanh x$ |
| $\text{csch}\, x$ | $-\text{csch}\, x \coth x$ |

**Table 2.2** Derivatives of the Hyperbolic Functions

Let's take a moment to compare the derivatives of the hyperbolic functions with the derivatives of the standard trigonometric functions. There are a lot of similarities, but differences as well. For example, the derivatives of the sine functions match: $(d/dx)\sin x = \cos x$ and $(d/dx)\sinh x = \cosh x$. The derivatives of the cosine functions, however, differ in sign: $(d/dx)\cos x = -\sin x$, but $(d/dx)\cosh x = \sinh x$. As we continue our examination of the hyperbolic functions, we must be mindful of their similarities and differences to the standard trigonometric functions.

These differentiation formulas for the hyperbolic functions lead directly to the following integral formulas.

$$\begin{aligned}\int \sinh u\, du &= \cosh u + C & \int \text{csch}^2\, u\, du &= -\coth u + C \\ \int \cosh u\, du &= \sinh u + C & \int \text{sech}\, u \tanh u\, du &= -\text{sech}\, u + C \\ \int \text{sech}^2 u\, du &= \tanh u + C & \int \text{csch}\, u \coth u\, du &= -\text{csch}\, u + C\end{aligned}$$

## Example 2.47

### Differentiating Hyperbolic Functions

Evaluate the following derivatives:

a. $\frac{d}{dx}\left(\sinh\left(x^2\right)\right)$

b. $\frac{d}{dx}(\cosh x)^2$

### Solution

Using the formulas in **Table 2.2** and the chain rule, we get

a. $\frac{d}{dx}\left(\sinh\left(x^2\right)\right) = \cosh\left(x^2\right) \cdot 2x$

b. $\frac{d}{dx}(\cosh x)^2 = 2 \cosh x \sinh x$

**2.47** Evaluate the following derivatives:

a. $\frac{d}{dx}\left(\tanh\left(x^2 + 3x\right)\right)$

b. $\frac{d}{dx}\left(\frac{1}{(\sinh x)^2}\right)$

## Example 2.48

### Integrals Involving Hyperbolic Functions

Evaluate the following integrals:

a. $\int x \cosh\left(x^2\right) dx$

b. $\int \tanh x \, dx$

### Solution

We can use $u$-substitution in both cases.

a. Let $u = x^2$. Then, $du = 2x\,dx$ and

$$\int x \cosh\left(x^2\right) dx = \int \frac{1}{2} \cosh u \, du = \frac{1}{2} \sinh u + C = \frac{1}{2} \sinh\left(x^2\right) + C.$$

b. Let $u = \cosh x$. Then, $du = \sinh x \, dx$ and

$$\int \tanh x \, dx = \int \frac{\sinh x}{\cosh x} dx = \int \frac{1}{u} du = \ln|u| + C = \ln|\cosh x| + C.$$

Note that $\cosh x > 0$ for all $x$, so we can eliminate the absolute value signs and obtain

$$\int \tanh x \, dx = \ln(\cosh x) + C.$$

**2.48** Evaluate the following integrals:

a. $\int \sinh^3 x \cosh x \, dx$

b. $\int \text{sech}^2 (3x) dx$

## Calculus of Inverse Hyperbolic Functions

Looking at the graphs of the hyperbolic functions, we see that with appropriate range restrictions, they all have inverses. Most of the necessary range restrictions can be discerned by close examination of the graphs. The domains and ranges of the inverse hyperbolic functions are summarized in the following table.

| Function | Domain | Range |
|---|---|---|
| $\sinh^{-1} x$ | $(-\infty, \infty)$ | $(-\infty, \infty)$ |
| $\cosh^{-1} x$ | $(1, \infty)$ | $[0, \infty)$ |
| $\tanh^{-1} x$ | $(-1, 1)$ | $(-\infty, \infty)$ |
| $\coth^{-1} x$ | $(-\infty, -1) \cup (1, \infty)$ | $(-\infty, 0) \cup (0, \infty)$ |
| $\text{sech}^{-1} x$ | $(0, 1)$ | $[0, \infty)$ |
| $\text{csch}^{-1} x$ | $(-\infty, 0) \cup (0, \infty)$ | $(-\infty, 0) \cup (0, \infty)$ |

**Table 2.3** Domains and Ranges of the Inverse Hyperbolic Functions

The graphs of the inverse hyperbolic functions are shown in the following figure.

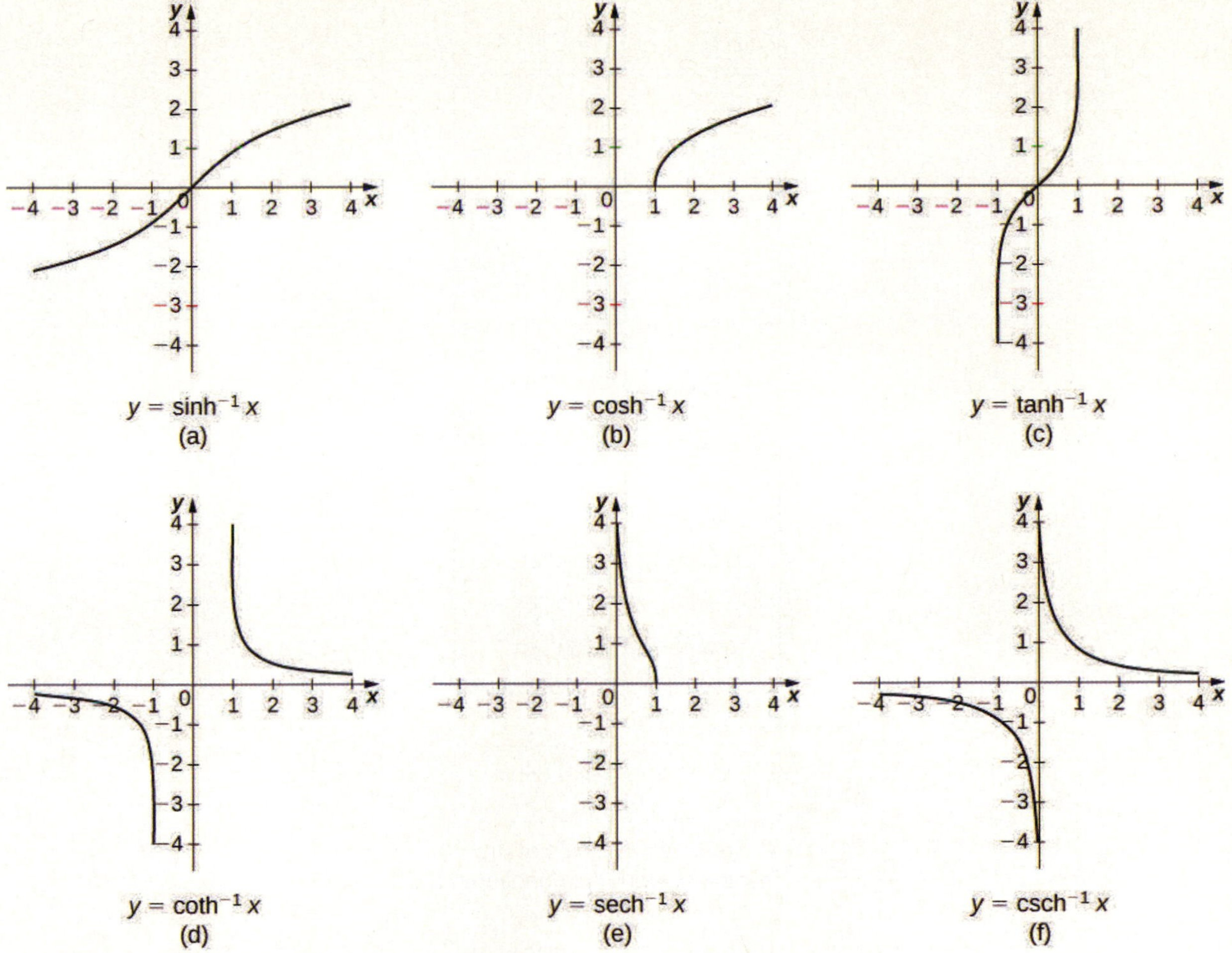


**Figure 2.82** Graphs of the inverse hyperbolic functions.

To find the derivatives of the inverse functions, we use implicit differentiation. We have

$$\begin{aligned} y &= \sinh^{-1} x \\ \sinh y &= x \\ \frac{d}{dx}\sinh y &= \frac{d}{dx}x \\ \cosh y\frac{dy}{dx} &= 1. \end{aligned}$$

Recall that $\cosh^2 y - \sinh^2 y = 1,$ so $\cosh y = \sqrt{1 + \sinh^2 y}.$ Then,

$$\frac{dy}{dx} = \frac{1}{\cosh y} = \frac{1}{\sqrt{1 + \sinh^2 y}} = \frac{1}{\sqrt{1 + x^2}}.$$

We can derive differentiation formulas for the other inverse hyperbolic functions in a similar fashion. These differentiation formulas are summarized in the following table.

| $f(x)$ | $\frac{d}{dx}f(x)$ |
|---|---|
| $\sinh^{-1} x$ | $\frac{1}{\sqrt{1+x^2}}$ |
| $\cosh^{-1} x$ | $\frac{1}{\sqrt{x^2-1}}$ |
| $\tanh^{-1} x$ | $\frac{1}{1-x^2}$ |
| $\coth^{-1} x$ | $\frac{1}{1-x^2}$ |
| $\text{sech}^{-1} x$ | $\frac{-1}{x\sqrt{1-x^2}}$ |
| $\text{csch}^{-1} x$ | $\frac{-1}{\lvert x\rvert\sqrt{1+x^2}}$ |

**Table 2.4** Derivatives of the Inverse Hyperbolic Functions

Note that the derivatives of $\tanh^{-1} x$ and $\coth^{-1} x$ are the same. Thus, when we integrate $1/\left(1-x^2\right)$, we need to select the proper antiderivative based on the domain of the functions and the values of $x$. Integration formulas involving the inverse hyperbolic functions are summarized as follows.

$$\int \frac{1}{\sqrt{1+u^2}}du = \sinh^{-1} u + C \qquad \int \frac{1}{u\sqrt{1-u^2}}du = -\text{sech}^{-1}\lvert u\rvert + C$$

$$\int \frac{1}{\sqrt{u^2-1}}du = \cosh^{-1} u + C \qquad \int \frac{1}{u\sqrt{1+u^2}}du = -\text{csch}^{-1}\lvert u\rvert + C$$

$$\int \frac{1}{1-u^2}du = \begin{cases} \tanh^{-1} u + C \text{ if } \lvert u\rvert < 1 \\ \coth^{-1} u + C \text{ if } \lvert u\rvert > 1 \end{cases}$$

## Example 2.49

### Differentiating Inverse Hyperbolic Functions

Evaluate the following derivatives:

a. $\frac{d}{dx}\left(\sinh^{-1}\left(\frac{x}{3}\right)\right)$

b. $\frac{d}{dx}\left(\tanh^{-1} x\right)^2$

### Solution

Using the formulas in **Table 2.4** and the chain rule, we obtain the following results:

a. $\frac{d}{dx}\left(\sinh^{-1}\left(\frac{x}{3}\right)\right) = \frac{1}{3\sqrt{1+\frac{x^2}{9}}} = \frac{1}{\sqrt{9+x^2}}$

b. $\frac{d}{dx}\left(\tanh^{-1} x\right)^2 = \frac{2\left(\tanh^{-1} x\right)}{1-x^2}$

**2.49** Evaluate the following derivatives:

a. $\frac{d}{dx}\left(\cosh^{-1}(3x)\right)$

b. $\frac{d}{dx}\left(\coth^{-1} x\right)^3$

## Example 2.50

### Integrals Involving Inverse Hyperbolic Functions

Evaluate the following integrals:

a. $\int \frac{1}{\sqrt{4x^2-1}}dx$

b. $\int \frac{1}{2x\sqrt{1-9x^2}}dx$

### Solution

We can use $u$-substitution in both cases.

a. Let $u = 2x$. Then, $du = 2dx$ and we have

$$\int \frac{1}{\sqrt{4x^2-1}}dx = \int \frac{1}{2\sqrt{u^2-1}}du = \frac{1}{2}\cosh^{-1} u + C = \frac{1}{2}\cosh^{-1}(2x) + C.$$

b. Let $u = 3x$. Then, $du = 3dx$ and we obtain

$$\int \frac{1}{2x\sqrt{1-9x^2}}dx = \frac{1}{2}\int \frac{1}{u\sqrt{1-u^2}}du = -\frac{1}{2}\text{sech}^{-1}|u| + C = -\frac{1}{2}\text{sech}^{-1}|3x| + C.$$

**2.50** Evaluate the following integrals:

a. $\int \frac{1}{\sqrt{x^2-4}}dx, \quad x > 2$

b. $\int \frac{1}{\sqrt{1-e^{2x}}}dx$

## Applications

One physical application of hyperbolic functions involves hanging cables. If a cable of uniform density is suspended between two supports without any load other than its own weight, the cable forms a curve called a **catenary**. High-voltage power lines, chains hanging between two posts, and strands of a spider's web all form catenaries. The following figure shows chains hanging from a row of posts.

**Figure 2.83** Chains between these posts take the shape of a catenary. (credit: modification of work by OKFoundryCompany, Flickr)

Hyperbolic functions can be used to model catenaries. Specifically, functions of the form $y = a\cosh(x/a)$ are catenaries. **Figure 2.84** shows the graph of $y = 2\cosh(x/2)$.

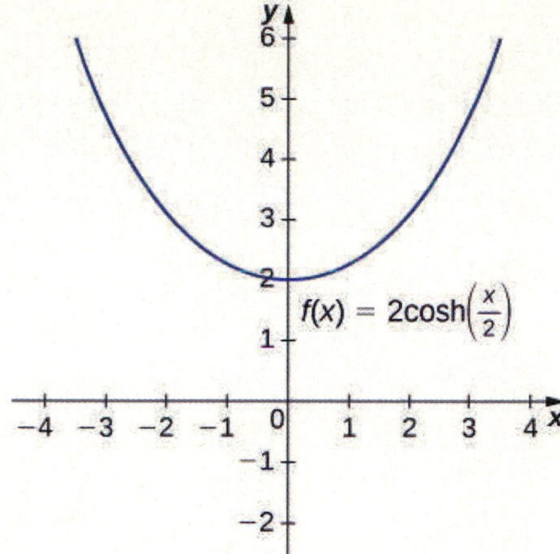


**Figure 2.84** A hyperbolic cosine function forms the shape of a catenary.

## Example 2.51

### Using a Catenary to Find the Length of a Cable

Assume a hanging cable has the shape $10\cosh(x/10)$ for $-15 \le x \le 15$, where $x$ is measured in feet. Determine the length of the cable (in feet).

#### Solution

Recall from Section 6.4 that the formula for arc length is

$$\text{Arc Length} = \int_a^b \sqrt{1 + [f'(x)]^2}\, dx.$$

We have $f(x) = 10\cosh(x/10)$, so $f'(x) = \sinh(x/10)$. Then

$$\begin{aligned}\text{Arc Length} &= \int_a^b \sqrt{1 + [f'(x)]^2}\, dx \\ &= \int_{-15}^{15} \sqrt{1 + \sinh^2\left(\frac{x}{10}\right)}\, dx.\end{aligned}$$

Now recall that $1 + \sinh^2 x = \cosh^2 x$, so we have

$$\begin{aligned}\text{Arc Length} &= \int_{-15}^{15} \sqrt{1 + \sinh^2\left(\frac{x}{10}\right)}\, dx \\ &= \int_{-15}^{15} \cosh\left(\frac{x}{10}\right) dx \\ &= 10\sinh\left(\frac{x}{10}\right)\Big|_{-15}^{15} = 10\left[\sinh\left(\frac{3}{2}\right) - \sinh\left(-\frac{3}{2}\right)\right] = 20\sinh\left(\frac{3}{2}\right) \\ &\approx 42.586 \text{ ft.}\end{aligned}$$

**2.51** Assume a hanging cable has the shape $15\cosh(x/15)$ for $-20 \le x \le 20$. Determine the length of the cable (in feet).

# 2.9 EXERCISES

377. **[T]** Find expressions for $\cosh x + \sinh x$ and $\cosh x - \sinh x$. Use a calculator to graph these functions and ensure your expression is correct.

378. From the definitions of $\cosh(x)$ and $\sinh(x)$, find their antiderivatives.

379. Show that $\cosh(x)$ and $\sinh(x)$ satisfy $y'' = y$.

380. Use the quotient rule to verify that $\tanh(x)' = \text{sech}^2(x)$.

381. Derive $\cosh^2(x) + \sinh^2(x) = \cosh(2x)$ from the definition.

382. Take the derivative of the previous expression to find an expression for $\sinh(2x)$.

383. Prove $\sinh(x + y) = \sinh(x)\cosh(y) + \cosh(x)\sinh(y)$ by changing the expression to exponentials.

384. Take the derivative of the previous expression to find an expression for $\cosh(x + y)$.

For the following exercises, find the derivatives of the given functions and graph along with the function to ensure your answer is correct.

385. **[T]** $\cosh(3x + 1)$

386. **[T]** $\sinh\left(x^2\right)$

387. **[T]** $\dfrac{1}{\cosh(x)}$

388. **[T]** $\sinh(\ln(x))$

389. **[T]** $\cosh^2(x) + \sinh^2(x)$

390. **[T]** $\cosh^2(x) - \sinh^2(x)$

391. **[T]** $\tanh\left(\sqrt{x^2 + 1}\right)$

392. **[T]** $\dfrac{1 + \tanh(x)}{1 - \tanh(x)}$

393. **[T]** $\sinh^6(x)$

394. **[T]** $\ln(\text{sech}(x) + \tanh(x))$

For the following exercises, find the antiderivatives for the given functions.

395. $\cosh(2x + 1)$

396. $\tanh(3x + 2)$

397. $x\cosh\left(x^2\right)$

398. $3x^3\tanh\left(x^4\right)$

399. $\cosh^2(x)\sinh(x)$

400. $\tanh^2(x)\text{sech}^2(x)$

401. $\dfrac{\sinh(x)}{1 + \cosh(x)}$

402. $\coth(x)$

403. $\cosh(x) + \sinh(x)$

404. $(\cosh(x) + \sinh(x))^n$

For the following exercises, find the derivatives for the functions.

405. $\tanh^{-1}(4x)$

406. $\sinh^{-1}\left(x^2\right)$

407. $\sinh^{-1}(\cosh(x))$

408. $\cosh^{-1}\left(x^3\right)$

409. $\tanh^{-1}(\cos(x))$

410. $e^{\sinh^{-1}(x)}$

411. $\ln\left(\tanh^{-1}(x)\right)$

For the following exercises, find the antiderivatives for the functions.

412. $\displaystyle\int \frac{dx}{4 - x^2}$

413. $\displaystyle\int \frac{dx}{a^2 - x^2}$

414. $\int \frac{dx}{\sqrt{x^2+1}}$

415. $\int \frac{x\,dx}{\sqrt{x^2+1}}$

416. $\int -\frac{dx}{x\sqrt{1-x^2}}$

417. $\int \frac{e^x}{\sqrt{e^{2x}-1}}$

418. $\int -\frac{2x}{x^4-1}$

For the following exercises, use the fact that a falling body with friction equal to velocity squared obeys the equation $dv/dt = g - v^2$.

419. Show that $v(t) = \sqrt{g}\tanh(\sqrt{gt})$ satisfies this equation.

420. Derive the previous expression for $v(t)$ by integrating $\frac{dv}{g-v^2} = dt$.

421. **[T]** Estimate how far a body has fallen in 12 seconds by finding the area underneath the curve of $v(t)$.

For the following exercises, use this scenario: A cable hanging under its own weight has a slope $S = dy/dx$ that satisfies $dS/dx = c\sqrt{1+S^2}$. The constant $c$ is the ratio of cable density to tension.

422. Show that $S = \sinh(cx)$ satisfies this equation.

423. Integrate $dy/dx = \sinh(cx)$ to find the cable height $y(x)$ if $y(0) = 1/c$.

424. Sketch the cable and determine how far down it sags at $x = 0$.

For the following exercises, solve each problem.

425. **[T]** A chain hangs from two posts 2 m apart to form a catenary described by the equation $y = 2\cosh(x/2) - 1$. Find the slope of the catenary at the left fence post.

426. **[T]** A chain hangs from two posts four meters apart to form a catenary described by the equation $y = 4\cosh(x/4) - 3$. Find the total length of the catenary (arc length).

427. **[T]** A high-voltage power line is a catenary described by $y = 10\cosh(x/10)$. Find the ratio of the area under the catenary to its arc length. What do you notice?

428. A telephone line is a catenary described by $y = a\cosh(x/a)$. Find the ratio of the area under the catenary to its arc length. Does this confirm your answer for the previous question?

429. Prove the formula for the derivative of $y = \sinh^{-1}(x)$ by differentiating $x = \sinh(y)$. (*Hint:* Use hyperbolic trigonometric identities.)

430. Prove the formula for the derivative of $y = \cosh^{-1}(x)$ by differentiating $x = \cosh(y)$. (*Hint:* Use hyperbolic trigonometric identities.)

431. Prove the formula for the derivative of $y = \text{sech}^{-1}(x)$ by differentiating $x = \text{sech}(y)$. (*Hint:* Use hyperbolic trigonometric identities.)

432. Prove that $(\cosh(x) + \sinh(x))^n = \cosh(nx) + \sinh(nx)$.

433. Prove the expression for $\sinh^{-1}(x)$. Multiply $x = \sinh(y) = (1/2)(e^y - e^{-y})$ by $2e^y$ and solve for $y$. Does your expression match the textbook?

434. Prove the expression for $\cosh^{-1}(x)$. Multiply $x = \cosh(y) = (1/2)(e^y - e^{-y})$ by $2e^y$ and solve for $y$. Does your expression match the textbook?

# CHAPTER 2 REVIEW

## KEY TERMS

**arc length** the arc length of a curve can be thought of as the distance a person would travel along the path of the curve

**catenary** a curve in the shape of the function $y = a\cosh(x/a)$ is a catenary; a cable of uniform density suspended between two supports assumes the shape of a catenary

**center of mass** the point at which the total mass of the system could be concentrated without changing the moment

**centroid** the centroid of a region is the geometric center of the region; laminas are often represented by regions in the plane; if the lamina has a constant density, the center of mass of the lamina depends only on the shape of the corresponding planar region; in this case, the center of mass of the lamina corresponds to the centroid of the representative region

**cross-section** the intersection of a plane and a solid object

**density function** a density function describes how mass is distributed throughout an object; it can be a linear density, expressed in terms of mass per unit length; an area density, expressed in terms of mass per unit area; or a volume density, expressed in terms of mass per unit volume; weight-density is also used to describe weight (rather than mass) per unit volume

**disk method** a special case of the slicing method used with solids of revolution when the slices are disks

**doubling time** if a quantity grows exponentially, the doubling time is the amount of time it takes the quantity to double, and is given by $(\ln 2)/k$

**exponential decay** systems that exhibit exponential decay follow a model of the form $y = y_0 e^{-kt}$

**exponential growth** systems that exhibit exponential growth follow a model of the form $y = y_0 e^{kt}$

**frustum** a portion of a cone; a frustum is constructed by cutting the cone with a plane parallel to the base

**half-life** if a quantity decays exponentially, the half-life is the amount of time it takes the quantity to be reduced by half. It is given by $(\ln 2)/k$

**Hooke's law** this law states that the force required to compress (or elongate) a spring is proportional to the distance the spring has been compressed (or stretched) from equilibrium; in other words, $F = kx,$ where $k$ is a constant

**hydrostatic pressure** the pressure exerted by water on a submerged object

**lamina** a thin sheet of material; laminas are thin enough that, for mathematical purposes, they can be treated as if they are two-dimensional

**method of cylindrical shells** a method of calculating the volume of a solid of revolution by dividing the solid into nested cylindrical shells; this method is different from the methods of disks or washers in that we integrate with respect to the opposite variable

**moment** if $n$ masses are arranged on a number line, the moment of the system with respect to the origin is given by $M = \sum_{i=1}^{n} m_i x_i;$ if, instead, we consider a region in the plane, bounded above by a function $f(x)$ over an interval $[a, b],$ then the moments of the region with respect to the $x$- and $y$-axes are given by $M_x = \rho\int_a^b \frac{[f(x)]^2}{2}dx$ and $M_y = \rho\int_a^b xf(x)dx,$ respectively

**slicing method** a method of calculating the volume of a solid that involves cutting the solid into pieces, estimating the volume of each piece, then adding these estimates to arrive at an estimate of the total volume; as the number of slices goes to infinity, this estimate becomes an integral that gives the exact value of the volume

**solid of revolution** a solid generated by revolving a region in a plane around a line in that plane

**surface area** the surface area of a solid is the total area of the outer layer of the object; for objects such as cubes or bricks, the surface area of the object is the sum of the areas of all of its faces

**symmetry principle** the symmetry principle states that if a region $R$ is symmetric about a line $l$, then the centroid of $R$ lies on $l$

**theorem of Pappus for volume** this theorem states that the volume of a solid of revolution formed by revolving a region around an external axis is equal to the area of the region multiplied by the distance traveled by the centroid of the region

**washer method** a special case of the slicing method used with solids of revolution when the slices are washers

**work** the amount of energy it takes to move an object; in physics, when a force is constant, work is expressed as the product of force and distance

# KEY EQUATIONS

- **Area between two curves, integrating on the $x$-axis**

  $$A = \int_a^b [f(x) - g(x)]dx$$

- **Area between two curves, integrating on the $y$-axis**

  $$A = \int_c^d [u(y) - v(y)]dy$$

- **Disk Method along the $x$-axis**

  $$V = \int_a^b \pi[f(x)]^2 dx$$

- **Disk Method along the $y$-axis**

  $$V = \int_c^d \pi[g(y)]^2 dy$$

- **Washer Method**

  $$V = \int_a^b \pi\left[(f(x))^2 - (g(x))^2\right]dx$$

- **Method of Cylindrical Shells**

  $$V = \int_a^b (2\pi x f(x))dx$$

- **Arc Length of a Function of $x$**

  $$\text{Arc Length} = \int_a^b \sqrt{1 + [f'(x)]^2}\, dx$$

- **Arc Length of a Function of $y$**

  $$\text{Arc Length} = \int_c^d \sqrt{1 + [g'(y)]^2}\, dy$$

- **Surface Area of a Function of $x$**

  $$\text{Surface Area} = \int_a^b \left(2\pi f(x)\sqrt{1 + (f'(x))^2}\right)dx$$

- **Mass of a one-dimensional object**

  $$m = \int_a^b \rho(x)dx$$

- **Mass of a circular object**

  $$m = \int_0^r 2\pi x\rho(x)dx$$

- **Work done on an object**
  $W = \int_a^b F(x)dx$
- **Hydrostatic force on a plate**
  $F = \int_a^b \rho w(x)s(x)dx$
- **Mass of a lamina**
  $m = \rho \int_a^b f(x)dx$
- **Moments of a lamina**
  $M_x = \rho \int_a^b \frac{[f(x)]^2}{2} dx$ and $M_y = \rho \int_a^b x f(x)dx$
- **Center of mass of a lamina**
  $\bar{x} = \frac{M_y}{m}$ and $\bar{y} = \frac{M_x}{m}$
- **Natural logarithm function**
- $\ln x = \int_1^x \frac{1}{t} dt$ Z
- **Exponential function** $y = e^x$
- $\ln y = \ln(e^x) = x$ Z

# KEY CONCEPTS

## 2.1 Areas between Curves

- Just as definite integrals can be used to find the area under a curve, they can also be used to find the area between two curves.
- To find the area between two curves defined by functions, integrate the difference of the functions.
- If the graphs of the functions cross, or if the region is complex, use the absolute value of the difference of the functions. In this case, it may be necessary to evaluate two or more integrals and add the results to find the area of the region.
- Sometimes it can be easier to integrate with respect to $y$ to find the area. The principles are the same regardless of which variable is used as the variable of integration.

## 2.2 Determining Volumes by Slicing

- Definite integrals can be used to find the volumes of solids. Using the slicing method, we can find a volume by integrating the cross-sectional area.
- For solids of revolution, the volume slices are often disks and the cross-sections are circles. The method of disks involves applying the method of slicing in the particular case in which the cross-sections are circles, and using the formula for the area of a circle.
- If a solid of revolution has a cavity in the center, the volume slices are washers. With the method of washers, the area of the inner circle is subtracted from the area of the outer circle before integrating.

## 2.3 Volumes of Revolution: Cylindrical Shells

- The method of cylindrical shells is another method for using a definite integral to calculate the volume of a solid of revolution. This method is sometimes preferable to either the method of disks or the method of washers because we integrate with respect to the other variable. In some cases, one integral is substantially more complicated than the other.

- The geometry of the functions and the difficulty of the integration are the main factors in deciding which integration method to use.

## 2.4 Arc Length of a Curve and Surface Area

- The arc length of a curve can be calculated using a definite integral.
- The arc length is first approximated using line segments, which generates a Riemann sum. Taking a limit then gives us the definite integral formula. The same process can be applied to functions of $y$.
- The concepts used to calculate the arc length can be generalized to find the surface area of a surface of revolution.
- The integrals generated by both the arc length and surface area formulas are often difficult to evaluate. It may be necessary to use a computer or calculator to approximate the values of the integrals.

## 2.5 Physical Applications

- Several physical applications of the definite integral are common in engineering and physics.
- Definite integrals can be used to determine the mass of an object if its density function is known.
- Work can also be calculated from integrating a force function, or when counteracting the force of gravity, as in a pumping problem.
- Definite integrals can also be used to calculate the force exerted on an object submerged in a liquid.

## 2.6 Moments and Centers of Mass

- Mathematically, the center of mass of a system is the point at which the total mass of the system could be concentrated without changing the moment. Loosely speaking, the center of mass can be thought of as the balancing point of the system.
- For point masses distributed along a number line, the moment of the system with respect to the origin is $M = \sum_{i=1}^{n} m_i x_i$. For point masses distributed in a plane, the moments of the system with respect to the $x$- and $y$-axes, respectively, are $M_x = \sum_{i=1}^{n} m_i y_i$ and $M_y = \sum_{i=1}^{n} m_i x_i$, respectively.
- For a lamina bounded above by a function $f(x)$, the moments of the system with respect to the $x$- and $y$-axes, respectively, are $M_x = \rho \int_a^b \frac{[f(x)]^2}{2} dx$ and $M_y = \rho \int_a^b x f(x) dx$.
- The $x$- and $y$-coordinates of the center of mass can be found by dividing the moments around the $y$-axis and around the $x$-axis, respectively, by the total mass. The symmetry principle says that if a region is symmetric with respect to a line, then the centroid of the region lies on the line.
- The theorem of Pappus for volume says that if a region is revolved around an external axis, the volume of the resulting solid is equal to the area of the region multiplied by the distance traveled by the centroid of the region.

## 2.7 Integrals, Exponential Functions, and Logarithms

- The earlier treatment of logarithms and exponential functions did not define the functions precisely and formally. This section develops the concepts in a mathematically rigorous way.
- The cornerstone of the development is the definition of the natural logarithm in terms of an integral.
- The function $e^x$ is then defined as the inverse of the natural logarithm.
- General exponential functions are defined in terms of $e^x$, and the corresponding inverse functions are general logarithms.

- Familiar properties of logarithms and exponents still hold in this more rigorous context.

### 2.8 Exponential Growth and Decay

- Exponential growth and exponential decay are two of the most common applications of exponential functions.
- Systems that exhibit exponential growth follow a model of the form $y = y_0 e^{kt}$.
- In exponential growth, the rate of growth is proportional to the quantity present. In other words, $y' = ky$.
- Systems that exhibit exponential growth have a constant doubling time, which is given by $(\ln 2)/k$.
- Systems that exhibit exponential decay follow a model of the form $y = y_0 e^{-kt}$.
- Systems that exhibit exponential decay have a constant half-life, which is given by $(\ln 2)/k$.

### 2.9 Calculus of the Hyperbolic Functions

- Hyperbolic functions are defined in terms of exponential functions.
- Term-by-term differentiation yields differentiation formulas for the hyperbolic functions. These differentiation formulas give rise, in turn, to integration formulas.
- With appropriate range restrictions, the hyperbolic functions all have inverses.
- Implicit differentiation yields differentiation formulas for the inverse hyperbolic functions, which in turn give rise to integration formulas.
- The most common physical applications of hyperbolic functions are calculations involving catenaries.

## CHAPTER 2 REVIEW EXERCISES

*True or False?* Justify your answer with a proof or a counterexample.

**435.** The amount of work to pump the water out of a half-full cylinder is half the amount of work to pump the water out of the full cylinder.

**436.** If the force is constant, the amount of work to move an object from $x = a$ to $x = b$ is $F(b - a)$.

**437.** The disk method can be used in any situation in which the washer method is successful at finding the volume of a solid of revolution.

**438.** If the half-life of seaborgium-266 is 360 ms, then $k = (\ln(2))/360$.

For the following exercises, use the requested method to determine the volume of the solid.

**439.** The volume that has a base of the ellipse $x^2/4 + y^2/9 = 1$ and cross-sections of an equilateral triangle perpendicular to the $y$-axis. Use the method of slicing.

**440.** $y = x^2 - x$, from $x = 1$ to $x = 4$, rotated around the$y$-axis using the washer method

**441.** $x = y^2$ and $x = 3y$ rotated around the $y$-axis using the washer method

**442.** $x = 2y^2 - y^3$, $x = 0$, and $y = 0$ rotated around the $x$-axis using cylindrical shells

For the following exercises, find

a. the area of the region,
b. the volume of the solid when rotated around the $x$-axis, and
c. the volume of the solid when rotated around the $y$-axis. Use whichever method seems most appropriate to you.

**443.** $y = x^3$, $x = 0$, $y = 0$, and $x = 2$

**444.** $y = x^2 - x$ and $x = 0$

**445.** **[T]** $y = \ln(x) + 2$ and $y = x$

**446.** $y = x^2$ and $y = \sqrt{x}$

**447.** $y = 5 + x$, $y = x^2$, $x = 0$, and $x = 1$

**448.** Below $x^2 + y^2 = 1$ and above $y = 1 - x$

**449.** Find the mass of $\rho = e^{-x}$ on a disk centered at the origin with radius $4$.

**450.** Find the center of mass for $\rho = \tan^2 x$ on $x \in \left(-\frac{\pi}{4}, \frac{\pi}{4}\right)$.

**451.** Find the mass and the center of mass of $\rho = 1$ on the region bounded by $y = x^5$ and $y = \sqrt{x}$.

For the following exercises, find the requested arc lengths.

**452.** The length of $x$ for $y = \cosh(x)$ from $x = 0$ to $x = 2$.

**453.** The length of $y$ for $x = 3 - \sqrt{y}$ from $y = 0$ to $y = 4$

For the following exercises, find the surface area and volume when the given curves are revolved around the specified axis.

**454.** The shape created by revolving the region between $y = 4 + x$, $y = 3 - x$, $x = 0$, and $x = 2$ rotated around the $y$-axis.

**455.** The loudspeaker created by revolving $y = 1/x$ from $x = 1$ to $x = 4$ around the $x$-axis.

For the following exercises, consider the Karun-3 dam in Iran. Its shape can be approximated as an isosceles triangle with height $205$ m and width $388$ m. Assume the current depth of the water is $180$ m. The density of water is $1000$ kg/m $^3$.

**456.** Find the total force on the wall of the dam.

**457.** You are a crime scene investigator attempting to determine the time of death of a victim. It is noon and $45°$F outside and the temperature of the body is $78°$F. You know the cooling constant is $k = 0.00824°$F/min. When did the victim die, assuming that a human's temperature is $98°$F ?

For the following exercise, consider the stock market crash in $1929$ in the United States. The table lists the Dow Jones industrial average per year leading up to the crash.

| Years after 1920 | Value ($) |
|---|---|
| 1 | 63.90 |
| 3 | 100 |
| 5 | 110 |
| 7 | 160 |
| 9 | 381.17 |

*Source*: http://stockcharts.com/freecharts/historical/djia19201940.html

**458.** **[T]** The best-fit exponential curve to these data is given by $y = 40.71 + 1.224^x$. Why do you think the gains of the market were unsustainable? Use first and second derivatives to help justify your answer. What would this model predict the Dow Jones industrial average to be in $2014$ ?

For the following exercises, consider the catenoid, the only solid of revolution that has a minimal surface, or zero mean curvature. A catenoid in nature can be found when stretching soap between two rings.

**459.** Find the volume of the catenoid $y = \cosh(x)$ from $x = -1$ to $x = 1$ that is created by rotating this curve around the $x$-axis, as shown here.

**460.** Find surface area of the catenoid $y = \cosh(x)$ from $x = -1$ to $x = 1$ that is created by rotating this curve around the $x$-axis.

# 3 | TECHNIQUES OF INTEGRATION

**Figure 3.1** Careful planning of traffic signals can prevent or reduce the number of accidents at busy intersections. (credit: modification of work by David McKelvey, Flickr)

## Chapter Outline



## Introduction

In a large city, accidents occurred at an average rate of one every three months at a particularly busy intersection. After residents complained, changes were made to the traffic lights at the intersection. It has now been eight months since the changes were made and there have been no accidents. Were the changes effective or is the eight-month interval without an accident a result of chance? We explore this question later in this chapter and see that integration is an essential part of determining the answer (see **Example 3.49**).

We saw in the previous chapter how important integration can be for all kinds of different topics—from calculations of volumes to flow rates, and from using a velocity function to determine a position to locating centers of mass. It is no surprise, then, that techniques for finding antiderivatives (or indefinite integrals) are important to know for everyone who uses them. We have already discussed some basic integration formulas and the method of integration by substitution. In this chapter, we study some additional techniques, including some ways of approximating definite integrals when normal techniques do not work.

# 3.1 | Integration by Parts

## Learning Objectives

- **3.1.1** Recognize when to use integration by parts.
- **3.1.2** Use the integration-by-parts formula to solve integration problems.
- **3.1.3** Use the integration-by-parts formula for definite integrals.

By now we have a fairly thorough procedure for how to evaluate many basic integrals. However, although we can integrate $\int x\sin(x^2)dx$ by using the substitution, $u = x^2$, something as simple looking as $\int x\sin x\,dx$ defies us. Many students want to know whether there is a product rule for integration. There isn't, but there is a technique based on the product rule for differentiation that allows us to exchange one integral for another. We call this technique **integration by parts**.

## The Integration-by-Parts Formula

If, $h(x) = f(x)g(x)$, then by using the product rule, we obtain $h'(x) = f'(x)g(x) + g'(x)f(x)$. Although at first it may seem counterproductive, let's now integrate both sides of this equation: $\int h'(x)dx = \int (g(x)f'(x) + f(x)g'(x))dx$.

This gives us

$$h(x) = f(x)g(x) = \int g(x)f'(x)dx + \int f(x)g'(x)dx.$$

Now we solve for $\int f(x)g'(x)dx$ :

$$\int f(x)g'(x)dx = f(x)g(x) - \int g(x)f'(x)dx.$$

By making the substitutions $u = f(x)$ and $v = g(x)$, which in turn make $du = f'(x)dx$ and $dv = g'(x)dx$, we have the more compact form

$$\int u\,dv = uv - \int v\,du.$$

### Theorem 3.1: Integration by Parts

Let $u = f(x)$ and $v = g(x)$ be functions with continuous derivatives. Then, the integration-by-parts formula for the integral involving these two functions is:

$$\int u\,dv = uv - \int v\,du. \tag{3.1}$$

The advantage of using the integration-by-parts formula is that we can use it to exchange one integral for another, possibly easier, integral. The following example illustrates its use.

### Example 3.1

#### Using Integration by Parts

Use integration by parts with $u = x$ and $dv = \sin x\,dx$ to evaluate $\int x\sin x\,dx$.

### Solution

By choosing $u = x$, we have $du = 1dx$. Since $dv = \sin x\, dx$, we get $v = \int \sin x\, dx = -\cos x$. It is handy to keep track of these values as follows:

$$\begin{aligned} u &= x & dv &= \sin x\, dx \\ du &= 1dx & v &= \int \sin x\, dx = -\cos x. \end{aligned}$$

Applying the integration-by-parts formula results in

$$\begin{aligned} \int x \sin x\, dx &= (x)(-\cos x) - \int(-\cos x)(1dx) && \text{Substitute.} \\ &= -x\cos x + \int \cos x\, dx && \text{Simplify.} \\ &= -x\cos x + \sin x + C. && \text{Use } \int \cos x\, dx = \sin x + C. \end{aligned}$$

### Analysis

At this point, there are probably a few items that need clarification. First of all, you may be curious about what would have happened if we had chosen $u = \sin x$ and $dv = x$. If we had done so, then we would have $du = \cos x$ and $v = \frac{1}{2}x^2$. Thus, after applying integration by parts, we have $\int x \sin x\, dx = \frac{1}{2}x^2 \sin x - \int \frac{1}{2}x^2 \cos x\, dx$. Unfortunately, with the new integral, we are in no better position than before. It is important to keep in mind that when we apply integration by parts, we may need to try several choices for $u$ and $dv$ before finding a choice that works.

Second, you may wonder why, when we find $v = \int \sin x\, dx = -\cos x$, we do not use $v = -\cos x + K$. To see that it makes no difference, we can rework the problem using $v = -\cos x + K$:

$$\begin{aligned} \int x \sin x\, dx &= (x)(-\cos x + K) - \int(-\cos x + K)(1dx) \\ &= -x\cos x + Kx + \int \cos x\, dx - \int K dx \\ &= -x\cos x + Kx + \sin x - Kx + C \\ &= -x\cos x + \sin x + C. \end{aligned}$$

As you can see, it makes no difference in the final solution.

Last, we can check to make sure that our antiderivative is correct by differentiating $-x\cos x + \sin x + C$:

$$\begin{aligned} \frac{d}{dx}(-x\cos x + \sin x + C) &= (-1)\cos x + (-x)(-\sin x) + \cos x \\ &= x \sin x. \end{aligned}$$

Therefore, the antiderivative checks out.

Watch this **video (http://www.openstaxcollege.org/l/20_intbyparts1)** and visit this **website (http://www.openstaxcollege.org/l/20_intbyparts2)** for examples of integration by parts.

**3.1** Evaluate $\int xe^{2x} dx$ using the integration-by-parts formula with $u = x$ and $dv = e^{2x} dx$.

The natural question to ask at this point is: How do we know how to choose $u$ and $dv$? Sometimes it is a matter of trial and error; however, the acronym LIATE can often help to take some of the guesswork out of our choices. This acronym stands for **L**ogarithmic Functions, **I**nverse Trigonometric Functions, **A**lgebraic Functions, **T**rigonometric Functions, and **E**xponential Functions. This mnemonic serves as an aid in determining an appropriate choice for $u$.

The type of function in the integral that appears first in the list should be our first choice of $u$. For example, if an integral contains a logarithmic function and an algebraic function, we should choose $u$ to be the logarithmic function, because L comes before A in LIATE. The integral in **Example 3.1** has a trigonometric function $(\sin x)$ and an algebraic function $(x)$. Because A comes before T in LIATE, we chose $u$ to be the algebraic function. When we have chosen $u$, $dv$ is selected to be the remaining part of the function to be integrated, together with $dx$.

Why does this mnemonic work? Remember that whatever we pick to be $dv$ must be something we can integrate. Since we do not have integration formulas that allow us to integrate simple logarithmic functions and inverse trigonometric functions, it makes sense that they should not be chosen as values for $dv$. Consequently, they should be at the head of the list as choices for $u$. Thus, we put LI at the beginning of the mnemonic. (We could just as easily have started with IL, since these two types of functions won't appear together in an integration-by-parts problem.) The exponential and trigonometric functions are at the end of our list because they are fairly easy to integrate and make good choices for $dv$. Thus, we have TE at the end of our mnemonic. (We could just as easily have used ET at the end, since when these types of functions appear together it usually doesn't really matter which one is $u$ and which one is $dv$.) Algebraic functions are generally easy both to integrate and to differentiate, and they come in the middle of the mnemonic.

## Example 3.2

### Using Integration by Parts

Evaluate $\int \frac{\ln x}{x^3} dx.$

#### Solution

Begin by rewriting the integral:

$$\int \frac{\ln x}{x^3} dx = \int x^{-3} \ln x \, dx.$$

Since this integral contains the algebraic function $x^{-3}$ and the logarithmic function $\ln x$, choose $u = \ln x$, since L comes before A in LIATE. After we have chosen $u = \ln x$, we must choose $dv = x^{-3} dx$.

Next, since $u = \ln x$, we have $du = \frac{1}{x} dx$. Also, $v = \int x^{-3} dx = -\frac{1}{2} x^{-2}$. Summarizing,

$$\begin{aligned} u &= \ln x & dv &= x^{-3} dx \\ du &= \tfrac{1}{x} dx & v &= \int x^{-3} dx = -\tfrac{1}{2} x^{-2}. \end{aligned}$$

Substituting into the integration-by-parts formula (**Equation 3.1**) gives

$$\begin{aligned} \int \frac{\ln x}{x^3} dx &= \int x^{-3} \ln x \, dx = (\ln x)\left(-\tfrac{1}{2} x^{-2}\right) - \int \left(-\tfrac{1}{2} x^{-2}\right)\left(\tfrac{1}{x} dx\right) \\ &= -\tfrac{1}{2} x^{-2} \ln x + \int \tfrac{1}{2} x^{-3} dx && \text{Simplify.} \\ &= -\tfrac{1}{2} x^{-2} \ln x - \tfrac{1}{4} x^{-2} + C && \text{Integrate.} \\ &= -\frac{1}{2x^2} \ln x - \frac{1}{4x^2} + C. && \text{Rewrite with positive integers.} \end{aligned}$$

**3.2** Evaluate $\int x \ln x \, dx.$

In some cases, as in the next two examples, it may be necessary to apply integration by parts more than once.

## Example 3.3

### Applying Integration by Parts More Than Once

Evaluate $\int x^2 e^{3x} dx.$

#### Solution

Using LIATE, choose $u = x^2$ and $dv = e^{3x} dx$. Thus, $du = 2x \, dx$ and $v = \int e^{3x} dx = \left(\frac{1}{3}\right)e^{3x}$. Therefore,

$$\begin{aligned} u &= x^2 & dv &= e^{3x} dx \\ du &= 2x \, dx & v &= \int e^{3x} dx = \tfrac{1}{3}e^{3x}. \end{aligned}$$

Substituting into **Equation 3.1** produces

$$\int x^2 e^{3x} dx = \frac{1}{3}x^2 e^{3x} - \int \frac{2}{3}xe^{3x} dx.$$

We still cannot integrate $\int \frac{2}{3}xe^{3x} dx$ directly, but the integral now has a lower power on $x$. We can evaluate this new integral by using integration by parts again. To do this, choose $u = x$ and $dv = \frac{2}{3}e^{3x} dx$. Thus, $du = dx$ and $v = \int \left(\frac{2}{3}\right)e^{3x} dx = \left(\frac{2}{9}\right)e^{3x}$. Now we have

$$\begin{aligned} u &= x & dv &= \tfrac{2}{3}e^{3x} dx \\ du &= dx & v &= \int \tfrac{2}{3}e^{3x} dx = \tfrac{2}{9}e^{3x}. \end{aligned}$$

Substituting back into the previous equation yields

$$\int x^2 e^{3x} dx = \frac{1}{3}x^2 e^{3x} - \left(\frac{2}{9}xe^{3x} - \int \frac{2}{9}e^{3x} dx\right).$$

After evaluating the last integral and simplifying, we obtain

$$\int x^2 e^{3x} dx = \frac{1}{3}x^2 e^{3x} - \frac{2}{9}xe^{3x} + \frac{2}{27}e^{3x} + C.$$

## Example 3.4

### Applying Integration by Parts When LIATE Doesn't Quite Work

Evaluate $\int t^3 e^{t^2} dt.$

### Solution

If we use a strict interpretation of the mnemonic LIATE to make our choice of $u,$ we end up with $u = t^3$ and $dv = e^{t^2}dt.$ Unfortunately, this choice won't work because we are unable to evaluate $\int e^{t^2}dt.$ However, since we can evaluate $\int te^{t^2}dx,$ we can try choosing $u = t^2$ and $dv = te^{t^2}dt.$ With these choices we have

$$\begin{aligned} u &= t^2 & dv &= te^{t^2}dt \\ du &= 2t\,dt & v &= \int te^{t^2}dt = \tfrac{1}{2}e^{t^2}. \end{aligned}$$

Thus, we obtain

$$\begin{aligned} \int t^3 e^{t^2}dt &= \tfrac{1}{2}t^2 e^{t^2} - \int \tfrac{1}{2}e^{t^2}2tdt \\ &= \tfrac{1}{2}t^2 e^{t^2} - \tfrac{1}{2}e^{t^2} + C. \end{aligned}$$

## Example 3.5

### Applying Integration by Parts More Than Once

Evaluate $\int \sin(\ln x)dx.$

### Solution

This integral appears to have only one function—namely, $\sin(\ln x)$ —however, we can always use the constant function 1 as the other function. In this example, let's choose $u = \sin(\ln x)$ and $dv = 1dx.$ (The decision to use $u = \sin(\ln x)$ is easy. We can't choose $dv = \sin(\ln x)dx$ because if we could integrate it, we wouldn't be using integration by parts in the first place!) Consequently, $du = (1/x)\cos(\ln x)dx$ and $v = \int 1dx = x.$ After applying integration by parts to the integral and simplifying, we have

$$\int \sin(\ln x)dx = x\sin(\ln x) - \int \cos(\ln x)dx.$$

Unfortunately, this process leaves us with a new integral that is very similar to the original. However, let's see what happens when we apply integration by parts again. This time let's choose $u = \cos(\ln x)$ and $dv = 1dx,$ making $du = -(1/x)\sin(\ln x)dx$ and $v = \int 1dx = x.$ Substituting, we have

$$\int \sin(\ln x)dx = x\sin(\ln x) - \left(x\cos(\ln x) - \int -\sin(\ln x)dx\right).$$

After simplifying, we obtain

$$\int \sin(\ln x)dx = x\sin(\ln x) - x\cos(\ln x) - \int \sin(\ln x)dx.$$

The last integral is now the same as the original. It may seem that we have simply gone in a circle, but now we can actually evaluate the integral. To see how to do this more clearly, substitute $I = \int \sin(\ln x)dx.$ Thus, the equation becomes

$$I = x\sin(\ln x) - x\cos(\ln x) - I.$$

First, add $I$ to both sides of the equation to obtain

$$2I = x\sin(\ln x) - x\cos(\ln x).$$

Next, divide by 2:

$$I = \frac{1}{2}x\sin(\ln x) - \frac{1}{2}x\cos(\ln x).$$

Substituting $I = \int \sin(\ln x)dx$ again, we have

$$\int \sin(\ln x)dx = \frac{1}{2}x\sin(\ln x) - \frac{1}{2}x\cos(\ln x).$$

From this we see that $(1/2)x\sin(\ln x) - (1/2)x\cos(\ln x)$ is an antiderivative of $\sin(\ln x)dx$. For the most general antiderivative, add $+C$:

$$\int \sin(\ln x)dx = \frac{1}{2}x\sin(\ln x) - \frac{1}{2}x\cos(\ln x) + C.$$

**Analysis**

If this method feels a little strange at first, we can check the answer by differentiation:

$$\begin{aligned}&\frac{d}{dx}\left(\frac{1}{2}x\sin(\ln x) - \frac{1}{2}x\cos(\ln x)\right)\\ &= \frac{1}{2}(\sin(\ln x)) + \cos(\ln x)\cdot\frac{1}{x}\cdot\frac{1}{2}x - \left(\frac{1}{2}\cos(\ln x) - \sin(\ln x)\cdot\frac{1}{x}\cdot\frac{1}{2}x\right)\\ &= \sin(\ln x).\end{aligned}$$

**3.3** Evaluate $\int x^2 \sin x\, dx$.

## Integration by Parts for Definite Integrals

Now that we have used integration by parts successfully to evaluate indefinite integrals, we turn our attention to definite integrals. The integration technique is really the same, only we add a step to evaluate the integral at the upper and lower limits of integration.

### Theorem 3.2: Integration by Parts for Definite Integrals

Let $u = f(x)$ and $v = g(x)$ be functions with continuous derivatives on $[a, b]$. Then

$$\int_a^b u\, dv = uv|_a^b - \int_a^b v\, du. \tag{3.2}$$

### Example 3.6

**Finding the Area of a Region**

Find the area of the region bounded above by the graph of $y = \tan^{-1} x$ and below by the $x$-axis over the interval $[0, 1]$.

### Solution

This region is shown in **Figure 3.2**. To find the area, we must evaluate $\int_0^1 \tan^{-1} x\, dx.$

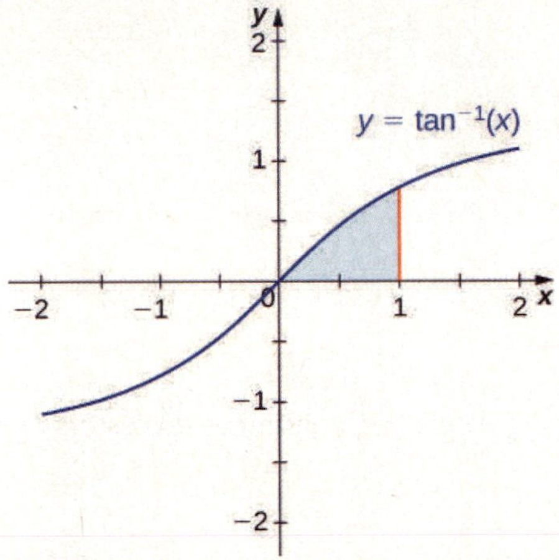


**Figure 3.2** To find the area of the shaded region, we have to use integration by parts.

For this integral, let's choose $u = \tan^{-1} x$ and $dv = dx$, thereby making $du = \frac{1}{x^2 + 1} dx$ and $v = x$. After applying the integration-by-parts formula (**Equation 3.2**) we obtain

$$\text{Area} = x \tan^{-1} x|_0^1 - \int_0^1 \frac{x}{x^2 + 1} dx.$$

Use $u$-substitution to obtain

$$\int_0^1 \frac{x}{x^2 + 1} dx = \frac{1}{2} \ln|x^2 + 1|\Big|_0^1.$$

Thus,

$$\text{Area} = x \tan^{-1} x\Big|_0^1 - \frac{1}{2} \ln|x^2 + 1|\Big|_0^1 = \frac{\pi}{4} - \frac{1}{2} \ln 2.$$

At this point it might not be a bad idea to do a "reality check" on the reasonableness of our solution. Since $\frac{\pi}{4} - \frac{1}{2} \ln 2 \approx 0.4388,$ and from **Figure 3.2** we expect our area to be slightly less than 0.5, this solution appears to be reasonable.

## Example 3.7

### Finding a Volume of Revolution

Find the volume of the solid obtained by revolving the region bounded by the graph of $f(x) = e^{-x}$, the $x$-axis, the $y$-axis, and the line $x = 1$ about the $y$-axis.

#### Solution

The best option to solving this problem is to use the shell method. Begin by sketching the region to be revolved, along with a typical rectangle (see the following graph).

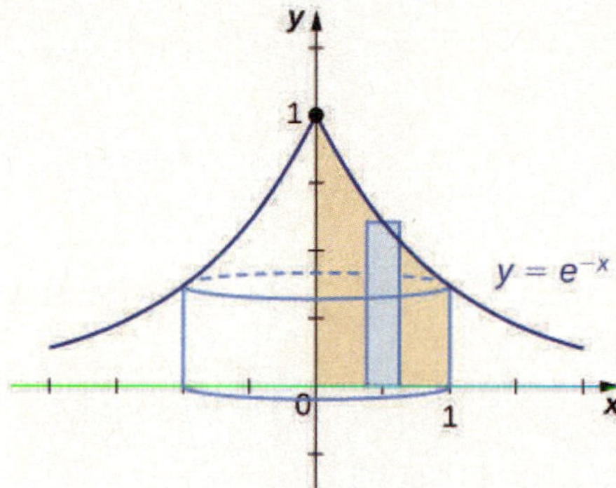


**Figure 3.3** We can use the shell method to find a volume of revolution.

To find the volume using shells, we must evaluate $2\pi\int_0^1 xe^{-x}\,dx$. To do this, let $u = x$ and $dv = e^{-x}$. These choices lead to $du = dx$ and $v = \int e^{-x} = -e^{-x}$. Substituting into **Equation 3.2**, we obtain

$$\begin{aligned} \text{Volume} &= 2\pi\int_0^1 xe^{-x}\,dx = 2\pi\left(-xe^{-x}\Big|_0^1 + \int_0^1 e^{-x}\,dx\right) && \text{Use integration by parts.} \\ &= -2\pi xe^{-x}\big|_0^1 - 2\pi e^{-x}\Big|_0^1 && \text{Evaluate } \int_0^1 e^{-x}\,dx = -e^{-x}\Big|_0^1. \\ &= 2\pi - \frac{4\pi}{e}. && \text{Evaluate and simplify.} \end{aligned}$$

#### Analysis

Again, it is a good idea to check the reasonableness of our solution. We observe that the solid has a volume slightly less than that of a cylinder of radius 1 and height of $1/e$ added to the volume of a cone of base radius 1 and height of $1 - \frac{1}{3}$. Consequently, the solid should have a volume a bit less than

$$\pi(1)^2\frac{1}{e} + \left(\frac{\pi}{3}\right)(1)^2\left(1 - \frac{1}{e}\right) = \frac{2\pi}{3e} - \frac{\pi}{3} \approx 1.8177.$$

Since $2\pi - \frac{4\pi}{e} \approx 1.6603$, we see that our calculated volume is reasonable.

**3.4** Evaluate $\int_0^{\pi/2} x\cos x\,dx$.

# 3.1 EXERCISES

In using the technique of integration by parts, you must carefully choose which expression is *u*. For each of the following problems, use the guidelines in this section to choose *u*. Do **not** evaluate the integrals.

1. $\int x^3 e^{2x} dx$

2. $\int x^3 \ln(x) dx$

3. $\int y^3 \cos y dx$

4. $\int x^2 \arctan x \, dx$

5. $\int e^{3x} \sin(2x) dx$

Find the integral by using the simplest method. Not all problems require integration by parts.

6. $\int v \sin v dv$

7. $\int \ln x \, dx$ (*Hint:* $\int \ln x \, dx$ is equivalent to $\int 1 \cdot \ln(x) dx$.)

8. $\int x \cos x \, dx$

9. $\int \tan^{-1} x \, dx$

10. $\int x^2 e^x dx$

11. $\int x \sin(2x) dx$

12. $\int xe^{4x} dx$

13. $\int xe^{-x} dx$

14. $\int x \cos 3x \, dx$

15. $\int x^2 \cos x \, dx$

16. $\int x \ln x \, dx$

17. $\int \ln(2x + 1) dx$

18. $\int x^2 e^{4x} dx$

19. $\int e^x \sin x \, dx$

20. $\int e^x \cos x \, dx$

21. $\int xe^{-x^2} dx$

22. $\int x^2 e^{-x} dx$

23. $\int \sin(\ln(2x)) dx$

24. $\int cos(\ln x) dx$

25. $\int (\ln x)^2 dx$

26. $\int \ln(x^2) dx$

27. $\int x^2 \ln x \, dx$

28. $\int \sin^{-1} x \, dx$

29. $\int \cos^{-1}(2x) dx$

30. $\int x \arctan x \, dx$

31. $\int x^2 \sin x \, dx$

32. $\int x^3 \cos x \, dx$

33. $\int x^3 \sin x \, dx$

34. $\int x^3 e^x dx$

35. $\int x \sec^{-1} x \, dx$

36. $\int x \sec^2 x \, dx$

37. $\int x \cosh x \, dx$

Compute the definite integrals. Use a graphing utility to confirm your answers.

38. $\int_{1/e}^{1} \ln x\, dx$

39. $\int_{0}^{1} xe^{-2x}\, dx$ (Express the answer in exact form.)

40. $\int_{0}^{1} e^{\sqrt{x}}\, dx (\text{let } u = \sqrt{x})$

41. $\int_{1}^{e} \ln(x^2) dx$

42. $\int_{0}^{\pi} x \cos x\, dx$

43. $\int_{-\pi}^{\pi} x \sin x\, dx$ (Express the answer in exact form.)

44. $\int_{0}^{3} \ln(x^2 + 1) dx$ (Express the answer in exact form.)

45. $\int_{0}^{\pi/2} x^2 \sin x\, dx$ (Express the answer in exact form.)

46. $\int_{0}^{1} x5^x\, dx$ (Express the answer using five significant digits.)

47. Evaluate $\int \cos x \ln(\sin x) dx$

Derive the following formulas using the technique of integration by parts. Assume that $n$ is a positive integer. These formulas are called *reduction formulas* because the exponent in the $x$ term has been reduced by one in each case. The second integral is simpler than the original integral.

48. $\int x^n e^x\, dx = x^n e^x - n \int x^{n-1} e^x\, dx$

49. $\int x^n \cos x\, dx = x^n \sin x - n \int x^{n-1} \sin x\, dx$

50. $\int x^n \sin x\, dx =$ ______

51. Integrate $\int 2x\sqrt{2x-3}\, dx$ using two methods:

a. Using parts, letting $dv = \sqrt{2x-3}\, dx$
b. Substitution, letting $u = 2x - 3$

State whether you would use integration by parts to evaluate the integral. If so, identify $u$ and $dv$. If not, describe the technique used to perform the integration without actually doing the problem.

52. $\int x \ln x\, dx$

53. $\int \frac{\ln^2 x}{x} dx$

54. $\int xe^x\, dx$

55. $\int xe^{x^2 - 3}\, dx$

56. $\int x^2 \sin x\, dx$

57. $\int x^2 \sin(3x^3 + 2) dx$

Sketch the region bounded above by the curve, the $x$-axis, and $x = 1$, and find the area of the region. Provide the exact form or round answers to the number of places indicated.

58. $y = 2xe^{-x}$ (Approximate answer to four decimal places.)

59. $y = e^{-x} \sin(\pi x)$ (Approximate answer to five decimal places.)

Find the volume generated by rotating the region bounded by the given curves about the specified line. Express the answers in exact form or approximate to the number of decimal places indicated.

60. $y = \sin x,\ y = 0,\ x = 2\pi,\ x = 3\pi$ about the y-axis (Express the answer in exact form.)

61. $y = e^{-x}$ $y = 0,\ x = -1 x = 0;$ about $x = 1$ (Express the answer in exact form.)

62. A particle moving along a straight line has a velocity of $v(t) = t^2 e^{-t}$ after $t$ sec. How far does it travel in the first 2 sec? (Assume the units are in feet and express the answer in exact form.)

63. Find the area under the graph of $y = \sec^3 x$ from $x = 0$ to $x = 1$. (Round the answer to two significant digits.)

64. Find the area between $y = (x - 2)e^x$ and the $x$-axis from $x = 2$ to $x = 5$. (Express the answer in exact form.)

65. Find the area of the region enclosed by the curve $y = x\cos x$ and the $x$-axis for $\frac{11\pi}{2} \le x \le \frac{13\pi}{2}$. (Express the answer in exact form.)

66. Find the volume of the solid generated by revolving the region bounded by the curve $y = \ln x$, the $x$-axis, and the vertical line $x = e^2$ about the $x$-axis. (Express the answer in exact form.)

67. Find the volume of the solid generated by revolving the region bounded by the curve $y = 4\cos x$ and the $x$-axis, $\frac{\pi}{2} \le x \le \frac{3\pi}{2}$, about the $x$-axis. (Express the answer in exact form.)

68. Find the volume of the solid generated by revolving the region in the first quadrant bounded by $y = e^x$ and the $x$-axis, from $x = 0$ to $x = \ln(7)$, about the $y$-axis. (Express the answer in exact form.)

# 3.2 | Trigonometric Integrals

## Learning Objectives

**3.2.1** Solve integration problems involving products and powers of $\sin x$ and $\cos x$.
**3.2.2** Solve integration problems involving products and powers of $\tan x$ and $\sec x$.
**3.2.3** Use reduction formulas to solve trigonometric integrals.

In this section we look at how to integrate a variety of products of trigonometric functions. These integrals are called **trigonometric integrals**. They are an important part of the integration technique called *trigonometric substitution*, which is featured in **Trigonometric Substitution**. This technique allows us to convert algebraic expressions that we may not be able to integrate into expressions involving trigonometric functions, which we may be able to integrate using the techniques described in this section. In addition, these types of integrals appear frequently when we study polar, cylindrical, and spherical coordinate systems later. Let's begin our study with products of $\sin x$ and $\cos x$.

## Integrating Products and Powers of sinx and cosx

A key idea behind the strategy used to integrate combinations of products and powers of $\sin x$ and $\cos x$ involves rewriting these expressions as sums and differences of integrals of the form $\int \sin^j x \cos x\, dx$ or $\int \cos^j x \sin x\, dx$. After rewriting these integrals, we evaluate them using $u$-substitution. Before describing the general process in detail, let's take a look at the following examples.

### Example 3.8

**Integrating $\int \cos^j x \sin x\, dx$**

Evaluate $\int \cos^3 x \sin x\, dx$.

**Solution**

Use $u$-substitution and let $u = \cos x$. In this case, $du = -\sin x\, dx$. Thus,

$$\begin{aligned}\int \cos^3 x \sin x\, dx &= -\int u^3\, du \\ &= -\frac{1}{4}u^4 + C \\ &= -\frac{1}{4}\cos^4 x + C.\end{aligned}$$

**3.5** Evaluate $\int \sin^4 x \cos x\, dx$.

### Example 3.9

**A Preliminary Example: Integrating $\int \cos^j x \sin^k x\, dx$ Where $k$ is Odd**

Evaluate $\int \cos^2 x \sin^3 x\,dx.$

### Solution

To convert this integral to integrals of the form $\int \cos^j x \sin x\,dx,$ rewrite $\sin^3 x = \sin^2 x \sin x$ and make the substitution $\sin^2 x = 1 - \cos^2 x.$ Thus,

$$\begin{aligned}\int \cos^2 x \sin^3 x\,dx &= \int \cos^2 x(1 - \cos^2 x)\sin x\,dx \quad \text{Let } u = \cos x; \text{ then } du = -\sin x\,dx.\\ &= -\int u^2\left(1 - u^2\right)du\\ &= \int\left(u^4 - u^2\right)du\\ &= \tfrac{1}{5}u^5 - \tfrac{1}{3}u^3 + C\\ &= \tfrac{1}{5}\cos^5 x - \tfrac{1}{3}\cos^3 x + C.\end{aligned}$$

**3.6** Evaluate $\int \cos^3 x \sin^2 x\,dx.$

In the next example, we see the strategy that must be applied when there are only even powers of $\sin x$ and $\cos x.$ For integrals of this type, the identities

$$\sin^2 x = \frac{1}{2} - \frac{1}{2}\cos(2x) = \frac{1 - \cos(2x)}{2}$$

and

$$\cos^2 x = \frac{1}{2} + \frac{1}{2}\cos(2x) = \frac{1 + \cos(2x)}{2}$$

are invaluable. These identities are sometimes known as *power-reducing identities* and they may be derived from the double-angle identity $\cos(2x) = \cos^2 x - \sin^2 x$ and the Pythagorean identity $\cos^2 x + \sin^2 x = 1.$

## Example 3.10

### Integrating an Even Power of $\sin x$

Evaluate $\int \sin^2 x\,dx.$

### Solution

To evaluate this integral, let's use the trigonometric identity $\sin^2 x = \frac{1}{2} - \frac{1}{2}\cos(2x).$ Thus,

$$\begin{aligned}\int \sin^2 x\,dx &= \int\left(\tfrac{1}{2} - \tfrac{1}{2}\cos(2x)\right)dx\\ &= \tfrac{1}{2}x - \tfrac{1}{4}\sin(2x) + C.\end{aligned}$$

**3.7** Evaluate $\int \cos^2 x\, dx$.

The general process for integrating products of powers of $\sin x$ and $\cos x$ is summarized in the following set of guidelines.

### Problem-Solving Strategy: Integrating Products and Powers of sin *x* and cos *x*

To integrate $\int \cos^j x \sin^k x\, dx$ use the following strategies:

1. If $k$ is odd, rewrite $\sin^k x = \sin^{k-1} x \sin x$ and use the identity $\sin^2 x = 1 - \cos^2 x$ to rewrite $\sin^{k-1} x$ in terms of $\cos x$. Integrate using the substitution $u = \cos x$. This substitution makes $du = -\sin x\, dx$.
2. If $j$ is odd, rewrite $\cos^j x = \cos^{j-1} x \cos x$ and use the identity $\cos^2 x = 1 - \sin^2 x$ to rewrite $\cos^{j-1} x$ in terms of $\sin x$. Integrate using the substitution $u = \sin x$. This substitution makes $du = \cos x\, dx$. (*Note*: If both $j$ and $k$ are odd, either strategy 1 or strategy 2 may be used.)
3. If both $j$ and $k$ are even, use $\sin^2 x = (1/2) - (1/2)\cos(2x)$ and $\cos^2 x = (1/2) + (1/2)\cos(2x)$. After applying these formulas, simplify and reapply strategies 1 through 3 as appropriate.

## Example 3.11

### Integrating $\int \cos^j x \sin^k x\, dx$ where *k* is Odd

Evaluate $\int \cos^8 x \sin^5 x\, dx$.

#### Solution

Since the power on $\sin x$ is odd, use strategy 1. Thus,

$$\begin{aligned}
\int \cos^8 x \sin^5 x\, dx &= \int \cos^8 x \sin^4 x \sin x\, dx && \text{Break off } \sin x. \\
&= \int \cos^8 x (\sin^2 x)^2 \sin x\, dx && \text{Rewrite } \sin^4 x = (\sin^2 x)^2. \\
&= \int \cos^8 x (1 - \cos^2 x)^2 \sin x\, dx && \text{Substitute } \sin^2 x = 1 - \cos^2 x. \\
&= \int u^8 (1 - u^2)^2 (-du) && \text{Let } u = \cos x \text{ and } du = -\sin x\, dx. \\
&= \int \left(-u^8 + 2u^{10} - u^{12}\right) du && \text{Expand.} \\
&= -\frac{1}{9}u^9 + \frac{2}{11}u^{11} - \frac{1}{13}u^{13} + C && \text{Evaluate the integral.} \\
&= -\frac{1}{9}\cos^9 x + \frac{2}{11}\cos^{11} x - \frac{1}{13}\cos^{13} x + C. && \text{Substitute } u = \cos x.
\end{aligned}$$

## Example 3.12

### Integrating $\int \cos^j x \sin^k x\, dx$ where *k* and *j* are Even

Evaluate $\int \sin^4 x\, dx$.

#### Solution

Since the power on $\sin x$ is even $(k = 4)$ and the power on $\cos x$ is even $(j = 0)$, we must use strategy 3. Thus,

$$\begin{aligned}
\int \sin^4 x\, dx &= \int \left(\sin^2 x\right)^2 dx && \text{Rewrite } \sin^4 x = \left(\sin^2 x\right)^2. \\
&= \int \left(\tfrac{1}{2} - \tfrac{1}{2}\cos(2x)\right)^2 dx && \text{Substitute } \sin^2 x = \tfrac{1}{2} - \tfrac{1}{2}\cos(2x). \\
&= \int \left(\tfrac{1}{4} - \tfrac{1}{2}\cos(2x) + \tfrac{1}{4}\cos^2(2x)\right) dx && \text{Expand} \left(\tfrac{1}{2} - \tfrac{1}{2}\cos(2x)\right)^2. \\
&= \int \left(\tfrac{1}{4} - \tfrac{1}{2}\cos(2x) + \tfrac{1}{4}\left(\tfrac{1}{2} + \tfrac{1}{2}\cos(4x)\right)\right) dx.
\end{aligned}$$

Since $\cos^2(2x)$ has an even power, substitute $\cos^2(2x) = \frac{1}{2} + \frac{1}{2}\cos(4x)$:

$$\begin{aligned}
&= \int \left(\tfrac{3}{8} - \tfrac{1}{2}\cos(2x) + \tfrac{1}{8}\cos(4x)\right) dx && \text{Simplify.} \\
&= \tfrac{3}{8}x - \tfrac{1}{4}\sin(2x) + \tfrac{1}{32}\sin(4x) + C && \text{Evaluate the integral.}
\end{aligned}$$

**3.8** Evaluate $\int \cos^3 x\, dx$.

**3.9** Evaluate $\int \cos^2(3x) dx$.

In some areas of physics, such as quantum mechanics, signal processing, and the computation of Fourier series, it is often necessary to integrate products that include $\sin(ax)$, $\sin(bx)$, $\cos(ax)$, and $\cos(bx)$. These integrals are evaluated by applying trigonometric identities, as outlined in the following rule.

#### Rule: Integrating Products of Sines and Cosines of Different Angles

To integrate products involving $\sin(ax)$, $\sin(bx)$, $\cos(ax)$, and $\cos(bx)$, use the substitutions

$$\sin(ax)\sin(bx) = \frac{1}{2}\cos((a-b)x) - \frac{1}{2}\cos((a+b)x) \tag{3.3}$$

$$\sin(ax)\cos(bx) = \frac{1}{2}\sin((a-b)x) + \frac{1}{2}\sin((a+b)x) \tag{3.4}$$

$$\cos(ax)\cos(bx) = \frac{1}{2}\cos((a-b)x) + \frac{1}{2}\cos((a+b)x) \tag{3.5}$$

These formulas may be derived from the sum-of-angle formulas for sine and cosine.

## Example 3.13

### Evaluating $\int \sin(ax)\cos(bx)dx$

Evaluate $\int \sin(5x)\cos(3x)dx.$

#### Solution

Apply the identity $\sin(5x)\cos(3x) = \frac{1}{2}\sin(2x) - \frac{1}{2}\cos(8x).$ Thus,

$$\begin{aligned}\int \sin(5x)\cos(3x)dx &= \int \frac{1}{2}\sin(2x) - \frac{1}{2}\cos(8x)dx \\ &= -\frac{1}{4}\cos(2x) - \frac{1}{16}\sin(8x) + C.\end{aligned}$$

 **3.10** Evaluate $\int \cos(6x)\cos(5x)dx.$

## Integrating Products and Powers of tanx and secx

Before discussing the integration of products and powers of $\tan x$ and $\sec x,$ it is useful to recall the integrals involving $\tan x$ and $\sec x$ we have already learned:

1. $\int \sec^2 x\,dx = \tan x + C$
2. $\int \sec x \tan x\,dx = \sec x + C$
3. $\int \tan x\,dx = \ln|\sec x| + C$
4. $\int \sec x\,dx = \ln|\sec x + \tan x| + C.$

For most integrals of products and powers of $\tan x$ and $\sec x,$ we rewrite the expression we wish to integrate as the sum or difference of integrals of the form $\int \tan^j x \sec^2 x\,dx$ or $\int \sec^j x \tan x\,dx.$ As we see in the following example, we can evaluate these new integrals by using $u$-substitution.

## Example 3.14

### Evaluating $\int \sec^j x \tan x\,dx$

Evaluate $\int \sec^5 x \tan x\,dx.$

#### Solution

Start by rewriting $\sec^5 x \tan x$ as $\sec^4 x \sec x \tan x.$

$$\begin{aligned}\int \sec^5 x \tan x\,dx &= \int \sec^4 x \sec x \tan x\,dx && \text{Let } u = \sec x;\text{ then, } du = \sec x \tan x\,dx.\\ &= \int u^4\,du && \text{Evaluate the integral.}\\ &= \tfrac{1}{5}u^5 + C && \text{Substitute } \sec x = u.\\ &= \tfrac{1}{5}\sec^5 x + C\end{aligned}$$

You can read some interesting information at this **website (http://www.openstaxcollege.org/l/20_intseccube)** to learn about a common integral involving the secant.

**3.11** Evaluate $\int \tan^5 x \sec^2 x\,dx.$

We now take a look at the various strategies for integrating products and powers of $\sec x$ and $\tan x.$

### Problem-Solving Strategy: Integrating $\int \tan^k x \sec^j x\,dx$

To integrate $\int \tan^k x \sec^j x\,dx,$ use the following strategies:

1. If $j$ is even and $j \geq 2,$ rewrite $\sec^j x = \sec^{j-2} x \sec^2 x$ and use $\sec^2 x = \tan^2 x + 1$ to rewrite $\sec^{j-2} x$ in terms of $\tan x.$ Let $u = \tan x$ and $du = \sec^2 x.$
2. If $k$ is odd and $j \geq 1,$ rewrite $\tan^k x \sec^j x = \tan^{k-1} x \sec^{j-1} x \sec x \tan x$ and use $\tan^2 x = \sec^2 x - 1$ to rewrite $\tan^{k-1} x$ in terms of $\sec x.$ Let $u = \sec x$ and $du = \sec x \tan x\,dx.$ (*Note*: If $j$ is even and $k$ is odd, then either strategy 1 or strategy 2 may be used.)
3. If $k$ is odd where $k \geq 3$ and $j = 0,$ rewrite $\tan^k x = \tan^{k-2} x \tan^2 x = \tan^{k-2} x(\sec^2 x - 1) = \tan^{k-2} x \sec^2 x - \tan^{k-2} x.$ It may be necessary to repeat this process on the $\tan^{k-2} x$ term.
4. If $k$ is even and $j$ is odd, then use $\tan^2 x = \sec^2 x - 1$ to express $\tan^k x$ in terms of $\sec x.$ Use integration by parts to integrate odd powers of $\sec x.$

## Example 3.15

### Integrating $\int \tan^k x \sec^j x\,dx$ when $j$ is Even

Evaluate $\int \tan^6 x \sec^4 x\,dx.$

### Solution

Since the power on $\sec x$ is even, rewrite $\sec^4 x = \sec^2 x \sec^2 x$ and use $\sec^2 x = \tan^2 x + 1$ to rewrite the first $\sec^2 x$ in terms of $\tan x$. Thus,

$$\begin{aligned}
\int \tan^6 x \sec^4 x\,dx &= \int \tan^6 x\left(\tan^2 x + 1\right)\sec^2 x\,dx && \text{Let } u = \tan x \text{ and } du = \sec^2 x. \\
&= \int u^6\left(u^2 + 1\right)du && \text{Expand.} \\
&= \int (u^8 + u^6)du && \text{Evaluate the integral.} \\
&= \frac{1}{9}u^9 + \frac{1}{7}u^7 + C && \text{Substitute } \tan x = u. \\
&= \frac{1}{9}\tan^9 x + \frac{1}{7}\tan^7 x + C.
\end{aligned}$$

## Example 3.16

### Integrating $\int \tan^k x \sec^j x\,dx$ when $k$ is Odd

Evaluate $\int \tan^5 x \sec^3 x\,dx$.

### Solution

Since the power on $\tan x$ is odd, begin by rewriting $\tan^5 x \sec^3 x = \tan^4 x \sec^2 x \sec x \tan x$. Thus,

$$\begin{aligned}
\tan^5 x \sec^3 x &= \tan^4 x \sec^2 x \sec x \tan x. && \text{Write } \tan^4 x = (\tan^2 x)^2. \\
\int \tan^5 x \sec^3 x\,dx &= \int (\tan^2 x)^2 \sec^2 x \sec x \tan x\,dx && \text{Use } \tan^2 x = \sec^2 x - 1. \\
&= \int (\sec^2 x - 1)^2 \sec^2 x \sec x \tan x\,dx && \text{Let } u = \sec x \text{ and } du = \sec x \tan x\,dx. \\
&= \int (u^2 - 1)^2 u^2\,du && \text{Expand.} \\
&= \int \left(u^6 - 2u^4 + u^2\right)du && \text{Integrate.} \\
&= \frac{1}{7}u^7 - \frac{2}{5}u^5 + \frac{1}{3}u^3 + C && \text{Substitute } \sec x = u. \\
&= \frac{1}{7}\sec^7 x - \frac{2}{5}\sec^5 x + \frac{1}{3}\sec^3 x + C.
\end{aligned}$$

## Example 3.17

### Integrating $\int \tan^k x\,dx$ where $k$ is Odd and $k \geq 3$

Evaluate $\int \tan^3 x\,dx$.

### Solution

Begin by rewriting $\tan^3 x = \tan x \tan^2 x = \tan x\left(\sec^2 x - 1\right) = \tan x \sec^2 x - \tan x$. Thus,

$$\begin{aligned} \int \tan^3 x\,dx &= \int\left(\tan x \sec^2 x - \tan x\right)dx \\ &= \int \tan x \sec^2 x\,dx - \int \tan x\,dx \\ &= \frac{1}{2}\tan^2 x - \ln|\sec x| + C. \end{aligned}$$

For the first integral, use the substitution $u = \tan x$. For the second integral, use the formula.

## Example 3.18

### Integrating $\int \sec^3 x\,dx$

Integrate $\int \sec^3 x\,dx$.

### Solution

This integral requires integration by parts. To begin, let $u = \sec x$ and $dv = \sec^2 x$. These choices make $du = \sec x \tan x$ and $v = \tan x$. Thus,

$$\begin{aligned} \int \sec^3 x\,dx &= \sec x \tan x - \int \tan x \sec x \tan x\,dx \\ &= \sec x \tan x - \int \tan^2 x \sec x\,dx && \text{Simplify.} \\ &= \sec x \tan x - \int\left(\sec^2 x - 1\right)\sec x\,dx && \text{Substitute } \tan^2 x = \sec^2 x - 1. \\ &= \sec x \tan x + \int \sec x\,dx - \int \sec^3 x\,dx && \text{Rewrite.} \\ &= \sec x \tan x + \ln|\sec x + \tan x| - \int \sec^3 x\,dx. && \text{Evaluate } \int \sec x\,dx. \end{aligned}$$

We now have

$$\int \sec^3 x\,dx = \sec x \tan x + \ln|\sec x + \tan x| - \int \sec^3 x\,dx.$$

Since the integral $\int \sec^3 x\,dx$ has reappeared on the right-hand side, we can solve for $\int \sec^3 x\,dx$ by adding it to both sides. In doing so, we obtain

$$2\int \sec^3 x\,dx = \sec x \tan x + \ln|\sec x + \tan x|.$$

Dividing by 2, we arrive at

$$\int \sec^3 x\,dx = \frac{1}{2}\sec x \tan x + \frac{1}{2}\ln|\sec x + \tan x| + C.$$

**3.12** Evaluate $\int \tan^3 x \sec^7 x\,dx$.

## Reduction Formulas

Evaluating $\int \sec^n x\,dx$ for values of $n$ where $n$ is odd requires integration by parts. In addition, we must also know the value of $\int \sec^{n-2} x\,dx$ to evaluate $\int \sec^n x\,dx$. The evaluation of $\int \tan^n x\,dx$ also requires being able to integrate $\int \tan^{n-2} x\,dx$. To make the process easier, we can derive and apply the following **power reduction formulas**. These rules allow us to replace the integral of a power of $\sec x$ or $\tan x$ with the integral of a lower power of $\sec x$ or $\tan x$.

### Rule: Reduction Formulas for $\int \sec^n x\,dx$ and $\int \tan^n x\,dx$

$$\int \sec^n x\,dx = \frac{1}{n-1}\sec^{n-2} x\tan x + \frac{n-2}{n-1}\int \sec^{n-2} x\,dx \quad (3.6)$$

$$\int \tan^n x\,dx = \frac{1}{n-1}\tan^{n-1} x - \int \tan^{n-2} x\,dx \quad (3.7)$$

The first power reduction rule may be verified by applying integration by parts. The second may be verified by following the strategy outlined for integrating odd powers of $\tan x$.

### Example 3.19

#### Revisiting $\int \sec^3 x\,dx$

Apply a reduction formula to evaluate $\int \sec^3 x\,dx$.

#### Solution

By applying the first reduction formula, we obtain

$$\begin{aligned}\int \sec^3 x\,dx &= \frac{1}{2}\sec x\tan x + \frac{1}{2}\int \sec x\,dx \\ &= \frac{1}{2}\sec x\tan x + \frac{1}{2}\ln|\sec x + \tan x| + C.\end{aligned}$$

### Example 3.20

#### Using a Reduction Formula

Evaluate $\int \tan^4 x\,dx$.

#### Solution

Applying the reduction formula for $\int \tan^4 x\,dx$ we have

$$\begin{aligned}\int \tan^4 x\,dx &= \tfrac{1}{3}\tan^3 x - \int \tan^2 x\,dx \\ &= \tfrac{1}{3}\tan^3 x - \left(\tan x - \int \tan^0 x\,dx\right) && \text{Apply the reduction formula to } \int \tan^2 x\,dx. \\ &= \tfrac{1}{3}\tan^3 x - \tan x + \int 1\,dx && \text{Simplify.} \\ &= \tfrac{1}{3}\tan^3 x - \tan x + x + C. && \text{Evaluate } \int 1dx.\end{aligned}$$

**3.13** Apply the reduction formula to $\int \sec^5 x\,dx$.

# 3.2 EXERCISES

Fill in the blank to make a true statement.

69. $\sin^2 x +$ _______ $= 1$

70. $\sec^2 x - 1 =$ _______

Use an identity to reduce the power of the trigonometric function to a trigonometric function raised to the first power.

71. $\sin^2 x =$ _______

72. $\cos^2 x =$ _______

Evaluate each of the following integrals by *u*-substitution.

73. $\int \sin^3 x \cos x\, dx$

74. $\int \sqrt{\cos x} \sin x\, dx$

75. $\int \tan^5(2x)\sec^2(2x)dx$

76. $\int \sin^7(2x)\cos(2x)dx$

77. $\int \tan\left(\frac{x}{2}\right)\sec^2\left(\frac{x}{2}\right)dx$

78. $\int \tan^2 x \sec^2 x\, dx$

Compute the following integrals using the guidelines for integrating powers of trigonometric functions. Use a CAS to check the solutions. (*Note*: Some of the problems may be done using techniques of integration learned previously.)

79. $\int \sin^3 x\, dx$

80. $\int \cos^3 x\, dx$

81. $\int \sin x \cos x\, dx$

82. $\int \cos^5 x\, dx$

83. $\int \sin^5 x \cos^2 x\, dx$

84. $\int \sin^3 x \cos^3 x\, dx$

85. $\int \sqrt{\sin x} \cos x\, dx$

86. $\int \sqrt{\sin x} \cos^3 x\, dx$

87. $\int \sec x \tan x\, dx$

88. $\int \tan(5x)dx$

89. $\int \tan^2 x \sec x\, dx$

90. $\int \tan x \sec^3 x\, dx$

91. $\int \sec^4 x\, dx$

92. $\int \cot x\, dx$

93. $\int \csc x\, dx$

94. $\int \frac{\tan^3 x}{\sqrt{\sec x}}dx$

For the following exercises, find a general formula for the integrals.

95. $\int \sin^2 ax \cos ax\, dx$

96. $\int \sin ax \cos ax\, dx.$

Use the double-angle formulas to evaluate the following integrals.

97. $\int_0^\pi \sin^2 x\, dx$

98. $\int_0^\pi \sin^4 x\, dx$

99. $\int \cos^2 3x\, dx$

100. $\int \sin^2 x \cos^2 x\, dx$

101. $\int \sin^2 x\, dx + \int \cos^2 x\, dx$

102. $\int \sin^2 x \cos^2(2x)dx$

For the following exercises, evaluate the definite integrals. Express answers in exact form whenever possible.

103. $\int_0^{2\pi} \cos x \sin 2x\, dx$

104. $\int_0^{\pi} \sin 3x \sin 5x\, dx$

105. $\int_0^{\pi} \cos(99x)\sin(101x)dx$

106. $\int_{-\pi}^{\pi} \cos^2(3x)dx$

107. $\int_0^{2\pi} \sin x \sin(2x)\sin(3x)dx$

108. $\int_0^{4\pi} \cos(x/2)\sin(x/2)dx$

109. $\int_{\pi/6}^{\pi/3} \frac{\cos^3 x}{\sqrt{\sin x}}dx$ (Round this answer to three decimal places.)

110. $\int_{-\pi/3}^{\pi/3} \sqrt{\sec^2 x - 1}\, dx$

111. $\int_0^{\pi/2} \sqrt{1 - \cos(2x)}\, dx$

112. Find the area of the region bounded by the graphs of the equations $y = \sin x,\ y = \sin^3 x,\ x = 0,$ and $x = \frac{\pi}{2}.$

113. Find the area of the region bounded by the graphs of the equations $y = \cos^2 x,\ y = \sin^2 x,\ x = -\frac{\pi}{4},$ and $x = \frac{\pi}{4}.$

114. A particle moves in a straight line with the velocity function $v(t) = \sin(\omega t)\cos^2(\omega t).$ Find its position function $x = f(t)$ if $f(0) = 0.$

115. Find the average value of the function $f(x) = \sin^2 x \cos^3 x$ over the interval $[-\pi, \pi].$

For the following exercises, solve the differential equations.

116. $\frac{dy}{dx} = \sin^2 x.$ The curve passes through point $(0, 0).$

117. $\frac{dy}{d\theta} = \sin^4(\pi\theta)$

118. Find the length of the curve $y = \ln(\csc x),\ \frac{\pi}{4} \le x \le \frac{\pi}{2}.$

119. Find the length of the curve $y = \ln(\sin x),\ \frac{\pi}{3} \le x \le \frac{\pi}{2}.$

120. Find the volume generated by revolving the curve $y = \cos(3x)$ about the $x$-axis, $0 \le x \le \frac{\pi}{36}.$

For the following exercises, use this information: The inner product of two functions $f$ and $g$ over $[a, b]$ is defined by $f(x) \cdot g(x) = \langle f, g \rangle = \int_a^b f \cdot g dx.$ Two distinct functions $f$ and $g$ are said to be orthogonal if $\langle f, g \rangle = 0.$

121. Show that $\{\sin(2x), \cos(3x)\}$ are orthogonal over the interval $[-\pi, \pi].$

122. Evaluate $\int_{-\pi}^{\pi} \sin(mx)\cos(nx)dx.$

123. Integrate $y' = \sqrt{\tan x}\sec^4 x.$

For each pair of integrals, determine which one is more difficult to evaluate. Explain your reasoning.

124. $\int \sin^{456} x \cos x\, dx$ or $\int \sin^2 x \cos^2 x\, dx$

125. $\int \tan^{350} x \sec^2 x\, dx$ or $\int \tan^{350} x \sec x\, dx$

# 3.3 | Trigonometric Substitution

**Learning Objectives**

**3.3.1** Solve integration problems involving the square root of a sum or difference of two squares.

In this section, we explore integrals containing expressions of the form $\sqrt{a^2 - x^2}$, $\sqrt{a^2 + x^2}$, and $\sqrt{x^2 - a^2}$, where the values of $a$ are positive. We have already encountered and evaluated integrals containing some expressions of this type, but many still remain inaccessible. The technique of **trigonometric substitution** comes in very handy when evaluating these integrals. This technique uses substitution to rewrite these integrals as trigonometric integrals.

## Integrals Involving $\sqrt{a^2 - x^2}$

Before developing a general strategy for integrals containing $\sqrt{a^2 - x^2}$, consider the integral $\int \sqrt{9 - x^2}dx$. This integral cannot be evaluated using any of the techniques we have discussed so far. However, if we make the substitution $x = 3\sin\theta$, we have $dx = 3\cos\theta d\theta$. After substituting into the integral, we have

$$\int \sqrt{9 - x^2}dx = \int \sqrt{9 - (3\sin\theta)^2}3\cos\theta d\theta.$$

After simplifying, we have

$$\int \sqrt{9 - x^2}dx = \int 9\sqrt{1 - \sin^2\theta}\cos\theta d\theta.$$

Letting $1 - \sin^2\theta = \cos^2\theta$, we now have

$$\int \sqrt{9 - x^2}dx = \int 9\sqrt{\cos^2\theta}\cos\theta d\theta.$$

Assuming that $\cos\theta \ge 0$, we have

$$\int \sqrt{9 - x^2}dx = \int 9\cos^2\theta d\theta.$$

At this point, we can evaluate the integral using the techniques developed for integrating powers and products of trigonometric functions. Before completing this example, let's take a look at the general theory behind this idea.

To evaluate integrals involving $\sqrt{a^2 - x^2}$, we make the substitution $x = a\sin\theta$ and $dx = a\cos\theta$. To see that this actually makes sense, consider the following argument: The domain of $\sqrt{a^2 - x^2}$ is $[-a, a]$. Thus, $-a \le x \le a$. Consequently, $-1 \le \frac{x}{a} \le 1$. Since the range of $\sin x$ over $[-(\pi/2), \pi/2]$ is $[-1, 1]$, there is a unique angle $\theta$ satisfying $-(\pi/2) \le \theta \le \pi/2$ so that $\sin\theta = x/a$, or equivalently, so that $x = a\sin\theta$. If we substitute $x = a\sin\theta$ into $\sqrt{a^2 - x^2}$, we get

$$\begin{aligned}
\sqrt{a^2 - x^2} &= \sqrt{a^2 - (a\sin\theta)^2} && \text{Let } x = a\sin\theta \text{ where } -\tfrac{\pi}{2} \le \theta \le \tfrac{\pi}{2}. \text{ Simplify.} \\
&= \sqrt{a^2 - a^2\sin^2\theta} && \text{Factor out } a^2. \\
&= \sqrt{a^2(1 - \sin^2\theta)} && \text{Substitute } 1 - \sin^2 x = \cos^2 x. \\
&= \sqrt{a^2\cos^2\theta} && \text{Take the square root.} \\
&= |a\cos\theta| \\
&= a\cos\theta.
\end{aligned}$$

Since $\cos x \ge 0$ on $-\frac{\pi}{2} \le \theta \le \frac{\pi}{2}$ and $a > 0$, $|a\cos\theta| = a\cos\theta$. We can see, from this discussion, that by making the substitution $x = a\sin\theta$, we are able to convert an integral involving a radical into an integral involving trigonometric functions. After we evaluate the integral, we can convert the solution back to an expression involving $x$. To see how to do this, let's begin by assuming that $0 < x < a$. In this case, $0 < \theta < \frac{\pi}{2}$. Since $\sin\theta = \frac{x}{a}$, we can draw the reference triangle in **Figure 3.4** to assist in expressing the values of $\cos\theta$, $\tan\theta$, and the remaining trigonometric functions in terms of $x$. It can be shown that this triangle actually produces the correct values of the trigonometric functions evaluated at $\theta$ for all $\theta$ satisfying $-\frac{\pi}{2} \le \theta \le \frac{\pi}{2}$. It is useful to observe that the expression $\sqrt{a^2 - x^2}$ actually appears as the length of one side of the triangle. Last, should $\theta$ appear by itself, we use $\theta = \sin^{-1}\left(\frac{x}{a}\right)$.

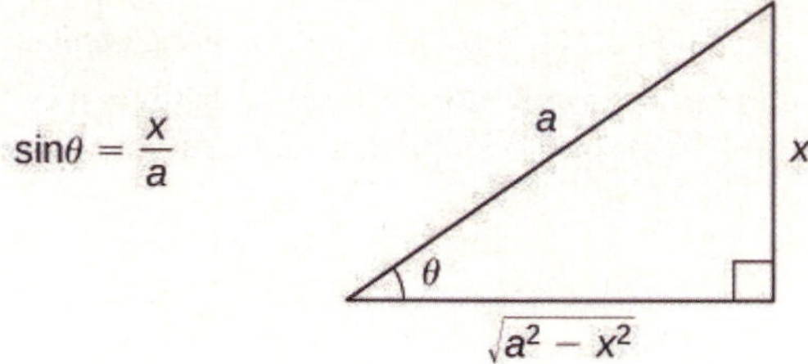


**Figure 3.4** A reference triangle can help express the trigonometric functions evaluated at $\theta$ in terms of $x$.

The essential part of this discussion is summarized in the following problem-solving strategy.

### Problem-Solving Strategy: Integrating Expressions Involving $\sqrt{a^2 - x^2}$

1. It is a good idea to make sure the integral cannot be evaluated easily in another way. For example, although this method can be applied to integrals of the form $\int \frac{1}{\sqrt{a^2 - x^2}}dx$, $\int \frac{x}{\sqrt{a^2 - x^2}}dx$, and $\int x\sqrt{a^2 - x^2}dx$, they can each be integrated directly either by formula or by a simple $u$-substitution.
2. Make the substitution $x = a\sin\theta$ and $dx = a\cos\theta d\theta$. *Note*: This substitution yields $\sqrt{a^2 - x^2} = a\cos\theta$.
3. Simplify the expression.
4. Evaluate the integral using techniques from the section on trigonometric integrals.
5. Use the reference triangle from **Figure 3.4** to rewrite the result in terms of $x$. You may also need to use some trigonometric identities and the relationship $\theta = \sin^{-1}\left(\frac{x}{a}\right)$.

The following example demonstrates the application of this problem-solving strategy.

## Example 3.21

### Integrating an Expression Involving $\sqrt{a^2 - x^2}$

Evaluate $\int \sqrt{9 - x^2}dx$.

#### Solution

Begin by making the substitutions $x = 3\sin\theta$ and $dx = 3\cos\theta d\theta$. Since $\sin\theta = \frac{x}{3}$, we can construct the reference triangle shown in the following figure.

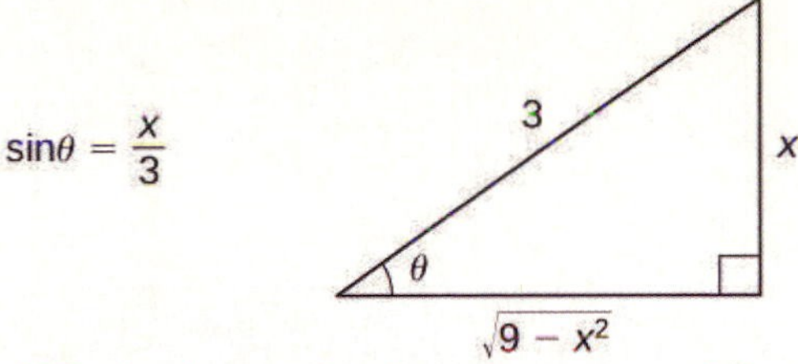


**Figure 3.5** A reference triangle can be constructed for **Example 3.21**.

Thus,

$$\begin{aligned}
\int \sqrt{9-x^2}\,dx &= \int \sqrt{9-(3\sin\theta)^2}\,3\cos\theta d\theta && \text{Substitute } x = 3\sin\theta \text{ and } dx = 3\cos\theta d\theta. \\
&= \int \sqrt{9(1-\sin^2\theta)}\,3\cos\theta d\theta && \text{Simplify.} \\
&= \int \sqrt{9\cos^2\theta}\,3\cos\theta d\theta && \text{Substitute } \cos^2\theta = 1-\sin^2\theta. \\
&= \int 3|\cos\theta| 3\cos\theta d\theta && \text{Take the square root.} \\
&= \int 9\cos^2\theta d\theta && \text{Simplify. Since } -\tfrac{\pi}{2} \le \theta \le \tfrac{\pi}{2},\ \cos\theta \ge 0 \text{ and } |\cos\theta| = \cos\theta. \\
&= \int 9\left(\tfrac{1}{2} + \tfrac{1}{2}\cos(2\theta)\right)d\theta && \text{Use the strategy for integrating an even power of } \cos\theta. \\
&= \tfrac{9}{2}\theta + \tfrac{9}{4}\sin(2\theta) + C && \text{Evaluate the integral.} \\
&= \tfrac{9}{2}\theta + \tfrac{9}{4}(2\sin\theta\cos\theta) + C && \text{Substitute } \sin(2\theta) = 2\sin\theta\cos\theta. \\
&= \tfrac{9}{2}\sin^{-1}\left(\tfrac{x}{3}\right) + \tfrac{9}{2}\cdot\tfrac{x}{3}\cdot\tfrac{\sqrt{9-x^2}}{3} + C && \text{Substitute } \sin^{-1}\left(\tfrac{x}{3}\right) = \theta \text{ and } \sin\theta = \tfrac{x}{3}. \text{ Use the reference triangle to see that } \cos\theta = \tfrac{\sqrt{9-x^2}}{3} \text{ and make this substitution.} \\
&= \tfrac{9}{2}\sin^{-1}\left(\tfrac{x}{3}\right) + \tfrac{x\sqrt{9-x^2}}{2} + C. && \text{Simplify.}
\end{aligned}$$

## Example 3.22

### Integrating an Expression Involving $\sqrt{a^2-x^2}$

Evaluate $\int \frac{\sqrt{4-x^2}}{x}dx.$

### Solution

First make the substitutions $x = 2\sin\theta$ and $dx = 2\cos\theta d\theta.$ Since $\sin\theta = \frac{x}{2},$ we can construct the reference triangle shown in the following figure.

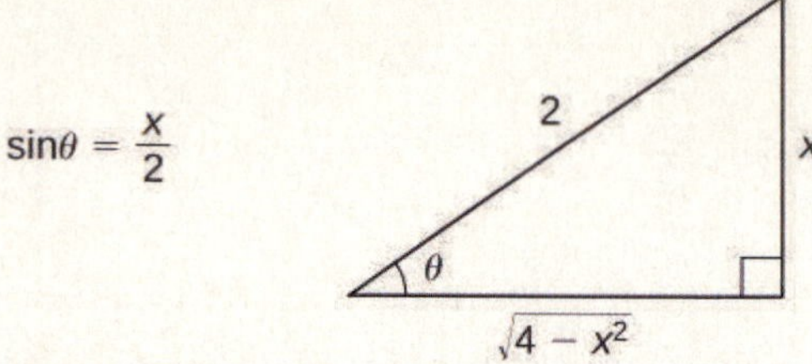


**Figure 3.6** A reference triangle can be constructed for **Example 3.22**.

Thus,

$$\begin{aligned}
\int \frac{\sqrt{4-x^2}}{x}dx &= \int \frac{\sqrt{4-(2\sin\theta)^2}}{2\sin\theta}2\cos\theta d\theta && \text{Substitute } x = 2\sin\theta \text{ and } = 2\cos\theta d\theta. \\
&= \int \frac{2\cos^2\theta}{\sin\theta}d\theta && \text{Substitute } \cos^2\theta = 1-\sin^2\theta \text{ and simplify.} \\
&= \int \frac{2(1-\sin^2\theta)}{\sin\theta}d\theta && \text{Substitute } \sin^2\theta = 1-\cos^2\theta. \\
&= \int (2\csc\theta - 2\sin\theta)d\theta && \text{Separate the numerator, simplify, and use } \csc\theta = \frac{1}{\sin\theta}. \\
&= 2\ln|\csc\theta - \cot\theta| + 2\cos\theta + C && \text{Evaluate the integral.} \\
&= 2\ln\left|\frac{2}{x} - \frac{\sqrt{4-x^2}}{x}\right| + \sqrt{4-x^2} + C. && \text{Use the reference triangle to rewrite the expression in terms of } x \text{ and simplify.}
\end{aligned}$$

In the next example, we see that we sometimes have a choice of methods.

## Example 3.23

### Integrating an Expression Involving $\sqrt{a^2-x^2}$ Two Ways

Evaluate $\int x^3\sqrt{1-x^2}dx$ two ways: first by using the substitution $u = 1-x^2$ and then by using a trigonometric substitution.

### Solution

**Method 1**

Let $u = 1-x^2$ and hence $x^2 = 1-u$. Thus, $du = -2xdx$. In this case, the integral becomes

$$\begin{aligned}\int x^3\sqrt{1-x^2}dx &= -\frac{1}{2}\int x^2\sqrt{1-x^2}(-2x\,dx) && \text{Make the substitution.}\\ &= -\frac{1}{2}\int (1-u)\sqrt{u}\,du && \text{Expand the expression.}\\ &= -\frac{1}{2}\int \left(u^{1/2}-u^{3/2}\right)du && \text{Evaluate the integral.}\\ &= -\frac{1}{2}\left(\frac{2}{3}u^{3/2}-\frac{2}{5}u^{5/2}\right)+C && \text{Rewrite in terms of } x.\\ &= -\frac{1}{3}\left(1-x^2\right)^{3/2}+\frac{1}{5}\left(1-x^2\right)^{5/2}+C.\end{aligned}$$

**Method 2**

Let $x=\sin\theta$. In this case, $dx=\cos\theta d\theta$. Using this substitution, we have

$$\begin{aligned}\int x^3\sqrt{1-x^2}dx &= \int \sin^3\theta\cos^2\theta d\theta\\ &= \int\left(1-\cos^2\theta\right)\cos^2\theta\sin\theta d\theta && \text{Let } u=\cos\theta. \text{ Thus, } du=-\sin\theta d\theta.\\ &= \int\left(u^4-u^2\right)du\\ &= \frac{1}{5}u^5-\frac{1}{3}u^3+C && \text{Substitute } \cos\theta=u.\\ &= \frac{1}{5}\cos^5\theta-\frac{1}{3}\cos^3\theta+C && \text{Use a reference triangle to see that } \cos\theta=\sqrt{1-x^2}.\\ &= \frac{1}{5}\left(1-x^2\right)^{5/2}-\frac{1}{3}\left(1-x^2\right)^{3/2}+C.\end{aligned}$$

**3.14** Rewrite the integral $\int \frac{x^3}{\sqrt{25-x^2}}dx$ using the appropriate trigonometric substitution (do not evaluate the integral).

## Integrating Expressions Involving $\sqrt{a^2+x^2}$

For integrals containing $\sqrt{a^2+x^2}$, let's first consider the domain of this expression. Since $\sqrt{a^2+x^2}$ is defined for all real values of $x$, we restrict our choice to those trigonometric functions that have a range of all real numbers. Thus, our choice is restricted to selecting either $x=a\tan\theta$ or $x=a\cot\theta$. Either of these substitutions would actually work, but the standard substitution is $x=a\tan\theta$ or, equivalently, $\tan\theta=x/a$. With this substitution, we make the assumption that $-(\pi/2)<\theta<\pi/2$, so that we also have $\theta=\tan^{-1}(x/a)$. The procedure for using this substitution is outlined in the following problem-solving strategy.

### Problem-Solving Strategy: Integrating Expressions Involving $\sqrt{a^2+x^2}$

1. Check to see whether the integral can be evaluated easily by using another method. In some cases, it is more convenient to use an alternative method.
2. Substitute $x=a\tan\theta$ and $dx=a\sec^2\theta d\theta$. This substitution yields $\sqrt{a^2+x^2}=\sqrt{a^2+(a\tan\theta)^2}=\sqrt{a^2(1+\tan^2\theta)}=\sqrt{a^2\sec^2\theta}=|a\sec\theta|=a\sec\theta$. (Since $-\frac{\pi}{2}<\theta<\frac{\pi}{2}$ and $\sec\theta>0$ over this interval, $|a\sec\theta|=a\sec\theta$.)

3. Simplify the expression.
4. Evaluate the integral using techniques from the section on trigonometric integrals.
5. Use the reference triangle from **Figure 3.7** to rewrite the result in terms of $x$. You may also need to use some trigonometric identities and the relationship $\theta = \tan^{-1}\left(\frac{x}{a}\right)$. (*Note*: The reference triangle is based on the assumption that $x > 0$; however, the trigonometric ratios produced from the reference triangle are the same as the ratios for which $x \le 0$.)

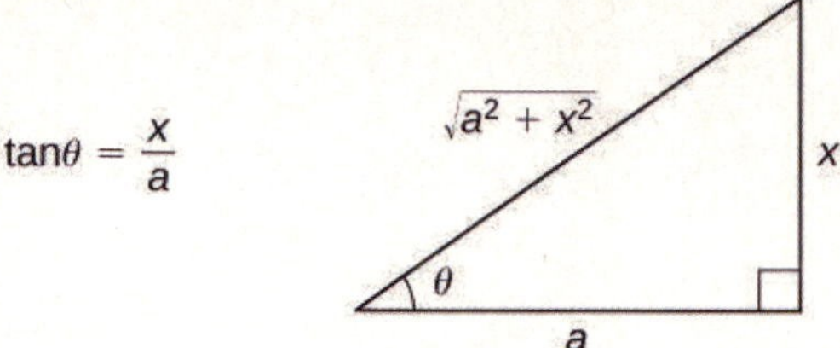


**Figure 3.7** A reference triangle can be constructed to express the trigonometric functions evaluated at $\theta$ in terms of $x$.

## Example 3.24

### Integrating an Expression Involving $\sqrt{a^2+x^2}$

Evaluate $\int \frac{dx}{\sqrt{1+x^2}}$ and check the solution by differentiating.

### Solution

Begin with the substitution $x = \tan\theta$ and $dx = \sec^2\theta d\theta$. Since $\tan\theta = x$, draw the reference triangle in the following figure.

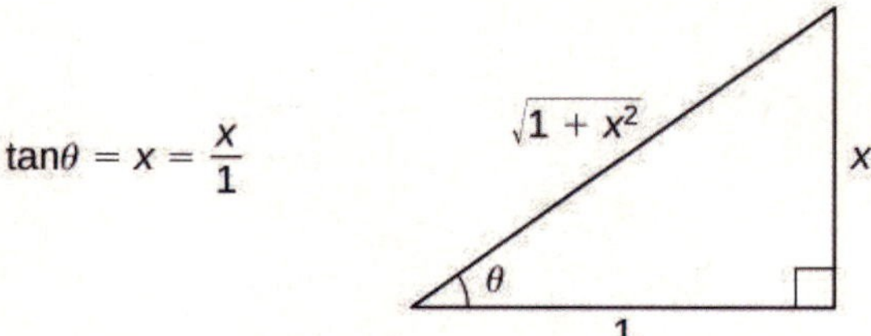


**Figure 3.8** The reference triangle for **Example 3.24**.

Thus,

$$\int \frac{dx}{\sqrt{1+x^2}} = \int \frac{\sec^2\theta}{\sec\theta} d\theta$$

Substitute $x = \tan\theta$ and $dx = \sec^2\theta d\theta$. This substitution makes $\sqrt{1+x^2} = \sec\theta$. Simplify.

$$= \int \sec\theta d\theta$$

Evaluate the integral.

$$= \ln|\sec\theta + \tan\theta| + C$$

Use the reference triangle to express the result in terms of $x$.

$$= \ln\left|\sqrt{1+x^2} + x\right| + C.$$

To check the solution, differentiate:

$$\begin{aligned}\frac{d}{dx}\left(\ln\left|\sqrt{1+x^2}+x\right|\right) &= \frac{1}{\sqrt{1+x^2}+x}\cdot\left(\frac{x}{\sqrt{1+x^2}}+1\right) \\ &= \frac{1}{\sqrt{1+x^2}+x}\cdot\frac{x+\sqrt{1+x^2}}{\sqrt{1+x^2}} \\ &= \frac{1}{\sqrt{1+x^2}}.\end{aligned}$$

Since $\sqrt{1+x^2}+x>0$ for all values of $x$, we could rewrite $\ln\left|\sqrt{1+x^2}+x\right|+C=\ln\left(\sqrt{1+x^2}+x\right)+C$, if desired.

## Example 3.25

### Evaluating $\int \frac{dx}{\sqrt{1+x^2}}$ Using a Different Substitution

Use the substitution $x=\sinh\theta$ to evaluate $\int \frac{dx}{\sqrt{1+x^2}}$.

### Solution

Because $\sinh\theta$ has a range of all real numbers, and $1+\sinh^2\theta=\cosh^2\theta$, we may also use the substitution $x=\sinh\theta$ to evaluate this integral. In this case, $dx=\cosh\theta d\theta$. Consequently,

$$\begin{aligned}\int\frac{dx}{\sqrt{1+x^2}} &= \int\frac{\cosh\theta}{\sqrt{1+\sinh^2\theta}}d\theta && \text{Substitute } x=\sinh\theta \text{ and } dx=\cosh\theta d\theta. \\ & && \text{Substitute } 1+\sinh^2\theta=\cosh^2\theta. \\ &= \int\frac{\cosh\theta}{\sqrt{\cosh^2\theta}}d\theta && \sqrt{\cosh^2\theta}=|\cosh\theta| \\ &= \int\frac{\cosh\theta}{|\cosh\theta|}d\theta && |\cosh\theta|=\cosh\theta \text{ since } \cosh\theta>0 \text{ for all } \theta. \\ &= \int\frac{\cosh\theta}{\cosh\theta}d\theta && \text{Simplify.} \\ &= \int 1d\theta && \text{Evaluate the integral.} \\ &= \theta+C && \text{Since } x=\sinh\theta, \text{ we know } \theta=\sinh^{-1}x. \\ &= \sinh^{-1}x+C.\end{aligned}$$

### Analysis

This answer looks quite different from the answer obtained using the substitution $x=\tan\theta$. To see that the solutions are the same, set $y=\sinh^{-1}x$. Thus, $\sinh y=x$. From this equation we obtain:

$$\frac{e^y-e^{-y}}{2}=x.$$

After multiplying both sides by $2e^y$ and rewriting, this equation becomes:

$$e^{2y} - 2xe^y - 1 = 0.$$

Use the quadratic equation to solve for $e^y$:

$$e^y = \frac{2x \pm \sqrt{4x^2 + 4}}{2}.$$

Simplifying, we have:

$$e^y = x \pm \sqrt{x^2 + 1}.$$

Since $x - \sqrt{x^2 + 1} < 0,$ it must be the case that $e^y = x + \sqrt{x^2 + 1}.$ Thus,

$$y = \ln\left(x + \sqrt{x^2 + 1}\right).$$

Last, we obtain

$$\sinh^{-1} x = \ln\left(x + \sqrt{x^2 + 1}\right).$$

After we make the final observation that, since $x + \sqrt{x^2 + 1} > 0,$

$$\ln\left(x + \sqrt{x^2 + 1}\right) = \ln\left|\sqrt{1 + x^2} + x\right|,$$

we see that the two different methods produced equivalent solutions.

## Example 3.26

### Finding an Arc Length

Find the length of the curve $y = x^2$ over the interval $[0, \frac{1}{2}]$.

#### Solution

Because $\frac{dy}{dx} = 2x,$ the arc length is given by

$$\int_0^{1/2} \sqrt{1 + (2x)^2} dx = \int_0^{1/2} \sqrt{1 + 4x^2} dx.$$

To evaluate this integral, use the substitution $x = \frac{1}{2}\tan\theta$ and $dx = \frac{1}{2}\sec^2\theta d\theta.$ We also need to change the limits of integration. If $x = 0,$ then $\theta = 0$ and if $x = \frac{1}{2},$ then $\theta = \frac{\pi}{4}.$ Thus,

$$\int_0^{1/2} \sqrt{1+4x^2}dx = \int_0^{\pi/4} \sqrt{1+\tan^2\theta}\frac{1}{2}\sec^2\theta d\theta$$

After substitution, $\sqrt{1+4x^2} = \tan\theta$. Substitute $1+\tan^2\theta = \sec^2\theta$ and simplify.

$$= \frac{1}{2}\int_0^{\pi/4} \sec^3\theta d\theta$$

We derived this integral in the previous section.

$$= \frac{1}{2}\left(\frac{1}{2}\sec\theta\tan\theta + \ln|\sec\theta + \tan\theta|\right)\Big|_0^{\pi/4}$$

Evaluate and simplify.

$$= \frac{1}{4}(\sqrt{2} + \ln(\sqrt{2}+1)).$$

**3.15** Rewrite $\int x^3\sqrt{x^2+4}dx$ by using a substitution involving $\tan\theta$.

## Integrating Expressions Involving $\sqrt{x^2-a^2}$

The domain of the expression $\sqrt{x^2-a^2}$ is $(-\infty, -a] \cup [a, +\infty)$. Thus, either $x < -a$ or $x > a$. Hence, $\frac{x}{a} \le -1$ or $\frac{x}{a} \ge 1$. Since these intervals correspond to the range of $\sec\theta$ on the set $\left[0, \frac{\pi}{2}\right) \cup \left(\frac{\pi}{2}, \pi\right]$, it makes sense to use the substitution $\sec\theta = \frac{x}{a}$ or, equivalently, $x = a\sec\theta$, where $0 \le \theta < \frac{\pi}{2}$ or $\frac{\pi}{2} < \theta \le \pi$. The corresponding substitution for $dx$ is $dx = a\sec\theta\tan\theta d\theta$. The procedure for using this substitution is outlined in the following problem-solving strategy.

### Problem-Solving Strategy: Integrals Involving $\sqrt{x^2-a^2}$

1. Check to see whether the integral cannot be evaluated using another method. If so, we may wish to consider applying an alternative technique.
2. Substitute $x = a\sec\theta$ and $dx = a\sec\theta\tan\theta d\theta$. This substitution yields

$$\sqrt{x^2-a^2} = \sqrt{(a\sec\theta)^2 - a^2} = \sqrt{a^2(\sec^2\theta+1)} = \sqrt{a^2\tan^2\theta} = |a\tan\theta|.$$

   For $x \ge a$, $|a\tan\theta| = a\tan\theta$ and for $x \le -a$, $|a\tan\theta| = -a\tan\theta$.
3. Simplify the expression.
4. Evaluate the integral using techniques from the section on trigonometric integrals.
5. Use the reference triangles from **Figure 3.9** to rewrite the result in terms of $x$. You may also need to use some trigonometric identities and the relationship $\theta = \sec^{-1}\left(\frac{x}{a}\right)$. (*Note*: We need both reference triangles, since the values of some of the trigonometric ratios are different depending on whether $x > a$ or $x < -a$.)

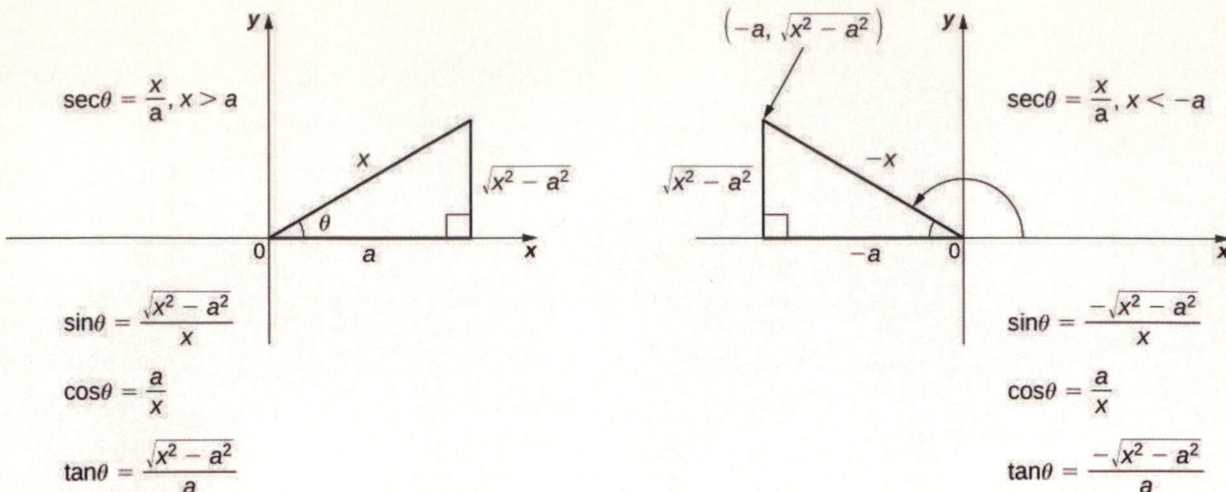


**Figure 3.9** Use the appropriate reference triangle to express the trigonometric functions evaluated at $\theta$ in terms of $x$.

## Example 3.27

### Finding the Area of a Region

Find the area of the region between the graph of $f(x) = \sqrt{x^2 - 9}$ and the $x$-axis over the interval $[3, 5]$.

#### Solution

First, sketch a rough graph of the region described in the problem, as shown in the following figure.

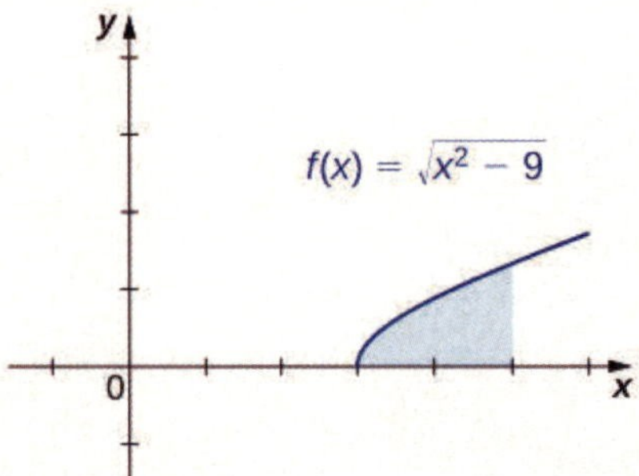


**Figure 3.10** Calculating the area of the shaded region requires evaluating an integral with a trigonometric substitution.

We can see that the area is $A = \int_3^5 \sqrt{x^2 - 9}\,dx$. To evaluate this definite integral, substitute $x = 3\sec\theta$ and $dx = 3\sec\theta\tan\theta d\theta$. We must also change the limits of integration. If $x = 3$, then $3 = 3\sec\theta$ and hence $\theta = 0$. If $x = 5$, then $\theta = \sec^{-1}\left(\frac{5}{3}\right)$. After making these substitutions and simplifying, we have

$$\begin{aligned}
\text{Area} &= \int_3^5 \sqrt{x^2 - 9}\,dx \\
&= \int_0^{\sec^{-1}(5/3)} 9\tan^2\theta \sec\theta d\theta && \text{Use } \tan^2\theta = 1 - \sec^2\theta. \\
&= \int_0^{\sec^{-1}(5/3)} 9(\sec^2\theta - 1)\sec\theta d\theta && \text{Expand.} \\
&= \int_0^{\sec^{-1}(5/3)} 9(\sec^3\theta - \sec\theta)d\theta && \text{Evaluate the integral.} \\
&= \left(\frac{9}{2}\ln|\sec\theta + \tan\theta| + \frac{9}{2}\sec\theta\tan\theta\right) - 9\ln|\sec\theta + \tan\theta|\Big|_0^{\sec^{-1}(5/3)} && \text{Simplify.} \\
&= \frac{9}{2}\sec\theta\tan\theta - \frac{9}{2}\ln|\sec\theta + \tan\theta|\Big|_0^{\sec^{-1}(5/3)} && \text{Evaluate. Use } \sec\left(\sec^{-1}\frac{5}{3}\right) = \frac{5}{3} \text{ and } \tan\left(\sec^{-1}\frac{5}{3}\right) = \frac{4}{3}. \\
&= \frac{9}{2}\cdot\frac{5}{3}\cdot\frac{4}{3} - \frac{9}{2}\ln\left|\frac{5}{3} + \frac{4}{3}\right| - \left(\frac{9}{2}\cdot 1\cdot 0 - \frac{9}{2}\ln|1 + 0|\right) \\
&= 10 - \frac{9}{2}\ln 3.
\end{aligned}$$

**3.16** Evaluate $\int \frac{dx}{\sqrt{x^2 - 4}}$. Assume that $x > 2$.

# 3.3 EXERCISES

Simplify the following expressions by writing each one using a single trigonometric function.

126. $4 - 4\sin^2\theta$

127. $9\sec^2\theta - 9$

128. $a^2 + a^2\tan^2\theta$

129. $a^2 + a^2\sinh^2\theta$

130. $16\cosh^2\theta - 16$

Use the technique of completing the square to express each trinomial as the square of a binomial.

131. $4x^2 - 4x + 1$

132. $2x^2 - 8x + 3$

133. $-x^2 - 2x + 4$

Integrate using the method of trigonometric substitution. Express the final answer in terms of the variable.

134. $\int \frac{dx}{\sqrt{4 - x^2}}$

135. $\int \frac{dx}{\sqrt{x^2 - a^2}}$

136. $\int \sqrt{4 - x^2}dx$

137. $\int \frac{dx}{\sqrt{1 + 9x^2}}$

138. $\int \frac{x^2 dx}{\sqrt{1 - x^2}}$

139. $\int \frac{dx}{x^2\sqrt{1 - x^2}}$

140. $\int \frac{dx}{(1 + x^2)^2}$

141. $\int \sqrt{x^2 + 9}dx$

142. $\int \frac{\sqrt{x^2 - 25}}{x}dx$

143. $\int \frac{\theta^3 d\theta}{\sqrt{9 - \theta^2}}d\theta$

144. $\int \frac{dx}{\sqrt{x^6 - x^2}}$

145. $\int \sqrt{x^6 - x^8}dx$

146. $\int \frac{dx}{\left(1 + x^2\right)^{3/2}}$

147. $\int \frac{dx}{\left(x^2 - 9\right)^{3/2}}$

148. $\int \frac{\sqrt{1 + x^2}dx}{x}$

149. $\int \frac{x^2 dx}{\sqrt{x^2 - 1}}$

150. $\int \frac{x^2 dx}{x^2 + 4}$

151. $\int \frac{dx}{x^2\sqrt{x^2 + 1}}$

152. $\int \frac{x^2 dx}{\sqrt{1 + x^2}}$

153. $\int_{-1}^{1} (1 - x^2)^{3/2} dx$

In the following exercises, use the substitutions $x = \sinh\theta, \cosh\theta,$ or $\tanh\theta.$ Express the final answers in terms of the variable $x$.

154. $\int \frac{dx}{\sqrt{x^2 - 1}}$

155. $\int \frac{dx}{x\sqrt{1 - x^2}}$

156. $\int \sqrt{x^2 - 1}dx$

157. $\int \frac{\sqrt{x^2 - 1}}{x^2}dx$

158. $\int \frac{dx}{1 - x^2}$

159. $\int \frac{\sqrt{1 + x^2}}{x^2} dx$

Use the technique of completing the square to evaluate the following integrals.

160. $\int \frac{1}{x^2 - 6x} dx$

161. $\int \frac{1}{x^2 + 2x + 1} dx$

162. $\int \frac{1}{\sqrt{-x^2 + 2x + 8}} dx$

163. $\int \frac{1}{\sqrt{-x^2 + 10x}} dx$

164. $\int \frac{1}{\sqrt{x^2 + 4x - 12}} dx$

165. Evaluate the integral without using calculus: $\int_{-3}^{3} \sqrt{9 - x^2} dx.$

166. Find the area enclosed by the ellipse $\frac{x^2}{4} + \frac{y^2}{9} = 1.$

167. Evaluate the integral $\int \frac{dx}{\sqrt{1 - x^2}}$ using two different substitutions. First, let $x = \cos\theta$ and evaluate using trigonometric substitution. Second, let $x = \sin\theta$ and use trigonometric substitution. Are the answers the same?

168. Evaluate the integral $\int \frac{dx}{x\sqrt{x^2 - 1}}$ using the substitution $x = \sec\theta$. Next, evaluate the same integral using the substitution $x = \csc\theta$. Show that the results are equivalent.

169. Evaluate the integral $\int \frac{x}{x^2 + 1} dx$ using the form $\int \frac{1}{u} du$. Next, evaluate the same integral using $x = \tan\theta$. Are the results the same?

170. State the method of integration you would use to evaluate the integral $\int x\sqrt{x^2 + 1}\, dx$. Why did you choose this method?

171. State the method of integration you would use to evaluate the integral $\int x^2 \sqrt{x^2 - 1}\, dx$. Why did you choose this method?

172. Evaluate $\int_{-1}^{1} \frac{x dx}{x^2 + 1}$

173. Find the length of the arc of the curve over the specified interval: $y = \ln x$, $[1, 5]$. Round the answer to three decimal places.

174. Find the surface area of the solid generated by revolving the region bounded by the graphs of $y = x^2$, $y = 0$, $x = 0$, and $x = \sqrt{2}$ about the $x$-axis. (Round the answer to three decimal places).

175. The region bounded by the graph of $f(x) = \frac{1}{1 + x^2}$ and the $x$-axis between $x = 0$ and $x = 1$ is revolved about the $x$-axis. Find the volume of the solid that is generated.

Solve the initial-value problem for $y$ as a function of $x$.

176. $(x^2 + 36)\frac{dy}{dx} = 1,\ y(6) = 0$

177. $(64 - x^2)\frac{dy}{dx} = 1,\ y(0) = 3$

178. Find the area bounded by $y = \frac{2}{\sqrt{64 - 4x^2}}$, $x = 0$, $y = 0$, and $x = 2$.

179. An oil storage tank can be described as the volume generated by revolving the area bounded by $y = \frac{16}{\sqrt{64 + x^2}}$, $x = 0$, $y = 0$, $x = 2$ about the $x$-axis. Find the volume of the tank (in cubic meters).

180. During each cycle, the velocity $v$ (in feet per second) of a robotic welding device is given by $v = 2t - \frac{14}{4 + t^2}$, where $t$ is time in seconds. Find the expression for the displacement $s$ (in feet) as a function of $t$ if $s = 0$ when $t = 0$.

181. Find the length of the curve $y = \sqrt{16 - x^2}$ between $x = 0$ and $x = 2$.

# 3.4 | Partial Fractions

## Learning Objectives

**3.4.1** Integrate a rational function using the method of partial fractions.
**3.4.2** Recognize simple linear factors in a rational function.
**3.4.3** Recognize repeated linear factors in a rational function.
**3.4.4** Recognize quadratic factors in a rational function.

We have seen some techniques that allow us to integrate specific rational functions. For example, we know that

$$\int \frac{du}{u} = \ln|u| + C \text{ and } \int \frac{du}{u^2 + a^2} = \frac{1}{a}\tan^{-1}\left(\frac{u}{a}\right) + C.$$

However, we do not yet have a technique that allows us to tackle arbitrary quotients of this type. Thus, it is not immediately obvious how to go about evaluating $\int \frac{3x}{x^2 - x - 2}dx.$ However, we know from material previously developed that

$$\int \left(\frac{1}{x+1} + \frac{2}{x-2}\right)dx = \ln|x+1| + 2\ln|x-2| + C.$$

In fact, by getting a common denominator, we see that

$$\frac{1}{x+1} + \frac{2}{x-2} = \frac{3x}{x^2 - x - 2}.$$

Consequently,

$$\int \frac{3x}{x^2 - x - 2}dx = \int \left(\frac{1}{x+1} + \frac{2}{x-2}\right)dx.$$

In this section, we examine the method of **partial fraction decomposition**, which allows us to decompose rational functions into sums of simpler, more easily integrated rational functions. Using this method, we can rewrite an expression such as: $\frac{3x}{x^2 - x - 2}$ as an expression such as $\frac{1}{x+1} + \frac{2}{x-2}.$

The key to the method of partial fraction decomposition is being able to anticipate the form that the decomposition of a rational function will take. As we shall see, this form is both predictable and highly dependent on the factorization of the denominator of the rational function. It is also extremely important to keep in mind that partial fraction decomposition can be applied to a rational function $\frac{P(x)}{Q(x)}$ only if $\deg(P(x)) < \deg(Q(x))$. In the case when $\deg(P(x)) \geq \deg(Q(x))$, we must first perform long division to rewrite the quotient $\frac{P(x)}{Q(x)}$ in the form $A(x) + \frac{R(x)}{Q(x)},$ where $\deg(R(x)) < \deg(Q(x))$. We then do a partial fraction decomposition on $\frac{R(x)}{Q(x)}$. The following example, although not requiring partial fraction decomposition, illustrates our approach to integrals of rational functions of the form $\int \frac{P(x)}{Q(x)}dx,$ where $\deg(P(x)) \geq \deg(Q(x))$.

## Example 3.28

### Integrating $\int \frac{P(x)}{Q(x)}dx,$ where $\deg(P(x)) \geq \deg(Q(x))$

Evaluate $\int \frac{x^2 + 3x + 5}{x+1}dx.$

### Solution

Since $\deg(x^2 + 3x + 5) \geq \deg(x + 1)$, we perform long division to obtain

$$\frac{x^2 + 3x + 5}{x + 1} = x + 2 + \frac{3}{x + 1}.$$

Thus,

$$\begin{aligned} \int \frac{x^2 + 3x + 5}{x + 1} dx &= \int \left(x + 2 + \frac{3}{x + 1}\right) dx \\ &= \frac{1}{2}x^2 + 2x + 3\ln|x + 1| + C. \end{aligned}$$

Visit this **website (http://www.openstaxcollege.org/l/20_polylongdiv)** for a review of long division of polynomials.

**3.17** Evaluate $\int \frac{x - 3}{x + 2} dx.$

To integrate $\int \frac{P(x)}{Q(x)} dx$, where $\deg(P(x)) < \deg(Q(x))$, we must begin by factoring $Q(x)$.

## Nonrepeated Linear Factors

If $Q(x)$ can be factored as $(a_1 x + b_1)(a_2 x + b_2) \ldots (a_n x + b_n)$, where each linear factor is distinct, then it is possible to find constants $A_1, A_2, \ldots A_n$ satisfying

$$\frac{P(x)}{Q(x)} = \frac{A_1}{a_1 x + b_1} + \frac{A_2}{a_2 x + b_2} + \cdots + \frac{A_n}{a_n x + b_n}.$$

The proof that such constants exist is beyond the scope of this course.

In this next example, we see how to use partial fractions to integrate a rational function of this type.

## Example 3.29

### Partial Fractions with Nonrepeated Linear Factors

Evaluate $\int \frac{3x + 2}{x^3 - x^2 - 2x} dx.$

### Solution

Since $\deg(3x + 2) < \deg(x^3 - x^2 - 2x)$, we begin by factoring the denominator of $\frac{3x + 2}{x^3 - x^2 - 2x}$. We can see that $x^3 - x^2 - 2x = x(x - 2)(x + 1)$. Thus, there are constants $A$, $B$, and $C$ satisfying

$$\frac{3x + 2}{x(x - 2)(x + 1)} = \frac{A}{x} + \frac{B}{x - 2} + \frac{C}{x + 1}.$$

We must now find these constants. To do so, we begin by getting a common denominator on the right. Thus,

$$\frac{3x+2}{x(x-2)(x+1)} = \frac{A(x-2)(x+1) + Bx(x+1) + Cx(x-2)}{x(x-2)(x+1)}.$$

Now, we set the numerators equal to each other, obtaining

$$3x + 2 = A(x-2)(x+1) + Bx(x+1) + Cx(x-2). \tag{3.8}$$

There are two different strategies for finding the coefficients $A$, $B$, and $C$. We refer to these as the *method of equating coefficients* and the *method of strategic substitution*.

### Rule: Method of Equating Coefficients

Rewrite **Equation 3.8** in the form

$$3x + 2 = (A + B + C)x^2 + (-A + B - 2C)x + (-2A).$$

Equating coefficients produces the system of equations

$$\begin{aligned} A + B + C &= 0 \\ -A + B - 2C &= 3 \\ -2A &= 2. \end{aligned}$$

To solve this system, we first observe that $-2A = 2 \Rightarrow A = -1$. Substituting this value into the first two equations gives us the system

$$\begin{aligned} B + C &= 1 \\ B - 2C &= 2. \end{aligned}$$

Multiplying the second equation by $-1$ and adding the resulting equation to the first produces

$$-3C = 1,$$

which in turn implies that $C = -\frac{1}{3}$. Substituting this value into the equation $B + C = 1$ yields $B = \frac{4}{3}$. Thus, solving these equations yields $A = -1$, $B = \frac{4}{3}$, and $C = -\frac{1}{3}$.

It is important to note that the system produced by this method is consistent if and only if we have set up the decomposition correctly. If the system is inconsistent, there is an error in our decomposition.

### Rule: Method of Strategic Substitution

The method of strategic substitution is based on the assumption that we have set up the decomposition correctly. If the decomposition is set up correctly, then there must be values of $A$, $B$, and $C$ that satisfy **Equation 3.8** for *all* values of $x$. That is, this equation must be true for any value of $x$ we care to substitute into it. Therefore, by choosing values of $x$ carefully and substituting them into the equation, we may find $A$, $B$, and $C$ easily. For example, if we substitute $x = 0$, the equation reduces to $2 = A(-2)(1)$. Solving for $A$ yields $A = -1$. Next, by substituting $x = 2$, the equation reduces to $8 = B(2)(3)$, or equivalently $B = 4/3$. Last, we substitute $x = -1$ into the equation and obtain $-1 = C(-1)(-3)$. Solving, we have $C = -\frac{1}{3}$.

It is important to keep in mind that if we attempt to use this method with a decomposition that has not been set up correctly, we are still able to find values for the constants, but these constants are meaningless. If we do opt to use the method of strategic substitution, then it is a good idea to check the result by recombining the terms algebraically.

Now that we have the values of $A,\quad B,$ and $C,\quad$ we rewrite the original integral:

$$\int \frac{3x+2}{x^3-x^2-2x}dx = \int \left(-\frac{1}{x} + \frac{4}{3}\cdot\frac{1}{(x-2)} - \frac{1}{3}\cdot\frac{1}{(x+1)}\right)dx.$$

Evaluating the integral gives us

$$\int \frac{3x+2}{x^3-x^2-2x}dx = -\ln|x| + \frac{4}{3}\ln|x-2| - \frac{1}{3}\ln|x+1| + C.$$

In the next example, we integrate a rational function in which the degree of the numerator is not less than the degree of the denominator.

## Example 3.30

### Dividing before Applying Partial Fractions

Evaluate $\int \frac{x^2+3x+1}{x^2-4}dx.$

#### Solution

Since $\text{degree}(x^2+3x+1) \geq \text{degree}(x^2-4),\quad$ we must perform long division of polynomials. This results in

$$\frac{x^2+3x+1}{x^2-4} = 1 + \frac{3x+5}{x^2-4}.$$

Next, we perform partial fraction decomposition on $\frac{3x+5}{x^2-4} = \frac{3x+5}{(x+2)(x-2)}.$ We have

$$\frac{3x+5}{(x-2)(x+2)} = \frac{A}{x-2} + \frac{B}{x+2}.$$

Thus,

$$3x+5 = A(x+2) + B(x-2).$$

Solving for $A$ and $B$ using either method, we obtain $A = 11/4$ and $B = 1/4.$

Rewriting the original integral, we have

$$\int \frac{x^2+3x+1}{x^2-4}dx = \int \left(1 + \frac{11}{4}\cdot\frac{1}{x-2} + \frac{1}{4}\cdot\frac{1}{x+2}\right)dx.$$

Evaluating the integral produces

$$\int \frac{x^2+3x+1}{x^2-4}dx = x + \frac{11}{4}\ln|x-2| + \frac{1}{4}\ln|x+2| + C.$$

As we see in the next example, it may be possible to apply the technique of partial fraction decomposition to a nonrational function. The trick is to convert the nonrational function to a rational function through a substitution.

## Example 3.31

### Applying Partial Fractions after a Substitution

Evaluate $\int \frac{\cos x}{\sin^2 x - \sin x} dx.$

#### Solution

Let's begin by letting $u = \sin x.$ Consequently, $du = \cos x dx.$ After making these substitutions, we have

$$\int \frac{\cos x}{\sin^2 x - \sin x} dx = \int \frac{du}{u^2 - u} = \int \frac{du}{u(u-1)}.$$

Applying partial fraction decomposition to $1/u(u-1)$ gives $\frac{1}{u(u-1)} = -\frac{1}{u} + \frac{1}{u-1}.$

Thus,

$$\begin{aligned} \int \frac{\cos x}{\sin^2 x - \sin x} dx &= -\ln|u| + \ln|u-1| + C \\ &= -\ln|\sin x| + \ln|\sin x - 1| + C. \end{aligned}$$

**3.18** Evaluate $\int \frac{x+1}{(x+3)(x-2)} dx.$

## Repeated Linear Factors

For some applications, we need to integrate rational expressions that have denominators with repeated linear factors—that is, rational functions with at least one factor of the form $(ax+b)^n,$ where $n$ is a positive integer greater than or equal to 2. If the denominator contains the repeated linear factor $(ax+b)^n,$ then the decomposition must contain

$$\frac{A_1}{ax+b} + \frac{A_2}{(ax+b)^2} + \cdots + \frac{A_n}{(ax+b)^n}.$$

As we see in our next example, the basic technique used for solving for the coefficients is the same, but it requires more algebra to determine the numerators of the partial fractions.

## Example 3.32

### Partial Fractions with Repeated Linear Factors

Evaluate $\int \frac{x-2}{(2x-1)^2(x-1)} dx.$

#### Solution

We have $\text{degree}(x-2) < \text{degree}\left((2x-1)^2(x-1)\right),$ so we can proceed with the decomposition. Since

$(2x-1)^2$ is a repeated linear factor, include $\frac{A}{2x-1}+\frac{B}{(2x-1)^2}$ in the decomposition. Thus,

$$\frac{x-2}{(2x-1)^2(x-1)}=\frac{A}{2x-1}+\frac{B}{(2x-1)^2}+\frac{C}{x-1}.$$

After getting a common denominator and equating the numerators, we have

$$x-2=A(2x-1)(x-1)+B(x-1)+C(2x-1)^2. \tag{3.9}$$

We then use the method of equating coefficients to find the values of $A,\ B,$ and $C.$

$$x-2=(2A+4C)x^2+(-3A+B-4C)x+(A-B+C).$$

Equating coefficients yields $2A+4C=0,\ -3A+B-4C=1,$ and $A-B+C=-2.$ Solving this system yields $A=2,\ B=3,$ and $C=-1.$

Alternatively, we can use the method of strategic substitution. In this case, substituting $x=1$ and $x=1/2$ into **Equation 3.9** easily produces the values $B=3$ and $C=-1.$ At this point, it may seem that we have run out of good choices for $x,$ however, since we already have values for $B$ and $C,$ we can substitute in these values and choose any value for $x$ not previously used. The value $x=0$ is a good option. In this case, we obtain the equation $-2=A(-1)(-1)+3(-1)+(-1)(-1)^2$ or, equivalently, $A=2.$

Now that we have the values for $A,\ B,$ and $C,$ we rewrite the original integral and evaluate it:

$$\begin{aligned}\int\frac{x-2}{(2x-1)^2(x-1)}dx &= \int\left(\frac{2}{2x-1}+\frac{3}{(2x-1)^2}-\frac{1}{x-1}\right)dx \\ &= \ln|2x-1|-\frac{3}{2(2x-1)}-\ln|x-1|+C.\end{aligned}$$

**3.19** Set up the partial fraction decomposition for $\int\frac{x+2}{(x+3)^3(x-4)^2}dx.$ (Do not solve for the coefficients or complete the integration.)

## The General Method

Now that we are beginning to get the idea of how the technique of partial fraction decomposition works, let's outline the basic method in the following problem-solving strategy.

### Problem-Solving Strategy: Partial Fraction Decomposition

To decompose the rational function $P(x)/Q(x),$ use the following steps:

1. Make sure that $\text{degree}(P(x))<\text{degree}(Q(x)).$ If not, perform long division of polynomials.
2. Factor $Q(x)$ into the product of linear and irreducible quadratic factors. An irreducible quadratic is a quadratic that has no real zeros.
3. Assuming that $\deg(P(x))<\deg(Q(x)),$ the factors of $Q(x)$ determine the form of the decomposition of $P(x)/Q(x).$
    a. If $Q(x)$ can be factored as $(a_1x+b_1)(a_2x+b_2)\ldots(a_nx+b_n),$ where each linear factor is distinct,

then it is possible to find constants $A_1, A_2, ...A_n$ satisfying

$$\frac{P(x)}{Q(x)} = \frac{A_1}{a_1x + b_1} + \frac{A_2}{a_2x + b_2} + \cdots + \frac{A_n}{a_nx + b_n}.$$

b. If $Q(x)$ contains the repeated linear factor $(ax + b)^n$, then the decomposition must contain

$$\frac{A_1}{ax + b} + \frac{A_2}{(ax + b)^2} + \cdots + \frac{A_n}{(ax + b)^n}.$$

c. For each irreducible quadratic factor $ax^2 + bx + c$ that $Q(x)$ contains, the decomposition must include

$$\frac{Ax + B}{ax^2 + bx + c}.$$

d. For each repeated irreducible quadratic factor $\left(ax^2 + bx + c\right)^n$, the decomposition must include

$$\frac{A_1x + B_1}{ax^2 + bx + c} + \frac{A_2x + B_2}{(ax^2 + bx + c)^2} + \cdots + \frac{A_nx + B_n}{(ax^2 + bx + c)^n}.$$

e. After the appropriate decomposition is determined, solve for the constants.

f. Last, rewrite the integral in its decomposed form and evaluate it using previously developed techniques or integration formulas.

## Simple Quadratic Factors

Now let's look at integrating a rational expression in which the denominator contains an irreducible quadratic factor. Recall that the quadratic $ax^2 + bx + c$ is irreducible if $ax^2 + bx + c = 0$ has no real zeros—that is, if $b^2 - 4ac < 0$.

### Example 3.33

#### Rational Expressions with an Irreducible Quadratic Factor

Evaluate $\int \frac{2x - 3}{x^3 + x}dx.$

#### Solution

Since $\deg(2x - 3) < \deg(x^3 + x)$, factor the denominator and proceed with partial fraction decomposition. Since $x^3 + x = x(x^2 + 1)$ contains the irreducible quadratic factor $x^2 + 1$, include $\frac{Ax + B}{x^2 + 1}$ as part of the decomposition, along with $\frac{C}{x}$ for the linear term $x$. Thus, the decomposition has the form

$$\frac{2x - 3}{x(x^2 + 1)} = \frac{Ax + B}{x^2 + 1} + \frac{C}{x}.$$

After getting a common denominator and equating the numerators, we obtain the equation

$$2x - 3 = (Ax + B)x + C\left(x^2 + 1\right).$$

Solving for $A, B,$ and $C,$ we get $A = 3,$ $B = 2,$ and $C = -3.$

Thus,

$$\frac{2x-3}{x^3+x} = \frac{3x+2}{x^2+1} - \frac{3}{x}.$$

Substituting back into the integral, we obtain

$$\begin{aligned} \int \frac{2x-3}{x^3+x}dx &= \int \left(\frac{3x+2}{x^2+1} - \frac{3}{x}\right)dx \\ &= 3\int \frac{x}{x^2+1}dx + 2\int \frac{1}{x^2+1}dx - 3\int \frac{1}{x}dx && \text{Split up the integral.} \\ &= \frac{3}{2}\ln\left|x^2+1\right| + 2\tan^{-1}x - 3\ln|x| + C. && \text{Evaluate each integral.} \end{aligned}$$

*Note*: We may rewrite $\ln\left|x^2+1\right| = \ln(x^2+1)$, if we wish to do so, since $x^2+1>0$.

## Example 3.34

### Partial Fractions with an Irreducible Quadratic Factor

Evaluate $\int \frac{dx}{x^3-8}$.

### Solution

We can start by factoring $x^3-8=(x-2)(x^2+2x+4)$. We see that the quadratic factor $x^2+2x+4$ is irreducible since $2^2-4(1)(4)=-12<0$. Using the decomposition described in the problem-solving strategy, we get

$$\frac{1}{(x-2)(x^2+2x+4)} = \frac{A}{x-2} + \frac{Bx+C}{x^2+2x+4}.$$

After obtaining a common denominator and equating the numerators, this becomes

$$1 = A\left(x^2+2x+4\right) + (Bx+C)(x-2).$$

Applying either method, we get $A=\frac{1}{12}$, $B=-\frac{1}{12}$, and $C=-\frac{1}{3}$.

Rewriting $\int \frac{dx}{x^3-8}$, we have

$$\int \frac{dx}{x^3-8} = \frac{1}{12}\int \frac{1}{x-2}dx - \frac{1}{12}\int \frac{x+4}{x^2+2x+4}dx.$$

We can see that

$\int \frac{1}{x-2}dx = \ln|x-2| + C$, but $\int \frac{x+4}{x^2+2x+4}dx$ requires a bit more effort. Let's begin by completing the square on $x^2+2x+4$ to obtain

$$x^2+2x+4 = (x+1)^2+3.$$

By letting $u = x + 1$ and consequently $du = dx,$ we see that

$$\begin{aligned}
\int \frac{x+4}{x^2+2x+4}dx &= \int \frac{x+4}{(x+1)^2+3}dx && \text{Complete the square on the denominator.} \\
&= \int \frac{u+3}{u^2+3}du && \text{Substitute } u = x+1,\ x = u-1, \text{ and } du = dx. \\
&= \int \frac{u}{u^2+3}du + \int \frac{3}{u^2+3}du && \text{Split the numerator apart.} \\
&= \frac{1}{2}\ln\left|u^2+3\right| + \frac{3}{\sqrt{3}}\tan^{-1}\frac{u}{\sqrt{3}} + C && \text{Evaluate each integral.} \\
&= \frac{1}{2}\ln\left|x^2+2x+4\right| + \sqrt{3}\tan^{-1}\left(\frac{x+1}{\sqrt{3}}\right) + C. && \text{Rewrite in terms of } x \text{ and simplify.}
\end{aligned}$$

Substituting back into the original integral and simplifying gives

$$\int \frac{dx}{x^3-8} = \frac{1}{12}\ln|x-2| - \frac{1}{24}\ln\left|x^2+2x+4\right| - \frac{\sqrt{3}}{12}\tan^{-1}\left(\frac{x+1}{\sqrt{3}}\right) + C.$$

Here again, we can drop the absolute value if we wish to do so, since $x^2 + 2x + 4 > 0$ for all $x$.

## Example 3.35

### Finding a Volume

Find the volume of the solid of revolution obtained by revolving the region enclosed by the graph of $f(x) = \frac{x^2}{\left(x^2+1\right)^2}$ and the $x$-axis over the interval $[0, 1]$ about the $y$-axis.

### Solution

Let's begin by sketching the region to be revolved (see **Figure 3.11**). From the sketch, we see that the shell method is a good choice for solving this problem.

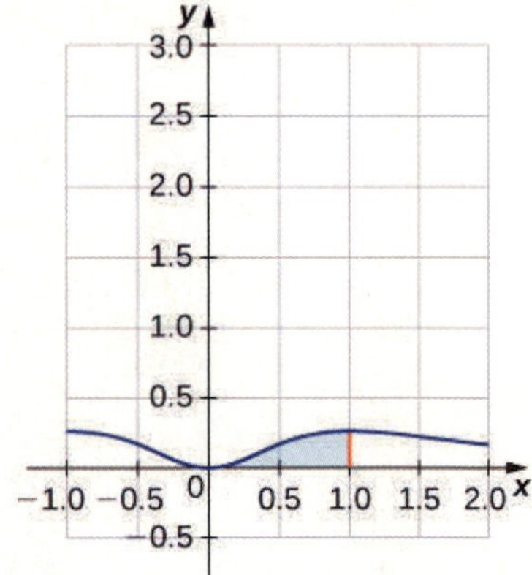


**Figure 3.11** We can use the shell method to find the volume of revolution obtained by revolving the region shown about the $y$-axis.

The volume is given by

$$V = 2\pi \int_0^1 x \cdot \frac{x^2}{\left(x^2+1\right)^2} dx = 2\pi \int_0^1 \frac{x^3}{(x^2+1)^2} dx.$$

Since $\deg\left(\left(x^2+1\right)^2\right) = 4 > 3 = \deg(x^3)$, we can proceed with partial fraction decomposition. Note that $(x^2+1)^2$ is a repeated irreducible quadratic. Using the decomposition described in the problem-solving strategy, we get

$$\frac{x^3}{(x^2+1)^2} = \frac{Ax+B}{x^2+1} + \frac{Cx+D}{(x^2+1)^2}.$$

Finding a common denominator and equating the numerators gives

$$x^3 = (Ax+B)\left(x^2+1\right) + Cx + D.$$

Solving, we obtain $A = 1$, $B = 0$, $C = -1$, and $D = 0$. Substituting back into the integral, we have

$$\begin{aligned} V &= 2\pi \int_0^1 \frac{x^3}{(x^2+1)^2} dx \\ &= 2\pi \int_0^1 \left( \frac{x}{x^2+1} - \frac{x}{(x^2+1)^2} \right) dx \\ &= 2\pi \left( \frac{1}{2}\ln(x^2+1) + \frac{1}{2} \cdot \frac{1}{x^2+1} \right) \Bigg|_0^1 \\ &= \pi\left(\ln 2 - \frac{1}{2}\right). \end{aligned}$$

**3.20** Set up the partial fraction decomposition for $\displaystyle\int \frac{x^2+3x+1}{(x+2)(x-3)^2(x^2+4)^2} dx.$

# 3.4 EXERCISES

Express the rational function as a sum or difference of two simpler rational expressions.

182. $\dfrac{1}{(x-3)(x-2)}$

183. $\dfrac{x^2+1}{x(x+1)(x+2)}$

184. $\dfrac{1}{x^3-x}$

185. $\dfrac{3x+1}{x^2}$

186. $\dfrac{3x^2}{x^2+1}$ (*Hint:* Use long division first.)

187. $\dfrac{2x^4}{x^2-2x}$

188. $\dfrac{1}{(x-1)(x^2+1)}$

189. $\dfrac{1}{x^2(x-1)}$

190. $\dfrac{x}{x^2-4}$

191. $\dfrac{1}{x(x-1)(x-2)(x-3)}$

192. $\dfrac{1}{x^4-1}=\dfrac{1}{(x+1)(x-1)\left(x^2+1\right)}$

193. $\dfrac{3x^2}{x^3-1}=\dfrac{3x^2}{(x-1)(x^2+x+1)}$

194. $\dfrac{2x}{(x+2)^2}$

195. $\dfrac{3x^4+x^3+20x^2+3x+31}{(x+1)\left(x^2+4\right)^2}$

Use the method of partial fractions to evaluate each of the following integrals.

196. $\int \dfrac{dx}{(x-3)(x-2)}$

197. $\int \dfrac{3x}{x^2+2x-8}dx$

198. $\int \dfrac{dx}{x^3-x}$

199. $\int \dfrac{x}{x^2-4}dx$

200. $\int \dfrac{dx}{x(x-1)(x-2)(x-3)}$

201. $\int \dfrac{2x^2+4x+22}{x^2+2x+10}dx$

202. $\int \dfrac{dx}{x^2-5x+6}$

203. $\int \dfrac{2-x}{x^2+x}dx$

204. $\int \dfrac{2}{x^2-x-6}dx$

205. $\int \dfrac{dx}{x^3-2x^2-4x+8}$

206. $\int \dfrac{dx}{x^4-10x^2+9}$

Evaluate the following integrals, which have irreducible quadratic factors.

207. $\int \dfrac{2}{(x-4)\left(x^2+2x+6\right)}dx$

208. $\int \dfrac{x^2}{x^3-x^2+4x-4}dx$

209. $\int \dfrac{x^3+6x^2+3x+6}{x^3+2x^2}dx$

210. $\int \dfrac{x}{(x-1)\left(x^2+2x+2\right)^2}dx$

Use the method of partial fractions to evaluate the following integrals.

211. $\int \dfrac{3x+4}{\left(x^2+4\right)(3-x)}dx$

212. $\int \dfrac{2}{(x+2)^2(2-x)}dx$

213. $\int \frac{3x+4}{x^3-2x-4}dx$ (*Hint:* Use the rational root theorem.)

Use substitution to convert the integrals to integrals of rational functions. Then use partial fractions to evaluate the integrals.

214. $\int_0^1 \frac{e^x}{36-e^{2x}}dx$ (Give the exact answer and the decimal equivalent. Round to five decimal places.)

215. $\int \frac{e^x dx}{e^{2x}-e^x}dx$

216. $\int \frac{\sin x dx}{1-\cos^2 x}$

217. $\int \frac{\sin x}{\cos^2 x+\cos x-6}dx$

218. $\int \frac{1-\sqrt{x}}{1+\sqrt{x}}dx$

219. $\int \frac{dt}{(e^t-e^{-t})^2}$

220. $\int \frac{1+e^x}{1-e^x}dx$

221. $\int \frac{dx}{1+\sqrt{x+1}}$

222. $\int \frac{dx}{\sqrt{x}+\sqrt[4]{x}}$

223. $\int \frac{\cos x}{\sin x(1-\sin x)}dx$

224. $\int \frac{e^x}{\left(e^{2x}-4\right)^2}dx$

225. $\int_1^2 \frac{1}{x^2\sqrt{4-x^2}}dx$

226. $\int \frac{1}{2+e^{-x}}dx$

227. $\int \frac{1}{1+e^x}dx$

Use the given substitution to convert the integral to an integral of a rational function, then evaluate.

228. $\int \frac{1}{t-\sqrt[3]{t}}dt t=x^3$

229. $\int \frac{1}{\sqrt{x}+\sqrt[3]{x}}dx;\ x=u^6$

230. Graph the curve $y=\frac{x}{1+x}$ over the interval $[0,\ 5]$. Then, find the area of the region bounded by the curve, the $x$-axis, and the line $x=4$.

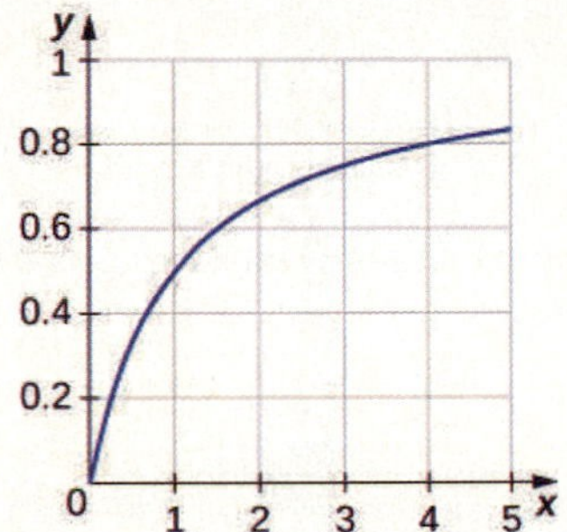


231. Find the volume of the solid generated when the region bounded by $y=1/\sqrt{x(3-x)}$, $y=0$, $x=1$, and $x=2$ is revolved about the $x$-axis.

232. The velocity of a particle moving along a line is a function of time given by $v(t)=\frac{88t^2}{t^2+1}$. Find the distance that the particle has traveled after $t=5$ sec.

Solve the initial-value problem for $x$ as a function of $t$.

233. $\left(t^2-7t+12\right)\frac{dx}{dt}=1,\ (t>4,\ x(5)=0)$

234. $(t+5)\frac{dx}{dt}=x^2+1,\ t>-5,\ x(1)=\tan 1$

235. $\left(2t^3-2t^2+t-1\right)\frac{dx}{dt}=3,\ x(2)=0$

236. Find the $x$-coordinate of the centroid of the area bounded by $y\left(x^2-9\right)=1$, $y=0$, $x=4$, and $x=5$. (Round the answer to two decimal places.)

237. Find the volume generated by revolving the area bounded by $y=\frac{1}{x^3+7x^2+6x}x=1$, $x=7$, and $y=0$ about the $y$-axis.

238. Find the area bounded by $y=\frac{x-12}{x^2-8x-20}$, $y=0$, $x=2$, and $x=4$. (Round the answer to the nearest hundredth.)

239. Evaluate the integral $\int \frac{dx}{x^3 + 1}$.

For the following problems, use the substitutions $\tan\left(\frac{x}{2}\right) = t,$ $dx = \frac{2}{1 + t^2}dt,$ $\sin x = \frac{2t}{1 + t^2},$ and $\cos x = \frac{1 - t^2}{1 + t^2}.$

240. $\int \frac{dx}{3 - 5\sin x}$

241. Find the area under the curve $y = \frac{1}{1 + \sin x}$ between $x = 0$ and $x = \pi.$ (Assume the dimensions are in inches.)

242. Given $\tan\left(\frac{x}{2}\right) = t,$ derive the formulas $dx = \frac{2}{1 + t^2}dt,$ $\sin x = \frac{2t}{1 + t^2},$ and $\cos x = \frac{1 - t^2}{1 + t^2}.$

243. Evaluate $\int \frac{\sqrt[3]{x - 8}}{x}dx.$

# 3.5 | Other Strategies for Integration

## Learning Objectives

**3.5.1** Use a table of integrals to solve integration problems.

**3.5.2** Use a computer algebra system (CAS) to solve integration problems.

In addition to the techniques of integration we have already seen, several other tools are widely available to assist with the process of integration. Among these tools are **integration tables**, which are readily available in many books, including the appendices to this one. Also widely available are **computer algebra systems (CAS)**, which are found on calculators and in many campus computer labs, and are free online.

## Tables of Integrals

Integration tables, if used in the right manner, can be a handy way either to evaluate or check an integral quickly. Keep in mind that when using a table to check an answer, it is possible for two completely correct solutions to look very different. For example, in **Trigonometric Substitution**, we found that, by using the substitution $x = \tan\theta$, we can arrive at

$$\int \frac{dx}{\sqrt{1+x^2}} = \ln\left(x + \sqrt{x^2+1}\right) + C.$$

However, using $x = \sinh\theta$, we obtained a different solution—namely,

$$\int \frac{dx}{\sqrt{1+x^2}} = \sinh^{-1} x + C.$$

We later showed algebraically that the two solutions are equivalent. That is, we showed that $\sinh^{-1} x = \ln\left(x + \sqrt{x^2+1}\right)$. In this case, the two antiderivatives that we found were actually equal. This need not be the case. However, as long as the difference in the two antiderivatives is a constant, they are equivalent.

### Example 3.36

#### Using a Formula from a Table to Evaluate an Integral

Use the table formula

$$\int \frac{\sqrt{a^2-u^2}}{u^2} du = -\frac{\sqrt{a^2-u^2}}{u} - \sin^{-1}\frac{u}{a} + C$$

to evaluate $\int \frac{\sqrt{16-e^{2x}}}{e^x} dx.$

#### Solution

If we look at integration tables, we see that several formulas contain expressions of the form $\sqrt{a^2-u^2}$. This expression is actually similar to $\sqrt{16-e^{2x}}$, where $a = 4$ and $u = e^x$. Keep in mind that we must also have $du = e^x$. Multiplying the numerator and the denominator of the given integral by $e^x$ should help to put this integral in a useful form. Thus, we now have

$$\int \frac{\sqrt{16-e^{2x}}}{e^x} dx = \int \frac{\sqrt{16-e^{2x}}}{e^{2x}} e^x\, dx.$$

Substituting $u = e^x$ and $du = e^x$ produces $\int \frac{\sqrt{a^2 - u^2}}{u^2} du$. From the integration table (#88 in **Appendix A**),

$$\int \frac{\sqrt{a^2 - u^2}}{u^2} du = -\frac{\sqrt{a^2 - u^2}}{u} - \sin^{-1}\frac{u}{a} + C.$$

Thus,

$$\begin{aligned}
\int \frac{\sqrt{16 - e^{2x}}}{e^x} dx &= \int \frac{\sqrt{16 - e^{2x}}}{e^{2x}} e^x \, dx && \text{Substitute } u = e^x \text{ and } du = e^x \, dx. \\
&= \int \frac{\sqrt{4^2 - u^2}}{u^2} du && \text{Apply the formula using } a = 4. \\
&= -\frac{\sqrt{4^2 - u^2}}{u} - \sin^{-1}\frac{u}{4} + C && \text{Substitute } u = e^x. \\
&= -\frac{\sqrt{16 - e^{2x}}}{u} - \sin^{-1}\left(\frac{e^x}{4}\right) + C.
\end{aligned}$$

## Computer Algebra Systems

If available, a CAS is a faster alternative to a table for solving an integration problem. Many such systems are widely available and are, in general, quite easy to use.

### Example 3.37

#### Using a Computer Algebra System to Evaluate an Integral

Use a computer algebra system to evaluate $\int \frac{dx}{\sqrt{x^2 - 4}}$. Compare this result with $\ln\left|\frac{\sqrt{x^2 - 4}}{2} + \frac{x}{2}\right| + C$, a result we might have obtained if we had used trigonometric substitution.

#### Solution

Using Wolfram Alpha, we obtain

$$\int \frac{dx}{\sqrt{x^2 - 4}} = \ln\left|\sqrt{x^2 - 4} + x\right| + C.$$

Notice that

$$\ln\left|\frac{\sqrt{x^2 - 4}}{2} + \frac{x}{2}\right| + C = \ln\left|\frac{\sqrt{x^2 - 4} + x}{2}\right| + C = \ln\left|\sqrt{x^2 - 4} + x\right| - \ln 2 + C.$$

Since these two antiderivatives differ by only a constant, the solutions are equivalent. We could have also demonstrated that each of these antiderivatives is correct by differentiating them.

You can access an **integral calculator (http://www.openstaxcollege.org/l/20_intcalc)** for more examples.

## Example 3.38

### Using a CAS to Evaluate an Integral

Evaluate $\int \sin^3 x dx$ using a CAS. Compare the result to $\frac{1}{3}\cos^3 x - \cos x + C,$ the result we might have obtained using the technique for integrating odd powers of $\sin x$ discussed earlier in this chapter.

#### Solution

Using Wolfram Alpha, we obtain

$$\int \sin^3 x dx = \frac{1}{12}(\cos(3x) - 9\cos x) + C.$$

This looks quite different from $\frac{1}{3}\cos^3 x - \cos x + C.$ To see that these antiderivatives are equivalent, we can make use of a few trigonometric identities:

$$\begin{aligned}
\frac{1}{12}(\cos(3x) - 9\cos x) &= \frac{1}{12}(\cos(x + 2x) - 9\cos x) \\
&= \frac{1}{12}(\cos(x)\cos(2x) - \sin(x)\sin(2x) - 9\cos x) \\
&= \frac{1}{12}\left(\cos x\left(2\cos^2 x - 1\right) - \sin x(2\sin x\cos x) - 9\cos x\right) \\
&= \frac{1}{12}\left(2\cos x - \cos x - 2\cos x\left(1 - \cos^2 x\right) - 9\cos x\right) \\
&= \frac{1}{12}(4\cos x - 12\cos x) \\
&= \frac{1}{3}\cos x - \cos x.
\end{aligned}$$

Thus, the two antiderivatives are identical.

We may also use a CAS to compare the graphs of the two functions, as shown in the following figure.

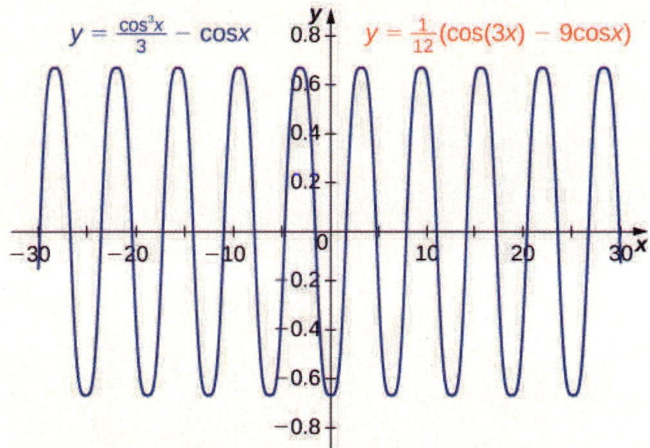


**Figure 3.12** The graphs of $y = \frac{1}{3}\cos^3 x - \cos x$ and $y = \frac{1}{12}(\cos(3x) - 9\cos x)$ are identical.

**3.21** Use a CAS to evaluate $\int \frac{dx}{\sqrt{x^2 + 4}}.$

# 3.5 EXERCISES

Use a table of integrals to evaluate the following integrals.

244. $\int_0^4 \frac{x}{\sqrt{1+2x}}dx$

245. $\int \frac{x+3}{x^2+2x+2}dx$

246. $\int x^3\sqrt{1+2x^2}dx$

247. $\int \frac{1}{\sqrt{x^2+6x}}dx$

248. $\int \frac{x}{x+1}dx$

249. $\int x\cdot 2^{x^2}dx$

250. $\int \frac{1}{4x^2+25}dx$

251. $\int \frac{dy}{\sqrt{4-y^2}}$

252. $\int \sin^3(2x)\cos(2x)dx$

253. $\int \csc(2w)\cot(2w)dw$

254. $\int 2^y dy$

255. $\int_0^1 \frac{3x\,dx}{\sqrt{x^2+8}}$

256. $\int_{-1/4}^{1/4} \sec^2(\pi x)\tan(\pi x)dx$

257. $\int_0^{\pi/2} \tan^2\left(\frac{x}{2}\right)dx$

258. $\int \cos^3 x\,dx$

259. $\int \tan^5(3x)dx$

260. $\int \sin^2 y\cos^3 y\,dy$

Use a CAS to evaluate the following integrals. Tables can also be used to verify the answers.

261. **[T]** $\int \frac{dw}{1+\sec\left(\frac{w}{2}\right)}$

262. **[T]** $\int \frac{dw}{1-\cos(7w)}$

263. **[T]** $\int_0^t \frac{dt}{4\cos t+3\sin t}$

264. **[T]** $\int \frac{\sqrt{x^2-9}}{3x}dx$

265. **[T]** $\int \frac{dx}{x^{1/2}+x^{1/3}}$

266. **[T]** $\int \frac{dx}{x\sqrt{x-1}}$

267. **[T]** $\int x^3\sin x\,dx$

268. **[T]** $\int x\sqrt{x^4-9}\,dx$

269. **[T]** $\int \frac{x}{1+e^{-x^2}}dx$

270. **[T]** $\int \frac{\sqrt{3-5x}}{2x}dx$

271. **[T]** $\int \frac{dx}{x\sqrt{x-1}}$

272. **[T]** $\int e^x\cos^{-1}(e^x)dx$

Use a calculator or CAS to evaluate the following integrals.

273. **[T]** $\int_0^{\pi/4} \cos(2x)dx$

274. **[T]** $\int_0^1 x\cdot e^{-x^2}dx$

275. **[T]** $\int_0^8 \frac{2x}{\sqrt{x^2+36}}dx$

276. **[T]** $\int_0^{2/\sqrt{3}} \frac{1}{4+9x^2}dx$

277. **[T]** $\int \frac{dx}{x^2 + 4x + 13}$

278. **[T]** $\int \frac{dx}{1 + \sin x}$

Use tables to evaluate the integrals. You may need to complete the square or change variables to put the integral into a form given in the table.

279. $\int \frac{dx}{x^2 + 2x + 10}$

280. $\int \frac{dx}{\sqrt{x^2 - 6x}}$

281. $\int \frac{e^x}{\sqrt{e^{2x} - 4}} dx$

282. $\int \frac{\cos x}{\sin^2 x + 2\sin x} dx$

283. $\int \frac{\arctan\left(x^3\right)}{x^4} dx$

284. $\int \frac{\ln|x| \arcsin(\ln|x|)}{x} dx$

Use tables to perform the integration.

285. $\int \frac{dx}{\sqrt{x^2 + 16}}$

286. $\int \frac{3x}{2x + 7} dx$

287. $\int \frac{dx}{1 - \cos(4x)}$

288. $\int \frac{dx}{\sqrt{4x + 1}}$

289. Find the area bounded by $y\left(4 + 25x^2\right) = 5,\ x = 0,\ y = 0,$ and $x = 4.$ Use a table of integrals or a CAS.

290. The region bounded between the curve $y = \frac{1}{\sqrt{1 + \cos x}},\ 0.3 \le x \le 1.1,$ and the $x$-axis is revolved about the $x$-axis to generate a solid. Use a table of integrals to find the volume of the solid generated. (Round the answer to two decimal places.)

291. Use substitution and a table of integrals to find the area of the surface generated by revolving the curve $y = e^x,\ 0 \le x \le 3,$ about the $x$-axis. (Round the answer to two decimal places.)

292. **[T]** Use an integral table and a calculator to find the area of the surface generated by revolving the curve $y = \frac{x^2}{2},\ 0 \le x \le 1,$ about the $x$-axis. (Round the answer to two decimal places.)

293. **[T]** Use a CAS or tables to find the area of the surface generated by revolving the curve $y = \cos x,\ 0 \le x \le \frac{\pi}{2},$ about the $x$-axis. (Round the answer to two decimal places.)

294. Find the length of the curve $y = \frac{x^2}{4}$ over $[0, 8]$.

295. Find the length of the curve $y = e^x$ over $[0, \ln(2)]$.

296. Find the area of the surface formed by revolving the graph of $y = 2\sqrt{x}$ over the interval $[0, 9]$ about the $x$-axis.

297. Find the average value of the function $f(x) = \frac{1}{x^2 + 1}$ over the interval $[-3, 3]$.

298. Approximate the arc length of the curve $y = \tan(\pi x)$ over the interval $\left[0, \frac{1}{4}\right]$. (Round the answer to three decimal places.)

# 3.6 | Numerical Integration

## Learning Objectives

**3.6.1** Approximate the value of a definite integral by using the midpoint and trapezoidal rules.
**3.6.2** Determine the absolute and relative error in using a numerical integration technique.
**3.6.3** Estimate the absolute and relative error using an error-bound formula.
**3.6.4** Recognize when the midpoint and trapezoidal rules over- or underestimate the true value of an integral.
**3.6.5** Use Simpson's rule to approximate the value of a definite integral to a given accuracy.

The antiderivatives of many functions either cannot be expressed or cannot be expressed easily in closed form (that is, in terms of known functions). Consequently, rather than evaluate definite integrals of these functions directly, we resort to various techniques of **numerical integration** to approximate their values. In this section we explore several of these techniques. In addition, we examine the process of estimating the error in using these techniques.

## The Midpoint Rule

Earlier in this text we defined the definite integral of a function over an interval as the limit of Riemann sums. In general, any Riemann sum of a function $f(x)$ over an interval $[a, b]$ may be viewed as an estimate of $\int_a^b f(x)dx$. Recall that a Riemann sum of a function $f(x)$ over an interval $[a, b]$ is obtained by selecting a partition

$$P = \{x_0, x_1, x_2, \ldots, x_n\}, \text{ where } a = x_0 < x_1 < x_2 < \cdots < x_n = b$$

and a set

$$S = \{x_1^*, x_2^*, \ldots, x_n^*\}, \text{ where } x_{i-1} \le x_i^* \le x_i \text{ for all } i.$$

The Riemann sum corresponding to the partition $P$ and the set $S$ is given by $\sum_{i=1}^{n} f(x_i^*)\Delta x_i,$ where $\Delta x_i = x_i - x_{i-1},$ the length of the $i$th subinterval.

The **midpoint rule** for estimating a definite integral uses a Riemann sum with subintervals of equal width and the midpoints, $m_i,$ of each subinterval in place of $x_i^*$. Formally, we state a theorem regarding the convergence of the midpoint rule as follows.

### Theorem 3.3: The Midpoint Rule

Assume that $f(x)$ is continuous on $[a, b]$. Let $n$ be a positive integer and $\Delta x = \frac{b-a}{n}$. If $[a, b]$ is divided into $n$ subintervals, each of length $\Delta x,$ and $m_i$ is the midpoint of the $i$th subinterval, set

$$M_n = \sum_{i=1}^{n} f(m_i)\Delta x. \tag{3.10}$$

Then $\lim_{n \to \infty} M_n = \int_a^b f(x)dx.$

As we can see in **Figure 3.13**, if $f(x) \ge 0$ over $[a, b],$ then $\sum_{i=1}^{n} f(m_i)\Delta x$ corresponds to the sum of the areas of rectangles approximating the area between the graph of $f(x)$ and the $x$-axis over $[a, b]$. The graph shows the rectangles corresponding to $M_4$ for a nonnegative function over a closed interval $[a, b]$.

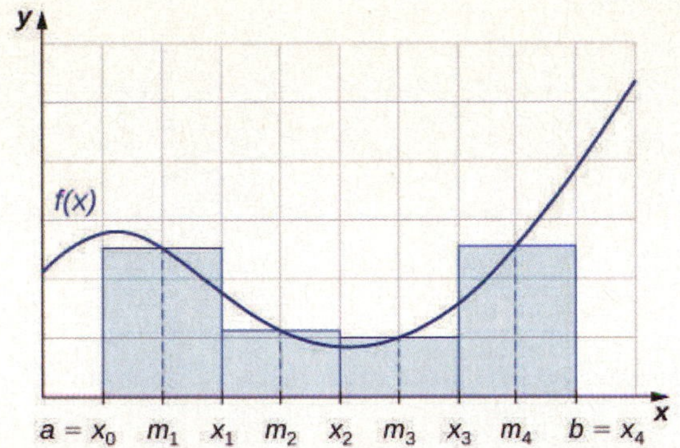


**Figure 3.13** The midpoint rule approximates the area between the graph of $f(x)$ and the $x$-axis by summing the areas of rectangles with midpoints that are points on $f(x)$.

## Example 3.39

### Using the Midpoint Rule with $M_4$

Use the midpoint rule to estimate $\int_0^1 x^2\,dx$ using four subintervals. Compare the result with the actual value of this integral.

#### Solution

Each subinterval has length $\Delta x = \frac{1-0}{4} = \frac{1}{4}$. Therefore, the subintervals consist of

$$\left[0, \frac{1}{4}\right], \left[\frac{1}{4}, \frac{1}{2}\right], \left[\frac{1}{2}, \frac{3}{4}\right], \text{ and} \left[\frac{3}{4}, 1\right].$$

The midpoints of these subintervals are $\left\{\frac{1}{8}, \frac{3}{8}, \frac{5}{8}, \frac{7}{8}\right\}$. Thus,

$$M_4 = \frac{1}{4}f\left(\frac{1}{8}\right) + \frac{1}{4}f\left(\frac{3}{8}\right) + \frac{1}{4}f\left(\frac{5}{8}\right) + \frac{1}{4}f\left(\frac{7}{8}\right) = \frac{1}{4} \cdot \frac{1}{64} + \frac{1}{4} \cdot \frac{9}{64} + \frac{1}{4} \cdot \frac{25}{64} + \frac{1}{4} \cdot \frac{21}{64} = \frac{21}{64}.$$

Since

$$\int_0^1 x^2\,dx = \frac{1}{3} \text{ and } \left|\frac{1}{3} - \frac{21}{64}\right| = \frac{1}{192} \approx 0.0052,$$

we see that the midpoint rule produces an estimate that is somewhat close to the actual value of the definite integral.

## Example 3.40

### Using the Midpoint Rule with $M_6$

Use $M_6$ to estimate the length of the curve $y = \frac{1}{2}x^2$ on $[1, 4]$.

### Solution

The length of $y = \frac{1}{2}x^2$ on $[1, 4]$ is

$$\int_1^4 \sqrt{1 + \left(\frac{dy}{dx}\right)^2}\,dx.$$

Since $\frac{dy}{dx} = x$, this integral becomes $\int_1^4 \sqrt{1 + x^2}\,dx.$

If $[1, 4]$ is divided into six subintervals, then each subinterval has length $\Delta x = \frac{4-1}{6} = \frac{1}{2}$ and the midpoints of the subintervals are $\left\{\frac{5}{4}, \frac{7}{4}, \frac{9}{4}, \frac{11}{4}, \frac{13}{4}, \frac{15}{4}\right\}$. If we set $f(x) = \sqrt{1 + x^2}$,

$$\begin{aligned} M_6 &= \tfrac{1}{2}f\left(\tfrac{5}{4}\right) + \tfrac{1}{2}f\left(\tfrac{7}{4}\right) + \tfrac{1}{2}f\left(\tfrac{9}{4}\right) + \tfrac{1}{2}f\left(\tfrac{11}{4}\right) + \tfrac{1}{2}f\left(\tfrac{13}{4}\right) + \tfrac{1}{2}f\left(\tfrac{15}{4}\right) \\ &\approx \tfrac{1}{2}(1.6008 + 2.0156 + 2.4622 + 2.9262 + 3.4004 + 3.8810) = 8.1431. \end{aligned}$$

**3.22** Use the midpoint rule with $n = 2$ to estimate $\int_1^2 \frac{1}{x}\,dx.$

## The Trapezoidal Rule

We can also approximate the value of a definite integral by using trapezoids rather than rectangles. In **Figure 3.14**, the area beneath the curve is approximated by trapezoids rather than by rectangles.

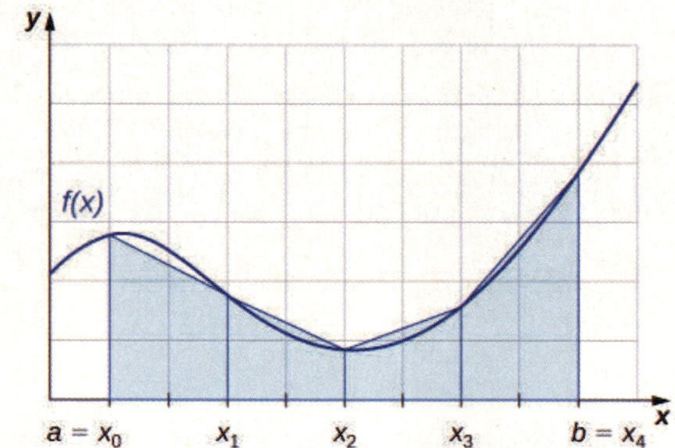


**Figure 3.14** Trapezoids may be used to approximate the area under a curve, hence approximating the definite integral.

The **trapezoidal rule** for estimating definite integrals uses trapezoids rather than rectangles to approximate the area under a curve. To gain insight into the final form of the rule, consider the trapezoids shown in **Figure 3.14**. We assume that the length of each subinterval is given by $\Delta x$. First, recall that the area of a trapezoid with a height of $h$ and bases of length $b_1$ and $b_2$ is given by $\text{Area} = \frac{1}{2}h(b_1 + b_2)$. We see that the first trapezoid has a height $\Delta x$ and parallel bases of length $f(x_0)$ and $f(x_1)$. Thus, the area of the first trapezoid in **Figure 3.14** is

$$\frac{1}{2}\Delta x\big(f(x_0) + f(x_1)\big).$$

The areas of the remaining three trapezoids are

$$\frac{1}{2}\Delta x(f(x_1) + f(x_2)),\ \frac{1}{2}\Delta x(f(x_2) + f(x_3)),\text{ and }\frac{1}{2}\Delta x(f(x_3) + f(x_4)).$$

Consequently,

$$\int_a^b f(x)dx \approx \frac{1}{2}\Delta x(f(x_0) + f(x_1)) + \frac{1}{2}\Delta x(f(x_1) + f(x_2)) + \frac{1}{2}\Delta x(f(x_2) + f(x_3)) + \frac{1}{2}\Delta x(f(x_3) + f(x_4)).$$

After taking out a common factor of $\frac{1}{2}\Delta x$ and combining like terms, we have

$$\int_a^b f(x)dx \approx \frac{1}{2}\Delta x\big(f(x_0) + 2f(x_1) + 2f(x_2) + 2f(x_3) + f(x_4)\big).$$

Generalizing, we formally state the following rule.

## Theorem 3.4: The Trapezoidal Rule

Assume that $f(x)$ is continuous over $[a, b]$. Let $n$ be a positive integer and $\Delta x = \frac{b-a}{n}$. Let $[a, b]$ be divided into $n$ subintervals, each of length $\Delta x$, with endpoints at $P = \{x_0, x_1, x_2 \ldots, x_n\}$. Set

$$T_n = \frac{1}{2}\Delta x\big(f(x_0) + 2f(x_1) + 2f(x_2) + \cdots + 2f(x_{n-1}) + f(x_n)\big). \tag{3.11}$$

Then, $\lim\limits_{n \to +\infty} T_n = \int_a^b f(x)dx.$

Before continuing, let's make a few observations about the trapezoidal rule. First of all, it is useful to note that

$$T_n = \frac{1}{2}(L_n + R_n)\text{ where } L_n = \sum_{i=1}^{n} f(x_{i-1})\Delta x \text{ and } R_n = \sum_{i=1}^{n} f(x_i)\Delta x.$$

That is, $L_n$ and $R_n$ approximate the integral using the left-hand and right-hand endpoints of each subinterval, respectively. In addition, a careful examination of **Figure 3.15** leads us to make the following observations about using the trapezoidal rules and midpoint rules to estimate the definite integral of a nonnegative function. The trapezoidal rule tends to overestimate the value of a definite integral systematically over intervals where the function is concave up and to underestimate the value of a definite integral systematically over intervals where the function is concave down. On the other hand, the midpoint rule tends to average out these errors somewhat by partially overestimating and partially underestimating the value of the definite integral over these same types of intervals. This leads us to hypothesize that, in general, the midpoint rule tends to be more accurate than the trapezoidal rule.

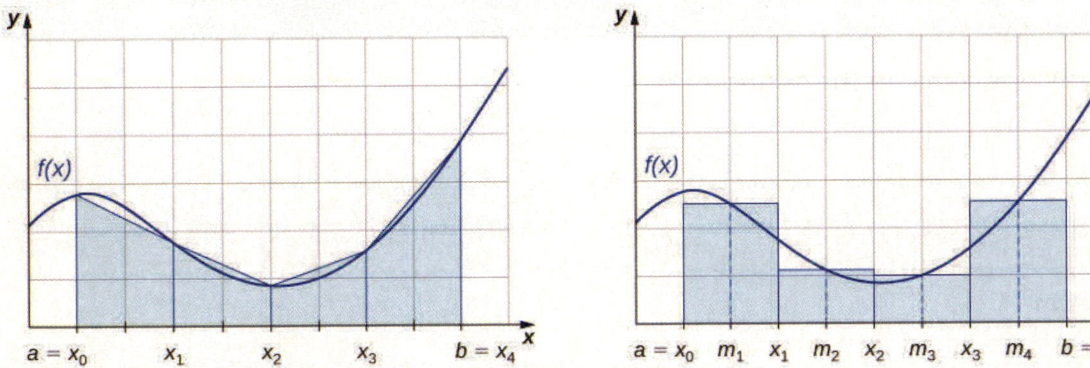


**Figure 3.15** The trapezoidal rule tends to be less accurate than the midpoint rule.

## Example 3.41

### Using the Trapezoidal Rule

Use the trapezoidal rule to estimate $\int_0^1 x^2\,dx$ using four subintervals.

#### Solution

The endpoints of the subintervals consist of elements of the set $P = \left\{0, \frac{1}{4}, \frac{1}{2}, \frac{3}{4}, 1\right\}$ and $\Delta x = \frac{1-0}{4} = \frac{1}{4}$. Thus,

$$\begin{aligned}\int_0^1 x^2\,dx &\approx \frac{1}{2}\cdot\frac{1}{4}\left(f(0) + 2f\left(\frac{1}{4}\right) + 2f\left(\frac{1}{2}\right) + 2f\left(\frac{3}{4}\right) + f(1)\right)\\ &= \frac{1}{8}\left(0 + 2\cdot\frac{1}{16} + 2\cdot\frac{1}{4} + 2\cdot\frac{9}{16} + 1\right)\\ &= \frac{11}{32}.\end{aligned}$$

**3.23** Use the trapezoidal rule with $n = 2$ to estimate $\int_1^2 \frac{1}{x}dx$.

## Absolute and Relative Error

An important aspect of using these numerical approximation rules consists of calculating the error in using them for estimating the value of a definite integral. We first need to define **absolute error** and **relative error**.

### Definition

If $B$ is our estimate of some quantity having an actual value of $A$, then the absolute error is given by $|A - B|$. The relative error is the error as a percentage of the absolute value and is given by $\left|\frac{A-B}{A}\right| = \left|\frac{A-B}{A}\right| \cdot 100\%$.

## Example 3.42

### Calculating Error in the Midpoint Rule

Calculate the absolute and relative error in the estimate of $\int_0^1 x^2\,dx$ using the midpoint rule, found in **Example 3.39**.

#### Solution

The calculated value is $\int_0^1 x^2\,dx = \frac{1}{3}$ and our estimate from the example is $M_4 = \frac{21}{64}$. Thus, the absolute error is given by $\left|\left(\frac{1}{3}\right) - \left(\frac{21}{64}\right)\right| = \frac{1}{192} \approx 0.0052$. The relative error is

$$\frac{1/192}{1/3} = \frac{1}{64} \approx 0.015625 \approx 1.6\%.$$

## Example 3.43

### Calculating Error in the Trapezoidal Rule

Calculate the absolute and relative error in the estimate of $\int_0^1 x^2\,dx$ using the trapezoidal rule, found in **Example 3.41**.

### Solution

The calculated value is $\int_0^1 x^2\,dx = \frac{1}{3}$ and our estimate from the example is $T_4 = \frac{11}{32}$. Thus, the absolute error is given by $\left|\frac{1}{3} - \frac{11}{32}\right| = \frac{1}{96} \approx 0.0104$. The relative error is given by

$$\frac{1/96}{1/3} = 0.03125 \approx 3.1\%.$$

**3.24** In an earlier checkpoint, we estimated $\int_1^2 \frac{1}{x}dx$ to be $\frac{24}{35}$ using $T_2$. The actual value of this integral is $\ln 2$. Using $\frac{24}{35} \approx 0.6857$ and $\ln 2 \approx 0.6931$, calculate the absolute error and the relative error.

In the two previous examples, we were able to compare our estimate of an integral with the actual value of the integral; however, we do not typically have this luxury. In general, if we are approximating an integral, we are doing so because we cannot compute the exact value of the integral itself easily. Therefore, it is often helpful to be able to determine an upper bound for the error in an approximation of an integral. The following theorem provides error bounds for the midpoint and trapezoidal rules. The theorem is stated without proof.

### Theorem 3.5: Error Bounds for the Midpoint and Trapezoidal Rules

Let $f(x)$ be a continuous function over $[a, b]$, having a second derivative $f''(x)$ over this interval. If $M$ is the maximum value of $|f''(x)|$ over $[a, b]$, then the upper bounds for the error in using $M_n$ and $T_n$ to estimate $\int_a^b f(x)dx$ are

$$\text{Error in } M_n \le \frac{M(b-a)^3}{24n^2} \quad (3.12)$$

and

$$\text{Error in } T_n \le \frac{M(b-a)^3}{12n^2}. \quad (3.13)$$

We can use these bounds to determine the value of $n$ necessary to guarantee that the error in an estimate is less than a specified value.

## Example 3.44

### Determining the Number of Intervals to Use

What value of $n$ should be used to guarantee that an estimate of $\int_0^1 e^{x^2}\,dx$ is accurate to within 0.01 if we use the midpoint rule?

#### Solution

We begin by determining the value of $M$, the maximum value of $|f''(x)|$ over $[0,\ 1]$ for $f(x) = e^{x^2}$. Since $f'(x) = 2xe^{x^2}$, we have

$$f''(x) = 2e^{x^2} + 4x^2 e^{x^2}.$$

Thus,

$$|f''(x)| = 2e^{x^2}\left(1 + 2x^2\right) \le 2 \cdot e \cdot 3 = 6e.$$

From the error-bound **Equation 3.12**, we have

$$\text{Error in } M_n \le \frac{M(b-a)^3}{24n^2} \le \frac{6e(1-0)^3}{24n^2} = \frac{6e}{24n^2}.$$

Now we solve the following inequality for $n$:

$$\frac{6e}{24n^2} \le 0.01.$$

Thus, $n \ge \sqrt{\frac{600e}{24}} \approx 8.24$. Since $n$ must be an integer satisfying this inequality, a choice of $n = 9$ would guarantee that $\left|\int_0^1 e^{x^2}\,dx - M_n\right| < 0.01$.

#### Analysis

We might have been tempted to round $8.24$ down and choose $n = 8$, but this would be incorrect because we must have an integer greater than or equal to $8.24$. We need to keep in mind that the error estimates provide an upper bound only for the error. The actual estimate may, in fact, be a much better approximation than is indicated by the error bound.

**3.25** Use **Equation 3.13** to find an upper bound for the error in using $M_4$ to estimate $\int_0^1 x^2\,dx$.

## Simpson's Rule

With the midpoint rule, we estimated areas of regions under curves by using rectangles. In a sense, we approximated the curve with piecewise constant functions. With the trapezoidal rule, we approximated the curve by using piecewise linear functions. What if we were, instead, to approximate a curve using piecewise quadratic functions? With **Simpson's rule**, we do just this. We partition the interval into an even number of subintervals, each of equal width. Over the first pair of subintervals we approximate $\int_{x_0}^{x_2} f(x)dx$ with $\int_{x_0}^{x_2} p(x)dx$, where $p(x) = Ax^2 + Bx + C$ is the quadratic function passing through $(x_0, f(x_0))$, $(x_1, f(x_1))$, and $(x_2, f(x_2))$ (**Figure 3.16**). Over the next pair of subintervals we approximate $\int_{x_2}^{x_4} f(x)dx$ with the integral of another quadratic function passing through $(x_2, f(x_2))$, $(x_3, f(x_3))$, and $(x_4, f(x_4))$. This process is continued with each successive pair of subintervals.

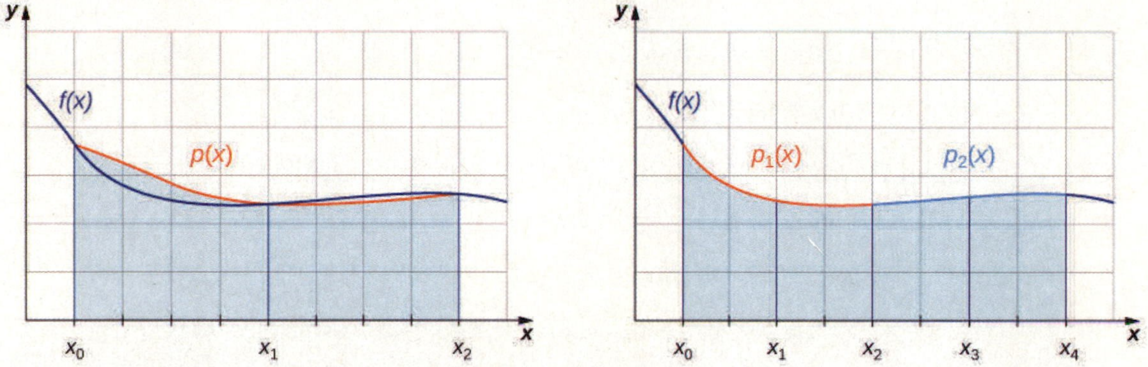


**Figure 3.16** With Simpson's rule, we approximate a definite integral by integrating a piecewise quadratic function.

To understand the formula that we obtain for Simpson's rule, we begin by deriving a formula for this approximation over the first two subintervals. As we go through the derivation, we need to keep in mind the following relationships:

$$f(x_0) = p(x_0) = Ax_0{}^2 + Bx_0 + C$$
$$f(x_1) = p(x_1) = Ax_1{}^2 + Bx_1 + C$$
$$f(x_2) = p(x_2) = Ax_2{}^2 + Bx_2 + C$$

$x_2 - x_0 = 2\Delta x$, where $\Delta x$ is the length of a subinterval.

$$x_2 + x_0 = 2x_1, \text{ since } x_1 = \frac{(x_2 + x_0)}{2}.$$

Thus,

$$\begin{aligned}
\int_{x_0}^{x_2} f(x)dx &\approx \int_{x_0}^{x_2} p(x)dx \\
&= \int_{x_0}^{x_2} (Ax^2 + Bx + C)dx \\
&= \frac{A}{3}x^3 + \frac{B}{2}x^2 + Cx\Big|_{x_0}^{x_2} && \text{Find the antiderivative.} \\
&= \frac{A}{3}\left(x_2{}^3 - x_0{}^3\right) + \frac{B}{2}\left(x_2{}^2 - x_0{}^2\right) + C(x_2 - x_0) && \text{Evaluate the antiderivative.} \\
&= \frac{A}{3}(x_2 - x_0)\left(x_2{}^2 + x_2x_0 + x_0{}^2\right) \\
&\quad + \frac{B}{2}(x_2 - x_0)(x_2 + x_0) + C(x_2 - x_0) \\
&= \frac{x_2 - x_0}{6}\left(2A\left(x_2{}^2 + x_2x_0 + x_0{}^2\right) + 3B(x_2 + x_0) + 6C\right) && \text{Factor out } \frac{x_2 - x_0}{6}. \\
&= \frac{\Delta x}{3}\left(\left(Ax_2{}^2 + Bx_2 + C\right) + (Ax_0{}^2 + Bx_0 + C\right) \\
&\quad + A\left(x_2{}^2 + 2x_2x_0 + x_0{}^2\right) + 2B(x_2 + x_0) + 4C) \\
&= \frac{\Delta x}{3}\left(f(x_2) + f(x_0) + A(x_2 + x_0)^2 + 2B(x_2 + x_0) + 4C\right) && \text{Rearrange the terms.} \\
& && \text{Factor and substitute.} \\
& && f(x_2) = Ax_0{}^2 + Bx_0 + C \text{ and} \\
& && f(x_0) = Ax_0{}^2 + Bx_0 + C. \\
&= \frac{\Delta x}{3}\left(f(x_2) + f(x_0) + A(2x_1)^2 + 2B(2x_1) + 4C\right) && \text{Substitute } x_2 + x_0 = 2x_1. \\
&= \frac{\Delta x}{3}(f(x_2) + 4f(x_1) + f(x_0)). && \text{Expand and substitute} \\
& && f(x_1) = Ax_1{}^2 + Bx_1 + .
\end{aligned}$$

If we approximate $\int_{x_2}^{x_4} f(x)dx$ using the same method, we see that we have

$$\int_{x_0}^{x_4} f(x)dx \approx \frac{\Delta x}{3}(f(x_4) + 4f(x_3) + f(x_2)).$$

Combining these two approximations, we get

$$\int_{x_0}^{x_4} f(x)dx = \frac{\Delta x}{3}(f(x_0) + 4f(x_1) + 2f(x_2) + 4f(x_3) + f(x_4)).$$

The pattern continues as we add pairs of subintervals to our approximation. The general rule may be stated as follows.

### Theorem 3.6: Simpson's Rule

Assume that $f(x)$ is continuous over $[a, b]$. Let $n$ be a positive even integer and $\Delta x = \frac{b - a}{n}$. Let $[a, b]$ be divided into $n$ subintervals, each of length $\Delta x$, with endpoints at $P = \{x_0, x_1, x_2, \ldots, x_n\}$. Set

$$S_n = \frac{\Delta x}{3}(f(x_0) + 4f(x_1) + 2f(x_2) + 4f(x_3) + 2f(x_4) + \cdots + 2f(x_{n-2}) + 4f(x_{n-1}) + f(x_n)). \tag{3.14}$$

Then,

$$\lim_{n \to +\infty} S_n = \int_a^b f(x)dx.$$

Just as the trapezoidal rule is the average of the left-hand and right-hand rules for estimating definite integrals, Simpson's rule may be obtained from the midpoint and trapezoidal rules by using a weighted average. It can be shown that $S_{2n} = \left(\frac{2}{3}\right)M_n + \left(\frac{1}{3}\right)T_n.$

It is also possible to put a bound on the error when using Simpson's rule to approximate a definite integral. The bound in the error is given by the following rule:

### Rule: Error Bound for Simpson's Rule

Let $f(x)$ be a continuous function over $[a, b]$ having a fourth derivative, $f^{(4)}(x),$ over this interval. If $M$ is the maximum value of $\left|f^{(4)}(x)\right|$ over $[a, b],$ then the upper bound for the error in using $S_n$ to estimate $\int_a^b f(x)dx$ is given by

$$\text{Error in } S_n \le \frac{M(b-a)^5}{180n^4}. \quad (3.15)$$

## Example 3.45

### Applying Simpson's Rule 1

Use $S_2$ to approximate $\int_0^1 x^3\,dx.$ Estimate a bound for the error in $S_2.$

#### Solution

Since $[0, 1]$ is divided into two intervals, each subinterval has length $\Delta x = \frac{1-0}{2} = \frac{1}{2}.$ The endpoints of these subintervals are $\left\{0, \frac{1}{2}, 1\right\}.$ If we set $f(x) = x^3,$ then

$S_4 = \frac{1}{3} \cdot \frac{1}{2}\left(f(0) + 4f\left(\frac{1}{2}\right) + f(1)\right) = \frac{1}{6}\left(0 + 4 \cdot \frac{1}{8} + 1\right) = \frac{1}{4}.$ Since $f^{(4)}(x) = 0$ and consequently $M = 0,$ we see that

$$\text{Error in } S_2 \le \frac{0(1)^5}{180 \cdot 2^4} = 0.$$

This bound indicates that the value obtained through Simpson's rule is exact. A quick check will verify that, in fact, $\int_0^1 x^3\,dx = \frac{1}{4}.$

## Example 3.46

### Applying Simpson's Rule 2

Use $S_6$ to estimate the length of the curve $y = \frac{1}{2}x^2$ over $[1, 4].$

#### Solution

The length of $y = \frac{1}{2}x^2$ over $[1, 4]$ is $\int_1^4 \sqrt{1 + x^2}\,dx.$ If we divide $[1, 4]$ into six subintervals, then each subinterval has length $\Delta x = \frac{4 - 1}{6} = \frac{1}{2},$ and the endpoints of the subintervals are $\left\{1, \frac{3}{2}, 2, \frac{5}{2}, 3, \frac{7}{2}, 4\right\}.$ Setting $f(x) = \sqrt{1 + x^2},$

$$S_6 = \frac{1}{3} \cdot \frac{1}{2}\left(f(1) + 4f\left(\frac{3}{2}\right) + 2f(2) + 4f\left(\frac{5}{2}\right) + 2f(3) + 4f\left(\frac{7}{2}\right) + f(4)\right).$$

After substituting, we have

$$\begin{aligned} S_6 &= \frac{1}{6}(1.4142 + 4 \cdot 1.80278 + 2 \cdot 2.23607 + 4 \cdot 2.69258 + 2 \cdot 3.16228 + 4 \cdot 3.64005 + 4.12311) \\ &\approx 8.14594. \end{aligned}$$

**3.26** Use $S_2$ to estimate $\int_1^2 \frac{1}{x}dx.$

# 3.6 EXERCISES

Approximate the following integrals using either the midpoint rule, trapezoidal rule, or Simpson's rule as indicated. (Round answers to three decimal places.)

299. $\int_1^2 \frac{dx}{x}$; trapezoidal rule; $n = 5$

300. $\int_0^3 \sqrt{4 + x^3}\,dx$; trapezoidal rule; $n = 6$

301. $\int_0^3 \sqrt{4 + x^3}\,dx$; Simpson's rule; $n = 3$

302. $\int_0^{12} x^2\,dx$; midpoint rule; $n = 6$

303. $\int_0^1 \sin^2(\pi x)dx$; midpoint rule; $n = 3$

304. Use the midpoint rule with eight subdivisions to estimate $\int_2^4 x^2\,dx$.

305. Use the trapezoidal rule with four subdivisions to estimate $\int_2^4 x^2\,dx$.

306. Find the exact value of $\int_2^4 x^2\,dx$. Find the error of approximation between the exact value and the value calculated using the trapezoidal rule with four subdivisions. Draw a graph to illustrate.

Approximate the integral to three decimal places using the indicated rule.

307. $\int_0^1 \sin^2(\pi x)dx$; trapezoidal rule; $n = 6$

308. $\int_0^3 \frac{1}{1 + x^3}dx$; trapezoidal rule; $n = 6$

309. $\int_0^3 \frac{1}{1 + x^3}dx$; Simpson's rule; $n = 3$

310. $\int_0^{0.8} e^{-x^2}\,dx$; trapezoidal rule; $n = 4$

311. $\int_0^{0.8} e^{-x^2}\,dx$; Simpson's rule; $n = 4$

312. $\int_0^{0.4} \sin(x^2)dx$; trapezoidal rule; $n = 4$

313. $\int_0^{0.4} \sin(x^2)dx$; Simpson's rule; $n = 4$

314. $\int_{0.1}^{0.5} \frac{\cos x}{x}dx$; trapezoidal rule; $n = 4$

315. $\int_{0.1}^{0.5} \frac{\cos x}{x}dx$; Simpson's rule; $n = 4$

316. Evaluate $\int_0^1 \frac{dx}{1 + x^2}$ exactly and show that the result is $\pi/4$. Then, find the approximate value of the integral using the trapezoidal rule with $n = 4$ subdivisions. Use the result to approximate the value of $\pi$.

317. Approximate $\int_2^4 \frac{1}{\ln x}dx$ using the midpoint rule with four subdivisions to four decimal places.

318. Approximate $\int_2^4 \frac{1}{\ln x}dx$ using the trapezoidal rule with eight subdivisions to four decimal places.

319. Use the trapezoidal rule with four subdivisions to estimate $\int_0^{0.8} x^3\,dx$ to four decimal places.

320. Use the trapezoidal rule with four subdivisions to estimate $\int_0^{0.8} x^3\,dx$. Compare this value with the exact value and find the error estimate.

321. Using Simpson's rule with four subdivisions, find $\int_0^{\pi/2} \cos(x)dx$.

322. Show that the exact value of $\int_0^1 xe^{-x}\,dx = 1 - \frac{2}{e}$. Find the absolute error if you approximate the integral using the midpoint rule with 16 subdivisions.

323. Given $\int_0^1 xe^{-x}\,dx = 1 - \frac{2}{e}$, use the trapezoidal rule with 16 subdivisions to approximate the integral and find the absolute error.

324. Find an upper bound for the error in estimating $\int_0^3 (5x+4)dx$ using the trapezoidal rule with six steps.

325. Find an upper bound for the error in estimating $\int_4^5 \frac{1}{(x-1)^2}dx$ using the trapezoidal rule with seven subdivisions.

326. Find an upper bound for the error in estimating $\int_0^3 (6x^2-1)dx$ using Simpson's rule with $n=10$ steps.

327. Find an upper bound for the error in estimating $\int_2^5 \frac{1}{x-1}dx$ using Simpson's rule with $n=10$ steps.

328. Find an upper bound for the error in estimating $\int_0^{\pi} 2x\cos(x)dx$ using Simpson's rule with four steps.

329. Estimate the minimum number of subintervals needed to approximate the integral $\int_1^4 \left(5x^2+8\right)dx$ with an error magnitude of less than 0.0001 using the trapezoidal rule.

330. Determine a value of $n$ such that the trapezoidal rule will approximate $\int_0^1 \sqrt{1+x^2}dx$ with an error of no more than 0.01.

331. Estimate the minimum number of subintervals needed to approximate the integral $\int_2^3 \left(2x^3+4x\right)dx$ with an error of magnitude less than 0.0001 using the trapezoidal rule.

332. Estimate the minimum number of subintervals needed to approximate the integral $\int_3^4 \frac{1}{(x-1)^2}dx$ with an error magnitude of less than 0.0001 using the trapezoidal rule.

333. Use Simpson's rule with four subdivisions to approximate the area under the probability density function $y=\frac{1}{\sqrt{2\pi}}e^{-x^2/2}$ from $x=0$ to $x=0.4$.

334. Use Simpson's rule with $n=14$ to approximate (to three decimal places) the area of the region bounded by the graphs of $y=0$, $x=0$, and $x=\pi/2$.

335. The length of one arch of the curve $y=3\sin(2x)$ is given by $L=\int_0^{\pi/2}\sqrt{1+36\cos^2(2x)}\,dx$. Estimate $L$ using the trapezoidal rule with $n=6$.

336. The length of the ellipse $x=a\cos(t)$, $y=b\sin(t)$, $0\le t\le 2\pi$ is given by $L=4a\int_0^{\pi/2}\sqrt{1-e^2\cos^2(t)}\,dt$, where $e$ is the eccentricity of the ellipse. Use Simpson's rule with $n=6$ subdivisions to estimate the length of the ellipse when $a=2$ and $e=1/3$.

337. Estimate the area of the surface generated by revolving the curve $y=\cos(2x)$, $0\le x\le\frac{\pi}{4}$ about the $x$-axis. Use the trapezoidal rule with six subdivisions.

338. Estimate the area of the surface generated by revolving the curve $y=2x^2$, $0\le x\le 3$ about the $x$-axis. Use Simpson's rule with $n=6$.

339. The growth rate of a certain tree (in feet) is given by $y=\frac{2}{t+1}+e^{-t^2/2}$, where $t$ is time in years. Estimate the growth of the tree through the end of the second year by using Simpson's rule, using two subintervals. (Round the answer to the nearest hundredth.)

340. **[T]** Use a calculator to approximate $\int_0^1 \sin(\pi x)dx$ using the midpoint rule with 25 subdivisions. Compute the relative error of approximation.

341. **[T]** Given $\int_1^5 \left(3x^2-2x\right)dx=100$, approximate the value of this integral using the midpoint rule with 16 subdivisions and determine the absolute error.

342. Given that we know the Fundamental Theorem of Calculus, why would we want to develop numerical methods for definite integrals?

343. The table represents the coordinates $(x, y)$ that give the boundary of a lot. The units of measurement are meters. Use the trapezoidal rule to estimate the number of square meters of land that is in this lot.

| x | y | x | y |
|---|---|---|---|
| 0 | 125 | 600 | 95 |
| 100 | 125 | 700 | 88 |
| 200 | 120 | 800 | 75 |
| 300 | 112 | 900 | 35 |
| 400 | 90 | 1000 | 0 |
| 500 | 90 | | |

344. Choose the correct answer. When Simpson's rule is used to approximate the definite integral, it is necessary that the number of partitions be____

a. an even number
b. odd number
c. either an even or an odd number
d. a multiple of 4

345. The "Simpson" sum is based on the area under a ____.

346. The error formula for Simpson's rule depends on___.

a. $f(x)$
b. $f'(x)$
c. $f^{(4)}(x)$
d. the number of steps

# 3.7 | Improper Integrals

## Learning Objectives

**3.7.1** Evaluate an integral over an infinite interval.
**3.7.2** Evaluate an integral over a closed interval with an infinite discontinuity within the interval.
**3.7.3** Use the comparison theorem to determine whether a definite integral is convergent.

Is the area between the graph of $f(x) = \frac{1}{x}$ and the $x$-axis over the interval $[1, +\infty)$ finite or infinite? If this same region is revolved about the $x$-axis, is the volume finite or infinite? Surprisingly, the area of the region described is infinite, but the volume of the solid obtained by revolving this region about the $x$-axis is finite.

In this section, we define integrals over an infinite interval as well as integrals of functions containing a discontinuity on the interval. Integrals of these types are called improper integrals. We examine several techniques for evaluating improper integrals, all of which involve taking limits.

## Integrating over an Infinite Interval

How should we go about defining an integral of the type $\int_a^{+\infty} f(x)dx$? We can integrate $\int_a^t f(x)dx$ for any value of $t$, so it is reasonable to look at the behavior of this integral as we substitute larger values of $t$. **Figure 3.17** shows that $\int_a^t f(x)dx$ may be interpreted as area for various values of $t$. In other words, we may define an improper integral as a limit, taken as one of the limits of integration increases or decreases without bound.

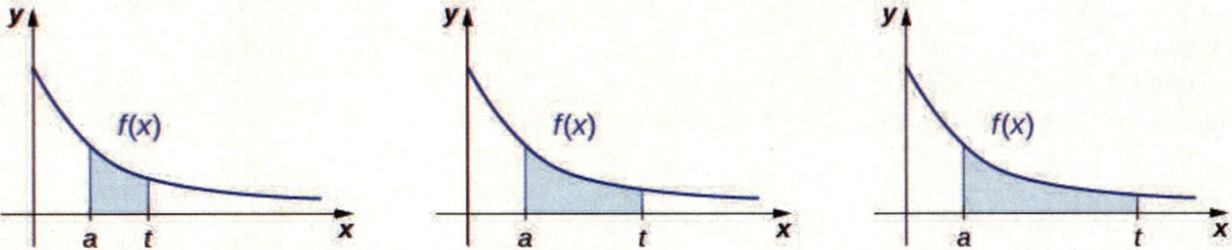


**Figure 3.17** To integrate a function over an infinite interval, we consider the limit of the integral as the upper limit increases without bound.

### Definition

1. Let $f(x)$ be continuous over an interval of the form $[a, +\infty)$. Then

$$\int_a^{+\infty} f(x)dx = \lim_{t \to +\infty} \int_a^t f(x)dx, \quad (3.16)$$

provided this limit exists.

2. Let $f(x)$ be continuous over an interval of the form $(-\infty, b]$. Then

$$\int_{-\infty}^{b} f(x)dx = \lim_{t \to -\infty} \int_t^b f(x)dx, \quad (3.17)$$

provided this limit exists.
In each case, if the limit exists, then the **improper integral** is said to converge. If the limit does not exist, then the improper integral is said to diverge.

3. Let $f(x)$ be continuous over $(-\infty, +\infty)$. Then

$$\int_{-\infty}^{+\infty} f(x)dx = \int_{-\infty}^{0} f(x)dx + \int_{0}^{+\infty} f(x)dx, \tag{3.18}$$

provided that $\int_{-\infty}^{0} f(x)dx$ and $\int_{0}^{+\infty} f(x)dx$ both converge. If either of these two integrals diverge, then $\int_{-\infty}^{+\infty} f(x)dx$ diverges. (It can be shown that, in fact, $\int_{-\infty}^{+\infty} f(x)dx = \int_{-\infty}^{a} f(x)dx + \int_{a}^{+\infty} f(x)dx$ for any value of $a$.)

In our first example, we return to the question we posed at the start of this section: Is the area between the graph of $f(x) = \frac{1}{x}$ and the $x$-axis over the interval $[1, +\infty)$ finite or infinite?

## Example 3.47

### Finding an Area

Determine whether the area between the graph of $f(x) = \frac{1}{x}$ and the $x$-axis over the interval $[1, +\infty)$ is finite or infinite.

#### Solution

We first do a quick sketch of the region in question, as shown in the following graph.

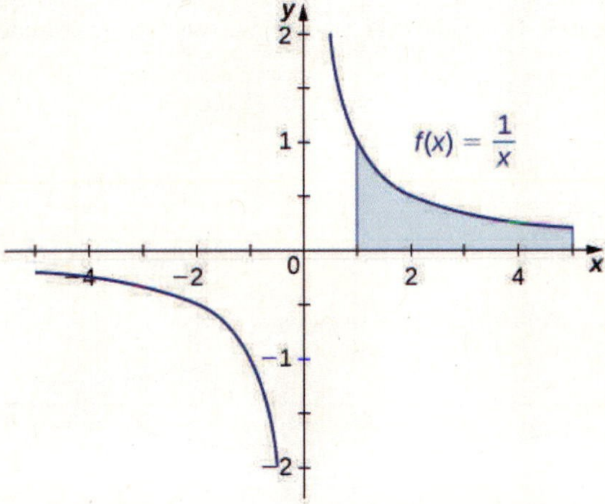


**Figure 3.18** We can find the area between the curve $f(x) = 1/x$ and the $x$-axis on an infinite interval.

We can see that the area of this region is given by $A = \int_{1}^{\infty} \frac{1}{x}dx$. Then we have

$$\begin{aligned} A &= \int_1^{\infty} \frac{1}{x}dx \\ &= \lim_{t \to +\infty} \int_1^t \frac{1}{x}dx && \text{Rewrite the improper integral as a limit.} \\ &= \lim_{t \to +\infty} \ln|x| \Big|_1^t && \text{Find the antiderivative.} \\ &= \lim_{t \to +\infty} (\ln|t| - \ln 1) && \text{Evaluate the antiderivative.} \\ &= +\infty. && \text{Evaluate the limit.} \end{aligned}$$

Since the improper integral diverges to $+\infty$, the area of the region is infinite.

## Example 3.48

### Finding a Volume

Find the volume of the solid obtained by revolving the region bounded by the graph of $f(x) = \frac{1}{x}$ and the $x$-axis over the interval $[1, +\infty)$ about the $x$-axis.

### Solution

The solid is shown in **Figure 3.19**. Using the disk method, we see that the volume $V$ is

$$V = \pi \int_1^{+\infty} \frac{1}{x^2}dx.$$

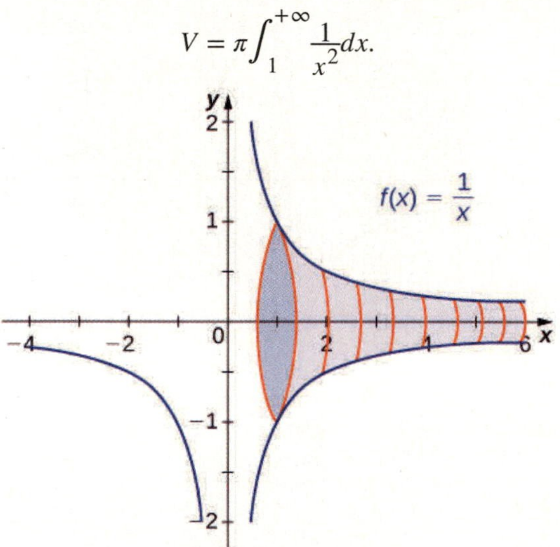


**Figure 3.19** The solid of revolution can be generated by rotating an infinite area about the $x$-axis.

Then we have

$$\begin{aligned} V &= \pi \int_1^{+\infty} \frac{1}{x^2} dx \\ &= \pi \lim_{t \to +\infty} \int_1^t \frac{1}{x^2} dx && \text{Rewrite as a limit.} \\ &= \pi \lim_{t \to +\infty} -\frac{1}{x}\Big|_1^t && \text{Find the antiderivative.} \\ &= \pi \lim_{t \to +\infty} \left(-\frac{1}{t} + 1\right) && \text{Evaluate the antiderivative.} \\ &= \pi. \end{aligned}$$

The improper integral converges to $\pi$. Therefore, the volume of the solid of revolution is $\pi$.

In conclusion, although the area of the region between the $x$-axis and the graph of $f(x) = 1/x$ over the interval $[1, +\infty)$ is infinite, the volume of the solid generated by revolving this region about the $x$-axis is finite. The solid generated is known as *Gabriel's Horn*.

Visit this **website (http://www.openstaxcollege.org/l/20_GabrielsHorn)** to read more about Gabriel's Horn.

## Example 3.49

### Chapter Opener: Traffic Accidents in a City

**Figure 3.20** (credit: modification of work by David McKelvey, Flickr)

In the chapter opener, we stated the following problem: Suppose that at a busy intersection, traffic accidents occur at an average rate of one every three months. After residents complained, changes were made to the traffic lights at the intersection. It has now been eight months since the changes were made and there have been no accidents. Were the changes effective or is the 8-month interval without an accident a result of chance?

Probability theory tells us that if the average time between events is $k$, the probability that $X$, the time between events, is between $a$ and $b$ is given by

$$P(a \le x \le b) = \int_a^b f(x)dx \text{ where } f(x) = \begin{cases} 0 \text{ if } x < 0 \\ ke^{-kx} \text{ if } x \ge 0 \end{cases}.$$

Thus, if accidents are occurring at a rate of one every 3 months, then the probability that $X$, the time between accidents, is between $a$ and $b$ is given by

$$P(a \le x \le b) = \int_a^b f(x)dx \text{ where } f(x) = \begin{cases} 0 \text{ if } x < 0 \\ 3e^{-3x} \text{ if } x \ge 0 \end{cases}.$$

To answer the question, we must compute $P(X \ge 8) = \int_8^{+\infty} 3e^{-3x}\,dx$ and decide whether it is likely that 8 months could have passed without an accident if there had been no improvement in the traffic situation.

### Solution

We need to calculate the probability as an improper integral:

$$\begin{aligned} P(X \ge 8) &= \int_8^{+\infty} 3e^{-3x}\,dx \\ &= \lim_{t \to +\infty} \int_8^t 3e^{-3x}\,dx \\ &= \lim_{t \to +\infty} -e^{-3x}\Big|_8^t \\ &= \lim_{t \to +\infty} (-e^{-3t} + e^{-24}) \\ &\approx 3.8 \times 10^{-11}. \end{aligned}$$

The value $3.8 \times 10^{-11}$ represents the probability of no accidents in 8 months under the initial conditions. Since this value is very, very small, it is reasonable to conclude the changes were effective.

## Example 3.50

### Evaluating an Improper Integral over an Infinite Interval

Evaluate $\int_{-\infty}^{0} \frac{1}{x^2+4}dx.$ State whether the improper integral converges or diverges.

### Solution

Begin by rewriting $\int_{-\infty}^{0} \frac{1}{x^2+4}dx$ as a limit using **Equation 3.17** from the definition. Thus,

$$\begin{aligned} \int_{-\infty}^{0} \frac{1}{x^2+4}dx &= \lim_{t \to -\infty} \int_t^0 \frac{1}{x^2+4}dx && \text{Rewrite as a limit.} \\ &= \lim_{t \to -\infty} \tan^{-1}\frac{x}{2}\Big|_t^0 && \text{Find the antiderivative.} \\ &= \lim_{t \to -\infty} \left(\tan^{-1} 0 - \tan^{-1}\frac{t}{2}\right) && \text{Evaluate the antiderivative.} \\ &= \frac{\pi}{2}. && \text{Evaluate the limit and simplify.} \end{aligned}$$

The improper integral converges to $\frac{\pi}{2}$.

## Example 3.51

### Evaluating an Improper Integral on $(-\infty, +\infty)$

Evaluate $\int_{-\infty}^{+\infty} xe^x\,dx$. State whether the improper integral converges or diverges.

#### Solution

Start by splitting up the integral:

$$\int_{-\infty}^{+\infty} xe^x\,dx = \int_{-\infty}^{0} xe^x\,dx + \int_{0}^{+\infty} xe^x\,dx.$$

If either $\int_{-\infty}^{0} xe^x\,dx$ or $\int_{0}^{+\infty} xe^x\,dx$ diverges, then $\int_{-\infty}^{+\infty} xe^x\,dx$ diverges. Compute each integral separately.

For the first integral,

$$\begin{aligned}
\int_{-\infty}^{0} xe^x\,dx &= \lim_{t \to -\infty} \int_{t}^{0} xe^x\,dx && \text{Rewrite as a limit.} \\
&= \lim_{t \to -\infty} (xe^x - e^x)\Big|_{t}^{0} && \text{Use integration by parts to find the antiderivative. (Here } u = x \text{ and } dv = e^x.) \\
&= \lim_{t \to -\infty} \left(-1 - te^t + e^t\right) && \text{Evaluate the antiderivative.} \\
&= -1. && \text{Evaluate the limit. } \textit{Note: } \lim_{t \to -\infty} te^t \text{ is indeterminate of the form } 0 \cdot \infty. \text{ Thus, } \lim_{t \to -\infty} te^t = \lim_{t \to -\infty} \frac{t}{e^{-t}} = \lim_{t \to -\infty} \frac{-1}{e^{-t}} = \lim_{t \to -\infty} -e^t = 0 \text{ by L'Hôpital's Rule.}
\end{aligned}$$

The first improper integral converges. For the second integral,

$$\begin{aligned}
\int_{0}^{+\infty} xe^x\,dx &= \lim_{t \to +\infty} \int_{0}^{t} xe^x\,dx && \text{Rewrite as a limit.} \\
&= \lim_{t \to +\infty} (xe^x - e^x)\Big|_{0}^{t} && \text{Find the antiderivative.} \\
&= \lim_{t \to +\infty} \left(te^t - e^t + 1\right) && \text{Evaluate the antiderivative.} \\
&= \lim_{t \to +\infty} \left((t-1)e^t + 1\right) && \text{Rewrite. } (te^t - e^t \text{ is indeterminate.}) \\
&= +\infty. && \text{Evaluate the limit.}
\end{aligned}$$

Thus, $\int_{0}^{+\infty} xe^x\,dx$ diverges. Since this integral diverges, $\int_{-\infty}^{+\infty} xe^x\,dx$ diverges as well.

**3.27** Evaluate $\int_{-3}^{+\infty} e^{-x}\,dx$. State whether the improper integral converges or diverges.

## Integrating a Discontinuous Integrand

Now let's examine integrals of functions containing an infinite discontinuity in the interval over which the integration occurs. Consider an integral of the form $\int_a^b f(x)dx,$ where $f(x)$ is continuous over $[a, b)$ and discontinuous at $b$. Since the function $f(x)$ is continuous over $[a, t]$ for all values of $t$ satisfying $a < t < b,$ the integral $\int_a^t f(x)dx$ is defined for all such values of $t$. Thus, it makes sense to consider the values of $\int_a^t f(x)dx$ as $t$ approaches $b$ for $a < t < b$. That is, we define $\int_a^b f(x)dx = \lim_{t \to b^-} \int_a^t f(x)dx,$ provided this limit exists. **Figure 3.21** illustrates $\int_a^t f(x)dx$ as areas of regions for values of $t$ approaching $b$.

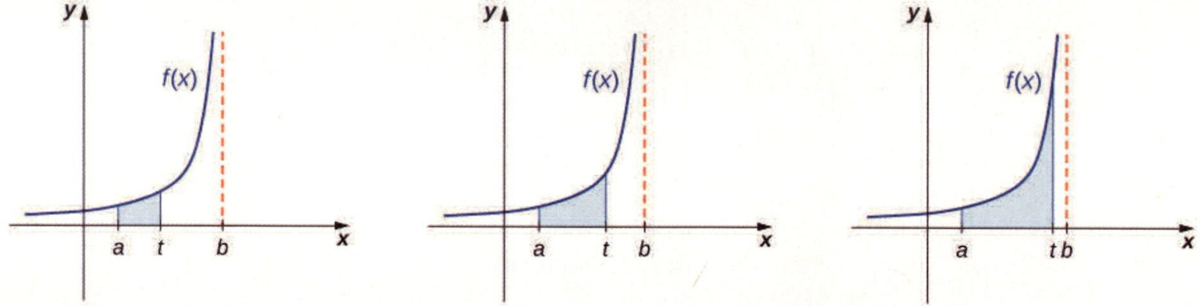


**Figure 3.21** As $t$ approaches $b$ from the left, the value of the area from $a$ to $t$ approaches the area from $a$ to $b$.

We use a similar approach to define $\int_a^b f(x)dx,$ where $f(x)$ is continuous over $(a, b]$ and discontinuous at $a$. We now proceed with a formal definition.

## Definition

1. Let $f(x)$ be continuous over $[a, b)$. Then,

$$\int_a^b f(x)dx = \lim_{t \to b^-} \int_a^t f(x)dx. \quad (3.19)$$

2. Let $f(x)$ be continuous over $(a, b]$. Then,

$$\int_a^b f(x)dx = \lim_{t \to a^+} \int_t^b f(x)dx. \quad (3.20)$$

   In each case, if the limit exists, then the improper integral is said to converge. If the limit does not exist, then the improper integral is said to diverge.

3. If $f(x)$ is continuous over $[a, b]$ except at a point $c$ in $(a, b),$ then

$$\int_a^b f(x)dx = \int_a^c f(x)dx + \int_c^b f(x)dx, \quad (3.21)$$

   provided both $\int_a^c f(x)dx$ and $\int_c^b f(x)dx$ converge. If either of these integrals diverges, then $\int_a^b f(x)dx$ diverges.

The following examples demonstrate the application of this definition.

## Example 3.52

### Integrating a Discontinuous Integrand

Evaluate $\int_0^4 \frac{1}{\sqrt{4-x}}dx,$ if possible. State whether the integral converges or diverges.

### Solution

The function $f(x) = \frac{1}{\sqrt{4-x}}$ is continuous over $[0, 4)$ and discontinuous at 4. Using **Equation 3.19** from the definition, rewrite $\int_0^4 \frac{1}{\sqrt{4-x}}dx$ as a limit:

$$\begin{aligned} \int_0^4 \frac{1}{\sqrt{4-x}}dx &= \lim_{t \to 4^-} \int_0^t \frac{1}{\sqrt{4-x}}dx && \text{Rewrite as a limit.} \\ &= \lim_{t \to 4^-} \left(-2\sqrt{4-x}\right)\Big|_0^t && \text{Find the antiderivative.} \\ &= \lim_{t \to 4^-} \left(-2\sqrt{4-t}+4\right) && \text{Evaluate the antiderivative.} \\ &= 4. && \text{Evaluate the limit.} \end{aligned}$$

The improper integral converges.

## Example 3.53

### Integrating a Discontinuous Integrand

Evaluate $\int_0^2 x\ln x\,dx.$ State whether the integral converges or diverges.

### Solution

Since $f(x) = x\ln x$ is continuous over $(0, 2]$ and is discontinuous at zero, we can rewrite the integral in limit form using **Equation 3.20**:

$$\begin{aligned} \int_0^2 x\ln x\,dx &= \lim_{t \to 0^+} \int_t^2 x\ln x\,dx && \text{Rewrite as a limit.} \\ &= \lim_{t \to 0^+} \left(\tfrac{1}{2}x^2\ln x - \tfrac{1}{4}x^2\right)\Big|_t^2 && \text{Evaluate } \textstyle\int x\ln x\,dx \text{ using integration by parts with } u = \ln x \text{ and } dv = x. \\ &= \lim_{t \to 0^+} \left(2\ln 2 - 1 - \tfrac{1}{2}t^2\ln t + \tfrac{1}{4}t^2\right). && \text{Evaluate the antiderivative.} \\ &= 2\ln 2 - 1. && \text{Evaluate the limit. } \lim_{t \to 0^+} t^2\ln t \text{ is indeterminate. To evaluate it, rewrite as a quotient and apply L'Hôpital's rule.} \end{aligned}$$

The improper integral converges.

## Example 3.54

### Integrating a Discontinuous Integrand

Evaluate $\int_{-1}^{1} \frac{1}{x^3}dx$. State whether the improper integral converges or diverges.

### Solution

Since $f(x) = 1/x^3$ is discontinuous at zero, using **Equation 3.21**, we can write

$$\int_{-1}^{1} \frac{1}{x^3}dx = \int_{-1}^{0} \frac{1}{x^3}dx + \int_{0}^{1} \frac{1}{x^3}dx.$$

If either of the two integrals diverges, then the original integral diverges. Begin with $\int_{-1}^{0} \frac{1}{x^3}dx$ :

$$\begin{aligned}
\int_{-1}^{0} \frac{1}{x^3}dx &= \lim_{t \to 0^-} \int_{-1}^{t} \frac{1}{x^3}dx && \text{Rewrite as a limit.} \\
&= \lim_{t \to 0^-} \left(-\frac{1}{2x^2}\right)\Bigg|_{-1}^{t} && \text{Find the antiderivative.} \\
&= \lim_{t \to 0^-} \left(-\frac{1}{2t^2} + \frac{1}{2}\right) && \text{Evaluate the antiderivative.} \\
&= +\infty. && \text{Evaluate the limit.}
\end{aligned}$$

Therefore, $\int_{-1}^{0} \frac{1}{x^3}dx$ diverges. Since $\int_{-1}^{0} \frac{1}{x^3}dx$ diverges, $\int_{-1}^{1} \frac{1}{x^3}dx$ diverges.

**3.28** Evaluate $\int_{0}^{2} \frac{1}{x}dx$. State whether the integral converges or diverges.

## A Comparison Theorem

It is not always easy or even possible to evaluate an improper integral directly; however, by comparing it with another carefully chosen integral, it may be possible to determine its convergence or divergence. To see this, consider two continuous functions $f(x)$ and $g(x)$ satisfying $0 \le f(x) \le g(x)$ for $x \ge a$ (**Figure 3.22**). In this case, we may view integrals of these functions over intervals of the form $[a, t]$ as areas, so we have the relationship

$$0 \le \int_{a}^{t} f(x)dx \le \int_{a}^{t} g(x)dx \text{ for } t \ge a.$$

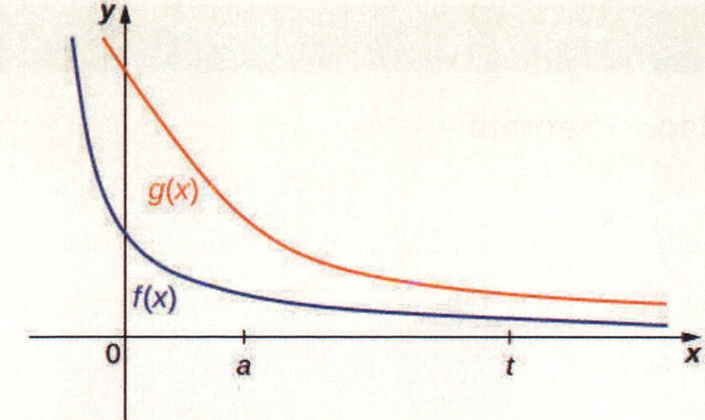


**Figure 3.22** If $0 \le f(x) \le g(x)$ for $x \ge a$, then for $t \ge a$, $\int_a^t f(x)dx \le \int_a^t g(x)dx$.

Thus, if

$$\int_a^{+\infty} f(x)dx = \lim_{t \to +\infty} \int_a^t f(x)dx = +\infty,$$

then

$\int_a^{+\infty} g(x)dx = \lim_{t \to +\infty} \int_a^t g(x)dx = +\infty$ as well. That is, if the area of the region between the graph of $f(x)$ and the $x$-axis over $[a, +\infty)$ is infinite, then the area of the region between the graph of $g(x)$ and the $x$-axis over $[a, +\infty)$ is infinite too.

On the other hand, if

$\int_a^{+\infty} g(x)dx = \lim_{t \to +\infty} \int_a^t g(x)dx = L$ for some real number $L$, then

$\int_a^{+\infty} f(x)dx = \lim_{t \to +\infty} \int_a^t f(x)dx$ must converge to some value less than or equal to $L$, since $\int_a^t f(x)dx$ increases as $t$ increases and $\int_a^t f(x)dx \le L$ for all $t \ge a$.

If the area of the region between the graph of $g(x)$ and the $x$-axis over $[a, +\infty)$ is finite, then the area of the region between the graph of $f(x)$ and the $x$-axis over $[a, +\infty)$ is also finite.

These conclusions are summarized in the following theorem.

## Theorem 3.7: A Comparison Theorem

Let $f(x)$ and $g(x)$ be continuous over $[a, +\infty)$. Assume that $0 \le f(x) \le g(x)$ for $x \ge a$.

i. If $\int_a^{+\infty} f(x)dx = \lim_{t \to +\infty} \int_a^t f(x)dx = +\infty$, then $\int_a^{+\infty} g(x)dx = \lim_{t \to +\infty} \int_a^t g(x)dx = +\infty$.

ii. If $\int_a^{+\infty} g(x)dx = \lim_{t \to +\infty} \int_a^t g(x)dx = L$, where $L$ is a real number, then $\int_a^{+\infty} f(x)dx = \lim_{t \to +\infty} \int_a^t f(x)dx = M$ for some real number $M \le L$.

## Example 3.55

### Applying the Comparison Theorem

Use a comparison to show that $\int_1^{+\infty} \frac{1}{xe^x}dx$ converges.

#### Solution

We can see that

$$0 \le \frac{1}{xe^x} \le \frac{1}{e^x} = e^{-x},$$

so if $\int_1^{+\infty} e^{-x}\,dx$ converges, then so does $\int_1^{+\infty} \frac{1}{xe^x}dx$. To evaluate $\int_1^{+\infty} e^{-x}\,dx$, first rewrite it as a limit:

$$\begin{aligned}\int_1^{+\infty} e^{-x}dx &= \lim_{t \to +\infty} \int_1^t e^{-x}\,dx \\ &= \lim_{t \to +\infty} (-e^{-x})\Big|_1^t \\ &= \lim_{t \to +\infty} \left(-e^{-t} + e^1\right) \\ &= e^1.\end{aligned}$$

Since $\int_1^{+\infty} e^{-x}\,dx$ converges, so does $\int_1^{+\infty} \frac{1}{xe^x}dx$.

## Example 3.56

### Applying the Comparison Theorem

Use the comparison theorem to show that $\int_1^{+\infty} \frac{1}{x^p}dx$ diverges for all $p < 1$.

#### Solution

For $p < 1$, $1/x \le 1/(x^p)$ over $[1, +\infty)$. In **Example 3.47**, we showed that $\int_1^{+\infty} \frac{1}{x}dx = +\infty$. Therefore, $\int_1^{+\infty} \frac{1}{x^p}dx$ diverges for all $p < 1$.

**3.29** Use a comparison to show that $\int_e^{+\infty} \frac{\ln x}{x}dx$ diverges.

# Student PROJECT

## Laplace Transforms

In the last few chapters, we have looked at several ways to use integration for solving real-world problems. For this next project, we are going to explore a more advanced application of integration: integral transforms. Specifically, we describe the Laplace transform and some of its properties. The Laplace transform is used in engineering and physics to simplify the computations needed to solve some problems. It takes functions expressed in terms of time and *transforms* them to functions expressed in terms of frequency. It turns out that, in many cases, the computations needed to solve problems in the frequency domain are much simpler than those required in the time domain.

The Laplace transform is defined in terms of an integral as

$$L\{f(t)\} = F(s) = \int_0^\infty e^{-st} f(t)dt.$$

Note that the input to a Laplace transform is a function of time, $f(t)$, and the output is a function of frequency, $F(s)$. Although many real-world examples require the use of complex numbers (involving the imaginary number $i = \sqrt{-1}$), in this project we limit ourselves to functions of real numbers.

Let's start with a simple example. Here we calculate the Laplace transform of $f(t) = t$. We have

$$L\{t\} = \int_0^\infty te^{-st} dt.$$

This is an improper integral, so we express it in terms of a limit, which gives

$$L\{t\} = \int_0^\infty te^{-st} dt = \lim_{z \to \infty} \int_0^z te^{-st} dt.$$

Now we use integration by parts to evaluate the integral. Note that we are integrating with respect to $t$, so we treat the variable $s$ as a constant. We have

$$\begin{aligned} u &= t & dv &= e^{-st} dt \\ du &= dt & v &= -\tfrac{1}{s}e^{-st}. \end{aligned}$$

Then we obtain

$$\begin{aligned} \lim_{z \to \infty} \int_0^z te^{-st} dt &= \lim_{z \to \infty} \left[ \left[ -\tfrac{t}{s}e^{-st} \right]_0^z + \tfrac{1}{s} \int_0^z e^{-st} dt \right] \\ &= \lim_{z \to \infty} \left[ \left[ -\tfrac{z}{s}e^{-sz} + \tfrac{0}{s}e^{-0s} \right] + \tfrac{1}{s} \int_0^z e^{-st} dt \right] \\ &= \lim_{z \to \infty} \left[ \left[ -\tfrac{z}{s}e^{-sz} + 0 \right] - \tfrac{1}{s} \left[ \frac{e^{-st}}{s} \right]_0^z \right] \\ &= \lim_{z \to \infty} \left[ \left[ -\tfrac{z}{s}e^{-sz} \right] - \frac{1}{s^2} \left[ e^{-sz} - 1 \right] \right] \\ &= \lim_{z \to \infty} \left[ -\frac{z}{se^{sz}} \right] - \lim_{z \to \infty} \left[ \frac{1}{s^2 e^{sz}} \right] + \lim_{z \to \infty} \frac{1}{s^2} \\ &= 0 - 0 + \frac{1}{s^2} \\ &= \frac{1}{s^2}. \end{aligned}$$

1. Calculate the Laplace transform of $f(t) = 1$.

2. Calculate the Laplace transform of $f(t) = e^{-3t}$.

3. Calculate the Laplace transform of $f(t) = t^2$. (Note, you will have to integrate by parts twice.)

   Laplace transforms are often used to solve differential equations. Differential equations are not covered in detail until later in this book; but, for now, let's look at the relationship between the Laplace transform of a function and the Laplace transform of its derivative.
   Let's start with the definition of the Laplace transform. We have

$$L\{f(t)\} = \int_0^{\infty} e^{-st} f(t)dt = \lim_{z \to \infty} \int_0^z e^{-st} f(t)dt.$$

4. Use integration by parts to evaluate $\lim_{z \to \infty} \int_0^z e^{-st} f(t)dt$. (Let $u = f(t)$ and $dv = e^{-st} dt$.)

   After integrating by parts and evaluating the limit, you should see that

$$L\{f(t)\} = \frac{f(0)}{s} + \frac{1}{s}[L\{f'(t)\}].$$

   Then,

$$L\{f'(t)\} = sL\{f(t)\} - f(0).$$

   Thus, differentiation in the time domain simplifies to multiplication by $s$ in the frequency domain.
   The final thing we look at in this project is how the Laplace transforms of $f(t)$ and its antiderivative are related. Let $g(t) = \int_0^t f(u)du$. Then,

$$L\{g(t)\} = \int_0^{\infty} e^{-st} g(t)dt = \lim_{z \to \infty} \int_0^z e^{-st} g(t)dt.$$

5. Use integration by parts to evaluate $\lim_{z \to \infty} \int_0^z e^{-st} g(t)dt$. (Let $u = g(t)$ and $dv = e^{-st} dt$. Note, by the way, that we have defined $g(t)$, $du = f(t)dt$.)

   As you might expect, you should see that

$$L\{g(t)\} = \frac{1}{s} \cdot L\{f(t)\}.$$

   Integration in the time domain simplifies to division by $s$ in the frequency domain.

# 3.7 EXERCISES

Evaluate the following integrals. If the integral is not convergent, answer "divergent."

347. $\int_2^4 \frac{dx}{(x-3)^2}$

348. $\int_0^\infty \frac{1}{4+x^2}dx$

349. $\int_0^2 \frac{1}{\sqrt{4-x^2}}dx$

350. $\int_1^\infty \frac{1}{x\ln x}dx$

351. $\int_1^\infty xe^{-x}\,dx$

352. $\int_{-\infty}^\infty \frac{x}{x^2+1}dx$

353. Without integrating, determine whether the integral $\int_1^\infty \frac{1}{\sqrt{x^3+1}}dx$ converges or diverges by comparing the function $f(x) = \frac{1}{\sqrt{x^3+1}}$ with $g(x) = \frac{1}{\sqrt{x^3}}$.

354. Without integrating, determine whether the integral $\int_1^\infty \frac{1}{\sqrt{x+1}}dx$ converges or diverges.

Determine whether the improper integrals converge or diverge. If possible, determine the value of the integrals that converge.

355. $\int_0^\infty e^{-x}\cos x\,dx$

356. $\int_1^\infty \frac{\ln x}{x}dx$

357. $\int_0^1 \frac{\ln x}{\sqrt{x}}dx$

358. $\int_0^1 \ln x\,dx$

359. $\int_{-\infty}^\infty \frac{1}{x^2+1}dx$

360. $\int_1^5 \frac{dx}{\sqrt{x-1}}$

361. $\int_{-2}^2 \frac{dx}{(1+x)^2}$

362. $\int_0^\infty e^{-x}\,dx$

363. $\int_0^\infty \sin x\,dx$

364. $\int_{-\infty}^\infty \frac{e^x}{1+e^{2x}}dx$

365. $\int_0^1 \frac{dx}{\sqrt[3]{x}}$

366. $\int_0^2 \frac{dx}{x^3}$

367. $\int_{-1}^2 \frac{dx}{x^3}$

368. $\int_0^1 \frac{dx}{\sqrt{1-x^2}}$

369. $\int_0^3 \frac{1}{x-1}dx$

370. $\int_1^\infty \frac{5}{x^3}dx$

371. $\int_3^5 \frac{5}{(x-4)^2}dx$

Determine the convergence of each of the following integrals by comparison with the given integral. If the integral converges, find the number to which it converges.

372. $\int_1^\infty \frac{dx}{x^2+4x}$; compare with $\int_1^\infty \frac{dx}{x^2}$.

373. $\int_1^\infty \frac{dx}{\sqrt{x}+1}$; compare with $\int_1^\infty \frac{dx}{2\sqrt{x}}$.

Evaluate the integrals. If the integral diverges, answer "diverges."

374. $\int_1^{\infty} \frac{dx}{x^e}$

375. $\int_0^1 \frac{dx}{x^{\pi}}$

376. $\int_0^1 \frac{dx}{\sqrt{1-x}}$

377. $\int_0^1 \frac{dx}{1-x}$

378. $\int_{-\infty}^0 \frac{dx}{x^2+1}$

379. $\int_{-1}^1 \frac{dx}{\sqrt{1-x^2}}$

380. $\int_0^1 \frac{\ln x}{x} dx$

381. $\int_0^e \ln(x) dx$

382. $\int_0^{\infty} xe^{-x} dx$

383. $\int_{-\infty}^{\infty} \frac{x}{\left(x^2+1\right)^2} dx$

384. $\int_0^{\infty} e^{-x} dx$

Evaluate the improper integrals. Each of these integrals has an infinite discontinuity either at an endpoint or at an interior point of the interval.

385. $\int_0^9 \frac{dx}{\sqrt{9-x}}$

386. $\int_{-27}^1 \frac{dx}{x^{2/3}}$

387. $\int_0^3 \frac{dx}{\sqrt{9-x^2}}$

388. $\int_6^{24} \frac{dt}{t\sqrt{t^2-36}}$

389. $\int_0^4 x\ln(4x) dx$

390. $\int_0^3 \frac{x}{\sqrt{9-x^2}} dx$

391. Evaluate $\int_{.5}^t \frac{dx}{\sqrt{1-x^2}}$. (Be careful!) (Express your answer using three decimal places.)

392. Evaluate $\int_1^4 \frac{dx}{\sqrt{x^2-1}}$. (Express the answer in exact form.)

393. Evaluate $\int_2^{\infty} \frac{dx}{(x^2-1)^{3/2}}$.

394. Find the area of the region in the first quadrant between the curve $y = e^{-6x}$ and the $x$-axis.

395. Find the area of the region bounded by the curve $y = \frac{7}{x^2}$, the $x$-axis, and on the left by $x = 1$.

396. Find the area under the curve $y = \frac{1}{(x+1)^{3/2}}$, bounded on the left by $x = 3$.

397. Find the area under $y = \frac{5}{1+x^2}$ in the first quadrant.

398. Find the volume of the solid generated by revolving about the $x$-axis the region under the curve $y = \frac{3}{x}$ from $x = 1$ to $x = \infty$.

399. Find the volume of the solid generated by revolving about the $y$-axis the region under the curve $y = 6e^{-2x}$ in the first quadrant.

400. Find the volume of the solid generated by revolving about the $x$-axis the area under the curve $y = 3e^{-x}$ in the first quadrant.

The Laplace transform of a continuous function over the interval $[0, \infty)$ is defined by $F(s) = \int_0^{\infty} e^{-sx} f(x) dx$ (see the Student Project). This definition is used to solve some important initial-value problems in differential equations, as discussed later. The domain of $F$ is the set of all real numbers $s$ such that the improper integral converges. Find the Laplace transform $F$ of each of the following functions and give the domain of $F$.

401. $f(x) = 1$

402. $f(x) = x$

403. $f(x) = \cos(2x)$

404. $f(x) = e^{ax}$

405. Use the formula for arc length to show that the circumference of the circle $x^2 + y^2 = 1$ is $2\pi$.

A function is a probability density function if it satisfies the following definition: $\int_{-\infty}^{\infty} f(t)dt = 1$. The probability that a random variable $x$ lies between $a$ and $b$ is given by $P(a \le x \le b) = \int_a^b f(t)dt$.

406. Show that $f(x) = \begin{cases} 0 \text{ if } x < 0 \\ 7e^{-7x} \text{ if } x \ge 0 \end{cases}$ is a probability density function.

407. Find the probability that $x$ is between 0 and 0.3. (Use the function defined in the preceding problem.) Use four-place decimal accuracy.

# CHAPTER 3 REVIEW

## KEY TERMS

**absolute error** if $B$ is an estimate of some quantity having an actual value of $A,$ then the absolute error is given by $|A - B|$

**computer algebra system (CAS)** technology used to perform many mathematical tasks, including integration

**improper integral** an integral over an infinite interval or an integral of a function containing an infinite discontinuity on the interval; an improper integral is defined in terms of a limit. The improper integral converges if this limit is a finite real number; otherwise, the improper integral diverges

**integration by parts** a technique of integration that allows the exchange of one integral for another using the formula $\int u\,dv = uv - \int v\,du$

**integration table** a table that lists integration formulas

**midpoint rule** a rule that uses a Riemann sum of the form $M_n = \sum_{i=1}^{n} f(m_i)\Delta x,$ where $m_i$ is the midpoint of the $i$th subinterval to approximate $\int_a^b f(x)dx$

**numerical integration** the variety of numerical methods used to estimate the value of a definite integral, including the midpoint rule, trapezoidal rule, and Simpson's rule

**partial fraction decomposition** a technique used to break down a rational function into the sum of simple rational functions

**power reduction formula** a rule that allows an integral of a power of a trigonometric function to be exchanged for an integral involving a lower power

**relative error** error as a percentage of the absolute value, given by $\left|\frac{A-B}{A}\right| = \left|\frac{A-B}{A}\right| \cdot 100\%$

**Simpson's rule** a rule that approximates $\int_a^b f(x)dx$ using the integrals of a piecewise quadratic function. The approximation $S_n$ to $\int_a^b f(x)dx$ is given by $S_n = \frac{\Delta x}{3}\begin{pmatrix} f(x_0) + 4f(x_1) + 2f(x_2) + 4f(x_3) + 2f(x_4) + 4f(x_5) \\ + \cdots + 2f(x_{n-2}) + 4f(x_{n-1}) + f(x_n) \end{pmatrix}$

trapezoidal rule a rule that approximates $\int_a^b f(x)dx$ using trapezoids

**trigonometric integral** an integral involving powers and products of trigonometric functions

**trigonometric substitution** an integration technique that converts an algebraic integral containing expressions of the form $\sqrt{a^2 - x^2},$ $\sqrt{a^2 + x^2},$ or $\sqrt{x^2 - a^2}$ into a trigonometric integral

## KEY EQUATIONS

- **Integration by parts formula**
  $\int u\,dv = uv - \int v\,du$
- **Integration by parts for definite integrals**
  $\int_a^b u\,dv = uv|_a^b - \int_a^b v\,du$

To integrate products involving $\sin(ax),$ $\sin(bx),$ $\cos(ax),$ and $\cos(bx),$ use the substitutions.

- **Sine Products**
  $\sin(ax)\sin(bx) = \frac{1}{2}\cos((a-b)x) - \frac{1}{2}\cos((a+b)x)$
- **Sine and Cosine Products**
  $\sin(ax)\cos(bx) = \frac{1}{2}\sin((a-b)x) + \frac{1}{2}\sin((a+b)x)$
- **Cosine Products**
  $\cos(ax)\cos(bx) = \frac{1}{2}\cos((a-b)x) + \frac{1}{2}\cos((a+b)x)$
- **Power Reduction Formula**
  $\int \sec^n x\,dx = \frac{1}{n-1}\sec^{n-1} x + \frac{n-2}{n-1}\int \sec^{n-2} x\,dx$
- **Power Reduction Formula**
  $\int \tan^n x\,dx = \frac{1}{n-1}\tan^{n-1} x - \int \tan^{n-2} x\,dx$
- **Midpoint rule**
  $M_n = \sum_{i=1}^{n} f(m_i)\Delta x$
- **Trapezoidal rule**
  $T_n = \frac{1}{2}\Delta x\big(f(x_0) + 2f(x_1) + 2f(x_2) + \cdots + 2f(x_{n-1}) + f(x_n)\big)$
- **Simpson's rule**
  $S_n = \frac{\Delta x}{3}\big(f(x_0) + 4f(x_1) + 2f(x_2) + 4f(x_3) + 2f(x_4) + 4f(x_5) + \cdots + 2f(x_{n-2}) + 4f(x_{n-1}) + f(x_n)\big)$
- **Error bound for midpoint rule**
  Error in $M_n \le \frac{M(b-a)^3}{24n^2}$
- **Error bound for trapezoidal rule**
  Error in $T_n \le \frac{M(b-a)^3}{12n^2}$
- **Error bound for Simpson's rule**
  Error in $S_n \le \frac{M(b-a)^5}{180n^4}$
- **Improper integrals**
  $\int_a^{+\infty} f(x)dx = \lim_{t \to +\infty} \int_a^t f(x)dx$
  $\int_{-\infty}^b f(x)dx = \lim_{t \to -\infty} \int_t^b f(x)dx$
  $\int_{-\infty}^{+\infty} f(x)dx = \int_{-\infty}^0 f(x)dx + \int_0^{+\infty} f(x)dx$

# KEY CONCEPTS

## 3.1 Integration by Parts

- The integration-by-parts formula allows the exchange of one integral for another, possibly easier, integral.
- Integration by parts applies to both definite and indefinite integrals.

## 3.2 Trigonometric Integrals

- Integrals of trigonometric functions can be evaluated by the use of various strategies. These strategies include
  1. Applying trigonometric identities to rewrite the integral so that it may be evaluated by $u$-substitution
  2. Using integration by parts
  3. Applying trigonometric identities to rewrite products of sines and cosines with different arguments as the sum of individual sine and cosine functions
  4. Applying reduction formulas

## 3.3 Trigonometric Substitution

- For integrals involving $\sqrt{a^2 - x^2}$, use the substitution $x = a\sin\theta$ and $dx = a\cos\theta d\theta$.
- For integrals involving $\sqrt{a^2 + x^2}$, use the substitution $x = a\tan\theta$ and $dx = a\sec^2\theta d\theta$.
- For integrals involving $\sqrt{x^2 - a^2}$, substitute $x = a\sec\theta$ and $dx = a\sec\theta\tan\theta d\theta$.

## 3.4 Partial Fractions

- Partial fraction decomposition is a technique used to break down a rational function into a sum of simple rational functions that can be integrated using previously learned techniques.
- When applying partial fraction decomposition, we must make sure that the degree of the numerator is less than the degree of the denominator. If not, we need to perform long division before attempting partial fraction decomposition.
- The form the decomposition takes depends on the type of factors in the denominator. The types of factors include nonrepeated linear factors, repeated linear factors, nonrepeated irreducible quadratic factors, and repeated irreducible quadratic factors.

## 3.5 Other Strategies for Integration

- An integration table may be used to evaluate indefinite integrals.
- A CAS (or computer algebra system) may be used to evaluate indefinite integrals.
- It may require some effort to reconcile equivalent solutions obtained using different methods.

## 3.6 Numerical Integration

- We can use numerical integration to estimate the values of definite integrals when a closed form of the integral is difficult to find or when an approximate value only of the definite integral is needed.
- The most commonly used techniques for numerical integration are the midpoint rule, trapezoidal rule, and Simpson's rule.
- The midpoint rule approximates the definite integral using rectangular regions whereas the trapezoidal rule approximates the definite integral using trapezoidal approximations.
- Simpson's rule approximates the definite integral by first approximating the original function using piecewise quadratic functions.

## 3.7 Improper Integrals

- Integrals of functions over infinite intervals are defined in terms of limits.
- Integrals of functions over an interval for which the function has a discontinuity at an endpoint may be defined in terms of limits.

- The convergence or divergence of an improper integral may be determined by comparing it with the value of an improper integral for which the convergence or divergence is known.

## CHAPTER 3 REVIEW EXERCISES

For the following exercises, determine whether the statement is true or false. Justify your answer with a proof or a counterexample.

**408.** $\int e^x \sin(x)dx$ cannot be integrated by parts.

**409.** $\int \frac{1}{x^4+1}dx$ cannot be integrated using partial fractions.

**410.** In numerical integration, increasing the number of points decreases the error.

**411.** Integration by parts can always yield the integral.

For the following exercises, evaluate the integral using the specified method.

**412.** $\int x^2 \sin(4x)dx$ using integration by parts

**413.** $\int \frac{1}{x^2\sqrt{x^2+16}}dx$ using trigonometric substitution

**414.** $\int \sqrt{x}\ln(x)dx$ using integration by parts

**415.** $\int \frac{3x}{x^3+2x^2-5x-6}dx$ using partial fractions

**416.** $\int \frac{x^5}{\left(4x^2+4\right)^{5/2}}dx$ using trigonometric substitution

**417.** $\int \frac{\sqrt{4-\sin^2(x)}}{\sin^2(x)}\cos(x)dx$ using a table of integrals or a CAS

For the following exercises, integrate using whatever method you choose.

**418.** $\int \sin^2(x)\cos^2(x)dx$

**419.** $\int x^3\sqrt{x^2+2}dx$

**420.** $\int \frac{3x^2+1}{x^4-2x^3-x^2+2x}dx$

**421.** $\int \frac{1}{x^4+4}dx$

**422.** $\int \frac{\sqrt{3+16x^4}}{x^4}dx$

For the following exercises, approximate the integrals using the midpoint rule, trapezoidal rule, and Simpson's rule using four subintervals, rounding to three decimals.

**423. [T]** $\int_1^2 \sqrt{x^5+2}dx$

**424. [T]** $\int_0^{\sqrt{\pi}} e^{-\sin(x^2)}dx$

**425. [T]** $\int_1^4 \frac{\ln(1/x)}{x}dx$

For the following exercises, evaluate the integrals, if possible.

**426.** $\int_1^\infty \frac{1}{x^n}dx,$ for what values of $n$ does this integral converge or diverge?

**427.** $\int_1^\infty \frac{e^{-x}}{x}dx$

For the following exercises, consider the gamma function given by $\Gamma(a) = \int_0^\infty e^{-y}y^{a-1}dy.$

**428.** Show that $\Gamma(a) = (a-1)\Gamma(a-1).$

**429.** Extend to show that $\Gamma(a) = (a-1)!,$ assuming $a$ is a positive integer.

The fastest car in the world, the Bugati Veyron, can reach a top speed of 408 km/h. The graph represents its velocity.

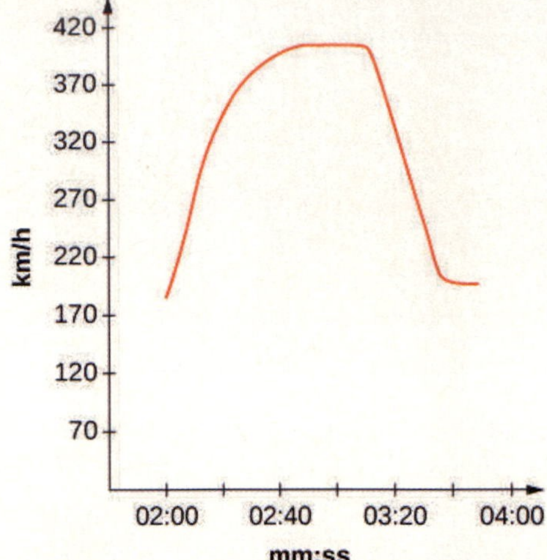


**430.** **[T]** Use the graph to estimate the velocity every 20 sec and fit to a graph of the form $v(t) = a\exp^{bx}\sin(cx) + d.$ (*Hint:* Consider the time units.)

**431.** **[T]** Using your function from the previous problem, find exactly how far the Bugati Veyron traveled in the 1 min 40 sec included in the graph.

# 4 | INTRODUCTION TO DIFFERENTIAL EQUATIONS

**Figure 4.1** The white-tailed deer (*Odocoileus virginianus*) of the eastern United States. Differential equations can be used to study animal populations. (credit: modification of work by Rachel Kramer, Flickr)

## Chapter Outline



## Introduction

Many real-world phenomena can be modeled mathematically by using differential equations. Population growth, radioactive decay, predator-prey models, and spring-mass systems are four examples of such phenomena. In this chapter we study some of these applications.

Suppose we wish to study a population of deer over time and determine the total number of animals in a given area. We can first observe the population over a period of time, estimate the total number of deer, and then use various assumptions to derive a mathematical model for different scenarios. Some factors that are often considered are environmental impact, threshold population values, and predators. In this chapter we see how differential equations can be used to predict populations over time (see **Example 4.14**).

Another goal of this chapter is to develop solution techniques for different types of differential equations. As the equations become more complicated, the solution techniques also become more complicated, and in fact an entire course could be dedicated to the study of these equations. In this chapter we study several types of differential equations and their corresponding methods of solution.

# 4.1 | Basics of Differential Equations

## Learning Objectives

**4.1.1** Identify the order of a differential equation.
**4.1.2** Explain what is meant by a solution to a differential equation.
**4.1.3** Distinguish between the general solution and a particular solution of a differential equation.
**4.1.4** Identify an initial-value problem.
**4.1.5** Identify whether a given function is a solution to a differential equation or an initial-value problem.

Calculus is the mathematics of change, and rates of change are expressed by derivatives. Thus, one of the most common ways to use calculus is to set up an equation containing an unknown function $y = f(x)$ and its derivative, known as a *differential equation*. Solving such equations often provides information about how quantities change and frequently provides insight into how and why the changes occur.

Techniques for solving differential equations can take many different forms, including direct solution, use of graphs, or computer calculations. We introduce the main ideas in this chapter and describe them in a little more detail later in the course. In this section we study what differential equations are, how to verify their solutions, some methods that are used for solving them, and some examples of common and useful equations.

## General Differential Equations

Consider the equation $y' = 3x^2$, which is an example of a differential equation because it includes a derivative. There is a relationship between the variables $x$ and $y$: $y$ is an unknown function of $x$. Furthermore, the left-hand side of the equation is the derivative of $y$. Therefore we can interpret this equation as follows: Start with some function $y = f(x)$ and take its derivative. The answer must be equal to $3x^2$. What function has a derivative that is equal to $3x^2$? One such function is $y = x^3$, so this function is considered a **solution to a differential equation**.

### Definition

A **differential equation** is an equation involving an unknown function $y = f(x)$ and one or more of its derivatives. A solution to a differential equation is a function $y = f(x)$ that satisfies the differential equation when $f$ and its derivatives are substituted into the equation.

Go to this **website (http://www.openstaxcollege.org/l/20_Differential)** to explore more on this topic.

Some examples of differential equations and their solutions appear in **Table 4.1**.

| Equation | Solution |
|---|---|
| $y' = 2x$ | $y = x^2$ |
| $y' + 3y = 6x + 11$ | $y = e^{-3x} + 2x + 3$ |
| $y'' - 3y' + 2y = 24e^{-2x}$ | $y = 3e^x - 4e^{2x} + 2e^{-2x}$ |

**Table 4.1** Examples of Differential Equations and Their Solutions

Note that a solution to a differential equation is not necessarily unique, primarily because the derivative of a constant is zero. For example, $y = x^2 + 4$ is also a solution to the first differential equation in **Table 4.1**. We will return to this idea a little bit later in this section. For now, let's focus on what it means for a function to be a solution to a differential equation.

## Example 4.1

### Verifying Solutions of Differential Equations

Verify that the function $y = e^{-3x} + 2x + 3$ is a solution to the differential equation $y' + 3y = 6x + 11$.

#### Solution

To verify the solution, we first calculate $y'$ using the chain rule for derivatives. This gives $y' = -3e^{-3x} + 2$. Next we substitute $y$ and $y'$ into the left-hand side of the differential equation:

$$(-3e^{-2x} + 2) + 3(e^{-2x} + 2x + 3).$$

The resulting expression can be simplified by first distributing to eliminate the parentheses, giving

$$-3e^{-2x} + 2 + 3e^{-2x} + 6x + 9.$$

Combining like terms leads to the expression $6x + 11,$ which is equal to the right-hand side of the differential equation. This result verifies that $y = e^{-3x} + 2x + 3$ is a solution of the differential equation.

**4.1** Verify that $y = 2e^{3x} - 2x - 2$ is a solution to the differential equation $y' - 3y = 6x + 4$.

It is convenient to define characteristics of differential equations that make it easier to talk about them and categorize them. The most basic characteristic of a differential equation is its order.

#### Definition

The **order of a differential equation** is the highest order of any derivative of the unknown function that appears in the equation.

## Example 4.2

### Identifying the Order of a Differential Equation

What is the order of each of the following differential equations?

a. $y' - 4y = x^2 - 3x + 4$

b. $x^2 y''' - 3xy'' + xy' - 3y = \sin x$

c. $\frac{4}{x}y^{(4)} - \frac{6}{x^2}y'' + \frac{12}{x^4}y = x^3 - 3x^2 + 4x - 12$

#### Solution

a. The highest derivative in the equation is $y'$, so the order is $1$.

b. The highest derivative in the equation is $y'''$, so the order is $3$.

c. The highest derivative in the equation is $y^{(4)}$, so the order is $4$.

**4.2** What is the order of the following differential equation?

$$\left(x^4 - 3x\right)y^{(5)} - \left(3x^2 + 1\right)y' + 3y = \sin x \cos x$$

## General and Particular Solutions

We already noted that the differential equation $y' = 2x$ has at least two solutions: $y = x^2$ and $y = x^2 + 4$. The only difference between these two solutions is the last term, which is a constant. What if the last term is a different constant? Will this expression still be a solution to the differential equation? In fact, any function of the form $y = x^2 + C$, where $C$ represents any constant, is a solution as well. The reason is that the derivative of $x^2 + C$ is $2x$, regardless of the value of $C$. It can be shown that any solution of this differential equation must be of the form $y = x^2 + C$. This is an example of a **general solution** to a differential equation. A graph of some of these solutions is given in Figure 4.2. (*Note*: in this graph we used even integer values for $C$ ranging between $-4$ and $4$. In fact, there is no restriction on the value of $C$; it can be an integer or not.)

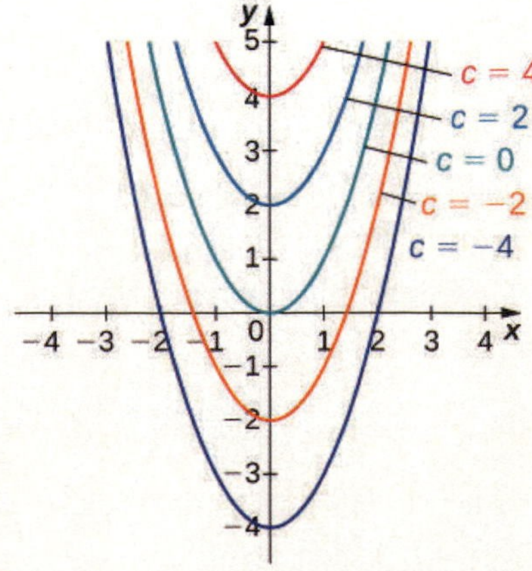


Figure 4.2 Family of solutions to the differential equation $y' = 2x$.

In this example, we are free to choose any solution we wish; for example, $y = x^2 - 3$ is a member of the family of solutions to this differential equation. This is called a **particular solution** to the differential equation. A particular solution can often be uniquely identified if we are given additional information about the problem.

## Example 4.3

### Finding a Particular Solution

Find the particular solution to the differential equation $y' = 2x$ passing through the point $(2, 7)$.

#### Solution

Any function of the form $y = x^2 + C$ is a solution to this differential equation. To determine the value of $C$, we substitute the values $x = 2$ and $y = 7$ into this equation and solve for $C$:

$$\begin{aligned} y &= x^2 + C \\ 7 &= 2^2 + C = 4 + C \\ C &= 3. \end{aligned}$$

Therefore the particular solution passing through the point $(2, 7)$ is $y = x^2 + 3$.

**4.3** Find the particular solution to the differential equation

$$y' = 4x + 3$$

passing through the point $(1, 7)$, given that $y = 2x^2 + 3x + C$ is a general solution to the differential equation.

## Initial-Value Problems

Usually a given differential equation has an infinite number of solutions, so it is natural to ask which one we want to use. To choose one solution, more information is needed. Some specific information that can be useful is an **initial value**, which is an ordered pair that is used to find a particular solution.

A differential equation together with one or more initial values is called an **initial-value problem**. The general rule is that the number of initial values needed for an initial-value problem is equal to the order of the differential equation. For example, if we have the differential equation $y' = 2x$, then $y(3) = 7$ is an initial value, and when taken together, these equations form an initial-value problem. The differential equation $y'' - 3y' + 2y = 4e^x$ is second order, so we need two initial values. With initial-value problems of order greater than one, the same value should be used for the independent variable. An example of initial values for this second-order equation would be $y(0) = 2$ and $y'(0) = -1$. These two initial values together with the differential equation form an initial-value problem. These problems are so named because often the independent variable in the unknown function is $t$, which represents time. Thus, a value of $t = 0$ represents the beginning of the problem.

## Example 4.4

### Verifying a Solution to an Initial-Value Problem

Verify that the function $y = 2e^{-2t} + e^t$ is a solution to the initial-value problem

$$y' + 2y = 3e^t, \quad y(0) = 3.$$

### Solution

For a function to satisfy an initial-value problem, it must satisfy both the differential equation and the initial condition. To show that $y$ satisfies the differential equation, we start by calculating $y'$. This gives $y' = -4e^{-2t} + e^t$. Next we substitute both $y$ and $y'$ into the left-hand side of the differential equation and simplify:

$$\begin{aligned} y' + 2y &= \left(-4e^{-2t} + e^t\right) + 2\left(2e^{-2t} + e^t\right) \\ &= -4e^{-2t} + e^t + 4e^{-2t} + 2e^t \\ &= 3e^t. \end{aligned}$$

This is equal to the right-hand side of the differential equation, so $y = 2e^{-2t} + e^t$ solves the differential equation. Next we calculate $y(0)$:

$$\begin{aligned} y(0) &= 2e^{-2(0)} + e^0 \\ &= 2 + 1 \\ &= 3. \end{aligned}$$

This result verifies the initial value. Therefore the given function satisfies the initial-value problem.

**4.4** Verify that $y = 3e^{2t} + 4\sin t$ is a solution to the initial-value problem

$$y' - 2y = 4\cos t - 8\sin t, \quad y(0) = 3.$$

In **Example 4.4**, the initial-value problem consisted of two parts. The first part was the differential equation $y' + 2y = 3e^x$, and the second part was the initial value $y(0) = 3$. These two equations together formed the initial-value problem.

The same is true in general. An initial-value problem will consists of two parts: the differential equation and the initial condition. The differential equation has a family of solutions, and the initial condition determines the value of $C$. The family of solutions to the differential equation in **Example 4.4** is given by $y = 2e^{-2t} + Ce^t$. This family of solutions is shown in **Figure 4.3**, with the particular solution $y = 2e^{-2t} + e^t$ labeled.

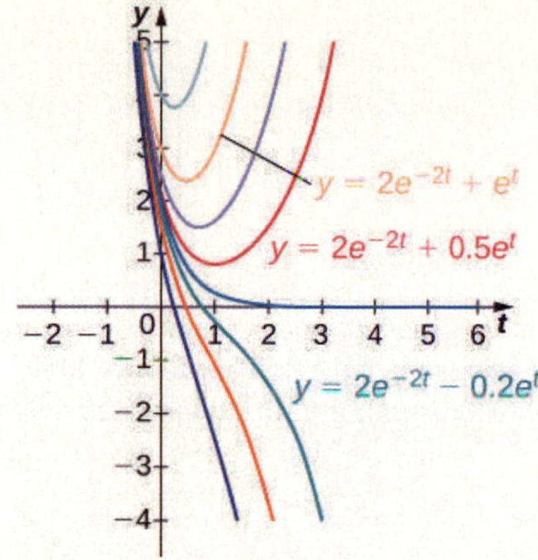


**Figure 4.3** A family of solutions to the differential equation $y' + 2y = 3e^t$. The particular solution $y = 2e^{-2t} + e^t$ is labeled.

## Example 4.5

### Solving an Initial-value Problem

Solve the following initial-value problem:

$$y' = 3e^x + x^2 - 4, \quad y(0) = 5.$$

#### Solution

The first step in solving this initial-value problem is to find a general family of solutions. To do this, we find an antiderivative of both sides of the differential equation

$$\int y'\,dx = \int \left(3e^x + x^2 - 4\right)dx,$$

namely,

$$y + C_1 = 3e^x + \frac{1}{3}x^3 - 4x + C_2. \tag{4.1}$$

We are able to integrate both sides because the $y$ term appears by itself. Notice that there are two integration constants: $C_1$ and $C_2$. Solving **Equation 4.1** for $y$ gives

$$y = 3e^x + \frac{1}{3}x^3 - 4x + C_2 - C_1.$$

Because $C_1$ and $C_2$ are both constants, $C_2 - C_1$ is also a constant. We can therefore define $C = C_2 - C_1$, which leads to the equation

$$y = 3e^x + \frac{1}{3}x^3 - 4x + C.$$

Next we determine the value of $C$. To do this, we substitute $x = 0$ and $y = 5$ into **Equation 4.1** and solve for $C$:

$$\begin{aligned} 5 &= 3e^0 + \frac{1}{3}0^3 - 4(0) + C \\ 5 &= 3 + C \\ C &= 2. \end{aligned}$$

Now we substitute the value $C = 2$ into **Equation 4.1**. The solution to the initial-value problem is $y = 3e^x + \frac{1}{3}x^3 - 4x + 2.$

**Analysis**

The difference between a general solution and a particular solution is that a general solution involves a family of functions, either explicitly or implicitly defined, of the independent variable. The initial value or values determine which particular solution in the family of solutions satisfies the desired conditions.

**4.5** Solve the initial-value problem

$$y' = x^2 - 4x + 3 - 6e^x, \quad y(0) = 8.$$

In physics and engineering applications, we often consider the forces acting upon an object, and use this information to understand the resulting motion that may occur. For example, if we start with an object at Earth's surface, the primary force acting upon that object is gravity. Physicists and engineers can use this information, along with Newton's second law of motion (in equation form $F = ma$, where $F$ represents force, $m$ represents mass, and $a$ represents acceleration), to derive an equation that can be solved.

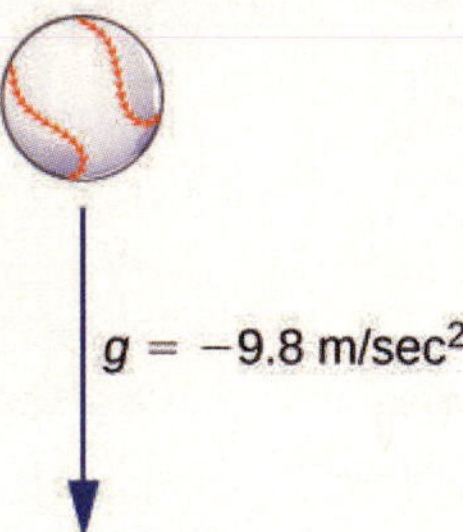


**Figure 4.4** For a baseball falling in air, the only force acting on it is gravity (neglecting air resistance).

In **Figure 4.4** we assume that the only force acting on a baseball is the force of gravity. This assumption ignores air resistance. (The force due to air resistance is considered in a later discussion.) The acceleration due to gravity at Earth's surface, $g$, is approximately $9.8 \text{ m/s}^2$. We introduce a frame of reference, where Earth's surface is at a height of 0 meters. Let $v(t)$ represent the velocity of the object in meters per second. If $v(t) > 0$, the ball is rising, and if $v(t) < 0$, the ball is falling (**Figure 4.5**).

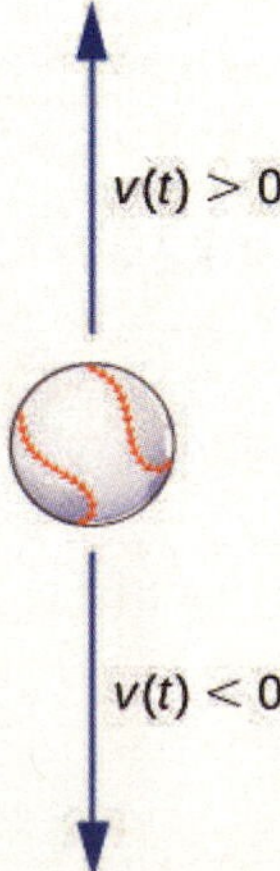


**Figure 4.5** Possible velocities for the rising/falling baseball.

Our goal is to solve for the velocity $v(t)$ at any time $t$. To do this, we set up an initial-value problem. Suppose the mass of the ball is $m$, where $m$ is measured in kilograms. We use Newton's second law, which states that the force acting on an object is equal to its mass times its acceleration $(F = ma)$. Acceleration is the derivative of velocity, so $a(t) = v'(t)$. Therefore the force acting on the baseball is given by $F = m\,v'(t)$. However, this force must be equal to the force of gravity acting on the object, which (again using Newton's second law) is given by $F_g = -mg$, since this force acts in a downward direction. Therefore we obtain the equation $F = F_g$, which becomes $m\,v'(t) = -mg$. Dividing both sides of the equation by $m$ gives the equation

$$v'(t) = -g.$$

Notice that this differential equation remains the same regardless of the mass of the object.

We now need an initial value. Because we are solving for velocity, it makes sense in the context of the problem to assume that we know the **initial velocity**, or the velocity at time $t = 0$. This is denoted by $v(0) = v_0$.

## Example 4.6

### Velocity of a Moving Baseball

A baseball is thrown upward from a height of $3$ meters above Earth's surface with an initial velocity of $10$ m/s, and the only force acting on it is gravity. The ball has a mass of $0.15$ kg at Earth's surface.

a. Find the velocity $v(t)$ of the baseball at time $t$.

b. What is its velocity after $2$ seconds?

### Solution

a. From the preceding discussion, the differential equation that applies in this situation is

$$v'(t) = -g,$$

where $g = 9.8\text{ m/s}^2$. The initial condition is $v(0) = v_0$, where $v_0 = 10$ m/s. Therefore the initial-value problem is $v'(t) = -9.8\text{ m/s}^2$, $v(0) = 10$ m/s.

The first step in solving this initial-value problem is to take the antiderivative of both sides of the differential equation. This gives

$$\begin{aligned} \int v'(t)\,dt &= \int -9.8\,dt \\ v(t) &= -9.8t + C. \end{aligned}$$

The next step is to solve for $C$. To do this, substitute $t = 0$ and $v(0) = 10$:

$$\begin{aligned} v(t) &= -9.8t + C \\ v(0) &= -9.8(0) + C \\ 10 &= C. \end{aligned}$$

Therefore $C = 10$ and the velocity function is given by $v(t) = -9.8t + 10$.

b. To find the velocity after $2$ seconds, substitute $t = 2$ into $v(t)$.

$$\begin{aligned} v(t) &= -9.8t + 10 \\ v(2) &= -9.8(2) + 10 \\ v(2) &= -9.6. \end{aligned}$$

The units of velocity are meters per second. Since the answer is negative, the object is falling at a speed of $9.6$ m/s.

**4.6** Suppose a rock falls from rest from a height of $100$ meters and the only force acting on it is gravity. Find an equation for the velocity $v(t)$ as a function of time, measured in meters per second.

A natural question to ask after solving this type of problem is how high the object will be above Earth's surface at a given point in time. Let $s(t)$ denote the height above Earth's surface of the object, measured in meters. Because velocity is the derivative of position (in this case height), this assumption gives the equation $s'(t) = v(t)$. An initial value is necessary; in this case the initial height of the object works well. Let the initial height be given by the equation $s(0) = s_0$. Together these assumptions give the initial-value problem

$$s'(t) = v(t), \quad s(0) = s_0.$$

If the velocity function is known, then it is possible to solve for the position function as well.

## Example 4.7

### Height of a Moving Baseball

A baseball is thrown upward from a height of $3$ meters above Earth's surface with an initial velocity of $10$ m/s, and the only force acting on it is gravity. The ball has a mass of $0.15$ kilogram at Earth's surface.

a. Find the position $s(t)$ of the baseball at time $t$.

b. What is its height after $2$ seconds?

### Solution

a. We already know the velocity function for this problem is $v(t) = -9.8t + 10$. The initial height of the baseball is $3$ meters, so $s_0 = 3$. Therefore the initial-value problem for this example is

To solve the initial-value problem, we first find the antiderivatives:

$$\begin{aligned} \int s'(t)\,dt &= \int -9.8t + 10\,dt \\ s(t) &= -4.9t^2 + 10t + C. \end{aligned}$$

Next we substitute $t = 0$ and solve for $C$:

$$\begin{aligned} s(t) &= -4.9t^2 + 10t + C \\ s(0) &= -4.9(0)^2 + 10(0) + C \\ 3 &= C. \end{aligned}$$

Therefore the position function is $s(t) = -4.9t^2 + 10t + 3.$

b. The height of the baseball after $2$ s is given by $s(2)$:

$$\begin{aligned} s(2) &= -4.9(2)^2 + 10(2) + 3 \\ &= -4.9(4) + 23 \\ &= 3.4. \end{aligned}$$

Therefore the baseball is $3.4$ meters above Earth's surface after $2$ seconds. It is worth noting that the mass of the ball cancelled out completely in the process of solving the problem.

# 4.1 EXERCISES

Determine the order of the following differential equations.

1. $y' + y = 3y^2$

2. $(y')^2 = y' + 2y$

3. $y''' + y''y' = 3x^2$

4. $y' = y'' + 3t^2$

5. $\frac{dy}{dt} = t$

6. $\frac{dy}{dx} + \frac{d^2y}{dx^2} = 3x^4$

7. $\left(\frac{dy}{dt}\right)^2 + 8\frac{dy}{dt} + 3y = 4t$

Verify that the following functions are solutions to the given differential equation.

8. $y = \frac{x^3}{3}$ solves $y' = x^2$

9. $y = 2e^{-x} + x - 1$ solves $y' = x - y$

10. $y = e^{3x} - \frac{e^x}{2}$ solves $y' = 3y + e^x$

11. $y = \frac{1}{1 - x}$ solves $y' = y^2$

12. $y = e^{x^2/2}$ solves $y' = xy$

13. $y = 4 + \ln x$ solves $xy' = 1$

14. $y = 3 - x + x\ln x$ solves $y' = \ln x$

15. $y = 2e^x - x - 1$ solves $y' = y + x$

16. $y = e^x + \frac{\sin x}{2} - \frac{\cos x}{2}$ solves $y' = \cos x + y$

17. $y = \pi e^{-\cos x}$ solves $y' = y\sin x$

Verify the following general solutions and find the particular solution.

18. Find the particular solution to the differential equation $y' = 4x^2$ that passes through $(-3, -30)$, given that $y = C + \frac{4x^3}{3}$ is a general solution.

19. Find the particular solution to the differential equation $y' = 3x^3$ that passes through $(1, 4.75)$, given that $y = C + \frac{3x^4}{4}$ is a general solution.

20. Find the particular solution to the differential equation $y' = 3x^2 y$ that passes through $(0, 12)$, given that $y = Ce^{x^3}$ is a general solution.

21. Find the particular solution to the differential equation $y' = 2xy$ that passes through $\left(0, \frac{1}{2}\right)$, given that $y = Ce^{x^2}$ is a general solution.

22. Find the particular solution to the differential equation $y' = (2xy)^2$ that passes through $\left(1, -\frac{1}{2}\right)$, given that $y = -\frac{3}{C + 4x^3}$ is a general solution.

23. Find the particular solution to the differential equation $y'x^2 = y$ that passes through $\left(1, \frac{2}{e}\right)$, given that $y = Ce^{-1/x}$ is a general solution.

24. Find the particular solution to the differential equation $8\frac{dx}{dt} = -2\cos(2t) - \cos(4t)$ that passes through $(\pi, \pi)$, given that $x = C - \frac{1}{8}\sin(2t) - \frac{1}{32}\sin(4t)$ is a general solution.

25. Find the particular solution to the differential equation $\frac{du}{dt} = \tan u$ that passes through $\left(1, \frac{\pi}{2}\right)$, given that $u = \sin^{-1}\left(e^{C + t}\right)$ is a general solution.

26. Find the particular solution to the differential equation $\frac{dy}{dt} = e^{(t + y)}$ that passes through $(1, 0)$, given that $y = -\ln(C - e^t)$ is a general solution.

27. Find the particular solution to the differential equation $y'(1 - x^2) = 1 + y$ that passes through $(0, -2)$, given that $y = C\frac{\sqrt{x + 1}}{\sqrt{1 - x}} - 1$ is a general solution.

For the following problems, find the general solution to the differential equation.

28. $y' = 3x + e^x$

29. $y' = \ln x + \tan x$

30. $y' = \sin x e^{\cos x}$

31. $y' = 4^x$

32. $y' = \sin^{-1}(2x)$

33. $y' = 2t\sqrt{t^2 + 16}$

34. $x' = \coth t + \ln t + 3t^2$

35. $x' = t\sqrt{4 + t}$

36. $y' = y$

37. $y' = \frac{y}{x}$

Solve the following initial-value problems starting from $y(t = 0) = 1$ and $y(t = 0) = -1$. Draw both solutions on the same graph.

38. $\frac{dy}{dt} = 2t$

39. $\frac{dy}{dt} = -t$

40. $\frac{dy}{dt} = 2y$

41. $\frac{dy}{dt} = -y$

42. $\frac{dy}{dt} = 2$

Solve the following initial-value problems starting from $y_0 = 10$. At what time does $y$ increase to $100$ or drop to $1$?

43. $\frac{dy}{dt} = 4t$

44. $\frac{dy}{dt} = 4y$

45. $\frac{dy}{dt} = -2y$

46. $\frac{dy}{dt} = e^{4t}$

47. $\frac{dy}{dt} = e^{-4t}$

Recall that a family of solutions includes solutions to a differential equation that differ by a constant. For the following problems, use your calculator to graph a family of solutions to the given differential equation. Use initial conditions from $y(t = 0) = -10$ to $y(t = 0) = 10$ increasing by $2$. Is there some critical point where the behavior of the solution begins to change?

48. **[T]** $y' = y(x)$

49. **[T]** $xy' = y$

50. **[T]** $y' = t^3$

51. **[T]** $y' = x + y$ (*Hint:* $y = Ce^x - x - 1$ is the general solution)

52. **[T]** $y' = x \ln x + \sin x$

53. Find the general solution to describe the velocity of a ball of mass $1$ lb that is thrown upward at a rate $a$ ft/sec.

54. In the preceding problem, if the initial velocity of the ball thrown into the air is $a = 25$ ft/s, write the particular solution to the velocity of the ball. Solve to find the time when the ball hits the ground.

55. You throw two objects with differing masses $m_1$ and $m_2$ upward into the air with the same initial velocity $a$ ft/s. What is the difference in their velocity after $1$ second?

56. **[T]** You throw a ball of mass $1$ kilogram upward with a velocity of $a = 25$ m/s on Mars, where the force of gravity is $g = -3.711$ m/s$^2$. Use your calculator to approximate how much longer the ball is in the air on Mars.

57. **[T]** For the previous problem, use your calculator to approximate how much higher the ball went on Mars.

58. **[T]** A car on the freeway accelerates according to $a = 15\cos(\pi t)$, where $t$ is measured in hours. Set up and solve the differential equation to determine the velocity of the car if it has an initial speed of $51$ mph. After $40$ minutes of driving, what is the driver's velocity?

59. **[T]** For the car in the preceding problem, find the expression for the distance the car has traveled in time $t$, assuming an initial distance of $0$. How long does it take the car to travel $100$ miles? Round your answer to hours and minutes.

60. **[T]** For the previous problem, find the total distance traveled in the first hour.

61. Substitute $y = Be^{3t}$ into $y' - y = 8e^{3t}$ to find a particular solution.

62. Substitute $y = a\cos(2t) + b\sin(2t)$ into $y' + y = 4\sin(2t)$ to find a particular solution.

63. Substitute $y = a + bt + ct^2$ into $y' + y = 1 + t^2$ to find a particular solution.

64. Substitute $y = ae^t\cos t + be^t\sin t$ into $y' = 2e^t\cos t$ to find a particular solution.

65. Solve $y' = e^{kt}$ with the initial condition $y(0) = 0$ and solve $y' = 1$ with the same initial condition. As $k$ approaches $0,$ what do you notice?

# 4.2 | Direction Fields and Numerical Methods

**Learning Objectives**

- **4.2.1** Draw the direction field for a given first-order differential equation.
- **4.2.2** Use a direction field to draw a solution curve of a first-order differential equation.
- **4.2.3** Use Euler's Method to approximate the solution to a first-order differential equation.

For the rest of this chapter we will focus on various methods for solving differential equations and analyzing the behavior of the solutions. In some cases it is possible to predict properties of a solution to a differential equation without knowing the actual solution. We will also study numerical methods for solving differential equations, which can be programmed by using various computer languages or even by using a spreadsheet program, such as Microsoft Excel.

## Creating Direction Fields

Direction fields (also called slope fields) are useful for investigating first-order differential equations. In particular, we consider a first-order differential equation of the form

$$y' = f(x, y).$$

An applied example of this type of differential equation appears in Newton's law of cooling, which we will solve explicitly later in this chapter. First, though, let us create a direction field for the differential equation

$$T'(t) = -0.4(T - 72).$$

Here $T(t)$ represents the temperature (in degrees Fahrenheit) of an object at time $t$, and the ambient temperature is $72°\text{F}$. **Figure 4.6** shows the direction field for this equation.

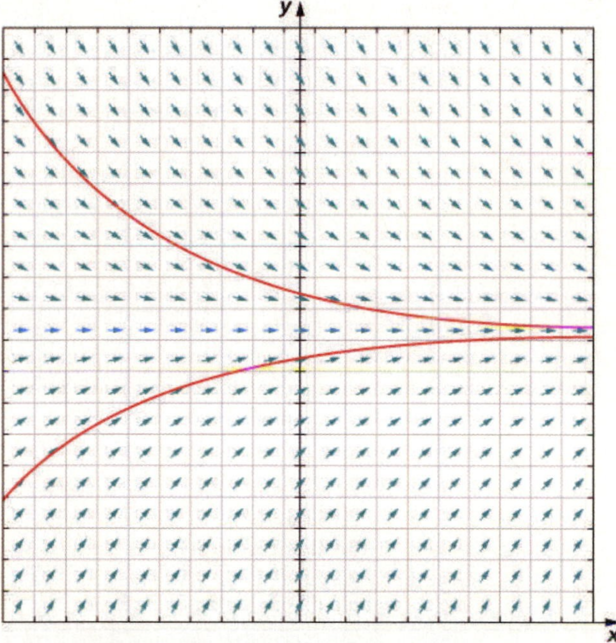


**Figure 4.6** Direction field for the differential equation $T'(t) = -0.4(T - 72)$. Two solutions are plotted: one with initial temperature less than $72°\text{F}$ and the other with initial temperature greater than $72°\text{F}$.

The idea behind a direction field is the fact that the derivative of a function evaluated at a given point is the slope of the tangent line to the graph of that function at the same point. Other examples of differential equations for which we can create a direction field include

$$y' = 3x + 2y - 4$$
$$y' = x^2 - y^2$$
$$y' = \frac{2x + 4}{y - 2}.$$

To create a direction field, we start with the first equation: $y' = 3x + 2y - 4$. We let $(x_0, y_0)$ be any ordered pair, and we substitute these numbers into the right-hand side of the differential equation. For example, if we choose $x = 1$ and $y = 2$, substituting into the right-hand side of the differential equation yields

$$\begin{aligned} y' &= 3x + 2y - 4 \\ &= 3(1) + 2(2) - 4 = 3. \end{aligned}$$

This tells us that if a solution to the differential equation $y' = 3x + 2y - 4$ passes through the point $(1, 2)$, then the slope of the solution at that point must equal $3$. To start creating the direction field, we put a short line segment at the point $(1, 2)$ having slope $3$. We can do this for any point in the domain of the function $f(x, y) = 3x + 2y - 4$, which consists of all ordered pairs $(x, y)$ in $\mathbb{R}^2$. Therefore any point in the Cartesian plane has a slope associated with it, assuming that a solution to the differential equation passes through that point. The direction field for the differential equation $y' = 3x + 2y - 4$ is shown in **Figure 4.7**.

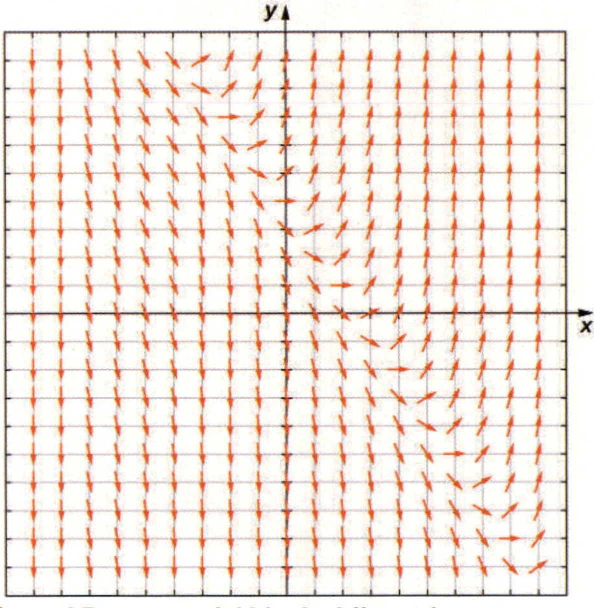


**Figure 4.7** Direction field for the differential equation $y' = 3x + 2y - 4$.

We can generate a direction field of this type for any differential equation of the form $y' = f(x, y)$.

### Definition

A **direction field (slope field)** is a mathematical object used to graphically represent solutions to a first-order differential equation. At each point in a direction field, a line segment appears whose slope is equal to the slope of a solution to the differential equation passing through that point.

## Using Direction Fields

We can use a direction field to predict the behavior of solutions to a differential equation without knowing the actual solution. For example, the direction field in **Figure 4.7** serves as a guide to the behavior of solutions to the differential equation $y' = 3x + 2y - 4$.

To use a direction field, we start by choosing any point in the field. The line segment at that point serves as a signpost telling us what direction to go from there. For example, if a solution to the differential equation passes through the point $(0, 1)$, then the slope of the solution passing through that point is given by $y' = 3(0) + 2(1) - 4 = -2$. Now let $x$ increase slightly, say to $x = 0.1$. Using the method of linear approximations gives a formula for the approximate value of $y$ for $x = 0.1$. In particular,

$$\begin{aligned} L(x) &= y_0 + f'(x_0)(x - x_0) \\ &= 1 - 2(x_0 - 0) \\ &= 1 - 2x_0. \end{aligned}$$

Substituting $x_0 = 0.1$ into $L(x)$ gives an approximate $y$ value of $0.8$.

At this point the slope of the solution changes (again according to the differential equation). We can keep progressing, recalculating the slope of the solution as we take small steps to the right, and watching the behavior of the solution. **Figure 4.8** shows a graph of the solution passing through the point $(0, 1)$.

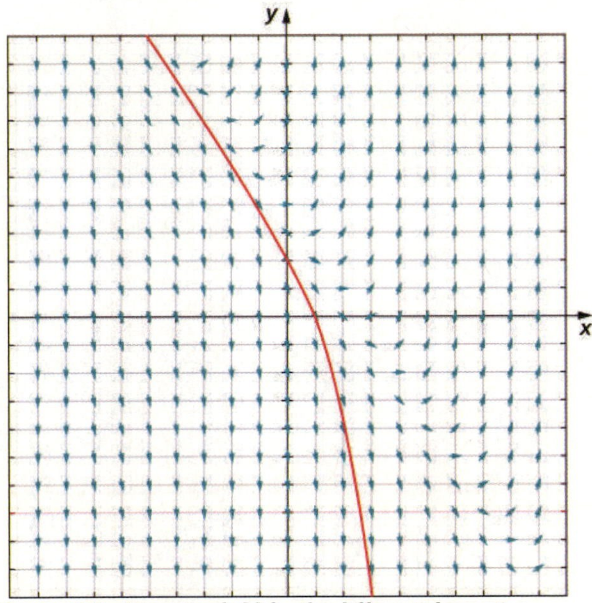


**Figure 4.8** Direction field for the differential equation $y' = 3x + 2y - 4$ with the solution passing through the point $(0, 1)$.

The curve is the graph of the solution to the initial-value problem

$$y' = 3x + 2y - 4, \quad y(0) = 1.$$

This curve is called a **solution curve** passing through the point $(0, 1)$. The exact solution to this initial-value problem is

$$y = -\frac{3}{2}x + \frac{5}{4} - \frac{1}{4}e^{2x},$$

and the graph of this solution is identical to the curve in **Figure 4.8**.

**4.7** Create a direction field for the differential equation $y' = x^2 - y^2$ and sketch a solution curve passing through the point $(-1, 2)$.

Go to this **Java applet (http://www.openstaxcollege.org/l/20_DifferEq)** and this **website (http://www.openstaxcollege.org/l/20_SlopeFields)** to see more about slope fields.

Now consider the direction field for the differential equation $y' = (x-3)(y^2-4)$, shown in **Figure 4.9**. This direction field has several interesting properties. First of all, at $y=-2$ and $y=2$, horizontal dashes appear all the way across the graph. This means that if $y=-2$, then $y'=0$. Substituting this expression into the right-hand side of the differential equation gives

$$\begin{aligned}(x-3)(y^2-4) &= (x-3)((^{-2}-4) \\ &= (x-3)(0) \\ &= 0 \\ &= y'.\end{aligned}$$

Therefore $y=-2$ is a solution to the differential equation. Similarly, $y=2$ is a solution to the differential equation. These are the only constant-valued solutions to the differential equation, as we can see from the following argument. Suppose $y=k$ is a constant solution to the differential equation. Then $y'=0$. Substituting this expression into the differential equation yields $0=(x-3)\left(k^2-4\right)$. This equation must be true for all values of $x$, so the second factor must equal zero. This result yields the equation $k^2-4=0$. The solutions to this equation are $k=-2$ and $k=2$, which are the constant solutions already mentioned. These are called the equilibrium solutions to the differential equation.

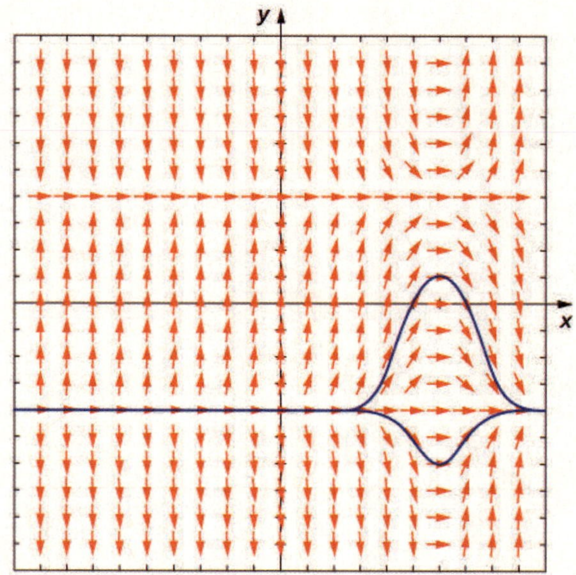


**Figure 4.9** Direction field for the differential equation $y' = (x-3)(y^2-4)$ showing two solutions. These solutions are very close together, but one is barely above the equilibrium solution $x=-2$ and the other is barely below the same equilibrium solution.

### Definition

Consider the differential equation $y' = f(x, y)$. An **equilibrium solution** is any solution to the differential equation of the form $y=c$, where $c$ is a constant.

To determine the equilibrium solutions to the differential equation $y' = f(x, y)$, set the right-hand side equal to zero. An equilibrium solution of the differential equation is any function of the form $y=k$ such that $f(x, k)=0$ for all values of $x$ in the domain of $f$.

An important characteristic of equilibrium solutions concerns whether or not they approach the line $y=k$ as an asymptote for large values of $x$.

### Definition

Consider the differential equation $y' = f(x, y)$, and assume that all solutions to this differential equation are defined for $x \geq x_0$. Let $y = k$ be an equilibrium solution to the differential equation.

1. $y = k$ is an **asymptotically stable solution** to the differential equation if there exists $\varepsilon > 0$ such that for any value $c \in (k - \varepsilon, k + \varepsilon)$ the solution to the initial-value problem

$$y' = f(x, y), \quad y(x_0) = c$$

approaches $k$ as $x$ approaches infinity.

2. $y = k$ is an **asymptotically unstable solution** to the differential equation if there exists $\varepsilon > 0$ such that for any value $c \in (k - \varepsilon, k + \varepsilon)$ the solution to the initial-value problem

$$y' = f(x, y), \quad y(x_0) = c$$

never approaches $k$ as $x$ approaches infinity.

3. $y = k$ is an **asymptotically semi-stable solution** to the differential equation if it is neither asymptotically stable nor asymptotically unstable.

Now we return to the differential equation $y' = (x - 3)(y^2 - 4)$, with the initial condition $y(0) = 0.5$. The direction field for this initial-value problem, along with the corresponding solution, is shown in **Figure 4.10**.

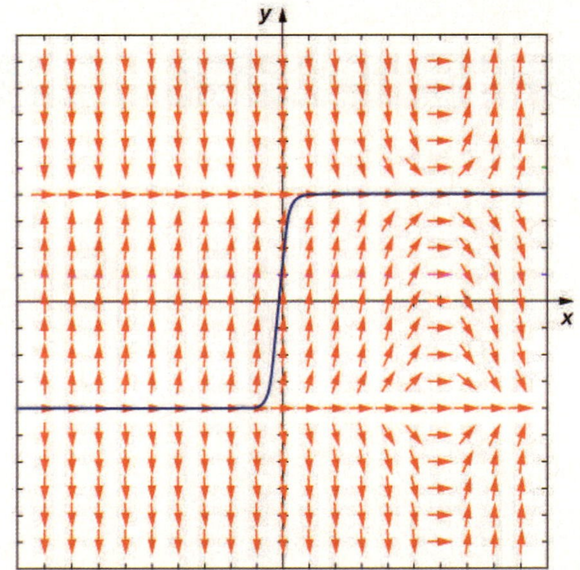


**Figure 4.10** Direction field for the initial-value problem $y' = (x - 3)(y^2 - 4), y(0) = 0.5$.

The values of the solution to this initial-value problem stay between $y = -2$ and $y = 2$, which are the equilibrium solutions to the differential equation. Furthermore, as $x$ approaches infinity, $y$ approaches 2. The behavior of solutions is similar if the initial value is higher than 2, for example, $y(0) = 2.3$. In this case, the solutions decrease and approach $y = 2$ as $x$ approaches infinity. Therefore $y = 2$ is an asymptotically stable solution to the differential equation.

What happens when the initial value is below $y = -2$? This scenario is illustrated in **Figure 4.11**, with the initial value $y(0) = -3$.

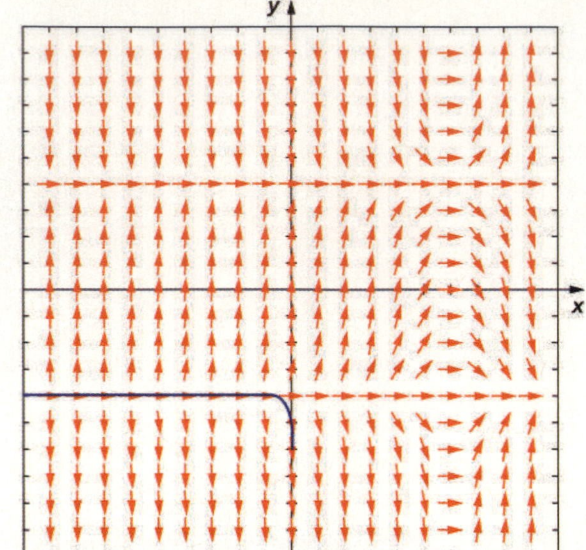


**Figure 4.11** Direction field for the initial-value problem $y' = (x-3)(y^2-4), \quad y(0) = -3$.

The solution decreases rapidly toward negative infinity as $x$ approaches infinity. Furthermore, if the initial value is slightly higher than $-2$, then the solution approaches $2$, which is the other equilibrium solution. Therefore in neither case does the solution approach $y = -2$, so $y = -2$ is called an asymptotically unstable, or unstable, equilibrium solution.

## Example 4.8

### Stability of an Equilibrium Solution

Create a direction field for the differential equation $y' = (y-3)^2(y^2+y-2)$ and identify any equilibrium solutions. Classify each of the equilibrium solutions as stable, unstable, or semi-stable.

#### Solution

The direction field is shown in **Figure 4.12**.

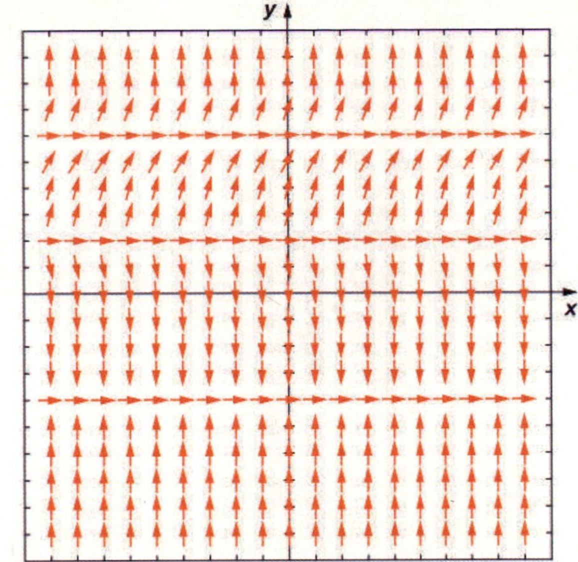


**Figure 4.12** Direction field for the differential equation $y' = (y-3)^2(y^2+y-2)$.

The equilibrium solutions are $y = -2$, $y = 1$, and $y = 3$. To classify each of the solutions, look at an arrow directly above or below each of these values. For example, at $y = -2$ the arrows directly below this solution point up, and the arrows directly above the solution point down. Therefore all initial conditions close to $y = -2$ approach $y = -2$, and the solution is stable. For the solution $y = 1$, all initial conditions above and below $y = 1$ are repelled (pushed away) from $y = 1$, so this solution is unstable. The solution $y = 3$ is semi-stable, because for initial conditions slightly greater than $3$, the solution approaches infinity, and for initial conditions slightly less than $3$, the solution approaches $y = 1$.

### Analysis

It is possible to find the equilibrium solutions to the differential equation by setting the right-hand side equal to zero and solving for $y$. This approach gives the same equilibrium solutions as those we saw in the direction field.

**4.8** Create a direction field for the differential equation $y' = (x+5)(y+2)(y^2-4y+4)$ and identify any equilibrium solutions. Classify each of the equilibrium solutions as stable, unstable, or semi-stable.

## Euler's Method

Consider the initial-value problem

$$y' = 2x - 3, \quad y(0) = 3.$$

Integrating both sides of the differential equation gives $y = x^2 - 3x + C$, and solving for $C$ yields the particular solution $y = x^2 - 3x + 3$. The solution for this initial-value problem appears as the parabola in **Figure 4.13**.

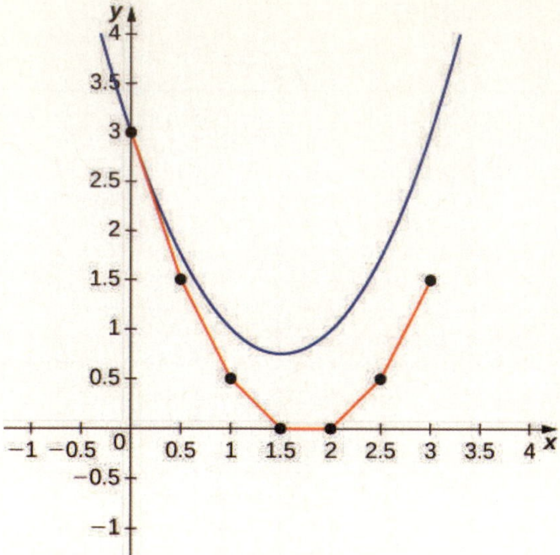


**Figure 4.13** Euler's Method for the initial-value problem $y' = 2x - 3, \quad y(0) = 3.$

The red graph consists of line segments that approximate the solution to the initial-value problem. The graph starts at the same initial value of $(0, 3)$. Then the slope of the solution at any point is determined by the right-hand side of the differential equation, and the length of the line segment is determined by increasing the $x$ value by $0.5$ each time (the *step size*). This approach is the basis of Euler's Method.

Before we state Euler's Method as a theorem, let's consider another initial-value problem:

$$y' = x^2 - y^2, \quad y(-1) = 2.$$

The idea behind direction fields can also be applied to this problem to study the behavior of its solution. For example, at the point $(-1, 2),$ the slope of the solution is given by $y' = (-1)^2 - 2^2 = -3,$ so the slope of the tangent line to the solution at that point is also equal to $-3.$ Now we define $x_0 = -1$ and $y_0 = 2.$ Since the slope of the solution at this point is equal to $-3,$ we can use the method of linear approximation to approximate $y$ near $(-1, 2).$

$$L(x) = y_0 + f'(x_0)(x - x_0).$$

Here $x_0 = -1, y_0 = 2,$ and $f'(x_0) = -3,$ so the linear approximation becomes

$$\begin{aligned} L(x) &= 2 - 3(x - (-1)) \\ &= 2 - 3x - 3 \\ &= -3x - 1. \end{aligned}$$

Now we choose a **step size**. The step size is a small value, typically $0.1$ or less, that serves as an increment for $x;$ it is represented by the variable $h.$ In our example, let $h = 0.1.$ Incrementing $x_0$ by $h$ gives our next $x$ value:

$$x_1 = x_0 + h = -1 + 0.1 = -0.9.$$

We can substitute $x_1 = -0.9$ into the linear approximation to calculate $y_1.$

$$\begin{aligned} y_1 &= L(x_1) \\ &= -3(-0.9) - 1 \\ &= 1.7. \end{aligned}$$

Therefore the approximate $y$ value for the solution when $x = -0.9$ is $y = 1.7.$ We can then repeat the process, using $x_1 = -0.9$ and $y_1 = 1.7$ to calculate $x_2$ and $y_2.$ The new slope is given by $y' = (-0.9)^2 - (1.7)^2 = -2.08.$ First, $x_2 = x_1 + h = -0.9 + 0.1 = -0.8.$ Using linear approximation gives

$$\begin{aligned} L(x) &= y_1 + f'(x_1)(x - x_1) \\ &= 1.7 - 2.08(x - (-0.9)) \\ &= 1.7 - 2.08x - 1.872 \\ &= -2.08x - 0.172. \end{aligned}$$

Finally, we substitute $x_2 = -0.8$ into the linear approximation to calculate $y_2$.

$$\begin{aligned} y_2 &= L(x_2) \\ &= -2.08x_2 - 0.172 \\ &= -2.08(-0.8) - 0.172 \\ &= 1.492. \end{aligned}$$

Therefore the approximate value of the solution to the differential equation is $y = 1.492$ when $x = -0.8$.

What we have just shown is the idea behind **Euler's Method**. Repeating these steps gives a list of values for the solution. These values are shown in **Table 4.2**, rounded off to four decimal places.

| $n$ | 0 | 1 | 2 | 3 | 4 | 5 |
|---|---|---|---|---|---|---|
| $x_n$ | −1 | −0.9 | −0.8 | −0.7 | −0.6 | −0.5 |
| $y_n$ | 2 | 1.7 | 1.492 | 1.3334 | 1.2046 | 1.0955 |
| $n$ | 6 | 7 | 8 | 9 | 10 | |
| $x_n$ | −0.4 | −0.3 | −0.2 | −0.1 | 0 | |
| $y_n$ | 1.0004 | 1.9164 | 1.8414 | 1.7746 | 1.7156 | |

**Table 4.2** Using Euler's Method to Approximate Solutions to a Differential Equation

### Theorem 4.1: Euler's Method

Consider the initial-value problem

$y' = f(x, y), \quad y(x_0) = y_0.$

To approximate a solution to this problem using Euler's method, define

$$\begin{aligned} x_n &= x_0 + nh \\ y_n &= y_{n-1} + hf(x_{n-1}, y_{n-1}). \end{aligned} \tag{4.2}$$

Here $h > 0$ represents the step size and $n$ is an integer, starting with $1$. The number of steps taken is counted by the variable $n$.

Typically $h$ is a small value, say $0.1$ or $0.05$. The smaller the value of $h$, the more calculations are needed. The higher the value of $h$, the fewer calculations are needed. However, the tradeoff results in a lower degree of accuracy for larger step size, as illustrated in **Figure 4.14**.

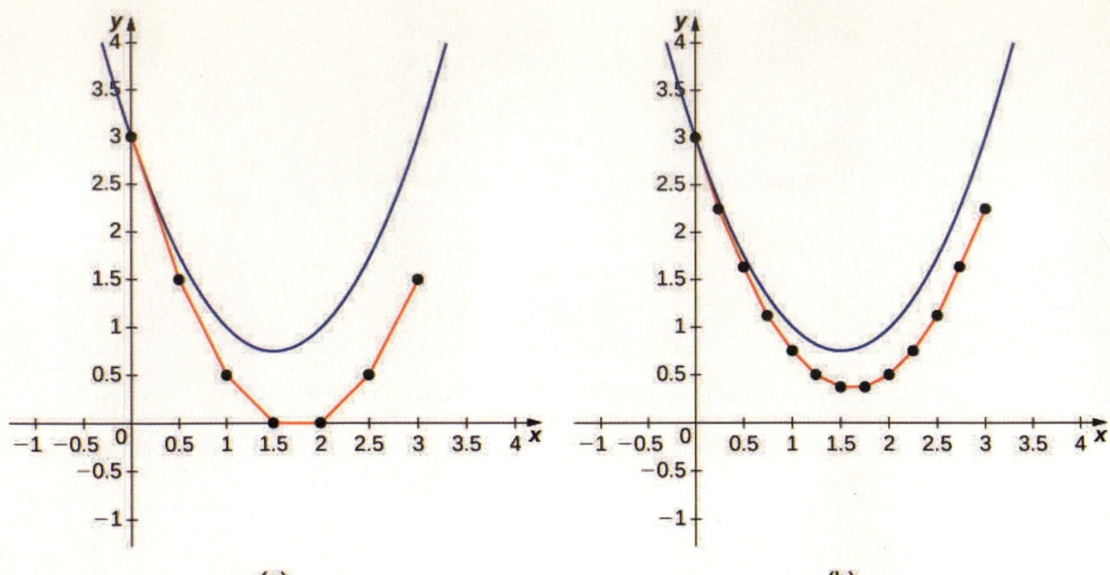


**Figure 4.14** Euler's method for the initial-value problem $y' = 2x - 3,\ y(0) = 3$ with (a) a step size of $h = 0.5$; and (b) a step size of $h = 0.25$.

## Example 4.9

### Using Euler's Method

Consider the initial-value problem

$$y' = 3x^2 - y^2 + 1, \quad y(0) = 2.$$

Use Euler's method with a step size of $0.1$ to generate a table of values for the solution for values of $x$ between $0$ and $1$.

#### Solution

We are given $h = 0.1$ and $f(x, y) = 3x^2 - y^2 + 1$. Furthermore, the initial condition $y(0) = 2$ gives $x_0 = 0$ and $y_0 = 2$. Using **Equation 4.2** with $n = 0$, we can generate **Table 4.3**.

| $n$ | $x_n$ | $y_n = y_{n-1} + hf(x_{n-1}, y_{n-1})$ |
|---|---|---|
| 0 | 0 | 2 |
| 1 | 0.1 | $y_1 = y_0 + hf(x_0, y_0) = 1.7$ |
| 2 | 0.2 | $y_2 = y_1 + hf(x_1, y_1) = 1.514$ |
| 3 | 0.3 | $y_3 = y_2 + hf(x_2, y_2) = 1.3968$ |
| 4 | 0.4 | $y_4 = y_3 + hf(x_3, y_3) = 1.3287$ |
| 5 | 0.5 | $y_5 = y_4 + hf(x_4, y_4) = 1.3001$ |
| 6 | 0.6 | $y_6 = y_5 + hf(x_5, y_5) = 1.3061$ |
| 7 | 0.7 | $y_7 = y_6 + hf(x_6, y_6) = 1.3435$ |
| 8 | 0.8 | $y_8 = y_7 + hf(x_7, y_7) = 1.4100$ |
| 9 | 0.9 | $y_9 = y_8 + hf(x_8, y_8) = 1.5032$ |
| 10 | 1.0 | $y_{10} = y_9 + hf(x_9, y_9) = 1.6202$ |

**Table 4.3**
Using Euler's Method to Approximate Solutions to a Differential Equation

With ten calculations, we are able to approximate the values of the solution to the initial-value problem for values of $x$ between $0$ and $1.$

Go to this **website (http://www.openstaxcollege.org/l/20_EulersMethod)** for more information on Euler's method.

**4.9** Consider the initial-value problem

$$y' = x^3 + y^2, \quad y(1) = -2.$$

Using a step size of $0.1$, generate a table with approximate values for the solution to the initial-value problem for values of $x$ between $1$ and $2$.

Visit this **website (http://www.openstaxcollege.org/l/20_EulerMethod2)** for a practical application of the material in this section.

# 4.2 EXERCISES

For the following problems, use the direction field below from the differential equation $y' = -2y$. Sketch the graph of the solution for the given initial conditions.

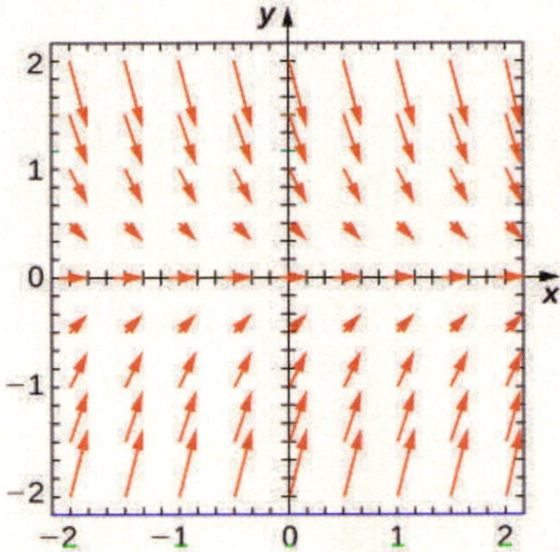

66. $y(0) = 1$

67. $y(0) = 0$

68. $y(0) = -1$

69. Are there any equilibria? What are their stabilities?

For the following problems, use the direction field below from the differential equation $y' = y^2 - 2y$. Sketch the graph of the solution for the given initial conditions.

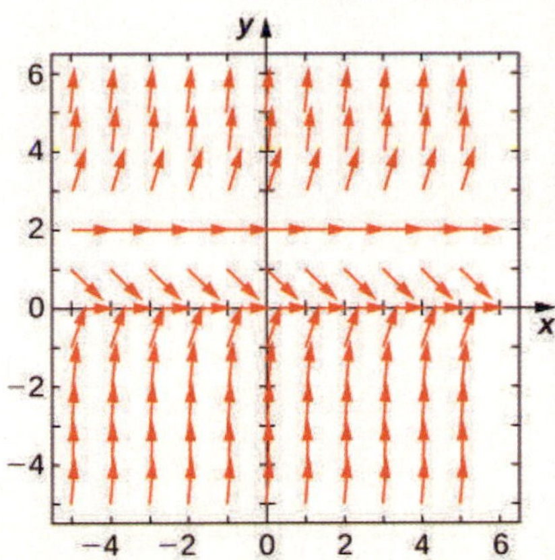

70. $y(0) = 3$

71. $y(0) = 1$

72. $y(0) = -1$

73. Are there any equilibria? What are their stabilities?

Draw the direction field for the following differential equations, then solve the differential equation. Draw your solution on top of the direction field. Does your solution follow along the arrows on your direction field?

74. $y' = t^3$

75. $y' = e^t$

76. $\dfrac{dy}{dx} = x^2 \cos x$

77. $\dfrac{dy}{dt} = te^t$

78. $\dfrac{dx}{dt} = \cosh(t)$

Draw the directional field for the following differential equations. What can you say about the behavior of the solution? Are there equilibria? What stability do these equilibria have?

79. $y' = y^2 - 1$

80. $y' = y - x$

81. $y' = 1 - y^2 - x^2$

82. $y' = t^2 \sin y$

83. $y' = 3y + xy$

Match the direction field with the given differential equations. Explain your selections.

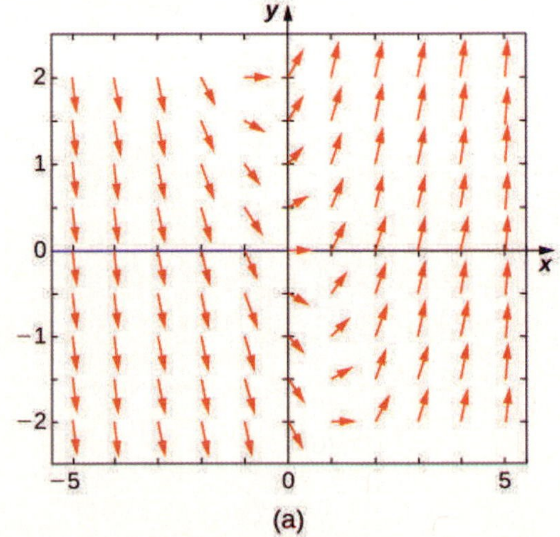
(a)

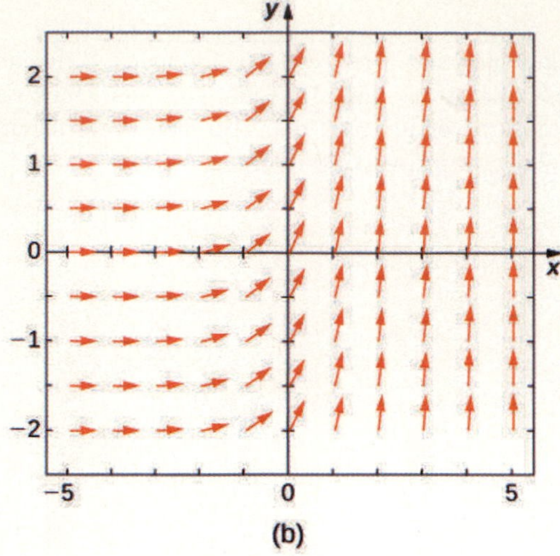

(b)

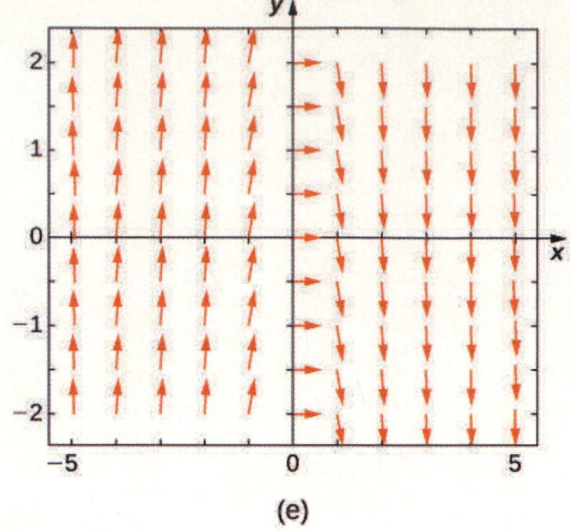

(e)

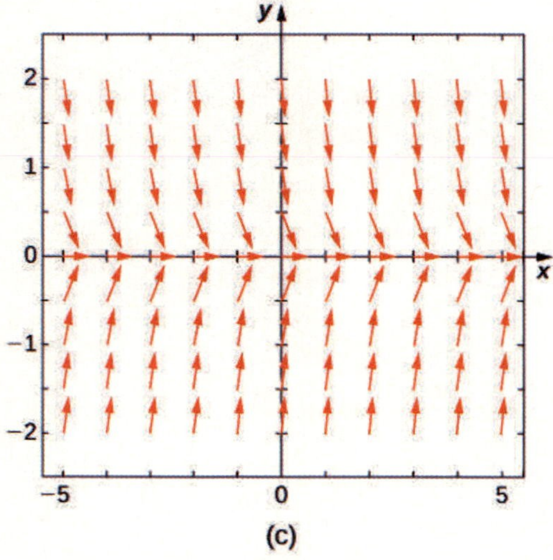

(c)

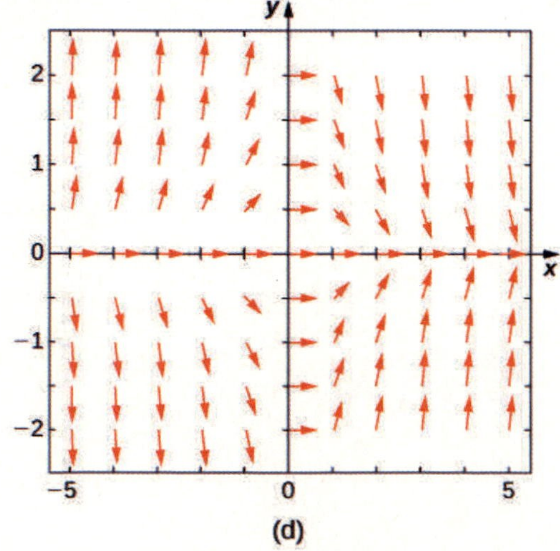

(d)

84. $y' = -3y$

85. $y' = -3t$

86. $y' = e^t$

87. $y' = \frac{1}{2}y + t$

88. $y' = -ty$

Match the direction field with the given differential equations. Explain your selections.

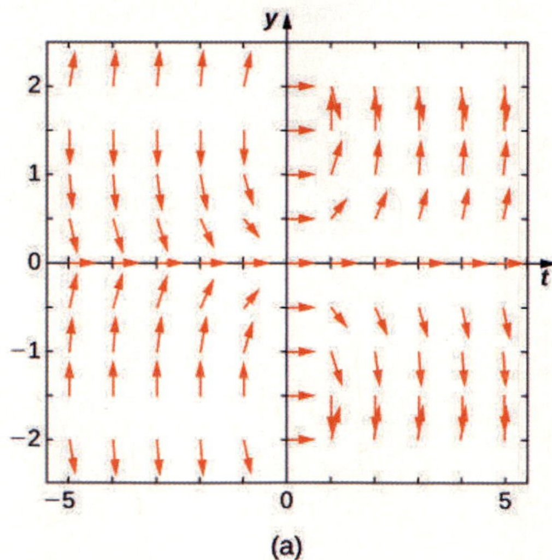

(a)

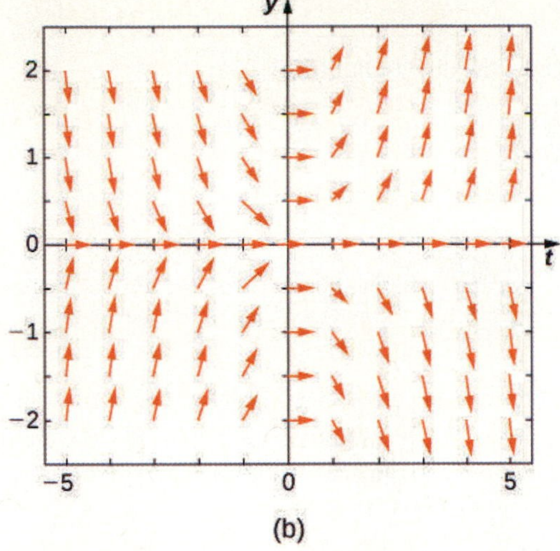

(b)

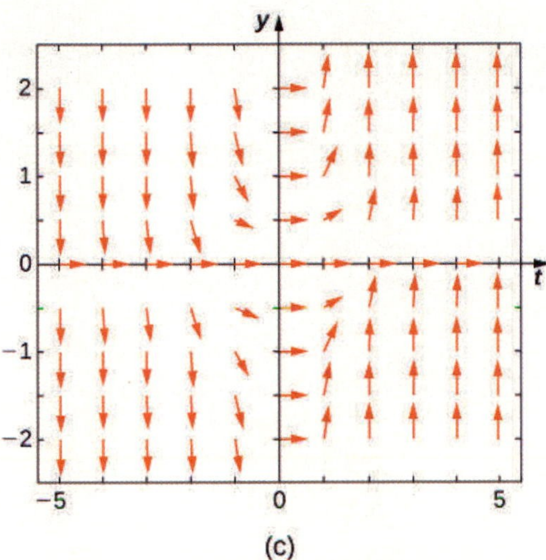

(c)

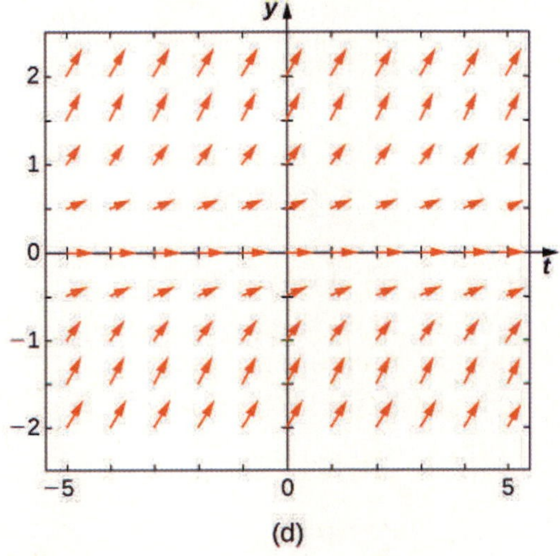

(d)

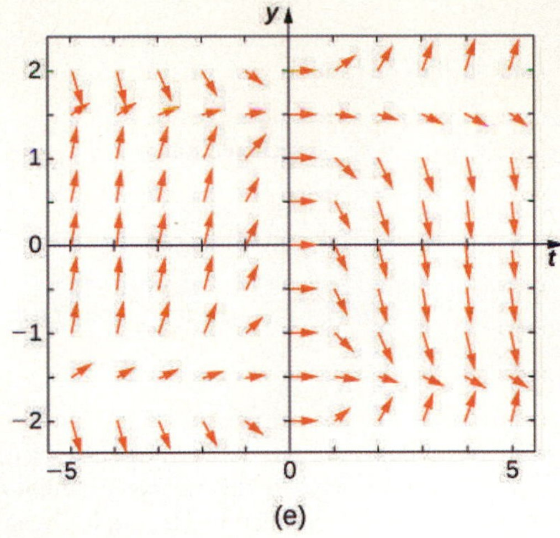

(e)

89. $y' = t \sin y$

90. $y' = -t \cos y$

91. $y' = t \tan y$

92. $y' = \sin^2 y$

93. $y' = y^2 t^3$

Estimate the following solutions using Euler's method with $n = 5$ steps over the interval $t = [0, 1]$. If you are able to solve the initial-value problem exactly, compare your solution with the exact solution. If you are unable to solve the initial-value problem, the exact solution will be provided for you to compare with Euler's method. How accurate is Euler's method?

94. $y' = -3y, \quad y(0) = 1$

95. $y' = t^2$

96. $y' = 3t - y$, $y(0) = 1$. Exact solution is $y = 3t + 4e^{-t} - 3$

97. $y' = y + t^2$, $y(0) = 3$. Exact solution is $y = 5e^t - 2 - t^2 - 2t$

98. $y' = 2t$, $y(0) = 0$

99. **[T]** $y' = e^{(x + y)}$, $y(0) = -1$. Exact solution is $y = -\ln(e + 1 - e^x)$

100. $y' = y^2 \ln(x+1)$, $y(0) = 1$. Exact solution is $y = -\frac{1}{(x+1)(\ln(x+1)-1)}$

101. $y' = 2^x$, $y(0) = 0$, Exact solution is $y = \frac{2^x - 1}{\ln(2)}$

102. $y' = y$, $y(0) = -1$. Exact solution is $y = -e^x$.

103. $y' = -5t$, $y(0) = -2$. Exact solution is $y = -\frac{5}{2}t^2 - 2$

Differential equations can be used to model disease epidemics. In the next set of problems, we examine the change of size of two sub-populations of people living in a city: individuals who are infected and individuals who are susceptible to infection. $S$ represents the size of the susceptible population, and $I$ represents the size of the infected population. We assume that if a susceptible person interacts with an infected person, there is a probability $c$ that the susceptible person will become infected. Each infected person recovers from the infection at a rate $r$ and becomes susceptible again. We consider the case of influenza, where we assume that no one dies from the disease, so we assume that the total population size of the two sub-populations is a constant number, $N$. The differential equations that model these population sizes are

$$S' = rI - cSI \quad \text{and}$$
$$I' = cSI - rI.$$

Here $c$ represents the contact rate and $r$ is the recovery rate.

104. Show that, by our assumption that the total population size is constant $(S + I = N)$, you can reduce the system to a single differential equation in $I: I' = c(N - I)I - rI$.

105. Assuming the parameters are $c = 0.5$, $N = 5$, and $r = 0.5$, draw the resulting directional field.

106. **[T]** Use computational software or a calculator to compute the solution to the initial-value problem $y' = ty$, $y(0) = 2$ using Euler's Method with the given step size $h$. Find the solution at $t = 1$. For a hint, here is "pseudo-code" for how to write a computer program to perform Euler's Method for $y' = f(t, y)$, $y(0) = 2$: Create function $f(t, y)$ Define parameters $y(1) = y_0$, $t(0) = 0$, step size $h$, and total number of steps, $N$ Write a for loop: for k = 1 to N fn = f(t(k), y(k)) y(k+1) = y(k) + h*fn t(k+1) = t(k) + h

107. Solve the initial-value problem for the exact solution.

108. Draw the directional field

109. $h = 1$

110. **[T]** $h = 10$

111. **[T]** $h = 100$

112. **[T]** $h = 1000$

113. **[T]** Evaluate the exact solution at $t = 1$. Make a table of errors for the relative error between the Euler's method solution and the exact solution. How much does the error change? Can you explain?

Consider the initial-value problem $y' = -2y$, $y(0) = 2$.

114. Show that $y = 2e^{-2x}$ solves this initial-value problem.

115. Draw the directional field of this differential equation.

116. **[T]** By hand or by calculator or computer, approximate the solution using Euler's Method at $t = 10$ using $h = 5$.

117. **[T]** By calculator or computer, approximate the solution using Euler's Method at $t = 10$ using $h = 100$.

118. **[T]** Plot exact answer and each Euler approximation (for $h = 5$ and $h = 100$) at each $h$ on the directional field. What do you notice?

# 4.3 | Separable Equations

## Learning Objectives

**4.3.1** Use separation of variables to solve a differential equation.
**4.3.2** Solve applications using separation of variables.

We now examine a solution technique for finding exact solutions to a class of differential equations known as separable differential equations. These equations are common in a wide variety of disciplines, including physics, chemistry, and engineering. We illustrate a few applications at the end of the section.

## Separation of Variables

We start with a definition and some examples.

### Definition

A **separable differential equation** is any equation that can be written in the form

$$y' = f(x)g(y). \tag{4.3}$$

The term 'separable' refers to the fact that the right-hand side of the equation can be separated into a function of $x$ times a function of $y$. Examples of separable differential equations include

$$\begin{aligned} y' &= \left(x^2 - 4\right)(3y + 2) \\ y' &= 6x^2 + 4x \\ y' &= \sec y + \tan y \\ y' &= xy + 3x - 2y - 6. \end{aligned}$$

The second equation is separable with $f(x) = 6x^2 + 4x$ and $g(y) = 1,$ the third equation is separable with $f(x) = 1$ and $g(y) = \sec y + \tan y,$ and the right-hand side of the fourth equation can be factored as $(x + 3)(y - 2),$ so it is separable as well. The third equation is also called an **autonomous differential equation** because the right-hand side of the equation is a function of $y$ alone. If a differential equation is separable, then it is possible to solve the equation using the method of **separation of variables**.

### Problem-Solving Strategy: Separation of Variables

1. Check for any values of $y$ that make $g(y) = 0.$ These correspond to constant solutions.
2. Rewrite the differential equation in the form $\dfrac{dy}{g(y)} = f(x)dx.$
3. Integrate both sides of the equation.
4. Solve the resulting equation for $y$ if possible.
5. If an initial condition exists, substitute the appropriate values for $x$ and $y$ into the equation and solve for the constant.

Note that Step 4. states "Solve the resulting equation for $y$ if possible." It is not always possible to obtain $y$ as an explicit function of $x.$ Quite often we have to be satisfied with finding $y$ as an implicit function of $x.$

## Example 4.10

### Using Separation of Variables

Find a general solution to the differential equation $y' = (x^2 - 4)(3y + 2)$ using the method of separation of variables.

### Solution

Follow the five-step method of separation of variables.

1. In this example, $f(x) = x^2 - 4$ and $g(y) = 3y + 2$. Setting $g(y) = 0$ gives $y = -\frac{2}{3}$ as a constant solution.
2. Rewrite the differential equation in the form
$$\frac{dy}{3y+2} = (x^2 - 4)dx.$$
3. Integrate both sides of the equation:
$$\int \frac{dy}{3y+2} = \int (x^2 - 4)dx.$$
Let $u = 3y + 2$. Then $du = 3\frac{dy}{dx}dx$, so the equation becomes
$$\begin{aligned} \frac{1}{3}\int \frac{1}{u}du &= \frac{1}{3}x^3 - 4x + C \\ \frac{1}{3}\ln|u| &= \frac{1}{3}x^3 - 4x + C \\ \frac{1}{3}\ln|3y+2| &= \frac{1}{3}x^3 - 4x + C. \end{aligned}$$
4. To solve this equation for $y$, first multiply both sides of the equation by $3$.
$$\ln|3y+2| = x^3 - 12x + 3C$$
Now we use some logic in dealing with the constant $C$. Since $C$ represents an arbitrary constant, $3C$ also represents an arbitrary constant. If we call the second arbitrary constant $C_1$, the equation becomes
$$\ln|3y+2| = x^3 - 12x + C_1.$$
Now exponentiate both sides of the equation (i.e., make each side of the equation the exponent for the base $e$).
$$\begin{aligned} e^{\ln|3y+2|} &= e^{x^3 - 12x + C_1} \\ |3y+2| &= e^{C_1}e^{x^3 - 12x} \end{aligned}$$
Again define a new constant $C_2 = e^{c_1}$ (note that $C_2 > 0$):
$$|3y+2| = C_2 e^{x^3 - 12x}.$$

This corresponds to two separate equations: $3y + 2 = C_2 e^{x^3 - 12x}$ and $3y + 2 = -C_2 e^{x^3 - 12x}$.

The solution to either equation can be written in the form $y = \frac{-2 \pm C_2 e^{x^3 - 12x}}{3}$.

Since $C_2 > 0,$ it does not matter whether we use plus or minus, so the constant can actually have either sign. Furthermore, the subscript on the constant $C$ is entirely arbitrary, and can be dropped. Therefore the solution can be written as

$$y = \frac{-2 + Ce^{x^3 - 12x}}{3}.$$

5. No initial condition is imposed, so we are finished.

**4.10** Use the method of separation of variables to find a general solution to the differential equation $y' = 2xy + 3y - 4x - 6.$

## Example 4.11

### Solving an Initial-Value Problem

Using the method of separation of variables, solve the initial-value problem

$$y' = (2x + 3)(y^2 - 4), \quad y(0) = -3.$$

### Solution

Follow the five-step method of separation of variables.

1. In this example, $f(x) = 2x + 3$ and $g(y) = y^2 - 4.$ Setting $g(y) = 0$ gives $y = \pm 2$ as constant solutions.
2. Divide both sides of the equation by $y^2 - 4$ and multiply by $dx.$ This gives the equation
$$\frac{dy}{y^2 - 4} = (2x + 3)dx.$$
3. Next integrate both sides:
$$\int \frac{1}{y^2 - 4} dy = \int (2x + 3)dx. \quad (4.4)$$
To evaluate the left-hand side, use the method of partial fraction decomposition. This leads to the identity
$$\frac{1}{y^2 - 4} = \frac{1}{4}\left(\frac{1}{y - 2} - \frac{1}{y + 2}\right).$$
Then **Equation 4.4** becomes

$$\begin{aligned} \frac{1}{4}\int\left(\frac{1}{y-2}-\frac{1}{y+2}\right)dy &= \int(2x+3)\,dx \\ \frac{1}{4}(\ln|y-2|-\ln|y+2|) &= x^2+3x+C. \end{aligned}$$

Multiplying both sides of this equation by $4$ and replacing $4C$ with $C_1$ gives

$$\begin{aligned} \ln|y-2|-\ln|y+2| &= 4x^2+12x+C_1 \\ \ln\left|\frac{y-2}{y+2}\right| &= 4x^2+12x+C_1. \end{aligned}$$

4. It is possible to solve this equation for $y$. First exponentiate both sides of the equation and define $C_2=e^{C_1}$:

$$\left|\frac{y-2}{y+2}\right| = C_2e^{4x^2+12x}.$$

Next we can remove the absolute value and let $C_2$ be either positive or negative. Then multiply both sides by $y+2$.

$$\begin{aligned} y-2 &= C_2(y+2)e^{4x^2+12x} \\ y-2 &= C_2ye^{4x^2+12x}+2C_2e^{4x^2+12x}. \end{aligned}$$

Now collect all terms involving $y$ on one side of the equation, and solve for $y$:

$$\begin{aligned} y-C_2ye^{4x^2+12x} &= 2+2C_2e^{4x^2+12x} \\ y(1-C_2e^{4x^2+12x}) &= 2+2C_2e^{4x^2+12x} \\ y &= \frac{2+2C_2e^{4x^2+12x}}{1-C_2e^{4x^2+12x}}. \end{aligned}$$

5. To determine the value of $C_2$, substitute $x=0$ and $y=-1$ into the general solution. Alternatively, we can put the same values into an earlier equation, namely the equation $\frac{y-2}{y+2}=C_2e^{4x^2+12}$. This is much easier to solve for $C_2$:

$$\begin{aligned} \frac{y-2}{y+2} &= C_2e^{4x^2+12x} \\ \frac{-1-2}{-1+2} &= C_2e^{4(0)^2+12(0)} \\ C_2 &= -3. \end{aligned}$$

Therefore the solution to the initial-value problem is

$$y=\frac{2-6e^{4x^2+12x}}{1+3e^{4x^2+12x}}.$$

A graph of this solution appears in **Figure 4.15**.

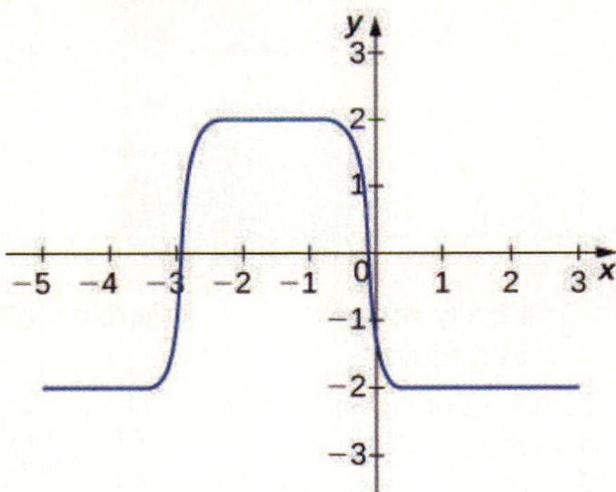


**Figure 4.15** Graph of the solution to the initial-value problem $y' = (2x+3)(y^2-4), \quad y(0) = -3.$

**4.11** Find the solution to the initial-value problem

$$6y' = (2x+1)(y^2-2y-8), \quad y(0) = -3$$

using the method of separation of variables.

## Applications of Separation of Variables

Many interesting problems can be described by separable equations. We illustrate two types of problems: solution concentrations and Newton's law of cooling.

### Solution concentrations

Consider a tank being filled with a salt solution. We would like to determine the amount of salt present in the tank as a function of time. We can apply the process of separation of variables to solve this problem and similar problems involving solution concentrations.

## Example 4.12

### Determining Salt Concentration over Time

A tank containing $100\text{ L}$ of a brine solution initially has $4\text{ kg}$ of salt dissolved in the solution. At time $t = 0,$ another brine solution flows into the tank at a rate of $2\text{ L/min}.$ This brine solution contains a concentration of $0.5\text{ kg/L}$ of salt. At the same time, a stopcock is opened at the bottom of the tank, allowing the combined solution to flow out at a rate of $2\text{ L/min},$ so that the level of liquid in the tank remains constant (**Figure 4.16**). Find the amount of salt in the tank as a function of time (measured in minutes), and find the limiting amount of salt in the tank, assuming that the solution in the tank is well mixed at all times.

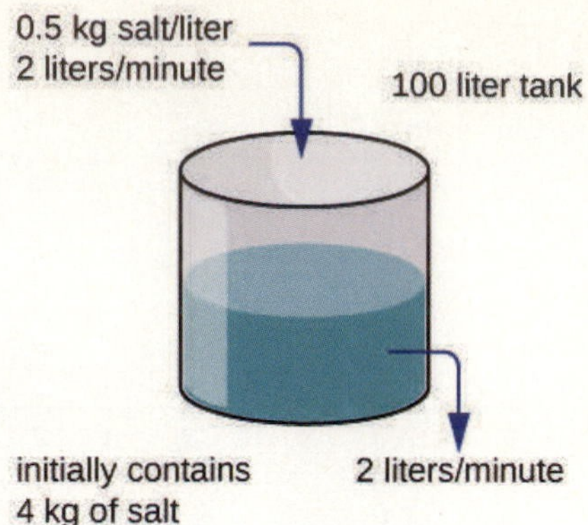


**Figure 4.16** A brine tank with an initial amount of salt solution accepts an input flow and delivers an output flow. How does the amount of salt change with time?

### Solution

First we define a function $u(t)$ that represents the amount of salt in kilograms in the tank as a function of time. Then $\frac{du}{dt}$ represents the rate at which the amount of salt in the tank changes as a function of time. Also, $u(0)$ represents the amount of salt in the tank at time $t = 0,$ which is $4$ kilograms.

The general setup for the differential equation we will solve is of the form

$$\frac{du}{dt} = \text{INFLOW RATE} - \text{OUTFLOW RATE}. \tag{4.5}$$

INFLOW RATE represents the rate at which salt enters the tank, and OUTFLOW RATE represents the rate at which salt leaves the tank. Because solution enters the tank at a rate of $2$ L/min, and each liter of solution contains $0.5$ kilogram of salt, every minute $2(0.5) = 1$ kilogram of salt enters the tank. Therefore INFLOW RATE = $1$.

To calculate the rate at which salt leaves the tank, we need the concentration of salt in the tank at any point in time. Since the actual amount of salt varies over time, so does the concentration of salt. However, the volume of the solution remains fixed at 100 liters. The number of kilograms of salt in the tank at time $t$ is equal to $u(t)$. Thus, the concentration of salt is $\frac{u(t)}{100}$ kg/L, and the solution leaves the tank at a rate of $2$ L/min. Therefore salt leaves the tank at a rate of $\frac{u(t)}{100} \cdot 2 = \frac{u(t)}{50}$ kg/min, and OUTFLOW RATE is equal to $\frac{u(t)}{50}$. Therefore the differential equation becomes $\frac{du}{dt} = 1 - \frac{u}{50},$ and the initial condition is $u(0) = 4.$ The initial-value problem to be solved is

$$\frac{du}{dt} = 1 - \frac{u}{50}, \quad u(0) = 4.$$

The differential equation is a separable equation, so we can apply the five-step strategy for solution.

Step 1. Setting $1 - \frac{u}{50} = 0$ gives $u = 50$ as a constant solution. Since the initial amount of salt in the tank is $4$ kilograms, this solution does not apply.

Step 2. Rewrite the equation as

$$\frac{du}{dt} = \frac{50 - u}{50}.$$

Then multiply both sides by $dt$ and divide both sides by $50 - u$:

$$\frac{du}{50 - u} = \frac{dt}{50}.$$

Step 3. Integrate both sides:

$$\begin{aligned} \int \frac{du}{50 - u} &= \int \frac{dt}{50} \\ -\ln|50 - u| &= \frac{t}{50} + C. \end{aligned}$$

Step 4. Solve for $u(t)$:

$$\begin{aligned} \ln|50 - u| &= -\frac{t}{50} - C \\ e^{\ln|50 - u|} &= e^{-(t/50) - C} \\ |50 - u| &= C_1 e^{-t/50}. \end{aligned}$$

Eliminate the absolute value by allowing the constant to be either positive or negative:

$$50 - u = C_1 e^{-t/50}.$$

Finally, solve for $u(t)$:

$$u(t) = 50 - C_1 e^{-t/50}.$$

Step 5. Solve for $C_1$:

$$\begin{aligned} u(0) &= 50 - C_1 e^{-0/50} \\ 4 &= 50 - C_1 \\ C_1 &= 46. \end{aligned}$$

The solution to the initial value problem is $u(t) = 50 - 46e^{-t/50}$. To find the limiting amount of salt in the tank, take the limit as $t$ approaches infinity:

$$\begin{aligned} \lim_{t \to \infty} u(t) &= 50 - 46e^{-t/50} \\ &= 50 - 46(0) \\ &= 50. \end{aligned}$$

Note that this was the constant solution to the differential equation. If the initial amount of salt in the tank is 50 kilograms, then it remains constant. If it starts at less than 50 kilograms, then it approaches 50 kilograms over time.

**4.12** A tank contains 3 kilograms of salt dissolved in 75 liters of water. A salt solution of 0.4 kg salt/L is pumped into the tank at a rate of 6 L/min and is drained at the same rate. Solve for the salt concentration at time $t$. Assume the tank is well mixed at all times.

## Newton's law of cooling

Newton's law of cooling states that the rate of change of an object's temperature is proportional to the difference between its own temperature and the ambient temperature (i.e., the temperature of its surroundings). If we let $T(t)$ represent the temperature of an object as a function of time, then $\frac{dT}{dt}$ represents the rate at which that temperature changes. The temperature of the object's surroundings can be represented by $T_s$. Then Newton's law of cooling can be written in the form

$$\frac{dT}{dt} = k(T(t) - T_s)$$

or simply

$$\frac{dT}{dt} = k(T - T_s). \tag{4.6}$$

The temperature of the object at the beginning of any experiment is the initial value for the initial-value problem. We call this temperature $T_0$. Therefore the initial-value problem that needs to be solved takes the form

$$\frac{dT}{dt} = k(T - T_s), \quad T(0) = T_0, \tag{4.7}$$

where $k$ is a constant that needs to be either given or determined in the context of the problem. We use these equations in **Example 4.13**.

## Example 4.13

### Waiting for a Pizza to Cool

A pizza is removed from the oven after baking thoroughly, and the temperature of the oven is $350°\text{F}$. The temperature of the kitchen is $75°\text{F}$, and after $5$ minutes the temperature of the pizza is $340°\text{F}$. We would like to wait until the temperature of the pizza reaches $300°\text{F}$ before cutting and serving it (**Figure 4.17**). How much longer will we have to wait?

**Figure 4.17** From Newton's law of cooling, if the pizza cools $10°\text{F}$ in $5$ minutes, how long before it cools to $300°\text{F}$?

#### Solution

The ambient temperature (surrounding temperature) is $75°\text{F}$, so $T_s = 75$. The temperature of the pizza when it comes out of the oven is $350°\text{F}$, which is the initial temperature (i.e., initial value), so $T_0 = 350$. Therefore **Equation 4.4** becomes

$$\frac{dT}{dt} = k(T - 75), \quad T(0) = 350.$$

To solve the differential equation, we use the five-step technique for solving separable equations.

1. Setting the right-hand side equal to zero gives $T = 75$ as a constant solution. Since the pizza starts at $350°\text{F}$, this is not the solution we are seeking.

2. Rewrite the differential equation by multiplying both sides by $dt$ and dividing both sides by $T - 75$:

$$\frac{dT}{T - 75} = kdt.$$

3. Integrate both sides:

$$\begin{aligned} \int \frac{dT}{T - 75} &= \int kdt \\ \ln|T - 75| &= kt + C. \end{aligned}$$

4. Solve for $T$ by first exponentiating both sides:

$$\begin{aligned} e^{\ln|T - 75|} &= e^{kt + C} \\ |T - 75| &= C_1 e^{kt} \\ T - 75 &= C_1 e^{kt} \\ T(t) &= 75 + C_1 e^{kt}. \end{aligned}$$

5. Solve for $C_1$ by using the initial condition $T(0) = 350$:

$$\begin{aligned} T(t) &= 75 + C_1 e^{kt} \\ T(0) &= 75 + C_1 e^{k(0)} \\ 350 &= 75 + C_1 \\ C_1 &= 275. \end{aligned}$$

Therefore the solution to the initial-value problem is

$$T(t) = 75 + 275e^{kt}.$$

To determine the value of $k$, we need to use the fact that after $5$ minutes the temperature of the pizza is $340°F$. Therefore $T(5) = 340$. Substituting this information into the solution to the initial-value problem, we have

$$\begin{aligned} T(t) &= 75 + 275e^{kt} \\ T(5) &= 340 = 75 + 275e^{5k} \\ 265 &= 275e^{5k} \\ e^{5k} &= \frac{53}{55} \\ \ln e^{5k} &= \ln\left(\frac{53}{55}\right) \\ 5k &= \ln\left(\frac{53}{55}\right) \\ k &= \frac{1}{5}\ln\left(\frac{53}{55}\right) \approx -0.007408. \end{aligned}$$

So now we have $T(t) = 75 + 275e^{-0.007048t}$. When is the temperature $300°F$? Solving for $t$, we find

$$\begin{aligned} T(t) &= 75 + 275e^{-0.007048t} \\ 300 &= 75 + 275e^{-0.007048t} \\ 225 &= 275e^{-0.007048t} \\ e^{-0.007048t} &= \frac{9}{11} \\ \ln e^{-0.007048t} &= \ln \frac{9}{11} \\ -0.007048t &= \ln \frac{9}{11} \\ t &= -\frac{1}{0.007048} \ln \frac{9}{11} \approx 28.5. \end{aligned}$$

Therefore we need to wait an additional 23.5 minutes (after the temperature of the pizza reached 340°F). That should be just enough time to finish this calculation.

**4.13** A cake is removed from the oven after baking thoroughly, and the temperature of the oven is 450°F. The temperature of the kitchen is 70°F, and after 10 minutes the temperature of the cake is 430°F.

a. Write the appropriate initial-value problem to describe this situation.

b. Solve the initial-value problem for $T(t)$.

c. How long will it take until the temperature of the cake is within 5°F of room temperature?

# 4.3 EXERCISES

Solve the following initial-value problems with the initial condition $y_0 = 0$ and graph the solution.

119. $\frac{dy}{dt} = y + 1$

120. $\frac{dy}{dt} = y - 1$

121. $\frac{dy}{dt} = y + 1$

122. $\frac{dy}{dt} = -y - 1$

Find the general solution to the differential equation.

123. $x^2 y' = (x + 1)y$

124. $y' = \tan(y)x$

125. $y' = 2xy^2$

126. $\frac{dy}{dt} = y\cos(3t + 2)$

127. $2x\frac{dy}{dx} = y^2$

128. $y' = e^y x^2$

129. $(1 + x)y' = (x + 2)(y - 1)$

130. $\frac{dx}{dt} = 3t^2\left(x^2 + 4\right)$

131. $t\frac{dy}{dt} = \sqrt{1 - y^2}$

132. $y' = e^x e^y$

Find the solution to the initial-value problem.

133. $y' = e^{y - x}, \ y(0) = 0$

134. $y' = y^2(x + 1), \ y(0) = 2$

135. $\frac{dy}{dx} = y^3 xe^{x^2}, \ y(0) = 1$

136. $\frac{dy}{dt} = y^2 e^x \sin(3x), \ y(0) = 1$

137. $y' = \frac{x}{\operatorname{sech}^2 y}, \ y(0) = 0$

138. $y' = 2xy(1 + 2y), \ y(0) = -1$

139. $\frac{dx}{dt} = \ln(t)\sqrt{1 - x^2}, \ x(0) = 0$

140. $y' = 3x^2(y^2 + 4), \ y(0) = 0$

141. $y' = e^y 5^x, \ y(0) = \ln(\ln(5))$

142. $y' = -2x\tan(y), \ y(0) = \frac{\pi}{2}$

For the following problems, use a software program or your calculator to generate the directional fields. Solve explicitly and draw solution curves for several initial conditions. Are there some critical initial conditions that change the behavior of the solution?

143. **[T]** $y' = 1 - 2y$

144. **[T]** $y' = y^2 x^3$

145. **[T]** $y' = y^3 e^x$

146. **[T]** $y' = e^y$

147. **[T]** $y' = y\ln(x)$

148. Most drugs in the bloodstream decay according to the equation $y' = cy,$ where $y$ is the concentration of the drug in the bloodstream. If the half-life of a drug is $2$ hours, what fraction of the initial dose remains after $6$ hours?

149. A drug is administered intravenously to a patient at a rate $r$ mg/h and is cleared from the body at a rate proportional to the amount of drug still present in the body, $d$ Set up and solve the differential equation, assuming there is no drug initially present in the body.

150. **[T]** How often should a drug be taken if its dose is $3$ mg, it is cleared at a rate $c = 0.1$ mg/h, and $1$ mg is required to be in the bloodstream at all times?

151. A tank contains $1$ kilogram of salt dissolved in $100$ liters of water. A salt solution of $0.1$ kg salt/L is pumped into the tank at a rate of $2$ L/min and is drained at the same rate. Solve for the salt concentration at time $t.$ Assume the tank is well mixed.

152. A tank containing $10$ kilograms of salt dissolved in $1000$ liters of water has two salt solutions pumped in. The first solution of $0.2$ kg salt/L is pumped in at a rate of $20$ L/min and the second solution of $0.05$ kg salt/L is pumped in at a rate of $5$ L/min. The tank drains at $25$ L/min. Assume the tank is well mixed. Solve for the salt concentration at time $t$.

153. **[T]** For the preceding problem, find how much salt is in the tank $1$ hour after the process begins.

154. Torricelli's law states that for a water tank with a hole in the bottom that has a cross-section of $A$ and with a height of water $h$ above the bottom of the tank, the rate of change of volume of water flowing from the tank is proportional to the square root of the height of water, according to $\frac{dV}{dt} = -A\sqrt{2gh},$ where $g$ is the acceleration due to gravity. Note that $\frac{dV}{dt} = A\frac{dh}{dt}.$ Solve the resulting initial-value problem for the height of the water, assuming a tank with a hole of radius $2$ ft. The initial height of water is $100$ ft.

155. For the preceding problem, determine how long it takes the tank to drain.

For the following problems, use Newton's law of cooling.

156. The liquid base of an ice cream has an initial temperature of $200°F$ before it is placed in a freezer with a constant temperature of $0°F.$ After $1$ hour, the temperature of the ice-cream base has decreased to $140°F.$ Formulate and solve the initial-value problem to determine the temperature of the ice cream.

157. **[T]** The liquid base of an ice cream has an initial temperature of $210°F$ before it is placed in a freezer with a constant temperature of $20°F.$ After $2$ hours, the temperature of the ice-cream base has decreased to $170°F.$ At what time will the ice cream be ready to eat? (Assume $30°F$ is the optimal eating temperature.)

158. **[T]** You are organizing an ice cream social. The outside temperature is $80°F$ and the ice cream is at $10°F.$ After $10$ minutes, the ice cream temperature has risen by $10°F.$ How much longer can you wait before the ice cream melts at $40°F$?

159. You have a cup of coffee at temperature $70°C$ and the ambient temperature in the room is $20°C.$ Assuming a cooling rate $k$ of $0.125,$ write and solve the differential equation to describe the temperature of the coffee with respect to time.

160. **[T]** You have a cup of coffee at temperature $70°C$ that you put outside, where the ambient temperature is $0°C.$ After $5$ minutes, how much colder is the coffee?

161. You have a cup of coffee at temperature $70°C$ and you immediately pour in $1$ part milk to $5$ parts coffee. The milk is initially at temperature $1°C.$ Write and solve the differential equation that governs the temperature of this coffee.

162. You have a cup of coffee at temperature $70°C,$ which you let cool $10$ minutes before you pour in the same amount of milk at $1°C$ as in the preceding problem. How does the temperature compare to the previous cup after $10$ minutes?

163. Solve the generic problem $y' = ay + b$ with initial condition $y(0) = c.$

164. Prove the basic continual compounded interest equation. Assuming an initial deposit of $P_0$ and an interest rate of $r,$ set up and solve an equation for continually compounded interest.

165. Assume an initial nutrient amount of $I$ kilograms in a tank with $L$ liters. Assume a concentration of $c$ kg/L being pumped in at a rate of $r$ L/min. The tank is well mixed and is drained at a rate of $r$ L/min. Find the equation describing the amount of nutrient in the tank.

166. Leaves accumulate on the forest floor at a rate of $2$ g/cm$^2$/yr and also decompose at a rate of $90\%$ per year. Write a differential equation governing the number of grams of leaf litter per square centimeter of forest floor, assuming at time $0$ there is no leaf litter on the ground. Does this amount approach a steady value? What is that value?

167. Leaves accumulate on the forest floor at a rate of $4$ g/cm$^2$/yr. These leaves decompose at a rate of $10\%$ per year. Write a differential equation governing the number of grams of leaf litter per square centimeter of forest floor. Does this amount approach a steady value? What is that value?

# 4.4 | The Logistic Equation

## Learning Objectives

**4.4.1** Describe the concept of environmental carrying capacity in the logistic model of population growth.

**4.4.2** Draw a direction field for a logistic equation and interpret the solution curves.

**4.4.3** Solve a logistic equation and interpret the results.

Differential equations can be used to represent the size of a population as it varies over time. We saw this in an earlier chapter in the section on exponential growth and decay, which is the simplest model. A more realistic model includes other factors that affect the growth of the population. In this section, we study the logistic differential equation and see how it applies to the study of population dynamics in the context of biology.

## Population Growth and Carrying Capacity

To model population growth using a differential equation, we first need to introduce some variables and relevant terms. The variable $t$. will represent time. The units of time can be hours, days, weeks, months, or even years. Any given problem must specify the units used in that particular problem. The variable $P$ will represent population. Since the population varies over time, it is understood to be a function of time. Therefore we use the notation $P(t)$ for the population as a function of time. If $P(t)$ is a differentiable function, then the first derivative $\frac{dP}{dt}$ represents the instantaneous rate of change of the population as a function of time.

In Exponential Growth and Decay, we studied the exponential growth and decay of populations and radioactive substances. An example of an exponential growth function is $P(t) = P_0 e^{rt}$. In this function, $P(t)$ represents the population at time $t$, $P_0$ represents the **initial population** (population at time $t = 0$), and the constant $r > 0$ is called the **growth rate**. Figure 4.18 shows a graph of $P(t) = 100e^{0.03t}$. Here $P_0 = 100$ and $r = 0.03$.

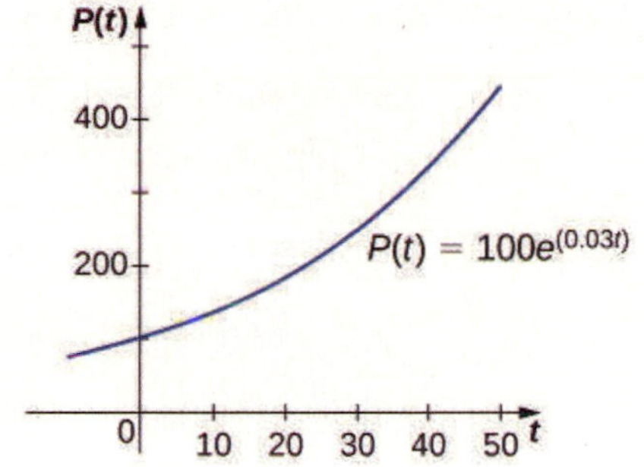

Figure 4.18 An exponential growth model of population.

We can verify that the function $P(t) = P_0 e^{rt}$ satisfies the initial-value problem

$$\frac{dP}{dt} = rP, \quad P(0) = P_0.$$

This differential equation has an interesting interpretation. The left-hand side represents the rate at which the population increases (or decreases). The right-hand side is equal to a positive constant multiplied by the current population. Therefore the differential equation states that the rate at which the population increases is proportional to the population at that point in time. Furthermore, it states that the constant of proportionality never changes.

One problem with this function is its prediction that as time goes on, the population grows without bound. This is unrealistic in a real-world setting. Various factors limit the rate of growth of a particular population, including birth rate, death rate, food supply, predators, and so on. The growth constant $r$ usually takes into consideration the birth and death rates but none of the other factors, and it can be interpreted as a net (birth minus death) percent growth rate per unit time. A natural question to ask is whether the population growth rate stays constant, or whether it changes over time. Biologists have found that in many biological systems, the population grows until a certain steady-state population is reached. This possibility is not taken into account with exponential growth. However, the concept of carrying capacity allows for the possibility that in a given area, only a certain number of a given organism or animal can thrive without running into resource issues.

### Definition

The **carrying capacity** of an organism in a given environment is defined to be the maximum population of that organism that the environment can sustain indefinitely.

We use the variable $K$ to denote the carrying capacity. The growth rate is represented by the variable $r.$ Using these variables, we can define the logistic differential equation.

### Definition

Let $K$ represent the carrying capacity for a particular organism in a given environment, and let $r$ be a real number that represents the growth rate. The function $P(t)$ represents the population of this organism as a function of time $t,$ and the constant $P_0$ represents the initial population (population of the organism at time $t = 0$). Then the **logistic differential equation** is

$$\frac{dP}{dt} = rP\left(1 - \frac{P}{K}\right) - \ = rP. \qquad (4.8)$$

See this website (http://www.openstaxcollege.org/l/20_logisticEq) for more information on the logistic equation.

The logistic equation was first published by Pierre Verhulst in $1845.$ This differential equation can be coupled with the initial condition $P(0) = P_0$ to form an initial-value problem for $P(t).$

Suppose that the initial population is small relative to the carrying capacity. Then $\frac{P}{K}$ is small, possibly close to zero. Thus, the quantity in parentheses on the right-hand side of Equation 4.8 is close to $1,$ and the right-hand side of this equation is close to $rP.$ If $r > 0,$ then the population grows rapidly, resembling exponential growth.

However, as the population grows, the ratio $\frac{P}{K}$ also grows, because $K$ is constant. If the population remains below the carrying capacity, then $\frac{P}{K}$ is less than $1,$ so $1 - \frac{P}{K} > 0.$ Therefore the right-hand side of Equation 4.8 is still positive, but the quantity in parentheses gets smaller, and the growth rate decreases as a result. If $P = K$ then the right-hand side is equal to zero, and the population does not change.

Now suppose that the population starts at a value higher than the carrying capacity. Then $\frac{P}{K} > 1,$ and $1 - \frac{P}{K} < 0.$ Then the right-hand side of Equation 4.8 is negative, and the population decreases. As long as $P > K,$ the population decreases. It never actually reaches $K$ because $\frac{dP}{dt}$ will get smaller and smaller, but the population approaches the carrying capacity as $t$ approaches infinity. This analysis can be represented visually by way of a phase line. A **phase line** describes the general behavior of a solution to an autonomous differential equation, depending on the initial condition. For the case of a carrying capacity in the logistic equation, the phase line is as shown in Figure 4.19.

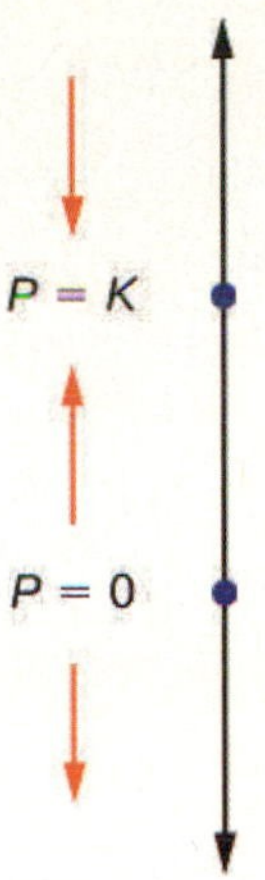


**Figure 4.19** A phase line for the differential equation $\frac{dP}{dt} = rP\left(1 - \frac{P}{K}\right)$.

This phase line shows that when $P$ is less than zero or greater than $K$, the population decreases over time. When $P$ is between $0$ and $K$, the population increases over time.

## Example 4.14

### Chapter Opener: Examining the Carrying Capacity of a Deer Population

**Figure 4.20** (credit: modification of work by Rachel Kramer, Flickr)

Let's consider the population of white-tailed deer (*Odocoileus virginianus*) in the state of Kentucky. The Kentucky Department of Fish and Wildlife Resources (KDFWR) sets guidelines for hunting and fishing in the state. Before the hunting season of $2004$, it estimated a population of $900{,}000$ deer. Johnson notes: "A deer population that has plenty to eat and is not hunted by humans or other predators will double every three years." (George Johnson, "The Problem of Exploding Deer Populations Has No Attractive Solutions," January $12$, $2001$, accessed April 9, 2015, http://www.txtwriter.com/onscience/Articles/deerpops.html.) This observation corresponds to a rate of increase $r = \frac{\ln(2)}{3} = 0.2311$, so the approximate growth rate is $23.11\%$ per year. (This assumes that the population grows exponentially, which is reasonable—at least in the short term—with plentiful food supply and no predators.) The KDFWR also reports deer population densities for $32$ counties in Kentucky, the average of which is approximately $27$ deer per square mile. Suppose this is the deer density for the whole state ($39{,}732$ square miles). The carrying capacity $K$ is $39{,}732$ square miles times $27$ deer per square mile, or $1{,}072{,}764$ deer.

a. For this application, we have $P_0 = 900{,}000,\ K = 1{,}072{,}764,$ and $r = 0.2311$. Substitute these values into **Equation 4.8** and form the initial-value problem.

b. Solve the initial-value problem from part a.

c. According to this model, what will be the population in 3 years? Recall that the doubling time predicted by Johnson for the deer population was 3 years. How do these values compare?

d. Suppose the population managed to reach 1,200,000 deer. What does the logistic equation predict will happen to the population in this scenario?

### Solution

a. The initial value problem is

$$\frac{dP}{dt} = 0.2311P\left(1 - \frac{P}{1{,}072{,}764}\right), \quad P(0) = 900{,}000.$$

b. The logistic equation is an autonomous differential equation, so we can use the method of separation of variables.

Step 1: Setting the right-hand side equal to zero gives $P = 0$ and $P = 1{,}072{,}764$. This means that if the population starts at zero it will never change, and if it starts at the carrying capacity, it will never change.

Step 2: Rewrite the differential equation and multiply both sides by:

$$\begin{aligned} \frac{dP}{dt} &= 0.2311P\left(\frac{1{,}072{,}764 - P}{1{,}072{,}764}\right) \\ dP &= 0.2311P\left(\frac{1{,}072{,}764 - P}{1{,}072{,}764}\right)dt. \end{aligned}$$

Divide both sides by $P(1{,}072{,}764 - P)$:

$$\frac{dP}{P(1{,}072{,}764 - P)} = \frac{0.2311}{1{,}072{,}764}dt.$$

Step 3: Integrate both sides of the equation using partial fraction decomposition:

$$\begin{aligned} \int \frac{dP}{P(1{,}072{,}764 - P)} &= \int \frac{0.2311}{1{,}072{,}764}dt \\ \frac{1}{1{,}072{,}764}\int\left(\frac{1}{P} + \frac{1}{1{,}072{,}764 - P}\right)dP &= \frac{0.2311t}{1{,}072{,}764} + C \\ \frac{1}{1{,}072{,}764}(\ln|P| - \ln|1{,}072{,}764 - P|) &= \frac{0.2311t}{1{,}072{,}764} + C. \end{aligned}$$

Step 4: Multiply both sides by 1,072,764 and use the quotient rule for logarithms:

$$\ln\left|\frac{P}{1{,}072{,}764 - P}\right| = 0.2311t + C_1.$$

Here $C_1 = 1{,}072{,}764C$. Next exponentiate both sides and eliminate the absolute value:

$$\begin{aligned} e^{\ln\left|\frac{P}{1{,}072{,}764 - P}\right|} &= e^{0.2311t + C_1} \\ \left|\frac{P}{1{,}072{,}764 - P}\right| &= C_2e^{0.2311t} \\ \frac{P}{1{,}072{,}764 - P} &= C_2e^{0.2311t}. \end{aligned}$$

Here $C_2 = e^{C_1}$ but after eliminating the absolute value, it can be negative as well. Now solve for:

$$\begin{aligned}
P &= C_2 e^{0.2311t}(1{,}072{,}764 - P). \\
P &= 1{,}072{,}764 C_2 e^{0.2311t} - C_2 P e^{0.2311t} \\
P + C_2 P e^{0.2311t} &= 1{,}072{,}764 C_2 e^{0.2311t} \\
P\left(1 + C_2 e^{0.2311t}\right) &= 1{,}072{,}764 C_2 e^{0.2311t} \\
P(t) &= \frac{1{,}072{,}764 C_2 e^{0.2311t}}{1 + C_2 e^{0.2311t}}.
\end{aligned}$$

Step 5: To determine the value of $C_2,$ it is actually easier to go back a couple of steps to where $C_2$ was defined. In particular, use the equation

$$\frac{P}{1{,}072{,}764 - P} = C_2 e^{0.2311t}.$$

The initial condition is $P(0) = 900{,}000.$ Replace $P$ with $900{,}000$ and $t$ with zero:

$$\begin{aligned}
\frac{P}{1{,}072{,}764 - P} &= C_2 e^{0.2311t} \\
\frac{900{,}000}{1{,}072{,}764 - 900{,}000} &= C_2 e^{0.2311(0)} \\
\frac{900{,}000}{172{,}764} &= C_2 \\
C_2 &= \frac{25{,}000}{4{,}799} \approx 5.209.
\end{aligned}$$

Therefore

$$\begin{aligned}
P(t) &= \frac{1{,}072{,}764\left(\frac{25000}{4799}\right)e^{0.2311t}}{1 + \left(\frac{25000}{4799}\right)e^{0.2311t}} \\
&= \frac{1{,}072{,}764(25000)e^{0.2311t}}{4799 + 25000e^{0.2311t}}.
\end{aligned}$$

Dividing the numerator and denominator by $25{,}000$ gives

$$P(t) = \frac{1{,}072{,}764 e^{0.2311t}}{0.19196 + e^{0.2311t}}.$$

**Figure 4.21** is a graph of this equation.

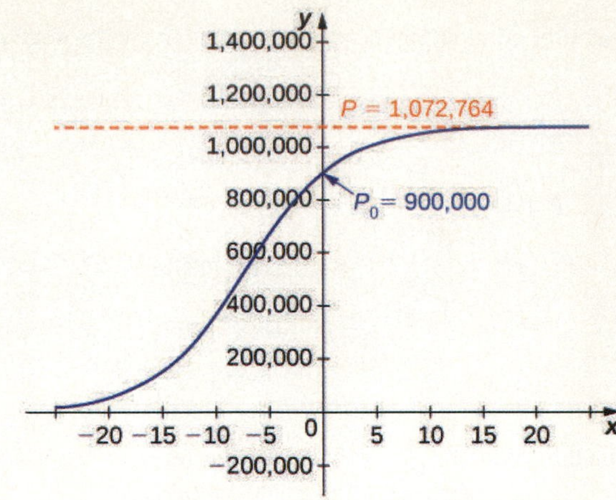


**Figure 4.21** Logistic curve for the deer population with an initial population of 900,000 deer.

c. Using this model we can predict the population in 3 years.

$$P(3) = \frac{1{,}072{,}764e^{0.2311(3)}}{0.19196 + e^{0.2311(3)}} \approx 978{,}830 \text{ deer}$$

This is far short of twice the initial population of 900,000. Remember that the doubling time is based on the assumption that the growth rate never changes, but the logistic model takes this possibility into account.

d. If the population reached 1,200,000 deer, then the new initial-value problem would be

$$\frac{dP}{dt} = 0.2311P\left(1 - \frac{P}{1{,}072{,}764}\right), \quad P(0) = 1{,}200{,}000.$$

The general solution to the differential equation would remain the same.

$$P(t) = \frac{1{,}072{,}764C_2 e^{0.2311t}}{1 + C_2 e^{0.2311t}}$$

To determine the value of the constant, return to the equation

$$\frac{P}{1{,}072{,}764 - P} = C_2 e^{0.2311t}.$$

Substituting the values $t = 0$ and $P = 1{,}200{,}000,$ you get

$$\begin{aligned} C_2 e^{0.2311(0)} &= \frac{1{,}200{,}000}{1{,}072{,}764 - 1{,}200{,}000} \\ C_2 &= -\frac{100{,}000}{10{,}603} \approx -9.431. \end{aligned}$$

Therefore

$$\begin{aligned} P(t) &= \frac{1{,}072{,}764C_2e^{0.2311t}}{1 + C_2e^{0.2311t}} \\ &= \frac{1{,}072{,}764\left(-\frac{100{,}000}{10{,}603}\right)e^{0.2311t}}{1 + \left(-\frac{100{,}000}{10{,}603}\right)e^{0.2311t}} \\ &= -\frac{107{,}276{,}400{,}000e^{0.2311t}}{100{,}000e^{0.2311t} - 10{,}603} \\ &\approx \frac{10{,}117{,}551e^{0.2311t}}{9.43129e^{0.2311t} - 1}. \end{aligned}$$

This equation is graphed in **Figure 4.22**.

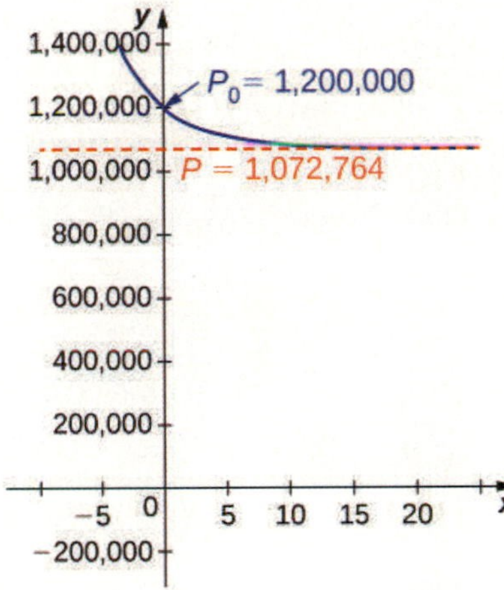


**Figure 4.22** Logistic curve for the deer population with an initial population of $1{,}200{,}000$ deer.

## Solving the Logistic Differential Equation

The logistic differential equation is an autonomous differential equation, so we can use separation of variables to find the general solution, as we just did in **Example 4.14**.

Step 1: Setting the right-hand side equal to zero leads to $P = 0$ and $P = K$ as constant solutions. The first solution indicates that when there are no organisms present, the population will never grow. The second solution indicates that when the population starts at the carrying capacity, it will never change.

Step 2: Rewrite the differential equation in the form

$$\frac{dP}{dt} = \frac{rP(K - P)}{K}.$$

Then multiply both sides by $dt$ and divide both sides by $P(K - P)$. This leads to

$$\frac{dP}{P(K - P)} = \frac{r}{K}dt.$$

Multiply both sides of the equation by $K$ and integrate:

$$\int \frac{K}{P(K - P)}dP = \int rdt.$$

The left-hand side of this equation can be integrated using partial fraction decomposition. We leave it to you to verify that

$$\frac{K}{P(K-P)} = \frac{1}{P} + \frac{1}{K-P}.$$

Then the equation becomes

$$\begin{aligned} \int \frac{1}{P} + \frac{1}{K-P} dP &= \int r dt \\ \ln|P| - \ln|K-P| &= rt + C \\ \ln\left|\frac{P}{K-P}\right| &= rt + C. \end{aligned}$$

Now exponentiate both sides of the equation to eliminate the natural logarithm:

$$\begin{aligned} e^{\ln\left|\frac{P}{K-P}\right|} &= e^{rt+C} \\ \left|\frac{P}{K-P}\right| &= e^C e^{rt}. \end{aligned}$$

We define $C_1 = e^c$ so that the equation becomes

$$\frac{P}{K-P} = C_1 e^{rt}. \tag{4.9}$$

To solve this equation for $P(t)$, first multiply both sides by $K-P$ and collect the terms containing $P$ on the left-hand side of the equation:

$$\begin{aligned} P &= C_1 e^{rt}(K-P) \\ P &= C_1 Ke^{rt} - C_1 Pe^{rt} \\ P + C_1 Pe^{rt} &= C_1 Ke^{rt}. \end{aligned}$$

Next, factor $P$ from the left-hand side and divide both sides by the other factor:

$$\begin{aligned} P\left(1 + C_1 e^{rt}\right) &= C_1 Ke^{rt} \\ P(t) &= \frac{C_1 Ke^{rt}}{1 + C_1 e^{rt}}. \end{aligned} \tag{4.10}$$

The last step is to determine the value of $C_1$. The easiest way to do this is to substitute $t = 0$ and $P_0$ in place of $P$ in **Equation 4.9** and solve for $C_1$:

$$\begin{aligned} \frac{P}{K-P} &= C_1 e^{rt} \\ \frac{P_0}{K-P_0} &= C_1 e^{r(0)} \\ C_1 &= \frac{P_0}{K-P_0}. \end{aligned}$$

Finally, substitute the expression for $C_1$ into **Equation 4.10**:

$$P(t) = \frac{C_1 Ke^{rt}}{1 + C_1 e^{rt}} = \frac{\frac{P_0}{K-P_0} Ke^{rt}}{1 + \frac{P_0}{K-P_0} e^{rt}}$$

Now multiply the numerator and denominator of the right-hand side by $(K - P_0)$ and simplify:

$$\begin{aligned} P(t) &= \frac{\frac{P_0}{K-P_0}Ke^{rt}}{1+\frac{P_0}{K-P_0}e^{rt}} \\ &= \frac{\frac{P_0}{K-P_0}Ke^{rt}}{1+\frac{P_0}{K-P_0}e^{rt}} \cdot \frac{K-P_0}{K-P_0} \\ &= \frac{P_0Ke^{rt}}{(K-P_0)+P_0e^{rt}}. \end{aligned}$$

We state this result as a theorem.

### Theorem 4.2: Solution of the Logistic Differential Equation

Consider the logistic differential equation subject to an initial population of $P_0$ with carrying capacity $K$ and growth rate $r$. The solution to the corresponding initial-value problem is given by

$$P(t) = \frac{P_0Ke^{rt}}{(K-P_0)+P_0e^{rt}}. \qquad (4.11)$$

Now that we have the solution to the initial-value problem, we can choose values for $P_0$, $r$, and $K$ and study the solution curve. For example, in **Example 4.14** we used the values $r = 0.2311$, $K = 1{,}072{,}764$, and an initial population of $900{,}000$ deer. This leads to the solution

$$\begin{aligned} P(t) &= \frac{P_0Ke^{rt}}{(K-P_0)+P_0e^{rt}} \\ &= \frac{900{,}000(1{,}072{,}764)e^{0.2311t}}{(1{,}072{,}764-900{,}000)+900{,}000e^{0.2311t}} \\ &= \frac{900{,}000(1{,}072{,}764)e^{0.2311t}}{172{,}764+900{,}000e^{0.2311t}}. \end{aligned}$$

Dividing top and bottom by $900{,}000$ gives

$$P(t) = \frac{1{,}072{,}764e^{0.2311t}}{0.19196+e^{0.2311t}}.$$

This is the same as the original solution. The graph of this solution is shown again in blue in **Figure 4.23**, superimposed over the graph of the exponential growth model with initial population $900{,}000$ and growth rate $0.2311$ (appearing in green). The red dashed line represents the carrying capacity, and is a horizontal asymptote for the solution to the logistic equation.

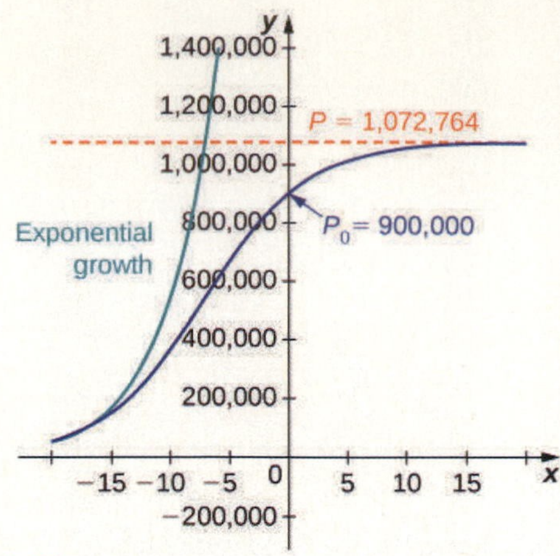


**Figure 4.23** A comparison of exponential versus logistic growth for the same initial population of $900{,}000$ organisms and growth rate of $23.11\%$.

Working under the assumption that the population grows according to the logistic differential equation, this graph predicts that approximately $20$ years earlier $(1984),$ the growth of the population was very close to exponential. The net growth rate at that time would have been around $23.1\%$ per year. As time goes on, the two graphs separate. This happens because the population increases, and the logistic differential equation states that the growth rate decreases as the population increases. At the time the population was measured $(2004),$ it was close to carrying capacity, and the population was starting to level off.

The solution to the logistic differential equation has a point of inflection. To find this point, set the second derivative equal to zero:

$$\begin{aligned} P(t) &= \frac{P_0 K e^{rt}}{(K - P_0) + P_0 e^{rt}} \\ P'(t) &= \frac{rP_0 K(K - P_0)e^{rt}}{((K - P_0) + P_0 e^{rt})^2} \\ P''(t) &= \frac{r^2 P_0 K(K - P_0)^2 e^{rt} - r^2 P_0{}^2 K(K - P_0)e^{2rt}}{((K - P_0) + P_0 e^{rt})^3} \\ &= \frac{r^2 P_0 K(K - P_0)e^{rt}((K - P_0) - P_0 e^{rt})}{((K - P_0) + P_0 e^{rt})^3}. \end{aligned}$$

Setting the numerator equal to zero,

$$r^2 P_0 K(K - P_0)e^{rt}((K - P_0) - P_0 e^{rt}) = 0.$$

As long as $P_0 \neq K,$ the entire quantity before and including $e^{rt}$ is nonzero, so we can divide it out:

$$(K - P_0) - P_0 e^{rt} = 0.$$

Solving for $t,$

$$\begin{aligned} P_0 e^{rt} &= K - P_0 \\ e^{rt} &= \frac{K - P_0}{P_0} \\ \ln e^{rt} &= \ln \frac{K - P_0}{P_0} \\ rt &= \ln \frac{K - P_0}{P_0} \\ t &= \frac{1}{r} \ln \frac{K - P_0}{P_0}. \end{aligned}$$

Notice that if $P_0 > K,$ then this quantity is undefined, and the graph does not have a point of inflection. In the logistic graph, the point of inflection can be seen as the point where the graph changes from concave up to concave down. This is where the "leveling off" starts to occur, because the net growth rate becomes slower as the population starts to approach the carrying capacity.

**4.14** A population of rabbits in a meadow is observed to be $200$ rabbits at time $t = 0.$ After a month, the rabbit population is observed to have increased by $4\%.$ Using an initial population of $200$ and a growth rate of $0.04,$ with a carrying capacity of $750$ rabbits,

a. Write the logistic differential equation and initial condition for this model.

b. Draw a slope field for this logistic differential equation, and sketch the solution corresponding to an initial population of $200$ rabbits.

c. Solve the initial-value problem for $P(t).$

d. Use the solution to predict the population after $1$ year.

Student PROJECT

## Student Project: Logistic Equation with a Threshold Population

An improvement to the logistic model includes a **threshold population**. The threshold population is defined to be the minimum population that is necessary for the species to survive. We use the variable $T$ to represent the threshold population. A differential equation that incorporates both the threshold population $T$ and carrying capacity $K$ is

$$\frac{dP}{dt} = -rP\left(1 - \frac{P}{K}\right)\left(1 - \frac{P}{T}\right) \quad (4.12)$$

where $r$ represents the growth rate, as before.

1. The threshold population is useful to biologists and can be utilized to determine whether a given species should be placed on the endangered list. A group of Australian researchers say they have determined the threshold population for any species to survive: $5000$ adults. (Catherine Clabby, "A Magic Number," *American Scientist* 98(1): 24, doi:10.1511/2010.82.24. accessed April 9, 2015, http://www.americanscientist.org/issues/pub/a-magic-number). Therefore we use $T = 5000$ as the threshold population in this project. Suppose that the environmental carrying capacity in Montana for elk is $25{,}000$. Set up Equation 4.12 using the carrying capacity of $25{,}000$ and threshold population of $5000$. Assume an annual net growth rate of $18\%$.
2. Draw the direction field for the differential equation from step $1$, along with several solutions for different initial populations. What are the constant solutions of the differential equation? What do these solutions correspond to in the original population model (i.e., in a biological context)?
3. What is the limiting population for each initial population you chose in step $2$? (Hint: use the slope field to see what happens for various initial populations, i.e., look for the horizontal asymptotes of your solutions.)
4. This equation can be solved using the method of separation of variables. However, it is very difficult to get the solution as an explicit function of $t$. Using an initial population of $18{,}000$ elk, solve the initial-value problem and express the solution as an implicit function of $t$, or solve the general initial-value problem, finding a solution in terms of $r$, $K$, $T$, and $P_0$.

# 4.4 EXERCISES

For the following problems, consider the logistic equation in the form $P' = CP - P^2$. Draw the directional field and find the stability of the equilibria.

168. $C = 3$

169. $C = 0$

170. $C = -3$

171. Solve the logistic equation for $C = 10$ and an initial condition of $P(0) = 2$.

172. Solve the logistic equation for $C = -10$ and an initial condition of $P(0) = 2$.

173. A population of deer inside a park has a carrying capacity of $200$ and a growth rate of $2\%$. If the initial population is $50$ deer, what is the population of deer at any given time?

174. A population of frogs in a pond has a growth rate of $5\%$. If the initial population is $1000$ frogs and the carrying capacity is $6000$, what is the population of frogs at any given time?

175. **[T]** Bacteria grow at a rate of $20\%$ per hour in a petri dish. If there is initially one bacterium and a carrying capacity of $1$ million cells, how long does it take to reach $500{,}000$ cells?

176. **[T]** Rabbits in a park have an initial population of $10$ and grow at a rate of $4\%$ per year. If the carrying capacity is $500$, at what time does the population reach $100$ rabbits?

177. **[T]** Two monkeys are placed on an island. After $5$ years, there are $8$ monkeys, and the estimated carrying capacity is $25$ monkeys. When does the population of monkeys reach $16$ monkeys?

178. **[T]** A butterfly sanctuary is built that can hold $2000$ butterflies, and $400$ butterflies are initially moved in. If after $2$ months there are now $800$ butterflies, when does the population get to $1500$ butterflies?

The following problems consider the logistic equation with an added term for depletion, either through death or emigration.

179. **[T]** The population of trout in a pond is given by $P' = 0.4P\left(1 - \frac{P}{10000}\right) - 400$, where $400$ trout are caught per year. Use your calculator or computer software to draw a directional field and draw a few sample solutions. What do you expect for the behavior?

180. In the preceding problem, what are the stabilities of the equilibria $0 < P_1 < P_2$?

181. **[T]** For the preceding problem, use software to generate a directional field for the value $f = 400$. What are the stabilities of the equilibria?

182. **[T]** For the preceding problems, use software to generate a directional field for the value $f = 600$. What are the stabilities of the equilibria?

183. **[T]** For the preceding problems, consider the case where a certain number of fish are added to the pond, or $f = -200$. What are the nonnegative equilibria and their stabilities?

It is more likely that the amount of fishing is governed by the current number of fish present, so instead of a constant number of fish being caught, the rate is proportional to the current number of fish present, with proportionality constant $k$, as

$$P' = 0.4P\left(1 - \frac{P}{10000}\right) - kP.$$

184. **[T]** For the previous fishing problem, draw a directional field assuming $k = 0.1$. Draw some solutions that exhibit this behavior. What are the equilibria and what are their stabilities?

185. **[T]** Use software or a calculator to draw directional fields for $k = 0.4$. What are the nonnegative equilibria and their stabilities?

186. **[T]** Use software or a calculator to draw directional fields for $k = 0.6$. What are the equilibria and their stabilities?

187. Solve this equation, assuming a value of $k = 0.05$ and an initial condition of $2000$ fish.

188. Solve this equation, assuming a value of $k = 0.05$ and an initial condition of $5000$ fish.

The following problems add in a minimal threshold value for the species to survive, $T$, which changes the differential equation to $P'(t) = rP\left(1 - \frac{P}{K}\right)\left(1 - \frac{T}{P}\right)$.

189. Draw the directional field of the threshold logistic equation, assuming $K = 10$, $r = 0.1$, $T = 2$. When does the population survive? When does it go extinct?

190. For the preceding problem, solve the logistic threshold equation, assuming the initial condition $P(0) = P_0$.

191. Bengal tigers in a conservation park have a carrying capacity of $100$ and need a minimum of $10$ to survive. If they grow in population at a rate of $1\%$ per year, with an initial population of $15$ tigers, solve for the number of tigers present.

192. A forest containing ring-tailed lemurs in Madagascar has the potential to support $5000$ individuals, and the lemur population grows at a rate of $5\%$ per year. A minimum of $500$ individuals is needed for the lemurs to survive. Given an initial population of $600$ lemurs, solve for the population of lemurs.

193. The population of mountain lions in Northern Arizona has an estimated carrying capacity of $250$ and grows at a rate of $0.25\%$ per year and there must be $25$ for the population to survive. With an initial population of $30$ mountain lions, how many years will it take to get the mountain lions off the endangered species list (at least $100$)?

The following questions consider the Gompertz equation, a modification for logistic growth, which is often used for modeling cancer growth, specifically the number of tumor cells.

194. The Gompertz equation is given by $P(t)' = \alpha \ln\left(\frac{K}{P(t)}\right)P(t)$. Draw the directional fields for this equation assuming all parameters are positive, and given that $K = 1$.

195. Assume that for a population, $K = 1000$ and $\alpha = 0.05$. Draw the directional field associated with this differential equation and draw a few solutions. What is the behavior of the population?

196. Solve the Gompertz equation for generic $\alpha$ and $K$ and $P(0) = P_0$.

197. **[T]** The Gompertz equation has been used to model tumor growth in the human body. Starting from one tumor cell on day $1$ and assuming $\alpha = 0.1$ and a carrying capacity of $10$ million cells, how long does it take to reach "detection" stage at $5$ million cells?

198. **[T]** It is estimated that the world human population reached $3$ billion people in $1959$ and $6$ billion in $1999$. Assuming a carrying capacity of $16$ billion humans, write and solve the differential equation for logistic growth, and determine what year the population reached $7$ billion.

199. **[T]** It is estimated that the world human population reached $3$ billion people in $1959$ and $6$ billion in $1999$. Assuming a carrying capacity of $16$ billion humans, write and solve the differential equation for Gompertz growth, and determine what year the population reached $7$ billion. Was logistic growth or Gompertz growth more accurate, considering world population reached $7$ billion on October $31, 2011$?

200. Show that the population grows fastest when it reaches half the carrying capacity for the logistic equation $P' = rP\left(1 - \frac{P}{K}\right)$.

201. When does population increase the fastest in the threshold logistic equation $P'(t) = rP\left(1 - \frac{P}{K}\right)\left(1 - \frac{T}{P}\right)$?

202. When does population increase the fastest for the Gompertz equation $P(t)' = \alpha \ln\left(\frac{K}{P(t)}\right)P(t)$?

Below is a table of the populations of whooping cranes in the wild from 1940 to 2000. The population rebounded from near extinction after conservation efforts began. The following problems consider applying population models to fit the data. Assume a carrying capacity of 10,000 cranes. Fit the data assuming years since $1940$ (so your initial population at time $0$ would be $22$ cranes).

| Year (years since conservation began) | Whooping Crane Population |
|---|---|
| 1940(0) | 22 |
| 1950(10) | 31 |
| 1960(20) | 36 |
| 1970(30) | 57 |
| 1980(40) | 91 |
| 1990(50) | 159 |
| 2000(60) | 256 |

*Source:* https://www.savingcranes.org/images/stories/site_images/conservation/whooping_crane/pdfs/historic_wc_numbers.pdf

203. Find the equation and parameter $r$ that best fit the data for the logistic equation.

204. Find the equation and parameters $r$ and $T$ that best fit the data for the threshold logistic equation.

205. Find the equation and parameter $\alpha$ that best fit the data for the Gompertz equation.

206. Graph all three solutions and the data on the same graph. Which model appears to be most accurate?

207. Using the three equations found in the previous problems, estimate the population in $2010$ (year $70$ after conservation). The real population measured at that time was $437$. Which model is most accurate?

# 4.5 | First-order Linear Equations

**Learning Objectives**

- **4.5.1** Write a first-order linear differential equation in standard form.
- **4.5.2** Find an integrating factor and use it to solve a first-order linear differential equation.
- **4.5.3** Solve applied problems involving first-order linear differential equations.

Earlier, we studied an application of a first-order differential equation that involved solving for the velocity of an object. In particular, if a ball is thrown upward with an initial velocity of $v_0$ ft/s, then an initial-value problem that describes the velocity of the ball after $t$ seconds is given by

$$\frac{dv}{dt} = -32, \quad v(0) = v_0.$$

This model assumes that the only force acting on the ball is gravity. Now we add to the problem by allowing for the possibility of air resistance acting on the ball.

Air resistance always acts in the direction opposite to motion. Therefore if an object is rising, air resistance acts in a downward direction. If the object is falling, air resistance acts in an upward direction (**Figure 4.24**). There is no exact relationship between the velocity of an object and the air resistance acting on it. For very small objects, air resistance is proportional to velocity; that is, the force due to air resistance is numerically equal to some constant $k$ times $v$. For larger (e.g., baseball-sized) objects, depending on the shape, air resistance can be approximately proportional to the square of the velocity. In fact, air resistance may be proportional to $v^{1.5}$, or $v^{0.9}$, or some other power of $v$.

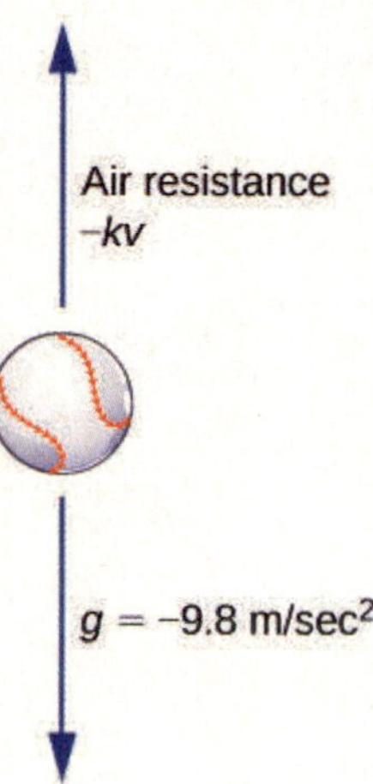


**Figure 4.24** Forces acting on a moving baseball: gravity acts in a downward direction and air resistance acts in a direction opposite to the direction of motion.

We will work with the linear approximation for air resistance. If we assume $k > 0$, then the expression for the force $F_A$ due to air resistance is given by $F_A = -kv$. Therefore the sum of the forces acting on the object is equal to the sum of the gravitational force and the force due to air resistance. This, in turn, is equal to the mass of the object multiplied by its acceleration at time $t$ (Newton's second law). This gives us the differential equation

$$m\frac{dv}{dt} = -kv - mg.$$

Finally, we impose an initial condition $v(0) = v_0$, where $v_0$ is the initial velocity measured in meters per second. This makes $g = 9.8 \text{ m/s}^2$. The initial-value problem becomes

$$m\frac{dv}{dt} = -kv - mg, \quad v(0) = v_0. \tag{4.13}$$

The differential equation in this initial-value problem is an example of a first-order linear differential equation. (Recall that a differential equation is first-order if the highest-order derivative that appears in the equation is $1$.) In this section, we study first-order linear equations and examine a method for finding a general solution to these types of equations, as well as solving initial-value problems involving them.

### Definition

A first-order differential equation is **linear** if it can be written in the form

$$a(x)y' + b(x)y = c(x), \tag{4.14}$$

where $a(x)$, $b(x)$, and $c(x)$ are arbitrary functions of $x$.

Remember that the unknown function $y$ depends on the variable $x$; that is, $x$ is the independent variable and $y$ is the dependent variable. Some examples of first-order linear differential equations are

$$\begin{aligned}\left(3x^2 - 4\right)y' + (x-3)y &= \sin x \\ (\sin x)y' - (\cos x)y &= \cot x \\ 4xy' + (3\ln x)y &= x^3 - 4x.\end{aligned}$$

Examples of first-order nonlinear differential equations include

$$\begin{aligned}(y')^4 - (y')^3 &= (3x-2)(y+4) \\ 4y' + 3y^3 &= 4x - 5 \\ (y')^2 &= \sin y + \cos x.\end{aligned}$$

These equations are nonlinear because of terms like $(y')^4$, $y^3$, etc. Due to these terms, it is impossible to put these equations into the same form as **Equation 4.14**.

## Standard Form

Consider the differential equation

$$\left(3x^2 - 4\right)y' + (x-3)y = \sin x.$$

Our main goal in this section is to derive a solution method for equations of this form. It is useful to have the coefficient of $y'$ be equal to $1$. To make this happen, we divide both sides by $3x^2 - 4$.

$$y' + \left(\frac{x-3}{3x^2-4}\right)y = \frac{\sin x}{3x^2-4}$$

This is called the **standard form** of the differential equation. We will use it later when finding the solution to a general first-order linear differential equation. Returning to **Equation 4.14**, we can divide both sides of the equation by $a(x)$. This leads to the equation

$$y' + \frac{b(x)}{a(x)}y = \frac{c(x)}{a(x)}. \tag{4.15}$$

Now define $p(x) = \dfrac{b(x)}{a(x)}$ and $q(x) = \dfrac{c(x)}{a(x)}$. Then **Equation 4.14** becomes

$$y' + p(x)y = q(x). \tag{4.16}$$

We can write any first-order linear differential equation in this form, and this is referred to as the standard form for a first-order linear differential equation.

## Example 4.15

### Writing First-Order Linear Equations in Standard Form

Put each of the following first-order linear differential equations into standard form. Identify $p(x)$ and $q(x)$ for each equation.

a. $y' = 3x - 4y$

b. $\frac{3xy'}{4y - 3} = 2$ (here $x > 0$)

c. $y = 3y' - 4x^2 + 5$

### Solution

a. Add $4y$ to both sides:

$$y' + 4y = 3x.$$

In this equation, $p(x) = 4$ and $q(x) = 3x$.

b. Multiply both sides by $4y - 3,$ then subtract $8y$ from each side:

$$\begin{aligned} \frac{3xy'}{4y - 3} &= 2 \\ 3xy' &= 2(4y - 3) \\ 3xy' &= 8y - 6 \\ 3xy' - 8y &= -6. \end{aligned}$$

Finally, divide both sides by $3x$ to make the coefficient of $y'$ equal to $1$:

$$y' - \frac{8}{3x}y = -\frac{2}{3x}. \qquad (4.17)$$

This is allowable because in the original statement of this problem we assumed that $x > 0$. (If $x = 0$ then the original equation becomes $0 = 2,$ which is clearly a false statement.)

In this equation, $p(x) = -\frac{8}{3x}$ and $q(x) = -\frac{2}{3x}$.

c. Subtract $y$ from each side and add $4x^2 - 5$:

$$3y' - y = 4x^2 - 5.$$

Next divide both sides by $3$:

$$y' - \frac{1}{3}y = \frac{4}{3}x^2 - \frac{5}{3}.$$

In this equation, $p(x) = -\frac{1}{3}$ and $q(x) = \frac{4}{3}x^2 - \frac{5}{3}$.

**4.15** Put the equation $\frac{(x + 3)y'}{2x - 3y - 4} = 5$ into standard form and identify $p(x)$ and $q(x)$.

## Integrating Factors

We now develop a solution technique for any first-order linear differential equation. We start with the standard form of a first-order linear differential equation:

$$y' + p(x)y = q(x). \tag{4.18}$$

The first term on the left-hand side of **Equation 4.15** is the derivative of the unknown function, and the second term is the product of a known function with the unknown function. This is somewhat reminiscent of the power rule from the **Differentiation Rules (http://cnx.org/content/m53575/latest/)** section. If we multiply **Equation 4.16** by a yet-to-be-determined function $\mu(x)$, then the equation becomes

$$\mu(x)y' + \mu(x)p(x)y = \mu(x)q(x). \tag{4.19}$$

The left-hand side **Equation 4.18** can be matched perfectly to the product rule:

$$\frac{d}{dx}[f(x)g(x)] = f'(x)g(x) + f(x)g'(x).$$

Matching term by term gives $y = f(x)$, $g(x) = \mu(x)$, and $g'(x) = \mu(x)p(x)$. Taking the derivative of $g(x) = \mu(x)$ and setting it equal to the right-hand side of $g'(x) = \mu(x)p(x)$ leads to

$$\mu'(x) = \mu(x)p(x).$$

This is a first-order, separable differential equation for $\mu(x)$. We know $p(x)$ because it appears in the differential equation we are solving. Separating variables and integrating yields

$$\begin{aligned} \frac{\mu'(x)}{\mu(x)} &= p(x) \\ \int \frac{\mu'(x)}{\mu(x)} dx &= \int p(x)\,dx \\ \ln|\mu(x)| &= \int p(x)\,dx + C \\ e^{\ln|\mu(x)|} &= e^{\int p(x)\,dx + C} \\ |\mu(x)| &= C_1 e^{\int p(x)\,dx} \\ \mu(x) &= C_2 e^{\int p(x)\,dx}. \end{aligned}$$

Here $C_2$ can be an arbitrary (positive or negative) constant. This leads to a general method for solving a first-order linear differential equation. We first multiply both sides of **Equation 4.16** by the **integrating factor** $\mu(x)$. This gives

$$\mu(x)y' + \mu(x)p(x)y = \mu(x)q(x). \tag{4.20}$$

The left-hand side of **Equation 4.19** can be rewritten as $\frac{d}{dx}(\mu(x)y)$.

$$\frac{d}{dx}(\mu(x)y) = \mu(x)q(x). \tag{4.21}$$

Next integrate both sides of **Equation 4.20** with respect to $x$.

$$\begin{aligned} \int \frac{d}{dx}(\mu(x)y)dx &= \int \mu(x)q(x)\,dx \\ \mu(x)y &= \int \mu(x)q(x)\,dx. \end{aligned} \tag{4.22}$$

Divide both sides of **Equation 4.21** by $\mu(x)$:

$$y = \frac{1}{\mu(x)}\left[\int \mu(x)q(x)\,dx + C\right]. \tag{4.23}$$

Since $\mu(x)$ was previously calculated, we are now finished. An important note about the integrating constant $C$: It may seem that we are inconsistent in the usage of the integrating constant. However, the integral involving $p(x)$ is necessary in order to find an integrating factor for **Equation 4.15**. Only one integrating factor is needed in order to solve the equation; therefore, it is safe to assign a value for $C$ for this integral. We chose $C = 0.$ When calculating the integral inside the brackets in **Equation 4.21**, it is necessary to keep our options open for the value of the integrating constant, because our goal is to find a general family of solutions to **Equation 4.15**. This integrating factor guarantees just that.

### Problem-Solving Strategy: Solving a First-order Linear Differential Equation

1. Put the equation into standard form and identify $p(x)$ and $q(x)$.
2. Calculate the integrating factor $\mu(x) = e^{\int p(x)\,dx}$.
3. Multiply both sides of the differential equation by $\mu(x)$.
4. Integrate both sides of the equation obtained in step $3,$ and divide both sides by $\mu(x)$.
5. If there is an initial condition, determine the value of $C$.

## Example 4.16

### Solving a First-order Linear Equation

Find a general solution for the differential equation $xy' + 3y = 4x^2 - 3x.$ Assume $x > 0.$

#### Solution

1. To put this differential equation into standard form, divide both sides by $x$:

$$y' + \frac{3}{x}y = 4x - 3.$$

Therefore $p(x) = \frac{3}{x}$ and $q(x) = 4x - 3.$

2. The integrating factor is $\mu(x) = e^{\int (3/x)\,dx} = e^{3\ln x} = x^3.$
3. Multiplying both sides of the differential equation by $\mu(x)$ gives us

$$\begin{aligned} x^3 y' + x^3\left(\frac{3}{x}\right)y &= x^3(4x - 3) \\ x^3 y' + 3x^2 y &= 4x^4 - 3x^3 \\ \frac{d}{dx}\left(x^3 y\right) &= 4x^4 - 3x^3. \end{aligned}$$

4. Integrate both sides of the equation.

$$\begin{aligned} \int \frac{d}{dx}\left(x^3 y\right)dx &= \int 4x^4 - 3x^3 dx \\ x^3 y &= \frac{4x^5}{5} - \frac{3x^4}{4} + C \\ y &= \frac{4x^2}{5} - \frac{3x}{4} + Cx^{-3}. \end{aligned}$$

5. There is no initial value, so the problem is complete.

#### Analysis

You may have noticed the condition that was imposed on the differential equation; namely, $x > 0$. For any nonzero value of $C$, the general solution is not defined at $x = 0$. Furthermore, when $x < 0$, the integrating factor changes. The integrating factor is given by **Equation 4.19** as $f(x) = e^{\int p(x)dx}$. For this $p(x)$ we get

$$e^{\int p(x)\,dx} = e^{\int (3/x)dx} = e^{3\ln|x|} = |x|^3,$$

since $x < 0$. The behavior of the general solution changes at $x = 0$ largely due to the fact that $p(x)$ is not defined there.

**4.16** Find the general solution to the differential equation $(x-2)y' + y = 3x^2 + 2x$. Assume $x > 2$.

Now we use the same strategy to find the solution to an initial-value problem.

## Example 4.17

### A First-order Linear Initial-Value Problem

Solve the initial-value problem

$$y' + 3y = 2x - 1, \quad y(0) = 3.$$

### Solution

1. This differential equation is already in standard form with $p(x) = 3$ and $q(x) = 2x - 1$.
2. The integrating factor is $\mu(x) = e^{\int 3dx} = e^{3x}$.
3. Multiplying both sides of the differential equation by $\mu(x)$ gives

$$\begin{aligned} e^{3x}y' + 3e^{3x}y &= (2x-1)e^{3x} \\ \frac{d}{dx}\left[ye^{3x}\right] &= (2x-1)e^{3x}. \end{aligned}$$

Integrate both sides of the equation:

$$\begin{aligned} \int \frac{d}{dx}\left[ye^{3x}\right]dx &= \int (2x-1)e^{3x}\,dx \\ ye^{3x} &= \frac{e^{3x}}{3}(2x-1) - \int \frac{2}{3}e^{3x}\,dx \\ ye^{3x} &= \frac{e^{3x}(2x-1)}{3} - \frac{2e^{3x}}{9} + C \\ y &= \frac{2x-1}{3} - \frac{2}{9} + Ce^{-3x} \\ y &= \frac{2x}{3} - \frac{5}{9} + Ce^{-3x}. \end{aligned}$$

4. Now substitute $x = 0$ and $y = 3$ into the general solution and solve for $C$:

$$\begin{aligned} y &= \frac{2}{3}x - \frac{5}{9} + Ce^{-3x} \\ 3 &= \frac{2}{3}(0) - \frac{5}{9} + Ce^{-3(0)} \\ 3 &= -\frac{5}{9} + C \\ C &= \frac{32}{9}. \end{aligned}$$

Therefore the solution to the initial-value problem is

$$y = \frac{2}{3}x - \frac{5}{9} + \frac{32}{9}e^{-3x}.$$

**4.17** Solve the initial-value problem $y' - 2y = 4x + 3 \quad y(0) = -2.$

## Applications of First-order Linear Differential Equations

We look at two different applications of first-order linear differential equations. The first involves air resistance as it relates to objects that are rising or falling; the second involves an electrical circuit. Other applications are numerous, but most are solved in a similar fashion.

### Free fall with air resistance

We discussed air resistance at the beginning of this section. The next example shows how to apply this concept for a ball in vertical motion. Other factors can affect the force of air resistance, such as the size and shape of the object, but we ignore them here.

### Example 4.18

#### A Ball with Air Resistance

A racquetball is hit straight upward with an initial velocity of $2$ m/s. The mass of a racquetball is approximately $0.0427$ kg. Air resistance acts on the ball with a force numerically equal to $0.5v,$ where $v$ represents the velocity of the ball at time $t$.

a. Find the velocity of the ball as a function of time.
b. How long does it take for the ball to reach its maximum height?
c. If the ball is hit from an initial height of $1$ meter, how high will it reach?

#### Solution

a. The mass $m = 0.0427\,\text{kg},\ k = 0.5,$ and $g = 9.8\,\text{m/s}^2$. The initial velocity is $v_0 = 2$ m/s. Therefore the initial-value problem is

$$0.0427\frac{dv}{dt} = -0.5v - 0.0427(9.8), \qquad v_0 = 2.$$

Dividing the differential equation by $0.0427$ gives

$$\frac{dv}{dt} = -11.7096v - 9.8, \quad v_0 = 2.$$

The differential equation is linear. Using the problem-solving strategy for linear differential equations:

Step 1. Rewrite the differential equation as $\frac{dv}{dt} + 11.7096v = -9.8$. This gives $p(t) = 11.7096$ and $q(t) = -9.8$

Step 2. The integrating factor is $\mu(t) = e^{\int 11.7096dt} = e^{11.7096t}$.

Step 3. Multiply the differential equation by $\mu(t)$:

$$\begin{aligned} e^{11.7096t}\frac{dv}{dt} + 11.7096ve^{11.7096t} &= -9.8e^{11.7096t} \\ \frac{d}{dt}\left[ve^{11.7096t}\right] &= -9.8e^{11.7096t}. \end{aligned}$$

Step 4. Integrate both sides:

$$\begin{aligned} \int \frac{d}{dt}\left[ve^{11.7096t}\right]dt &= \int -9.8e^{11.7096t}dt \\ ve^{11.7096t} &= \frac{-9.8}{11.7096}e^{11.7096t} + C \\ v(t) &= -0.8369 + Ce^{-11.7096t}. \end{aligned}$$

Step 5. Solve for $C$ using the initial condition $v_0 = v(0) = 2$:

$$\begin{aligned} v(t) &= -0.8369 + Ce^{-11.7096t} \\ v(0) &= -0.8369 + Ce^{-11.7096(0)} \\ 2 &= -0.8369 + C \\ C &= 2.8369. \end{aligned}$$

Therefore the solution to the initial-value problem is $v(t) = 2.8369e^{-11.7096t} - 0.8369$.

b. The ball reaches its maximum height when the velocity is equal to zero. The reason is that when the velocity is positive, it is rising, and when it is negative, it is falling. Therefore when it is zero, it is neither rising nor falling, and is at its maximum height:

$$\begin{aligned} 2.8369e^{-11.7096t} - 0.8369 &= 0 \\ 2.8369e^{-11.7096t} &= 0.8369 \\ e^{-11.7096t} &= \frac{0.8369}{2.8369} \approx 0.295 \\ \ln e^{-11.7096t} &= \ln 0.295 \approx -1.221 \\ -11.7096t &= -1.221 \\ t &\approx 0.104. \end{aligned}$$

Therefore it takes approximately $0.104$ second to reach maximum height.

c. To find the height of the ball as a function of time, use the fact that the derivative of position is velocity, i.e., if $h(t)$ represents the height at time $t$, then $h'(t) = v(t)$. Because we know $v(t)$ and the initial height, we can form an initial-value problem:

$$h'(t) = 2.8369e^{-11.7096t} - 0.8369, \quad h(0) = 1.$$

Integrating both sides of the differential equation with respect to $t$ gives

$$\begin{aligned} \int h'(t)\,dt &= \int 2.8369e^{-11.7096t} - 0.8369dt \\ h(t) &= -\frac{2.8369}{11.7096}e^{-11.7096t} - 0.8369t + C \\ h(t) &= -0.2423e^{-11.7096t} - 0.8369t + C. \end{aligned}$$

Solve for $C$ by using the initial condition:

$$\begin{aligned} h(t) &= -0.2423e^{-11.7096t} - 0.8369t + C \\ h(0) &= -0.2423e^{-11.7096(0)} - 0.8369(0) + C \\ 1 &= -0.2423 + C \\ C &= 1.2423. \end{aligned}$$

Therefore

$$h(t) = -0.2423e^{-11.7096t} - 0.8369t + 1.2423.$$

After $0.104$ second, the height is given by

$h(0.2) = -0.2423e^{-11.7096t} - 0.8369t + 1.2423 \approx 1.0836$ meter.

**4.18** The weight of a penny is $2.5$ grams (United States Mint, “Coin Specifications,” accessed April 9, 2015, http://www.usmint.gov/about_the_mint/?action=coin_specifications), and the upper observation deck of the Empire State Building is $369$ meters above the street. Since the penny is a small and relatively smooth object, air resistance acting on the penny is actually quite small. We assume the air resistance is numerically equal to $0.0025v$. Furthermore, the penny is dropped with no initial velocity imparted to it.

a. Set up an initial-value problem that represents the falling penny.

b. Solve the problem for $v(t)$.

c. What is the terminal velocity of the penny (i.e., calculate the limit of the velocity as $t$ approaches infinity)?

## Electrical Circuits

A source of electromotive force (e.g., a battery or generator) produces a flow of current in a closed circuit, and this current produces a voltage drop across each resistor, inductor, and capacitor in the circuit. Kirchhoff’s Loop Rule states that the sum of the voltage drops across resistors, inductors, and capacitors is equal to the total electromotive force in a closed circuit. We have the following three results:

1. The voltage drop across a resistor is given by

$$E_R = Ri,$$

where $R$ is a constant of proportionality called the *resistance,* and $i$ is the current.

2. The voltage drop across an inductor is given by

$$E_L = Li',$$

where $L$ is a constant of proportionality called the *inductance*, and $i$ again denotes the current.

3. The voltage drop across a capacitor is given by

$$E_C = \frac{1}{C}q,$$

where $C$ is a constant of proportionality called the *capacitance*, and $q$ is the instantaneous charge on the capacitor. The relationship between $i$ and $q$ is $i = q'$.

We use units of volts (V) to measure voltage $E$, amperes (A) to measure current $i$, coulombs (C) to measure charge $q$, ohms (Ω) to measure resistance $R$, henrys (H) to measure inductance $L$, and farads (F) to measure capacitance $C$. Consider the circuit in **Figure 4.25**.

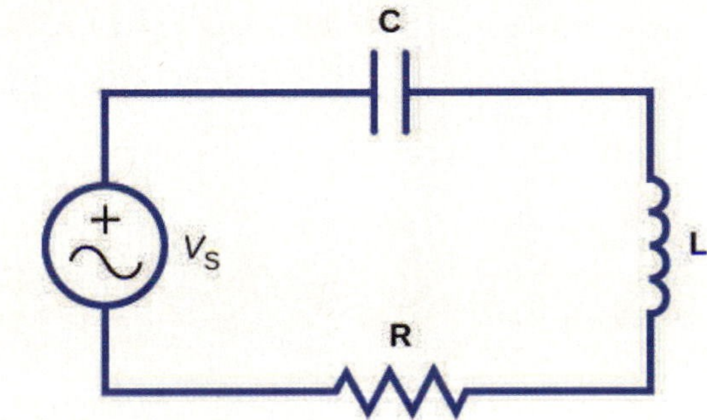


**Figure 4.25** A typical electric circuit, containing a voltage generator $(V_S)$, capacitor $(C)$, inductor $(L)$, and resistor $(R)$.

Applying Kirchhoff's Loop Rule to this circuit, we let $E$ denote the electromotive force supplied by the voltage generator. Then

$$E_L + E_R + E_C = E.$$

Substituting the expressions for $E_L$, $E_R$, and $E_C$ into this equation, we obtain

$$Li' + Ri + \frac{1}{C}q = E. \tag{4.24}$$

If there is no capacitor in the circuit, then the equation becomes

$$Li' + Ri = E. \tag{4.25}$$

This is a first-order differential equation in $i$. The circuit is referred to as an $LR$ circuit.

Next, suppose there is no inductor in the circuit, but there is a capacitor and a resistor, so $L = 0$, $R \neq 0$, and $C \neq 0$. Then **Equation 4.23** can be rewritten as

$$Rq' + \frac{1}{C}q = E, \tag{4.26}$$

which is a first-order linear differential equation. This is referred to as an *RC* circuit. In either case, we can set up and solve an initial-value problem.

## Example 4.19

### Finding Current in an *RL* Electric Circuit

A circuit has in series an electromotive force given by $E = 50\sin 20t$ V, a resistor of 5Ω, and an inductor of 0.4 H. If the initial current is 0, find the current at time $t > 0$.

### Solution

We have a resistor and an inductor in the circuit, so we use **Equation 4.24**. The voltage drop across the resistor is given by $E_R = Ri = 5i$. The voltage drop across the inductor is given by $E_L = Li' = 0.4i'$. The electromotive force becomes the right-hand side of **Equation 4.24**. Therefore **Equation 4.24** becomes

$$0.4i' + 5i = 50\sin 20t.$$

Dividing both sides by $0.4$ gives the equation

$$i' + 12.5i = 125\sin 20t.$$

Since the initial current is 0, this result gives an initial condition of $i(0) = 0$. We can solve this initial-value problem using the five-step strategy for solving first-order differential equations.

Step 1. Rewrite the differential equation as $i' + 12.5i = 125\sin 20t$. This gives $p(t) = 12.5$ and $q(t) = 125\sin 20t$.

Step 2. The integrating factor is $\mu(t) = e^{\int 12.5dt} = e^{12.5t}$.

Step 3. Multiply the differential equation by $\mu(t)$:

$$\begin{aligned} e^{12.5t}i' + 12.5e^{12.5t}i &= 125e^{12.5t}\sin 20t \\ \frac{d}{dt}\left[ie^{12.5t}\right] &= 125e^{12.5t}\sin 20t. \end{aligned}$$

Step 4. Integrate both sides:

$$\begin{aligned} \int \frac{d}{dt}\left[ie^{12.5t}\right]dt &= \int 125e^{12.5t}\sin 20t\,dt \\ ie^{12.5t} &= \left(\frac{250\sin 20t - 400\cos 20t}{89}\right)e^{12.5t} + C \\ i(t) &= \frac{250\sin 20t - 400\cos 20t}{89} + Ce^{-12.5t}. \end{aligned}$$

Step 5. Solve for $C$ using the initial condition $v(0) = 2$:

$$\begin{aligned} i(t) &= \frac{250\sin 20t - 400\cos 20t}{89} + Ce^{-12.5t} \\ i(0) &= \frac{250\sin 20(0) - 400\cos 20(0)}{89} + Ce^{-12.5(0)} \\ 0 &= -\frac{400}{89} + C \\ C &= \frac{400}{89}. \end{aligned}$$

Therefore the solution to the initial-value problem is $i(t) = \frac{250\sin 20t - 400\cos 20t + 400e^{-12.5t}}{89} = \frac{250\sin 20t - 400\cos 20t}{89} + \frac{400e^{-12.5t}}{89}.$

The first term can be rewritten as a single cosine function. First, multiply and divide by $\sqrt{250^2 + 400^2} = 50\sqrt{89}$:

$$\begin{aligned} \frac{250\sin 20t - 400\cos 20t}{89} &= \frac{50\sqrt{89}}{89}\left(\frac{250\sin 20t - 400\cos 20t}{50\sqrt{89}}\right) \\ &= -\frac{50\sqrt{89}}{89}\left(\frac{8\cos 20t}{\sqrt{89}} - \frac{5\sin 20t}{\sqrt{89}}\right). \end{aligned}$$

Next, define $\varphi$ to be an acute angle such that $\cos\varphi = \frac{8}{\sqrt{89}}$. Then $\sin\varphi = \frac{5}{\sqrt{89}}$ and

$$-\frac{50\sqrt{89}}{89}\left(\frac{8\cos 20t}{\sqrt{89}} - \frac{5\sin 20t}{\sqrt{89}}\right) = -\frac{50\sqrt{89}}{89}(\cos\varphi\cos 20t - \sin\varphi\sin 20t)$$

$$= -\frac{50\sqrt{89}}{89}\cos(20t + \varphi).$$

Therefore the solution can be written as

$$i(t) = -\frac{50\sqrt{89}}{89}\cos(20t + \varphi) + \frac{400e^{-12.5t}}{89}.$$

The second term is called the *attenuation* term, because it disappears rapidly as $t$ grows larger. The phase shift is given by $\varphi,$ and the amplitude of the steady-state current is given by $\frac{50\sqrt{89}}{89}.$ The graph of this solution appears in **Figure 4.26**:

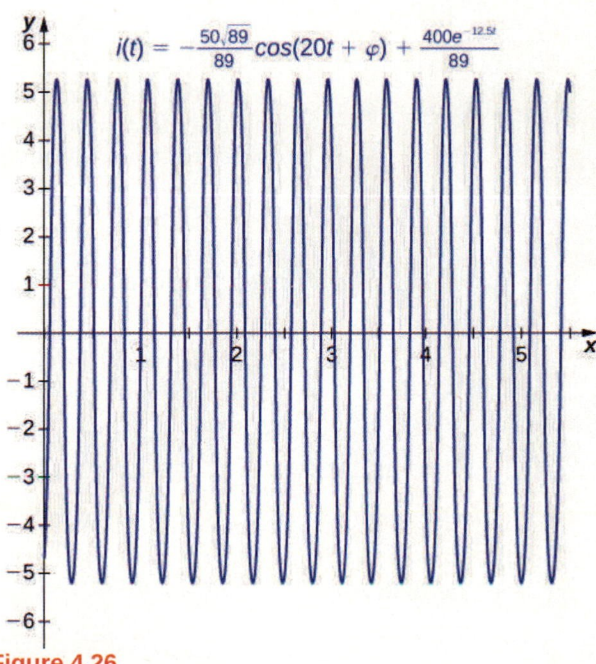


**Figure 4.26**

**4.19** A circuit has in series an electromotive force given by $E = 20\sin 5t$ V, a capacitor with capacitance $0.02$ F, and a resistor of $8\,\Omega$. If the initial charge is $4$ C, find the charge at time $t > 0$.

# 4.5 EXERCISES

Are the following differential equations linear? Explain your reasoning.

208. $\frac{dy}{dx} = x^2 y + \sin x$

209. $\frac{dy}{dt} = ty$

210. $\frac{dy}{dt} + y^2 = x$

211. $y' = x^3 + e^x$

212. $y' = y + e^y$

Write the following first-order differential equations in standard form.

213. $y' = x^3 y + \sin x$

214. $y' + 3y - \ln x = 0$

215. $-xy' = (3x + 2)y + xe^x$

216. $\frac{dy}{dt} = 4y + ty + \tan t$

217. $\frac{dy}{dt} = yx(x + 1)$

What are the integrating factors for the following differential equations?

218. $y' = xy + 3$

219. $y' + e^x y = \sin x$

220. $y' = x\ln(x)y + 3x$

221. $\frac{dy}{dx} = \tanh(x)y + 1$

222. $\frac{dy}{dt} + 3ty = e^t y$

Solve the following differential equations by using integrating factors.

223. $y' = 3y + 2$

224. $y' = 2y - x^2$

225. $xy' = 3y - 6x^2$

226. $(x + 2)y' = 3x + y$

227. $y' = 3x + xy$

228. $xy' = x + y$

229. $\sin(x)y' = y + 2x$

230. $y' = y + e^x$

231. $xy' = 3y + x^2$

232. $y' + \ln x = \frac{y}{x}$

Solve the following differential equations. Use your calculator to draw a family of solutions. Are there certain initial conditions that change the behavior of the solution?

233. **[T]** $(x + 2)y' = 2y - 1$

234. **[T]** $y' = 3e^{t/3} - 2y$

235. **[T]** $xy' + \frac{y}{2} = \sin(3t)$

236. **[T]** $xy' = 2\frac{\cos x}{x} - 3y$

237. **[T]** $(x + 1)y' = 3y + x^2 + 2x + 1$

238. **[T]** $\sin(x)y' + \cos(x)y = 2x$

239. **[T]** $\sqrt{x^2 + 1}y' = y + 2$

240. **[T]** $x^3 y' + 2x^2 y = x + 1$

Solve the following initial-value problems by using integrating factors.

241. $y' + y = x,\ y(0) = 3$

242. $y' = y + 2x^2,\ y(0) = 0$

243. $xy' = y - 3x^3,\ y(1) = 0$

244. $x^2 y' = xy - \ln x,\ y(1) = 1$

245. $\left(1 + x^2\right)y' = y - 1,\ y(0) = 0$

246. $xy' = y + 2x\ln x,\ y(1) = 5$

247. $(2 + x)y' = y + 2 + x,\ y(0) = 0$

248. $y' = xy + 2xe^x,\ y(0) = 2$

249. $\sqrt{x}y' = y + 2x,\ y(0) = 1$

250. $y' = 2y + xe^x,\ y(0) = -1$

251. A falling object of mass $m$ can reach terminal velocity when the drag force is proportional to its velocity, with proportionality constant $k$. Set up the differential equation and solve for the velocity given an initial velocity of $0$.

252. Using your expression from the preceding problem, what is the terminal velocity? (*Hint:* Examine the limiting behavior; does the velocity approach a value?)

253. **[T]** Using your equation for terminal velocity, solve for the distance fallen. How long does it take to fall $5000$ meters if the mass is $100$ kilograms, the acceleration due to gravity is $9.8\ \text{m/s}^2$ and the proportionality constant is $4$?

254. A more accurate way to describe terminal velocity is that the drag force is proportional to the square of velocity, with a proportionality constant $k$. Set up the differential equation and solve for the velocity.

255. Using your expression from the preceding problem, what is the terminal velocity? (*Hint:* Examine the limiting behavior: Does the velocity approach a value?)

256. **[T]** Using your equation for terminal velocity, solve for the distance fallen. How long does it take to fall $5000$ meters if the mass is $100$ kilograms, the acceleration due to gravity is $9.8\,\text{m/s}^2$ and the proportionality constant is $4$? Does it take more or less time than your initial estimate?

For the following problems, determine how parameter $a$ affects the solution.

257. Solve the generic equation $y' = ax + y$. How does varying $a$ change the behavior?

258. Solve the generic equation $y' = ax + y$. How does varying $a$ change the behavior?

259. Solve the generic equation $y' = ax + xy$. How does varying $a$ change the behavior?

260. Solve the generic equation $y' = x + axy$. How does varying $a$ change the behavior?

261. Solve $y' - y = e^{kt}$ with the initial condition $y(0) = 0$. As $k$ approaches $1$, what happens to your formula?

# CHAPTER 4 REVIEW

## KEY TERMS

**asymptotically semi-stable solution** $y = k$ if it is neither asymptotically stable nor asymptotically unstable

**asymptotically stable solution** $y = k$ if there exists $\varepsilon > 0$ such that for any value $c \in (k - \varepsilon, k + \varepsilon)$ the solution to the initial-value problem $y' = f(x, y), \quad y(x_0) = c$ approaches $k$ as $x$ approaches infinity

**asymptotically unstable solution** $y = k$ if there exists $\varepsilon > 0$ such that for any value $c \in (k - \varepsilon, k + \varepsilon)$ the solution to the initial-value problem $y' = f(x, y), \quad y(x_0) = c$ never approaches $k$ as $x$ approaches infinity

**autonomous differential equation** an equation in which the right-hand side is a function of $y$ alone

**carrying capacity** the maximum population of an organism that the environment can sustain indefinitely

**differential equation** an equation involving a function $y = y(x)$ and one or more of its derivatives

**direction field (slope field)** a mathematical object used to graphically represent solutions to a first-order differential equation; at each point in a direction field, a line segment appears whose slope is equal to the slope of a solution to the differential equation passing through that point

**equilibrium solution** any solution to the differential equation of the form $y = c$, where $c$ is a constant

**Euler's Method** a numerical technique used to approximate solutions to an initial-value problem

**general solution (or family of solutions)** the entire set of solutions to a given differential equation

**growth rate** the constant $r > 0$ in the exponential growth function $P(t) = P_0 e^{rt}$

**initial population** the population at time $t = 0$

**initial value(s)** a value or set of values that a solution of a differential equation satisfies for a fixed value of the independent variable

**initial velocity** the velocity at time $t = 0$

**initial-value problem** a differential equation together with an initial value or values

**integrating factor** any function $f(x)$ that is multiplied on both sides of a differential equation to make the side involving the unknown function equal to the derivative of a product of two functions

**linear** description of a first-order differential equation that can be written in the form $a(x)y' + b(x)y = c(x)$

**logistic differential equation** a differential equation that incorporates the carrying capacity $K$ and growth rate $r$ into a population model

**order of a differential equation** the highest order of any derivative of the unknown function that appears in the equation

**particular solution** member of a family of solutions to a differential equation that satisfies a particular initial condition

**phase line** a visual representation of the behavior of solutions to an autonomous differential equation subject to various initial conditions

**separable differential equation** any equation that can be written in the form $y' = f(x)g(y)$

**separation of variables** a method used to solve a separable differential equation

**solution curve** a curve graphed in a direction field that corresponds to the solution to the initial-value problem passing through a given point in the direction field

**solution to a differential equation** a function $y = f(x)$ that satisfies a given differential equation

**standard form** the form of a first-order linear differential equation obtained by writing the differential equation in the form $y' + p(x)y = q(x)$

**step size** the increment $h$ that is added to the $x$ value at each step in Euler's Method

**threshold population** the minimum population that is necessary for a species to survive

# KEY EQUATIONS

- **Euler's Method**
  $x_n = x_0 + nh$
  $y_n = y_{n-1} + hf(x_{n-1}, y_{n-1})$, where $h$ is the step size
- **Separable differential equation**
  $y' = f(x)g(y)$
- **Solution concentration**
  $\frac{du}{dt} = \text{INFLOW RATE} - \text{OUTFLOW RATE}$
- **Newton's law of cooling**
  $\frac{dT}{dt} = k(T - T_s)$
- **Logistic differential equation and initial-value problem**
  $\frac{dP}{dt} = rP\left(1 - \frac{P}{K}\right), \quad P(0) = P_0$
- **Solution to the logistic differential equation/initial-value problem**
  $P(t) = \frac{P_0 K e^{rt}}{(K - P_0) + P_0 e^{rt}}$
- **Threshold population model**
  $\frac{dP}{dt} = -rP\left(1 - \frac{P}{K}\right)\left(1 - \frac{P}{T}\right)$
- **standard form**
  $y' + p(x)y = q(x)$
- **integrating factor**
  $\mu(x) = e^{\int p(x)dx}$

# KEY CONCEPTS

## 4.1 Basics of Differential Equations

- A differential equation is an equation involving a function $y = f(x)$ and one or more of its derivatives. A solution is a function $y = f(x)$ that satisfies the differential equation when $f$ and its derivatives are substituted into the equation.
- The order of a differential equation is the highest order of any derivative of the unknown function that appears in the equation.
- A differential equation coupled with an initial value is called an initial-value problem. To solve an initial-value problem, first find the general solution to the differential equation, then determine the value of the constant. Initial-value problems have many applications in science and engineering.

## 4.2 Direction Fields and Numerical Methods

- A direction field is a mathematical object used to graphically represent solutions to a first-order differential equation.

- Euler's Method is a numerical technique that can be used to approximate solutions to a differential equation.

### 4.3 Separable Equations

- A separable differential equation is any equation that can be written in the form $y' = f(x)g(y)$.
- The method of separation of variables is used to find the general solution to a separable differential equation.

### 4.4 The Logistic Equation

- When studying population functions, different assumptions—such as exponential growth, logistic growth, or threshold population—lead to different rates of growth.
- The logistic differential equation incorporates the concept of a carrying capacity. This value is a limiting value on the population for any given environment.
- The logistic differential equation can be solved for any positive growth rate, initial population, and carrying capacity.

### 4.5 First-order Linear Equations

- Any first-order linear differential equation can be written in the form $y' + p(x)y = q(x)$.
- We can use a five-step problem-solving strategy for solving a first-order linear differential equation that may or may not include an initial value.
- Applications of first-order linear differential equations include determining motion of a rising or falling object with air resistance and finding current in an electrical circuit.

## CHAPTER 4 REVIEW EXERCISES

*True or False?* Justify your answer with a proof or a counterexample.

**262.** The differential equation $y' = 3x^2 y - \cos(x)y''$ is linear.

**263.** The differential equation $y' = x - y$ is separable.

**264.** You can explicitly solve all first-order differential equations by separation or by the method of integrating factors.

**265.** You can determine the behavior of all first-order differential equations using directional fields or Euler's method.

For the following problems, find the general solution to the differential equations.

**266.** $y' = x^2 + 3e^x - 2x$

**267.** $y' = 2^x + \cos^{-1} x$

**268.** $y' = y\left(x^2 + 1\right)$

**269.** $y' = e^{-y} \sin x$

**270.** $y' = 3x - 2y$

**271.** $y' = y \ln y$

For the following problems, find the solution to the initial value problem.

**272.** $y' = 8x - \ln x - 3x^4,\ y(1) = 5$

**273.** $y' = 3x - \cos x + 2,\ y(0) = 4$

**274.** $xy' = y(x - 2),\ y(1) = 3$

**275.** $y' = 3y^2(x + \cos x),\ y(0) = -2$

**276.** $(x - 1)y' = y - 2,\ y(0) = 0$

**277.** $y' = 3y - x + 6x^2,\ y(0) = -1$

For the following problems, draw the directional field

associated with the differential equation, then solve the differential equation. Draw a sample solution on the directional field.

**278.** $y' = 2y - y^2$

**279.** $y' = \frac{1}{x} + \ln x - y, \quad \text{for } x > 0$

For the following problems, use Euler's Method with $n = 5$ steps over the interval $t = [0, 1]$. Then solve the initial-value problem exactly. How close is your Euler's Method estimate?

**280.** $y' = -4yx,\ y(0) = 1$

**281.** $y' = 3^x - 2y,\ y(0) = 0$

For the following problems, set up and solve the differential equations.

**282.** A car drives along a freeway, accelerating according to $a = 5\sin(\pi t)$, where $t$ represents time in minutes. Find the velocity at any time $t$, assuming the car starts with an initial speed of $60$ mph.

**283.** You throw a ball of mass $2$ kilograms into the air with an upward velocity of $8$ m/s. Find exactly the time the ball will remain in the air, assuming that gravity is given by $g = 9.8\text{ m/s}^2$.

**284.** You drop a ball with a mass of $5$ kilograms out an airplane window at a height of $5000$ m. How long does it take for the ball to reach the ground?

**285.** You drop the same ball of mass $5$ kilograms out of the same airplane window at the same height, except this time you assume a drag force proportional to the ball's velocity, using a proportionality constant of $3$ and the ball reaches terminal velocity. Solve for the distance fallen as a function of time. How long does it take the ball to reach the ground?

**286.** A drug is administered to a patient every $24$ hours and is cleared at a rate proportional to the amount of drug left in the body, with proportionality constant $0.2$. If the patient needs a baseline level of $5$ mg to be in the bloodstream at all times, how large should the dose be?

**287.** A $1000$ -liter tank contains pure water and a solution of $0.2$ kg salt/L is pumped into the tank at a rate of $1$ L/min and is drained at the same rate. Solve for total amount of salt in the tank at time $t$.

**288.** You boil water to make tea. When you pour the water into your teapot, the temperature is $100°\text{C}$. After $5$ minutes in your $15°\text{C}$ room, the temperature of the tea is $85°\text{C}$. Solve the equation to determine the temperatures of the tea at time $t$. How long must you wait until the tea is at a drinkable temperature $(72°\text{C})$?

**289.** The human population (in thousands) of Nevada in $1950$ was roughly $160$. If the carrying capacity is estimated at $10$ million individuals, and assuming a growth rate of $2\%$ per year, develop a logistic growth model and solve for the population in Nevada at any time (use $1950$ as time = 0). What population does your model predict for $2000$? How close is your prediction to the true value of $1,998,257$?

**290.** Repeat the previous problem but use Gompertz growth model. Which is more accurate?

# 5 | SEQUENCES AND SERIES

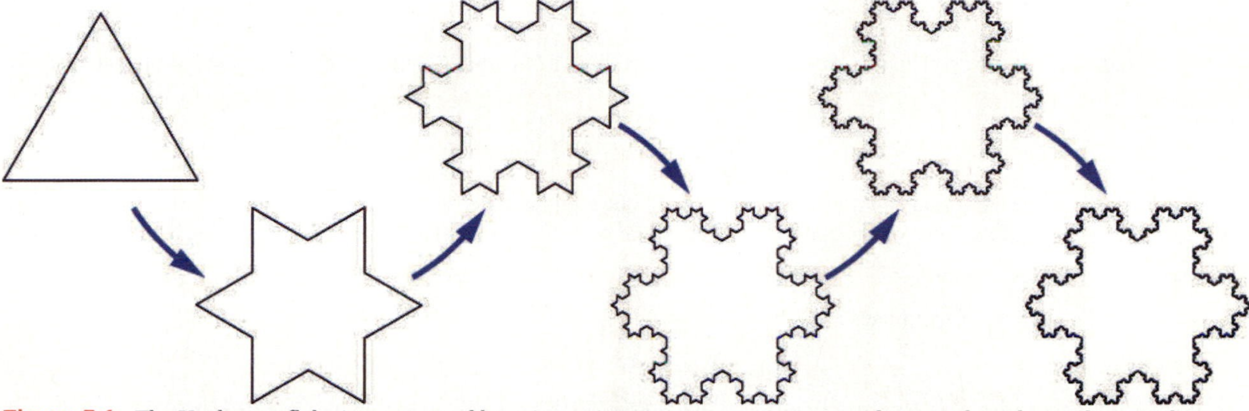

**Figure 5.1** The Koch snowflake is constructed by using an iterative process. Starting with an equilateral triangle, at each step of the process the middle third of each line segment is removed and replaced with an equilateral triangle pointing outward.

## Chapter Outline



## Introduction

The Koch snowflake is constructed from an infinite number of nonoverlapping equilateral triangles. Consequently, we can express its area as a sum of infinitely many terms. How do we add an infinite number of terms? Can a sum of an infinite number of terms be finite? To answer these questions, we need to introduce the concept of an infinite series, a sum with infinitely many terms. Having defined the necessary tools, we will be able to calculate the area of the Koch snowflake (see **Example 5.8**).

The topic of infinite series may seem unrelated to differential and integral calculus. In fact, an infinite series whose terms involve powers of a variable is a powerful tool that we can use to express functions as "infinite polynomials." We can use infinite series to evaluate complicated functions, approximate definite integrals, and create new functions. In addition, infinite series are used to solve differential equations that model physical behavior, from tiny electronic circuits to Earth-orbiting satellites.

## 5.1 | Sequences

### Learning Objectives

**5.1.1** Find the formula for the general term of a sequence.

**5.1.2** Calculate the limit of a sequence if it exists.

**5.1.3** Determine the convergence or divergence of a given sequence.

In this section, we introduce sequences and define what it means for a sequence to converge or diverge. We show how to find limits of sequences that converge, often by using the properties of limits for functions discussed earlier. We close this section with the Monotone Convergence Theorem, a tool we can use to prove that certain types of sequences converge.

## Terminology of Sequences

To work with this new topic, we need some new terms and definitions. First, an infinite sequence is an ordered list of numbers of the form

$$a_1, a_2, a_3, \ldots, a_n, \ldots .$$

Each of the numbers in the sequence is called a term. The symbol $n$ is called the index variable for the sequence. We use the notation

$$\{a_n\}_{n=1}^{\infty}, \text{ or simply } \{a_n\},$$

to denote this sequence. A similar notation is used for sets, but a sequence is an ordered list, whereas a set is not ordered. Because a particular number $a_n$ exists for each positive integer $n,$ we can also define a sequence as a function whose domain is the set of positive integers.

Let's consider the infinite, ordered list

$$2, 4, 8, 16, 32, \ldots .$$

This is a sequence in which the first, second, and third terms are given by $a_1 = 2,$ $a_2 = 4,$ and $a_3 = 8.$ You can probably see that the terms in this sequence have the following pattern:

$$a_1 = 2^1, \ a_2 = 2^2, \ a_3 = 2^3, \ a_4 = 2^4, \text{ and } a_5 = 2^5.$$

Assuming this pattern continues, we can write the $n$th term in the sequence by the explicit formula $a_n = 2^n.$ Using this notation, we can write this sequence as

$$\{2^n\}_{n=1}^{\infty} \text{ or } \{2^n\}.$$

Alternatively, we can describe this sequence in a different way. Since each term is twice the previous term, this sequence can be defined recursively by expressing the $n$th term $a_n$ in terms of the previous term $a_{n-1}.$ In particular, we can define this sequence as the sequence $\{a_n\}$ where $a_1 = 2$ and for all $n \geq 2,$ each term $a_n$ is defined by the **recurrence relation** $a_n = 2a_{n-1}.$

### Definition

An **infinite sequence** $\{a_n\}$ is an ordered list of numbers of the form

$$a_1, a_2, \ldots, a_n, \ldots .$$

The subscript $n$ is called the **index variable** of the sequence. Each number $a_n$ is a **term** of the sequence. Sometimes sequences are defined by **explicit formulas**, in which case $a_n = f(n)$ for some function $f(n)$ defined over the positive integers. In other cases, sequences are defined by using a **recurrence relation**. In a recurrence relation, one term (or more) of the sequence is given explicitly, and subsequent terms are defined in terms of earlier terms in the sequence.

Note that the index does not have to start at $n = 1$ but could start with other integers. For example, a sequence given by the explicit formula $a_n = f(n)$ could start at $n = 0,$ in which case the sequence would be

$$a_0, a_1, a_2, \ldots .$$

Similarly, for a sequence defined by a recurrence relation, the term $a_0$ may be given explicitly, and the terms $a_n$ for $n \geq 1$ may be defined in terms of $a_{n-1}.$ Since a sequence $\{a_n\}$ has exactly one value for each positive integer $n,$ it can be described as a function whose domain is the set of positive integers. As a result, it makes sense to discuss the graph of a sequence. The graph of a sequence $\{a_n\}$ consists of all points $(n,\ a_n)$ for all positive integers $n$. **Figure 5.2** shows the graph of $\{2^n\}$.

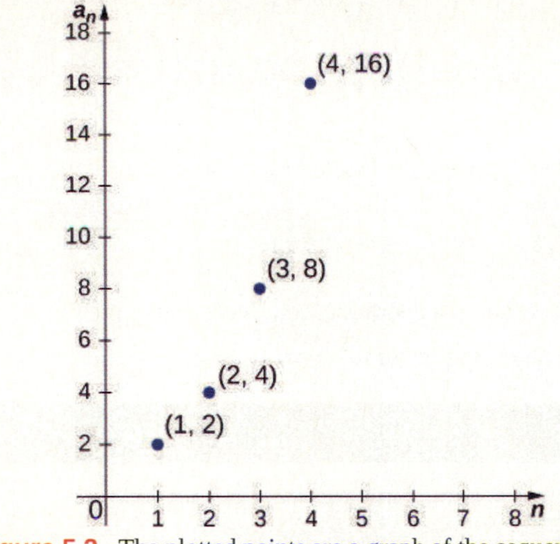


**Figure 5.2** The plotted points are a graph of the sequence $\{2^n\}$.

Two types of sequences occur often and are given special names: arithmetic sequences and geometric sequences. In an **arithmetic sequence**, the *difference* between every pair of consecutive terms is the same. For example, consider the sequence

$$3,\ 7,\ 11,\ 15,\ 19,\ldots.$$

You can see that the difference between every consecutive pair of terms is $4$. Assuming that this pattern continues, this sequence is an arithmetic sequence. It can be described by using the recurrence relation

$$\begin{cases} a_1 = 3 \\ a_n = a_{n-1} + 4 \text{ for } n \geq 2. \end{cases}$$

Note that

$$\begin{aligned} a_2 &= 3 + 4 \\ a_3 &= 3 + 4 + 4 = 3 + 2 \cdot 4 \\ a_4 &= 3 + 4 + 4 + 4 = 3 + 3 \cdot 4. \end{aligned}$$

Thus the sequence can also be described using the explicit formula

$$\begin{aligned} a_n &= 3 + 4(n - 1) \\ &= 4n - 1. \end{aligned}$$

In general, an arithmetic sequence is any sequence of the form $a_n = cn + b$.

In a **geometric sequence**, the *ratio* of every pair of consecutive terms is the same. For example, consider the sequence

$$2,\ -\frac{2}{3},\ \frac{2}{9},\ -\frac{2}{27},\ \frac{2}{81},\ldots.$$

We see that the ratio of any term to the preceding term is $-\frac{1}{3}$. Assuming this pattern continues, this sequence is a geometric sequence. It can be defined recursively as

$$\begin{aligned} a_1 &= 2 \\ a_n &= -\frac{1}{3} \cdot a_{n-1} \text{ for } n \geq 2. \end{aligned}$$

Alternatively, since

$$a_2 = -\frac{1}{3} \cdot 2$$
$$a_3 = \left(-\frac{1}{3}\right)\left(-\frac{1}{3}\right)(2) = \left(-\frac{1}{3}\right)^2 \cdot 2$$
$$a_4 = \left(-\frac{1}{3}\right)\left(-\frac{1}{3}\right)\left(-\frac{1}{3}\right)(2) = \left(-\frac{1}{3}\right)^3 \cdot 2,$$

we see that the sequence can be described by using the explicit formula

$$a_n = 2\left(-\frac{1}{3}\right)^{n-1}.$$

The sequence $\{2^n\}$ that we discussed earlier is a geometric sequence, where the ratio of any term to the previous term is 2. In general, a geometric sequence is any sequence of the form $a_n = cr^n$.

## Example 5.1

### Finding Explicit Formulas

For each of the following sequences, find an explicit formula for the $n$th term of the sequence.

a. $-\frac{1}{2}, \frac{2}{3}, -\frac{3}{4}, \frac{4}{5}, -\frac{5}{6}, \ldots$

b. $\frac{3}{4}, \frac{9}{7}, \frac{27}{10}, \frac{81}{13}, \frac{243}{16}, \ldots$

### Solution

a. First, note that the sequence is alternating from negative to positive. The odd terms in the sequence are negative, and the even terms are positive. Therefore, the $n$th term includes a factor of $(-1)^n$. Next, consider the sequence of numerators $\{1, 2, 3, \ldots\}$ and the sequence of denominators $\{2, 3, 4, \ldots\}$. We can see that both of these sequences are arithmetic sequences. The $n$th term in the sequence of numerators is $n$, and the $n$th term in the sequence of denominators is $n+1$. Therefore, the sequence can be described by the explicit formula

$$a_n = \frac{(-1)^n n}{n+1}.$$

b. The sequence of numerators $3, 9, 27, 81, 243, \ldots$ is a geometric sequence. The numerator of the $n$th term is $3^n$ The sequence of denominators $4, 7, 10, 13, 16, \ldots$ is an arithmetic sequence. The denominator of the $n$th term is $4 + 3(n-1) = 3n + 1$. Therefore, we can describe the sequence by the explicit formula $a_n = \frac{3^n}{3n+1}$.

**5.1** Find an explicit formula for the $n$th term of the sequence $\left\{\frac{1}{5}, -\frac{1}{7}, \frac{1}{9}, -\frac{1}{11}, \ldots\right\}$.

## Example 5.2

### Defined by Recurrence Relations

For each of the following recursively defined sequences, find an explicit formula for the sequence.

a. $a_1 = 2, \quad a_n = -3a_{n-1}$ for $n \geq 2$

b. $a_1 = \frac{1}{2}, \quad a_n = a_{n-1} + \left(\frac{1}{2}\right)^n$ for $n \geq 2$

#### Solution

a. Writing out the first few terms, we have

$$\begin{aligned} a_1 &= 2 \\ a_2 &= -3a_1 = -3(2) \\ a_3 &= -3a_2 = (-3)^2 2 \\ a_4 &= -3a_3 = (-3)^3 2. \end{aligned}$$

In general,

$$a_n = 2(-3)^{n-1}.$$

b. Write out the first few terms:

$$\begin{aligned} a_1 &= \frac{1}{2} \\ a_2 &= a_1 + \left(\frac{1}{2}\right)^2 = \frac{1}{2} + \frac{1}{4} = \frac{3}{4} \\ a_3 &= a_2 + \left(\frac{1}{2}\right)^3 = \frac{3}{4} + \frac{1}{8} = \frac{7}{8} \\ a_4 &= a_3 + \left(\frac{1}{2}\right)^4 = \frac{7}{8} + \frac{1}{16} = \frac{15}{16}. \end{aligned}$$

From this pattern, we derive the explicit formula

$$a_n = \frac{2^n - 1}{2^n} = 1 - \frac{1}{2^n}.$$

**5.2** Find an explicit formula for the sequence defined recursively such that $a_1 = -4$ and $a_n = a_{n-1} + 6$.

## Limit of a Sequence

A fundamental question that arises regarding infinite sequences is the behavior of the terms as $n$ gets larger. Since a sequence is a function defined on the positive integers, it makes sense to discuss the limit of the terms as $n \to \infty$. For example, consider the following four sequences and their different behaviors as $n \to \infty$ (see **Figure 5.3**):

a. $\{1 + 3n\} = \{4, 7, 10, 13, \ldots\}$. The terms $1 + 3n$ become arbitrarily large as $n \to \infty$. In this case, we say that $1 + 3n \to \infty$ as $n \to \infty$.

b. $\left\{1 - \left(\frac{1}{2}\right)^n\right\} = \left\{\frac{1}{2}, \frac{3}{4}, \frac{7}{8}, \frac{15}{16}, \ldots\right\}$. The terms $1 - \left(\frac{1}{2}\right)^n \to 1$ as $n \to \infty$.

c. $\{(-1)^n\} = \{-1, 1, -1, 1, \ldots\}$. The terms alternate but do not approach one single value as $n \to \infty$.

d. $\left\{\frac{(-1)^n}{n}\right\} = \left\{-1, \frac{1}{2}, -\frac{1}{3}, \frac{1}{4}, \ldots\right\}$. The terms alternate for this sequence as well, but $\frac{(-1)^n}{n} \to 0$ as $n \to \infty$.

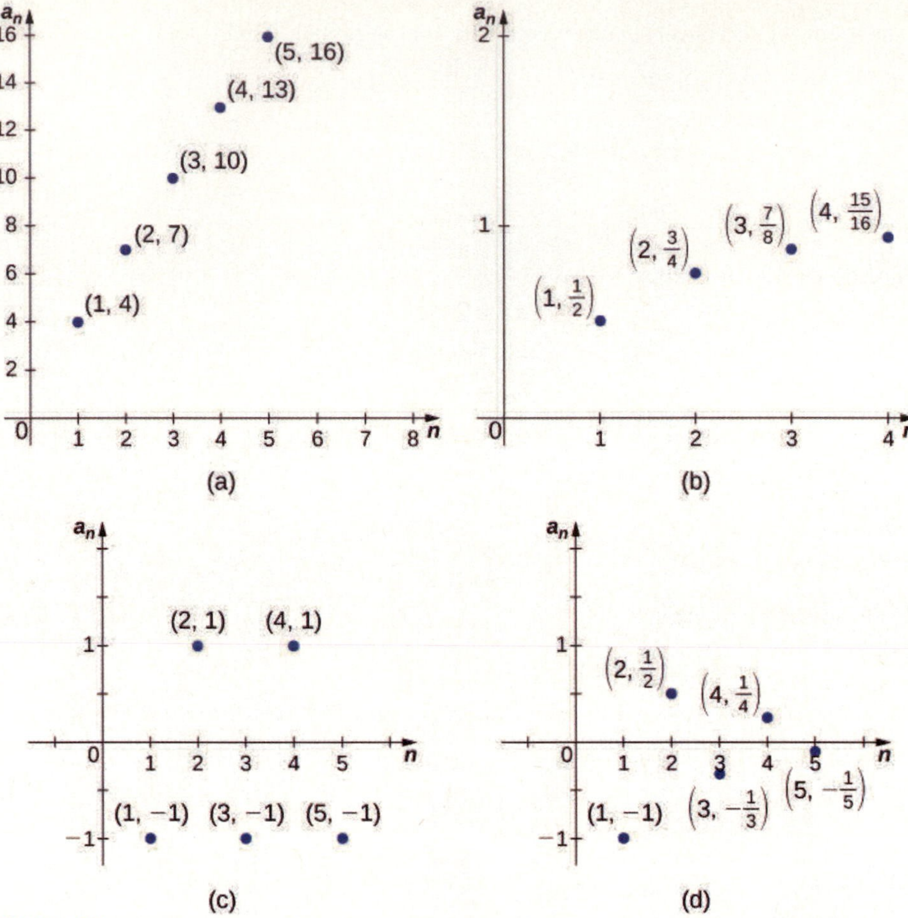


**Figure 5.3** (a) The terms in the sequence become arbitrarily large as $n \to \infty$. (b) The terms in the sequence approach $1$ as $n \to \infty$. (c) The terms in the sequence alternate between $1$ and $-1$ as $n \to \infty$. (d) The terms in the sequence alternate between positive and negative values but approach $0$ as $n \to \infty$.

From these examples, we see several possibilities for the behavior of the terms of a sequence as $n \to \infty$. In two of the sequences, the terms approach a finite number as $n \to \infty$. In the other two sequences, the terms do not. If the terms of a sequence approach a finite number $L$ as $n \to \infty$, we say that the sequence is a convergent sequence and the real number $L$ is the limit of the sequence. We can give an informal definition here.

### Definition

Given a sequence $\{a_n\}$, if the terms $a_n$ become arbitrarily close to a finite number $L$ as $n$ becomes sufficiently large, we say $\{a_n\}$ is a **convergent sequence** and $L$ is the **limit of the sequence**. In this case, we write

$$\lim_{n \to \infty} a_n = L.$$

If a sequence $\{a_n\}$ is not convergent, we say it is a **divergent sequence**.

From **Figure 5.3**, we see that the terms in the sequence $\left\{1 - \left(\frac{1}{2}\right)^n\right\}$ are becoming arbitrarily close to $1$ as $n$ becomes very large. We conclude that $\left\{1 - \left(\frac{1}{2}\right)^n\right\}$ is a convergent sequence and its limit is $1$. In contrast, from **Figure 5.3**, we see that the terms in the sequence $1 + 3n$ are not approaching a finite number as $n$ becomes larger. We say that $\{1 + 3n\}$ is a divergent sequence.

In the informal definition for the limit of a sequence, we used the terms "arbitrarily close" and "sufficiently large." Although these phrases help illustrate the meaning of a converging sequence, they are somewhat vague. To be more precise, we now present the more formal definition of limit for a sequence and show these ideas graphically in **Figure 5.4**.

### Definition

A sequence $\{a_n\}$ converges to a real number $L$ if for all $\varepsilon > 0,$ there exists an integer $N$ such that $|a_n - L| < \varepsilon$ if $n \geq N$. The number $L$ is the limit of the sequence and we write

$$\lim_{n \to \infty} a_n = L \, or \, a_n \to L.$$

In this case, we say the sequence $\{a_n\}$ is a convergent sequence. If a sequence does not converge, it is a divergent sequence, and we say the limit does not exist.

We remark that the convergence or divergence of a sequence $\{a_n\}$ depends only on what happens to the terms $a_n$ as $n \to \infty$. Therefore, if a finite number of terms $b_1, b_2, \ldots, b_N$ are placed before $a_1$ to create a new sequence

$$b_1, b_2, \ldots, b_N, a_1, a_2, \ldots,$$

this new sequence will converge if $\{a_n\}$ converges and diverge if $\{a_n\}$ diverges. Further, if the sequence $\{a_n\}$ converges to $L,$ this new sequence will also converge to $L$.

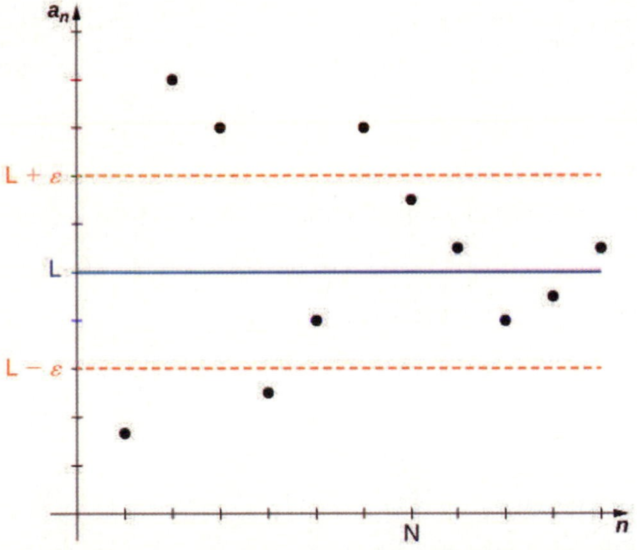


**Figure 5.4** As $n$ increases, the terms $a_n$ become closer to $L$. For values of $n \geq N,$ the distance between each point $(n, a_n)$ and the line $y = L$ is less than $\varepsilon$.

As defined above, if a sequence does not converge, it is said to be a divergent sequence. For example, the sequences $\{1 + 3n\}$ and $\{(-1)^n\}$ shown in **Figure 5.4** diverge. However, different sequences can diverge in different ways. The sequence $\{(-1)^n\}$ diverges because the terms alternate between $1$ and $-1,$ but do not approach one value as $n \to \infty$. On the other hand, the sequence $\{1 + 3n\}$ diverges because the terms $1 + 3n \to \infty$ as $n \to \infty$. We say the sequence $\{1 + 3n\}$ diverges to infinity and write $\lim_{n \to \infty}(1 + 3n) = \infty$. It is important to recognize that this notation does not imply the limit of the sequence $\{1 + 3n\}$ exists. The sequence is, in fact, divergent. Writing that the limit is infinity is intended only to provide more information about why the sequence is divergent. A sequence can also diverge to negative infinity. For example, the sequence $\{-5n+2\}$ diverges to negative infinity because $-5n+2 \to -\infty$ as $n \to -\infty$. We write this as $\lim_{n \to \infty}(-5n+2) = \to -\infty$.

Because a sequence is a function whose domain is the set of positive integers, we can use properties of limits of functions to determine whether a sequence converges. For example, consider a sequence $\{a_n\}$ and a related function $f$ defined on all positive real numbers such that $f(n) = a_n$ for all integers $n \geq 1$. Since the domain of the sequence is a subset of the domain of $f$, if $\lim_{x \to \infty} f(x)$ exists, then the sequence converges and has the same limit. For example, consider the sequence $\left\{\frac{1}{n}\right\}$ and the related function $f(x) = \frac{1}{x}$. Since the function $f$ defined on all real numbers $x > 0$ satisfies $f(x) = \frac{1}{x} \to 0$ as $x \to \infty$, the sequence $\left\{\frac{1}{n}\right\}$ must satisfy $\frac{1}{n} \to 0$ as $n \to \infty$.

### Theorem 5.1: Limit of a Sequence Defined by a Function

Consider a sequence $\{a_n\}$ such that $a_n = f(n)$ for all $n \geq 1$. If there exists a real number $L$ such that

$$\lim_{x \to \infty} f(x) = L,$$

then $\{a_n\}$ converges and

$$\lim_{n \to \infty} a_n = L.$$

We can use this theorem to evaluate $\lim_{n \to \infty} r^n$ for $0 \leq r \leq 1$. For example, consider the sequence $\{(1/2)^n\}$ and the related exponential function $f(x) = (1/2)^x$. Since $\lim_{x \to \infty}(1/2)^x = 0$, we conclude that the sequence $\{(1/2)^n\}$ converges and its limit is $0$. Similarly, for any real number $r$ such that $0 \leq r < 1$, $\lim_{x \to \infty} r^x = 0$, and therefore the sequence $\{r^n\}$ converges. On the other hand, if $r = 1$, then $\lim_{x \to \infty} r^x = 1$, and therefore the limit of the sequence $\{1^n\}$ is $1$. If $r > 1$, $\lim_{x \to \infty} r^x = \infty$, and therefore we cannot apply this theorem. However, in this case, just as the function $r^x$ grows without bound as $n \to \infty$, the terms $r^n$ in the sequence become arbitrarily large as $n \to \infty$, and we conclude that the sequence $\{r^n\}$ diverges to infinity if $r > 1$.

We summarize these results regarding the geometric sequence $\{r^n\}$:

$$\begin{aligned} r^n &\to 0 \; if \; 0 < r < 1 \\ r^n &\to 1 \; if \; r = 1 \\ r^n &\to \infty \; if \; r > 1. \end{aligned}$$

Later in this section we consider the case when $r < 0$.

We now consider slightly more complicated sequences. For example, consider the sequence $\{(2/3)^n + (1/4)^n\}$. The terms in this sequence are more complicated than other sequences we have discussed, but luckily the limit of this sequence is determined by the limits of the two sequences $\{(2/3)^n\}$ and $\{(1/4)^n\}$. As we describe in the following algebraic limit laws, since $\{(2/3)^n\}$ and $\{1/4)^n\}$ both converge to $0$, the sequence $\{(2/3)^n + (1/4)^n\}$ converges to $0 + 0 = 0$. Just as we were able to evaluate a limit involving an algebraic combination of functions $f$ and $g$ by looking at the limits of $f$ and $g$ (see **Introduction to Limits (http://cnx.org/content/m53483/latest/)** ), we are able to evaluate the limit of a sequence whose terms are algebraic combinations of $a_n$ and $b_n$ by evaluating the limits of $\{a_n\}$ and $\{b_n\}$.

### Theorem 5.2: Algebraic Limit Laws

Given sequences $\{a_n\}$ and $\{b_n\}$ and any real number $c$, if there exist constants $A$ and $B$ such that $\lim_{n \to \infty} a_n = A$ and $\lim_{n \to \infty} b_n = B$, then

i. $\lim_{n \to \infty} c = c$

ii. $\lim_{n \to \infty} ca_n = c \lim_{n \to \infty} a_n = cA$

iii. $\lim_{n \to \infty} (a_n \pm b_n) = \lim_{n \to \infty} a_n \pm \lim_{n \to \infty} b_n = A \pm B$

iv. $\lim_{n \to \infty} (a_n \cdot b_n) = \left(\lim_{n \to \infty} a_n\right) \cdot \left(\lim_{n \to \infty} b_n\right) = A \cdot B$

v. $\lim_{n \to \infty} \left(\frac{a_n}{b_n}\right) = \frac{\lim_{n \to \infty} a_n}{\lim_{n \to \infty} b_n} = \frac{A}{B}$, provided $B \neq 0$ and each $b_n \neq 0$.

### Proof

We prove part iii.

Let $\epsilon > 0$. Since $\lim_{n \to \infty} a_n = A$, there exists a constant positive integer $N_1$ such that for all $n \geq N_1$. Since $\lim_{n \to \infty} b_n = B$, there exists a constant $N_2$ such that $|b_n - B| < \varepsilon/2$ for all $n \geq N_2$. Let $N$ be the largest of $N_1$ and $N_2$. Therefore, for all $n \geq N$,

$$|(a_n + b_n) - (A + B)| \leq |a_n - A| + |b_n - B| < \frac{\varepsilon}{2} + \frac{\varepsilon}{2} = \varepsilon.$$

□

The algebraic limit laws allow us to evaluate limits for many sequences. For example, consider the sequence $\left\{\frac{1}{n^2}\right\}$. As shown earlier, $\lim_{n \to \infty} 1/n = 0$. Similarly, for any positive integer $k$, we can conclude that

$$\lim_{n \to \infty} \frac{1}{n^k} = 0.$$

In the next example, we make use of this fact along with the limit laws to evaluate limits for other sequences.

## Example 5.3

### Determining Convergence and Finding Limits

For each of the following sequences, determine whether or not the sequence converges. If it converges, find its limit.

a. $\left\{5 - \frac{3}{n^2}\right\}$

b. $\left\{\frac{3n^4 - 7n^2 + 5}{6 - 4n^4}\right\}$

c. $\left\{\frac{2^n}{n^2}\right\}$

d. $\left\{\left(1+\frac{4}{n}\right)^n\right\}$

### Solution

a. We know that $1/n \to 0$. Using this fact, we conclude that

$$\lim_{n \to \infty} \frac{1}{n^2} = \lim_{n \to \infty}\left(\frac{1}{n}\right) \cdot \lim_{n \to \infty}\left(\frac{1}{n}\right) = 0.$$

Therefore,

$$\lim_{n \to \infty}\left(5 - \frac{3}{n^2}\right) = \lim_{n \to \infty} 5 - 3 \lim_{n \to \infty} \frac{1}{n^2} = 5 - 3.0 = 5.$$

The sequence converges and its limit is $5$.

b. By factoring $n^4$ out of the numerator and denominator and using the limit laws above, we have

$$\begin{aligned}
\lim_{n \to \infty} \frac{3n^4 - 7n^2 + 5}{6 - 4n^4} &= \lim_{n \to \infty} \frac{3 - \frac{7}{n^2} + \frac{5}{n^4}}{\frac{6}{n^4} - 4} \\
&= \frac{\lim_{n \to \infty}\left(3 - \frac{7}{n^2} + \frac{5}{n^4}\right)}{\lim_{n \to \infty}\left(\frac{6}{n^4} - 4\right)} \\
&= \frac{\left(\lim_{n \to \infty}(3) - \lim_{n \to \infty} \frac{7}{n^2} + \lim_{n \to \infty} \frac{5}{n^4}\right)}{\left(\lim_{n \to \infty} \frac{6}{n^4} - \lim_{n \to \infty}(4)\right)} \\
&= \frac{\left(\lim_{n \to \infty}(3) - 7 \cdot \lim_{n \to \infty} \frac{1}{n^2} + 5 \cdot \lim_{n \to \infty} \frac{1}{n^4}\right)}{\left(6 \cdot \lim_{n \to \infty} \frac{1}{n^4} - \lim_{n \to \infty}(4)\right)} \\
&= \frac{3 - 7 \cdot 0 + 5 \cdot 0}{6 \cdot 0 - 4} = -\frac{3}{4}.
\end{aligned}$$

The sequence converges and its limit is $-3/4$.

c. Consider the related function $f(x) = 2^x/x^2$ defined on all real numbers $x > 0$. Since $2^x \to \infty$ and $x^2 \to \infty$ as $x \to \infty$, apply L'Hôpital's rule and write

$$\begin{aligned}
\lim_{x \to \infty} \frac{2^x}{x^2} &= \lim_{x \to \infty} \frac{2^x \ln 2}{2x} && \text{Take the derivatives of the numerator and denominator.} \\
&= \lim_{x \to \infty} \frac{2^x (\ln 2)^2}{2} && \text{Take the derivatives again.} \\
&= \infty.
\end{aligned}$$

We conclude that the sequence diverges.

d. Consider the function $f(x) = \left(1 + \frac{4}{x}\right)^x$ defined on all real numbers $x > 0$. This function has the indeterminate form $1^\infty$ as $x \to \infty$. Let

$$y = \lim_{x \to \infty}\left(1 + \frac{4}{x}\right)^x.$$

Now taking the natural logarithm of both sides of the equation, we obtain

$$\ln(y) = \ln\left[\lim_{x \to \infty}\left(1 + \frac{4}{x}\right)^x\right].$$

Since the function $f(x) = \ln x$ is continuous on its domain, we can interchange the limit and the natural logarithm. Therefore,

$$\ln(y) = \lim_{x \to \infty}\left[\ln\left(1 + \frac{4}{x}\right)^x\right].$$

Using properties of logarithms, we write

$$\lim_{x \to \infty}\left[\ln\left(1 + \frac{4}{x}\right)^x\right] = \lim_{x \to \infty} x \ln\left(1 + \frac{4}{x}\right).$$

Since the right-hand side of this equation has the indeterminate form $\infty \cdot 0,$ rewrite it as a fraction to apply L'Hôpital's rule. Write

$$\lim_{x \to \infty} x \ln\left(1 + \frac{4}{x}\right) = \lim_{x \to \infty} \frac{\ln(1 + 4/x)}{1/x}.$$

Since the right-hand side is now in the indeterminate form $0/0,$ we are able to apply L'Hôpital's rule. We conclude that

$$\lim_{x \to \infty} \frac{\ln(1 + 4/x)}{1/x} = \lim_{x \to \infty} \frac{4}{1 + 4/x} = 4.$$

Therefore, $\ln(y) = 4$ and $y = e^4$. Therefore, since $\lim_{x \to \infty}\left(1 + \frac{4}{x}\right)^x = e^4,$ we can conclude that the sequence $\left\{\left(1 + \frac{4}{n}\right)^n\right\}$ converges to $e^4$.

**5.3** Consider the sequence $\left\{\left(5n^2 + 1\right)/e^n\right\}$. Determine whether or not the sequence converges. If it converges, find its limit.

Recall that if $f$ is a continuous function at a value $L,$ then $f(x) \to f(L)$ as $x \to L$. This idea applies to sequences as well. Suppose a sequence $a_n \to L,$ and a function $f$ is continuous at $L$. Then $f(a_n) \to f(L)$. This property often enables us to find limits for complicated sequences. For example, consider the sequence $\sqrt{5 - \frac{3}{n^2}}$. From **Example 5.3**a. we know the sequence $5 - \frac{3}{n^2} \to 5$. Since $\sqrt{x}$ is a continuous function at $x = 5,$

$$\lim_{n \to \infty}\sqrt{5 - \frac{3}{n^2}} = \sqrt{\lim_{n \to \infty}\left(5 - \frac{3}{n^2}\right)} = \sqrt{5}.$$

### Theorem 5.3: Continuous Functions Defined on Convergent Sequences

Consider a sequence $\{a_n\}$ and suppose there exists a real number $L$ such that the sequence $\{a_n\}$ converges to $L$. Suppose $f$ is a continuous function at $L$. Then there exists an integer $N$ such that $f$ is defined at all values $a_n$ for $n \geq N$, and the sequence $\{f(a_n)\}$ converges to $f(L)$ (**Figure 5.5**).

### Proof

Let $\epsilon > 0$. Since $f$ is continuous at $L$, there exists $\delta > 0$ such that $|f(x) - f(L)| < \varepsilon$ if $|x - L| < \delta$. Since the sequence $\{a_n\}$ converges to $L$, there exists $N$ such that $|a_n - L| < \delta$ for all $n \geq N$. Therefore, for all $n \geq N$, $|a_n - L| < \delta$, which implies $|f(a_n) - f(L)| < \varepsilon$. We conclude that the sequence $\{f(a_n)\}$ converges to $f(L)$.

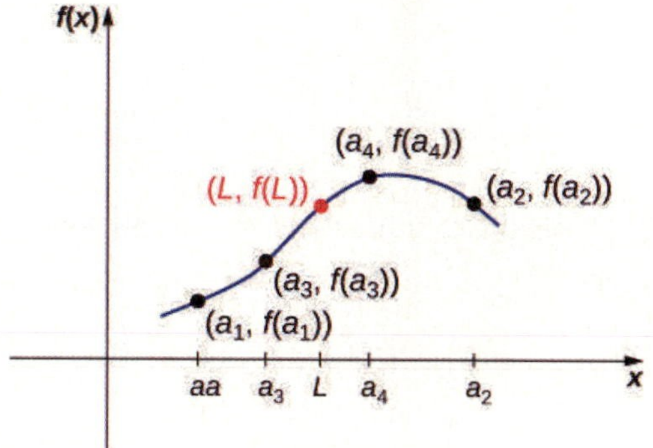


**Figure 5.5** Because $f$ is a continuous function as the inputs $a_1, a_2, a_3, \ldots$ approach $L$, the outputs $f(a_1), f(a_2), f(a_3), \ldots$ approach $f(L)$.

## Example 5.4

### Limits Involving Continuous Functions Defined on Convergent Sequences

Determine whether the sequence $\{\cos(3/n^2)\}$ converges. If it converges, find its limit.

#### Solution

Since the sequence $\{3/n^2\}$ converges to $0$ and $\cos x$ is continuous at $x = 0$, we can conclude that the sequence $\{\cos(3/n^2)\}$ converges and

$$\lim_{n \to \infty} \cos\left(\frac{3}{n^2}\right) = \cos(0) = 1.$$

**5.4** Determine if the sequence $\left\{\sqrt{\frac{2n+1}{3n+5}}\right\}$ converges. If it converges, find its limit.

Another theorem involving limits of sequences is an extension of the Squeeze Theorem for limits discussed in **Introduction to Limits (http://cnx.org/content/m53483/latest/)** .

### Theorem 5.4: Squeeze Theorem for Sequences

Consider sequences $\{a_n\}$, $\{b_n\}$, and $\{c_n\}$. Suppose there exists an integer $N$ such that

$$a_n \le b_n \le c_n \text{ for all } n \ge N.$$

If there exists a real number $L$ such that

$$\lim_{n \to \infty} a_n = L = \lim_{n \to \infty} c_n,$$

then $\{b_n\}$ converges and $\lim_{n \to \infty} b_n = L$ (**Figure 5.6**).

### Proof

Let $\varepsilon > 0$. Since the sequence $\{a_n\}$ converges to $L$, there exists an integer $N_1$ such that $|a_n - L| < \varepsilon$ for all $n \ge N_1$. Similarly, since $\{c_n\}$ converges to $L$, there exists an integer $N_2$ such that $|c_n - L| < \varepsilon$ for all $n \ge N_2$. By assumption, there exists an integer $N$ such that $a_n \le b_n \le c_n$ for all $n \ge N$. Let $M$ be the largest of $N_1$, $N_2$, and $N$. We must show that $|b_n - L| < \varepsilon$ for all $n \ge M$. For all $n \ge M$,

$$-\varepsilon < -|a_n - L| \le a_n - L \le b_n - L \le c_n - L \le |c_n - L| < \varepsilon.$$

Therefore, $-\varepsilon < b_n - L < \varepsilon$, and we conclude that $|b_n - L| < \varepsilon$ for all $n \ge M$, and we conclude that the sequence $\{b_n\}$ converges to $L$.

□

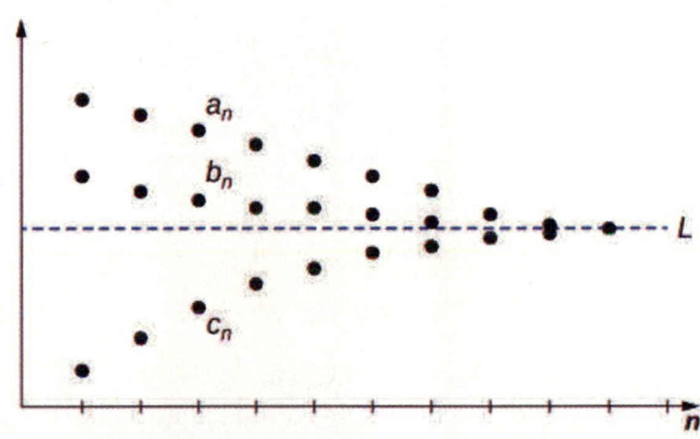


**Figure 5.6** Each term $b_n$ satisfies $a_n \le b_n \le c_n$ and the sequences $\{a_n\}$ and $\{c_n\}$ converge to the same limit, so the sequence $\{b_n\}$ must converge to the same limit as well.

## Example 5.5

### Using the Squeeze Theorem

Use the Squeeze Theorem to find the limit of each of the following sequences.

a. $\left\{\dfrac{\cos n}{n^2}\right\}$

b. $\left\{\left(-\dfrac{1}{2}\right)^n\right\}$

**Solution**

a. Since $-1 \leq \cos n \leq 1$ for all integers $n,$ we have

$$-\frac{1}{n^2} \leq \frac{\cos n}{n^2} \leq \frac{1}{n^2}.$$

Since $-1/n^2 \to 0$ and $1/n^2 \to 0,$ we conclude that $\cos n/n^2 \to 0$ as well.

b. Since

$$-\frac{1}{2^n} \leq \left(-\frac{1}{2}\right)^n \leq \frac{1}{2^n}$$

for all positive integers $n,$ $-1/2^n \to 0$ and $1/2^n \to 0,$ we can conclude that $(-1/2)^n \to 0.$

**5.5** Find $\lim_{n \to \infty} \frac{2n - \sin n}{n}.$

Using the idea from **Example 5.5**b. we conclude that $r^n \to 0$ for any real number $r$ such that $-1 < r < 0.$ If $r < -1,$ the sequence $\{r^n\}$ diverges because the terms oscillate and become arbitrarily large in magnitude. If $r = -1,$ the sequence $\{r^n\} = \{(-1)^n\}$ diverges, as discussed earlier. Here is a summary of the properties for geometric sequences.

$$r^n \to 0 \text{ if } |r| < 1 \tag{5.1}$$

$$r^n \to 1 \text{ if } r = 1 \tag{5.2}$$

$$r^n \to \infty \text{ if } r > 1 \tag{5.3}$$

$$\{r^n\} \text{ diverges if } r \leq -1 \tag{5.4}$$

## Bounded Sequences

We now turn our attention to one of the most important theorems involving sequences: the Monotone Convergence Theorem. Before stating the theorem, we need to introduce some terminology and motivation. We begin by defining what it means for a sequence to be bounded.

**Definition**

A sequence $\{a_n\}$ is **bounded above** if there exists a real number $M$ such that

$$a_n \leq M$$

for all positive integers $n.$

A sequence $\{a_n\}$ is **bounded below** if there exists a real number $M$ such that

$$M \leq a_n$$

for all positive integers $n.$

A sequence $\{a_n\}$ is a **bounded sequence** if it is bounded above and bounded below.

If a sequence is not bounded, it is an **unbounded sequence**.

For example, the sequence $\{1/n\}$ is bounded above because $1/n \leq 1$ for all positive integers $n.$ It is also bounded below because $1/n \geq 0$ for all positive integers $n.$ Therefore, $\{1/n\}$ is a bounded sequence. On the other hand, consider the sequence $\{2^n\}$. Because $2^n \geq 2$ for all $n \geq 1$, the sequence is bounded below. However, the sequence is not bounded above. Therefore, $\{2^n\}$ is an unbounded sequence.

We now discuss the relationship between boundedness and convergence. Suppose a sequence $\{a_n\}$ is unbounded. Then it is not bounded above, or not bounded below, or both. In either case, there are terms $a_n$ that are arbitrarily large in magnitude as $n$ gets larger. As a result, the sequence $\{a_n\}$ cannot converge. Therefore, being bounded is a necessary condition for a sequence to converge.

### Theorem 5.5: Convergent Sequences Are Bounded

If a sequence $\{a_n\}$ converges, then it is bounded.

Note that a sequence being bounded is not a sufficient condition for a sequence to converge. For example, the sequence $\{(-1)^n\}$ is bounded, but the sequence diverges because the sequence oscillates between $1$ and $-1$ and never approaches a finite number. We now discuss a sufficient (but not necessary) condition for a bounded sequence to converge.

Consider a bounded sequence $\{a_n\}$. Suppose the sequence $\{a_n\}$ is increasing. That is, $a_1 \leq a_2 \leq a_3 \ldots$. Since the sequence is increasing, the terms are not oscillating. Therefore, there are two possibilities. The sequence could diverge to infinity, or it could converge. However, since the sequence is bounded, it is bounded above and the sequence cannot diverge to infinity. We conclude that $\{a_n\}$ converges. For example, consider the sequence

$$\left\{\frac{1}{2}, \frac{2}{3}, \frac{3}{4}, \frac{4}{5}, \ldots\right\}.$$

Since this sequence is increasing and bounded above, it converges. Next, consider the sequence

$$\left\{2, 0, 3, 0, 4, 0, 1, -\frac{1}{2}, -\frac{1}{3}, -\frac{1}{4}, \ldots\right\}.$$

Even though the sequence is not increasing for all values of $n$, we see that $-1/2 < -1/3 < -1/4 < \cdots$. Therefore, starting with the eighth term, $a_8 = -1/2$, the sequence is increasing. In this case, we say the sequence is *eventually* increasing. Since the sequence is bounded above, it converges. It is also true that if a sequence is decreasing (or eventually decreasing) and bounded below, it also converges.

### Definition

A sequence $\{a_n\}$ is increasing for all $n \geq n_0$ if

$$a_n \leq a_{n+1} \text{ for all } n \geq n_0.$$

A sequence $\{a_n\}$ is decreasing for all $n \geq n_0$ if

$$a_n \geq a_{n+1} \text{ for all } n \geq n_0.$$

A sequence $\{a_n\}$ is a **monotone sequence** for all $n \geq n_0$ if it is increasing for all $n \geq n_0$ or decreasing for all $n \geq n_0$.

We now have the necessary definitions to state the Monotone Convergence Theorem, which gives a sufficient condition for convergence of a sequence.

### Theorem 5.6: Monotone Convergence Theorem

If $\{a_n\}$ is a bounded sequence and there exists a positive integer $n_0$ such that $\{a_n\}$ is monotone for all $n \geq n_0$, then $\{a_n\}$ converges.

The proof of this theorem is beyond the scope of this text. Instead, we provide a graph to show intuitively why this theorem makes sense (Figure 5.7).

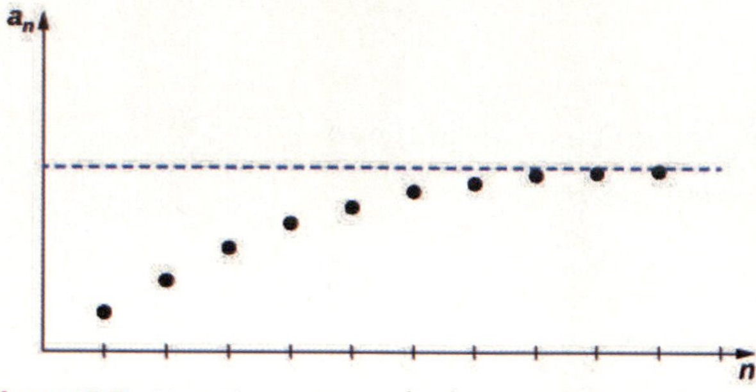


Figure 5.7 Since the sequence $\{a_n\}$ is increasing and bounded above, it must converge.

In the following example, we show how the Monotone Convergence Theorem can be used to prove convergence of a sequence.

## Example 5.6

### Using the Monotone Convergence Theorem

For each of the following sequences, use the Monotone Convergence Theorem to show the sequence converges and find its limit.

a. $\left\{\frac{4^n}{n!}\right\}$

b. $\{a_n\}$ defined recursively such that

$$a_1 = 2 \text{ and } a_{n+1} = \frac{a_n}{2} + \frac{1}{2a_n} \text{ for all } n \geq 2.$$

### Solution

a. Writing out the first few terms, we see that

$$\left\{\frac{4^n}{n!}\right\} = \left\{4, 8, \frac{32}{3}, \frac{32}{3}, \frac{128}{15}, \ldots\right\}.$$

At first, the terms increase. However, after the third term, the terms decrease. In fact, the terms decrease for all $n \geq 3$. We can show this as follows.

$$a_{n+1} = \frac{4^{n+1}}{(n+1)!} = \frac{4}{n+1} \cdot \frac{4^n}{n!} = \frac{4}{n+1} \cdot a_n \leq a_n \; if \; n \geq 3.$$

Therefore, the sequence is decreasing for all $n \geq 3$. Further, the sequence is bounded below by $0$ because $4^n/n! \geq 0$ for all positive integers $n$. Therefore, by the Monotone Convergence Theorem, the sequence converges.

To find the limit, we use the fact that the sequence converges and let $L = \lim_{n \to \infty} a_n$. Now note this important observation. Consider $\lim_{n \to \infty} a_{n+1}$. Since

$$\{a_{n+1}\} = \{a_2, a_3, a_4, \ldots\},$$

the only difference between the sequences $\{a_{n+1}\}$ and $\{a_n\}$ is that $\{a_{n+1}\}$ omits the first term. Since a finite number of terms does not affect the convergence of a sequence,

$$\lim_{n \to \infty} a_{n+1} = \lim_{n \to \infty} a_n = L.$$

Combining this fact with the equation

$$a_{n+1} = \frac{4}{n+1} a_n$$

and taking the limit of both sides of the equation

$$\lim_{n \to \infty} a_{n+1} = \lim_{n \to \infty} \frac{4}{n+1} a_n,$$

we can conclude that

$$L = 0 \cdot L = 0.$$

b. Writing out the first several terms,

$$\left\{2, \frac{5}{4}, \frac{41}{40}, \frac{3281}{3280}, \ldots\right\}.$$

we can conjecture that the sequence is decreasing and bounded below by $1$. To show that the sequence is bounded below by $1,$ we can show that

$$\frac{a_n}{2} + \frac{1}{2a_n} \geq 1.$$

To show this, first rewrite

$$\frac{a_n}{2} + \frac{1}{2a_n} = \frac{a_n^2 + 1}{2a_n}.$$

Since $a_1 > 0$ and $a_2$ is defined as a sum of positive terms, $a_2 > 0$. Similarly, all terms $a_n > 0$. Therefore,

$$\frac{a_n^2 + 1}{2a_n} \geq 1$$

if and only if

$$a_n^2 + 1 \geq 2a_n.$$

Rewriting the inequality $a_n^2 + 1 \geq 2a_n$ as $a_n^2 - 2a_n + 1 \geq 0,$ and using the fact that

$$a_n^2 - 2a_n + 1 = (a_n - 1)^2 \geq 0$$

because the square of any real number is nonnegative, we can conclude that

$$\frac{a_n}{2} + \frac{1}{2a_n} \geq 1.$$

To show that the sequence is decreasing, we must show that $a_{n+1} \leq a_n$ for all $n \geq 1$. Since $1 \leq a_n^2$, it follows that

$$a_n^2 + 1 \leq 2a_n^2.$$

Dividing both sides by $2a_n$, we obtain

$$\frac{a_n}{2} + \frac{1}{2a_n} \leq a_n.$$

Using the definition of $a_{n+1}$, we conclude that

$$a_{n+1} = \frac{a_n}{2} + \frac{1}{2a_n} \leq a_n.$$

Since $\{a_n\}$ is bounded below and decreasing, by the Monotone Convergence Theorem, it converges. To find the limit, let $L = \lim_{n \to \infty} a_n$. Then using the recurrence relation and the fact that $\lim_{n \to \infty} a_n = \lim_{n \to \infty} a_{n+1}$, we have

$$\lim_{n \to \infty} a_{n+1} = \lim_{n \to \infty}\left(\frac{a_n}{2} + \frac{1}{2a_n}\right),$$

and therefore

$$L = \frac{L}{2} + \frac{1}{2L}.$$

Multiplying both sides of this equation by $2L$, we arrive at the equation

$$2L^2 = L^2 + 1.$$

Solving this equation for $L$, we conclude that $L^2 = 1$, which implies $L = \pm 1$. Since all the terms are positive, the limit $L = 1$.

**5.6** Consider the sequence $\{a_n\}$ defined recursively such that $a_1 = 1$, $a_n = a_{n-1}/2$. Use the Monotone Convergence Theorem to show that this sequence converges and find its limit.

# Student PROJECT

## Fibonacci Numbers

The Fibonacci numbers are defined recursively by the sequence $\{F_n\}$ where $F_0 = 0,\quad F_1 = 1$ and for $n \geq 2,$

$$F_n = F_{n-1} + F_{n-2}.$$

Here we look at properties of the Fibonacci numbers.

1. Write out the first twenty Fibonacci numbers.
2. Find a closed formula for the Fibonacci sequence by using the following steps.
   a. Consider the recursively defined sequence $\{x_n\}$ where $x_o = c$ and $x_{n+1} = ax_n$. Show that this sequence can be described by the closed formula $x_n = ca^n$ for all $n \geq 0$.
   b. Using the result from part a. as motivation, look for a solution of the equation
   $$F_n = F_{n-1} + F_{n-2}$$
   of the form $F_n = c\lambda^n$. Determine what two values for $\lambda$ will allow $F_n$ to satisfy this equation.
   c. Consider the two solutions from part b.: $\lambda_1$ and $\lambda_2$. Let $F_n = c_1 {\lambda_1}^n + c_2 {\lambda_2}^n$. Use the initial conditions $F_0$ and $F_1$ to determine the values for the constants $c_1$ and $c_2$ and write the closed formula $F_n$.
3. Use the answer in 2 c. to show that
   $$\lim_{n \to \infty} \frac{F_{n+1}}{F_n} = \frac{1 + \sqrt{5}}{2}.$$

   The number $\phi = \left(1 + \sqrt{5}\right)/2$ is known as the golden ratio (**Figure 5.8** and **Figure 5.9**).

**Figure 5.8** The seeds in a sunflower exhibit spiral patterns curving to the left and to the right. The number of spirals in each direction is always a Fibonacci number—always. (credit: modification of work by Esdras Calderan, Wikimedia Commons)

**Figure 5.9** The proportion of the golden ratio appears in many famous examples of art and architecture. The ancient Greek temple known as the Parthenon was designed with these proportions, and the ratio appears again in many of the smaller details. (credit: modification of work by TravelingOtter, Flickr)

# 5.1 EXERCISES

Find the first six terms of each of the following sequences, starting with $n = 1$.

1. $a_n = 1 + (-1)^n$ for $n \geq 1$

2. $a_n = n^2 - 1$ for $n \geq 1$

3. $a_1 = 1$ and $a_n = a_{n-1} + n$ for $n \geq 2$

4. $a_1 = 1$, $a_2 = 1$ and $a_{n+2} = a_n + a_{n+1}$ for $n \geq 1$

5. Find an explicit formula for $a_n$ where $a_1 = 1$ and $a_n = a_{n-1} + n$ for $n \geq 2$.

6. Find a formula $a_n$ for the $n$th term of the arithmetic sequence whose first term is $a_1 = 1$ such that $a_{n-1} - a_n = 17$ for $n \geq 1$.

7. Find a formula $a_n$ for the $n$th term of the arithmetic sequence whose first term is $a_1 = -3$ such that $a_{n-1} - a_n = 4$ for $n \geq 1$.

8. Find a formula $a_n$ for the $n$th term of the geometric sequence whose first term is $a_1 = 1$ such that $\frac{a_{n+1}}{a_n} = 10$ for $n \geq 1$.

9. Find a formula $a_n$ for the $n$th term of the geometric sequence whose first term is $a_1 = 3$ such that $\frac{a_{n+1}}{a_n} = 1/10$ for $n \geq 1$.

10. Find an explicit formula for the $n$th term of the sequence whose first several terms are $\{0, 3, 8, 15, 24, 35, 48, 63, 80, 99, \ldots\}$. (*Hint:* First add one to each term.)

11. Find an explicit formula for the $n$th term of the sequence satisfying $a_1 = 0$ and $a_n = 2a_{n-1} + 1$ for $n \geq 2$.

Find a formula for the general term $a_n$ of each of the following sequences.

12. $\{1, 0, -1, 0, 1, 0, -1, 0, \ldots\}$ (*Hint:* Find where $\sin x$ takes these values)

13. $\{1, -1/3, 1/5, -1/7, \ldots\}$

Find a function $f(n)$ that identifies the $n$th term $a_n$ of the following recursively defined sequences, as $a_n = f(n)$.

14. $a_1 = 1$ and $a_{n+1} = -a_n$ for $n \geq 1$

15. $a_1 = 2$ and $a_{n+1} = 2a_n$ for $n \geq 1$

16. $a_1 = 1$ and $a_{n+1} = (n+1)a_n$ for $n \geq 1$

17. $a_1 = 2$ and $a_{n+1} = (n+1)a_n/2$ for $n \geq 1$

18. $a_1 = 1$ and $a_{n+1} = a_n/2^n$ for $n \geq 1$

Plot the first $N$ terms of each sequence. State whether the graphical evidence suggests that the sequence converges or diverges.

19. **[T]** $a_1 = 1$, $a_2 = 2$, and for $n \geq 2$, $a_n = \frac{1}{2}(a_{n-1} + a_{n-2})$; $N = 30$

20. **[T]** $a_1 = 1$, $a_2 = 2$, $a_3 = 3$ and for $n \geq 4$, $a_n = \frac{1}{3}(a_{n-1} + a_{n-2} + a_{n-3})$, $N = 30$

21. **[T]** $a_1 = 1$, $a_2 = 2$, and for $n \geq 3$, $a_n = \sqrt{a_{n-1}a_{n-2}}$; $N = 30$

22. **[T]** $a_1 = 1$, $a_2 = 2$, $a_3 = 3$, and for $n \geq 4$, $a_n = \sqrt{a_{n-1}a_{n-2}a_{n-3}}$; $N = 30$

Suppose that $\lim_{n \to \infty} a_n = 1$, $\lim_{n \to \infty} b_n = -1$, and $0 < -b_n < a_n$ for all $n$. Evaluate each of the following limits, or state that the limit does not exist, or state that there is not enough information to determine whether the limit exists.

23. $\lim_{n \to \infty} 3a_n - 4b_n$

24. $\lim_{n \to \infty} \frac{1}{2}b_n - \frac{1}{2}a_n$

25. $\lim_{n \to \infty} \frac{a_n + b_n}{a_n - b_n}$

26. $\lim_{n \to \infty} \frac{a_n - b_n}{a_n + b_n}$

Find the limit of each of the following sequences, using L'Hôpital's rule when appropriate.

27. $\frac{n^2}{2^n}$

28. $\frac{(n-1)^2}{(n+1)^2}$

29. $\frac{\sqrt{n}}{\sqrt{n+1}}$

30. $n^{1/n}$ (*Hint:* $n^{1/n} = e^{\frac{1}{n}\ln n}$)

For each of the following sequences, whose $n$th terms are indicated, state whether the sequence is bounded and whether it is eventually monotone, increasing, or decreasing.

31. $n/2^n, \quad n \geq 2$

32. $\ln\left(1 + \frac{1}{n}\right)$

33. $\sin n$

34. $\cos\left(n^2\right)$

35. $n^{1/n}, \quad n \geq 3$

36. $n^{-1/n}, \quad n \geq 3$

37. $\tan n$

38. Determine whether the sequence defined as follows has a limit. If it does, find the limit. $a_1 = \sqrt{2}$, $a_2 = \sqrt{2\sqrt{2}}$, $a_3 = \sqrt{2\sqrt{2\sqrt{2}}}$ etc.

39. Determine whether the sequence defined as follows has a limit. If it does, find the limit. $a_1 = 3$, $a_n = \sqrt{2a_{n-1}}$, $n = 2, 3,\ldots.$

Use the Squeeze Theorem to find the limit of each of the following sequences.

40. $n\sin(1/n)$

41. $\frac{\cos(1/n) - 1}{1/n}$

42. $a_n = \frac{n!}{n^n}$

43. $a_n = \sin n \sin(1/n)$

For the following sequences, plot the first 25 terms of the sequence and state whether the graphical evidence suggests that the sequence converges or diverges.

44. **[T]** $a_n = \sin n$

45. **[T]** $a_n = \cos n$

Determine the limit of the sequence or show that the sequence diverges. If it converges, find its limit.

46. $a_n = \tan^{-1}(n^2)$

47. $a_n = (2n)^{1/n} - n^{1/n}$

48. $a_n = \frac{\ln(n^2)}{\ln(2n)}$

49. $a_n = \left(1 - \frac{2}{n}\right)^n$

50. $a_n = \ln\left(\frac{n+2}{n^2-3}\right)$

51. $a_n = \frac{2^n + 3^n}{4^n}$

52. $a_n = \frac{(1000)^n}{n!}$

53. $a_n = \frac{(n!)^2}{(2n)!}$

Newton's method seeks to approximate a solution $f(x) = 0$ that starts with an initial approximation $x_0$ and successively defines a sequence $x_{n+1} = x_n - \frac{f(x_n)}{f'(x_n)}$. For the given choice of $f$ and $x_0$, write out the formula for $x_{n+1}$. If the sequence appears to converge, give an exact formula for the solution $x$, then identify the limit $x$ accurate to four decimal places and the smallest $n$ such that $x_n$ agrees with $x$ up to four decimal places.

54. **[T]** $f(x) = x^2 - 2, \quad x_0 = 1$

55. **[T]** $f(x) = (x-1)^2 - 2, \quad x_0 = 2$

56. **[T]** $f(x) = e^x - 2, \quad x_0 = 1$

57. **[T]** $f(x) = \ln x - 1, \quad x_0 = 2$

58. **[T]** Suppose you start with one liter of vinegar and repeatedly remove $0.1$ L, replace with water, mix, and repeat.

a. Find a formula for the concentration after $n$ steps.
b. After how many steps does the mixture contain less than $10\%$ vinegar?

59. **[T]** A lake initially contains $2000$ fish. Suppose that in the absence of predators or other causes of removal, the fish population increases by $6\%$ each month. However, factoring in all causes, $150$ fish are lost each month.

a. Explain why the fish population after $n$ months is modeled by $P_n = 1.06P_{n-1} - 150$ with $P_0 = 2000$.
b. How many fish will be in the pond after one year?

60. **[T]** A bank account earns $5\%$ interest compounded monthly. Suppose that $\$1000$ is initially deposited into the account, but that $\$10$ is withdrawn each month.

a. Show that the amount in the account after $n$ months is $A_n = (1 + .05/12)A_{n-1} - 10$; $A_0 = 1000$.
b. How much money will be in the account after $1$ year?
c. Is the amount increasing or decreasing?
d. Suppose that instead of $\$10$, a fixed amount $d$ dollars is withdrawn each month. Find a value of $d$ such that the amount in the account after each month remains $\$1000$.
e. What happens if $d$ is greater than this amount?

61. **[T]** A student takes out a college loan of $\$10,000$ at an annual percentage rate of $6\%$, compounded monthly.

a. If the student makes payments of $\$100$ per month, how much does the student owe after $12$ months?
b. After how many months will the loan be paid off?

62. **[T]** Consider a series combining geometric growth and arithmetic decrease. Let $a_1 = 1$. Fix $a > 1$ and $0 < b < a$. Set $a_{n+1} = a.a_n - b$. Find a formula for $a_{n+1}$ in terms of $a^n$, $a$, and $b$ and a relationship between $a$ and $b$ such that $a_n$ converges.

63. **[T]** The binary representation $x = 0.b_1 b_2 b_3 ...$ of a number $x$ between $0$ and $1$ can be defined as follows. Let $b_1 = 0$ if $x < 1/2$ and $b_1 = 1$ if $1/2 \le x < 1$. Let $x_1 = 2x - b_1$. Let $b_2 = 0$ if $x_1 < 1/2$ and $b_2 = 1$ if $1/2 \le x < 1$. Let $x_2 = 2x_1 - b_2$ and in general, $x_n = 2x_{n-1} - b_n$ and $b_{n-1} = 0$ if $x_n < 1/2$ and $b_{n-1} = 1$ if $1/2 \le x_n < 1$. Find the binary expansion of $1/3$.

64. **[T]** To find an approximation for $\pi$, set $a_0 = \sqrt{2+1}$, $a_1 = \sqrt{2+a_0}$, and, in general, $a_{n+1} = \sqrt{2+a_n}$. Finally, set $p_n = 3.2^n \sqrt{2-a_n}$. Find the first ten terms of $p_n$ and compare the values to $\pi$.

For the following two exercises, assume that you have access to a computer program or Internet source that can generate a list of zeros and ones of any desired length. Pseudorandom number generators (PRNGs) play an important role in simulating random noise in physical systems by creating sequences of zeros and ones that appear like the result of flipping a coin repeatedly. One of the simplest types of PRNGs recursively defines a random-looking sequence of $N$ integers $a_1, a_2, \ldots, a_N$ by fixing two special integers $K$ and $M$ and letting $a_{n+1}$ be the remainder after dividing $K.a_n$ into $M$, then creates a bit sequence of zeros and ones whose $n$th term $b_n$ is equal to one if $a_n$ is odd and equal to zero if $a_n$ is even. If the bits $b_n$ are pseudorandom, then the behavior of their average $(b_1 + b_2 + \cdots + b_N)/N$ should be similar to behavior of averages of truly randomly generated bits.

65. **[T]** Starting with $K = 16,807$ and $M = 2,147,483,647$, using ten different starting values of $a_1$, compute sequences of bits $b_n$ up to $n = 1000$, and compare their averages to ten such sequences generated by a random bit generator.

66. **[T]** Find the first $1000$ digits of $\pi$ using either a computer program or Internet resource. Create a bit sequence $b_n$ by letting $b_n = 1$ if the $n$th digit of $\pi$ is odd and $b_n = 0$ if the $n$th digit of $\pi$ is even. Compute the average value of $b_n$ and the average value of $d_n = |b_{n+1} - b_n|$, $n = 1,..., 999$. Does the sequence $b_n$ appear random? Do the differences between successive elements of $b_n$ appear random?

# 5.2 | Infinite Series

## Learning Objectives

**5.2.1** Explain the meaning of the sum of an infinite series.
**5.2.2** Calculate the sum of a geometric series.
**5.2.3** Evaluate a telescoping series.

We have seen that a sequence is an ordered set of terms. If you add these terms together, you get a series. In this section we define an infinite series and show how series are related to sequences. We also define what it means for a series to converge or diverge. We introduce one of the most important types of series: the geometric series. We will use geometric series in the next chapter to write certain functions as polynomials with an infinite number of terms. This process is important because it allows us to evaluate, differentiate, and integrate complicated functions by using polynomials that are easier to handle. We also discuss the harmonic series, arguably the most interesting divergent series because it just fails to converge.

## Sums and Series

An infinite series is a sum of infinitely many terms and is written in the form

$$\sum_{n=1}^{\infty} a_n = a_1 + a_2 + a_3 + \cdots.$$

But what does this mean? We cannot add an infinite number of terms in the same way we can add a finite number of terms. Instead, the value of an infinite series is defined in terms of the *limit* of partial sums. A partial sum of an infinite series is a finite sum of the form

$$\sum_{n=1}^{k} a_n = a_1 + a_2 + a_3 + \cdots + a_k.$$

To see how we use partial sums to evaluate infinite series, consider the following example. Suppose oil is seeping into a lake such that $1000$ gallons enters the lake the first week. During the second week, an additional $500$ gallons of oil enters the lake. The third week, $250$ more gallons enters the lake. Assume this pattern continues such that each week half as much oil enters the lake as did the previous week. If this continues forever, what can we say about the amount of oil in the lake? Will the amount of oil continue to get arbitrarily large, or is it possible that it approaches some finite amount? To answer this question, we look at the amount of oil in the lake after $k$ weeks. Letting $S_k$ denote the amount of oil in the lake (measured in thousands of gallons) after $k$ weeks, we see that

$$\begin{aligned}
S_1 &= 1 \\
S_2 &= 1 + 0.5 = 1 + \frac{1}{2} \\
S_3 &= 1 + 0.5 + 0.25 = 1 + \frac{1}{2} + \frac{1}{4} \\
S_4 &= 1 + 0.5 + 0.25 + 0.125 = 1 + \frac{1}{2} + \frac{1}{4} + \frac{1}{8} \\
S_5 &= 1 + 0.5 + 0.25 + 0.125 + 0.0625 = 1 + \frac{1}{2} + \frac{1}{4} + \frac{1}{8} + \frac{1}{16}.
\end{aligned}$$

Looking at this pattern, we see that the amount of oil in the lake (in thousands of gallons) after $k$ weeks is

$$S_k = 1 + \frac{1}{2} + \frac{1}{4} + \frac{1}{8} + \frac{1}{16} + \cdots + \frac{1}{2^{k-1}} = \sum_{n=1}^{k} \left(\frac{1}{2}\right)^{n-1}.$$

We are interested in what happens as $k \to \infty$. Symbolically, the amount of oil in the lake as $k \to \infty$ is given by the infinite series

$$\sum_{n=1}^{\infty} \left(\frac{1}{2}\right)^{n-1} = 1 + \frac{1}{2} + \frac{1}{4} + \frac{1}{8} + \frac{1}{16} + \cdots.$$

At the same time, as $k \to \infty,$ the amount of oil in the lake can be calculated by evaluating $\lim_{k \to \infty} S_k.$ Therefore, the behavior of the infinite series can be determined by looking at the behavior of the sequence of partial sums $\{S_k\}.$ If the sequence of partial sums $\{S_k\}$ converges, we say that the infinite series converges, and its sum is given by $\lim_{k \to \infty} S_k.$ If the sequence $\{S_k\}$ diverges, we say the infinite series diverges. We now turn our attention to determining the limit of this sequence $\{S_k\}.$

First, simplifying some of these partial sums, we see that

$$\begin{aligned} S_1 &= 1 \\ S_2 &= 1 + \frac{1}{2} = \frac{3}{2} \\ S_3 &= 1 + \frac{1}{2} + \frac{1}{4} = \frac{7}{4} \\ S_4 &= 1 + \frac{1}{2} + \frac{1}{4} + \frac{1}{8} = \frac{15}{8} \\ S_5 &= 1 + \frac{1}{2} + \frac{1}{4} + \frac{1}{8} + \frac{1}{16} = \frac{31}{16}. \end{aligned}$$

Plotting some of these values in **Figure 5.10**, it appears that the sequence $\{S_k\}$ could be approaching 2.

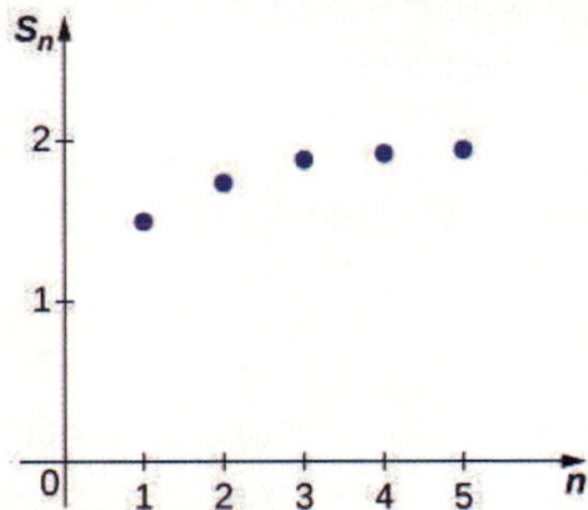


**Figure 5.10** The graph shows the sequence of partial sums $\{S_k\}.$ It appears that the sequence is approaching the value $2.$

Let’s look for more convincing evidence. In the following table, we list the values of $S_k$ for several values of $k.$

| $k$ | 5 | 10 | 15 | 20 |
|---|---|---|---|---|
| $S_k$ | 1.9375 | 1.998 | 1.999939 | 1.999998 |

These data supply more evidence suggesting that the sequence $\{S_k\}$ converges to $2.$ Later we will provide an analytic argument that can be used to prove that $\lim_{k \to \infty} S_k = 2.$ For now, we rely on the numerical and graphical data to convince ourselves that the sequence of partial sums does actually converge to $2.$ Since this sequence of partial sums converges to $2,$ we say the infinite series converges to $2$ and write

$$\sum_{n=1}^{\infty} \left(\frac{1}{2}\right)^{n-1} = 2.$$

Returning to the question about the oil in the lake, since this infinite series converges to $2,$ we conclude that the amount of oil in the lake will get arbitrarily close to $2000$ gallons as the amount of time gets sufficiently large.

This series is an example of a geometric series. We discuss geometric series in more detail later in this section. First, we summarize what it means for an infinite series to converge.

### Definition

An **infinite series** is an expression of the form

$$\sum_{n=1}^{\infty} a_n = a_1 + a_2 + a_3 + \cdots.$$

For each positive integer $k$, the sum

$$S_k = \sum_{n=1}^{k} a_n = a_1 + a_2 + a_3 + \cdots + a_k$$

is called the $k$th **partial sum** of the infinite series. The partial sums form a sequence $\{S_k\}$. If the sequence of partial sums converges to a real number $S$, the infinite series converges. If we can describe the **convergence of a series** to $S$, we call $S$ the sum of the series, and we write

$$\sum_{n=1}^{\infty} a_n = S.$$

If the sequence of partial sums diverges, we have the **divergence of a series**.

This **website (http://www.openstaxcollege.org/l/20_series)** shows a more whimsical approach to series.

Note that the index for a series need not begin with $n = 1$ but can begin with any value. For example, the series

$$\sum_{n=1}^{\infty} \left(\frac{1}{2}\right)^{n-1}$$

can also be written as

$$\sum_{n=0}^{\infty} \left(\frac{1}{2}\right)^{n} \text{ or } \sum_{n=5}^{\infty} \left(\frac{1}{2}\right)^{n-5}.$$

Often it is convenient for the index to begin at $1$, so if for some reason it begins at a different value, we can reindex by making a change of variables. For example, consider the series

$$\sum_{n=2}^{\infty} \frac{1}{n^2}.$$

By introducing the variable $m = n - 1$, so that $n = m + 1$, we can rewrite the series as

$$\sum_{m=1}^{\infty} \frac{1}{(m+1)^2}.$$

## Example 5.7

### Evaluating Limits of Sequences of Partial Sums

For each of the following series, use the sequence of partial sums to determine whether the series converges or diverges.

a. $\sum_{n=1}^{\infty} \frac{n}{n+1}$

b. $\sum_{n=1}^{\infty} (-1)^n$

c. $\sum_{n=1}^{\infty} \frac{1}{n(n+1)}$

### Solution

a. The sequence of partial sums $\{S_k\}$ satisfies

$$\begin{aligned} S_1 &= \tfrac{1}{2} \\ S_2 &= \tfrac{1}{2} + \tfrac{2}{3} \\ S_3 &= \tfrac{1}{2} + \tfrac{2}{3} + \tfrac{3}{4} \\ S_4 &= \tfrac{1}{2} + \tfrac{2}{3} + \tfrac{3}{4} + \tfrac{4}{5}. \end{aligned}$$

Notice that each term added is greater than $1/2$. As a result, we see that

$$\begin{aligned} S_1 &= \tfrac{1}{2} \\ S_2 &= \tfrac{1}{2} + \tfrac{2}{3} > \tfrac{1}{2} + \tfrac{1}{2} = 2\left(\tfrac{1}{2}\right) \\ S_3 &= \tfrac{1}{2} + \tfrac{2}{3} + \tfrac{3}{4} > \tfrac{1}{2} + \tfrac{1}{2} + \tfrac{1}{2} = 3\left(\tfrac{1}{2}\right) \\ S_4 &= \tfrac{1}{2} + \tfrac{2}{3} + \tfrac{3}{4} + \tfrac{4}{5} > \tfrac{1}{2} + \tfrac{1}{2} + \tfrac{1}{2} + \tfrac{1}{2} = 4\left(\tfrac{1}{2}\right). \end{aligned}$$

From this pattern we can see that $S_k > k\left(\frac{1}{2}\right)$ for every integer $k$. Therefore, $\{S_k\}$ is unbounded and consequently, diverges. Therefore, the infinite series $\sum_{n=1}^{\infty} n/(n+1)$ diverges.

b. The sequence of partial sums $\{S_k\}$ satisfies

$$\begin{aligned} S_1 &= -1 \\ S_2 &= -1 + 1 = 0 \\ S_3 &= -1 + 1 - 1 = -1 \\ S_4 &= -1 + 1 - 1 + 1 = 0. \end{aligned}$$

From this pattern we can see the sequence of partial sums is

$$\{S_k\} = \{-1, 0, -1, 0, \ldots\}.$$

Since this sequence diverges, the infinite series $\sum_{n=1}^{\infty} (-1)^n$ diverges.

c. The sequence of partial sums $\{S_k\}$ satisfies

$$\begin{aligned}
S_1 &= \frac{1}{1 \cdot 2} = \frac{1}{2} \\
S_2 &= \frac{1}{1 \cdot 2} + \frac{1}{2 \cdot 3} = \frac{1}{2} + \frac{1}{6} = \frac{2}{3} \\
S_3 &= \frac{1}{1 \cdot 2} + \frac{1}{2 \cdot 3} + \frac{1}{3 \cdot 4} = \frac{1}{2} + \frac{1}{6} + \frac{1}{12} = \frac{3}{4} \\
S_4 &= \frac{1}{1 \cdot 2} + \frac{1}{2 \cdot 3} + \frac{1}{3 \cdot 4} + \frac{1}{4 \cdot 5} = \frac{4}{5} \\
S_5 &= \frac{1}{1 \cdot 2} + \frac{1}{2 \cdot 3} + \frac{1}{3 \cdot 4} + \frac{1}{4 \cdot 5} + \frac{1}{5 \cdot 6} = \frac{5}{6}.
\end{aligned}$$

From this pattern, we can see that the $k$th partial sum is given by the explicit formula

$$S_k = \frac{k}{k+1}.$$

Since $k/(k+1) \to 1,$ we conclude that the sequence of partial sums converges, and therefore the infinite series converges to $1.$ We have

$$\sum_{n=1}^{\infty} \frac{1}{n(n+1)} = 1.$$

 **5.7** Determine whether the series $\sum_{n=1}^{\infty} (n+1)/n$ converges or diverges.

## The Harmonic Series

A useful series to know about is the **harmonic series**. The harmonic series is defined as

$$\sum_{n=1}^{\infty} \frac{1}{n} = 1 + \frac{1}{2} + \frac{1}{3} + \frac{1}{4} + \cdots. \tag{5.5}$$

This series is interesting because it diverges, but it diverges very slowly. By this we mean that the terms in the sequence of partial sums $\{S_k\}$ approach infinity, but do so very slowly. We will show that the series diverges, but first we illustrate the slow growth of the terms in the sequence $\{S_k\}$ in the following table.

| $k$ | 10 | 100 | 1000 | 10,000 | 100,000 | 1,000,000 |
|---|---|---|---|---|---|---|
| $S_k$ | 2.92897 | 5.18738 | 7.48547 | 9.78761 | 12.09015 | 14.39273 |

Even after $1{,}000{,}000$ terms, the partial sum is still relatively small. From this table, it is not clear that this series actually diverges. However, we can show analytically that the sequence of partial sums diverges, and therefore the series diverges.

To show that the sequence of partial sums diverges, we show that the sequence of partial sums is unbounded. We begin by writing the first several partial sums:

$$S_1 = 1$$
$$S_2 = 1 + \frac{1}{2}$$
$$S_3 = 1 + \frac{1}{2} + \frac{1}{3}$$
$$S_4 = 1 + \frac{1}{2} + \frac{1}{3} + \frac{1}{4}.$$

Notice that for the last two terms in $S_4$,

$$\frac{1}{3} + \frac{1}{4} > \frac{1}{4} + \frac{1}{4}.$$

Therefore, we conclude that

$$S_4 > 1 + \frac{1}{2} + \left(\frac{1}{4} + \frac{1}{4}\right) = 1 + \frac{1}{2} + \frac{1}{2} = 1 + 2\left(\frac{1}{2}\right).$$

Using the same idea for $S_8$, we see that

$$\begin{aligned} S_8 &= 1 + \frac{1}{2} + \frac{1}{3} + \frac{1}{4} + \frac{1}{5} + \frac{1}{6} + \frac{1}{7} + \frac{1}{8} > 1 + \frac{1}{2} + \left(\frac{1}{4} + \frac{1}{4}\right) + \left(\frac{1}{8} + \frac{1}{8} + \frac{1}{8} + \frac{1}{8}\right) \\ &= 1 + \frac{1}{2} + \frac{1}{2} + \frac{1}{2} = 1 + 3\left(\frac{1}{2}\right). \end{aligned}$$

From this pattern, we see that $S_1 = 1$, $S_2 = 1 + 1/2$, $S_4 > 1 + 2(1/2)$, and $S_8 > 1 + 3(1/2)$. More generally, it can be shown that $S_{2^j} > 1 + j(1/2)$ for all $j > 1$. Since $1 + j(1/2) \to \infty$, we conclude that the sequence $\{S_k\}$ is unbounded and therefore diverges. In the previous section, we stated that convergent sequences are bounded. Consequently, since $\{S_k\}$ is unbounded, it diverges. Thus, the harmonic series diverges.

## Algebraic Properties of Convergent Series

Since the sum of a convergent infinite series is defined as a limit of a sequence, the algebraic properties for series listed below follow directly from the algebraic properties for sequences.

### Theorem 5.7: Algebraic Properties of Convergent Series

Let $\sum_{n=1}^{\infty} a_n$ and $\sum_{n=1}^{\infty} b_n$ be convergent series. Then the following algebraic properties hold.

i. The series $\sum_{n=1}^{\infty} (a_n + b_n)$ converges and $\sum_{n=1}^{\infty} (a_n + b_n) = \sum_{n=1}^{\infty} a_n + \sum_{n=1}^{\infty} b_n$. (Sum Rule)

ii. The series $\sum_{n=1}^{\infty} (a_n - b_n)$ converges and $\sum_{n=1}^{\infty} (a_n - b_n) = \sum_{n=1}^{\infty} a_n - \sum_{n=1}^{\infty} b_n$. (Difference Rule)

iii. For any real number $c$, the series $\sum_{n=1}^{\infty} ca_n$ converges and $\sum_{n=1}^{\infty} ca_n = c\sum_{n=1}^{\infty} a_n$. (Constant Multiple Rule)

## Example 5.8

### Using Algebraic Properties of Convergent Series

Evaluate

$$\sum_{n=1}^{\infty}\left[\frac{3}{n(n+1)}+\left(\frac{1}{2}\right)^{n-2}\right].$$

### Solution

We showed earlier that

$$\sum_{n=1}^{\infty}\frac{1}{n(n+1)}$$

and

$$\sum_{n=1}^{\infty}\left(\frac{1}{2}\right)^{n-1}=2.$$

Since both of those series converge, we can apply the properties of **Algebraic Properties of Convergent Series** to evaluate

$$\sum_{n=1}^{\infty}\left[\frac{3}{n(n+1)}+\left(\frac{1}{2}\right)^{n-2}\right].$$

Using the sum rule, write

$$\sum_{n=1}^{\infty}\left[\frac{3}{n(n+1)}+\left(\frac{1}{2}\right)^{n-2}\right]=\sum_{n=1}^{\infty}\frac{3}{n(n+1)}+\sum_{n=1}^{\infty}\left(\frac{1}{2}\right)^{n-2}.$$

Then, using the constant multiple rule and the sums above, we can conclude that

$$\begin{aligned}\sum_{n=1}^{\infty}\frac{3}{n(n+1)}+\sum_{n=1}^{\infty}\left(\frac{1}{2}\right)^{n-2} &= 3\sum_{n=1}^{\infty}\frac{1}{n(n+1)}+\left(\frac{1}{2}\right)^{-1}\sum_{n=1}^{\infty}\left(\frac{1}{2}\right)^{n-1}\\ &= 3(1)+\left(\frac{1}{2}\right)^{-1}(2)=3+2(2)=7.\end{aligned}$$

 **5.8** Evaluate $\sum_{n=1}^{\infty}\frac{5}{2^{n-1}}$.

## Geometric Series

A **geometric series** is any series that we can write in the form

$$a+ar+ar^2+ar^3+\cdots=\sum_{n=1}^{\infty}ar^{n-1}. \quad (5.6)$$

Because the ratio of each term in this series to the previous term is $r$, the number $r$ is called the ratio. We refer to $a$ as the initial term because it is the first term in the series. For example, the series

$$\sum_{n=1}^{\infty}\left(\frac{1}{2}\right)^{n-1}=1+\frac{1}{2}+\frac{1}{4}+\frac{1}{8}+\cdots$$

is a geometric series with initial term $a=1$ and ratio $r=1/2$.

In general, when does a geometric series converge? Consider the geometric series

$$\sum_{n=1}^{\infty}ar^{n-1}$$

when $a>0$. Its sequence of partial sums $\{S_k\}$ is given by

$$S_k = \sum_{n=1}^{k} ar^{n-1} = a + ar + ar^2 + \cdots + ar^{k-1}.$$

Consider the case when $r = 1$. In that case,

$$S_k = a + a(1) + a(1)^2 + \cdots + a(1)^{k-1} = ak.$$

Since $a > 0$, we know $ak \to \infty$ as $k \to \infty$. Therefore, the sequence of partial sums is unbounded and thus diverges. Consequently, the infinite series diverges for $r = 1$. For $r \neq 1$, to find the limit of $\{S_k\}$, multiply **Equation 5.6** by $1 - r$. Doing so, we see that

$$\begin{aligned}(1-r)S_k &= a(1-r)\left(1 + r + r^2 + r^3 + \cdots + r^{k-1}\right) \\ &= a[(1 + r + r^2 + r^3 + \cdots + r^{k-1}) - (r + r^2 + r^3 + \cdots + r^k)] \\ &= a\left(1 - r^k\right).\end{aligned}$$

All the other terms cancel out.

Therefore,

$$S_k = \frac{a\left(1 - r^k\right)}{1 - r} \text{ for } r \neq 1.$$

From our discussion in the previous section, we know that the geometric sequence $r^k \to 0$ if $|r| < 1$ and that $r^k$ diverges if $|r| > 1$ or $r = \pm 1$. Therefore, for $|r| < 1$, $S_k \to a/(1 - r)$ and we have

$$\sum_{n=1}^{\infty} ar^{n-1} = \frac{a}{1-r} \text{ if } |r| < 1.$$

If $|r| \geq 1$, $S_k$ diverges, and therefore

$$\sum_{n=1}^{\infty} ar^{n-1} \text{ diverges if } |r| \geq 1.$$

### Definition

A geometric series is a series of the form

$$\sum_{n=1}^{\infty} ar^{n-1} = a + ar + ar^2 + ar^3 + \cdots.$$

If $|r| < 1$, the series converges, and

$$\sum_{n=1}^{\infty} ar^{n-1} = \frac{a}{1-r} \text{ for } |r| < 1. \quad (5.7)$$

If $|r| \geq 1$, the series diverges.

Geometric series sometimes appear in slightly different forms. For example, sometimes the index begins at a value other than $n = 1$ or the exponent involves a linear expression for $n$ other than $n - 1$. As long as we can rewrite the series in the form given by **Equation 5.5**, it is a geometric series. For example, consider the series

$$\sum_{n=0}^{\infty} \left(\frac{2}{3}\right)^{n+2}.$$

To see that this is a geometric series, we write out the first several terms:

$$\sum_{n=0}^{\infty}\left(\frac{2}{3}\right)^{n+2} = \left(\frac{2}{3}\right)^2 + \left(\frac{2}{3}\right)^3 + \left(\frac{2}{3}\right)^4 + \cdots$$
$$= \frac{4}{9} + \frac{4}{9}\cdot\left(\frac{2}{3}\right) + \frac{4}{9}\cdot\left(\frac{2}{3}\right)^2 + \cdots.$$

We see that the initial term is $a = 4/9$ and the ratio is $r = 2/3$. Therefore, the series can be written as

$$\sum_{n=1}^{\infty}\frac{4}{9}\cdot\left(\frac{2}{3}\right)^{n-1}.$$

Since $r = 2/3 < 1$, this series converges, and its sum is given by

$$\sum_{n=1}^{\infty}\frac{4}{9}\cdot\left(\frac{2}{3}\right)^{n-1} = \frac{4/9}{1 - 2/3} = \frac{4}{3}.$$

## Example 5.9

### Determining Convergence or Divergence of a Geometric Series

Determine whether each of the following geometric series converges or diverges, and if it converges, find its sum.

a. $\sum_{n=1}^{\infty}\frac{(-3)^{n+1}}{4^{n-1}}$

b. $\sum_{n=1}^{\infty} e^{2n}$

### Solution

a. Writing out the first several terms in the series, we have

$$\sum_{n=1}^{\infty}\frac{(-3)^{n+1}}{4^{n-1}} = \frac{(-3)^2}{4^0} + \frac{(-3)^3}{4} + \frac{(-3)^4}{4^2} + \cdots$$
$$= (-3)^2 + (-3)^2\cdot\left(\frac{-3}{4}\right) + (-3)^2\cdot\left(\frac{-3}{4}\right)^2 + \cdots$$
$$= 9 + 9\cdot\left(\frac{-3}{4}\right) + 9\cdot\left(\frac{-3}{4}\right)^2 + \cdots.$$

The initial term $a = -3$ and the ratio $r = -3/4$. Since $|r| = 3/4 < 1$, the series converges to

$$\frac{9}{1-(-3/4)} = \frac{9}{7/4} = \frac{36}{7}.$$

b. Writing this series as

$$e^2\sum_{n=1}^{\infty}\left(e^2\right)^{n-1}$$

we can see that this is a geometric series where $r = e^2 > 1$. Therefore, the series diverges.

**5.9** Determine whether the series $\sum_{n=1}^{\infty}\left(\frac{-2}{5}\right)^{n-1}$ converges or diverges. If it converges, find its sum.

We now turn our attention to a nice application of geometric series. We show how they can be used to write repeating decimals as fractions of integers.

## Example 5.10

### Writing Repeating Decimals as Fractions of Integers

Use a geometric series to write $3.\overline{26}$ as a fraction of integers.

### Solution

Since $3.\overline{26} = 3.262626\ldots,$ first we write

$$\begin{aligned} 3.262626\ldots &= 3 + \frac{26}{100} + \frac{26}{1000} + \frac{26}{100{,}000} + \cdots \\ &= 3 + \frac{26}{10^2} + \frac{26}{10^4} + \frac{26}{10^6} + \cdots. \end{aligned}$$

Ignoring the term 3, the rest of this expression is a geometric series with initial term $a = 26/10^2$ and ratio $r = 1/10^2$. Therefore, the sum of this series is

$$\frac{26/10^2}{1 - (1/10^2)} = \frac{26/10^2}{99/10^2} = \frac{26}{99}.$$

Thus,

$$3.262626\ldots = 3 + \frac{26}{99} = \frac{323}{99}.$$

**5.10** Write $5.2\overline{7}$ as a fraction of integers.

## Example 5.11

### Chapter Opener: Finding the Area of the Koch Snowflake

Define a sequence of figures $\{F_n\}$ recursively as follows (**Figure 5.11**). Let $F_0$ be an equilateral triangle with sides of length $1$. For $n \geq 1,$ let $F_n$ be the curve created by removing the middle third of each side of $F_{n-1}$ and replacing it with an equilateral triangle pointing outward. The limiting figure as $n \to \infty$ is known as Koch's snowflake.

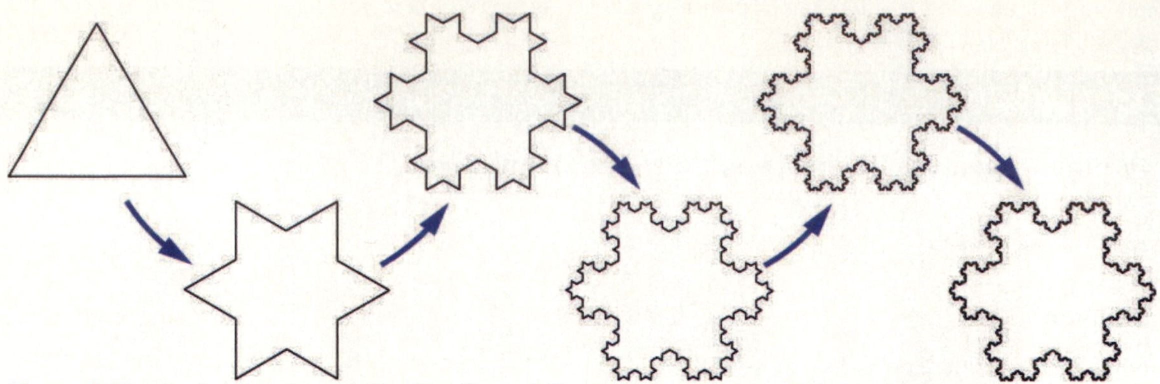

**Figure 5.11** The first four figures, $F_0, F_1, F_2,$ and $F_3,$ in the construction of the Koch snowflake.

a. Find the length $L_n$ of the perimeter of $F_n$. Evaluate $\lim_{n \to \infty} L_n$ to find the length of the perimeter of Koch's snowflake.

b. Find the area $A_n$ of figure $F_n$. Evaluate $\lim_{n \to \infty} A_n$ to find the area of Koch's snowflake.

### Solution

a. Let $N_n$ denote the number of sides of figure $F_n$. Since $F_0$ is a triangle, $N_0 = 3$. Let $l_n$ denote the length of each side of $F_n$. Since $F_0$ is an equilateral triangle with sides of length $l_0 = 1,$ we now need to determine $N_1$ and $l_1$. Since $F_1$ is created by removing the middle third of each side and replacing that line segment with two line segments, for each side of $F_0,$ we get four sides in $F_1$. Therefore, the number of sides for $F_1$ is

$$N_1 = 4 \cdot 3.$$

Since the length of each of these new line segments is $1/3$ the length of the line segments in $F_0,$ the length of the line segments for $F_1$ is given by

$$l_1 = \frac{1}{3} \cdot 1 = \frac{1}{3}.$$

Similarly, for $F_2,$ since the middle third of each side of $F_1$ is removed and replaced with two line segments, the number of sides in $F_2$ is given by

$$N_2 = 4N_1 = 4(4 \cdot 3) = 4^2 \cdot 3.$$

Since the length of each of these sides is $1/3$ the length of the sides of $F_1,$ the length of each side of figure $F_2$ is given by

$$l_2 = \frac{1}{3} \cdot l_1 = \frac{1}{3} \cdot \frac{1}{3} = \left(\frac{1}{3}\right)^2.$$

More generally, since $F_n$ is created by removing the middle third of each side of $F_{n-1}$ and replacing that line segment with two line segments of length $\frac{1}{3} l_{n-1}$ in the shape of an equilateral triangle, we know that $N_n = 4N_{n-1}$ and $l_n = \frac{l_{n-1}}{3}$. Therefore, the number of sides of figure $F_n$ is

$$N_n = 4^n \cdot 3$$

and the length of each side is

$$l_n = \left(\frac{1}{3}\right)^n.$$

Therefore, to calculate the perimeter of $F_n$, we multiply the number of sides $N_n$ and the length of each side $l_n$. We conclude that the perimeter of $F_n$ is given by

$$L_n = N_n \cdot l_n = 3 \cdot \left(\frac{4}{3}\right)^n.$$

Therefore, the length of the perimeter of Koch's snowflake is

$$L = \lim_{n \to \infty} L_n = \infty.$$

b. Let $T_n$ denote the area of each new triangle created when forming $F_n$. For $n = 0$, $T_0$ is the area of the original equilateral triangle. Therefore, $T_0 = A_0 = \sqrt{3}/4$. For $n \geq 1$, since the lengths of the sides of the new triangle are $1/3$ the length of the sides of $F_{n-1}$, we have

$$T_n = \left(\frac{1}{3}\right)^2 T_{n-1} = \frac{1}{9} \cdot T_{n-1}.$$

Therefore, $T_n = \left(\frac{1}{9}\right)^n \cdot \frac{\sqrt{3}}{4}$. Since a new triangle is formed on each side of $F_{n-1}$,

$$\begin{aligned} A_n &= A_{n-1} + N_{n-1} \cdot T_n \\ &= A_{n-1} + \left(3 \cdot 4^{n-1}\right) \cdot \left(\frac{1}{9}\right)^n \cdot \frac{\sqrt{3}}{4} \\ &= A_{n-1} + \frac{3}{4} \cdot \left(\frac{4}{9}\right)^n \cdot \frac{\sqrt{3}}{4}. \end{aligned}$$

Writing out the first few terms $A_0, A_1, A_2$, we see that

$$\begin{aligned} A_0 &= \frac{\sqrt{3}}{4} \\ A_1 &= A_0 + \frac{3}{4} \cdot \left(\frac{4}{9}\right) \cdot \frac{\sqrt{3}}{4} = \frac{\sqrt{3}}{4} + \frac{3}{4} \cdot \left(\frac{4}{9}\right) \cdot \frac{\sqrt{3}}{4} = \frac{\sqrt{3}}{4}\left[1 + \frac{3}{4} \cdot \left(\frac{4}{9}\right)\right] \\ A_2 &= A_1 + \frac{3}{4} \cdot \left(\frac{4}{9}\right)^2 \cdot \frac{\sqrt{3}}{4} = \frac{\sqrt{3}}{4}\left[1 + \frac{3}{4} \cdot \left(\frac{4}{9}\right)\right] + \frac{3}{4} \cdot \left(\frac{4}{9}\right)^2 \cdot \frac{\sqrt{3}}{4} = \frac{\sqrt{3}}{4}\left[1 + \frac{3}{4} \cdot \left(\frac{4}{9}\right) + \frac{3}{4} \cdot \left(\frac{4}{9}\right)^2\right]. \end{aligned}$$

More generally,

$$A_n = \frac{\sqrt{3}}{4}\left[1 + \frac{3}{4}\left(\frac{4}{9} + \left(\frac{4}{9}\right)^2 + \cdots + \left(\frac{4}{9}\right)^n\right)\right].$$

Factoring $4/9$ out of each term inside the inner parentheses, we rewrite our expression as

$$A_n = \frac{\sqrt{3}}{4}\left[1 + \frac{1}{3}\left(1 + \frac{4}{9} + \left(\frac{4}{9}\right)^2 + \cdots + \left(\frac{4}{9}\right)^{n-1}\right)\right].$$

The expression $1 + \left(\frac{4}{9}\right) + \left(\frac{4}{9}\right)^2 + \cdots + \left(\frac{4}{9}\right)^{n-1}$ is a geometric sum. As shown earlier, this sum satisfies

$$1 + \frac{4}{9} + \left(\frac{4}{9}\right)^2 + \cdots + \left(\frac{4}{9}\right)^{n-1} = \frac{1 - (4/9)^n}{1 - (4/9)}.$$

Substituting this expression into the expression above and simplifying, we conclude that

$$\begin{aligned} A_n &= \frac{\sqrt{3}}{4}\left[1 + \frac{1}{3}\left(\frac{1 - (4/9)^n}{1 - (4/9)}\right)\right] \\ &= \frac{\sqrt{3}}{4}\left[\frac{8}{5} - \frac{3}{5}\left(\frac{4}{9}\right)^n\right]. \end{aligned}$$

Therefore, the area of Koch's snowflake is

$$A = \lim_{n \to \infty} A_n = \frac{2\sqrt{3}}{5}.$$

### Analysis

The Koch snowflake is interesting because it has finite area, yet infinite perimeter. Although at first this may seem impossible, recall that you have seen similar examples earlier in the text. For example, consider the region bounded by the curve $y = 1/x^2$ and the $x$-axis on the interval $[1, \infty)$. Since the improper integral

$$\int_1^\infty \frac{1}{x^2} dx$$

converges, the area of this region is finite, even though the perimeter is infinite.

## Telescoping Series

Consider the series $\sum_{n=1}^{\infty} \frac{1}{n(n+1)}$. We discussed this series in **Example 5.7**, showing that the series converges by writing out the first several partial sums $S_1, S_2, \ldots, S_6$ and noticing that they are all of the form $S_k = \frac{k}{k+1}$. Here we use a different technique to show that this series converges. By using partial fractions, we can write

$$\frac{1}{n(n+1)} = \frac{1}{n} - \frac{1}{n+1}.$$

Therefore, the series can be written as

$$\sum_{n=1}^{\infty} \left[\frac{1}{n} - \frac{1}{n+1}\right] = \left(1 + \frac{1}{2}\right) + \left(\frac{1}{2} - \frac{1}{3}\right) + \left(\frac{1}{3} - \frac{1}{4}\right) + \cdots.$$

Writing out the first several terms in the sequence of partial sums $\{S_k\}$, we see that

$$\begin{aligned} S_1 &= 1 - \frac{1}{2} \\ S_2 &= \left(1 - \frac{1}{2}\right) + \left(\frac{1}{2} - \frac{1}{3}\right) = 1 - \frac{1}{3} \\ S_3 &= \left(1 - \frac{1}{2}\right) + \left(\frac{1}{2} - \frac{1}{3}\right) + \left(\frac{1}{3} - \frac{1}{4}\right) = 1 - \frac{1}{4}. \end{aligned}$$

In general,

$$S_k = \left(1 - \frac{1}{2}\right) + \left(\frac{1}{2} - \frac{1}{3}\right) + \left(\frac{1}{3} - \frac{1}{4}\right) + \cdots + \left(\frac{1}{k} - \frac{1}{k+1}\right) = 1 - \frac{1}{k+1}.$$

We notice that the middle terms cancel each other out, leaving only the first and last terms. In a sense, the series collapses like a spyglass with tubes that disappear into each other to shorten the telescope. For this reason, we call a series that has this property a telescoping series. For this series, since $S_k = 1 - 1/(k+1)$ and $1/(k+1) \to 0$ as $k \to \infty$, the sequence of partial sums converges to $1$, and therefore the series converges to $1$.

### Definition

A **telescoping series** is a series in which most of the terms cancel in each of the partial sums, leaving only some of the first terms and some of the last terms.

For example, any series of the form

$$\sum_{n=1}^{\infty} [b_n - b_{n+1}] = (b_1 - b_2) + (b_2 - b_3) + (b_3 - b_4) + \cdots$$

is a telescoping series. We can see this by writing out some of the partial sums. In particular, we see that

$$S_1 = b_1 - b_2$$
$$S_2 = (b_1 - b_2) + (b_2 - b_3) = b_1 - b_3$$
$$S_3 = (b_1 - b_2) + (b_2 - b_3) + (b_3 - b_4) = b_1 - b_4.$$

In general, the $k$th partial sum of this series is

$$S_k = b_1 - b_{k+1}.$$

Since the $k$th partial sum can be simplified to the difference of these two terms, the sequence of partial sums $\{S_k\}$ will converge if and only if the sequence $\{b_{k+1}\}$ converges. Moreover, if the sequence $b_{k+1}$ converges to some finite number $B$, then the sequence of partial sums converges to $b_1 - B$, and therefore

$$\sum_{n=1}^{\infty} [b_n - b_{n+1}] = b_1 - B.$$

In the next example, we show how to use these ideas to analyze a telescoping series of this form.

## Example 5.12

### Evaluating a Telescoping Series

Determine whether the telescoping series

$$\sum_{n=1}^{\infty} \left[\cos\left(\frac{1}{n}\right) - \cos\left(\frac{1}{n+1}\right)\right]$$

converges or diverges. If it converges, find its sum.

#### Solution

By writing out terms in the sequence of partial sums, we can see that

$$\begin{aligned} S_1 &= \cos(1) - \cos\left(\frac{1}{2}\right) \\ S_2 &= \left(\cos(1) - \cos\left(\frac{1}{2}\right)\right) + \left(\cos\left(\frac{1}{2}\right) - \cos\left(\frac{1}{3}\right)\right) = \cos(1) - \cos\left(\frac{1}{3}\right) \\ S_3 &= \left(\cos(1) - \cos\left(\frac{1}{2}\right)\right) + \left(\cos\left(\frac{1}{2}\right) - \cos\left(\frac{1}{3}\right)\right) + \left(\cos\left(\frac{1}{3}\right) - \cos\left(\frac{1}{4}\right)\right) \\ &= \cos(1) - \cos\left(\frac{1}{4}\right). \end{aligned}$$

In general,

$$S_k = \cos(1) - \cos\left(\frac{1}{k+1}\right).$$

Since $1/(k+1) \to 0$ as $k \to \infty$ and $\cos x$ is a continuous function, $\cos(1/(k+1)) \to \cos(0) = 1.$ Therefore, we conclude that $S_k \to \cos(1) - 1.$ The telescoping series converges and the sum is given by

$$\sum_{n=1}^{\infty} \left[\cos\left(\frac{1}{n}\right) - \cos\left(\frac{1}{n+1}\right)\right] = \cos(1) - 1.$$

**5.11** Determine whether $\sum_{n=1}^{\infty} \left[e^{1/n} - e^{1/(n+1)}\right]$ converges or diverges. If it converges, find its sum.

# Student PROJECT

## Euler's Constant

We have shown that the harmonic series $\sum_{n=1}^{\infty} \frac{1}{n}$ diverges. Here we investigate the behavior of the partial sums $S_k$ as $k \to \infty$. In particular, we show that they behave like the natural logarithm function by showing that there exists a constant $\gamma$ such that

$$\sum_{n=1}^{k} \frac{1}{n} - \ln k \to \gamma \text{ as } k \to \infty.$$

This constant $\gamma$ is known as Euler's constant.

1. Let $T_k = \sum_{n=1}^{k} \frac{1}{n} - \ln k$. Evaluate $T_k$ for various values of $k$.
2. For $T_k$ as defined in part 1. show that the sequence $\{T_k\}$ converges by using the following steps.
   a. Show that the sequence $\{T_k\}$ is monotone decreasing. (*Hint:* Show that $\ln(1 + 1/k > 1/(k+1))$
   b. Show that the sequence $\{T_k\}$ is bounded below by zero. (*Hint:* Express $\ln k$ as a definite integral.)
   c. Use the Monotone Convergence Theorem to conclude that the sequence $\{T_k\}$ converges. The limit $\gamma$ is Euler's constant.
3. Now estimate how far $T_k$ is from $\gamma$ for a given integer $k$. Prove that for $k \geq 1$, $0 < T_k - \gamma \leq 1/k$ by using the following steps.
   a. Show that $\ln(k+1) - \ln k < 1/k$.
   b. Use the result from part a. to show that for any integer $k$,
   $$T_k - T_{k+1} < \frac{1}{k} - \frac{1}{k+1}.$$
   c. For any integers $k$ and $j$ such that $j > k$, express $T_k - T_j$ as a telescoping sum by writing
   $$T_k - T_j = (T_k - T_{k+1}) + (T_{k+1} - T_{k+2}) + (T_{k+2} - T_{k+3}) + \cdots + (T_{j-1} - T_j).$$
   Use the result from part b. combined with this telescoping sum to conclude that
   $$T_k - T_j < \frac{1}{k} - \frac{1}{j}.$$
   d. Apply the limit to both sides of the inequality in part c. to conclude that
   $$T_k - \gamma \leq \frac{1}{k}.$$
   e. Estimate $\gamma$ to an accuracy of within $0.001$.

# 5.2 EXERCISES

Using sigma notation, write the following expressions as infinite series.

67. $1 + \frac{1}{2} + \frac{1}{3} + \frac{1}{4} + \cdots$

68. $1 - 1 + 1 - 1 + \cdots$

69. $1 - \frac{1}{2} + \frac{1}{3} - \frac{1}{4} + \ldots$

70. $\sin 1 + \sin 1/2 + \sin 1/3 + \sin 1/4 + \cdots$

Compute the first four partial sums $S_1, \ldots, S_4$ for the series having $n$th term $a_n$ starting with $n = 1$ as follows.

71. $a_n = n$

72. $a_n = 1/n$

73. $a_n = \sin(n\pi/2)$

74. $a_n = (-1)^n$

In the following exercises, compute the general term $a_n$ of the series with the given partial sum $S_n$. If the sequence of partial sums converges, find its limit $S$.

75. $S_n = 1 - \frac{1}{n}, \quad n \geq 2$

76. $S_n = \frac{n(n+1)}{2}, \quad n \geq 1$

77. $S_n = \sqrt{n}, \ n \geq 2$

78. $S_n = 2 - (n+2)/2^n, \ n \geq 1$

For each of the following series, use the sequence of partial sums to determine whether the series converges or diverges.

79. $\sum_{n=1}^{\infty} \frac{n}{n+2}$

80. $\sum_{n=1}^{\infty} (1 - (-1)^n))$

81. $\sum_{n=1}^{\infty} \frac{1}{(n+1)(n+2)}$ (*Hint:* Use a partial fraction decomposition like that for $\sum_{n=1}^{\infty} \frac{1}{n(n+1)}$.)

82. $\sum_{n=1}^{\infty} \frac{1}{2n+1}$ (*Hint:* Follow the reasoning for $\sum_{n=1}^{\infty} \frac{1}{n}$.)

Suppose that $\sum_{n=1}^{\infty} a_n = 1$, that $\sum_{n=1}^{\infty} b_n = -1$, that $a_1 = 2$, and $b_1 = -3$. Find the sum of the indicated series.

83. $\sum_{n=1}^{\infty} (a_n + b_n)$

84. $\sum_{n=1}^{\infty} (a_n - 2b_n)$

85. $\sum_{n=2}^{\infty} (a_n - b_n)$

86. $\sum_{n=1}^{\infty} (3a_{n+1} - 4b_{n+1})$

State whether the given series converges and explain why.

87. $\sum_{n=1}^{\infty} \frac{1}{n+1000}$ (*Hint:* Rewrite using a change of index.)

88. $\sum_{n=1}^{\infty} \frac{1}{n+10^{80}}$ (*Hint:* Rewrite using a change of index.)

89. $1 + \frac{1}{10} + \frac{1}{100} + \frac{1}{1000} + \cdots$

90. $1 + \frac{e}{\pi} + \frac{e^2}{\pi^2} + \frac{e^3}{\pi^3} + \cdots$

91. $1 + \frac{\pi}{e} + \frac{\pi^2}{e^4} + \frac{\pi^3}{e^6} + \frac{\pi^4}{e^8} + \cdots$

92. $1 - \sqrt{\frac{\pi}{3}} + \sqrt{\frac{\pi^2}{9}} - \sqrt{\frac{\pi^3}{27}} + \cdots$

For $a_n$ as follows, write the sum as a geometric series of the form $\sum_{n=1}^{\infty} ar^n$. State whether the series converges and if it does, find the value of $\sum a_n$.

93. $a_1 = -1$ and $a_n/a_{n+1} = -5$ for $n \geq 1$.

94. $a_1 = 2$ and $a_n/a_{n+1} = 1/2$ for $n \geq 1$.

95. $a_1 = 10$ and $a_n/a_{n+1} = 10$ for $n \geq 1$.

96. $a_1 = 1/10$ and $a_n/a_{n+1} = -10$ for $n \geq 1$.

Use the identity $\frac{1}{1-y} = \sum_{n=0}^{\infty} y^n$ to express the function as a geometric series in the indicated term.

97. $\frac{x}{1+x}$ in $x$

98. $\frac{\sqrt{x}}{1-x^{3/2}}$ in $\sqrt{x}$

99. $\frac{1}{1+\sin^2 x}$ in $\sin x$

100. $\sec^2 x$ in $\sin x$

Evaluate the following telescoping series or state whether the series diverges.

101. $\sum_{n=1}^{\infty} 2^{1/n} - 2^{1/(n+1)}$

102. $\sum_{n=1}^{\infty} \frac{1}{n^{13}} - \frac{1}{(n+1)^{13}}$

103. $\sum_{n=1}^{\infty} \left(\sqrt{n} - \sqrt{n+1}\right)$

104. $\sum_{n=1}^{\infty} (\sin n - \sin(n+1))$

Express the following series as a telescoping sum and evaluate its *n*th partial sum.

105. $\sum_{n=1}^{\infty} \ln\left(\frac{n}{n+1}\right)$

106. $\sum_{n=1}^{\infty} \frac{2n+1}{\left(n^2+n\right)^2}$ (*Hint:* Factor denominator and use partial fractions.)

107. $\sum_{n=2}^{\infty} \frac{\ln\left(1+\frac{1}{n}\right)}{\ln n \ln(n+1)}$

108. $\sum_{n=1}^{\infty} \frac{(n+2)}{n(n+1)2^{n+1}}$ (*Hint:* Look at $1/(n2^n)$.)

A general telescoping series is one in which all but the first few terms cancel out after summing a given number of successive terms.

109. Let $a_n = f(n) - 2f(n+1) + f(n+2)$, in which $f(n) \to 0$ as $n \to \infty$. Find $\sum_{n=1}^{\infty} a_n$.

110. $a_n = f(n) - f(n+1) - f(n+2) + f(n+3)$, in which $f(n) \to 0$ as $n \to \infty$. Find $\sum_{n=1}^{\infty} a_n$.

111. Suppose that $a_n = c_0 f(n) + c_1 f(n+1) + c_2 f(n+2) + c_3 f(n+3) + c_4 f(n+4)$, where $f(n) \to 0$ as $n \to \infty$. Find a condition on the coefficients $c_0, \ldots, c_4$ that make this a general telescoping series.

112. Evaluate $\sum_{n=1}^{\infty} \frac{1}{n(n+1)(n+2)}$ (*Hint:* $\frac{1}{n(n+1)(n+2)} = \frac{1}{2n} - \frac{1}{n+1} + \frac{1}{2(n+2)}$)

113. Evaluate $\sum_{n=2}^{\infty} \frac{2}{n^3 - n}$.

114. Find a formula for $\sum_{n=1}^{\infty} \frac{1}{n(n+N)}$ where $N$ is a positive integer.

115. **[T]** Define a sequence $t_k = \sum_{n=1}^{k-1} (1/k) - \ln k$. Use the graph of $1/x$ to verify that $t_k$ is increasing. Plot $t_k$ for $k = 1 \ldots 100$ and state whether it appears that the sequence converges.

116. **[T]** Suppose that $N$ equal uniform rectangular blocks are stacked one on top of the other, allowing for some overhang. Archimedes' law of the lever implies that the stack of $N$ blocks is stable as long as the center of mass of the top $(N-1)$ blocks lies at the edge of the bottom block. Let $x$ denote the position of the edge of the bottom block, and think of its position as relative to the center of the next-to-bottom block. This implies that $(N-1)x = \left(\frac{1}{2} - x\right)$ or $x = 1/(2N)$. Use this expression to compute the maximum overhang (the position of the edge of the top block over the edge of the bottom block.) See the following figure.

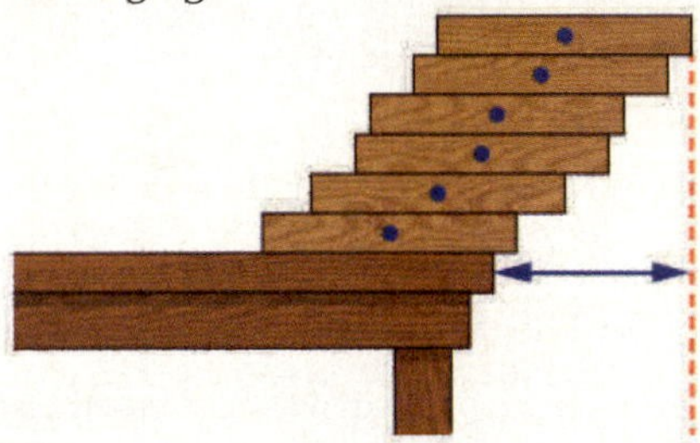

Each of the following infinite series converges to the given multiple of $\pi$ or $1/\pi$.

In each case, find the minimum value of $N$ such that the $N$th partial sum of the series accurately approximates the left-hand side to the given number of decimal places, and give the desired approximate value. Up to 15 decimals place, $\pi = 3.141592653589793....$

117. **[T]** $\pi = -3 + \sum_{n=1}^{\infty} \frac{n2^n n!^2}{(2n)!}$, error $< 0.0001$

118. **[T]** $\frac{\pi}{2} = \sum_{k=0}^{\infty} \frac{k!}{(2k+1)!!} = \sum_{k=0}^{\infty} \frac{2^k k!^2}{(2k+1)!}$, error $< 10^{-4}$

119. **[T]** $\frac{9801}{2\pi} = \frac{4}{9801} \sum_{k=0}^{\infty} \frac{(4k)!(1103 + 26390k)}{(k!)^4 396^{4k}}$, error $< 10^{-12}$

120. **[T]** $\frac{1}{12\pi} = \sum_{k=0}^{\infty} \frac{(-1)^k (6k)!(13591409 + 545140134k)}{(3k)!(k!)^3 640320^{3k+3/2}}$, error $< 10^{-15}$

121. **[T]** A fair coin is one that has probability $1/2$ of coming up heads when flipped.

a. What is the probability that a fair coin will come up tails $n$ times in a row?

b. Find the probability that a coin comes up heads for the first time after an even number of coin flips.

122. **[T]** Find the probability that a fair coin is flipped a multiple of three times before coming up heads.

123. **[T]** Find the probability that a fair coin will come up heads for the second time after an even number of flips.

124. **[T]** Find a series that expresses the probability that a fair coin will come up heads for the second time on a multiple of three flips.

125. **[T]** The expected number of times that a fair coin will come up heads is defined as the sum over $n = 1, 2,\ldots$ of $n$ times the probability that the coin will come up heads exactly $n$ times in a row, or $n/2^{n+1}$. Compute the expected number of consecutive times that a fair coin will come up heads.

126. **[T]** A person deposits $\$10$ at the beginning of each quarter into a bank account that earns $4\%$ annual interest compounded quarterly (four times a year).

a. Show that the interest accumulated after $n$ quarters is $\$10\left(\frac{1.01^{n+1} - 1}{0.01} - n\right)$.

b. Find the first eight terms of the sequence.

c. How much interest has accumulated after 2 years?

127. **[T]** Suppose that the amount of a drug in a patient's system diminishes by a multiplicative factor $r < 1$ each hour. Suppose that a new dose is administered every $N$ hours. Find an expression that gives the amount $A(n)$ in the patient's system after $n$ hours for each $n$ in terms of the dosage $d$ and the ratio $r$. (*Hint:* Write $n = mN + k$, where $0 \le k < N$, and sum over values from the different doses administered.)

128. **[T]** A certain drug is effective for an average patient only if there is at least 1 mg per kg in the patient's system, while it is safe only if there is at most 2 mg per kg in an average patient's system. Suppose that the amount in a patient's system diminishes by a multiplicative factor of 0.9 each hour after a dose is administered. Find the maximum interval $N$ of hours between doses, and corresponding dose range $d$ (in mg/kg) for this $N$ that will enable use of the drug to be both safe and effective in the long term.

129. Suppose that $a_n \ge 0$ is a sequence of numbers. Explain why the sequence of partial sums of $a_n$ is increasing.

130. **[T]** Suppose that $a_n$ is a sequence of positive numbers and the sequence $S_n$ of partial sums of $a_n$ is bounded above. Explain why $\sum_{n=1}^{\infty} a_n$ converges. Does the conclusion remain true if we remove the hypothesis $a_n \geq 0$?

131. **[T]** Suppose that $a_1 = S_1 = 1$ and that, for given numbers $S > 1$ and $0 < k < 1$, one defines $a_{n+1} = k(S - S_n)$ and $S_{n+1} = a_{n+1} + S_n$. Does $S_n$ converge? If so, to what? (*Hint:* First argue that $S_n < S$ for all $n$ and $S_n$ is increasing.)

132. **[T]** A version of von Bertalanffy growth can be used to estimate the age of an individual in a homogeneous species from its length if the annual increase in year $n+1$ satisfies $a_{n+1} = k(S - S_n)$, with $S_n$ as the length at year $n$, $S$ as a limiting length, and $k$ as a relative growth constant. If $S_1 = 3$, $S = 9$, and $k = 1/2$, numerically estimate the smallest value of $n$ such that $S_n \geq 8$. Note that $S_{n+1} = S_n + a_{n+1}$. Find the corresponding $n$ when $k = 1/4$.

133. **[T]** Suppose that $\sum_{n=1}^{\infty} a_n$ is a convergent series of positive terms. Explain why $\lim_{N \to \infty} \sum_{n=N+1}^{\infty} a_n = 0$.

134. **[T]** Find the length of the dashed zig-zag path in the following figure.

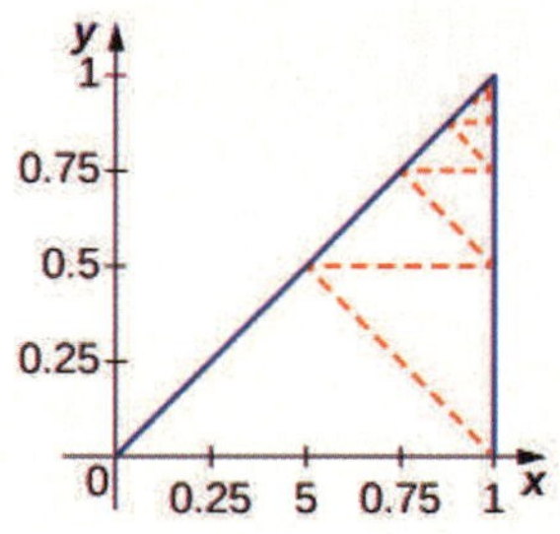


135. **[T]** Find the total length of the dashed path in the following figure.

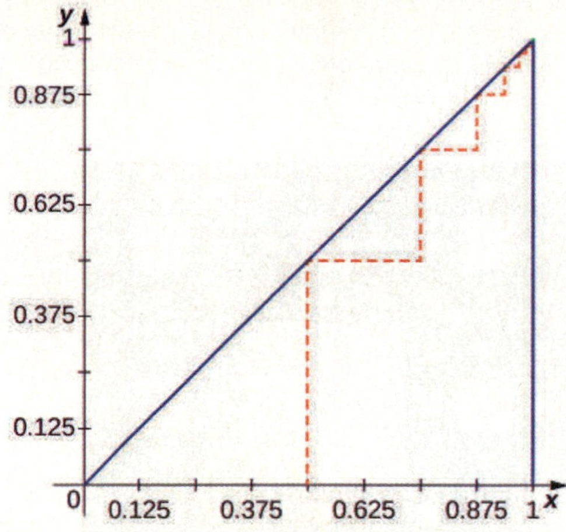


136. **[T]** The Sierpinski triangle is obtained from a triangle by deleting the middle fourth as indicated in the first step, by deleting the middle fourths of the remaining three congruent triangles in the second step, and in general deleting the middle fourths of the remaining triangles in each successive step. Assuming that the original triangle is shown in the figure, find the areas of the remaining parts of the original triangle after $N$ steps and find the total length of all of the boundary triangles after $N$ steps.

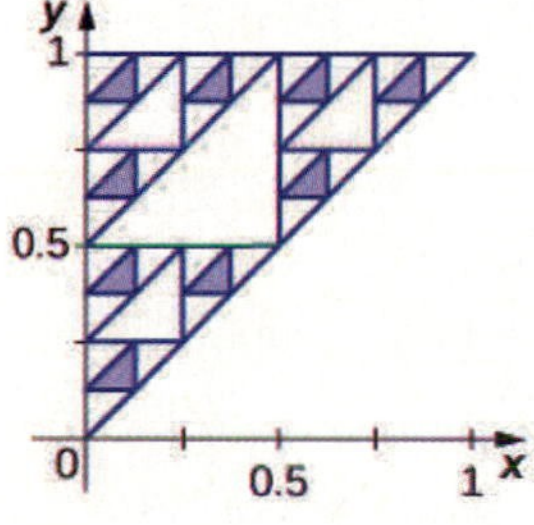

137. **[T]** The Sierpinski gasket is obtained by dividing the unit square into nine equal sub-squares, removing the middle square, then doing the same at each stage to the remaining sub-squares. The figure shows the remaining set after four iterations. Compute the total area removed after $N$ stages, and compute the length the total perimeter of the remaining set after $N$ stages.

# 5.3 | The Divergence and Integral Tests

## Learning Objectives

**5.3.1** Use the divergence test to determine whether a series converges or diverges.
**5.3.2** Use the integral test to determine the convergence of a series.
**5.3.3** Estimate the value of a series by finding bounds on its remainder term.

In the previous section, we determined the convergence or divergence of several series by explicitly calculating the limit of the sequence of partial sums $\{S_k\}$. In practice, explicitly calculating this limit can be difficult or impossible. Luckily, several tests exist that allow us to determine convergence or divergence for many types of series. In this section, we discuss two of these tests: the divergence test and the integral test. We will examine several other tests in the rest of this chapter and then summarize how and when to use them.

## Divergence Test

For a series $\sum_{n=1}^{\infty} a_n$ to converge, the $n$th term $a_n$ must satisfy $a_n \to 0$ as $n \to \infty$.

Therefore, from the algebraic limit properties of sequences,

$$\lim_{k \to \infty} a_k = \lim_{k \to \infty} (S_k - S_{k-1}) = \lim_{k \to \infty} S_k - \lim_{k \to \infty} S_{k-1} = S - S = 0.$$

Therefore, if $\sum_{n=1}^{\infty} a_n$ converges, the $n$th term $a_n \to 0$ as $n \to \infty$. An important consequence of this fact is the following statement:

$$\text{If } a_n \nrightarrow 0 \text{ as } n \to \infty, \sum_{n=1}^{\infty} a_n \text{ diverges.} \tag{5.8}$$

This test is known as the **divergence test** because it provides a way of proving that a series diverges.

### Theorem 5.8: Divergence Test

If $\lim_{n \to \infty} a_n = c \neq 0$ or $\lim_{n \to \infty} a_n$ does not exist, then the series $\sum_{n=1}^{\infty} a_n$ diverges.

It is important to note that the converse of this theorem is not true. That is, if $\lim_{n \to \infty} a_n = 0,$ we cannot make any conclusion about the convergence of $\sum_{n=1}^{\infty} a_n$. For example, $\lim_{n \to 0} (1/n) = 0,$ but the harmonic series $\sum_{n=1}^{\infty} 1/n$ diverges. In this section and the remaining sections of this chapter, we show many more examples of such series. Consequently, although we can use the divergence test to show that a series diverges, we cannot use it to prove that a series converges. Specifically, if $a_n \to 0,$ the divergence test is inconclusive.

### Example 5.13

#### Using the divergence test

For each of the following series, apply the divergence test. If the divergence test proves that the series diverges, state so. Otherwise, indicate that the divergence test is inconclusive.

a. $\sum_{n=1}^{\infty} \frac{n}{3n-1}$

b. $\sum_{n=1}^{\infty} \frac{1}{n^3}$

c. $\sum_{n=1}^{\infty} e^{1/n^2}$

### Solution

a. Since $n/(3n-1) \to 1/3 \neq 0,$ by the divergence test, we can conclude that

$$\sum_{n=1}^{\infty} \frac{n}{3n-1}$$

diverges.

b. Since $1/n^3 \to 0,$ the divergence test is inconclusive.

c. Since $e^{1/n^2} \to 1 \neq 0,$ by the divergence test, the series

$$\sum_{n=1}^{\infty} e^{1/n^2}$$

diverges.

**5.12** What does the divergence test tell us about the series $\sum_{n=1}^{\infty} \cos(1/n^2)$?

## Integral Test

In the previous section, we proved that the harmonic series diverges by looking at the sequence of partial sums $\{S_k\}$ and showing that $S_{2^k} > 1 + k/2$ for all positive integers $k.$ In this section we use a different technique to prove the divergence of the harmonic series. This technique is important because it is used to prove the divergence or convergence of many other series. This test, called the **integral test**, compares an infinite sum to an improper integral. It is important to note that this test can only be applied when we are considering a series whose terms are all positive.

To illustrate how the integral test works, use the harmonic series as an example. In **Figure 5.12**, we depict the harmonic series by sketching a sequence of rectangles with areas $1, 1/2, 1/3, 1/4, \ldots$ along with the function $f(x) = 1/x.$ From the graph, we see that

$$\sum_{n=1}^{k} \frac{1}{n} = 1 + \frac{1}{2} + \frac{1}{3} + \cdots + \frac{1}{k} > \int_{1}^{k+1} \frac{1}{x} dx.$$

Therefore, for each $k,$ the $k$th partial sum $S_k$ satisfies

$$S_k = \sum_{n=1}^{k} \frac{1}{n} > \int_{1}^{k+1} \frac{1}{x} dx = \ln x \Big|_{1}^{k+1} = \ln(k+1) - \ln(1) = \ln(k+1).$$

Since $\lim_{k \to \infty} \ln(k+1) = \infty,$ we see that the sequence of partial sums $\{S_k\}$ is unbounded. Therefore, $\{S_k\}$ diverges, and, consequently, the series $\sum_{n=1}^{\infty} \frac{1}{n}$ also diverges.

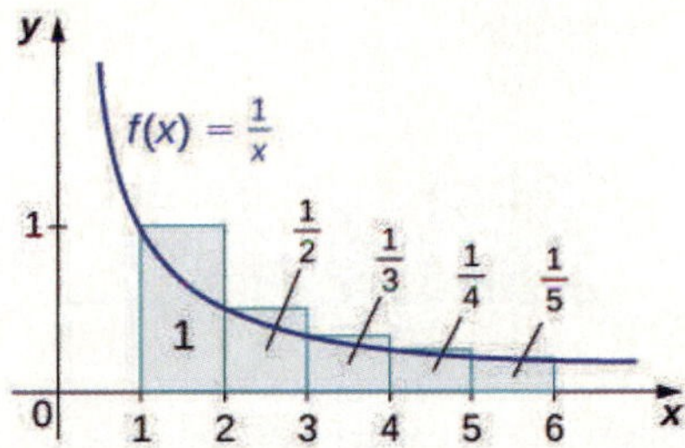


**Figure 5.12** The sum of the areas of the rectangles is greater than the area between the curve $f(x) = 1/x$ and the $x$-axis for $x \geq 1.$ Since the area bounded by the curve is infinite (as calculated by an improper integral), the sum of the areas of the rectangles is also infinite.

Now consider the series $\sum_{n=1}^{\infty} 1/n^2.$ We show how an integral can be used to prove that this series converges. In **Figure 5.13**, we sketch a sequence of rectangles with areas $1,\ 1/2^2,\ 1/3^2, \ldots$ along with the function $f(x) = 1/x^2.$ From the graph we see that

$$\sum_{n=1}^{k} \frac{1}{n^2} = 1 + \frac{1}{2^2} + \frac{1}{3^2} + \cdots + \frac{1}{k^2} < 1 + \int_1^k \frac{1}{x^2} dx.$$

Therefore, for each $k,$ the $k$th partial sum $S_k$ satisfies

$$S_k = \sum_{n=1}^{k} \frac{1}{n^2} < 1 + \int_1^k \frac{1}{x^2} dx = 1 - \frac{1}{x}\Big|_1^k = 1 - \frac{1}{k} + 1 = 2 - \frac{1}{k} < 2.$$

We conclude that the sequence of partial sums $\{S_k\}$ is bounded. We also see that $\{S_k\}$ is an increasing sequence:

$$S_k = S_{k-1} + \frac{1}{k^2} \text{ for } k \geq 2.$$

Since $\{S_k\}$ is increasing and bounded, by the Monotone Convergence Theorem, it converges. Therefore, the series $\sum_{n=1}^{\infty} 1/n^2$ converges.

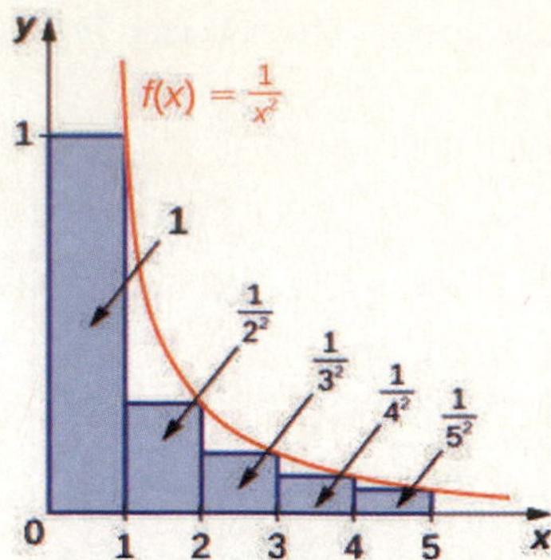


**Figure 5.13** The sum of the areas of the rectangles is less than the sum of the area of the first rectangle and the area between the curve $f(x) = 1/x^2$ and the $x$-axis for $x \geq 1$. Since the area bounded by the curve is finite, the sum of the areas of the rectangles is also finite.

We can extend this idea to prove convergence or divergence for many different series. Suppose $\sum_{n=1}^{\infty} a_n$ is a series with positive terms $a_n$ such that there exists a continuous, positive, decreasing function $f$ where $f(n) = a_n$ for all positive integers. Then, as in **Figure 5.14**(a), for any integer $k$, the $k$th partial sum $S_k$ satisfies

$$S_k = a_1 + a_2 + a_3 + \cdots + a_k < a_1 + \int_1^k f(x)dx < 1 + \int_1^{\infty} f(x)dx.$$

Therefore, if $\int_1^{\infty} f(x)dx$ converges, then the sequence of partial sums $\{S_k\}$ is bounded. Since $\{S_k\}$ is an increasing sequence, if it is also a bounded sequence, then by the Monotone Convergence Theorem, it converges. We conclude that if $\int_1^{\infty} f(x)dx$ converges, then the series $\sum_{n=1}^{\infty} a_n$ also converges. On the other hand, from **Figure 5.14**(b), for any integer $k$, the $k$th partial sum $S_k$ satisfies

$$S_k = a_1 + a_2 + a_3 + \cdots + a_k > \int_1^{k+1} f(x)dx.$$

If $\lim_{k \to \infty} \int_1^{k+1} f(x)dx = \infty$, then $\{S_k\}$ is an unbounded sequence and therefore diverges. As a result, the series $\sum_{n=1}^{\infty} a_n$ also diverges. Since $f$ is a positive function, if $\int_1^{\infty} f(x)dx$ diverges, then $\lim_{k \to \infty} \int_1^{k+1} f(x)dx = \infty$. We conclude that if $\int_1^{\infty} f(x)dx$ diverges, then $\sum_{n=1}^{\infty} a_n$ diverges.

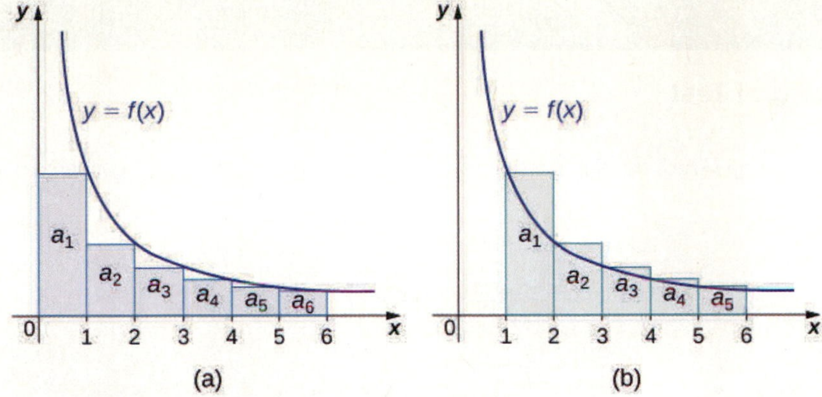


**Figure 5.14** (a) If we can inscribe rectangles inside a region bounded by a curve $y = f(x)$ and the $x$-axis, and the area bounded by those curves for $x \geq 1$ is finite, then the sum of the areas of the rectangles is also finite. (b) If a set of rectangles circumscribes the region bounded by $y = f(x)$ and the $x$ axis for $x \geq 1$ and the region has infinite area, then the sum of the areas of the rectangles is also infinite.

### Theorem 5.9: Integral Test

Suppose $\sum_{n=1}^{\infty} a_n$ is a series with positive terms $a_n$. Suppose there exists a function $f$ and a positive integer $N$ such that the following three conditions are satisfied:

i. $f$ is continuous,

ii. $f$ is decreasing, and

iii. $f(n) = a_n$ for all integers $n \geq N$.

Then

$$\sum_{n=1}^{\infty} a_n \text{ and} \int_N^{\infty} f(x)dx$$

both converge or both diverge (see **Figure 5.14**).

Although convergence of $\int_N^{\infty} f(x)dx$ implies convergence of the related series $\sum_{n=1}^{\infty} a_n,$ it does not imply that the value of the integral and the series are the same. They may be different, and often are. For example,

$$\sum_{n=1}^{\infty} \left(\frac{1}{e}\right)^n = \frac{1}{e} + \left(\frac{1}{e}\right)^2 + \left(\frac{1}{e}\right)^3 + \cdots$$

is a geometric series with initial term $a = 1/e$ and ratio $r = 1/e,$ which converges to

$$\frac{1/e}{1 - (1/e)} = \frac{1/e}{(e-1)/e} = \frac{1}{e-1}.$$

However, the related integral $\int_1^{\infty} (1/e)^x dx$ satisfies

$$\int_1^{\infty} \left(\frac{1}{e}\right)^x dx = \int_1^{\infty} e^{-x} dx = \lim_{b \to \infty} \int_1^b e^{-x} dx = \lim_{b \to \infty} -e^{-x} \Big|_1^b = \lim_{b \to \infty} \left[-e^{-b} + e^{-1}\right] = \frac{1}{e}.$$

## Example 5.14

### Using the Integral Test

For each of the following series, use the integral test to determine whether the series converges or diverges.

a. $\sum_{n=1}^{\infty} 1/n^3$

b. $\sum_{n=1}^{\infty} 1/\sqrt{2n-1}$

### Solution

a. Compare

$$\sum_{n=1}^{\infty} \frac{1}{n^3} \text{ and } \int_1^{\infty} \frac{1}{x^3} dx.$$

We have

$$\int_1^{\infty} \frac{1}{x^3} dx = \lim_{b \to \infty} \int_1^b \frac{1}{x^3} dx = \lim_{b \to \infty} \left[ -\frac{1}{2x^2} \Big|_1^b \right] = \lim_{b \to \infty} \left[ -\frac{1}{2b^2} + \frac{1}{2} \right] = \frac{1}{2}.$$

Thus the integral $\int_1^{\infty} 1/x^3\, dx$ converges, and therefore so does the series

$$\sum_{n=1}^{\infty} \frac{1}{n^3}.$$

b. Compare

$$\sum_{n=1}^{\infty} \frac{1}{\sqrt{2n-1}} \text{ and } \int_1^{\infty} \frac{1}{\sqrt{2x-1}} dx.$$

Since

$$\begin{aligned} \int_1^{\infty} \frac{1}{\sqrt{2x-1}} dx &= \lim_{b \to \infty} \int_1^b \frac{1}{\sqrt{2x-1}} dx = \lim_{b \to \infty} \sqrt{2x-1} \Big|_1^b \\ &= \lim_{b \to \infty} \left[ \sqrt{2b-1} - 1 \right] = \infty, \end{aligned}$$

the integral $\int_1^{\infty} 1/\sqrt{2x-1}\, dx$ diverges, and therefore

$$\sum_{n=1}^{\infty} \frac{1}{\sqrt{2n-1}}$$

diverges.

**5.13** Use the integral test to determine whether the series $\sum_{n=1}^{\infty} \frac{n}{3n^2+1}$ converges or diverges.

## The *p*-Series

The harmonic series $\sum_{n=1}^{\infty} 1/n$ and the series $\sum_{n=1}^{\infty} 1/n^2$ are both examples of a type of series called a *p*-series.

### Definition

For any real number $p,$ the series

$$\sum_{n=1}^{\infty} \frac{1}{n^p}$$

is called a ***p*-series**.

We know the *p*-series converges if $p = 2$ and diverges if $p = 1.$ What about other values of $p$? In general, it is difficult, if not impossible, to compute the exact value of most $p$-series. However, we can use the tests presented thus far to prove whether a $p$-series converges or diverges.

If $p < 0,$ then $1/n^p \to \infty,$ and if $p = 0,$ then $1/n^p \to 1.$ Therefore, by the divergence test,

$$\sum_{n=1}^{\infty} 1/n^p \text{ diverges if } p \le 0.$$

If $p > 0,$ then $f(x) = 1/x^p$ is a positive, continuous, decreasing function. Therefore, for $p > 0,$ we use the integral test, comparing

$$\sum_{n=1}^{\infty} \frac{1}{n^p} \text{ and } \int_1^{\infty} \frac{1}{x^p} dx.$$

We have already considered the case when $p = 1.$ Here we consider the case when $p > 0, p \ne 1.$ For this case,

$$\int_1^{\infty} \frac{1}{x^p} dx = \lim_{b \to \infty} \int_1^b \frac{1}{x^p} dx = \lim_{b \to \infty} \frac{1}{1-p} x^{1-p} \Big|_1^b = \lim_{b \to \infty} \frac{1}{1-p} \left[ b^{1-p} - 1 \right].$$

Because

$$b^{1-p} \to 0 \text{ if } p > 1 \text{ and } b^{1-p} \to \infty \text{ if } p < 1,$$

we conclude that

$$\int_1^{\infty} \frac{1}{x^p} dx = \begin{cases} \frac{1}{p-1} \text{ if } p > 1 \\ \infty \text{ if } p < 1 \end{cases}.$$

Therefore, $\sum_{n=1}^{\infty} 1/n^p$ converges if $p > 1$ and diverges if $0 < p < 1.$

In summary,

$$\sum_{n=1}^{\infty} \frac{1}{n^p} \begin{cases} \text{converges if } p > 1 \\ \text{diverges if } p \le 1 \end{cases}. \tag{5.9}$$

### Example 5.15

### Testing for Convergence of *p*-series

For each of the following series, determine whether it converges or diverges.

a. $\sum_{n=1}^{\infty} \frac{1}{n^4}$

b. $\sum_{n=1}^{\infty} \frac{1}{n^{2/3}}$

#### Solution

a. This is a $p$-series with $p = 4 > 1,$ so the series converges.

b. Since $p = 2/3 < 1,$ the series diverges.

 **5.14** Does the series $\sum_{n=1}^{\infty} \frac{1}{n^{5/4}}$ converge or diverge?

## Estimating the Value of a Series

Suppose we know that a series $\sum_{n=1}^{\infty} a_n$ converges and we want to estimate the sum of that series. Certainly we can approximate that sum using any finite sum $\sum_{n=1}^{N} a_n$ where $N$ is any positive integer. The question we address here is, for a convergent series $\sum_{n=1}^{\infty} a_n,$ how good is the approximation $\sum_{n=1}^{N} a_n$? More specifically, if we let

$$R_N = \sum_{n=1}^{\infty} a_n - \sum_{n=1}^{N} a_n$$

be the remainder when the sum of an infinite series is approximated by the $N$th partial sum, how large is $R_N$? For some types of series, we are able to use the ideas from the integral test to estimate $R_N$.

### Theorem 5.10: Remainder Estimate from the Integral Test

Suppose $\sum_{n=1}^{\infty} a_n$ is a convergent series with positive terms. Suppose there exists a function $f$ satisfying the following three conditions:

i. $f$ is continuous,

ii. $f$ is decreasing, and

iii. $f(n) = a_n$ for all integers $n \geq 1.$

Let $S_N$ be the $N$th partial sum of $\sum_{n=1}^{\infty} a_n.$ For all positive integers $N,$

$$S_N + \int_{N+1}^{\infty} f(x)dx < \sum_{n=1}^{\infty} a_n < S_N + \int_N^{\infty} f(x)dx.$$

In other words, the remainder $R_N = \sum_{n=1}^{\infty} a_n - S_N = \sum_{n=N+1}^{\infty} a_n$ satisfies the following estimate:

$$\int_{N+1}^{\infty} f(x)dx < R_N < \int_N^{\infty} f(x)dx. \quad (5.10)$$

This is known as the **remainder estimate**.

We illustrate **Remainder Estimate from the Integral Test** in **Figure 5.15**. In particular, by representing the remainder $R_N = a_{N+1} + a_{N+2} + a_{N+3} + \cdots$ as the sum of areas of rectangles, we see that the area of those rectangles is bounded above by $\int_N^{\infty} f(x)dx$ and bounded below by $\int_{N+1}^{\infty} f(x)dx.$ In other words,

$$R_N = a_{N+1} + a_{N+2} + a_{N+3} + \cdots > \int_{N+1}^{\infty} f(x)dx$$

and

$$R_N = a_{N+1} + a_{N+2} + a_{N+3} + \cdots < \int_N^{\infty} f(x)dx.$$

We conclude that

$$\int_{N+1}^{\infty} f(x)dx < R_N < \int_N^{\infty} f(x)dx.$$

Since

$$\sum_{n=1}^{\infty} a_n = S_N + R_N,$$

where $S_N$ is the $N$th partial sum, we conclude that

$$S_N + \int_{N+1}^{\infty} f(x)dx < \sum_{n=1}^{\infty} a_n < S_N + \int_N^{\infty} f(x)dx.$$

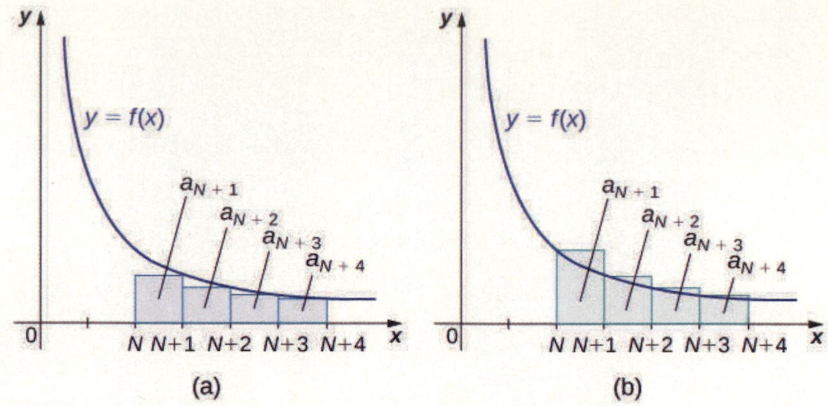


**Figure 5.15** Given a continuous, positive, decreasing function $f$ and a sequence of positive terms $a_n$ such that $a_n = f(n)$ for all positive integers $n$, (a) the areas $a_{N+1} + a_{N+2} + a_{N+3} + \cdots < \int_N^{\infty} f(x)dx$, or (b) the areas $a_{N+1} + a_{N+2} + a_{N+3} + \cdots > \int_{N+1}^{\infty} f(x)dx$. Therefore, the integral is either an overestimate or an underestimate of the error.

## Example 5.16

### Estimating the Value of a Series

Consider the series $\sum_{n=1}^{\infty} 1/n^3$.

a. Calculate $S_{10} = \sum_{n=1}^{10} 1/n^3$ and estimate the error.

b. Determine the least value of $N$ necessary such that $S_N$ will estimate $\sum_{n=1}^{\infty} 1/n^3$ to within $0.001$.

### Solution

a. Using a calculating utility, we have

$$S_{10} = 1 + \frac{1}{2^3} + \frac{1}{3^3} + \frac{1}{4^3} + \cdots + \frac{1}{10^3} \approx 1.19753.$$

By the remainder estimate, we know

$$R_N < \int_N^{\infty} \frac{1}{x^3} dx.$$

We have

$$\int_{10}^{\infty} \frac{1}{x^3} dx = \lim_{b \to \infty} \int_{10}^{b} \frac{1}{x^3} dx = \lim_{b \to \infty} \left[ -\frac{1}{2x^2} \right]_N^b = \lim_{b \to \infty} \left[ -\frac{1}{2b^2} + \frac{1}{2N^2} \right] = \frac{1}{2N^2}.$$

Therefore, the error is $R_{10} < 1/2(10)^2 = 0.005$.

b. Find $N$ such that $R_N < 0.001$. In part a. we showed that $R_N < 1/2N^2$. Therefore, the remainder $R_N < 0.001$ as long as $1/2N^2 < 0.001$. That is, we need $2N^2 > 1000$. Solving this inequality for $N$, we see that we need $N > 22.36$. To ensure that the remainder is within the desired amount, we need to round up to the nearest integer. Therefore, the minimum necessary value is $N = 23$.

**5.15** For $\sum_{n=1}^{\infty} \frac{1}{n^4}$, calculate $S_5$ and estimate the error $R_5$.

# 5.3 EXERCISES

For each of the following sequences, if the divergence test applies, either state that $\lim_{n \to \infty} a_n$ does not exist or find $\lim_{n \to \infty} a_n$. If the divergence test does not apply, state why.

138. $a_n = \frac{n}{n+2}$

139. $a_n = \frac{n}{5n^2 - 3}$

140. $a_n = \frac{n}{\sqrt{3n^2 + 2n + 1}}$

141. $a_n = \frac{(2n+1)(n-1)}{(n+1)^2}$

142. $a_n = \frac{(2n+1)^{2n}}{\left(3n^2 + 1\right)^n}$

143. $a_n = \frac{2^n}{3^{n/2}}$

144. $a_n = \frac{2^n + 3^n}{10^{n/2}}$

145. $a_n = e^{-2/n}$

146. $a_n = \cos n$

147. $a_n = \tan n$

148. $a_n = \frac{1 - \cos^2(1/n)}{\sin^2(2/n)}$

149. $a_n = \left(1 - \frac{1}{n}\right)^{2n}$

150. $a_n = \frac{\ln n}{n}$

151. $a_n = \frac{(\ln n)^2}{\sqrt{n}}$

State whether the given $p$-series converges.

152. $\sum_{n=1}^{\infty} \frac{1}{\sqrt{n}}$

153. $\sum_{n=1}^{\infty} \frac{1}{n\sqrt{n}}$

154. $\sum_{n=1}^{\infty} \frac{1}{\sqrt[3]{n^2}}$

155. $\sum_{n=1}^{\infty} \frac{1}{\sqrt[3]{n^4}}$

156. $\sum_{n=1}^{\infty} \frac{n^e}{n^{\pi}}$

157. $\sum_{n=1}^{\infty} \frac{n^{\pi}}{n^{2e}}$

Use the integral test to determine whether the following sums converge.

158. $\sum_{n=1}^{\infty} \frac{1}{\sqrt{n+5}}$

159. $\sum_{n=1}^{\infty} \frac{1}{\sqrt[3]{n+5}}$

160. $\sum_{n=2}^{\infty} \frac{1}{n \ln n}$

161. $\sum_{n=1}^{\infty} \frac{n}{1+n^2}$

162. $\sum_{n=1}^{\infty} \frac{e^n}{1+e^{2n}}$

163. $\sum_{n=1}^{\infty} \frac{2n}{1+n^4}$

164. $\sum_{n=2}^{\infty} \frac{1}{n \ln^2 n}$

Express the following sums as $p$-series and determine whether each converges.

165. $\sum_{n=1}^{\infty} 2^{-\ln n}$ (*Hint:* $2^{-\ln n} = 1/n^{\ln 2}$.)

166. $\sum_{n=1}^{\infty} 3^{-\ln n}$ (*Hint:* $3^{-\ln n} = 1/n^{\ln 3}$.)

167. $\sum_{n=1}^{\infty} n 2^{-2\ln n}$

168. $\sum_{n=1}^{\infty} n3^{-2\ln n}$

Use the estimate $R_N \le \int_N^{\infty} f(t)dt$ to find a bound for the remainder $R_N = \sum_{n=1}^{\infty} a_n - \sum_{n=1}^{N} a_n$ where $a_n = f(n)$.

169. $\sum_{n=1}^{1000} \frac{1}{n^2}$

170. $\sum_{n=1}^{1000} \frac{1}{n^3}$

171. $\sum_{n=1}^{1000} \frac{1}{1+n^2}$

172. $\sum_{n=1}^{100} n/2^n$

**[T]** Find the minimum value of $N$ such that the remainder estimate $\int_{N+1}^{\infty} f < R_N < \int_N^{\infty} f$ guarantees that $\sum_{n=1}^{N} a_n$ estimates $\sum_{n=1}^{\infty} a_n$, accurate to within the given error.

173. $a_n = \frac{1}{n^2}$, error $< 10^{-4}$

174. $a_n = \frac{1}{n^{1.1}}$, error $< 10^{-4}$

175. $a_n = \frac{1}{n^{1.01}}$, error $< 10^{-4}$

176. $a_n = \frac{1}{n\ln^2 n}$, error $< 10^{-3}$

177. $a_n = \frac{1}{1+n^2}$, error $< 10^{-3}$

In the following exercises, find a value of $N$ such that $R_N$ is smaller than the desired error. Compute the corresponding sum $\sum_{n=1}^{N} a_n$ and compare it to the given estimate of the infinite series.

178. $a_n = \frac{1}{n^{11}}$, error $< 10^{-4}$, $\sum_{n=1}^{\infty} \frac{1}{n^{11}} = 1.000494\ldots$

179. $a_n = \frac{1}{e^n}$, error $< 10^{-5}$, $\sum_{n=1}^{\infty} \frac{1}{e^n} = \frac{1}{e-1} = 0.581976\ldots$

180. $a_n = \frac{1}{e^{n^2}}$, error $< 10^{-5}$, $\sum_{n=1}^{\infty} n/e^{n^2} = 0.40488139857\ldots$

181. $a_n = 1/n^4$, error $< 10^{-4}$, $\sum_{n=1}^{\infty} 1/n^4 = \pi^4/90 = 1.08232...$

182. $a_n = 1/n^6$, error $< 10^{-6}$, $\sum_{n=1}^{\infty} 1/n^4 = \pi^6/945 = 1.01734306...$,

183. Find the limit as $n \to \infty$ of $\frac{1}{n} + \frac{1}{n+1} + \cdots + \frac{1}{2n}$. (*Hint:* Compare to $\int_n^{2n} \frac{1}{t}dt$.)

184. Find the limit as $n \to \infty$ of $\frac{1}{n} + \frac{1}{n+1} + \cdots + \frac{1}{3n}$

The next few exercises are intended to give a sense of applications in which partial sums of the harmonic series arise.

185. In certain applications of probability, such as the so-called Watterson estimator for predicting mutation rates in population genetics, it is important to have an accurate estimate of the number $H_k = \left(1 + \frac{1}{2} + \frac{1}{3} + \cdots + \frac{1}{k}\right)$. Recall that $T_k = H_k - \ln k$ is decreasing. Compute $T = \lim_{k\to\infty} T_k$ to four decimal places. (*Hint:* $\frac{1}{k+1} < \int_k^{k+1} \frac{1}{x}dx$.)

186. **[T]** Complete sampling with replacement, sometimes called the *coupon collector's problem,* is phrased as follows: Suppose you have $N$ unique items in a bin. At each step, an item is chosen at random, identified, and put back in the bin. The problem asks what is the expected number of steps $E(N)$ that it takes to draw each unique item at least once. It turns out that $E(N) = N.H_N = N\left(1 + \frac{1}{2} + \frac{1}{3} + \cdots + \frac{1}{N}\right).$ Find $E(N)$ for $N = 10$, 20, and 50.

187. **[T]** The simplest way to shuffle cards is to take the top card and insert it at a random place in the deck, called top random insertion, and then repeat. We will consider a deck to be randomly shuffled once enough top random insertions have been made that the card originally at the bottom has reached the top and then been randomly inserted. If the deck has $n$ cards, then the probability that the insertion will be below the card initially at the bottom (call this card $B$) is $1/n.$ Thus the expected number of top random insertions before $B$ is no longer at the bottom is $n.$ Once one card is below $B,$ there are two places below $B$ and the probability that a randomly inserted card will fall below $B$ is $2/n.$ The expected number of top random insertions before this happens is $n/2.$ The two cards below $B$ are now in random order. Continuing this way, find a formula for the expected number of top random insertions needed to consider the deck to be randomly shuffled.

188. Suppose a scooter can travel 100 km on a full tank of fuel. Assuming that fuel can be transferred from one scooter to another but can only be carried in the tank, present a procedure that will enable one of the scooters to travel $100H_N$ km, where $H_N = 1 + 1/2 + \cdots + 1/N.$

189. Show that for the remainder estimate to apply on $[N, \infty)$ it is sufficient that $f(x)$ be decreasing on $[N, \infty),$ but $f$ need not be decreasing on $[1, \infty).$

190. **[T]** Use the remainder estimate and integration by parts to approximate $\sum_{n=1}^{\infty} n/e^n$ within an error smaller than 0.0001.

191. Does $\sum_{n=2}^{\infty} \frac{1}{n(\ln n)^p}$ converge if $p$ is large enough? If so, for which $p$?

192. **[T]** Suppose a computer can sum one million terms per second of the divergent series $\sum_{n=1}^{N} \frac{1}{n}.$ Use the integral test to approximate how many seconds it will take to add up enough terms for the partial sum to exceed 100.

193. **[T]** A fast computer can sum one million terms per second of the divergent series $\sum_{n=2}^{N} \frac{1}{n \ln n}.$ Use the integral test to approximate how many seconds it will take to add up enough terms for the partial sum to exceed 100.

# 5.4 | Comparison Tests

## Learning Objectives

**5.4.1** Use the comparison test to test a series for convergence.

**5.4.2** Use the limit comparison test to determine convergence of a series.

We have seen that the integral test allows us to determine the convergence or divergence of a series by comparing it to a related improper integral. In this section, we show how to use comparison tests to determine the convergence or divergence of a series by comparing it to a series whose convergence or divergence is known. Typically these tests are used to determine convergence of series that are similar to geometric series or *p*-series.

## Comparison Test

In the preceding two sections, we discussed two large classes of series: geometric series and *p*-series. We know exactly when these series converge and when they diverge. Here we show how to use the convergence or divergence of these series to prove convergence or divergence for other series, using a method called the **comparison test**.

For example, consider the series

$$\sum_{n=1}^{\infty} \frac{1}{n^2+1}.$$

This series looks similar to the convergent series

$$\sum_{n=1}^{\infty} \frac{1}{n^2}.$$

Since the terms in each of the series are positive, the sequence of partial sums for each series is monotone increasing. Furthermore, since

$$0 < \frac{1}{n^2+1} < \frac{1}{n^2}$$

for all positive integers $n$, the $k$th partial sum $S_k$ of $\sum_{n=1}^{\infty} \frac{1}{n^2+1}$ satisfies

$$S_k = \sum_{n=1}^{k} \frac{1}{n^2+1} < \sum_{n=1}^{k} \frac{1}{n^2} < \sum_{n=1}^{\infty} \frac{1}{n^2}.$$

(See **Figure 5.16**(a) and **Table 5.1**.) Since the series on the right converges, the sequence $\{S_k\}$ is bounded above. We conclude that $\{S_k\}$ is a monotone increasing sequence that is bounded above. Therefore, by the Monotone Convergence Theorem, $\{S_k\}$ converges, and thus

$$\sum_{n=1}^{\infty} \frac{1}{n^2+1}$$

converges.

Similarly, consider the series

$$\sum_{n=1}^{\infty} \frac{1}{n-1/2}.$$

This series looks similar to the divergent series

$$\sum_{n=1}^{\infty} \frac{1}{n}.$$

The sequence of partial sums for each series is monotone increasing and

$$\frac{1}{n - 1/2} > \frac{1}{n} > 0$$

for every positive integer $n$. Therefore, the $k$th partial sum $S_k$ of $\sum_{n=1}^{\infty} \frac{1}{n - 1/2}$ satisfies

$$S_k = \sum_{n=1}^{k} \frac{1}{n - 1/2} > \sum_{n=1}^{k} \frac{1}{n}.$$

(See **Figure 5.16**(b) and **Table 5.2**.) Since the series $\sum_{n=1}^{\infty} 1/n$ diverges to infinity, the sequence of partial sums $\sum_{n=1}^{k} 1/n$ is unbounded. Consequently, $\{S_k\}$ is an unbounded sequence, and therefore diverges. We conclude that

$$\sum_{n=1}^{\infty} \frac{1}{n - 1/2}$$

diverges.

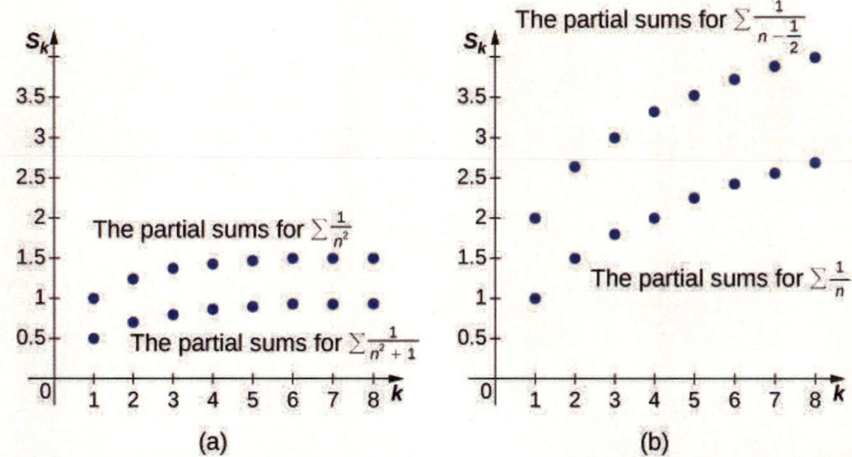


**Figure 5.16** (a) Each of the partial sums for the given series is less than the corresponding partial sum for the converging $p-$ series. (b) Each of the partial sums for the given series is greater than the corresponding partial sum for the diverging harmonic series.

| $k$ | 1 | 2 | 3 | 4 | 5 | 6 | 7 | 8 |
|---|---|---|---|---|---|---|---|---|
| $\sum_{n=1}^{k} \frac{1}{n^2+1}$ | 0.5 | 0.7 | 0.8 | 0.8588 | 0.8973 | 0.9243 | 0.9443 | 0.9597 |
| $\sum_{n=1}^{k} \frac{1}{n^2}$ | 1 | 1.25 | 1.3611 | 1.4236 | 1.4636 | 1.4914 | 1.5118 | 1.5274 |

**Table 5.1** Comparing a series with a $p$-series ($p = 2$)

| $k$ | 1 | 2 | 3 | 4 | 5 | 6 | 7 | 8 |
|---|---|---|---|---|---|---|---|---|
| $\sum_{n=1}^{k} \frac{1}{n-1/2}$ | 2 | 2.6667 | 3.0667 | 3.3524 | 3.5746 | 3.7564 | 3.9103 | 4.0436 |
| $\sum_{n=1}^{k} \frac{1}{n}$ | 1 | 1.5 | 1.8333 | 2.0933 | 2.2833 | 2.45 | 2.5929 | 2.7179 |

**Table 5.2** Comparing a series with the harmonic series

### Theorem 5.11: Comparison Test

i. Suppose there exists an integer $N$ such that $0 \leq a_n \leq b_n$ for all $n \geq N$. If $\sum_{n=1}^{\infty} b_n$ converges, then $\sum_{n=1}^{\infty} a_n$ converges.

ii. Suppose there exists an integer $N$ such that $a_n \geq b_n \geq 0$ for all $n \geq N$. If $\sum_{n=1}^{\infty} b_n$ diverges, then $\sum_{n=1}^{\infty} a_n$ diverges.

### Proof

We prove part i. The proof of part ii. is the contrapositive of part i. Let $\{S_k\}$ be the sequence of partial sums associated with $\sum_{n=1}^{\infty} a_n$, and let $L = \sum_{n=1}^{\infty} b_n$. Since the terms $a_n \geq 0$,

$$S_k = a_1 + a_2 + \cdots + a_k \leq a_1 + a_2 + \cdots + a_k + a_{k+1} = S_{k+1}.$$

Therefore, the sequence of partial sums is increasing. Further, since $a_n \leq b_n$ for all $n \geq N$, then

$$\sum_{n=N}^{k} a_n \leq \sum_{n=N}^{k} b_n \leq \sum_{n=1}^{\infty} b_n = L.$$

Therefore, for all $k \geq 1$,

$$S_k = (a_1 + a_2 + \cdots + a_{N-1}) + \sum_{n=N}^{k} a_n \leq (a_1 + a_2 + \cdots + a_{N-1}) + L.$$

Since $a_1 + a_2 + \cdots + a_{N-1}$ is a finite number, we conclude that the sequence $\{S_k\}$ is bounded above. Therefore, $\{S_k\}$ is an increasing sequence that is bounded above. By the Monotone Convergence Theorem, we conclude that $\{S_k\}$ converges, and therefore the series $\sum_{n=1}^{\infty} a_n$ converges.

□

To use the comparison test to determine the convergence or divergence of a series $\sum_{n=1}^{\infty} a_n$, it is necessary to find a suitable series with which to compare it. Since we know the convergence properties of geometric series and *p*-series, these series are often used. If there exists an integer $N$ such that for all $n \geq N,$ each term $a_n$ is less than each corresponding term of a known convergent series, then $\sum_{n=1}^{\infty} a_n$ converges. Similarly, if there exists an integer $N$ such that for all $n \geq N,$ each term $a_n$ is greater than each corresponding term of a known divergent series, then $\sum_{n=1}^{\infty} a_n$ diverges.

## Example 5.17

### Using the Comparison Test

For each of the following series, use the comparison test to determine whether the series converges or diverges.

a. $\sum_{n=1}^{\infty} \frac{1}{n^3 + 3n + 1}$

b. $\sum_{n=1}^{\infty} \frac{1}{2^n + 1}$

c. $\sum_{n=2}^{\infty} \frac{1}{\ln(n)}$

### Solution

a. Compare to $\sum_{n=1}^{\infty} \frac{1}{n^3}$ Since $\sum_{n=1}^{\infty} \frac{1}{n^3}$ is a $p$-series with $p = 3,$ it converges. Further,

$$\frac{1}{n^3 + 3n + 1} < \frac{1}{n^3}$$

for every positive integer $n$. Therefore, we can conclude that $\sum_{n=1}^{\infty} \frac{1}{n^3 + 3n + 1}$ converges.

b. Compare to $\sum_{n=1}^{\infty} \left(\frac{1}{2}\right)^n.$ Since $\sum_{n=1}^{\infty} \left(\frac{1}{2}\right)^n$ is a geometric series with $r = 1/2$ and $|1/2| < 1,$ it converges. Also,

$$\frac{1}{2^n + 1} < \frac{1}{2^n}$$

for every positive integer $n$. Therefore, we see that $\sum_{n=1}^{\infty} \frac{1}{2^n + 1}$ converges.

c. Compare to $\sum_{n=2}^{\infty} \frac{1}{n}.$ Since

$$\frac{1}{\ln(n)} > \frac{1}{n}$$

for every integer $n \geq 2$ and $\sum_{n=2}^{\infty} 1/n$ diverges, we have that $\sum_{n=2}^{\infty} \frac{1}{\ln(n)}$ diverges.

**5.16** Use the comparison test to determine if the series $\sum_{n=1}^{\infty} \frac{n}{n^3+n+1}$ converges or diverges.

## Limit Comparison Test

The comparison test works nicely if we can find a comparable series satisfying the hypothesis of the test. However, sometimes finding an appropriate series can be difficult. Consider the series

$$\sum_{n=2}^{\infty} \frac{1}{n^2-1}.$$

It is natural to compare this series with the convergent series

$$\sum_{n=2}^{\infty} \frac{1}{n^2}.$$

However, this series does not satisfy the hypothesis necessary to use the comparison test because

$$\frac{1}{n^2-1} > \frac{1}{n^2}$$

for all integers $n \geq 2$. Although we could look for a different series with which to compare $\sum_{n=2}^{\infty} 1/(n^2-1)$, instead we show how we can use the **limit comparison test** to compare

$$\sum_{n=2}^{\infty} \frac{1}{n^2-1} \text{ and } \sum_{n=2}^{\infty} \frac{1}{n^2}.$$

Let us examine the idea behind the limit comparison test. Consider two series $\sum_{n=1}^{\infty} a_n$ and $\sum_{n=1}^{\infty} b_n$. with positive terms $a_n$ and $b_n$ and evaluate

$$\lim_{n \to \infty} \frac{a_n}{b_n}.$$

If

$$\lim_{n \to \infty} \frac{a_n}{b_n} = L \neq 0,$$

then, for $n$ sufficiently large, $a_n \approx Lb_n$. Therefore, either both series converge or both series diverge. For the series $\sum_{n=2}^{\infty} 1/(n^2-1)$ and $\sum_{n=2}^{\infty} 1/n^2$, we see that

$$\lim_{n \to \infty} \frac{1/(n^2-1)}{1/n^2} = \lim_{n \to \infty} \frac{n^2}{n^2-1} = 1.$$

Since $\sum_{n=2}^{\infty} 1/n^2$ converges, we conclude that

$$\sum_{n=2}^{\infty} \frac{1}{n^2-1}$$

converges.

The limit comparison test can be used in two other cases. Suppose

$$\lim_{n \to \infty} \frac{a_n}{b_n} = 0.$$

In this case, $\{a_n/b_n\}$ is a bounded sequence. As a result, there exists a constant $M$ such that $a_n \le Mb_n$. Therefore, if $\sum_{n=1}^{\infty} b_n$ converges, then $\sum_{n=1}^{\infty} a_n$ converges. On the other hand, suppose

$$\lim_{n \to \infty} \frac{a_n}{b_n} = \infty.$$

In this case, $\{a_n/b_n\}$ is an unbounded sequence. Therefore, for every constant $M$ there exists an integer $N$ such that $a_n \ge Mb_n$ for all $n \ge N$. Therefore, if $\sum_{n=1}^{\infty} b_n$ diverges, then $\sum_{n=1}^{\infty} a_n$ diverges as well.

### Theorem 5.12: Limit Comparison Test

Let $a_n,\ b_n \ge 0$ for all $n \ge 1$.

i. If $\lim_{n \to \infty} a_n/b_n = L \ne 0,$ then $\sum_{n=1}^{\infty} a_n$ and $\sum_{n=1}^{\infty} b_n$ both converge or both diverge.

ii. If $\lim_{n \to \infty} a_n/b_n = 0$ and $\sum_{n=1}^{\infty} b_n$ converges, then $\sum_{n=1}^{\infty} a_n$ converges.

iii. If $\lim_{n \to \infty} a_n/b_n = \infty$ and $\sum_{n=1}^{\infty} b_n$ diverges, then $\sum_{n=1}^{\infty} a_n$ diverges.

Note that if $a_n/b_n \to 0$ and $\sum_{n=1}^{\infty} b_n$ diverges, the limit comparison test gives no information. Similarly, if $a_n/b_n \to \infty$ and $\sum_{n=1}^{\infty} b_n$ converges, the test also provides no information. For example, consider the two series $\sum_{n=1}^{\infty} 1/\sqrt{n}$ and $\sum_{n=1}^{\infty} 1/n^2$. These series are both *p*-series with $p = 1/2$ and $p = 2,$ respectively. Since $p = 1/2 > 1,$ the series $\sum_{n=1}^{\infty} 1/\sqrt{n}$ diverges. On the other hand, since $p = 2 < 1,$ the series $\sum_{n=1}^{\infty} 1/n^2$ converges. However, suppose we attempted to apply the limit comparison test, using the convergent $p-$ series $\sum_{n=1}^{\infty} 1/n^3$ as our comparison series. First, we see that

$$\frac{1/\sqrt{n}}{1/n^3} = \frac{n^3}{\sqrt{n}} = n^{5/2} \to \infty \text{ as } n \to \infty.$$

Similarly, we see that

$$\frac{1/n^2}{1/n^3} = n \to \infty \text{ as } n \to \infty.$$

Therefore, if $a_n/b_n \to \infty$ when $\sum_{n=1}^{\infty} b_n$ converges, we do not gain any information on the convergence or divergence of $\sum_{n=1}^{\infty} a_n.$

## Example 5.18

### Using the Limit Comparison Test

For each of the following series, use the limit comparison test to determine whether the series converges or diverges. If the test does not apply, say so.

a. $\sum_{n=1}^{\infty} \frac{1}{\sqrt{n}+1}$

b. $\sum_{n=1}^{\infty} \frac{2^n+1}{3^n}$

c. $\sum_{n=1}^{\infty} \frac{\ln(n)}{n^2}$

### Solution

a. Compare this series to $\sum_{n=1}^{\infty} \frac{1}{\sqrt{n}}$. Calculate

$$\lim_{n \to \infty} \frac{1/(\sqrt{n}+1)}{1/\sqrt{n}} = \lim_{n \to \infty} \frac{\sqrt{n}}{\sqrt{n}+1} = \lim_{n \to \infty} \frac{1/\sqrt{n}}{1+1/\sqrt{n}} = 1.$$

By the limit comparison test, since $\sum_{n=1}^{\infty} \frac{1}{\sqrt{n}}$ diverges, then $\sum_{n=1}^{\infty} \frac{1}{\sqrt{n}+1}$ diverges.

b. Compare this series to $\sum_{n=1}^{\infty} \left(\frac{2}{3}\right)^n$. We see that

$$\lim_{n \to \infty} \frac{(2^n+1)/3^n}{2^n/3^n} = \lim_{n \to \infty} \frac{2^n+1}{3^n} \cdot \frac{3^n}{2^n} = \lim_{n \to \infty} \frac{2^n+1}{2^n} = \lim_{n \to \infty} \left[1 + \left(\frac{1}{2}\right)^n\right] = 1.$$

Therefore,

$$\lim_{n \to \infty} \frac{(2^n+1)/3^n}{2^n/3^n} = 1.$$

Since $\sum_{n=1}^{\infty} \left(\frac{2}{3}\right)^n$ converges, we conclude that $\sum_{n=1}^{\infty} \frac{2^n+1}{3^n}$ converges.

c. Since $\ln n < n$, compare with $\sum_{n=1}^{\infty} \frac{1}{n}$. We see that

$$\lim_{n \to \infty} \frac{\ln n/n^2}{1/n} = \lim_{n \to \infty} \frac{\ln n}{n^2} \cdot \frac{n}{1} = \lim_{n \to \infty} \frac{\ln n}{n}.$$

In order to evaluate $\lim_{n \to \infty} \ln n/n$, evaluate the limit as $x \to \infty$ of the real-valued function $\ln(x)/x$. These two limits are equal, and making this change allows us to use L'Hôpital's rule. We obtain

$$\lim_{x \to \infty} \frac{\ln x}{x} = \lim_{x \to \infty} \frac{1}{x} = 0.$$

Therefore, $\lim_{n \to \infty} \ln n/n = 0,$ and, consequently,

$$\lim_{n \to \infty} \frac{\ln n/n^2}{1/n} = 0.$$

Since the limit is $0$ but $\sum_{n=1}^{\infty} \frac{1}{n}$ diverges, the limit comparison test does not provide any information.

Compare with $\sum_{n=1}^{\infty} \frac{1}{n^2}$ instead. In this case,

$$\lim_{n \to \infty} \frac{\ln n/n^2}{1/n^2} = \lim_{n \to \infty} \frac{\ln n}{n^2} \cdot \frac{n^2}{1} = \lim_{n \to \infty} \ln n = \infty.$$

Since the limit is $\infty$ but $\sum_{n=1}^{\infty} \frac{1}{n^2}$ converges, the test still does not provide any information.

So now we try a series between the two we already tried. Choosing the series $\sum_{n=1}^{\infty} \frac{1}{n^{3/2}},$ we see that

$$\lim_{n \to \infty} \frac{\ln n/n^2}{1/n^{3/2}} = \lim_{n \to \infty} \frac{\ln n}{n^2} \cdot \frac{n^{3/2}}{1} = \lim_{n \to \infty} \frac{\ln n}{\sqrt{n}}.$$

As above, in order to evaluate $\lim_{n \to \infty} \ln n/\sqrt{n},$ evaluate the limit as $x \to \infty$ of the real-valued function $\ln x/\sqrt{x}.$ Using L'Hôpital's rule,

$$\lim_{x \to \infty} \frac{\ln x}{\sqrt{x}} = \lim_{x \to \infty} \frac{2\sqrt{x}}{x} = \lim_{x \to \infty} \frac{2}{\sqrt{x}} = 0.$$

Since the limit is $0$ and $\sum_{n=1}^{\infty} \frac{1}{n^{3/2}}$ converges, we can conclude that $\sum_{n=1}^{\infty} \frac{\ln n}{n^2}$ converges.

**5.17** Use the limit comparison test to determine whether the series $\sum_{n=1}^{\infty} \frac{5^n}{3^n + 2}$ converges or diverges.

# 5.4 EXERCISES

Use the comparison test to determine whether the following series converge.

194. $\sum_{n=1}^{\infty} a_n$ where $a_n = \frac{2}{n(n+1)}$

195. $\sum_{n=1}^{\infty} a_n$ where $a_n = \frac{1}{n(n+1/2)}$

196. $\sum_{n=1}^{\infty} \frac{1}{2(n+1)}$

197. $\sum_{n=1}^{\infty} \frac{1}{2n-1}$

198. $\sum_{n=2}^{\infty} \frac{1}{(n \ln n)^2}$

199. $\sum_{n=1}^{\infty} \frac{n!}{(n+2)!}$

200. $\sum_{n=1}^{\infty} \frac{1}{n!}$

201. $\sum_{n=1}^{\infty} \frac{\sin(1/n)}{n}$

202. $\sum_{n=1}^{\infty} \frac{\sin^2 n}{n^2}$

203. $\sum_{n=1}^{\infty} \frac{\sin(1/n)}{\sqrt{n}}$

204. $\sum_{n=1}^{\infty} \frac{n^{1.2}-1}{n^{2.3}+1}$

205. $\sum_{n=1}^{\infty} \frac{\sqrt{n+1}-\sqrt{n}}{n}$

206. $\sum_{n=1}^{\infty} \frac{\sqrt[4]{n}}{\sqrt[3]{n^4+n^2}}$

Use the limit comparison test to determine whether each of the following series converges or diverges.

207. $\sum_{n=1}^{\infty} \left(\frac{\ln n}{n}\right)^2$

208. $\sum_{n=1}^{\infty} \left(\frac{\ln n}{n^{0.6}}\right)^2$

209. $\sum_{n=1}^{\infty} \frac{\ln\left(1+\frac{1}{n}\right)}{n}$

210. $\sum_{n=1}^{\infty} \ln\left(1+\frac{1}{n^2}\right)$

211. $\sum_{n=1}^{\infty} \frac{1}{4^n-3^n}$

212. $\sum_{n=1}^{\infty} \frac{1}{n^2 - n \sin n}$

213. $\sum_{n=1}^{\infty} \frac{1}{e^{(1.1)n} - 3^n}$

214. $\sum_{n=1}^{\infty} \frac{1}{e^{(1.01)n} - 3^n}$

215. $\sum_{n=1}^{\infty} \frac{1}{n^{1+1/n}}$

216. $\sum_{n=1}^{\infty} \frac{1}{2^{1+1/n} n^{1+1/n}}$

217. $\sum_{n=1}^{\infty} \left(\frac{1}{n} - \sin\left(\frac{1}{n}\right)\right)$

218. $\sum_{n=1}^{\infty} \left(1 - \cos\left(\frac{1}{n}\right)\right)$

219. $\sum_{n=1}^{\infty} \frac{1}{n}\left(\tan^{-1} n - \frac{\pi}{2}\right)$

220. $\sum_{n=1}^{\infty} \left(1-\frac{1}{n}\right)^{n.n}$ (*Hint:* $\left(1-\frac{1}{n}\right)^n \to 1/e$.)

221. $\sum_{n=1}^{\infty} \left(1-e^{-1/n}\right)$ (*Hint:* $1/e \approx (1-1/n)^n$, so $1-e^{-1/n} \approx 1/n$.)

222. Does $\sum_{n=2}^{\infty} \frac{1}{(\ln n)^p}$ converge if $p$ is large enough? If so, for which $p$?

223. Does $\sum_{n=1}^{\infty}\left(\frac{(\ln n)}{n}\right)^p$ converge if $p$ is large enough? If so, for which $p$?

224. For which $p$ does the series $\sum_{n=1}^{\infty} 2^{pn}/3^n$ converge?

225. For which $p > 0$ does the series $\sum_{n=1}^{\infty} \frac{n^p}{2^n}$ converge?

226. For which $r > 0$ does the series $\sum_{n=1}^{\infty} \frac{r^{n^2}}{2^n}$ converge?

227. For which $r > 0$ does the series $\sum_{n=1}^{\infty} \frac{2^n}{r^{n^2}}$ converge?

228. Find all values of $p$ and $q$ such that $\sum_{n=1}^{\infty} \frac{n^p}{(n!)^q}$ converges.

229. Does $\sum_{n=1}^{\infty} \frac{\sin^2(nr/2)}{n}$ converge or diverge? Explain.

230. Explain why, for each $n$, at least one of $\{|\sin n|, |\sin(n+1)|,..., |\sin n + 6|\}$ is larger than $1/2$. Use this relation to test convergence of $\sum_{n=1}^{\infty} \frac{|\sin n|}{\sqrt{n}}$.

231. Suppose that $a_n \geq 0$ and $b_n \geq 0$ and that $\sum_{n=1}^{\infty} a^2{}_n$ and $\sum_{n=1}^{\infty} b^2{}_n$ converge. Prove that $\sum_{n=1}^{\infty} a_n b_n$ converges and $\sum_{n=1}^{\infty} a_n b_n \leq \frac{1}{2}\left(\sum_{n=1}^{\infty} a_n^2 + \sum_{n=1}^{\infty} b_n^2\right)$.

232. Does $\sum_{n=1}^{\infty} 2^{-\ln\ln n}$ converge? (*Hint:* Write $2^{\ln\ln n}$ as a power of $\ln n$.)

233. Does $\sum_{n=1}^{\infty} (\ln n)^{-\ln n}$ converge? (*Hint:* Use $t = e^{\ln(t)}$ to compare to a $p-$ series.)

234. Does $\sum_{n=2}^{\infty} (\ln n)^{-\ln\ln n}$ converge? (*Hint:* Compare $a_n$ to $1/n$.)

235. Show that if $a_n \geq 0$ and $\sum_{n=1}^{\infty} a_n$ converges, then $\sum_{n=1}^{\infty} a^2{}_n$ converges. If $\sum_{n=1}^{\infty} a^2{}_n$ converges, does $\sum_{n=1}^{\infty} a_n$ necessarily converge?

236. Suppose that $a_n > 0$ for all $n$ and that $\sum_{n=1}^{\infty} a_n$ converges. Suppose that $b_n$ is an arbitrary sequence of zeros and ones. Does $\sum_{n=1}^{\infty} a_n b_n$ necessarily converge?

237. Suppose that $a_n > 0$ for all $n$ and that $\sum_{n=1}^{\infty} a_n$ diverges. Suppose that $b_n$ is an arbitrary sequence of zeros and ones with infinitely many terms equal to one. Does $\sum_{n=1}^{\infty} a_n b_n$ necessarily diverge?

238. Complete the details of the following argument: If $\sum_{n=1}^{\infty} \frac{1}{n}$ converges to a finite sum $s$, then $\frac{1}{2}s = \frac{1}{2} + \frac{1}{4} + \frac{1}{6} + \cdots$ and $s - \frac{1}{2}s = 1 + \frac{1}{3} + \frac{1}{5} + \cdots$. Why does this lead to a contradiction?

239. Show that if $a_n \geq 0$ and $\sum_{n=1}^{\infty} a^2{}_n$ converges, then $\sum_{n=1}^{\infty} \sin^2(a_n)$ converges.

240. Suppose that $a_n/b_n \to 0$ in the comparison test, where $a_n \geq 0$ and $b_n \geq 0$. Prove that if $\sum b_n$ converges, then $\sum a_n$ converges.

241. Let $b_n$ be an infinite sequence of zeros and ones. What is the largest possible value of $x = \sum_{n=1}^{\infty} b_n/2^n$?

242. Let $d_n$ be an infinite sequence of digits, meaning $d_n$ takes values in $\{0, 1,\ldots, 9\}$. What is the largest possible value of $x = \sum_{n=1}^{\infty} d_n/10^n$ that converges?

243. Explain why, if $x > 1/2$, then $x$ cannot be written $x = \sum_{n=2}^{\infty} \frac{b_n}{2^n}(b_n = 0 \text{ or } 1,\ b_1 = 0)$.

244. **[T]** Evelyn has a perfect balancing scale, an unlimited number of $1$ -kg weights, and one each of $1/2$ -kg, $1/4$ -kg, $1/8$ -kg, and so on weights. She wishes to weigh a meteorite of unspecified origin to arbitrary precision. Assuming the scale is big enough, can she do it? What does this have to do with infinite series?

245. **[T]** Robert wants to know his body mass to arbitrary precision. He has a big balancing scale that works perfectly, an unlimited collection of $1$ -kg weights, and nine each of $0.1$ -kg, $0.01$ -kg, $0.001$ -kg, and so on weights. Assuming the scale is big enough, can he do this? What does this have to do with infinite series?

246. The series $\sum_{n=1}^{\infty} \frac{1}{2n}$ is half the harmonic series and hence diverges. It is obtained from the harmonic series by deleting all terms in which $n$ is odd. Let $m > 1$ be fixed. Show, more generally, that deleting all terms $1/n$ where $n = mk$ for some integer $k$ also results in a divergent series.

247. In view of the previous exercise, it may be surprising that a subseries of the harmonic series in which about one in every five terms is deleted might converge. A *depleted harmonic series* is a series obtained from $\sum_{n=1}^{\infty} \frac{1}{n}$ by removing any term $1/n$ if a given digit, say $9$, appears in the decimal expansion of $n$. Argue that this depleted harmonic series converges by answering the following questions.

a. How many whole numbers $n$ have $d$ digits?

b. How many $d$-digit whole numbers $h(d)$. do not contain $9$ as one or more of their digits?

c. What is the smallest $d$-digit number $m(d)$?

d. Explain why the deleted harmonic series is bounded by $\sum_{d=1}^{\infty} \frac{h(d)}{m(d)}$.

e. Show that $\sum_{d=1}^{\infty} \frac{h(d)}{m(d)}$ converges.

248. Suppose that a sequence of numbers $a_n > 0$ has the property that $a_1 = 1$ and $a_{n+1} = \frac{1}{n+1}S_n$, where $S_n = a_1 + \cdots + a_n$. Can you determine whether $\sum_{n=1}^{\infty} a_n$ converges? (*Hint:* $S_n$ is monotone.)

249. Suppose that a sequence of numbers $a_n > 0$ has the property that $a_1 = 1$ and $a_{n+1} = \frac{1}{(n+1)^2}S_n$, where $S_n = a_1 + \cdots + a_n$. Can you determine whether $\sum_{n=1}^{\infty} a_n$ converges? (*Hint:* $S_2 = a_2 + a_1 = a_2 + S_1 = a_2 + 1 = 1 + 1/4 = (1 + 1/4)S_1$, $S_3 = \frac{1}{3^2}S_2 + S_2 = (1 + 1/9)S_2 = (1 + 1/9)(1 + 1/4)S_1$, etc. Look at $\ln(S_n)$, and use $\ln(1 + t) \le t$, $t > 0$.)

# 5.5 | Alternating Series

## Learning Objectives

**5.5.1** Use the alternating series test to test an alternating series for convergence.
**5.5.2** Estimate the sum of an alternating series.
**5.5.3** Explain the meaning of absolute convergence and conditional convergence.

So far in this chapter, we have primarily discussed series with positive terms. In this section we introduce alternating series—those series whose terms alternate in sign. We will show in a later chapter that these series often arise when studying power series. After defining alternating series, we introduce the alternating series test to determine whether such a series converges.

## The Alternating Series Test

A series whose terms alternate between positive and negative values is an **alternating series**. For example, the series

$$\sum_{n=1}^{\infty} \left(-\frac{1}{2}\right)^n = -\frac{1}{2} + \frac{1}{4} - \frac{1}{8} + \frac{1}{16} - \cdots \quad (5.11)$$

and

$$\sum_{n=1}^{\infty} \frac{(-1)^{n+1}}{n} = 1 - \frac{1}{2} + \frac{1}{3} - \frac{1}{4} + \cdots \quad (5.12)$$

are both alternating series.

### Definition

Any series whose terms alternate between positive and negative values is called an alternating series. An alternating series can be written in the form

$$\sum_{n=1}^{\infty} (-1)^{n+1} b_n = b_1 - b_2 + b_3 - b_4 + \cdots \quad (5.13)$$

or

$$\sum_{n-1}^{\infty} (-1)^n b_n = -b_1 + b_2 - b_3 + b_4 - \cdots \quad (5.14)$$

Where $b_n \geq 0$ for all positive integers *n*.

Series (1), shown in **Equation 5.11**, is a geometric series. Since $|r| = |-1/2| < 1,$ the series converges. Series (2), shown in **Equation 5.12**, is called the alternating harmonic series. We will show that whereas the harmonic series diverges, the alternating harmonic series converges.

To prove this, we look at the sequence of partial sums $\{S_k\}$ (**Figure 5.17**).

### Proof

Consider the odd terms $S_{2k+1}$ for $k \geq 0.$ Since $1/(2k+1) < 1/2k,$

$$S_{2k+1} = S_{2k-1} - \frac{1}{2k} + \frac{1}{2k+1} < S_{2k-1}.$$

Therefore, $\{S_{2k+1}\}$ is a decreasing sequence. Also,

$$S_{2k+1} = \left(1 - \frac{1}{2}\right) + \left(\frac{1}{3} - \frac{1}{4}\right) + \cdots + \left(\frac{1}{2k-1} - \frac{1}{2k}\right) + \frac{1}{2k+1} > 0.$$

Therefore, $\{S_{2k+1}\}$ is bounded below. Since $\{S_{2k+1}\}$ is a decreasing sequence that is bounded below, by the Monotone Convergence Theorem, $\{S_{2k+1}\}$ converges. Similarly, the even terms $\{S_{2k}\}$ form an increasing sequence that is bounded above because

$$S_{2k} = S_{2k-2} + \frac{1}{2k-1} - \frac{1}{2k} > S_{2k-2}$$

and

$$S_{2k} = 1 + \left(-\frac{1}{2} + \frac{1}{3}\right) + \cdots + \left(-\frac{1}{2k-2} + \frac{1}{2k-1}\right) - \frac{1}{2k} < 1.$$

Therefore, by the Monotone Convergence Theorem, the sequence $\{S_{2k}\}$ also converges. Since

$$S_{2k+1} = S_{2k} + \frac{1}{2k+1},$$

we know that

$$\lim_{k\to\infty} S_{2k+1} = \lim_{k\to\infty} S_{2k} + \lim_{k\to\infty} \frac{1}{2k+1}.$$

Letting $S = \lim_{k\to\infty} S_{2k+1}$ and using the fact that $1/(2k+1) \to 0,$ we conclude that $\lim_{k\to\infty} S_{2k} = S.$ Since the odd terms and the even terms in the sequence of partial sums converge to the same limit $S,$ it can be shown that the sequence of partial sums converges to $S,$ and therefore the alternating harmonic series converges to $S.$

It can also be shown that $S = \ln 2,$ and we can write

$$\sum_{n=1}^{\infty} \frac{(-1)^{n+1}}{n} = 1 - \frac{1}{2} + \frac{1}{3} - \frac{1}{4} + \cdots = \ln(2).$$

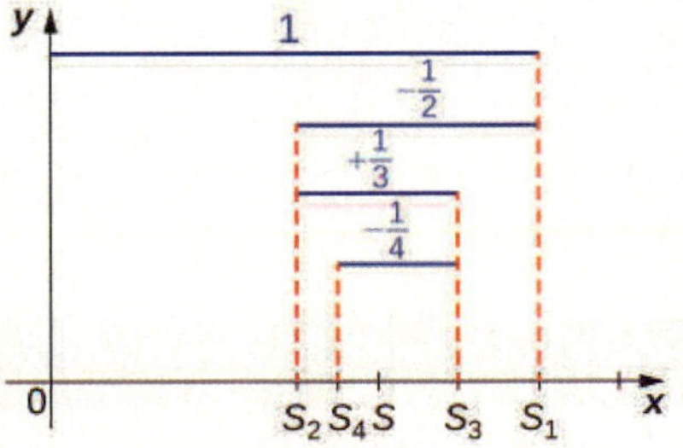

**Figure 5.17** For the alternating harmonic series, the odd terms $S_{2k+1}$ in the sequence of partial sums are decreasing and bounded below. The even terms $S_{2k}$ are increasing and bounded above.

□

More generally, any alternating series of form (3) (**Equation 5.13**) or (4) (**Equation 5.14**) converges as long as $b_1 \geq b_2 \geq b_3 \geq \cdots$ and $b_n \to 0$ (**Figure 5.18**). The proof is similar to the proof for the alternating harmonic series.

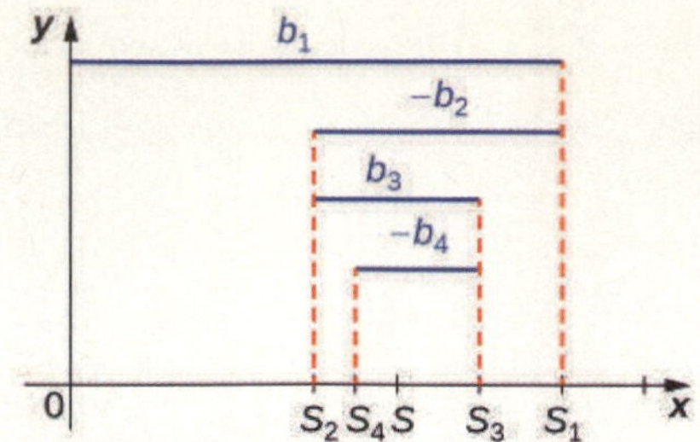


**Figure 5.18** For an alternating series $b_1 - b_2 + b_3 - \cdots$ in which $b_1 > b_2 > b_3 > \cdots,$ the odd terms $S_{2k+1}$ in the sequence of partial sums are decreasing and bounded below. The even terms $S_{2k}$ are increasing and bounded above.

### Theorem 5.13: Alternating Series Test

An alternating series of the form

$$\sum_{n=1}^{\infty} (-1)^{n+1} b_n \text{ or } \sum_{n=1}^{\infty} (-1)^n b_n$$

converges if

i. $0 \le b_{n+1} \le b_n$ for all $n \ge 1$ and

ii. $\lim_{n \to \infty} b_n = 0.$

This is known as the **alternating series test**.

We remark that this theorem is true more generally as long as there exists some integer $N$ such that $0 \le b_{n+1} \le b_n$ for all $n \ge N$.

## Example 5.19

### Convergence of Alternating Series

For each of the following alternating series, determine whether the series converges or diverges.

a. $\sum_{n=1}^{\infty} (-1)^{n+1}/n^2$

b. $\sum_{n=1}^{\infty} (-1)^{n+1} n/(n+1)$

#### Solution

a. Since
$$\frac{1}{(n+1)^2} < \frac{1}{n^2} \text{ and } \frac{1}{n^2} \to 0,$$
the series converges.

b. Since $n/(n+1) \nrightarrow 0$ as $n \to \infty,$ we cannot apply the alternating series test. Instead, we use the *n*th term test for divergence. Since

$$\lim_{n \to \infty} \frac{(-1)^{n+1} n}{n+1} \neq 0,$$

the series diverges.

**5.18** Determine whether the series $\sum_{n=1}^{\infty} (-1)^{n+1} n/2^n$ converges or diverges.

## Remainder of an Alternating Series

It is difficult to explicitly calculate the sum of most alternating series, so typically the sum is approximated by using a partial sum. When doing so, we are interested in the amount of error in our approximation. Consider an alternating series

$$\sum_{n=1}^{\infty} (-1)^{n+1} b_n$$

satisfying the hypotheses of the alternating series test. Let $S$ denote the sum of this series and $\{S_k\}$ be the corresponding sequence of partial sums. From **Figure 5.18**, we see that for any integer $N \geq 1,$ the remainder $R_N$ satisfies

$$|R_N| = |S - S_N| \leq |S_{N+1} - S_N| = b_{n+1}.$$

**Theorem 5.14: Remainders in Alternating Series**

Consider an alternating series of the form

$$\sum_{n=1}^{\infty} (-1)^{n+1} b_n \text{or} \sum_{n=1}^{\infty} (-1)^n b_n$$

that satisfies the hypotheses of the alternating series test. Let $S$ denote the sum of the series and $S_N$ denote the $N$th partial sum. For any integer $N \geq 1,$ the remainder $R_N = S - S_N$ satisfies

$$|R_N| \leq b_{N+1}.$$

In other words, if the conditions of the alternating series test apply, then the error in approximating the infinite series by the $N$th partial sum $S_N$ is in magnitude at most the size of the next term $b_{N+1}$.

**Example 5.20**

### Estimating the Remainder of an Alternating Series

Consider the alternating series

$$\sum_{n=1}^{\infty} \frac{(-1)^{n+1}}{n^2}.$$

Use the remainder estimate to determine a bound on the error $R_{10}$ if we approximate the sum of the series by the partial sum $S_{10}$.

**Solution**

From the theorem stated above,

$$|R_{10}| \leq b_{11} = \frac{1}{11^2} \approx 0.008265.$$

**5.19** Find a bound for $R_{20}$ when approximating $\sum_{n=1}^{\infty} (-1)^{n+1}/n$ by $S_{20}$.

## Absolute and Conditional Convergence

Consider a series $\sum_{n=1}^{\infty} a_n$ and the related series $\sum_{n=1}^{\infty} |a_n|$. Here we discuss possibilities for the relationship between the convergence of these two series. For example, consider the alternating harmonic series $\sum_{n=1}^{\infty} (-1)^{n+1}/n$. The series whose terms are the absolute value of these terms is the harmonic series, since $\sum_{n=1}^{\infty} |(-1)^{n+1}/n| = \sum_{n=1}^{\infty} 1/n$. Since the alternating harmonic series converges, but the harmonic series diverges, we say the alternating harmonic series exhibits conditional convergence.

By comparison, consider the series $\sum_{n=1}^{\infty} (-1)^{n+1}/n^2$. The series whose terms are the absolute values of the terms of this series is the series $\sum_{n=1}^{\infty} 1/n^2$. Since both of these series converge, we say the series $\sum_{n=1}^{\infty} (-1)^{n+1}/n^2$ exhibits absolute convergence.

### Definition

A series $\sum_{n=1}^{\infty} a_n$ exhibits **absolute convergence** if $\sum_{n=1}^{\infty} |a_n|$ converges. A series $\sum_{n=1}^{\infty} a_n$ exhibits **conditional convergence** if $\sum_{n=1}^{\infty} a_n$ converges but $\sum_{n=1}^{\infty} |a_n|$ diverges.

As shown by the alternating harmonic series, a series $\sum_{n=1}^{\infty} a_n$ may converge, but $\sum_{n=1}^{\infty} |a_n|$ may diverge. In the following theorem, however, we show that if $\sum_{n=1}^{\infty} |a_n|$ converges, then $\sum_{n=1}^{\infty} a_n$ converges.

### Theorem 5.15: Absolute Convergence Implies Convergence

If $\sum_{n=1}^{\infty} |a_n|$ converges, then $\sum_{n=1}^{\infty} a_n$ converges.

### Proof

Suppose that $\sum_{n=1}^{\infty} |a_n|$ converges. We show this by using the fact that $a_n = |a_n|$ or $a_n = -|a_n|$ and therefore $|a_n| + a_n = 2|a_n|$ or $|a_n| + a_n = 0$. Therefore, $0 \le |a_n| + a_n \le 2|a_n|$. Consequently, by the comparison test, since $2\sum_{n=1}^{\infty} |a_n|$ converges, the series

$$\sum_{n=1}^{\infty} (|a_n| + a_n)$$

converges. By using the algebraic properties for convergent series, we conclude that

$$\sum_{n=1}^{\infty} a_n = \sum_{n=1}^{\infty} (|a_n| + a_n) - \sum_{n=1}^{\infty} |a_n|$$

converges.

□

## Example 5.21

### Absolute versus Conditional Convergence

For each of the following series, determine whether the series converges absolutely, converges conditionally, or diverges.

a. $\sum_{n=1}^{\infty} (-1)^{n+1}/(3n+1)$

b. $\sum_{n=1}^{\infty} \cos(n)/n^2$

### Solution

a. We can see that

$$\sum_{n=1}^{\infty} \left| \frac{(-1)^{n+1}}{3n+1} \right| = \sum_{n=1}^{\infty} \frac{1}{3n+1}$$

diverges by using the limit comparison test with the harmonic series. In fact,

$$\lim_{n\to\infty} \frac{1/(3n+1)}{1/n} = \frac{1}{3}.$$

Therefore, the series does not converge absolutely. However, since

$$\frac{1}{3(n+1)+1} < \frac{1}{3n+1} \text{ and } \frac{1}{3n+1} \to 0,$$

the series converges. We can conclude that $\sum_{n=1}^{\infty} (-1)^{n+1}/(3n+1)$ converges conditionally.

b. Noting that $|\cos n| \le 1$, to determine whether the series converges absolutely, compare

$$\sum_{n=1}^{\infty} \left|\frac{\cos n}{n^2}\right|$$

with the series $\sum_{n=1}^{\infty} 1/n^2$. Since $\sum_{n=1}^{\infty} 1/n^2$ converges, by the comparison test, $\sum_{n=1}^{\infty} |\cos n/n^2|$ converges, and therefore $\sum_{n=1}^{\infty} \cos n/n^2$ converges absolutely.

**5.20** Determine whether the series $\sum_{n=1}^{\infty} (-1)^{n+1} n/(2n^3+1)$ converges absolutely, converges conditionally, or diverges.

To see the difference between absolute and conditional convergence, look at what happens when we *rearrange* the terms of the alternating harmonic series $\sum_{n=1}^{\infty} (-1)^{n+1}/n$. We show that we can rearrange the terms so that the new series diverges. Certainly if we rearrange the terms of a finite sum, the sum does not change. When we work with an infinite sum, however, interesting things can happen.

Begin by adding enough of the positive terms to produce a sum that is larger than some real number $M > 0$. For example, let $M = 10$, and find an integer $k$ such that

$$1 + \frac{1}{3} + \frac{1}{5} + \cdots + \frac{1}{2k-1} > 10.$$

(We can do this because the series $\sum_{n=1}^{\infty} 1/(2n-1)$ diverges to infinity.) Then subtract $1/2$. Then add more positive terms until the sum reaches 100. That is, find another integer $j > k$ such that

$$1 + \frac{1}{3} + \cdots + \frac{1}{2k-1} - \frac{1}{2} + \frac{1}{2k+1} + \cdots + \frac{1}{2j+1} > 100.$$

Then subtract $1/4$. Continuing in this way, we have found a way of rearranging the terms in the alternating harmonic series so that the sequence of partial sums for the rearranged series is unbounded and therefore diverges.

The terms in the alternating harmonic series can also be rearranged so that the new series converges to a different value. In **Example 5.22**, we show how to rearrange the terms to create a new series that converges to $3\ln(2)/2$. We point out that the alternating harmonic series can be rearranged to create a series that converges to any real number $r$; however, the proof of that fact is beyond the scope of this text.

In general, any series $\sum_{n=1}^{\infty} a_n$ that converges conditionally can be rearranged so that the new series diverges or converges to a different real number. A series that converges absolutely does not have this property. For any series $\sum_{n=1}^{\infty} a_n$ that converges absolutely, the value of $\sum_{n=1}^{\infty} a_n$ is the same for any rearrangement of the terms. This result is known as the Riemann Rearrangement Theorem, which is beyond the scope of this book.

## Example 5.22

### Rearranging Series

Use the fact that

$$1-\frac{1}{2}+\frac{1}{3}-\frac{1}{4}+\frac{1}{5}-\cdots=\ln 2$$

to rearrange the terms in the alternating harmonic series so the sum of the rearranged series is $3\ln(2)/2$.

### Solution

Let

$$\sum_{n=1}^{\infty} a_n = 1-\frac{1}{2}+\frac{1}{3}-\frac{1}{4}+\frac{1}{5}-\frac{1}{6}+\frac{1}{7}-\frac{1}{8}+\cdots.$$

Since $\sum_{n=1}^{\infty} a_n = \ln(2)$, by the algebraic properties of convergent series,

$$\sum_{n=1}^{\infty} \frac{1}{2}a_n = \frac{1}{2}-\frac{1}{4}+\frac{1}{6}-\frac{1}{8}+\cdots=\frac{1}{2}\sum_{n=1}^{\infty} a_n = \frac{\ln 2}{2}.$$

Now introduce the series $\sum_{n=1}^{\infty} b_n$ such that for all $n \geq 1$, $b_{2n-1}=0$ and $b_{2n}=a_n/2$. Then

$$\sum_{n=1}^{\infty} b_n = 0+\frac{1}{2}+0-\frac{1}{4}+0+\frac{1}{6}+0-\frac{1}{8}+\cdots=\frac{\ln 2}{2}.$$

Then using the algebraic limit properties of convergent series, since $\sum_{n=1}^{\infty} a_n$ and $\sum_{n=1}^{\infty} b_n$ converge, the series $\sum_{n=1}^{\infty} (a_n+b_n)$ converges and

$$\sum_{n=1}^{\infty} (a_n+b_n) = \sum_{n=1}^{\infty} a_n + \sum_{n=1}^{\infty} b_n = \ln 2+\frac{\ln 2}{2}=\frac{3\ln 2}{2}.$$

Now adding the corresponding terms, $a_n$ and $b_n$, we see that

$$\begin{aligned}\sum_{n=1}^{\infty} (a_n+b_n) &= (1+0)+\left(-\frac{1}{2}+\frac{1}{2}\right)+\left(\frac{1}{3}+0\right)+\left(-\frac{1}{4}-\frac{1}{4}\right)+\left(\frac{1}{5}+0\right)+\left(-\frac{1}{6}+\frac{1}{6}\right)\\ &\quad+\left(\frac{1}{7}+0\right)+\left(\frac{1}{8}-\frac{1}{8}\right)+\cdots\\ &= 1+\frac{1}{3}-\frac{1}{2}+\frac{1}{5}+\frac{1}{7}-\frac{1}{4}+\cdots.\end{aligned}$$

We notice that the series on the right side of the equal sign is a rearrangement of the alternating harmonic series. Since $\sum_{n=1}^{\infty} (a_n+b_n) = 3\ln(2)/2$, we conclude that

$$1+\frac{1}{3}-\frac{1}{2}+\frac{1}{5}+\frac{1}{7}-\frac{1}{4}+\cdots=\frac{3\ln(2)}{2}.$$

Therefore, we have found a rearrangement of the alternating harmonic series having the desired property.

# 5.5 EXERCISES

State whether each of the following series converges absolutely, conditionally, or not at all.

250. $\sum_{n=1}^{\infty} (-1)^{n+1} \frac{n}{n+3}$

251. $\sum_{n=1}^{\infty} (-1)^{n+1} \frac{\sqrt{n}+1}{\sqrt{n}+3}$

252. $\sum_{n=1}^{\infty} (-1)^{n+1} \frac{1}{\sqrt{n+3}}$

253. $\sum_{n=1}^{\infty} (-1)^{n+1} \frac{\sqrt{n+3}}{n}$

254. $\sum_{n=1}^{\infty} (-1)^{n+1} \frac{1}{n!}$

255. $\sum_{n=1}^{\infty} (-1)^{n+1} \frac{3^n}{n!}$

256. $\sum_{n=1}^{\infty} (-1)^{n+1} \left(\frac{n-1}{n}\right)^n$

257. $\sum_{n=1}^{\infty} (-1)^{n+1} \left(\frac{n+1}{n}\right)^n$

258. $\sum_{n=1}^{\infty} (-1)^{n+1} \sin^2 n$

259. $\sum_{n=1}^{\infty} (-1)^{n+1} \cos^2 n$

260. $\sum_{n=1}^{\infty} (-1)^{n+1} \sin^2 (1/n)$

261. $\sum_{n=1}^{\infty} (-1)^{n+1} \cos^2 (1/n)$

262. $\sum_{n=1}^{\infty} (-1)^{n+1} \ln(1/n)$

263. $\sum_{n=1}^{\infty} (-1)^{n+1} \ln\left(1+\frac{1}{n}\right)$

264. $\sum_{n=1}^{\infty} (-1)^{n+1} \frac{n^2}{1+n^4}$

265. $\sum_{n=1}^{\infty} (-1)^{n+1} \frac{n^e}{1+n^{\pi}}$

266. $\sum_{n=1}^{\infty} (-1)^{n+1} 2^{1/n}$

267. $\sum_{n=1}^{\infty} (-1)^{n+1} n^{1/n}$

268. $\sum_{n=1}^{\infty} (-1)^n \left(1-n^{1/n}\right)$ (*Hint:* $n^{1/n} \approx 1 + \ln(n)/n$ for large $n$.)

269. $\sum_{n=1}^{\infty} (-1)^{n+1} n\left(1-\cos\left(\frac{1}{n}\right)\right)$ (*Hint:* $\cos(1/n) \approx 1 - 1/n^2$ for large $n$.)

270. $\sum_{n=1}^{\infty} (-1)^{n+1} \left(\sqrt{n+1}-\sqrt{n}\right)$ (*Hint:* Rationalize the numerator.)

271. $\sum_{n=1}^{\infty} (-1)^{n+1} \left(\frac{1}{\sqrt{n}}-\frac{1}{\sqrt{n+1}}\right)$ (*Hint:* Cross-multiply then rationalize numerator.)

272. $\sum_{n=1}^{\infty} (-1)^{n+1} (\ln(n+1)-\ln n)$

273. $\sum_{n=1}^{\infty} (-1)^{n+1} n\left(\tan^{-1}(n+1)-\tan^{-1} n\right)$ (*Hint:* Use Mean Value Theorem.)

274. $\sum_{n=1}^{\infty} (-1)^{n+1} \left((n+1)^2-n^2\right)$

275. $\sum_{n=1}^{\infty} (-1)^{n+1} \left(\frac{1}{n}-\frac{1}{n+1}\right)$

276. $\sum_{n=1}^{\infty} \frac{\cos(n\pi)}{n}$

277. $\sum_{n=1}^{\infty} \frac{\cos(n\pi)}{n^{1/n}}$

278. $\sum_{n=1}^{\infty} \frac{1}{n}\sin\left(\frac{n\pi}{2}\right)$

279. $\sum_{n=1}^{\infty} \sin(n\pi/2)\sin(1/n)$

In each of the following problems, use the estimate $|R_N| \le b_{N+1}$ to find a value of $N$ that guarantees that the sum of the first $N$ terms of the alternating series $\sum_{n=1}^{\infty} (-1)^{n+1} b_n$ differs from the infinite sum by at most the given error. Calculate the partial sum $S_N$ for this $N$.

280. **[T]** $b_n = 1/n$, error $< 10^{-5}$

281. **[T]** $b_n = 1/\ln(n)$, $n \ge 2$, error $< 10^{-1}$

282. **[T]** $b_n = 1/\sqrt{n}$, error $< 10^{-3}$

283. **[T]** $b_n = 1/2^n$, error $< 10^{-6}$

284. **[T]** $b_n = \ln\left(1 + \frac{1}{n}\right)$, error $< 10^{-3}$

285. **[T]** $b_n = 1/n^2$, error $< 10^{-6}$

For the following exercises, indicate whether each of the following statements is true or false. If the statement is false, provide an example in which it is false.

286. If $b_n \ge 0$ is decreasing and $\lim_{n \to \infty} b_n = 0$, then $\sum_{n=1}^{\infty} (b_{2n-1} - b_{2n})$ converges absolutely.

287. If $b_n \ge 0$ is decreasing, then $\sum_{n=1}^{\infty} (b_{2n-1} - b_{2n})$ converges absolutely.

288. If $b_n \ge 0$ and $\lim_{n \to \infty} b_n = 0$ then $\sum_{n=1}^{\infty} (\frac{1}{2}(b_{3n-2} + b_{3n-1}) - b_{3n})$ converges.

289. If $b_n \ge 0$ is decreasing and $\sum_{n=1}^{\infty} (b_{3n-2} + b_{3n-1} - b_{3n})$ converges then $\sum_{n=1}^{\infty} b_{3n-2}$ converges.

290. If $b_n \ge 0$ is decreasing and $\sum_{n=1}^{\infty} (-1)^{n-1} b_n$ converges conditionally but not absolutely, then $b_n$ does not tend to zero.

291. Let $a_n^+ = a_n$ if $a_n \ge 0$ and $a_n^- = -a_n$ if $a_n < 0$. (Also, $a_n^+ = 0$ if $a_n < 0$ and $a_n^- = 0$ if $a_n \ge 0$.) If $\sum_{n=1}^{\infty} a_n$ converges conditionally but not absolutely, then neither $\sum_{n=1}^{\infty} a_n^+$ nor $\sum_{n=1}^{\infty} a_n^-$ converge.

292. Suppose that $a_n$ is a sequence of positive real numbers and that $\sum_{n=1}^{\infty} a_n$ converges. Suppose that $b_n$ is an arbitrary sequence of ones and minus ones. Does $\sum_{n=1}^{\infty} a_n b_n$ necessarily converge?

293. Suppose that $a_n$ is a sequence such that $\sum_{n=1}^{\infty} a_n b_n$ converges for every possible sequence $b_n$ of zeros and ones. Does $\sum_{n=1}^{\infty} a_n$ converge absolutely?

The following series do not satisfy the hypotheses of the alternating series test as stated.

In each case, state which hypothesis is not satisfied. State whether the series converges absolutely.

294. $\sum_{n=1}^{\infty} (-1)^{n+1} \frac{\sin^2 n}{n}$

295. $\sum_{n=1}^{\infty} (-1)^{n+1} \frac{\cos^2 n}{n}$

296. $1 + \frac{1}{2} - \frac{1}{3} - \frac{1}{4} + \frac{1}{5} + \frac{1}{6} - \frac{1}{7} - \frac{1}{8} + \cdots$

297. $1 + \frac{1}{2} - \frac{1}{3} + \frac{1}{4} + \frac{1}{5} - \frac{1}{6} + \frac{1}{7} + \frac{1}{8} - \frac{1}{9} + \cdots$

298. Show that the alternating series $1 - \frac{1}{2} + \frac{1}{2} - \frac{1}{4} + \frac{1}{3} - \frac{1}{6} + \frac{1}{4} - \frac{1}{8} + \cdots$ does not converge. What hypothesis of the alternating series test is not met?

299. Suppose that $\sum a_n$ converges absolutely. Show that the series consisting of the positive terms $a_n$ also converges.

300. Show that the alternating series $\frac{2}{3}-\frac{3}{5}+\frac{4}{7}-\frac{5}{9}+\cdots$ does not converge. What hypothesis of the alternating series test is not met?

301. The formula $\cos\theta = 1-\frac{\theta^2}{2!}+\frac{\theta^4}{4!}-\frac{\theta^6}{6!}+\cdots$ will be derived in the next chapter. Use the remainder $|R_N| \le b_{N+1}$ to find a bound for the error in estimating $\cos\theta$ by the fifth partial sum $1-\theta^2/2!+\theta^4/4!-\theta^6/6!+\theta^8/8!$ for $\theta=1$, $\theta=\pi/6$, and $\theta=\pi$.

302. The formula $\sin\theta = \theta-\frac{\theta^3}{3!}+\frac{\theta^5}{5!}-\frac{\theta^7}{7!}+\cdots$ will be derived in the next chapter. Use the remainder $|R_N| \le b_{N+1}$ to find a bound for the error in estimating $\sin\theta$ by the fifth partial sum $\theta-\theta^3/3!+\theta^5/5!-\theta^7/7!+\theta^9/9!$ for $\theta=1$, $\theta=\pi/6$, and $\theta=\pi$.

303. How many terms in $\cos\theta = 1-\frac{\theta^2}{2!}+\frac{\theta^4}{4!}-\frac{\theta^6}{6!}+\cdots$ are needed to approximate $\cos 1$ accurate to an error of at most 0.00001?

304. How many terms in $\sin\theta = \theta-\frac{\theta^3}{3!}+\frac{\theta^5}{5!}-\frac{\theta^7}{7!}+\cdots$ are needed to approximate $\sin 1$ accurate to an error of at most 0.00001?

305. Sometimes the alternating series $\sum_{n=1}^{\infty}(-1)^{n-1}b_n$ converges to a certain fraction of an absolutely convergent series $\sum_{n=1}^{\infty}b_n$ at a faster rate. Given that $\sum_{n=1}^{\infty}\frac{1}{n^2}=\frac{\pi^2}{6}$, find $S=1-\frac{1}{2^2}+\frac{1}{3^2}-\frac{1}{4^2}+\cdots$. Which of the series $6\sum_{n=1}^{\infty}\frac{1}{n^2}$ and $S\sum_{n=1}^{\infty}\frac{(-1)^{n-1}}{n^2}$ gives a better estimation of $\pi^2$ using 1000 terms?

The following alternating series converge to given multiples of $\pi$. Find the value of $N$ predicted by the remainder estimate such that the $N$th partial sum of the series accurately approximates the left-hand side to within the given error. Find the minimum $N$ for which the error bound holds, and give the desired approximate value in each case. Up to 15 decimals places, $\pi = 3.141592653589793\ldots$.

306. **[T]** $\frac{\pi}{4}=\sum_{n=0}^{\infty}\frac{(-1)^n}{2n+1}$, error $< 0.0001$

307. **[T]** $\frac{\pi}{\sqrt{12}}=\sum_{k=0}^{\infty}\frac{(-3)^{-k}}{2k+1}$, error $< 0.0001$

308. **[T]** The series $\sum_{n=0}^{\infty}\frac{\sin(x+\pi n)}{x+\pi n}$ plays an important role in signal processing. Show that $\sum_{n=0}^{\infty}\frac{\sin(x+\pi n)}{x+\pi n}$ converges whenever $0<x<\pi$. (*Hint:* Use the formula for the sine of a sum of angles.)

309. **[T]** If $\sum_{n=1}^{N}(-1)^{n-1}\frac{1}{n}\to\ln 2$, what is $1+\frac{1}{3}+\frac{1}{5}-\frac{1}{2}-\frac{1}{4}-\frac{1}{6}+\frac{1}{7}+\frac{1}{9}+\frac{1}{11}-\frac{1}{8}-\frac{1}{10}-\frac{1}{12}+\cdots$?

310. **[T]** Plot the series $\sum_{n=1}^{100}\frac{\cos(2\pi nx)}{n}$ for $0\le x<1$. Explain why $\sum_{n=1}^{100}\frac{\cos(2\pi nx)}{n}$ diverges when $x=0, 1$. How does the series behave for other $x$?

311. **[T]** Plot the series $\sum_{n=1}^{100}\frac{\sin(2\pi nx)}{n}$ for $0\le x<1$ and comment on its behavior

312. **[T]** Plot the series $\sum_{n=1}^{100}\frac{\cos(2\pi nx)}{n^2}$ for $0\le x<1$ and describe its graph.

313. **[T]** The alternating harmonic series converges because of cancellation among its terms. Its sum is known because the cancellation can be described explicitly. A random harmonic series is one of the form $\sum_{n=1}^{\infty}\frac{S_n}{n}$, where $s_n$ is a randomly generated sequence of $\pm1$'s in which the values $\pm1$ are equally likely to occur. Use a random number generator to produce 1000 random $\pm1$s and plot the partial sums $S_N=\sum_{n=1}^{N}\frac{s_n}{n}$ of your random harmonic sequence for $N=1$ to 1000. Compare to a plot of the first 1000 partial sums of the harmonic series.

314. **[T]** Estimates of $\sum_{n=1}^{\infty} \frac{1}{n^2}$ can be *accelerated* by writing its partial sums as $\sum_{n=1}^{N} \frac{1}{n^2} = \sum_{n=1}^{N} \frac{1}{n(n+1)} + \sum_{n=1}^{N} \frac{1}{n^2(n+1)}$ and recalling that $\sum_{n=1}^{N} \frac{1}{n(n+1)} = 1 - \frac{1}{N+1}$ converges to one as $N \to \infty$. Compare the estimate of $\pi^2/6$ using the sums $\sum_{n=1}^{1000} \frac{1}{n^2}$ with the estimate using $1 + \sum_{n=1}^{1000} \frac{1}{n^2(n+1)}$.

315. **[T]** The *Euler transform* rewrites $S = \sum_{n=0}^{\infty} (-1)^n b_n$ as $S = \sum_{n=0}^{\infty} (-1)^n 2^{-n-1} \sum_{m=0}^{n} \binom{n}{m} b_{n-m}$. For the alternating harmonic series, it takes the form $\ln(2) = \sum_{n=1}^{\infty} \frac{(-1)^{n-1}}{n} = \sum_{n=1}^{\infty} \frac{1}{n2^n}$. Compute partial sums of $\sum_{n=1}^{\infty} \frac{1}{n2^n}$ until they approximate $\ln(2)$ accurate to within $0.0001$. How many terms are needed? Compare this answer to the number of terms of the alternating harmonic series are needed to estimate $\ln(2)$.

316. **[T]** In the text it was stated that a conditionally convergent series can be rearranged to converge to any number. Here is a slightly simpler, but similar, fact. If $a_n \geq 0$ is such that $a_n \to 0$ as $n \to \infty$ but $\sum_{n=1}^{\infty} a_n$ diverges, then, given any number $A$ there is a sequence $s_n$ of $\pm 1$'s such that $\sum_{n=1}^{\infty} a_n s_n \to A$. Show this for $A > 0$ as follows.

a. Recursively define $s_n$ by $s_n = 1$ if $S_{n-1} = \sum_{k=1}^{n-1} a_k s_k < A$ and $s_n = -1$ otherwise.

b. Explain why eventually $S_n \geq A$, and for any $m$ larger than this $n$, $A - a_m \leq S_m \leq A + a_m$.

c. Explain why this implies that $S_n \to A$ as $n \to \infty$.

# 5.6 | Ratio and Root Tests

## Learning Objectives

**5.6.1** Use the ratio test to determine absolute convergence of a series.
**5.6.2** Use the root test to determine absolute convergence of a series.
**5.6.3** Describe a strategy for testing the convergence of a given series.

In this section, we prove the last two series convergence tests: the ratio test and the root test. These tests are particularly nice because they do not require us to find a comparable series. The ratio test will be especially useful in the discussion of power series in the next chapter.

Throughout this chapter, we have seen that no single convergence test works for all series. Therefore, at the end of this section we discuss a strategy for choosing which convergence test to use for a given series.

## Ratio Test

Consider a series $\sum_{n=1}^{\infty} a_n$. From our earlier discussion and examples, we know that $\lim_{n \to \infty} a_n = 0$ is not a sufficient condition for the series to converge. Not only do we need $a_n \to 0$, but we need $a_n \to 0$ quickly enough. For example, consider the series $\sum_{n=1}^{\infty} 1/n$ and the series $\sum_{n=1}^{\infty} 1/n^2$. We know that $1/n \to 0$ and $1/n^2 \to 0$. However, only the series $\sum_{n=1}^{\infty} 1/n^2$ converges. The series $\sum_{n=1}^{\infty} 1/n$ diverges because the terms in the sequence $\{1/n\}$ do not approach zero fast enough as $n \to \infty$. Here we introduce the **ratio test**, which provides a way of measuring how fast the terms of a series approach zero.

### Theorem 5.16: Ratio Test

Let $\sum_{n=1}^{\infty} a_n$ be a series with nonzero terms. Let

$$\rho = \lim_{n \to \infty} \left| \frac{a_{n+1}}{a_n} \right|.$$

i. If $0 \le \rho < 1$, then $\sum_{n=1}^{\infty} a_n$ converges absolutely.

ii. If $\rho > 1$ or $\rho = \infty$, then $\sum_{n=1}^{\infty} a_n$ diverges.

iii. If $\rho = 1$, the test does not provide any information.

### Proof

Let $\sum_{n=1}^{\infty} a_n$ be a series with nonzero terms.

We begin with the proof of part i. In this case, $\rho = \lim_{n \to \infty} \left| \frac{a_{n+1}}{a_n} \right| < 1$. Since $0 \le \rho < 1$, there exists $R$ such that $0 \le \rho < R < 1$. Let $\varepsilon = R - \rho > 0$. By the definition of limit of a sequence, there exists some integer $N$ such that

$$\left| \left| \frac{a_{n+1}}{a_n} \right| - \rho \right| < \varepsilon \text{ for all } n \ge N.$$

Therefore,

$$\left|\frac{a_{n+1}}{a_n}\right| < \rho + \varepsilon = R \text{ for all } n \ge N$$

and, thus,

$$\begin{aligned}
&|a_{N+1}| < R|a_N| \\
&|a_{N+2}| < R|a_{N+1}| < R^2|a_N| \\
&|a_{N+3}| < R|a_{N+2}| < R^2|a_{N+1}| < R^3|a_N| \\
&|a_{N+4}| < R|a_{N+3}| < R^2|a_{N+2}| < R^3|a_{N+1}| < R^4|a_N| \\
&\vdots .
\end{aligned}$$

Since $R < 1,$ the geometric series

$$R|a_N| + R^2|a_N| + R^3|a_N| + \cdots$$

converges. Given the inequalities above, we can apply the comparison test and conclude that the series

$$|a_{N+1}| + |a_{N+2}| + |a_{N+3}| + |a_{N+4}| + \cdots$$

converges. Therefore, since

$$\sum_{n=1}^{\infty} |a_n| = \sum_{n=1}^{N} |a_n| + \sum_{n=N+1}^{\infty} |a_n|$$

where $\sum_{n=1}^{N} |a_n|$ is a finite sum and $\sum_{n=N+1}^{\infty} |a_n|$ converges, we conclude that $\sum_{n=1}^{\infty} |a_n|$ converges.

For part ii.

$$\rho = \lim_{n \to \infty}\left|\frac{a_{n+1}}{a_n}\right| > 1.$$

Since $\rho > 1,$ there exists $R$ such that $\rho > R > 1.$ Let $\varepsilon = \rho - R > 0.$ By the definition of the limit of a sequence, there exists an integer $N$ such that

$$\left|\left|\frac{a_{n+1}}{a_n}\right| - \rho\right| < \varepsilon \text{ for all } n \ge N.$$

Therefore,

$$R = \rho - \varepsilon < \left|\frac{a_{n+1}}{a_n}\right| \text{ for all } n \ge N,$$

and, thus,

$$\begin{aligned}
&|a_{N+1}| > R|a_N| \\
&|a_{N+2}| > R|a_{N+1}| > R^2|a_N| \\
&|a_{N+3}| > R|a_{N+2}| > R^2|a_{N+1}| > R^3|a_N| \\
&|a_{N+4}| > R|a_{N+3}| > R^2|a_{N+2}| > R^3|a_{N+1}| > R^4|a_N|.
\end{aligned}$$

Since $R > 1,$ the geometric series

$$R|a_N| + R^2|a_N| + R^3|a_N| + \cdots$$

diverges. Applying the comparison test, we conclude that the series

$$|a_{N+1}| + |a_{N+2}| + |a_{N+3}| + \cdots$$

diverges, and therefore the series $\sum_{n=1}^{\infty} |a_n|$ diverges.

For part iii. we show that the test does not provide any information if $\rho = 1$ by considering the $p-$series $\sum_{n=1}^{\infty} 1/n^p.$

For any real number $p$,

$$\rho = \lim_{n \to \infty} \frac{1/(n+1)^p}{1/n^p} = \lim_{n \to \infty} \frac{n^p}{(n+1)^p} = 1.$$

However, we know that if $p \leq 1,$ the $p-$series $\sum_{n=1}^{\infty} 1/n^p$ diverges, whereas $\sum_{n=1}^{\infty} 1/n^p$ converges if $p > 1.$

□

The ratio test is particularly useful for series whose terms contain factorials or exponentials, where the ratio of terms simplifies the expression. The ratio test is convenient because it does not require us to find a comparative series. The drawback is that the test sometimes does not provide any information regarding convergence.

## Example 5.23

### Using the Ratio Test

For each of the following series, use the ratio test to determine whether the series converges or diverges.

a. $\sum_{n=1}^{\infty} \frac{2^n}{n!}$

b. $\sum_{n=1}^{\infty} \frac{n^n}{n!} \sum_{n=1}^{\infty} \frac{(-1)^n (n!)^2}{(2n)!}$

c. $\sum_{n=1}^{\infty} \frac{(-1)^n (n!)^2}{(2n)!}$

### Solution

a. From the ratio test, we can see that

$$\rho = \lim_{n \to \infty} \frac{2^{n+1}/(n+1)!}{2^n/n!} = \lim_{n \to \infty} \frac{2^{n+1}}{(n+1)!} \cdot \frac{n!}{2^n}.$$

Since $(n+1)! = (n+1) \cdot n!,$

$$\rho = \lim_{n \to \infty} \frac{2}{n+1} = 0.$$

Since $\rho < 1,$ the series converges.

b. We can see that

$$\begin{aligned}\rho &= \lim_{n\to\infty}\frac{(n+1)^{n+1}/(n+1)!}{n^n/n!}\\ &= \lim_{n\to\infty}\frac{(n+1)^{n+1}}{(n+1)!}\cdot\frac{n!}{n^n}\\ &= \lim_{n\to\infty}\left(\frac{n+1}{n}\right)^n = \lim_{n\to\infty}\left(1+\frac{1}{n}\right)^n = e.\end{aligned}$$

Since $\rho > 1,$ the series diverges.

c. Since

$$\begin{aligned}\left|\frac{(-1)^{n+1}((n+1)!)^2/(2(n+1))!}{(-1)^n(n!)^2/(2n)!}\right| &= \frac{(n+1)!(n+1)!}{(2n+2)!}\cdot\frac{(2n)!}{n!n!}\\ &= \frac{(n+1)(n+1)}{(2n+2)(2n+1)}\end{aligned}$$

we see that

$$\rho = \lim_{n\to\infty}\frac{(n+1)(n+1)}{(2n+2)(2n+1)} = \frac{1}{4}.$$

Since $\rho < 1,$ the series converges.

**5.21** Use the ratio test to determine whether the series $\sum_{n=1}^{\infty}\frac{n^3}{3^n}$ converges or diverges.

## Root Test

The approach of the **root test** is similar to that of the ratio test. Consider a series $\sum_{n=1}^{\infty} a_n$ such that $\lim_{n\to\infty}\sqrt[n]{|a_n|} = \rho$ for some real number $\rho$. Then for $N$ sufficiently large, $|a_N| \approx \rho^N$. Therefore, we can approximate $\sum_{n=N}^{\infty}|a_n|$ by writing

$$|a_N| + |a_{N+1}| + |a_{N+2}| + \cdots \approx \rho^N + \rho^{N+1} + \rho^{N+2} + \cdots.$$

The expression on the right-hand side is a geometric series. As in the ratio test, the series $\sum_{n=1}^{\infty} a_n$ converges absolutely if $0 \le \rho < 1$ and the series diverges if $\rho \ge 1$. If $\rho = 1,$ the test does not provide any information. For example, for any $p$-series, $\sum_{n=1}^{\infty} 1/n^p,$ we see that

$$\rho = \lim_{n\to\infty}\sqrt[n]{\left|\frac{1}{n^p}\right|} = \lim_{n\to\infty}\frac{1}{n^{p/n}}.$$

To evaluate this limit, we use the natural logarithm function. Doing so, we see that

$$\ln\rho = \ln\left(\lim_{n\to\infty}\frac{1}{n^{p/n}}\right) = \lim_{n\to\infty}\ln\left(\frac{1}{n}\right)^{p/n} = \lim_{n\to\infty}\frac{p}{n}\cdot\ln\left(\frac{1}{n}\right) = \lim_{n\to\infty}\frac{p\ln(1/n)}{n}.$$

Using L'Hôpital's rule, it follows that $\ln \rho = 0,$ and therefore $\rho = 1$ for all $p$. However, we know that the $p$-series only converges if $p > 1$ and diverges if $p < 1$.

### Theorem 5.17: Root Test

Consider the series $\sum_{n=1}^{\infty} a_n$. Let

$$\rho = \lim_{n \to \infty} \sqrt[n]{|a_n|}.$$

i. If $0 \le \rho < 1,$ then $\sum_{n=1}^{\infty} a_n$ converges absolutely.

ii. If $\rho > 1$ or $\rho = \infty,$ then $\sum_{n=1}^{\infty} a_n$ diverges.

iii. If $\rho = 1,$ the test does not provide any information.

The root test is useful for series whose terms involve exponentials. In particular, for a series whose terms $a_n$ satisfy $|a_n| = b_n^n,$ then $\sqrt[n]{|a_n|} = b_n$ and we need only evaluate $\lim_{n \to \infty} b_n$.

## Example 5.24

### Using the Root Test

For each of the following series, use the root test to determine whether the series converges or diverges.

a. $\sum_{n=1}^{\infty} \frac{(n^2 + 3n)^n}{(4n^2 + 5)^n}$

b. $\sum_{n=1}^{\infty} \frac{n^n}{(\ln(n))^n}$

#### Solution

a. To apply the root test, we compute

$$\rho = \lim_{n \to \infty} \sqrt[n]{(n^2 + 3n)^n / (4n^2 + 5)^n} = \lim_{n \to \infty} \frac{n^2 + 3n}{4n^2 + 5} = \frac{1}{4}.$$

Since $\rho < 1,$ the series converges absolutely.

b. We have

$$\rho = \lim_{n \to \infty} \sqrt[n]{n^n / (\ln n)^n} = \lim_{n \to \infty} \frac{n}{\ln n} = \infty \text{ by L'Hôpital's rule}.$$

Since $\rho = \infty,$ the series diverges.

**5.22** Use the root test to determine whether the series $\sum_{n=1}^{\infty} 1/n^n$ converges or diverges.

## Choosing a Convergence Test

At this point, we have a long list of convergence tests. However, not all tests can be used for all series. When given a series, we must determine which test is the best to use. Here is a strategy for finding the best test to apply.

### Problem-Solving Strategy: Choosing a Convergence Test for a Series

Consider a series $\sum_{n=1}^{\infty} a_n$. In the steps below, we outline a strategy for determining whether the series converges.

1. Is $\sum_{n=1}^{\infty} a_n$ a familiar series? For example, is it the harmonic series (which diverges) or the alternating harmonic series (which converges)? Is it a $p-$series or geometric series? If so, check the power $p$ or the ratio $r$ to determine if the series converges.
2. Is it an alternating series? Are we interested in absolute convergence or just convergence? If we are just interested in whether the series converges, apply the alternating series test. If we are interested in absolute convergence, proceed to step $3,$ considering the series of absolute values $\sum_{n=1}^{\infty} |a_n|.$
3. Is the series similar to a $p-$series or geometric series? If so, try the comparison test or limit comparison test.
4. Do the terms in the series contain a factorial or power? If the terms are powers such that $a_n = b_n^n,$ try the root test first. Otherwise, try the ratio test first.
5. Use the divergence test. If this test does not provide any information, try the integral test.

Visit this **website (http://www.openstaxcollege.org/l/20_series2)** for more information on testing series for convergence, plus general information on sequences and series.

## Example 5.25

### Using Convergence Tests

For each of the following series, determine which convergence test is the best to use and explain why. Then determine if the series converges or diverges. If the series is an alternating series, determine whether it converges absolutely, converges conditionally, or diverges.

a. $\sum_{n=1}^{\infty} \frac{n^2 + 2n}{n^3 + 3n^2 + 1}$

b. $\sum_{n=1}^{\infty} \frac{(-1)^{n+1}(3n+1)}{n!}$

c. $\sum_{n=1}^{\infty} \frac{e^n}{n^3}$

d. $\sum_{n=1}^{\infty} \frac{3^n}{(n+1)^n}$

### Solution

a. Step 1. The series is not a $p-$ series or geometric series.

Step 2. The series is not alternating.
Step 3. For large values of $n,$ we approximate the series by the expression

$$\frac{n^2+2n}{n^3+3n^2+1} \approx \frac{n^2}{n^3} = \frac{1}{n}.$$

Therefore, it seems reasonable to apply the comparison test or limit comparison test using the series $\sum_{n=1}^{\infty} 1/n.$ Using the limit comparison test, we see that

$$\lim_{n \to \infty} \frac{(n^2+2n)/(n^3+3n^2+1)}{1/n} = \lim_{n \to \infty} \frac{n^3+2n^2}{n^3+3n^2+1} = 1.$$

Since the series $\sum_{n=1}^{\infty} 1/n$ diverges, this series diverges as well.

b. Step 1.The series is not a familiar series.
Step 2. The series is alternating. Since we are interested in absolute convergence, consider the series

$$\sum_{n=1}^{\infty} \frac{3n}{(n+1)!}.$$

Step 3. The series is not similar to a $p$-series or geometric series.
Step 4. Since each term contains a factorial, apply the ratio test. We see that

$$\lim_{n \to \infty} \frac{(3(n+1))/(n+1)!}{(3n+1)/n!} = \lim_{n \to \infty} \frac{3n+3}{(n+1)!} \cdot \frac{n!}{3n+1} = \lim_{n \to \infty} \frac{3n+3}{(n+1)(3n+1)} = 0.$$

Therefore, this series converges, and we conclude that the original series converges absolutely, and thus converges.

c. Step 1. The series is not a familiar series.
Step 2. It is not an alternating series.
Step 3. There is no obvious series with which to compare this series.
Step 4. There is no factorial. There is a power, but it is not an ideal situation for the root test.
Step 5. To apply the divergence test, we calculate that

$$\lim_{n \to \infty} \frac{e^n}{n^3} = \infty.$$

Therefore, by the divergence test, the series diverges.

d. Step 1. This series is not a familiar series.
Step 2. It is not an alternating series.
Step 3. There is no obvious series with which to compare this series.
Step 4. Since each term is a power of $n,$ we can apply the root test. Since

$$\lim_{n \to \infty} \sqrt[n]{\left(\frac{3}{n+1}\right)^n} = \lim_{n \to \infty} \frac{3}{n+1} = 0,$$

by the root test, we conclude that the series converges.

**5.23** For the series $\sum_{n=1}^{\infty} \frac{2^n}{3^n + n}$, determine which convergence test is the best to use and explain why.

In **Table 5.3**, we summarize the convergence tests and when each can be applied. Note that while the comparison test, limit comparison test, and integral test require the series $\sum_{n=1}^{\infty} a_n$ to have nonnegative terms, if $\sum_{n=1}^{\infty} a_n$ has negative terms, these tests can be applied to $\sum_{n=1}^{\infty} |a_n|$ to test for absolute convergence.

| Series or Test | Conclusions | Comments |
|---|---|---|
| **Divergence Test**<br>For any series $\sum_{n=1}^{\infty} a_n,$ evaluate $\lim_{n \to \infty} a_n.$ | If $\lim_{n \to \infty} a_n = 0,$ the test is inconclusive.<br><br>If $\lim_{n \to \infty} a_n \neq 0,$ the series diverges. | This test cannot prove convergence of a series. |
| **Geometric Series**<br>$\sum_{n=1}^{\infty} ar^{n-1}$ | If $\lvert r \rvert < 1,$ the series converges to $a/(1-r).$<br><br>If $\lvert r \rvert \geq 1,$ the series diverges. | Any geometric series can be reindexed to be written in the form $a + ar + ar^2 + \cdots,$ where $a$ is the initial term and $r$ is the ratio. |
| ***p*-Series**<br>$\sum_{n=1}^{\infty} \frac{1}{n^p}$ | If $p > 1,$ the series converges.<br><br>If $p \leq 1,$ the series diverges. | For $p = 1,$ we have the harmonic series $\sum_{n=1}^{\infty} 1/n.$ |
| **Comparison Test**<br>For $\sum_{n=1}^{\infty} a_n$ with nonnegative terms, compare with a known series $\sum_{n=1}^{\infty} b_n.$ | If $a_n \leq b_n$ for all $n \geq N$ and $\sum_{n=1}^{\infty} b_n$ converges, then $\sum_{n=1}^{\infty} a_n$ converges.<br><br>If $a_n \geq b_n$ for all $n \geq N$ and $\sum_{n=1}^{\infty} b_n$ diverges, then $\sum_{n=1}^{\infty} a_n$ diverges. | Typically used for a series similar to a geometric or $p$-series. It can sometimes be difficult to find an appropriate series. |
| **Limit Comparison Test**<br>For $\sum_{n=1}^{\infty} a_n$ with positive terms, compare with a series $\sum_{n=1}^{\infty} b_n$ by evaluating $L = \lim_{n \to \infty} \frac{a_n}{b_n}.$ | If $L$ is a real number and $L \neq 0,$ then $\sum_{n=1}^{\infty} a_n$ and $\sum_{n=1}^{\infty} b_n$ both converge or both diverge. | Typically used for a series similar to a geometric or $p$-series. Often easier to apply than the comparison test. |

Table 5.3 Summary of Convergence Tests

| Series or Test | Conclusions | Comments |
|---|---|---|
| | If $L = 0$ and $\sum_{n=1}^{\infty} b_n$ converges, then $\sum_{n=1}^{\infty} a_n$ converges. | |
| | If $L = \infty$ and $\sum_{n=1}^{\infty} b_n$ diverges, then $\sum_{n=1}^{\infty} a_n$ diverges. | |
| **Integral Test** If there exists a positive, continuous, decreasing function $f$ such that $a_n = f(n)$ for all $n \geq N$, evaluate $\int_N^{\infty} f(x)dx.$ | $\int_N^{\infty} f(x)dx$ and $\sum_{n=1}^{\infty} a_n$ both converge or both diverge. | Limited to those series for which the corresponding function $f$ can be easily integrated. |
| **Alternating Series** $\sum_{n=1}^{\infty} (-1)^{n+1} b_n$ or $\sum_{n=1}^{\infty} (-1)^n b_n$ | If $b_{n+1} \leq b_n$ for all $n \geq 1$ and $b_n \to 0,$ then the series converges. | Only applies to alternating series. |
| **Ratio Test** For any series $\sum_{n=1}^{\infty} a_n$ with nonzero terms, let $\rho = \lim_{n \to \infty} \left\lvert \frac{a_{n+1}}{a_n} \right\rvert.$ | If $0 \leq \rho < 1,$ the series converges absolutely. | Often used for series involving factorials or exponentials. |
| | If $\rho > 1 \text{ or } \rho = \infty,$ the series diverges. | |
| | If $\rho = 1,$ the test is inconclusive. | |
| **Root Test** For any series $\sum_{n=1}^{\infty} a_n,$ let $\rho = \lim_{n \to \infty} \sqrt[n]{\lvert a_n \rvert}.$ | If $0 \leq \rho < 1,$ the series converges absolutely. | Often used for series where $\lvert a_n \rvert = b_n^n.$ |
| | If $\rho > 1 \text{ or } \rho = \infty,$ the series diverges. | |

**Table 5.3** Summary of Convergence Tests

| Series or Test | Conclusions | Comments |
|---|---|---|
| | If $\rho = 1,$ the test is inconclusive. | |

**Table 5.3** Summary of Convergence Tests

# Student PROJECT

## Series Converging to $\pi$ and $1/\pi$

Dozens of series exist that converge to $\pi$ or an algebraic expression containing $\pi$. Here we look at several examples and compare their rates of convergence. By rate of convergence, we mean the number of terms necessary for a partial sum to be within a certain amount of the actual value. The series representations of $\pi$ in the first two examples can be explained using Maclaurin series, which are discussed in the next chapter. The third example relies on material beyond the scope of this text.

1. The series

$$\pi = 4\sum_{n=1}^{\infty} \frac{(-1)^{n+1}}{2n-1} = 4 - \frac{4}{3} + \frac{4}{5} - \frac{4}{7} + \frac{4}{9} - \cdots$$

was discovered by Gregory and Leibniz in the late 1600s. This result follows from the Maclaurin series for $f(x) = \tan^{-1} x$. We will discuss this series in the next chapter.

   a. Prove that this series converges.
   b. Evaluate the partial sums $S_n$ for $n = 10, 20, 50, 100$.
   c. Use the remainder estimate for alternating series to get a bound on the error $R_n$.
   d. What is the smallest value of $N$ that guarantees $|R_N| < 0.01$? Evaluate $S_N$.

2. The series

$$\begin{aligned}\pi &= 6\sum_{n=0}^{\infty} \frac{(2n)!}{2^{4n+1}(n!)^2(2n+1)} \\ &= 6\left(\frac{1}{2} + \frac{1}{2\cdot 3}\left(\frac{1}{2}\right)^3 + \frac{1\cdot 3}{2\cdot 4\cdot 5}\cdot\left(\frac{1}{2}\right)^5 + \frac{1\cdot 3\cdot 5}{2\cdot 4\cdot 6\cdot 7}\left(\frac{1}{2}\right)^7 + \cdots\right)\end{aligned}$$

has been attributed to Newton in the late 1600s. The proof of this result uses the Maclaurin series for $f(x) = \sin^{-1} x$.

   a. Prove that the series converges.
   b. Evaluate the partial sums $S_n$ for $n = 5, 10, 20$.
   c. Compare $S_n$ to $\pi$ for $n = 5, 10, 20$ and discuss the number of correct decimal places.

3. The series

$$\frac{1}{\pi} = \frac{\sqrt{8}}{9801}\sum_{n=0}^{\infty} \frac{(4n)!(1103 + 26390n)}{(n!)^4 396^{4n}}$$

was discovered by Ramanujan in the early 1900s. William Gosper, Jr., used this series to calculate $\pi$ to an accuracy of more than 17 million digits in the mid-1980s. At the time, that was a world record. Since that time, this series and others by Ramanujan have led mathematicians to find many other series representations for $\pi$ and $1/\pi$.

   a. Prove that this series converges.
   b. Evaluate the first term in this series. Compare this number with the value of $\pi$ from a calculating

utility. To how many decimal places do these two numbers agree? What if we add the first two terms in the series?

c. Investigate the life of Srinivasa Ramanujan (1887–1920) and write a brief summary. Ramanujan is one of the most fascinating stories in the history of mathematics. He was basically self-taught, with no formal training in mathematics, yet he contributed in highly original ways to many advanced areas of mathematics.

# 5.6 EXERCISES

Use the ratio test to determine whether $\sum_{n=1}^{\infty} a_n$ converges, where $a_n$ is given in the following problems. State if the ratio test is inconclusive.

317. $a_n = 1/n!$

318. $a_n = 10^n/n!$

319. $a_n = n^2/2^n$

320. $a_n = n^{10}/2^n$

321. $\sum_{n=1}^{\infty} \frac{(n!)^3}{(3n!)}$

322. $\sum_{n=1}^{\infty} \frac{2^{3n}(n!)^3}{(3n!)}$

323. $\sum_{n=1}^{\infty} \frac{(2n)!}{n^{2n}}$

324. $\sum_{n=1}^{\infty} \frac{(2n)!}{(2n)^n}$

325. $\sum_{n=1}^{\infty} \frac{n!}{(n/e)^n}$

326. $\sum_{n=1}^{\infty} \frac{(2n)!}{(n/e)^{2n}}$

327. $\sum_{n=1}^{\infty} \frac{(2^n n!)^2}{(2n)^{2n}}$

Use the root test to determine whether $\sum_{n=1}^{\infty} a_n$ converges, where $a_n$ is as follows.

328. $a_k = \left(\frac{k-1}{2k+3}\right)^k$

329. $a_k = \left(\frac{2k^2-1}{k^2+3}\right)^k$

330. $a_n = \frac{(\ln n)^{2n}}{n^n}$

331. $a_n = n/2^n$

332. $a_n = n/e^n$

333. $a_k = \frac{k^e}{e^k}$

334. $a_k = \frac{\pi^k}{k^\pi}$

335. $a_n = \left(\frac{1}{e} + \frac{1}{n}\right)^n$

336. $a_k = \frac{1}{(1+\ln k)^k}$

337. $a_n = \frac{(\ln(1+\ln n))^n}{(\ln n)^n}$

In the following exercises, use either the ratio test or the root test as appropriate to determine whether the series $\sum_{k=1}^{\infty} a_k$ with given terms $a_k$ converges, or state if the test is inconclusive.

338. $a_k = \frac{k!}{1 \cdot 3 \cdot 5 \cdots (2k-1)}$

339. $a_k = \frac{2 \cdot 4 \cdot 6 \cdots 2k}{(2k)!}$

340. $a_k = \frac{1 \cdot 4 \cdot 7 \cdots (3k-2)}{3^k k!}$

341. $a_n = \left(1 - \frac{1}{n}\right)^{n^2}$

342. $a_k = \left(\frac{1}{k+1} + \frac{1}{k+2} + \cdots + \frac{1}{2k}\right)^k$ (*Hint:* Compare $a_k^{1/k}$ to $\int_k^{2k} \frac{dt}{t}$.)

343. $a_k = \left(\frac{1}{k+1} + \frac{1}{k+2} + \cdots + \frac{1}{3k}\right)^k$

344. $a_n = (n^{1/n} - 1)^n$

Use the ratio test to determine whether $\sum_{n=1}^{\infty} a_n$ converges, or state if the ratio test is inconclusive.

345. $\sum_{n=1}^{\infty} \frac{3^{n^2}}{2^{n^3}}$

346. $\sum_{n=1}^{\infty} \frac{2^{n^2}}{n^n n!}$

Use the root and limit comparison tests to determine whether $\sum_{n=1}^{\infty} a_n$ converges.

347. $a_n = 1/x_n^n$ where $x_{n+1} = \frac{1}{2}x_n + \frac{1}{x_n}$, $x_1 = 1$ (*Hint:* Find limit of $\{x_n\}$.)

In the following exercises, use an appropriate test to determine whether the series converges.

348. $\sum_{n=1}^{\infty} \frac{(n+1)}{n^3 + n^2 + n + 1}$

349. $\sum_{n=1}^{\infty} \frac{(-1)^{n+1}(n+1)}{n^3 + 3n^2 + 3n + 1}$

350. $\sum_{n=1}^{\infty} \frac{(n+1)^2}{n^3 + (1.1)^n}$

351. $\sum_{n=1}^{\infty} \frac{(n-1)^n}{(n+1)^n}$

352. $a_n = \left(1 + \frac{1}{n^2}\right)^n$ (*Hint:* $\left(1 + \frac{1}{n^2}\right)^{n^2} \approx e$.)

353. $a_k = 1/2^{\sin^2 k}$

354. $a_k = 2^{-\sin(1/k)}$

355. $a_n = 1/\binom{n+2}{n}$ where $\binom{n}{k} = \frac{n!}{k!(n-k)!}$

356. $a_k = 1/\binom{2k}{k}$

357. $a_k = 2^k/\binom{3k}{k}$

358. $a_k = \left(\frac{k}{k + \ln k}\right)^k$ (*Hint:* $a_k = \left(1 + \frac{\ln k}{k}\right)^{-(k/\ln k)\ln k} \approx e^{-\ln k}$.)

359. $a_k = \left(\frac{k}{k + \ln k}\right)^{2k}$ (*Hint:* $a_k = \left(1 + \frac{\ln k}{k}\right)^{-(k/\ln k)\ln k^2}$.)

The following series converge by the ratio test. Use summation by parts, $\sum_{k=1}^{n} a_k(b_{k+1} - b_k) = [a_{n+1}b_{n+1} - a_1 b_1] - \sum_{k=1}^{n} b_{k+1}(a_{k+1} - a_k)$, to find the sum of the given series.

360. $\sum_{k=1}^{\infty} \frac{k}{2^k}$ (*Hint:* Take $a_k = k$ and $b_k = 2^{1-k}$.)

361. $\sum_{k=1}^{\infty} \frac{k}{c^k}$, where $c > 1$ (*Hint:* Take $a_k = k$ and $b_k = c^{1-k}/(c-1)$.)

362. $\sum_{n=1}^{\infty} \frac{n^2}{2^n}$

363. $\sum_{n=1}^{\infty} \frac{(n+1)^2}{2^n}$

The $k$th term of each of the following series has a factor $x^k$. Find the range of $x$ for which the ratio test implies that the series converges.

364. $\sum_{k=1}^{\infty} \frac{x^k}{k^2}$

365. $\sum_{k=1}^{\infty} \frac{x^{2k}}{k^2}$

366. $\sum_{k=1}^{\infty} \frac{x^{2k}}{3^k}$

367. $\sum_{k=1}^{\infty} \frac{x^k}{k!}$

368. Does there exist a number $p$ such that $\sum_{n=1}^{\infty} \frac{2^n}{n^p}$ converges?

369. Let $0 < r < 1$. For which real numbers $p$ does $\sum_{n=1}^{\infty} n^p r^n$ converge?

370. Suppose that $\lim_{n \to \infty} \left| \frac{a_{n+1}}{a_n} \right| = p.$ For which values of $p$ must $\sum_{n=1}^{\infty} 2^n a_n$ converge?

371. Suppose that $\lim_{n \to \infty} \left| \frac{a_{n+1}}{a_n} \right| = p.$ For which values of $r > 0$ is $\sum_{n=1}^{\infty} r^n a_n$ guaranteed to converge?

372. Suppose that $\left| \frac{a_{n+1}}{a_n} \right| \le (n+1)^p$ for all $n = 1, 2, \ldots$ where $p$ is a fixed real number. For which values of $p$ is $\sum_{n=1}^{\infty} n!\, a_n$ guaranteed to converge?

373. For which values of $r > 0,$ if any, does $\sum_{n=1}^{\infty} r^{\sqrt{n}}$ converge? (*Hint:* $\sum_{n=1}^{\infty} a_n = \sum_{k=1}^{\infty} \sum_{n=k^2}^{(k+1)^2 - 1} a_n.$)

374. Suppose that $\left| \frac{a_{n+2}}{a_n} \right| \le r < 1$ for all $n.$ Can you conclude that $\sum_{n=1}^{\infty} a_n$ converges?

375. Let $a_n = 2^{-[n/2]}$ where $[x]$ is the greatest integer less than or equal to $x.$ Determine whether $\sum_{n=1}^{\infty} a_n$ converges and justify your answer.

The following *advanced* exercises use a generalized ratio test to determine convergence of some series that arise in particular applications when tests in this chapter, including the ratio and root test, are not powerful enough to determine their convergence. The test states that if $\lim_{n \to \infty} \frac{a_{2n}}{a_n} < 1/2,$ then $\sum a_n$ converges, while if $\lim_{n \to \infty} \frac{a_{2n+1}}{a_n} > 1/2,$ then $\sum a_n$ diverges.

376. Let $a_n = \frac{1}{4} \frac{3}{6} \frac{5}{8} \cdots \frac{2n-1}{2n+2} = \frac{1 \cdot 3 \cdot 5 \cdots (2n-1)}{2^n (n+1)!}.$ Explain why the ratio test cannot determine convergence of $\sum_{n=1}^{\infty} a_n.$ Use the fact that $1 - 1/(4k)$ is increasing $k$ to estimate $\lim_{n \to \infty} \frac{a_{2n}}{a_n}.$

377. Let $a_n = \frac{1}{1+x} \frac{2}{2+x} \cdots \frac{n}{n+x} \frac{1}{n} = \frac{(n-1)!}{(1+x)(2+x)\cdots(n+x)}.$ Show that $a_{2n}/a_n \le e^{-x/2}/2.$ For which $x > 0$ does the generalized ratio test imply convergence of $\sum_{n=1}^{\infty} a_n?$ (*Hint:* Write $2a_{2n}/a_n$ as a product of $n$ factors each smaller than $1/(1 + x/(2n)).$)

378. Let $a_n = \frac{n^{\ln n}}{(\ln n)^n}.$ Show that $\frac{a_{2n}}{a_n} \to 0$ as $n \to \infty.$

# CHAPTER 5 REVIEW

## KEY TERMS

**absolute convergence** if the series $\sum_{n=1}^{\infty} |a_n|$ converges, the series $\sum_{n=1}^{\infty} a_n$ is said to converge absolutely

**alternating series** a series of the form $\sum_{n=1}^{\infty} (-1)^{n+1} b_n$ or $\sum_{n=1}^{\infty} (-1)^n b_n,$ where $b_n \geq 0,$ is called an alternating series

**alternating series test** for an alternating series of either form, if $b_{n+1} \leq b_n$ for all integers $n \geq 1$ and $b_n \to 0,$ then an alternating series converges

**arithmetic sequence** a sequence in which the difference between every pair of consecutive terms is the same is called an arithmetic sequence

**bounded above** a sequence $\{a_n\}$ is bounded above if there exists a constant $M$ such that $a_n \leq M$ for all positive integers $n$

**bounded below** a sequence $\{a_n\}$ is bounded below if there exists a constant $M$ such that $M \leq a_n$ for all positive integers $n$

**bounded sequence** a sequence $\{a_n\}$ is bounded if there exists a constant $M$ such that $|a_n| \leq M$ for all positive integers $n$

**comparison test** if $0 \leq a_n \leq b_n$ for all $n \geq N$ and $\sum_{n=1}^{\infty} b_n$ converges, then $\sum_{n=1}^{\infty} a_n$ converges; if $a_n \geq b_n \geq 0$ for all $n \geq N$ and $\sum_{n=1}^{\infty} b_n$ diverges, then $\sum_{n=1}^{\infty} a_n$ diverges

**conditional convergence** if the series $\sum_{n=1}^{\infty} a_n$ converges, but the series $\sum_{n=1}^{\infty} |a_n|$ diverges, the series $\sum_{n=1}^{\infty} a_n$ is said to converge conditionally

**convergence of a series** a series converges if the sequence of partial sums for that series converges

**convergent sequence** a convergent sequence is a sequence $\{a_n\}$ for which there exists a real number $L$ such that $a_n$ is arbitrarily close to $L$ as long as $n$ is sufficiently large

**divergence of a series** a series diverges if the sequence of partial sums for that series diverges

**divergence test** if $\lim_{n \to \infty} a_n \neq 0,$ then the series $\sum_{n=1}^{\infty} a_n$ diverges

**divergent sequence** a sequence that is not convergent is divergent

**explicit formula** a sequence may be defined by an explicit formula such that $a_n = f(n)$

**geometric sequence** a sequence $\{a_n\}$ in which the ratio $a_{n+1}/a_n$ is the same for all positive integers $n$ is called a geometric sequence

**geometric series** a geometric series is a series that can be written in the form

$$\sum_{n=1}^{\infty} ar^{n-1} = a + ar + ar^2 + ar^3 + \cdots$$

**harmonic series** the harmonic series takes the form

$$\sum_{n=1}^{\infty} \frac{1}{n} = 1 + \frac{1}{2} + \frac{1}{3} + \cdots$$

**index variable** the subscript used to define the terms in a sequence is called the index

**infinite series** an infinite series is an expression of the form

$$a_1 + a_2 + a_3 + \cdots = \sum_{n=1}^{\infty} a_n$$

**integral test** for a series $\sum_{n=1}^{\infty} a_n$ with positive terms $a_n,$ if there exists a continuous, decreasing function $f$ such that $f(n) = a_n$ for all positive integers $n,$ then

$$\sum_{n=1}^{\infty} a_n \text{and} \int_1^{\infty} f(x)dx$$

either both converge or both diverge

**limit comparison test** suppose $a_n,\ b_n \geq 0$ for all $n \geq 1.$ If $\lim_{n \to \infty} a_n/b_n \to L \neq 0,$ then $\sum_{n=1}^{\infty} a_n$ and $\sum_{n=1}^{\infty} b_n$ both converge or both diverge; if $\lim_{n \to \infty} a_n/b_n \to 0$ and $\sum_{n=1}^{\infty} b_n$ converges, then $\sum_{n=1}^{\infty} a_n$ converges. If $\lim_{n \to \infty} a_n/b_n \to \infty,$ and $\sum_{n=1}^{\infty} b_n$ diverges, then $\sum_{n=1}^{\infty} a_n$ diverges

**limit of a sequence** the real number $L$ to which a sequence converges is called the limit of the sequence

**monotone sequence** an increasing or decreasing sequence

***p*-series** a series of the form $\sum_{n=1}^{\infty} 1/n^p$

**partial sum** the $k$th partial sum of the infinite series $\sum_{n=1}^{\infty} a_n$ is the finite sum

$$S_k = \sum_{n=1}^{k} a_n = a_1 + a_2 + a_3 + \cdots + a_k$$

**ratio test** for a series $\sum_{n=1}^{\infty} a_n$ with nonzero terms, let $\rho = \lim_{n \to \infty} |a_{n+1}/a_n|;$ if $0 \leq \rho < 1,$ the series converges absolutely; if $\rho > 1,$ the series diverges; if $\rho = 1,$ the test is inconclusive

**recurrence relation** a recurrence relation is a relationship in which a term $a_n$ in a sequence is defined in terms of earlier terms in the sequence

**remainder estimate** for a series $\sum_{n=1}^{\infty} a_n$ with positive terms $a_n$ and a continuous, decreasing function $f$ such that $f(n) = a_n$ for all positive integers $n,$ the remainder $R_N = \sum_{n=1}^{\infty} a_n - \sum_{n=1}^{N} a_n$ satisfies the following estimate:

$$\int_{N+1}^{\infty} f(x)dx < R_N < \int_N^{\infty} f(x)dx$$

**root test** for a series $\sum_{n=1}^{\infty} a_n,$ let $\rho = \lim_{n \to \infty} \sqrt[n]{|a_n|};$ if $0 \le \rho < 1,$ the series converges absolutely; if $\rho > 1,$ the series diverges; if $\rho = 1,$ the test is inconclusive

**sequence** an ordered list of numbers of the form $a_1, a_2, a_3,\ldots$ is a sequence

**telescoping series** a telescoping series is one in which most of the terms cancel in each of the partial sums

**term** the number $a_n$ in the sequence $\{a_n\}$ is called the $n$th term of the sequence

**unbounded sequence** a sequence that is not bounded is called unbounded

# KEY EQUATIONS

- **Harmonic series**

  $$\sum_{n=1}^{\infty} \frac{1}{n} = 1 + \frac{1}{2} + \frac{1}{3} + \frac{1}{4} + \cdots$$

- **Sum of a geometric series**

  $$\sum_{n=1}^{\infty} ar^{n-1} = \frac{a}{1-r} \text{ for } |r| < 1$$

- **Divergence test**

  $$\text{If } a_n \nrightarrow 0 \text{ as } n \to \infty, \sum_{n=1}^{\infty} a_n \text{ diverges.}$$

- ***p*-series**

  $$\sum_{n=1}^{\infty} \frac{1}{n^p} \begin{cases} \text{converges if } p > 1 \\ \text{diverges if } p \le 1 \end{cases}$$

- **Remainder estimate from the integral test**

  $$\int_{N+1}^{\infty} f(x)dx < R_N < \int_{N}^{\infty} f(x)dx$$

- **Alternating series**

  $$\sum_{n=1}^{\infty} (-1)^{n+1} b_n = b_1 - b_2 + b_3 - b_4 + \cdots \text{ or}$$

  $$\sum_{n=1}^{\infty} (-1)^{n} b_n = -b_1 + b_2 - b_3 + b_4 - \cdots$$

# KEY CONCEPTS

## 5.1 Sequences

- To determine the convergence of a sequence given by an explicit formula $a_n = f(n),$ we use the properties of limits for functions.
- If $\{a_n\}$ and $\{b_n\}$ are convergent sequences that converge to $A$ and $B,$ respectively, and $c$ is any real number, then the sequence $\{ca_n\}$ converges to $c \cdot A,$ the sequences $\{a_n \pm b_n\}$ converge to $A \pm B,$ the sequence $\{a_n \cdot b_n\}$ converges to $A \cdot B,$ and the sequence $\{a_n / b_n\}$ converges to $A/B,$ provided $B \ne 0.$
- If a sequence is bounded and monotone, then it converges, but not all convergent sequences are monotone.
- If a sequence is unbounded, it diverges, but not all divergent sequences are unbounded.
- The geometric sequence $\{r^n\}$ converges if and only if $|r| < 1$ or $r = 1.$

## 5.2 Infinite Series

- Given the infinite series

$$\sum_{n=1}^{\infty} a_n = a_1 + a_2 + a_3 + \cdots$$

and the corresponding sequence of partial sums $\{S_k\}$ where

$$S_k = \sum_{n=1}^{k} a_n = a_1 + a_2 + a_3 + \cdots + a_k,$$

the series converges if and only if the sequence $\{S_k\}$ converges.

- The geometric series $\sum_{n=1}^{\infty} ar^{n-1}$ converges if $|r| < 1$ and diverges if $|r| \geq 1$. For $|r| < 1$,

$$\sum_{n=1}^{\infty} ar^{n-1} = \frac{a}{1-r}.$$

- The harmonic series

$$\sum_{n=1}^{\infty} \frac{1}{n} = 1 + \frac{1}{2} + \frac{1}{3} + \cdots$$

diverges.

- A series of the form $\sum_{n=1}^{\infty} [b_n - b_{n+1}] = [b_1 - b_2] + [b_2 - b_3] + [b_3 - b_4] + \cdots + [b_n - b_{n+1}] + \cdots$ is a telescoping series. The $k$th partial sum of this series is given by $S_k = b_1 - b_{k+1}$. The series will converge if and only if $\lim_{k \to \infty} b_{k+1}$ exists. In that case,

$$\sum_{n=1}^{\infty} [b_n - b_{n+1}] = b_1 - \lim_{k \to \infty} (b_{k+1}).$$

## 5.3 The Divergence and Integral Tests

- If $\lim_{n \to \infty} a_n \neq 0$, then the series $\sum_{n=1}^{\infty} a_n$ diverges.

- If $\lim_{n \to \infty} a_n = 0$, the series $\sum_{n=1}^{\infty} a_n$ may converge or diverge.

- If $\sum_{n=1}^{\infty} a_n$ is a series with positive terms $a_n$ and $f$ is a continuous, decreasing function such that $f(n) = a_n$ for all positive integers $n$, then

$$\sum_{n=1}^{\infty} a_n \text{ and} \int_1^{\infty} f(x)dx$$

either both converge or both diverge. Furthermore, if $\sum_{n=1}^{\infty} a_n$ converges, then the $N$th partial sum approximation

$S_N$ is accurate up to an error $R_N$ where $\int_{N+1}^{\infty} f(x)dx < R_N < \int_{N}^{\infty} f(x)dx.$

- The $p$-series $\sum_{n=1}^{\infty} 1/n^p$ converges if $p > 1$ and diverges if $p \leq 1$.

## 5.4 Comparison Tests

- The comparison tests are used to determine convergence or divergence of series with positive terms.
- When using the comparison tests, a series $\sum_{n=1}^{\infty} a_n$ is often compared to a geometric or $p$-series.

## 5.5 Alternating Series

- For an alternating series $\sum_{n=1}^{\infty} (-1)^{n+1} b_n,$ if $b_{k+1} \leq b_k$ for all $k$ and $b_k \to 0$ as $k \to \infty,$ the alternating series converges.
- If $\sum_{n=1}^{\infty} |a_n|$ converges, then $\sum_{n=1}^{\infty} a_n$ converges.

## 5.6 Ratio and Root Tests

- For the ratio test, we consider

$$\rho = \lim_{n \to \infty} \left|\frac{a_{n+1}}{a_n}\right|.$$

If $\rho < 1,$ the series $\sum_{n=1}^{\infty} a_n$ converges absolutely. If $\rho > 1,$ the series diverges. If $\rho = 1,$ the test does not provide any information. This test is useful for series whose terms involve factorials.

- For the root test, we consider

$$\rho = \lim_{n \to \infty} \sqrt[n]{|a_n|}.$$

If $\rho < 1,$ the series $\sum_{n=1}^{\infty} a_n$ converges absolutely. If $\rho > 1,$ the series diverges. If $\rho = 1,$ the test does not provide any information. The root test is useful for series whose terms involve powers.

- For a series that is similar to a geometric series or $p-$ series, consider one of the comparison tests.

# CHAPTER 5 REVIEW EXERCISES

*True or False?* Justify your answer with a proof or a counterexample.

**379.** If $\lim_{n \to \infty} a_n = 0,$ then $\sum_{n=1}^{\infty} a_n$ converges.

**380.** If $\lim_{n \to \infty} a_n \neq 0,$ then $\sum_{n=1}^{\infty} a_n$ diverges.

**381.** If $\sum_{n=1}^{\infty} |a_n|$ converges, then $\sum_{n=1}^{\infty} a_n$ converges.

**382.** If $\sum_{n=1}^{\infty} 2^n a_n$ converges, then $\sum_{n=1}^{\infty} (-2)^n a_n$ converges.

Is the sequence bounded, monotone, and convergent or divergent? If it is convergent, find the limit.

**383.** $a_n = \frac{3 + n^2}{1 - n}$

**384.** $a_n = \ln\left(\frac{1}{n}\right)$

**385.** $a_n = \frac{\ln(n + 1)}{\sqrt{n + 1}}$

**386.** $a_n = \frac{2^{n + 1}}{5^n}$

**387.** $a_n = \frac{\ln(\cos n)}{n}$

Is the series convergent or divergent?

**388.** $\sum_{n = 1}^{\infty} \frac{1}{n^2 + 5n + 4}$

**389.** $\sum_{n = 1}^{\infty} \ln\left(\frac{n + 1}{n}\right)$

**390.** $\sum_{n = 1}^{\infty} \frac{2^n}{n^4}$

**391.** $\sum_{n = 1}^{\infty} \frac{e^n}{n!}$

**392.** $\sum_{n = 1}^{\infty} n^{-(n + 1/n)}$

Is the series convergent or divergent? If convergent, is it absolutely convergent?

**393.** $\sum_{n = 1}^{\infty} \frac{(-1)^n}{\sqrt{n}}$

**394.** $\sum_{n = 1}^{\infty} \frac{(-1)^n n!}{3^n}$

**395.** $\sum_{n = 1}^{\infty} \frac{(-1)^n n!}{n^n}$

**396.** $\sum_{n = 1}^{\infty} \sin\left(\frac{n\pi}{2}\right)$

**397.** $\sum_{n = 1}^{\infty} \cos(\pi n)e^{-n}$

Evaluate

**398.** $\sum_{n = 1}^{\infty} \frac{2^{n + 4}}{7^n}$

**399.** $\sum_{n = 1}^{\infty} \frac{1}{(n + 1)(n + 2)}$

**400.** A legend from India tells that a mathematician invented chess for a king. The king enjoyed the game so much he allowed the mathematician to demand any payment. The mathematician asked for one grain of rice for the first square on the chessboard, two grains of rice for the second square on the chessboard, and so on. Find an exact expression for the total payment (in grains of rice) requested by the mathematician. Assuming there are 30,000 grains of rice in 1 pound, and 2000 pounds in 1 ton, how many tons of rice did the mathematician attempt to receive?

The following problems consider a simple population model of the housefly, which can be exhibited by the recursive formula $x_{n + 1} = bx_n$, where $x_n$ is the population of houseflies at generation $n$, and $b$ is the average number of offspring per housefly who survive to the next generation. Assume a starting population $x_0$.

**401.** Find $\lim_{n \to \infty} x_n$ if $b > 1$, $b < 1$, and $b = 1$.

**402.** Find an expression for $S_n = \sum_{i = 0}^{n} x_i$ in terms of $b$ and $x_0$. What does it physically represent?

**403.** If $b = \frac{3}{4}$ and $x_0 = 100$, find $S_{10}$ and $\lim_{n \to \infty} S_n$

**404.** For what values of $b$ will the series converge and diverge? What does the series converge to?

# 6 | POWER SERIES

Figure 6.1 If you win a lottery, do you get more money by taking a lump-sum payment or by accepting fixed payments over time? (credit: modification of work by Robert Huffstutter, Flickr)

## Chapter Outline



# Introduction

When winning a lottery, sometimes an individual has an option of receiving winnings in one lump-sum payment or receiving smaller payments over fixed time intervals. For example, you might have the option of receiving 20 million dollars today or receiving 1.5 million dollars each year for the next 20 years. Which is the better deal? Certainly 1.5 million dollars over 20 years is equivalent to 30 million dollars. However, receiving the 20 million dollars today would allow you to invest the money.

Alternatively, what if you were guaranteed to receive 1 million dollars every year indefinitely (extending to your heirs) or receive 20 million dollars today. Which would be the better deal? To answer these questions, you need to know how to use infinite series to calculate the value of periodic payments over time in terms of today's dollars (see **Example 6.7**).

An infinite series of the form $\sum_{n=0}^{\infty} c_n x^n$ is known as a power series. Since the terms contain the variable x, power series can be used to define functions. They can be used to represent given functions, but they are also important because they allow us to write functions that cannot be expressed any other way than as “infinite polynomials.” In addition, power series can be easily differentiated and integrated, thus being useful in solving differential equations and integrating complicated functions. An infinite series can also be truncated, resulting in a finite polynomial that we can use to approximate functional values. Power series have applications in a variety of fields, including physics, chemistry, biology, and economics. As we will see in this chapter, representing functions using power series allows us to solve mathematical problems that cannot be solved with other techniques.

# 6.1 | Power Series and Functions

**Learning Objectives**

- **6.1.1** Identify a power series and provide examples of them.
- **6.1.2** Determine the radius of convergence and interval of convergence of a power series.
- **6.1.3** Use a power series to represent a function.

A power series is a type of series with terms involving a variable. More specifically, if the variable is $x$, then all the terms of the series involve powers of $x$. As a result, a power series can be thought of as an infinite polynomial. Power series are used to represent common functions and also to define new functions. In this section we define power series and show how to determine when a power series converges and when it diverges. We also show how to represent certain functions using power series.

## Form of a Power Series

A series of the form

$$\sum_{n=0}^{\infty} c_n x^n = c_0 + c_1 x + c_2 x^2 + \cdots,$$

where $x$ is a variable and the coefficients $c_n$ are constants, is known as a **power series**. The series

$$1 + x + x^2 + \cdots = \sum_{n=0}^{\infty} x^n$$

is an example of a power series. Since this series is a geometric series with ratio $r = |x|$, we know that it converges if $|x| < 1$ and diverges if $|x| \geq 1$.

**Definition**

A series of the form

$$\sum_{n=0}^{\infty} c_n x^n = c_0 + c_1 x + c_2 x^2 + \cdots \tag{6.1}$$

is a power series centered at $x = 0$. A series of the form

$$\sum_{n=0}^{\infty} c_n (x-a)^n = c_0 + c_1 (x-a) + c_2 (x-a)^2 + \cdots \tag{6.2}$$

is a power series centered at $x = a$.

To make this definition precise, we stipulate that $x^0 = 1$ and $(x-a)^0 = 1$ even when $x = 0$ and $x = a$, respectively.

The series

$$\sum_{n=0}^{\infty} \frac{x^n}{n!} = 1 + x + \frac{x^2}{2!} + \frac{x^3}{3!} + \cdots$$

and

$$\sum_{n=0}^{\infty} n!x^n = 1 + x + 2!x^2 + 3!x^3 + \cdots$$

are both power series centered at $x = 0.$ The series

$$\sum_{n=0}^{\infty} \frac{(x-2)^n}{(n+1)3^n} = 1 + \frac{x-2}{2 \cdot 3} + \frac{(x-2)^2}{3 \cdot 3^2} + \frac{(x-2)^3}{4 \cdot 3^3} + \cdots$$

is a power series centered at $x = 2.$

## Convergence of a Power Series

Since the terms in a power series involve a variable $x$, the series may converge for certain values of $x$ and diverge for other values of $x$. For a power series centered at $x = a,$ the value of the series at $x = a$ is given by $c_0.$ Therefore, a power series always converges at its center. Some power series converge only at that value of $x$. Most power series, however, converge for more than one value of $x$. In that case, the power series either converges for all real numbers $x$ or converges for all $x$ in a finite interval. For example, the geometric series $\sum_{n=0}^{\infty} x^n$ converges for all $x$ in the interval $(-1, 1),$ but diverges for all $x$ outside that interval. We now summarize these three possibilities for a general power series.

### Theorem 6.1: Convergence of a Power Series

Consider the power series $\sum_{n=0}^{\infty} c_n (x-a)^n.$ The series satisfies exactly one of the following properties:

i. The series converges at $x = a$ and diverges for all $x \neq a.$
ii. The series converges for all real numbers $x$.
iii. There exists a real number $R > 0$ such that the series converges if $|x-a| < R$ and diverges if $|x-a| > R.$ At the values $x$ where $|x-a| = R,$ the series may converge or diverge.

### Proof

Suppose that the power series is centered at $a = 0.$ (For a series centered at a value of $a$ other than zero, the result follows by letting $y = x - a$ and considering the series $\sum_{n=1}^{\infty} c_n y^n.$) We must first prove the following fact:

If there exists a real number $d \neq 0$ such that $\sum_{n=0}^{\infty} c_n d^n$ converges, then the series $\sum_{n=0}^{\infty} c_n x^n$ converges absolutely for all $x$ such that $|x| < |d|.$

Since $\sum_{n=0}^{\infty} c_n d^n$ converges, the $n$th term $c_n d^n \to 0$ as $n \to \infty.$ Therefore, there exists an integer $N$ such that $|c_n d^n| \leq 1$ for all $n \geq N.$ Writing

$$|c_n x^n| = |c_n d^n| \left|\frac{x}{d}\right|^n,$$

we conclude that, for all $n \geq N,$

$$|c_n x^n| \leq \left|\frac{x}{d}\right|^n.$$

The series

$$\sum_{n=N}^{\infty} \left|\frac{x}{d}\right|^n$$

is a geometric series that converges if $\left|\frac{x}{d}\right| < 1$. Therefore, by the comparison test, we conclude that $\sum_{n=N}^{\infty} c_n x^n$ also converges for $|x| < |d|$. Since we can add a finite number of terms to a convergent series, we conclude that $\sum_{n=0}^{\infty} c_n x^n$ converges for $|x| < |d|$.

With this result, we can now prove the theorem. Consider the series

$$\sum_{n=0}^{\infty} a_n x^n$$

and let *S* be the set of real numbers for which the series converges. Suppose that the set $S = \{0\}$. Then the series falls under case i. Suppose that the set *S* is the set of all real numbers. Then the series falls under case ii. Suppose that $S \neq \{0\}$ and *S* is not the set of real numbers. Then there exists a real number $x^* \neq 0$ such that the series does not converge. Thus, the series cannot converge for any *x* such that $|x| > |x^*|$. Therefore, the set *S* must be a bounded set, which means that it must have a smallest upper bound. (This fact follows from the Least Upper Bound Property for the real numbers, which is beyond the scope of this text and is covered in real analysis courses.) Call that smallest upper bound *R*. Since $S \neq \{0\}$, the number $R > 0$. Therefore, the series converges for all *x* such that $|x| < R$, and the series falls into case iii.

□

If a series $\sum_{n=0}^{\infty} c_n (x-a)^n$ falls into case iii. of **Convergence of a Power Series**, then the series converges for all *x* such that $|x-a| < R$ for some $R > 0$, and diverges for all *x* such that $|x-a| > R$. The series may converge or diverge at the values *x* where $|x-a| = R$. The set of values *x* for which the series $\sum_{n=0}^{\infty} c_n (x-a)^n$ converges is known as the **interval of convergence**. Since the series diverges for all values *x* where $|x-a| > R$, the length of the interval is 2*R*, and therefore, the radius of the interval is *R*. The value *R* is called the **radius of convergence**. For example, since the series $\sum_{n=0}^{\infty} x^n$ converges for all values *x* in the interval $(-1, 1)$ and diverges for all values *x* such that $|x| \geq 1$, the interval of convergence of this series is $(-1, 1)$. Since the length of the interval is 2, the radius of convergence is 1.

### Definition

Consider the power series $\sum_{n=0}^{\infty} c_n (x-a)^n$. The set of real numbers *x* where the series converges is the interval of convergence. If there exists a real number $R > 0$ such that the series converges for $|x-a| < R$ and diverges for $|x-a| > R$, then *R* is the radius of convergence. If the series converges only at $x = a$, we say the radius of convergence is $R = 0$. If the series converges for all real numbers *x*, we say the radius of convergence is $R = \infty$ (**Figure 6.2**).

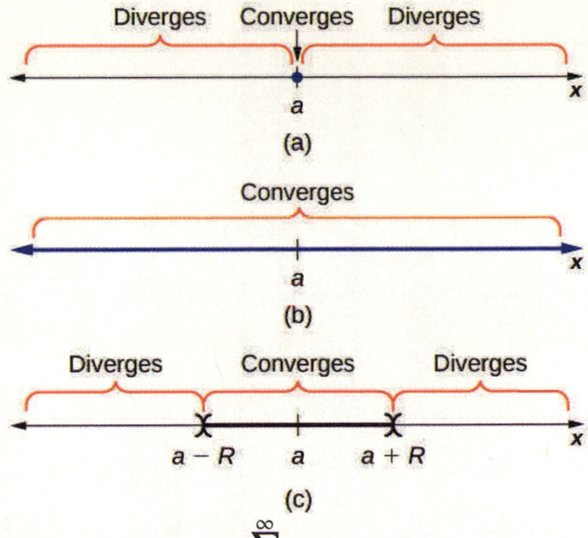


**Figure 6.2** For a series $\sum_{n=0}^{\infty} c_n (x-a)^n$ graph (a) shows a radius of convergence at $R=0,$ graph (b) shows a radius of convergence at $R=\infty,$ and graph (c) shows a radius of convergence at $R$. For graph (c) we note that the series may or may not converge at the endpoints $x=a+R$ and $x=a-R$.

To determine the interval of convergence for a power series, we typically apply the ratio test. In **Example 6.1**, we show the three different possibilities illustrated in **Figure 6.2**.

## Example 6.1

### Finding the Interval and Radius of Convergence

For each of the following series, find the interval and radius of convergence.

a. $\sum_{n=0}^{\infty} \frac{x^n}{n!}$

b. $\sum_{n=0}^{\infty} n!x^n$

c. $\sum_{n=0}^{\infty} \frac{(x-2)^n}{(n+1)3^n}$

### Solution

a. To check for convergence, apply the ratio test. We have

$$\begin{aligned}
\rho &= \lim_{n\to\infty}\left|\frac{\frac{x^{n+1}}{(n+1)!}}{\frac{x^n}{n!}}\right| \\
&= \lim_{n\to\infty}\left|\frac{x^{n+1}}{(n+1)!}\cdot\frac{n!}{x^n}\right| \\
&= \lim_{n\to\infty}\left|\frac{x^{n+1}}{(n+1)\cdot n!}\cdot\frac{n!}{x^n}\right| \\
&= \lim_{n\to\infty}\left|\frac{x}{n+1}\right| \\
&= |x|\lim_{n\to\infty}\frac{1}{n+1} \\
&= 0 < 1
\end{aligned}$$

for all values of $x$. Therefore, the series converges for all real numbers $x$. The interval of convergence is $(-\infty, \infty)$ and the radius of convergence is $R = \infty$.

b. Apply the ratio test. For $x \neq 0$, we see that

$$\begin{aligned}
\rho &= \lim_{n\to\infty}\left|\frac{(n+1)!x^{n+1}}{n!x^n}\right| \\
&= \lim_{n\to\infty}|(n+1)x| \\
&= |x|\lim_{n\to\infty}(n+1) \\
&= \infty.
\end{aligned}$$

Therefore, the series diverges for all $x \neq 0$. Since the series is centered at $x = 0$, it must converge there, so the series converges only for $x \neq 0$. The interval of convergence is the single value $x = 0$ and the radius of convergence is $R = 0$.

c. In order to apply the ratio test, consider

$$\begin{aligned}
\rho &= \lim_{n\to\infty}\left|\frac{\frac{(x-2)^{n+1}}{(n+2)3^{n+1}}}{\frac{(x-2)^n}{(n+1)3^n}}\right| \\
&= \lim_{n\to\infty}\left|\frac{(x-2)^{n+1}}{(n+2)3^{n+1}}\cdot\frac{(n+1)3^n}{(x-2)^n}\right| \\
&= \lim_{n\to\infty}\left|\frac{(x-2)(n+1)}{3(n+2)}\right| \\
&= \frac{|x-2|}{3}.
\end{aligned}$$

The ratio $\rho < 1$ if $|x-2| < 3$. Since $|x-2| < 3$ implies that $-3 < x-2 < 3$, the series converges absolutely if $-1 < x < 5$. The ratio $\rho > 1$ if $|x-2| > 3$. Therefore, the series diverges if $x < -1$ or $x > 5$. The ratio test is inconclusive if $\rho = 1$. The ratio $\rho = 1$ if and only if $x = -1$ or $x = 5$. We need to test these values of $x$ separately. For $x = -1$, the series is given by

$$\sum_{n=0}^{\infty}\frac{(-1)^n}{n+1} = 1 - \frac{1}{2} + \frac{1}{3} - \frac{1}{4} + \cdots.$$

Since this is the alternating harmonic series, it converges. Thus, the series converges at $x = -1$. For $x = 5$, the series is given by

$$\sum_{n=0}^{\infty} \frac{1}{n+1} = 1 + \frac{1}{2} + \frac{1}{3} + \frac{1}{4} + \cdots.$$

This is the harmonic series, which is divergent. Therefore, the power series diverges at $x = 5$. We conclude that the interval of convergence is $[-1, 5)$ and the radius of convergence is $R = 3$.

**6.1** Find the interval and radius of convergence for the series $\sum_{n=1}^{\infty} \frac{x^n}{\sqrt{n}}$.

## Representing Functions as Power Series

Being able to represent a function by an "infinite polynomial" is a powerful tool. Polynomial functions are the easiest functions to analyze, since they only involve the basic arithmetic operations of addition, subtraction, multiplication, and division. If we can represent a complicated function by an infinite polynomial, we can use the polynomial representation to differentiate or integrate it. In addition, we can use a truncated version of the polynomial expression to approximate values of the function. So, the question is, when can we represent a function by a power series?

Consider again the geometric series

$$1 + x + x^2 + x^3 + \cdots = \sum_{n=0}^{\infty} x^n. \tag{6.3}$$

Recall that the geometric series

$$a + ar + ar^2 + ar^3 + \cdots$$

converges if and only if $|r| < 1$. In that case, it converges to $\frac{a}{1-r}$. Therefore, if $|x| < 1$, the series in **Example 6.3** converges to $\frac{1}{1-x}$ and we write

$$1 + x + x^2 + x^3 + \cdots = \frac{1}{1-x} \text{ for } |x| < 1.$$

As a result, we are able to represent the function $f(x) = \frac{1}{1-x}$ by the power series

$$1 + x + x^2 + x^3 + \cdots \text{ when } |x| < 1.$$

We now show graphically how this series provides a representation for the function $f(x) = \frac{1}{1-x}$ by comparing the graph of $f$ with the graphs of several of the partial sums of this infinite series.

### Example 6.2

**Graphing a Function and Partial Sums of its Power Series**

Sketch a graph of $f(x) = \frac{1}{1-x}$ and the graphs of the corresponding partial sums $S_N(x) = \sum_{n=0}^{N} x^n$ for $N = 2, 4, 6$ on the interval $(-1, 1)$. Comment on the approximation $S_N$ as $N$ increases.

### Solution

From the graph in **Figure 6.3** you see that as $N$ increases, $S_N$ becomes a better approximation for $f(x) = \frac{1}{1-x}$ for $x$ in the interval $(-1, 1)$.

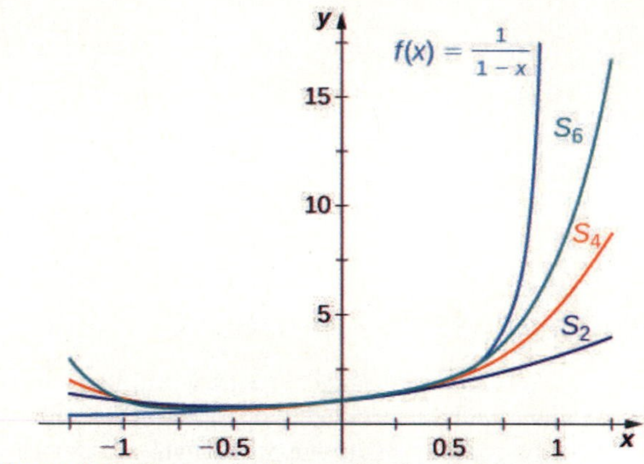


**Figure 6.3** The graph shows a function and three approximations of it by partial sums of a power series.

**6.2** Sketch a graph of $f(x) = \frac{1}{1-x^2}$ and the corresponding partial sums $S_N(x) = \sum_{n=0}^{N} x^{2n}$ for $N = 2, 4, 6$ on the interval $(-1, 1)$.

Next we consider functions involving an expression similar to the sum of a geometric series and show how to represent these functions using power series.

## Example 6.3

### Representing a Function with a Power Series

Use a power series to represent each of the following functions $f$. Find the interval of convergence.

a. $f(x) = \frac{1}{1+x^3}$

b. $f(x) = \frac{x^2}{4-x^2}$

### Solution

a. You should recognize this function $f$ as the sum of a geometric series, because

$$\frac{1}{1+x^3} = \frac{1}{1-\left(-x^3\right)}.$$

Using the fact that, for $|r| < 1,\ \frac{a}{1-r}$ is the sum of the geometric series

$$\sum_{n=0}^{\infty} ar^n = a + ar + ar^2 + \cdots,$$

we see that, for $\left|-x^3\right| < 1,$

$$\begin{aligned}\frac{1}{1+x^3} &= \frac{1}{1-\left(-x^3\right)} \\ &= \sum_{n=0}^{\infty} \left(-x^3\right)^n \\ &= 1 - x^3 + x^6 - x^9 + \cdots.\end{aligned}$$

Since this series converges if and only if $\left|-x^3\right| < 1,$ the interval of convergence is $(-1, 1),$ and we have

$$\frac{1}{1+x^3} = 1 - x^3 + x^6 - x^9 + \cdots \text{ for } |x| < 1.$$

b. This function is not in the exact form of a sum of a geometric series. However, with a little algebraic manipulation, we can relate $f$ to a geometric series. By factoring 4 out of the two terms in the denominator, we obtain

$$\begin{aligned}\frac{x^2}{4-x^2} &= \frac{x^2}{4\left(\frac{1-x^2}{4}\right)} \\ &= \frac{x^2}{4\left(1-\left(\frac{x}{2}\right)^2\right)}.\end{aligned}$$

Therefore, we have

$$\begin{aligned}\frac{x^2}{4-x^2} &= \frac{x^2}{4\left(1-\left(\frac{x}{2}\right)^2\right)} \\ &= \frac{\frac{x^2}{4}}{1-\left(\frac{x}{2}\right)^2} \\ &= \sum_{n=0}^{\infty} \frac{x^2}{4}\left(\frac{x}{2}\right)^{2n}.\end{aligned}$$

The series converges as long as $\left|\left(\frac{x}{2}\right)^2\right| < 1$ (note that when $\left|\left(\frac{x}{2}\right)^2\right| = 1$ the series does not converge). Solving this inequality, we conclude that the interval of convergence is $(-2, 2)$ and

$$\begin{aligned}\frac{x^2}{4-x^2} &= \sum_{n=0}^{\infty} \frac{x^{2n+2}}{4^{n+1}} \\ &= \frac{x^2}{4} + \frac{x^4}{4^2} + \frac{x^6}{4^3} + \cdots\end{aligned}$$

for $|x| < 2$.

**6.3** Represent the function $f(x) = \frac{x^3}{2-x}$ using a power series and find the interval of convergence.

In the remaining sections of this chapter, we will show ways of deriving power series representations for many other functions, and how we can make use of these representations to evaluate, differentiate, and integrate various functions.

# 6.1 EXERCISES

In the following exercises, state whether each statement is true, or give an example to show that it is false.

1. If $\sum_{n=1}^{\infty} a_n x^n$ converges, then $a_n x^n \to 0$ as $n \to \infty$.

2. $\sum_{n=1}^{\infty} a_n x^n$ converges at $x = 0$ for any real numbers $a_n$.

3. Given any sequence $a_n$, there is always some $R > 0$, possibly very small, such that $\sum_{n=1}^{\infty} a_n x^n$ converges on $(-R, R)$.

4. If $\sum_{n=1}^{\infty} a_n x^n$ has radius of convergence $R > 0$ and if $|b_n| \le |a_n|$ for all $n$, then the radius of convergence of $\sum_{n=1}^{\infty} b_n x^n$ is greater than or equal to $R$.

5. Suppose that $\sum_{n=0}^{\infty} a_n (x-3)^n$ converges at $x = 6$. At which of the following points must the series also converge? Use the fact that if $\sum a_n (x-c)^n$ converges at $x$, then it converges at any point closer to $c$ than $x$.
   a. $x = 1$
   b. $x = 2$
   c. $x = 3$
   d. $x = 0$
   e. $x = 5.99$
   f. $x = 0.000001$

6. Suppose that $\sum_{n=0}^{\infty} a_n (x+1)^n$ converges at $x = -2$. At which of the following points must the series also converge? Use the fact that if $\sum a_n (x-c)^n$ converges at $x$, then it converges at any point closer to $c$ than $x$.
   a. $x = 2$
   b. $x = -1$
   c. $x = -3$
   d. $x = 0$
   e. $x = 0.99$
   f. $x = 0.000001$

In the following exercises, suppose that $\left|\frac{a_{n+1}}{a_n}\right| \to 1$ as $n \to \infty$. Find the radius of convergence for each series.

7. $\sum_{n=0}^{\infty} a_n 2^n x^n$

8. $\sum_{n=0}^{\infty} \frac{a_n x^n}{2^n}$

9. $\sum_{n=0}^{\infty} \frac{a_n \pi^n x^n}{e^n}$

10. $\sum_{n=0}^{\infty} \frac{a_n (-1)^n x^n}{10^n}$

11. $\sum_{n=0}^{\infty} a_n (-1)^n x^{2n}$

12. $\sum_{n=0}^{\infty} a_n (-4)^n x^{2n}$

In the following exercises, find the radius of convergence $R$ and interval of convergence for $\sum a_n x^n$ with the given coefficients $a_n$.

13. $\sum_{n=1}^{\infty} \frac{(2x)^n}{n}$

14. $\sum_{n=1}^{\infty} (-1)^n \frac{x^n}{\sqrt{n}}$

15. $\sum_{n=1}^{\infty} \frac{n x^n}{2^n}$

16. $\sum_{n=1}^{\infty} \frac{n x^n}{e^n}$

17. $\sum_{n=1}^{\infty} \frac{n^2 x^n}{2^n}$

18. $\sum_{k=1}^{\infty} \frac{k^e x^k}{e^k}$

19. $\sum_{k=1}^{\infty} \frac{\pi^k x^k}{k^\pi}$

20. $\sum_{n=1}^{\infty} \frac{x^n}{n!}$

21. $\sum_{n=1}^{\infty} \frac{10^n x^n}{n!}$

22. $\sum_{n=1}^{\infty} (-1)^n \frac{x^n}{\ln(2n)}$

In the following exercises, find the radius of convergence of each series.

23. $\sum_{k=1}^{\infty} \frac{(k!)^2 x^k}{(2k)!}$

24. $\sum_{n=1}^{\infty} \frac{(2n)! x^n}{n^{2n}}$

25. $\sum_{k=1}^{\infty} \frac{k!}{1 \cdot 3 \cdot 5 \cdots (2k-1)} x^k$

26. $\sum_{k=1}^{\infty} \frac{2 \cdot 4 \cdot 6 \cdots 2k}{(2k)!} x^k$

27. $\sum_{n=1}^{\infty} \frac{x^n}{\binom{2n}{n}}$ where $\binom{n}{k} = \frac{n!}{k!(n-k)!}$

28. $\sum_{n=1}^{\infty} \sin^2 n x^n$

In the following exercises, use the ratio test to determine the radius of convergence of each series.

29. $\sum_{n=1}^{\infty} \frac{(n!)^3}{(3n)!} x^n$

30. $\sum_{n=1}^{\infty} \frac{2^{3n} (n!)^3}{(3n)!} x^n$

31. $\sum_{n=1}^{\infty} \frac{n!}{n^n} x^n$

32. $\sum_{n=1}^{\infty} \frac{(2n)!}{n^{2n}} x^n$

In the following exercises, given that $\frac{1}{1-x} = \sum_{n=0}^{\infty} x^n$ with convergence in $(-1, 1)$, find the power series for each function with the given center $a$, and identify its interval of convergence.

33. $f(x) = \frac{1}{x}; a = 1$ (*Hint:* $\frac{1}{x} = \frac{1}{1-(1-x)}$)

34. $f(x) = \frac{1}{1-x^2}; a = 0$

35. $f(x) = \frac{x}{1-x^2}; a = 0$

36. $f(x) = \frac{1}{1+x^2}; a = 0$

37. $f(x) = \frac{x^2}{1+x^2}; a = 0$

38. $f(x) = \frac{1}{2-x}; a = 1$

39. $f(x) = \frac{1}{1-2x}; a = 0.$

40. $f(x) = \frac{1}{1-4x^2}; a = 0$

41. $f(x) = \frac{x^2}{1-4x^2}; a = 0$

42. $f(x) = \frac{x^2}{5-4x+x^2}; a = 2$

Use the next exercise to find the radius of convergence of the given series in the subsequent exercises.

43. Explain why, if $|a_n|^{1/n} \to r > 0,$ then $|a_n x^n|^{1/n} \to |x|r < 1$ whenever $|x| < \frac{1}{r}$ and, therefore, the radius of convergence of $\sum_{n=1}^{\infty} a_n x^n$ is $R = \frac{1}{r}.$

44. $\sum_{n=1}^{\infty} \frac{x^n}{n^n}$

45. $\sum_{k=1}^{\infty} \left(\frac{k-1}{2k+3}\right)^k x^k$

46. $\sum_{k=1}^{\infty} \left(\frac{2k^2-1}{k^2+3}\right)^k x^k$

47. $\sum_{n=1}^{\infty} a_n = \left(n^{1/n} - 1\right)^n x^n$

48. Suppose that $p(x) = \sum_{n=0}^{\infty} a_n x^n$ such that $a_n = 0$ if $n$ is even. Explain why $p(x) = p(-x)$.

49. Suppose that $p(x) = \sum_{n=0}^{\infty} a_n x^n$ such that $a_n = 0$ if $n$ is odd. Explain why $p(x) = -p(-x)$.

50. Suppose that $p(x) = \sum_{n=0}^{\infty} a_n x^n$ converges on $(-1, 1]$. Find the interval of convergence of $p(Ax)$.

51. Suppose that $p(x) = \sum_{n=0}^{\infty} a_n x^n$ converges on $(-1, 1]$. Find the interval of convergence of $p(2x-1)$.

In the following exercises, suppose that $p(x) = \sum_{n=0}^{\infty} a_n x^n$ satisfies $\lim_{n \to \infty} \frac{a_{n+1}}{a_n} = 1$ where $a_n \geq 0$ for each $n$. State whether each series converges on the full interval $(-1, 1)$, or if there is not enough information to draw a conclusion. Use the comparison test when appropriate.

52. $\sum_{n=0}^{\infty} a_n x^{2n}$

53. $\sum_{n=0}^{\infty} a_{2n} x^{2n}$

54. $\sum_{n=0}^{\infty} a_{2n} x^n \left(Hint: x = \pm\sqrt{x^2}\right)$

55. $\sum_{n=0}^{\infty} a_{n^2} x^{n^2}$ (*Hint:* Let $b_k = a_k$ if $k = n^2$ for some $n$, otherwise $b_k = 0$.)

56. Suppose that $p(x)$ is a polynomial of degree $N$. Find the radius and interval of convergence of $\sum_{n=1}^{\infty} p(n)x^n$.

57. **[T]** Plot the graphs of $\frac{1}{1-x}$ and of the partial sums $S_N = \sum_{n=0}^{N} x^n$ for $n = 10, 20, 30$ on the interval $[-0.99, 0.99]$. Comment on the approximation of $\frac{1}{1-x}$ by $S_N$ near $x = -1$ and near $x = 1$ as $N$ increases.

58. **[T]** Plot the graphs of $-\ln(1-x)$ and of the partial sums $S_N = \sum_{n=1}^{N} \frac{x^n}{n}$ for $n = 10, 50, 100$ on the interval $[-0.99, 0.99]$. Comment on the behavior of the sums near $x = -1$ and near $x = 1$ as $N$ increases.

59. **[T]** Plot the graphs of the partial sums $S_n = \sum_{n=1}^{N} \frac{x^n}{n^2}$ for $n = 10, 50, 100$ on the interval $[-0.99, 0.99]$. Comment on the behavior of the sums near $x = -1$ and near $x = 1$ as $N$ increases.

60. **[T]** Plot the graphs of the partial sums $S_N = \sum_{n=1}^{N} \sin nx^n$ for $n = 10, 50, 100$ on the interval $[-0.99, 0.99]$. Comment on the behavior of the sums near $x = -1$ and near $x = 1$ as $N$ increases.

61. **[T]** Plot the graphs of the partial sums $S_N = \sum_{n=0}^{N} (-1)^n \frac{x^{2n+1}}{(2n+1)!}$ for $n = 3, 5, 10$ on the interval $[-2\pi, 2\pi]$. Comment on how these plots approximate $\sin x$ as $N$ increases.

62. **[T]** Plot the graphs of the partial sums $S_N = \sum_{n=0}^{N} (-1)^n \frac{x^{2n}}{(2n)!}$ for $n = 3, 5, 10$ on the interval $[-2\pi, 2\pi]$. Comment on how these plots approximate $\cos x$ as $N$ increases.

# 6.2 | Properties of Power Series

## Learning Objectives

**6.2.1** Combine power series by addition or subtraction.

**6.2.2** Create a new power series by multiplication by a power of the variable or a constant, or by substitution.

**6.2.3** Multiply two power series together.

**6.2.4** Differentiate and integrate power series term-by-term.

In the preceding section on power series and functions we showed how to represent certain functions using power series. In this section we discuss how power series can be combined, differentiated, or integrated to create new power series. This capability is particularly useful for a couple of reasons. First, it allows us to find power series representations for certain elementary functions, by writing those functions in terms of functions with known power series. For example, given the power series representation for $f(x) = \frac{1}{1-x}$, we can find a power series representation for $f'(x) = \frac{1}{(1-x)^2}$. Second, being able to create power series allows us to define new functions that cannot be written in terms of elementary functions. This capability is particularly useful for solving differential equations for which there is no solution in terms of elementary functions.

## Combining Power Series

If we have two power series with the same interval of convergence, we can add or subtract the two series to create a new power series, also with the same interval of convergence. Similarly, we can multiply a power series by a power of $x$ or evaluate a power series at $x^m$ for a positive integer $m$ to create a new power series. Being able to do this allows us to find power series representations for certain functions by using power series representations of other functions. For example, since we know the power series representation for $f(x) = \frac{1}{1-x}$, we can find power series representations for related functions, such as

$$y = \frac{3x}{1-x^2} \text{ and } y = \frac{1}{(x-1)(x-3)}.$$

In **Combining Power Series** we state results regarding addition or subtraction of power series, composition of a power series, and multiplication of a power series by a power of the variable. For simplicity, we state the theorem for power series centered at $x = 0$. Similar results hold for power series centered at $x = a$.

### Theorem 6.2: Combining Power Series

Suppose that the two power series $\sum_{n=0}^{\infty} c_n x^n$ and $\sum_{n=0}^{\infty} d_n x^n$ converge to the functions *f* and *g*, respectively, on a common interval *I*.

i. The power series $\sum_{n=0}^{\infty} (c_n x^n \pm d_n x^n)$ converges to $f \pm g$ on *I*.

ii. For any integer $m \geq 0$ and any real number *b*, the power series $\sum_{n=0}^{\infty} bx^m c_n x^n$ converges to $bx^m f(x)$ on *I*.

iii. For any integer $m \geq 0$ and any real number *b*, the series $\sum_{n=0}^{\infty} c_n (bx^m)^n$ converges to $f(bx^m)$ for all *x* such that $bx^m$ is in *I*.

### Proof

We prove i. in the case of the series $\sum_{n=0}^{\infty}(c_n x^n + d_n x^n)$. Suppose that $\sum_{n=0}^{\infty} c_n x^n$ and $\sum_{n=0}^{\infty} d_n x^n$ converge to the functions *f* and *g*, respectively, on the interval *I*. Let *x* be a point in *I* and let $S_N(x)$ and $T_N(x)$ denote the *N*th partial sums of the series $\sum_{n=0}^{\infty} c_n x^n$ and $\sum_{n=0}^{\infty} d_n x^n$, respectively. Then the sequence $\{S_N(x)\}$ converges to $f(x)$ and the sequence $\{T_N(x)\}$ converges to $g(x)$. Furthermore, the *N*th partial sum of $\sum_{n=0}^{\infty}(c_n x^n + d_n x^n)$ is

$$\begin{aligned}\sum_{n=0}^{N}(c_n x^n + d_n x^n) &= \sum_{n=0}^{N} c_n x^n + \sum_{n=0}^{N} d_n x^n \\ &= S_N(x) + T_N(x).\end{aligned}$$

Because

$$\begin{aligned}\lim_{N\to\infty}(S_N(x) + T_N(x)) &= \lim_{N\to\infty} S_N(x) + \lim_{N\to\infty} T_N(x) \\ &= f(x) + g(x),\end{aligned}$$

we conclude that the series $\sum_{n=0}^{\infty}(c_n x^n + d_n x^n)$ converges to $f(x) + g(x)$.

□

We examine products of power series in a later theorem. First, we show several applications of **Combining Power Series** and how to find the interval of convergence of a power series given the interval of convergence of a related power series.

## Example 6.4

### Combining Power Series

Suppose that $\sum_{n=0}^{\infty} a_n x^n$ is a power series whose interval of convergence is $(-1, 1)$, and suppose that $\sum_{n=0}^{\infty} b_n x^n$ is a power series whose interval of convergence is $(-2, 2)$.

a. Find the interval of convergence of the series $\sum_{n=0}^{\infty}(a_n x^n + b_n x^n)$.

b. Find the interval of convergence of the series $\sum_{n=0}^{\infty} a_n 3^n x^n$.

### Solution

a. Since the interval $(-1, 1)$ is a common interval of convergence of the series $\sum_{n=0}^{\infty} a_n x^n$ and $\sum_{n=0}^{\infty} b_n x^n$, the interval of convergence of the series $\sum_{n=0}^{\infty}(a_n x^n + b_n x^n)$ is $(-1, 1)$.

b. Since $\sum_{n=0}^{\infty} a_n x^n$ is a power series centered at zero with radius of convergence 1, it converges for all $x$ in the interval $(-1, 1)$. By **Combining Power Series**, the series

$$\sum_{n=0}^{\infty} a_n 3^n x^n = \sum_{n=0}^{\infty} a_n (3x)^n$$

converges if $3x$ is in the interval $(-1, 1)$. Therefore, the series converges for all $x$ in the interval $\left(-\frac{1}{3}, \frac{1}{3}\right)$.

**6.4** Suppose that $\sum_{n=0}^{\infty} a_n x^n$ has an interval of convergence of $(-1, 1)$. Find the interval of convergence of $\sum_{n=0}^{\infty} a_n \left(\frac{x}{2}\right)^n$.

In the next example, we show how to use **Combining Power Series** and the power series for a function $f$ to construct power series for functions related to $f$. Specifically, we consider functions related to the function $f(x) = \frac{1}{1-x}$ and we use the fact that

$$\frac{1}{1-x} = \sum_{n=0}^{\infty} x^n = 1 + x + x^2 + x^3 + \cdots$$

for $|x| < 1$.

## Example 6.5

### Constructing Power Series from Known Power Series

Use the power series representation for $f(x) = \frac{1}{1-x}$ combined with **Combining Power Series** to construct a power series for each of the following functions. Find the interval of convergence of the power series.

a. $f(x) = \frac{3x}{1+x^2}$

b. $f(x) = \frac{1}{(x-1)(x-3)}$

#### Solution

a. First write $f(x)$ as

$$f(x) = 3x\left(\frac{1}{1-\left(-x^2\right)}\right).$$

Using the power series representation for $f(x) = \frac{1}{1-x}$ and parts ii. and iii. of **Combining Power Series**, we find that a power series representation for $f$ is given by

$$\sum_{n=0}^{\infty} 3x\left(-x^2\right)^n = \sum_{n=0}^{\infty} 3(-1)^n x^{2n+1}.$$

Since the interval of convergence of the series for $\frac{1}{1-x}$ is $(-1, 1)$, the interval of convergence for this new series is the set of real numbers $x$ such that $\left|x^2\right| < 1$. Therefore, the interval of convergence is $(-1, 1)$.

b. To find the power series representation, use partial fractions to write $f(x) = \frac{1}{(1-x)(x-3)}$ as the sum of two fractions. We have

$$\begin{aligned}\frac{1}{(x-1)(x-3)} &= \frac{-1/2}{x-1} + \frac{1/2}{x-3} \\ &= \frac{1/2}{1-x} - \frac{1/2}{3-x} \\ &= \frac{1/2}{1-x} - \frac{1/6}{1-\frac{x}{3}}.\end{aligned}$$

First, using part ii. of **Combining Power Series**, we obtain

$$\frac{1/2}{1-x} = \sum_{n=0}^{\infty} \frac{1}{2}x^n \text{ for } |x| < 1.$$

Then, using parts ii. and iii. of **Combining Power Series**, we have

$$\frac{1/6}{1-x/3} = \sum_{n=0}^{\infty} \frac{1}{6}\left(\frac{x}{3}\right)^n \text{ for } |x| < 3.$$

Since we are combining these two power series, the interval of convergence of the difference must be the smaller of these two intervals. Using this fact and part i. of **Combining Power Series**, we have

$$\frac{1}{(x-1)(x-3)} = \sum_{n=0}^{\infty}\left(\frac{1}{2} - \frac{1}{6\cdot 3^n}\right)x^n$$

where the interval of convergence is $(-1, 1)$.

**6.5** Use the series for $f(x) = \frac{1}{1-x}$ on $|x| < 1$ to construct a series for $\frac{1}{(1-x)(x-2)}$. Determine the interval of convergence.

In **Example 6.5**, we showed how to find power series for certain functions. In **Example 6.6** we show how to do the opposite: given a power series, determine which function it represents.

## Example 6.6

### Finding the Function Represented by a Given Power Series

Consider the power series $\sum_{n=0}^{\infty} 2^n x^n$. Find the function $f$ represented by this series. Determine the interval of convergence of the series.

#### Solution

Writing the given series as

$$\sum_{n=0}^{\infty} 2^n x^n = \sum_{n=0}^{\infty} (2x)^n,$$

we can recognize this series as the power series for

$$f(x) = \frac{1}{1-2x}.$$

Since this is a geometric series, the series converges if and only if $|2x| < 1$. Therefore, the interval of convergence is $\left(-\frac{1}{2}, \frac{1}{2}\right)$.

**6.6** Find the function represented by the power series $\sum_{n=0}^{\infty} \frac{1}{3^n} x^n$. Determine its interval of convergence.

Recall the questions posed in the chapter opener about which is the better way of receiving payouts from lottery winnings. We now revisit those questions and show how to use series to compare values of payments over time with a lump sum payment today. We will compute how much future payments are worth in terms of today's dollars, assuming we have the ability to invest winnings and earn interest. The value of future payments in terms of today's dollars is known as the *present value* of those payments.

## Example 6.7

### Chapter Opener: Present Value of Future Winnings

**Figure 6.4** (credit: modification of work by Robert Huffstutter, Flickr)

Suppose you win the lottery and are given the following three options: (1) Receive 20 million dollars today; (2) receive 1.5 million dollars per year over the next 20 years; or (3) receive 1 million dollars per year indefinitely (being passed on to your heirs). Which is the best deal, assuming that the annual interest rate is 5%? We answer this by working through the following sequence of questions.

a. How much is the 1.5 million dollars received annually over the course of 20 years worth in terms of today's dollars, assuming an annual interest rate of 5%?

b. Use the answer to part a. to find a general formula for the present value of payments of $C$ dollars received each year over the next $n$ years, assuming an average annual interest rate $r$.

c. Find a formula for the present value if annual payments of $C$ dollars continue indefinitely, assuming an average annual interest rate $r$.

d. Use the answer to part c. to determine the present value of 1 million dollars paid annually indefinitely.

e. Use your answers to parts a. and d. to determine which of the three options is best.

### Solution

a. Consider the payment of 1.5 million dollars made at the end of the first year. If you were able to receive that payment today instead of one year from now, you could invest that money and earn 5% interest. Therefore, the present value of that money $P_1$ satisfies $P_1(1+0.05)=1.5$ million dollars. We conclude that

$$P_1=\frac{1.5}{1.05}=\$1.429 \text{ million dollars.}$$

Similarly, consider the payment of 1.5 million dollars made at the end of the second year. If you were able to receive that payment today, you could invest that money for two years, earning 5% interest, compounded annually. Therefore, the present value of that money $P_2$ satisfies $P_2(1+0.05)^2=1.5$ million dollars. We conclude that

$$P_2=\frac{1.5}{(1.05)^2}=\$1.361 \text{ million dollars.}$$

The value of the future payments today is the sum of the present values $P_1, P_2, \ldots, P_{20}$ of each of those annual payments. The present value $P_k$ satisfies

$$P_k=\frac{1.5}{(1.05)^k}.$$

Therefore,

$$\begin{aligned} P &= \frac{1.5}{1.05}+\frac{1.5}{(1.05)^2}+\cdots+\frac{1.5}{(1.05)^{20}} \\ &= \$18.693 \text{ million dollars.} \end{aligned}$$

b. Using the result from part a. we see that the present value $P$ of $C$ dollars paid annually over the course of $n$ years, assuming an annual interest rate $r$, is given by

$$P=\frac{C}{1+r}+\frac{C}{(1+r)^2}+\cdots+\frac{C}{(1+r)^n} \text{ dollars.}$$

c. Using the result from part b. we see that the present value of an annuity that continues indefinitely is given by the infinite series

$$P=\sum_{n=0}^{\infty}\frac{C}{(1+r)^{n+1}}.$$

We can view the present value as a power series in $r$, which converges as long as $\left|\frac{1}{1+r}\right|<1$. Since $r>0$, this series converges. Rewriting the series as

$$P = \frac{C}{(1+r)} \sum_{n=0}^{\infty} \left(\frac{1}{1+r}\right)^n,$$

we recognize this series as the power series for

$$f(r) = \frac{1}{1 - \left(\frac{1}{1+r}\right)} = \frac{1}{\left(\frac{r}{1+r}\right)} = \frac{1+r}{r}.$$

We conclude that the present value of this annuity is

$$P = \frac{C}{1+r} \cdot \frac{1+r}{r} = \frac{C}{r}.$$

d. From the result to part c. we conclude that the present value $P$ of $C = 1$ million dollars paid out every year indefinitely, assuming an annual interest rate $r = 0.05$, is given by

$$P = \frac{1}{0.05} = 20 \text{ million dollars.}$$

e. From part a. we see that receiving \$1.5 million dollars over the course of 20 years is worth \$18.693 million dollars in today's dollars. From part d. we see that receiving \$1 million dollars per year indefinitely is worth \$20 million dollars in today's dollars. Therefore, either receiving a lump-sum payment of \$20 million dollars today or receiving \$1 million dollars indefinitely have the same present value.

## Multiplication of Power Series

We can also create new power series by multiplying power series. Being able to multiply two power series provides another way of finding power series representations for functions.

The way we multiply them is similar to how we multiply polynomials. For example, suppose we want to multiply

$$\sum_{n=0}^{\infty} c_n x^n = c_0 + c_1 x + c_2 x^2 + \cdots$$

and

$$\sum_{n=0}^{\infty} d_n x^n = d_0 + d_1 x + d_2 x^2 + \cdots.$$

It appears that the product should satisfy

$$\begin{aligned}\left(\sum_{n=0}^{\infty} c_n x^n\right)\left(\sum_{n=-0}^{\infty} d_n x^n\right) &= \left(c_0 + c_1 x + c_2 x^2 + \cdots\right) \cdot \left(d_0 + d_1 x + d_2 x^2 + \cdots\right) \\ &= c_0 d_0 + (c_1 d_0 + c_0 d_1)x + (c_2 d_0 + c_1 d_1 + c_0 d_2)x^2 + \cdots.\end{aligned}$$

In **Multiplying Power Series**, we state the main result regarding multiplying power series, showing that if $\sum_{n=0}^{\infty} c_n x^n$ and $\sum_{n=0}^{\infty} d_n x^n$ converge on a common interval $I$, then we can multiply the series in this way, and the resulting series also converges on the interval $I$.

### Theorem 6.3: Multiplying Power Series

Suppose that the power series $\sum_{n=0}^{\infty} c_n x^n$ and $\sum_{n=0}^{\infty} d_n x^n$ converge to $f$ and $g$, respectively, on a common interval $I$. Let

$$\begin{aligned} e_n &= c_0 d_n + c_1 d_{n-1} + c_2 d_{n-2} + \cdots + c_{n-1} d_1 + c_n d_0 \\ &= \sum_{k=0}^{n} c_k d_{n-k}. \end{aligned}$$

Then

$$\left(\sum_{n=0}^{\infty} c_n x^n\right)\left(\sum_{n=0}^{\infty} d_n x^n\right) = \sum_{n=0}^{\infty} e_n x^n$$

and

$$\sum_{n=0}^{\infty} e_n x^n \text{ converges to } f(x) \cdot g(x) \text{ on } I.$$

The series $\sum_{n=0}^{\infty} e_n x^n$ is known as the Cauchy product of the series $\sum_{n=0}^{\infty} c_n x^n$ and $\sum_{n=0}^{\infty} d_n x^n$.

We omit the proof of this theorem, as it is beyond the level of this text and is typically covered in a more advanced course. We now provide an example of this theorem by finding the power series representation for

$$f(x) = \frac{1}{(1-x)\left(1-x^2\right)}$$

using the power series representations for

$$y = \frac{1}{1-x} \text{ and } y = \frac{1}{1-x^2}.$$

## Example 6.8

### Multiplying Power Series

Multiply the power series representation

$$\begin{aligned} \frac{1}{1-x} &= \sum_{n=0}^{\infty} x^n \\ &= 1 + x + x^2 + x^3 + \cdots \end{aligned}$$

for $|x| < 1$ with the power series representation

$$\begin{aligned} \frac{1}{1-x^2} &= \sum_{n=0}^{\infty} \left(x^2\right)^n \\ &= 1 + x^2 + x^4 + x^6 + \cdots \end{aligned}$$

for $|x| < 1$ to construct a power series for $f(x) = \frac{1}{(1-x)\left(1-x^2\right)}$ on the interval $(-1,\ 1)$.

**Solution**

We need to multiply

$$\left(1 + x + x^2 + x^3 + \cdots\right)\left(1 + x^2 + x^4 + x^6 + \cdots\right).$$

Writing out the first several terms, we see that the product is given by

$$\begin{aligned}&\left(1 + x^2 + x^4 + x^6 + \cdots\right) + \left(x + x^3 + x^5 + x^7 + \cdots\right) + \left(x^2 + x^4 + x^6 + x^8 + \cdots\right) + \left(x^3 + x^5 + x^7 + x^9 + \cdots\right)\\ &= 1 + x + (1+1)x^2 + (1+1)x^3 + (1+1+1)x^4 + (1+1+1)x^5 + \cdots\\ &= 1 + x + 2x^2 + 2x^3 + 3x^4 + 3x^5 + \cdots.\end{aligned}$$

Since the series for $y = \frac{1}{1-x}$ and $y = \frac{1}{1-x^2}$ both converge on the interval $(-1, 1)$, the series for the product also converges on the interval $(-1, 1)$.

**6.7** Multiply the series $\frac{1}{1-x} = \sum_{n=0}^{\infty} x^n$ by itself to construct a series for $\frac{1}{(1-x)(1-x)}$.

## Differentiating and Integrating Power Series

Consider a power series $\sum_{n=0}^{\infty} c_n x^n = c_0 + c_1 x + c_2 x^2 + \cdots$ that converges on some interval *I*, and let $f$ be the function defined by this series. Here we address two questions about $f$.

- Is $f$ differentiable, and if so, how do we determine the derivative $f'$?
- How do we evaluate the indefinite integral $\int f(x)dx$?

We know that, for a polynomial with a finite number of terms, we can evaluate the derivative by differentiating each term separately. Similarly, we can evaluate the indefinite integral by integrating each term separately. Here we show that we can do the same thing for convergent power series. That is, if

$$f(x) = c_n x^n = c_0 + c_1 x + c_2 x^2 + \cdots$$

converges on some interval *I*, then

$$f'(x) = c_1 + 2c_2 x + 3c_3 x^2 + \cdots$$

and

$$\int f(x)dx = C + c_0 x + c_1 \frac{x^2}{2} + c_2 \frac{x^3}{3} + \cdots.$$

Evaluating the derivative and indefinite integral in this way is called **term-by-term differentiation of a power series** and **term-by-term integration of a power series**, respectively. The ability to differentiate and integrate power series term-by-term also allows us to use known power series representations to find power series representations for other functions. For example, given the power series for $f(x) = \frac{1}{1-x}$, we can differentiate term-by-term to find the power series for $f'(x) = \frac{1}{(1-x)^2}$. Similarly, using the power series for $g(x) = \frac{1}{1+x}$, we can integrate term-by-term to find the power series for $G(x) = \ln(1+x)$, an antiderivative of $g$. We show how to do this in Example 6.9 and Example 6.10. First, we state Term-by-Term Differentiation and Integration for Power Series, which provides the main result regarding differentiation and integration of power series.

### Theorem 6.4: Term-by-Term Differentiation and Integration for Power Series

Suppose that the power series $\sum_{n=0}^{\infty} c_n (x-a)^n$ converges on the interval $(a-R, a+R)$ for some $R > 0$. Let $f$ be the function defined by the series

$$\begin{aligned} f(x) &= \sum_{n=0}^{\infty} c_n (x-a)^n \\ &= c_0 + c_1(x-a) + c_2(x-a)^2 + c_3(x-a)^3 + \cdots \end{aligned}$$

for $|x-a| < R$. Then $f$ is differentiable on the interval $(a-R, a+R)$ and we can find $f'$ by differentiating the series term-by-term:

$$\begin{aligned} f'(x) &= \sum_{n=1}^{\infty} n c_n (x-a)^{n-1} \\ &= c_1 + 2c_2(x-a) + 3c_3(x-a)^2 + \cdots \end{aligned}$$

for $|x-a| < R$. Also, to find $\int f(x)dx,$ we can integrate the series term-by-term. The resulting series converges on $(a-R, a+R),$ and we have

$$\begin{aligned} \int f(x)dx &= C + \sum_{n=0}^{\infty} c_n \frac{(x-a)^{n+1}}{n+1} \\ &= C + c_0(x-a) + c_1 \frac{(x-a)^2}{2} + c_2 \frac{(x-a)^3}{3} + \cdots \end{aligned}$$

for $|x-a| < R.$

The proof of this result is beyond the scope of the text and is omitted. Note that although **Term-by-Term Differentiation and Integration for Power Series** guarantees the same radius of convergence when a power series is differentiated or integrated term-by-term, it says nothing about what happens at the endpoints. It is possible that the differentiated and integrated power series have different behavior at the endpoints than does the original series. We see this behavior in the next examples.

## Example 6.9

### Differentiating Power Series

a. Use the power series representation

$$\begin{aligned} f(x) &= \frac{1}{1-x} \\ &= \sum_{n=0}^{\infty} x^n \\ &= 1 + x + x^2 + x^3 + \cdots \end{aligned}$$

for $|x| < 1$ to find a power series representation for

$$g(x) = \frac{1}{(1-x)^2}$$

on the interval $(-1, 1)$. Determine whether the resulting series converges at the endpoints.

b. Use the result of part a. to evaluate the sum of the series $\sum_{n=0}^{\infty} \frac{n+1}{4^n}$.

### Solution

a. Since $g(x) = \frac{1}{(1-x)^2}$ is the derivative of $f(x) = \frac{1}{1-x}$, we can find a power series representation for $g$ by differentiating the power series for $f$ term-by-term. The result is

$$\begin{aligned} g(x) &= \frac{1}{(1-x)^2} \\ &= \frac{d}{dx}\left(\frac{1}{1-x}\right) \\ &= \sum_{n=0}^{\infty} \frac{d}{dx}(x^n) \\ &= \frac{d}{dx}\left(1 + x + x^2 + x^3 + \cdots\right) \\ &= 0 + 1 + 2x + 3x^2 + 4x^3 + \cdots \\ &= \sum_{n=0}^{\infty} (n+1)x^n \end{aligned}$$

for $|x| < 1$. **Term-by-Term Differentiation and Integration for Power Series** does not guarantee anything about the behavior of this series at the endpoints. Testing the endpoints by using the divergence test, we find that the series diverges at both endpoints $x = \pm 1$. Note that this is the same result found in **Example 6.8**.

b. From part a. we know that

$$\sum_{n=0}^{\infty} (n+1)x^n = \frac{1}{(1-x)^2}.$$

Therefore,

$$\begin{aligned} \sum_{n=0}^{\infty} \frac{n+1}{4^n} &= \sum_{n=0}^{\infty} (n+1)\left(\frac{1}{4}\right)^n \\ &= \frac{1}{\left(1 - \frac{1}{4}\right)^2} \\ &= \frac{1}{\left(\frac{3}{4}\right)^2} \\ &= \frac{16}{9}. \end{aligned}$$

**6.8** Differentiate the series $\frac{1}{(1-x)^2} = \sum_{n=0}^{\infty} (n+1)x^n$ term-by-term to find a power series representation for $\frac{2}{(1-x)^3}$ on the interval $(-1, 1)$.

## Example 6.10

### Integrating Power Series

For each of the following functions $f$, find a power series representation for $f$ by integrating the power series for $f'$ and find its interval of convergence.

a. $f(x) = \ln(1 + x)$

b. $f(x) = \tan^{-1} x$

### Solution

a. For $f(x) = \ln(1 + x)$, the derivative is $f'(x) = \frac{1}{1 + x}$. We know that

$$\begin{aligned} \frac{1}{1+x} &= \frac{1}{1-(-x)} \\ &= \sum_{n=0}^{\infty} (-x)^n \\ &= 1 - x + x^2 - x^3 + \cdots \end{aligned}$$

for $|x| < 1$. To find a power series for $f(x) = \ln(1 + x)$, we integrate the series term-by-term.

$$\begin{aligned} \int f'(x)dx &= \int \left(1 - x + x^2 - x^3 + \cdots\right)dx \\ &= C + x - \frac{x^2}{2} + \frac{x^3}{3} - \frac{x^4}{4} + \cdots \end{aligned}$$

Since $f(x) = \ln(1 + x)$ is an antiderivative of $\frac{1}{1 + x}$, it remains to solve for the constant $C$. Since $\ln(1 + 0) = 0$, we have $C = 0$. Therefore, a power series representation for $f(x) = \ln(1 + x)$ is

$$\begin{aligned} \ln(1 + x) &= x - \frac{x^2}{2} + \frac{x^3}{3} - \frac{x^4}{4} + \cdots \\ &= \sum_{n=1}^{\infty} (-1)^{n+1} \frac{x^n}{n} \end{aligned}$$

for $|x| < 1$. **Term-by-Term Differentiation and Integration for Power Series** does not guarantee anything about the behavior of this power series at the endpoints. However, checking the endpoints, we find that at $x = 1$ the series is the alternating harmonic series, which converges. Also, at $x = -1$, the series is the harmonic series, which diverges. It is important to note that, even though this series converges at $x = 1$, **Term-by-Term Differentiation and Integration for Power Series** does not guarantee that the series actually converges to $\ln(2)$. In fact, the series does converge to $\ln(2)$, but showing this fact requires more advanced techniques. (Abel's theorem, covered in more advanced texts, deals with this more technical point.) The interval of convergence is $(-1, 1]$.

b. The derivative of $f(x) = \tan^{-1} x$ is $f'(x) = \frac{1}{1 + x^2}$. We know that

$$\begin{aligned}\frac{1}{1+x^2} &= \frac{1}{1-\left(-x^2\right)} \\ &= \sum_{n=0}^{\infty}\left(-x^2\right)^n \\ &= 1 - x^2 + x^4 - x^6 + \cdots\end{aligned}$$

for $|x| < 1.$ To find a power series for $f(x) = \tan^{-1} x,$ we integrate this series term-by-term.

$$\begin{aligned}\int f'(x)dx &= \int\left(1 - x^2 + x^4 - x^6 + \cdots\right)dx \\ &= C + x - \frac{x^3}{3} + \frac{x^5}{5} - \frac{x^7}{7} + \cdots\end{aligned}$$

Since $\tan^{-1}(0) = 0,$ we have $C = 0.$ Therefore, a power series representation for $f(x) = \tan^{-1} x$ is

$$\begin{aligned}\tan^{-1} x &= x - \frac{x^3}{3} + \frac{x^5}{5} - \frac{x^7}{7} + \cdots \\ &= \sum_{n=0}^{\infty}(-1)^n \frac{x^{2n+1}}{2n+1}\end{aligned}$$

for $|x| < 1.$ Again, **Term-by-Term Differentiation and Integration for Power Series** does not guarantee anything about the convergence of this series at the endpoints. However, checking the endpoints and using the alternating series test, we find that the series converges at $x = 1$ and $x = -1.$ As discussed in part a., using Abel's theorem, it can be shown that the series actually converges to $\tan^{-1}(1)$ and $\tan^{-1}(-1)$ at $x = 1$ and $x = -1,$ respectively. Thus, the interval of convergence is $[-1, 1].$

**6.9** Integrate the power series $\ln(1 + x) = \sum_{n=1}^{\infty}(-1)^{n+1}\frac{x^n}{n}$ term-by-term to evaluate $\int \ln(1 + x)dx.$

Up to this point, we have shown several techniques for finding power series representations for functions. However, how do we know that these power series are unique? That is, given a function *f* and a power series for *f* at *a*, is it possible that there is a different power series for *f* at *a* that we could have found if we had used a different technique? The answer to this question is no. This fact should not seem surprising if we think of power series as polynomials with an infinite number of terms. Intuitively, if

$$c_0 + c_1 x + c_2 x^2 + \cdots = d_0 + d_1 x + d_2 x^2 + \cdots$$

for all values *x* in some open interval *I* about zero, then the coefficients $c_n$ should equal $d_n$ for $n \geq 0.$ We now state this result formally in **Uniqueness of Power Series**.

### Theorem 6.5: Uniqueness of Power Series

Let $\sum_{n=0}^{\infty} c_n(x - a)^n$ and $\sum_{n=0}^{\infty} d_n(x - a)^n$ be two convergent power series such that

$$\sum_{n=0}^{\infty} c_n(x - a)^n = \sum_{n=0}^{\infty} d_n(x - a)^n$$

for all $x$ in an open interval containing $a$. Then $c_n = d_n$ for all $n \geq 0$.

### Proof

Let

$$\begin{aligned} f(x) &= c_0 + c_1(x-a) + c_2(x-a)^2 + c_3(x-a)^3 + \cdots \\ &= d_0 + d_1(x-a) + d_2(x-a)^2 + d_3(x-a)^3 + \cdots. \end{aligned}$$

Then $f(a) = c_0 = d_0$. By **Term-by-Term Differentiation and Integration for Power Series**, we can differentiate both series term-by-term. Therefore,

$$\begin{aligned} f'(x) &= c_1 + 2c_2(x-a) + 3c_3(x-a)^2 + \cdots \\ &= d_1 + 2d_2(x-a) + 3d_3(x-a)^2 + \cdots, \end{aligned}$$

and thus, $f'(a) = c_1 = d_1$. Similarly,

$$\begin{aligned} f''(x) &= 2c_2 + 3 \cdot 2c_3(x-a) + \cdots \\ &= 2d_2 + 3 \cdot 2d_3(x-a) + \cdots \end{aligned}$$

implies that $f''(a) = 2c_2 = 2d_2$, and therefore, $c_2 = d_2$. More generally, for any integer $n \geq 0$, $f^{(n)}(a) = n!c_n = n!d_n$, and consequently, $c_n = d_n$ for all $n \geq 0$.

□

In this section we have shown how to find power series representations for certain functions using various algebraic operations, differentiation, or integration. At this point, however, we are still limited as to the functions for which we can find power series representations. Next, we show how to find power series representations for many more functions by introducing Taylor series.

# 6.2 EXERCISES

63. If $f(x) = \sum_{n=0}^{\infty} \frac{x^n}{n!}$ and $g(x) = \sum_{n=0}^{\infty} (-1)^n \frac{x^n}{n!}$, find the power series of $\frac{1}{2}(f(x) + g(x))$ and of $\frac{1}{2}(f(x) - g(x))$.

64. If $C(x) = \sum_{n=0}^{\infty} \frac{x^{2n}}{(2n)!}$ and $S(x) = \sum_{n=0}^{\infty} \frac{x^{2n+1}}{(2n+1)!}$, find the power series of $C(x) + S(x)$ and of $C(x) - S(x)$.

In the following exercises, use partial fractions to find the power series of each function.

65. $\frac{4}{(x-3)(x+1)}$

66. $\frac{3}{(x+2)(x-1)}$

67. $\frac{5}{\left(x^2+4\right)\left(x^2-1\right)}$

68. $\frac{30}{\left(x^2+1\right)\left(x^2-9\right)}$

In the following exercises, express each series as a rational function.

69. $\sum_{n=1}^{\infty} \frac{1}{x^n}$

70. $\sum_{n=1}^{\infty} \frac{1}{x^{2n}}$

71. $\sum_{n=1}^{\infty} \frac{1}{(x-3)^{2n-1}}$

72. $\sum_{n=1}^{\infty} \left(\frac{1}{(x-3)^{2n-1}} - \frac{1}{(x-2)^{2n-1}}\right)$

The following exercises explore applications of annuities.

73. Calculate the present values $P$ of an annuity in which \$10,000 is to be paid out annually for a period of 20 years, assuming interest rates of $r = 0.03$, $r = 0.05$, and $r = 0.07$.

74. Calculate the present values $P$ of annuities in which \$9,000 is to be paid out annually perpetually, assuming interest rates of $r = 0.03$, $r = 0.05$ and $r = 0.07$.

75. Calculate the annual payouts $C$ to be given for 20 years on annuities having present value \$100,000 assuming respective interest rates of $r = 0.03$, $r = 0.05$, and $r = 0.07$.

76. Calculate the annual payouts $C$ to be given perpetually on annuities having present value \$100,000 assuming respective interest rates of $r = 0.03$, $r = 0.05$, and $r = 0.07$.

77. Suppose that an annuity has a present value $P = 1$ million dollars. What interest rate $r$ would allow for perpetual annual payouts of \$50,000?

78. Suppose that an annuity has a present value $P = 10$ million dollars. What interest rate $r$ would allow for perpetual annual payouts of \$100,000?

In the following exercises, express the sum of each power series in terms of geometric series, and then express the sum as a rational function.

79. $x + x^2 - x^3 + x^4 + x^5 - x^6 + \cdots$ (*Hint:* Group powers $x^{3k}$, $x^{3k-1}$, and $x^{3k-2}$.)

80. $x + x^2 - x^3 - x^4 + x^5 + x^6 - x^7 - x^8 + \cdots$ (*Hint:* Group powers $x^{4k}$, $x^{4k-1}$, etc.)

81. $x - x^2 - x^3 + x^4 - x^5 - x^6 + x^7 - \cdots$ (*Hint:* Group powers $x^{3k}$, $x^{3k-1}$, and $x^{3k-2}$.)

82. $\frac{x}{2} + \frac{x^2}{4} - \frac{x^3}{8} + \frac{x^4}{16} + \frac{x^5}{32} - \frac{x^6}{64} + \cdots$ (*Hint:* Group powers $\left(\frac{x}{2}\right)^{3k}$, $\left(\frac{x}{2}\right)^{3k-1}$, and $\left(\frac{x}{2}\right)^{3k-2}$.)

In the following exercises, find the power series of $f(x)g(x)$ given $f$ and $g$ as defined.

83. $f(x) = 2\sum_{n=0}^{\infty} x^n$, $g(x) = \sum_{n=0}^{\infty} nx^n$

84. $f(x) = \sum_{n=1}^{\infty} x^n$, $g(x) = \sum_{n=1}^{\infty} \frac{1}{n}x^n$. Express the coefficients of $f(x)g(x)$ in terms of $H_n = \sum_{k=1}^{n} \frac{1}{k}$.

85. $f(x) = g(x) = \sum_{n=1}^{\infty} \left(\frac{x}{2}\right)^n$

86. $f(x) = g(x) = \sum_{n=1}^{\infty} nx^n$

In the following exercises, differentiate the given series expansion of $f$ term-by-term to obtain the corresponding series expansion for the derivative of $f$.

87. $f(x) = \frac{1}{1+x} = \sum_{n=0}^{\infty} (-1)^n x^n$

88. $f(x) = \frac{1}{1-x^2} = \sum_{n=0}^{\infty} x^{2n}$

In the following exercises, integrate the given series expansion of $f$ term-by-term from zero to $x$ to obtain the corresponding series expansion for the indefinite integral of $f$.

89. $f(x) = \frac{2x}{\left(1+x^2\right)^2} = \sum_{n=1}^{\infty} (-1)^n (2n)x^{2n-1}$

90. $f(x) = \frac{2x}{1+x^2} = 2\sum_{n=0}^{\infty} (-1)^n x^{2n+1}$

In the following exercises, evaluate each infinite series by identifying it as the value of a derivative or integral of geometric series.

91. Evaluate $\sum_{n=1}^{\infty} \frac{n}{2^n}$ as $f'\left(\frac{1}{2}\right)$ where $f(x) = \sum_{n=0}^{\infty} x^n$.

92. Evaluate $\sum_{n=1}^{\infty} \frac{n}{3^n}$ as $f'\left(\frac{1}{3}\right)$ where $f(x) = \sum_{n=0}^{\infty} x^n$.

93. Evaluate $\sum_{n=2}^{\infty} \frac{n(n-1)}{2^n}$ as $f''\left(\frac{1}{2}\right)$ where $f(x) = \sum_{n=0}^{\infty} x^n$.

94. Evaluate $\sum_{n=0}^{\infty} \frac{(-1)^n}{n+1}$ as $\int_0^1 f(t)dt$ where $f(x) = \sum_{n=0}^{\infty} (-1)^n x^{2n} = \frac{1}{1+x^2}$.

In the following exercises, given that $\frac{1}{1-x} = \sum_{n=0}^{\infty} x^n$, use term-by-term differentiation or integration to find power series for each function centered at the given point.

95. $f(x) = \ln x$ centered at $x = 1$ (*Hint:* $x = 1 - (1 - x)$)

96. $\ln(1 - x)$ at $x = 0$

97. $\ln\left(1 - x^2\right)$ at $x = 0$

98. $f(x) = \frac{2x}{\left(1 - x^2\right)^2}$ at $x = 0$

99. $f(x) = \tan^{-1}\left(x^2\right)$ at $x = 0$

100. $f(x) = \ln\left(1 + x^2\right)$ at $x = 0$

101. $f(x) = \int_0^x \ln t dt$ where $\ln(x) = \sum_{n=1}^{\infty} (-1)^{n-1} \frac{(x-1)^n}{n}$

102. **[T]** Evaluate the power series expansion $\ln(1+x) = \sum_{n=1}^{\infty} (-1)^{n-1} \frac{x^n}{n}$ at $x = 1$ to show that $\ln(2)$ is the sum of the alternating harmonic series. Use the alternating series test to determine how many terms of the sum are needed to estimate $\ln(2)$ accurate to within 0.001, and find such an approximation.

103. **[T]** Subtract the infinite series of $\ln(1-x)$ from $\ln(1+x)$ to get a power series for $\ln\left(\frac{1+x}{1-x}\right)$. Evaluate at $x = \frac{1}{3}$. What is the smallest $N$ such that the $N$th partial sum of this series approximates $\ln(2)$ with an error less than 0.001?

In the following exercises, using a substitution if indicated, express each series in terms of elementary functions and find the radius of convergence of the sum.

104. $\sum_{k=0}^{\infty} \left(x^k - x^{2k+1}\right)$

105. $\sum_{k=1}^{\infty} \frac{x^{3k}}{6k}$

106. $\sum_{k=1}^{\infty} \left(1 + x^2\right)^{-k}$ using $y = \frac{1}{1+x^2}$

107. $\sum_{k=1}^{\infty} 2^{-kx}$ using $y = 2^{-x}$

108. Show that, up to powers $x^3$ and $y^3$, $E(x) = \sum_{n=0}^{\infty} \frac{x^n}{n!}$ satisfies $E(x+y) = E(x)E(y)$.

109. Differentiate the series $E(x) = \sum_{n=0}^{\infty} \frac{x^n}{n!}$ term-by-term to show that $E(x)$ is equal to its derivative.

110. Show that if $f(x) = \sum_{n=0}^{\infty} a_n x^n$ is a sum of even powers, that is, $a_n = 0$ if $n$ is odd, then $F = \int_0^x f(t)dt$ is a sum of odd powers, while if $f$ is a sum of odd powers, then $F$ is a sum of even powers.

111. **[T]** Suppose that the coefficients $a_n$ of the series $\sum_{n=0}^{\infty} a_n x^n$ are defined by the recurrence relation $a_n = \frac{a_{n-1}}{n} + \frac{a_{n-2}}{n(n-1)}$. For $a_0 = 0$ and $a_1 = 1$, compute and plot the sums $S_N = \sum_{n=0}^{N} a_n x^n$ for $N = 2, 3, 4, 5$ on $[-1, 1]$.

112. **[T]** Suppose that the coefficients $a_n$ of the series $\sum_{n=0}^{\infty} a_n x^n$ are defined by the recurrence relation $a_n = \frac{a_{n-1}}{\sqrt{n}} - \frac{a_{n-2}}{\sqrt{n(n-1)}}$. For $a_0 = 1$ and $a_1 = 0$, compute and plot the sums $S_N = \sum_{n=0}^{N} a_n x^n$ for $N = 2, 3, 4, 5$ on $[-1, 1]$.

113. **[T]** Given the power series expansion $\ln(1+x) = \sum_{n=1}^{\infty} (-1)^{n-1} \frac{x^n}{n}$, determine how many terms $N$ of the sum evaluated at $x = -1/2$ are needed to approximate $\ln(2)$ accurate to within 1/1000. Evaluate the corresponding partial sum $\sum_{n=1}^{N} (-1)^{n-1} \frac{x^n}{n}$.

114. **[T]** Given the power series expansion $\tan^{-1}(x) = \sum_{k=0}^{\infty} (-1)^k \frac{x^{2k+1}}{2k+1}$, use the alternating series test to determine how many terms $N$ of the sum evaluated at $x = 1$ are needed to approximate $\tan^{-1}(1) = \frac{\pi}{4}$ accurate to within 1/1000. Evaluate the corresponding partial sum $\sum_{k=0}^{N} (-1)^k \frac{x^{2k+1}}{2k+1}$.

115. **[T]** Recall that $\tan^{-1}\left(\frac{1}{\sqrt{3}}\right) = \frac{\pi}{6}$. Assuming an exact value of $\left(\frac{1}{\sqrt{3}}\right)$, estimate $\frac{\pi}{6}$ by evaluating partial sums $S_N\left(\frac{1}{\sqrt{3}}\right)$ of the power series expansion $\tan^{-1}(x) = \sum_{k=0}^{\infty} (-1)^k \frac{x^{2k+1}}{2k+1}$ at $x = \frac{1}{\sqrt{3}}$. What is the smallest number $N$ such that $6S_N\left(\frac{1}{\sqrt{3}}\right)$ approximates $\pi$ accurately to within 0.001? How many terms are needed for accuracy to within 0.00001?

# 6.3 | Taylor and Maclaurin Series

**Learning Objectives**

**6.3.1** Describe the procedure for finding a Taylor polynomial of a given order for a function.
**6.3.2** Explain the meaning and significance of Taylor's theorem with remainder.
**6.3.3** Estimate the remainder for a Taylor series approximation of a given function.

In the previous two sections we discussed how to find power series representations for certain types of functions—specifically, functions related to geometric series. Here we discuss power series representations for other types of functions. In particular, we address the following questions: Which functions can be represented by power series and how do we find such representations? If we can find a power series representation for a particular function $f$ and the series converges on some interval, how do we prove that the series actually converges to $f$?

## Overview of Taylor/Maclaurin Series

Consider a function $f$ that has a power series representation at $x = a.$ Then the series has the form

$$\sum_{n=0}^{\infty} c_n (x-a)^n = c_0 + c_1(x-a) + c_2(x-a)^2 + \cdots. \tag{6.4}$$

What should the coefficients be? For now, we ignore issues of convergence, but instead focus on what the series should be, if one exists. We return to discuss convergence later in this section. If the series **Equation 6.4** is a representation for $f$ at $x = a,$ we certainly want the series to equal $f(a)$ at $x = a.$ Evaluating the series at $x = a,$ we see that

$$\begin{aligned}\sum_{n=0}^{\infty} c_n (x-a)^n &= c_0 + c_1(a-a) + c_2(a-a)^2 + \cdots \\ &= c_0.\end{aligned}$$

Thus, the series equals $f(a)$ if the coefficient $c_0 = f(a).$ In addition, we would like the first derivative of the power series to equal $f'(a)$ at $x = a.$ Differentiating **Equation 6.4** term-by-term, we see that

$$\frac{d}{dx}\left(\sum_{n=0}^{\infty} c_n (x-a)^n\right) = c_1 + 2c_2(x-a) + 3c_3(x-a)^2 + \cdots.$$

Therefore, at $x = a,$ the derivative is

$$\begin{aligned}\frac{d}{dx}\left(\sum_{n=0}^{\infty} c_n (x-a)^n\right) &= c_1 + 2c_2(a-a) + 3c_3(a-a)^2 + \cdots \\ &= c_1.\end{aligned}$$

Therefore, the derivative of the series equals $f'(a)$ if the coefficient $c_1 = f'(a).$ Continuing in this way, we look for coefficients $c_n$ such that all the derivatives of the power series **Equation 6.4** will agree with all the corresponding derivatives of $f$ at $x = a.$ The second and third derivatives of **Equation 6.4** are given by

$$\frac{d^2}{dx^2}\left(\sum_{n=0}^{\infty} c_n (x-a)^n\right) = 2c_2 + 3\cdot 2c_3(x-a) + 4\cdot 3c_4(x-a)^2 + \cdots$$

and

$$\frac{d^3}{dx^3}\left(\sum_{n=0}^{\infty} c_n (x-a)^n\right) = 3\cdot 2c_3 + 4\cdot 3\cdot 2c_4(x-a) + 5\cdot 4\cdot 3c_5(x-a)^2 + \cdots.$$

Therefore, at $x = a,$ the second and third derivatives

$$\frac{d^2}{dx^2}\left(\sum_{n=0}^{\infty} c_n(x-a)^n\right) = 2c_2 + 3\cdot 2c_3(a-a) + 4\cdot 3c_4(a-a)^2 + \cdots$$
$$= 2c_2$$

and

$$\frac{d^3}{dx^3}\left(\sum_{n=0}^{\infty} c_n(x-a)^n\right) = 3\cdot 2c_3 + 4\cdot 3\cdot 2c_4(a-a) + 5\cdot 4\cdot 3c_5(a-a)^2 + \cdots$$
$$= 3\cdot 2c_3$$

equal $f''(a)$ and $f'''(a)$, respectively, if $c_2 = \frac{f''(a)}{2}$ and $c_3 = \frac{f'''(a)}{3}\cdot 2$. More generally, we see that if $f$ has a power series representation at $x = a$, then the coefficients should be given by $c_n = \frac{f^{(n)}(a)}{n!}$. That is, the series should be

$$\sum_{n=0}^{\infty} \frac{f^{(n)}(a)}{n!}(x-a)^n = f(a) + f'(a)(x-a) + \frac{f''(a)}{2!}(x-a)^2 + \frac{f'''(a)}{3!}(x-a)^3 + \cdots.$$

This power series for $f$ is known as the Taylor series for $f$ at $a$. If $x = 0$, then this series is known as the Maclaurin series for $f$.

**Definition**

If $f$ has derivatives of all orders at $x = a$, then the **Taylor series** for the function $f$ at $a$ is

$$\sum_{n=0}^{\infty} \frac{f^{(n)}(a)}{n!}(x-a)^n = f(a) + f'(a)(x-a) + \frac{f''(a)}{2!}(x-a)^2 + \cdots + \frac{f^{(n)}(a)}{n!}(x-a)^n + \cdots. \quad (6.5)$$

The Taylor series for $f$ at 0 is known as the **Maclaurin series** for $f$.

Later in this section, we will show examples of finding Taylor series and discuss conditions under which the Taylor series for a function will converge to that function. Here, we state an important result. Recall from **Uniqueness of Power Series** that power series representations are unique. Therefore, if a function $f$ has a power series at $a$, then it must be the Taylor series for $f$ at $a$.

**Theorem 6.6: Uniqueness of Taylor Series**

If a function $f$ has a power series at *a* that converges to $f$ on some open interval containing *a*, then that power series is the Taylor series for $f$ at *a*.

The proof follows directly from **Uniqueness of Power Series**.

To determine if a Taylor series converges, we need to look at its sequence of partial sums. These partial sums are finite polynomials, known as **Taylor polynomials**.

Visit the MacTutor History of Mathematics archive to read brief biographies of **Brook Taylor (http://www.openstaxcollege.org/l/20_BTaylor)** and **Colin Maclaurin (http://www.openstaxcollege.org/l/20_CMaclaurin)** and how they developed the concepts named after them.

## Taylor Polynomials

The *n*th partial sum of the Taylor series for a function $f$ at $a$ is known as the *n*th Taylor polynomial. For example, the 0th,

1st, 2nd, and 3rd partial sums of the Taylor series are given by

$$p_0(x) = f(a),$$
$$p_1(x) = f(a) + f'(a)(x-a),$$
$$p_2(x) = f(a) + f'(a)(x-a) + \frac{f''(a)}{2!}(x-a)^2,$$
$$p_3(x) = f(a) + f'(a)(x-a) + \frac{f''(a)}{2!}(x-a)^2 + \frac{f'''(a)}{3!}(x-a)^3,$$

respectively. These partial sums are known as the 0th, 1st, 2nd, and 3rd Taylor polynomials of $f$ at $a$, respectively. If $x = a$, then these polynomials are known as **Maclaurin polynomials** for $f$. We now provide a formal definition of Taylor and Maclaurin polynomials for a function $f$.

### Definition

If $f$ has $n$ derivatives at $x = a$, then the $n$th Taylor polynomial for $f$ at $a$ is

$$p_n(x) = f(a) + f'(a)(x-a) + \frac{f''(a)}{2!}(x-a)^2 + \frac{f'''(a)}{3!}(x-a)^3 + \cdots + \frac{f^{(n)}(a)}{n!}(x-a)^n.$$

The $n$th Taylor polynomial for $f$ at 0 is known as the $n$th Maclaurin polynomial for $f$.

We now show how to use this definition to find several Taylor polynomials for $f(x) = \ln x$ at $x = 1$.

## Example 6.11

### Finding Taylor Polynomials

Find the Taylor polynomials $p_0, p_1, p_2$ and $p_3$ for $f(x) = \ln x$ at $x = 1$. Use a graphing utility to compare the graph of $f$ with the graphs of $p_0, p_1, p_2$ and $p_3$.

### Solution

To find these Taylor polynomials, we need to evaluate $f$ and its first three derivatives at $x = 1$.

$$\begin{aligned} f(x) &= \ln x & f(1) &= 0 \\ f'(x) &= \frac{1}{x} & f'(1) &= 1 \\ f''(x) &= -\frac{1}{x^2} & f''(1) &= -1 \\ f'''(x) &= \frac{2}{x^3} & f'''(1) &= 2 \end{aligned}$$

Therefore,

$$\begin{aligned} p_0(x) &= f(1) = 0, \\ p_1(x) &= f(1) + f'(1)(x-1) = x - 1, \\ p_2(x) &= f(1) + f'(1)(x-1) + \frac{f''(1)}{2}(x-1)^2 = (x-1) - \frac{1}{2}(x-1)^2, \\ p_3(x) &= f(1) + f'(1)(x-1) + \frac{f''(1)}{2}(x-1)^2 + \frac{f'''(1)}{3!}(x-1)^3 \\ &= (x-1) - \frac{1}{2}(x-1)^2 + \frac{1}{3}(x-1)^3. \end{aligned}$$

The graphs of $y = f(x)$ and the first three Taylor polynomials are shown in **Figure 6.5**.

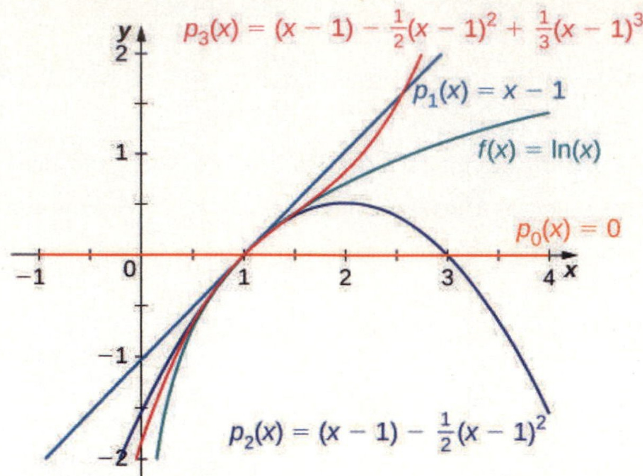


**Figure 6.5** The function $y = \ln x$ and the Taylor polynomials $p_0, p_1, p_2$ and $p_3$ at $x = 1$ are plotted on this graph.

**6.10** Find the Taylor polynomials $p_0, p_1, p_2$ and $p_3$ for $f(x) = \frac{1}{x^2}$ at $x = 1$.

We now show how to find Maclaurin polynomials for $e^x$, $\sin x$, and $\cos x$. As stated above, Maclaurin polynomials are Taylor polynomials centered at zero.

## Example 6.12

### Finding Maclaurin Polynomials

For each of the following functions, find formulas for the Maclaurin polynomials $p_0, p_1, p_2$ and $p_3$. Find a formula for the *n*th Maclaurin polynomial and write it using sigma notation. Use a graphing utilty to compare the graphs of $p_0, p_1, p_2$ and $p_3$ with $f$.

a. $f(x) = e^x$

b. $f(x) = \sin x$

c. $f(x) = \cos x$

### Solution

a. Since $f(x) = e^x$, we know that $f(x) = f'(x) = f''(x) = \cdots = f^{(n)}(x) = e^x$ for all positive integers $n$. Therefore,

$$f(0) = f'(0) = f''(0) = \cdots = f^{(n)}(0) = 1$$

for all positive integers $n$. Therefore, we have

$$\begin{aligned}
p_0(x) &= f(0) = 1, \\
p_1(x) &= f(0) + f'(0)x = 1 + x, \\
p_2(x) &= f(0) + f'(0)x + \frac{f''(0)}{2!}x^2 = 1 + x + \frac{1}{2}x^2, \\
p_3(x) &= f(0) + f'(0)x + \frac{f''(0)}{2}x^2 + \frac{f'''(0)}{3!}x^3 \\
&= 1 + x + \frac{1}{2}x^2 + \frac{1}{3!}x^3, \\
p_n(x) &= f(0) + f'(0)x + \frac{f''(0)}{2}x^2 + \frac{f'''(0)}{3!}x^3 + \cdots + \frac{f^{(n)}(0)}{n!}x^n \\
&= 1 + x + \frac{x^2}{2!} + \frac{x^3}{3!} + \cdots + \frac{x^n}{n!} \\
&= \sum_{k=0}^{n} \frac{x^k}{k!}.
\end{aligned}$$

The function and the first three Maclaurin polynomials are shown in **Figure 6.6**.

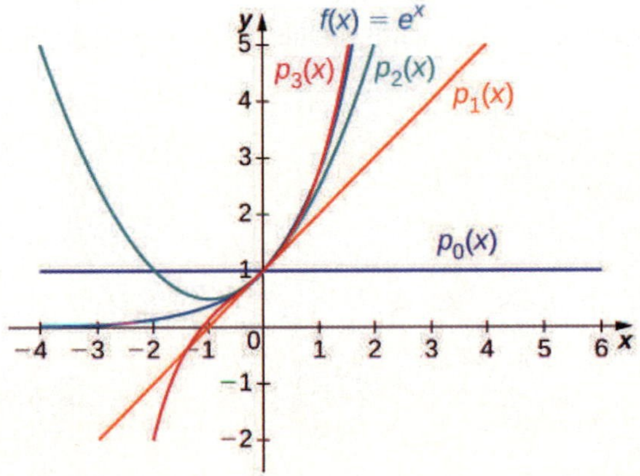


**Figure 6.6** The graph shows the function $y = e^x$ and the Maclaurin polynomials $p_0$, $p_1$, $p_2$ and $p_3$.

b. For $f(x) = \sin x$, the values of the function and its first four derivatives at $x = 0$ are given as follows:

$$\begin{aligned}
f(x) &= \sin x & f(0) &= 0 \\
f'(x) &= \cos x & f'(0) &= 1 \\
f''(x) &= -\sin x & f''(0) &= 0 \\
f'''(x) &= -\cos x & f'''(0) &= -1 \\
f^{(4)}(x) &= \sin x & f^{(4)}(0) &= 0.
\end{aligned}$$

Since the fourth derivative is $\sin x$, the pattern repeats. That is, $f^{(2m)}(0) = 0$ and $f^{(2m+1)}(0) = (-1)^m$ for $m \geq 0$. Thus, we have

$$\begin{aligned}
p_0(x) &= 0, \\
p_1(x) &= 0 + x = x, \\
p_2(x) &= 0 + x + 0 = x, \\
p_3(x) &= 0 + x + 0 - \frac{1}{3!}x^3 = x - \frac{x^3}{3!}, \\
p_4(x) &= 0 + x + 0 - \frac{1}{3!}x^3 + 0 = x - \frac{x^3}{3!}, \\
p_5(x) &= 0 + x + 0 - \frac{1}{3!}x^3 + 0 + \frac{1}{5!}x^5 = x - \frac{x^3}{3!} + \frac{x^5}{5!},
\end{aligned}$$

and for $m \geq 0,$

$$\begin{aligned}
p_{2m+1}(x) &= p_{2m+2}(x) \\
&= x - \frac{x^3}{3!} + \frac{x^5}{5!} - \cdots + (-1)^m \frac{x^{2m+1}}{(2m+1)!} \\
&= \sum_{k=0}^{m} (-1)^k \frac{x^{2k+1}}{(2k+1)!}.
\end{aligned}$$

Graphs of the function and its Maclaurin polynomials are shown in **Figure 6.7**.

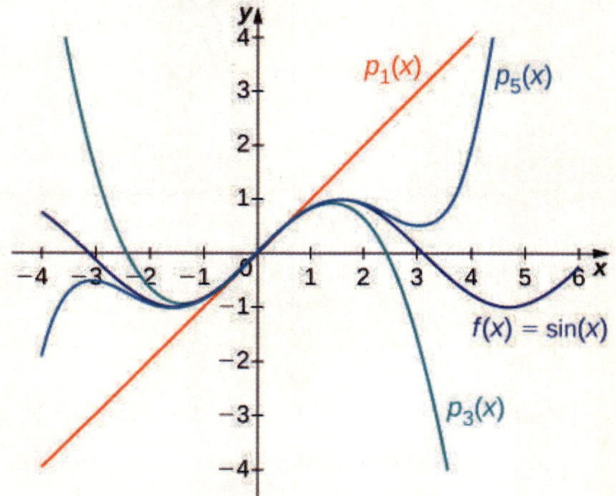


**Figure 6.7** The graph shows the function $y = \sin x$ and the Maclaurin polynomials $p_1$, $p_3$ and $p_5$.

c. For $f(x) = \cos x,$ the values of the function and its first four derivatives at $x = 0$ are given as follows:

$$\begin{aligned}
f(x) &= \cos x & f(0) &= 1 \\
f'(x) &= -\sin x & f'(0) &= 0 \\
f''(x) &= -\cos x & f''(0) &= -1 \\
f'''(x) &= \sin x & f'''(0) &= 0 \\
f^{(4)}(x) &= \cos x & f^{(4)}(0) &= 1.
\end{aligned}$$

Since the fourth derivative is $\sin x,$ the pattern repeats. In other words, $f^{(2m)}(0) = (-1)^m$ and

$f^{(2m+1)} = 0$ for $m \geq 0$. Therefore,

$$\begin{aligned} p_0(x) &= 1, \\ p_1(x) &= 1 + 0 = 1, \\ p_2(x) &= 1 + 0 - \frac{1}{2!}x^2 = 1 - \frac{x^2}{2!}, \\ p_3(x) &= 1 + 0 - \frac{1}{2!}x^2 + 0 = 1 - \frac{x^2}{2!}, \\ p_4(x) &= 1 + 0 - \frac{1}{2!}x^2 + 0 + \frac{1}{4!}x^4 = 1 - \frac{x^2}{2!} + \frac{x^4}{4!}, \\ p_5(x) &= 1 + 0 - \frac{1}{2!}x^2 + 0 + \frac{1}{4!}x^4 + 0 = 1 - \frac{x^2}{2!} + \frac{x^4}{4!}, \end{aligned}$$

and for $n \geq 0$,

$$\begin{aligned} p_{2m}(x) &= p_{2m+1}(x) \\ &= 1 - \frac{x^2}{2!} + \frac{x^4}{4!} - \cdots + (-1)^m \frac{x^{2m}}{(2m)!} \\ &= \sum_{k=0}^{m} (-1)^k \frac{x^{2k}}{(2k)!}. \end{aligned}$$

Graphs of the function and the Maclaurin polynomials appear in **Figure 6.8**.

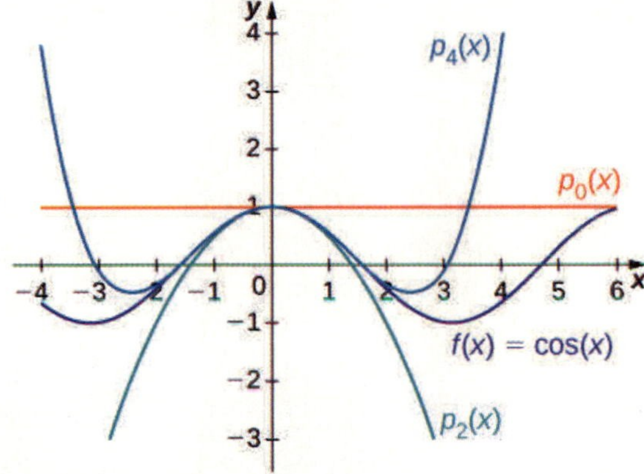


**Figure 6.8** The function $y = \cos x$ and the Maclaurin polynomials $p_0$, $p_2$ and $p_4$ are plotted on this graph.

**6.11** Find formulas for the Maclaurin polynomials $p_0$, $p_1$, $p_2$ and $p_3$ for $f(x) = \frac{1}{1+x}$. Find a formula for the $n$th Maclaurin polynomial. Write your anwer using sigma notation.

## Taylor's Theorem with Remainder

Recall that the $n$th Taylor polynomial for a function $f$ at $a$ is the $n$th partial sum of the Taylor series for $f$ at $a$. Therefore, to determine if the Taylor series converges, we need to determine whether the sequence of Taylor polynomials $\{p_n\}$ converges. However, not only do we want to know if the sequence of Taylor polynomials converges, we want to know if it converges to $f$. To answer this question, we define the remainder $R_n(x)$ as

$$R_n(x) = f(x) - p_n(x).$$

For the sequence of Taylor polynomials to converge to $f$, we need the remainder $R_n$ to converge to zero. To determine if $R_n$ converges to zero, we introduce **Taylor's theorem with remainder**. Not only is this theorem useful in proving that a Taylor series converges to its related function, but it will also allow us to quantify how well the *n*th Taylor polynomial approximates the function.

Here we look for a bound on $|R_n|$. Consider the simplest case: $n = 0$. Let $p_0$ be the 0th Taylor polynomial at $a$ for a function $f$. The remainder $R_0$ satisfies

$$\begin{aligned} R_0(x) &= f(x) - p_0(x) \\ &= f(x) - f(a). \end{aligned}$$

If $f$ is differentiable on an interval $I$ containing $a$ and $x$, then by the Mean Value Theorem there exists a real number $c$ between $a$ and $x$ such that $f(x) - f(a) = f'(c)(x - a)$. Therefore,

$$R_0(x) = f'(c)(x - a).$$

Using the Mean Value Theorem in a similar argument, we can show that if $f$ is $n$ times differentiable on an interval $I$ containing $a$ and $x$, then the *n*th remainder $R_n$ satisfies

$$R_n(x) = \frac{f^{(n+1)}(c)}{(n+1)!}(x - a)^{n+1}$$

for some real number $c$ between $a$ and $x$. It is important to note that the value $c$ in the numerator above is not the center $a$, but rather an unknown value $c$ between $a$ and $x$. This formula allows us to get a bound on the remainder $R_n$. If we happen to know that $\left|f^{(n+1)}(x)\right|$ is bounded by some real number $M$ on this interval $I$, then

$$|R_n(x)| \le \frac{M}{(n+1)!}|x - a|^{n+1}$$

for all $x$ in the interval $I$.

We now state Taylor's theorem, which provides the formal relationship between a function $f$ and its *n*th degree Taylor polynomial $p_n(x)$. This theorem allows us to bound the error when using a Taylor polynomial to approximate a function value, and will be important in proving that a Taylor series for $f$ converges to $f$.

### Theorem 6.7: Taylor's Theorem with Remainder

Let $f$ be a function that can be differentiated $n + 1$ times on an interval $I$ containing the real number $a$. Let $p_n$ be the *n*th Taylor polynomial of $f$ at $a$ and let

$$R_n(x) = f(x) - p_n(x)$$

be the *n*th remainder. Then for each $x$ in the interval $I$, there exists a real number $c$ between $a$ and $x$ such that

$$R_n(x) = \frac{f^{(n+1)}(c)}{(n+1)!}(x - a)^{n+1}.$$

If there exists a real number $M$ such that $\left|f^{(n+1)}(x)\right| \le M$ for all $x \in I$, then

$$|R_n(x)| \le \frac{M}{(n+1)!}|x - a|^{n+1}$$

for all $x$ in $I$.

### Proof

Fix a point $x \in I$ and introduce the function $g$ such that

$$g(t) = f(x) - f(t) - f'(t)(x-t) - \frac{f''(t)}{2!}(x-t)^2 - \cdots - \frac{f^{(n)}(t)}{n!}(x-t)^n - R_n(x)\frac{(x-t)^{n+1}}{(x-a)^{n+1}}.$$

We claim that $g$ satisfies the criteria of Rolle's theorem. Since $g$ is a polynomial function (in $t$), it is a differentiable function. Also, $g$ is zero at $t = a$ and $t = x$ because

$$\begin{aligned} g(a) &= f(x) - f(a) - f'(a)(x-a) - \frac{f''(a)}{2!}(x-a)^2 + \cdots + \frac{f^{(n)}(a)}{n!}(x-a)^n - R_n(x) \\ &= f(x) - p_n(x) - R_n(x) \\ &= 0, \\ g(x) &= f(x) - f(x) - 0 - \cdots - 0 \\ &= 0. \end{aligned}$$

Therefore, $g$ satisfies Rolle's theorem, and consequently, there exists $c$ between $a$ and $x$ such that $g'(c) = 0.$ We now calculate $g'$. Using the product rule, we note that

$$\frac{d}{dt}\left[\frac{f^{(n)}(t)}{n!}(x-t)^n\right] = \frac{-f^{(n)}(t)}{(n-1)!}(x-t)^{n-1} + \frac{f^{(n+1)}(t)}{n!}(x-t)^n.$$

Consequently,

$$\begin{aligned} g'(t) &= -f'(t) + [f'(t) - f''(t)(x-t)] + \left[f''(t)(x-t) - \frac{f'''(t)}{2!}(x-t)^2\right] + \cdots \\ &\quad + \left[\frac{f^{(n)}(t)}{(n-1)!}(x-t)^{n-1} - \frac{f^{(n+1)}(t)}{n!}(x-t)^n\right] + (n+1)R_n(x)\frac{(x-t)^n}{(x-a)^{n+1}}. \end{aligned}$$

Notice that there is a telescoping effect. Therefore,

$$g'(t) = -\frac{f^{(n+1)}(t)}{n!}(x-t)^n + (n+1)R_n(x)\frac{(x-t)^n}{(x-a)^{n+1}}.$$

By Rolle's theorem, we conclude that there exists a number $c$ between $a$ and $x$ such that $g'(c) = 0.$ Since

$$g'(c) = -\frac{f^{(n+1)}(c)}{n!}(x-c)^n + (n+1)R_n(x)\frac{(x-c)^n}{(x-a)^{n+1}}$$

we conclude that

$$-\frac{f^{(n+1)}(c)}{n!}(x-c)^n + (n+1)R_n(x)\frac{(x-c)^n}{(x-a)^{n+1}} = 0.$$

Adding the first term on the left-hand side to both sides of the equation and dividing both sides of the equation by $n+1,$ we conclude that

$$R_n(x) = \frac{f^{(n+1)}(c)}{(n+1)!}(x-a)^{n+1}$$

as desired. From this fact, it follows that if there exists $M$ such that $\left|f^{(n+1)}(x)\right| \leq M$ for all $x$ in $I$, then

$$|R_n(x)| \leq \frac{M}{(n+1)!}|x-a|^{n+1}.$$

□

Not only does Taylor's theorem allow us to prove that a Taylor series converges to a function, but it also allows us to estimate the accuracy of Taylor polynomials in approximating function values. We begin by looking at linear and quadratic approximations of $f(x) = \sqrt[3]{x}$ at $x = 8$ and determine how accurate these approximations are at estimating $\sqrt[3]{11}$.

## Example 6.13

### Using Linear and Quadratic Approximations to Estimate Function Values

Consider the function $f(x) = \sqrt[3]{x}$.

a. Find the first and second Taylor polynomials for $f$ at $x = 8$. Use a graphing utility to compare these polynomials with $f$ near $x = 8$.

b. Use these two polynomials to estimate $\sqrt[3]{11}$.

c. Use Taylor's theorem to bound the error.

### Solution

a. For $f(x) = \sqrt[3]{x}$, the values of the function and its first two derivatives at $x = 8$ are as follows:

$$\begin{aligned} f(x) &= \sqrt[3]{x} & f(8) &= 2 \\ f'(x) &= \frac{1}{3x^{2/3}} & f'(8) &= \frac{1}{12} \\ f''(x) &= \frac{-2}{9x^{5/3}} & f''(8) &= -\frac{1}{144}. \end{aligned}$$

Thus, the first and second Taylor polynomials at $x = 8$ are given by

$$\begin{aligned} p_1(x) &= f(8) + f'(8)(x-8) \\ &= 2 + \frac{1}{12}(x-8) \\ p_2(x) &= f(8) + f'(8)(x-8) + \frac{f''(8)}{2!}(x-8)^2 \\ &= 2 + \frac{1}{12}(x-8) - \frac{1}{288}(x-8)^2. \end{aligned}$$

The function and the Taylor polynomials are shown in **Figure 6.9**.

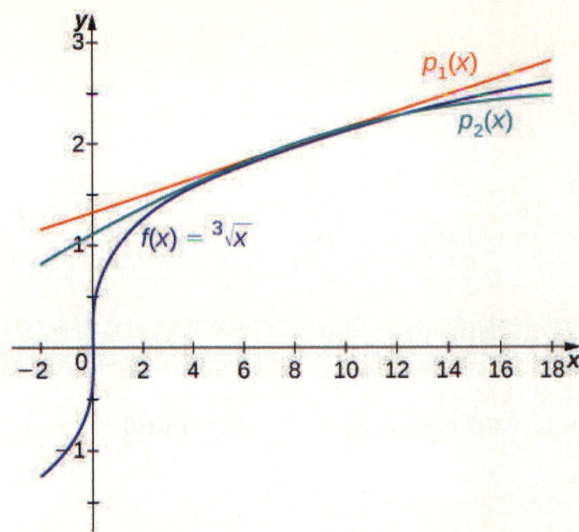


**Figure 6.9** The graphs of $f(x) = \sqrt[3]{x}$ and the linear and quadratic approximations $p_1(x)$ and $p_2(x)$.

b. Using the first Taylor polynomial at $x = 8$, we can estimate

$$\sqrt[3]{11} \approx p_1(11) = 2 + \frac{1}{12}(11 - 8) = 2.25.$$

Using the second Taylor polynomial at $x = 8$, we obtain

$$\sqrt[3]{11} \approx p_2(11) = 2 + \frac{1}{12}(11 - 8) - \frac{1}{288}(11 - 8)^2 = 2.21875.$$

c. By **Uniqueness of Taylor Series**, there exists a $c$ in the interval $(8, 11)$ such that the remainder when approximating $\sqrt[3]{11}$ by the first Taylor polynomial satisfies

$$R_1(11) = \frac{f''(c)}{2!}(11 - 8)^2.$$

We do not know the exact value of $c$, so we find an upper bound on $R_1(11)$ by determining the maximum value of $f''$ on the interval $(8, 11)$. Since $f''(x) = -\frac{2}{9x^{5/3}}$, the largest value for $|f''(x)|$ on that interval occurs at $x = 8$. Using the fact that $f''(8) = -\frac{1}{144}$, we obtain

$$|R_1(11)| \le \frac{1}{144 \cdot 2!}(11 - 8)^2 = 0.03125.$$

Similarly, to estimate $R_2(11)$, we use the fact that

$$R_2(11) = \frac{f'''(c)}{3!}(11 - 8)^3.$$

Since $f'''(x) = \frac{10}{27x^{8/3}}$, the maximum value of $f'''$ on the interval $(8, 11)$ is $f'''(8) \approx 0.0014468$. Therefore, we have

$$|R_2(11)| \leq \frac{0.0011468}{3!}(11-8)^3 \approx 0.0065104.$$

**6.12** Find the first and second Taylor polynomials for $f(x) = \sqrt{x}$ at $x = 4$. Use these polynomials to estimate $\sqrt{6}$. Use Taylor's theorem to bound the error.

## Example 6.14

### Approximating sin *x* Using Maclaurin Polynomials

From **Example 6.12**b., the Maclaurin polynomials for $\sin x$ are given by

$$\begin{aligned} p_{2m+1}(x) &= p_{2m+2}(x) \\ &= x - \frac{x^3}{3!} + \frac{x^5}{5!} - \frac{x^7}{7!} + \cdots + (-1)^m \frac{x^{2m+1}}{(2m+1)!} \end{aligned}$$

for $m = 0, 1, 2, \ldots$.

a. Use the fifth Maclaurin polynomial for $\sin x$ to approximate $\sin\left(\frac{\pi}{18}\right)$ and bound the error.

b. For what values of *x* does the fifth Maclaurin polynomial approximate $\sin x$ to within 0.0001?

### Solution

a. The fifth Maclaurin polynomial is

$$p_5(x) = x - \frac{x^3}{3!} + \frac{x^5}{5!}.$$

Using this polynomial, we can estimate as follows:

$$\begin{aligned} \sin\left(\frac{\pi}{18}\right) &\approx p_5\left(\frac{\pi}{18}\right) \\ &= \frac{\pi}{18} - \frac{1}{3!}\left(\frac{\pi}{18}\right)^3 + \frac{1}{5!}\left(\frac{\pi}{18}\right)^5 \\ &\approx 0.173648. \end{aligned}$$

To estimate the error, use the fact that the sixth Maclaurin polynomial is $p_6(x) = p_5(x)$ and calculate a bound on $R_6\left(\frac{\pi}{18}\right)$. By **Uniqueness of Taylor Series**, the remainder is

$$R_6\left(\frac{\pi}{18}\right) = \frac{f^{(7)}(c)}{7!}\left(\frac{\pi}{18}\right)^7$$

for some *c* between 0 and $\frac{\pi}{18}$. Using the fact that $\left|f^{(7)}(x)\right| \leq 1$ for all *x*, we find that the magnitude of the error is at most

$$\frac{1}{7!} \cdot \left(\frac{\pi}{18}\right)^7 \leq 9.8 \times 10^{-10}.$$

b. We need to find the values of $x$ such that

$$\frac{1}{7!}|x|^7 \leq 0.0001.$$

Solving this inequality for $x$, we have that the fifth Maclaurin polynomial gives an estimate to within 0.0001 as long as $|x| < 0.907$.

**6.13** Use the fourth Maclaurin polynomial for $\cos x$ to approximate $\cos\left(\frac{\pi}{12}\right)$.

Now that we are able to bound the remainder $R_n(x)$, we can use this bound to prove that a Taylor series for $f$ at $a$ converges to $f$.

## Representing Functions with Taylor and Maclaurin Series

We now discuss issues of convergence for Taylor series. We begin by showing how to find a Taylor series for a function, and how to find its interval of convergence.

### Example 6.15

#### Finding a Taylor Series

Find the Taylor series for $f(x) = \frac{1}{x}$ at $x = 1$. Determine the interval of convergence.

#### Solution

For $f(x) = \frac{1}{x}$, the values of the function and its first four derivatives at $x = 1$ are

$$\begin{aligned} f(x) &= \frac{1}{x} & f(1) &= 1 \\ f'(x) &= -\frac{1}{x^2} & f'(1) &= -1 \\ f''(x) &= \frac{2}{x^3} & f''(1) &= 2! \\ f'''(x) &= -\frac{3 \cdot 2}{x^4} & f'''(1) &= -3! \\ f^{(4)}(x) &= \frac{4 \cdot 3 \cdot 2}{x^5} & f^{(4)}(1) &= 4!. \end{aligned}$$

That is, we have $f^{(n)}(1) = (-1)^n n!$ for all $n \geq 0$. Therefore, the Taylor series for $f$ at $x = 1$ is given by

$$\sum_{n=0}^{\infty} \frac{f^{(n)}(1)}{n!}(x-1)^n = \sum_{n=0}^{\infty} (-1)^n (x-1)^n.$$

To find the interval of convergence, we use the ratio test. We find that

$$\frac{|a_{n+1}|}{|a_n|} = \frac{\left|(-1)^{n+1}(x-1)^{n+1}\right|}{\left|(-1)^n (x-1)^n\right|} = |x-1|.$$

Thus, the series converges if $|x-1| < 1$. That is, the series converges for $0 < x < 2$. Next, we need to check the endpoints. At $x = 2$, we see that

$$\sum_{n=0}^{\infty} (-1)^n (2-1)^n = \sum_{n=0}^{\infty} (-1)^n$$

diverges by the divergence test. Similarly, at $x = 0$,

$$\sum_{n=0}^{\infty} (-1)^n (0-1)^n = \sum_{n=0}^{\infty} (-1)^{2n} = \sum_{n=0}^{\infty} 1$$

diverges. Therefore, the interval of convergence is $(0, 2)$.

**6.14** Find the Taylor series for $f(x) = \frac{1}{2}$ at $x = 2$ and determine its interval of convergence.

We know that the Taylor series found in this example converges on the interval $(0, 2)$, but how do we know it actually converges to $f$? We consider this question in more generality in a moment, but for this example, we can answer this question by writing

$$f(x) = \frac{1}{x} = \frac{1}{1-(1-x)}.$$

That is, $f$ can be represented by the geometric series $\sum_{n=0}^{\infty} (1-x)^n$. Since this is a geometric series, it converges to $\frac{1}{x}$ as long as $|1-x| < 1$. Therefore, the Taylor series found in **Example 6.15** does converge to $f(x) = \frac{1}{x}$ on $(0, 2)$.

We now consider the more general question: if a Taylor series for a function $f$ converges on some interval, how can we determine if it actually converges to $f$? To answer this question, recall that a series converges to a particular value if and only if its sequence of partial sums converges to that value. Given a Taylor series for $f$ at $a$, the $n$th partial sum is given by the $n$th Taylor polynomial $p_n$. Therefore, to determine if the Taylor series converges to $f$, we need to determine whether

$$\lim_{n \to \infty} p_n(x) = f(x).$$

Since the remainder $R_n(x) = f(x) - p_n(x)$, the Taylor series converges to $f$ if and only if

$$\lim_{n \to \infty} R_n(x) = 0.$$

We now state this theorem formally.

### Theorem 6.8: Convergence of Taylor Series

Suppose that $f$ has derivatives of all orders on an interval $I$ containing $a$. Then the Taylor series

$$\sum_{n=0}^{\infty} \frac{f^{(n)}(a)}{n!}(x-a)^n$$

converges to $f(x)$ for all $x$ in $I$ if and only if

$$\lim_{n \to \infty} R_n(x) = 0$$

for all $x$ in $I$.

With this theorem, we can prove that a Taylor series for $f$ at $a$ converges to $f$ if we can prove that the remainder $R_n(x) \to 0$. To prove that $R_n(x) \to 0$, we typically use the bound

$$|R_n(x)| \leq \frac{M}{(n+1)!}|x-a|^{n+1}$$

from Taylor's theorem with remainder.

In the next example, we find the Maclaurin series for $e^x$ and $\sin x$ and show that these series converge to the corresponding functions for all real numbers by proving that the remainders $R_n(x) \to 0$ for all real numbers $x$.

## Example 6.16

### Finding Maclaurin Series

For each of the following functions, find the Maclaurin series and its interval of convergence. Use **Taylor's Theorem with Remainder** to prove that the Maclaurin series for $f$ converges to $f$ on that interval.

a. $e^x$

b. $\sin x$

### Solution

a. Using the $n$th Maclaurin polynomial for $e^x$ found in **Example 6.12**a., we find that the Maclaurin series for $e^x$ is given by

$$\sum_{n=0}^{\infty} \frac{x^n}{n!}.$$

To determine the interval of convergence, we use the ratio test. Since

$$\frac{|a_{n+1}|}{|a_n|} = \frac{|x|^{n+1}}{(n+1)!} \cdot \frac{n!}{|x|^n} = \frac{|x|}{n+1},$$

we have

$$\lim_{n \to \infty} \frac{|a_{n+1}|}{|a_n|} = \lim_{n \to \infty} \frac{|x|}{n+1} = 0$$

for all $x$. Therefore, the series converges absolutely for all $x$, and thus, the interval of convergence is $(-\infty, \infty)$. To show that the series converges to $e^x$ for all $x$, we use the fact that $f^{(n)}(x) = e^x$ for all $n \geq 0$ and $e^x$ is an increasing function on $(-\infty, \infty)$. Therefore, for any real number $b$, the maximum value of $e^x$ for all $|x| \leq b$ is $e^b$. Thus,

$$|R_n(x)| \leq \frac{e^b}{(n+1)!}|x|^{n+1}.$$

Since we just showed that

$$\sum_{n=0}^{\infty} \frac{|x|^n}{n!}$$

converges for all $x$, by the divergence test, we know that

$$\lim_{n \to \infty} \frac{|x|^{n+1}}{(n+1)!} = 0$$

for any real number $x$. By combining this fact with the squeeze theorem, the result is $\lim_{n \to \infty} R_n(x) = 0$.

b. Using the $n$th Maclaurin polynomial for $\sin x$ found in **Example 6.12**b., we find that the Maclaurin series for $\sin x$ is given by

$$\sum_{n=0}^{\infty} (-1)^n \frac{x^{2n+1}}{(2n+1)!}.$$

In order to apply the ratio test, consider

$$\frac{|a_{n+1}|}{|a_n|} = \frac{|x|^{2n+3}}{(2n+3)!} \cdot \frac{(2n+1)!}{|x|^{2n+1}} = \frac{|x|^2}{(2n+3)(2n+2)}.$$

Since

$$\lim_{n \to \infty} \frac{|x|^2}{(2n+3)(2n+2)} = 0$$

for all $x$, we obtain the interval of convergence as $(-\infty, \infty)$. To show that the Maclaurin series converges to $\sin x$, look at $R_n(x)$. For each $x$ there exists a real number $c$ between 0 and $x$ such that

$$R_n(x) = \frac{f^{(n+1)}(c)}{(n+1)!} x^{n+1}.$$

Since $\left|f^{(n+1)}(c)\right| \leq 1$ for all integers $n$ and all real numbers $c$, we have

$$|R_n(x)| \leq \frac{|x|^{n+1}}{(n+1)!}$$

for all real numbers $x$. Using the same idea as in part a., the result is $\lim_{n \to \infty} R_n(x) = 0$ for all $x$, and therefore, the Maclaurin series for $\sin x$ converges to $\sin x$ for all real $x$.

**6.15** Find the Maclaurin series for $f(x) = \cos x$. Use the ratio test to show that the interval of convergence is $(-\infty, \infty)$. Show that the Maclaurin series converges to $\cos x$ for all real numbers $x$.

# Student PROJECT

## Proving that $e$ is Irrational

In this project, we use the Maclaurin polynomials for $e^x$ to prove that $e$ is irrational. The proof relies on supposing that $e$ is rational and arriving at a contradiction. Therefore, in the following steps, we suppose $e = r/s$ for some integers $r$ and $s$ where $s \neq 0$.

1. Write the Maclaurin polynomials $p_0(x), p_1(x), p_2(x), p_3(x), p_4(x)$ for $e^x$. Evaluate $p_0(1), p_1(1), p_2(1), p_3(1), p_4(1)$ to estimate $e$.
2. Let $R_n(x)$ denote the remainder when using $p_n(x)$ to estimate $e^x$. Therefore, $R_n(x) = e^x - p_n(x)$, and $R_n(1) = e - p_n(1)$. Assuming that $e = \frac{r}{s}$ for integers $r$ and $s$, evaluate $R_0(1), R_1(1), R_2(1), R_3(1), R_4(1)$.
3. Using the results from part 2, show that for each remainder $R_0(1), R_1(1), R_2(1), R_3(1), R_4(1)$, we can find an integer $k$ such that $kR_n(1)$ is an integer for $n = 0, 1, 2, 3, 4$.
4. Write down the formula for the $n$th Maclaurin polynomial $p_n(x)$ for $e^x$ and the corresponding remainder $R_n(x)$. Show that $sn!R_n(1)$ is an integer.
5. Use Taylor's theorem to write down an explicit formula for $R_n(1)$. Conclude that $R_n(1) \neq 0$, and therefore, $sn!R_n(1) \neq 0$.
6. Use Taylor's theorem to find an estimate on $R_n(1)$. Use this estimate combined with the result from part 5 to show that $|sn!R_n(1)| < \frac{se}{n+1}$. Conclude that if $n$ is large enough, then $|sn!R_n(1)| < 1$. Therefore, $sn!R_n(1)$ is an integer with magnitude less than 1. Thus, $sn!R_n(1) = 0$. But from part 5, we know that $sn!R_n(1) \neq 0$. We have arrived at a contradiction, and consequently, the original supposition that $e$ is rational must be false.

# 6.3 EXERCISES

In the following exercises, find the Taylor polynomials of degree two approximating the given function centered at the given point.

116. $f(x) = 1 + x + x^2$ at $a = 1$

117. $f(x) = 1 + x + x^2$ at $a = -1$

118. $f(x) = \cos(2x)$ at $a = \pi$

119. $f(x) = \sin(2x)$ at $a = \frac{\pi}{2}$

120. $f(x) = \sqrt{x}$ at $a = 4$

121. $f(x) = \ln x$ at $a = 1$

122. $f(x) = \frac{1}{x}$ at $a = 1$

123. $f(x) = e^x$ at $a = 1$

In the following exercises, verify that the given choice of $n$ in the remainder estimate $|R_n| \le \frac{M}{(n+1)!}(x-a)^{n+1}$, where $M$ is the maximum value of $\left|f^{(n+1)}(z)\right|$ on the interval between $a$ and the indicated point, yields $|R_n| \le \frac{1}{1000}$. Find the value of the Taylor polynomial $p_n$ of $f$ at the indicated point.

124. **[T]** $\sqrt{10}$; $a = 9$, $n = 3$

125. **[T]** $(28)^{1/3}$; $a = 27$, $n = 1$

126. **[T]** $\sin(6)$; $a = 2\pi$, $n = 5$

127. **[T]** $e^2$; $a = 0$, $n = 9$

128. **[T]** $\cos\left(\frac{\pi}{5}\right)$; $a = 0$, $n = 4$

129. **[T]** $\ln(2)$; $a = 1$, $n = 1000$

130. Integrate the approximation $\sin t \approx t - \frac{t^3}{6} + \frac{t^5}{120} - \frac{t^7}{5040}$ evaluated at $\pi t$ to approximate $\int_0^1 \frac{\sin \pi t}{\pi t} dt$.

131. Integrate the approximation $e^x \approx 1 + x + \frac{x^2}{2} + \cdots + \frac{x^6}{720}$ evaluated at $-x^2$ to approximate $\int_0^1 e^{-x^2} dx$.

In the following exercises, find the smallest value of $n$ such that the remainder estimate $|R_n| \le \frac{M}{(n+1)!}(x-a)^{n+1}$, where $M$ is the maximum value of $\left|f^{(n+1)}(z)\right|$ on the interval between $a$ and the indicated point, yields $|R_n| \le \frac{1}{1000}$ on the indicated interval.

132. $f(x) = \sin x$ on $[-\pi, \pi]$, $a = 0$

133. $f(x) = \cos x$ on $\left[-\frac{\pi}{2}, \frac{\pi}{2}\right]$, $a = 0$

134. $f(x) = e^{-2x}$ on $[-1, 1]$, $a = 0$

135. $f(x) = e^{-x}$ on $[-3, 3]$, $a = 0$

In the following exercises, the maximum of the right-hand side of the remainder estimate $|R_1| \le \frac{\max|f''(z)|}{2} R^2$ on $[a - R, a + R]$ occurs at $a$ or $a \pm R$. Estimate the maximum value of $R$ such that $\frac{\max|f''(z)|}{2} R^2 \le 0.1$ on $[a - R, a + R]$ by plotting this maximum as a function of $R$.

136. **[T]** $e^x$ approximated by $1 + x$, $a = 0$

137. **[T]** $\sin x$ approximated by $x$, $a = 0$

138. **[T]** $\ln x$ approximated by $x - 1$, $a = 1$

139. **[T]** $\cos x$ approximated by $1$, $a = 0$

In the following exercises, find the Taylor series of the given function centered at the indicated point.

140. $x^4$ at $a = -1$

141. $1 + x + x^2 + x^3$ at $a = -1$

142. $\sin x$ at $a = \pi$

143. $\cos x$ at $a = 2\pi$

144. $\sin x$ at $x = \frac{\pi}{2}$

145. $\cos x$ at $x = \frac{\pi}{2}$

146. $e^x$ at $a = -1$

147. $e^x$ at $a = 1$

148. $\frac{1}{(x-1)^2}$ at $a = 0$ (*Hint:* Differentiate $\frac{1}{1-x}$.)

149. $\frac{1}{(x-1)^3}$ at $a = 0$

150. $F(x) = \int_0^x \cos(\sqrt{t})dt$; $f(t) = \sum_{n=0}^{\infty} (-1)^n \frac{t^n}{(2n)!}$ at $a = 0$ (*Note:* $f$ is the Taylor series of $\cos(\sqrt{t})$.)

In the following exercises, compute the Taylor series of each function around $x = 1$.

151. $f(x) = 2 - x$

152. $f(x) = x^3$

153. $f(x) = (x-2)^2$

154. $f(x) = \ln x$

155. $f(x) = \frac{1}{x}$

156. $f(x) = \frac{1}{2x - x^2}$

157. $f(x) = \frac{x}{4x - 2x^2 - 1}$

158. $f(x) = e^{-x}$

159. $f(x) = e^{2x}$

**[T]** In the following exercises, identify the value of $x$ such that the given series $\sum_{n=0}^{\infty} a_n$ is the value of the Maclaurin series of $f(x)$ at $x$. Approximate the value of $f(x)$ using $S_{10} = \sum_{n=0}^{10} a_n$.

160. $\sum_{n=0}^{\infty} \frac{1}{n!}$

161. $\sum_{n=0}^{\infty} \frac{2^n}{n!}$

162. $\sum_{n=0}^{\infty} \frac{(-1)^n (2\pi)^{2n}}{(2n)!}$

163. $\sum_{n=0}^{\infty} \frac{(-1)^n (2\pi)^{2n+1}}{(2n+1)!}$

The following exercises make use of the functions $S_5(x) = x - \frac{x^3}{6} + \frac{x^5}{120}$ and $C_4(x) = 1 - \frac{x^2}{2} + \frac{x^4}{24}$ on $[-\pi, \pi]$.

164. **[T]** Plot $\sin^2 x - (S_5(x))^2$ on $[-\pi, \pi]$. Compare the maximum difference with the square of the Taylor remainder estimate for $\sin x$.

165. **[T]** Plot $\cos^2 x - (C_4(x))^2$ on $[-\pi, \pi]$. Compare the maximum difference with the square of the Taylor remainder estimate for $\cos x$.

166. **[T]** Plot $|2S_5(x)C_4(x) - \sin(2x)|$ on $[-\pi, \pi]$.

167. **[T]** Compare $\frac{S_5(x)}{C_4(x)}$ on $[-1, 1]$ to $\tan x$. Compare this with the Taylor remainder estimate for the approximation of $\tan x$ by $x + \frac{x^3}{3} + \frac{2x^5}{15}$.

168. **[T]** Plot $e^x - e_4(x)$ where $e_4(x) = 1 + x + \frac{x^2}{2} + \frac{x^3}{6} + \frac{x^4}{24}$ on $[0, 2]$. Compare the maximum error with the Taylor remainder estimate.

169. (Taylor approximations and root finding.) Recall that Newton's method $x_{n+1} = x_n - \frac{f(x_n)}{f'(x_n)}$ approximates solutions of $f(x) = 0$ near the input $x_0$.

a. If $f$ and $g$ are inverse functions, explain why a solution of $g(x) = a$ is the value $f(a)$ of $f$.

b. Let $p_N(x)$ be the $N$th degree Maclaurin polynomial of $e^x$. Use Newton's method to approximate solutions of $p_N(x) - 2 = 0$ for $N = 4, 5, 6$.

c. Explain why the approximate roots of $p_N(x) - 2 = 0$ are approximate values of $\ln(2)$.

In the following exercises, use the fact that if

$q(x) = \sum_{n=1}^{\infty} a_n (x - c)^n$ converges in an interval containing $c$, then $\lim_{x \to c} q(x) = a_0$ to evaluate each limit using Taylor series.

170. $\lim_{x \to 0} \frac{\cos x - 1}{x^2}$

171. $\lim_{x \to 0} \frac{\ln\left(1 - x^2\right)}{x^2}$

172. $\lim_{x \to 0} \frac{e^{x^2} - x^2 - 1}{x^4}$

173. $\lim_{x \to 0^+} \frac{\cos(\sqrt{x}) - 1}{2x}$

# 6.4 | Working with Taylor Series

## Learning Objectives

6.4.1 Write the terms of the binomial series.
6.4.2 Recognize the Taylor series expansions of common functions.
6.4.3 Recognize and apply techniques to find the Taylor series for a function.
6.4.4 Use Taylor series to solve differential equations.
6.4.5 Use Taylor series to evaluate nonelementary integrals.

In the preceding section, we defined Taylor series and showed how to find the Taylor series for several common functions by explicitly calculating the coefficients of the Taylor polynomials. In this section we show how to use those Taylor series to derive Taylor series for other functions. We then present two common applications of power series. First, we show how power series can be used to solve differential equations. Second, we show how power series can be used to evaluate integrals when the antiderivative of the integrand cannot be expressed in terms of elementary functions. In one example, we consider $\int e^{-x^2}dx,$ an integral that arises frequently in probability theory.

## The Binomial Series

Our first goal in this section is to determine the Maclaurin series for the function $f(x) = (1+x)^r$ for all real numbers $r.$ The Maclaurin series for this function is known as the **binomial series**. We begin by considering the simplest case: $r$ is a nonnegative integer. We recall that, for $r = 0, 1, 2, 3, 4,$ $f(x) = (1+x)^r$ can be written as

$$\begin{aligned}
f(x) &= (1+x)^0 = 1, \\
f(x) &= (1+x)^1 = 1+x, \\
f(x) &= (1+x)^2 = 1+2x+x^2, \\
f(x) &= (1+x)^3 = 1+3x+3x^2+x^3, \\
f(x) &= (1+x)^4 = 1+4x+6x^2+4x^3+x^4.
\end{aligned}$$

The expressions on the right-hand side are known as binomial expansions and the coefficients are known as binomial coefficients. More generally, for any nonnegative integer $r,$ the binomial coefficient of $x^n$ in the binomial expansion of $(1+x)^r$ is given by

$$\binom{r}{n} = \frac{r!}{n!(r-n)!} \tag{6.6}$$

and

$$\begin{aligned}
f(x) &= (1+x)^r \\
&= \binom{r}{0}1 + \binom{r}{1}x + \binom{r}{2}x^2 + \binom{r}{3}x^3 + \cdots + \binom{r}{r-1}x^{r-1} + \binom{r}{r}x^r \\
&= \sum_{n=0}^{r} \binom{r}{n}x^n.
\end{aligned} \tag{6.7}$$

For example, using this formula for $r = 5,$ we see that

$$\begin{aligned}
f(x) &= (1+x)^5 \\
&= \binom{5}{0}1 + \binom{5}{1}x + \binom{5}{2}x^2 + \binom{5}{3}x^3 + \binom{5}{4}x^4 + \binom{5}{5}x^5 \\
&= \frac{5!}{0!5!}1 + \frac{5!}{1!4!}x + \frac{5!}{2!3!}x^2 + \frac{5!}{3!2!}x^3 + \frac{5!}{4!1!}x^4 + \frac{5!}{5!0!}x^5 \\
&= 1 + 5x + 10x^2 + 10x^3 + 5x^4 + x^5.
\end{aligned}$$

We now consider the case when the exponent $r$ is any real number, not necessarily a nonnegative integer. If $r$ is not a nonnegative integer, then $f(x) = (1+x)^r$ cannot be written as a finite polynomial. However, we can find a power series for $f$. Specifically, we look for the Maclaurin series for $f$. To do this, we find the derivatives of $f$ and evaluate them at $x = 0$.

$$\begin{aligned} f(x) &= (1+x)^r & f(0) &= 1 \\ f'(x) &= r(1+x)^{r-1} & f'(0) &= r \\ f''(x) &= r(r-1)(1+x)^{r-2} & f''(0) &= r(r-1) \\ f'''(x) &= r(r-1)(r-2)(1+x)^{r-3} & f'''(0) &= r(r-1)(r-2) \\ f^{(n)}(x) &= r(r-1)(r-2)\cdots(r-n+1)(1+x)^{r-n} & f^{(n)}(0) &= r(r-1)(r-2)\cdots(r-n+1) \end{aligned}$$

We conclude that the coefficients in the binomial series are given by

$$\frac{f^{(n)}(0)}{n!} = \frac{r(r-1)(r-2)\cdots(r-n+1)}{n!}. \tag{6.8}$$

We note that if $r$ is a nonnegative integer, then the $(r+1)$st derivative $f^{(r+1)}$ is the zero function, and the series terminates. In addition, if $r$ is a nonnegative integer, then **Equation 6.8** for the coefficients agrees with **Equation 6.6** for the coefficients, and the formula for the binomial series agrees with **Equation 6.7** for the finite binomial expansion. More generally, to denote the binomial coefficients for any real number $r$, we define

$$\binom{r}{n} = \frac{r(r-1)(r-2)\cdots(r-n+1)}{n!}.$$

With this notation, we can write the binomial series for $(1+x)^r$ as

$$\sum_{n=0}^{\infty} \binom{r}{n} x^n = 1 + rx + \frac{r(r-1)}{2!}x^2 + \cdots + \frac{r(r-1)\cdots(r-n+1)}{n!}x^n + \cdots. \tag{6.9}$$

We now need to determine the interval of convergence for the binomial series **Equation 6.9**. We apply the ratio test. Consequently, we consider

$$\begin{aligned} \frac{|a_{n+1}|}{|a_n|} &= \frac{|r(r-1)(r-2)\cdots(r-n)||x|^{n+1}}{(n+1)!} \cdot \frac{n}{|r(r-1)(r-2)\cdots(r-n+1)||x|^n} \\ &= \frac{|r-n||x|}{|n+1|}. \end{aligned}$$

Since

$$\lim_{n\to\infty} \frac{|a_{n+1}|}{|a_n|} = |x| < 1$$

if and only if $|x| < 1$, we conclude that the interval of convergence for the binomial series is $(-1, 1)$. The behavior at the endpoints depends on $r$. It can be shown that for $r \geq 0$ the series converges at both endpoints; for $-1 < r < 0$, the series converges at $x = 1$ and diverges at $x = -1$; and for $r < -1$, the series diverges at both endpoints. The binomial series does converge to $(1+x)^r$ in $(-1, 1)$ for all real numbers $r$, but proving this fact by showing that the remainder $R_n(x) \to 0$ is difficult.

### Definition

For any real number $r$, the Maclaurin series for $f(x) = (1+x)^r$ is the binomial series. It converges to $f$ for $|x| < 1$, and we write

$$(1+x)^r = \sum_{n=0}^{\infty} \binom{r}{n} x^n$$
$$= 1 + rx + \frac{r(r-1)}{2!}x^2 + \cdots + \frac{r(r-1)\cdots(r-n+1)}{n!}x^n + \cdots$$

for $|x| < 1$.

We can use this definition to find the binomial series for $f(x) = \sqrt{1+x}$ and use the series to approximate $\sqrt{1.5}$.

## Example 6.17

### Finding Binomial Series

a. Find the binomial series for $f(x) = \sqrt{1+x}$.

b. Use the third-order Maclaurin polynomial $p_3(x)$ to estimate $\sqrt{1.5}$. Use Taylor's theorem to bound the error. Use a graphing utility to compare the graphs of $f$ and $p_3$.

### Solution

a. Here $r = \frac{1}{2}$. Using the definition for the binomial series, we obtain

$$\sqrt{1+x} = 1 + \frac{1}{2}x + \frac{(1/2)(-1/2)}{2!}x^2 + \frac{(1/2)(-1/2)(-3/2)}{3!}x^3 + \cdots$$
$$= 1 + \frac{1}{2}x - \frac{1}{2!}\frac{1}{2^2}x^2 + \frac{1}{3!}\frac{1\cdot 3}{2^3}x^3 - \cdots + \frac{(-1)^{n+1}}{n!}\frac{1\cdot 3\cdot 5\cdots(2n-3)}{2^n}x^n + \cdots$$
$$= 1 + \sum_{n=1}^{\infty} \frac{(-1)^{n+1}}{n!}\frac{1\cdot 3\cdot 5\cdots(2n-3)}{2^n}x^n.$$

b. From the result in part a. the third-order Maclaurin polynomial is

$$p_3(x) = 1 + \frac{1}{2}x - \frac{1}{8}x^2 + \frac{1}{16}x^3.$$

Therefore,

$$\sqrt{1.5} = \sqrt{1+0.5}$$
$$\approx 1 + \frac{1}{2}(0.5) - \frac{1}{8}(0.5)^2 + \frac{1}{16}(0.5)^3$$
$$\approx 1.2266.$$

From Taylor's theorem, the error satisfies

$$R_3(0.5) = \frac{f^{(4)}(c)}{4!}(0.5)^4$$

for some $c$ between 0 and 0.5. Since $f^{(4)}(x) = -\frac{15}{2^4(1+x)^{7/2}},$ and the maximum value of $\left|f^{(4)}(x)\right|$ on the interval $(0, 0.5)$ occurs at $x = 0,$ we have

$$|R_3(0.5)| \le \frac{15}{4!2^4}(0.5)^4 \approx 0.00244.$$

The function and the Maclaurin polynomial $p_3$ are graphed in **Figure 6.10**.

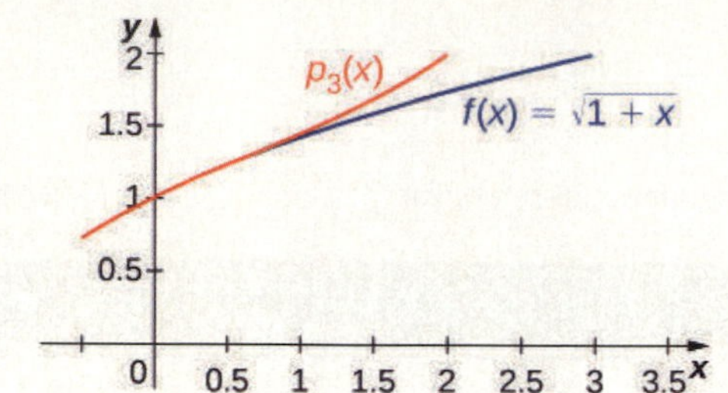


**Figure 6.10** The third-order Maclaurin polynomial $p_3(x)$ provides a good approximation for $f(x) = \sqrt{1+x}$ for $x$ near zero.

**6.16** Find the binomial series for $f(x) = \dfrac{1}{(1+x)^2}$.

## Common Functions Expressed as Taylor Series

At this point, we have derived Maclaurin series for exponential, trigonometric, and logarithmic functions, as well as functions of the form $f(x) = (1+x)^r$. In **Table 6.1**, we summarize the results of these series. We remark that the convergence of the Maclaurin series for $f(x) = \ln(1+x)$ at the endpoint $x = 1$ and the Maclaurin series for $f(x) = \tan^{-1} x$ at the endpoints $x = 1$ and $x = -1$ relies on a more advanced theorem than we present here. (Refer to Abel's theorem for a discussion of this more technical point.)

| Function | Maclaurin Series | Interval of Convergence |
|---|---|---|
| $f(x) = \frac{1}{1-x}$ | $\sum_{n=0}^{\infty} x^n$ | $-1 < x < 1$ |
| $f(x) = e^x$ | $\sum_{n=0}^{\infty} \frac{x^n}{n!}$ | $-\infty < x < \infty$ |
| $f(x) = \sin x$ | $\sum_{n=0}^{\infty} (-1)^n \frac{x^{2n+1}}{(2n+1)!}$ | $-\infty < x < \infty$ |
| $f(x) = \cos x$ | $\sum_{n=0}^{\infty} (-1)^n \frac{x^{2n}}{(2n)!}$ | $-\infty < x < \infty$ |
| $f(x) = \ln(1+x)$ | $\sum_{n=0}^{\infty} (-1)^{n+1} \frac{x^n}{n}$ | $-1 < x \leq 1$ |
| $f(x) = \tan^{-1} x$ | $\sum_{n=0}^{\infty} (-1)^n \frac{x^{2n+1}}{2n+1}$ | $-1 < x \leq 1$ |
| $f(x) = (1+x)^r$ | $\sum_{n=0}^{\infty} \binom{r}{n} x^n$ | $-1 < x < 1$ |

**Table 6.1** Maclaurin Series for Common Functions

Earlier in the chapter, we showed how you could combine power series to create new power series. Here we use these properties, combined with the Maclaurin series in **Table 6.1**, to create Maclaurin series for other functions.

## Example 6.18

### Deriving Maclaurin Series from Known Series

Find the Maclaurin series of each of the following functions by using one of the series listed in **Table 6.1**.

a. $f(x) = \cos\sqrt{x}$

b. $f(x) = \sinh x$

### Solution

a. Using the Maclaurin series for $\cos x$ we find that the Maclaurin series for $\cos\sqrt{x}$ is given by

$$\sum_{n=0}^{\infty} \frac{(-1)^n (\sqrt{x})^{2n}}{(2n)!} = \sum_{n=0}^{\infty} \frac{(-1)^n x^n}{(2n)!}$$
$$= 1 - \frac{x}{2!} + \frac{x^2}{4!} - \frac{x^3}{6!} + \frac{x^4}{8!} - \cdots.$$

This series converges to $\cos\sqrt{x}$ for all $x$ in the domain of $\cos\sqrt{x}$; that is, for all $x \geq 0$.

b. To find the Maclaurin series for $\sinh x$, we use the fact that

$$\sinh x = \frac{e^x - e^{-x}}{2}.$$

Using the Maclaurin series for $e^x$, we see that the $n$th term in the Maclaurin series for $\sinh x$ is given by

$$\frac{x^n}{n!} - \frac{(-x)^n}{n!}.$$

For $n$ even, this term is zero. For $n$ odd, this term is $\frac{2x^n}{n!}$. Therefore, the Maclaurin series for $\sinh x$ has only odd-order terms and is given by

$$\sum_{n=0}^{\infty} \frac{x^{2n+1}}{(2n+1)!} = x + \frac{x^3}{3!} + \frac{x^5}{5!} + \cdots.$$

**6.17** Find the Maclaurin series for $\sin\left(x^2\right)$.

We also showed previously in this chapter how power series can be differentiated term by term to create a new power series. In **Example 6.19**, we differentiate the binomial series for $\sqrt{1+x}$ term by term to find the binomial series for $\frac{1}{\sqrt{1+x}}$. Note that we could construct the binomial series for $\frac{1}{\sqrt{1+x}}$ directly from the definition, but differentiating the binomial series for $\sqrt{1+x}$ is an easier calculation.

## Example 6.19

### Differentiating a Series to Find a New Series

Use the binomial series for $\sqrt{1+x}$ to find the binomial series for $\frac{1}{\sqrt{1+x}}$.

#### Solution

The two functions are related by

$$\frac{d}{dx}\sqrt{1+x} = \frac{1}{2\sqrt{1+x}},$$

so the binomial series for $\frac{1}{\sqrt{1+x}}$ is given by

$$\begin{aligned}\frac{1}{\sqrt{1+x}} &= 2\frac{d}{dx}\sqrt{1+x} \\ &= 1 + \sum_{n=1}^{\infty} \frac{(-1)^n}{n!} \frac{1 \cdot 3 \cdot 5 \cdots (2n-1)}{2^n} x^n.\end{aligned}$$

**6.18** Find the binomial series for $f(x) = \frac{1}{(1+x)^{3/2}}$

In this example, we differentiated a known Taylor series to construct a Taylor series for another function. The ability to differentiate power series term by term makes them a powerful tool for solving differential equations. We now show how this is accomplished.

## Solving Differential Equations with Power Series

Consider the differential equation

$$y'(x) = y.$$

Recall that this is a first-order separable equation and its solution is $y = Ce^x$. This equation is easily solved using techniques discussed earlier in the text. For most differential equations, however, we do not yet have analytical tools to solve them. Power series are an extremely useful tool for solving many types of differential equations. In this technique, we look for a solution of the form $y = \sum_{n=0}^{\infty} c_n x^n$ and determine what the coefficients would need to be. In the next example, we consider an initial-value problem involving $y' = y$ to illustrate the technique.

### Example 6.20

#### Power Series Solution of a Differential Equation

Use power series to solve the initial-value problem

$$y' = y, \quad y(0) = 3.$$

#### Solution

Suppose that there exists a power series solution

$$y(x) = \sum_{n=0}^{\infty} c_n x^n = c_0 + c_1 x + c_2 x^2 + c_3 x^3 + c_4 x^4 + \cdots.$$

Differentiating this series term by term, we obtain

$$y' = c_1 + 2c_2 x + 3c_3 x^2 + 4c_4 x^3 + \cdots.$$

If $y$ satisfies the differential equation, then

$$c_0 + c_1 x + c_2 x^2 + c_3 x^3 + \cdots = c_1 + 2c_2 x + 3c_3 x^2 + 4c_3 x^3 + \cdots.$$

Using **Uniqueness of Power Series** on the uniqueness of power series representations, we know that these series can only be equal if their coefficients are equal. Therefore,

$$\begin{aligned} c_0 &= c_1, \\ c_1 &= 2c_2, \\ c_2 &= 3c_3, \\ c_3 &= 4c_4, \\ &\vdots. \end{aligned}$$

Using the initial condition $y(0) = 3$ combined with the power series representation

$$y(x) = c_0 + c_1 x + c_2 x^2 + c_3 x^3 + \cdots,$$

we find that $c_0 = 3$. We are now ready to solve for the rest of the coefficients. Using the fact that $c_0 = 3,$ we have

$$\begin{aligned} c_1 &= c_0 = 3 = \frac{3}{1!}, \\ c_2 &= \frac{c_1}{2} = \frac{3}{2} = \frac{3}{2!}, \\ c_3 &= \frac{c_2}{3} = \frac{3}{3 \cdot 2} = \frac{3}{3!}, \\ c_4 &= \frac{c_3}{4} = \frac{3}{4 \cdot 3 \cdot 2} = \frac{3}{4!}. \end{aligned}$$

Therefore,

$$\begin{aligned} y &= 3\left[1 + \frac{1}{1!}x + \frac{1}{2!}x^2 + \frac{1}{3!}x^3 \frac{1}{4!}x^4 + \cdots\right] \\ &= 3\sum_{n=0}^{\infty} \frac{x^n}{n!}. \end{aligned}$$

You might recognize

$$\sum_{n=0}^{\infty} \frac{x^n}{n!}$$

as the Taylor series for $e^x$. Therefore, the solution is $y = 3e^x$.

 **6.19** Use power series to solve $y' = 2y, \quad y(0) = 5.$

We now consider an example involving a differential equation that we cannot solve using previously discussed methods. This differential equation

$$y' - xy = 0$$

is known as Airy's equation. It has many applications in mathematical physics, such as modeling the diffraction of light. Here we show how to solve it using power series.

## Example 6.21

## Power Series Solution of Airy's Equation

Use power series to solve

$$y'' - xy = 0$$

with the initial conditions $y(0) = a$ and $y'(0) = b$.

### Solution

We look for a solution of the form

$$y = \sum_{n=0}^{\infty} c_n x^n = c_0 + c_1 x + c_2 x^2 + c_3 x^3 + c_4 x^4 + \cdots.$$

Differentiating this function term by term, we obtain

$$\begin{aligned} y' &= c_1 + 2c_2 x + 3c_3 x^2 + 4c_4 x^3 + \cdots, \\ y'' &= 2 \cdot 1 c_2 + 3 \cdot 2 c_3 x + 4 \cdot 3 c_4 x^2 + \cdots. \end{aligned}$$

If $y$ satisfies the equation $y'' = xy$, then

$$2 \cdot 1c_2 + 3 \cdot 2c_3 x + 4 \cdot 3c_4 x^2 + \cdots = x\left(c_0 + c_1 x + c_2 x^2 + c_3 x^3 + \cdots\right).$$

Using **Uniqueness of Power Series** on the uniqueness of power series representations, we know that coefficients of the same degree must be equal. Therefore,

$$\begin{aligned} 2 \cdot 1c_2 &= 0, \\ 3 \cdot 2c_3 &= c_0, \\ 4 \cdot 3c_4 &= c_1, \\ 5 \cdot 4c_5 &= c_2, \\ &\vdots. \end{aligned}$$

More generally, for $n \geq 3$, we have $n \cdot (n-1)c_n = c_{n-3}$. In fact, all coefficients can be written in terms of $c_0$ and $c_1$. To see this, first note that $c_2 = 0$. Then

$$\begin{aligned} c_3 &= \frac{c_0}{3 \cdot 2}, \\ c_4 &= \frac{c_1}{4 \cdot 3}. \end{aligned}$$

For $c_5, c_6, c_7,$ we see that

$$\begin{aligned} c_5 &= \frac{c_2}{5 \cdot 4} = 0, \\ c_6 &= \frac{c_3}{6 \cdot 5} = \frac{c_0}{6 \cdot 5 \cdot 3 \cdot 2}, \\ c_7 &= \frac{c_4}{7 \cdot 6} = \frac{c_1}{7 \cdot 6 \cdot 4 \cdot 3}. \end{aligned}$$

Therefore, the series solution of the differential equation is given by

$$y = c_0 + c_1 x + 0 \cdot x^2 + \frac{c_0}{3 \cdot 2}x^3 + \frac{c_1}{4 \cdot 3}x^4 + 0 \cdot x^5 + \frac{c_0}{6 \cdot 5 \cdot 3 \cdot 2}x^6 + \frac{c_1}{7 \cdot 6 \cdot 4 \cdot 3}x^7 + \cdots.$$

The initial condition $y(0) = a$ implies $c_0 = a$. Differentiating this series term by term and using the fact that

$y'(0) = b,$ we conclude that $c_1 = b.$ Therefore, the solution of this initial-value problem is

$$y = a\left(1 + \frac{x^3}{3 \cdot 2} + \frac{x^6}{6 \cdot 5 \cdot 3 \cdot 2} + \cdots\right) + b\left(x + \frac{x^4}{4 \cdot 3} + \frac{x^7}{7 \cdot 6 \cdot 4 \cdot 3} + \cdots\right).$$

**6.20** Use power series to solve $y'' + x^2 y = 0$ with the initial condition $y(0) = a$ and $y'(0) = b.$

## Evaluating Nonelementary Integrals

Solving differential equations is one common application of power series. We now turn to a second application. We show how power series can be used to evaluate integrals involving functions whose antiderivatives cannot be expressed using elementary functions.

One integral that arises often in applications in probability theory is $\int e^{-x^2} dx.$ Unfortunately, the antiderivative of the integrand $e^{-x^2}$ is not an elementary function. By elementary function, we mean a function that can be written using a finite number of algebraic combinations or compositions of exponential, logarithmic, trigonometric, or power functions. We remark that the term "elementary function" is not synonymous with noncomplicated function. For example, the function $f(x) = \sqrt{x^2 - 3x} + e^{x^3} - \sin(5x + 4)$ is an elementary function, although not a particularly simple-looking function. Any integral of the form $\int f(x)dx$ where the antiderivative of $f$ cannot be written as an elementary function is considered a **nonelementary integral**.

Nonelementary integrals cannot be evaluated using the basic integration techniques discussed earlier. One way to evaluate such integrals is by expressing the integrand as a power series and integrating term by term. We demonstrate this technique by considering $\int e^{-x^2} dx.$

### Example 6.22

### Using Taylor Series to Evaluate a Definite Integral

a. Express $\int e^{-x^2} dx$ as an infinite series.

b. Evaluate $\int_0^1 e^{-x^2} dx$ to within an error of $0.01.$

### Solution

a. The Maclaurin series for $e^{-x^2}$ is given by

$$\begin{aligned} e^{-x^2} &= \sum_{n=0}^{\infty} \frac{\left(-x^2\right)^n}{n!} \\ &= 1 - x^2 + \frac{x^4}{2!} - \frac{x^6}{3!} + \cdots + (-1)^n \frac{x^{2n}}{n!} + \cdots \\ &= \sum_{n=0}^{\infty} (-1)^n \frac{x^{2n}}{n!}. \end{aligned}$$

Therefore,

$$\begin{aligned} \int e^{-x^2} dx &= \int \left(1 - x^2 + \frac{x^4}{2!} - \frac{x^6}{3!} + \cdots + (-1)^n \frac{x^{2n}}{n!} + \cdots\right) dx \\ &= C + x - \frac{x^3}{3} + \frac{x^5}{5.2!} - \frac{x^7}{7.3!} + \cdots + (-1)^n \frac{x^{2n+1}}{(2n+1)n!} + \cdots. \end{aligned}$$

b. Using the result from part a. we have

$$\int_0^1 e^{-x^2} dx = 1 - \frac{1}{3} + \frac{1}{10} - \frac{1}{42} + \frac{1}{216} - \cdots.$$

The sum of the first four terms is approximately $0.74$. By the alternating series test, this estimate is accurate to within an error of less than $\frac{1}{216} \approx 0.0046296 < 0.01$.

**6.21** Express $\int \cos\sqrt{x}dx$ as an infinite series. Evaluate $\int_0^1 \cos\sqrt{x}dx$ to within an error of $0.01$.

As mentioned above, the integral $\int e^{-x^2} dx$ arises often in probability theory. Specifically, it is used when studying data sets that are normally distributed, meaning the data values lie under a bell-shaped curve. For example, if a set of data values is normally distributed with mean $\mu$ and standard deviation $\sigma$, then the probability that a randomly chosen value lies between $x = a$ and $x = b$ is given by

$$\frac{1}{\sigma\sqrt{2\pi}} \int_a^b e^{-(x-\mu)^2/\left(2\sigma^2\right)} dx. \tag{6.10}$$

(See **Figure 6.11**.)

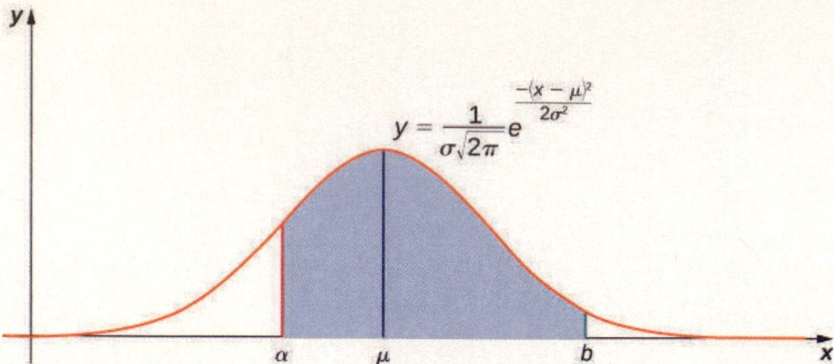


**Figure 6.11** If data values are normally distributed with mean $\mu$ and standard deviation $\sigma,$ the probability that a randomly selected data value is between $a$ and $b$ is the area under the curve $y = \frac{1}{\sigma\sqrt{2\pi}} e^{-(x-\mu)^2/\left(2\sigma^2\right)}$ between $x = a$ and $x = b.$

To simplify this integral, we typically let $z = \frac{x - \mu}{\sigma}.$ This quantity $z$ is known as the $z$ score of a data value. With this simplification, integral **Equation 6.10** becomes

$$\frac{1}{\sqrt{2\pi}} \int_{(a-\mu)/\sigma}^{(b-\mu)/\sigma} e^{-z^2/2} dz. \tag{6.11}$$

In **Example 6.23**, we show how we can use this integral in calculating probabilities.

## Example 6.23

### Using Maclaurin Series to Approximate a Probability

Suppose a set of standardized test scores are normally distributed with mean $\mu = 100$ and standard deviation $\sigma = 50.$ Use **Equation 6.11** and the first six terms in the Maclaurin series for $e^{-x^2/2}$ to approximate the probability that a randomly selected test score is between $x = 100$ and $x = 200.$ Use the alternating series test to determine how accurate your approximation is.

#### Solution

Since $\mu = 100, \sigma = 50,$ and we are trying to determine the area under the curve from $a = 100$ to $b = 200,$ integral **Equation 6.11** becomes

$$\frac{1}{\sqrt{2\pi}} \int_0^2 e^{-z^2/2} dz.$$

The Maclaurin series for $e^{-x^2/2}$ is given by

$$e^{-x^2/2} = \sum_{n=0}^{\infty} \frac{\left(-\frac{x^2}{2}\right)^n}{n!}$$
$$= 1 - \frac{x^2}{2^1 \cdot 1!} + \frac{x^4}{2^2 \cdot 2!} - \frac{x^6}{2^3 \cdot 3!} + \cdots + (-1)^n \frac{x^{2n}}{2^n \cdot n!} + \cdots$$
$$= \sum_{n=0}^{\infty} (-1)^n \frac{x^{2n}}{2^n \cdot n!}.$$

Therefore,

$$\frac{1}{\sqrt{2\pi}} \int e^{-z^2/2} dz = \frac{1}{\sqrt{2\pi}} \int \left(1 - \frac{z^2}{2^1 \cdot 1!} + \frac{z^4}{2^2 \cdot 2!} - \frac{z^6}{2^3 \cdot 3!} + \cdots + (-1)^n \frac{z^{2n}}{2^n \cdot n!} + \cdots\right) dz$$
$$= \frac{1}{\sqrt{2\pi}} \left(C + z - \frac{z^3}{3 \cdot 2^1 \cdot 1!} + \frac{z^5}{5 \cdot 2^2 \cdot 2!} - \frac{z^7}{7 \cdot 2^3 \cdot 3!} + \cdots + (-1)^n \frac{z^{2n+1}}{(2n+1)2^n \cdot n!} + \cdots\right)$$
$$\frac{1}{\sqrt{2\pi}} \int_0^2 e^{-z^2/2} dz = \frac{1}{\sqrt{2\pi}} \left(2 - \frac{8}{6} + \frac{32}{40} - \frac{128}{336} + \frac{512}{3456} - \frac{2^{11}}{11 \cdot 2^5 \cdot 5!} + \cdots\right).$$

Using the first five terms, we estimate that the probability is approximately $0.4922$. By the alternating series test, we see that this estimate is accurate to within

$$\frac{1}{\sqrt{2\pi}} \frac{2^{13}}{13 \cdot 2^6 \cdot 6!} \approx 0.00546.$$

### Analysis

If you are familiar with probability theory, you may know that the probability that a data value is within two standard deviations of the mean is approximately $95\%$. Here we calculated the probability that a data value is between the mean and two standard deviations above the mean, so the estimate should be around $47.5\%$. The estimate, combined with the bound on the accuracy, falls within this range.

**6.22** Use the first five terms of the Maclaurin series for $e^{-x^2/2}$ to estimate the probability that a randomly selected test score is between $100$ and $150$. Use the alternating series test to determine the accuracy of this estimate.

Another application in which a nonelementary integral arises involves the period of a pendulum. The integral is

$$\int_0^{\pi/2} \frac{d\theta}{\sqrt{1 - k^2 \sin^2 \theta}}.$$

An integral of this form is known as an elliptic integral of the first kind. Elliptic integrals originally arose when trying to calculate the arc length of an ellipse. We now show how to use power series to approximate this integral.

## Example 6.24

### Period of a Pendulum

The period of a pendulum is the time it takes for a pendulum to make one complete back-and-forth swing. For a pendulum with length $L$ that makes a maximum angle $\theta_{max}$ with the vertical, its period $T$ is given by

$$T = 4\sqrt{\frac{L}{g}}\int_0^{\pi/2} \frac{d\theta}{\sqrt{1 - k^2 \sin^2\theta}}$$

where $g$ is the acceleration due to gravity and $k = \sin\left(\frac{\theta_{max}}{2}\right)$ (see **Figure 6.12**). (We note that this formula for the period arises from a non-linearized model of a pendulum. In some cases, for simplification, a linearized model is used and $\sin\theta$ is approximated by $\theta$.) Use the binomial series

$$\frac{1}{\sqrt{1+x}} = 1 + \sum_{n=1}^{\infty} \frac{(-1)^n}{n!} \frac{1 \cdot 3 \cdot 5 \cdots (2n-1)}{2^n} x^n$$

to estimate the period of this pendulum. Specifically, approximate the period of the pendulum if

a. you use only the first term in the binomial series, and

b. you use the first two terms in the binomial series.

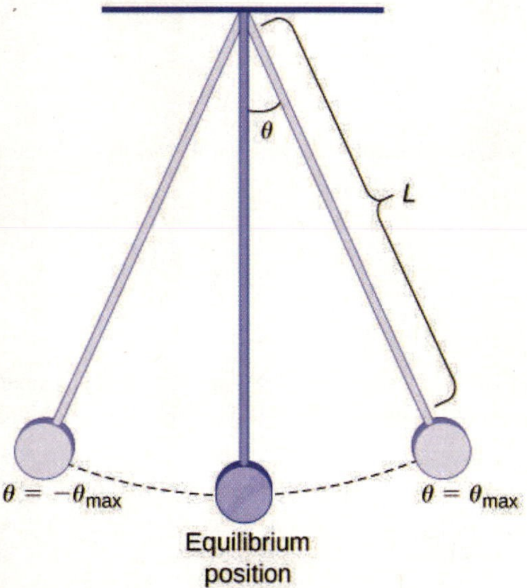


**Figure 6.12** This pendulum has length $L$ and makes a maximum angle $\theta_{max}$ with the vertical.

## Solution

We use the binomial series, replacing $x$ with $-k^2 \sin^2\theta$. Then we can write the period as

$$T = 4\sqrt{\frac{L}{g}}\int_0^{\pi/2} \left(1 + \frac{1}{2}k^2 \sin^2\theta + \frac{1 \cdot 3}{2!2^2}k^4 \sin^4\theta + \cdots\right)d\theta.$$

a. Using just the first term in the integrand, the first-order estimate is

$$T \approx 4\sqrt{\frac{L}{g}}\int_0^{\pi/2} d\theta = 2\pi\sqrt{\frac{L}{g}}.$$

If $\theta_{max}$ is small, then $k = \sin\left(\frac{\theta_{max}}{2}\right)$ is small. We claim that when $k$ is small, this is a good estimate. To justify this claim, consider

$$\int_0^{\pi/2}\left(1+\frac{1}{2}k^2\sin^2\theta+\frac{1\cdot 3}{2!2^2}k^4\sin^4\theta+\cdots\right)d\theta.$$

Since $|\sin x| \leq 1,$ this integral is bounded by

$$\int_0^{\pi/2}\left(\frac{1}{2}k^2+\frac{1.3}{2!2^2}k^4+\cdots\right)d\theta < \frac{\pi}{2}\left(\frac{1}{2}k^2+\frac{1\cdot 3}{2!2^2}k^4+\cdots\right).$$

Furthermore, it can be shown that each coefficient on the right-hand side is less than $1$ and, therefore, that this expression is bounded by

$$\frac{\pi k^2}{2}\left(1+k^2+k^4+\cdots\right)=\frac{\pi k^2}{2}\cdot\frac{1}{1-k^2},$$

which is small for $k$ small.

b. For larger values of $\theta_{\text{max}},$ we can approximate $T$ by using more terms in the integrand. By using the first two terms in the integral, we arrive at the estimate

$$\begin{aligned} T &\approx 4\sqrt{\frac{L}{g}}\int_0^{\pi/2}\left(1+\frac{1}{2}k^2\sin^2\theta\right)d\theta \\ &= 2\pi\sqrt{\frac{L}{g}}\left(1+\frac{k^2}{4}\right). \end{aligned}$$

The applications of Taylor series in this section are intended to highlight their importance. In general, Taylor series are useful because they allow us to represent known functions using polynomials, thus providing us a tool for approximating function values and estimating complicated integrals. In addition, they allow us to define new functions as power series, thus providing us with a powerful tool for solving differential equations.

# 6.4 EXERCISES

In the following exercises, use appropriate substitutions to write down the Maclaurin series for the given binomial.

174. $(1-x)^{1/3}$

175. $\left(1+x^2\right)^{-1/3}$

176. $(1-x)^{1.01}$

177. $(1-2x)^{2/3}$

In the following exercises, use the substitution $(b+x)^r = (b+a)^r\left(1+\frac{x-a}{b+a}\right)^r$ in the binomial expansion to find the Taylor series of each function with the given center.

178. $\sqrt{x+2}$ at $a=0$

179. $\sqrt{x^2+2}$ at $a=0$

180. $\sqrt{x+2}$ at $a=1$

181. $\sqrt{2x-x^2}$ at $a=1$ (*Hint:* $2x-x^2 = 1-(x-1)^2$)

182. $(x-8)^{1/3}$ at $a=9$

183. $\sqrt{x}$ at $a=4$

184. $x^{1/3}$ at $a=27$

185. $\sqrt{x}$ at $x=9$

In the following exercises, use the binomial theorem to estimate each number, computing enough terms to obtain an estimate accurate to an error of at most $1/1000$.

186. **[T]** $(15)^{1/4}$ using $(16-x)^{1/4}$

187. **[T]** $(1001)^{1/3}$ using $(1000+x)^{1/3}$

In the following exercises, use the binomial approximation $\sqrt{1-x} \approx 1-\frac{x}{2}-\frac{x^2}{8}-\frac{x^3}{16}-\frac{5x^4}{128}-\frac{7x^5}{256}$ for $|x|<1$ to approximate each number. Compare this value to the value given by a scientific calculator.

188. **[T]** $\frac{1}{\sqrt{2}}$ using $x=\frac{1}{2}$ in $(1-x)^{1/2}$

189. **[T]** $\sqrt{5} = 5\times\frac{1}{\sqrt{5}}$ using $x=\frac{4}{5}$ in $(1-x)^{1/2}$

190. **[T]** $\sqrt{3} = \frac{3}{\sqrt{3}}$ using $x=\frac{2}{3}$ in $(1-x)^{1/2}$

191. **[T]** $\sqrt{6}$ using $x=\frac{5}{6}$ in $(1-x)^{1/2}$

192. Integrate the binomial approximation of $\sqrt{1-x}$ to find an approximation of $\int_0^x \sqrt{1-t}\,dt$.

193. **[T]** Recall that the graph of $\sqrt{1-x^2}$ is an upper semicircle of radius 1. Integrate the binomial approximation of $\sqrt{1-x^2}$ up to order 8 from $x=-1$ to $x=1$ to estimate $\frac{\pi}{2}$.

In the following exercises, use the expansion $(1+x)^{1/3} = 1+\frac{1}{3}x-\frac{1}{9}x^2+\frac{5}{81}x^3-\frac{10}{243}x^4+\cdots$ to write the first five terms (not necessarily a quartic polynomial) of each expression.

194. $(1+4x)^{1/3}$; $a=0$

195. $(1+4x)^{4/3}$; $a=0$

196. $(3+2x)^{1/3}$; $a=-1$

197. $\left(x^2+6x+10\right)^{1/3}$; $a=-3$

198. Use $(1+x)^{1/3} = 1+\frac{1}{3}x-\frac{1}{9}x^2+\frac{5}{81}x^3-\frac{10}{243}x^4+\cdots$ with $x=1$ to approximate $2^{1/3}$.

199. Use the approximation $(1-x)^{2/3} = 1-\frac{2x}{3}-\frac{x^2}{9}-\frac{4x^3}{81}-\frac{7x^4}{243}-\frac{14x^5}{729}+\cdots$ for $|x|<1$ to approximate $2^{1/3} = 2.2^{-2/3}$.

200. Find the 25th derivative of $f(x) = \left(1+x^2\right)^{13}$ at $x=0$.

201. Find the 99 th derivative of $f(x) = \left(1+x^4\right)^{25}$.

In the following exercises, find the Maclaurin series of each function.

202. $f(x) = xe^{2x}$

203. $f(x) = 2^x$

204. $f(x) = \frac{\sin x}{x}$

205. $f(x) = \frac{\sin(\sqrt{x})}{\sqrt{x}}$, $(x > 0)$,

206. $f(x) = \sin\left(x^2\right)$

207. $f(x) = e^{x^3}$

208. $f(x) = \cos^2 x$ using the identity $\cos^2 x = \frac{1}{2} + \frac{1}{2}\cos(2x)$

209. $f(x) = \sin^2 x$ using the identity $\sin^2 x = \frac{1}{2} - \frac{1}{2}\cos(2x)$

In the following exercises, find the Maclaurin series of $F(x) = \int_0^x f(t)dt$ by integrating the Maclaurin series of $f$ term by term. If $f$ is not strictly defined at zero, you may substitute the value of the Maclaurin series at zero.

210. $F(x) = \int_0^x e^{-t^2} dt;\ f(t) = e^{-t^2} = \sum_{n=0}^{\infty} (-1)^n \frac{t^{2n}}{n!}$

211. $F(x) = \tan^{-1} x;\ \ f(t) = \frac{1}{1+t^2} = \sum_{n=0}^{\infty} (-1)^n t^{2n}$

212. $F(x) = \tanh^{-1} x;\ \ f(t) = \frac{1}{1-t^2} = \sum_{n=0}^{\infty} t^{2n}$

213. $F(x) = \sin^{-1} x;\ \ f(t) = \frac{1}{\sqrt{1-t^2}} = \sum_{k=0}^{\infty} \binom{\frac{1}{2}}{k} \frac{t^{2k}}{k!}$

214.
$F(x) = \int_0^x \frac{\sin t}{t} dt;\ \ f(t) = \frac{\sin t}{t} = \sum_{n=0}^{\infty} (-1)^n \frac{t^{2n}}{(2n+1)!}$

215. $F(x) = \int_0^x \cos(\sqrt{t})dt;\ \ f(t) = \sum_{n=0}^{\infty} (-1)^n \frac{x^n}{(2n)!}$

216.
$F(x) = \int_0^x \frac{1-\cos t}{t^2} dt;\ \ f(t) = \frac{1-\cos t}{t^2} = \sum_{n=0}^{\infty} (-1)^n \frac{t^{2n}}{(2n+2)!}$

217. $F(x) = \int_0^x \frac{\ln(1+t)}{t} dt;\ \ f(t) = \sum_{n=0}^{\infty} (-1)^n \frac{t^n}{n+1}$

In the following exercises, compute at least the first three nonzero terms (not necessarily a quadratic polynomial) of the Maclaurin series of $f$.

218. $f(x) = \sin\left(x + \frac{\pi}{4}\right) = \sin x \cos\left(\frac{\pi}{4}\right) + \cos x \sin\left(\frac{\pi}{4}\right)$

219. $f(x) = \tan x$

220. $f(x) = \ln(\cos x)$

221. $f(x) = e^x \cos x$

222. $f(x) = e^{\sin x}$

223. $f(x) = \sec^2 x$

224. $f(x) = \tanh x$

225. $f(x) = \frac{\tan\sqrt{x}}{\sqrt{x}}$ (see expansion for $\tan x$)

In the following exercises, find the radius of convergence of the Maclaurin series of each function.

226. $\ln(1+x)$

227. $\frac{1}{1+x^2}$

228. $\tan^{-1} x$

229. $\ln\left(1+x^2\right)$

230. Find the Maclaurin series of $\sinh x = \frac{e^x - e^{-x}}{2}$.

231. Find the Maclaurin series of $\cosh x = \frac{e^x + e^{-x}}{2}$.

232. Differentiate term by term the Maclaurin series of $\sinh x$ and compare the result with the Maclaurin series of $\cosh x$.

233. **[T]** Let $S_n(x) = \sum_{k=0}^{n} (-1)^k \frac{x^{2k+1}}{(2k+1)!}$ and $C_n(x) = \sum_{n=0}^{n} (-1)^k \frac{x^{2k}}{(2k)!}$ denote the respective Maclaurin polynomials of degree $2n+1$ of $\sin x$ and degree $2n$ of $\cos x$. Plot the errors $\frac{S_n(x)}{C_n(x)} - \tan x$ for $n = 1, .., 5$ and compare them to $x + \frac{x^3}{3} + \frac{2x^5}{15} + \frac{17x^7}{315} - \tan x$ on $\left(-\frac{\pi}{4}, \frac{\pi}{4}\right)$.

234. Use the identity $2\sin x \cos x = \sin(2x)$ to find the power series expansion of $\sin^2 x$ at $x = 0$. (*Hint:* Integrate the Maclaurin series of $\sin(2x)$ term by term.)

235. If $y = \sum_{n=0}^{\infty} a_n x^n$, find the power series expansions of $xy'$ and $x^2 y''$.

236. **[T]** Suppose that $y = \sum_{k=0}^{\infty} a_k x^k$ satisfies $y' = -2xy$ and $y(0) = 0$. Show that $a_{2k+1} = 0$ for all $k$ and that $a_{2k+2} = \frac{-a_{2k}}{k+1}$. Plot the partial sum $S_{20}$ of $y$ on the interval $[-4, 4]$.

237. **[T]** Suppose that a set of standardized test scores is normally distributed with mean $\mu = 100$ and standard deviation $\sigma = 10$. Set up an integral that represents the probability that a test score will be between 90 and 110 and use the integral of the degree 10 Maclaurin polynomial of $\frac{1}{\sqrt{2\pi}} e^{-x^2/2}$ to estimate this probability.

238. **[T]** Suppose that a set of standardized test scores is normally distributed with mean $\mu = 100$ and standard deviation $\sigma = 10$. Set up an integral that represents the probability that a test score will be between 70 and 130 and use the integral of the degree 50 Maclaurin polynomial of $\frac{1}{\sqrt{2\pi}} e^{-x^2/2}$ to estimate this probability.

239. **[T]** Suppose that $\sum_{n=0}^{\infty} a_n x^n$ converges to a function $f(x)$ such that $f(0) = 1, f'(0) = 0,$ and $f''(x) = -f(x)$. Find a formula for $a_n$ and plot the partial sum $S_N$ for $N = 20$ on $[-5, 5]$.

240. **[T]** Suppose that $\sum_{n=0}^{\infty} a_n x^n$ converges to a function $f(x)$ such that $f(0) = 0,$ $f'(0) = 1,$ and $f''(x) = -f(x)$. Find a formula for $a_n$ and plot the partial sum $S_N$ for $N = 10$ on $[-5, 5]$.

241. Suppose that $\sum_{n=0}^{\infty} a_n x^n$ converges to a function $y$ such that $y'' - y' + y = 0$ where $y(0) = 1$ and $y'(0) = 0$. Find a formula that relates $a_{n+2}$, $a_{n+1}$, and $a_n$ and compute $a_0, ..., a_5$.

242. Suppose that $\sum_{n=0}^{\infty} a_n x^n$ converges to a function $y$ such that $y'' - y' + y = 0$ where $y(0) = 0$ and $y'(0) = 1$. Find a formula that relates $a_{n+2}$, $a_{n+1}$, and $a_n$ and compute $a_1, ..., a_5$.

The error in approximating the integral $\int_a^b f(t)dt$ by that of a Taylor approximation $\int_a^b P_n(t)dt$ is at most $\int_a^b R_n(t)dt$. In the following exercises, the Taylor remainder estimate $R_n \le \frac{M}{(n+1)!}|x - a|^{n+1}$ guarantees that the integral of the Taylor polynomial of the given order approximates the integral of $f$ with an error less than $\frac{1}{10}$.

a. Evaluate the integral of the appropriate Taylor polynomial and verify that it approximates the CAS value with an error less than $\frac{1}{100}$.

b. Compare the accuracy of the polynomial integral estimate with the remainder estimate.

243. **[T]** $\int_0^{\pi} \frac{\sin t}{t} dt;\ P_s = 1 - \frac{x^2}{3!} + \frac{x^4}{5!} - \frac{x^6}{7!} + \frac{x^8}{9!}$ (You may assume that the absolute value of the ninth derivative of $\frac{\sin t}{t}$ is bounded by 0.1.)

244. **[T]** $\int_0^2 e^{-x^2} dx;\ p_{11} = 1 - x^2 + \frac{x^4}{2} - \frac{x^6}{3!} + \cdots - \frac{x^{22}}{11!}$ (You may assume that the absolute value of the 23rd derivative of $e^{-x^2}$ is less than $2 \times 10^{14}$.)

The following exercises deal with Fresnel integrals.

245. The Fresnel integrals are defined by $C(x) = \int_0^x \cos(t^2)dt$ and $S(x) = \int_0^x \sin(t^2)dt$. Compute the power series of $C(x)$ and $S(x)$ and plot the sums $C_N(x)$ and $S_N(x)$ of the first $N = 50$ nonzero terms on $[0, 2\pi]$.

246. **[T]** The Fresnel integrals are used in design applications for roadways and railways and other applications because of the curvature properties of the curve with coordinates $(C(t), S(t))$. Plot the curve $(C_{50}, S_{50})$ for $0 \le t \le 2\pi$, the coordinates of which were computed in the previous exercise.

247. Estimate $\int_0^{1/4} \sqrt{x - x^2}dx$ by approximating $\sqrt{1 - x}$ using the binomial approximation $1 - \frac{x}{2} - \frac{x^2}{8} - \frac{x^3}{16} - \frac{5x^4}{2128} - \frac{7x^5}{256}$.

248. **[T]** Use Newton's approximation of the binomial $\sqrt{1 - x^2}$ to approximate $\pi$ as follows. The circle centered at $\left(\frac{1}{2}, 0\right)$ with radius $\frac{1}{2}$ has upper semicircle $y = \sqrt{x}\sqrt{1 - x}$. The sector of this circle bounded by the $x$ -axis between $x = 0$ and $x = \frac{1}{2}$ and by the line joining $\left(\frac{1}{4}, \frac{\sqrt{3}}{4}\right)$ corresponds to $\frac{1}{6}$ of the circle and has area $\frac{\pi}{24}$. This sector is the union of a right triangle with height $\frac{\sqrt{3}}{4}$ and base $\frac{1}{4}$ and the region below the graph between $x = 0$ and $x = \frac{1}{4}$. To find the area of this region you can write $y = \sqrt{x}\sqrt{1 - x} = \sqrt{x} \times (\text{binomial expansion of} \sqrt{1 - x})$ and integrate term by term. Use this approach with the binomial approximation from the previous exercise to estimate $\pi$.

249. Use the approximation $T \approx 2\pi\sqrt{\frac{L}{g}}\left(1 + \frac{k^2}{4}\right)$ to approximate the period of a pendulum having length 10 meters and maximum angle $\theta_{max} = \frac{\pi}{6}$ where $k = \sin\left(\frac{\theta_{max}}{2}\right)$. Compare this with the small angle estimate $T \approx 2\pi\sqrt{\frac{L}{g}}$.

250. Suppose that a pendulum is to have a period of 2 seconds and a maximum angle of $\theta_{max} = \frac{\pi}{6}$. Use $T \approx 2\pi\sqrt{\frac{L}{g}}\left(1 + \frac{k^2}{4}\right)$ to approximate the desired length of the pendulum. What length is predicted by the small angle estimate $T \approx 2\pi\sqrt{\frac{L}{g}}$?

251. Evaluate $\int_0^{\pi/2} \sin^4 \theta d\theta$ in the approximation $T = 4\sqrt{\frac{L}{g}}\int_0^{\pi/2}\left(1 + \frac{1}{2}k^2 \sin^2\theta + \frac{3}{8}k^4 \sin^4\theta + \cdots\right)d\theta$ to obtain an improved estimate for $T$.

252. **[T]** An equivalent formula for the period of a pendulum with amplitude $\theta_{max}$ is $T(\theta_{max}) = 2\sqrt{2}\sqrt{\frac{L}{g}}\int_0^{\theta_{max}} \frac{d\theta}{\sqrt{\cos\theta - \cos(\theta_{max})}}$ where $L$ is the pendulum length and $g$ is the gravitational acceleration constant. When $\theta_{max} = \frac{\pi}{3}$ we get $\frac{1}{\sqrt{\cos t - 1/2}} \approx \sqrt{2}\left(1 + \frac{t^2}{2} + \frac{t^4}{3} + \frac{181t^6}{720}\right)$. Integrate this approximation to estimate $T\left(\frac{\pi}{3}\right)$ in terms of $L$ and $g$. Assuming $g = 9.806$ meters per second squared, find an approximate length $L$ such that $T\left(\frac{\pi}{3}\right) = 2$ seconds.

# CHAPTER 6 REVIEW

## KEY TERMS

**binomial series** the Maclaurin series for $f(x) = (1 + x)^r$; it is given by

$$(1 + x)^r = \sum_{n=0}^{\infty} \binom{r}{n} x^n = 1 + rx + \frac{r(r-1)}{2!}x^2 + \cdots + \frac{r(r-1)\cdots(r-n+1)}{n!}x^n + \cdots \text{ for } |x| < 1$$

**interval of convergence** the set of real numbers $x$ for which a power series converges

**Maclaurin polynomial** a Taylor polynomial centered at 0; the $n$th Taylor polynomial for $f$ at 0 is the $n$th Maclaurin polynomial for $f$

**Maclaurin series** a Taylor series for a function $f$ at $x = 0$ is known as a Maclaurin series for $f$

**nonelementary integral** an integral for which the antiderivative of the integrand cannot be expressed as an elementary function

**power series** a series of the form $\sum_{n=0}^{\infty} c_n x^n$ is a power series centered at $x = 0$; a series of the form $\sum_{n=0}^{\infty} c_n (x-a)^n$ is a power series centered at $x = a$

**radius of convergence** if there exists a real number $R > 0$ such that a power series centered at $x = a$ converges for $|x - a| < R$ and diverges for $|x - a| > R$, then $R$ is the radius of convergence; if the power series only converges at $x = a$, the radius of convergence is $R = 0$; if the power series converges for all real numbers $x$, the radius of convergence is $R = \infty$

**Taylor polynomials** the $n$th Taylor polynomial for $f$ at $x = a$ is $p_n(x) = f(a) + f'(a)(x-a) + \frac{f''(a)}{2!}(x-a)^2 + \cdots + \frac{f^{(n)}(a)}{n!}(x-a)^n$

**Taylor series** a power series at $a$ that converges to a function $f$ on some open interval containing $a$

**Taylor's theorem with remainder** for a function $f$ and the $n$th Taylor polynomial for $f$ at $x = a$, the remainder $R_n(x) = f(x) - p_n(x)$ satisfies $R_n(x) = \frac{f^{(n+1)}(c)}{(n+1)!}(x-a)^{n+1}$

for some $c$ between $x$ and $a$; if there exists an interval $I$ containing $a$ and a real number $M$ such that $\left|f^{(n+1)}(x)\right| \le M$ for all $x$ in $I$, then $|R_n(x)| \le \frac{M}{(n+1)!}|x-a|^{n+1}$

**term-by-term differentiation of a power series** a technique for evaluating the derivative of a power series $\sum_{n=0}^{\infty} c_n (x-a)^n$ by evaluating the derivative of each term separately to create the new power series $\sum_{n=1}^{\infty} n c_n (x-a)^{n-1}$

**term-by-term integration of a power series** a technique for integrating a power series $\sum_{n=0}^{\infty} c_n (x-a)^n$ by integrating each term separately to create the new power series $C + \sum_{n=0}^{\infty} c_n \frac{(x-a)^{n+1}}{n+1}$

## KEY EQUATIONS

- **Power series centered at $x = 0$**

  $$\sum_{n=0}^{\infty} c_n x^n = c_0 + c_1 x + c_2 x^2 + \cdots$$

- **Power series centered at $x = a$**

  $$\sum_{n=0}^{\infty} c_n (x-a)^n = c_0 + c_1 (x-a) + c_2 (x-a)^2 + \cdots$$

- **Taylor series for the function $f$ at the point $x = a$**

  $$\sum_{n=0}^{\infty} \frac{f^{(n)}(a)}{n!}(x-a)^n = f(a) + f'(a)(x-a) + \frac{f''(a)}{2!}(x-a)^2 + \cdots + \frac{f^{(n)}(a)}{n!}(x-a)^n + \cdots$$

## KEY CONCEPTS

### 6.1 Power Series and Functions

- For a power series centered at $x = a$, one of the following three properties hold:
  i. The power series converges only at $x = a$. In this case, we say that the radius of convergence is $R = 0$.
  ii. The power series converges for all real numbers $x$. In this case, we say that the radius of convergence is $R = \infty$.
  iii. There is a real number $R$ such that the series converges for $|x-a| < R$ and diverges for $|x-a| > R$. In this case, the radius of convergence is $R$.
- If a power series converges on a finite interval, the series may or may not converge at the endpoints.
- The ratio test may often be used to determine the radius of convergence.
- The geometric series $\sum_{n=0}^{\infty} x^n = \frac{1}{1-x}$ for $|x| < 1$ allows us to represent certain functions using geometric series.

### 6.2 Properties of Power Series

- Given two power series $\sum_{n=0}^{\infty} c_n x^n$ and $\sum_{n=0}^{\infty} d_n x^n$ that converge to functions $f$ and $g$ on a common interval $I$, the sum and difference of the two series converge to $f \pm g$, respectively, on $I$. In addition, for any real number $b$ and integer $m \geq 0$, the series $\sum_{n=0}^{\infty} bx^m c_n x^n$ converges to $bx^m f(x)$ and the series $\sum_{n=0}^{\infty} c_n (bx^m)^n$ converges to $f(bx^m)$ whenever $bx^m$ is in the interval $I$.
- Given two power series that converge on an interval $(-R, R)$, the Cauchy product of the two power series converges on the interval $(-R, R)$.
- Given a power series that converges to a function $f$ on an interval $(-R, R)$, the series can be differentiated term-by-term and the resulting series converges to $f'$ on $(-R, R)$. The series can also be integrated term-by-term and the resulting series converges to $\int f(x)dx$ on $(-R, R)$.

### 6.3 Taylor and Maclaurin Series

- Taylor polynomials are used to approximate functions near a value $x = a$. Maclaurin polynomials are Taylor polynomials at $x = 0$.

- The $n$th degree Taylor polynomials for a function $f$ are the partial sums of the Taylor series for $f$.
- If a function $f$ has a power series representation at $x = a$, then it is given by its Taylor series at $x = a$.
- A Taylor series for $f$ converges to $f$ if and only if $\lim_{n \to \infty} R_n(x) = 0$ where $R_n(x) = f(x) - p_n(x)$.
- The Taylor series for $e^x$, $\sin x$, and $\cos x$ converge to the respective functions for all real $x$.

### 6.4 Working with Taylor Series

- The binomial series is the Maclaurin series for $f(x) = (1 + x)^r$. It converges for $|x| < 1$.
- Taylor series for functions can often be derived by algebraic operations with a known Taylor series or by differentiating or integrating a known Taylor series.
- Power series can be used to solve differential equations.
- Taylor series can be used to help approximate integrals that cannot be evaluated by other means.

# CHAPTER 6 REVIEW EXERCISES

*True or False?* In the following exercises, justify your answer with a proof or a counterexample.

**253.** If the radius of convergence for a power series $\sum_{n=0}^{\infty} a_n x^n$ is 5, then the radius of convergence for the series $\sum_{n=1}^{\infty} n a_n x^{n-1}$ is also 5.

**254.** Power series can be used to show that the derivative of $e^x$ is $e^x$. (*Hint:* Recall that $e^x = \sum_{n=0}^{\infty} \frac{1}{n!} x^n$.)

**255.** For small values of $x$, $\sin x \approx x$.

**256.** The radius of convergence for the Maclaurin series of $f(x) = 3^x$ is 3.

In the following exercises, find the radius of convergence and the interval of convergence for the given series.

**257.** $\sum_{n=0}^{\infty} n^2 (x-1)^n$

**258.** $\sum_{n=0}^{\infty} \frac{x^n}{n^n}$

**259.** $\sum_{n=0}^{\infty} \frac{3nx^n}{12^n}$

**260.** $\sum_{n=0}^{\infty} \frac{2^n}{e^n} (x-e)^n$

In the following exercises, find the power series representation for the given function. Determine the radius of convergence and the interval of convergence for that series.

**261.** $f(x) = \frac{x^2}{x+3}$

**262.** $f(x) = \frac{8x+2}{2x^2 - 3x + 1}$

In the following exercises, find the power series for the given function using term-by-term differentiation or integration.

**263.** $f(x) = \tan^{-1}(2x)$

**264.** $f(x) = \frac{x}{\left(2 + x^2\right)^2}$

In the following exercises, evaluate the Taylor series expansion of degree four for the given function at the specified point. What is the error in the approximation?

**265.** $f(x) = x^3 - 2x^2 + 4$, $a = -3$

**266.** $f(x) = e^{1/(4x)}$, $a = 4$

In the following exercises, find the Maclaurin series for the given function.

**267.** $f(x) = \cos(3x)$

**268.** $f(x) = \ln(x + 1)$

In the following exercises, find the Taylor series at the given value.

**269.** $f(x) = \sin x,\ a = \frac{\pi}{2}$

**270.** $f(x) = \frac{3}{x},\ a = 1$

In the following exercises, find the Maclaurin series for the given function.

**271.** $f(x) = e^{-x^2} - 1$

**272.** $f(x) = \cos x - x\sin x$

In the following exercises, find the Maclaurin series for $F(x) = \int_0^x f(t)dt$ by integrating the Maclaurin series of $f(x)$ term by term.

**273.** $f(x) = \frac{\sin x}{x}$

**274.** $f(x) = 1 - e^x$

**275.** Use power series to prove Euler's formula: $e^{ix} = \cos x + i\sin x$

The following exercises consider problems of annuity payments.

**276.** For annuities with a present value of $\$1$ million, calculate the annual payouts given over $25$ years assuming interest rates of $1\%,\ 5\%,$ and $10\%.$

**277.** A lottery winner has an annuity that has a present value of $\$10$ million. What interest rate would they need to live on perpetual annual payments of $\$250{,}000$?

**278.** Calculate the necessary present value of an annuity in order to support annual payouts of $\$15{,}000$ given over $25$ years assuming interest rates of $1\%,\ 5\%,$ and $10\%.$

# 7 | PARAMETRIC EQUATIONS AND POLAR COORDINATES

**Figure 7.1** The chambered nautilus is a marine animal that lives in the tropical Pacific Ocean. Scientists think they have existed mostly unchanged for about 500 million years.(credit: modification of work by Jitze Couperus, Flickr)

## Chapter Outline



# Introduction

The chambered nautilus is a fascinating creature. This animal feeds on hermit crabs, fish, and other crustaceans. It has a hard outer shell with many chambers connected in a spiral fashion, and it can retract into its shell to avoid predators. When part of the shell is cut away, a perfect spiral is revealed, with chambers inside that are somewhat similar to growth rings in a tree.

The mathematical function that describes a spiral can be expressed using rectangular (or Cartesian) coordinates. However, if we change our coordinate system to something that works a bit better with circular patterns, the function becomes much simpler to describe. The polar coordinate system is well suited for describing curves of this type. How can we use this coordinate system to describe spirals and other radial figures? (See **Example 7.14**.)

In this chapter we also study parametric equations, which give us a convenient way to describe curves, or to study the position of a particle or object in two dimensions as a function of time. We will use parametric equations and polar coordinates for describing many topics later in this text.

# 7.1 | Parametric Equations

## Learning Objectives

**7.1.1** Plot a curve described by parametric equations.
**7.1.2** Convert the parametric equations of a curve into the form $y = f(x)$.
**7.1.3** Recognize the parametric equations of basic curves, such as a line and a circle.
**7.1.4** Recognize the parametric equations of a cycloid.

In this section we examine parametric equations and their graphs. In the two-dimensional coordinate system, parametric equations are useful for describing curves that are not necessarily functions. The parameter is an independent variable that both $x$ and $y$ depend on, and as the parameter increases, the values of $x$ and $y$ trace out a path along a plane curve. For example, if the parameter is $t$ (a common choice), then $t$ might represent time. Then $x$ and $y$ are defined as functions of time, and $(x(t),\ y(t))$ can describe the position in the plane of a given object as it moves along a curved path.

## Parametric Equations and Their Graphs

Consider the orbit of Earth around the Sun. Our year lasts approximately 365.25 days, but for this discussion we will use 365 days. On January 1 of each year, the physical location of Earth with respect to the Sun is nearly the same, except for leap years, when the lag introduced by the extra $\frac{1}{4}$ day of orbiting time is built into the calendar. We call January 1 “day 1” of the year. Then, for example, day 31 is January 31, day 59 is February 28, and so on.

The number of the day in a year can be considered a variable that determines Earth’s position in its orbit. As Earth revolves around the Sun, its physical location changes relative to the Sun. After one full year, we are back where we started, and a new year begins. According to Kepler’s laws of planetary motion, the shape of the orbit is elliptical, with the Sun at one focus of the ellipse. We study this idea in more detail in **Conic Sections**.

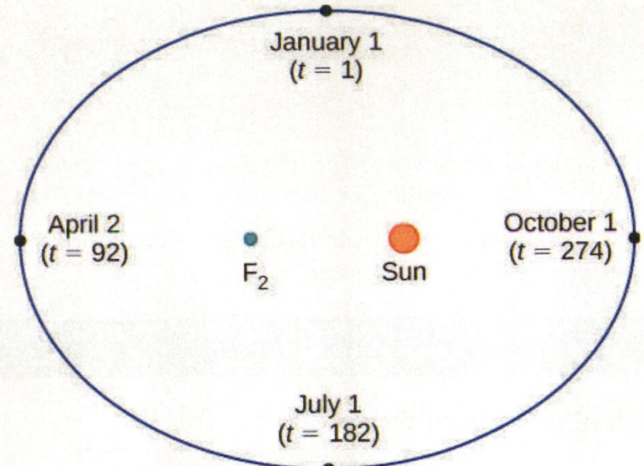


**Figure 7.2** Earth's orbit around the Sun in one year.

**Figure 7.2** depicts Earth's orbit around the Sun during one year. The point labeled $F_2$ is one of the foci of the ellipse; the other focus is occupied by the Sun. If we superimpose coordinate axes over this graph, then we can assign ordered pairs to each point on the ellipse (**Figure 7.3**). Then each *x* value on the graph is a value of position as a function of time, and each *y* value is also a value of position as a function of time. Therefore, each point on the graph corresponds to a value of Earth's position as a function of time.

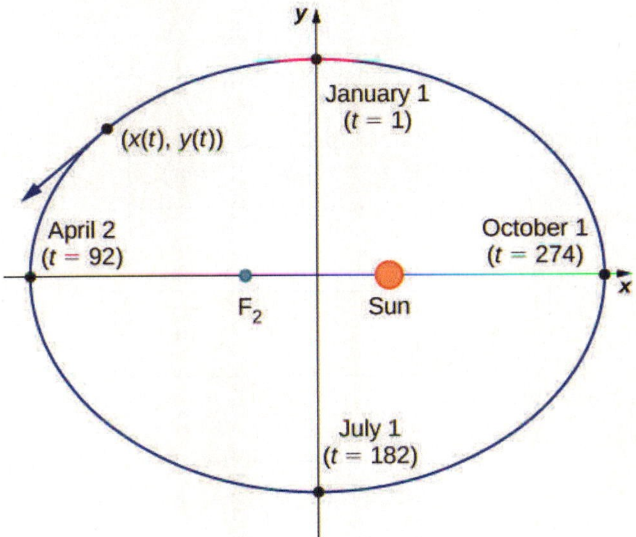


**Figure 7.3** Coordinate axes superimposed on the orbit of Earth.

We can determine the functions for $x(t)$ and $y(t),$ thereby parameterizing the orbit of Earth around the Sun. The variable $t$ is called an independent parameter and, in this context, represents time relative to the beginning of each year.

A curve in the $(x, y)$ plane can be represented parametrically. The equations that are used to define the curve are called **parametric equations**.

### Definition

If *x* and *y* are continuous functions of *t* on an interval *I*, then the equations

$$x = x(t) \text{ and } y = y(t)$$

are called parametric equations and *t* is called the **parameter**. The set of points $(x, y)$ obtained as *t* varies over the interval $I$ is called the graph of the parametric equations. The graph of parametric equations is called a **parametric curve** or *plane curve*, and is denoted by $C$.

Notice in this definition that $x$ and $y$ are used in two ways. The first is as functions of the independent variable $t$. As $t$ varies over the interval $I$, the functions $x(t)$ and $y(t)$ generate a set of ordered pairs $(x, y)$. This set of ordered pairs generates the graph of the parametric equations. In this second usage, to designate the ordered pairs, $x$ and $y$ are variables. It is important to distinguish the variables $x$ and $y$ from the functions $x(t)$ and $y(t)$.

## Example 7.1

### Graphing a Parametrically Defined Curve

Sketch the curves described by the following parametric equations:

a. $x(t) = t - 1, \quad y(t) = 2t + 4, \quad -3 \le t \le 2$

b. $x(t) = t^2 - 3, \quad y(t) = 2t + 1, \quad -2 \le t \le 3$

c. $x(t) = 4\cos t, \quad y(t) = 4\sin t, \quad 0 \le t \le 2\pi$

### Solution

a. To create a graph of this curve, first set up a table of values. Since the independent variable in both $x(t)$ and $y(t)$ is $t$, let $t$ appear in the first column. Then $x(t)$ and $y(t)$ will appear in the second and third columns of the table.

| $t$ | $x(t)$ | $y(t)$ |
|---|---|---|
| −3 | −4 | −2 |
| −2 | −3 | 0 |
| −1 | −2 | 2 |
| 0 | −1 | 4 |
| 1 | 0 | 6 |
| 2 | 1 | 8 |

The second and third columns in this table provide a set of points to be plotted. The graph of these points appears in Figure 7.4. The arrows on the graph indicate the **orientation** of the graph, that is, the direction that a point moves on the graph as $t$ varies from −3 to 2.

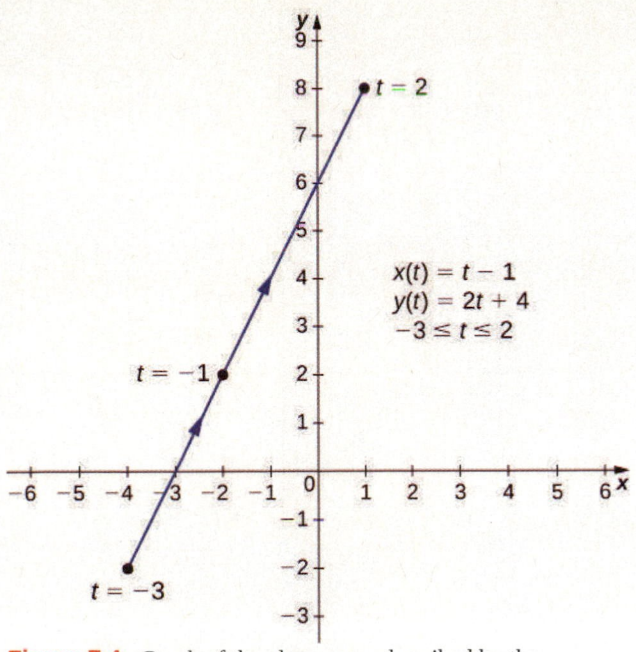


**Figure 7.4** Graph of the plane curve described by the parametric equations in part a.

b. To create a graph of this curve, again set up a table of values.

| $t$ | $x(t)$ | $y(t)$ |
|---|---|---|
| −2 | 1 | −3 |
| −1 | −2 | −1 |
| 0 | −3 | 1 |
| 1 | −2 | 3 |
| 2 | 1 | 5 |
| 3 | 6 | 7 |

The second and third columns in this table give a set of points to be plotted (**Figure 7.5**). The first point on the graph (corresponding to $t = -2$) has coordinates $(1, -3)$, and the last point (corresponding to $t = 3$) has coordinates $(6, 7)$. As $t$ progresses from −2 to 3, the point on the curve travels along a parabola. The direction the point moves is again called the orientation and is indicated on the graph.

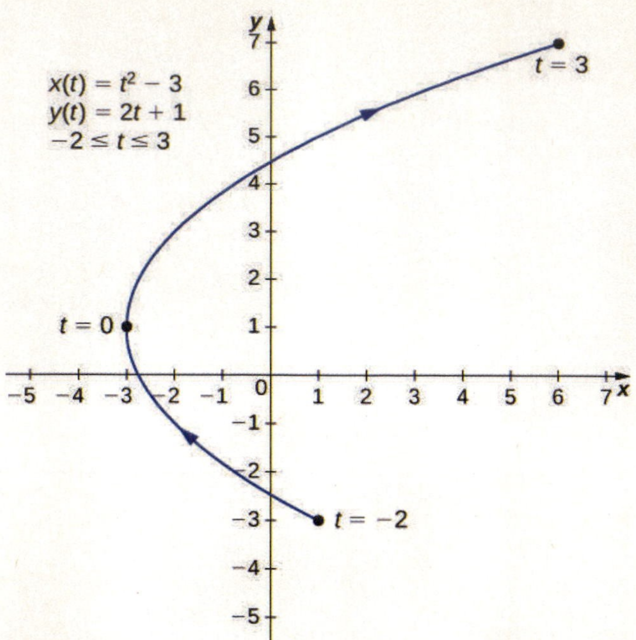


**Figure 7.5** Graph of the plane curve described by the parametric equations in part b.

c. In this case, use multiples of $\pi/6$ for $t$ and create another table of values:

| $t$ | $x(t)$ | $y(t)$ | | $t$ | $x(t)$ | $y(t)$ |
|---|---|---|---|---|---|---|
| 0 | 4 | 0 | | $\frac{7\pi}{6}$ | $-2\sqrt{3} \approx -3.5$ | 2 |
| $\frac{\pi}{6}$ | $2\sqrt{3} \approx 3.5$ | 2 | | $\frac{4\pi}{3}$ | −2 | $-2\sqrt{3} \approx -3.5$ |
| $\frac{\pi}{3}$ | 2 | $2\sqrt{3} \approx 3.5$ | | $\frac{3\pi}{2}$ | 0 | −4 |
| $\frac{\pi}{2}$ | 0 | 4 | | $\frac{5\pi}{3}$ | 2 | $-2\sqrt{3} \approx -3.5$ |
| $\frac{2\pi}{3}$ | −2 | $2\sqrt{3} \approx 3.5$ | | $\frac{11\pi}{6}$ | $2\sqrt{3} \approx 3.5$ | 2 |
| $\frac{5\pi}{6}$ | $-2\sqrt{3} \approx -3.5$ | 2 | | $2\pi$ | 4 | 0 |
| $\pi$ | −4 | 0 | | | | |

The graph of this plane curve appears in the following graph.

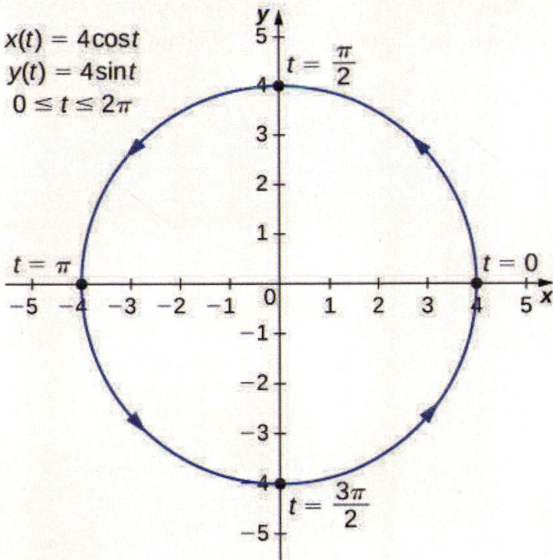


**Figure 7.6** Graph of the plane curve described by the parametric equations in part c.

This is the graph of a circle with radius 4 centered at the origin, with a counterclockwise orientation. The starting point and ending points of the curve both have coordinates $(4, 0)$.

**7.1** Sketch the curve described by the parametric equations

$$x(t) = 3t + 2, \quad y(t) = t^2 - 1, \quad -3 \le t \le 2.$$

## Eliminating the Parameter

To better understand the graph of a curve represented parametrically, it is useful to rewrite the two equations as a single equation relating the variables $x$ and $y$. Then we can apply any previous knowledge of equations of curves in the plane to identify the curve. For example, the equations describing the plane curve in **Example 7.1**b. are

$$x(t) = t^2 - 3, \quad y(t) = 2t + 1, \quad -2 \le t \le 3.$$

Solving the second equation for $t$ gives

$$t = \frac{y - 1}{2}.$$

This can be substituted into the first equation:

$$x = \left(\frac{y - 1}{2}\right)^2 - 3 = \frac{y^2 - 2y + 1}{4} - 3 = \frac{y^2 - 2y - 11}{4}.$$

This equation describes $x$ as a function of $y$. These steps give an example of *eliminating the parameter*. The graph of this function is a parabola opening to the right. Recall that the plane curve started at $(1, -3)$ and ended at $(6, 7)$. These terminations were due to the restriction on the parameter $t$.

## Example 7.2

### Eliminating the Parameter

Eliminate the parameter for each of the plane curves described by the following parametric equations and describe the resulting graph.

a. $x(t) = \sqrt{2t+4}, \quad y(t) = 2t+1, \quad -2 \le t \le 6$

b. $x(t) = 4\cos t, \quad y(t) = 3\sin t, \quad 0 \le t \le 2\pi$

### Solution

a. To eliminate the parameter, we can solve either of the equations for $t$. For example, solving the first equation for $t$ gives

$$\begin{aligned} x &= \sqrt{2t+4} \\ x^2 &= 2t+4 \\ x^2-4 &= 2t \\ t &= \frac{x^2-4}{2}. \end{aligned}$$

Note that when we square both sides it is important to observe that $x \ge 0$. Substituting $t = \frac{x^2-4}{2}$ this into $y(t)$ yields

$$\begin{aligned} y(t) &= 2t+1 \\ y &= 2\left(\frac{x^2-4}{2}\right)+1 \\ y &= x^2-4+1 \\ y &= x^2-3. \end{aligned}$$

This is the equation of a parabola opening upward. There is, however, a domain restriction because of the limits on the parameter $t$. When $t=-2$, $x = \sqrt{2(-2)+4} = 0$, and when $t=6$, $x = \sqrt{2(6)+4} = 4$. The graph of this plane curve follows.

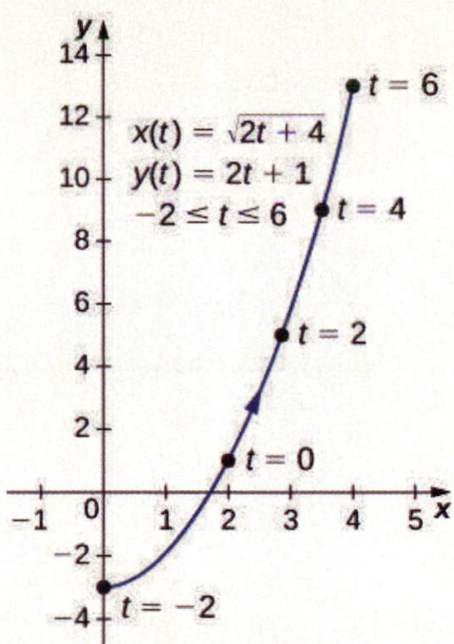


**Figure 7.7** Graph of the plane curve described by the parametric equations in part a.

b. Sometimes it is necessary to be a bit creative in eliminating the parameter. The parametric equations for this example are

$$x(t) = 4\cos t \text{ and } y(t) = 3\sin t.$$

Solving either equation for $t$ directly is not advisable because sine and cosine are not one-to-one functions. However, dividing the first equation by 4 and the second equation by 3 (and suppressing the $t$) gives us

$$\cos t = \frac{x}{4} \text{ and } \sin t = \frac{y}{3}.$$

Now use the Pythagorean identity $\cos^2 t + \sin^2 t = 1$ and replace the expressions for $\sin t$ and $\cos t$ with the equivalent expressions in terms of $x$ and $y$. This gives

$$\begin{aligned} \left(\frac{x}{4}\right)^2 + \left(\frac{y}{3}\right)^2 &= 1 \\ \frac{x^2}{16} + \frac{y^2}{9} &= 1. \end{aligned}$$

This is the equation of a horizontal ellipse centered at the origin, with semimajor axis 4 and semiminor axis 3 as shown in the following graph.

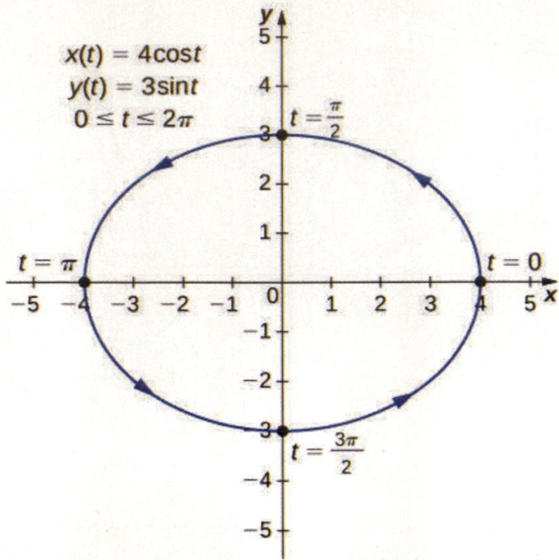


**Figure 7.8** Graph of the plane curve described by the parametric equations in part b.

As $t$ progresses from $0$ to $2\pi,$ a point on the curve traverses the ellipse once, in a counterclockwise direction. Recall from the section opener that the orbit of Earth around the Sun is also elliptical. This is a perfect example of using parameterized curves to model a real-world phenomenon.

**7.2** Eliminate the parameter for the plane curve defined by the following parametric equations and describe the resulting graph.

$$x(t) = 2 + \frac{3}{t}, \quad y(t) = t - 1, \quad 2 \le t \le 6$$

So far we have seen the method of eliminating the parameter, assuming we know a set of parametric equations that describe a plane curve. What if we would like to start with the equation of a curve and determine a pair of parametric equations for that curve? This is certainly possible, and in fact it is possible to do so in many different ways for a given curve. The process is known as **parameterization of a curve**.

## Example 7.3

### Parameterizing a Curve

Find two different pairs of parametric equations to represent the graph of $y = 2x^2 - 3.$

### Solution

First, it is always possible to parameterize a curve by defining $x(t) = t,$ then replacing $x$ with $t$ in the equation for $y(t).$ This gives the parameterization

$$x(t) = t, \quad y(t) = 2t^2 - 3.$$

Since there is no restriction on the domain in the original graph, there is no restriction on the values of $t$.

We have complete freedom in the choice for the second parameterization. For example, we can choose $x(t) = 3t - 2$. The only thing we need to check is that there are no restrictions imposed on $x$; that is, the range of $x(t)$ is all real numbers. This is the case for $x(t) = 3t - 2$. Now since $y = 2x^2 - 3$, we can substitute $x(t) = 3t - 2$ for $x$. This gives

$$\begin{aligned} y(t) &= 2(3t-2)^2 - 2 \\ &= 2\left(9t^2 - 12t + 4\right) - 2 \\ &= 18t^2 - 24t + 8 - 2 \\ &= 18t^2 - 24t + 6. \end{aligned}$$

Therefore, a second parameterization of the curve can be written as

$$x(t) = 3t - 2 \text{ and } y(t) = 18t^2 - 24t + 6.$$

**7.3** Find two different sets of parametric equations to represent the graph of $y = x^2 + 2x$.

## Cycloids and Other Parametric Curves

Imagine going on a bicycle ride through the country. The tires stay in contact with the road and rotate in a predictable pattern. Now suppose a very determined ant is tired after a long day and wants to get home. So he hangs onto the side of the tire and gets a free ride. The path that this ant travels down a straight road is called a **cycloid** (**Figure 7.9**). A cycloid generated by a circle (or bicycle wheel) of radius $a$ is given by the parametric equations

$$x(t) = a(t - \sin t), \quad y(t) = a(1 - \cos t).$$

To see why this is true, consider the path that the center of the wheel takes. The center moves along the $x$-axis at a constant height equal to the radius of the wheel. If the radius is $a$, then the coordinates of the center can be given by the equations

$$x(t) = at, \quad y(t) = a$$

for any value of $t$. Next, consider the ant, which rotates around the center along a circular path. If the bicycle is moving from left to right then the wheels are rotating in a clockwise direction. A possible parameterization of the circular motion of the ant (relative to the center of the wheel) is given by

$$x(t) = -a \sin t, \quad y(t) = -a \cos t.$$

(The negative sign is needed to reverse the orientation of the curve. If the negative sign were not there, we would have to imagine the wheel rotating counterclockwise.) Adding these equations together gives the equations for the cycloid.

$$x(t) = a(t - \sin t), \quad y(t) = a(1 - \cos t).$$

**Figure 7.9** A wheel traveling along a road without slipping; the point on the edge of the wheel traces out a cycloid.

Now suppose that the bicycle wheel doesn't travel along a straight road but instead moves along the inside of a larger wheel, as in **Figure 7.10**. In this graph, the green circle is traveling around the blue circle in a counterclockwise direction. A point on the edge of the green circle traces out the red graph, which is called a hypocycloid.

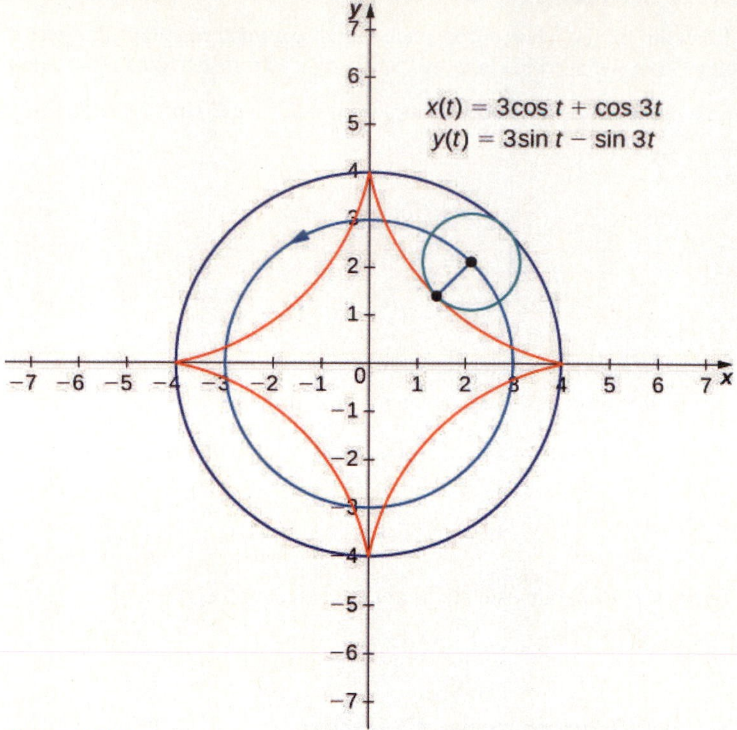


**Figure 7.10** Graph of the hypocycloid described by the parametric equations shown.

The general parametric equations for a hypocycloid are

$$x(t) = (a - b)\cos t + b\cos\left(\frac{a-b}{b}\right)t$$
$$y(t) = (a - b)\sin t - b\sin\left(\frac{a-b}{b}\right)t.$$

These equations are a bit more complicated, but the derivation is somewhat similar to the equations for the cycloid. In this case we assume the radius of the larger circle is $a$ and the radius of the smaller circle is $b$. Then the center of the wheel travels along a circle of radius $a - b$. This fact explains the first term in each equation above. The period of the second trigonometric function in both $x(t)$ and $y(t)$ is equal to $\frac{2\pi b}{a-b}$.

The ratio $\frac{a}{b}$ is related to the number of **cusps** on the graph (cusps are the corners or pointed ends of the graph), as illustrated in **Figure 7.11**. This ratio can lead to some very interesting graphs, depending on whether or not the ratio is rational. **Figure 7.10** corresponds to $a = 4$ and $b = 1$. The result is a hypocycloid with four cusps. **Figure 7.11** shows some other possibilities. The last two hypocycloids have irrational values for $\frac{a}{b}$. In these cases the hypocycloids have an infinite number of cusps, so they never return to their starting point. These are examples of what are known as *space-filling curves*.

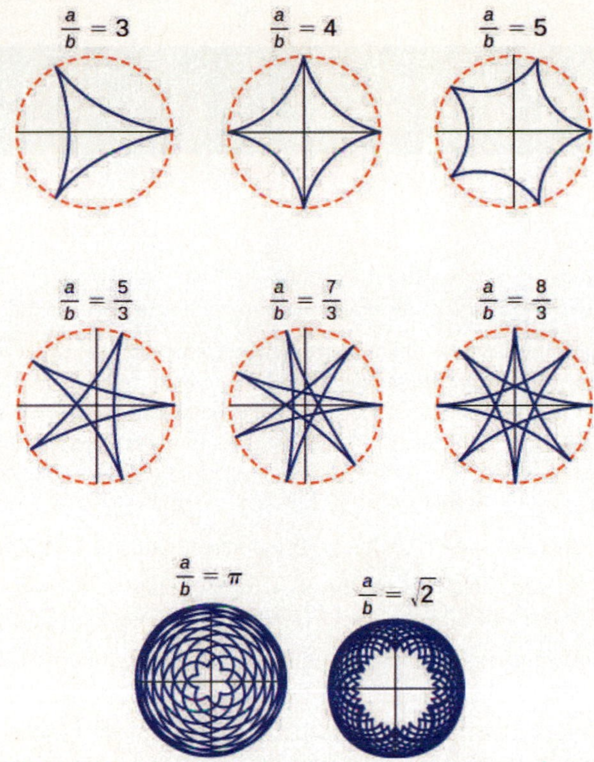


**Figure 7.11** Graph of various hypocycloids corresponding to different values of $a/b$.

# Student PROJECT

## The Witch of Agnesi

Many plane curves in mathematics are named after the people who first investigated them, like the folium of Descartes or the spiral of Archimedes. However, perhaps the strangest name for a curve is the witch of Agnesi. Why a witch?

Maria Gaetana Agnesi (1718–1799) was one of the few recognized women mathematicians of eighteenth-century Italy. She wrote a popular book on analytic geometry, published in 1748, which included an interesting curve that had been studied by Fermat in 1630. The mathematician Guido Grandi showed in 1703 how to construct this curve, which he later called the "versoria," a Latin term for a rope used in sailing. Agnesi used the Italian term for this rope, "versiera," but in Latin, this same word means a "female goblin." When Agnesi's book was translated into English in 1801, the translator used the term "witch" for the curve, instead of rope. The name "witch of Agnesi" has stuck ever since.

The witch of Agnesi is a curve defined as follows: Start with a circle of radius $a$ so that the points $(0, 0)$ and $(0, 2a)$ are points on the circle (**Figure 7.12**). Let $O$ denote the origin. Choose any other point $A$ on the circle, and draw the secant line $OA$. Let $B$ denote the point at which the line $OA$ intersects the horizontal line through $(0, 2a)$. The vertical line through $B$ intersects the horizontal line through $A$ at the point $P$. As the point $A$ varies, the path that the point $P$ travels is the witch of Agnesi curve for the given circle.

Witch of Agnesi curves have applications in physics, including modeling water waves and distributions of spectral lines. In probability theory, the curve describes the probability density function of the Cauchy distribution. In this project you will parameterize these curves.

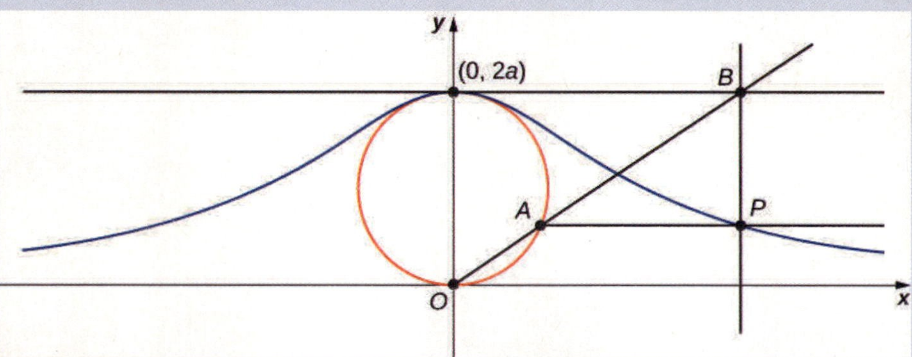


**Figure 7.12** As the point $A$ moves around the circle, the point $P$ traces out the witch of Agnesi curve for the given circle.

1. On the figure, label the following points, lengths, and angle:
   a. $C$ is the point on the $x$-axis with the same $x$-coordinate as $A$.
   b. $x$ is the $x$-coordinate of $P$, and $y$ is the $y$-coordinate of $P$.
   c. $E$ is the point $(0, a)$.
   d. $F$ is the point on the line segment $OA$ such that the line segment $EF$ is perpendicular to the line segment $OA$.
   e. $b$ is the distance from $O$ to $F$.
   f. $c$ is the distance from $F$ to $A$.
   g. $d$ is the distance from $O$ to $B$.
   h. $\theta$ is the measure of angle $\angle COA$.

The goal of this project is to parameterize the witch using $\theta$ as a parameter. To do this, write equations for $x$ and $y$ in terms of only $\theta$.

2. Show that $d = \frac{2a}{\sin\theta}$.
3. Note that $x = d\cos\theta$. Show that $x = 2a\cot\theta$. When you do this, you will have parameterized the $x$-coordinate of the curve with respect to $\theta$. If you can get a similar equation for $y$, you will have parameterized the curve.
4. In terms of $\theta$, what is the angle $\angle EOA$?
5. Show that $b + c = 2a\cos\left(\frac{\pi}{2} - \theta\right)$.
6. Show that $y = 2a\cos\left(\frac{\pi}{2} - \theta\right)\sin\theta$.
7. Show that $y = 2a\sin^2\theta$. You have now parameterized the $y$-coordinate of the curve with respect to $\theta$.
8. Conclude that a parameterization of the given witch curve is

$$x = 2a\cot\theta,\ y = 2a\sin^2\theta,\ \ -\infty < \theta < \infty.$$

9. Use your parameterization to show that the given witch curve is the graph of the function $f(x) = \frac{8a^3}{x^2 + 4a^2}$.

# Student PROJECT

## Travels with My Ant: The Curtate and Prolate Cycloids

Earlier in this section, we looked at the parametric equations for a cycloid, which is the path a point on the edge of a wheel traces as the wheel rolls along a straight path. In this project we look at two different variations of the cycloid, called the curtate and prolate cycloids.

First, let's revisit the derivation of the parametric equations for a cycloid. Recall that we considered a tenacious ant trying to get home by hanging onto the edge of a bicycle tire. We have assumed the ant climbed onto the tire at the very edge, where the tire touches the ground. As the wheel rolls, the ant moves with the edge of the tire (**Figure 7.13**).

As we have discussed, we have a lot of flexibility when parameterizing a curve. In this case we let our parameter $t$ represent the angle the tire has rotated through. Looking at **Figure 7.13**, we see that after the tire has rotated through an angle of $t$, the position of the center of the wheel, $C = (x_C, y_C)$, is given by

$$x_C = at \text{ and } y_C = a.$$

Furthermore, letting $A = (x_A, y_A)$ denote the position of the ant, we note that

$$x_C - x_A = a \sin t \text{ and } y_C - y_A = a \cos t.$$

Then

$$\begin{aligned} x_A &= x_C - a \sin t = at - a \sin t = a(t - \sin t) \\ y_A &= y_C - a \cos t = a - a \cos t = a(1 - \cos t). \end{aligned}$$

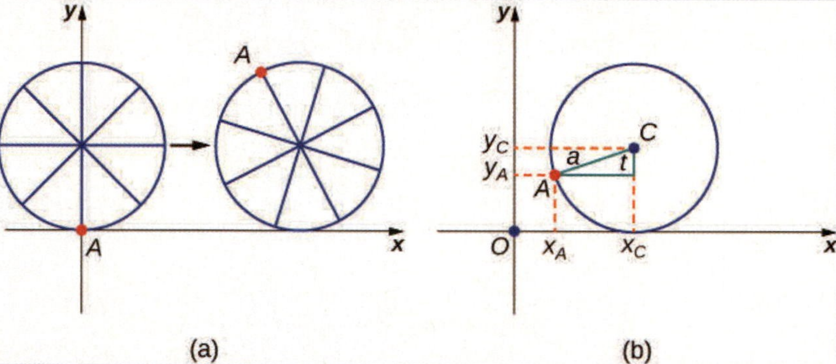


**Figure 7.13** (a) The ant clings to the edge of the bicycle tire as the tire rolls along the ground. (b) Using geometry to determine the position of the ant after the tire has rotated through an angle of $t$.

Note that these are the same parametric representations we had before, but we have now assigned a physical meaning to the parametric variable $t$.

After a while the ant is getting dizzy from going round and round on the edge of the tire. So he climbs up one of the spokes toward the center of the wheel. By climbing toward the center of the wheel, the ant has changed his path of motion. The new path has less up-and-down motion and is called a curtate cycloid (**Figure 7.14**). As shown in the figure, we let $b$ denote the distance along the spoke from the center of the wheel to the ant. As before, we let $t$ represent the angle the tire has rotated through. Additionally, we let $C = (x_C, y_C)$ represent the position of the center of the wheel and $A = (x_A, y_A)$ represent the position of the ant.

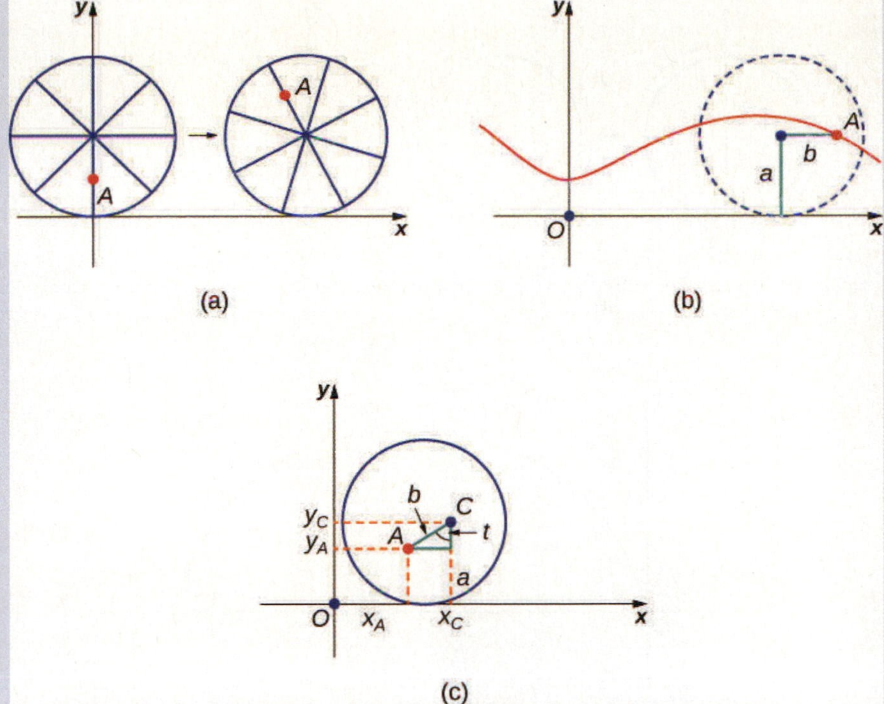


**Figure 7.14** (a) The ant climbs up one of the spokes toward the center of the wheel. (b) The ant's path of motion after he climbs closer to the center of the wheel. This is called a curtate cycloid. (c) The new setup, now that the ant has moved closer to the center of the wheel.

1. What is the position of the center of the wheel after the tire has rotated through an angle of $t$?
2. Use geometry to find expressions for $x_C - x_A$ and for $y_C - y_A$.
3. On the basis of your answers to parts 1 and 2, what are the parametric equations representing the curtate cycloid?
   Once the ant's head clears, he realizes that the bicyclist has made a turn, and is now traveling away from his home. So he drops off the bicycle tire and looks around. Fortunately, there is a set of train tracks nearby, headed back in the right direction. So the ant heads over to the train tracks to wait. After a while, a train goes by, heading in the right direction, and he manages to jump up and just catch the edge of the train wheel (without getting squished!).
   The ant is still worried about getting dizzy, but the train wheel is slippery and has no spokes to climb, so he decides to just hang on to the edge of the wheel and hope for the best. Now, train wheels have a flange to keep the wheel running on the tracks. So, in this case, since the ant is hanging on to the very edge of the flange, the distance from the center of the wheel to the ant is actually greater than the radius of the wheel (**Figure 7.15**). The setup here is essentially the same as when the ant climbed up the spoke on the bicycle wheel. We let $b$ denote the distance from the center of the wheel to the ant, and we let $t$ represent the angle the tire has rotated through. Additionally, we let $C = (x_C, y_C)$ represent the position of the center of the wheel and $A = (x_A, y_A)$ represent the position of the ant (**Figure 7.15**).

   When the distance from the center of the wheel to the ant is greater than the radius of the wheel, his path of motion is called a prolate cycloid. A graph of a prolate cycloid is shown in the figure.

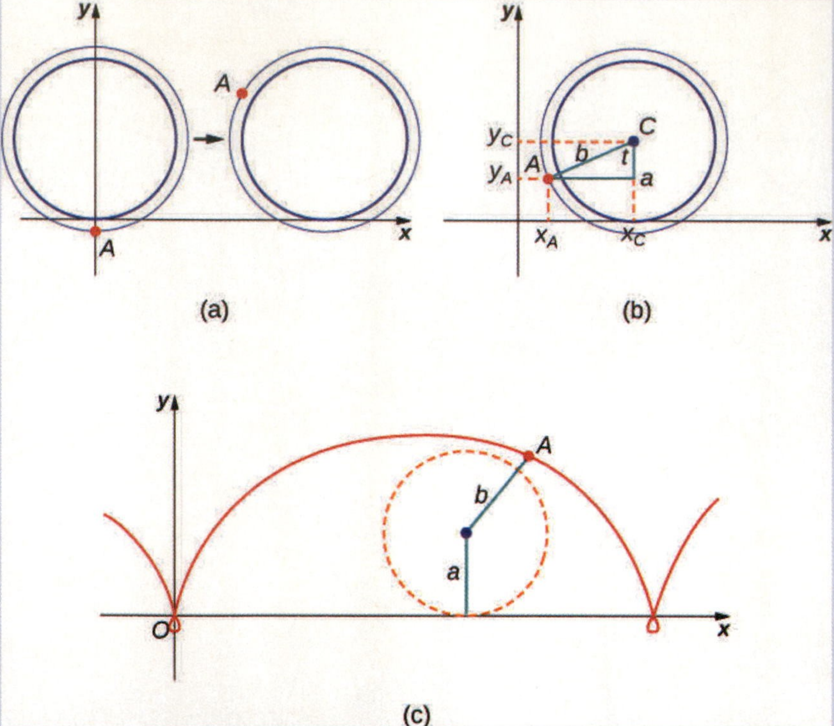


**Figure 7.15** (a) The ant is hanging onto the flange of the train wheel. (b) The new setup, now that the ant has jumped onto the train wheel. (c) The ant travels along a prolate cycloid.

4. Using the same approach you used in parts 1– 3, find the parametric equations for the path of motion of the ant.
5. What do you notice about your answer to part 3 and your answer to part 4?
Notice that the ant is actually traveling backward at times (the "loops" in the graph), even though the train continues to move forward. He is probably going to be *really* dizzy by the time he gets home!

## 7.1 EXERCISES

For the following exercises, sketch the curves below by eliminating the parameter $t$. Give the orientation of the curve.

1. $x = t^2 + 2t, \quad y = t + 1$

2. $x = \cos(t),\ y = \sin(t),\ (0, 2\pi]$

3. $x = 2t + 4,\ y = t - 1$

4. $x = 3 - t,\ y = 2t - 3,\ 1.5 \le t \le 3$

For the following exercises, eliminate the parameter and sketch the graphs.

5. $x = 2t^2, \quad y = t^4 + 1$

For the following exercises, use technology (CAS or calculator) to sketch the parametric equations.

6. **[T]** $x = t^2 + t, \quad y = t^2 - 1$

7. **[T]** $x = e^{-t}, \quad y = e^{2t} - 1$

8. **[T]** $x = 3\cos t, \quad y = 4\sin t$

9. **[T]** $x = \sec t, \quad y = \cos t$

For the following exercises, sketch the parametric equations by eliminating the parameter. Indicate any asymptotes of the graph.

10. $x = e^t, \quad y = e^{2t} + 1$

11. $x = 6\sin(2\theta),\ y = 4\cos(2\theta)$

12. $x = \cos\theta, \quad y = 2\sin(2\theta)$

13. $x = 3 - 2\cos\theta, \quad y = -5 + 3\sin\theta$

14. $x = 4 + 2\cos\theta, \quad y = -1 + \sin\theta$

15. $x = \sec t, \quad y = \tan t$

16. $x = \ln(2t), \quad y = t^2$

17. $x = e^t,\ y = e^{2t}$

18. $x = e^{-2t}, \quad y = e^{3t}$

19. $x = t^3, \quad y = 3\ln t$

20. $x = 4\sec\theta, \quad y = 3\tan\theta$

For the following exercises, convert the parametric equations of a curve into rectangular form. No sketch is necessary. State the domain of the rectangular form.

21. $x = t^2 - 1, \quad y = \frac{t}{2}$

22. $x = \frac{1}{\sqrt{t+1}}, \quad y = \frac{t}{1+t}, t > -1$

23. $x = 4\cos\theta,\ y = 3\sin\theta,\ t \in (0, 2\pi]$

24. $x = \cosh t, \quad y = \sinh t$

25. $x = 2t - 3, \quad y = 6t - 7$

26. $x = t^2, \quad y = t^3$

27. $x = 1 + \cos t, \quad y = 3 - \sin t$

28. $x = \sqrt{t}, \quad y = 2t + 4$

29. $x = \sec t, \quad y = \tan t,\ \pi \le t < \frac{3\pi}{2}$

30. $x = 2\cosh t, \quad y = 4\sinh t$

31. $x = \cos(2t), \quad y = \sin t$

32. $x = 4t + 3,\ y = 16t^2 - 9$

33. $x = t^2, \quad y = 2\ln t,\ t \ge 1$

34. $x = t^3, \quad y = 3\ln t,\ t \ge 1$

35. $x = t^n, \quad y = n\ln t,\ t \ge 1,$ where $n$ is a natural number

36. $\begin{array}{l} x = \ln(5t) \\ y = \ln(t^2) \end{array}$ where $1 \le t \le e$

37. $\begin{array}{l} x = 2\sin(8t) \\ y = 2\cos(8t) \end{array}$

38. $\begin{array}{l} x = \tan t \\ y = \sec^2 t - 1 \end{array}$

For the following exercises, the pairs of parametric equations represent lines, parabolas, circles, ellipses, or hyperbolas. Name the type of basic curve that each pair of equations represents.

39. $x = 3t + 4$
$y = 5t - 2$

40. $x - 4 = 5t$
$y + 2 = t$

41. $x = 2t + 1$
$y = t^2 - 3$

42. $x = 3\cos t$
$y = 3\sin t$

43. $x = 2\cos(3t)$
$y = 2\sin(3t)$

44. $x = \cosh t$
$y = \sinh t$

45. $x = 3\cos t$
$y = 4\sin t$

46. $x = 2\cos(3t)$
$y = 5\sin(3t)$

47. $x = 3\cosh(4t)$
$y = 4\sinh(4t)$

48. $x = 2\cosh t$
$y = 2\sinh t$

49. Show that $\begin{array}{l} x = h + r\cos\theta \\ y = k + r\sin\theta \end{array}$ represents the equation of a circle.

50. Use the equations in the preceding problem to find a set of parametric equations for a circle whose radius is 5 and whose center is $(-2, 3)$.

For the following exercises, use a graphing utility to graph the curve represented by the parametric equations and identify the curve from its equation.

51. **[T]** $x = \theta + \sin\theta$
$y = 1 - \cos\theta$

52. **[T]** $x = 2t - 2\sin t$
$y = 2 - 2\cos t$

53. **[T]** $x = t - 0.5\sin t$
$y = 1 - 1.5\cos t$

54. An airplane traveling horizontally at 100 m/s over flat ground at an elevation of 4000 meters must drop an emergency package on a target on the ground. The trajectory of the package is given by $x = 100t,\ y = -4.9t^2 + 4000,\ t \geq 0$ where the origin is the point on the ground directly beneath the plane at the moment of release. How many horizontal meters before the target should the package be released in order to hit the target?

55. The trajectory of a bullet is given by $x = v_0 (\cos\alpha)\, t y = v_0 (\sin\alpha)\, t - \frac{1}{2}gt^2$ where $v_0 = 500\ \text{m/s}$, $g = 9.8 = 9.8\ \text{m/s}^2$, and $\alpha = 30\ \text{degrees}$. When will the bullet hit the ground? How far from the gun will the bullet hit the ground?

56. **[T]** Use technology to sketch the curve represented by $x = \sin(4t),\ y = \sin(3t),\ 0 \leq t \leq 2\pi$.

57. **[T]** Use technology to sketch $x = 2\tan(t),\ y = 3\sec(t),\ -\pi < t < \pi$.

58. Sketch the curve known as an *epitrochoid*, which gives the path of a point on a circle of radius $b$ as it rolls on the outside of a circle of radius $a$. The equations are

$$x = (a + b)\cos t - c \cdot \cos\left[\frac{(a + b)t}{b}\right]$$
$$y = (a + b)\sin t - c \cdot \sin\left[\frac{(a + b)t}{b}\right].$$

Let $a = 1,\ b = 2,\ c = 1$.

59. **[T]** Use technology to sketch the spiral curve given by $x = t\cos(t),\ y = t\sin(t)$ from $-2\pi \leq t \leq 2\pi$.

60. **[T]** Use technology to graph the curve given by the parametric equations $x = 2\cot(t),\ y = 1 - \cos(2t),\ -\pi/2 \leq t \leq \pi/2$. This curve is known as the witch of Agnesi.

61. **[T]** Sketch the curve given by parametric equations $\begin{array}{l} x = \cosh(t) \\ y = \sinh(t), \end{array}$ where $-2 \leq t \leq 2$.

# 7.2 | Calculus of Parametric Curves

## Learning Objectives

7.2.1 Determine derivatives and equations of tangents for parametric curves.
7.2.2 Find the area under a parametric curve.
7.2.3 Use the equation for arc length of a parametric curve.
7.2.4 Apply the formula for surface area to a volume generated by a parametric curve.

Now that we have introduced the concept of a parameterized curve, our next step is to learn how to work with this concept in the context of calculus. For example, if we know a parameterization of a given curve, is it possible to calculate the slope of a tangent line to the curve? How about the arc length of the curve? Or the area under the curve?

Another scenario: Suppose we would like to represent the location of a baseball after the ball leaves a pitcher's hand. If the position of the baseball is represented by the plane curve $(x(t), y(t)),$ then we should be able to use calculus to find the speed of the ball at any given time. Furthermore, we should be able to calculate just how far that ball has traveled as a function of time.

## Derivatives of Parametric Equations

We start by asking how to calculate the slope of a line tangent to a parametric curve at a point. Consider the plane curve defined by the parametric equations

$$x(t) = 2t + 3, \quad y(t) = 3t - 4, \quad -2 \leq t \leq 3.$$

The graph of this curve appears in **Figure 7.16**. It is a line segment starting at $(-1, -10)$ and ending at $(9, 5)$.

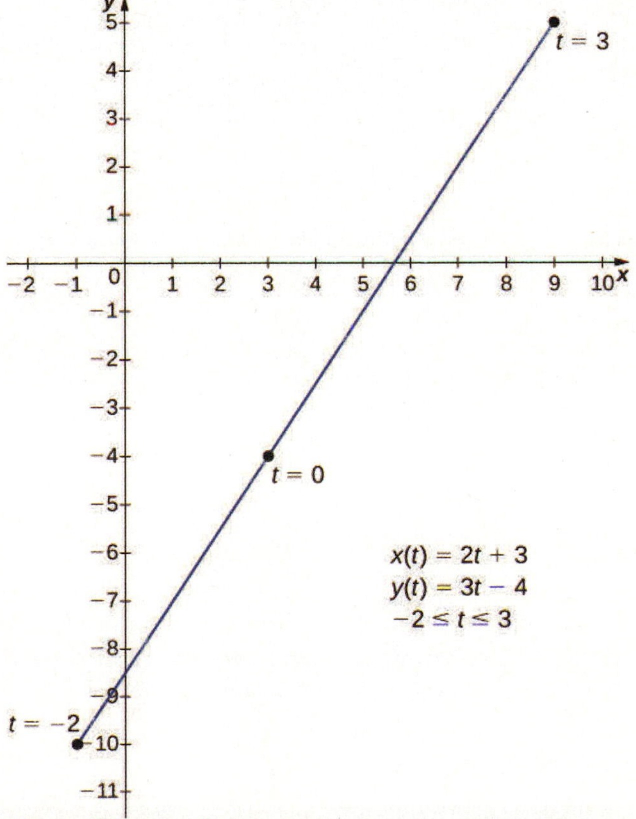


**Figure 7.16** Graph of the line segment described by the given parametric equations.

We can eliminate the parameter by first solving the equation $x(t) = 2t + 3$ for $t$:

$$\begin{aligned} x(t) &= 2t + 3 \\ x - 3 &= 2t \\ t &= \frac{x-3}{2}. \end{aligned}$$

Substituting this into $y(t)$, we obtain

$$\begin{aligned} y(t) &= 3t - 4 \\ y &= 3\left(\frac{x-3}{2}\right) - 4 \\ y &= \frac{3x}{2} - \frac{9}{2} - 4 \\ y &= \frac{3x}{2} - \frac{17}{2}. \end{aligned}$$

The slope of this line is given by $\frac{dy}{dx} = \frac{3}{2}$. Next we calculate $x'(t)$ and $y'(t)$. This gives $x'(t) = 2$ and $y'(t) = 3$. Notice that $\frac{dy}{dx} = \frac{dy/dt}{dx/dt} = \frac{3}{2}$. This is no coincidence, as outlined in the following theorem.

### Theorem 7.1: Derivative of Parametric Equations

Consider the plane curve defined by the parametric equations $x = x(t)$ and $y = y(t)$. Suppose that $x'(t)$ and $y'(t)$ exist, and assume that $x'(t) \neq 0$. Then the derivative $\frac{dy}{dx}$ is given by

$$\frac{dy}{dx} = \frac{dy/dt}{dx/dt} = \frac{y'(t)}{x'(t)}. \quad (7.1)$$

### Proof

This theorem can be proven using the Chain Rule. In particular, assume that the parameter $t$ can be eliminated, yielding a differentiable function $y = F(x)$. Then $y(t) = F(x(t))$. Differentiating both sides of this equation using the Chain Rule yields

$$y'(t) = F'(x(t))x'(t),$$

so

$$F'(x(t)) = \frac{y'(t)}{x'(t)}.$$

But $F'(x(t)) = \frac{dy}{dx}$, which proves the theorem.

□

**Equation 7.1** can be used to calculate derivatives of plane curves, as well as critical points. Recall that a critical point of a differentiable function $y = f(x)$ is any point $x = x_0$ such that either $f'(x_0) = 0$ or $f'(x_0)$ does not exist. **Equation 7.1** gives a formula for the slope of a tangent line to a curve defined parametrically regardless of whether the curve can be described by a function $y = f(x)$ or not.

## Example 7.4

## Finding the Derivative of a Parametric Curve

Calculate the derivative $\frac{dy}{dx}$ for each of the following parametrically defined plane curves, and locate any critical points on their respective graphs.

a. $x(t) = t^2 - 3, \quad y(t) = 2t - 1, \quad -3 \le t \le 4$

b. $x(t) = 2t + 1, \quad y(t) = t^3 - 3t + 4, \quad -2 \le t \le 5$

c. $x(t) = 5\cos t, \quad y(t) = 5\sin t, \quad 0 \le t \le 2\pi$

### Solution

a. To apply **Equation 7.1**, first calculate $x'(t)$ and $y'(t)$:

$$x'(t) = 2t$$
$$y'(t) = 2.$$

Next substitute these into the equation:

$$\frac{dy}{dx} = \frac{dy/dt}{dx/dt}$$
$$\frac{dy}{dx} = \frac{2}{2t}$$
$$\frac{dy}{dx} = \frac{1}{t}.$$

This derivative is undefined when $t = 0$. Calculating $x(0)$ and $y(0)$ gives $x(0) = (0)^2 - 3 = -3$ and $y(0) = 2(0) - 1 = -1$, which corresponds to the point $(-3, -1)$ on the graph. The graph of this curve is a parabola opening to the right, and the point $(-3, -1)$ is its vertex as shown.

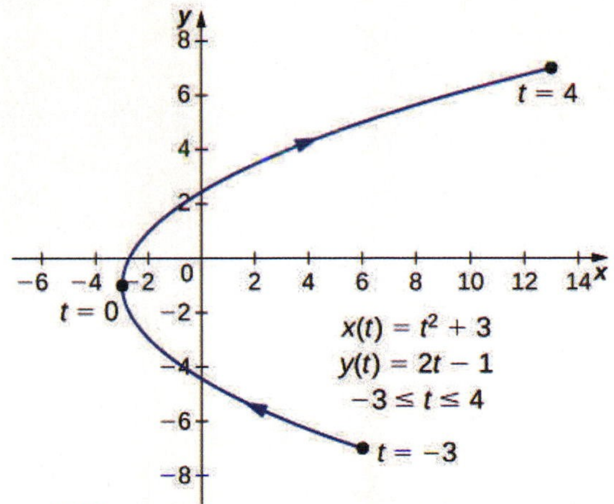


**Figure 7.17** Graph of the parabola described by parametric equations in part a.

b. To apply **Equation 7.1**, first calculate $x'(t)$ and $y'(t)$:

$$x'(t) = 2$$
$$y'(t) = 3t^2 - 3.$$

Next substitute these into the equation:

$$\frac{dy}{dx} = \frac{dy/dt}{dx/dt}$$
$$\frac{dy}{dx} = \frac{3t^2 - 3}{2}.$$

This derivative is zero when $t = \pm 1.$ When $t = -1$ we have

$$x(-1) = 2(-1) + 1 = -1 \text{ and } y(-1) = (-1)^3 - 3(-1) + 4 = -1 + 3 + 4 = 6,$$

which corresponds to the point $(-1, 6)$ on the graph. When $t = 1$ we have

$$x(1) = 2(1) + 1 = 3 \text{ and } y(1) = (1)^3 - 3(1) + 4 = 1 - 3 + 4 = 2,$$

which corresponds to the point $(3, 2)$ on the graph. The point $(3, 2)$ is a relative minimum and the point $(-1, 6)$ is a relative maximum, as seen in the following graph.

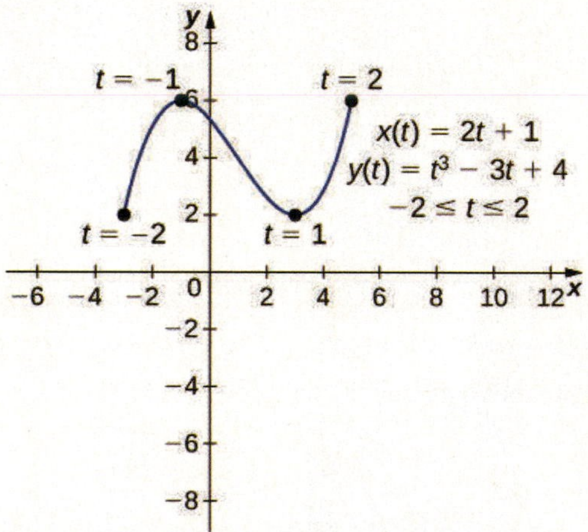


**Figure 7.18** Graph of the curve described by parametric equations in part b.

c. To apply **Equation 7.1**, first calculate $x'(t)$ and $y'(t)$:

$$x'(t) = -5 \sin t$$
$$y'(t) = 5 \cos t.$$

Next substitute these into the equation:

$$\frac{dy}{dx} = \frac{dy/dt}{dx/dt}$$
$$\frac{dy}{dx} = \frac{5 \cos t}{-5 \sin t}$$
$$\frac{dy}{dx} = -\cot t.$$

This derivative is zero when $\cos t = 0$ and is undefined when $\sin t = 0.$ This gives $t = 0, \frac{\pi}{2}, \pi, \frac{3\pi}{2},$ and $2\pi$ as critical points for $t$. Substituting each of these into $x(t)$ and $y(t),$ we obtain

| $t$ | $x(t)$ | $y(t)$ |
|---|---|---|
| 0 | 5 | 0 |
| $\frac{\pi}{2}$ | 0 | 5 |
| $\pi$ | −5 | 0 |
| $\frac{3\pi}{2}$ | 0 | −5 |
| $2\pi$ | 5 | 0 |

These points correspond to the sides, top, and bottom of the circle that is represented by the parametric equations (**Figure 7.19**). On the left and right edges of the circle, the derivative is undefined, and on the top and bottom, the derivative equals zero.

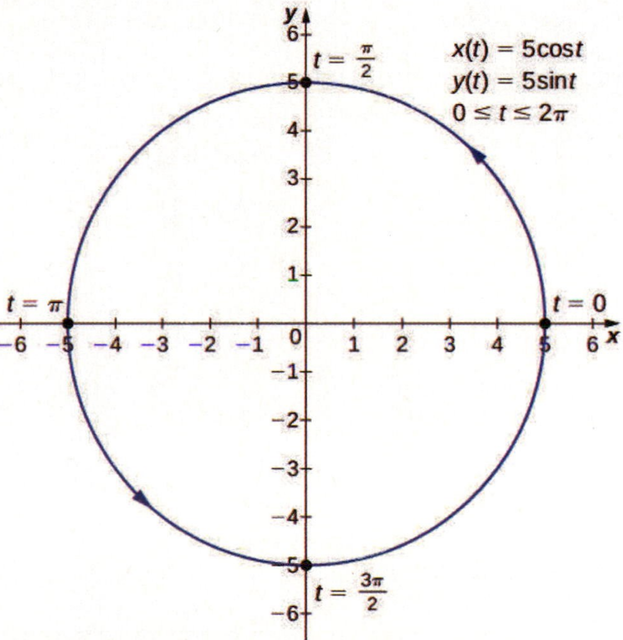


**Figure 7.19** Graph of the curve described by parametric equations in part c.

**7.4** Calculate the derivative $dy/dx$ for the plane curve defined by the equations

$$x(t) = t^2 - 4t, \quad y(t) = 2t^3 - 6t, \quad -2 \le t \le 3$$

and locate any critical points on its graph.

## Example 7.5

### Finding a Tangent Line

Find the equation of the tangent line to the curve defined by the equations

$$x(t) = t^2 - 3, \quad y(t) = 2t - 1, \quad -3 \le t \le 4 \text{ when } t = 2.$$

### Solution

First find the slope of the tangent line using **Equation 7.1**, which means calculating $x'(t)$ and $y'(t)$:

$$x'(t) = 2t$$
$$y'(t) = 2.$$

Next substitute these into the equation:

$$\frac{dy}{dx} = \frac{dy/dt}{dx/dt}$$
$$\frac{dy}{dx} = \frac{2}{2t}$$
$$\frac{dy}{dx} = \frac{1}{t}.$$

When $t = 2$, $\frac{dy}{dx} = \frac{1}{2}$, so this is the slope of the tangent line. Calculating $x(2)$ and $y(2)$ gives

$$x(2) = (2)^2 - 3 = 1 \text{ and } y(2) = 2(2) - 1 = 3,$$

which corresponds to the point $(1, 3)$ on the graph (**Figure 7.20**). Now use the point-slope form of the equation of a line to find the equation of the tangent line:

$$\begin{aligned} y - y_0 &= m(x - x_0) \\ y - 3 &= \frac{1}{2}(x - 1) \\ y - 3 &= \frac{1}{2}x - \frac{1}{2} \\ y &= \frac{1}{2}x + \frac{5}{2}. \end{aligned}$$

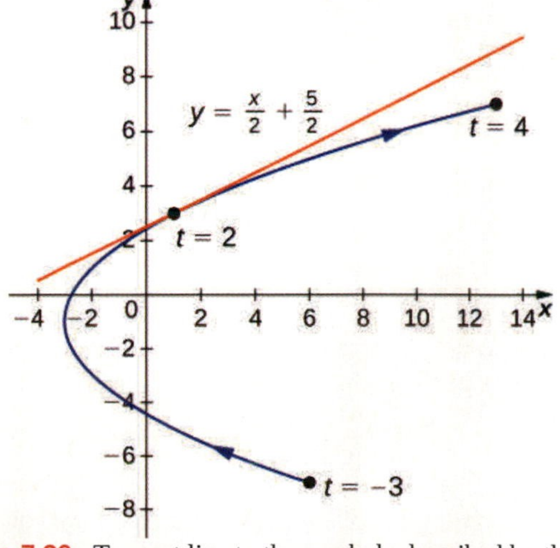


**Figure 7.20** Tangent line to the parabola described by the given parametric equations when $t = 2$.

**7.5** Find the equation of the tangent line to the curve defined by the equations

$$x(t) = t^2 - 4t, \quad y(t) = 2t^3 - 6t, \quad -2 \le t \le 3 \text{ when } t = 5.$$

## Second-Order Derivatives

Our next goal is to see how to take the second derivative of a function defined parametrically. The second derivative of a function $y = f(x)$ is defined to be the derivative of the first derivative; that is,

$$\frac{d^2y}{dx^2} = \frac{d}{dx}\left[\frac{dy}{dx}\right].$$

Since $\frac{dy}{dx} = \frac{dy/dt}{dx/dt}$, we can replace the $y$ on both sides of this equation with $\frac{dy}{dx}$. This gives us

$$\frac{d^2y}{dx^2} = \frac{d}{dx}\left(\frac{dy}{dx}\right) = \frac{(d/dt)(dy/dx)}{dx/dt}. \quad (7.2)$$

If we know $dy/dx$ as a function of $t$, then this formula is straightforward to apply.

### Example 7.6

#### Finding a Second Derivative

Calculate the second derivative $d^2y/dx^2$ for the plane curve defined by the parametric equations $x(t) = t^2 - 3$, $y(t) = 2t - 1$, $-3 \le t \le 4$.

#### Solution

From **Example 7.4** we know that $\frac{dy}{dx} = \frac{2}{2t} = \frac{1}{t}$. Using **Equation 7.2**, we obtain

$$\frac{d^2y}{dx^2} = \frac{(d/dt)(dy/dx)}{dx/dt} = \frac{(d/dt)(1/t)}{2t} = \frac{-t^{-2}}{2t} = -\frac{1}{2t^3}.$$

**7.6** Calculate the second derivative $d^2y/dx^2$ for the plane curve defined by the equations

$$x(t) = t^2 - 4t, \quad y(t) = 2t^3 - 6t, \quad -2 \le t \le 3$$

and locate any critical points on its graph.

## Integrals Involving Parametric Equations

Now that we have seen how to calculate the derivative of a plane curve, the next question is this: How do we find the area under a curve defined parametrically? Recall the cycloid defined by the equations $x(t) = t - \sin t$, $y(t) = 1 - \cos t$. Suppose we want to find the area of the shaded region in the following graph.

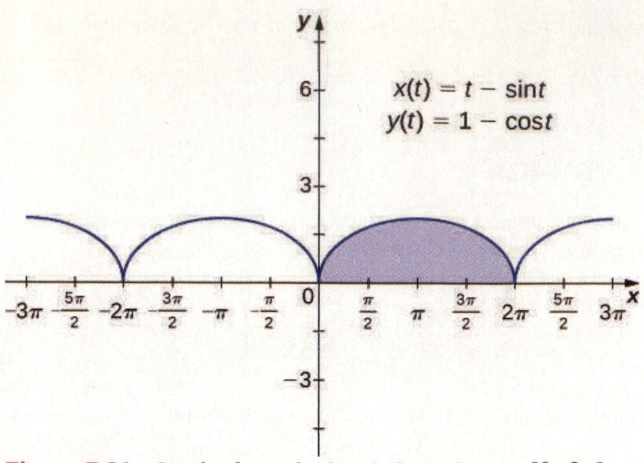


**Figure 7.21** Graph of a cycloid with the arch over $[0, 2\pi]$ highlighted.

To derive a formula for the area under the curve defined by the functions

$$x = x(t), \quad y = y(t), \quad a \le t \le b,$$

we assume that $x(t)$ is differentiable and start with an equal partition of the interval $a \le t \le b$. Suppose $t_0 = a < t_1 < t_2 < \cdots < t_n = b$ and consider the following graph.

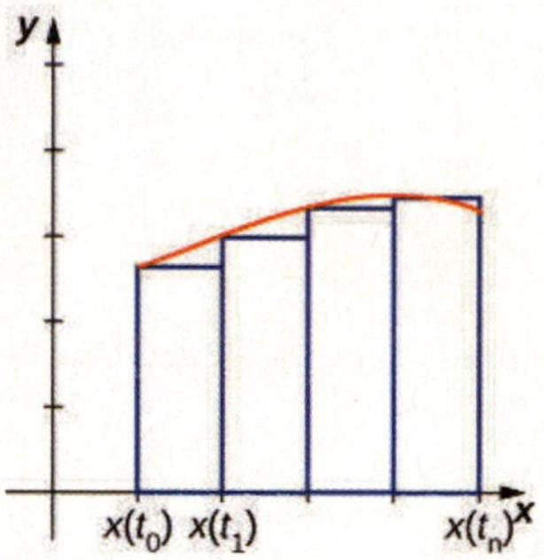


**Figure 7.22** Approximating the area under a parametrically defined curve.

We use rectangles to approximate the area under the curve. The height of a typical rectangle in this parametrization is $y(x(\bar{t}_i))$ for some value $\bar{t}_i$ in the $i$th subinterval, and the width can be calculated as $x(t_i) - x(t_{i-1})$. Thus the area of the $i$th rectangle is given by

$$A_i = y(x(\bar{t}_i))(x(t_i) - x(t_{i-1})).$$

Then a Riemann sum for the area is

$$A_n = \sum_{i=1}^{n} y(x(\bar{t}_i))(x(t_i) - x(t_{i-1})).$$

Multiplying and dividing each area by $t_i - t_{i-1}$ gives

$$A_n = \sum_{i=1}^{n} y(x(\bar{t}_i))\left(\frac{x(t_i) - x(t_{i-1})}{t_i - t_{i-1}}\right)(t_i - t_{i-1}) = \sum_{i=1}^{n} y(x(\bar{t}_i))\left(\frac{x(t_i) - x(t_{i-1})}{\Delta t}\right)\Delta t.$$

Taking the limit as $n$ approaches infinity gives

$$A = \lim_{n \to \infty} A_n = \int_a^b y(t)x'(t)\,dt.$$

This leads to the following theorem.

**Theorem 7.2: Area under a Parametric Curve**

Consider the non-self-intersecting plane curve defined by the parametric equations

$$x = x(t), \quad y = y(t), \quad a \le t \le b$$

and assume that $x(t)$ is differentiable. The area under this curve is given by

$$A = \int_a^b y(t)x'(t)\,dt. \tag{7.3}$$

## Example 7.7

### Finding the Area under a Parametric Curve

Find the area under the curve of the cycloid defined by the equations

$$x(t) = t - \sin t, \quad y(t) = 1 - \cos t, \quad 0 \le t \le 2\pi.$$

**Solution**

Using **Equation 7.3**, we have

$$\begin{aligned} A &= \int_a^b y(t)x'(t)\,dt \\ &= \int_0^{2\pi} (1 - \cos t)(1 - \cos t)\,dt \\ &= \int_0^{2\pi} (1 - 2\cos t + \cos^2 t)dt \\ &= \int_0^{2\pi} \left(1 - 2\cos t + \frac{1 + \cos 2t}{2}\right)dt \\ &= \int_0^{2\pi} \left(\frac{3}{2} - 2\cos t + \frac{\cos 2t}{2}\right)dt \\ &= \frac{3t}{2} - 2\sin t + \frac{\sin 2t}{4}\Big|_0^{2\pi} \\ &= 3\pi. \end{aligned}$$

**7.7** Find the area under the curve of the hypocycloid defined by the equations

$$x(t) = 3\cos t + \cos 3t, \quad y(t) = 3\sin t - \sin 3t, \quad 0 \le t \le \pi.$$

## Arc Length of a Parametric Curve

In addition to finding the area under a parametric curve, we sometimes need to find the arc length of a parametric curve. In the case of a line segment, arc length is the same as the distance between the endpoints. If a particle travels from point $A$ to point $B$ along a curve, then the distance that particle travels is the arc length. To develop a formula for arc length, we start with an approximation by line segments as shown in the following graph.

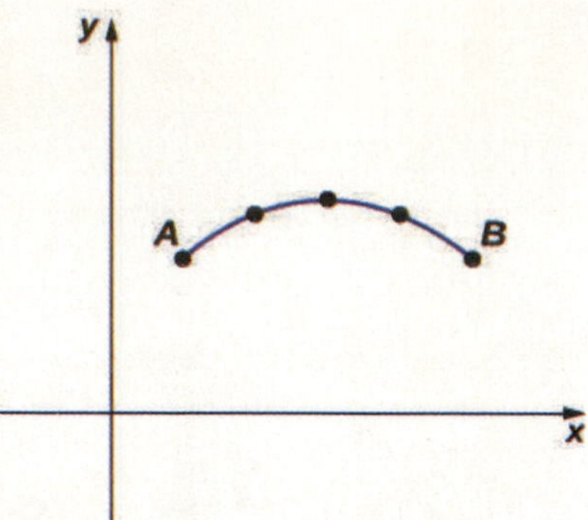


**Figure 7.23** Approximation of a curve by line segments.

Given a plane curve defined by the functions $x = x(t), y = y(t), a \le t \le b,$ we start by partitioning the interval $[a, b]$ into $n$ equal subintervals: $t_0 = a < t_1 < t_2 < \cdots < t_n = b.$ The width of each subinterval is given by $\Delta t = (b - a)/n.$ We can calculate the length of each line segment:

$$d_1 = \sqrt{(x(t_1) - x(t_0))^2 + (y(t_1) - y(t_0))^2}$$
$$d_2 = \sqrt{(x(t_2) - x(t_1))^2 + (y(t_2) - y(t_1))^2} \text{ etc.}$$

Then add these up. We let $s$ denote the exact arc length and $s_n$ denote the approximation by $n$ line segments:

$$s \approx \sum_{k=1}^{n} s_k = \sum_{k=1}^{n} \sqrt{(x(t_k) - x(t_{k-1}))^2 + (y(t_k) - y(t_{k-1}))^2}. \tag{7.4}$$

If we assume that $x(t)$ and $y(t)$ are differentiable functions of $t$, then the Mean Value Theorem (**Introduction to the Applications of Derivatives (http://cnx.org/content/m53602/latest/)** ) applies, so in each subinterval $[t_{k-1}, t_k]$ there exist $\hat{t}_k$ and $\tilde{t}_k$ such that

$$x(t_k) - x(t_{k-1}) = x'\left(\hat{t}_k\right)(t_k - t_{k-1}) = x'\left(\hat{t}_k\right)\Delta t$$
$$y(t_k) - y(t_{k-1}) = y'\left(\tilde{t}_k\right)(t_k - t_{k-1}) = y'\left(\tilde{t}_k\right)\Delta t.$$

Therefore **Equation 7.4** becomes

$$\begin{aligned} s &\approx \sum_{k=1}^{n} s_k \\ &= \sum_{k=1}^{n} \sqrt{\left(x'\left(\hat{t}_k\right)\Delta t\right)^2 + \left(y'\left(\tilde{t}_k\right)\Delta t\right)^2} \\ &= \sum_{k=1}^{n} \sqrt{\left(x'\left(\hat{t}_k\right)\right)^2 (\Delta t)^2 + \left(y'\left(\tilde{t}_k\right)\right)^2 (\Delta t)^2} \\ &= \left(\sum_{k=1}^{n} \sqrt{\left(x'\left(\hat{t}_k\right)\right)^2 + \left(y'\left(\tilde{t}_k\right)\right)^2}\right)\Delta t. \end{aligned}$$

This is a Riemann sum that approximates the arc length over a partition of the interval $[a, b]$. If we further assume that the derivatives are continuous and let the number of points in the partition increase without bound, the approximation approaches the exact arc length. This gives

$$\begin{aligned} s &= \lim_{n \to \infty} \sum_{k=1}^{n} s_k \\ &= \lim_{n \to \infty} \left( \sum_{k=1}^{n} \sqrt{\left(x'\left(\hat{t}_k\right)\right)^2 + \left(y'\left(\tilde{t}_k\right)\right)^2} \Delta t \right) \\ &= \int_a^b \sqrt{(x'(t))^2 + (y'(t))^2} dt. \end{aligned}$$

When taking the limit, the values of $\hat{t}_k$ and $\tilde{t}_k$ are both contained within the same ever-shrinking interval of width $\Delta t$, so they must converge to the same value.

We can summarize this method in the following theorem.

### Theorem 7.3: Arc Length of a Parametric Curve

Consider the plane curve defined by the parametric equations

$$x = x(t), \quad y = y(t), \quad t_1 \le t \le t_2$$

and assume that $x(t)$ and $y(t)$ are differentiable functions of $t$. Then the arc length of this curve is given by

$$s = \int_{t_1}^{t_2} \sqrt{\left(\frac{dx}{dt}\right)^2 + \left(\frac{dy}{dt}\right)^2} dt. \quad \textbf{(7.5)}$$

At this point a side derivation leads to a previous formula for arc length. In particular, suppose the parameter can be eliminated, leading to a function $y = F(x)$. Then $y(t) = F(x(t))$ and the Chain Rule gives $y'(t) = F'(x(t))x'(t)$. Substituting this into **Equation 7.5** gives

$$\begin{aligned} s &= \int_{t_1}^{t_2} \sqrt{\left(\frac{dx}{dt}\right)^2 + \left(\frac{dy}{dt}\right)^2} dt \\ &= \int_{t_1}^{t_2} \sqrt{\left(\frac{dx}{dt}\right)^2 + \left(F'(x)\frac{dx}{dt}\right)^2} dt \\ &= \int_{t_1}^{t_2} \sqrt{\left(\frac{dx}{dt}\right)^2 \left(1 + (F'(x))^2\right)} dt \\ &= \int_{t_1}^{t_2} x'(t) \sqrt{1 + \left(\frac{dy}{dx}\right)^2} dt. \end{aligned}$$

Here we have assumed that $x'(t) > 0,$ which is a reasonable assumption. The Chain Rule gives $dx = x'(t)\,dt,$ and letting $a = x(t_1)$ and $b = x(t_2)$ we obtain the formula

$$s = \int_a^b \sqrt{1 + \left(\frac{dy}{dx}\right)^2} dx,$$

which is the formula for arc length obtained in the **Introduction to the Applications of Integration**.

## Example 7.8

### Finding the Arc Length of a Parametric Curve

Find the arc length of the semicircle defined by the equations

$$x(t) = 3\cos t, \quad y(t) = 3\sin t, \quad 0 \le t \le \pi.$$

### Solution

The values $t = 0$ to $t = \pi$ trace out the red curve in **Figure 7.23**. To determine its length, use **Equation 7.5**:

$$\begin{aligned} s &= \int_{t_1}^{t_2} \sqrt{\left(\frac{dx}{dt}\right)^2 + \left(\frac{dy}{dt}\right)^2}\, dt \\ &= \int_0^{\pi} \sqrt{(-3\sin t)^2 + (3\cos t)^2}\, dt \\ &= \int_0^{\pi} \sqrt{9\sin^2 t + 9\cos^2 t}\, dt \\ &= \int_0^{\pi} \sqrt{9\left(\sin^2 t + \cos^2 t\right)}\, dt \\ &= \int_0^{\pi} 3\, dt = 3t\big|_0^{\pi} = 3\pi. \end{aligned}$$

Note that the formula for the arc length of a semicircle is $\pi r$ and the radius of this circle is 3. This is a great example of using calculus to derive a known formula of a geometric quantity.

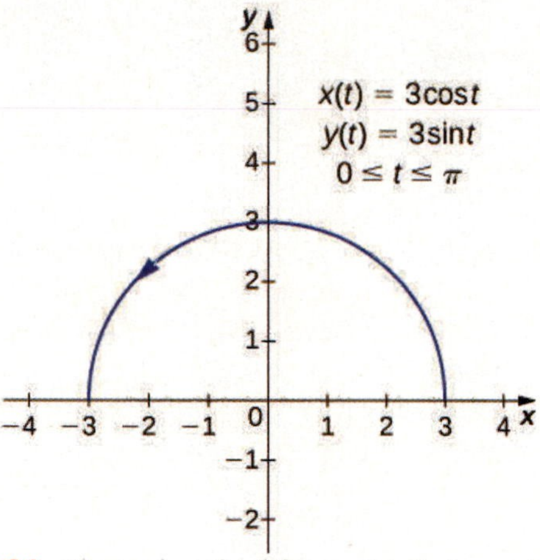


**Figure 7.24** The arc length of the semicircle is equal to its radius times $\pi$.

**7.8** Find the arc length of the curve defined by the equations

$$x(t) = 3t^2, \quad y(t) = 2t^3, \quad 1 \le t \le 3.$$

We now return to the problem posed at the beginning of the section about a baseball leaving a pitcher's hand. Ignoring the effect of air resistance (unless it is a curve ball!), the ball travels a parabolic path. Assuming the pitcher's hand is at the origin and the ball travels left to right in the direction of the positive $x$-axis, the parametric equations for this curve can be written as

$$x(t) = 140t, \quad y(t) = -16t^2 + 2t$$

where $t$ represents time. We first calculate the distance the ball travels as a function of time. This distance is represented by the arc length. We can modify the arc length formula slightly. First rewrite the functions $x(t)$ and $y(t)$ using $v$ as an independent variable, so as to eliminate any confusion with the parameter $t$:

$$x(v) = 140v, \quad y(v) = -16v^2 + 2v.$$

Then we write the arc length formula as follows:

$$\begin{aligned} s(t) &= \int_0^t \sqrt{\left(\frac{dx}{dv}\right)^2 + \left(\frac{dy}{dv}\right)^2}\, dv \\ &= \int_0^t \sqrt{140^2 + (-32v+2)^2} dv. \end{aligned}$$

The variable $v$ acts as a dummy variable that disappears after integration, leaving the arc length as a function of time $t$. To integrate this expression we can use a formula from **Appendix A**,

$$\int \sqrt{a^2+u^2} du = \frac{u}{2}\sqrt{a^2+u^2} + \frac{a^2}{2}\ln\left|u+\sqrt{a^2+u^2}\right| + C.$$

We set $a = 140$ and $u = -32v+2$. This gives $du = -32dv$, so $dv = -\frac{1}{32}du$. Therefore

$$\begin{aligned} \int \sqrt{140^2+(-32v+2)^2} dv &= -\frac{1}{32}\int \sqrt{a^2+u^2} du \\ &= -\frac{1}{32}\left[\begin{array}{l}\frac{(-32v+2)}{2}\sqrt{140^2+(-32v+2)^2} \\ +\frac{140^2}{2}\ln\left|(-32v+2)+\sqrt{140^2+(-32v+2)^2}\right|\end{array}\right] + C \end{aligned}$$

and

$$\begin{aligned} s(t) &= -\frac{1}{32}\left[\frac{(-32t+2)}{2}\sqrt{140^2+(-32t+2)^2} + \frac{140^2}{2}\ln\left|(-32t+2)+\sqrt{140^2+(-32t+2)^2}\right|\right] \\ &\quad +\frac{1}{32}\left[\sqrt{140^2+2^2} + \frac{140^2}{2}\ln\left|2+\sqrt{140^2+2^2}\right|\right] \\ &= \left(\frac{t}{2}-\frac{1}{32}\right)\sqrt{1024t^2-128t+19604} - \frac{1225}{4}\ln\left|(-32t+2)+\sqrt{1024t^2-128t+19604}\right| \\ &\quad +\frac{\sqrt{19604}}{32} + \frac{1225}{4}\ln\left(2+\sqrt{19604}\right). \end{aligned}$$

This function represents the distance traveled by the ball as a function of time. To calculate the speed, take the derivative of this function with respect to $t$. While this may seem like a daunting task, it is possible to obtain the answer directly from the Fundamental Theorem of Calculus:

$$\frac{d}{dx}\int_a^x f(u)\, du = f(x).$$

Therefore

$$\begin{aligned} s'(t) &= \frac{d}{dt}[s(t)] \\ &= \frac{d}{dt}\left[\int_0^t \sqrt{140^2+(-32v+2)^2} dv\right] \\ &= \sqrt{140^2+(-32t+2)^2} \\ &= \sqrt{1024t^2-128t+19604} \\ &= 2\sqrt{256t^2-32t+4901}. \end{aligned}$$

One third of a second after the ball leaves the pitcher's hand, the distance it travels is equal to

$$\begin{aligned} s\left(\frac{1}{3}\right) &= \left(\frac{1/3}{2} - \frac{1}{32}\right)\sqrt{1024\left(\frac{1}{3}\right)^2 - 128\left(\frac{1}{3}\right) + 19604} \\ &\quad - \frac{1225}{4}\ln\left|\left(-32\left(\frac{1}{3}\right) + 2\right) + \sqrt{1024\left(\frac{1}{3}\right)^2 - 128\left(\frac{1}{3}\right) + 19604}\right| \\ &\quad + \frac{\sqrt{19604}}{32} + \frac{1225}{4}\ln\left(2 + \sqrt{19604}\right) \\ &\approx 46.69 \text{ feet.} \end{aligned}$$

This value is just over three quarters of the way to home plate. The speed of the ball is

$$s'\left(\frac{1}{3}\right) = 2\sqrt{256\left(\frac{1}{3}\right)^2 - 16\left(\frac{1}{3}\right) + 4901} \approx 140.34 \text{ ft/s.}$$

This speed translates to approximately 95 mph—a major-league fastball.

## Surface Area Generated by a Parametric Curve

Recall the problem of finding the surface area of a volume of revolution. In **Curve Length and Surface Area**, we derived a formula for finding the surface area of a volume generated by a function $y = f(x)$ from $x = a$ to $x = b$, revolved around the $x$-axis:

$$S = 2\pi \int_a^b f(x)\sqrt{1 + (f'(x))^2}\,dx.$$

We now consider a volume of revolution generated by revolving a parametrically defined curve $x = x(t),\ y = y(t),\ a \le t \le b$ around the $x$-axis as shown in the following figure.

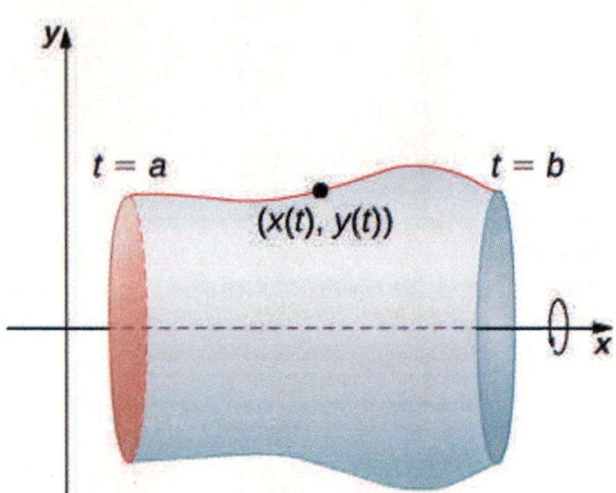


**Figure 7.25** A surface of revolution generated by a parametrically defined curve.

The analogous formula for a parametrically defined curve is

$$S = 2\pi \int_a^b y(t)\sqrt{(x'(t))^2 + (y'(t))^2}\,dt \qquad \textbf{(7.6)}$$

provided that $y(t)$ is not negative on $[a, b]$.

### Example 7.9

#### Finding Surface Area

Find the surface area of a sphere of radius $r$ centered at the origin.

### Solution

We start with the curve defined by the equations

$$x(t) = r\cos t, \quad y(t) = r\sin t, \quad 0 \le t \le \pi.$$

This generates an upper semicircle of radius $r$ centered at the origin as shown in the following graph.

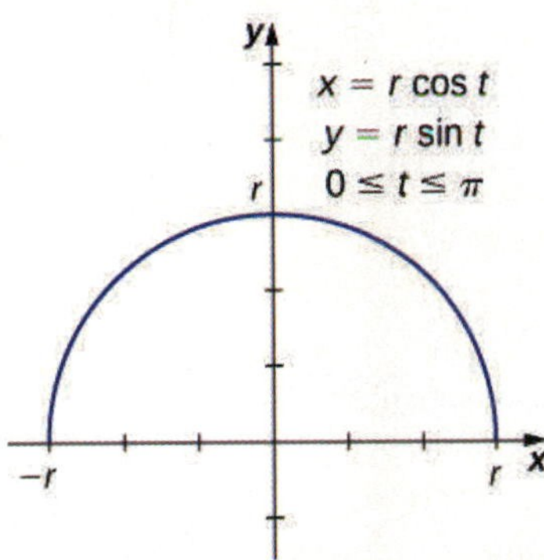


**Figure 7.26** A semicircle generated by parametric equations.

When this curve is revolved around the $x$-axis, it generates a sphere of radius $r$. To calculate the surface area of the sphere, we use **Equation 7.6**:

$$\begin{aligned} S &= 2\pi \int_a^b y(t)\sqrt{(x'(t))^2 + (y'(t))^2}\,dt \\ &= 2\pi \int_0^\pi r\sin t\sqrt{(-r\sin t)^2 + (r\cos t)^2}\,dt \\ &= 2\pi \int_0^\pi r\sin t\sqrt{r^2\sin^2 t + r^2\cos^2 t}\,dt \\ &= 2\pi \int_0^\pi r\sin t\sqrt{r^2\left(\sin^2 t + \cos^2 t\right)}\,dt \\ &= 2\pi \int_0^\pi r^2 \sin t\,dt \\ &= 2\pi r^2 (-\cos t|_0^\pi) \\ &= 2\pi r^2 (-\cos \pi + \cos 0) \\ &= 4\pi r^2. \end{aligned}$$

This is, in fact, the formula for the surface area of a sphere.

**7.9** Find the surface area generated when the plane curve defined by the equations

$$x(t) = t^3, \quad y(t) = t^2, \quad 0 \le t \le 1$$

is revolved around the $x$-axis.

## 7.2 EXERCISES

For the following exercises, each set of parametric equations represents a line. Without eliminating the parameter, find the slope of each line.

62. $x = 3 + t, \quad y = 1 - t$

63. $x = 8 + 2t, \quad y = 1$

64. $x = 4 - 3t, \quad y = -2 + 6t$

65. $x = -5t + 7, \quad y = 3t - 1$

For the following exercises, determine the slope of the tangent line, then find the equation of the tangent line at the given value of the parameter.

66. $x = 3\sin t, \quad y = 3\cos t, \quad t = \frac{\pi}{4}$

67. $x = \cos t, \quad y = 8\sin t, \ t = \frac{\pi}{2}$

68. $x = 2t, \quad y = t^3, \quad t = -1$

69. $x = t + \frac{1}{t}, \quad y = t - \frac{1}{t}, \quad t = 1$

70. $x = \sqrt{t}, \quad y = 2t, \quad t = 4$

For the following exercises, find all points on the curve that have the given slope.

71. $x = 4\cos t, \quad y = 4\sin t, \quad \text{slope} = 0.5$

72. $x = 2\cos t, \quad y = 8\sin t, \ \text{slope} = -1$

73. $x = t + \frac{1}{t}, \quad y = t - \frac{1}{t}, \ \text{slope} = 1$

74. $x = 2 + \sqrt{t}, \quad y = 2 - 4t, \ \text{slope} = 0$

For the following exercises, write the equation of the tangent line in Cartesian coordinates for the given parameter $t$.

75. $x = e^{\sqrt{t}}, \quad y = 1 - \ln t^2, \quad t = 1$

76. $x = t\ln t, \quad y = \sin^2 t, \ t = \frac{\pi}{4}$

77. $x = e^t, \quad y = (t - 1)^2, \quad \text{at}(1, 1)$

78. For $x = \sin(2t),\ y = 2\sin t$ where $0 \le t < 2\pi$. Find all values of $t$ at which a horizontal tangent line exists.

79. For $x = \sin(2t),\ y = 2\sin t$ where $0 \le t < 2\pi$. Find all values of $t$ at which a vertical tangent line exists.

80. Find all points on the curve $x = 4\cos(t),\ y = 4\sin(t)$ that have the slope of $\frac{1}{2}$.

81. Find $\frac{dy}{dx}$ for $x = \sin(t),\ y = \cos(t)$.

82. Find the equation of the tangent line to $x = \sin(t),\ y = \cos(t)$ at $t = \frac{\pi}{4}$.

83. For the curve $x = 4t,\ y = 3t - 2,$ find the slope and concavity of the curve at $t = 3$.

84. For the parametric curve whose equation is $x = 4\cos\theta,\ y = 4\sin\theta,$ find the slope and concavity of the curve at $\theta = \frac{\pi}{4}$.

85. Find the slope and concavity for the curve whose equation is $x = 2 + \sec\theta,\ y = 1 + 2\tan\theta$ at $\theta = \frac{\pi}{6}$.

86. Find all points on the curve $x = t + 4,\ y = t^3 - 3t$ at which there are vertical and horizontal tangents.

87. Find all points on the curve $x = \sec\theta,\ y = \tan\theta$ at which horizontal and vertical tangents exist.

For the following exercises, find $d^2y/dx^2$.

88. $x = t^4 - 1, \quad y = t - t^2$

89. $x = \sin(\pi t), \quad y = \cos(\pi t)$

90. $x = e^{-t}, \quad y = te^{2t}$

For the following exercises, find points on the curve at which tangent line is horizontal or vertical.

91. $x = t(t^2 - 3), \quad y = 3(t^2 - 3)$

92. $x = \frac{3t}{1 + t^3}, \quad y = \frac{3t^2}{1 + t^3}$

For the following exercises, find $dy/dx$ at the value of the parameter.

93. $x = \cos t, \quad y = \sin t, \quad t = \frac{3\pi}{4}$

94. $x = \sqrt{t}, \quad y = 2t + 4, \quad t = 9$

95. $x = 4\cos(2\pi s), \quad y = 3\sin(2\pi s), \quad s = -\frac{1}{4}$

For the following exercises, find $d^2y/dx^2$ at the given point without eliminating the parameter.

96. $x = \frac{1}{2}t^2, \quad y = \frac{1}{3}t^3, \quad t = 2$

97. $x = \sqrt{t}, \quad y = 2t + 4, \quad t = 1$

98. Find $t$ intervals on which the curve $x = 3t^2,\ y = t^3 - t$ is concave up as well as concave down.

99. Determine the concavity of the curve $x = 2t + \ln t,\ y = 2t - \ln t$.

100. Sketch and find the area under one arch of the cycloid $x = r(\theta - \sin\theta),\ y = r(1 - \cos\theta)$.

101. Find the area bounded by the curve $x = \cos t,\ y = e^t,\ 0 \le t \le \frac{\pi}{2}$ and the lines $y = 1$ and $x = 0$.

102. Find the area enclosed by the ellipse $x = a\cos\theta,\ y = b\sin\theta,\ 0 \le \theta < 2\pi$.

103. Find the area of the region bounded by $x = 2\sin^2\theta,\ y = 2\sin^2\theta\tan\theta$, for $0 \le \theta \le \frac{\pi}{2}$.

For the following exercises, find the area of the regions bounded by the parametric curves and the indicated values of the parameter.

104. $x = 2\cot\theta,\ y = 2\sin^2\theta,\ 0 \le \theta \le \pi$

105. **[T]** $x = 2a\cos t - a\cos(2t),\ y = 2a\sin t - a\sin(2t),\ 0 \le t < 2\pi$

106. **[T]** $x = a\sin(2t),\ y = b\sin(t),\ 0 \le t < 2\pi$ (the "hourglass")

107. **[T]** $x = 2a\cos t - a\sin(2t),\ y = b\sin t,\ 0 \le t < 2\pi$ (the "teardrop")

For the following exercises, find the arc length of the curve on the indicated interval of the parameter.

108. $x = 4t + 3, \quad y = 3t - 2, \quad 0 \le t \le 2$

109. $x = \frac{1}{3}t^3, \quad y = \frac{1}{2}t^2, \quad 0 \le t \le 1$

110. $x = \cos(2t), \quad y = \sin(2t), \quad 0 \le t \le \frac{\pi}{2}$

111. $x = 1 + t^2, \quad y = (1 + t)^3, \quad 0 \le t \le 1$

112. $x = e^t\cos t, \quad y = e^t\sin t, \quad 0 \le t \le \frac{\pi}{2}$ (express answer as a decimal rounded to three places)

113. $x = a\cos^3\theta,\ y = a\sin^3\theta$ on the interval $[0, 2\pi)$ (the hypocycloid)

114. Find the length of one arch of the cycloid $x = 4(t - \sin t),\ y = 4(1 - \cos t)$.

115. Find the distance traveled by a particle with position $(x, y)$ as $t$ varies in the given time interval: $x = \sin^2 t, \quad y = \cos^2 t, \quad 0 \le t \le 3\pi$.

116. Find the length of one arch of the cycloid $x = \theta - \sin\theta,\ y = 1 - \cos\theta$.

117. Show that the total length of the ellipse $x = 4\sin\theta,\ y = 3\cos\theta$ is $L = 16\int_0^{\pi/2}\sqrt{1 - e^2\sin^2\theta}\,d\theta$, where $e = \frac{c}{a}$ and $c = \sqrt{a^2 - b^2}$.

118. Find the length of the curve $x = e^t - t,\ y = 4e^{t/2},\ -8 \le t \le 3$.

For the following exercises, find the area of the surface obtained by rotating the given curve about the $x$-axis.

119. $x = t^3, \quad y = t^2, \quad 0 \le t \le 1$

120. $x = a\cos^3\theta, \quad y = a\sin^3\theta, \quad 0 \le \theta \le \frac{\pi}{2}$

121. **[T]** Use a CAS to find the area of the surface generated by rotating $x = t + t^3,\ y = t - \frac{1}{t^2},\ 1 \le t \le 2$ about the $x$-axis. (Answer to three decimal places.)

122. Find the surface area obtained by rotating $x = 3t^2,\ y = 2t^3,\ 0 \le t \le 5$ about the $y$-axis.

123. Find the area of the surface generated by revolving $x = t^2,\ y = 2t,\ 0 \le t \le 4$ about the $x$-axis.

124. Find the surface area generated by revolving $x = t^2,\ y = 2t^2,\ 0 \le t \le 1$ about the $y$-axis.

# 7.3 | Polar Coordinates

## Learning Objectives

- **7.3.1** Locate points in a plane by using polar coordinates.
- **7.3.2** Convert points between rectangular and polar coordinates.
- **7.3.3** Sketch polar curves from given equations.
- **7.3.4** Convert equations between rectangular and polar coordinates.
- **7.3.5** Identify symmetry in polar curves and equations.

The rectangular coordinate system (or Cartesian plane) provides a means of mapping points to ordered pairs and ordered pairs to points. This is called a *one-to-one mapping* from points in the plane to ordered pairs. The polar coordinate system provides an alternative method of mapping points to ordered pairs. In this section we see that in some circumstances, polar coordinates can be more useful than rectangular coordinates.

## Defining Polar Coordinates

To find the coordinates of a point in the polar coordinate system, consider **Figure 7.27**. The point $P$ has Cartesian coordinates $(x, y)$. The line segment connecting the origin to the point $P$ measures the distance from the origin to $P$ and has length $r$. The angle between the positive $x$-axis and the line segment has measure $\theta$. This observation suggests a natural correspondence between the coordinate pair $(x, y)$ and the values $r$ and $\theta$. This correspondence is the basis of the **polar coordinate system**. Note that every point in the Cartesian plane has two values (hence the term *ordered pair*) associated with it. In the polar coordinate system, each point also two values associated with it: $r$ and $\theta$.

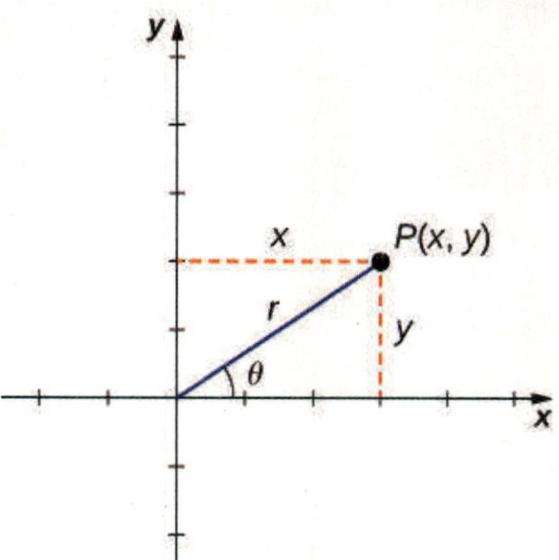


**Figure 7.27** An arbitrary point in the Cartesian plane.

Using right-triangle trigonometry, the following equations are true for the point $P$:

$$\cos\theta = \frac{x}{r} \text{ so } x = r\cos\theta$$
$$\sin\theta = \frac{y}{r} \text{ so } y = r\sin\theta.$$

Furthermore,

$$r^2 = x^2 + y^2 \text{ and } \tan\theta = \frac{y}{x}.$$

Each point $(x, y)$ in the Cartesian coordinate system can therefore be represented as an ordered pair $(r, \theta)$ in the polar coordinate system. The first coordinate is called the **radial coordinate** and the second coordinate is called the **angular coordinate**. Every point in the plane can be represented in this form.

Note that the equation $\tan\theta = y/x$ has an infinite number of solutions for any ordered pair $(x, y)$. However, if we restrict the solutions to values between $0$ and $2\pi$ then we can assign a unique solution to the quadrant in which the original point $(x, y)$ is located. Then the corresponding value of r is positive, so $r^2 = x^2 + y^2$.

### Theorem 7.4: Converting Points between Coordinate Systems

Given a point $P$ in the plane with Cartesian coordinates $(x, y)$ and polar coordinates $(r, \theta)$, the following conversion formulas hold true:

$$x = r\cos\theta \text{ and } y = r\sin\theta, \quad (7.7)$$

$$r^2 = x^2 + y^2 \text{ and } \tan\theta = \frac{y}{x}. \quad (7.8)$$

These formulas can be used to convert from rectangular to polar or from polar to rectangular coordinates.

## Example 7.10

### Converting between Rectangular and Polar Coordinates

Convert each of the following points into polar coordinates.

a. $(1, 1)$

b. $(-3, 4)$

c. $(0, 3)$

d. $(5\sqrt{3}, -5)$

Convert each of the following points into rectangular coordinates.

e. $(3, \pi/3)$

f. $(2, 3\pi/2)$

g. $(6, -5\pi/6)$

#### Solution

a. Use $x = 1$ and $y = 1$ in **Equation 7.8**:

$$\begin{aligned} r^2 &= x^2 + y^2 \\ &= 1^2 + 1^2 \\ r &= \sqrt{2} \end{aligned} \quad \text{and} \quad \begin{aligned} \tan\theta &= \frac{y}{x} \\ &= \frac{1}{1} = 1 \\ \theta &= \frac{\pi}{4}. \end{aligned}$$

Therefore this point can be represented as $\left(\sqrt{2}, \frac{\pi}{4}\right)$ in polar coordinates.

b. Use $x = -3$ and $y = 4$ in **Equation 7.8**:

$$\begin{aligned} r^2 &= x^2 + y^2 \\ &= (-3)^2 + (4)^2 \\ r &= 5 \end{aligned} \quad \text{and} \quad \begin{aligned} \tan\theta &= \frac{y}{x} \\ &= -\frac{4}{3} \\ \theta &= -\arctan\left(\frac{4}{3}\right) \\ &\approx 2.21. \end{aligned}$$

Therefore this point can be represented as $(5, 2.21)$ in polar coordinates.

c. Use $x = 0$ and $y = 3$ in **Equation 7.8**:

$$\begin{aligned} r^2 &= x^2 + y^2 \\ &= (3)^2 + (0)^2 \\ &= 9 + 0 \\ r &= 3 \end{aligned} \quad \text{and} \quad \begin{aligned} \tan\theta &= \frac{y}{x} \\ &= \frac{3}{0}. \end{aligned}$$

Direct application of the second equation leads to division by zero. Graphing the point $(0, 3)$ on the rectangular coordinate system reveals that the point is located on the positive y-axis. The angle between the positive x-axis and the positive y-axis is $\frac{\pi}{2}$. Therefore this point can be represented as $\left(3, \frac{\pi}{2}\right)$ in polar coordinates.

d. Use $x = 5\sqrt{3}$ and $y = -5$ in **Equation 7.8**:

$$\begin{aligned} r^2 &= x^2 + y^2 \\ &= \left(5\sqrt{3}\right)^2 + (-5)^2 \\ &= 75 + 25 \\ r &= 10 \end{aligned} \quad \text{and} \quad \begin{aligned} \tan\theta &= \frac{y}{x} \\ &= \frac{-5}{5\sqrt{3}} = -\frac{\sqrt{3}}{3} \\ \theta &= -\frac{\pi}{6}. \end{aligned}$$

Therefore this point can be represented as $\left(10, -\frac{\pi}{6}\right)$ in polar coordinates.

e. Use $r = 3$ and $\theta = \frac{\pi}{3}$ in **Equation 7.7**:

$$\begin{aligned} x &= r\cos\theta \\ &= 3\cos\left(\frac{\pi}{3}\right) \\ &= 3\left(\frac{1}{2}\right) = \frac{3}{2} \end{aligned} \quad \text{and} \quad \begin{aligned} y &= r\sin\theta \\ &= 3\sin\left(\frac{\pi}{3}\right) \\ &= 3\left(\frac{\sqrt{3}}{2}\right) = \frac{3\sqrt{3}}{2}. \end{aligned}$$

Therefore this point can be represented as $\left(\frac{3}{2}, \frac{3\sqrt{3}}{2}\right)$ in rectangular coordinates.

f. Use $r = 2$ and $\theta = \frac{3\pi}{2}$ in **Equation 7.7**:

$$\begin{aligned} x &= r\cos\theta \\ &= 2\cos\left(\frac{3\pi}{2}\right) \\ &= 2(0) = 0 \end{aligned} \quad \text{and} \quad \begin{aligned} y &= r\sin\theta \\ &= 2\sin\left(\frac{3\pi}{2}\right) \\ &= 2(-1) = -2. \end{aligned}$$

Therefore this point can be represented as $(0, -2)$ in rectangular coordinates.

g. Use $r = 6$ and $\theta = -\frac{5\pi}{6}$ in **Equation 7.7**:

$$\begin{aligned} x &= r\cos\theta \\ &= 6\cos\left(-\frac{5\pi}{6}\right) \\ &= 6\left(-\frac{\sqrt{3}}{2}\right) \\ &= -3\sqrt{3} \end{aligned} \quad \text{and} \quad \begin{aligned} y &= r\sin\theta \\ &= 6\sin\left(-\frac{5\pi}{6}\right) \\ &= 6\left(-\frac{1}{2}\right) \\ &= -3. \end{aligned}$$

Therefore this point can be represented as $\left(-3\sqrt{3}, -3\right)$ in rectangular coordinates.

**7.10** Convert $(-8, -8)$ into polar coordinates and $\left(4, \frac{2\pi}{3}\right)$ into rectangular coordinates.

The polar representation of a point is not unique. For example, the polar coordinates $\left(2, \frac{\pi}{3}\right)$ and $\left(2, \frac{7\pi}{3}\right)$ both represent the point $\left(1, \sqrt{3}\right)$ in the rectangular system. Also, the value of $r$ can be negative. Therefore, the point with polar coordinates $\left(-2, \frac{4\pi}{3}\right)$ also represents the point $\left(1, \sqrt{3}\right)$ in the rectangular system, as we can see by using **Equation 7.8**:

$$\begin{aligned} x &= r\cos\theta \\ &= -2\cos\left(\frac{4\pi}{3}\right) \\ &= -2\left(-\frac{1}{2}\right) = 1 \end{aligned} \quad \text{and} \quad \begin{aligned} y &= r\sin\theta \\ &= -2\sin\left(\frac{4\pi}{3}\right) \\ &= -2\left(-\frac{\sqrt{3}}{2}\right) = \sqrt{3}. \end{aligned}$$

Every point in the plane has an infinite number of representations in polar coordinates. However, each point in the plane has only one representation in the rectangular coordinate system.

Note that the polar representation of a point in the plane also has a visual interpretation. In particular, $r$ is the directed distance that the point lies from the origin, and $\theta$ measures the angle that the line segment from the origin to the point makes with the positive $x$-axis. Positive angles are measured in a counterclockwise direction and negative angles are measured in a clockwise direction. The polar coordinate system appears in the following figure.

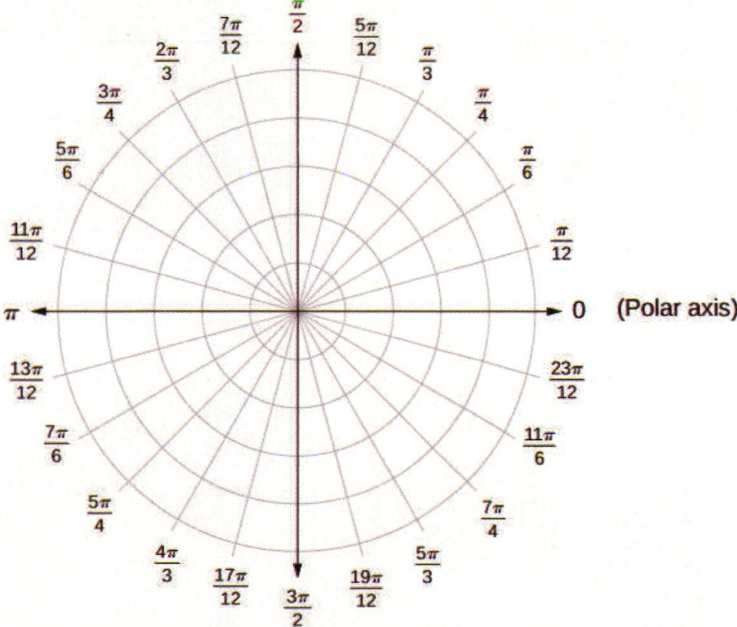

**Figure 7.28** The polar coordinate system.

The line segment starting from the center of the graph going to the right (called the positive $x$-axis in the Cartesian system) is the **polar axis**. The center point is the **pole**, or origin, of the coordinate system, and corresponds to $r = 0$. The innermost circle shown in **Figure 7.28** contains all points a distance of 1 unit from the pole, and is represented by the equation $r = 1$.

Then $r = 2$ is the set of points 2 units from the pole, and so on. The line segments emanating from the pole correspond to fixed angles. To plot a point in the polar coordinate system, start with the angle. If the angle is positive, then measure the angle from the polar axis in a counterclockwise direction. If it is negative, then measure it clockwise. If the value of $r$ is positive, move that distance along the terminal ray of the angle. If it is negative, move along the ray that is opposite the terminal ray of the given angle.

## Example 7.11

### Plotting Points in the Polar Plane

Plot each of the following points on the polar plane.

a. $\left(2, \frac{\pi}{4}\right)$

b. $\left(-3, \frac{2\pi}{3}\right)$

c. $\left(4, \frac{5\pi}{4}\right)$

### Solution

The three points are plotted in the following figure.

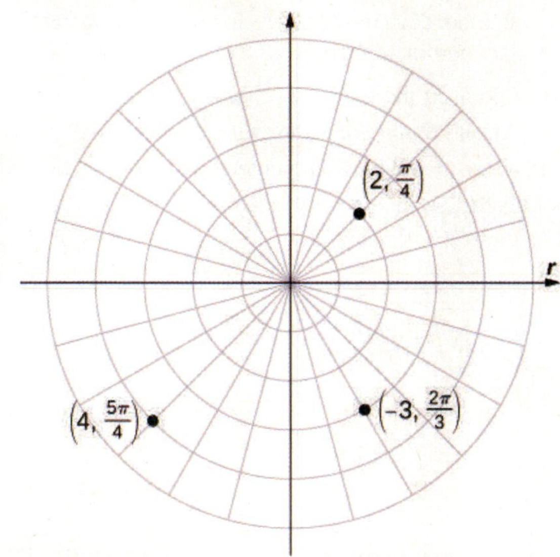


**Figure 7.29** Three points plotted in the polar coordinate system.

**7.11** Plot $\left(4, \frac{5\pi}{3}\right)$ and $\left(-3, -\frac{7\pi}{2}\right)$ on the polar plane.

## Polar Curves

Now that we know how to plot points in the polar coordinate system, we can discuss how to plot curves. In the rectangular coordinate system, we can graph a function $y = f(x)$ and create a curve in the Cartesian plane. In a similar fashion, we can graph a curve that is generated by a function $r = f(\theta)$.

The general idea behind graphing a function in polar coordinates is the same as graphing a function in rectangular coordinates. Start with a list of values for the independent variable ($\theta$ in this case) and calculate the corresponding values of the dependent variable $r$. This process generates a list of ordered pairs, which can be plotted in the polar coordinate system. Finally, connect the points, and take advantage of any patterns that may appear. The function may be periodic, for example, which indicates that only a limited number of values for the independent variable are needed.

### Problem-Solving Strategy: Plotting a Curve in Polar Coordinates

1. Create a table with two columns. The first column is for $\theta$, and the second column is for $r$.
2. Create a list of values for $\theta$.
3. Calculate the corresponding $r$ values for each $\theta$.
4. Plot each ordered pair $(r, \theta)$ on the coordinate axes.
5. Connect the points and look for a pattern.

Watch this **video (http://www.openstaxcollege.org/l/20_polarcurves)** for more information on sketching polar curves.

## Example 7.12

### Graphing a Function in Polar Coordinates

Graph the curve defined by the function $r = 4 \sin \theta$. Identify the curve and rewrite the equation in rectangular coordinates.

#### Solution

Because the function is a multiple of a sine function, it is periodic with period $2\pi$, so use values for $\theta$ between 0 and $2\pi$. The result of steps 1–3 appear in the following table. **Figure 7.30** shows the graph based on this table.

| $\theta$ | $r = 4\sin\theta$ | $\theta$ | $r = 4\sin\theta$ |
|---|---|---|---|
| 0 | 0 | $\pi$ | 0 |
| $\frac{\pi}{6}$ | 2 | $\frac{7\pi}{6}$ | −2 |
| $\frac{\pi}{4}$ | $2\sqrt{2} \approx 2.8$ | $\frac{5\pi}{4}$ | $-2\sqrt{2} \approx -2.8$ |
| $\frac{\pi}{3}$ | $2\sqrt{3} \approx 3.4$ | $\frac{4\pi}{3}$ | $-2\sqrt{3} \approx -3.4$ |
| $\frac{\pi}{2}$ | 4 | $\frac{3\pi}{2}$ | 4 |
| $\frac{2\pi}{3}$ | $2\sqrt{3} \approx 3.4$ | $\frac{5\pi}{3}$ | $-2\sqrt{3} \approx -3.4$ |
| $\frac{3\pi}{4}$ | $2\sqrt{2} \approx 2.8$ | $\frac{7\pi}{4}$ | $-2\sqrt{2} \approx -2.8$ |
| $\frac{5\pi}{6}$ | 2 | $\frac{11\pi}{6}$ | −2 |
| | | $2\pi$ | 0 |

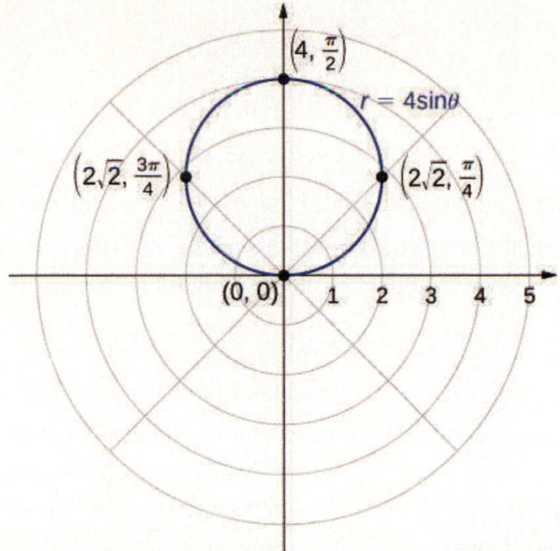


**Figure 7.30** The graph of the function $r = 4\sin\theta$ is a circle.

This is the graph of a circle. The equation $r = 4\sin\theta$ can be converted into rectangular coordinates by first multiplying both sides by $r$. This gives the equation $r^2 = 4r\sin\theta$. Next use the facts that $r^2 = x^2 + y^2$ and $y = r\sin\theta$. This gives $x^2 + y^2 = 4y$. To put this equation into standard form, subtract $4y$ from both sides of the equation and complete the square:

$$\begin{aligned} x^2 + y^2 - 4y &= 0 \\ x^2 + \left(y^2 - 4y\right) &= 0 \\ x^2 + \left(y^2 - 4y + 4\right) &= 0 + 4 \\ x^2 + (y-2)^2 &= 4. \end{aligned}$$

This is the equation of a circle with radius 2 and center $(0, 2)$ in the rectangular coordinate system.

**7.12** Create a graph of the curve defined by the function $r = 4 + 4\cos\theta$.

The graph in **Example 7.12** was that of a circle. The equation of the circle can be transformed into rectangular coordinates using the coordinate transformation formulas in **Equation 7.8**. **Example 7.14** gives some more examples of functions for transforming from polar to rectangular coordinates.

## Example 7.13

### Transforming Polar Equations to Rectangular Coordinates

Rewrite each of the following equations in rectangular coordinates and identify the graph.

a. $\theta = \frac{\pi}{3}$

b. $r = 3$

c. $r = 6\cos\theta - 8\sin\theta$

### Solution

a. Take the tangent of both sides. This gives $\tan\theta = \tan(\pi/3) = \sqrt{3}$. Since $\tan\theta = y/x$ we can replace the left-hand side of this equation by $y/x$. This gives $y/x = \sqrt{3}$, which can be rewritten as $y = x\sqrt{3}$. This is the equation of a straight line passing through the origin with slope $\sqrt{3}$. In general, any polar equation of the form $\theta = K$ represents a straight line through the pole with slope equal to $\tan K$.

b. First, square both sides of the equation. This gives $r^2 = 9$. Next replace $r^2$ with $x^2 + y^2$. This gives the equation $x^2 + y^2 = 9$, which is the equation of a circle centered at the origin with radius 3. In general, any polar equation of the form $r = k$ where $k$ is a positive constant represents a circle of radius $k$ centered at the origin. (*Note*: when squaring both sides of an equation it is possible to introduce new points unintentionally. This should always be taken into consideration. However, in this case we do not introduce new points. For example, $\left(-3, \frac{\pi}{3}\right)$ is the same point as $\left(3, \frac{4\pi}{3}\right)$.)

c. Multiply both sides of the equation by $r$. This leads to $r^2 = 6r\cos\theta - 8r\sin\theta$. Next use the formulas

$$r^2 = x^2 + y^2, \quad x = r\cos\theta, \quad y = r\sin\theta.$$

This gives

$$\begin{aligned} r^2 &= 6(r\cos\theta) - 8(r\sin\theta) \\ x^2 + y^2 &= 6x - 8y. \end{aligned}$$

To put this equation into standard form, first move the variables from the right-hand side of the equation to the left-hand side, then complete the square.

$$\begin{aligned} x^2 + y^2 &= 6x - 8y \\ x^2 - 6x + y^2 + 8y &= 0 \\ \left(x^2 - 6x\right) + \left(y^2 + 8y\right) &= 0 \\ \left(x^2 - 6x + 9\right) + \left(y^2 + 8y + 16\right) &= 9 + 16 \\ (x-3)^2 + (y+4)^2 &= 25. \end{aligned}$$

This is the equation of a circle with center at $(3, -4)$ and radius 5. Notice that the circle passes through the origin since the center is 5 units away.

**7.13** Rewrite the equation $r = \sec\theta\tan\theta$ in rectangular coordinates and identify its graph.

We have now seen several examples of drawing graphs of curves defined by **polar equations**. A summary of some common curves is given in the tables below. In each equation, $a$ and $b$ are arbitrary constants.

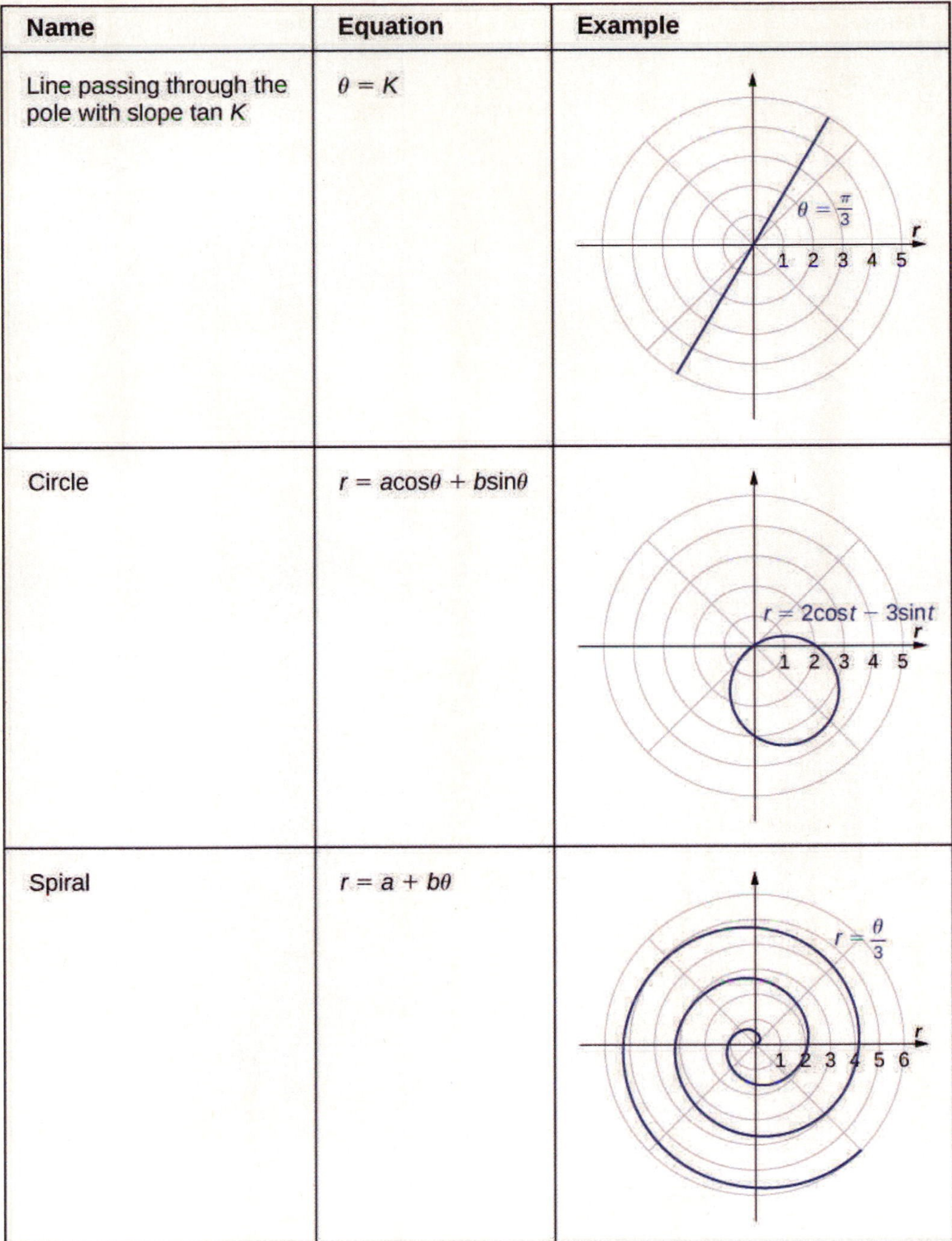

| Name | Equation | Example |
|---|---|---|
| Line passing through the pole with slope tan *K* | $\theta = K$ | $\theta = \frac{\pi}{3}$ |
| Circle | $r = a\cos\theta + b\sin\theta$ | $r = 2\cos t - 3\sin t$ |
| Spiral | $r = a + b\theta$ | $r = \frac{\theta}{3}$ |

Figure 7.31

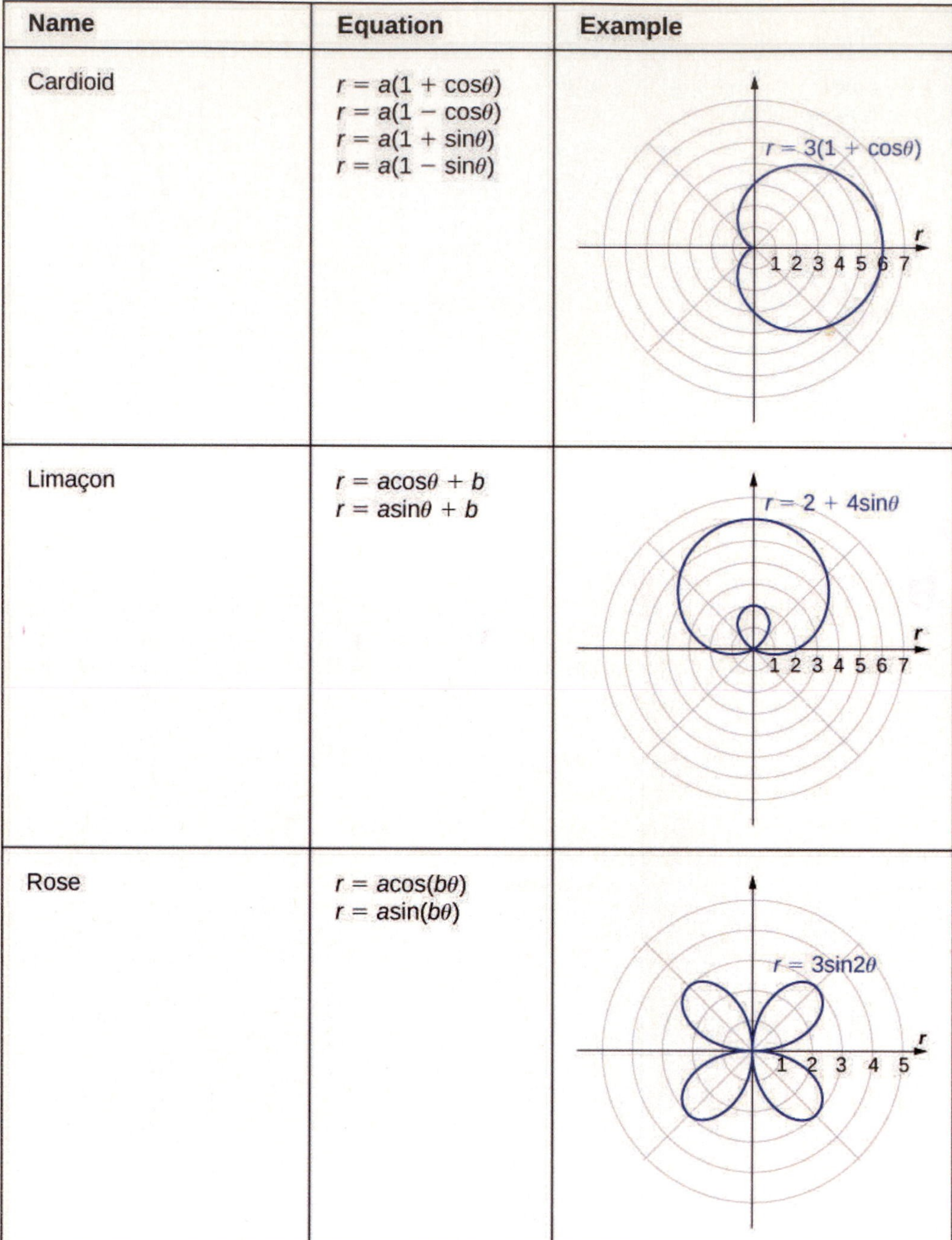

| Name | Equation | Example |
|---|---|---|
| Cardioid | $r = a(1 + \cos\theta)$<br>$r = a(1 - \cos\theta)$<br>$r = a(1 + \sin\theta)$<br>$r = a(1 - \sin\theta)$ | $r = 3(1 + \cos\theta)$ |
| Limaçon | $r = a\cos\theta + b$<br>$r = a\sin\theta + b$ | $r = 2 + 4\sin\theta$ |
| Rose | $r = a\cos(b\theta)$<br>$r = a\sin(b\theta)$ | $r = 3\sin2\theta$ |



Figure 7.32

A **cardioid** is a special case of a **limaçon** (pronounced "lee-mah-son"), in which $a = b$ or $a = -b$. The **rose** is a very interesting curve. Notice that the graph of $r = 3 \sin 2\theta$ has four petals. However, the graph of $r = 3 \sin 3\theta$ has three petals as shown.

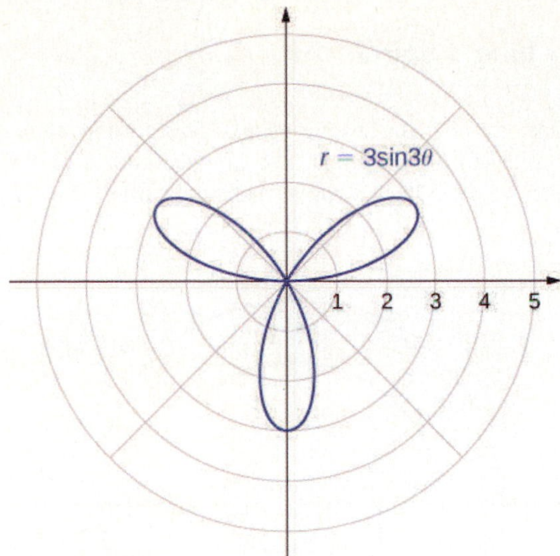


**Figure 7.33** Graph of $r = 3\sin 3\theta$.

If the coefficient of $\theta$ is even, the graph has twice as many petals as the coefficient. If the coefficient of $\theta$ is odd, then the number of petals equals the coefficient. You are encouraged to explore why this happens. Even more interesting graphs emerge when the coefficient of $\theta$ is not an integer. For example, if it is rational, then the curve is closed; that is, it eventually ends where it started (**Figure 7.34**(a)). However, if the coefficient is irrational, then the curve never closes (**Figure 7.34**(b)). Although it may appear that the curve is closed, a closer examination reveals that the petals just above the positive *x* axis are slightly thicker. This is because the petal does not quite match up with the starting point.

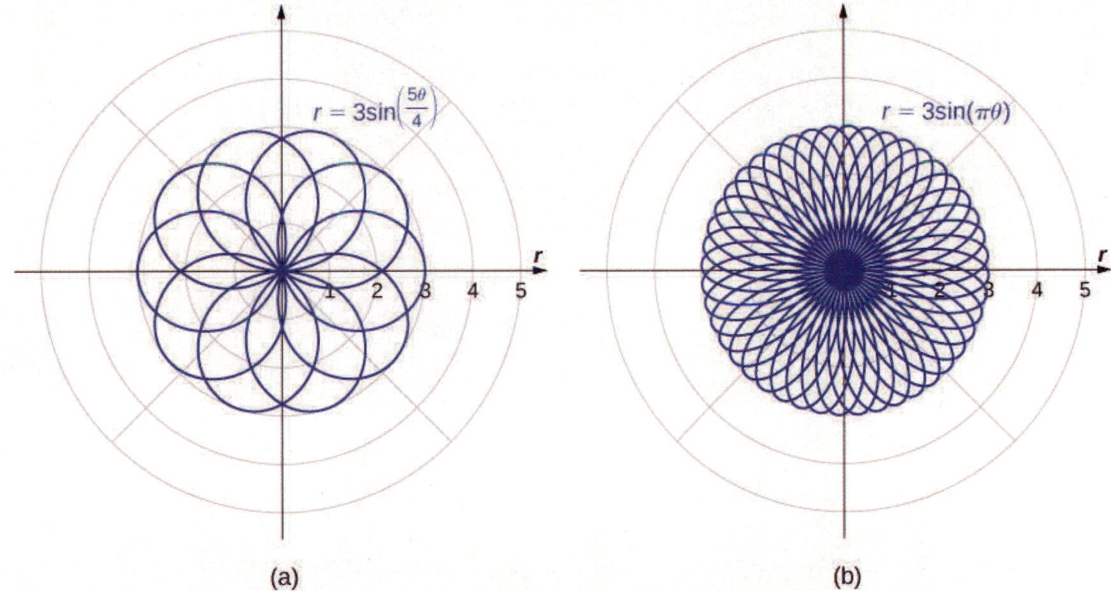


**Figure 7.34** Polar rose graphs of functions with (a) rational coefficient and (b) irrational coefficient. Note that the rose in part (b) would actually fill the entire circle if plotted in full.

Since the curve defined by the graph of $r = 3\sin(\pi\theta)$ never closes, the curve depicted in **Figure 7.34**(b) is only a partial depiction. In fact, this is an example of a **space-filling curve**. A space-filling curve is one that in fact occupies a two-dimensional subset of the real plane. In this case the curve occupies the circle of radius 3 centered at the origin.

## Example 7.14

## Chapter Opener: Describing a Spiral

Recall the chambered nautilus introduced in the chapter opener. This creature displays a spiral when half the outer shell is cut away. It is possible to describe a spiral using rectangular coordinates. **Figure 7.35** shows a spiral in rectangular coordinates. How can we describe this curve mathematically?

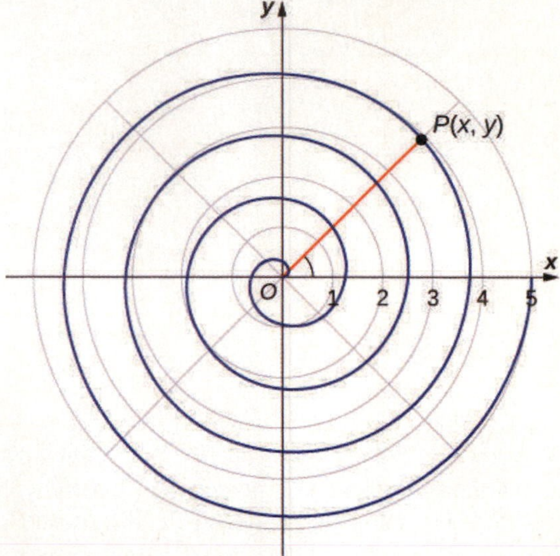


**Figure 7.35** How can we describe a spiral graph mathematically?

### Solution

As the point $P$ travels around the spiral in a counterclockwise direction, its distance $d$ from the origin increases. Assume that the distance $d$ is a constant multiple $k$ of the angle $\theta$ that the line segment $OP$ makes with the positive $x$-axis. Therefore $d(P, O) = k\theta,$ where $O$ is the origin. Now use the distance formula and some trigonometry:

$$\begin{aligned} d(P, O) &= k\theta \\ \sqrt{(x-0)^2 + (y-0)^2} &= k \arctan\left(\frac{y}{x}\right) \\ \sqrt{x^2 + y^2} &= k \arctan\left(\frac{y}{x}\right) \\ \arctan\left(\frac{y}{x}\right) &= \frac{\sqrt{x^2 + y^2}}{k} \\ y &= x \tan\left(\frac{\sqrt{x^2 + y^2}}{k}\right). \end{aligned}$$

Although this equation describes the spiral, it is not possible to solve it directly for either $x$ or $y$. However, if we use polar coordinates, the equation becomes much simpler. In particular, $d(P, O) = r,$ and $\theta$ is the second coordinate. Therefore the equation for the spiral becomes $r = k\theta.$ Note that when $\theta = 0$ we also have $r = 0,$ so the spiral emanates from the origin. We can remove this restriction by adding a constant to the equation. Then the equation for the spiral becomes $r = a + k\theta$ for arbitrary constants $a$ and $k.$ This is referred to as an Archimedean spiral, after the Greek mathematician Archimedes.

Another type of spiral is the logarithmic spiral, described by the function $r = a \cdot b^{\theta}.$ A graph of the function $r = 1.2\left(1.25^{\theta}\right)$ is given in **Figure 7.36**. This spiral describes the shell shape of the chambered nautilus.

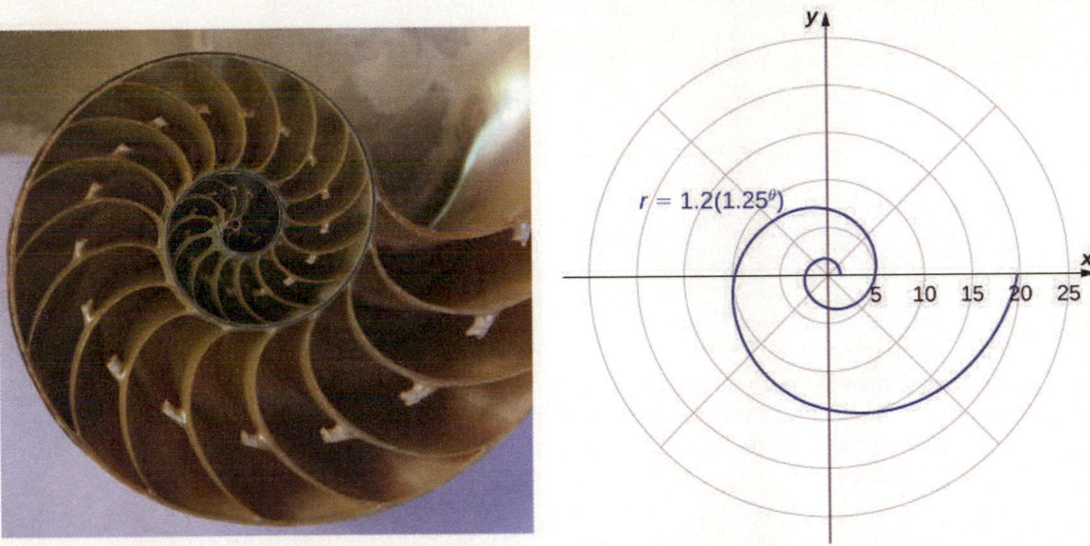


**Figure 7.36** A logarithmic spiral is similar to the shape of the chambered nautilus shell. (credit: modification of work by Jitze Couperus, Flickr)

Suppose a curve is described in the polar coordinate system via the function $r = f(\theta)$. Since we have conversion formulas from polar to rectangular coordinates given by

$$x = r\cos\theta$$
$$y = r\sin\theta,$$

it is possible to rewrite these formulas using the function

$$x = f(\theta)\cos\theta$$
$$y = f(\theta)\sin\theta.$$

This step gives a parameterization of the curve in rectangular coordinates using $\theta$ as the parameter. For example, the spiral formula $r = a + b\theta$ from **Figure 7.31** becomes

$$x = (a + b\theta)\cos\theta$$
$$y = (a + b\theta)\sin\theta.$$

Letting $\theta$ range from $-\infty$ to $\infty$ generates the entire spiral.

## Symmetry in Polar Coordinates

When studying symmetry of functions in rectangular coordinates (i.e., in the form $y = f(x)$), we talk about symmetry with respect to the *y*-axis and symmetry with respect to the origin. In particular, if $f(-x) = f(x)$ for all $x$ in the domain of $f$, then $f$ is an even function and its graph is symmetric with respect to the *y*-axis. If $f(-x) = -f(x)$ for all $x$ in the domain of $f$, then $f$ is an odd function and its graph is symmetric with respect to the origin. By determining which types of symmetry a graph exhibits, we can learn more about the shape and appearance of the graph. Symmetry can also reveal other properties of the function that generates the graph. Symmetry in polar curves works in a similar fashion.

### Theorem 7.5: Symmetry in Polar Curves and Equations

Consider a curve generated by the function $r = f(\theta)$ in polar coordinates.

i. The curve is symmetric about the polar axis if for every point $(r, \theta)$ on the graph, the point $(r, -\theta)$ is also on the graph. Similarly, the equation $r = f(\theta)$ is unchanged by replacing $\theta$ with $-\theta$.

ii. The curve is symmetric about the pole if for every point $(r, \theta)$ on the graph, the point $(r, \pi + \theta)$ is also on the graph. Similarly, the equation $r = f(\theta)$ is unchanged when replacing $r$ with $-r$, or $\theta$ with $\pi + \theta$.

iii. The curve is symmetric about the vertical line $\theta = \frac{\pi}{2}$ if for every point $(r, \theta)$ on the graph, the point $(r, \pi - \theta)$ is also on the graph. Similarly, the equation $r = f(\theta)$ is unchanged when $\theta$ is replaced by $\pi - \theta$.

The following table shows examples of each type of symmetry.

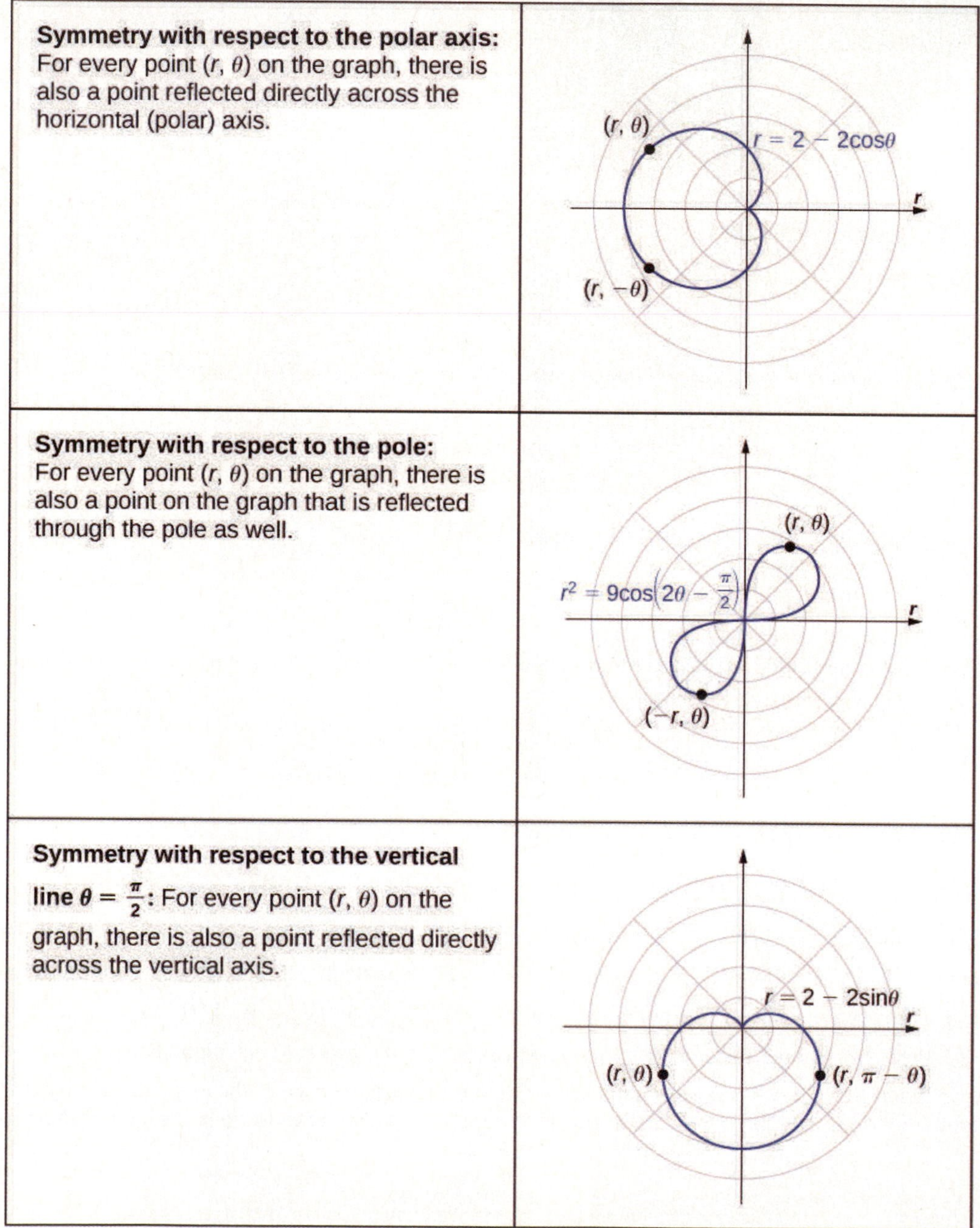

## Example 7.15

### Using Symmetry to Graph a Polar Equation

Find the symmetry of the rose defined by the equation $r = 3\sin(2\theta)$ and create a graph.

### Solution

Suppose the point $(r, \theta)$ is on the graph of $r = 3\sin(2\theta)$.

i. To test for symmetry about the polar axis, first try replacing $\theta$ with $-\theta$. This gives $r = 3\sin(2(-\theta)) = -3\sin(2\theta)$. Since this changes the original equation, this test is not satisfied. However, returning to the original equation and replacing $r$ with $-r$ and $\theta$ with $\pi - \theta$ yields

$$\begin{aligned} -r &= 3\sin(2(\pi - \theta)) \\ -r &= 3\sin(2\pi - 2\theta) \\ -r &= 3\sin(-2\theta) \\ -r &= -3\sin 2\theta. \end{aligned}$$

Multiplying both sides of this equation by $-1$ gives $r = 3\sin 2\theta$, which is the original equation. This demonstrates that the graph is symmetric with respect to the polar axis.

ii. To test for symmetry with respect to the pole, first replace $r$ with $-r$, which yields $-r = 3\sin(2\theta)$. Multiplying both sides by $-1$ gives $r = -3\sin(2\theta)$, which does not agree with the original equation. Therefore the equation does not pass the test for this symmetry. However, returning to the original equation and replacing $\theta$ with $\theta + \pi$ gives

$$\begin{aligned} r &= 3\sin(2(\theta + \pi)) \\ &= 3\sin(2\theta + 2\pi) \\ &= 3(\sin 2\theta \cos 2\pi + \cos 2\theta \sin 2\pi) \\ &= 3\sin 2\theta. \end{aligned}$$

Since this agrees with the original equation, the graph is symmetric about the pole.

iii. To test for symmetry with respect to the vertical line $\theta = \frac{\pi}{2}$, first replace both $r$ with $-r$ and $\theta$ with $-\theta$.

$$\begin{aligned} -r &= 3\sin(2(-\theta)) \\ -r &= 3\sin(-2\theta) \\ -r &= -3\sin 2\theta. \end{aligned}$$

Multiplying both sides of this equation by $-1$ gives $r = 3\sin 2\theta$, which is the original equation. Therefore the graph is symmetric about the vertical line $\theta = \frac{\pi}{2}$.

This graph has symmetry with respect to the polar axis, the origin, and the vertical line going through the pole. To graph the function, tabulate values of $\theta$ between 0 and $\pi/2$ and then reflect the resulting graph.

| $\theta$ | $r$ |
|---|---|
| 0 | 0 |
| $\frac{\pi}{6}$ | $\frac{3\sqrt{3}}{2} \approx 2.6$ |
| $\frac{\pi}{4}$ | 3 |
| $\frac{\pi}{3}$ | $\frac{3\sqrt{3}}{2} \approx 2.6$ |
| $\frac{\pi}{2}$ | 0 |

This gives one petal of the rose, as shown in the following graph.

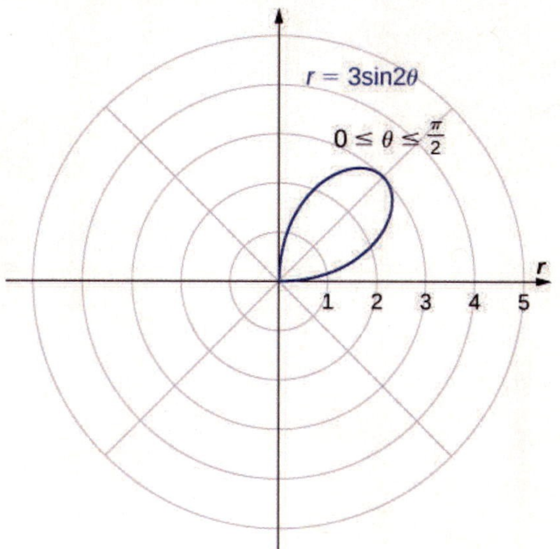


**Figure 7.37** The graph of the equation between $\theta = 0$ and $\theta = \pi/2$.

Reflecting this image into the other three quadrants gives the entire graph as shown.

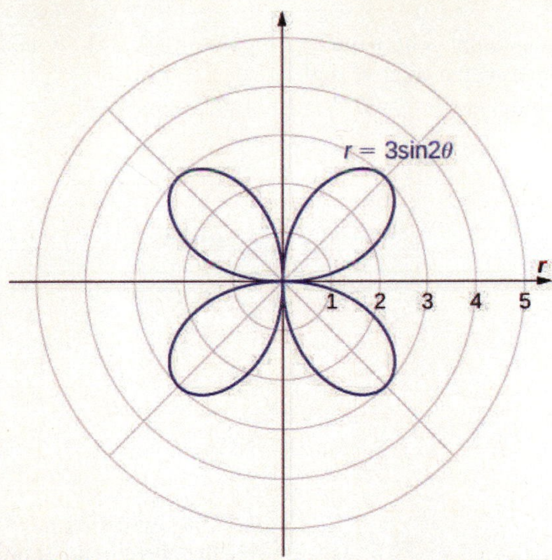


**Figure 7.38** The entire graph of the equation is called a four-petaled rose.

**7.14** Determine the symmetry of the graph determined by the equation $r = 2\cos(3\theta)$ and create a graph.

# 7.3 EXERCISES

In the following exercises, plot the point whose polar coordinates are given by first constructing the angle $\theta$ and then marking off the distance $r$ along the ray.

125. $\left(3, \frac{\pi}{6}\right)$

126. $\left(-2, \frac{5\pi}{3}\right)$

127. $\left(0, \frac{7\pi}{6}\right)$

128. $\left(-4, \frac{3\pi}{4}\right)$

129. $\left(1, \frac{\pi}{4}\right)$

130. $\left(2, \frac{5\pi}{6}\right)$

131. $\left(1, \frac{\pi}{2}\right)$

For the following exercises, consider the polar graph below. Give two sets of polar coordinates for each point.

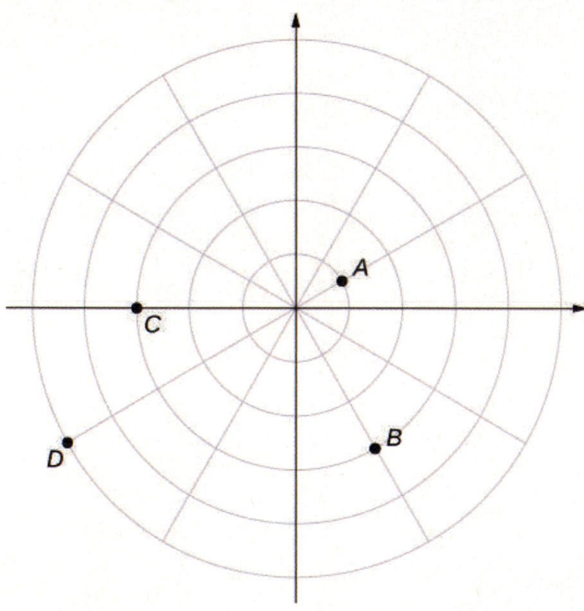


132. Coordinates of point $A$.

133. Coordinates of point $B$.

134. Coordinates of point $C$.

135. Coordinates of point $D$.

For the following exercises, the rectangular coordinates of a point are given. Find two sets of polar coordinates for the point in $(0, 2\pi]$. Round to three decimal places.

136. $(2, 2)$

137. $(3, -4)$ $(3, -4)$

138. $(8, 15)$

139. $(-6, 8)$

140. $(4, 3)$

141. $\left(3, -\sqrt{3}\right)$

For the following exercises, find rectangular coordinates for the given point in polar coordinates.

142. $\left(2, \frac{5\pi}{4}\right)$

143. $\left(-2, \frac{\pi}{6}\right)$

144. $\left(5, \frac{\pi}{3}\right)$

145. $\left(1, \frac{7\pi}{6}\right)$

146. $\left(-3, \frac{3\pi}{4}\right)$

147. $\left(0, \frac{\pi}{2}\right)$

148. $(-4.5, 6.5)$

For the following exercises, determine whether the graphs of the polar equation are symmetric with respect to the $x$ -axis, the $y$ -axis, or the origin.

149. $r = 3\sin(2\theta)$

150. $r^2 = 9\cos\theta$

151. $r = \cos\left(\frac{\theta}{5}\right)$

152. $r = 2\sec\theta$

153. $r = 1 + \cos\theta$

For the following exercises, describe the graph of each polar equation. Confirm each description by converting into a rectangular equation.

154. $r = 3$

155. $\theta = \frac{\pi}{4}$

156. $r = \sec\theta$

157. $r = \csc\theta$

For the following exercises, convert the rectangular equation to polar form and sketch its graph.

158. $x^2 + y^2 = 16$

159. $x^2 - y^2 = 16$

160. $x = 8$

For the following exercises, convert the rectangular equation to polar form and sketch its graph.

161. $3x - y = 2$

162. $y^2 = 4x$

For the following exercises, convert the polar equation to rectangular form and sketch its graph.

163. $r = 4\sin\theta$

164. $r = 6\cos\theta$

165. $r = \theta$

166. $r = \cot\theta\csc\theta$

For the following exercises, sketch a graph of the polar equation and identify any symmetry.

167. $r = 1 + \sin\theta$

168. $r = 3 - 2\cos\theta$

169. $r = 2 - 2\sin\theta$

170. $r = 5 - 4\sin\theta$

171. $r = 3\cos(2\theta)$

172. $r = 3\sin(2\theta)$

173. $r = 2\cos(3\theta)$

174. $r = 3\cos\left(\frac{\theta}{2}\right)$

175. $r^2 = 4\cos(2\theta)$

176. $r^2 = 4\sin\theta$

177. $r = 2\theta$

178. **[T]** The graph of $r = 2\cos(2\theta)\sec(\theta)$. is called a *strophoid*. Use a graphing utility to sketch the graph, and, from the graph, determine the asymptote.

179. **[T]** Use a graphing utility and sketch the graph of $r = \frac{6}{2\sin\theta - 3\cos\theta}$.

180. **[T]** Use a graphing utility to graph $r = \frac{1}{1 - \cos\theta}$.

181. **[T]** Use technology to graph $r = e^{\sin(\theta)} - 2\cos(4\theta)$.

182. **[T]** Use technology to plot $r = \sin\left(\frac{3\theta}{7}\right)$ (use the interval $0 \le \theta \le 14\pi$).

183. Without using technology, sketch the polar curve $\theta = \frac{2\pi}{3}$.

184. **[T]** Use a graphing utility to plot $r = \theta\sin\theta$ for $-\pi \le \theta \le \pi$.

185. **[T]** Use technology to plot $r = e^{-0.1\theta}$ for $-10 \le \theta \le 10$.

186. **[T]** There is a curve known as the "*Black Hole*." Use technology to plot $r = e^{-0.01\theta}$ for $-100 \le \theta \le 100$.

187. **[T]** Use the results of the preceding two problems to explore the graphs of $r = e^{-0.001\theta}$ and $r = e^{-0.0001\theta}$ for $|\theta| > 100$.

# 7.4 | Area and Arc Length in Polar Coordinates

## Learning Objectives

7.4.1 Apply the formula for area of a region in polar coordinates.
7.4.2 Determine the arc length of a polar curve.

In the rectangular coordinate system, the definite integral provides a way to calculate the area under a curve. In particular, if we have a function $y = f(x)$ defined from $x = a$ to $x = b$ where $f(x) > 0$ on this interval, the area between the curve and the *x*-axis is given by $A = \int_a^b f(x)\,dx.$ This fact, along with the formula for evaluating this integral, is summarized in the Fundamental Theorem of Calculus. Similarly, the arc length of this curve is given by $L = \int_a^b \sqrt{1 + (f'(x))^2}dx.$ In this section, we study analogous formulas for area and arc length in the polar coordinate system.

## Areas of Regions Bounded by Polar Curves

We have studied the formulas for area under a curve defined in rectangular coordinates and parametrically defined curves. Now we turn our attention to deriving a formula for the area of a region bounded by a polar curve. Recall that the proof of the Fundamental Theorem of Calculus used the concept of a Riemann sum to approximate the area under a curve by using rectangles. For polar curves we use the Riemann sum again, but the rectangles are replaced by sectors of a circle.

Consider a curve defined by the function $r = f(\theta),$ where $\alpha \le \theta \le \beta.$ Our first step is to partition the interval $[\alpha, \beta]$ into $n$ equal-width subintervals. The width of each subinterval is given by the formula $\Delta\theta = (\beta - \alpha)/n,$ and the $i$th partition point $\theta_i$ is given by the formula $\theta_i = \alpha + i\Delta\theta.$ Each partition point $\theta = \theta_i$ defines a line with slope $\tan\theta_i$ passing through the pole as shown in the following graph.

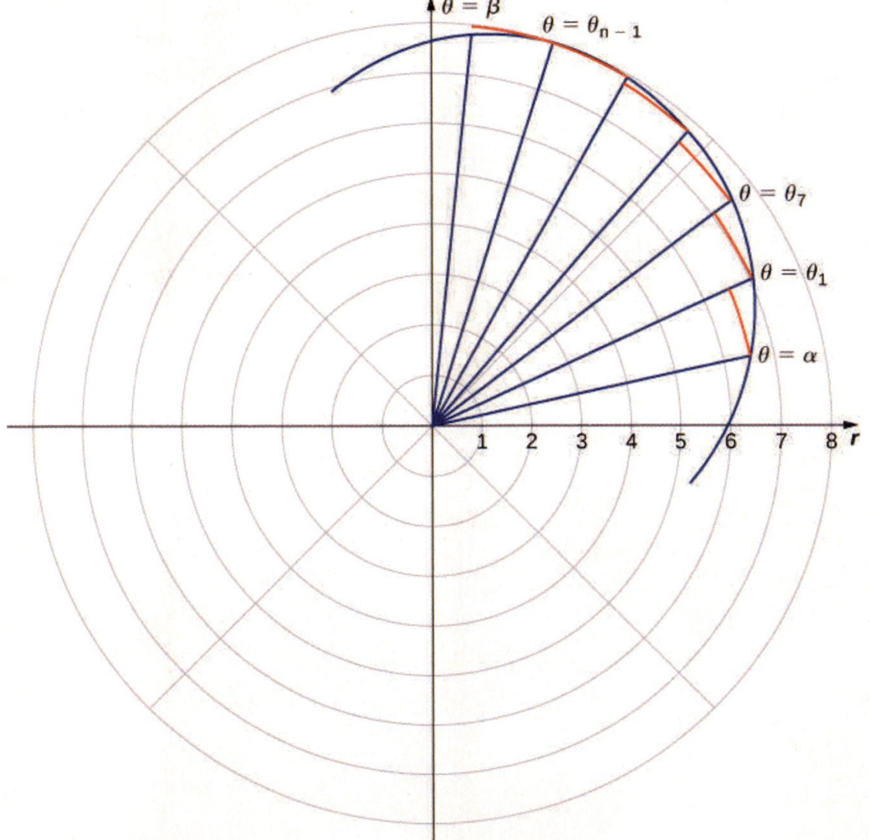


**Figure 7.39** A partition of a typical curve in polar coordinates.

The line segments are connected by arcs of constant radius. This defines sectors whose areas can be calculated by using a geometric formula. The area of each sector is then used to approximate the area between successive line segments. We then sum the areas of the sectors to approximate the total area. This approach gives a Riemann sum approximation for the total area. The formula for the area of a sector of a circle is illustrated in the following figure.

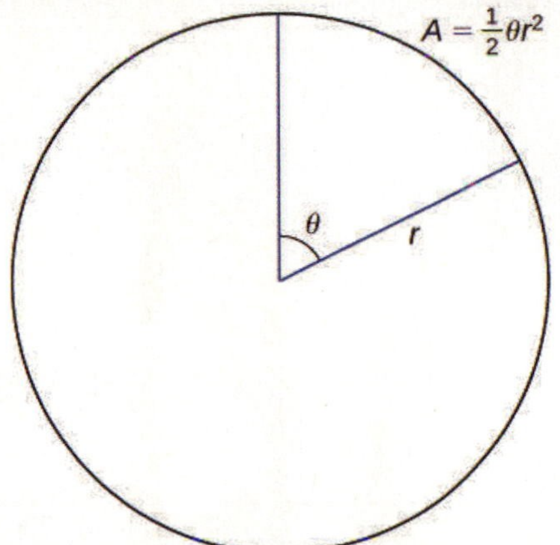


**Figure 7.40** The area of a sector of a circle is given by $A = \frac{1}{2}\theta r^2$.

Recall that the area of a circle is $A = \pi r^2$. When measuring angles in radians, 360 degrees is equal to $2\pi$ radians. Therefore a fraction of a circle can be measured by the central angle $\theta$. The fraction of the circle is given by $\frac{\theta}{2\pi}$, so the area of the sector is this fraction multiplied by the total area:

$$A = \left(\frac{\theta}{2\pi}\right)\pi r^2 = \frac{1}{2}\theta r^2.$$

Since the radius of a typical sector in **Figure 7.39** is given by $r_i = f(\theta_i)$, the area of the $i$th sector is given by

$$A_i = \frac{1}{2}(\Delta\theta)(f(\theta_i))^2.$$

Therefore a Riemann sum that approximates the area is given by

$$A_n = \sum_{i=1}^{n} A_i \approx \sum_{i=1}^{n} \frac{1}{2}(\Delta\theta)(f(\theta_i))^2.$$

We take the limit as $n \to \infty$ to get the exact area:

$$A = \lim_{n \to \infty} A_n = \frac{1}{2}\int_{\alpha}^{\beta} (f(\theta))^2 \, d\theta.$$

This gives the following theorem.

### Theorem 7.6: Area of a Region Bounded by a Polar Curve

Suppose $f$ is continuous and nonnegative on the interval $\alpha \le \theta \le \beta$ with $0 < \beta - \alpha \le 2\pi$. The area of the region bounded by the graph of $r = f(\theta)$ between the radial lines $\theta = \alpha$ and $\theta = \beta$ is

$$A = \frac{1}{2}\int_{\alpha}^{\beta} [f(\theta)]^2 \, d\theta = \frac{1}{2}\int_{\alpha}^{\beta} r^2 \, d\theta. \tag{7.9}$$

## Example 7.16

### Finding an Area of a Polar Region

Find the area of one petal of the rose defined by the equation $r = 3\sin(2\theta)$.

#### Solution

The graph of $r = 3\sin(2\theta)$ follows.

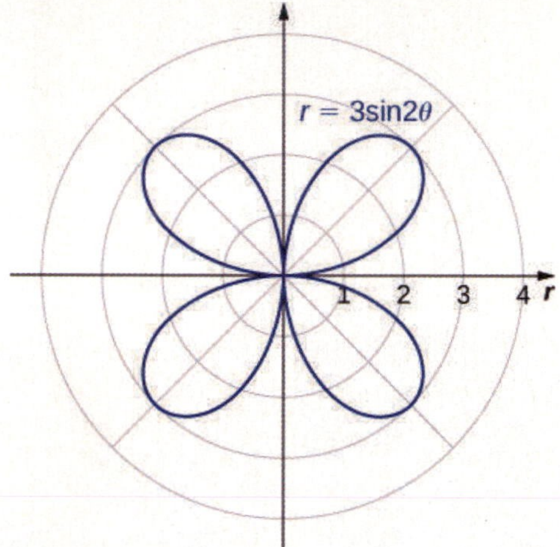


**Figure 7.41** The graph of $r = 3\sin(2\theta)$.

When $\theta = 0$ we have $r = 3\sin(2(0)) = 0$. The next value for which $r = 0$ is $\theta = \pi/2$. This can be seen by solving the equation $3\sin(2\theta) = 0$ for $\theta$. Therefore the values $\theta = 0$ to $\theta = \pi/2$ trace out the first petal of the rose. To find the area inside this petal, use **Equation 7.9** with $f(\theta) = 3\sin(2\theta)$, $\alpha = 0$, and $\beta = \pi/2$:

$$\begin{aligned} A &= \frac{1}{2}\int_{\alpha}^{\beta} [f(\theta)]^2 \, d\theta \\ &= \frac{1}{2}\int_{0}^{\pi/2} [3\sin(2\theta)]^2 \, d\theta \\ &= \frac{1}{2}\int_{0}^{\pi/2} 9\sin^2(2\theta) \, d\theta. \end{aligned}$$

To evaluate this integral, use the formula $\sin^2\alpha = (1 - \cos(2\alpha))/2$ with $\alpha = 2\theta$:

$$\begin{aligned} A &= \frac{1}{2}\int_0^{\pi/2} 9\sin^2(2\theta)\,d\theta \\ &= \frac{9}{2}\int_0^{\pi/2} \frac{(1-\cos(4\theta))}{2}d\theta \\ &= \frac{9}{4}\left(\int_0^{\pi/2} 1-\cos(4\theta)\,d\theta\right) \\ &= \frac{9}{4}\left(\theta - \frac{\sin(4\theta)}{4}\Big|_0^{\pi/2}\right. \\ &= \frac{9}{4}\left(\frac{\pi}{2} - \frac{\sin 2\pi}{4}\right) - \frac{9}{4}\left(0 - \frac{\sin 4(0)}{4}\right) \\ &= \frac{9\pi}{8}. \end{aligned}$$

 **7.15** Find the area inside the cardioid defined by the equation $r = 1 - \cos\theta$.

**Example 7.16** involved finding the area inside one curve. We can also use **Area of a Region Bounded by a Polar Curve** to find the area between two polar curves. However, we often need to find the points of intersection of the curves and determine which function defines the outer curve or the inner curve between these two points.

## Example 7.17

### Finding the Area between Two Polar Curves

Find the area outside the cardioid $r = 2 + 2\sin\theta$ and inside the circle $r = 6\sin\theta$.

#### Solution

First draw a graph containing both curves as shown.

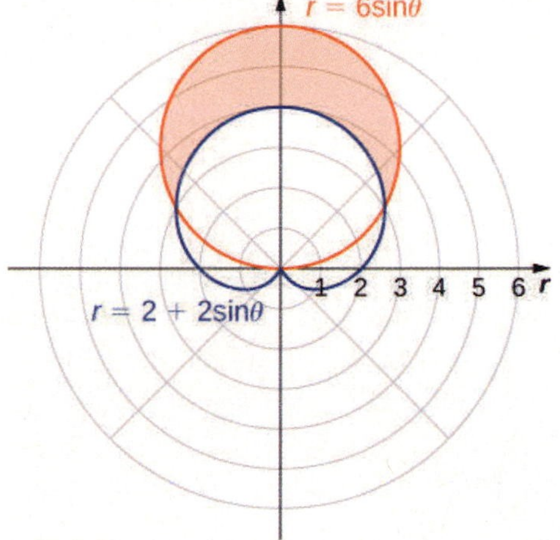


**Figure 7.42** The region between the curves $r = 2 + 2\sin\theta$ and $r = 6\sin\theta$.

To determine the limits of integration, first find the points of intersection by setting the two functions equal to each other and solving for $\theta$:

$$\begin{aligned} 6\sin\theta &= 2+2\sin\theta \\ 4\sin\theta &= 2 \\ \sin\theta &= \frac{1}{2}. \end{aligned}$$

This gives the solutions $\theta = \frac{\pi}{6}$ and $\theta = \frac{5\pi}{6}$, which are the limits of integration. The circle $r = 3\sin\theta$ is the red graph, which is the outer function, and the cardioid $r = 2+2\sin\theta$ is the blue graph, which is the inner function. To calculate the area between the curves, start with the area inside the circle between $\theta = \frac{\pi}{6}$ and $\theta = \frac{5\pi}{6}$, then subtract the area inside the cardioid between $\theta = \frac{\pi}{6}$ and $\theta = \frac{5\pi}{6}$:

$$\begin{aligned} A &= \text{circle} - \text{cardioid} \\ &= \frac{1}{2}\int_{\pi/6}^{5\pi/6} [6\sin\theta]^2\,d\theta - \frac{1}{2}\int_{\pi/6}^{5\pi/6} [2+2\sin\theta]^2\,d\theta \\ &= \frac{1}{2}\int_{\pi/6}^{5\pi/6} 36\sin^2\theta\,d\theta - \frac{1}{2}\int_{\pi/6}^{5\pi/6} 4+8\sin\theta+4\sin^2\theta\,d\theta \\ &= 18\int_{\pi/6}^{5\pi/6} \frac{1-\cos(2\theta)}{2}\,d\theta - 2\int_{\pi/6}^{5\pi/6} 1+2\sin\theta+\frac{1-\cos(2\theta)}{2}\,d\theta \\ &= 9\left[\theta - \frac{\sin(2\theta)}{2}\right]_{\pi/6}^{5\pi/6} - 2\left[\frac{3\theta}{2} - 2\cos\theta - \frac{\sin(2\theta)}{4}\right]_{\pi/6}^{5\pi/6} \\ &= 9\left(\frac{5\pi}{6} - \frac{\sin 2(5\pi/6)}{2}\right) - 9\left(\frac{\pi}{6} - \frac{\sin 2(\pi/6)}{2}\right) \\ &\quad -\left(3\left(\frac{5\pi}{6}\right) - 4\cos\frac{5\pi}{6} - \frac{\sin 2(5\pi/6)}{2}\right) + \left(3\left(\frac{\pi}{6}\right) - 4\cos\frac{\pi}{6} - \frac{\sin 2(\pi/6)}{2}\right) \\ &= 4\pi. \end{aligned}$$

**7.16** Find the area inside the circle $r = 4\cos\theta$ and outside the circle $r = 2$.

In **Example 7.17** we found the area inside the circle and outside the cardioid by first finding their intersection points. Notice that solving the equation directly for $\theta$ yielded two solutions: $\theta = \frac{\pi}{6}$ and $\theta = \frac{5\pi}{6}$. However, in the graph there are three intersection points. The third intersection point is the origin. The reason why this point did not show up as a solution is because the origin is on both graphs but for different values of $\theta$. For example, for the cardioid we get

$$\begin{aligned} 2+2\sin\theta &= 0 \\ \sin\theta &= -1, \end{aligned}$$

so the values for $\theta$ that solve this equation are $\theta = \frac{3\pi}{2} + 2n\pi$, where $n$ is any integer. For the circle we get

$$6\sin\theta = 0.$$

The solutions to this equation are of the form $\theta = n\pi$ for any integer value of $n$. These two solution sets have no points in common. Regardless of this fact, the curves intersect at the origin. This case must always be taken into consideration.

## Arc Length in Polar Curves

Here we derive a formula for the arc length of a curve defined in polar coordinates.

In rectangular coordinates, the arc length of a parameterized curve $(x(t), y(t))$ for $a \le t \le b$ is given by

$$L = \int_a^b \sqrt{\left(\frac{dx}{dt}\right)^2 + \left(\frac{dy}{dt}\right)^2}\, dt.$$

In polar coordinates we define the curve by the equation $r = f(\theta)$, where $\alpha \le \theta \le \beta$. In order to adapt the arc length formula for a polar curve, we use the equations

$$x = r\cos\theta = f(\theta)\cos\theta \text{ and } y = r\sin\theta = f(\theta)\sin\theta,$$

and we replace the parameter $t$ by $\theta$. Then

$$\frac{dx}{d\theta} = f'(\theta)\cos\theta - f(\theta)\sin\theta$$
$$\frac{dy}{d\theta} = f'(\theta)\sin\theta + f(\theta)\cos\theta.$$

We replace $dt$ by $d\theta$, and the lower and upper limits of integration are $\alpha$ and $\beta$, respectively. Then the arc length formula becomes

$$\begin{aligned}
L &= \int_a^b \sqrt{\left(\frac{dx}{dt}\right)^2 + \left(\frac{dy}{dt}\right)^2}\, dt \\
&= \int_\alpha^\beta \sqrt{\left(\frac{dx}{d\theta}\right)^2 + \left(\frac{dy}{d\theta}\right)^2}\, d\theta \\
&= \int_\alpha^\beta \sqrt{(f'(\theta)\cos\theta - f(\theta)\sin\theta)^2 + (f'(\theta)\sin\theta + f(\theta)\cos\theta)^2}\, d\theta \\
&= \int_\alpha^\beta \sqrt{(f'(\theta))^2\left(\cos^2\theta + \sin^2\theta\right) + (f(\theta))^2\left(\cos^2\theta + \sin^2\theta\right)}\, d\theta \\
&= \int_\alpha^\beta \sqrt{(f'(\theta))^2 + (f(\theta))^2}\, d\theta \\
&= \int_\alpha^\beta \sqrt{r^2 + \left(\frac{dr}{d\theta}\right)^2}\, d\theta.
\end{aligned}$$

This gives us the following theorem.

### Theorem 7.7: Arc Length of a Curve Defined by a Polar Function

Let $f$ be a function whose derivative is continuous on an interval $\alpha \le \theta \le \beta$. The length of the graph of $r = f(\theta)$ from $\theta = \alpha$ to $\theta = \beta$ is

$$L = \int_\alpha^\beta \sqrt{[f(\theta)]^2 + [f'(\theta)]^2}\, d\theta = \int_\alpha^\beta \sqrt{r^2 + \left(\frac{dr}{d\theta}\right)^2}\, d\theta. \tag{7.10}$$

### Example 7.18

#### Finding the Arc Length of a Polar Curve

Find the arc length of the cardioid $r = 2 + 2\cos\theta$.

### Solution

When $\theta = 0,\ r = 2 + 2\cos 0 = 4.$ Furthermore, as $\theta$ goes from $0$ to $2\pi,$ the cardioid is traced out exactly once. Therefore these are the limits of integration. Using $f(\theta) = 2 + 2\cos\theta,\quad \alpha = 0,\quad$ and $\beta = 2\pi,$ **Equation 7.10** becomes

$$\begin{aligned} L &= \int_\alpha^\beta \sqrt{[f(\theta)]^2 + [f'(\theta)]^2}\, d\theta \\ &= \int_0^{2\pi} \sqrt{[2 + 2\cos\theta]^2 + [-2\sin\theta]^2}\, d\theta \\ &= \int_0^{2\pi} \sqrt{4 + 8\cos\theta + 4\cos^2\theta + 4\sin^2\theta}\, d\theta \\ &= \int_0^{2\pi} \sqrt{4 + 8\cos\theta + 4\left(\cos^2\theta + \sin^2\theta\right)}\, d\theta \\ &= \int_0^{2\pi} \sqrt{8 + 8\cos\theta}\, d\theta \\ &= 2\int_0^{2\pi} \sqrt{2 + 2\cos\theta}\, d\theta. \end{aligned}$$

Next, using the identity $\cos(2\alpha) = 2\cos^2\alpha - 1,$ add 1 to both sides and multiply by 2. This gives $2 + 2\cos(2\alpha) = 4\cos^2\alpha.$ Substituting $\alpha = \theta/2$ gives $2 + 2\cos\theta = 4\cos^2(\theta/2),$ so the integral becomes

$$\begin{aligned} L &= 2\int_0^{2\pi} \sqrt{2 + 2\cos\theta}\, d\theta \\ &= 2\int_0^{2\pi} \sqrt{4\cos^2\left(\frac{\theta}{2}\right)}\, d\theta \\ &= 2\int_0^{2\pi} \left|\cos\left(\frac{\theta}{2}\right)\right| d\theta. \end{aligned}$$

The absolute value is necessary because the cosine is negative for some values in its domain. To resolve this issue, change the limits from $0$ to $\pi$ and double the answer. This strategy works because cosine is positive between $0$ and $\frac{\pi}{2}$. Thus,

$$\begin{aligned} L &= 4\int_0^{2\pi} \left|\cos\left(\frac{\theta}{2}\right)\right| d\theta \\ &= 8\int_0^{\pi} \cos\left(\frac{\theta}{2}\right) d\theta \\ &= 8\left(2\sin\left(\frac{\theta}{2}\right)\right)\Big|_0^{\pi} \\ &= 16. \end{aligned}$$

**7.17** Find the total arc length of $r = 3\sin\theta.$

# 7.4 EXERCISES

For the following exercises, determine a definite integral that represents the area.

188. Region enclosed by $r = 4$

189. Region enclosed by $r = 3 \sin \theta$

190. Region in the first quadrant within the cardioid $r = 1 + \sin \theta$

191. Region enclosed by one petal of $r = 8 \sin(2\theta)$

192. Region enclosed by one petal of $r = \cos(3\theta)$

193. Region below the polar axis and enclosed by $r = 1 - \sin \theta$

194. Region in the first quadrant enclosed by $r = 2 - \cos \theta$

195. Region enclosed by the inner loop of $r = 2 - 3 \sin \theta$

196. Region enclosed by the inner loop of $r = 3 - 4 \cos \theta$

197. Region enclosed by $r = 1 - 2 \cos \theta$ and outside the inner loop

198. Region common to $r = 3 \sin \theta$ and $r = 2 - \sin \theta$

199. Region common to $r = 2$ and $r = 4 \cos \theta$

200. Region common to $r = 3 \cos \theta$ and $r = 3 \sin \theta$

For the following exercises, find the area of the described region.

201. Enclosed by $r = 6 \sin \theta$

202. Above the polar axis enclosed by $r = 2 + \sin \theta$

203. Below the polar axis and enclosed by $r = 2 - \cos \theta$

204. Enclosed by one petal of $r = 4 \cos(3\theta)$

205. Enclosed by one petal of $r = 3 \cos(2\theta)$

206. Enclosed by $r = 1 + \sin \theta$

207. Enclosed by the inner loop of $r = 3 + 6 \cos \theta$

208. Enclosed by $r = 2 + 4 \cos \theta$ and outside the inner loop

209. Common interior of $r = 4 \sin(2\theta)$ and $r = 2$

210. Common interior of $r = 3 - 2 \sin \theta$ and $r = -3 + 2 \sin \theta$

211. Common interior of $r = 6 \sin \theta$ and $r = 3$

212. Inside $r = 1 + \cos \theta$ and outside $r = \cos \theta$

213. Common interior of $r = 2 + 2 \cos \theta$ and $r = 2 \sin \theta$

For the following exercises, find a definite integral that represents the arc length.

214. $r = 4 \cos \theta$ on the interval $0 \le \theta \le \frac{\pi}{2}$

215. $r = 1 + \sin \theta$ on the interval $0 \le \theta \le 2\pi$

216. $r = 2 \sec \theta$ on the interval $0 \le \theta \le \frac{\pi}{3}$

217. $r = e^{\theta}$ on the interval $0 \le \theta \le 1$

For the following exercises, find the length of the curve over the given interval.

218. $r = 6$ on the interval $0 \le \theta \le \frac{\pi}{2}$

219. $r = e^{3\theta}$ on the interval $0 \le \theta \le 2$

220. $r = 6 \cos \theta$ on the interval $0 \le \theta \le \frac{\pi}{2}$

221. $r = 8 + 8 \cos \theta$ on the interval $0 \le \theta \le \pi$

222. $r = 1 - \sin \theta$ on the interval $0 \le \theta \le 2\pi$

For the following exercises, use the integration capabilities of a calculator to approximate the length of the curve.

223. **[T]** $r = 3\theta$ on the interval $0 \le \theta \le \frac{\pi}{2}$

224. **[T]** $r = \frac{2}{\theta}$ on the interval $\pi \le \theta \le 2\pi$

225. **[T]** $r = \sin^2\left(\frac{\theta}{2}\right)$ on the interval $0 \le \theta \le \pi$

226. **[T]** $r = 2\theta^2$ on the interval $0 \le \theta \le \pi$

227. **[T]** $r = \sin(3 \cos \theta)$ on the interval $0 \le \theta \le \pi$

For the following exercises, use the familiar formula from

geometry to find the area of the region described and then confirm by using the definite integral.

228. $r = 3\sin\theta$ on the interval $0 \le \theta \le \pi$

229. $r = \sin\theta + \cos\theta$ on the interval $0 \le \theta \le \pi$

230. $r = 6\sin\theta + 8\cos\theta$ on the interval $0 \le \theta \le \pi$

For the following exercises, use the familiar formula from geometry to find the length of the curve and then confirm using the definite integral.

231. $r = 3\sin\theta$ on the interval $0 \le \theta \le \pi$

232. $r = \sin\theta + \cos\theta$ on the interval $0 \le \theta \le \pi$

233. $r = 6\sin\theta + 8\cos\theta$ on the interval $0 \le \theta \le \pi$

234. Verify that if $y = r\sin\theta = f(\theta)\sin\theta$ then $\frac{dy}{d\theta} = f'(\theta)\sin\theta + f(\theta)\cos\theta.$

For the following exercises, find the slope of a tangent line to a polar curve $r = f(\theta)$. Let $x = r\cos\theta = f(\theta)\cos\theta$ and $y = r\sin\theta = f(\theta)\sin\theta,$ so the polar equation $r = f(\theta)$ is now written in parametric form.

235. Use the definition of the derivative $\frac{dy}{dx} = \frac{dy/d\theta}{dx/d\theta}$ and the product rule to derive the derivative of a polar equation.

236. $r = 1 - \sin\theta;\ \left(\frac{1}{2}, \frac{\pi}{6}\right)$

237. $r = 4\cos\theta;\ \left(2, \frac{\pi}{3}\right)$

238. $r = 8\sin\theta;\ \left(4, \frac{5\pi}{6}\right)$

239. $r = 4 + \sin\theta;\ \left(3, \frac{3\pi}{2}\right)$

240. $r = 6 + 3\cos\theta;\ (3, \pi)$

241. $r = 4\cos(2\theta);$ tips of the leaves

242. $r = 2\sin(3\theta);$ tips of the leaves

243. $r = 2\theta;\ \left(\frac{\pi}{2}, \frac{\pi}{4}\right)$

244. Find the points on the interval $-\pi \le \theta \le \pi$ at which the cardioid $r = 1 - \cos\theta$ has a vertical or horizontal tangent line.

245. For the cardioid $r = 1 + \sin\theta,$ find the slope of the tangent line when $\theta = \frac{\pi}{3}.$

For the following exercises, find the slope of the tangent line to the given polar curve at the point given by the value of $\theta.$

246. $r = 3\cos\theta,\ \theta = \frac{\pi}{3}$

247. $r = \theta,\quad \theta = \frac{\pi}{2}$

248. $r = \ln\theta,\quad \theta = e$

249. **[T]** Use technology: $r = 2 + 4\cos\theta$ at $\theta = \frac{\pi}{6}$

For the following exercises, find the points at which the following polar curves have a horizontal or vertical tangent line.

250. $r = 4\cos\theta$

251. $r^2 = 4\cos(2\theta)$

252. $r = 2\sin(2\theta)$

253. The cardioid $r = 1 + \sin\theta$

254. Show that the curve $r = \sin\theta\tan\theta$ (called a *cissoid of Diocles*) has the line $x = 1$ as a vertical asymptote.

# 7.5 | Conic Sections

## Learning Objectives

7.5.1 Identify the equation of a parabola in standard form with given focus and directrix.
7.5.2 Identify the equation of an ellipse in standard form with given foci.
7.5.3 Identify the equation of a hyperbola in standard form with given foci.
7.5.4 Recognize a parabola, ellipse, or hyperbola from its eccentricity value.
7.5.5 Write the polar equation of a conic section with eccentricity $e$.
7.5.6 Identify when a general equation of degree two is a parabola, ellipse, or hyperbola.

Conic sections have been studied since the time of the ancient Greeks, and were considered to be an important mathematical concept. As early as 320 BCE, such Greek mathematicians as Menaechmus, Appollonius, and Archimedes were fascinated by these curves. Appollonius wrote an entire eight-volume treatise on conic sections in which he was, for example, able to derive a specific method for identifying a conic section through the use of geometry. Since then, important applications of conic sections have arisen (for example, in astronomy), and the properties of conic sections are used in radio telescopes, satellite dish receivers, and even architecture. In this section we discuss the three basic conic sections, some of their properties, and their equations.

Conic sections get their name because they can be generated by intersecting a plane with a cone. A cone has two identically shaped parts called **nappes**. One nappe is what most people mean by "cone," having the shape of a party hat. A right circular cone can be generated by revolving a line passing through the origin around the *y*-axis as shown.

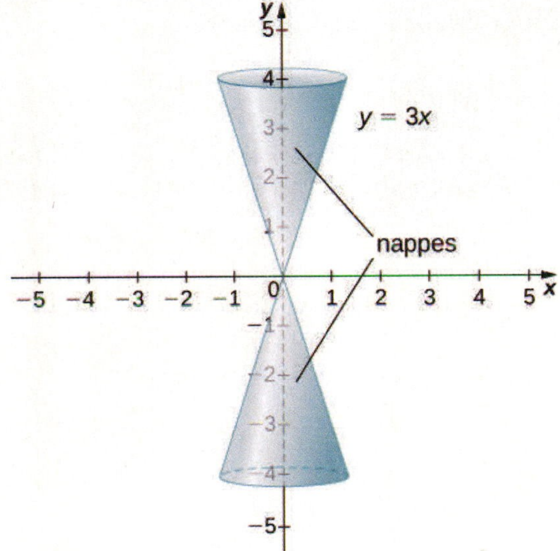


**Figure 7.43** A cone generated by revolving the line $y = 3x$ around the $y$-axis.

Conic sections are generated by the intersection of a plane with a cone (**Figure 7.44**). If the plane is parallel to the axis of revolution (the *y*-axis), then the **conic section** is a hyperbola. If the plane is parallel to the generating line, the conic section is a parabola. If the plane is perpendicular to the axis of revolution, the conic section is a circle. If the plane intersects one nappe at an angle to the axis (other than $90°$), then the conic section is an ellipse.

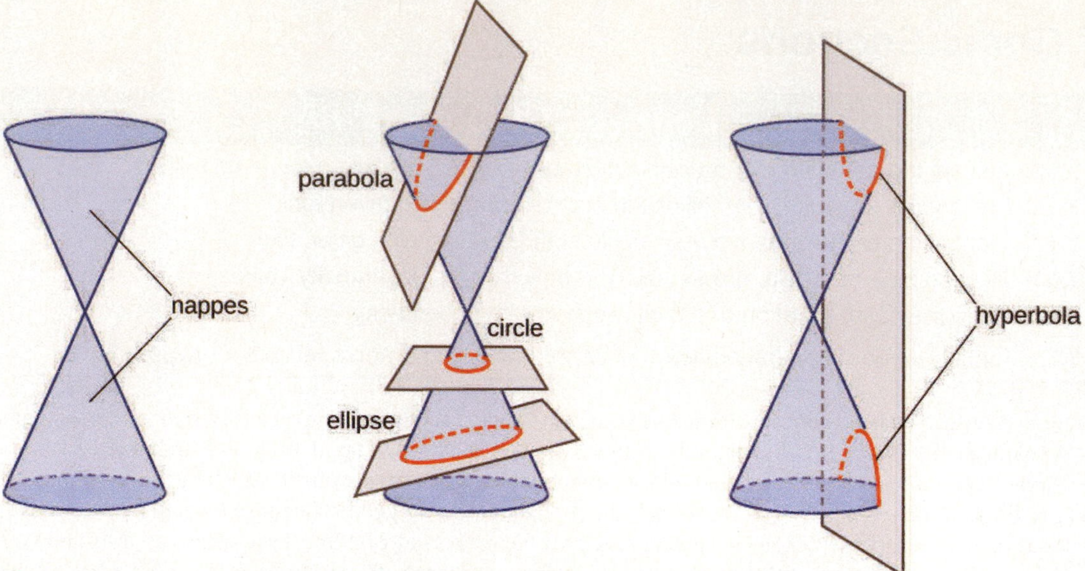


**Figure 7.44** The four conic sections. Each conic is determined by the angle the plane makes with the axis of the cone.

## Parabolas

A parabola is generated when a plane intersects a cone parallel to the generating line. In this case, the plane intersects only one of the nappes. A parabola can also be defined in terms of distances.

### Definition

A parabola is the set of all points whose distance from a fixed point, called the **focus**, is equal to the distance from a fixed line, called the **directrix**. The point halfway between the focus and the directrix is called the **vertex** of the parabola.

A graph of a typical parabola appears in **Figure 7.45**. Using this diagram in conjunction with the distance formula, we can derive an equation for a parabola. Recall the distance formula: Given point $P$ with coordinates $(x_1, y_1)$ and point $Q$ with coordinates $(x_2, y_2)$, the distance between them is given by the formula

$$d(P, Q) = \sqrt{(x_2 - x_1)^2 + (y_2 - y_1)^2}.$$

Then from the definition of a parabola and **Figure 7.45**, we get

$$\begin{aligned} d(F, P) &= d(P, Q) \\ \sqrt{(0 - x)^2 + (p - y)^2} &= \sqrt{(x - x)^2 + (-p - y)^2}. \end{aligned}$$

Squaring both sides and simplifying yields

$$\begin{aligned} x^2 + (p - y)^2 &= 0^2 + (-p - y)^2 \\ x^2 + p^2 - 2py + y^2 &= p^2 + 2py + y^2 \\ x^2 - 2py &= 2py \\ x^2 &= 4py. \end{aligned}$$

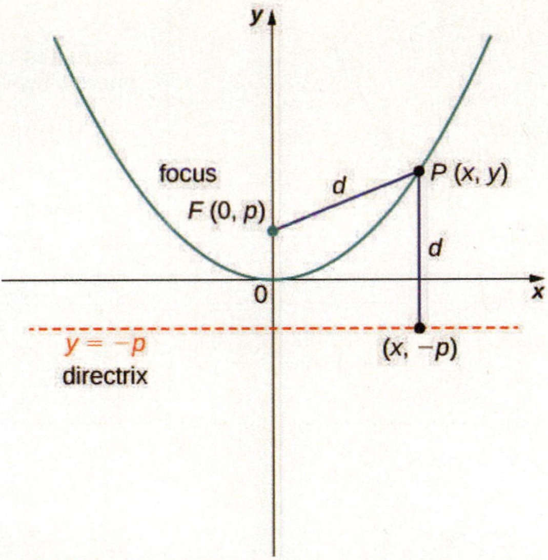


**Figure 7.45** A typical parabola in which the distance from the focus to the vertex is represented by the variable $p$.

Now suppose we want to relocate the vertex. We use the variables $(h,\ k)$ to denote the coordinates of the vertex. Then if the focus is directly above the vertex, it has coordinates $(h,\ k+p)$ and the directrix has the equation $y=k-p$. Going through the same derivation yields the formula $(x-h)^2=4p(y-k)$. Solving this equation for $y$ leads to the following theorem.

### Theorem 7.8: Equations for Parabolas

Given a parabola opening upward with vertex located at $(h,\ k)$ and focus located at $(h,\ k+p)$, where $p$ is a constant, the equation for the parabola is given by

$$y=\frac{1}{4p}(x-h)^2+k. \tag{7.11}$$

This is the **standard form** of a parabola.

We can also study the cases when the parabola opens down or to the left or the right. The equation for each of these cases can also be written in standard form as shown in the following graphs.

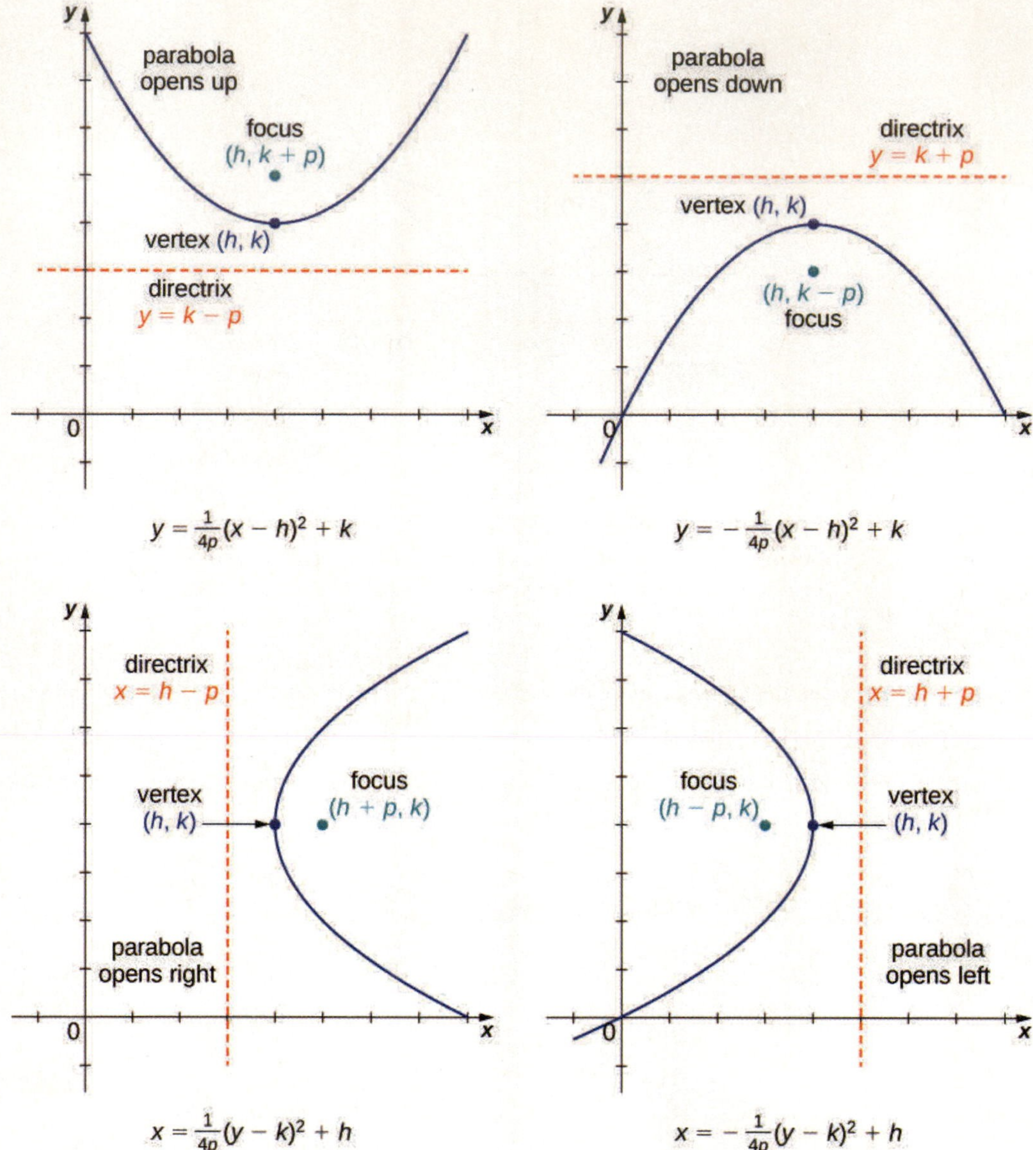


**Figure 7.46** Four parabolas, opening in various directions, along with their equations in standard form.

In addition, the equation of a parabola can be written in the **general form**, though in this form the values of $h$, $k$, and $p$ are not immediately recognizable. The general form of a parabola is written as

$$ax^2 + bx + cy + d = 0 \quad \text{or} \quad ay^2 + bx + cy + d = 0.$$

The first equation represents a parabola that opens either up or down. The second equation represents a parabola that opens either to the left or to the right. To put the equation into standard form, use the method of completing the square.

## Example 7.19

### Converting the Equation of a Parabola from General into Standard Form

Put the equation $x^2 - 4x - 8y + 12 = 0$ into standard form and graph the resulting parabola.

### Solution

Since $y$ is not squared in this equation, we know that the parabola opens either upward or downward. Therefore we need to solve this equation for $y$, which will put the equation into standard form. To do that, first add $8y$ to both sides of the equation:

$$8y = x^2 - 4x + 12.$$

The next step is to complete the square on the right-hand side. Start by grouping the first two terms on the right-hand side using parentheses:

$$8y = \left(x^2 - 4x\right) + 12.$$

Next determine the constant that, when added inside the parentheses, makes the quantity inside the parentheses a perfect square trinomial. To do this, take half the coefficient of $x$ and square it. This gives $\left(\frac{-4}{2}\right)^2 = 4.$ Add 4 inside the parentheses and subtract 4 outside the parentheses, so the value of the equation is not changed:

$$8y = \left(x^2 - 4x + 4\right) + 12 - 4.$$

Now combine like terms and factor the quantity inside the parentheses:

$$8y = (x - 2)^2 + 8.$$

Finally, divide by 8:

$$y = \frac{1}{8}(x - 2)^2 + 1.$$

This equation is now in standard form. Comparing this to **Equation 7.11** gives $h = 2,$ $k = 1,$ and $p = 2.$ The parabola opens up, with vertex at $(2, 1),$ focus at $(2, 3),$ and directrix $y = -1.$ The graph of this parabola appears as follows.

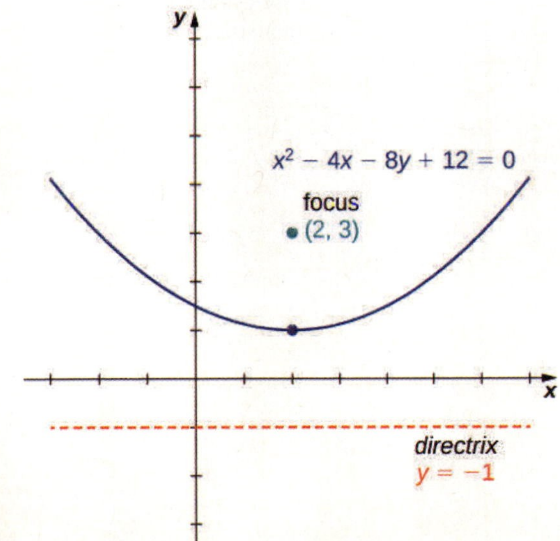


**Figure 7.47** The parabola in **Example 7.19**.

**7.18** Put the equation $2y^2 - x + 12y + 16 = 0$ into standard form and graph the resulting parabola.

The axis of symmetry of a vertical (opening up or down) parabola is a vertical line passing through the vertex. The parabola has an interesting reflective property. Suppose we have a satellite dish with a parabolic cross section. If a beam of electromagnetic waves, such as light or radio waves, comes into the dish in a straight line from a satellite (parallel to the axis of symmetry), then the waves reflect off the dish and collect at the focus of the parabola as shown.

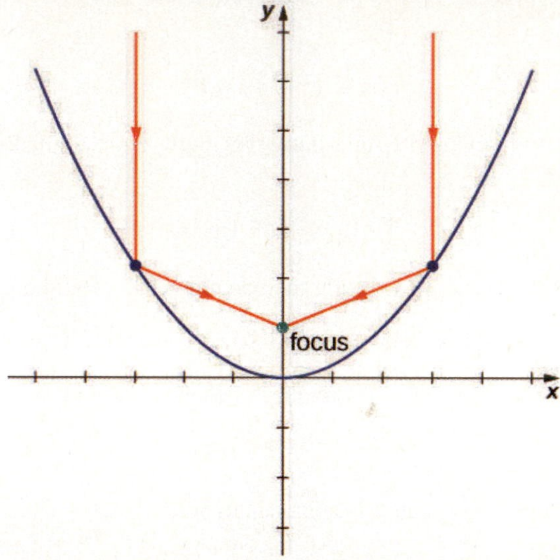


Consider a parabolic dish designed to collect signals from a satellite in space. The dish is aimed directly at the satellite, and a receiver is located at the focus of the parabola. Radio waves coming in from the satellite are reflected off the surface of the parabola to the receiver, which collects and decodes the digital signals. This allows a small receiver to gather signals from a wide angle of sky. Flashlights and headlights in a car work on the same principle, but in reverse: the source of the light (that is, the light bulb) is located at the focus and the reflecting surface on the parabolic mirror focuses the beam straight ahead. This allows a small light bulb to illuminate a wide angle of space in front of the flashlight or car.

## Ellipses

An ellipse can also be defined in terms of distances. In the case of an ellipse, there are two foci (plural of focus), and two directrices (plural of directrix). We look at the directrices in more detail later in this section.

### Definition

An *ellipse* is the set of all points for which the sum of their distances from two fixed points (the foci) is constant.

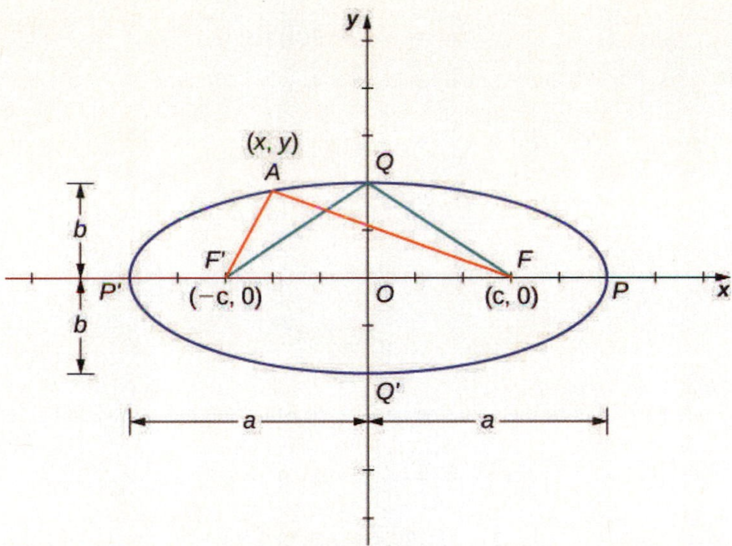


**Figure 7.48** A typical ellipse in which the sum of the distances from any point on the ellipse to the foci is constant.

A graph of a typical ellipse is shown in **Figure 7.48**. In this figure the foci are labeled as $F$ and $F'$. Both are the same fixed distance from the origin, and this distance is represented by the variable $c$. Therefore the coordinates of $F$ are $(c, 0)$ and the coordinates of $F'$ are $(-c, 0)$. The points $P$ and $P'$ are located at the ends of the **major axis** of the ellipse, and have coordinates $(a, 0)$ and $(-a, 0)$, respectively. The major axis is always the longest distance across the ellipse, and can be horizontal or vertical. Thus, the length of the major axis in this ellipse is $2a$. Furthermore, $P$ and $P'$ are called the vertices of the ellipse. The points $Q$ and $Q'$ are located at the ends of the **minor axis** of the ellipse, and have coordinates $(0, b)$ and $(0, -b)$, respectively. The minor axis is the shortest distance across the ellipse. The minor axis is perpendicular to the major axis.

According to the definition of the ellipse, we can choose any point on the ellipse and the sum of the distances from this point to the two foci is constant. Suppose we choose the point $P$. Since the coordinates of point $P$ are $(a, 0)$, the sum of the distances is

$$d(P, F) + d(P, F') = (a - c) + (a + c) = 2a.$$

Therefore the sum of the distances from an arbitrary point $A$ with coordinates $(x, y)$ is also equal to $2a$. Using the distance formula, we get

$$\begin{aligned} d(A, F) + d(A, F') &= 2a \\ \sqrt{(x-c)^2 + y^2} + \sqrt{(x+c)^2 + y^2} &= 2a. \end{aligned}$$

Subtract the second radical from both sides and square both sides:

$$\begin{aligned} \sqrt{(x-c)^2 + y^2} &= 2a - \sqrt{(x+c)^2 + y^2} \\ (x-c)^2 + y^2 &= 4a^2 - 4a\sqrt{(x+c)^2 + y^2} + (x+c)^2 + y^2 \\ x^2 - 2cx + c^2 + y^2 &= 4a^2 - 4a\sqrt{(x+c)^2 + y^2} + x^2 + 2cx + c^2 + y^2 \\ -2cx &= 4a^2 - 4a\sqrt{(x+c)^2 + y^2} + 2cx. \end{aligned}$$

Now isolate the radical on the right-hand side and square again:

$$\begin{aligned}
-2cx &= 4a^2 - 4a\sqrt{(x+c)^2 + y^2} + 2cx \\
4a\sqrt{(x+c)^2 + y^2} &= 4a^2 + 4cx \\
\sqrt{(x+c)^2 + y^2} &= a + \frac{cx}{a} \\
(x+c)^2 + y^2 &= a^2 + 2cx + \frac{c^2x^2}{a^2} \\
x^2 + 2cx + c^2 + y^2 &= a^2 + 2cx + \frac{c^2x^2}{a^2} \\
x^2 + c^2 + y^2 &= a^2 + \frac{c^2x^2}{a^2}.
\end{aligned}$$

Isolate the variables on the left-hand side of the equation and the constants on the right-hand side:

$$\begin{aligned}
x^2 - \frac{c^2x^2}{a^2} + y^2 &= a^2 - c^2 \\
\frac{\left(a^2 - c^2\right)x^2}{a^2} + y^2 &= a^2 - c^2.
\end{aligned}$$

Divide both sides by $a^2 - c^2$. This gives the equation

$$\frac{x^2}{a^2} + \frac{y^2}{a^2 - c^2} = 1.$$

If we refer back to **Figure 7.48**, then the length of each of the two green line segments is equal to $a$. This is true because the sum of the distances from the point $Q$ to the foci $F$ and $F'$ is equal to $2a$, and the lengths of these two line segments are equal. This line segment forms a right triangle with hypotenuse length $a$ and leg lengths $b$ and $c$. From the Pythagorean theorem, $a^2 + b^2 = c^2$ and $b^2 = a^2 - c^2$. Therefore the equation of the ellipse becomes

$$\frac{x^2}{a^2} + \frac{y^2}{b^2} = 1.$$

Finally, if the center of the ellipse is moved from the origin to a point $(h, k)$, we have the following standard form of an ellipse.

### Theorem 7.9: Equation of an Ellipse in Standard Form

Consider the ellipse with center $(h, k)$, a horizontal major axis with length $2a$, and a vertical minor axis with length $2b$. Then the equation of this ellipse in standard form is

$$\frac{(x-h)^2}{a^2} + \frac{(y-k)^2}{b^2} = 1 \tag{7.12}$$

and the foci are located at $(h \pm c, k)$, where $c^2 = a^2 - b^2$. The equations of the directrices are $x = h \pm \frac{a^2}{c}$.

If the major axis is vertical, then the equation of the ellipse becomes

$$\frac{(x-h)^2}{b^2} + \frac{(y-k)^2}{a^2} = 1 \tag{7.13}$$

and the foci are located at $(h, k \pm c)$, where $c^2 = a^2 - b^2$. The equations of the directrices in this case are $y = k \pm \frac{a^2}{c}$.

If the major axis is horizontal, then the ellipse is called horizontal, and if the major axis is vertical, then the ellipse is called vertical. The equation of an ellipse is in general form if it is in the form $Ax^2 + By^2 + Cx + Dy + E = 0,$ where $A$ and $B$ are either both positive or both negative. To convert the equation from general to standard form, use the method of completing the square.

## Example 7.20

### Finding the Standard Form of an Ellipse

Put the equation $9x^2 + 4y^2 - 36x + 24y + 36 = 0$ into standard form and graph the resulting ellipse.

#### Solution

First subtract 36 from both sides of the equation:

$$9x^2 + 4y^2 - 36x + 24y = -36.$$

Next group the $x$ terms together and the $y$ terms together, and factor out the common factor:

$$\begin{aligned}(9x^2 - 36x) + (4y^2 + 24y) &= -36 \\ 9(x^2 - 4x) + 4(y^2 + 6y) &= -36.\end{aligned}$$

We need to determine the constant that, when added inside each set of parentheses, results in a perfect square. In the first set of parentheses, take half the coefficient of $x$ and square it. This gives $\left(\frac{-4}{2}\right)^2 = 4.$ In the second set of parentheses, take half the coefficient of $y$ and square it. This gives $\left(\frac{6}{2}\right)^2 = 9.$ Add these inside each pair of parentheses. Since the first set of parentheses has a 9 in front, we are actually adding 36 to the left-hand side. Similarly, we are adding 36 to the second set as well. Therefore the equation becomes

$$\begin{aligned}9(x^2 - 4x + 4) + 4(y^2 + 6y + 9) &= -36 + 36 + 36 \\ 9(x^2 - 4x + 4) + 4(y^2 + 6y + 9) &= 36.\end{aligned}$$

Now factor both sets of parentheses and divide by 36:

$$\begin{aligned}9(x-2)^2 + 4(y+3)^2 &= 36 \\ \frac{9(x-2)^2}{36} + \frac{4(y+3)^2}{36} &= 1 \\ \frac{(x-2)^2}{4} + \frac{(y+3)^2}{9} &= 1.\end{aligned}$$

The equation is now in standard form. Comparing this to **Equation 7.14** gives $h = 2,$ $k = -3,$ $a = 3,$ and $b = 2.$ This is a vertical ellipse with center at $(2, -3),$ major axis 6, and minor axis 4. The graph of this ellipse appears as follows.

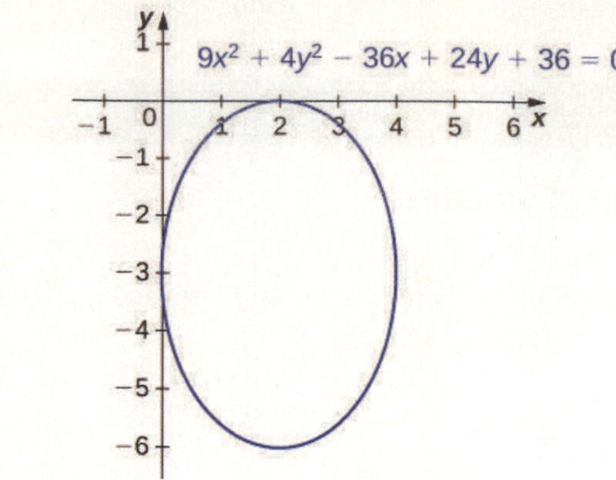


**Figure 7.49** The ellipse in **Example 7.20**.

**7.19** Put the equation $9x^2 + 16y^2 + 18x - 64y - 71 = 0$ into standard form and graph the resulting ellipse.

According to Kepler's first law of planetary motion, the orbit of a planet around the Sun is an ellipse with the Sun at one of the foci as shown in **Figure 7.50**(a). Because Earth's orbit is an ellipse, the distance from the Sun varies throughout the year. A commonly held misconception is that Earth is closer to the Sun in the summer. In fact, in summer for the northern hemisphere, Earth is farther from the Sun than during winter. The difference in season is caused by the tilt of Earth's axis in the orbital plane. Comets that orbit the Sun, such as Halley's Comet, also have elliptical orbits, as do moons orbiting the planets and satellites orbiting Earth.

Ellipses also have interesting reflective properties: A light ray emanating from one focus passes through the other focus after mirror reflection in the ellipse. The same thing occurs with a sound wave as well. The National Statuary Hall in the U.S. Capitol in Washington, DC, is a famous room in an elliptical shape as shown in **Figure 7.50**(b). This hall served as the meeting place for the U.S. House of Representatives for almost fifty years. The location of the two foci of this semi-elliptical room are clearly identified by marks on the floor, and even if the room is full of visitors, when two people stand on these spots and speak to each other, they can hear each other much more clearly than they can hear someone standing close by. Legend has it that John Quincy Adams had his desk located on one of the foci and was able to eavesdrop on everyone else in the House without ever needing to stand. Although this makes a good story, it is unlikely to be true, because the original ceiling produced so many echoes that the entire room had to be hung with carpets to dampen the noise. The ceiling was rebuilt in 1902 and only then did the now-famous whispering effect emerge. Another famous whispering gallery—the site of many marriage proposals—is in Grand Central Station in New York City.

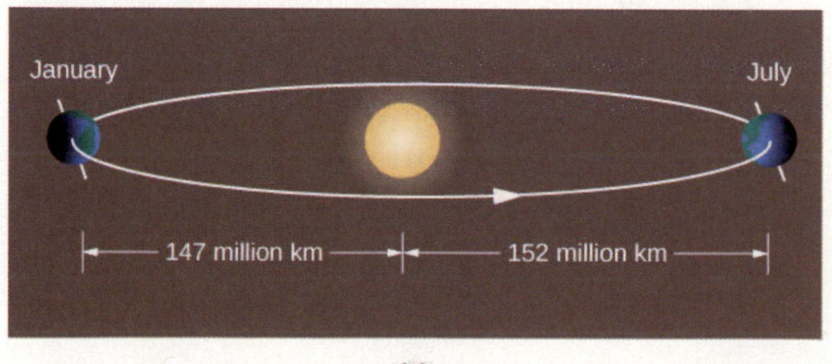


(a)

(b)

**Figure 7.50** (a) Earth's orbit around the Sun is an ellipse with the Sun at one focus. (b) Statuary Hall in the U.S. Capitol is a whispering gallery with an elliptical cross section.

## Hyperbolas

A hyperbola can also be defined in terms of distances. In the case of a hyperbola, there are two foci and two directrices. Hyperbolas also have two asymptotes.

### Definition

A hyperbola is the set of all points where the difference between their distances from two fixed points (the foci) is constant.

A graph of a typical hyperbola appears as follows.

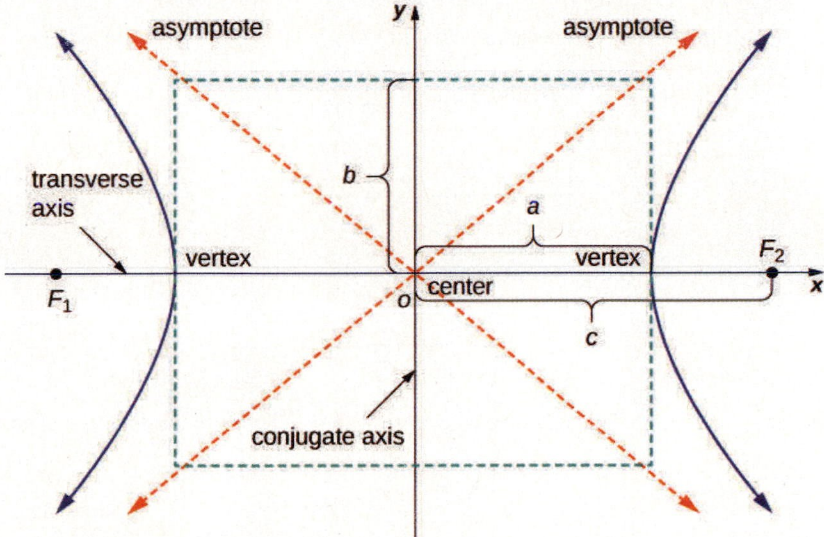


**Figure 7.51** A typical hyperbola in which the difference of the distances from any point on the ellipse to the foci is constant. The transverse axis is also called the major axis, and the conjugate axis is also called the minor axis.

The derivation of the equation of a hyperbola in standard form is virtually identical to that of an ellipse. One slight hitch lies in the definition: The difference between two numbers is always positive. Let $P$ be a point on the hyperbola with coordinates $(x, y)$. Then the definition of the hyperbola gives $|d(P, F_1) - d(P, F_2)| = \text{constant}$. To simplify the derivation, assume that $P$ is on the right branch of the hyperbola, so the absolute value bars drop. If it is on the left branch, then the subtraction is reversed. The vertex of the right branch has coordinates $(a, 0)$, so

$$d(P, F_1) - d(P, F_2) = (c + a) - (c - a) = 2a.$$

This equation is therefore true for any point on the hyperbola. Returning to the coordinates $(x, y)$ for $P$:

$$\begin{aligned} d(P, F_1) - d(P, F_2) &= 2a \\ \sqrt{(x+c)^2 + y^2} - \sqrt{(x-c)^2 + y^2} &= 2a. \end{aligned}$$

Add the second radical from both sides and square both sides:

$$\begin{aligned} \sqrt{(x-c)^2 + y^2} &= 2a + \sqrt{(x+c)^2 + y^2} \\ (x-c)^2 + y^2 &= 4a^2 + 4a\sqrt{(x+c)^2 + y^2} + (x+c)^2 + y^2 \\ x^2 - 2cx + c^2 + y^2 &= 4a^2 + 4a\sqrt{(x+c)^2 + y^2} + x^2 + 2cx + c^2 + y^2 \\ -2cx &= 4a^2 + 4a\sqrt{(x+c)^2 + y^2} + 2cx. \end{aligned}$$

Now isolate the radical on the right-hand side and square again:

$$\begin{aligned}
-2cx &= 4a^2 + 4a\sqrt{(x+c)^2 + y^2} + 2cx \\
4a\sqrt{(x+c)^2 + y^2} &= -4a^2 - 4cx \\
\sqrt{(x+c)^2 + y^2} &= -a - \frac{cx}{a} \\
(x+c)^2 + y^2 &= a^2 + 2cx + \frac{c^2x^2}{a^2} \\
x^2 + 2cx + c^2 + y^2 &= a^2 + 2cx + \frac{c^2x^2}{a^2} \\
x^2 + c^2 + y^2 &= a^2 + \frac{c^2x^2}{a^2}.
\end{aligned}$$

Isolate the variables on the left-hand side of the equation and the constants on the right-hand side:

$$\begin{aligned}
x^2 - \frac{c^2x^2}{a^2} + y^2 &= a^2 - c^2 \\
\frac{(a^2 - c^2)x^2}{a^2} + y^2 &= a^2 - c^2.
\end{aligned}$$

Finally, divide both sides by $a^2 - c^2$. This gives the equation

$$\frac{x^2}{a^2} + \frac{y^2}{a^2 - c^2} = 1.$$

We now define $b$ so that $b^2 = c^2 - a^2$. This is possible because $c > a$. Therefore the equation of the ellipse becomes

$$\frac{x^2}{a^2} - \frac{y^2}{b^2} = 1.$$

Finally, if the center of the hyperbola is moved from the origin to the point $(h, k)$, we have the following standard form of a hyperbola.

## Theorem 7.10: Equation of a Hyperbola in Standard Form

Consider the hyperbola with center $(h, k)$, a horizontal major axis, and a vertical minor axis. Then the equation of this ellipse is

$$\frac{(x-h)^2}{a^2} - \frac{(y-k)^2}{b^2} = 1 \tag{7.14}$$

and the foci are located at $(h \pm c, k)$, where $c^2 = a^2 + b^2$. The equations of the asymptotes are given by $y = k \pm \frac{b}{a}(x - h)$. The equations of the directrices are

$$x = k \pm \frac{a^2}{\sqrt{a^2 + b^2}} = h \pm \frac{a^2}{c}.$$

If the major axis is vertical, then the equation of the hyperbola becomes

$$\frac{(y-k)^2}{a^2} - \frac{(x-h)^2}{b^2} = 1 \tag{7.15}$$

and the foci are located at $(h, k \pm c)$, where $c^2 = a^2 + b^2$. The equations of the asymptotes are given by $y = k \pm \frac{a}{b}(x - h)$. The equations of the directrices are

$$y = k \pm \frac{a^2}{\sqrt{a^2+b^2}} = k \pm \frac{a^2}{c}.$$

If the major axis (transverse axis) is horizontal, then the hyperbola is called horizontal, and if the major axis is vertical then the hyperbola is called vertical. The equation of a hyperbola is in general form if it is in the form $Ax^2 + By^2 + Cx + Dy + E = 0,$ where $A$ and $B$ have opposite signs. In order to convert the equation from general to standard form, use the method of completing the square.

## Example 7.21

### Finding the Standard Form of a Hyperbola

Put the equation $9x^2 - 16y^2 + 36x + 32y - 124 = 0$ into standard form and graph the resulting hyperbola. What are the equations of the asymptotes?

#### Solution

First add 124 to both sides of the equation:

$$9x^2 - 16y^2 + 36x + 32y = 124.$$

Next group the $x$ terms together and the $y$ terms together, then factor out the common factors:

$$\begin{aligned} \left(9x^2 + 36x\right) - \left(16y^2 - 32y\right) &= 124 \\ 9\left(x^2 + 4x\right) - 16\left(y^2 - 2y\right) &= 124. \end{aligned}$$

We need to determine the constant that, when added inside each set of parentheses, results in a perfect square. In the first set of parentheses, take half the coefficient of $x$ and square it. This gives $\left(\frac{4}{2}\right)^2 = 4.$ In the second set of parentheses, take half the coefficient of $y$ and square it. This gives $\left(\frac{-2}{2}\right)^2 = 1.$ Add these inside each pair of parentheses. Since the first set of parentheses has a 9 in front, we are actually adding 36 to the left-hand side. Similarly, we are subtracting 16 from the second set of parentheses. Therefore the equation becomes

$$\begin{aligned} 9\left(x^2 + 4x + 4\right) - 16\left(y^2 - 2y + 1\right) &= 124 + 36 - 16 \\ 9\left(x^2 + 4x + 4\right) - 16\left(y^2 - 2y + 1\right) &= 144. \end{aligned}$$

Next factor both sets of parentheses and divide by 144:

$$\begin{aligned} 9(x+2)^2 - 16(y-1)^2 &= 144 \\ \frac{9(x+2)^2}{144} - \frac{16(y-1)^2}{144} &= 1 \\ \frac{(x+2)^2}{16} - \frac{(y-1)^2}{9} &= 1. \end{aligned}$$

The equation is now in standard form. Comparing this to **Equation 7.15** gives $h = -2,$ $k = 1,$ $a = 4,$ and $b = 3.$ This is a horizontal hyperbola with center at $(-2, 1)$ and asymptotes given by the equations $y = 1 \pm \frac{3}{4}(x+2).$ The graph of this hyperbola appears in the following figure.

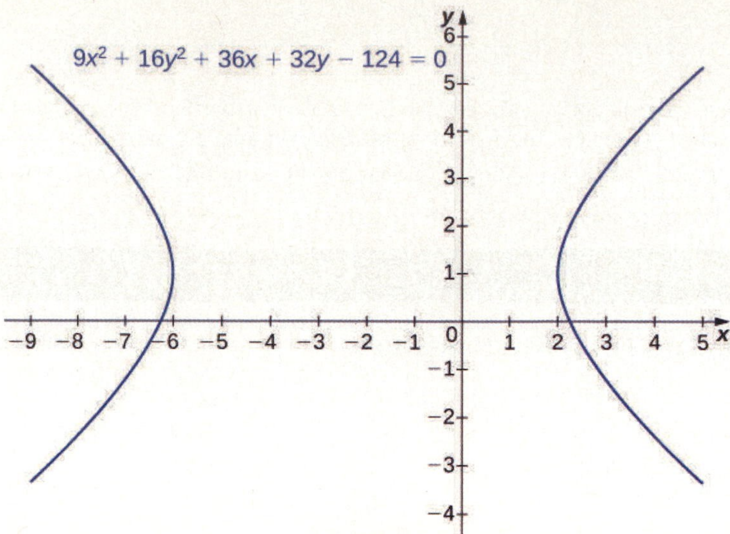


Figure 7.52 Graph of the hyperbola in Example 7.21.

**7.20** Put the equation $4y^2 - 9x^2 + 16y + 18x - 29 = 0$ into standard form and graph the resulting hyperbola. What are the equations of the asymptotes?

Hyperbolas also have interesting reflective properties. A ray directed toward one focus of a hyperbola is reflected by a hyperbolic mirror toward the other focus. This concept is illustrated in the following figure.

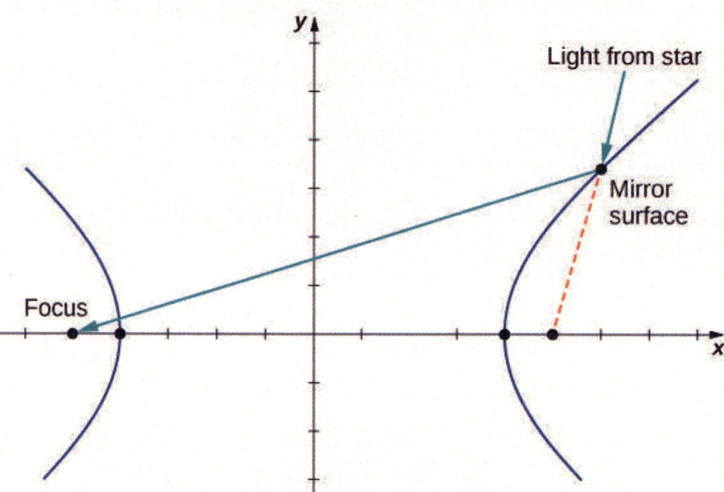


Figure 7.53 A hyperbolic mirror used to collect light from distant stars.

This property of the hyperbola has important applications. It is used in radio direction finding (since the difference in signals from two towers is constant along hyperbolas), and in the construction of mirrors inside telescopes (to reflect light coming from the parabolic mirror to the eyepiece). Another interesting fact about hyperbolas is that for a comet entering the solar system, if the speed is great enough to escape the Sun's gravitational pull, then the path that the comet takes as it passes through the solar system is hyperbolic.

## Eccentricity and Directrix

An alternative way to describe a conic section involves the directrices, the foci, and a new property called eccentricity. We will see that the value of the eccentricity of a conic section can uniquely define that conic.

### Definition

The **eccentricity** $e$ of a conic section is defined to be the distance from any point on the conic section to its focus, divided by the perpendicular distance from that point to the nearest directrix. This value is constant for any conic section, and can define the conic section as well:

1. If $e = 1,$ the conic is a parabola.
2. If $e < 1,$ it is an ellipse.
3. If $e > 1,$ it is a hyperbola.

The eccentricity of a circle is zero. The directrix of a conic section is the line that, together with the point known as the focus, serves to define a conic section. Hyperbolas and noncircular ellipses have two foci and two associated directrices. Parabolas have one focus and one directrix.

The three conic sections with their directrices appear in the following figure.

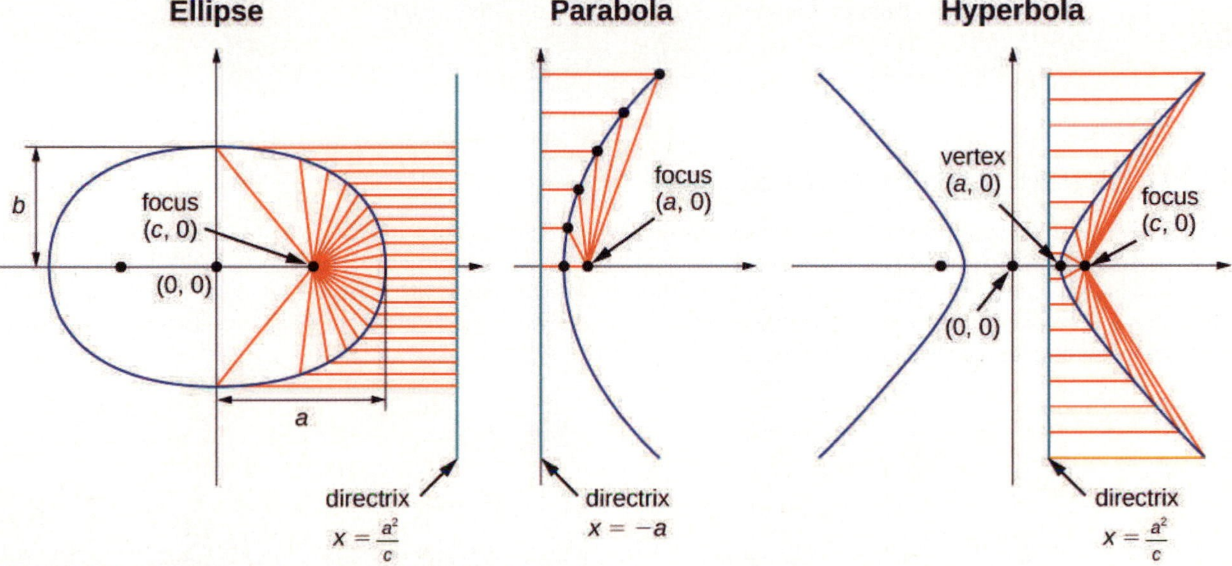


**Figure 7.54** The three conic sections with their foci and directrices.

Recall from the definition of a parabola that the distance from any point on the parabola to the focus is equal to the distance from that same point to the directrix. Therefore, by definition, the eccentricity of a parabola must be 1. The equations of the directrices of a horizontal ellipse are $x = \pm\frac{a^2}{c}.$ The right vertex of the ellipse is located at $(a, 0)$ and the right focus is $(c, 0).$ Therefore the distance from the vertex to the focus is $a - c$ and the distance from the vertex to the right directrix is $\frac{a^2}{c} - c.$ This gives the eccentricity as

$$e = \frac{a - c}{\frac{a^2}{c} - a} = \frac{c(a - c)}{a^2 - ac} = \frac{c(a - c)}{a(a - c)} = \frac{c}{a}.$$

Since $c < a,$ this step proves that the eccentricity of an ellipse is less than 1. The directrices of a horizontal hyperbola are also located at $x = \pm\frac{a^2}{c},$ and a similar calculation shows that the eccentricity of a hyperbola is also $e = \frac{c}{a}.$ However in this case we have $c > a,$ so the eccentricity of a hyperbola is greater than 1.

## Example 7.22

### Determining Eccentricity of a Conic Section

Determine the eccentricity of the ellipse described by the equation

$$\frac{(x-3)^2}{16}+\frac{(y+2)^2}{25}=1.$$

#### Solution

From the equation we see that $a=5$ and $b=4$. The value of $c$ can be calculated using the equation $a^2=b^2+c^2$ for an ellipse. Substituting the values of $a$ and $b$ and solving for $c$ gives $c=3$. Therefore the eccentricity of the ellipse is $e=\frac{c}{a}=\frac{3}{5}=0.6$.

**7.21** Determine the eccentricity of the hyperbola described by the equation

$$\frac{(y-3)^2}{49}-\frac{(x+2)^2}{25}=1.$$

## Polar Equations of Conic Sections

Sometimes it is useful to write or identify the equation of a conic section in polar form. To do this, we need the concept of the focal parameter. The **focal parameter** of a conic section $p$ is defined as the distance from a focus to the nearest directrix. The following table gives the focal parameters for the different types of conics, where $a$ is the length of the semi-major axis (i.e., half the length of the major axis), $c$ is the distance from the origin to the focus, and $e$ is the eccentricity. In the case of a parabola, $a$ represents the distance from the vertex to the focus.

| Conic | e | p |
|---|---|---|
| Ellipse | $0<e<1$ | $\frac{a^2-c^2}{c}=\frac{a(1-e^2)}{c}$ |
| Parabola | $e=1$ | $2a$ |
| Hyperbola | $e>1$ | $\frac{c^2-a^2}{c}=\frac{a(e^2-1)}{e}$ |

**Table 7.7** Eccentricities and Focal Parameters of the Conic Sections

Using the definitions of the focal parameter and eccentricity of the conic section, we can derive an equation for any conic section in polar coordinates. In particular, we assume that one of the foci of a given conic section lies at the pole. Then using the definition of the various conic sections in terms of distances, it is possible to prove the following theorem.

### Theorem 7.11: Polar Equation of Conic Sections

The polar equation of a conic section with focal parameter $p$ is given by

$$r=\frac{ep}{1\pm e\cos\theta}\text{ or }r=\frac{ep}{1\pm e\sin\theta}.$$

In the equation on the left, the major axis of the conic section is horizontal, and in the equation on the right, the major axis is vertical. To work with a conic section written in polar form, first make the constant term in the denominator equal to 1. This can be done by dividing both the numerator and the denominator of the fraction by the constant that appears in front of the plus or minus in the denominator. Then the coefficient of the sine or cosine in the denominator is the eccentricity. This value identifies the conic. If cosine appears in the denominator, then the conic is horizontal. If sine appears, then the conic is vertical. If both appear then the axes are rotated. The center of the conic is not necessarily at the origin. The center is at the origin only if the conic is a circle (i.e., $e = 0$).

## Example 7.23

### Graphing a Conic Section in Polar Coordinates

Identify and create a graph of the conic section described by the equation

$$r = \frac{3}{1 + 2\cos\theta}.$$

### Solution

The constant term in the denominator is 1, so the eccentricity of the conic is 2. This is a hyperbola. The focal parameter $p$ can be calculated by using the equation $ep = 3$. Since $e = 2$, this gives $p = \frac{3}{2}$. The cosine function appears in the denominator, so the hyperbola is horizontal. Pick a few values for $\theta$ and create a table of values. Then we can graph the hyperbola (**Figure 7.55**).

| $\theta$ | $r$ | $\theta$ | $r$ |
|---|---|---|---|
| 0 | 1 | $\pi$ | −3 |
| $\frac{\pi}{4}$ | $\frac{3}{1+\sqrt{2}} \approx 1.2426$ | $\frac{5\pi}{4}$ | $\frac{3}{1-\sqrt{2}} \approx -7.2426$ |
| $\frac{\pi}{2}$ | 3 | $\frac{3\pi}{2}$ | 3 |
| $\frac{3\pi}{4}$ | $\frac{3}{1-\sqrt{2}} \approx -7.2426$ | $\frac{7\pi}{4}$ | $\frac{3}{1+\sqrt{2}} \approx 1.2426$ |

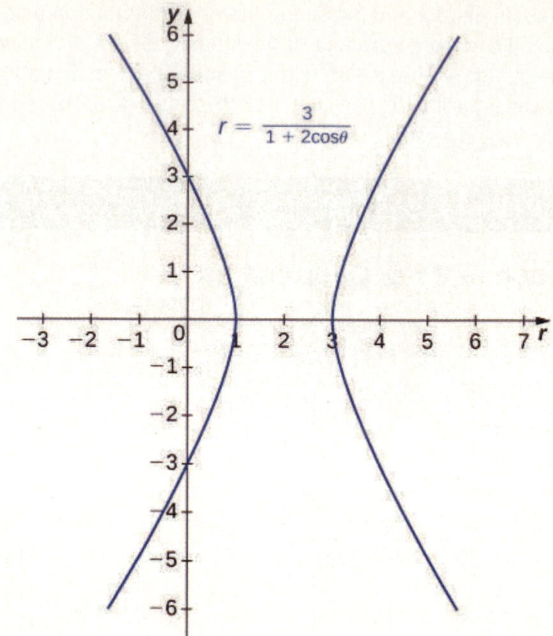


**Figure 7.55** Graph of the hyperbola described in **Example 7.23**.

**7.22** Identify and create a graph of the conic section described by the equation

$$r = \frac{4}{1 - 0.8 \sin \theta}.$$

## General Equations of Degree Two

A general equation of degree two can be written in the form

$$Ax^2 + Bxy + Cy^2 + Dx + Ey + F = 0.$$

The graph of an equation of this form is a conic section. If $B \neq 0$ then the coordinate axes are rotated. To identify the conic section, we use the **discriminant** of the conic section $4AC - B^2$. One of the following cases must be true:

1. $4AC - B^2 > 0$. If so, the graph is an ellipse.
2. $4AC - B^2 = 0$. If so, the graph is a parabola.
3. $4AC - B^2 < 0$. If so, the graph is a hyperbola.

The simplest example of a second-degree equation involving a cross term is $xy = 1$. This equation can be solved for $y$ to obtain $y = \frac{1}{x}$. The graph of this function is called a *rectangular hyperbola* as shown.

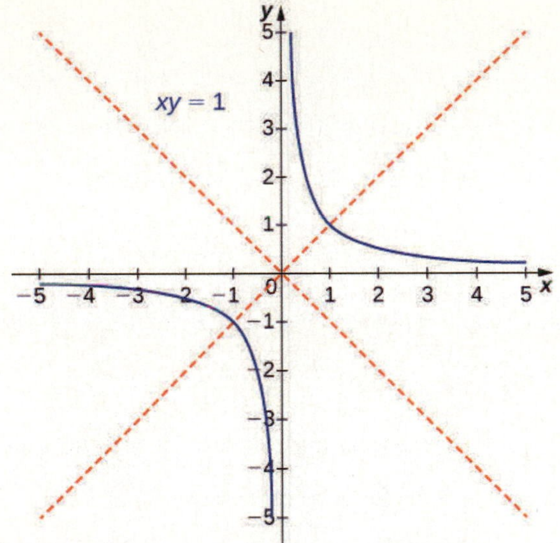


**Figure 7.56** Graph of the equation $xy = 1$; The red lines indicate the rotated axes.

The asymptotes of this hyperbola are the *x* and *y* coordinate axes. To determine the angle $\theta$ of rotation of the conic section, we use the formula $\cot 2\theta = \frac{A - C}{B}$. In this case $A = C = 0$ and $B = 1$, so $\cot 2\theta = (0 - 0)/1 = 0$ and $\theta = 45°$.

The method for graphing a conic section with rotated axes involves determining the coefficients of the conic in the rotated coordinate system. The new coefficients are labeled $A', B', C', D', E',$ and $F'$, and are given by the formulas

$$\begin{aligned} A' &= A\cos^2\theta + B\cos\theta\sin\theta + C\sin^2\theta \\ B' &= 0 \\ C' &= A\sin^2\theta - B\sin\theta\cos\theta + C\cos^2\theta \\ D' &= D\cos\theta + E\sin\theta \\ E' &= -D\sin\theta + E\cos\theta \\ F' &= F. \end{aligned}$$

The procedure for graphing a rotated conic is the following:

1. Identify the conic section using the discriminant $4AC - B^2$.
2. Determine $\theta$ using the formula $\cot 2\theta = \frac{A - C}{B}$.
3. Calculate $A', B', C', D', E',$ and $F'$.
4. Rewrite the original equation using $A', B', C', D', E',$ and $F'$.
5. Draw a graph using the rotated equation.

## Example 7.24

### Identifying a Rotated Conic

Identify the conic and calculate the angle of rotation of axes for the curve described by the equation

$$13x^2 - 6\sqrt{3}xy + 7y^2 - 256 = 0.$$

#### Solution

In this equation, $A = 13, B = -6\sqrt{3}, C = 7, D = 0, E = 0,$ and $F = -256.$ The discriminant of this equation is $4AC - B^2 = 4(13)(7) - (-6\sqrt{3})^2 = 364 - 108 = 256.$ Therefore this conic is an ellipse. To calculate the angle of rotation of the axes, use $\cot 2\theta = \frac{A - C}{B}.$ This gives

$$\begin{aligned} \cot 2\theta &= \frac{A - C}{B} \\ &= \frac{13 - 7}{-6\sqrt{3}} \\ &= -\frac{\sqrt{3}}{3}. \end{aligned}$$

Therefore $2\theta = 120^{\circ}$ and $\theta = 60^{\circ},$ which is the angle of the rotation of the axes.

To determine the rotated coefficients, use the formulas given above:

$$\begin{aligned} A' &= A\cos^2\theta + B\cos\theta\sin\theta + C\sin^2\theta \\ &= 13\cos^2 60 + (-6\sqrt{3})\cos 60\sin 60 + 7\sin^2 60 \\ &= 13\left(\frac{1}{2}\right)^2 - 6\sqrt{3}\left(\frac{1}{2}\right)\left(\frac{\sqrt{3}}{2}\right) + 7\left(\frac{\sqrt{3}}{2}\right)^2 \\ &= 4, \\ B' &= 0, \\ C' &= A\sin^2\theta - B\sin\theta\cos\theta + C\cos^2\theta \\ &= 13\sin^2 60 + (-6\sqrt{3})\sin 60\cos 60 = 7\cos^2 60 \\ &= \left(\frac{\sqrt{3}}{2}\right)^2 + 6\sqrt{3}\left(\frac{\sqrt{3}}{2}\right)\left(\frac{1}{2}\right) + 7\left(\frac{1}{2}\right)^2 \\ &= 16, \\ D' &= D\cos\theta + E\sin\theta \\ &= (0)\cos 60 + (0)\sin 60 \\ &= 0, \\ E' &= -D\sin\theta + E\cos\theta \\ &= -(0)\sin 60 + (0)\cos 60 \\ &= 0, \\ F' &= F \\ &= -256. \end{aligned}$$

The equation of the conic in the rotated coordinate system becomes

$$\begin{aligned} 4(x')^2 + 16(y')^2 &= 256 \\ \frac{(x')^2}{64} + \frac{(y')^2}{16} &= 1. \end{aligned}$$

A graph of this conic section appears as follows.

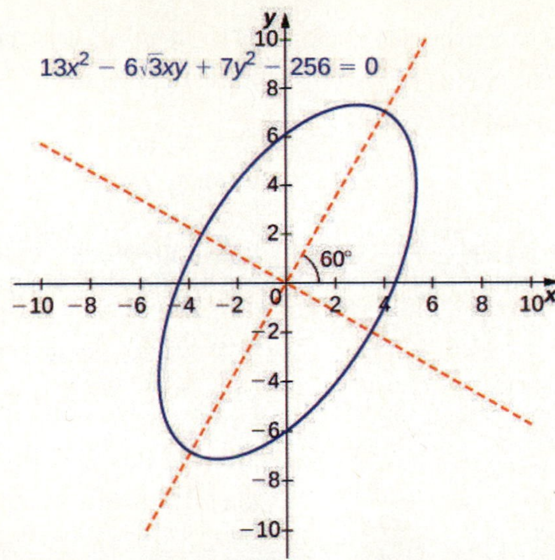


**Figure 7.57** Graph of the ellipse described by the equation $13x^2 - 6\sqrt{3}xy + 7y^2 - 256 = 0$. The axes are rotated $60°$. The red dashed lines indicate the rotated axes.

**7.23** Identify the conic and calculate the angle of rotation of axes for the curve described by the equation

$$3x^2 + 5xy - 2y^2 - 125 = 0.$$

# 7.5 EXERCISES

For the following exercises, determine the equation of the parabola using the information given.

255. Focus $(4, 0)$ and directrix $x = -4$

256. Focus $(0, -3)$ and directrix $y = 3$

257. Focus $(0, 0.5)$ and directrix $y = -0.5$

258. Focus $(2, 3)$ and directrix $x = -2$

259. Focus $(0, 2)$ and directrix $y = 4$

260. Focus $(-1, 4)$ and directrix $x = 5$

261. Focus $(-3, 5)$ and directrix $y = 1$

262. Focus $\left(\frac{5}{2}, -4\right)$ and directrix $x = \frac{7}{2}$

For the following exercises, determine the equation of the ellipse using the information given.

263. Endpoints of major axis at $(4, 0), (-4, 0)$ and foci located at $(2, 0), (-2, 0)$

264. Endpoints of major axis at $(0, 5), (0, -5)$ and foci located at $(0, 3), (0, -3)$

265. Endpoints of major axis at $(0, 2), (0, -2)$ and foci located at $(3, 0), (-3, 0)$

266. Endpoints of major axis at $(-3, 3), (7, 3)$ and foci located at $(-2, 3), (6, 3)$

267. Endpoints of major axis at $(-3, 5), (-3, -3)$ and foci located at $(-3, 3), (-3, -1)$

268. Endpoints of major axis at $(0, 0), (0, 4)$ and foci located at $(5, 2), (-5, 2)$

269. Foci located at $(2, 0), (-2, 0)$ and eccentricity of $\frac{1}{2}$

270. Foci located at $(0, -3), (0, 3)$ and eccentricity of $\frac{3}{4}$

For the following exercises, determine the equation of the hyperbola using the information given.

271. Vertices located at $(5, 0), (-5, 0)$ and foci located at $(6, 0), (-6, 0)$

272. Vertices located at $(0, 2), (0, -2)$ and foci located at $(0, 3), (0, -3)$

273. Endpoints of the conjugate axis located at $(0, 3), (0, -3)$ and foci located $(4, 0), (-4, 0)$

274. Vertices located at $(0, 1), (6, 1)$ and focus located at $(8, 1)$

275. Vertices located at $(-2, 0), (-2, -4)$ and focus located at $(-2, -8)$

276. Endpoints of the conjugate axis located at $(3, 2), (3, 4)$ and focus located at $(3, 7)$

277. Foci located at $(6, -0), (6, 0)$ and eccentricity of 3

278. $(0, 10), (0, -10)$ and eccentricity of 2.5

For the following exercises, consider the following polar equations of conics. Determine the eccentricity and identify the conic.

279. $r = \frac{-1}{1 + \cos\theta}$

280. $r = \frac{8}{2 - \sin\theta}$

281. $r = \frac{5}{2 + \sin\theta}$

282. $r = \frac{5}{-1 + 2\sin\theta}$

283. $r = \frac{3}{2 - 6\sin\theta}$

284. $r = \frac{3}{-4 + 3\sin\theta}$

For the following exercises, find a polar equation of the conic with focus at the origin and eccentricity and directrix as given.

285. Directrix: $x = 4$; $e = \frac{1}{5}$

286. Directrix: $x = -4$; $e = 5$

287. Directrix: $y = 2$; $e = 2$

288. Directrix: $y = -2$; $e = \frac{1}{2}$

For the following exercises, sketch the graph of each conic.

289. $r = \frac{1}{1 + \sin\theta}$

290. $r = \frac{1}{1 - \cos\theta}$

291. $r = \frac{4}{1 + \cos\theta}$

292. $r = \frac{10}{5 + 4\sin\theta}$

293. $r = \frac{15}{3 - 2\cos\theta}$

294. $r = \frac{32}{3 + 5\sin\theta}$

295. $r(2 + \sin\theta) = 4$

296. $r = \frac{3}{2 + 6\sin\theta}$

297. $r = \frac{3}{-4 + 2\sin\theta}$

298. $\frac{x^2}{9} + \frac{y^2}{4} = 1$

299. $\frac{x^2}{4} + \frac{y^2}{16} = 1$

300. $4x^2 + 9y^2 = 36$

301. $25x^2 - 4y^2 = 100$

302. $\frac{x^2}{16} - \frac{y^2}{9} = 1$

303. $x^2 = 12y$

304. $y^2 = 20x$

305. $12x = 5y^2$

For the following equations, determine which of the conic sections is described.

306. $xy = 4$

307. $x^2 + 4xy - 2y^2 - 6 = 0$

308. $x^2 + 2\sqrt{3}xy + 3y^2 - 6 = 0$

309. $x^2 - xy + y^2 - 2 = 0$

310. $34x^2 - 24xy + 41y^2 - 25 = 0$

311. $52x^2 - 72xy + 73y^2 + 40x + 30y - 75 = 0$

312. The mirror in an automobile headlight has a parabolic cross section, with the lightbulb at the focus. On a schematic, the equation of the parabola is given as $x^2 = 4y$. At what coordinates should you place the lightbulb?

313. A satellite dish is shaped like a paraboloid of revolution. The receiver is to be located at the focus. If the dish is 12 feet across at its opening and 4 feet deep at its center, where should the receiver be placed?

314. Consider the satellite dish of the preceding problem. If the dish is 8 feet across at the opening and 2 feet deep, where should we place the receiver?

315. A searchlight is shaped like a paraboloid of revolution. A light source is located 1 foot from the base along the axis of symmetry. If the opening of the searchlight is 3 feet across, find the depth.

316. Whispering galleries are rooms designed with elliptical ceilings. A person standing at one focus can whisper and be heard by a person standing at the other focus because all the sound waves that reach the ceiling are reflected to the other person. If a whispering gallery has a length of 120 feet and the foci are located 30 feet from the center, find the height of the ceiling at the center.

317. A person is standing 8 feet from the nearest wall in a whispering gallery. If that person is at one focus and the other focus is 80 feet away, what is the length and the height at the center of the gallery?

For the following exercises, determine the polar equation form of the orbit given the length of the major axis and eccentricity for the orbits of the comets or planets. Distance is given in astronomical units (AU).

318. Halley's Comet: length of major axis = 35.88, eccentricity = 0.967

319. Hale-Bopp Comet: length of major axis = 525.91, eccentricity = 0.995

320. Mars: length of major axis = 3.049, eccentricity = 0.0934

321. Jupiter: length of major axis = 10.408, eccentricity = 0.0484

# CHAPTER 7 REVIEW

## KEY TERMS

**angular coordinate** $\theta$ the angle formed by a line segment connecting the origin to a point in the polar coordinate system with the positive radial ($x$) axis, measured counterclockwise

**cardioid** a plane curve traced by a point on the perimeter of a circle that is rolling around a fixed circle of the same radius; the equation of a cardioid is $r = a(1 + \sin\theta)$ or $r = a(1 + \cos\theta)$

**conic section** a conic section is any curve formed by the intersection of a plane with a cone of two nappes

**cusp** a pointed end or part where two curves meet

**cycloid** the curve traced by a point on the rim of a circular wheel as the wheel rolls along a straight line without slippage

**directrix** a directrix (plural: directrices) is a line used to construct and define a conic section; a parabola has one directrix; ellipses and hyperbolas have two

**discriminant** the value $4AC - B^2$, which is used to identify a conic when the equation contains a term involving $xy$, is called a discriminant

**eccentricity** the eccentricity is defined as the distance from any point on the conic section to its focus divided by the perpendicular distance from that point to the nearest directrix

**focal parameter** the focal parameter is the distance from a focus of a conic section to the nearest directrix

**focus** a focus (plural: foci) is a point used to construct and define a conic section; a parabola has one focus; an ellipse and a hyperbola have two

**general form** an equation of a conic section written as a general second-degree equation

**limaçon** the graph of the equation $r = a + b\sin\theta$ or $r = a + b\cos\theta$. If $a = b$ then the graph is a cardioid

**major axis** the major axis of a conic section passes through the vertex in the case of a parabola or through the two vertices in the case of an ellipse or hyperbola; it is also an axis of symmetry of the conic; also called the transverse axis

**minor axis** the minor axis is perpendicular to the major axis and intersects the major axis at the center of the conic, or at the vertex in the case of the parabola; also called the conjugate axis

**nappe** a nappe is one half of a double cone

**orientation** the direction that a point moves on a graph as the parameter increases

**parameter** an independent variable that both $x$ and $y$ depend on in a parametric curve; usually represented by the variable $t$

**parameterization of a curve** rewriting the equation of a curve defined by a function $y = f(x)$ as parametric equations

**parametric curve** the graph of the parametric equations $x(t)$ and $y(t)$ over an interval $a \le t \le b$ combined with the equations

**parametric equations** the equations $x = x(t)$ and $y = y(t)$ that define a parametric curve

**polar axis** the horizontal axis in the polar coordinate system corresponding to $r \ge 0$

**polar coordinate system** a system for locating points in the plane. The coordinates are $r$, the radial coordinate, and $\theta$, the angular coordinate

**polar equation** an equation or function relating the radial coordinate to the angular coordinate in the polar coordinate system

**pole** the central point of the polar coordinate system, equivalent to the origin of a Cartesian system

**radial coordinate** $r$ the coordinate in the polar coordinate system that measures the distance from a point in the plane to the pole

**rose** graph of the polar equation $r = a\cos 2\theta$ or $r = a\sin 2\theta$ for a positive constant $a$

**space-filling curve** a curve that completely occupies a two-dimensional subset of the real plane

**standard form** an equation of a conic section showing its properties, such as location of the vertex or lengths of major and minor axes

**vertex** a vertex is an extreme point on a conic section; a parabola has one vertex at its turning point. An ellipse has two vertices, one at each end of the major axis; a hyperbola has two vertices, one at the turning point of each branch

# KEY EQUATIONS

- **Derivative of parametric equations**
  $$\frac{dy}{dx} = \frac{dy/dt}{dx/dt} = \frac{y'(t)}{x'(t)}$$
- **Second-order derivative of parametric equations**
  $$\frac{d^2y}{dx^2} = \frac{d}{dx}\left(\frac{dy}{dx}\right) = \frac{(d/dt)(dy/dx)}{dx/dt}$$
- **Area under a parametric curve**
  $$A = \int_a^b y(t)x'(t)\,dt$$
- **Arc length of a parametric curve**
  $$s = \int_{t_1}^{t_2} \sqrt{\left(\frac{dx}{dt}\right)^2 + \left(\frac{dy}{dt}\right)^2}\,dt$$
- **Surface area generated by a parametric curve**
  $$S = 2\pi \int_a^b y(t)\sqrt{(x'(t))^2 + (y'(t))^2}\,dt$$
- **Area of a region bounded by a polar curve**
  $$A = \frac{1}{2}\int_\alpha^\beta [f(\theta)]^2\,d\theta = \frac{1}{2}\int_\alpha^\beta r^2\,d\theta$$
- **Arc length of a polar curve**
  $$L = \int_\alpha^\beta \sqrt{[f(\theta)]^2 + [f'(\theta)]^2}\,d\theta = \int_\alpha^\beta \sqrt{r^2 + \left(\frac{dr}{d\theta}\right)^2}\,d\theta$$

# KEY CONCEPTS

## 7.1 Parametric Equations

- Parametric equations provide a convenient way to describe a curve. A parameter can represent time or some other meaningful quantity.
- It is often possible to eliminate the parameter in a parameterized curve to obtain a function or relation describing that curve.
- There is always more than one way to parameterize a curve.
- Parametric equations can describe complicated curves that are difficult or perhaps impossible to describe using rectangular coordinates.

## 7.2 Calculus of Parametric Curves

- The derivative of the parametrically defined curve $x = x(t)$ and $y = y(t)$ can be calculated using the formula $\frac{dy}{dx} = \frac{y'(t)}{x'(t)}$. Using the derivative, we can find the equation of a tangent line to a parametric curve.
- The area between a parametric curve and the $x$-axis can be determined by using the formula $A = \int_{t_1}^{t_2} y(t)x'(t)\,dt$.
- The arc length of a parametric curve can be calculated by using the formula $s = \int_{t_1}^{t_2} \sqrt{\left(\frac{dx}{dt}\right)^2 + \left(\frac{dy}{dt}\right)^2}\,dt$.
- The surface area of a volume of revolution revolved around the $x$-axis is given by $S = 2\pi \int_a^b y(t)\sqrt{(x'(t))^2 + (y'(t))^2}\,dt$. If the curve is revolved around the $y$-axis, then the formula is $S = 2\pi \int_a^b x(t)\sqrt{(x'(t))^2 + (y'(t))^2}\,dt$.

## 7.3 Polar Coordinates

- The polar coordinate system provides an alternative way to locate points in the plane.
- Convert points between rectangular and polar coordinates using the formulas

$$x = r\cos\theta \text{ and } y = r\sin\theta$$

  and

$$r = \sqrt{x^2 + y^2} \text{ and } \tan\theta = \frac{y}{x}.$$

- To sketch a polar curve from a given polar function, make a table of values and take advantage of periodic properties.
- Use the conversion formulas to convert equations between rectangular and polar coordinates.
- Identify symmetry in polar curves, which can occur through the pole, the horizontal axis, or the vertical axis.

## 7.4 Area and Arc Length in Polar Coordinates

- The area of a region in polar coordinates defined by the equation $r = f(\theta)$ with $\alpha \le \theta \le \beta$ is given by the integral $A = \frac{1}{2}\int_\alpha^\beta [f(\theta)]^2\,d\theta$.
- To find the area between two curves in the polar coordinate system, first find the points of intersection, then subtract the corresponding areas.
- The arc length of a polar curve defined by the equation $r = f(\theta)$ with $\alpha \le \theta \le \beta$ is given by the integral $L = \int_\alpha^\beta \sqrt{[f(\theta)]^2 + [f'(\theta)]^2}\,d\theta = \int_\alpha^\beta \sqrt{r^2 + \left(\frac{dr}{d\theta}\right)^2}\,d\theta$.

## 7.5 Conic Sections

- The equation of a vertical parabola in standard form with given focus and directrix is $y = \frac{1}{4p}(x - h)^2 + k$ where $p$ is the distance from the vertex to the focus and $(h, k)$ are the coordinates of the vertex.

- The equation of a horizontal ellipse in standard form is $\frac{(x-h)^2}{a^2}+\frac{(y-k)^2}{b^2}=1$ where the center has coordinates $(h, k)$, the major axis has length $2a$, the minor axis has length $2b$, and the coordinates of the foci are $(h \pm c, k)$, where $c^2 = a^2 - b^2$.
- The equation of a horizontal hyperbola in standard form is $\frac{(x-h)^2}{a^2}-\frac{(y-k)^2}{b^2}=1$ where the center has coordinates $(h, k)$, the vertices are located at $(h \pm a, k)$, and the coordinates of the foci are $(h \pm c, k)$, where $c^2 = a^2 + b^2$.
- The eccentricity of an ellipse is less than 1, the eccentricity of a parabola is equal to 1, and the eccentricity of a hyperbola is greater than 1. The eccentricity of a circle is 0.
- The polar equation of a conic section with eccentricity $e$ is $r = \frac{ep}{1 \pm e\cos\theta}$ or $r = \frac{ep}{1 \pm e\sin\theta}$, where $p$ represents the focal parameter.
- To identify a conic generated by the equation $Ax^2 + Bxy + Cy^2 + Dx + Ey + F = 0$, first calculate the discriminant $D = 4AC - B^2$. If $D > 0$ then the conic is an ellipse, if $D = 0$ then the conic is a parabola, and if $D < 0$ then the conic is a hyperbola.

## CHAPTER 7 REVIEW EXERCISES

*True or False?* Justify your answer with a proof or a counterexample.

**322.** The rectangular coordinates of the point $\left(4, \frac{5\pi}{6}\right)$ are $(2\sqrt{3}, -2)$.

**323.** The equations $x = \cosh(3t)$, $y = 2\sinh(3t)$ represent a hyperbola.

**324.** The arc length of the spiral given by $r = \frac{\theta}{2}$ for $0 \le \theta \le 3\pi$ is $\frac{9}{4}\pi^3$.

**325.** Given $x = f(t)$ and $y = g(t)$, if $\frac{dx}{dy} = \frac{dy}{dx}$, then $f(t) = g(t) + \text{C}$, where C is a constant.

For the following exercises, sketch the parametric curve and eliminate the parameter to find the Cartesian equation of the curve.

**326.** $x = 1 + t$, $y = t^2 - 1$, $-1 \le t \le 1$

**327.** $x = e^t$, $y = 1 - e^{3t}$, $0 \le t \le 1$

**328.** $x = \sin\theta$, $y = 1 - \csc\theta$, $0 \le \theta \le 2\pi$

**329.** $x = 4\cos\phi$, $y = 1 - \sin\phi$, $0 \le \phi \le 2\pi$

For the following exercises, sketch the polar curve and determine what type of symmetry exists, if any.

**330.** $r = 4\sin\left(\frac{\theta}{3}\right)$

**331.** $r = 5\cos(5\theta)$

For the following exercises, find the polar equation for the curve given as a Cartesian equation.

**332.** $x + y = 5$

**333.** $y^2 = 4 + x^2$

For the following exercises, find the equation of the tangent line to the given curve. Graph both the function and its tangent line.

**334.** $x = \ln(t)$, $y = t^2 - 1$, $t = 1$

**335.** $r = 3 + \cos(2\theta)$, $\theta = \frac{3\pi}{4}$

**336.** Find $\frac{dy}{dx}$, $\frac{dx}{dy}$, and $\frac{d^2x}{dy^2}$ of $y = \left(2 + e^{-t}\right)$, $x = 1 - \sin(t)$

For the following exercises, find the area of the region.

**337.** $x = t^2$, $y = \ln(t)$, $0 \le t \le e$

**338.** $r = 1 - \sin\theta$ in the first quadrant

For the following exercises, find the arc length of the curve over the given interval.

**339.** $x = 3t + 4, \quad y = 9t - 2, \quad 0 \le t \le 3$

**340.** $r = 6\cos\theta, \quad 0 \le \theta \le 2\pi.$ Check your answer by geometry.

For the following exercises, find the Cartesian equation describing the given shapes.

**341.** A parabola with focus $(2, -5)$ and directrix $x = 6$

**342.** An ellipse with a major axis length of 10 and foci at $(-7, 2)$ and $(1, 2)$

**343.** A hyperbola with vertices at $(3, -2)$ and $(-5, -2)$ and foci at $(-2, -6)$ and $(-2, 4)$

For the following exercises, determine the eccentricity and identify the conic. Sketch the conic.

**344.** $r = \dfrac{6}{1 + 3\cos(\theta)}$

**345.** $r = \dfrac{4}{3 - 2\cos\theta}$

**346.** $r = \dfrac{7}{5 - 5\cos\theta}$

**347.** Determine the Cartesian equation describing the orbit of Pluto, the most eccentric orbit around the Sun. The length of the major axis is 39.26 AU and minor axis is 38.07 AU. What is the eccentricity?

**348.** The C/1980 E1 comet was observed in 1980. Given an eccentricity of 1.057 and a perihelion (point of closest approach to the Sun) of 3.364 AU, find the Cartesian equations describing the comet's trajectory. Are we guaranteed to see this comet again? (*Hint*: Consider the Sun at point $(0, 0)$.)

# APPENDIX A | TABLE OF INTEGRALS

## Basic Integrals

1. $\int u^n\, du = \frac{u^{n+1}}{n+1} + C,\ n \neq -1$

2. $\int \frac{du}{u} = \ln|u| + C$

3. $\int e^u\, du = e^u + C$

4. $\int a^u\, du = \frac{a^u}{\ln a} + C$

5. $\int \sin u\, du = -\cos u + C$

6. $\int \cos u\, du = \sin u + C$

7. $\int \sec^2 u\, du = \tan u + C$

8. $\int \csc^2 u\, du = -\cot u + C$

9. $\int \sec u \tan u\, du = \sec u + C$

10. $\int \csc u \cot u\, du = -\csc u + C$

11. $\int \tan u\, du = \ln|\sec u| + C$

12. $\int \cot u\, du = \ln|\sin u| + C$

13. $\int \sec u\, du = \ln|\sec u + \tan u| + C$

14. $\int \csc u\, du = \ln|\csc u - \cot u| + C$

15. $\int \frac{du}{\sqrt{a^2 - u^2}} = \sin^{-1}\frac{u}{a} + C$

16. $\int \frac{du}{a^2 + u^2} = \frac{1}{a}\tan^{-1}\frac{u}{a} + C$

17. $\int \frac{du}{u\sqrt{u^2 - a^2}} = \frac{1}{a}\sec^{-1}\frac{u}{a} + C$

## Trigonometric Integrals

18. $\int \sin^2 u\, du = \frac{1}{2}u - \frac{1}{4}\sin 2u + C$

19. $\int \cos^2 u\,du = \frac{1}{2}u + \frac{1}{4}\sin 2u + C$

20. $\int \tan^2 u\,du = \tan u - u + C$

21. $\int \cot^2 u\,du = -\cot u - u + C$

22. $\int \sin^3 u\,du = -\frac{1}{3}\left(2 + \sin^2 u\right)\cos u + C$

23. $\int \cos^3 u\,du = \frac{1}{3}\left(2 + \cos^2 u\right)\sin u + C$

24. $\int \tan^3 u\,du = \frac{1}{2}\tan^2 u + \ln|\cos u| + C$

25. $\int \cot^3 u\,du = -\frac{1}{2}\cot^2 u - \ln|\sin u| + C$

26. $\int \sec^3 u\,du = \frac{1}{2}\sec u \tan u + \frac{1}{2}\ln|\sec u + \tan u| + C$

27. $\int \csc^3 u\,du = -\frac{1}{2}\csc u \cot u + \frac{1}{2}\ln|\csc u - \cot u| + C$

28. $\int \sin^n u\,du = -\frac{1}{n}\sin^{n-1} u \cos u + \frac{n-1}{n}\int \sin^{n-2} u\,du$

29. $\int \cos^n u\,du = \frac{1}{n}\cos^{n-1} u \sin u + \frac{n-1}{n}\int \cos^{n-2} u\,du$

30. $\int \tan^n u\,du = \frac{1}{n-1}\tan^{n-1} u - \int \tan^{n-2} u\,du$

31. $\int \cot^n u\,du = \frac{-1}{n-1}\cot^{n-1} u - \int \cot^{n-2} u\,du$

32. $\int \sec^n u\,du = \frac{1}{n-1}\tan u \sec^{n-2} u + \frac{n-2}{n-1}\int \sec^{n-2} u\,du$

33. $\int \csc^n u\,du = \frac{-1}{n-1}\cot u \csc^{n-2} u + \frac{n-2}{n-1}\int \csc^{n-2} u\,du$

34. $\int \sin au \sin bu\,du = \frac{\sin(a-b)u}{2(a-b)} - \frac{\sin(a+b)u}{2(a+b)} + C$

35. $\int \cos au \cos bu\,du = \frac{\sin(a-b)u}{2(a-b)} + \frac{\sin(a+b)u}{2(a+b)} + C$

36. $\int \sin au \cos bu\,du = -\frac{\cos(a-b)u}{2(a-b)} - \frac{\cos(a+b)u}{2(a+b)} + C$

37. $\int u \sin u\,du = \sin u - u \cos u + C$

38. $\int u \cos u\,du = \cos u + u \sin u + C$

39. $\int u^n \sin u\,du = -u^n \cos u + n\int u^{n-1} \cos u\,du$

40. $\int u^n \cos u\,du = u^n \sin u - n\int u^{n-1} \sin u\,du$

41. $$\begin{aligned}\int \sin^n u \cos^m u\,du &= -\frac{\sin^{n-1} u \cos^{m+1} u}{n+m} + \frac{n-1}{n+m}\int \sin^{n-2} u \cos^m u\,du \\ &= \frac{\sin^{n+1} u \cos^{m-1} u}{n+m} + \frac{m-1}{n+m}\int \sin^n u \cos^{m-2} u\,du\end{aligned}$$

## Exponential and Logarithmic Integrals

42. $\int ue^{au}\,du = \frac{1}{a^2}(au - 1)e^{au} + C$

43. $\int u^n e^{au}\,du = \frac{1}{a}u^n e^{au} - \frac{n}{a}\int u^{n-1} e^{au}\,du$

44. $\int e^{au}\sin bu\,du = \frac{e^{au}}{a^2 + b^2}(a\sin bu - b\cos bu) + C$

45. $\int e^{au}\cos bu\,du = \frac{e^{au}}{a^2 + b^2}(a\cos bu + b\sin bu) + C$

46. $\int \ln u\,du = u\ln u - u + C$

47. $\int u^n \ln u\,du = \frac{u^{n+1}}{(n+1)^2}[(n+1)\ln u - 1] + C$

48. $\int \frac{1}{u\ln u}\,du = \ln|\ln u| + C$

## Hyperbolic Integrals

49. $\int \sinh u\,du = \cosh u + C$

50. $\int \cosh u\,du = \sinh u + C$

51. $\int \tanh u\,du = \ln\cosh u + C$

52. $\int \coth u\,du = \ln|\sinh u| + C$

53. $\int \operatorname{sech} u\,du = \tan^{-1}|\sinh u| + C$

54. $\int \operatorname{csch} u\,du = \ln\left|\tanh\frac{1}{2}u\right| + C$

55. $\int \operatorname{sech}^2 u\,du = \tanh u + C$

56. $\int \operatorname{csch}^2 u\,du = -\coth u + C$

57. $\int \operatorname{sech} u\tanh u\,du = -\operatorname{sech} u + C$

58. $\int \operatorname{csch} u\coth u\,du = -\operatorname{csch} u + C$

## Inverse Trigonometric Integrals

59. $\int \sin^{-1}u\,du = u\sin^{-1}u + \sqrt{1 - u^2} + C$

60. $\int \cos^{-1}u\,du = u\cos^{-1}u - \sqrt{1 - u^2} + C$

61. $\int \tan^{-1}u\,du = u\tan^{-1}u - \frac{1}{2}\ln\left(1 + u^2\right) + C$

62. $\int u\sin^{-1}u\,du = \frac{2u^2 - 1}{4}\sin^{-1}u + \frac{u\sqrt{1 - u^2}}{4} + C$

63. $\int u \cos^{-1} u\, du = \frac{2u^2 - 1}{4} \cos^{-1} u - \frac{u\sqrt{1 - u^2}}{4} + C$

64. $\int u \tan^{-1} u\, du = \frac{u^2 + 1}{2} \tan^{-1} u - \frac{u}{2} + C$

65. $\int u^n \sin^{-1} u\, du = \frac{1}{n+1}\left[u^{n+1} \sin^{-1} u - \int \frac{u^{n+1}\, du}{\sqrt{1 - u^2}}\right], n \neq -1$

66. $\int u^n \cos^{-1} u\, du = \frac{1}{n+1}\left[u^{n+1} \cos^{-1} u + \int \frac{u^{n+1}\, du}{\sqrt{1 - u^2}}\right], n \neq -1$

67. $\int u^n \tan^{-1} u\, du = \frac{1}{n+1}\left[u^{n+1} \tan^{-1} u - \int \frac{u^{n+1}\, du}{1 + u^2}\right], n \neq -1$

## Integrals Involving $a^2 + u^2$, $a > 0$

68. $\int \sqrt{a^2 + u^2}\, du = \frac{u}{2}\sqrt{a^2 + u^2} + \frac{a^2}{2} \ln\left(u + \sqrt{a^2 + u^2}\right) + C$

69. $\int u^2 \sqrt{a^2 + u^2}\, du = \frac{u}{8}\left(a^2 + 2u^2\right)\sqrt{a^2 + u^2} - \frac{a^4}{8} \ln\left(u + \sqrt{a^2 + u^2}\right) + C$

70. $\int \frac{\sqrt{a^2 + u^2}}{u}\, du = \sqrt{a^2 + u^2} - a \ln\left|\frac{a + \sqrt{a^2 + u^2}}{u}\right| + C$

71. $\int \frac{\sqrt{a^2 + u^2}}{u^2}\, du = -\frac{\sqrt{a^2 + u^2}}{u} + \ln\left(u + \sqrt{a^2 + u^2}\right) + C$

72. $\int \frac{du}{\sqrt{a^2 + u^2}} = \ln\left(u + \sqrt{a^2 + u^2}\right) + C$

73. $\int \frac{u^2\, du}{\sqrt{a^2 + u^2}} = \frac{u}{2}\left(\sqrt{a^2 + u^2}\right) - \frac{a^2}{2} \ln\left(u + \sqrt{a^2 + u^2}\right) + C$

74. $\int \frac{du}{u\sqrt{a^2 + u^2}} = -\frac{1}{a} \ln\left|\frac{\sqrt{a^2 + u^2} + a}{u}\right| + C$

75. $\int \frac{du}{u^2\sqrt{a^2 + u^2}} = -\frac{\sqrt{a^2 + u^2}}{a^2 u} + C$

76. $\int \frac{du}{\left(a^2 + u^2\right)^{3/2}} = \frac{u}{a^2\sqrt{a^2 + u^2}} + C$

## Integrals Involving $u^2 - a^2$, $a > 0$

77. $\int \sqrt{u^2 - a^2}\, du = \frac{u}{2}\sqrt{u^2 - a^2} - \frac{a^2}{2} \ln\left|u + \sqrt{u^2 - a^2}\right| + C$

78. $\int u^2 \sqrt{u^2 - a^2}\, du = \frac{u}{8}\left(2u^2 - a^2\right)\sqrt{u^2 - a^2} - \frac{a^4}{8} \ln\left|u + \sqrt{u^2 - a^2}\right| + C$

79. $\int \frac{\sqrt{u^2 - a^2}}{u}\, du = \sqrt{u^2 - a^2} - a\cos^{-1} \frac{a}{|u|} + C$

80. $\int \frac{\sqrt{u^2 - a^2}}{u^2}\, du = -\frac{\sqrt{u^2 - a^2}}{u} + \ln\left|u + \sqrt{u^2 - a^2}\right| + C$

81. $\int \frac{du}{\sqrt{u^2 - a^2}} = \ln\left|u + \sqrt{u^2 - a^2}\right| + C$

82. $\int \frac{u^2\,du}{\sqrt{u^2 - a^2}} = \frac{u}{2}\sqrt{u^2 - a^2} + \frac{a^2}{2}\ln\left|u + \sqrt{u^2 - a^2}\right| + C$

83. $\int \frac{du}{u^2\sqrt{u^2 - a^2}} = \frac{\sqrt{u^2 - a^2}}{a^2 u} + C$

84. $\int \frac{du}{\left(u^2 - a^2\right)^{3/2}} = -\frac{u}{a^2\sqrt{u^2 - a^2}} + C$

## Integrals Involving $a^2 - u^2$, $a > 0$

85. $\int \sqrt{a^2 - u^2}\,du = \frac{u}{2}\sqrt{a^2 - u^2} + \frac{a^2}{2}\sin^{-1}\frac{u}{a} + C$

86. $\int u^2\sqrt{a^2 - u^2}\,du = \frac{u}{8}\left(2u^2 - a^2\right)\sqrt{a^2 - u^2} + \frac{a^4}{8}\sin^{-1}\frac{u}{a} + C$

87. $\int \frac{\sqrt{a^2 - u^2}}{u}\,du = \sqrt{a^2 - u^2} - a\ln\left|\frac{a + \sqrt{a^2 - u^2}}{u}\right| + C$

88. $\int \frac{\sqrt{a^2 - u^2}}{u^2}\,du = -\frac{1}{u}\sqrt{a^2 - u^2} - \sin^{-1}\frac{u}{a} + C$

89. $\int \frac{u^2\,du}{\sqrt{a^2 - u^2}} = -\frac{u}{u}\sqrt{a^2 - u^2} + \frac{a^2}{2}\sin^{-1}\frac{u}{a} + C$

90. $\int \frac{du}{u\sqrt{a^2 - u^2}} = -\frac{1}{a}\ln\left|\frac{a + \sqrt{a^2 - u^2}}{u}\right| + C$

91. $\int \frac{du}{u^2\sqrt{a^2 - u^2}} = -\frac{1}{a^2 u}\sqrt{a^2 - u^2} + C$

92. $\int \left(a^2 - u^2\right)^{3/2}\,du = -\frac{u}{8}\left(2u^2 - 5a^2\right)\sqrt{a^2 - u^2} + \frac{3a^4}{8}\sin^{-1}\frac{u}{a} + C$

93. $\int \frac{du}{\left(a^2 - u^2\right)^{3/2}} = -\frac{u}{a^2\sqrt{a^2 - u^2}} + C$

## Integrals Involving $2au - u^2$, $a > 0$

94. $\int \sqrt{2au - u^2}\,du = \frac{u - a}{2}\sqrt{2au - u^2} + \frac{a^2}{2}\cos^{-1}\left(\frac{a - u}{a}\right) + C$

95. $\int \frac{du}{\sqrt{2au - u^2}} = \cos^{-1}\left(\frac{a - u}{a}\right) + C$

96. $\int u\sqrt{2au - u^2}\,du = \frac{2u^2 - au - 3a^2}{6}\sqrt{2au - u^2} + \frac{a^3}{2}\cos^{-1}\left(\frac{a - u}{a}\right) + C$

97. $\int \frac{du}{u\sqrt{2au - u^2}} = -\frac{\sqrt{2au - u^2}}{au} + C$

## Integrals Involving $a + bu$, $a \neq 0$

98. $\int \frac{u\,du}{a+bu} = \frac{1}{b^2}(a + bu - a\ln|a+bu|) + C$

99. $\int \frac{u^2\,du}{a+bu} = \frac{1}{2b^3}\left[(a+bu)^2 - 4a(a+bu) + 2a^2\ln|a+bu|\right] + C$

100. $\int \frac{du}{u(a+bu)} = \frac{1}{a}\ln\left|\frac{u}{a+bu}\right| + C$

101. $\int \frac{du}{u^2(a+bu)} = -\frac{1}{au} + \frac{b}{a^2}\ln\left|\frac{a+bu}{u}\right| + C$

102. $\int \frac{u\,du}{(a+bu)^2} = \frac{a}{b^2(a+bu)} + \frac{1}{b^2}\ln|a+bu| + C$

103. $\int \frac{u\,du}{u(a+bu)^2} = \frac{1}{a(a+bu)} - \frac{1}{a^2}\ln\left|\frac{a+bu}{u}\right| + C$

104. $\int \frac{u^2\,du}{(a+bu)^2} = \frac{1}{b^3}\left(a + bu - \frac{a^2}{a+bu} - 2a\ln|a+bu|\right) + C$

105. $\int u\sqrt{a+bu}\,du = \frac{2}{15b^2}(3bu - 2a)(a+bu)^{3/2} + C$

106. $\int \frac{u\,du}{\sqrt{a+bu}} = \frac{2}{3b^2}(bu - 2a)\sqrt{a+bu} + C$

107. $\int \frac{u^2\,du}{\sqrt{a+bu}} = \frac{2}{15b^3}\left(8a^2 + 3b^2u^2 - 4abu\right)\sqrt{a+bu} + C$

108. $\int \frac{du}{u\sqrt{a+bu}} = \frac{1}{\sqrt{a}}\ln\left|\frac{\sqrt{a+bu}-\sqrt{a}}{\sqrt{a+bu}+\sqrt{a}}\right| + C, \quad \text{if } a > 0$

$= \frac{2}{\sqrt{-a}}\tan - 1\sqrt{\frac{a+bu}{-a}} + C, \quad \text{if } a < 0$

109. $\int \frac{\sqrt{a+bu}}{u}\,du = 2\sqrt{a+bu} + a\int \frac{du}{u\sqrt{a+bu}}$

110. $\int \frac{\sqrt{a+bu}}{u^2}\,du = -\frac{\sqrt{a+bu}}{u} + \frac{b}{2}\int \frac{du}{u\sqrt{a+bu}}$

111. $\int u^n\sqrt{a+bu}\,du = \frac{2}{b(2n+3)}\left[u^n(a+bu)^{3/2} - na\int u^{n-1}\sqrt{a+bu}\,du\right]$

112. $\int \frac{u^n\,du}{\sqrt{a+bu}} = \frac{2u^n\sqrt{a+bu}}{b(2n+1)} - \frac{2na}{b(2n+1)}\int \frac{u^{n-1}\,du}{\sqrt{a+bu}}$

113. $\int \frac{du}{u^n\sqrt{a+bu}} = -\frac{\sqrt{a+bu}}{a(n-1)u^{n-1}} - \frac{b(2n-3)}{2a(n-1)}\int \frac{du}{u^{n-1}\sqrt{a+bu}}$

# APPENDIX B | TABLE OF DERIVATIVES

## General Formulas

1. $\frac{d}{dx}(c) = 0$

2. $\frac{d}{dx}(f(x) + g(x)) = f'(x) + g'(x)$

3. $\frac{d}{dx}(f(x)g(x)) = f'(x)g(x) + f(x)g'(x)$

4. $\frac{d}{dx}(x^n) = nx^{n-1}$, for real numbers $n$

5. $\frac{d}{dx}(cf(x)) = cf'(x)$

6. $\frac{d}{dx}(f(x) - g(x)) = f'(x) - g'(x)$

7. $\frac{d}{dx}\left(\frac{f(x)}{g(x)}\right) = \frac{g(x)f'(x) - f(x)g'(x)}{(g(x))^2}$

8. $\frac{d}{dx}[f(g(x))] = f'(g(x)) \cdot g'(x)$

## Trigonometric Functions

9. $\frac{d}{dx}(\sin x) = \cos x$

10. $\frac{d}{dx}(\tan x) = \sec^2 x$

11. $\frac{d}{dx}(\sec x) = \sec x \tan x$

12. $\frac{d}{dx}(\cos x) = -\sin x$

13. $\frac{d}{dx}(\cot x) = -\csc^2 x$

14. $\frac{d}{dx}(\csc x) = -\csc x \cot x$

## Inverse Trigonometric Functions

15. $\frac{d}{dx}\left(\sin^{-1} x\right) = \frac{1}{\sqrt{1 - x^2}}$

16. $\frac{d}{dx}\left(\tan^{-1} x\right) = \frac{1}{1 + x^2}$

17. $\frac{d}{dx}\left(\sec^{-1} x\right) = \frac{1}{|x|\sqrt{x^2 - 1}}$

18. $\frac{d}{dx}\left(\cos^{-1} x\right) = -\frac{1}{\sqrt{1 - x^2}}$

19. $\frac{d}{dx}\left(\cot^{-1} x\right) = -\frac{1}{1 + x^2}$

20. $\frac{d}{dx}\left(\csc^{-1} x\right) = -\frac{1}{|x|\sqrt{x^2 - 1}}$

## Exponential and Logarithmic Functions

21. $\frac{d}{dx}(e^x) = e^x$

22. $\frac{d}{dx}(\ln|x|) = \frac{1}{x}$

23. $\frac{d}{dx}(b^x) = b^x \ln b$

24. $\frac{d}{dx}\left(\log_b x\right) = \frac{1}{x \ln b}$

## Hyperbolic Functions

25. $\frac{d}{dx}(\sinh x) = \cosh x$

26. $\frac{d}{dx}(\tanh x) = \operatorname{sech}^2 x$

27. $\frac{d}{dx}(\operatorname{sech} x) = -\operatorname{sech} x \tanh x$

28. $\frac{d}{dx}(\cosh x) = \sinh x$

29. $\frac{d}{dx}(\coth x) = -\operatorname{csch}^2 x$

30. $\frac{d}{dx}(\operatorname{csch} x) = -\operatorname{csch} x \coth x$

## Inverse Hyperbolic Functions

31. $\frac{d}{dx}\left(\sinh^{-1} x\right) = \frac{1}{\sqrt{x^2 + 1}}$

32. $\frac{d}{dx}\left(\tanh^{-1} x\right) = \frac{1}{1 - x^2} (|x| < 1)$

33. $\frac{d}{dx}\left(\operatorname{sech}^{-1} x\right) = -\frac{1}{x\sqrt{1 - x^2}} \quad (0 < x < 1)$

34. $\frac{d}{dx}\left(\cosh^{-1} x\right) = \frac{1}{\sqrt{x^2 - 1}} \quad (x > 1)$

35. $\frac{d}{dx}\left(\coth^{-1} x\right) = \frac{1}{1 - x^2} \quad (|x| > 1)$

36. $\frac{d}{dx}\left(\operatorname{csch}^{-1} x\right) = -\frac{1}{|x|\sqrt{1 + x^2}} (x \neq 0)$

# APPENDIX C | REVIEW OF PRE-CALCULUS

## Formulas from Geometry

$A =$ area, $V =$ Volume, and $S =$ lateral surface area

Parallelogram

$A = bh$

Triangle

$A = \frac{1}{2}bh$

Trapezoid

$A = \frac{1}{2}(a + b)h$

Circle

$A = \pi r^2$
$C = 2\pi r$

Sector

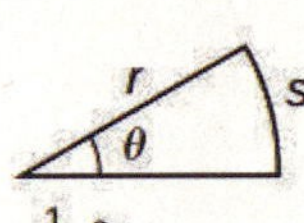


$A = \frac{1}{2}r^2\theta$
$s = r\theta$ ($\theta$ in radians)

Cylinder

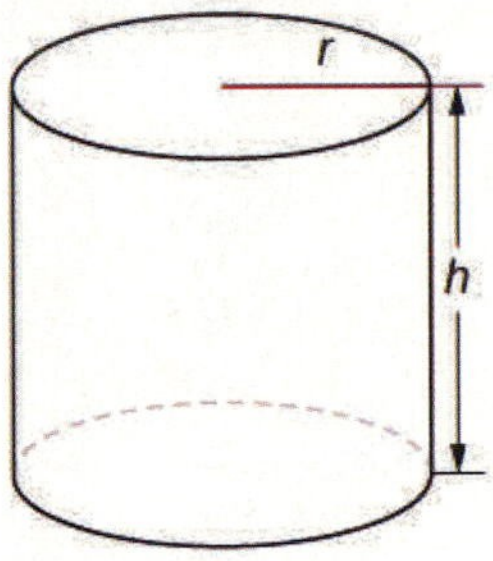


$V = \pi r^2 h$
$S = 2\pi rh$

Cone

$V = \frac{1}{3}\pi r^2 h$
$S = \pi rl$

Sphere

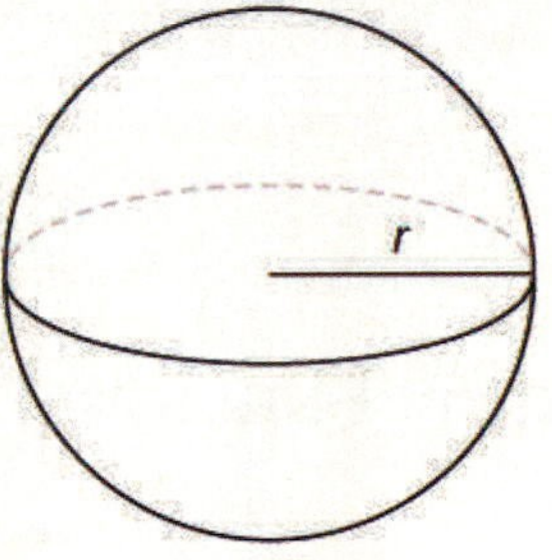


$V = \frac{4}{3}\pi r^3$
$S = 4\pi r^2$

## Formulas from Algebra

### Laws of Exponents

$$x^m x^n = x^{m+n} \qquad \frac{x^m}{x^n} = x^{m-n} \qquad (x^m)^n = x^{mn}$$

$$x^{-n} = \frac{1}{x^n} \qquad (xy)^n = x^n y^n \qquad \left(\frac{x}{y}\right)^n = \frac{x^n}{y^n}$$

$$x^{1/n} = \sqrt[n]{x} \qquad \sqrt[n]{xy} = \sqrt[n]{x}\sqrt[n]{y} \qquad \sqrt[n]{\frac{x}{y}} = \frac{\sqrt[n]{x}}{\sqrt[n]{y}}$$

$$x^{m/n} = \sqrt[n]{x^m} = (\sqrt[n]{x})^m$$

### Special Factorizations

$$x^2 - y^2 = (x + y)(x - y)$$
$$x^3 + y^3 = (x + y)\left(x^2 - xy + y^2\right)$$
$$x^3 - y^3 = (x - y)\left(x^2 + xy + y^2\right)$$

### Quadratic Formula

If $ax^2 + bx + c = 0$, then $x = \dfrac{-b \pm \sqrt{b^2 - 4ca}}{2a}$.

## Binomial Theorem

$$(a+b)^n = a^n + \binom{n}{1}a^{n-1}b + \binom{n}{2}a^{n-2}b^2 + \cdots + \binom{n}{n-1}ab^{n-1} + b^n,$$

where $\binom{n}{k} = \dfrac{n(n-1)(n-2)\cdots(n-k+1)}{k(k-1)(k-2)\cdots 3\cdot 2\cdot 1} = \dfrac{n!}{k!(n-k)!}$

# Formulas from Trigonometry

## Right-Angle Trigonometry

$\sin\theta = \dfrac{\text{opp}}{\text{hyp}}$ $\quad \csc\theta = \dfrac{\text{hyp}}{\text{opp}}$

$\cos\theta = \dfrac{\text{adj}}{\text{hyp}}$ $\quad \sec\theta = \dfrac{\text{hyp}}{\text{adj}}$

$\tan\theta = \dfrac{\text{opp}}{\text{adj}}$ $\quad \cot\theta = \dfrac{\text{adj}}{\text{opp}}$

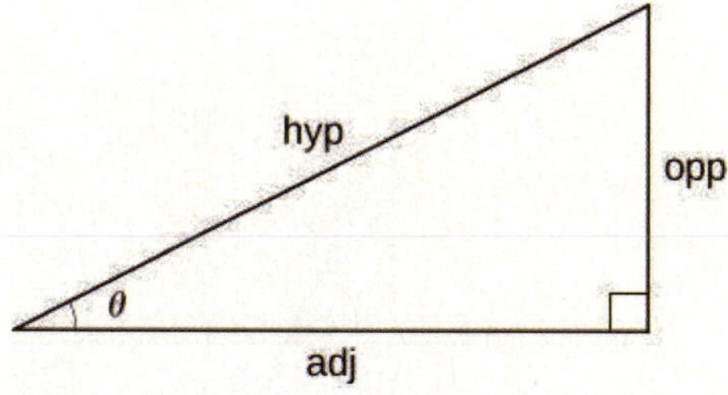


## Trigonometric Functions of Important Angles

| $\theta$ | Radians | $\sin\theta$ | $\cos\theta$ | $\tan\theta$ |
|---|---|---|---|---|
| 0° | 0 | 0 | 1 | 0 |
| 30° | $\pi/6$ | 1/2 | $\sqrt{3}/2$ | $\sqrt{3}/3$ |
| 45° | $\pi/4$ | $\sqrt{2}/2$ | $\sqrt{2}/2$ | 1 |
| 60° | $\pi/3$ | $\sqrt{3}/2$ | 1/2 | $\sqrt{3}$ |
| 90° | $\pi/2$ | 1 | 0 | — |

## Fundamental Identities

$$
\begin{aligned}
\sin^2\theta + \cos^2\theta &= 1 & \sin(-\theta) &= -\sin\theta \\
1 + \tan^2\theta &= \sec^2\theta & \cos(-\theta) &= \cos\theta \\
1 + \cot^2\theta &= \csc^2\theta & \tan(-\theta) &= -\tan\theta \\
\sin\left(\frac{\pi}{2} - \theta\right) &= \cos\theta & \sin(\theta + 2\pi) &= \sin\theta \\
\cos\left(\frac{\pi}{2} - \theta\right) &= \sin\theta & \cos(\theta + 2\pi) &= \cos\theta \\
\tan\left(\frac{\pi}{2} - \theta\right) &= \cot\theta & \tan(\theta + \pi) &= \tan\theta
\end{aligned}
$$

## Law of Sines

$$\frac{\sin A}{a} = \frac{\sin B}{b} = \frac{\sin C}{c}$$

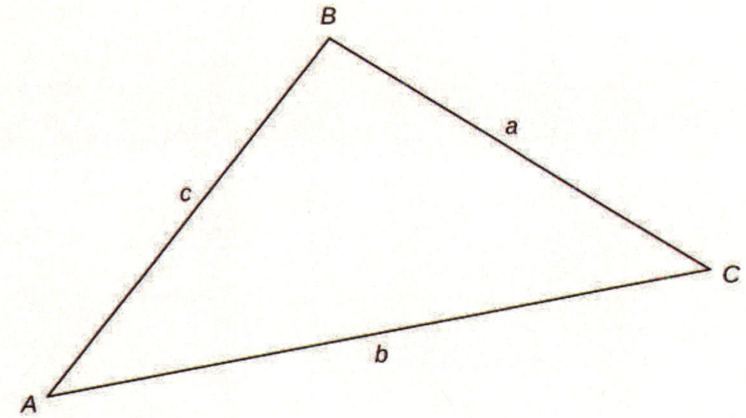


## Law of Cosines

$$
\begin{aligned}
a^2 &= b^2 + c^2 - 2bc\cos A \\
b^2 &= a^2 + c^2 - 2ac\cos B \\
c^2 &= a^2 + b^2 - 2ab\cos C
\end{aligned}
$$

## Addition and Subtraction Formulas

$$
\begin{aligned}
\sin(x + y) &= \sin x\cos y + \cos x\sin y \\
\sin(x - y) &= \sin x\cos y - \cos x\sin y \\
\cos(x + y) &= \cos x\cos y - \sin x\sin y \\
\cos(x - y) &= \cos x\cos y + \sin x\sin y \\
\tan(x + y) &= \frac{\tan x + \tan y}{1 - \tan x\tan y} \\
\tan(x - y) &= \frac{\tan x - \tan y}{1 + \tan x\tan y}
\end{aligned}
$$

## Double-Angle Formulas

$$
\begin{aligned}
\sin 2x &= 2\sin x\cos x \\
\cos 2x &= \cos^2 x - \sin^2 x = 2\cos^2 x - 1 = 1 - 2\sin^2 x \\
\tan 2x &= \frac{2\tan x}{1 - \tan^2 x}
\end{aligned}
$$

## Half-Angle Formulas

$$\sin^2 x = \frac{1 - \cos 2x}{2}$$

$$\cos^2 x = \frac{1 + \cos 2x}{2}$$

# ANSWER KEY

## Chapter 1

### Checkpoint

**1.1.** $\sum_{i=3}^{6} 2^i = 2^3 + 2^4 + 2^5 + 2^6 = 120$

**1.2.** 15,550

**1.3.** 440

**1.4.** The left-endpoint approximation is 0.7595. The right-endpoint approximation is 0.6345. See the below **image**.

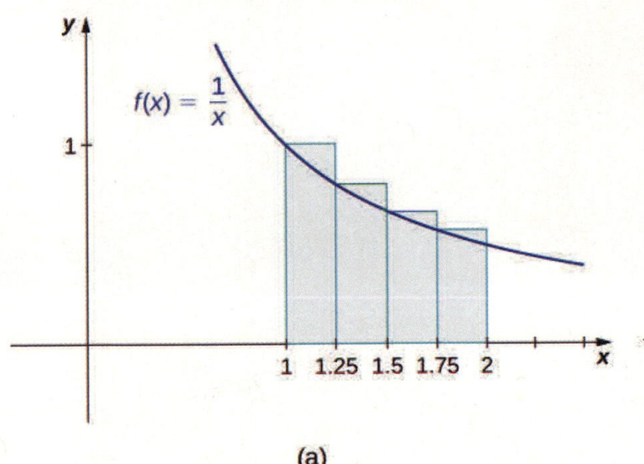


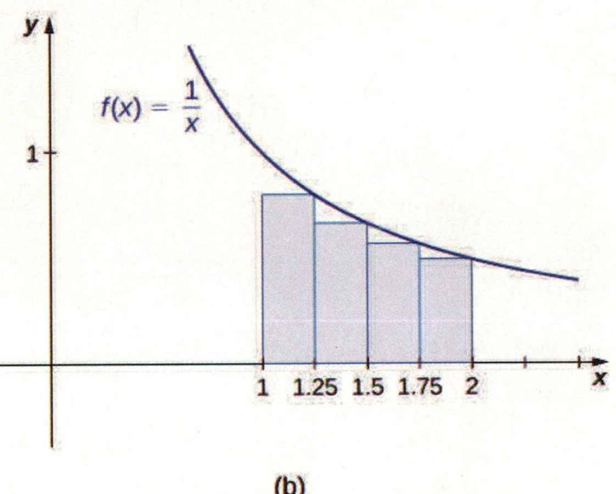


**1.5.**

a. Upper sum $= 8.0313$.

b.

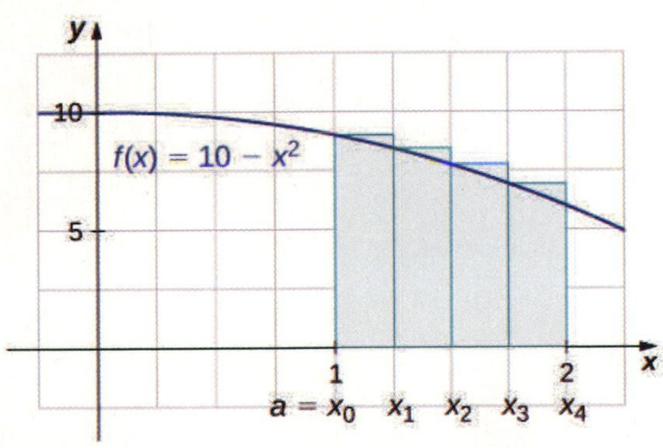


**1.6.** $A \approx 1.125$

**1.7.** 6

**1.8.** 18 square units

**1.9.** 6

**1.10.** 18

**1.11.** $6\int_1^3 x^3\,dx - 4\int_1^3 x^2\,dx + 2\int_1^3 x\,dx - \int_1^3 3\,dx$

**1.12.** −7

**1.13.** 3

**1.14.** Average value $= 1.5$; $c = 3$

**1.15**. $c = \sqrt{3}$

**1.16**. $g'(r) = \sqrt{r^2 + 4}$

**1.17**. $F'(x) = 3x^2 \cos x^3$

**1.18**. $F'(x) = 2x \cos x^2 - \cos x$

**1.19**. $\frac{7}{24}$

**1.20**. Kathy still wins, but by a much larger margin: James skates 24 ft in 3 sec, but Kathy skates 29.3634 ft in 3 sec.

**1.21**. $-\frac{10}{3}$

**1.22**. Net displacement: $\frac{e^2 - 9}{2} \approx -0.8055$ m; total distance traveled: $4 \ln 4 - 7.5 + \frac{e^2}{2} \approx 1.740$ m

**1.23**. 17.5 mi

**1.24**. $\frac{64}{5}$

**1.25**. $\int 3x^2 \left(x^3 - 3\right)^2 dx = \frac{1}{3}\left(x^3 - 3\right)^3 + C$

**1.26**. $\frac{\left(x^3 + 5\right)^{10}}{30} + C$

**1.27**. $-\frac{1}{\sin t} + C$

**1.28**. $-\frac{\cos^4 t}{4} + C$

**1.29**. $\frac{91}{3}$

**1.30**. $\frac{2}{3\pi} \approx 0.2122$

**1.31**. $\int x^2 e^{-2x^3} dx = -\frac{1}{6}e^{-2x^3} + C$

**1.32**. $\int e^x (3e^x - 2)^2 dx = \frac{1}{9}(3e^x - 2)^3$

**1.33**. $\int 2x^3 e^{x^4} dx = \frac{1}{2}e^{x^4}$

**1.34**. $\frac{1}{2}\int_0^4 e^u du = \frac{1}{2}\left(e^4 - 1\right)$

**1.35**. $Q(t) = \frac{2^t}{\ln 2} + 8.557.$ There are 20,099 bacteria in the dish after 3 hours.

**1.36**. There are 116 flies.

**1.37**. $\int_1^2 \frac{1}{x^3} e^{4x^{-2}} dx = \frac{1}{8}\left[e^4 - e\right]$

**1.38**. $\ln|x + 2| + C$

**1.39**. $\frac{x}{\ln 3}(\ln x - 1) + C$

**1.40**. $\frac{1}{4}\sin^{-1}(4x) + C$

**1.41**. $\sin^{-1}\left(\frac{x}{3}\right) + C$

**1.42**. $\frac{1}{10}\tan^{-1}\left(\frac{2x}{5}\right) + C$

**1.43**. $\frac{1}{4}\tan^{-1}\left(\frac{x}{4}\right) + C$

**1.44**. $\frac{\pi}{8}$

## Section Exercises

**1**. a. They are equal; both represent the sum of the first 10 whole numbers. b. They are equal; both represent the sum of the first 10 whole numbers. c. They are equal by substituting $j = i - 1$. d. They are equal; the first sum factors the terms of the second.

**3**. $385 - 30 = 355$

**5**. $15 - (-12) = 27$

**7**. $5(15) + 4(-12) = 27$

**9**. $\sum_{j=1}^{50} j^2 - 2\sum_{j=1}^{50} j = \frac{(50)(51)(101)}{6} - \frac{2(50)(51)}{2} = 40,375$

**11**. $4\sum_{k=1}^{25} k^2 - 100\sum_{k=1}^{25} k = \frac{4(25)(26)(51)}{9} - 50(25)(26) = -10,400$

**13**. $R_4 = 0.25$

**15**. $R_6 = 0.372$

**17**. $L_4 = 2.20$

**19**. $L_8 = 0.6875$

**21**. $L_6 = 9.000 = R_6$. The graph of $f$ is a triangle with area 9.

**23**. $L_6 = 13.12899 = R_6$. They are equal.

**25**. $L_{10} = \frac{4}{10}\sum_{i=1}^{10}\sqrt{4 - \left(-2 + 4\frac{(i-1)}{10}\right)}$

**27**. $R_{100} = \frac{e-1}{100}\sum_{i=1}^{100}\ln\left(1 + (e-1)\frac{i}{100}\right)$

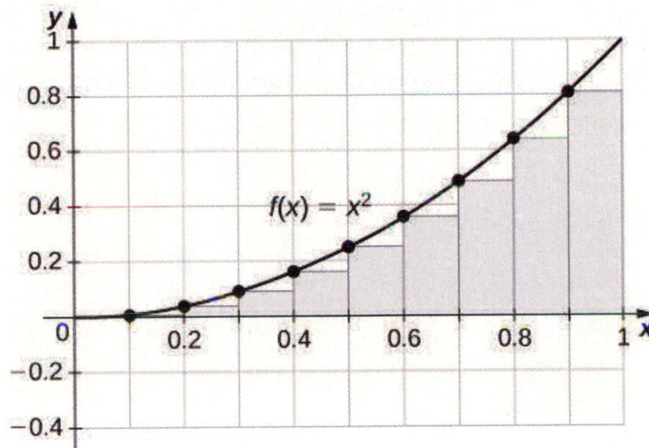


**29**.
$R_{100} = 0.33835$, $L_{100} = 0.32835$. The plot shows that the left Riemann sum is an underestimate because the function is increasing. Similarly, the right Riemann sum is an overestimate. The area lies between the left and right Riemann sums. Ten rectangles are shown for visual clarity. This behavior persists for more rectangles.

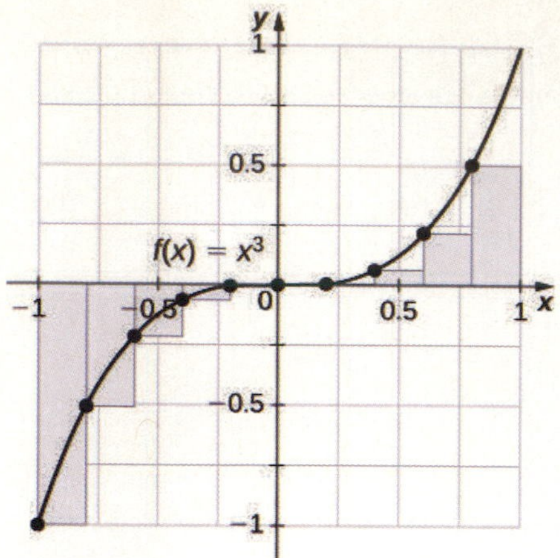


**31.**
$L_{100} = -0.02,\ R_{100} = 0.02.$ The left endpoint sum is an underestimate because the function is increasing. Similarly, a right endpoint approximation is an overestimate. The area lies between the left and right endpoint estimates.

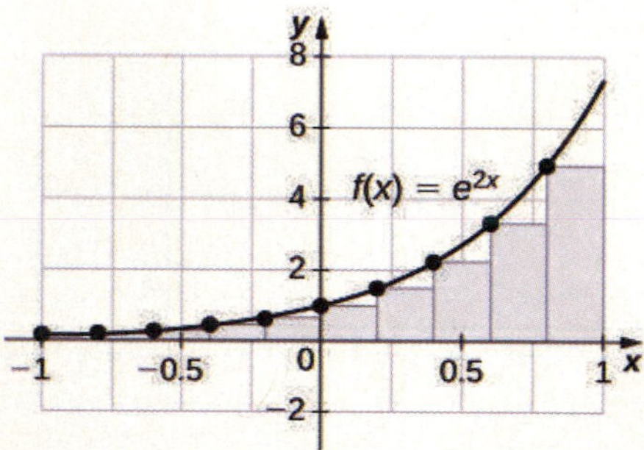


**33.**
$L_{100} = 3.555,\ R_{100} = 3.670.$ The plot shows that the left Riemann sum is an underestimate because the function is increasing. Ten rectangles are shown for visual clarity. This behavior persists for more rectangles.
**35.** The sum represents the cumulative rainfall in January 2009.
**37.** The total mileage is $7 \times \sum_{i=1}^{25} \left(1 + \frac{(i-1)}{10}\right) = 7 \times 25 + \frac{7}{10} \times 12 \times 25 = 385$ mi.
**39.** Add the numbers to get 8.1-in. net increase.
**41.** 309,389,957
**43.** $L_8 = 3 + 2 + 1 + 2 + 3 + 4 + 5 + 4 = 24$
**45.** $L_8 = 3 + 5 + 7 + 6 + 8 + 6 + 5 + 4 = 44$
**47.** $L_{10} \approx 1.7604,\ L_{30} \approx 1.7625,\ L_{50} \approx 1.76265$
**49.** $R_1 = -1,\ L_1 = 1,\ R_{10} = -0.1,\ L_{10} = 0.1,\ L_{100} = 0.01,$ and $R_{100} = -0.1.$ By symmetry of the graph, the exact area is zero.
**51.** $R_1 = 0,\ L_1 = 0,\ R_{10} = 2.4499,\ L_{10} = 2.4499,\ R_{100} = 2.1365,\ L_{100} = 2.1365$
**53.** If $[c, d]$ is a subinterval of $[a, b]$ under one of the left-endpoint sum rectangles, then the area of the rectangle contributing to the left-endpoint estimate is $f(c)(d - c)$. But, $f(c) \le f(x)$ for $c \le x \le d,$ so the area under the graph of $f$ between $c$ and $d$ is $f(c)(d - c)$ plus the area below the graph of $f$ but above the horizontal line segment at height $f(c),$ which is positive. As this is true for each left-endpoint sum interval, it follows that the left Riemann sum is less than or equal to the area below the graph of $f$ on $[a, b]$.
**55.** $L_N = \frac{b-a}{N} \sum_{i=1}^{N} f\left(a + (b - a)\frac{i-1}{N}\right) = \frac{b-a}{N} \sum_{i=0}^{N-1} f\left(a + (b - a)\frac{i}{N}\right)$ and $R_N = \frac{b-a}{N} \sum_{i=1}^{N} f\left(a + (b - a)\frac{i}{N}\right)$. The left sum has a term corresponding to $i = 0$ and the right sum has a term corresponding to $i = N$. In $R_N - L_N,$ any term corresponding to $i = 1, 2, \ldots, N - 1$ occurs once with a plus sign and once with a minus sign, so each such term cancels and one

is left with $R_N - L_N = \frac{b-a}{N}\left(f\left(a + (b-a)\frac{N}{N}\right) - \left(f(a) + (b-a)\frac{0}{N}\right)\right) = \frac{b-a}{N}(f(b) - f(a))$.

**57**. Graph 1: a. $L(A) = 0$, $B(A) = 20$; b. $U(A) = 20$. Graph 2: a. $L(A) = 9$; b. $B(A) = 11$, $U(A) = 20$. Graph 3: a. $L(A) = 11.0$; b. $B(A) = 4.5$, $U(A) = 15.5$.

**59**. Let $A$ be the area of the unit circle. The circle encloses $n$ congruent triangles each of area $\frac{\sin\left(\frac{2\pi}{n}\right)}{2}$, so $\frac{n}{2}\sin\left(\frac{2\pi}{n}\right) \le A$. Similarly, the circle is contained inside $n$ congruent triangles each of area $\frac{BH}{2} = \frac{1}{2}\left(\cos\left(\frac{\pi}{n}\right) + \sin\left(\frac{\pi}{n}\right)\tan\left(\frac{\pi}{n}\right)\right)\sin\left(\frac{2\pi}{n}\right)$, so $A \le \frac{n}{2}\sin\left(\frac{2\pi}{n}\right)\left(\cos\left(\frac{\pi}{n}\right)\right) + \sin\left(\frac{\pi}{n}\right)\tan\left(\frac{\pi}{n}\right)$. As $n \to \infty$, $\frac{n}{2}\sin\left(\frac{2\pi}{n}\right) = \frac{\pi\sin\left(\frac{2\pi}{n}\right)}{\left(\frac{2\pi}{n}\right)} \to \pi$, so we conclude $\pi \le A$. Also, as $n \to \infty$, $\cos\left(\frac{\pi}{n}\right) + \sin\left(\frac{\pi}{n}\right)\tan\left(\frac{\pi}{n}\right) \to 1$, so we also have $A \le \pi$. By the squeeze theorem for limits, we conclude that $A = \pi$.

**61**. $\int_0^2 \left(5x^2 - 3x^3\right)dx$

**63**. $\int_0^1 \cos^2(2\pi x)dx$

**65**. $\int_0^1 xdx$

**67**. $\int_3^6 xdx$

**69**. $\int_1^2 x\log\left(x^2\right)dx$

**71**. $1 + 2\cdot 2 + 3\cdot 3 = 14$

**73**. $1 - 4 + 9 = 6$

**75**. $1 - 2\pi + 9 = 10 - 2\pi$

**77**. The integral is the area of the triangle, $\frac{1}{2}$

**79**. The integral is the area of the triangle, 9.

**81**. The integral is the area $\frac{1}{2}\pi r^2 = 2\pi$.

**83**. The integral is the area of the “big” triangle less the “missing” triangle, $9 - \frac{1}{2}$.

**85**. $L = 2 + 0 + 10 + 5 + 4 = 21$, $R = 0 + 10 + 10 + 2 + 0 = 22$, $\frac{L+R}{2} = 21.5$

**87**. $L = 0 + 4 + 0 + 4 + 2 = 10$, $R = 4 + 0 + 2 + 4 + 0 = 10$, $\frac{L+R}{2} = 10$

**89**. $\int_2^4 f(x)dx + \int_2^4 g(x)dx = 8 - 3 = 5$

**91**. $\int_2^4 f(x)dx - \int_2^4 g(x)dx = 8 + 3 = 11$

**93**. $4\int_2^4 f(x)dx - 3\int_2^4 g(x)dx = 32 + 9 = 41$

**95**. The integrand is odd; the integral is zero.

**97**. The integrand is antisymmetric with respect to $x = 3$. The integral is zero.

**99**. $1 - \frac{1}{2} + \frac{1}{3} - \frac{1}{4} = \frac{7}{12}$

**101**. $\int_0^1 \left(1 - 2x + 4x^2 - 8x^3\right)dx = 1 - 1 + \frac{4}{3} - 2 = -\frac{2}{3}$

**103**. $7 - \frac{5}{4} = \frac{23}{4}$

**105**. The integrand is negative over $[-2, 3]$.

**107**. $x \le x^2$ over $[1, 2]$, so $\sqrt{1+x} \le \sqrt{1+x^2}$ over $[1, 2]$.

**109**. $\cos(t) \ge \frac{\sqrt{2}}{2}$. Multiply by the length of the interval to get the inequality.

**111**. $f_{\text{ave}} = 0; c = 0$

**113**. $\frac{3}{2}$ when $c = \pm\frac{3}{2}$

**115**. $f_{\text{ave}} = 0; c = \frac{\pi}{2}, \frac{3\pi}{2}$

**117**. $L_{100} = 1.294$, $R_{100} = 1.301$; the exact average is between these values.

**119**. $L_{100} \times \left(\frac{1}{2}\right) = 0.5178$, $R_{100} \times \left(\frac{1}{2}\right) = 0.5294$

**121**. $L_1 = 0$, $L_{10} \times \left(\frac{1}{2}\right) = 8.743493$, $L_{100} \times \left(\frac{1}{2}\right) = 12.861728$. The exact answer $\approx 26.799$, so $L_{100}$ is not accurate.

**123**. $L_1 \times \left(\frac{1}{\pi}\right) = 1.352$, $L_{10} \times \left(\frac{1}{\pi}\right) = -0.1837$, $L_{100} \times \left(\frac{1}{\pi}\right) = -0.2956$. The exact answer $\approx -0.303$, so $L_{100}$ is not accurate to first decimal.

**125**. Use $\tan^2\theta + 1 = \sec^2\theta$. Then, $B - A = \int_{-\pi/4}^{\pi/4} 1dx = \frac{\pi}{2}$.

**127**. $\int_0^{2\pi} \cos^2 tdt = \pi$, so divide by the length $2\pi$ of the interval. $\cos^2 t$ has period $\pi$, so yes, it is true.

**129**. The integral is maximized when one uses the largest interval on which $p$ is nonnegative. Thus, $A = \frac{-b - \sqrt{b^2 - 4ac}}{2a}$ and $B = \frac{-b + \sqrt{b^2 - 4ac}}{2a}$.

**131**. If $f(t_0) > g(t_0)$ for some $t_0 \in [a, b]$, then since $f - g$ is continuous, there is an interval containing $t_0$ such that $f(t) > g(t)$ over the interval $[c, d]$, and then $\int_d^d f(t)dt > \int_c^d g(t)dt$ over this interval.

**133**. The integral of $f$ over an interval is the same as the integral of the average of $f$ over that interval. Thus, $\int_a^b f(t)dt = \int_{a_0}^{a_1} f(t)dt + \int_{a_1}^{a_2} f(t)dt + \cdots + \int_{a_{N+1}}^{a_N} f(t)dt = \int_{a_0}^{a_1} 1dt + \int_{a_1}^{a_2} 1dt + \cdots + \int_{a_{N+1}}^{a_N} 1dt$ $= (a_1 - a_0) + (a_2 - a_1) + \cdots + (a_N - a_{N-1}) = a_N - a_0 = b - a$. Dividing through by $b - a$ gives the desired identity.

**135**. $\int_0^N f(t)dt = \sum_{i=1}^{N} \int_{i-1}^{i} f(t)dt = \sum_{i=1}^{N} i^2 = \frac{N(N+1)(2N+1)}{6}$

**137**. $L_{10} = 1.815$, $R_{10} = 1.515$, $\frac{L_{10} + R_{10}}{2} = 1.665$, so the estimate is accurate to two decimal places.

**139**. The average is $1/2$, which is equal to the integral in this case.

**141**. a. The graph is antisymmetric with respect to $t = \frac{1}{2}$ over $[0, 1]$, so the average value is zero. b. For any value of $a$, the graph between $[a, a+1]$ is a shift of the graph over $[0, 1]$, so the net areas above and below the axis do not change and the average remains zero.

**143**. Yes, the integral over any interval of length 1 is the same.

**145**. Yes. It is implied by the Mean Value Theorem for Integrals.

**147**. $F'(2) = -1$; average value of $F'$ over $[1, 2]$ is $-1/2$.

**149**. $e^{\cos t}$

**151**. $\frac{1}{\sqrt{16 - x^2}}$

**153**. $\sqrt{x}\frac{d}{dx}\sqrt{x} = \frac{1}{2}$

**155**. $-\sqrt{1-\cos^2 x}\frac{d}{dx}\cos x = |\sin x|\sin x$

**157**. $2x\frac{|x|}{1+x^2}$

**159**. $\ln(e^{2x})\frac{d}{dx}e^x = 2xe^x$

**161**. a. $f$ is positive over $[1, 2]$ and $[5, 6]$, negative over $[0, 1]$ and $[3, 4]$, and zero over $[2, 3]$ and $[4, 5]$. b. The maximum value is 2 and the minimum is −3. c. The average value is 0.

**163**. a. $\ell$ is positive over $[0, 1]$ and $[3, 6]$, and negative over $[1, 3]$. b. It is increasing over $[0, 1]$ and $[3, 5]$, and it is constant over $[1, 3]$ and $[5, 6]$. c. Its average value is $\frac{1}{3}$.

**165**. $T_{10} = 49.08$, $\int_{-2}^{3} x^3 + 6x^2 + x - 5dx = 48$

**167**. $T_{10} = 260.836$, $\int_{1}^{9}\left(\sqrt{x} + x^2\right)dx = 260$

**169**. $T_{10} = 3.058$, $\int_{1}^{4}\frac{4}{x^2}dx = 3$

**171**. $F(x) = \frac{x^3}{3} + \frac{3x^2}{2} - 5x$, $F(3) - F(-2) = -\frac{35}{6}$

**173**. $F(x) = -\frac{t^5}{5} + \frac{13t^3}{3} - 36t$, $F(3) - F(2) = \frac{62}{15}$

**175**. $F(x) = \frac{x^{100}}{100}$, $F(1) - F(0) = \frac{1}{100}$

**177**. $F(x) = \frac{x^3}{3} + \frac{1}{x}$, $F(4) - F\left(\frac{1}{4}\right) = \frac{1125}{64}$

**179**. $F(x) = \sqrt{x}$, $F(4) - F(1) = 1$

**181**. $F(x) = \frac{4}{3}t^{3/4}$, $F(16) - F(1) = \frac{28}{3}$

**183**. $F(x) = -\cos x$, $F\left(\frac{\pi}{2}\right) - F(0) = 1$

**185**. $F(x) = \sec x$, $F\left(\frac{\pi}{4}\right) - F(0) = \sqrt{2} - 1$

**187**. $F(x) = -\cot(x)$, $F\left(\frac{\pi}{2}\right) - F\left(\frac{\pi}{4}\right) = 1$

**189**. $F(x) = -\frac{1}{x} + \frac{1}{2x^2}$, $F(-1) - F(-2) = \frac{7}{8}$

**191**. $F(x) = e^x - e$

**193**. $F(x) = 0$

**195**. $\int_{-2}^{-1}\left(t^2 - 2t - 3\right)dt - \int_{-1}^{3}\left(t^2 - 2t - 3\right)dt + \int_{3}^{4}\left(t^2 - 2t - 3\right)dt = \frac{46}{3}$

**197**. $-\int_{-\pi/2}^{0} \sin t dt + \int_{0}^{\pi/2} \sin t dt = 2$

**199**. a. The average is $11.21 \times 10^9$ since $\cos\left(\frac{\pi t}{6}\right)$ has period 12 and integral 0 over any period. Consumption is equal to the average when $\cos\left(\frac{\pi t}{6}\right) = 0$, when $t = 3$, and when $t = 9$. b. Total consumption is the average rate times duration: $11.21 \times 12 \times 10^9 = 1.35 \times 10^{11}$ c. $10^9\left(11.21 - \frac{1}{6}\int_{3}^{9}\cos\left(\frac{\pi t}{6}\right)dt\right) = 10^9\left(11.21 + \frac{2}{\pi}\right) = 11.84x10^9$

**201**. If $f$ is not constant, then its average is strictly smaller than the maximum and larger than the minimum, which are attained over $[a, b]$ by the extreme value theorem.

**203**. a. $d^2\theta = (a\cos\theta + c)^2 + b^2\sin^2\theta = a^2 + c^2\cos^2\theta + 2ac\cos\theta = (a + c\cos\theta)^2$; b. $\bar{d} = \frac{1}{2\pi}\int_0^{2\pi}(a + 2c\cos\theta)d\theta = a$

**205**. Mean gravitational force = $\frac{GmM}{2}\int_0^{2\pi}\frac{1}{\left(a + 2\sqrt{a^2 - b^2}\cos\theta\right)^2}d\theta.$

**207**. $\int\left(\sqrt{x} - \frac{1}{\sqrt{x}}\right)dx = \int x^{1/2}dx - \int x^{-1/2}dx = \frac{2}{3}x^{3/2} + C_1 - 2x^{1/2} + C_2 = \frac{2}{3}x^{3/2} - 2x^{1/2} + C$

**209**. $\int\frac{dx}{2x} = \frac{1}{2}\ln|x| + C$

**211**. $\int_0^{\pi}\sin x dx - \int_0^{\pi}\cos x dx = -\cos x|_0^{\pi} - (\sin x)|_0^{\pi} = (-(-1) + 1) - (0 - 0) = 2$

**213**. $P(s) = 4s,$ so $\frac{dP}{ds} = 4$ and $\int_2^4 4ds = 8.$

**215**. $\int_1^2 Nds = N$

**217**. With $p$ as in the previous exercise, each of the 12 pentagons increases in area from $2p$ to $4p$ units so the net increase in the area of the dodecahedron is $36p$ units.

**219**. $18s^2 = 6\int_s^{2s} 2xdx$

**221**. $12\pi R^2 = 8\pi\int_R^{2R} rdr$

**223**. $d(t) = \int_0^t v(s)ds = 4t - t^2.$ The total distance is $d(2) = 4$ m.

**225**. $d(t) = \int_0^t v(s)ds.$ For $t < 3,\ d(t) = \int_0^t(6 - 2t)dt = 6t - t^2.$ For $t > 3,\ d(t) = d(3) + \int_3^t(2t - 6)dt = 9 + (t^2 - 6t).$ The total distance is $d(6) = 9$ m.

**227**. $v(t) = 40 - 9.8t;\ h(t) = 1.5 + 40t - 4.9t^2$ m/s

**229**. The net increase is 1 unit.

**231**. At $t = 5,$ the height of water is $x = \left(\frac{15}{\pi}\right)^{1/3}$ m.. The net change in height from $t = 5$ to $t = 10$ is $\left(\frac{30}{\pi}\right)^{1/3} - \left(\frac{15}{\pi}\right)^{1/3}$ m.

**233**. The total daily power consumption is estimated as the sum of the hourly power rates, or 911 gW-h.

**235**. 17 kJ

**237**. a. 54.3%; b. 27.00%; c. The curve in the following plot is $2.35(t + 3)e^{-0.15(t + 3)}$.

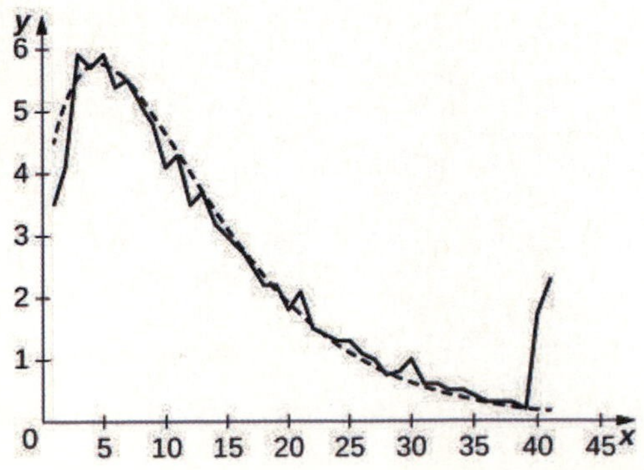

**239**. In dry conditions, with initial velocity $v_0 = 30$ m/s, $D = 64.3$ and, if $v_0 = 25, D = 44.64$. In wet conditions, if $v_0 = 30,$ and $D = 180$ and if $v_0 = 25, D = 125.$

**241**. 225 cal

**243**. $E(150) = 28,\ E(300) = 22,\ E(450) = 16$

**245**. a.

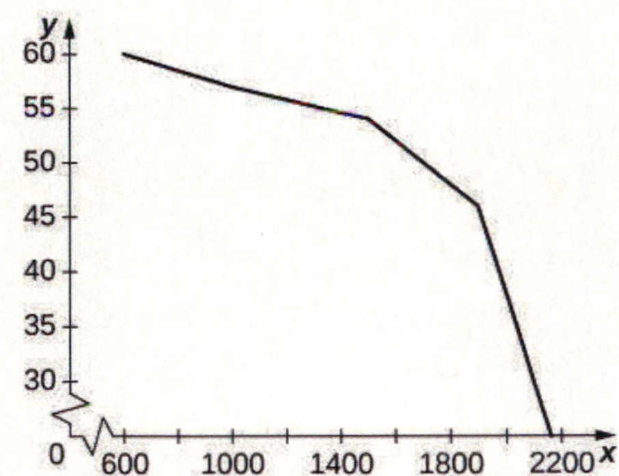


b. Between 600 and 1000 the average decrease in vehicles per hour per lane is −0.0075. Between 1000 and 1500 it is −0.006 per vehicles per hour per lane, and between 1500 and 2100 it is −0.04 vehicles per hour per lane. c.

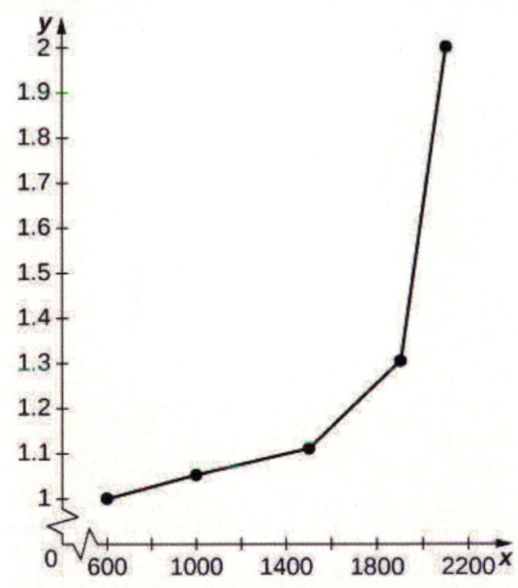


The graph is nonlinear, with minutes per mile increasing dramatically as vehicles per hour per lane reach 2000.

**247**. $\frac{1}{37}\int_0^{37} p(t)dt = \frac{0.07(37)^3}{4} + \frac{2.42(37)^2}{3} - \frac{25.63(37)}{2} + 521.23 \approx 2037$

**249**. Average acceleration is $A = \frac{1}{5}\int_0^5 a(t)dt = -\frac{0.7(5^2)}{3} + \frac{1.44(5)}{2} + 10.44 \approx 8.2$ mph/s

**251**. $d(t) = \int_0^1 |v(t)|dt = \int_0^t \left(\frac{7}{30}t^3 - 0.72t^2 - 10.44t + 41.033\right)dt = \frac{7}{120}t^4 - 0.24t^3 - 5.22t^3 + 41.033t.$ Then, $d(5) \approx 81.12$ mph $\times$ sec $\approx 119$ feet.

**253**. $\frac{1}{40}\int_0^{40} (-0.068t + 5.14)dt = -\frac{0.068(40)}{2} + 5.14 = 3.78$

**255**. $u = h(x)$

**257**. $f(u) = \frac{(u+1)^2}{\sqrt{u}}$

**259**. $du = 8x dx;\ f(u) = \frac{1}{8\sqrt{u}}$

**261**. $\frac{1}{5}(x+1)^5+C$

**263**. $-\frac{1}{12(3-2x)^6}+C$

**265**. $\sqrt{x^2+1}+C$

**267**. $\frac{1}{8}\left(x^2-2x\right)^4+C$

**269**. $\sin\theta-\frac{\sin^3\theta}{3}+C$

**271**. $\frac{(1-x)^{101}}{101}-\frac{(1-x)^{100}}{100}+C$

**273**. $-\frac{1}{22\left(7-11x^2\right)}+C$

**275**. $-\frac{\cos^4\theta}{4}+C$

**277**. $-\frac{\cos^3(\pi t)}{3\pi}+C$

**279**. $-\frac{1}{4}\cos^2\left(t^2\right)+C$

**281**. $-\frac{1}{3(x^3-3)}+C$

**283**. $-\frac{2\left(y^3-2\right)}{3\sqrt{1-y^3}}$

**285**. $\frac{1}{33}\left(1-\cos^3\theta\right)^{11}+C$

**287**. $\frac{1}{12}\left(\sin^3\theta-3\sin^2\theta\right)^4+C$

**289**. $L_{50}=-8.5779.$ The exact area is $\frac{-81}{8}$

**291**. $L_{50}=-0.006399$ … The exact area is 0.

**293**. $u=1+x^2,\ du=2xdx,\ \frac{1}{2}\int_1^2 u^{-1/2}du=\sqrt{2}-1$

**295**. $u=1+t^3,\ du=3t^2,\ \frac{1}{3}\int_1^2 u^{-1/2}du=\frac{2}{3}(\sqrt{2}-1)$

**297**. $u=\cos\theta,\ du=-\sin\theta d\theta,\ \int_{1/\sqrt{2}}^1 u^{-4}du=\frac{1}{3}(2\sqrt{2}-1)$

**299**.

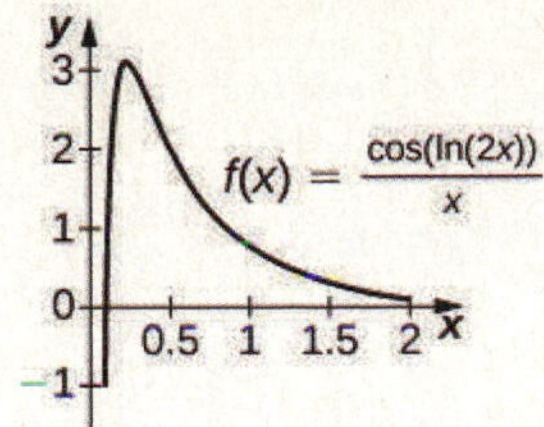


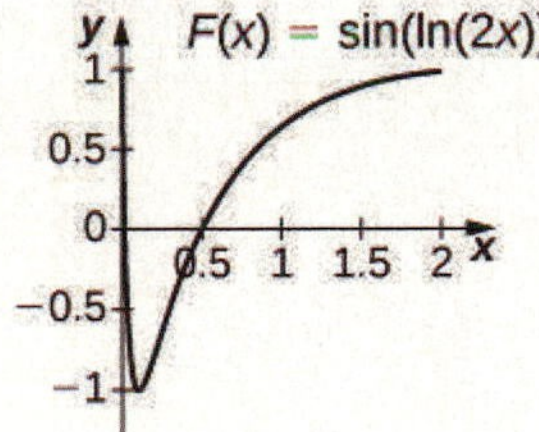


The antiderivative is $y = \sin(\ln(2x))$. Since the antiderivative is not continuous at $x = 0$, one cannot find a value of $C$ that would make $y = \sin(\ln(2x)) - C$ work as a definite integral.

**301**.

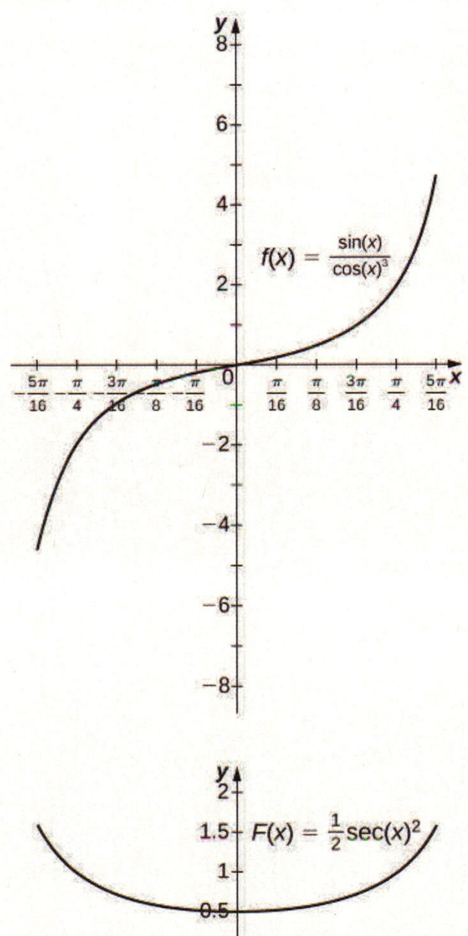


The antiderivative is $y = \frac{1}{2}\sec^2 x$. You should take $C = -2$ so that $F\left(-\frac{\pi}{3}\right) = 0$.

**303**.

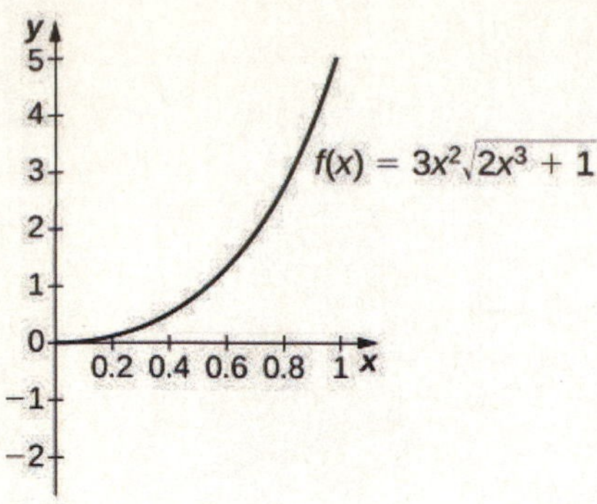


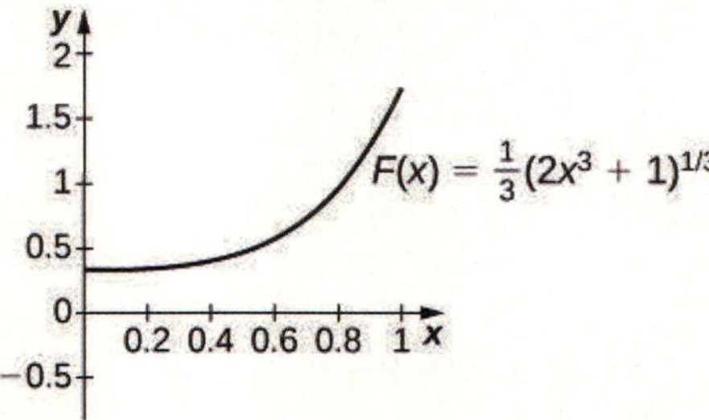


The antiderivative is $y = \frac{1}{3}\left(2x^3 + 1\right)^{3/2}$. One should take $C = -\frac{1}{3}$.

**305**. No, because the integrand is discontinuous at $x = 1$.

**307**. $u = \sin\left(t^2\right)$; the integral becomes $\frac{1}{2}\int_0^0 u\,du$.

**309**. $u = \left(1 + \left(t - \frac{1}{2}\right)^2\right)$; the integral becomes $-\int_{5/4}^{5/4} \frac{1}{u}du$.

**311**. $u = 1 - t$; the integral becomes

$$\begin{aligned}&\int_1^{-1} u\cos(\pi(1-u))du\\ &= \int_1^{-1} u[\cos\pi\cos u - \sin\pi\sin u]du\\ &= -\int_1^{-1} u\cos u\,du\\ &= \int_{-1}^{1} u\cos u\,du = 0\end{aligned}$$

since the integrand is odd.

**313**. Setting $u = cx$ and $du = cdx$ gets you $\frac{1}{\frac{b}{c} - \frac{a}{c}}\int_{a/c}^{b/c} f(cx)dx = \frac{c}{b-a}\int_{u=a}^{u=b} f(u)\frac{du}{c} = \frac{1}{b-a}\int_a^b f(u)du$.

**315**. $\displaystyle\int_0^x g(t)dt = \frac{1}{2}\int_{u=1-x^2}^{1} \frac{du}{u^a} = \frac{1}{2(1-a)}u^{1-a}\Big|_{u=1-x^2}^{1} = \frac{1}{2(1-a)}\left(1 - \left(1 - x^2\right)^{1-a}\right)$. As $x \to 1$ the limit is $\frac{1}{2(1-a)}$ if $a < 1$, and the limit diverges to $+\infty$ if $a > 1$.

**317**. $\displaystyle\int_{t=\pi}^{0} b\sqrt{1 - \cos^2 t} \times (-a\sin t)dt = \int_{t=0}^{\pi} ab\sin^2 t\,dt$

**319**. $f(t) = 2\cos(3t) - \cos(2t); \int_0^{\pi/2} (2\cos(3t) - \cos(2t)) = -\frac{2}{3}$

**321**. $\frac{-1}{3}e^{-3x} + C$

**323**. $-\frac{3^{-x}}{\ln 3} + C$

**325**. $\ln\left(x^2\right) + C$

**327**. $2\sqrt{x} + C$

**329**. $-\frac{1}{\ln x} + C$

**331**. $\ln(\ln(\ln x)) + C$

**333**. $\ln(x\cos x) + C$

**335**. $-\frac{1}{2}(\ln(\cos(x)))^2 + C$

**337**. $\frac{-e^{-x^3}}{3} + C$

**339**. $e^{\tan x} + C$

**341**. $t + C$

**343**. $\frac{1}{9}x^3\left(\ln\left(x^3\right) - 1\right) + C$

**345**. $2\sqrt{x}(\ln x - 2) + C$

**347**. $\int_0^{\ln x} e^t\, dt = e^t\Big|_0^{\ln x} = e^{\ln x} - e^0 = x - 1$

**349**. $-\frac{1}{3}\ln(\sin(3x) + \cos(3x))$

**351**. $-\frac{1}{2}\ln\left|\csc\left(x^2\right) + \cot\left(x^2\right)\right| + C$

**353**. $-\frac{1}{2}(\ln(\csc x))^2 + C$

**355**. $\frac{1}{3}\ln\left(\frac{26}{7}\right)$

**357**. $\ln\left(\sqrt{3} - 1\right)$

**359**. $\frac{1}{2}\ln\frac{3}{2}$

**361**. $y - 2\ln|y + 1| + C$

**363**. $\ln|\sin x - \cos x| + C$

**365**. $-\frac{1}{3}\left(1 - \left(\ln x^2\right)\right)^{3/2} + C$

**367**. Exact solution: $\frac{e-1}{e}$, $R_{50} = 0.6258$. Since $f$ is decreasing, the right endpoint estimate underestimates the area.

**369**. Exact solution: $\frac{2\ln(3) - \ln(6)}{2}$, $R_{50} = 0.2033$. Since $f$ is increasing, the right endpoint estimate overestimates the area.

**371**. Exact solution: $-\frac{1}{\ln(4)}$, $R_{50} = -0.7164$. Since $f$ is increasing, the right endpoint estimate overestimates the area (the actual area is a larger negative number).

**373**. $\frac{11}{2}\ln 2$

**375**. $\frac{1}{\ln(65, 536)}$

**377**. $\int_N^{N+1} xe^{-x^2}\, dx = \frac{1}{2}\left(e^{-N^2} - e^{-(N+1)^2}\right)$. The quantity is less than 0.01 when $N = 2$.

**379**. $\int_a^b \frac{dx}{x} = \ln(b) - \ln(a) = \ln\left(\frac{1}{a}\right) - \ln\left(\frac{1}{b}\right) = \int_{1/b}^{1/a} \frac{dx}{x}$

**381**. 23

**383**. We may assume that $x > 1$, so $\frac{1}{x} < 1$. Then, $\int_1^{1/x} \frac{dt}{t}$. Now make the substitution $u = \frac{1}{t}$, so $du = -\frac{dt}{t^2}$ and $\frac{du}{u} = -\frac{dt}{t}$, and change endpoints: $\int_1^{1/x} \frac{dt}{t} = -\int_1^{x} \frac{du}{u} = -\ln x.$

**387**. $x = E(\ln(x))$. Then, $1 = \frac{E'(\ln x)}{x}$ or $x = E'(\ln x)$. Since any number $t$ can be written $t = \ln x$ for some $x$, and for such $t$ we have $x = E(t)$, it follows that for any $t$, $E'(t) = E(t)$.

**389**. $R_{10} = 0.6811$, $R_{100} = 0.6827$

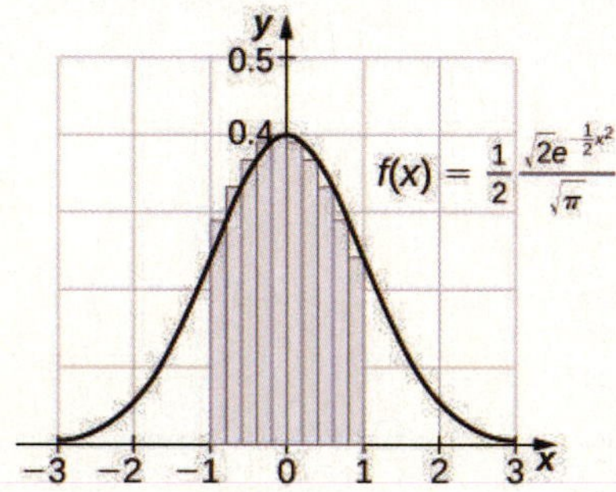


**391**. $\sin^{-1} x \Big|_0^{\sqrt{3}/2} = \frac{\pi}{3}$

**393**. $\tan^{-1} x \Big|_{\sqrt{3}}^{1} = -\frac{\pi}{12}$

**395**. $\sec^{-1} x \Big|_1^{\sqrt{2}} = \frac{\pi}{4}$

**397**. $\sin^{-1}\left(\frac{x}{3}\right) + C$

**399**. $\frac{1}{3}\tan^{-1}\left(\frac{x}{3}\right) + C$

**401**. $\frac{1}{3}\sec^{-1}\left(\frac{x}{3}\right) + C$

**403**. $\cos\left(\frac{\pi}{2} - \theta\right) = \sin\theta$. So, $\sin^{-1} t = \frac{\pi}{2} - \cos^{-1} t$. They differ by a constant.

**405**. $\sqrt{1 - t^2}$ is not defined as a real number when $t > 1$.

**407**.

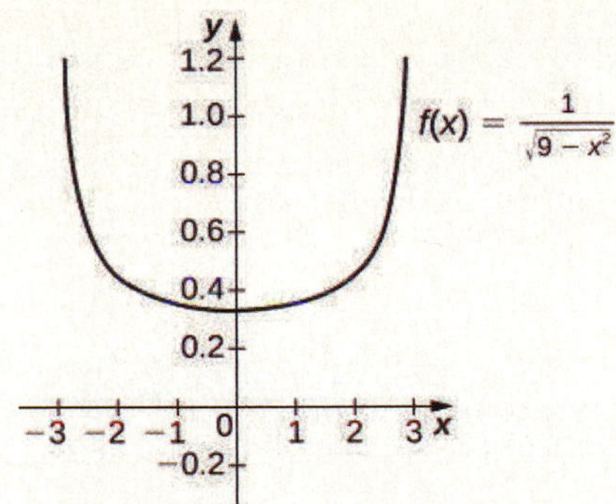


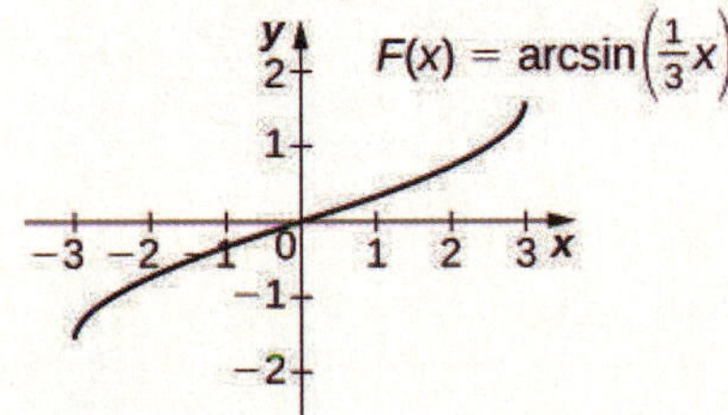


The antiderivative is $\sin^{-1}\left(\frac{x}{3}\right) + C$. Taking $C = \frac{\pi}{2}$ recovers the definite integral.

**409**.

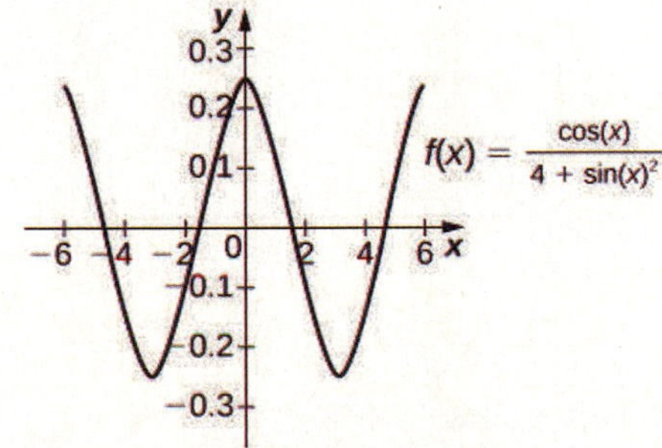


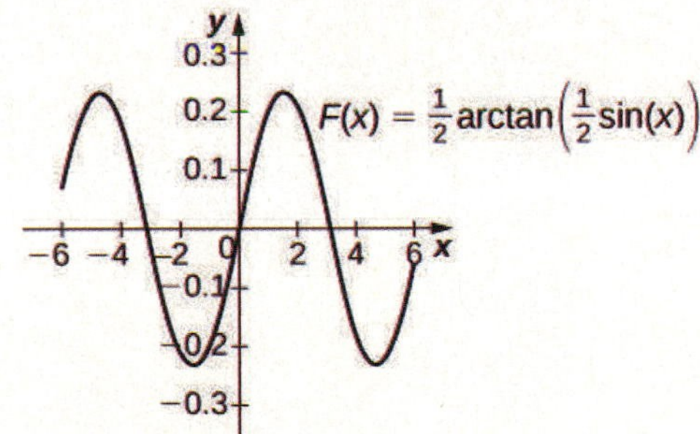


The antiderivative is $\frac{1}{2}\tan^{-1}\left(\frac{\sin x}{2}\right) + C$. Taking $C = \frac{1}{2}\tan^{-1}\left(\frac{\sin(6)}{2}\right)$ recovers the definite integral.

**411**. $\frac{1}{2}\left(\sin^{-1} t\right)^2 + C$

**413**. $\frac{1}{4}\left(\tan^{-1}(2t)\right)^2$

**415**. $\frac{1}{4}\left(\sec^{-1}\left(\frac{t}{2}\right)^2\right) + C$

**417**.

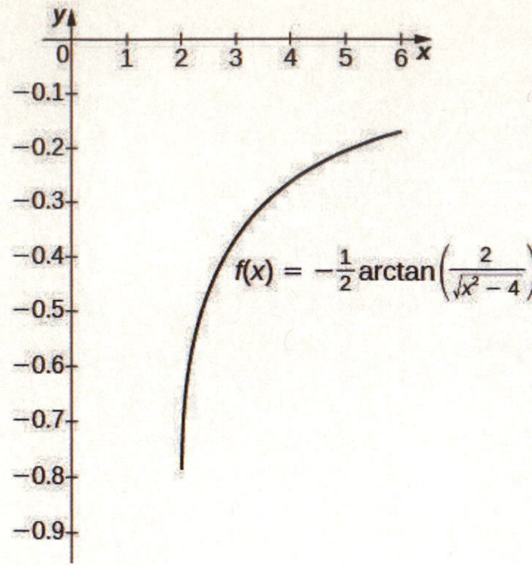


The antiderivative is $\frac{1}{2}\sec^{-1}\left(\frac{x}{2}\right) + C$. Taking $C = 0$ recovers the definite integral over $[2, 6]$.

**419**.

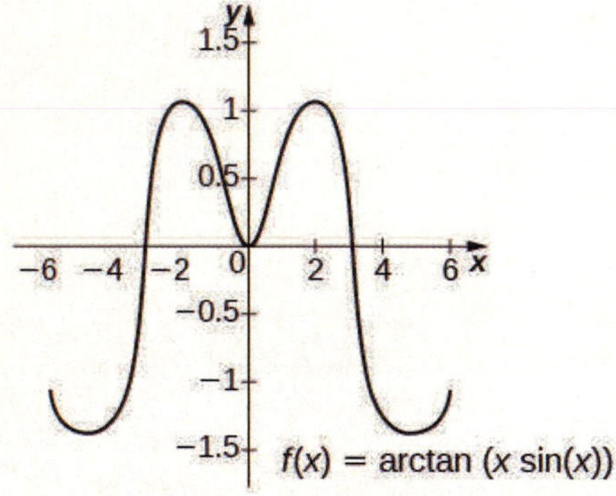


The general antiderivative is $\tan^{-1}(x\sin x) + C$. Taking $C = -\tan^{-1}(6\sin(6))$ recovers the definite integral.

**421**.

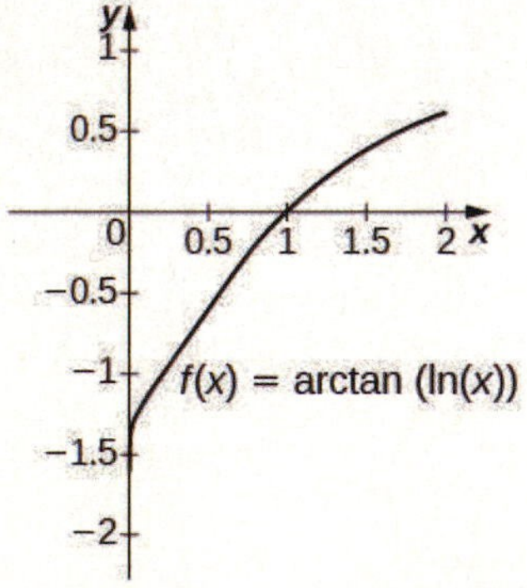


The general antiderivative is $\tan^{-1}(\ln x) + C$. Taking $C = \frac{\pi}{2} = \tan^{-1}\infty$ recovers the definite integral.

**423**. $\sin^{-1}(e^t) + C$

**425**. $\sin^{-1}(\ln t) + C$

**427**. $-\frac{1}{2}\left(\cos^{-1}(2t)\right)^2 + C$

**429**. $\frac{1}{2}\ln\left(\frac{4}{3}\right)$

**431**. $1 - \frac{2}{\sqrt{5}}$

**433**. $2\tan^{-1}(A) \to \pi$ as $A \to \infty$

**435**. Using the hint, one has $\int \frac{\csc^2 x}{\csc^2 x + \cot^2 x} dx = \int \frac{\csc^2 x}{1 + 2\cot^2 x} dx$. Set $u = \sqrt{2}\cot x$. Then, $du = -\sqrt{2}\csc^2 x$ and the integral is $-\frac{1}{\sqrt{2}} \int \frac{du}{1 + u^2} = -\frac{1}{\sqrt{2}}\tan^{-1} u + C = \frac{1}{\sqrt{2}}\tan^{-1}\left(\sqrt{2}\cot x\right) + C$. If one uses the identity $\tan^{-1} s + \tan^{-1}\left(\frac{1}{s}\right) = \frac{\pi}{2}$, then this can also be written $\frac{1}{\sqrt{2}}\tan^{-1}\left(\frac{\tan x}{\sqrt{2}}\right) + C$.

**437**. $x \approx \pm 1.13525$. The left endpoint estimate with $N = 100$ is 2.796 and these decimals persist for $N = 500$.

## Review Exercises

**439**. False

**441**. True

**443**. $L_4 = 5.25$, $R_4 = 3.25$, exact answer: 4

**445**. $L_4 = 5.364$, $R_4 = 5.364$, exact answer: 5.870

**447**. $-\frac{4}{3}$

**449**. 1

**451**. $-\frac{1}{2(x+4)^2} + C$

**453**. $\frac{4}{3}\sin^{-1}\left(x^3\right) + C$

**455**. $\frac{\sin t}{\sqrt{1 + t^2}}$

**457**. $4\frac{\ln x}{x} + 1$

**459**. $6,328,113

**461**. $73.36

**463**. $\frac{19117}{12}$ ft/sec, or 1593 ft/sec

# Chapter 2

## Checkpoint

**2.1**. 12 units$^2$

**2.2**. $\frac{3}{10}$ unit$^2$

**2.3**. $2 + 2\sqrt{2}$ units$^2$

**2.4**. $\frac{5}{3}$ units$^2$

**2.5**. $\frac{5}{3}$ units$^2$

**2.7**. $\frac{\pi}{2}$

**2.8**. $8\pi$ units$^3$

**2.9**. $21\pi$ units$^3$

**2.10**. $\frac{10\pi}{3}$ units$^3$

**2.11**. $60\pi$ units$^3$

**2.12**. $\frac{15\pi}{2}$ units$^3$

**2.13**. $8\pi$ units$^3$

**2.14**. $12\pi$ units$^3$

**2.15**. $\frac{11\pi}{6}$ units$^3$

**2.16**. $\frac{\pi}{6}$ units$^3$

**2.17**. Use the method of washers; $V = \int_{-1}^{1} \pi\left[\left(2 - x^2\right)^2 - \left(x^2\right)^2\right] dx$

**2.18**. $\frac{1}{6}(5\sqrt{5} - 1) \approx 1.697$

**2.19**. Arc Length $\approx 3.8202$

**2.20**. Arc Length $= 3.15018$

**2.21**. $\frac{\pi}{6}(5\sqrt{5} - 3\sqrt{3}) \approx 3.133$

**2.22**. $12\pi$

**2.23**. 70/3

**2.24**. $24\pi$

**2.25**. 8 ft-lb

**2.26**. Approximately 43,255.2 ft-lb

**2.27**. 156,800 N

**2.28**. Approximately 7,164,520,000 lb or 3,582,260 t

**2.29**. $M = 24, \ \bar{x} = \frac{2}{5}$ m

**2.30**. $(-1, -1)$ m

**2.31**. The centroid of the region is $(3/2, 6/5)$.

**2.32**. The centroid of the region is $(1, 13/5)$.

**2.33**. The centroid of the region is $(0, 2/5)$.

**2.34**. $6\pi^2$ units$^3$

**2.35**.

a. $\frac{d}{dx}\ln\left(2x^2 + x\right) = \frac{4x + 1}{2x^2 + x}$

b. $\frac{d}{dx}\left(\ln\left(x^3\right)\right)^2 = \frac{6\ln\left(x^3\right)}{x}$

**2.36**. $\int \frac{x^2}{x^3 + 6} dx = \frac{1}{3}\ln\left|x^3 + 6\right| + C$

**2.37**. $4 \ln 2$

**2.38**.

a. $\frac{d}{dx}\left(\frac{e^{x^2}}{e^{5x}}\right) = e^{x^2 - 5x}(2x - 5)$

b. $\frac{d}{dt}\left(e^{2t}\right)^3 = 6e^{6t}$

**2.39**. $\int \frac{4}{e^{3x}} dx = -\frac{4}{3}e^{-3x} + C$

**2.40**.

a. $\frac{d}{dt}4^{t^4} = 4^{t^4}(\ln 4)\left(4t^3\right)$

b. $\frac{d}{dx}\log_3\left(\sqrt{x^2 + 1}\right) = \frac{x}{(\ln 3)\left(x^2 + 1\right)}$

**2.41**. $\int x^2 2^{x^3} dx = \frac{1}{3\ln 2}2^{x^3} + C$

**2.42**. There are 81,377,396 bacteria in the population after 4 hours. The population reaches 100 million bacteria after

244.12 minutes.

**2.43**. At 5% interest, she must invest $223,130.16. At 6% interest, she must invest $165,298.89.

**2.44**. 38.90 months

**2.45**. The coffee is first cool enough to serve about 3.5 minutes after it is poured. The coffee is too cold to serve about 7 minutes after it is poured.

**2.46**. A total of 94.13 g of carbon remains. The artifact is approximately 13,300 years old.

**2.47**.

a. $\frac{d}{dx}(\tanh(x^2+3x)) = (\operatorname{sech}^2(x^2+3x))(2x+3)$

b. $\frac{d}{dx}\left(\frac{1}{(\sinh x)^2}\right) = \frac{d}{dx}(\sinh x)^{-2} = -2(\sinh x)^{-3}\cosh x$

**2.48**.

a. $\int \sinh^3 x \cosh x\, dx = \frac{\sinh^4 x}{4} + C$

b. $\int \operatorname{sech}^2(3x)dx = \frac{\tanh(3x)}{3} + C$

**2.49**.

a. $\frac{d}{dx}(\cosh^{-1}(3x)) = \frac{3}{\sqrt{9x^2-1}}$

b. $\frac{d}{dx}\left(\coth^{-1}x\right)^3 = \frac{3\left(\coth^{-1}x\right)^2}{1-x^2}$

**2.50**.

a. $\int \frac{1}{\sqrt{x^2-4}}dx = \cosh^{-1}\left(\frac{x}{2}\right) + C$

b. $\int \frac{1}{\sqrt{1-e^{2x}}}dx = -\operatorname{sech}^{-1}(e^x) + C$

**2.51**. 52.95 ft

## Section Exercises

**1**. $\frac{32}{3}$

**3**. $\frac{13}{12}$

**5**. 36

**7**.

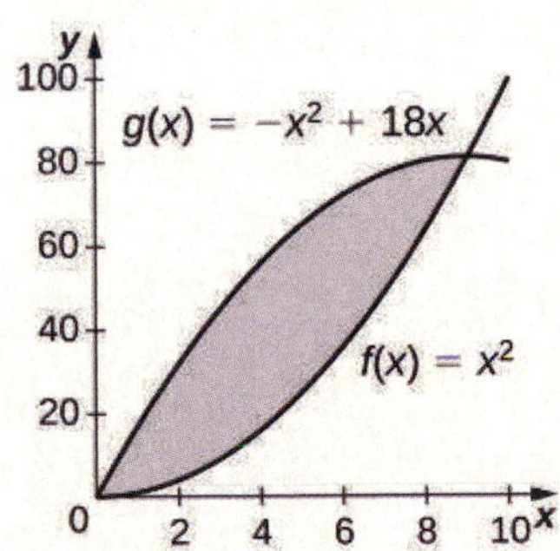


243 square units

**9**.

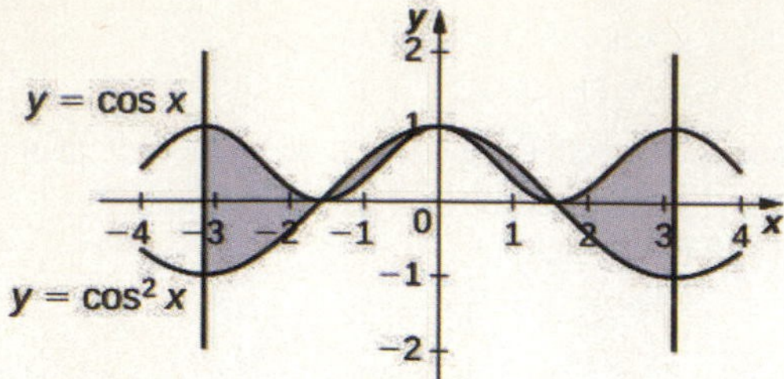


4

**11.**

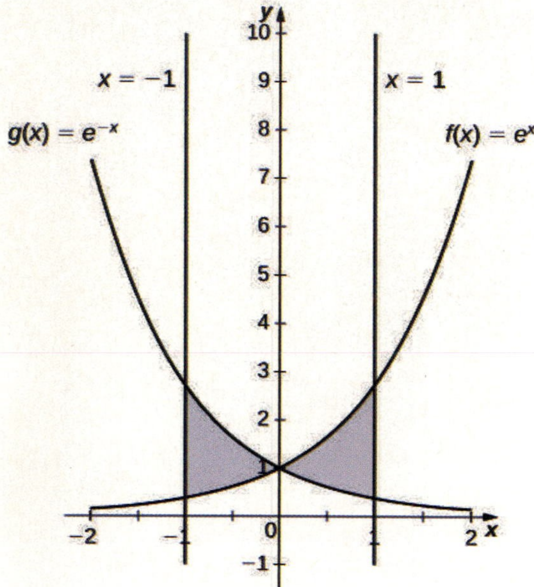


$\frac{2(e-1)^2}{e}$

**13.**

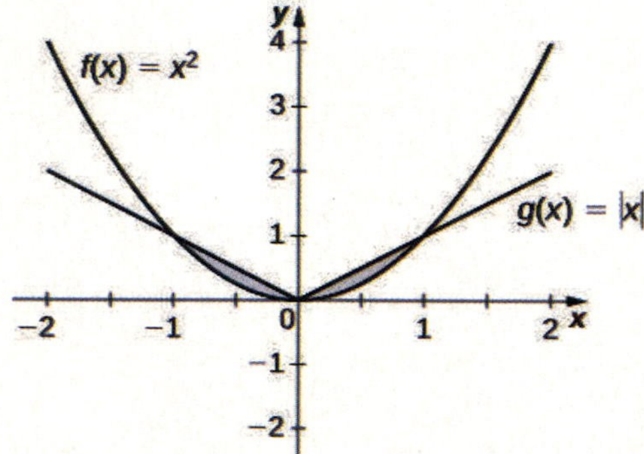


$\frac{1}{3}$

**15.**

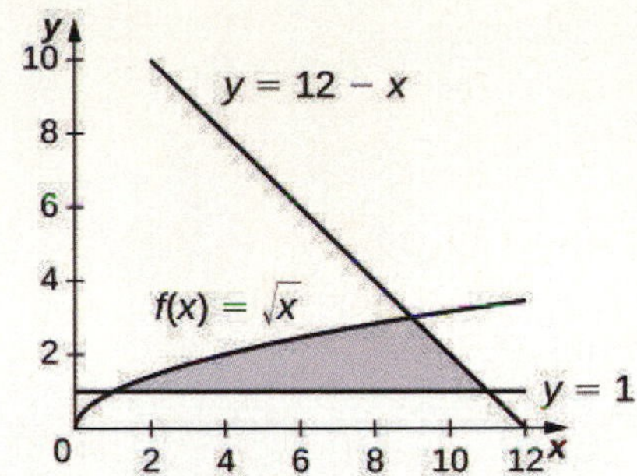


$\frac{34}{3}$

**17**.

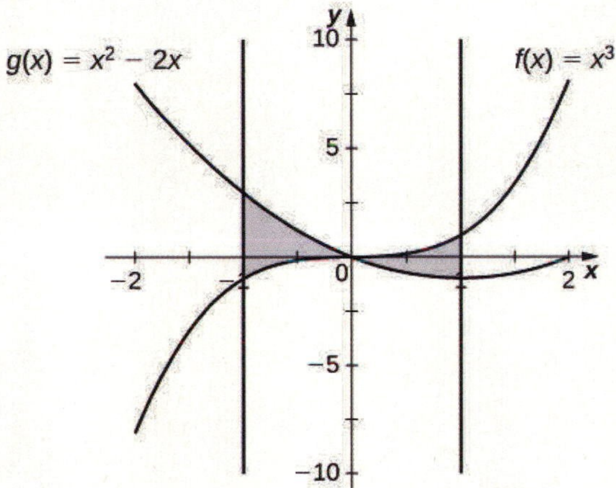


$\frac{5}{2}$

**19**.

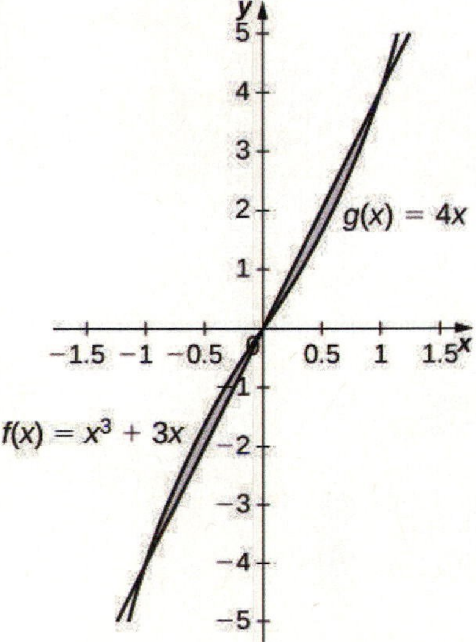


$\frac{1}{2}$

**21**.

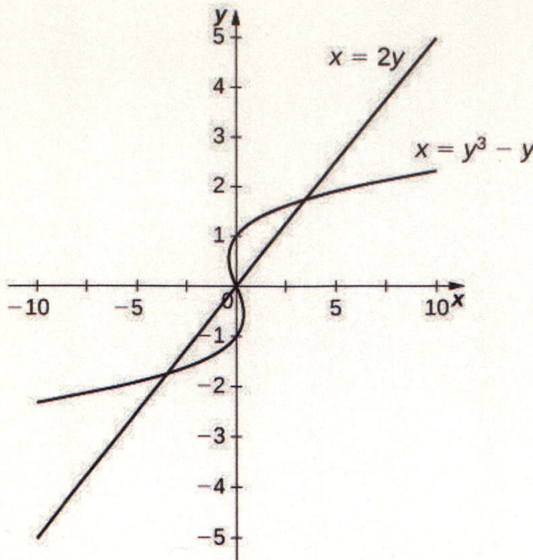


$\frac{9}{2}$

**23**.

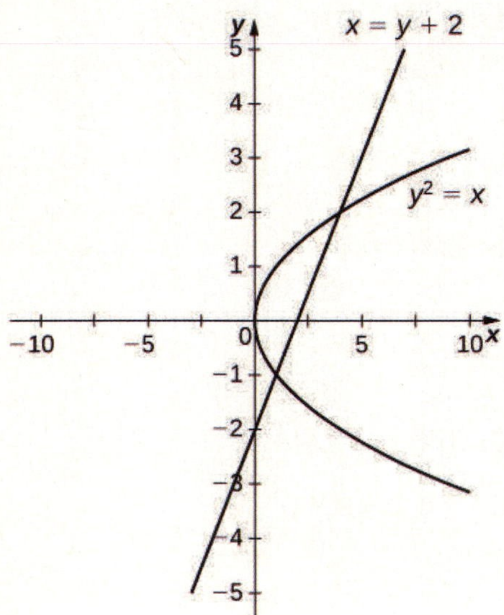


$\frac{9}{2}$

**25**.

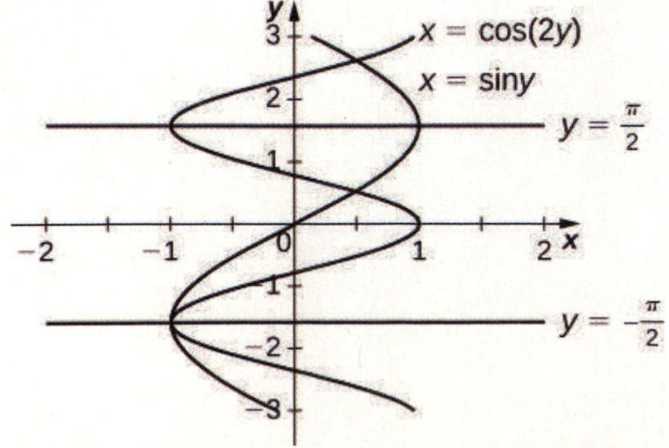

$\frac{3\sqrt{3}}{2}$

**27**.

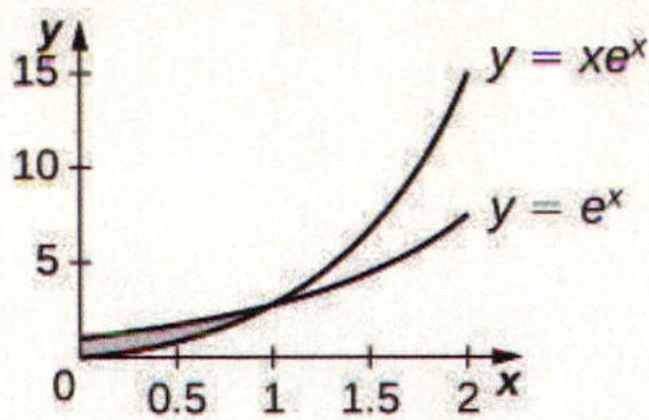


$e^{-2}$

**29**.

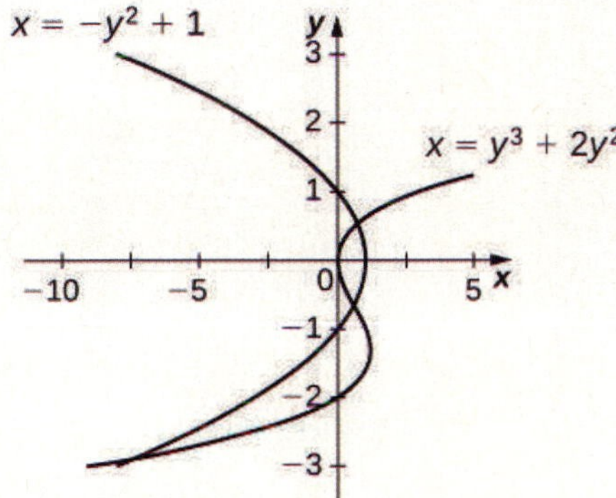


$\frac{27}{4}$

**31**.

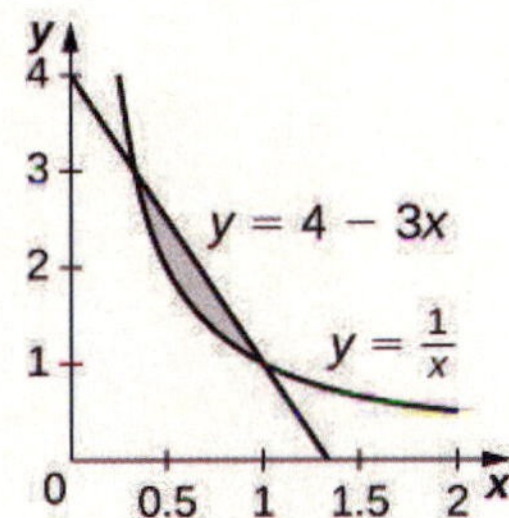


$\frac{4}{3} - \ln(3)$

**33**.

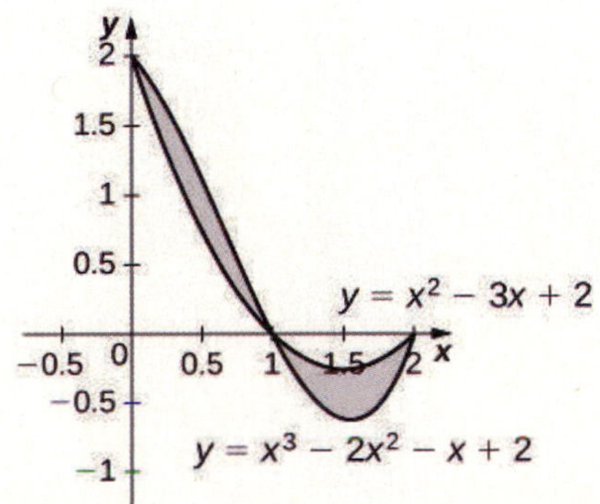


$\frac{1}{2}$

**35.**

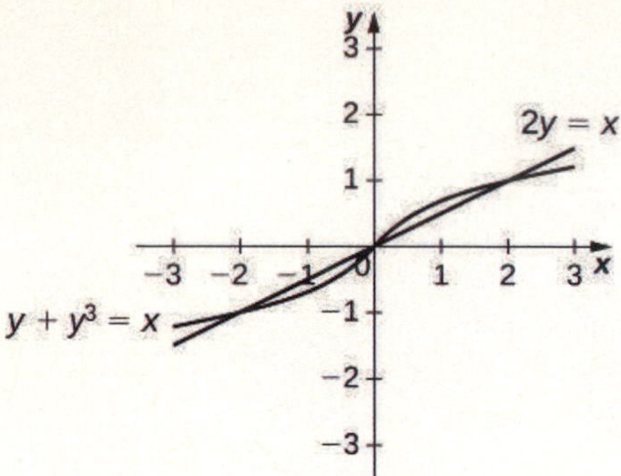


$\frac{1}{2}$

**37.**

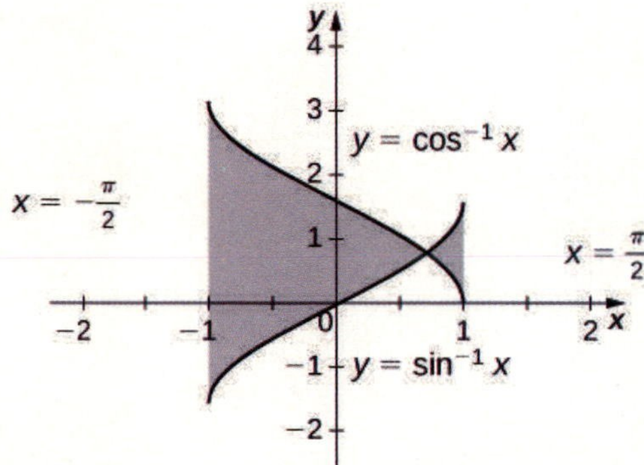


$-2(\sqrt{2}-\pi)$

**39.** 1.067

**41.** 0.852

**43.** 7.523

**45.** $\frac{3\pi - 4}{12}$

**47.** 1.429

**49.** $33,333.33 total profit for 200 cell phones sold

**51.** 3.263 mi represents how far ahead the hare is from the tortoise

**53.** $\frac{343}{24}$

**55.** $4\sqrt{3}$

**57.** $\pi - \frac{32}{25}$

**63.** 8 units$^3$

**65.** $\frac{32}{3\sqrt{2}}$ units$^3$

**67.** $\frac{7\pi}{12}hr^2$ units$^3$

**69.**

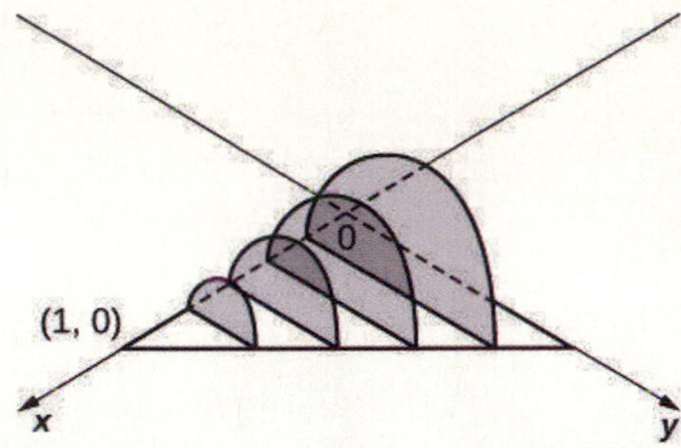


$\frac{\pi}{24}$ units$^3$

**71**.

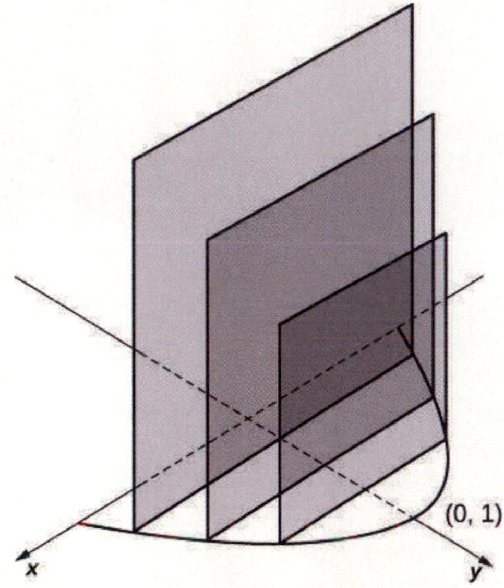


$2$ units$^3$

**73**.

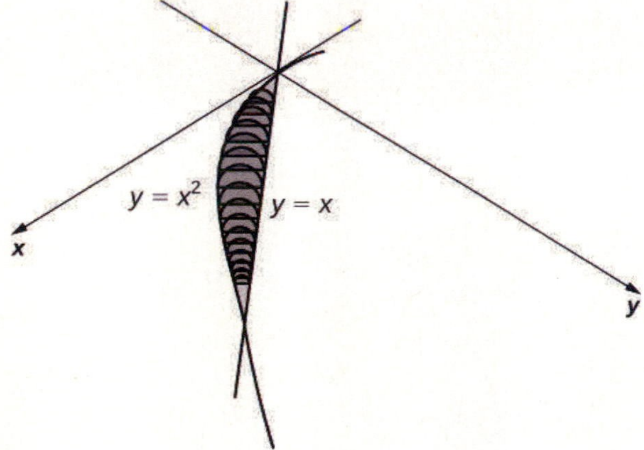


$\frac{\pi}{240}$ units$^3$

**75**.

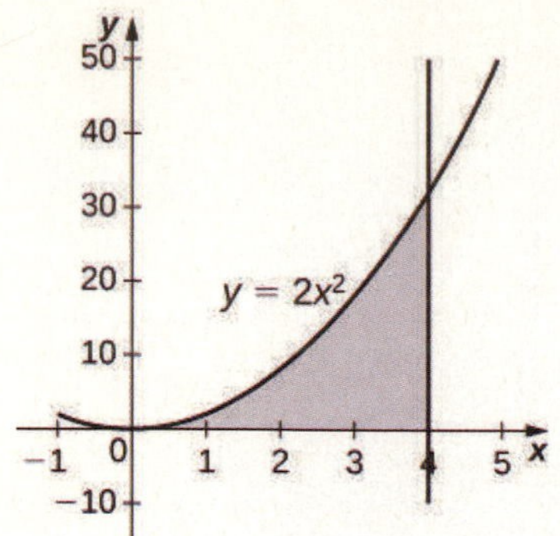


$\frac{4096\pi}{5}$ units$^3$

**77**.

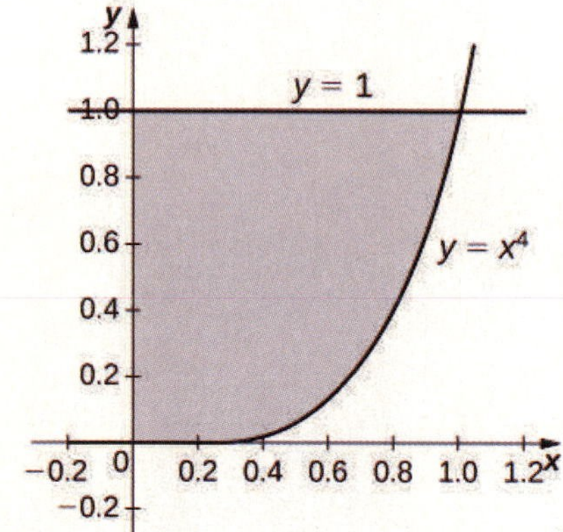


$\frac{8\pi}{9}$ units$^3$

**79**.

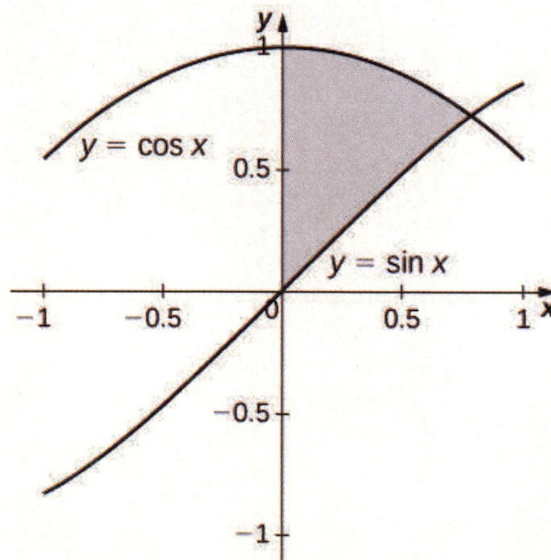


$\frac{\pi}{2}$ units$^3$

**81**.

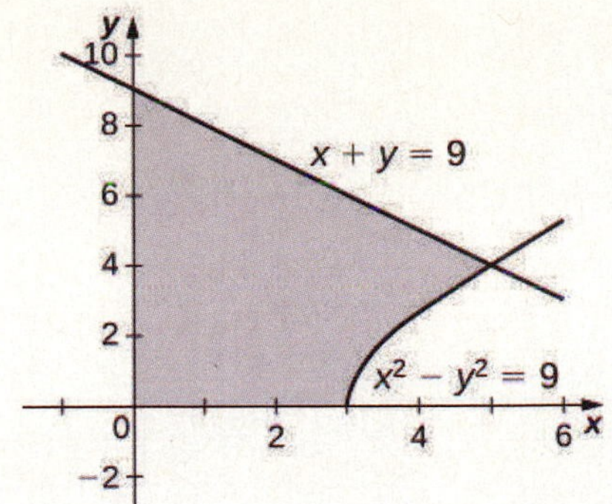


$207\pi$ units$^3$

**83**.

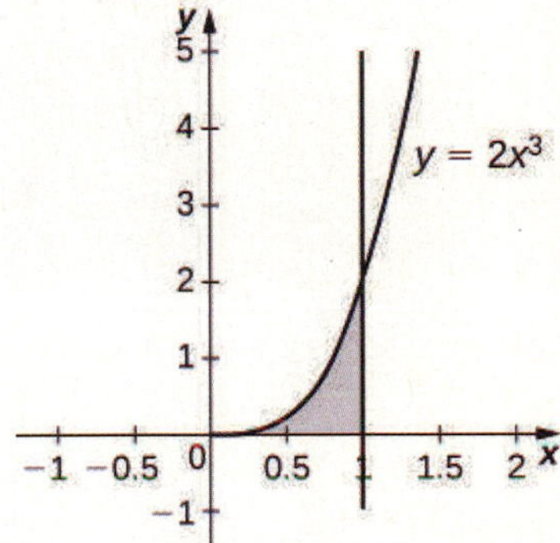


$\frac{4\pi}{5}$ units$^3$

**85**.

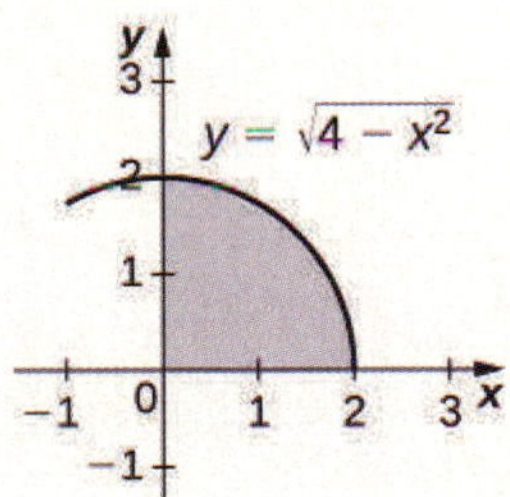


$\frac{16\pi}{3}$ units$^3$

**87**.

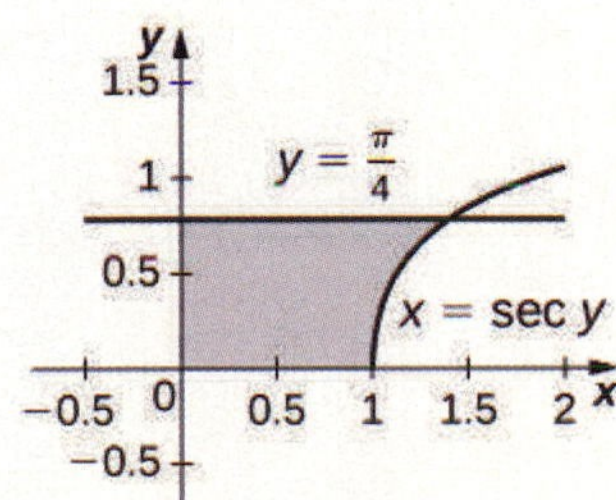


$\pi$ units$^3$

**89**.

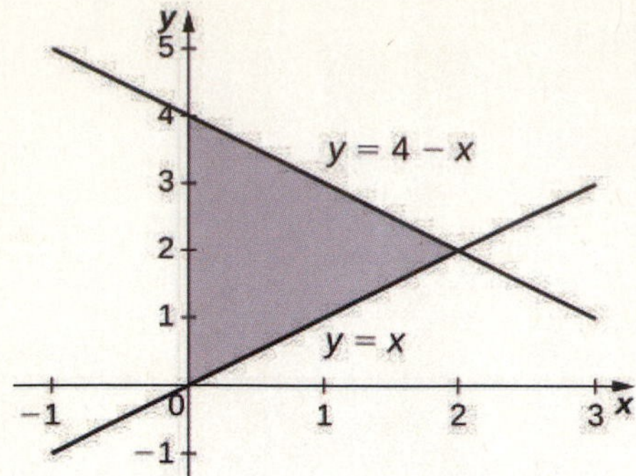


$\frac{16\pi}{3}$ units$^3$

**91**.

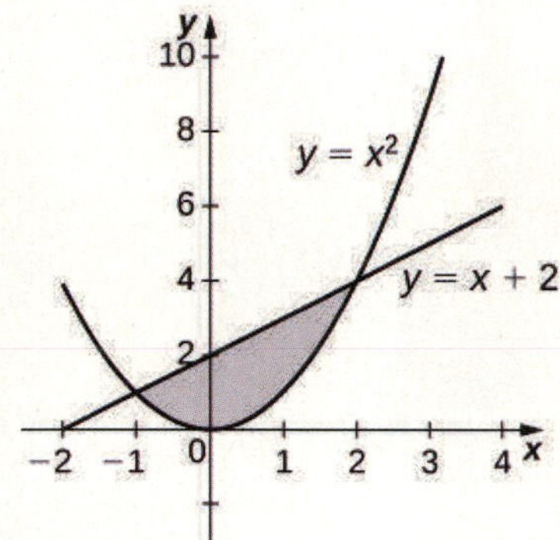


$\frac{72\pi}{5}$ units$^3$

**93**.

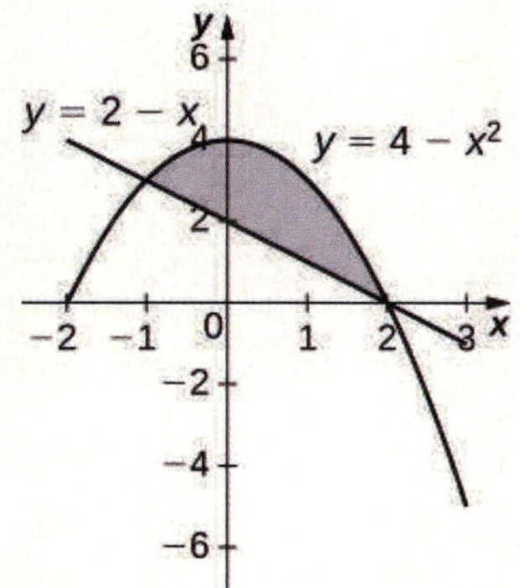


$\frac{108\pi}{5}$ units$^3$

**95**.

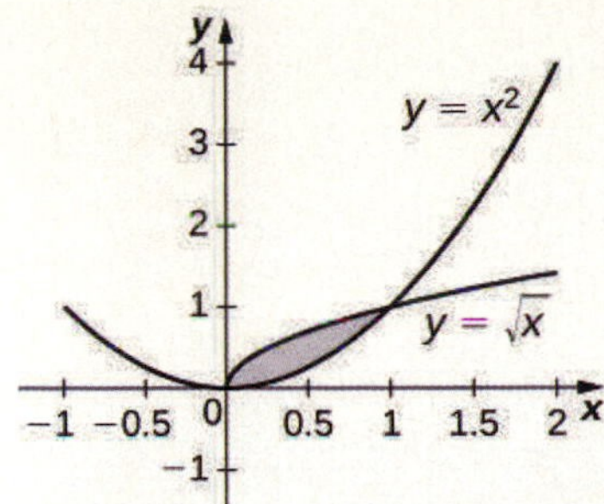


$\frac{3\pi}{10}$ units$^3$

**97**.

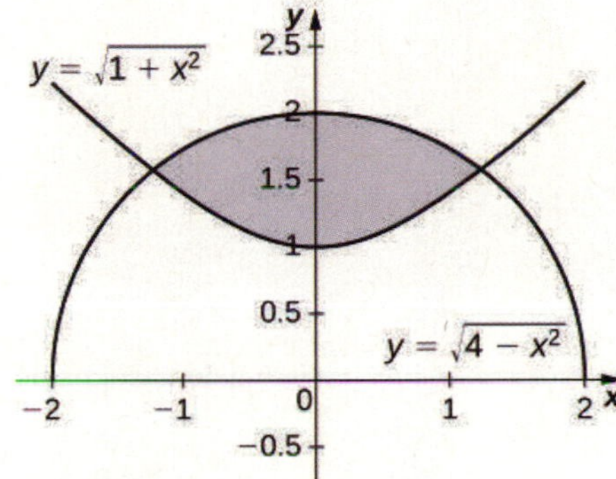


$2\sqrt{6}\pi$ units$^3$

**99**.

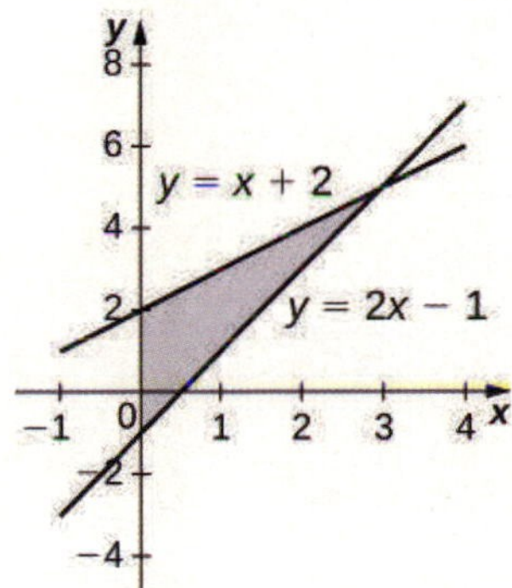


$9\pi$ units$^3$

**101**.

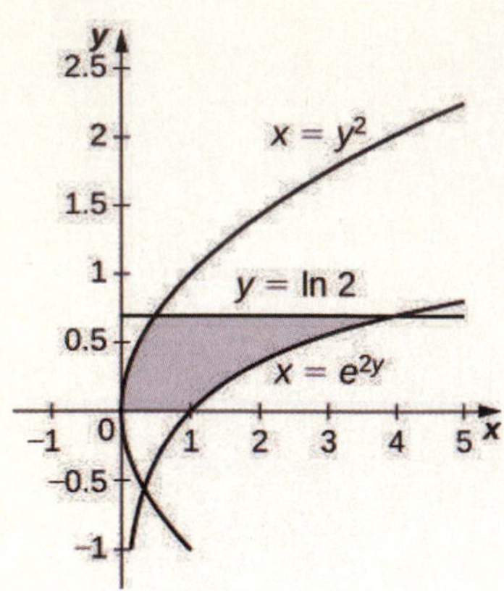


$\frac{\pi}{20}\left(75 - 4\ln^5(2)\right)$ units$^3$

**103**. $\frac{m^2\pi}{3}\left(b^3 - a^3\right)$ units$^3$

**105**. $\frac{4a^2 b\pi}{3}$ units$^3$

**107**. $2\pi^2$ units$^3$

**109**. $\frac{2ab^2\pi}{3}$ units$^3$

**111**. $\frac{\pi}{12}(r+h)^2(6r-h)$ units$^3$

**113**. $\frac{\pi}{3}(h+R)(h-2R)^2$ units$^3$

**115**.

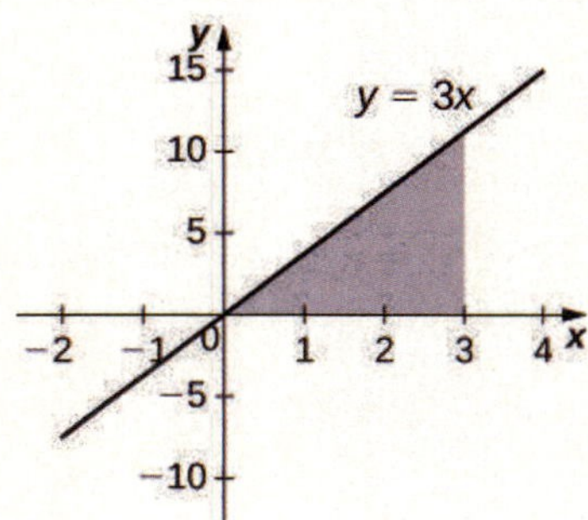


$54\pi$ units$^3$

**117**.

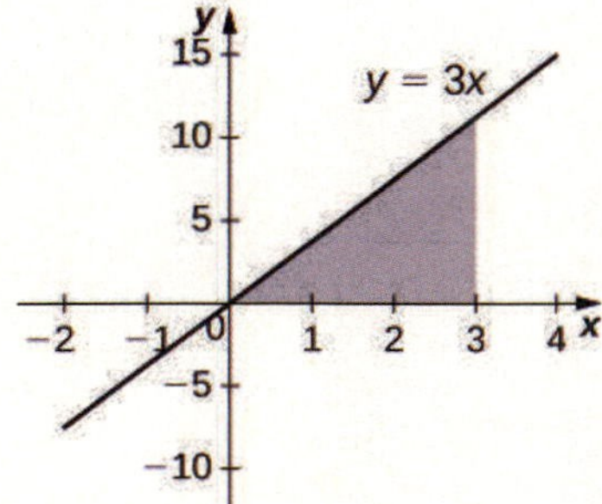


$81\pi$ units$^3$

**119**.

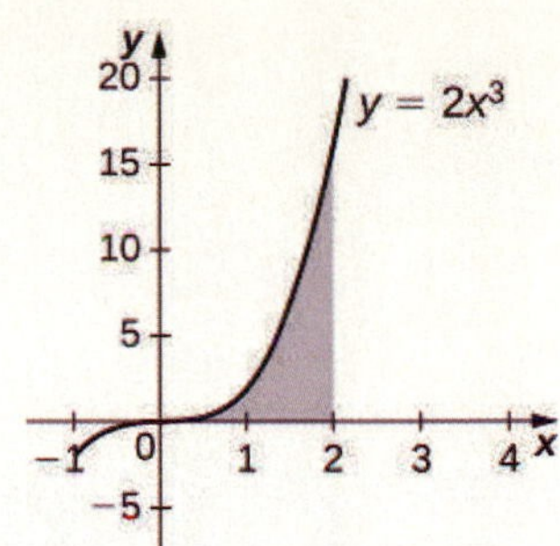


$\frac{512\pi}{7}$ units$^3$

**121**. $2\pi$ units$^3$

**123**. $\frac{2\pi}{3}$ units$^3$

**125**. $2\pi$ units$^3$

**127**. $\frac{4\pi}{5}$ units$^3$

**129**. $\frac{64\pi}{3}$ units$^3$

**131**. $\frac{32\pi}{5}$ units$^3$

**133**. $\pi(e-2)$ units$^3$

**135**. $\frac{28\pi}{3}$ units$^3$

**137**. $\frac{-84\pi}{5}$ units$^3$

**139**. $-e^{\pi}\pi^2$ units$^3$

**141**. $\frac{64\pi}{5}$ units$^3$

**143**. $\frac{28\pi}{15}$ units$^3$

**145**. $\frac{3\pi}{10}$ units$^3$

**147**. $\frac{52\pi}{5}$ units$^3$

**149**. $0.9876$ units$^3$

**151**.

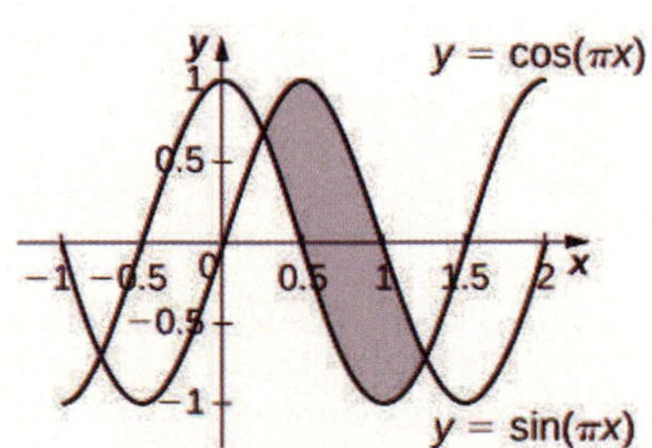


$3\sqrt{2}$ units$^3$

**153**.

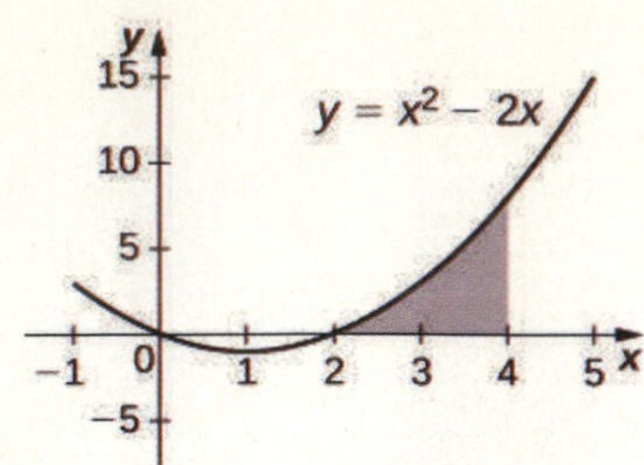


$\frac{496\pi}{15}$ units$^3$

**155**.

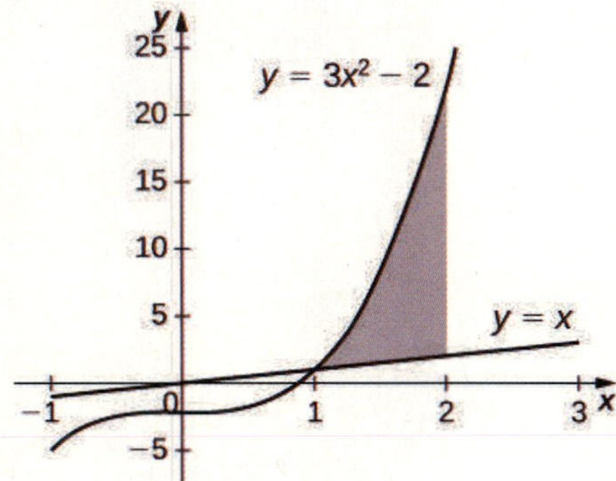


$\frac{398\pi}{15}$ units$^3$

**157**.

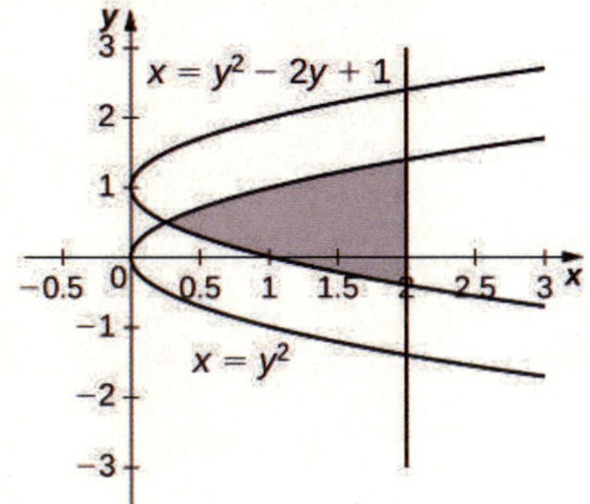


15.9074 units$^3$

**159**. $\frac{1}{3}\pi r^2 h$ units$^3$

**161**. $\pi r^2 h$ units$^3$

**163**. $\pi a^2$ units$^3$

**165**. $2\sqrt{26}$

**167**. $2\sqrt{17}$

**169**. $\frac{\pi}{6}\left(17\sqrt{17} - 5\sqrt{5}\right)$

**171**. $\frac{13\sqrt{13} - 8}{27}$

**173**. $\frac{4}{3}$

**175**. 2.0035

**177**. $\frac{123}{32}$

**179**. 10

**181**. $\frac{20}{3}$

**183**. $\frac{1}{675}\left(229\sqrt{229} - 8\right)$

**185**. $\frac{1}{8}\left(4\sqrt{5} + \ln\left(9 + 4\sqrt{5}\right)\right)$

**187**. 1.201

**189**. 15.2341

**191**. $\frac{49\pi}{3}$

**193**. $70\pi\sqrt{2}$

**195**. $8\pi$

**197**. $120\pi\sqrt{26}$

**199**. $\frac{\pi}{6}(17\sqrt{17} - 1)$

**201**. $9\sqrt{2}\pi$

**203**. $\frac{10\sqrt{10}\pi}{27}\left(73\sqrt{73} - 1\right)$

**205**. 25.645

**207**. $2\pi$

**209**. 10.5017

**211**. 23 ft

**213**. 2

**215**. Answers may vary

**217**. For more information, look up Gabriel's Horn.

**219**. 150 ft-lb

**221**. 200 J

**223**. 1 J

**225**. $\frac{39}{2}$

**227**. $\ln(243)$

**229**. $\frac{332\pi}{15}$

**231**. $100\pi$

**233**. $20\pi\sqrt{15}$

**235**. 6 J

**237**. 5 cm

**239**. 36 J

**241**. 18,750 ft-lb

**243**. $\frac{32}{3} \times 10^9$ ft-lb

**245**. $8.65 \times 10^5$ J

**247**. a. 3,000,000 lb, b. 749,000 lb

**249**. $23.25\pi$ million ft-lb

**251**. $\frac{A\rho H^2}{2}$

**253**. Answers may vary

**255**. $\frac{5}{4}$

**257**. $\left(\frac{2}{3}, \frac{2}{3}\right)$

**259**. $\left(\frac{7}{4}, \frac{3}{2}\right)$

**261**. $\frac{3L}{4}$

**263**. $\frac{\pi}{2}$

**265**. $\frac{e^2 + 1}{e^2 - 1}$

**267**. $\frac{\pi^2 - 4}{\pi}$

**269**. $\frac{1}{4}\left(1 + e^2\right)$

**271**. $\left(\frac{a}{3}, \frac{b}{3}\right)$

**273**. $\left(0, \frac{\pi}{8}\right)$

**275**. $(0, 3)$

**277**. $\left(0, \frac{4}{\pi}\right)$

**279**. $\left(\frac{5}{8}, \frac{1}{3}\right)$

**281**. $\frac{m\pi}{3}$

**283**. $\pi a^2 b$

**285**. $\left(\frac{4}{3\pi}, \frac{4}{3\pi}\right)$

**287**. $\left(\frac{1}{2}, \frac{2}{5}\right)$

**289**. $\left(0, \frac{28}{9\pi}\right)$

**291**. Center of mass: $\left(\frac{a}{6}, \frac{4a^2}{5}\right)$, volume: $\frac{2\pi a^4}{9}$

**293**. Volume: $2\pi^2 a^2 (b + a)$

**295**. $\frac{1}{x}$

**297**. $-\frac{1}{x(\ln x)^2}$

**299**. $\ln(x + 1) + C$

**301**. $\ln(x) + 1$

**303**. $\cot(x)$

**305**. $\frac{7}{x}$

**307**. $\csc(x)\sec x$

**309**. $-2\tan x$

**311**. $\frac{1}{2}\ln\left(\frac{5}{3}\right)$

**313**. $2 - \frac{1}{2}\ln(5)$

**315**. $\frac{1}{\ln(2)} - 1$

**317**. $\frac{1}{2}\ln(2)$

**319**. $\frac{1}{3}(\ln x)^3$

**321**. $\frac{2x^3}{\sqrt{x^2+1}\sqrt{x^2-1}}$

**323**. $x^{-2-(1/x)}(\ln x - 1)$

**325**. $ex^{e-1}$

**327**. 1

**329**. $-\frac{1}{x^2}$

**331**. $\pi - \ln(2)$

**333**. $\frac{1}{x}$

**335**. $e^5 - 6$ units$^2$

**337**. $\ln(4) - 1$ units$^2$

**339**. 2.8656

**341**. 3.1502

**349**. True

**351**. False; $k = \frac{\ln(2)}{t}$

**353**. 20 hours

**355**. No. The relic is approximately 871 years old.

**357**. 71.92 years

**359**. 5 days 6 hours 27 minutes

**361**. 12

**363**. 8.618%

**365**. $6766.76

**367**. 9 hours 13 minutes

**369**. 239,179 years

**371**. $P'(t) = 43e^{0.01604t}$. The population is always increasing.

**373**. The population reaches 10 billion people in 2027.

**375**. $P'(t) = 2.259e^{0.06407t}$. The population is always increasing.

**377**. $e^x$ and $e^{-x}$

**379**. Answers may vary

**381**. Answers may vary

**383**. Answers may vary

**385**. $3\sinh(3x+1)$

**387**. $-\tanh(x)\text{sech}(x)$

**389**. $4\cosh(x)\sinh(x)$

**391**. $\frac{x\,\text{sech}^2\left(\sqrt{x^2+1}\right)}{\sqrt{x^2+1}}$

**393**. $6\sinh^5(x)\cosh(x)$

**395**. $\frac{1}{2}\sinh(2x+1)+C$

**397**. $\frac{1}{2}\sinh^2\left(x^2\right)+C$

**399**. $\frac{1}{3}\cosh^3(x)+C$

**401**. $\ln(1+\cosh(x))+C$

**403**. $\cosh(x)+\sinh(x)+C$

**405**. $\frac{4}{1-16x^2}$

**407**. $\frac{\sinh(x)}{\sqrt{\cosh^2(x)+1}}$

**409**. $-\csc(x)$

**411**. $-\frac{1}{\left(x^2-1\right)\tanh^{-1}(x)}$

**413**. $\frac{1}{a}\tanh^{-1}\left(\frac{x}{a}\right)+C$

**415**. $\sqrt{x^2+1}+C$

**417**. $\cosh^{-1}(e^x)+C$

**419**. Answers may vary

**421**. $37.30$

**423**. $y=\frac{1}{c}\cosh(cx)$

**425**. $-0.521095$

**427**. $10$

## Review Exercises

**435**. False

**437**. False

**439**. $32\sqrt{3}$

**441**. $\frac{162\pi}{5}$

**443**. a. $4$, b. $\frac{128\pi}{7}$, c. $\frac{64\pi}{5}$

**445**. a. $1.949$, b. $21.952$, c. $17.099$

**447**. a. $\frac{31}{6}$, b. $\frac{452\pi}{15}$, c. $\frac{31\pi}{6}$

**449**. $245.282$

**451**. Mass: $\frac{1}{2}$, center of mass: $\left(\frac{18}{35},\frac{9}{11}\right)$

**453**. $\sqrt{17}+\frac{1}{8}\ln(33+8\sqrt{17})$

**455**. Volume: $\frac{3\pi}{4}$, surface area: $\pi\left(\sqrt{2}-\sinh^{-1}(1)+\sinh^{-1}(16)-\frac{\sqrt{257}}{16}\right)$

**457**. 11:02 a.m.

**459**. $\pi(1+\sinh(1)\cosh(1))$

# Chapter 3

## Checkpoint

**3.1**. $\int xe^{2x}\,dx=\frac{1}{2}xe^{2x}-\frac{1}{4}e^{2x}+C$

**3.2**. $\frac{1}{2}x^2\ln x-\frac{1}{4}x^2+C$

**3.3**. $-x^2\cos x+2x\sin x+2\cos x+C$

**3.4**. $\frac{\pi}{2}-1$

**3.5**. $\frac{1}{5}\sin^5 x+C$

**3.6**. $\frac{1}{3}\sin^3 x-\frac{1}{5}\sin^5 x+C$

**3.7**. $\frac{1}{2}x+\frac{1}{4}\sin(2x)+C$

**3.8**. $\sin x - \frac{1}{3}\sin^3 x + C$

**3.9**. $\frac{1}{2}x + \frac{1}{12}\sin(6x) + C$

**3.10**. $\frac{1}{2}\sin x + \frac{1}{22}\sin(11x) + C$

**3.11**. $\frac{1}{6}\tan^6 x + C$

**3.12**. $\frac{1}{9}\sec^9 x - \frac{1}{7}\sec^7 x + C$

**3.13**. $\int \sec^5 x\,dx = \frac{1}{4}\sec^3 x\tan x - \frac{3}{4}\int \sec^3 x$

**3.14**. $\int 125\sin^3 \theta d\theta$

**3.15**. $\int 32\tan^3 \theta \sec^3 \theta d\theta$

**3.16**. $\ln\left|\frac{x}{2} + \frac{\sqrt{x^2-4}}{2}\right| + C$

**3.17**. $x - 5\ln|x+2| + C$

**3.18**. $\frac{2}{5}\ln|x+3| + \frac{3}{5}\ln|x-2| + C$

**3.19**. $\frac{x+2}{(x+3)^3(x-4)^2} = \frac{A}{x+3} + \frac{B}{(x+3)^2} + \frac{C}{(x+3)^3} + \frac{D}{(x-4)} + \frac{E}{(x-4)^2}$

**3.20**. $\frac{x^2+3x+1}{(x+2)(x-3)^2(x^2+4)^2} = \frac{A}{x+2} + \frac{B}{x-3} + \frac{C}{(x-3)^2} + \frac{Dx+E}{x^2+4} + \frac{Fx+G}{(x^2+4)^2}$

**3.21**. Possible solutions include $\sinh^{-1}\left(\frac{x}{2}\right) + C$ and $\ln\left|\sqrt{x^2+4} + x\right| + C$.

**3.22**. $\frac{24}{35}$

**3.23**. $\frac{17}{24}$

**3.24**. 0.0074, 1.1%

**3.25**. $\frac{1}{192}$

**3.26**. $\frac{25}{36}$

**3.27**. $e^3$, converges

**3.28**. $+\infty$, diverges

**3.29**. Since $\int_e^{+\infty} \frac{1}{x}dx = +\infty$, $\int_e^{+\infty} \frac{\ln x}{x}dx$ diverges.

## Section Exercises

**1**. $u = x^3$

**3**. $u = y^3$

**5**. $u = \sin(2x)$

**7**. $-x + x\ln x + C$

**9**. $x\tan^{-1} x - \frac{1}{2}\ln(1+x^2) + C$

**11**. $-\frac{1}{2}x\cos(2x) + \frac{1}{4}\sin(2x) + C$

**13**. $e^{-x}(-1-x) + C$

**15**. $2x\cos x + \left(-2+x^2\right)\sin x + C$

**17**. $\frac{1}{2}(1+2x)(-1+\ln(1+2x))+C$

**19**. $\frac{1}{2}e^{x}(-\cos x+\sin x)+C$

**21**. $-\frac{e^{-x^2}}{2}+C$

**23**. $-\frac{1}{2}x\cos[\ln(2x)]+\frac{1}{2}x\sin[\ln(2x)]+C$

**25**. $2x-2x\ln x+x(\ln x)^2+C$

**27**. $\left(-\frac{x^3}{9}+\frac{1}{3}x^3\ln x\right)+C$

**29**. $-\frac{1}{2}\sqrt{1-4x^2}+x\cos^{-1}(2x)+C$

**31**. $-\left(-2+x^2\right)\cos x+2x\sin x+C$

**33**. $-x\left(-6+x^2\right)\cos x+3\left(-2+x^2\right)\sin x+C$

**35**. $\frac{1}{2}x\left(-\sqrt{1-\frac{1}{x^2}}+x\cdot\sec^{-1}x\right)+C$

**37**. $-\cosh x+x\sinh x+C$

**39**. $\frac{1}{4}-\frac{3}{4e^2}$

**41**. 2

**43**. $2\pi$

**45**. $-2+\pi$

**47**. $-\sin(x)+\ln[\sin(x)]\sin x+C$

**49**. Answers vary

**51**. a. $\frac{2}{5}(1+x)(-3+2x)^{3/2}+C$ b. $\frac{2}{5}(1+x)(-3+2x)^{3/2}+C$

**53**. Do not use integration by parts. Choose $u$ to be $\ln x$, and the integral is of the form $\int u^2\,du$.

**55**. Do not use integration by parts. Let $u=x^2-3$, and the integral can be put into the form $\int e^u\,du$.

**57**. Do not use integration by parts. Choose $u$ to be $u=3x^3+2$ and the integral can be put into the form $\int \sin(u)du$.

**59**. The area under graph is 0.39535.

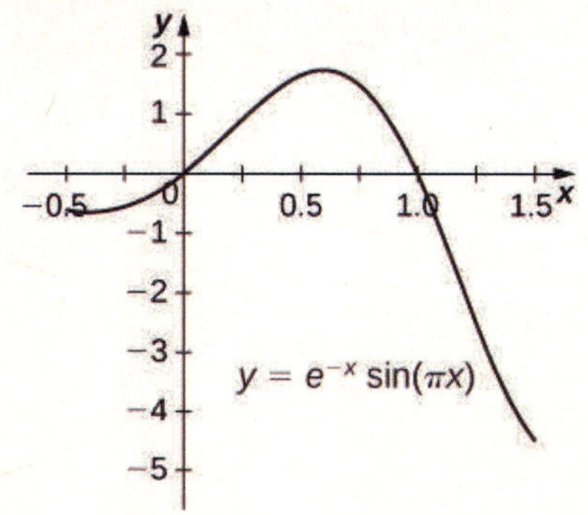


**61**. $2\pi e$

**63**. 2.05

**65**. $12\pi$

**67**. $8\pi^2$

**69**. $\cos^2 x$

**71.** $\frac{1-\cos(2x)}{2}$

**73.** $\frac{\sin^4 x}{4}+C$

**75.** $\frac{1}{12}\tan^6(2x)+C$

**77.** $\sec^2\left(\frac{x}{2}\right)+C$

**79.** $-\frac{3\cos x}{4}+\frac{1}{12}\cos(3x)+C=-\cos x+\frac{\cos^3 x}{3}+C$

**81.** $-\frac{1}{2}\cos^2 x+C$

**83.** $-\frac{5\cos x}{64}-\frac{1}{192}\cos(3x)+\frac{3}{320}\cos(5x)-\frac{1}{448}\cos(7x)+C$

**85.** $\frac{2}{3}(\sin x)^{2/3}+C$

**87.** $\sec x+C$

**89.** $\frac{1}{2}\sec x\tan x-\frac{1}{2}\ln(\sec x+\tan x)+C$

**91.** $\frac{2\tan x}{3}+\frac{1}{3}\sec(x)^2\tan x \ =\tan x+\frac{\tan^3 x}{3}+C$

**93.** $-\ln|\cot x+\csc x|+C$

**95.** $\frac{\sin^3(ax)}{3a}+C$

**97.** $\frac{\pi}{2}$

**99.** $\frac{x}{2}+\frac{1}{12}\sin(6x)+C$

**101.** $x+C$

**103.** 0

**105.** 0

**107.** 0

**109.** Approximately 0.239

**111.** $\sqrt{2}$

**113.** 1.0

**115.** 0

**117.** $\frac{3\theta}{8}-\frac{1}{4\pi}\sin(2\pi\theta)+\frac{1}{32\pi}\sin(4\pi\theta)+C=f(x)$

**119.** $\ln(\sqrt{3})$

**121.** $\int_{-\pi}^{\pi}\sin(2x)\cos(3x)dx=0$

**123.** $\sqrt{\tan(x)}x\left(\frac{8\tan x}{21}+\frac{2}{7}\sec x^2\tan x\right)+C=f(x)$

**125.** The second integral is more difficult because the first integral is simply a $u$-substitution type.

**127.** $9\tan^2\theta$

**129.** $a^2\cosh^2\theta$

**131.** $4\left(x-\frac{1}{2}\right)^2$

**133.** $-(x+1)^2+5$

**135.** $\ln\left|x+\sqrt{-a^2+x^2}\right|+C$

**137.** $\frac{1}{3}\ln\left|\sqrt{9x^2+1}+3x\right|+C$

**139**. $-\frac{\sqrt{1-x^2}}{x}+C$

**141**. $9\left[\frac{x\sqrt{x^2+9}}{18}+\frac{1}{2}ln\left|\frac{\sqrt{x^2+9}}{3}+\frac{x}{3}\right|\right]+C$

**143**. $-\frac{1}{3}\sqrt{9-\theta^2}\left(18+\theta^2\right)+C$

**145**. $\frac{\left(-1+x^2\right)\left(2+3x^2\right)\sqrt{x^6-x^8}}{15x^3}+C$

**147**. $-\frac{x}{9\sqrt{-9+x^2}}+C$

**149**. $\frac{1}{2}\left(\ln\left|x+\sqrt{x^2-1}\right|+x\sqrt{x^2-1}\right)+C$

**151**. $-\frac{\sqrt{1+x^2}}{x}+C$

**153**. $\frac{1}{8}\left(x\left(5-2x^2\right)\sqrt{1-x^2}+3\arcsin x\right)+C$

**155**. $\ln x-\ln\left|1+\sqrt{1-x^2}\right|+C$

**157**. $-\frac{\sqrt{-1+x^2}}{x}+\ln\left|x+\sqrt{-1+x^2}\right|+C$

**159**. $-\frac{\sqrt{1+x^2}}{x}+\operatorname{arcsinh} x+C$

**161**. $-\frac{1}{1+x}+C$

**163**. $\frac{2\sqrt{-10+x}\sqrt{x}\ln\left|\sqrt{-10+x}+\sqrt{x}\right|}{\sqrt{(10-x)x}}+C$

**165**. $\frac{9\pi}{2}$; area of a semicircle with radius 3

**167**. $\arcsin(x)+C$ is the common answer.

**169**. $\frac{1}{2}\ln\left(1+x^2\right)+C$ is the result using either method.

**171**. Use trigonometric substitution. Let $x=\sec(\theta)$.

**173**. 4.367

**175**. $\frac{\pi^2}{8}+\frac{\pi}{4}$

**177**. $y=\frac{1}{16}\ln\left|\frac{x+8}{x-8}\right|+3$

**179**. 24.6 $\text{m}^3$

**181**. $\frac{2\pi}{3}$

**183**. $-\frac{2}{x+1}+\frac{5}{2(x+2)}+\frac{1}{2x}$

**185**. $\frac{1}{x^2}+\frac{3}{x}$

**187**. $2x^2+4x+8+\frac{16}{x-2}$

**189**. $-\frac{1}{x^2}-\frac{1}{x}+\frac{1}{x-1}$

**191**. $-\frac{1}{2(x-2)}+\frac{1}{2(x-1)}-\frac{1}{6x}+\frac{1}{6(x-3)}$

**193**. $\frac{1}{x-1}+\frac{2x+1}{x^2+x+1}$

**195.** $\frac{2}{x+1} + \frac{x}{x^2+4} - \frac{1}{\left(x^2+4\right)^2}$

**197.** $-\ln|2-x| + 2\ln|4+x| + C$

**199.** $\frac{1}{2}\ln\left|4-x^2\right| + C$

**201.** $2\left(x + \frac{1}{3}\arctan\left(\frac{1+x}{3}\right)\right) + C$

**203.** $2\ln|x| - 3\ln|1+x| + C$

**205.** $\frac{1}{16}\left(-\frac{4}{-2+x} - \ln|-2+x| + \ln|2+x|\right) + C$

**207.** $\frac{1}{30}\left(-2\sqrt{5}\arctan\left[\frac{1+x}{\sqrt{5}}\right] + 2\ln|-4+x| - \ln\left|6+2x+x^2\right|\right) + C$

**209.** $-\frac{3}{x} + 4\ln|x+2| + x + C$

**211.** $-\ln|3-x| + \frac{1}{2}\ln\left|x^2+4\right| + C$

**213.** $\ln|x-2| - \frac{1}{2}\ln\left|x^2+2x+2\right| + C$

**215.** $-x + \ln\left|1-e^x\right| + C$

**217.** $\frac{1}{5}\ln\left|\frac{\cos x+3}{\cos x-2}\right| + C$

**219.** $\frac{1}{2-2e^{2t}} + C$

**221.** $2\sqrt{1+x} - 2\ln\left|1+\sqrt{1+x}\right| + C$

**223.** $\ln\left|\frac{\sin x}{1-\sin x}\right| + C$

**225.** $\frac{\sqrt{3}}{4}$

**227.** $x - \ln(1+e^x) + C$

**229.** $6x^{1/6} - 3x^{1/3} + 2\sqrt{x} - 6\ln\left(1+x^{1/6}\right) + C$

**231.** $\frac{4}{3}\pi\,\text{arctanh}\left[\frac{1}{3}\right] = \frac{1}{3}\pi\ln 4$

**233.** $x = -\ln|t-3| + \ln|t-4| + \ln 2$

**235.** $x = \ln|t-1| - \sqrt{2}\arctan(\sqrt{2}t) - \frac{1}{2}\ln\left(t^2+\frac{1}{2}\right) + \sqrt{2}\arctan(2\sqrt{2}) + \frac{1}{2}\ln 4.5$

**237.** $\frac{2}{5}\pi\ln\frac{28}{13}$

**239.** $\frac{\arctan\left[\frac{-1+2x}{\sqrt{3}}\right]}{\sqrt{3}} + \frac{1}{3}\ln|1+x| - \frac{1}{6}\ln\left|1-x+x^2\right| + C$

**241.** 2.0 in.$^2$

**243.** $3(-8+x)^{1/3}$

$-2\sqrt{3}\arctan\left[\frac{-1+(-8+x)^{1/3}}{\sqrt{3}}\right]$

$-2\ln\left[2+(-8+x)^{1/3}\right]$

$+\ln\left[4-2(-8+x)^{1/3}+(-8+x)^{2/3}\right] + C$

**245.** $\frac{1}{2}\ln\left|x^2+2x+2\right| + 2\arctan(x+1) + C$

**247.** $\cosh^{-1}\left(\frac{x+3}{3}\right) + C$

**249**. $\frac{2^{x^2-1}}{\ln 2}+C$

**251**. $\arcsin\left(\frac{y}{2}\right)+C$

**253**. $-\frac{1}{2}\csc(2w)+C$

**255**. $9-6\sqrt{2}$

**257**. $2-\frac{\pi}{2}$

**259**. $\frac{1}{12}\tan^4(3x)-\frac{1}{6}\tan^2(3x)+\frac{1}{3}\ln|\sec(3x)|+C$

**261**. $2\cot\left(\frac{w}{2}\right)-2\csc\left(\frac{w}{2}\right)+w+C$

**263**. $\frac{1}{5}\ln\left|\frac{2(5+4\sin t-3\cos t)}{4\cos t+3\sin t}\right|$

**265**. $6x^{1/6}-3x^{1/3}+2\sqrt{x}-6\ln\left[1+x^{1/6}\right]+C$

**267**. $-x^3\cos x+3x^2\sin x+6x\cos x-6\sin x+C$

**269**. $\frac{1}{2}\left(x^2+\ln\left|1+e^{-x^2}\right|\right)+C$

**271**. $2\arctan\left(\sqrt{x-1}\right)+C$

**273**. $0.5=\frac{1}{2}$

**275**. 8.0

**277**. $\frac{1}{3}\arctan\left(\frac{1}{3}(x+2)\right)+C$

**279**. $\frac{1}{3}\arctan\left(\frac{x+1}{3}\right)+C$

**281**. $\ln\left(e^x+\sqrt{4+e^{2x}}\right)+C$

**283**. $\ln x-\frac{1}{6}\ln\left(x^6+1\right)-\frac{\arctan\left(x^3\right)}{3x^3}+C$

**285**. $\ln\left|x+\sqrt{16+x^2}\right|+C$

**287**. $-\frac{1}{4}\cot(2x)+C$

**289**. $\frac{1}{2}\arctan 10$

**291**. 1276.14

**293**. 7.21

**295**. $\sqrt{5}-\sqrt{2}+\ln\left|\frac{2+2\sqrt{2}}{1+\sqrt{5}}\right|$

**297**. $\frac{1}{3}\arctan(3)\approx 0.416$

**299**. 0.696

**301**. 9.279

**303**. 0.5000

**305**. $T_4=18.75$

**307**. 0.500

**309**. 1.1614

**311**. 0.6577

**313**. 0.0213

**315**. 1.5629

**317**. 1.9133

**319**. $\text{T}(4)=0.1088$

**321**. 1.0
**323**. Approximate error is 0.000325.
**325**. $\frac{1}{7938}$
**327**. $\frac{81}{25,\,000}$
**329**. 475
**331**. 174
**333**. 0.1544
**335**. 6.2807
**337**. 4.606
**339**. 3.41 ft
**341**. $T_{16} = 100.125;$ absolute error = 0.125
**343**. about 89,250 $\text{m}^2$
**345**. parabola
**347**. divergent
**349**. $\frac{\pi}{2}$
**351**. $\frac{2}{e}$
**353**. Converges
**355**. Converges to 1/2.
**357**. −4
**359**. $\pi$
**361**. diverges
**363**. diverges
**365**. 1.5
**367**. diverges
**369**. diverges
**371**. diverges
**373**. Both integrals diverge.
**375**. diverges
**377**. diverges
**379**. $\pi$
**381**. 0.0
**383**. 0.0
**385**. 6.0
**387**. $\frac{\pi}{2}$
**389**. $8\ln(16) - 4$
**391**. $1.047$
**393**. $-1 + \frac{2}{\sqrt{3}}$
**395**. 7.0
**397**. $\frac{5\pi}{2}$
**399**. $3\pi$
**401**. $\frac{1}{s},\ s > 0$
**403**. $\frac{s}{s^2 + 4},\ s > 0$
**405**. Answers will vary.
**407**. 0.8775

## Review Exercises

**409**. False
**411**. False
**413**. $-\frac{\sqrt{x^2 + 16}}{16x} + C$

**415**. $\frac{1}{10}(4\ln(2-x)+5\ln(x+1)-9\ln(x+3))+C$

**417**. $-\frac{\sqrt{4-\sin^2(x)}}{\sin(x)}-\frac{x}{2}+C$

**419**. $\frac{1}{15}\left(x^2+2\right)^{3/2}\left(3x^2-4\right)+C$

**421**. $\frac{1}{16}\ln\left(\frac{x^2+2x+2}{x^2-2x+2}\right)-\frac{1}{8}\tan^{-1}(1-x)+\frac{1}{8}\tan^{-1}(x+1)+C$

**423**. $M_4=3.312,\ T_4=3.354,\ S_4=3.326$

**425**. $M_4=-0.982,\ T_4=-0.917,\ S_4=-0.952$

**427**. approximately 0.2194

**431**. Answers may vary. Ex: $9.405\ \text{km}$

# Chapter 4

## Checkpoint

**4.2**. $5$

**4.3**. $y=2x^2+3x+2$

**4.5**. $y=\frac{1}{3}x^3-2x^2+3x-6e^x+14$

**4.6**. $v(t)=-9.8t$

**4.7**.

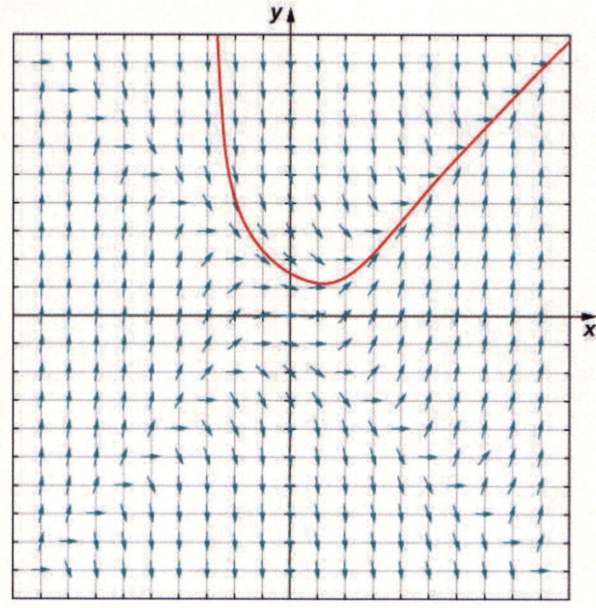


**4.8**.

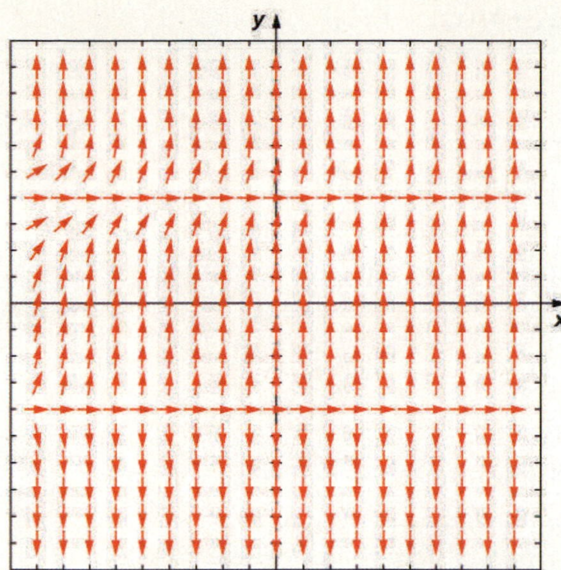


The equilibrium solutions are $y = -2$ and $y = 2.$ For this equation, $y = -2$ is an unstable equilibrium solution, and $y = 2$ is a semi-stable equilibrium solution.

**4.9**.

| $n$ | $x_n$ | $y_n = y_{n-1} + hf(x_{n-1}, y_{n-1})$ |
|---|---|---|
| 0 | 1 | −2 |
| 1 | 1.1 | $y_1 = y_0 + hf(x_0, y_0) = -1.5$ |
| 2 | 1.2 | $y_2 = y_1 + hf(x_1, y_1) = -1.1419$ |
| 3 | 1.3 | $y_3 = y_2 + hf(x_2, y_2) = -0.8387$ |
| 4 | 1.4 | $y_4 = y_3 + hf(x_3, y_3) = -0.5487$ |
| 5 | 1.5 | $y_5 = y_4 + hf(x_4, y_4) = -0.2442$ |
| 6 | 1.6 | $y_6 = y_5 + hf(x_5, y_5) = 0.0993$ |
| 7 | 1.7 | $y_7 = y_6 + hf(x_6, y_6) = 0.5099$ |
| 8 | 1.8 | $y_8 = y_7 + hf(x_7, y_7) = 1.0272$ |
| 9 | 1.9 | $y_9 = y_8 + hf(x_8, y_8) = 1.7159$ |
| 10 | 2 | $y_{10} = y_9 + hf(x_9, y_9) = 2.6962$ |

**4.10**. $y = 2 + Ce^{x^2 + 3x}$

**4.11**. $y = \dfrac{4 + 14e^{x^2 + x}}{1 - 7e^{x^2 + x}}$

**4.12**. Initial value problem: $\frac{du}{dt} = 2.4 - \frac{2u}{25}, \quad u(0) = 3$ Solution: $u(t) = 30 - 27e^{-t/50}$

**4.13**.

a. Initial-value problem
$$\frac{dT}{dt} = k(T - 70), \quad T(0) = 450$$

b. $T(t) = 70 + 380e^{kt}$

c. Approximately 114 minutes.

**4.14**.

a. $\frac{dP}{dt} = 0.04\left(1 - \frac{P}{750}\right), \quad P(0) = 200$

b.

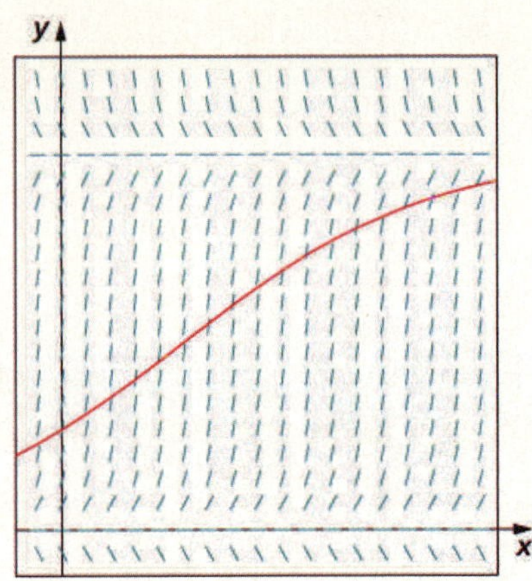


c. $P(t) = \dfrac{3000e^{.04t}}{11 + 4e^{.04t}}$

d. After 12 months, the population will be $P(12) \approx 278$ rabbits.

**4.15**. $y' + \dfrac{15}{x+3}y = \dfrac{10x-20}{x+3}$; $p(x) = \dfrac{15}{x+3}$ and $q(x) = \dfrac{10x-20}{x+3}$

**4.16**. $y = \dfrac{x^3 + x^2 + C}{x-2}$

**4.17**. $y = -2x - 4 + 2e^{2x}$

**4.18**.

a. $\begin{aligned} \frac{dv}{dt} &= -v - 9.8 \\ v(0) &= 0 \end{aligned}$

b. $v(t) = 9.8\left(e^{-t} - 1\right)$

c. $\lim_{t \to \infty} v(t) = \lim_{t \to \infty} \left(9.8\left(e^{-t} - 1\right)\right) = -9.8 \text{ m/s} \approx -21.922 \text{ mph}$

**4.19**. Initial-value problem: $8q' + \dfrac{1}{0.02}q = 20\sin 5t, \quad q(0) = 4$ $q(t) = \dfrac{10\sin 5t - 8\cos 5t + 172e^{-6.25t}}{41}$

## Section Exercises

**1**. 1

**3**. 3

**5**. 1

**7**. 1

**19**. $y = 4 + \dfrac{3x^4}{4}$

**21**. $y = \frac{1}{2}e^{x^2}$

**23**. $y = 2e^{-1/x}$

**25**. $u = \sin^{-1}\left(e^{-1+t}\right)$

**27**. $y = -\dfrac{\sqrt{x+1}}{\sqrt{1-x}} - 1$

**29**. $y = C - x + x\ln x - \ln(\cos x)$

**31**. $y = C + \dfrac{4^x}{\ln(4)}$

**33**. $y = \frac{2}{3}\sqrt{t^2 + 16}\left(t^2 + 16\right) + C$

35. $x = \frac{2}{15}\sqrt{4+t}\left(3t^2 + 4t - 32\right) + C$

37. $y = Cx$

39. $y = 1 - \frac{t^2}{2}, \ y = -\frac{t^2}{2} - 1$

41. $y = e^{-t}, \ y = -e^{-t}$

43. $y = 2\left(t^2 + 5\right), \ t = 3\sqrt{5}$

45. $y = 10e^{-2t}, \ t = -\frac{1}{2}\ln\left(\frac{1}{10}\right)$

47. $y = \frac{1}{4}\left(41 - e^{-4t}\right),$ never

49. Solution changes from increasing to decreasing at $y(0) = 0$

51. Solution changes from increasing to decreasing at $y(0) = 0$

53. $v(t) = -32t + a$

55. $0$ ft/s

57. $4.86$ meters

59. $x = 50t - \frac{15}{\pi^2}\cos(\pi t) + \frac{3}{\pi^2},$ $2$ hours $1$ minute

61. $y = 4e^{3t}$

63. $y = 1 - 2t + t^2$

65. $y = \frac{1}{k}\left(e^{kt} - 1\right)$ and $y = x$

67.

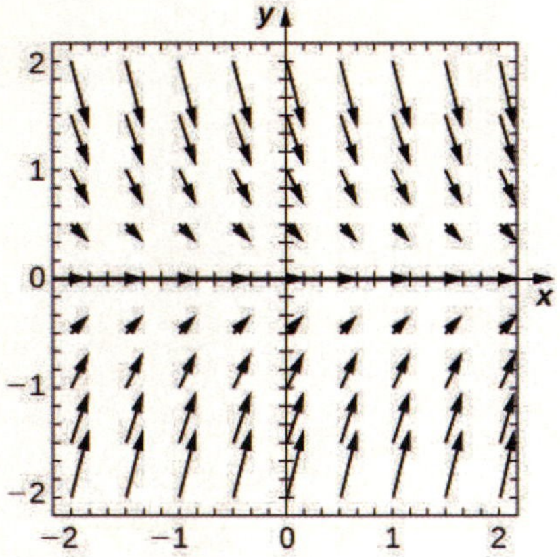


69. $y = 0$ is a stable equilibrium

71.

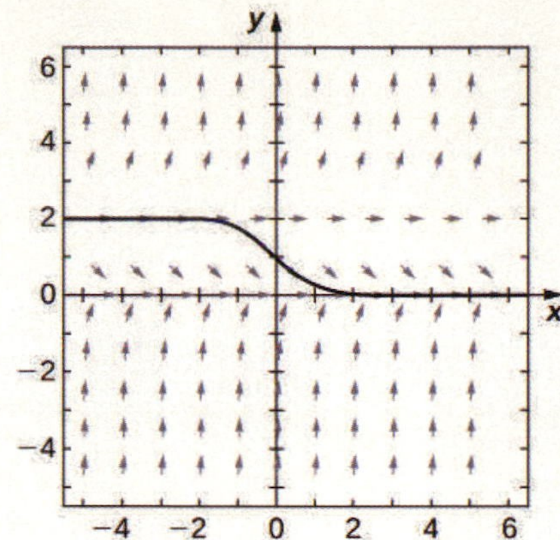


**73**. $y = 0$ is a stable equilibrium and $y = 2$ is unstable

**75**.

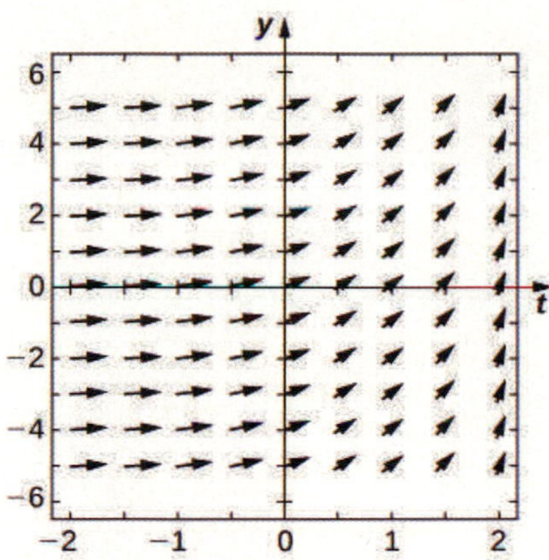


**77**.

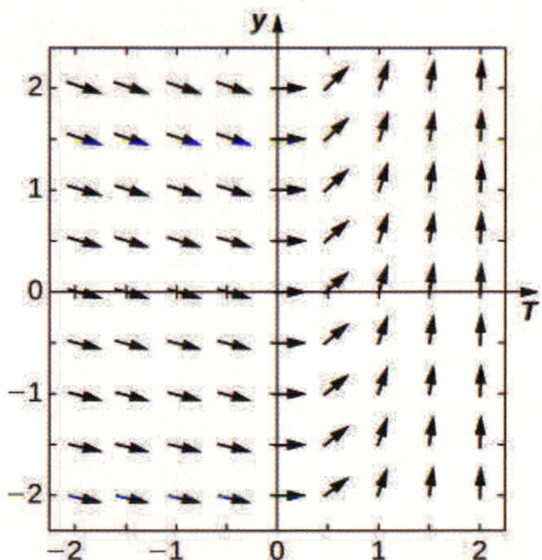


**79**.

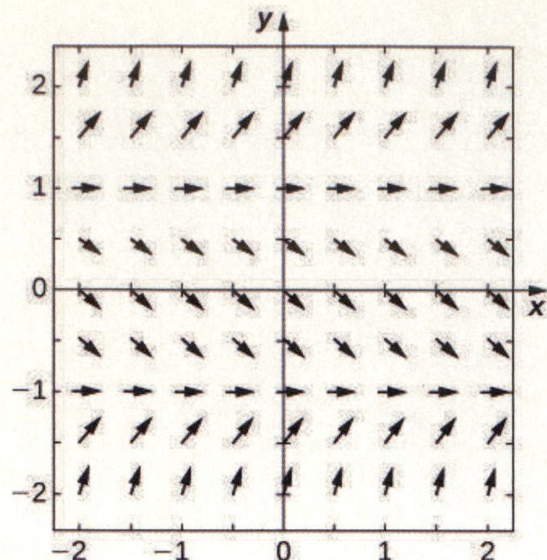


**81**.

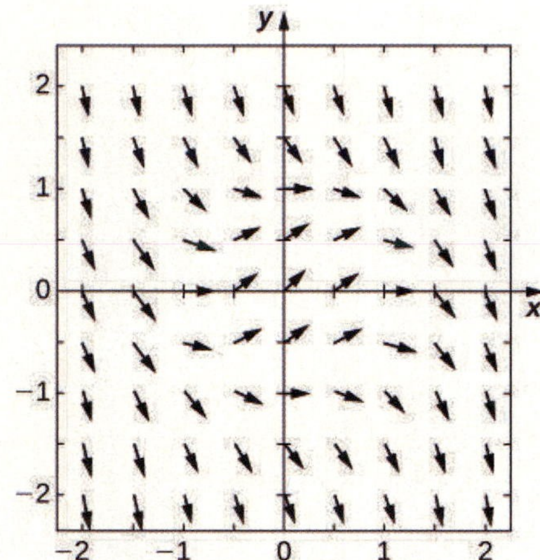


**83**.

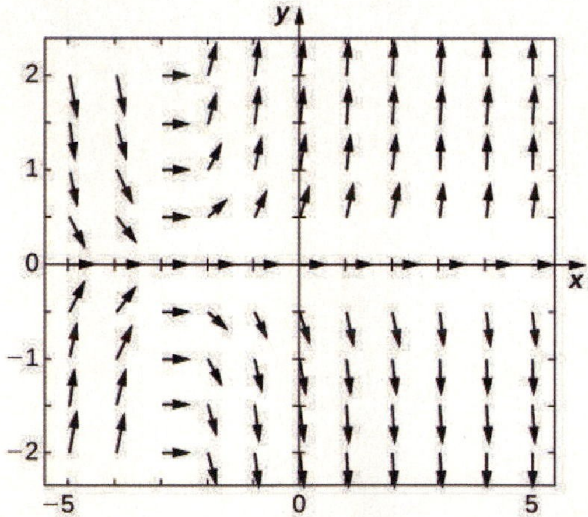


**85**. E
**87**. A
**89**. B
**91**. A
**93**. C
**95**. $2.24, \quad \text{exact: } 3$
**97**. $7.739364, \quad \text{exact: } 5(e-1)$
**99**. $-0.2535 \ \text{exact: } 0$

**101**. $1.345, \quad \text{exact: } \frac{1}{\ln(2)}$

**103**. $-4, \quad \text{exact: } -1/2$

**105**.

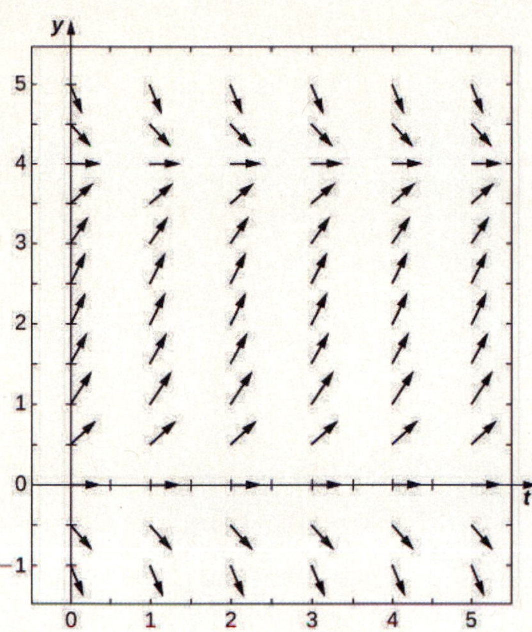


**107**. $y' = 2e^{t^2/2}$

**109**. $2$

**111**. $3.2756$

**113**. $2\sqrt{e}$

| Step Size | Error |
|---|---|
| $h = 1$ | 0.3935 |
| $h = 10$ | 0.06163 |
| $h = 100$ | 0.006612 |
| $h = 1000$ | 0.0006661 |

**115**.

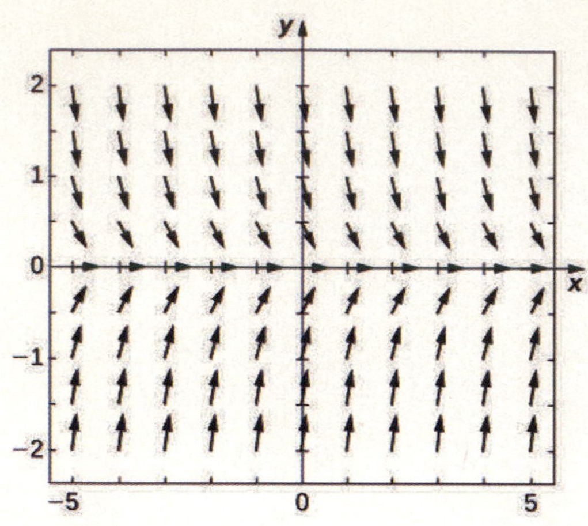


**117**. $4.0741e^{-10}$

**119**. $y = e^t - 1$

**121**. $y = 1 - e^{-t}$

**123**. $y = Cxe^{-1/x}$

**125**. $y = \dfrac{1}{C - x^2}$

**127**. $y = -\dfrac{2}{C + \ln x}$

**129**. $y = Ce^x(x + 1) + 1$

**131**. $y = \sin(\ln t + C)$

**133**. $y = -\ln(e^{-x})$

**135**. $y = \dfrac{1}{\sqrt{2 - e^{x^2}}}$

**137**. $y = \tanh^{-1}\left(\dfrac{x^2}{2}\right)$

**139**. $x = -\sin(t - t\ln t)$

**141**. $y = \ln(\ln(5)) - \ln(2 - 5^x)$

**143**. $y = Ce^{-2x} + \dfrac{1}{2}$

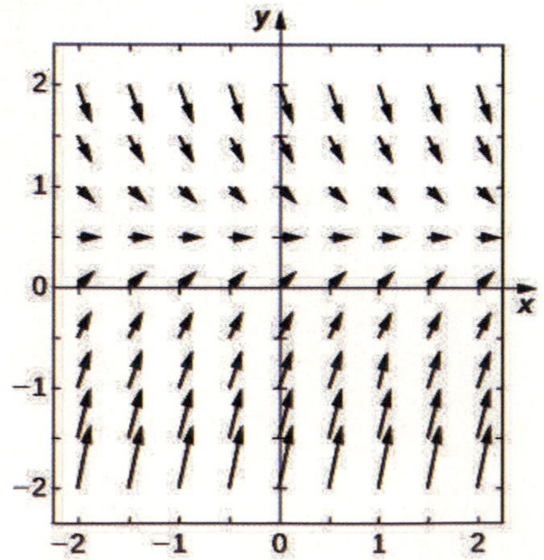


**145**. $y = \dfrac{1}{\sqrt{2}\sqrt{C - e^x}}$

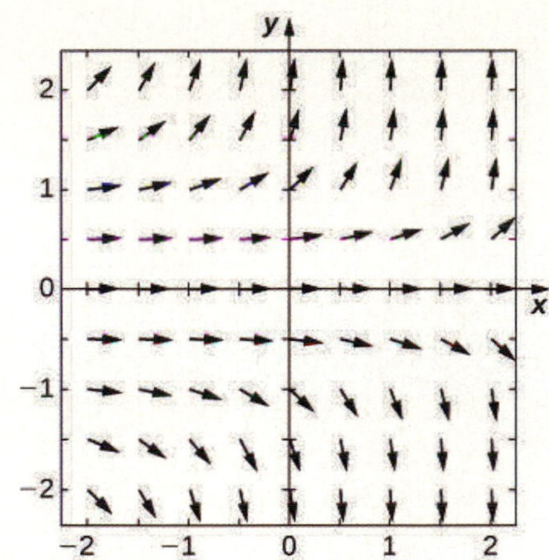


**147**. $y = Ce^{-x}x^{x}$

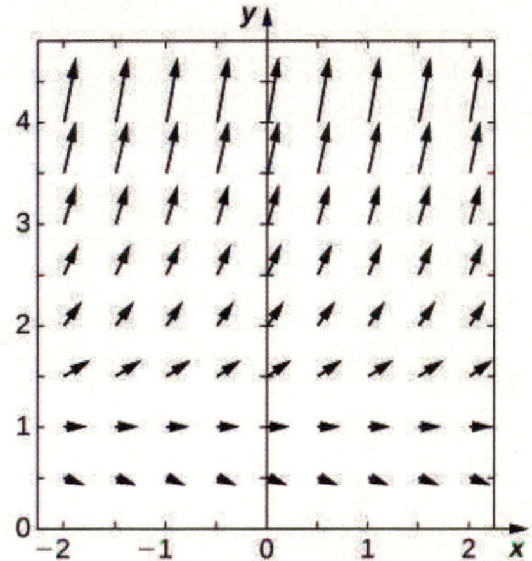


**149**. $y = \frac{r}{d}\left(1 - e^{-dt}\right)$

**151**. $y(t) = 10 - 9e^{-x/50}$

**153**. 134.3 kilograms

**155**. 720 seconds

**157**. 12 hours 14 minutes

**159**. $T(t) = 20 + 50e^{-0.125t}$

**161**. $T(t) = 20 + 38.5e^{-0.125t}$

**163**. $y = \left(c + \frac{b}{a}\right)e^{ax} - \frac{b}{a}$

**165**. $y(t) = cL + (I - cL)e^{-rt/L}$

**167**. $y = 40\left(1 - e^{-0.1t}\right)$, 40 g/cm$^2$

**169**.

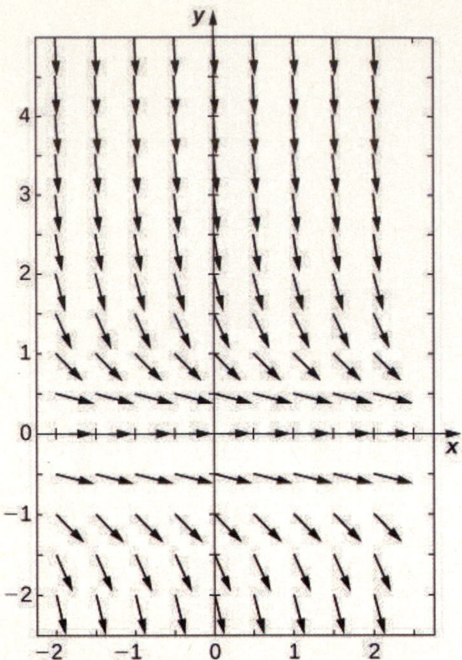


$P = 0$ semi-stable

**171**. $P = \dfrac{10e^{10x}}{e^{10x} + 4}$

**173**. $P(t) = \dfrac{10000e^{0.02t}}{150 + 50e^{0.02t}}$

**175**. 69 hours 5 minutes

**177**. 7 years 2 months

**179**.

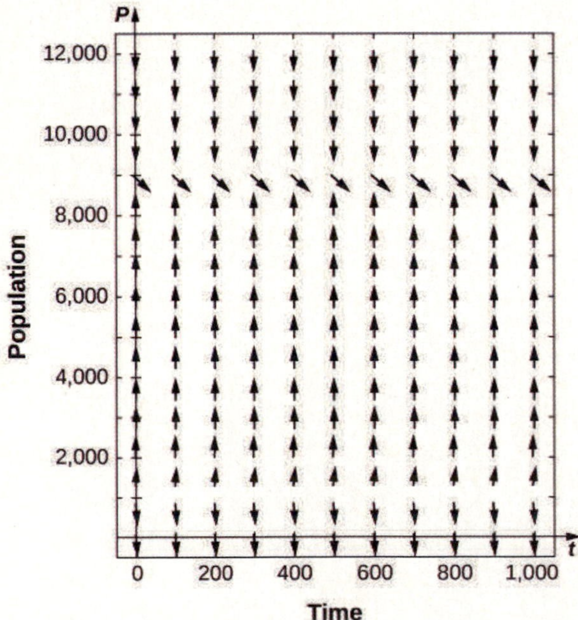


**181**.

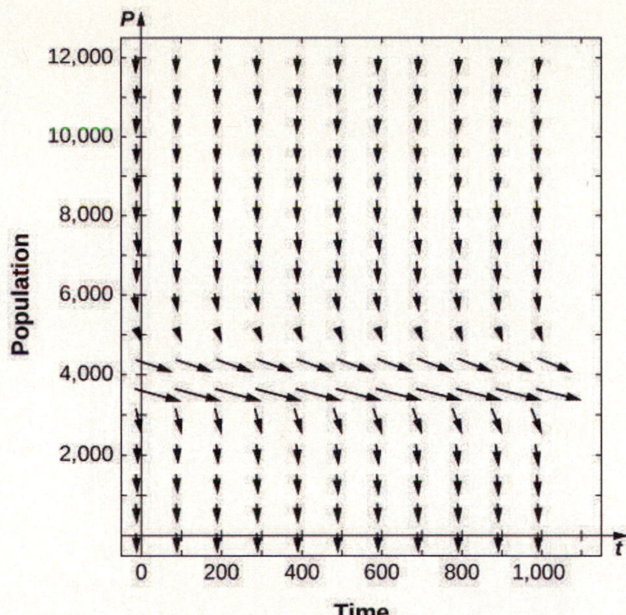


$P_1$ semi-stable

**183**.

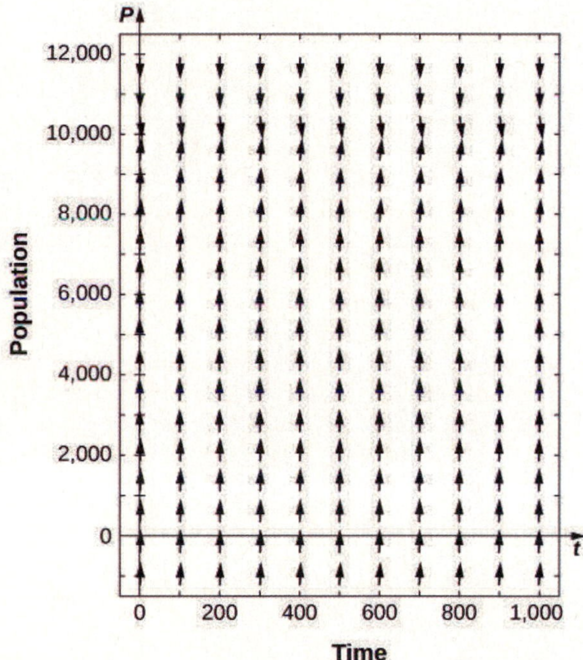


$P_2 > 0$ stable

**185**.

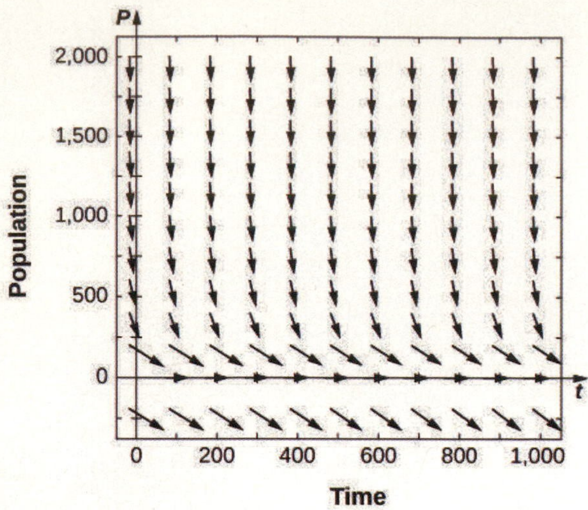


$P_1 = 0$ is semi-stable

**187**. $y = \dfrac{-20}{4 \times 10^{-6} - 0.002e^{0.01t}}$

**189**.

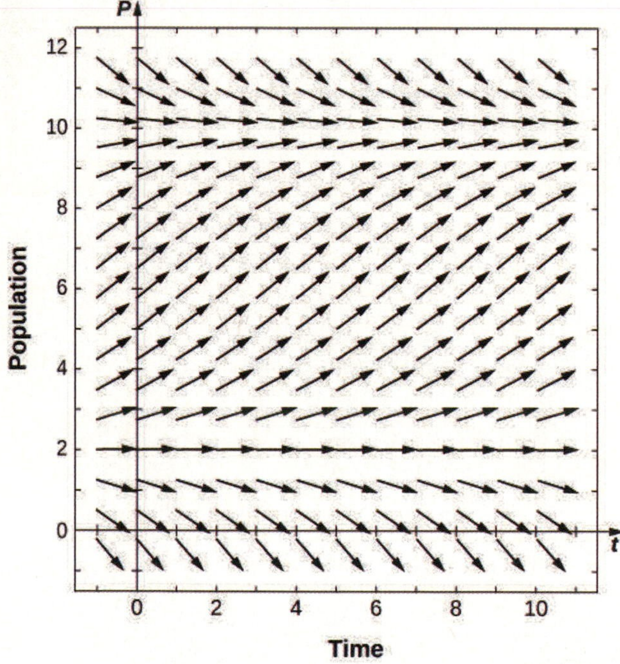


**191**. $P(t) = \dfrac{850 + 500e^{0.009t}}{85 + 5e^{0.009t}}$

**193**. 13 years months

**195**.

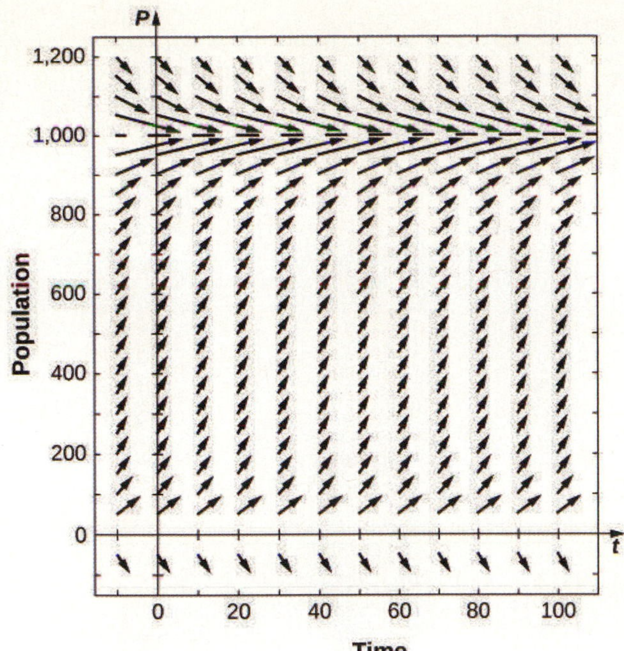


**197**. 31.465 days

**199**. September 2008

**201**. $\frac{K+T}{2}$

**203**. $r = 0.0405$

**205**. $\alpha = 0.0081$

**207**. Logistic: 361, Threshold: 436, Gompertz: 309.

**209**. Yes

**211**. Yes

**213**. $y' - x^3 y = \sin x$

**215**. $y' + \frac{(3x+2)}{x} y = -e^x$

**217**. $\frac{dy}{dt} - yx(x+1) = 0$

**219**. $e^x$

**221**. $-\ln(\cosh x)$

**223**. $y = Ce^{3x} - \frac{2}{3}$

**225**. $y = Cx^3 + 6x^2$

**227**. $y = Ce^{x^2/2} - 3$

**229**. $y = C\tan\left(\frac{x}{2}\right) - 2x + 4\tan\left(\frac{x}{2}\right)\ln\left(\sin\left(\frac{x}{2}\right)\right)$

**231**. $y = Cx^3 - x^2$

**233**. $y = C(x+2)^2 + \frac{1}{2}$

**235**. $y = \frac{C}{\sqrt{x}} + 2\sin(3t)$

**237**. $y = C(x+1)^3 - x^2 - 2x - 1$

**239**. $y = Ce^{\sinh^{-1} x} - 2$

**241**. $y = x + 4e^x - 1$

**243**. $y = -\frac{3x}{2}\left(x^2 - 1\right)$

**245**. $y = 1 - e^{\tan^{-1} x}$

**247**. $y = (x + 2)\ln\left(\frac{x + 2}{2}\right)$

**249**. $y = 2e^{2\sqrt{x}} - 2x - 2\sqrt{x} - 1$

**251**. $v(t) = \frac{gm}{k}\left(1 - e^{-kt/m}\right)$

**253**. $40.451$ seconds

**255**. $\sqrt{\frac{gm}{k}}$

**257**. $y = Ce^x - a(x + 1)$

**259**. $y = Ce^{x^2/2} - a$

**261**. $y = \frac{e^{kt} - e^t}{k - 1}$

## Review Exercises

**263**. F
**265**. T

**267**. $y(x) = \frac{2^x}{\ln(2)} + x\cos^{-1} x - \sqrt{1 - x^2} + C$

**269**. $y(x) = \ln(C - \cos x)$

**271**. $y(x) = e^{e^{C + x}}$

**273**. $y(x) = 4 + \frac{3}{2}x^2 + 2x - \sin x$

**275**. $y(x) = -\frac{2}{1 + 3\left(x^2 + 2\sin x\right)}$

**277**. $y(x) = -2x^2 - 2x - \frac{1}{3} - \frac{2}{3}e^{3x}$

**279**.

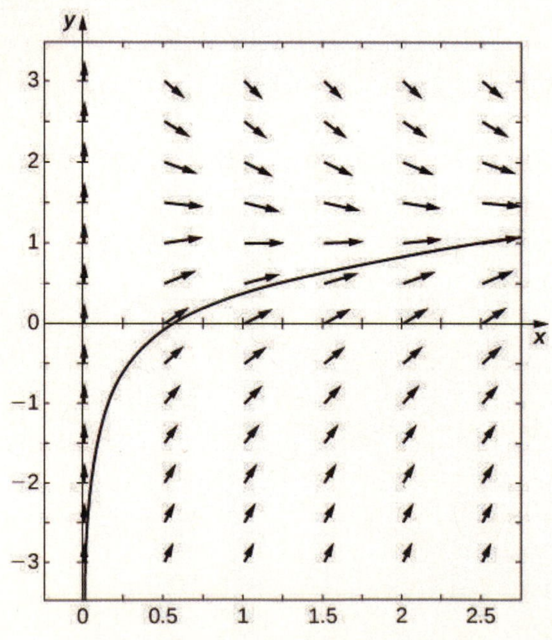

$y(x) = Ce^{-x} + \ln x$

**281**. Euler: $0.6939$, exact solution: $y(x) = \dfrac{3^x - e^{-2x}}{2 + \ln(3)}$

**283**. $\dfrac{40}{49}$ second

**285**. $x(t) = 5000 + \dfrac{245}{9} - \dfrac{49}{3}t - \dfrac{245}{9}e^{-5/3t}$, $t = 307.8$ seconds

**287**. $T(t) = 200\left(1 - e^{-t/1000}\right)$

**289**. $P(t) = \dfrac{1600000e^{0.02t}}{9840 + 160e^{0.02t}}$

## Chapter 5

## Checkpoint

**5.1**. $a_n = \dfrac{(-1)^{n+1}}{3 + 2n}$

**5.2**. $a_n = 6n - 10$

**5.3**. The sequence converges, and its limit is $0$.

**5.4**. The sequence converges, and its limit is $\sqrt{2/3}$.

**5.5**. 2

**5.6**. 0.

**5.7**. The series diverges because the $k$th partial sum $S_k > k$.

**5.8**. 10.

**5.9**. 5/7

**5.10**. 475/90

**5.11**. $e - 1$

**5.12**. The series diverges.

**5.13**. The series diverges.

**5.14**. The series converges.

**5.15**. $S_5 \approx 1.09035$, $R_5 < 0.00267$

**5.16**. The series converges.

**5.17**. The series diverges.

**5.18**. The series converges.

**5.19**. 0.04762

**5.20**. The series converges absolutely.

**5.21**. The series converges.

**5.22**. The series converges.

**5.23**. The comparison test because $2^n/(3^n + n) < 2^n/3^n$ for all positive integers $n$. The limit comparison test could also be used.

## Section Exercises

**1**. $a_n = 0$ if $n$ is odd and $a_n = 2$ if $n$ is even

**3**. $\{a_n\} = \{1, 3, 6, 10, 15, 21, \ldots\}$

**5**. $a_n = \dfrac{n(n+1)}{2}$

**7**. $a_n = 4n - 7$

**9**. $a_n = 3.10^{1-n} = 30.10^{-n}$

**11**. $a_n = 2^n - 1$

**13**. $a_n = \dfrac{(-1)^{n-1}}{2n - 1}$

**15**. $f(n) = 2^n$

**17**. $f(n) = n!/2^{n-2}$

**19**. Terms oscillate above and below $5/3$ and appear to converge to $5/3$.

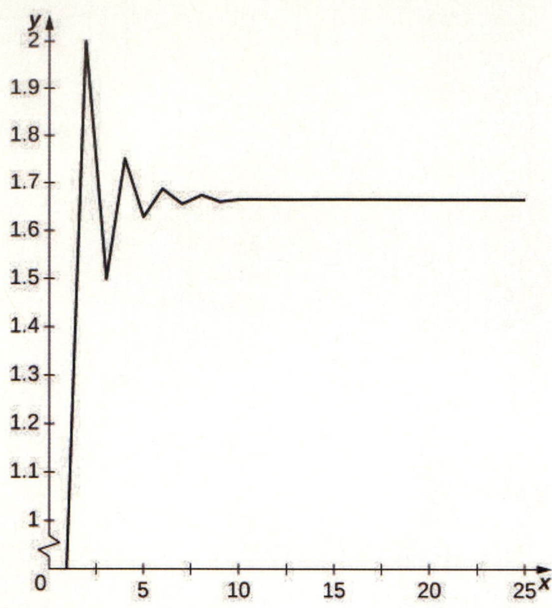


**21**. Terms oscillate above and below $y \approx 1.57...$ and appear to converge to a limit.

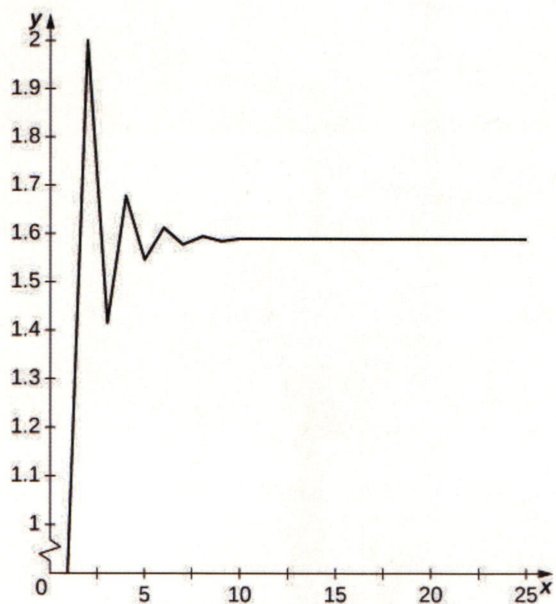


**23**. 7

**25**. 0

**27**. 0

**29**. 1

**31**. bounded, decreasing for $n \geq 1$

**33**. bounded, not monotone

**35**. bounded, decreasing

**37**. not monotone, not bounded

**39**. $a_n$ is decreasing and bounded below by 2. The limit $a$ must satisfy $a = \sqrt{2a}$ so $a = 2$, independent of the initial value.

**41**. 0

**43**. $0 : |\sin x| \le |x|$ and $|\sin x| \le 1$ so $-\frac{1}{n} \le a_n \le \frac{1}{n})$.

**45**. Graph oscillates and suggests no limit.

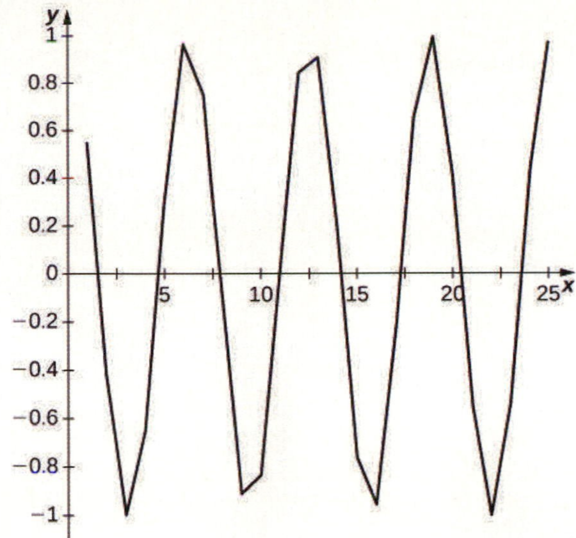


**47**. $n^{1/n} \to 1$ and $2^{1/n} \to 1,$ so $a_n \to 0$

**49**. Since $(1 + 1/n)^n \to e,$ one has $(1 - 2/n)^n \approx (1 + k)^{-2k} \to e^{-2}$ as $k \to \infty.$

**51**. $2^n + 3^n \le 2 \cdot 3^n$ and $3^n/4^n \to 0$ as $n \to \infty,$ so $a_n \to 0$ as $n \to \infty.$

**53**. $\frac{a_{n+1}}{a_n} = n!/(n+1)(n+2)\cdots(2n) = \frac{1 \cdot 2 \cdot 3 \cdots n}{(n+1)(n+2)\cdots(2n)} < 1/2^n.$ In particular, $a_{n+1}/a_n \le 1/2,$ so $a_n \to 0$ as $n \to \infty.$

**55**. $x_{n+1} = x_n - \left((x_n - 1)^2 - 2\right)/2(x_n - 1);$ $x = 1 + \sqrt{2},$ $x \approx 2.4142,$ $n = 5$

**57**. $x_{n+1} = x_n - x_n(\ln(x_n) - 1);$ $x = e,$ $x \approx 2.7183,$ $n = 5$

**59**. a. Without losses, the population would obey $P_n = 1.06P_{n-1}.$ The subtraction of $150$ accounts for fish losses. b. After $12$ months, we have $P_{12} \approx 1494.$

**61**. a. The student owes $\$9383$ after $12$ months. b. The loan will be paid in full after $139$ months or eleven and a half years.

**63**. $b_1 = 0,$ $x_1 = 2/3,$ $b_2 = 1,$ $x_2 = 4/3 - 1 = 1/3,$ so the pattern repeats, and $1/3 = 0.010101\ldots.$

**65**. For the starting values $a_1 = 1,$ $a_2 = 2, \ldots,$ $a_1 = 10,$ the corresponding bit averages calculated by the method indicated are $0.5220,$ $0.5000,$ $0.4960,$ $0.4870,$ $0.4860,$ $0.4680,$ $0.5130,$ $0.5210,$ $0.5040,$ and $0.4840.$ Here is an example of ten corresponding averages of strings of $1000$ bits generated by a random number generator: $0.4880,$ $0.4870,$ $0.5150,$ $0.5490,$ $0.5130,$ $0.5180,$ $0.4860,$ $0.5030,$ $0.5050,$ $0.4980.$ There is no real pattern in either type of average. The random-number-generated averages range between $0.4860$ and $0.5490,$ a range of $0.0630,$ whereas the calculated PRNG bit averages range between $0.4680$ and $0.5220,$ a range of $0.0540.$

**67**. $\sum_{n=1}^{\infty} \frac{1}{n}$

**69**. $\sum_{n=1}^{\infty} \frac{(-1)^{n-1}}{n}$

**71**. $1, 3, 6, 10$

**73**. $1, 1, 0, 0$

**75**. $a_n = S_n - S_{n-1} = \frac{1}{n-1} - \frac{1}{n}.$ Series converges to $S = 1.$

**77**. $a_n = S_n - S_{n-1} = \sqrt{n} - \sqrt{n-1} = \frac{1}{\sqrt{n-1} + \sqrt{n}}.$ Series diverges because partial sums are unbounded.

**79**. $S_1 = 1/3,\quad S_2 = 1/3 + 2/4 > 1/3 + 1/3 = 2/3,\quad S_3 = 1/3 + 2/4 + 3/5 > 3 \cdot (1/3) = 1.$ In general $S_k > k/3$. Series diverges.

**81**. $S_1 = 1/(2.3) = 1/6 = 2/3 - 1/2,$
$S_2 = 1/(2.3) + 1/(3.4) = 2/12 + 1/12 = 1/4 = 3/4 - 1/2,$
$S_3 = 1/(2.3) + 1/(3.4) + 1/(4.5) = 10/60 + 5/60 + 3/60 = 3/10 = 4/5 - 1/2,$
$S_4 = 1/(2.3) + 1/(3.4) + 1/(4.5) + 1/(5.6) = 10/60 + 5/60 + 3/60 + 2/60 = 1/3 = 5/6 - 1/2.$ The pattern is $S_k = (k+1)/(k+2) - 1/2$ and the series converges to $1/2$.

**83**. 0

**85**. $-3$

**87**. diverges, $\sum_{n=1001}^{\infty} \frac{1}{n}$

**89**. convergent geometric series, $r = 1/10 < 1$

**91**. convergent geometric series, $r = \pi/e^2 < 1$

**93**. $\sum_{n=1}^{\infty} 5 \cdot (-1/5)^n,$ converges to $-5/6$

**95**. $\sum_{n=1}^{\infty} 100 \cdot (1/10)^n,$ converges to $100/9$

**97**. $x \sum_{n=0}^{\infty} (-x)^n = \sum_{n=1}^{\infty} (-1)^{n-1} x^n$

**99**. $\sum_{n=0}^{\infty} (-1)^n \sin^{2n}(x)$

**101**. $S_k = 2 - 2^{1/(k+1)} \to 1$ as $k \to \infty$.

**103**. $S_k = 1 - \sqrt{k+1}$ diverges

**105**. $\sum_{n=1}^{\infty} \ln n - \ln(n+1),\ S_k = -\ln(k+1)$

**107**. $a_n = \frac{1}{\ln n} - \frac{1}{\ln(n+1)}$ and $S_k = \frac{1}{\ln(2)} - \frac{1}{\ln(k+1)} \to \frac{1}{\ln(2)}$

**109**. $\sum_{n=1}^{\infty} a_n = f(1) - f(2)$

**111**. $c_0 + c_1 + c_2 + c_3 + c_4 = 0$

**113**. $\frac{2}{n^3 - 1} = \frac{1}{n-1} - \frac{2}{n} + \frac{1}{n+1},$ $S_n = (1 - 1 + 1/3) + (1/2 - 2/3 + 1/4)$ $+ (1/3 - 2/4 + 1/5) + (1/4 - 2/5 + 1/6) + \cdots = 1/2$

**115**. $t_k$ converges to $0.57721\ldots t_k$ is a sum of rectangles of height $1/k$ over the interval $[k, k+1]$ which lie above the graph of $1/x$.

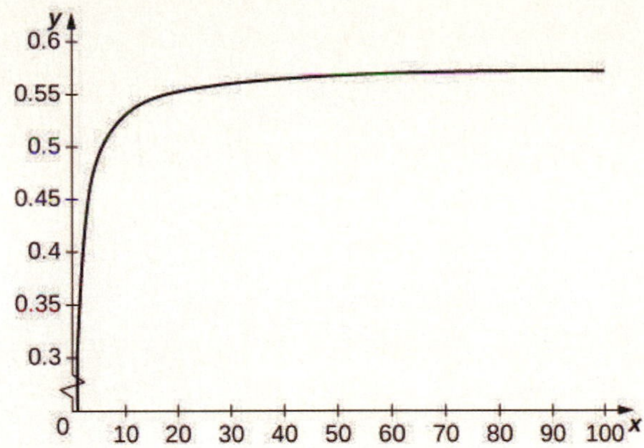


**117**. $N = 22, \quad S_N = 6.1415$

**119**. $N = 3, \quad S_N = 1.559877597243667...$

**121**. a. The probability of any given ordered sequence of outcomes for $n$ coin flips is $1/2^n$. b. The probability of coming up heads for the first time on the $n$ th flip is the probability of the sequence $TT...TH$ which is $1/2^n$. The probability of coming up heads for the first time on an even flip is $\sum_{n=1}^{\infty} 1/2^{2n}$ or $1/3$.

**123**. 5/9

**125**. $E = \sum_{n=1}^{\infty} n/2^{n+1} = 1,$ as can be shown using summation by parts

**127**. The part of the first dose after $n$ hours is $dr^n$, the part of the second dose is $dr^{n-N}$, and, in general, the part remaining of the $m$th dose is $dr^{n-mN}$, so $A(n) = \sum_{l=0}^{m} dr^{n-lN} = \sum_{l=0}^{m} dr^{k+(m-l)N} = \sum_{q=0}^{m} dr^{k+qN} = dr^k \sum_{q=0}^{m} r^{Nq} = dr^k \frac{1-r^{(m+1)N}}{1-r^N}, \ n = k + mN.$

**129**. $S_{N+1} = a_{N+1} + S_N \geq S_N$

**131**. Since $S > 1$, $a_2 > 0$, and since $k < 1$, $S_2 = 1 + a_2 < 1 + (S-1) = S$. If $S_n > S$ for some $n$, then there is a smallest $n$. For this $n$, $S > S_{n-1}$, so $S_n = S_{n-1} + k(S - S_{n-1}) \ = kS + (1-k)S_{n-1} < S$, a contradiction. Thus $S_n < S$ and $a_{n+1} > 0$ for all $n$, so $S_n$ is increasing and bounded by $S$. Let $S_* = \lim S_n$. If $S_* < S$, then $\delta = k(S - S_*) > 0$, but we can find $n$ such that $S_* - S_n < \delta/2$, which implies that $S_{n+1} = S_n + k(S - S_n)$ $> S_* + \delta/2$, contradicting that $S_n$ is increasing to $S_*$. Thus $S_n \to S$.

**133**. Let $S_k = \sum_{n=1}^{k} a_n$ and $S_k \to L$. Then $S_k$ eventually becomes arbitrarily close to $L$, which means that $L - S_N = \sum_{n=N+1}^{\infty} a_n$ becomes arbitrarily small as $N \to \infty$.

**135**. $L = \left(1 + \frac{1}{2}\right) \sum_{n=1}^{\infty} 1/2^n = \frac{3}{2}.$

**137**. At stage one a square of area $1/9$ is removed, at stage $2$ one removes $8$ squares of area $1/9^2$, at stage three one removes $8^2$ squares of area $1/9^3$, and so on. The total removed area after $N$ stages is $\sum_{n=0}^{N-1} 8^N/9^{N+1} = \frac{1}{8}(1 - (8/9)^N)/(1 - 8/9) \to 1$ as $N \to \infty$. The total perimeter is $4 + 4\sum_{n=0} 8^N/3^{N+1} \to \infty.$

**139**. $\lim_{n \to \infty} a_n = 0.$ Divergence test does not apply.

**141**. $\lim_{n \to \infty} a_n = 2.$ Series diverges.

**143**. $\lim_{n \to \infty} a_n = \infty$ (does not exist). Series diverges.

**145**. $\lim_{n \to \infty} a_n = 1.$ Series diverges.

**147**. $\lim_{n \to \infty} a_n$ does not exist. Series diverges.

**149**. $\lim_{n \to \infty} a_n = 1/e^2.$ Series diverges.

**151**. $\lim_{n \to \infty} a_n = 0.$ Divergence test does not apply.

**153**. Series converges, $p > 1.$

**155**. Series converges, $p = 4/3 > 1.$

**157**. Series converges, $p = 2e - \pi > 1.$

**159**. Series diverges by comparison with $\int_1^\infty \frac{dx}{(x+5)^{1/3}}.$

**161**. Series diverges by comparison with $\int_1^\infty \frac{x}{1+x^2} dx.$

**163**. Series converges by comparison with $\int_1^\infty \frac{2x}{1+x^4} dx.$

**165**. $2^{-\ln n} = 1/n^{\ln 2}.$ Since $\ln 2 < 1,$ diverges by $p$ -series.

**167**. $2^{-2\ln n} = 1/n^{2\ln 2}.$ Since $2\ln 2 - 1 < 1,$ diverges by $p$ -series.

**169**. $R_{1000} \le \int_{1000}^\infty \frac{dt}{t^2} = -\frac{1}{t}\Big|_{1000}^\infty = 0.001$

**171**. $R_{1000} \le \int_{1000}^\infty \frac{dt}{1+t^2} = \tan^{-1}\infty - \tan^{-1}(1000) = \pi/2 - \tan^{-1}(1000) \approx 0.000999$

**173**. $R_N < \int_N^\infty \frac{dx}{x^2} = 1/N,\ N > 10^4$

**175**. $R_N < \int_N^\infty \frac{dx}{x^{1.01}} = 100N^{-0.01},\ N > 10^{600}$

**177**. $R_N < \int_N^\infty \frac{dx}{1+x^2} = \pi/2 - \tan^{-1}(N),\ N > \tan\left(\pi/2 - 10^{-3}\right) \approx 1000$

**179**. $R_N < \int_N^\infty \frac{dx}{e^x} = e^{-N},\ N > 5\ln(10),$ okay if $N = 12;$ $\sum_{n=1}^{12} e^{-n} = 0.581973....$ Estimate agrees with $1/(e-1)$ to five decimal places.

**181**. $R_N < \int_N^\infty dx/x^4 = 4/N^3,\ N > \left(4.10^4\right)^{1/3},$ okay if $N = 35;$ $\sum_{n=1}^{35} 1/n^4 = 1.08231\ldots.$ Estimate agrees with the sum to four decimal places.

**183**. $\ln(2)$

**185**. $T = 0.5772...$

**187**. The expected number of random insertions to get $B$ to the top is $n + n/2 + n/3 + \cdots + n/(n-1).$ Then one more insertion puts $B$ back in at random. Thus, the expected number of shuffles to randomize the deck is $n(1 + 1/2 + \cdots + 1/n).$

**189**. Set $b_n = a_{n+N}$ and $g(t) = f(t+N)$ such that $f$ is decreasing on $[t, \infty).$

**191**. The series converges for $p > 1$ by integral test using change of variable.

**193**. $N = e^{e^{100}} \approx e^{10^{43}}$ terms are needed.

**195**. Converges by comparison with $1/n^2.$

**197**. Diverges by comparison with harmonic series, since $2n - 1 \ge n.$

**199**. $a_n = 1/(n+1)(n+2) < 1/n^2.$ Converges by comparison with *p*-series, $p = 2.$

**201**. $\sin(1/n) \le 1/n,$ so converges by comparison with *p*-series, $p = 2.$

**203**. $\sin(1/n) \le 1,$ so converges by comparison with *p*-series, $p = 3/2.$

**205**. Since $\sqrt{n+1} - \sqrt{n} = 1/\left(\sqrt{n+1} + \sqrt{n}\right) \le 2/\sqrt{n},$ series converges by comparison with *p*-series for $p = 1.5.$

**207**. Converges by limit comparison with *p*-series for $p > 1.$

**209**. Converges by limit comparison with *p*-series, $p = 2.$

**211**. Converges by limit comparison with $4^{-n}.$

**213**. Converges by limit comparison with $1/e^{1.1n}.$

**215**. Diverges by limit comparison with harmonic series.

**217**. Converges by limit comparison with *p*-series, $p = 3.$

**219**. Converges by limit comparison with *p*-series, $p = 3.$

**221**. Diverges by limit comparison with $1/n.$

**223**. Converges for $p > 1$ by comparison with a $p$ series for slightly smaller $p.$

**225**. Converges for all $p > 0.$

**227**. Converges for all $r > 1.$ If $r > 1$ then $r^n > 4,$ say, once $n > \ln(2)/\ln(r)$ and then the series converges by limit comparison with a geometric series with ratio $1/2.$

**229**. The numerator is equal to $1$ when $n$ is odd and $0$ when $n$ is even, so the series can be rewritten $\sum_{n=1}^{\infty} \frac{1}{2n+1},$ which diverges by limit comparison with the harmonic series.

**231**. $(a-b)^2 = a^2 - 2ab + b^2$ or $a^2 + b^2 \ge 2ab,$ so convergence follows from comparison of $2a_n b_n$ with $a^2{}_n + b^2{}_n.$ Since the partial sums on the left are bounded by those on the right, the inequality holds for the infinite series.

**233**. $(\ln n)^{-\ln n} = e^{-\ln(n)\ln\ln(n)}.$ If $n$ is sufficiently large, then $\ln\ln n > 2,$ so $(\ln n)^{-\ln n} < 1/n^2,$ and the series converges by comparison to a $p-$ series.

**235**. $a_n \to 0,$ so $a^2{}_n \le |a_n|$ for large $n.$ Convergence follows from limit comparison. $\sum 1/n^2$ converges, but $\sum 1/n$ does not, so the fact that $\sum_{n=1}^{\infty} a^2{}_n$ converges does not imply that $\sum_{n=1}^{\infty} a_n$ converges.

**237**. No. $\sum_{n=1}^{\infty} 1/n$ diverges. Let $b_k = 0$ unless $k = n^2$ for some $n.$ Then $\sum_k b_k/k = \sum 1/k^2$ converges.

**239**. $|\sin t| \le |t|,$ so the result follows from the comparison test.

**241**. By the comparison test, $x = \sum_{n=1}^{\infty} b_n/2^n \le \sum_{n=1}^{\infty} 1/2^n = 1.$

**243**. If $b_1 = 0,$ then, by comparison, $x \le \sum_{n=2}^{\infty} 1/2^n = 1/2.$

**245**. Yes. Keep adding $1$ -kg weights until the balance tips to the side with the weights. If it balances perfectly, with Robert standing on the other side, stop. Otherwise, remove one of the $1$ -kg weights, and add $0.1$ -kg weights one at a time. If it balances after adding some of these, stop. Otherwise if it tips to the weights, remove the last $0.1$ -kg weight. Start adding $0.01$ -kg weights. If it balances, stop. If it tips to the side with the weights, remove the last $0.01$ -kg weight that was added. Continue in this way for the $0.001$ -kg weights, and so on. After a finite number of steps, one has a finite series of the form $A + \sum_{n=1}^{N} s_n/10^n$ where $A$ is the number of full kg weights and $d_n$ is the number of $1/10^n$ -kg weights that were added. If at some state this series is Robert's exact weight, the process will stop. Otherwise it represents the $N$th partial sum of an infinite series that gives Robert's exact weight, and the error of this sum is at most $1/10^N.$

**247**. a. $10^d - 10^{d-1} < 10^d$ b. $h(d) < 9^d$ c. $m(d) = 10^{d-1} + 1$ d. Group the terms in the deleted harmonic series together by number of digits. $h(d)$ bounds the number of terms, and each term is at most $1/m(d).$

$\sum_{d=1}^{\infty} h(d)/m(d) \le \sum_{d=1}^{\infty} 9^d/(10)^{d-1} \le 90.$ One can actually use comparison to estimate the value to smaller than $80.$ The actual value is smaller than $23.$

**249**. Continuing the hint gives $S_N = \left(1 + 1/N^2\right)\left(1 + 1/(N-1)^2 \ldots(1 + 1/4)\right).$ Then $\ln(S_N) = \ln\left(1 + 1/N^2\right) + \ln\left(1 + 1/(N-1)^2\right) + \cdots + \ln(1 + 1/4).$ Since $\ln(1+t)$ is bounded by a constant times $t,$ when $0 < t < 1$ one has $\ln(S_N) \le C \sum_{n=1}^{N} \frac{1}{n^2},$ which converges by comparison to the $p$-series for $p = 2.$

**251**. Does not converge by divergence test. Terms do not tend to zero.

**253**. Converges conditionally by alternating series test, since $\sqrt{n+3}/n$ is decreasing. Does not converge absolutely by comparison with $p$-series, $p = 1/2.$

**255**. Converges absolutely by limit comparison to $3^n/4^n,$ for example.

**257**. Diverges by divergence test since $\lim_{n \to \infty} |a_n| = e.$

**259**. Does not converge. Terms do not tend to zero.

**261**. $\lim_{n \to \infty} \cos^2(1/n) = 1.$ Diverges by divergence test.

**263**. Converges by alternating series test.

**265**. Converges conditionally by alternating series test. Does not converge absolutely by limit comparison with $p$-series, $p = \pi - e$

**267**. Diverges; terms do not tend to zero.

**269**. Converges by alternating series test. Does not converge absolutely by limit comparison with harmonic series.

**271**. Converges absolutely by limit comparison with $p$-series, $p = 3/2,$ after applying the hint.

**273**. Converges by alternating series test since $n(\tan^{-1}(n+1) - \tan^{-1} n)$ is decreasing to zero for large $n.$ Does not converge absolutely by limit comparison with harmonic series after applying hint.

**275**. Converges absolutely, since $a_n = \frac{1}{n} - \frac{1}{n+1}$ are terms of a telescoping series.

**277**. Terms do not tend to zero. Series diverges by divergence test.

**279**. Converges by alternating series test. Does not converge absolutely by limit comparison with harmonic series.

**281**. $\ln(N+1) > 10, \quad N + 1 > e^{10}, \quad N \ge 22026; \quad S_{22026} = 0.0257\ldots$

**283**. $2^{N+1} > 10^6$ or $N + 1 > 6\ln(10)/\ln(2) = 19.93.$ or $N \ge 19;$ $S_{19} = 0.333333969\ldots$

**285**. $(N+1)^2 > 10^6$ or $N > 999;$ $S_{1000} \approx 0.822466.$

**287**. True. $b_n$ need not tend to zero since if $c_n = b_n - \lim b_n,$ then $c_{2n-1} - c_{2n} = b_{2n-1} - b_{2n}.$

**289**. True. $b_{3n-1} - b_{3n} \ge 0,$ so convergence of $\sum b_{3n-2}$ follows from the comparison test.

**291**. True. If one converges, then so must the other, implying absolute convergence.

**293**. Yes. Take $b_n = 1$ if $a_n \ge 0$ and $b_n = 0$ if $a_n < 0.$ Then $\sum_{n=1}^{\infty} a_n b_n = \sum_{n : a_n \ge 0} a_n$ converges. Similarly, one can show $\sum_{n : a_n < 0} a_n$ converges. Since both series converge, the series must converge absolutely.

**295**. Not decreasing. Does not converge absolutely.

**297**. Not alternating. Can be expressed as $\sum_{n=1}^{\infty} \left(\frac{1}{3n-2} + \frac{1}{3n-1} - \frac{1}{3n}\right),$ which diverges by comparison with $\sum \frac{1}{3n-2}.$

**299**. Let $a^+{}_n = a_n$ if $a_n \ge 0$ and $a^+{}_n = 0$ if $a_n < 0.$ Then $a^+{}_n \le |a_n|$ for all $n$ so the sequence of partial sums of $a^+{}_n$ is increasing and bounded above by the sequence of partial sums of $|a_n|,$ which converges; hence, $\sum_{n=1}^{\infty} a^+{}_n$ converges.

**301**. For $N = 5$ one has $\left|R_N\right| b_6 = \theta^{10}/10!.$ When $\theta = 1,$ $R_5 \le 1/10! \approx 2.75 \times 10^{-7}.$ When $\theta = \pi/6,$ $R_5 \le (\pi/6)^{10}/10! \approx 4.26 \times 10^{-10}.$ When $\theta = \pi,$ $R_5 \le \pi^{10}/10! = 0.0258.$

**303**. Let $b_n = 1/(2n-2)!$. Then $R_N \le 1/(2N)! < 0.00001$ when $(2N)! > 10^5$ or $N = 5$ and $1 - \frac{1}{2!} + \frac{1}{4!} - \frac{1}{6!} + \frac{1}{8!} = 0.540325\ldots$, whereas $\cos 1 = 0.5403023\ldots$

**305**. Let $T = \sum \frac{1}{n^2}$. Then $T - S = \frac{1}{2}T$, so $S = T/2$. $\sqrt{6 \times \sum_{n=1}^{1000} 1/n^2} = 3.140638\ldots$; $\sqrt{12 \times \sum_{n=1}^{1000} (-1)^{n-1}/n^2} = 3.141591\ldots$; $\pi = 3.141592\ldots$. The alternating series is more accurate for $1000$ terms.

**307**. $N = 6$, $S_N = 0.9068$

**309**. $\ln(2)$. The $3n$th partial sum is the same as that for the alternating harmonic series.

**311**. The series jumps rapidly near the endpoints. For $x$ away from the endpoints, the graph looks like $\pi(1/2 - x)$.

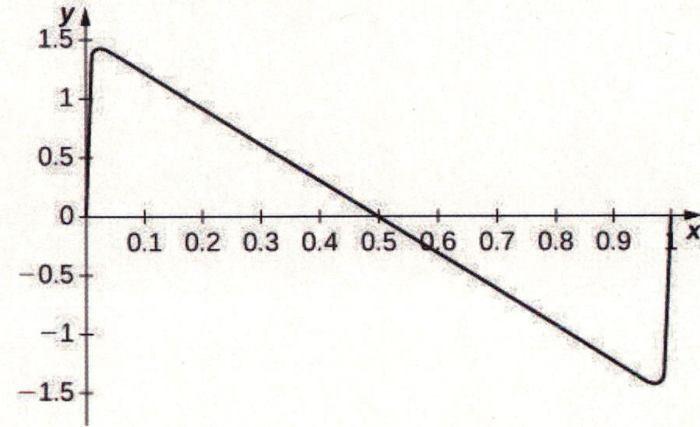


**313**. Here is a typical result. The top curve consists of partial sums of the harmonic series. The bottom curve plots partial sums of a random harmonic series.

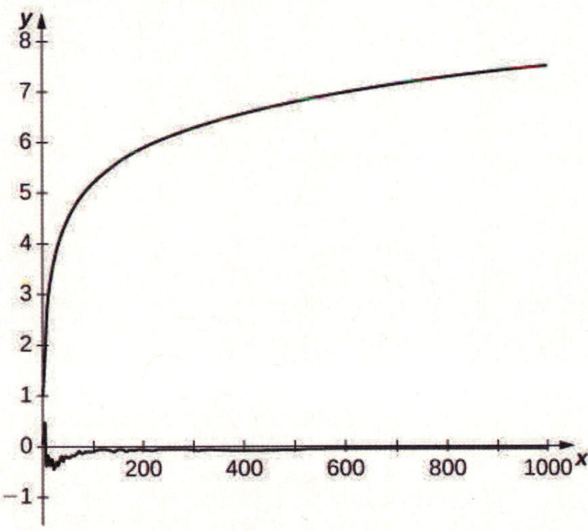


**315**. By the alternating series test, $|S_n - S| \le b_{n+1}$, so one needs $10^4$ terms of the alternating harmonic series to estimate $\ln(2)$ to within $0.0001$. The first $10$ partial sums of the series $\sum_{n=1}^{\infty} \frac{1}{n2^n}$ are (up to four decimals) $0.5000, 0.6250, 0.6667, 0.6823, 0.6885, 0.6911, 0.6923, 0.6928, 0.6930, 0.6931$ and the tenth partial sum is within $0.0001$ of $\ln(2) = 0.6931\ldots$.

**317**. $a_{n+1}/a_n \to 0$. Converges.

**319**. $\frac{a_{n+1}}{a_n} = \frac{1}{2}\left(\frac{n+1}{n}\right)^2 \to 1/2 < 1$. Converges.

**321**. $\frac{a_{n+1}}{a_n} \to 1/27 < 1.$ Converges.

**323**. $\frac{a_{n+1}}{a_n} \to 4/e^2 < 1.$ Converges.

**325**. $\frac{a_{n+1}}{a_n} \to 1.$ Ratio test is inconclusive.

**327**. $\frac{a_n}{a_{n+1}} \to 1/e^2.$ Converges.

**329**. $(a_k)^{1/k} \to 2 > 1.$ Diverges.

**331**. $(a_n)^{1/n} \to 1/2 < 1.$ Converges.

**333**. $(a_k)^{1/k} \to 1/e < 1.$ Converges.

**335**. $a_n^{1/n} = \frac{1}{e} + \frac{1}{n} \to \frac{1}{e} < 1.$ Converges.

**337**. $a_n^{1/n} = \frac{(\ln(1+\ln n))}{(\ln n)} \to 0$ by L'Hôpital's rule. Converges.

**339**. $\frac{a_{k+1}}{a_k} = \frac{1}{2k+1} \to 0.$ Converges by ratio test.

**341**. $(a_n)^{1/n} \to 1/e.$ Converges by root test.

**343**. $a_k^{1/k} \to \ln(3) > 1.$ Diverges by root test.

**345**. $\frac{a_{n+1}}{a_n} = \frac{3^{2n+1}}{2^{3n^2+3n+1}} \to 0.$ Converge.

**347**. Converges by root test and limit comparison test since $x_n \to \sqrt{2}.$

**349**. Converges absolutely by limit comparison with $p-$ series, $p = 2.$

**351**. $\lim_{n \to \infty} a_n = 1/e^2 \neq 0.$ Series diverges.

**353**. Terms do not tend to zero: $a_k \geq 1/2,$ since $\sin^2 x \leq 1.$

**355**. $a_n = \frac{2}{(n+1)(n+2)},$ which converges by comparison with $p-$ series for $p = 2.$

**357**. $a_k = \frac{2^k 1 \cdot 2 \cdots k}{(2k+1)(2k+2)\cdots 3k} \leq (2/3)^k$ converges by comparison with geometric series.

**359**. $a_k \approx e^{-\ln k^2} = 1/k^2.$ Series converges by limit comparison with $p-$ series, $p = 2.$

**361**. If $b_k = c^{1-k}/(c-1)$ and $a_k = k,$ then $b_{k+1} - b_k = -c^{-k}$ and $\sum_{n=1}^{\infty} \frac{k}{c^k} = a_1 b_1 + \frac{1}{c-1} \sum_{k=1}^{\infty} c^{-k} = \frac{c}{(c-1)^2}.$

**363**. $6 + 4 + 1 = 11$

**365**. $|x| \leq 1$

**367**. $|x| < \infty$

**369**. All real numbers $p$ by the ratio test.

**371**. $r < 1/p$

**373**. $0 < r < 1.$ Note that the ratio and root tests are inconclusive. Using the hint, there are $2k$ terms $r^{\sqrt{n}}$ for $k^2 \leq n < (k+1)^2,$ and for $r < 1$ each term is at least $r^k.$ Thus, $\sum_{n=1}^{\infty} r^{\sqrt{n}} = \sum_{k=1}^{\infty} \sum_{n=k^2}^{(k+1)^2-1} r^{\sqrt{n}} \geq \sum_{k=1}^{\infty} 2kr^k,$ which converges by the ratio test for $r < 1.$ For $r \geq 1$ the series diverges by the divergence test.

**375**. One has $a_1 = 1,$ $a_2 = a_3 = 1/2, \ldots a_{2n} = a_{2n+1} = 1/2^n.$ The ratio test does not apply because $a_{n+1}/a_n = 1$ if $n$ is even. However, $a_{n+2}/a_n = 1/2,$ so the series converges according to the previous exercise. Of course, the series is just a duplicated geometric series.

**377**. $a_{2n}/a_n = \frac{1}{2} \cdot \frac{n+1}{n+1+x} \frac{n+2}{n+2+x} \cdots \frac{2n}{2n+x}.$ The inverse of the $k$th factor is $(n+k+x)/(n+k) > 1 + x/(2n)$ so the product is less than $(1 + x/(2n))^{-n} \approx e^{-x/2}$. Thus for $x > 0$, $\frac{a_{2n}}{a_n} \leq \frac{1}{2}e^{-x/2}$. The series converges for $x > 0$.

## Review Exercises

**379**. false
**381**. true
**383**. unbounded, not monotone, divergent
**385**. bounded, monotone, convergent, $0$
**387**. unbounded, not monotone, divergent
**389**. diverges
**391**. converges
**393**. converges, but not absolutely
**395**. converges absolutely
**397**. converges absolutely
**399**. $\frac{1}{2}$
**401**. $\infty, \quad 0, \quad x_0$
**403**. $S_{10} \approx 383, \quad \lim_{n \to \infty} S_n = 400$

# Chapter 6

## Checkpoint

**6.1**. The interval of convergence is $[-1, 1)$. The radius of convergence is $R = 1$.

**6.2**.

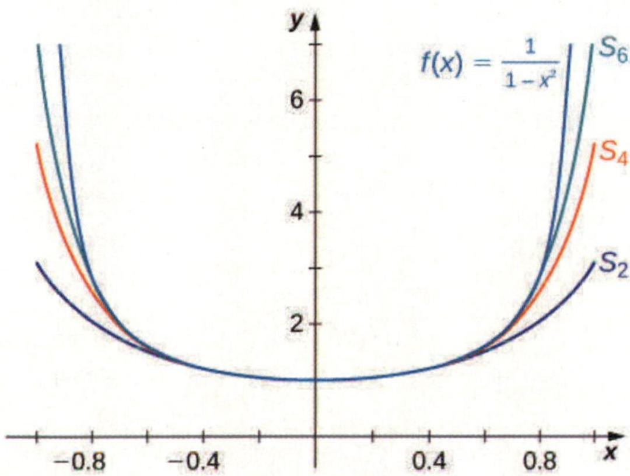


**6.3**. $\sum_{n=0}^{\infty} \frac{x^{n+3}}{2^{n+1}}$ with interval of convergence $(-2, 2)$

**6.4**. Interval of convergence is $(-2, 2)$.

**6.5**. $\sum_{n=0}^{\infty} \left(-1 + \frac{1}{2^{n+1}}\right)x^n$. The interval of convergence is $(-1, 1)$.

**6.6**. $f(x) = \frac{3}{3-x}$. The interval of convergence is $(-3, 3)$.

**6.7**. $1 + 2x + 3x^2 + 4x^3 + \cdots$

**6.8**. $\sum_{n=0}^{\infty} (n+2)(n+1)x^n$

**6.9**. $\sum_{n=2}^{\infty} \frac{(-1)^n x^n}{n(n-1)}$

**6.10**.

$p_0(x) = 1$; $p_1(x) = 1 - 2(x-1)$; $p_2(x) = 1 - 2(x-1) + 3(x-1)^2$; $p_3(x) = 1 - 2(x-1) + 3(x-1)^2 - 4(x-1)^3$

**6.11**.

$p_0(x) = 1$; $p_1(x) = 1 - x$; $p_2(x) = 1 - x + x^2$; $p_3(x) = 1 - x + x^2 - x^3$; $p_n(x) = 1 - x + x^2 - x^3 + \cdots + (-1)^n x^n = \sum_{k=0}^{n} (-1)^k x^k$

**6.12**. $p_1(x) = 2 + \frac{1}{4}(x-4)$; $p_2(x) = 2 + \frac{1}{4}(x-4) - \frac{1}{64}(x-4)^2$; $p_1(6) = 2.5$; $p_2(6) = 2.4375$; $|R_1(6)| \le 0.0625$; $|R_2(6)| \le 0.015625$

**6.13**. 0.96593

**6.14**. $\frac{1}{2}\sum_{n=0}^{\infty}\left(\frac{2-x}{2}\right)^n$. The interval of convergence is $(0, 4)$.

**6.15**. $\sum_{n=0}^{\infty}\frac{(-1)^n x^{2n}}{(2n)!}$ By the ratio test, the interval of convergence is $(-\infty, \infty)$. Since $|R_n(x)| \le \frac{|x|^{n+1}}{(n+1)!}$, the series converges to $\cos x$ for all real $x$.

**6.16**. $\sum_{n=0}^{\infty}(-1)^n(n+1)x^n$

**6.17**. $\sum_{n=0}^{\infty}\frac{(-1)^n x^{4n+2}}{(2n+1)!}$

**6.18**. $\sum_{n=1}^{\infty}\frac{(-1)^n}{n!}\frac{1\cdot 3\cdot 5\cdots(2n-1)}{2^n}x^n$

**6.19**. $y = 5e^{2x}$

**6.20**. $y = a\left(1 - \frac{x^4}{3\cdot 4} + \frac{x^8}{3\cdot 4\cdot 7\cdot 8} - \cdots\right) + b\left(x - \frac{x^5}{4\cdot 5} + \frac{x^9}{4\cdot 5\cdot 8\cdot 9} - \cdots\right)$

**6.21**. $C + \sum_{n=1}^{\infty}(-1)^{n+1}\frac{x^n}{n(2n-2)!}$ The definite integral is approximately $0.514$ to within an error of $0.01$.

**6.22**. The estimate is approximately $0.3414$. This estimate is accurate to within $0.0000094$.

## Section Exercises

**1**. True. If a series converges then its terms tend to zero.

**3**. False. It would imply that $a_n x^n \to 0$ for $|x| < R$. If $a_n = n^n$, then $a_n x^n = (nx)^n$ does not tend to zero for any $x \neq 0$.

**5**. It must converge on $(0, 6]$ and hence at: a. $x = 1$; b. $x = 2$; c. $x = 3$; d. $x = 0$; e. $x = 5.99$; and f. $x = 0.000001$.

**7**. $\left|\frac{a_{n+1}2^{n+1}x^{n+1}}{a_n 2^n x^n}\right| = 2|x|\left|\frac{a_{n+1}}{a_n}\right| \to 2|x|$ so $R = \frac{1}{2}$

**9**. $\left|\frac{a_{n+1}\left(\frac{\pi}{e}\right)^{n+1}x^{n+1}}{a_n\left(\frac{\pi}{e}\right)^n x^n}\right| = \frac{\pi|x|}{e}\left|\frac{a_{n+1}}{a_n}\right| \to \frac{\pi|x|}{e}$ so $R = \frac{e}{\pi}$

**11**. $\left|\frac{a_{n+1}(-1)^{n+1}x^{2n+2}}{a_n(-1)^n x^{2n}}\right| = \left|x^2\right|\left|\frac{a_{n+1}}{a_n}\right| \to \left|x^2\right|$ so $R = 1$

**13**. $a_n = \frac{2^n}{n}$ so $\frac{a_{n+1}x}{a_n} \to 2x$. so $R = \frac{1}{2}$. When $x = \frac{1}{2}$ the series is harmonic and diverges. When $x = -\frac{1}{2}$ the series is alternating harmonic and converges. The interval of convergence is $I = \left[-\frac{1}{2}, \frac{1}{2}\right)$.

**15**. $a_n = \frac{n}{2^n}$ so $\frac{a_{n+1}x}{a_n} \to \frac{x}{2}$ so $R = 2$. When $x = \pm 2$ the series diverges by the divergence test. The interval of convergence is $I = (-2, 2)$.

**17**. $a_n = \frac{n^2}{2^n}$ so $R = 2$. When $x = \pm 2$ the series diverges by the divergence test. The interval of convergence is $I = (-2, 2)$.

**19**. $a_k = \frac{\pi^k}{k^\pi}$ so $R = \frac{1}{\pi}$. When $x = \pm\frac{1}{\pi}$ the series is an absolutely convergent $p$-series. The interval of convergence is

$I = \left[-\frac{1}{\pi}, \frac{1}{\pi}\right]$.

**21**. $a_n = \frac{10^n}{n!}, \frac{a_{n+1}x}{a_n} = \frac{10x}{n+1} \to 0 < 1$ so the series converges for all $x$ by the ratio test and $I = (-\infty, \infty)$.

**23**. $a_k = \frac{(k!)^2}{(2k)!}$ so $\frac{a_{k+1}}{a_k} = \frac{(k+1)^2}{(2k+2)(2k+1)} \to \frac{1}{4}$ so $R = 4$

**25**. $a_k = \frac{k!}{1 \cdot 3 \cdot 5 \cdots (2k-1)}$ so $\frac{a_{k+1}}{a_k} = \frac{k+1}{2k+1} \to \frac{1}{2}$ so $R = 2$

**27**. $a_n = \frac{1}{\binom{2n}{n}}$ so $\frac{a_{n+1}}{a_n} = \frac{((n+1)!)^2}{(2n+2)!} \frac{2n!}{(n!)^2} = \frac{(n+1)^2}{(2n+2)(2n+1)} \to \frac{1}{4}$ so $R = 4$

**29**. $\frac{a_{n+1}}{a_n} = \frac{(n+1)^3}{(3n+3)(3n+2)(3n+1)} \to \frac{1}{27}$ so $R = 27$

**31**. $a_n = \frac{n!}{n^n}$ so $\frac{a_{n+1}}{a_n} = \frac{(n+1)!}{n!} \frac{n^n}{(n+1)^{n+1}} = \left(\frac{n}{n+1}\right)^n \to \frac{1}{e}$ so $R = e$

**33**. $f(x) = \sum_{n=0}^{\infty} (1-x)^n$ on $I = (0, 2)$

**35**. $\sum_{n=0}^{\infty} x^{2n+1}$ on $I = (-1, 1)$

**37**. $\sum_{n=0}^{\infty} (-1)^n x^{2n+2}$ on $I = (-1, 1)$

**39**. $\sum_{n=0}^{\infty} 2^n x^n$ on $\left(-\frac{1}{2}, \frac{1}{2}\right)$

**41**. $\sum_{n=0}^{\infty} 4^n x^{2n+2}$ on $\left(-\frac{1}{2}, \frac{1}{2}\right)$

**43**. $|a_n x^n|^{1/n} = |a_n|^{1/n}|x| \to |x|r$ as $n \to \infty$ and $|x|r < 1$ when $|x| < \frac{1}{r}$. Therefore, $\sum_{n=1}^{\infty} a_n x^n$ converges when $|x| < \frac{1}{r}$ by the $n$th root test.

**45**. $a_k = \left(\frac{k-1}{2k+3}\right)^k$ so $(a_k)^{1/k} \to \frac{1}{2} < 1$ so $R = 2$

**47**. $a_n = \left(n^{1/n} - 1\right)^n$ so $(a_n)^{1/n} \to 0$ so $R = \infty$

**49**. We can rewrite $p(x) = \sum_{n=0}^{\infty} a_{2n+1} x^{2n+1}$ and $p(x) = p(-x)$ since $x^{2n+1} = -(-x)^{2n+1}$.

**51**. If $x \in [0, 1]$, then $y = 2x - 1 \in [-1, 1]$ so $p(2x-1) = p(y) = \sum_{n=0}^{\infty} a_n y^n$ converges.

**53**. Converges on $(-1, 1)$ by the ratio test

**55**. Consider the series $\sum b_k x^k$ where $b_k = a_k$ if $k = n^2$ and $b_k = 0$ otherwise. Then $b_k \le a_k$ and so the series converges on $(-1, 1)$ by the comparison test.

**57**.

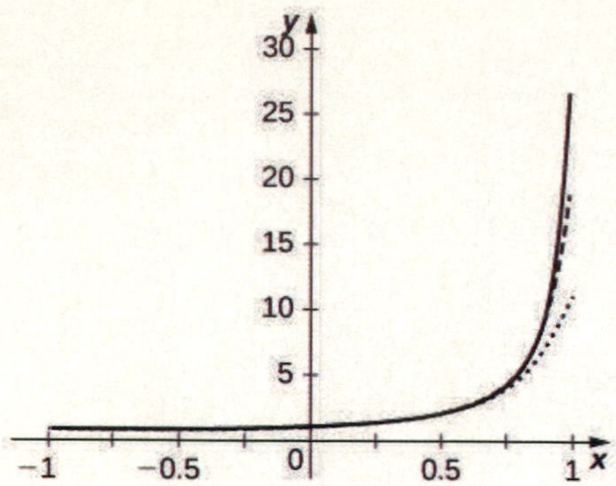


The approximation is more accurate near $x = -1$. The partial sums follow $\frac{1}{1-x}$ more closely as $N$ increases but are never accurate near $x = 1$ since the series diverges there.

**59**.

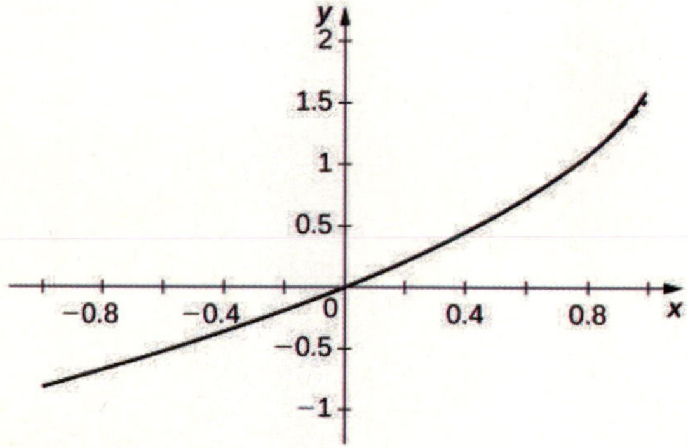


The approximation appears to stabilize quickly near both $x = \pm 1$.

**61**.

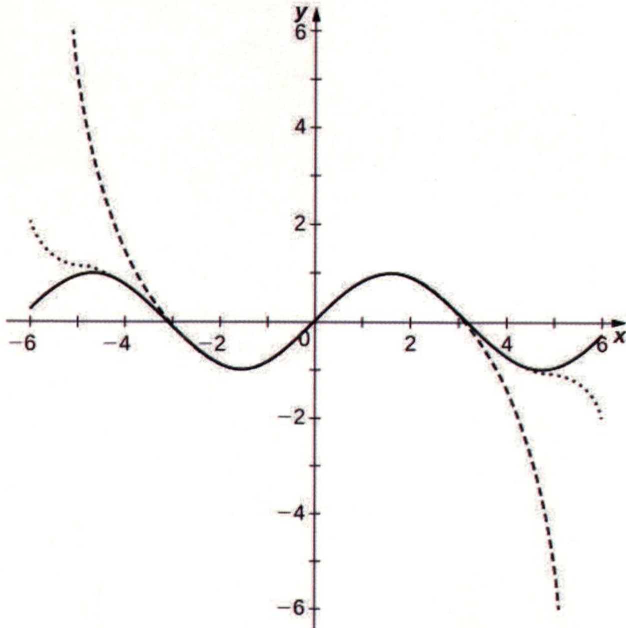


The polynomial curves have roots close to those of $\sin x$ up to their degree and then the polynomials diverge from $\sin x$.

**63.** $\frac{1}{2}(f(x)+g(x))=\sum_{n=0}^{\infty}\frac{x^{2n}}{(2n)!}$ and $\frac{1}{2}(f(x)-g(x))=\sum_{n=0}^{\infty}\frac{x^{2n+1}}{(2n+1)!}$.

**65.**

$$\frac{4}{(x-3)(x+1)}=\frac{1}{x-3}-\frac{1}{x+1}=-\frac{1}{3\left(1-\frac{x}{3}\right)}-\frac{1}{1-(-x)}=-\frac{1}{3}\sum_{n=0}^{\infty}\left(\frac{x}{3}\right)^n-\sum_{n=0}^{\infty}(-1)^n x^n=\sum_{n=0}^{\infty}\left((-1)^{n+1}-\frac{1}{3^{n+1}}\right)x^n$$

**67.** $\frac{5}{\left(x^2+4\right)\left(x^2-1\right)}=\frac{1}{x^2-1}-\frac{1}{4}\frac{1}{1+\left(\frac{x}{2}\right)^2}=-\sum_{n=0}^{\infty}x^{2n}-\frac{1}{4}\sum_{n=0}^{\infty}(-1)^n\left(\frac{x}{2}\right)^n=\sum_{n=0}^{\infty}\left((-1)+(-1)^{n+1}\frac{1}{2^{n+2}}\right)x^{2n}$

**69.** $\frac{1}{x}\sum_{n=0}^{\infty}\frac{1}{x^n}=\frac{1}{x}\frac{1}{1-\frac{1}{x}}=\frac{1}{x-1}$

**71.** $\frac{1}{x-3}\frac{1}{1-\frac{1}{(x-3)^2}}=\frac{x-3}{(x-3)^2-1}$

**73.** $P=P_1+\cdots+P_{20}$ where $P_k=10{,}000\frac{1}{(1+r)^k}$. Then $P=10{,}000\sum_{k=1}^{20}\frac{1}{(1+r)^k}=10{,}000\frac{1-(1+r)^{-20}}{r}$. When $r=0.03$, $P\approx 10{,}000\times 14.8775=148{,}775$. When $r=0.05$, $P\approx 10{,}000\times 12.4622=124{,}622$. When $r=0.07$, $P\approx 105{,}940$.

**75.** In general, $P=\frac{C\left(1-(1+r)^{-N}\right)}{r}$ for $N$ years of payouts, or $C=\frac{Pr}{1-(1+r)^{-N}}$. For $N=20$ and $P=100{,}000$, one has $C=6721.57$ when $r=0.03$; $C=8024.26$ when $r=0.05$; and $C\approx 9439.29$ when $r=0.07$.

**77.** In general, $P=\frac{C}{r}$. Thus, $r=\frac{C}{P}=5\times\frac{10^4}{10^6}=0.05$.

**79.** $\left(x+x^2-x^3\right)\left(1+x^3+x^6+\cdots\right)=\frac{x+x^2-x^3}{1-x^3}$

**81.** $\left(x-x^2-x^3\right)\left(1+x^3+x^6+\cdots\right)=\frac{x-x^2-x^3}{1-x^3}$

**83.** $a_n=2$, $b_n=n$ so $c_n=\sum_{k=0}^{n}b_k a_{n-k}=2\sum_{k=0}^{n}k=(n)(n+1)$ and $f(x)g(x)=\sum_{n=1}^{\infty}n(n+1)x^n$

**85.** $a_n=b_n=2^{-n}$ so $c_n=\sum_{k=1}^{n}b_k a_{n-k}=2^{-n}\sum_{k=1}^{n}1=\frac{n}{2^n}$ and $f(x)g(x)=\sum_{n=1}^{\infty}n\left(\frac{x}{2}\right)^n$

**87.** The derivative of $f$ is $-\frac{1}{(1+x)^2}=-\sum_{n=0}^{\infty}(-1)^n(n+1)x^n$.

**89.** The indefinite integral of $f$ is $\frac{1}{1+x^2}=\sum_{n=0}^{\infty}(-1)^n x^{2n}$.

**91.** $f(x)=\sum_{n=0}^{\infty}x^n=\frac{1}{1-x}$; $f'\left(\frac{1}{2}\right)=\sum_{n=1}^{\infty}\frac{n}{2^{n-1}}=\frac{d}{dx}(1-x)^{-1}\Big|_{x=1/2}=\frac{1}{(1-x)^2}\Big|_{x=1/2}=4$ so $\sum_{n=1}^{\infty}\frac{n}{2^n}=2$.

**93.** $f(x)=\sum_{n=0}^{\infty}x^n=\frac{1}{1-x}$; $f''\left(\frac{1}{2}\right)=\sum_{n=2}^{\infty}\frac{n(n-1)}{2^{n-2}}=\frac{d^2}{dx^2}(1-x)^{-1}\Big|_{x=1/2}=\frac{2}{(1-x)^3}\Big|_{x=1/2}=16$ so $\sum_{n=2}^{\infty}\frac{n(n-1)}{2^n}=4$.

**95.** $\int\sum(1-x)^n dx=\int\sum(-1)^n(x-1)^n dx=\sum\frac{(-1)^n(x-1)^{n+1}}{n+1}$

**97.** $-\int_{t=0}^{x^2}\frac{1}{1-t}dt=-\sum_{n=0}^{\infty}\int_0^{x^2}t^n dx-\sum_{n=0}^{\infty}\frac{x^{2(n+1)}}{n+1}=-\sum_{n=1}^{\infty}\frac{x^{2n}}{n}$

**99**. $\int_0^{x^2} \frac{dt}{1+t^2} = \sum_{n=0}^{\infty} (-1)^n \int_0^{x^2} t^{2n}\,dt = \sum_{n=0}^{\infty} (-1)^n \frac{t^{2n+1}}{2n+1}\Big|_{t=0}^{x^2} = \sum_{n=0}^{\infty} (-1)^n \frac{x^{4n+2}}{2n+1}$

**101**. Term-by-term integration gives $\int_0^x \ln t\,dt = \sum_{n=1}^{\infty} (-1)^{n-1} \frac{(x-1)^{n+1}}{n(n+1)} = \sum_{n=1}^{\infty} (-1)^{n-1}\left(\frac{1}{n} - \frac{1}{n+1}\right)(x-1)^{n+1} = (x-1)\ln x + \sum_{n=2}^{\infty} (-1)^n \frac{(x-1)^n}{n} = x\ln x - x.$

**103**. We have $\ln(1-x) = -\sum_{n=1}^{\infty} \frac{x^n}{n}$ so $\ln(1+x) = \sum_{n=1}^{\infty} (-1)^{n-1} \frac{x^n}{n}$. Thus, $\ln\left(\frac{1+x}{1-x}\right) = \sum_{n=1}^{\infty} \left(1 + (-1)^{n-1}\right)\frac{x^n}{n} = 2\sum_{n=1}^{\infty} \frac{x^{2n-1}}{2n-1}$. When $x = \frac{1}{3}$ we obtain $\ln(2) = 2\sum_{n=1}^{\infty} \frac{1}{3^{2n-1}(2n-1)}$. We have $2\sum_{n=1}^{3} \frac{1}{3^{2n-1}(2n-1)} = 0.69300\ldots$, while $2\sum_{n=1}^{4} \frac{1}{3^{2n-1}(2n-1)} = 0.69313\ldots$ and $\ln(2) = 0.69314\ldots$; therefore, $N = 4$.

**105**. $\sum_{k=1}^{\infty} \frac{x^k}{k} = -\ln(1-x)$ so $\sum_{k=1}^{\infty} \frac{x^{3k}}{6k} = -\frac{1}{6}\ln\left(1 - x^3\right)$. The radius of convergence is equal to 1 by the ratio test.

**107**. If $y = 2^{-x}$, then $\sum_{k=1}^{\infty} y^k = \frac{y}{1-y} = \frac{2^{-x}}{1-2^{-x}} = \frac{1}{2^x - 1}$. If $a_k = 2^{-kx}$, then $\frac{a_{k+1}}{a_k} = 2^{-x} < 1$ when $x > 0$. So the series converges for all $x > 0$.

**109**. Answers will vary.

**111**.

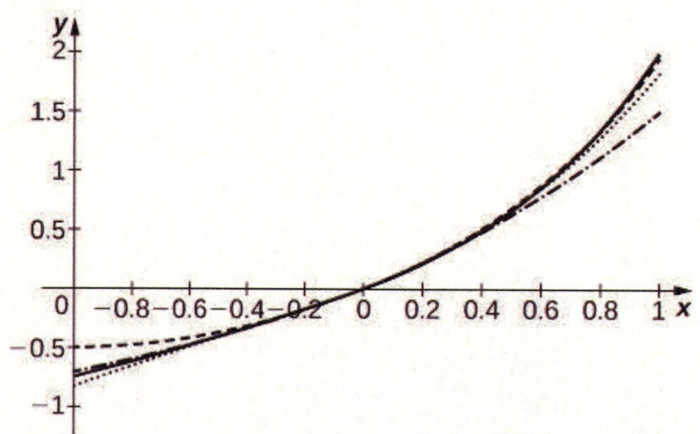


The solid curve is $S_5$. The dashed curve is $S_2$, dotted is $S_3$, and dash-dotted is $S_4$

**113**. When $x = -\frac{1}{2}$, $-\ln(2) = \ln\left(\frac{1}{2}\right) = -\sum_{n=1}^{\infty} \frac{1}{n2^n}$. Since $\sum_{n=11}^{\infty} \frac{1}{n2^n} < \sum_{n=11}^{\infty} \frac{1}{2^n} = \frac{1}{2^{10}}$, one has $\sum_{n=1}^{10} \frac{1}{n2^n} = 0.69306\ldots$ whereas $\ln(2) = 0.69314\ldots$; therefore, $N = 10$.

**115**. $6S_N\left(\frac{1}{\sqrt{3}}\right) = 2\sqrt{3}\sum_{n=0}^{N} (-1)^n \frac{1}{3^n(2n+1)}$. One has $\pi - 6S_4\left(\frac{1}{\sqrt{3}}\right) = 0.00101\ldots$ and $\pi - 6S_5\left(\frac{1}{\sqrt{3}}\right) = 0.00028\ldots$ so $N = 5$ is the smallest partial sum with accuracy to within 0.001. Also, $\pi - 6S_7\left(\frac{1}{\sqrt{3}}\right) = 0.00002\ldots$ while $\pi - 6S_8\left(\frac{1}{\sqrt{3}}\right) = -0.000007\ldots$ so $N = 8$ is the smallest $N$ to give accuracy to within 0.00001.

**117**. $f(-1) = 1$; $f'(-1) = -1$; $f''(-1) = 2$; $f(x) = 1 - (x+1) + (x+1)^2$

**119**. $f'(x) = 2\cos(2x)$; $f''(x) = -4\sin(2x)$; $p_2(x) = -2\left(x - \frac{\pi}{2}\right)$

**121**. $f'(x) = \frac{1}{x}$; $f''(x) = -\frac{1}{x^2}$; $p_2(x) = 0 + (x-1) - \frac{1}{2}(x-1)^2$

**123**. $p_2(x) = e + e(x-1) + \frac{e}{2}(x-1)^2$

**125**. $\frac{d^2}{dx^2}x^{1/3} = -\frac{2}{9x^{5/3}} \geq -0.00092\ldots$ when $x \geq 28$ so the remainder estimate applies to the linear approximation $x^{1/3} \approx p_1(27) = 3 + \frac{x-27}{27}$, which gives $(28)^{1/3} \approx 3 + \frac{1}{27} = 3.\overline{037}$, while $(28)^{1/3} \approx 3.03658$.

**127**. Using the estimate $\frac{2^{10}}{10!} < 0.000283$ we can use the Taylor expansion of order 9 to estimate $e^x$ at $x = 2$. as $e^2 \approx p_9(2) = 1 + 2 + \frac{2^2}{2} + \frac{2^3}{6} + \cdots + \frac{2^9}{9!} = 7.3887\ldots$ whereas $e^2 \approx 7.3891$.

**129**. Since $\frac{d^n}{dx^n}(\ln x) = (-1)^{n-1}\frac{(n-1)!}{x^n}$, $R_{1000} \approx \frac{1}{1001}$. One has $p_{1000}(1) = \sum_{n=1}^{1000} \frac{(-1)^{n-1}}{n} \approx 0.6936$ whereas $\ln(2) \approx 0.6931\cdots$.

**131**. $\int_0^1 \left(1 - x^2 + \frac{x^4}{2} - \frac{x^6}{6} + \frac{x^8}{24} - \frac{x^{10}}{120} + \frac{x^{12}}{720}\right)dx = 1 - \frac{1^3}{3} + \frac{1^5}{10} - \frac{1^7}{42} + \frac{1^9}{9\cdot 24} - \frac{1^{11}}{120\cdot 11} + \frac{1^{13}}{720\cdot 13} \approx 0.74683$ whereas $\int_0^1 e^{-x^2}dx \approx 0.74682$.

**133**. Since $f^{(n+1)}(z)$ is $\sin z$ or $\cos z$, we have $M = 1$. Since $|x - 0| \leq \frac{\pi}{2}$, we seek the smallest $n$ such that $\frac{\pi^{n+1}}{2^{n+1}(n+1)!} \leq 0.001$. The smallest such value is $n = 7$. The remainder estimate is $R_7 \leq 0.00092$.

**135**. Since $f^{(n+1)}(z) = \pm e^{-z}$ one has $M = e^3$. Since $|x - 0| \leq 3$, one seeks the smallest $n$ such that $\frac{3^{n+1}e^3}{(n+1)!} \leq 0.001$. The smallest such value is $n = 14$. The remainder estimate is $R_{14} \leq 0.000220$.

**137**.

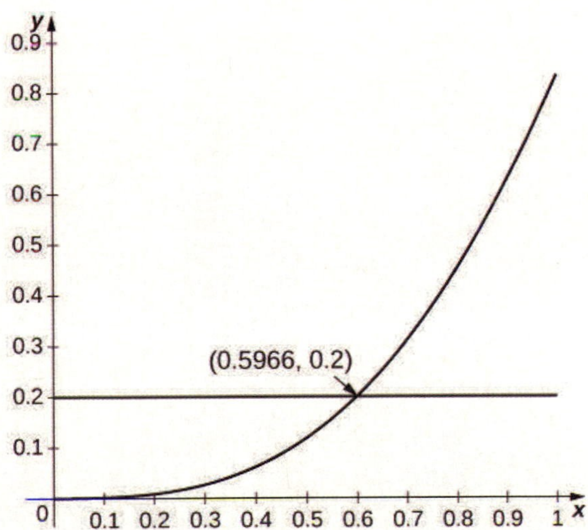


Since $\sin x$ is increasing for small $x$ and since $\sin''x = -\sin x$, the estimate applies whenever $R^2\sin(R) \leq 0.2$, which applies up to $R = 0.596$.

**139**.

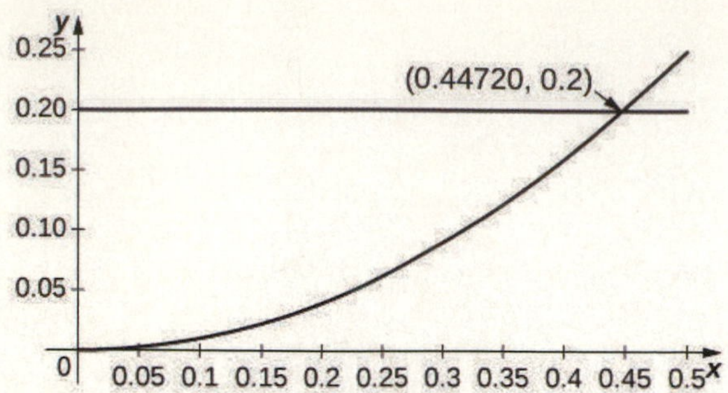


Since the second derivative of $\cos x$ is $-\cos x$ and since $\cos x$ is decreasing away from $x = 0,$ the estimate applies when $R^2 \cos R \leq 0.2$ or $R \leq 0.447$.

**141**. $(x+1)^3 - 2(x+1)^2 + 2(x+1)$

**143**. Values of derivatives are the same as for $x = 0$ so $\cos x = \sum_{n=0}^{\infty} (-1)^n \frac{(x - 2\pi)^{2n}}{(2n)!}$

**145**. $\cos\left(\frac{\pi}{2}\right) = 0,\ -\sin\left(\frac{\pi}{2}\right) = -1$ so $\cos x = \sum_{n=0}^{\infty} (-1)^{n+1} \frac{\left(x - \frac{\pi}{2}\right)^{2n+1}}{(2n+1)!},$ which is also $-\cos\left(x - \frac{\pi}{2}\right)$.

**147**. The derivatives are $f^{(n)}(1) = e$ so $e^x = e \sum_{n=0}^{\infty} \frac{(x-1)^n}{n!}$.

**149**. $\frac{1}{(x-1)^3} = -\left(\frac{1}{2}\right)\frac{d^2}{dx^2}\frac{1}{1-x} = -\sum_{n=0}^{\infty}\left(\frac{(n+2)(n+1)x^n}{2}\right)$

**151**. $2 - x = 1 - (x - 1)$

**153**. $((x-1)-1)^2 = (x-1)^2 - 2(x-1) + 1$

**155**. $\frac{1}{1-(1-x)} = \sum_{n=0}^{\infty} (-1)^n (x-1)^n$

**157**. $x \sum_{n=0}^{\infty} 2^n (1-x)^{2n} = \sum_{n=0}^{\infty} 2^n (x-1)^{2n+1} + \sum_{n=0}^{\infty} 2^n (x-1)^{2n}$

**159**. $e^{2x} = e^{2(x-1)+2} = e^2 \sum_{n=0}^{\infty} \frac{2^n (x-1)^n}{n!}$

**161**. $x = e^2;\ S_{10} = \frac{34{,}913}{4725} \approx 7.3889947$

**163**. $\sin(2\pi) = 0;\ S_{10} = 8.27 \times 10^{-5}$

**165**.

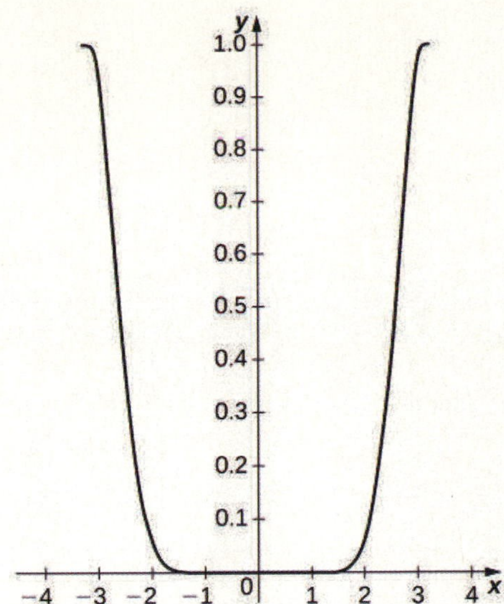

The difference is small on the interior of the interval but approaches $1$ near the endpoints. The remainder estimate is $|R_4| = \frac{\pi^5}{120} \approx 2.552.$

**167**.

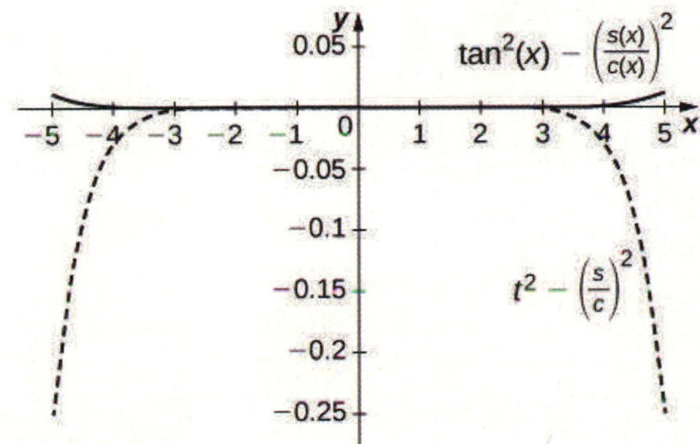


The difference is on the order of $10^{-4}$ on $[-1, 1]$ while the Taylor approximation error is around $0.1$ near $\pm 1$. The top curve is a plot of $\tan^2 x - \left(\frac{S_5(x)}{C_4(x)}\right)^2$ and the lower dashed plot shows $t^2 - \left(\frac{S_5}{C_4}\right)^2$.

**169**. a. Answers will vary. b. The following are the $x_n$ values after $10$ iterations of Newton's method to approximation a root of $p_N(x) - 2 = 0$: for $N = 4, x = 0.6939...$; for $N = 5, x = 0.6932...$; for $N = 6, x = 0.69315...$; . *(Note:* $\ln(2) = 0.69314...$) c. Answers will vary.

**171**. $\frac{\ln\left(1 - x^2\right)}{x^2} \to -1$

**173**. $\frac{\cos(\sqrt{x}) - 1}{2x} \approx \frac{\left(1 - \frac{x}{2} + \frac{x^2}{4!} - \cdots\right) - 1}{2x} \to -\frac{1}{4}$

**175**. $\left(1 + x^2\right)^{-1/3} = \sum_{n=0}^{\infty} \binom{-\frac{1}{3}}{n} x^{2n}$

**177**. $(1 - 2x)^{2/3} = \sum_{n=0}^{\infty} (-1)^n 2^n \binom{\frac{2}{3}}{n} x^n$

**179**. $\sqrt{2+x^2} = \sum_{n=0}^{\infty} 2^{(1/2)-n}\binom{\frac{1}{2}}{n}x^{2n};\ (|x^2| < 2)$

**181**. $\sqrt{2x-x^2} = \sqrt{1-(x-1)^2}$ so $\sqrt{2x-x^2} = \sum_{n=0}^{\infty}(-1)^n\binom{\frac{1}{2}}{n}(x-1)^{2n}$

**183**. $\sqrt{x} = 2\sqrt{1+\frac{x-4}{4}}$ so $\sqrt{x} = \sum_{n=0}^{\infty} 2^{1-2n}\binom{\frac{1}{2}}{n}(x-4)^n$

**185**. $\sqrt{x} = \sum_{n=0}^{\infty} 3^{1-3n}\binom{\frac{1}{2}}{n}(x-9)^n$

**187**. $10\left(1+\frac{x}{1000}\right)^{1/3} = \sum_{n=0}^{\infty} 10^{1-3n}\binom{\frac{1}{3}}{n}x^n$. Using, for example, a fourth-degree estimate at $x=1$ gives

$$(1001)^{1/3} \approx 10\left(1+\binom{\frac{1}{3}}{1}10^{-3}+\binom{\frac{1}{3}}{2}10^{-6}+\binom{\frac{1}{3}}{3}10^{-9}+\binom{\frac{1}{3}}{4}10^{-12}\right)$$

$$= 10\left(1+\frac{1}{3.10^3}-\frac{1}{9.10^6}+\frac{5}{81.10^9}-\frac{10}{243.10^{12}}\right) = 10.00333222...$$

whereas $(1001)^{1/3} = 10.00332222839093....$ Two terms would suffice for three-digit accuracy.

**189**. The approximation is $2.3152$; the CAS value is $2.23\ldots$.

**191**. The approximation is $2.583\ldots$; the CAS value is $2.449\ldots$.

**193**.

$\sqrt{1-x^2} = 1-\frac{x^2}{2}-\frac{x^4}{8}-\frac{x^6}{16}-\frac{5x^8}{128}+\cdots.$ Thus

$\int_{-1}^{1}\sqrt{1-x^2}dx = x-\frac{x^3}{6}-\frac{x^5}{40}-\frac{x^7}{7\cdot 16}-\frac{5x^9}{9\cdot 128}+\cdots\Big|_{-1}^{1} \approx 2-\frac{1}{3}-\frac{1}{20}-\frac{1}{56}-\frac{10}{9\cdot 128}+\text{error} = 1.590...$ whereas $\frac{\pi}{2} = 1.570...$

**195**. $(1+x)^{4/3} = (1+x)\left(1+\frac{1}{3}x-\frac{1}{9}x^2+\frac{5}{81}x^3-\frac{10}{243}x^4+\cdots\right) = 1+\frac{4x}{3}+\frac{2x^2}{9}-\frac{4x^3}{81}+\frac{5x^4}{243}+\cdots$

**197**. $\left(1+(x+3)^2\right)^{1/3} = 1+\frac{1}{3}(x+3)^2-\frac{1}{9}(x+3)^4+\frac{5}{81}(x+3)^6-\frac{10}{243}(x+3)^8+\cdots$

**199**. Twice the approximation is $1.260\ldots$ whereas $2^{1/3} = 1.2599....$

**201**. $f^{(99)}(0) = 0$

**203**. $\sum_{n=0}^{\infty}\frac{(\ln(2)x)^n}{n!}$

**205**. For $x > 0$, $\sin(\sqrt{x}) = \sum_{n=0}^{\infty}(-1)^n\frac{x^{(2n+1)/2}}{\sqrt{x}(2n+1)!} = \sum_{n=0}^{\infty}(-1)^n\frac{x^n}{(2n+1)!}$.

**207**. $e^{x^3} = \sum_{n=0}^{\infty}\frac{x^{3n}}{n!}$

**209**. $\sin^2 x = -\sum_{k=1}^{\infty}\frac{(-1)^k 2^{2k-1}x^{2k}}{(2k)!}$

**211**. $\tan^{-1}x = \sum_{k=0}^{\infty}\frac{(-1)^k x^{2k+1}}{2k+1}$

**213**. $\sin^{-1}x = \sum_{n=0}^{\infty}\binom{\frac{1}{2}}{n}\frac{x^{2n+1}}{(2n+1)n!}$

**215**. $F(x) = \sum_{n=0}^{\infty}(-1)^n\frac{x^{n+1}}{(n+1)(2n)!}$

**217**. $F(x) = \sum_{n=1}^{\infty} (-1)^{n+1} \frac{x^n}{n^2}$

**219**. $x + \frac{x^3}{3} + \frac{2x^5}{15} + \cdots$

**221**. $1 + x - \frac{x^3}{3} - \frac{x^4}{6} + \cdots$

**223**. $1 + x^2 + \frac{2x^4}{3} + \frac{17x^6}{45} + \cdots$

**225**. Using the expansion for $\tan x$ gives $1 + \frac{x}{3} + \frac{2x^2}{15}$.

**227**. $\frac{1}{1+x^2} = \sum_{n=0}^{\infty} (-1)^n x^{2n}$ so $R = 1$ by the ratio test.

**229**. $\ln(1 + x^2) = \sum_{n=1}^{\infty} \frac{(-1)^{n-1}}{n} x^{2n}$ so $R = 1$ by the ratio test.

**231**. Add series of $e^x$ and $e^{-x}$ term by term. Odd terms cancel and $\cosh x = \sum_{n=0}^{\infty} \frac{x^{2n}}{(2n)!}$.

**233**.

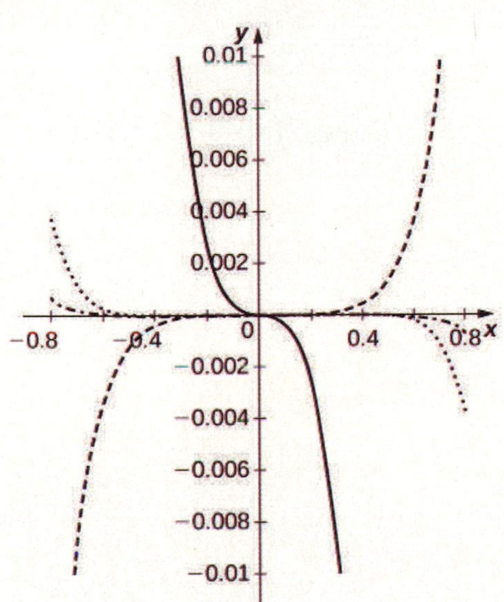


The ratio $\frac{S_n(x)}{C_n(x)}$ approximates $\tan x$ better than does $p_7(x) = x + \frac{x^3}{3} + \frac{2x^5}{15} + \frac{17x^7}{315}$ for $N \geq 3$. The dashed curves are $\frac{S_n}{C_n} - \tan$ for $n = 1, 2$. The dotted curve corresponds to $n = 3$, and the dash-dotted curve corresponds to $n = 4$. The solid curve is $p_7 - \tan x$.

**235**. By the term-by-term differentiation theorem, $y' = \sum_{n=1}^{\infty} n a_n x^{n-1}$ so $y' = \sum_{n=1}^{\infty} n a_n x^{n-1} xy' = \sum_{n=1}^{\infty} n a_n x^n$, whereas $y' = \sum_{n=2}^{\infty} n(n-1) a_n x^{n-2}$ so $xy'' = \sum_{n=2}^{\infty} n(n-1) a_n x^n$.

**237**. The probability is $p = \frac{1}{\sqrt{2\pi}} \int_{(a-\mu)/\sigma}^{(b-\mu)/\sigma} e^{-x^2/2} dx$ where $a = 90$ and $b = 100$, that is,

$$p = \frac{1}{\sqrt{2\pi}} \int_{-1}^{1} e^{-x^2/2} dx = \frac{1}{\sqrt{2\pi}} \int_{-1}^{1} \sum_{n=0}^{5} (-1)^n \frac{x^{2n}}{2^n n!} dx = \frac{2}{\sqrt{2\pi}} \sum_{n=0}^{5} (-1)^n \frac{1}{(2n+1)2^n n!} \approx 0.6827.$$

**239**.

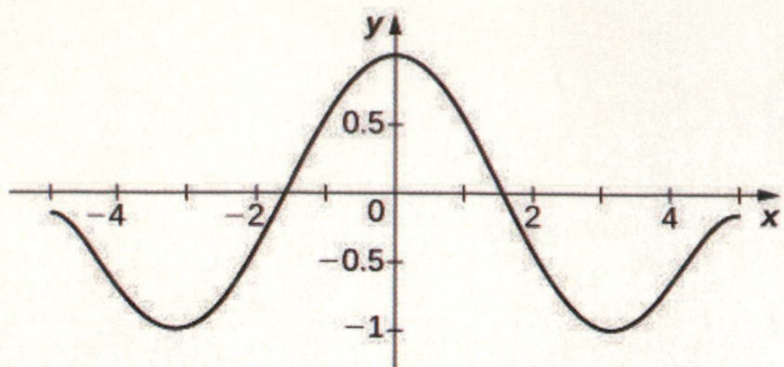


As in the previous problem one obtains $a_n = 0$ if $n$ is odd and $a_n = -(n+2)(n+1)a_{n+2}$ if $n$ is even, so $a_0 = 1$ leads to $a_{2n} = \frac{(-1)^n}{(2n)!}$.

**241**. $y'' = \sum_{n=0}^{\infty} (n+2)(n+1)a_{n+2}x^n$ and $y' = \sum_{n=0}^{\infty} (n+1)a_{n+1}x^n$ so $y'' - y' + y = 0$ implies that $(n+2)(n+1)a_{n+2} - (n+1)a_{n+1} + a_n = 0$ or $a_n = \frac{a_{n-1}}{n} - \frac{a_{n-2}}{n(n-1)}$ for all $n \cdot y(0) = a_0 = 1$ and $y'(0) = a_1 = 0,$ so $a_2 = \frac{1}{2}$, $a_3 = \frac{1}{6}$, $a_4 = 0,$ and $a_5 = -\frac{1}{120}$.

**243**. a. (Proof) b. We have $R_s \le \frac{0.1}{(9)!}\pi^9 \approx 0.0082 < 0.01.$ We have $\int_0^{\pi}\left(1 - \frac{x^2}{3!} + \frac{x^4}{5!} - \frac{x^6}{7!} + \frac{x^8}{9!}\right)dx = \pi - \frac{\pi^3}{3 \cdot 3!} + \frac{\pi^5}{5 \cdot 5!} - \frac{\pi^7}{7 \cdot 7!} + \frac{\pi^9}{9 \cdot 9!} = 1.852...,$ whereas $\int_0^{\pi} \frac{\sin t}{t} dt = 1.85194...,$ so the actual error is approximately $0.00006$.

**245**.

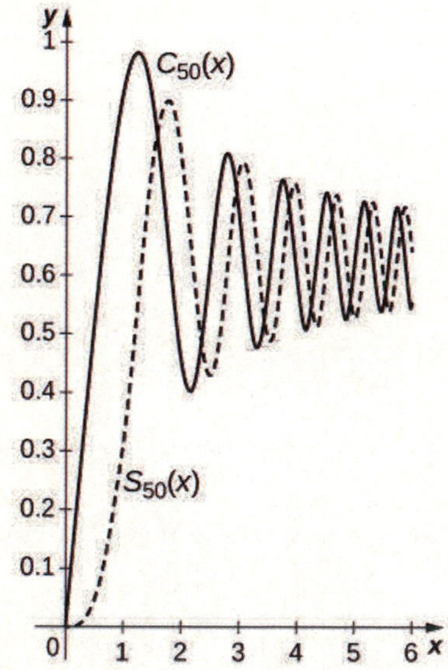


Since $\cos\left(t^2\right) = \sum_{n=0}^{\infty} (-1)^n \frac{t^{4n}}{(2n)!}$ and $\sin\left(t^2\right) = \sum_{n=0}^{\infty} (-1)^n \frac{t^{4n+2}}{(2n+1)!}$, one has $S(x) = \sum_{n=0}^{\infty} (-1)^n \frac{x^{4n+3}}{(4n+3)(2n+1)!}$ and $C(x) = \sum_{n=0}^{\infty} (-1)^n \frac{x^{4n+1}}{(4n+1)(2n)!}$. The sums of the first $50$ nonzero terms are plotted below with $C_{50}(x)$ the solid curve and $S_{50}(x)$ the dashed curve.

**247**. $\int_0^{1/4} \sqrt{x}\left(1 - \frac{x}{2} - \frac{x^2}{8} - \frac{x^3}{16} - \frac{5x^4}{128} - \frac{7x^5}{256}\right)dx$

$= \frac{2}{3}2^{-3} - \frac{1}{2}\frac{2}{5}2^{-5} - \frac{1}{8}\frac{2}{7}2^{-7} - \frac{1}{16}\frac{2}{9}2^{-9} - \frac{5}{128}\frac{2}{11}2^{-11} - \frac{7}{256}\frac{2}{13}2^{-13} = 0.0767732...$ whereas $\int_0^{1/4} \sqrt{x - x^2}dx = 0.076773.$

**249**. $T \approx 2\pi\sqrt{\frac{10}{9.8}}\left(1 + \frac{\sin^2(\theta/12)}{4}\right) \approx 6.453$ seconds. The small angle estimate is $T \approx 2\pi\sqrt{\frac{10}{9.8}} \approx 6.347$. The relative error is around $2$ percent.

**251**. $\int_0^{\pi/2} \sin^4 \theta d\theta = \frac{3\pi}{16}$. Hence $T \approx 2\pi\sqrt{\frac{L}{g}}\left(1 + \frac{k^2}{4} + \frac{9}{256}k^4\right)$.

## Review Exercises

**253**. True
**255**. True
**257**. ROC: $1$; IOC: $(0, 2)$
**259**. ROC: $12$; IOC: $(-16, 8)$
**261**. $\sum_{n=0}^{\infty} \frac{(-1)^n}{3^{n+1}}x^n$; ROC: $3$; IOC: $(-3, 3)$
**263**. integration: $\sum_{n=0}^{\infty} \frac{(-1)^n}{2n+1}(2x)^{2n+1}$
**265**. $p_4(x) = (x+3)^3 - 11(x+3)^2 + 39(x+3) - 41$; exact
**267**. $\sum_{n=0}^{\infty} \frac{(-1)^n (3x)^{2n}}{2n!}$
**269**. $\sum_{n=0}^{\infty} \frac{(-1)^n}{(2n)!}\left(x - \frac{\pi}{2}\right)^{2n}$
**271**. $\sum_{n=1}^{\infty} \frac{(-1)^n}{n!}x^{2n}$
**273**. $F(x) = \sum_{n=0}^{\infty} \frac{(-1)^n}{(2n+1)(2n+1)!}x^{2n+1}$
**275**. Answers may vary.
**277**. $2.5\%$

# Chapter 7

## Checkpoint

**7.1**.

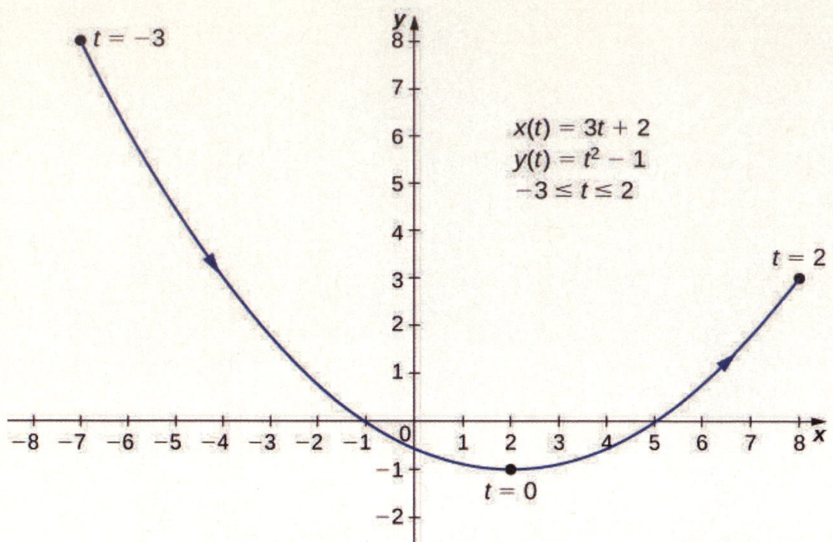


**7.2.** $x = 2 + \frac{3}{y+1}$, or $y = -1 + \frac{3}{x-2}$. This equation describes a portion of a rectangular hyperbola centered at $(2, -1)$.

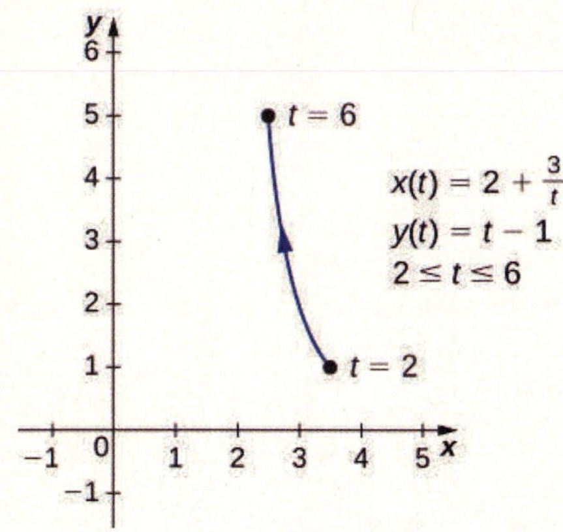


**7.3.** One possibility is $x(t) = t, \quad y(t) = t^2 + 2t$. Another possibility is $x(t) = 2t - 3, \quad y(t) = (2t-3)^2 + 2(2t-3) = 4t^2 - 8t + 3$. There are, in fact, an infinite number of possibilities.

**7.4.** $x'(t) = 2t - 4$ and $y'(t) = 6t^2 - 6$, so $\frac{dy}{dx} = \frac{6t^2 - 6}{2t - 4} = \frac{3t^2 - 3}{t - 2}$.

This expression is undefined when $t = 2$ and equal to zero when $t = \pm 1$.

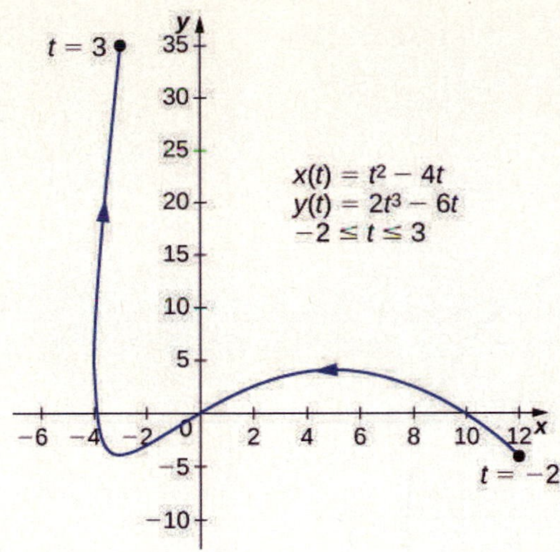


**7.5**. The equation of the tangent line is $y = 24x + 100.$

**7.6**. $\frac{d^2y}{dx^2} = \frac{3t^2 - 12t + 3}{2(t-2)^3}$. Critical points $(5, 4), (-3, -4),$ and $(-4, 6).$

**7.7**. $A = 3\pi$ (Note that the integral formula actually yields a negative answer. This is due to the fact that $x(t)$ is a decreasing function over the interval $[0, 2\pi];$ that is, the curve is traced from right to left.)

**7.8**. $s = 2\left(10^{3/2} - 2^{3/2}\right) \approx 57.589$

**7.9**. $A = \frac{\pi\left(494\sqrt{13} + 128\right)}{1215}$

**7.10**. $\left(8\sqrt{2}, \frac{5\pi}{4}\right)$ and $\left(-2, 2\sqrt{3}\right)$

**7.11**.

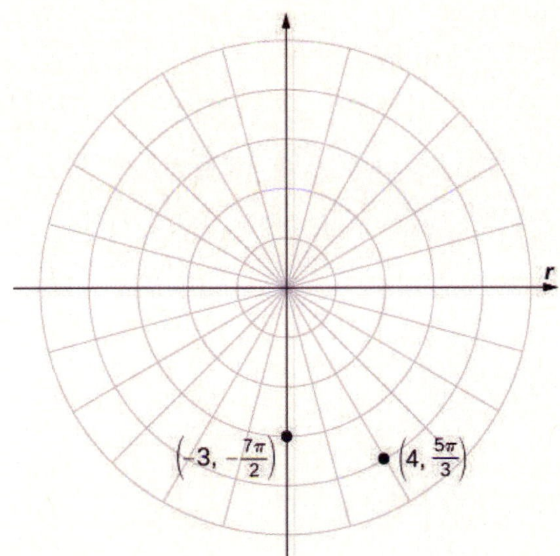


**7.12**.

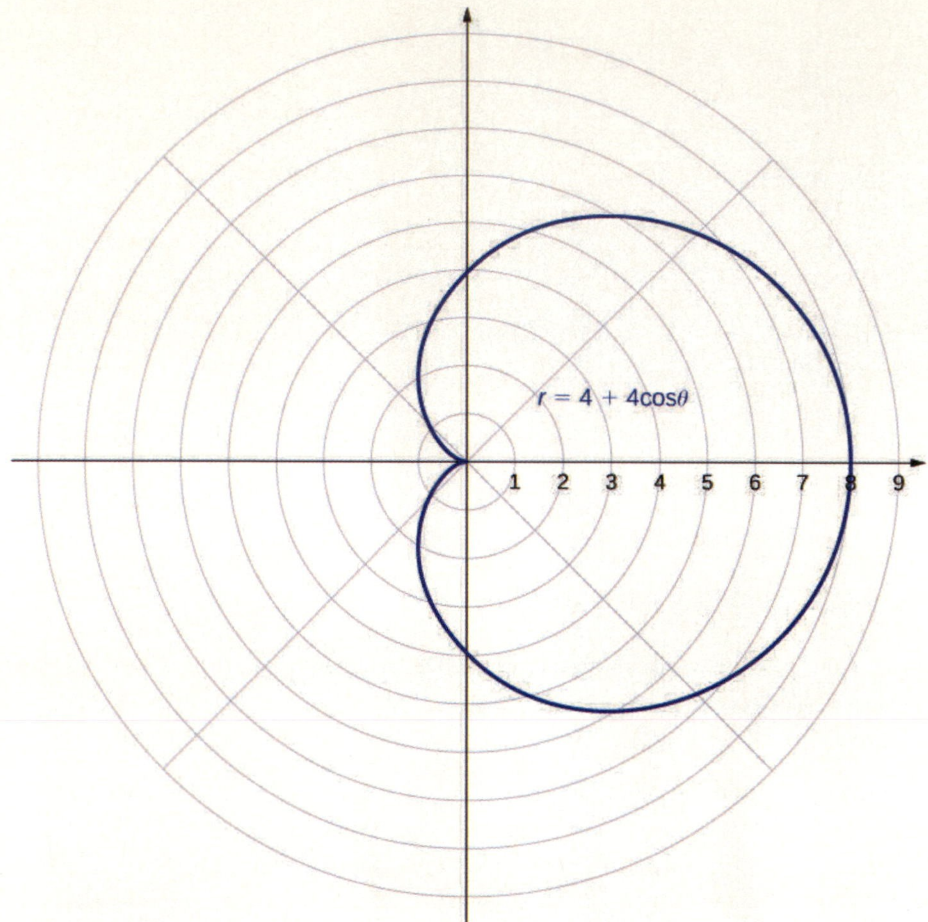


The name of this shape is a cardioid, which we will study further later in this section.

**7.13**. $y = x^2,$ which is the equation of a parabola opening upward.

**7.14**. Symmetric with respect to the polar axis.

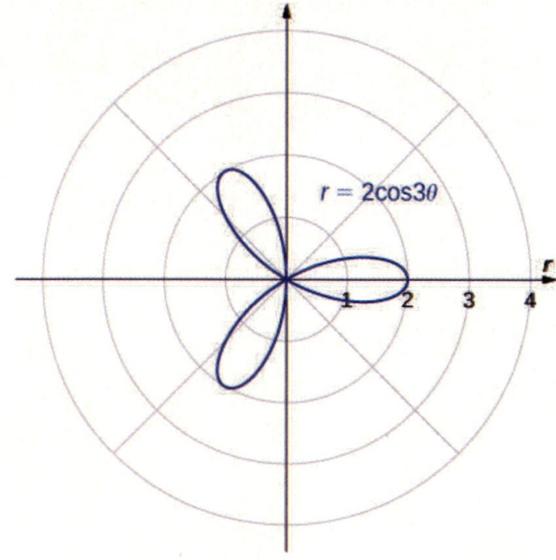


**7.15**. $A = 3\pi/2$

**7.16**. $A = \frac{4\pi}{3} + 4\sqrt{3}$

**7.17**. $s = 3\pi$

**7.18**. $x = 2(y + 3)^2 - 2$

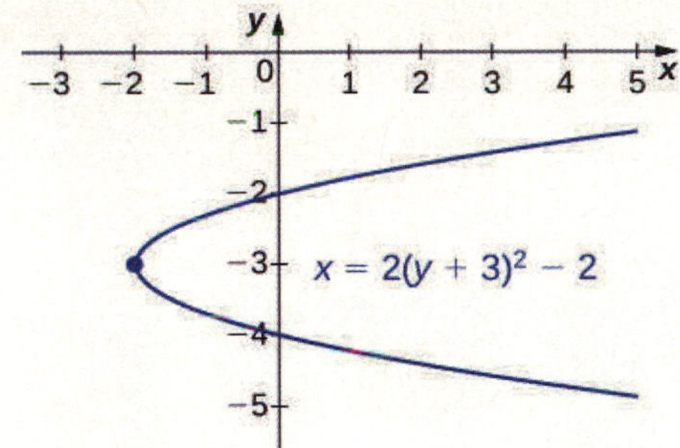


**7.19**. $\frac{(x + 1)^2}{16} + \frac{(y - 2)^2}{9} = 1$

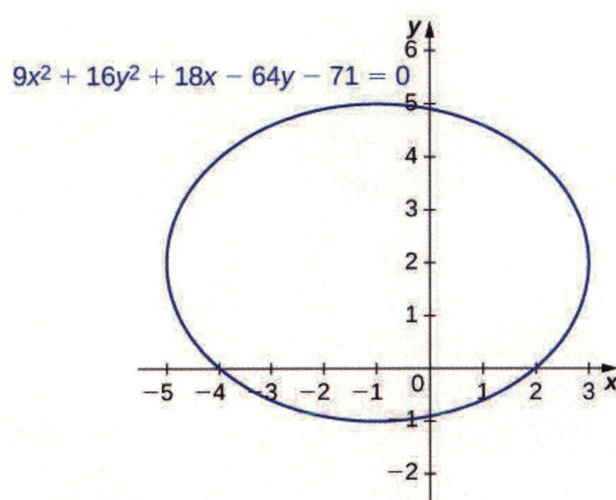


**7.20**. $\frac{(y + 2)^2}{9} - \frac{(x - 1)^2}{4} = 1$. This is a vertical hyperbola. Asymptotes $y = -2 \pm \frac{3}{2}(x - 1)$.

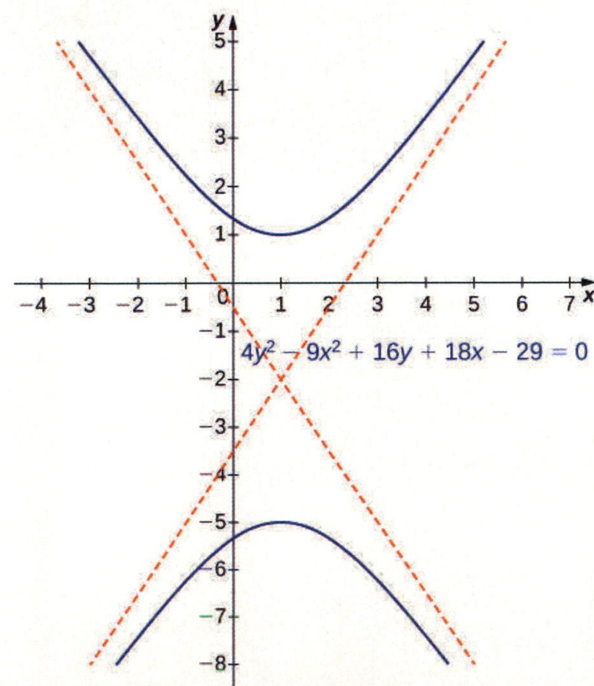

**7.21**. $e = \frac{c}{a} = \frac{\sqrt{74}}{7} \approx 1.229$

**7.22**. Here $e = 0.8$ and $p = 5$. This conic section is an ellipse.

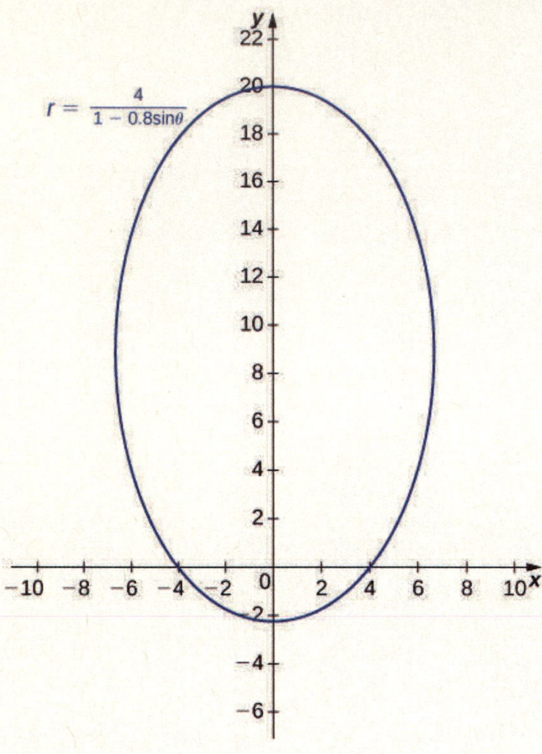


**7.23**. The conic is a hyperbola and the angle of rotation of the axes is $\theta = 22.5°$.

## Section Exercises

**1**.

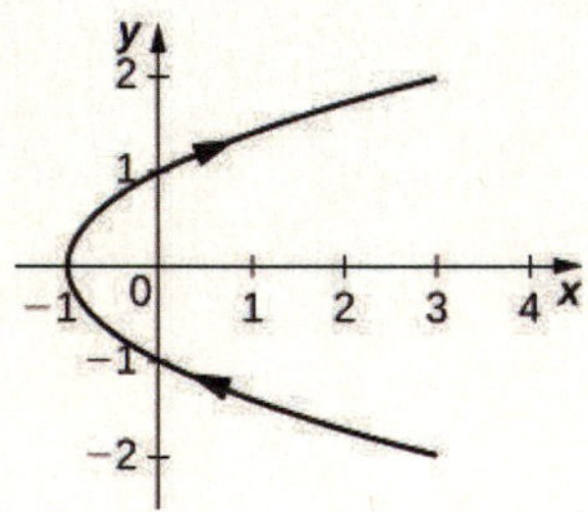

orientation: bottom to top

**3**.

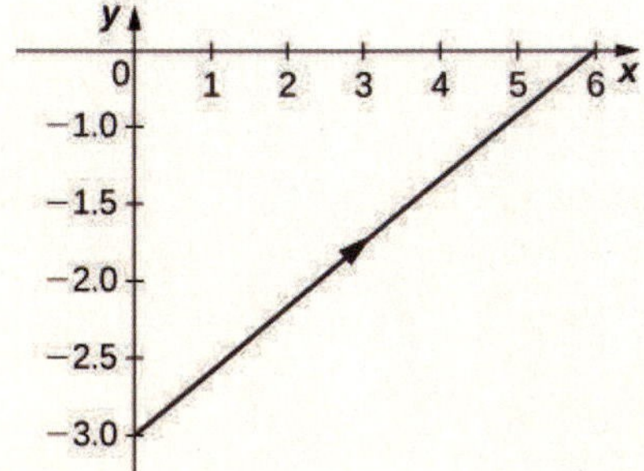

orientation: left to right

**5.** $y = \frac{x^2}{4} + 1$

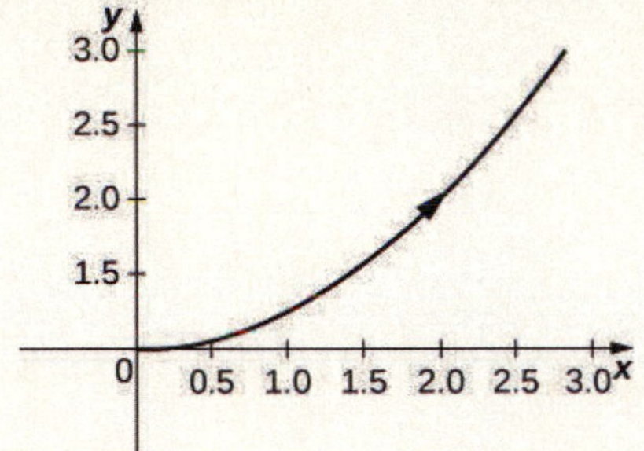


**7.**

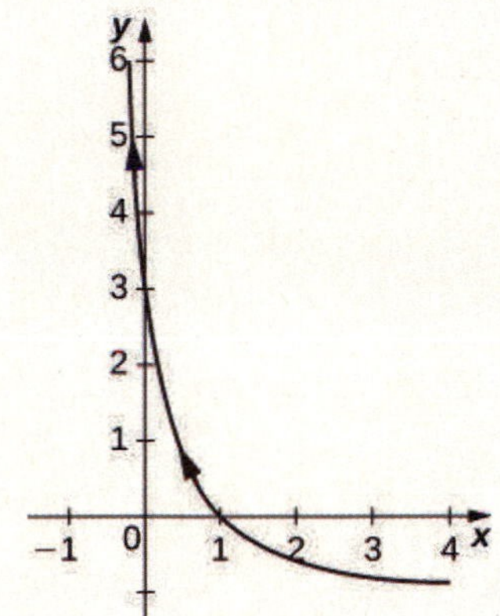


**9.**

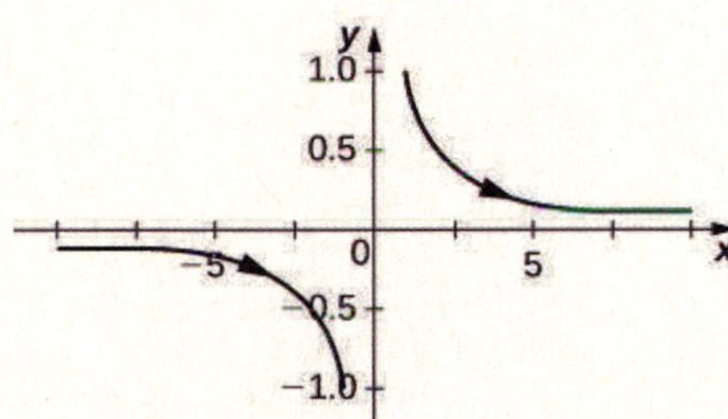


**11.**

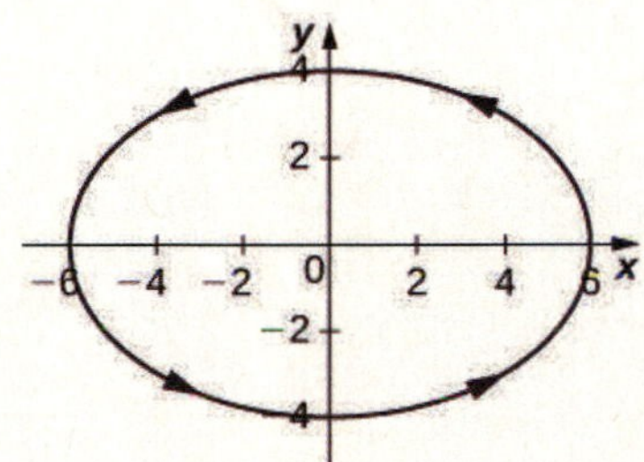


**13.**

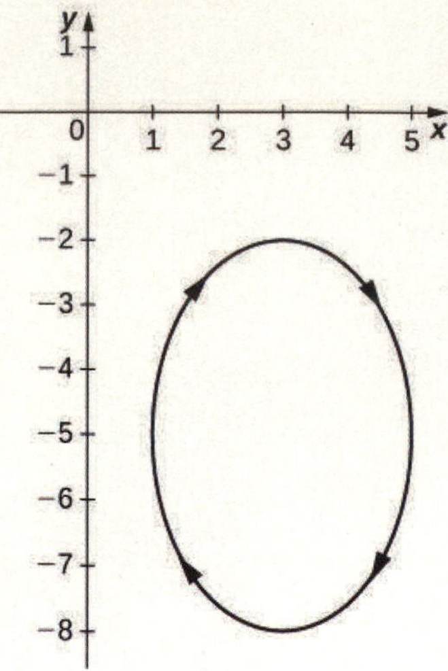


**15**.

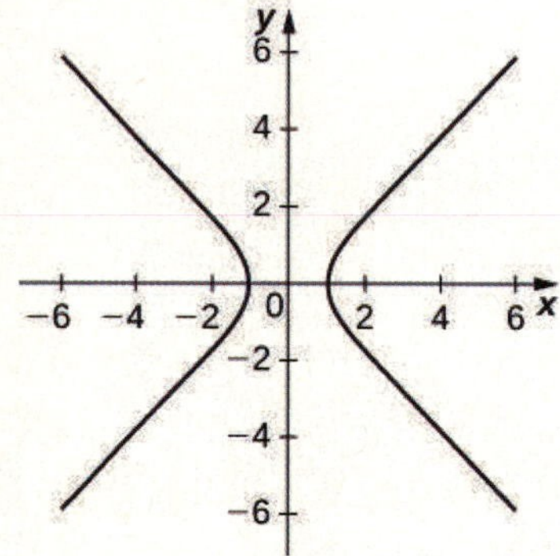


Asymptotes are $y = x$ and $y = -x$

**17**.

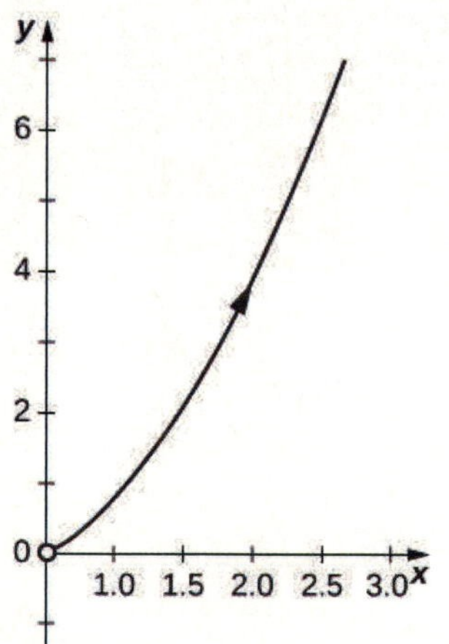


**19**.

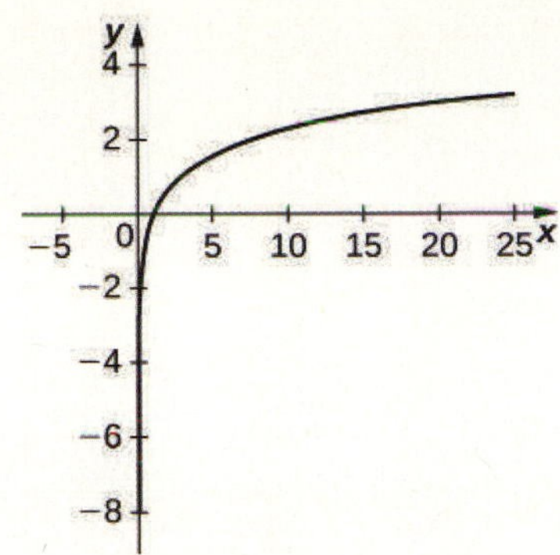


**21**. $x = 4y^2 - 1;$ domain: $x \in [1, \infty).$

**23**. $\frac{x^2}{16} + \frac{y^2}{9} = 1;$ domain $x \in [-4, 4].$

**25**. $y = 3x + 2;$ domain: all real numbers.

**27**. $(x - 1)^2 + (y - 3)^2 = 1;$ domain: $x \in [0, 2].$

**29**. $y = \sqrt{x^2 - 1};$ domain: $x \in [-1, 1].$

**31**. $y^2 = \frac{1 - x}{2};$ domain: $x \in [2, \infty) \cup (-\infty, -2].$

**33**. $y = \ln x;$ domain: $x \in (0, \infty).$

**35**. $y = \ln x;$ domain: $x \in (0, \infty).$

**37**. $x^2 + y^2 = 4;$ domain: $x \in [-2, 2].$

**39**. line
**41**. parabola
**43**. circle
**45**. ellipse
**47**. hyperbola
**51**. The equations represent a cycloid.

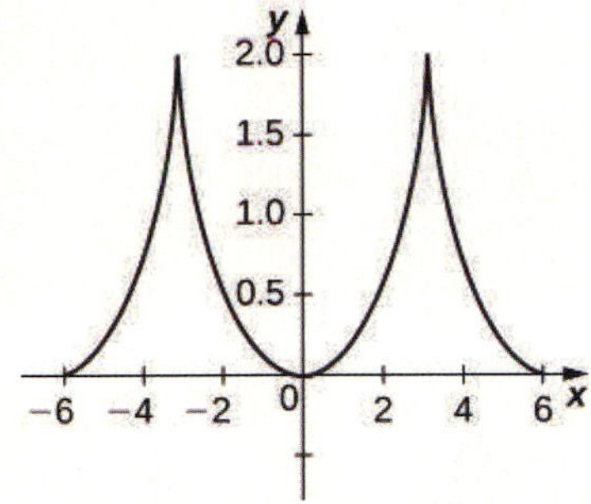


**53**.

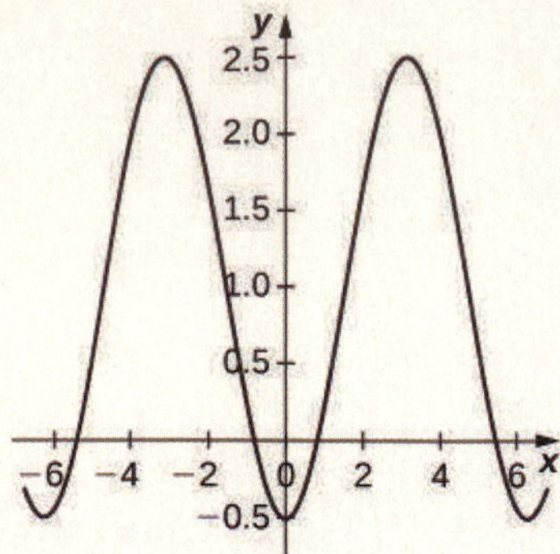


**55**. 22,092 meters at approximately 51 seconds.

**57**.

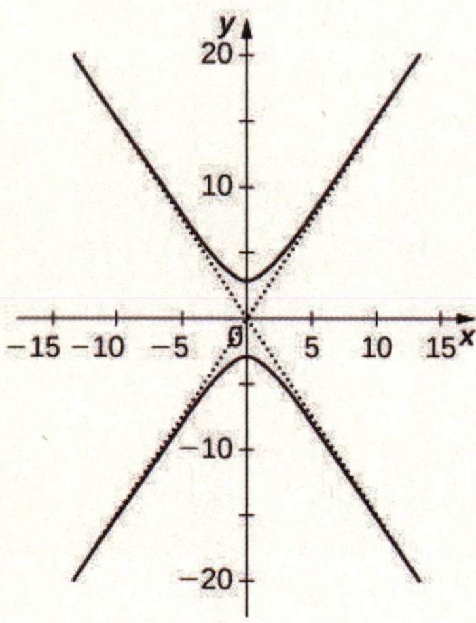


**59**.

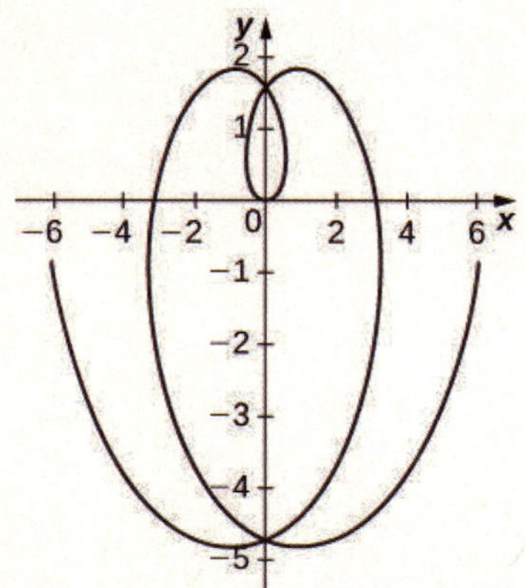


**61**.

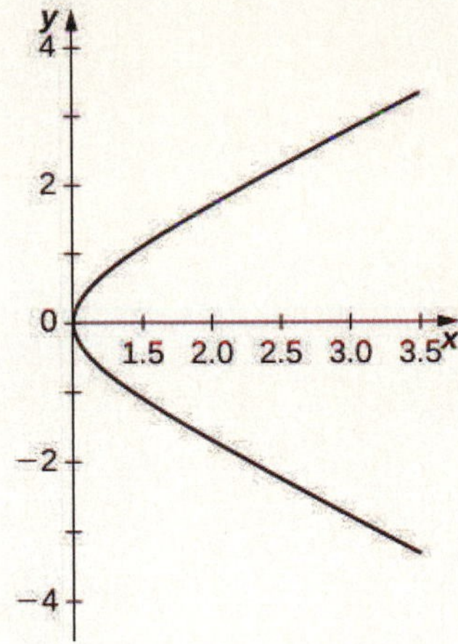


**63**. 0

**65**. $\frac{-3}{5}$

**67**. Slope $= 0$; $y = 8$.

**69**. Slope is undefined; $x = 2$.

**71**. $t = \arctan(-2)$; $\left(\frac{4}{\sqrt{5}}, \frac{-8}{\sqrt{5}}\right)$.

**73**. No points possible; undefined expression.

**75**. $y = -\left(\frac{2}{e}\right)x + 3$

**77**. $y = 2x - 7$

**79**. $\frac{\pi}{4}, \frac{5\pi}{4}, \frac{3\pi}{4}, \frac{7\pi}{4}$

**81**. $\frac{dy}{dx} = -\tan(t)$

**83**. $\frac{dy}{dx} = \frac{3}{4}$ and $\frac{d^2y}{dx^2} = 0$, so the curve is neither concave up nor concave down at $t = 3$. Therefore the graph is linear and has a constant slope but no concavity.

**85**. $\frac{dy}{dx} = 4$, $\frac{d^2y}{dx^2} = -6\sqrt{3}$; the curve is concave down at $\theta = \frac{\pi}{6}$.

**87**. No horizontal tangents. Vertical tangents at $(1, 0), (-1, 0)$.

**89**. $-\sec^3(\pi t)$

**91**. Horizontal $(0, -9)$; vertical $(\pm 2, -6)$.

**93**. 1

**95**. 0

**97**. 4

**99**. Concave up on $t > 0$.

**101**. 1

**103**. $\frac{3\pi}{2}$

**105**. $6\pi a^2$

**107**. $2\pi ab$

**109**. $\frac{1}{3}(2\sqrt{2} - 1)$

**111**. 7.075

**113**. $6a$

**115**. $6\sqrt{2}$

**119**. $\frac{2\pi\left(247\sqrt{13}+64\right)}{1215}$

**121**. 59.101

**123**. $\frac{8\pi}{3}(17\sqrt{17}-1)$

**125**.

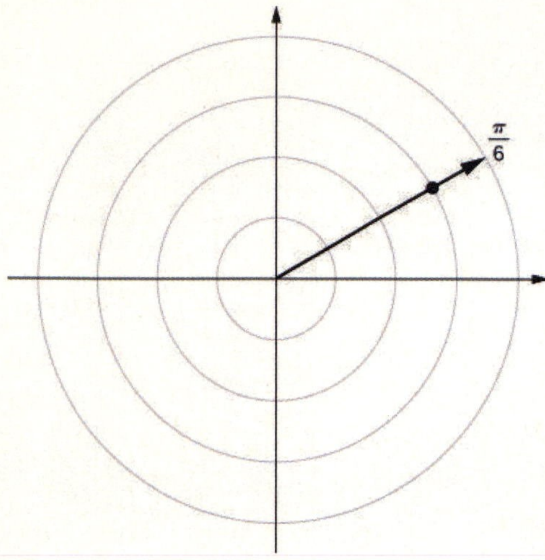


**127**.

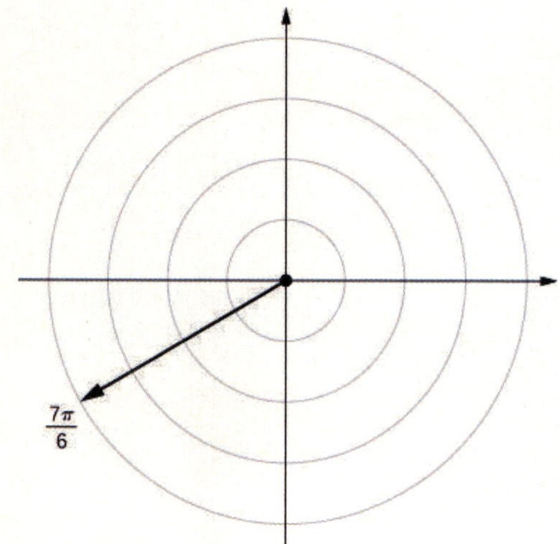


**129**.

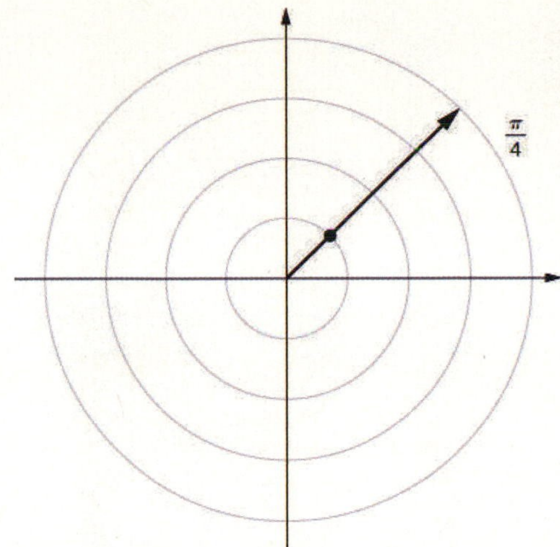


**131**.

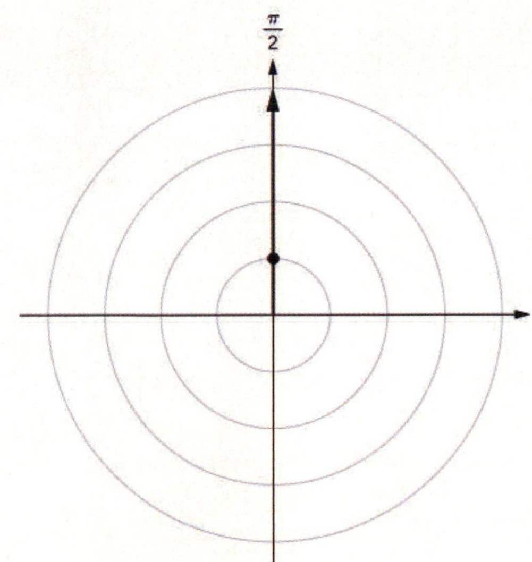


**133**. $B\left(3, \frac{-\pi}{3}\right)$ $B\left(-3, \frac{2\pi}{3}\right)$

**135**. $D\left(5, \frac{7\pi}{6}\right)D\left(-5, \frac{\pi}{6}\right)$

**137**. $(5, -0.927)$ $(-5, -0.927 + \pi)$

**139**. $(10, -0.927)(-10, -0.927 + \pi)$

**141**. $(2\sqrt{3}, -0.524)(-2\sqrt{3}, -0.524 + \pi)$

**143**. $(-\sqrt{3}, \ -1)$

**145**. $\left(-\frac{\sqrt{3}}{2}, \ \frac{-1}{2}\right)$

**147**. $(0, \ 0)$

**149**. Symmetry with respect to the $x$-axis, $y$-axis, and origin.
**151**. Symmetric with respect to $x$-axis only.
**153**. Symmetry with respect to $x$-axis only.
**155**. Line $y = x$

**157**. $y = 1$

**159**. Hyperbola; polar form $r^2 \cos(2\theta) = 16$ or $r^2 = 16 \sec \theta$.

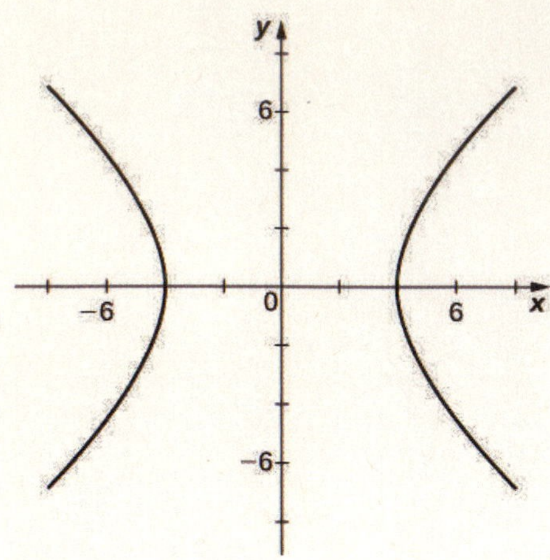


**161**. $r = \frac{2}{3\cos\theta - \sin\theta}$

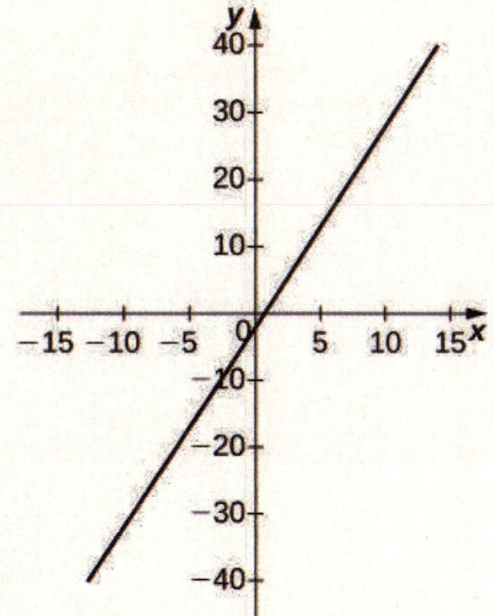


**163**. $x^2 + y^2 = 4y$

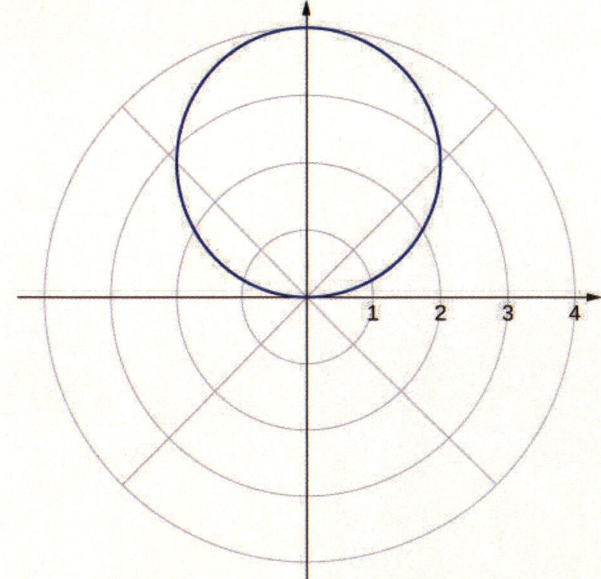


**165**. $x \tan\sqrt{x^2 + y^2} = y$

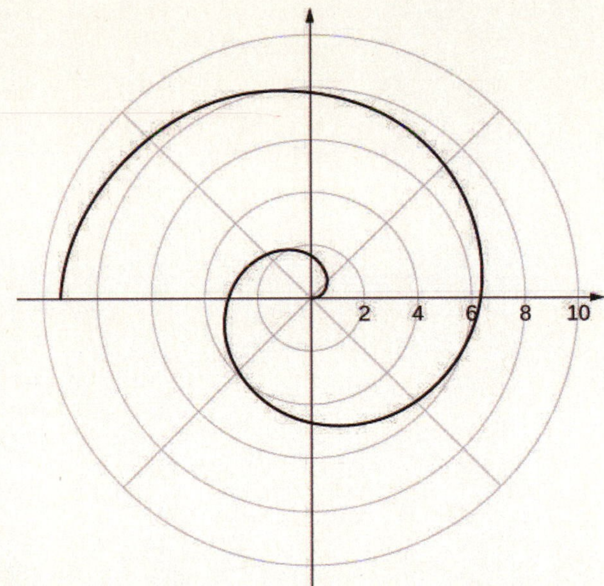


**167**.

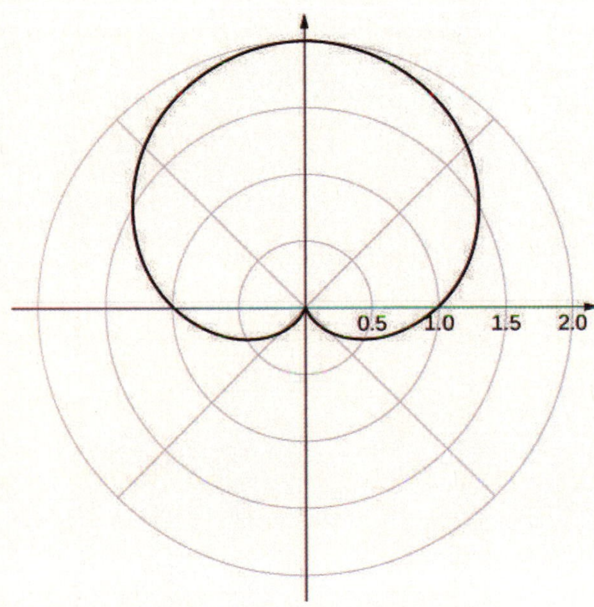


$y$-axis symmetry

**169**.

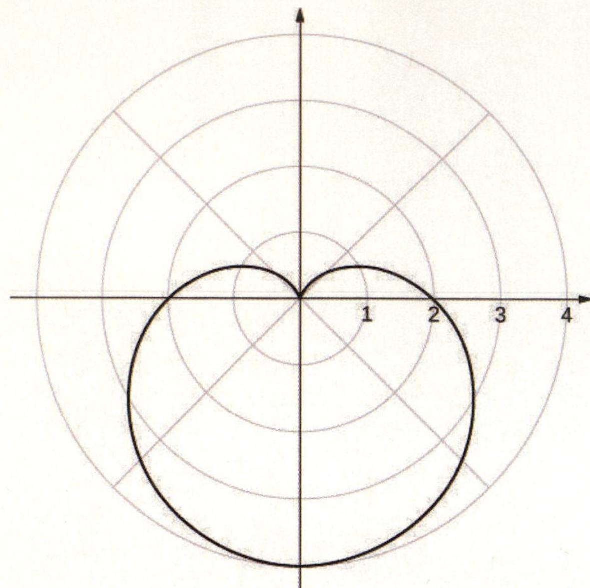


*y*-axis symmetry

**171**.

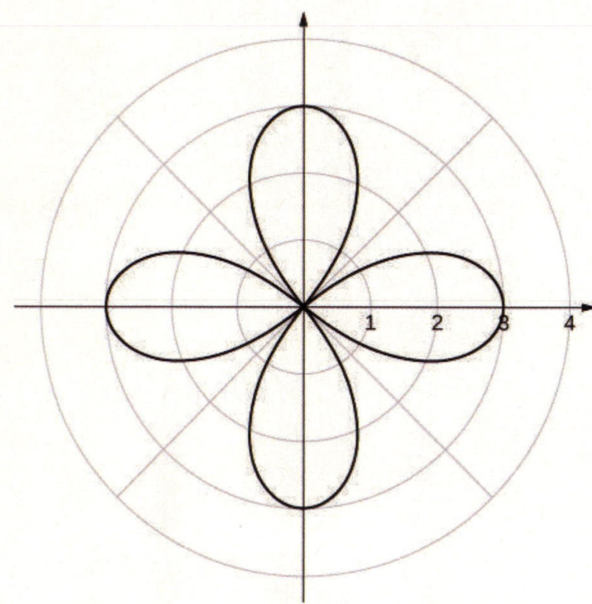


*x*- and *y*-axis symmetry and symmetry about the pole

**173**.

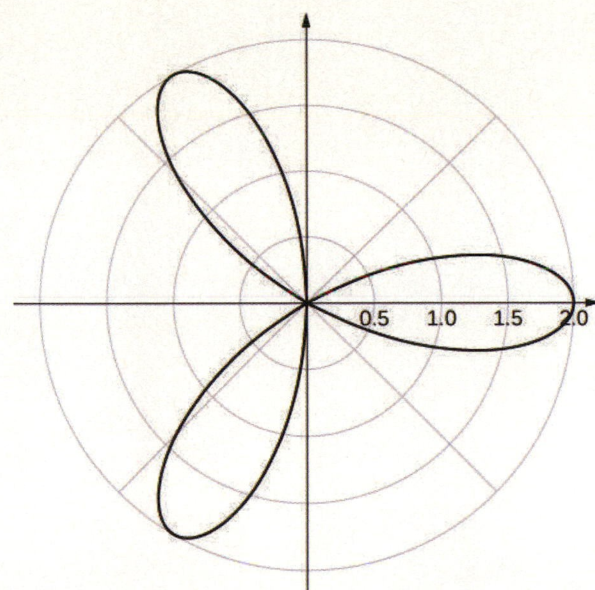


$x$-axis symmetry

**175**.

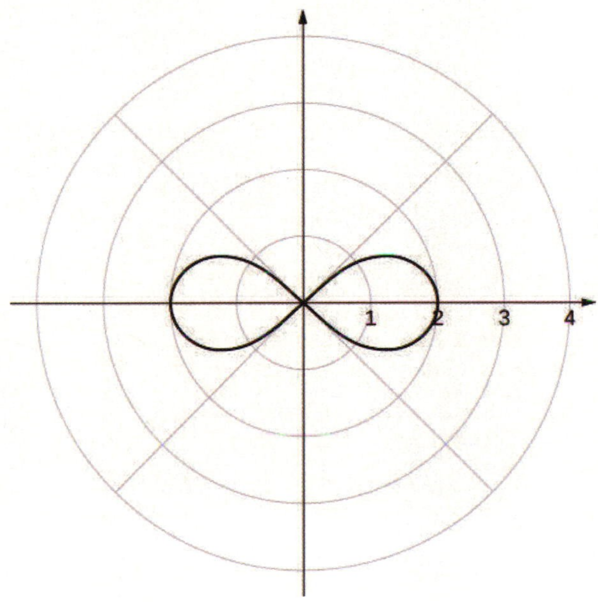


$x$- and $y$-axis symmetry and symmetry about the pole

**177**.

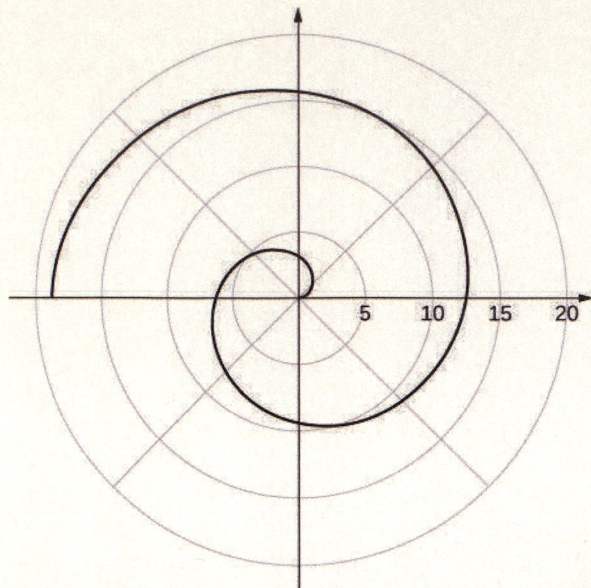


no symmetry

**179**.

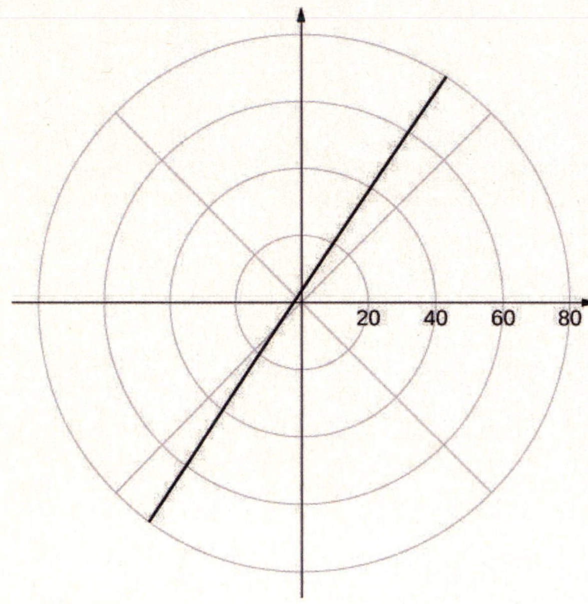


a line

**181**.

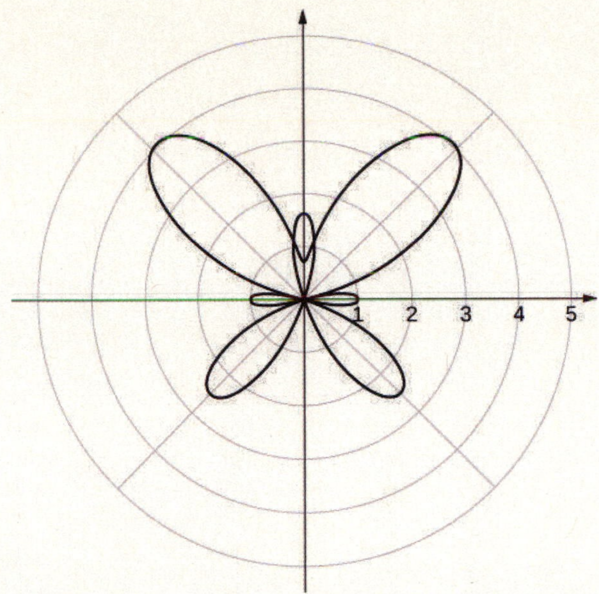


**183**.

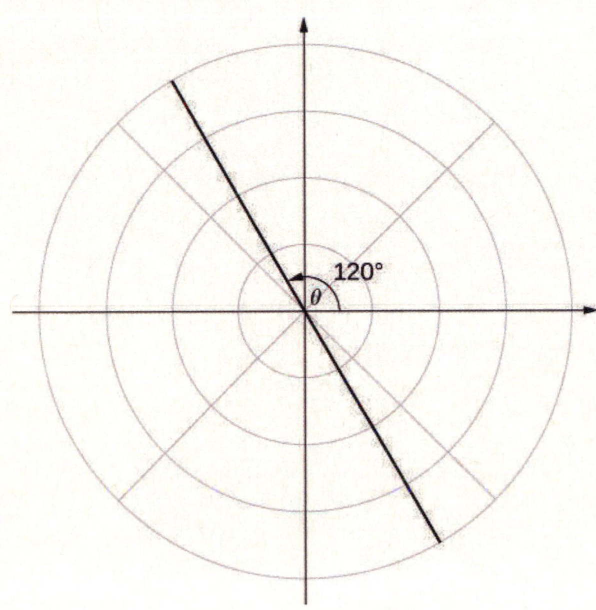


**185**.

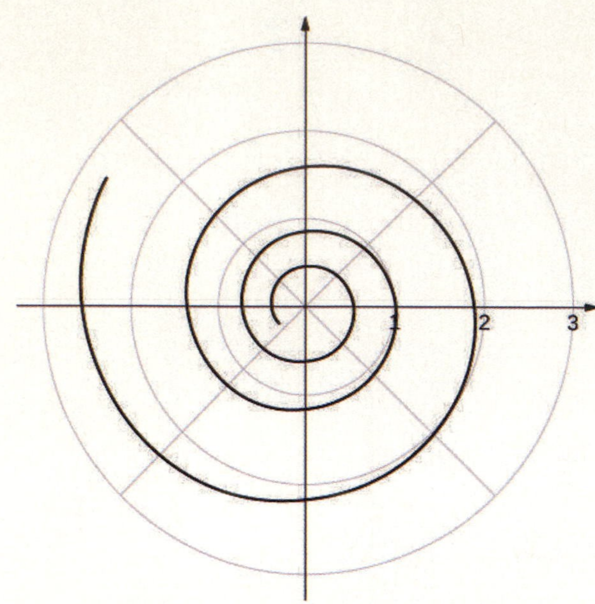


**187**. Answers vary. One possibility is the spiral lines become closer together and the total number of spirals increases.

**189**. $\frac{9}{2}\int_0^{\pi} \sin^2 \theta \, d\theta$

**191**. $32\int_0^{\pi/2} \sin^2(2\theta) d\theta$

**193**. $\frac{1}{2}\int_{\pi}^{2\pi} (1 - \sin \theta)^2 \, d\theta$

**195**. $\int_{\sin^{-1}(2/3)}^{\pi/2} (2 - 3 \sin \theta)^2 d\theta$

**197**. $\int_0^{\pi} (1 - 2 \cos \theta)^2 \, d\theta - \int_0^{\pi/3} (1 - 2 \cos \theta)^2 d\theta$

**199**. $4\int_0^{\pi/3} d\theta + 16\int_{\pi/3}^{\pi/2} \left(\cos^2 \theta\right) d\theta$

**201**. $9\pi$

**203**. $\frac{9\pi}{4}$

**205**. $\frac{9\pi}{8}$

**207**. $\frac{18\pi - 27\sqrt{3}}{2}$

**209**. $\frac{4}{3}\left(4\pi - 3\sqrt{3}\right)$

**211**. $\frac{3}{2}\left(4\pi - 3\sqrt{3}\right)$

**213**. $2\pi - 4$

**215**. $\int_0^{2\pi} \sqrt{(1 + \sin \theta)^2 + \cos^2 \theta} d\theta$

**217**. $\sqrt{2}\int_0^1 e^{\theta} \, d\theta$

**219**. $\frac{\sqrt{10}}{3}\left(e^6 - 1\right)$

**221**. 32

**223**. 6.238
**225**. 2
**227**. 4.39

**229**. $A = \pi\left(\frac{\sqrt{2}}{2}\right)^2 = \frac{\pi}{2}$ and $\frac{1}{2}\int_0^{\pi}(1 + 2\sin\theta\cos\theta)d\theta = \frac{\pi}{2}$

**231**. $C = 2\pi\left(\frac{3}{2}\right) = 3\pi$ and $\int_0^{\pi} 3d\theta = 3\pi$

**233**. $C = 2\pi(5) = 10\pi$ and $\int_0^{\pi} 10\, d\theta = 10\pi$

**235**. $\frac{dy}{dx} = \frac{f'(\theta)\sin\theta + f(\theta)\cos\theta}{f'(\theta)\cos\theta - f(\theta)\sin\theta}$

**237**. The slope is $\frac{1}{\sqrt{3}}$.

**239**. The slope is 0.

**241**. At $(4, 0)$, the slope is undefined. At $\left(-4, \frac{\pi}{2}\right)$, the slope is 0.

**243**. The slope is undefined at $\theta = \frac{\pi}{4}$.

**245**. Slope = −1.

**247**. Slope is $\frac{-2}{\pi}$.

**249**. Calculator answer: −0.836.

**251**. Horizontal tangent at $\left(\pm\sqrt{2}, \frac{\pi}{6}\right)$, $\left(\pm\sqrt{2}, -\frac{\pi}{6}\right)$.

**253**. Horizontal tangents at $\frac{\pi}{2}, \frac{7\pi}{6}, \frac{11\pi}{6}$. Vertical tangents at $\frac{\pi}{6}, \frac{5\pi}{6}$ and also at the pole $(0, 0)$.

**255**. $y^2 = 16x$

**257**. $x^2 = 2y$

**259**. $x^2 = -4(y - 3)$

**261**. $(x + 3)^2 = 8(y - 3)$

**263**. $\frac{x^2}{16} + \frac{y^2}{12} = 1$

**265**. $\frac{x^2}{13} + \frac{y^2}{4} = 1$

**267**. $\frac{(y - 1)^2}{16} + \frac{(x + 3)^2}{12} = 1$

**269**. $\frac{x^2}{16} + \frac{y^2}{12} = 1$

**271**. $\frac{x^2}{25} - \frac{y^2}{11} = 1$

**273**. $\frac{x^2}{7} - \frac{y^2}{9} = 1$

**275**. $\frac{(y + 2)^2}{4} - \frac{(x + 2)^2}{32} = 1$

**277**. $\frac{x^2}{4} - \frac{y^2}{32} = 1$

**279**. $e = 1$, parabola

**281**. $e = \frac{1}{2}$, ellipse

**283**. $e = 3$, hyperbola

**285**. $r = \dfrac{4}{5 + \cos\theta}$

**287**. $r = \dfrac{4}{1 + 2\sin\theta}$

**289**.

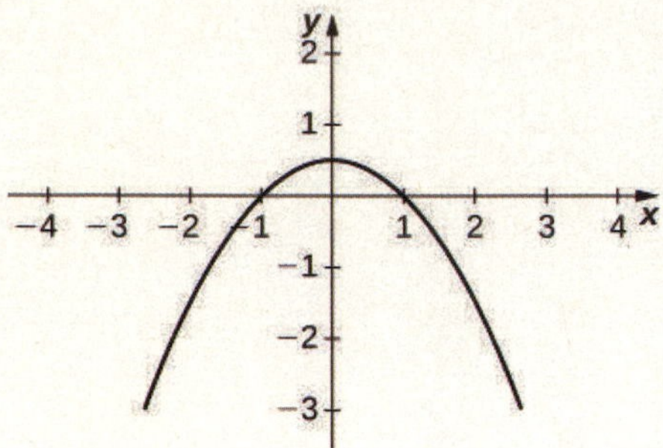

**291**.

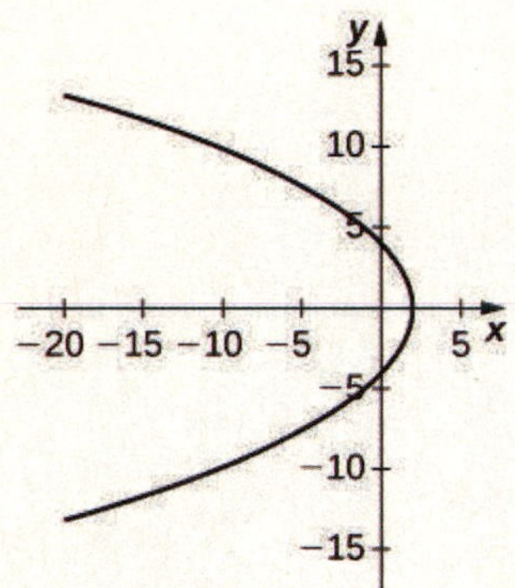

**293**.

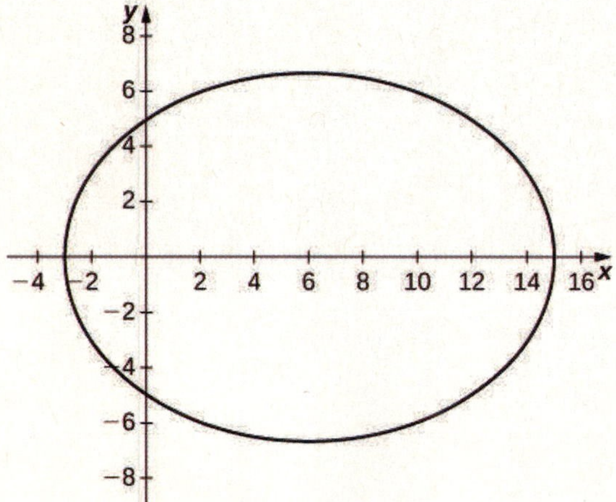

**295**.

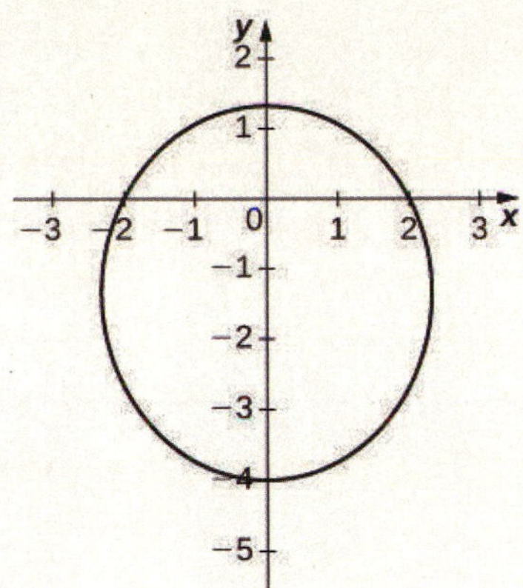
y
2
1
−3
−2
−1
0
1
2
3
x
−1
−2
−3
−4
−5

**297**.

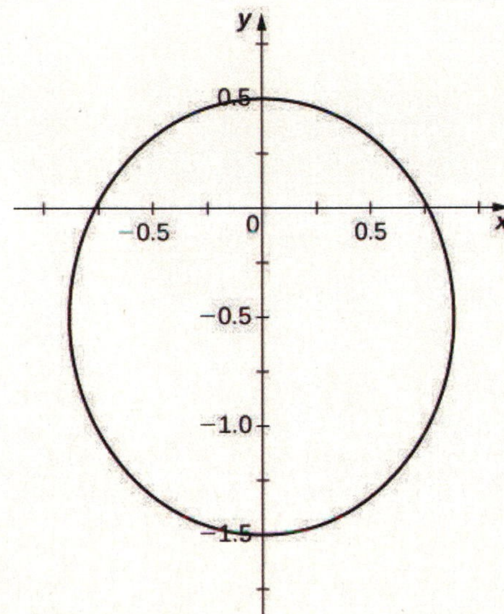
y
0.5
−0.5
0
0.5
x
−0.5
−1.0
−1.5

**299**.

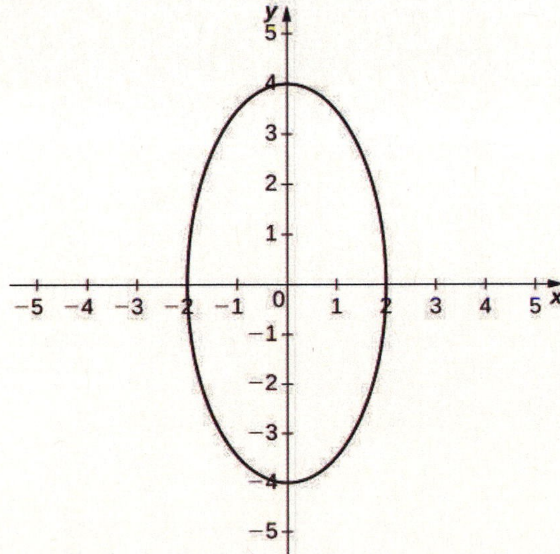
y
5
4
3
2
1
−5
−4
−3
−2
−1
0
1
2
3
4
5
x
−1
−2
−3
−4
−5

**301**.

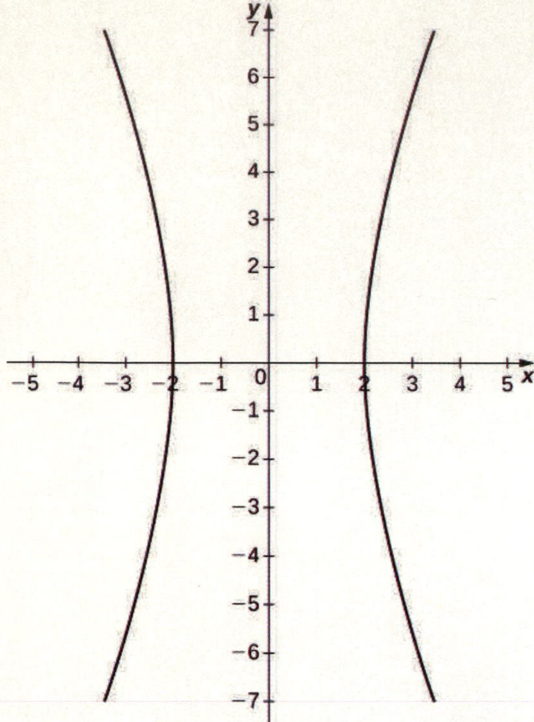


**303**.

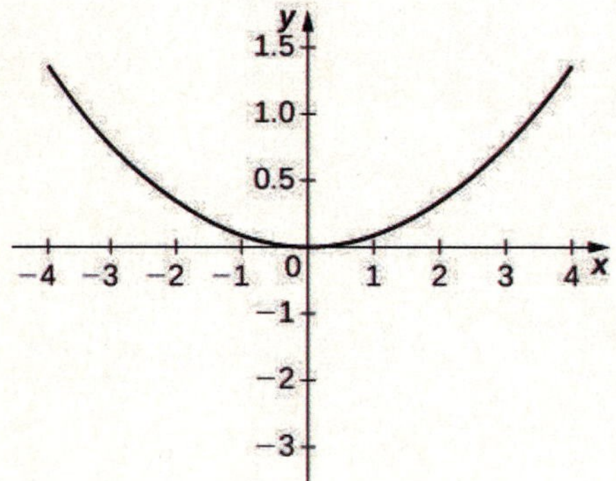


**305**.

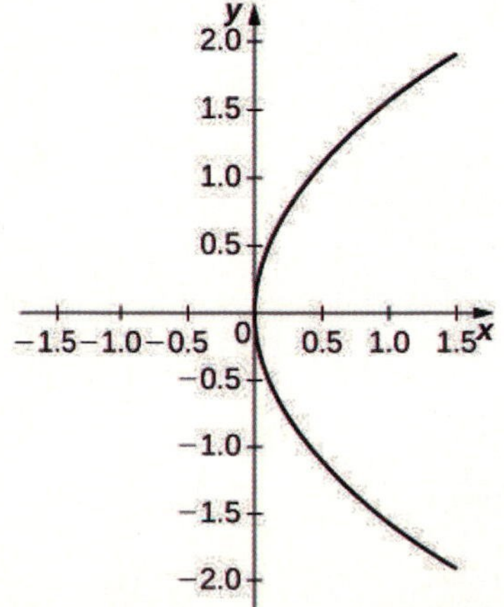


**307**. Hyperbola
**309**. Ellipse

**311**. Ellipse
**313**. At the point 2.25 feet above the vertex.
**315**. 0.5625 feet
**317**. Length is 96 feet and height is approximately 26.53 feet.
**319**. $r = \frac{2.616}{1 + 0.995 \cos \theta}$
**321**. $r = \frac{5.192}{1 + 0.0484 \cos \theta}$

## Review Exercises

**323**. True.
**325**. False. Imagine $y = t + 1, \quad x = -t + 1.$
**327**.

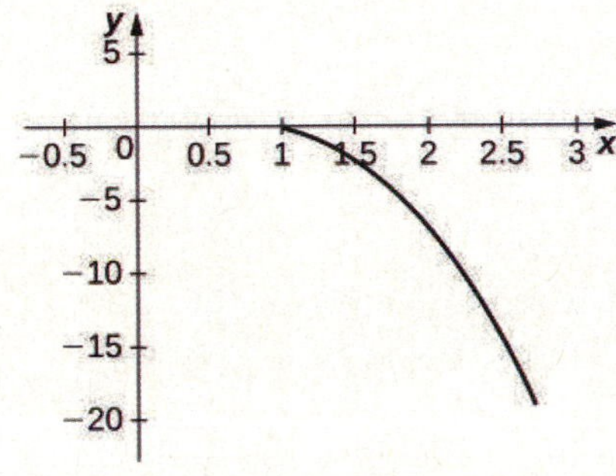


$y = 1 - x^3$

**329**.

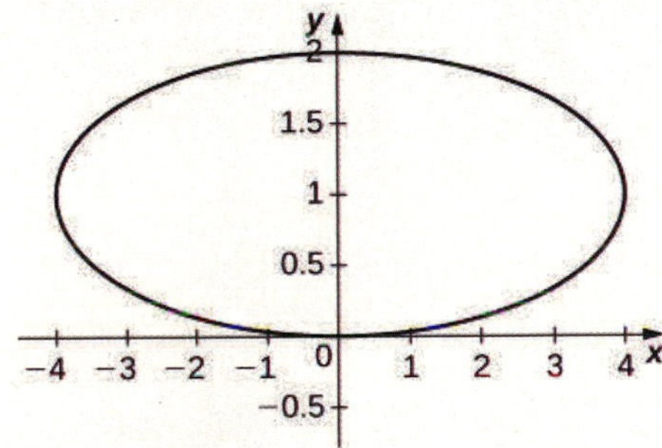


$\frac{x^2}{16} + (y-1)^2 = 1$

**331**.

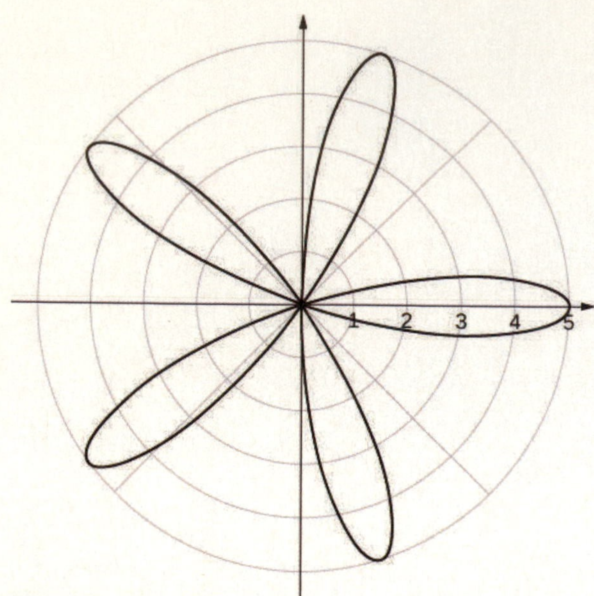


Symmetric about polar axis

**333**. $r^2 = \frac{4}{\sin^2\theta - \cos^2\theta}$

**335**.

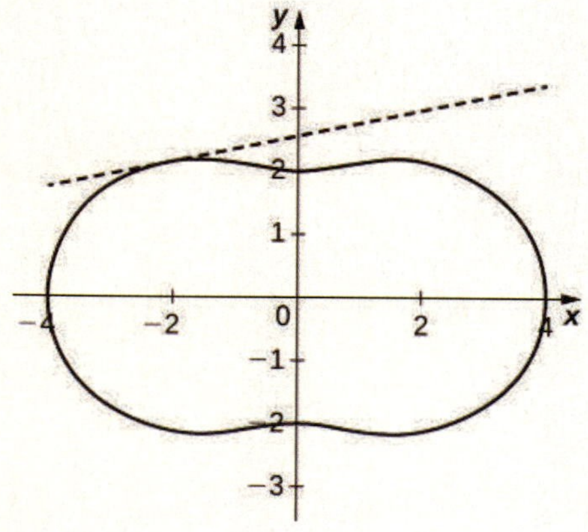


$y = \frac{3\sqrt{2}}{2} + \frac{1}{5}\left(x + \frac{3\sqrt{2}}{2}\right)$

**337**. $\frac{e^2}{2}$

**339**. $9\sqrt{10}$

**341**. $(y + 5)^2 = -8x + 32$

**343**. $\frac{(y+1)^2}{16} - \frac{(x+2)^2}{9} = 1$

**345**. $e = \frac{2}{3}$, ellipse

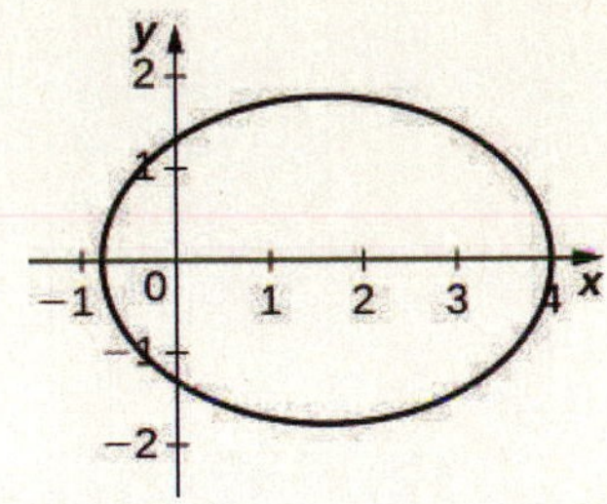


**347**. $\dfrac{y^2}{19.03^2} + \dfrac{x^2}{19.63^2} = 1, \quad e = 0.2447$

# INDEX

## U



## V



## W